W9-AFB-236

American
Jewish
Year Book

The American Jewish Committee acknowledges with appreciation the foresight and wisdom of the founders of the Jewish Publication Society (of America) in the creation of the AMERICAN JEWISH YEAR BOOK in 1899, a work committed to providing a continuous record of developments in the U.S. and world Jewish communities. For over a century JPS has occupied a special place in American Jewish life, publishing and disseminating important, enduring works of scholarship and general interest on Jewish subjects.

The American Jewish Committee assumed responsibility for the compilation and editing of the YEAR BOOK in 1908. The Society served as its publisher until 1949; from 1950 through 1993, the Committee and the Society were co-publishers. In 1994 the Committee became the sole publisher of the YEAR BOOK.

American

Jewish

Year Book 2000

VOLUME 100

Editors
DAVID SINGER
LAWRENCE GROSSMAN

THE AMERICAN JEWISH COMMITTEE
NEW YORK

ISBN 0-87495-115-1

Library of Congress Catalogue Number: 99-4040

PRINTED IN THE UNITED STATES OF AMERICA
BY MAPLE-VAIL BOOK MANUFACTURING GROUP, BINGHAMTON, N.Y.

Foreword

It is with great pride that the American Jewish Committee issues the centennial volume of the AMERICAN JEWISH YEAR BOOK. For a full century, the YEAR BOOK has been universally recognized as the authoritative source of information on Jewish life in the United States and around the world. As Jonathan D. Sarna and Jonathan J. Golden show in their superb feature article this year, "The Twentieth Century Through American Jewish Eyes: A History of the *American Jewish Year Book, 1899-1999*," the YEAR BOOK has not only served as a record of events and trends, but often also as a barometer of communal priorities and as a catalyst for change.

In the pages of the YEAR BOOK's 100 volumes one can trace the full trajectory of the Jewish experience over the last tumultuous century—the great migration of East European Jews to the United States and their difficult process of Americanization; the persistence of anti-Semitism around the world that culminated in the horrors of the Holocaust; the progress of Zionism from its meager origins to its great triumph in the creation of the State of Israel; the concern that Jewish communities have felt for each other, leading to heroic projects of rescue and relief; and the ongoing challenge, for American Jews, of developing a vibrant Jewish culture and a distinctive Jewish identity under conditions of acceptance and equality unprecedented in Jewish history.

On this auspicious occasion, I wish the AMERICAN JEWISH YEAR BOOK many more years of distinguished service as a lucid interpreter of the Jewish experience and an indispensable resource for Jewish life.

DAVID A. HARRIS
EXECUTIVE DIRECTOR, THE AMERICAN JEWISH COMMITTEE

Contributors

GREG CAPLAN: Doctoral candidate in modern German history, Georgetown University; Federal Chancellor Scholar, Berlin, Germany.

SERGIO DELLAPERGOLA: Professor and head, Division of Jewish Demography and Statistics, Avraham Harman Institute of Contemporary Jewry, Hebrew University of Jerusalem, Israel.

RICHARD T. FOLTIN: Legislative director and counsel, Office of Government and International Affairs, American Jewish Committee.

ZVI GITELMAN: Professor, political science, and Preston R. Tisch Professor of Judaic Studies, University of Michigan.

JONATHAN J. GOLDEN: Graduate student, Brandeis University.

MURRAY GORDON: Adjunct professor, Austrian Diplomatic Academy, Vienna, Austria.

LAWRENCE GROSSMAN: Editor, AMERICAN JEWISH YEAR BOOK; associate director of research, American Jewish Committee.

RUTH ELLEN GRUBER: European-based American journalist and author, specialist in contemporary Jewish affairs; Morre, Italy.

GEORGE E. GRUEN: Adjunct professor, international affairs, Middle East Institute and School of International and Public Affairs, Columbia University.

PETER HIRSCHBERG: Senior writer, *The Jerusalem Report;* Jerusalem, Israel.

LIONEL E. KOCHAN: Historian; Wolfson College, Oxford, England.

MIRIAM L. KOCHAN: Free-lance journalist and translator; Oxford, England.

UZI REBHUN: Lecturer, Division of Jewish Demography and Statistics, Avraham Harman Institute of Contemporary Jewry, Hebrew University of Jerusalem, Israel.

COLIN L. RUBENSTEIN: Executive director, Australia/Israel and Jewish Affairs Council; honorary associate, Monash University, Melbourne, Australia.

JONATHAN D. SARNA: Joseph H. and Belle R. Braun Professor of American Jewish History, and chair, Near Eastern and Judaic studies, Brandeis University.

JEFFREY SCHECKNER: Research consultant, United Jewish Communities; administrator, North American Jewish Data Bank, City University of New York.

JIM SCHWARTZ: Research director, United Jewish Communities; director, North American Jewish Data Bank, City University of New York.

RUTH R. SELDIN: Former executive editor, AMERICAN JEWISH YEAR BOOK.

MILTON SHAIN: Professor, Hebrew and Jewish studies, and director, Kaplan Centre for Jewish Studies and Research, University of Cape Town, South Africa.

BRIGITTE SION: Secretary general, CICAD, the Committee against anti-Semitism and Defamation; Geneva, Switzerland.

MARK TOLTS: Senior research associate, Division of Jewish Demography and Statistics, Avraham Harman Institute of Contemporary Jewry, Hebrew University of Jerusalem, Israel.

MEIR WAINTRATER: Editor in chief, *L'Arche,* the French Jewish monthly, Paris, France.

HAROLD M. WALLER: Professor, political science, McGill University; director, Canadian Centre for Jewish Community Studies, Montreal, Canada.

Contents

FOREWORD   *David A. Harris*   v

CONTRIBUTORS   vii

SPECIAL ARTICLES

The Twentieth Century Through American Jewish Eyes: A History of the *American Jewish Year Book*, 1899–1999	*Jonathan D. Sarna and Jonathan J. Golden*	3
A Photographic Retrospective of the Jewish Twentieth Century	*Ruth R. Seldin*	*following* 52
Prospecting the Jewish Future: Population Projections, 2000–2080	*Sergio DellaPergola, Uzi Rebhun, and Mark Tolts*	103

UNITED STATES

National Affairs	*Richard T. Foltin*	149
The United States, Israel, and the Middle East	*George E. Gruen*	189
Jewish Communal Affairs	*Lawrence Grossman*	208
Jewish Population in the United States, 1999	*Jim Schwartz and Jeffrey Scheckner*	242

ix

OTHER COUNTRIES

CANADA   *Harold M. Waller*   267

WESTERN EUROPE
Great Britain   *Miriam and Lionel
                                            Kochan*   289
France   *Meir Waintrater*   303
Italy   *Ruth Ellen Gruber*   317
Switzerland   *Brigitte Sion*   329

CENTRAL AND EASTERN EUROPE
Federal Republic of Germany   *Greg Caplan*   338
Austria   *Murray Gordon*   364
East-Central Europe   *Ruth Ellen Gruber*   373
Former Soviet Union   *Zvi Gitelman*   396

AUSTRALIA   *Colin L. Rubenstein*   405

SOUTH AFRICA   *Milton Shain*   416

ISRAEL   *Peter Hirschberg*   427

WORLD JEWISH POPULATION, 2000   *Sergio DellaPergola*   484

DIRECTORIES, LISTS, AND OBITUARIES

NATIONAL JEWISH ORGANIZATIONS
United States   499
Canada   557

JEWISH FEDERATIONS, WELFARE FUNDS,
COMMUNITY COUNCILS
United States   561
Canada   572

JEWISH PERIODICALS
United States   574
Canada   585

OBITUARIES: UNITED STATES   587

SUMMARY JEWISH CALENDAR,
5760-5764 (Sept. 1999–Aug. 2004)   596

CONDENSED MONTHLY CALENDAR,
5759-5762 (1999–2002)   598

INDEX   635

Special Articles

The Twentieth Century Through American Jewish Eyes: A History of the *American Jewish Year Book*, 1899-1999

BY JONATHAN D. SARNA AND JONATHAN J. GOLDEN

"EVERYTHING MUST HAVE A BEGINNING, and the beginning is necessarily imperfect."[1] With this modest disclaimer, the first volume of the *American Jewish Year Book* opened, appearing in time for Rosh Hashanah of the Hebrew year 5660 (1899–1900). American Jewry at that time boasted a population (according to the *Year Book*) of 1,043,800, making it the third largest Jewish population center in the world, after Russia and Austria-Hungary. New York, home to about half the nation's Jews, had ballooned into the world's most populous Jewish community, more than twice the size of its nearest rival, Warsaw. Over 40 percent of America's Jews were newcomers, in the country ten years or less. And more Jews were pouring into the country every day.

The publishers of the new *Year Book,* the Jewish Publication Society (JPS), founded in Philadelphia in 1888, understood the changing situation of the American Jewish community better than did most American Jews. JPS leaders, many of them longtime community activists, viewed America as the future center of world Jewry and boldly aimed to prepare American Jewry to assume its "manifest destiny." Germany, where many of their own parents had been born, had disappointed them by succumbing to "a revival of mediaeval prejudices." "It befits us as free citizens of the noblest of countries," they announced, "to take it up in their stead." Blending together American patriotism with concern for the welfare of their fellow Jews abroad, they looked to publish books that would both prepare American Jewry to assume the burden of Jewish leadership and, simultaneously, announce to the world that the American Jewish community had arrived.[2]

The *Year Book* would advance both of these goals. Its editor, 36-year-old Cyrus Adler, was something of a wunderkind. America's first Ph.D.

---

[1] *American Jewish Year Book,* vol. 1(1899–1900), p. ix. Subsequent references to the *Year Book* cite only volume, year(s), and page(s).

[2] Jonathan D. Sarna, *JPS: The Americanization of Jewish Culture, 1888–1988* (Philadelphia, 1989), pp. 13–26, 357.

3

in Semitics from an American university (Johns Hopkins), he had already helped found the Jewish Publication Society, the American Jewish Historical Society, and Gratz College, and he was an editor of the *American Hebrew*—all of which he managed to do while working full time in Washington as the librarian of the Smithsonian Institution, one of the highest ranking positions then held by a Jew in the federal bureaucracy. Apparently, he edited the *Year Book* in his spare time—and for no money. He did so, he later explained, to help provide American Jews with the facts they needed in order to "grapple successfully with the large problems of the Jewish situation."[3] At the same time, he clearly sought to counter the snobbish European Jewish view that American Jewry was backward. As recently as 1888, the English-Jewish textbook writer, Katie Magnus, had described American Judaism as "not always in a very much better state of preservation than among the semi-savage sects of ancient civilization."[4] The new *Year Book* offered a contrary view: "A cursory examination," Adler observed, " . . . will . . . convince the most pessimistic that Jewish ideals have a strong hold upon the Jews of the United States, especially in the direction of charitable and educational work."[5]

The same cursory examination would disclose that the *Year Book* drew upon two venerable traditions. First, like an almanac, it provided American Jews with a reliable Jewish calendar, carefully listing dates according to the Jewish lunar system, as well as Jewish holidays and fast days, the new moons, the weekly "Pentateuchal" and "Prophetical" portions, and related information critical to Jews who sought to organize their lives according to the traditional rhythms of the Jewish year. Jewish communities had been producing these kinds of annual calendars since the dawn of printing, and one had appeared in America (covering a period of 54 years!) as early as 1806.[6] Unlike secular almanacs, these volumes did not perpetuate beliefs in "astrology, prophecy, and mysterious occurrences in the natural world."[7] They did gradually expand to include useful information—everything from memorable dates to a list of the most important European highways. The *Year Book* would include some of these and other "useful" features. Second, the *Year Book* drew upon the 19th-

---

[3] Vol. 5 (1903–04), p. viii.
[4] Katie Magnus, *Outlines of Jewish History* (London, 1888), p. 313; Sarna, *JPS*, p. 30.
[5] Vol. 1 (1899–1900), p. x.
[6] "Almanac," *Jewish Encyclopedia*, vol. 1 (1901), pp. 426–28; Moses Lopez, *A Lunar Calendar, of the Festivals, and Other Days in the Year, Observed by the Israelites, Commencing Anno Mundi, 5566, and Ending in 5619 . . .* (Newport, 1806).
[7] Maureen Perkins, *Visions of the Future: Almanacs, Time, and Cultural Change, 1775–1870* (New York, 1996), p. 1.

century tradition of the literary yearbook, the German *Jahrbuch,* which featured annual articles of communal and scholarly concern. The Hebrew annual *Bikkure ha-'Ittim* (1820–31) and Isidor Busch's *Jahrbuch* (1842–1847), both published in Vienna, offered examples of this genre, while in the United States the more popular *American Jews' Annual,* published by Bloch Publishing Company from 1884 to 1896, similarly included literary articles in addition to an extensive calendar. The *Year Book* would include such material as well.

The most immediate model for the *Year Book,* however, was *The Jewish Year Book,* established in England in 1896 as "an annual record of matters Jewish." Its editor, the "critic, folklorist, historian, statistician, [and] communal worker" Joseph Jacobs, believed that "inadequate information" lay at the root of many of Anglo-Jewry's communal problems. Through his *Jewish Year Book* he sought to provide the facts and figures that the community needed to know about itself so that it might plan its future intelligently. He also provided additional data — a guide to Jewish reference books, a glossary of basic Jewish terms, lists of Jewish celebrities, and the like — to serve as a basis for Jewish home education and communal self-defense.[8] The handsomely bound and printed "English Jewish Year Book," as it came to be called, impressed American Jews, and in 1897 the influential New York Jewish newsweekly, the *American Hebrew,* urged JPS to produce a Jewish yearbook on the same model for American Jews. Cyrus Adler, who had actually proposed such a volume even before the British book appeared, heartily seconded the suggestion and offered his services. Unsurprisingly, when it finally appeared in 1899, the *American Jewish Year Book* followed its English predecessor in everything from its name and the spelling of "year book" as two words, to its size and its format. Later, it would far surpass its English older cousin and become the most important and enduring annual Jewish reference book in the world.

Setting the Course

The first two volumes of the *American Jewish Year Book* established patterns that lasted for many years. First, as noted, the volume opened with an extensive calendar — the only place in the volume that Hebrew words and letters appeared. This became, in time, the "official" calendar of the American Jewish community, and was widely consulted by non-Jews seeking to learn when Jewish holidays began and ended. In 1904 the *Year Book* added a multiyear listing of Jewish holidays for those who

---

[8]Sarna, *JPS,* p. 79.

sought to plan ahead, and in 1906, as a service for "those who observe the Sabbath in the traditional way," it began to print sunrise and sunset tables for various latitudes, so that Jews might know when the day of rest officially began and ended throughout the United States.[9] Any reader who opened the volume was thus transported at once into the world of "Jewish time," where days begin at sundown, and months are defined by the waxing and waning of the moon.

Following the calendar, the volume featured an extensive review of the previous year. In 1899 this was accomplished through two articles, one by Abram S. Isaacs on "The Jews of the United States," and the other by the English *Jewish Year Book*'s Joseph Jacobs on "The Jews of Europe." Isaacs's article began on a triumphalist note that characterized much of the *Year Book*'s early writing about America:

> The record of the Jews of the United States each succeeding year, as the population steadily increases, with corresponding growth in religious, charitable, and educational institutions, becomes more and more noteworthy . . . . While in many countries the mediaeval spirit prevails, making the Jew a wanderer and outcast, on American soil he seems to be preparing a distinctly new era . . . . [here] the genius of the Jew, his adaptativeness [*sic*], energy, persistency, is finding ample field for the highest and most varied endeavor.[10]

Jacobs offered a more sophisticated analysis, and in the process pointed to a problem that would regularly confront many a *Year Book* writer over the years. "Where the condition of Jews is favorable," he observed, "there is little or nothing to say, so that what one has to report gives a rather sombre tinge to the whole picture, which is liable to be misleading." He then went on to summarize the year "in two words—Zionism and Dreyfus," predicting (correctly) that the former would "divide the communities of this generation" just as Reform Judaism did earlier ones and (less correctly) that the collapse of the case against Captain Alfred Dreyfus in France would deal "a severe blow . . . to Anti-Semitism throughout Europe."[11]

The decision to separate American from European events was reversed in the second volume of the *Year Book*. Henrietta Szold, perhaps the most learned American Jewish woman of her day and best known for her later role as founder of Hadassah, was then "Secretary to the Publication Committee" at JPS—actually its de facto editor—and she greatly assisted Adler with this volume. Her "painstaking and indefatigable labors," Adler acknowledged in the preface, were responsible for "much of the ac-

---

[9]Vol. 8 (1906–07), p. vii.
[10]Vol. 1 (1899–1900), p. 14.
[11]Ibid., pp. 20–21.

curacy and many of the improvements" that the new *Year Book* introduced.[12]

One of these improvements was a different kind of review of the year, which Szold wrote by herself. A characteristically brilliant piece, it covered wide sections of the Jewish world in a single narrative that linked Europe and America together thematically. "In the annals of Jewish history, the closing year of the nineteenth century will occupy a prominent though not an honorable place," Szold began. Notwithstanding many tales of woe — from "ritual murder charges" to "distress" to "famine" — she found "the prevailing gloom" to be "shot through with gleams of light." A heightened degree of "self-respect," she argued, was manifesting itself throughout the Jewish world — in Zionism, in movements of Jewish self-defense, and in Jewish religious life. The Old and New Worlds were, to her mind, inexorably linked insofar as Jews were concerned: "The Old World," she wrote, "has for many years been setting the Jews of the New World difficult problems to solve. They must try to remedy in detail what the civilization of Europe perpetuates in the wholesale." Even as she warned against "the rosy view of Judaism in America," she predicted that "in the not too distant future the United States will become a centre of Jewish scholarship." Yet it was not with America that Szold ultimately concluded, but Zion. Choosing her words carefully — she knew that *Year Book* readers disagreed violently over the wisdom of political Zionism, and on all such divisive issues the *Year Book* took refuge in nonpartisanship — she declared that "in the habitations of the Jews there is light . . . . the Jew steps into the new century still conscious of his mission, occupied with the questions, political, social, ideal, that are at once summed up and solved in the word Zion." And then, to ensure that opponents of Zionism did not complain, she recalled for her readers the spiritual meaning of the word: "Zion, that is, the mountain of the house of the Lord, to which the nations shall flow to be taught the ways of the God of Jacob, and to walk in His paths."[13]

The essay, an engaging mixture of high intelligence and careful diplomacy, received accolades, but its solution to the question of *how* to review the year just past proved ephemeral. Over the next century the *Year Book* would grapple with this problem again and again, sometimes treating the Jewish world as a unified whole, sometimes focusing separately on some of it parts (notably the United States), sometimes creatively analyzing developments the way Szold did, and sometimes simply record-

---

[12]Vol. 2 (1900–01), p. ix.
[13]Ibid., pp. 14–39.

ing facts for posterity without analysis—all the while never fully resolving the function of the annual review.

The major portion of the first two *Year Books*—and a prominent feature of all subsequent ones down to the present day—consisted of listings and directories. American Jewish leaders, like their British counterparts and like Progressive-era Americans generally, deeply believed in the value of facts, research, and quantifiable information. Theirs was, in the words of historian Robert Wiebe, "an age that assumed an automatic connection between accurate data and rational action."[14] As a result, from the beginning the *Year Book* set itself up as American Jewry's central source for accurate data. It regularly apologized that its data was not accurate enough, and carefully marked unofficial data with a star (*), even as it offered assurances that "in a majority of cases it is entirely authentic."[15] Volume 1 featured a "Directory of National Organizations" providing extensive (and historically invaluable) information on the 19 nationwide American Jewish organizations then in existence, including, as available, when they were founded, their officers, membership, annual income, meeting date, objectives, activities, and branches. In the case of the then recently established "Orthodox Jewish Congregational Union of America"—today commonly known as the "OU," or Orthodox Union—the *Year Book* went so far as to print the proceedings of its first annual convention (1898), complete with statement of principles. The fact that Cyrus Adler served as a trustee of the new organization probably didn't hurt. A short report on the convention of the (Reform) Union of American Hebrew Congregations (UAHC), including the full text of its 1898 anti-Zionism resolution, also appeared in the volume.

The listing of national organizations was followed by a much longer 166-page "Directory of Local Organizations" listing synagogues, charitable organizations, women's organizations, burial societies, clubs, and more—all organized by city and state. Henrietta Szold knew that the list was inadequate, and the next year's *Year Book* (1900–1901) acknowledged that the original list "left so much to be desired" and replaced it with a list that was approximately twice as long. For students of American Jewry this second listing is of inestimable significance. For the linguist, Cyrus Adler dryly observed, there was "an almost infinite variety in the spelling of Hebrew names . . . found in the Directory." This was an indication of the many and varied sources of Jewish immigration to the United States. The community, he believed, reflected "most of the peculiarities of Hebrew pronunciation now in existence."[16] For the geogra-

---

[14]Robert H. Wiebe, *The Search for Order, 1877–1920* (New York, 1967), p. 181.
[15]Vol. 2 (1900–01), p. viii.
[16]Vol. 1 (1899–1900), p. x.

pher, the list also disclosed the remarkable spread of Jewish communities across the United States: Over 500 different cities and towns boasted some kind of Jewish congregation or organization at the turn of the century, including such unlikely places as Cripple Creek, Colorado, Pocahontas, Virginia, and Ponce, Puerto Rico. On the other hand, three states and one territory—Idaho, North Dakota, Wyoming, and Arizona—registered no Jewish organizational life at all, even though all but North Dakota were known to have Jewish residents. The Jewish Publication Society, whose membership was also listed for the first time in this second volume, reached further, embracing some 600 cities and towns (including Tucson, Arizona and "Indian territory"). Clearly, the JPS itself served as a link to some otherwise unaffiliated Jews who had no organized Jewish community around them.

The directory enumerated 791 Jewish congregations across the country. Yet only 91 of these belonged to the UAHC (Reform) and 50 to the OU (Orthodox). The other 650 were described as "barely organized," "composed of the recently immigrated population," and unable "to adapt themselves to the conditions of a national federation." Moreover, only ten United States cities housed nine or more congregations. They were, in ascending order, Newark and San Francisco (9 each), Cincinnati and Cleveland (13 each), Boston (14), Brooklyn (25), Baltimore (27), Chicago (47), Philadelphia (50), and New York (62).

In addition to the directories of institutions, the second volume of the *Year Book* introduced several other new features that endured for many years. Three of them had clear apologetic motives, designed to demonstrate the patriotism, public service, and charitableness of America's Jews—all virtues publicly called into question by critics of the Jews.

Ninety-four pages were occupied by an extensive "Preliminary List of Jewish Soldiers and Sailors who served in the Spanish-American War." Those eager to denigrate Jews had long charged that Jews failed to defend their country on the field of battle, and in the 1890s these allegations had been printed in the respected *North American Review* and repeated by no less a personage than Mark Twain (who later recanted). The Jewish community's leading apologist of that day, Simon Wolf, published a voluminous tome, *The American Jew as Patriot, Soldier and Citizen* (1895), designed to refute this ugly canard through a listing of all known Jews (and, it turned out, quite a number of non-Jews with Jewish-sounding names) who fought in American wars from the Revolution to the Civil War. The *Year Book*'s listing provided a continuation of this list to demonstrate the Jewish role in America's latest military action—one which many Jews had supported on patriotic grounds and as a kind of revenge against Spain for expelling Jews 400 years earlier. (For her part, Henrietta Szold, a pacifist, privately condemned the war as "all arrogance."[17]) Actually, Adler conceded that his list was no more accurate than Simon Wolf's. In an unusual effort to forestall critics, and perhaps in a fit of pique over the problems the list caused and the flood of angry letters he knew it would engender, Adler testily admitted to the list's faults himself—the only time readers were ever addressed in such a sneering tone in all of the *Year Book*'s history:

> To save persons who will be called upon to criticize this list any trouble or undue expenditure of time, I will point out some of its most glaring defects. It is inconsistent and inconvenient in arrangement; it contains names which should have been omitted, and omits names which should have been included; it frequently gives names incorrectly or with insufficient data or under wrong commands; and it even contains some repetitions. These faults are mentioned so that those who might otherwise be obliged to give their time in discovering them will use it in aiding me to correct them.[18]

By the time America next went to war, in World War I, there would be a whole organization to meet the needs of Jewish servicemen, and the latter would be identified with a great deal more accuracy.

A second listing with somewhat apologetic aims consisted of "Biographical Sketches of Jews who have served in the Congress of the United States." Eager to prove their "contribution" to American life, and doubtless proud of the fact that, in America, Jews could attain high political office, the *Year Book* maintained and even expanded this list through the years until it became a full-fledged list of "Jews in American Public Service" past and present (though a few non-Jews with Jewish-sounding names included on the list in the first years were subsequently dropped). In addition to senators and congressmen, the list came to include judges, governors, presidential advisors, ambassadors, and members of high-level commissions.

Still a third list introduced in 1900 was one of "Bequests and Gifts." American Jews had long enjoyed a reputation in some quarters for being charitable, but no central record of their largesse existed. In hostile circles Jews were often perceived as stingy and avaricious. The *Year Book,* through its listing, gave publicity to major individual gifts and ensured that they would be permanently recorded, thereby encouraging others to make similar gifts and at the same time refuting the negative stereotype. Initially, even some $500 gifts sufficed to make the list, but as time (and inflation) marched on, the bar rose. By 1929 the smallest gift listed was

---

[17]Jeanne Abrams, "Remembering the Maine: The Jewish Attitude Toward the Spanish-American War as Reflected in the *American Israelite*," *American Jewish History* 76, June 1987, pp. 439–55; Henrietta Szold to Joseph H. Hertz, August 8, 1899, Szold Papers, Hadassah Archives, NYC.

[18]Vol. 2 (1900–01), p. 528.

$15,000. The nature of the gifts also changed over time, reflecting the shifting worldviews and priorities of American Jews. In 1900 most were donations to American Jewish hospitals and synagogues, but three decades later many went to non-Jewish institutions (schools, museums, and universities), while a substantial number of others assisted the creation of Jewish institutions in Palestine.

Surprisingly, the first two volumes devoted only three pages each to what they called "Jewish Statistics" — the number of Jews in the United States and around the world. The reason, the editor confessed, was that these statistics rested largely "upon estimates repeated and added to by one statistical authority after another," that utilized "unsatisfactory" methods.[19] Official figures for Jewish immigration into the United States permitted some generalizations, and the first *Year Book* dutifully provided estimated population figures for each state and for the community as a whole (1,043,800). It then provided figures for the British Empire, broken down by country (148,130), and for 32 other countries where it claimed that Jews resided, ranging from Costa Rica (where it listed 35 Jews) to Russia (with 5,700,000). Several of these figures were reprinted unchanged for several years running, testimony to the sorry state of Jewish statistics when the *Year Book* began, and the editors' inability, at least initially, to improve upon them.

No Longer an Experiment

Notwithstanding these and other faults, however, the *Year Book* quickly proved its "usefulness" to the Americanized middle- and upper-class Jews of Central European descent who dominated the JPS membership. The JPS resolved to publish it annually and to incorporate its own annual report into each volume. But it also went further. In the preface to the second volume Cyrus Adler announced: "The policy of the Society with regard to the Year Book is that each issue shall in the main be made up of new material, and not consist of repetitions with additions of matter already published." That meant that each year the *Year Book* had to be planned afresh — no mean feat, given the small size of its staff, and made all the more difficult since the closest model available, the English *Jewish Year Book,* did repeat and update a great deal of material every year, much as most almanacs do to this day and the *Year Book* itself would do later. The decision not to repeat was partly dictated by costs. The 1900–01 *Year Book* had ballooned to 775 pages — a budget-breaker. The next year, by referring readers back to earlier volumes for some features, the vol-

---

[19]Vol. 1 (1899–1900), p. 283.

ume was kept down to 333 pages, including 18 pages of advertisements. At a deeper level, though, the decision to focus on "new material" sought—unsuccessfully as it turned out—to resolve an identity problem that the *Year Book* would grapple with for many years. Should it be a cumulative series of books, like the modern-day encyclopedia year book, each one focused on a single year, or should it be an annually updated reference work, each one essentially replacing its predecessor, much like the traditional almanac? In time, the *Year Book* became a hybrid. It positioned unique "special articles" and reviews of the year up front, and annually updated directories and reference lists in the back. To this day, some owners add a new volume to their shelf each year, while others discard each year's volume when its successor arrives. But that was not the plan back in 1900. Then, the Jewish Publication Society seems to have believed that each volume of the *Year Book* would be uniquely valuable, and it encouraged subscribers to acquire the full set.

How to make each volume uniquely valuable proved something of a challenge, especially in the Jewish year 5661 (1900–1901) when the *Year Book* candidly acknowledged that "there was no occurrence of supreme importance by which to characterize either the internal history of the Jewish people or their relations to the world at large."[20] That year the *Year Book* focused on the history of Romanian (then spelled "Roumanian") Jewry, because, it explained, the community's "unrelenting persecution ... has produced a condition of affairs which will inevitably bring about a considerable migration to the United States."[21] The prediction proved accurate—some 80,000 Romanian Jews came to America between 1881 and 1914, a quarter of them between 1899 and 1902[22]—and, writing in the *Year Book,* the expatriate Romanian historian Elias Schwarzfeld explained why. He described the Jewish condition in his homeland in the most lachrymose terms as a place where the Jew was "refused the rights of a man and a citizen," was "robbed of the means of living," was "persecuted by everybody," was "without land and without protection." In short, Romania was a "hellish country in which life had become intolerable."[23] Revealingly, the *Year Book* juxtaposed this portrait with a fascinating article on "The Roumanian Jews in America," which painted a far sunnier portrait. A gold mine of otherwise unavailable information on early Romanian Jewish immigrants, the article noted their success in the

---

[20]Vol. 3 (1901–02), p. 15.

[21]Ibid., p. ix.

[22]Simon Kuznets, "Immigration of Russian Jews to the United States: Background and Structure," *Perspectives in American History* 9, 1975, p. 39; Samuel Joseph, *Jewish Immigration to the United States from 1881 to 1910* (New York, 1914), pp. 105–08.

[23]Vol. 3 (1901–02), pp. 83, 86.

food business ("By a moderate estimate there are in New York one hundred and fifty restaurants, two hundred wine-cellars, with lunch rooms attached, and about thirty coffee-houses kept by Roumanian Jews"[24]), their distinctive religious and social lives, their contribution to the Yiddish theater, even their impact on Masonry. Written by the Romanian-American Yiddish journalist David Hermalin, the article also reflected, in part, the prejudices of the *Year Book*'s readership—Americanized Jews of Central European origin—particularly in its attack on Romanian political clubs, one of which was depicted as sinking "to the low degree occupied by the typical political organizations that infest the entire East Side of New York."[25] This description of Romanian Jews in America ended on a mawkishly apologetic note not seen in previous *Year Book* articles:

> On the whole, they are an industrious class of people, and grasp at every opportunity to Americanize themselves. They have a proper appreciation of American institutions, and learn to speak and read the English language in a shorter time than other foreigners. They regard the United States as their permanent home and do everything within the bounds of possibility to qualify themselves to be worthy citizens of the great Republic that has offered them a secure haven of rest.[26]

As we shall see, pious pronouncements of this sort would become ever more common in the *Year Book* as domestic support for immigration waned and anti-Semitism swelled. The larger significance of the articles on Romania, however, was that they viewed a world Jewish issue—the persecution of Jews in Romania—through an American prism. Over time, this became one of the *Year Book*'s most enduring legacies, its volumes recounting the central issues of 20th-century Jewish life from an American Jewish perspective.

Another example of how the *Year Book* reported through American Jewish eyes was its coverage of the infamous 1903 Kishinev pogrom in Russia. The Easter-time attack, which killed 47 Jews and wounded more than 400 others, dominated Jewish public life in 1903, so much so that Rabbi Maxmillian Heller, writing in the *Year Book,* dubbed 1903 "the year of Kishineff."[27] Instead of rehearsing the horrors, however, Heller focused on the response to them, especially in the United States. He described the "great meetings of protest . . . held all over the country," the "large sums of money . . . collected," President Theodore Roosevelt's "cordial and sincere address," and the petition to the czar that "an imposing array of the

---

[24]Ibid., p. 102.
[25]Ibid., p. 96.
[26]Ibid., p. 103.
[27]Vol. 5 (1903–04), p. 17.

most resplendent names in American public life" had signed and that the State Department had unsuccessfully attempted to deliver.[28] With British Jewry divided on how to deal with the pogrom, he argued, American Jewry had taken over the leadership of the cause. His conclusion, which certainly echoed what many American Jews of the time believed, was that the Kishinev affair:

> Gave to American Jewry the hegemony of the world's Judaism by proving that American Jews have the courage and the public spirit openly to espouse the cause of their brothers as they stand ready to make the sacrifice involved in keeping open to the Jewish refugee this last asylum of the oppressed; they not only showed themselves possessed of the statesmanship which is equal to a great emergency, but they demonstrated that they have a Government back of them for which the resentment of the greatest of autocracies has no terrors, that they are equally sure of the active sympathy of their best fellow-citizens whenever they turn to them in a humanitarian cause.[29]

This conviction that American Jewry had emerged from the periphery to stand at the very center of world Jewish life animated much of what the Jewish Publication Society and its leaders did during the late-19th and early-20th centuries, and was repeatedly reinforced by *Year Book* authors. In 1902, a woman with the arresting name of Martha Washington Levy quoted predictions, made in connection with the arrival on America's shores of the great Jewish scholar Solomon Schechter, that "in this country will lie, in the near future, the centre and focus of Jewish religious activity and the chosen home of Jewish learning." She went on to argue that "the centre of gravity of Judaism itself, in much that marks its highest aims, is tending toward this side of the water."[30] Two years later, the Jewish merchant and communal leader Cyrus Sulzberger, reviewing the year, listed a range of positive developments taking place throughout the United States and concluded that "American Jewry looks with confidence into the future."[31] Two years after that, the Jewish educator Julius Greenstone wrote of America's "blessed shores" for Jews and proudly pointed out that the year's "most important event in Jewish literary circles" transpired that year in America: "the publication of the last volume of the Jewish Encyclopedia."[32]

By then the *Year Book* had formally "taken for its province the assem-

---

[28]Ibid., pp. 21–22; Cyrus Adler, *The Voice of America on Kishineff* (Philadelphia, 1904), pp. 476–80.

[29]Vol. 5 (1903–04), p. 39. See also Philip E. Schoenberg, "The American Reaction to the Kishinev Pogrom of 1903," *American Jewish Historical Quarterly* 63, March 1974, pp. 262–83.

[30]Vol. 4 (1902–03), p. 15.

[31]Vol. 6 (1904–05), p. 39.

[32]Vol. 8 (1906–07), pp. 263, 274.

bling of some of the important facts of American Jewish life,"[33] and to that end it began to move beyond the year in review to offer both historical and reference articles about American Jews—a subject of enormous personal interest to editor Cyrus Adler. In 1902 it published "A Sketch of the History of the Jews in the United States," probably written by Adler himself, as well as an adulatory biographical article on the 19th-century American Jewish naval commodore Uriah P. Levy, authored by Simon Wolf. Later it gave space to popular historical articles (as distinct from the dry-as-dust scholarly articles that the American Jewish Historical Society published) on such early American Jewish heroes as Gershom Seixas, "the Patriot Jewish Minister of the American Revolution," and the antebellum Charleston poetess, Penina Moïse.

At the same time, the *Year Book* initiated in 1903 what Adler described as "the first installment of an American Jewish Who's Who." This consisted of 363 laboriously compiled sketches of "the spiritual guides of American Jewry"—rabbis and cantors—and was followed in subsequent volumes by hundreds more such treatments of Jews prominent in the professions, arts, sciences, journalism, business, and public life, and of Jewish communal workers. Adler and Henrietta Szold believed that this work would make American Jews more aware "of the forces at their disposal"—the many Jews who were making their mark on American and American Jewish life.[34] They therefore endlessly bewailed the large number of Jews who failed to return the circulars sent to them and who (unless information concerning them was available elsewhere) had therefore to be excluded. Today, of course, students of American Jewish history are grateful for the names that *were* included, since frequently the brief *Year Book* biographies provide information available nowhere else. By the time a more comprehensive *Who's Who in American Jewry* appeared, in 1926, many of these Jews had passed from the scene.

As it approached its tenth volume (1908–09), the *American Jewish Year Book* had proved its worth, receiving wide recognition as the leading reference work of its type. But it also proved to be an overwhelming administrative and financial burden, one far greater than the Jewish Publication Society had ever envisaged. The JPS recovered some costs by printing its own annual report and membership roster in the *Year Book,* instead of separately as heretofore, but the underlying problem admitted to no easy solution. Year after year, preparation of the *Year Book* pitted those who counted costs against those who strove for quality.

Henrietta Szold at the JPS usually came down on the side of quality,

---

[33] Vol. 5 (1903–04), pp. viii–ix.
[34] Vol. 6 (1904–05), p. vii.

and then volunteered to do the extra work necessary to guarantee it—without additional compensation. But as time went on the burden became too great even for her, especially when she became the *Year Book*'s coeditor with Cyrus Adler in 1904, and then sole editor two years later (the only time a woman edited the *Year Book* single-handedly). Her letters are filled with complaints about the "crazy orgy of work" and the "hated drudgery" involved in the annual labor; one evening in 1907 she "collapsed entirely" over it. In a particularly poignant letter to her then dear friend Dr. Louis Ginzberg, she described herself as a "veritable martinet, writing to certain organizations that would not answer, and writing again, and still again, all but sending . . . the sheriff after them." But to no avail: "The stars with which I conscientiously mark unofficial information remain numerous in spite of the eighteen hundred personal letters I have dictated . . . not to mention circulars galore." Still, individuals became angry when they found themselves or their organizations excluded from the *Year Book,* even if the exclusions resulted from their own neglect.

The fundamental question that the leaders of the Jewish Publication Society faced was whether all of this time, effort, energy, and money could be justified. Critics from among the membership of the JPS insisted that the answer was no. They found the massive amounts of data dull and repetitive, felt annoyed that the JPS produced the volume year in and year out even when it was one of only three volumes published during the year, and demanded that the *Year Book* be published, if at all, only once every few years so that it might prove less of a drain on limited resources. Community professionals, however, considered the *Year Book* essential, not only for Jews but for non-Jews. They noted that many libraries included the volume in their reference collections, and expected an updated edition annually—which, after all, is what made it a yearbook.

For a time, the JPS attempted to raise money for the *Year Book* separately, by raising the cover price to nonmembers and by selling advertisements on inside pages. There were ads for schools, books, magazines, clothing, railroads, insurance, even ads for Carmel wines "for the sick and convalescent" and for those who needed to "make blood."[35] By 1907, however, the *Year Book*'s annual cost, the enormous administrative burden of producing it, and the dissatisfaction of JPS members demanded a reexamination of the *Year Book.* Moreover, Henrietta Szold, emotionally distraught over her failed love affair with Louis Ginzberg, sought time off to travel abroad. She suggested to her boss, Judge Mayer Sulzberger—who was simultaneously chairman of the JPS Publication Committee and president of the newly organized American Jewish Com-

---

[35]Vol. 8 (1906–07), p. *29.

mittee—that AJC take over the time-consuming statistical and research aspects of the *Year Book*. Given the AJC's belief that, as a defense agency, its proper function was "enlightenment," and given, too, its emphasis on the need to base social planning upon "scientific inquiry," this division of labor seemed to make good sense.[36]

The Committee, however, went further—further, indeed, than Henrietta Szold herself wanted. Its leaders, many of whom were also active in JPS, agreed to take over total responsibility for compiling the *Year Book*, to supply an editor from within its own ranks (though JPS continued to supply editorial assistance, and Henrietta Szold continued to devote long hours to the work behind the scenes for several more years), and even to contribute $1,500 toward the *Year Book*'s publication costs. JPS, according to the new plan, would continue to serve as publisher, would pay the cost of printing its own report in the volume, and would assume responsibility for overall distribution. Both sides applauded the new agreement, and it came into effect in time to prepare the tenth *Year Book*, scheduled for 1908. For that issue, Herbert Friedenwald, secretary of the American Jewish Committee (and Cyrus Adler's brother-in-law), took over as editor, and with him a new era in *Year Book* history began.[37]

Year Book *as Advocate*

Herbert Friedenwald (1870–1944) was born into one of Baltimore's most illustrious Jewish families. He received a Ph.D. in American history, served as the first superintendent (1897–1900) of the manuscript division of the Library of Congress, and was a founder and deeply engaged member of the American Jewish Historical Society. At the American Jewish Committee he served as executive secretary—the chief administrative officer—providing the Jewish titans who ran the organization with the information they needed to formulate policy.[38] The *American Jewish Year Book* came to serve as the permanent repository for this data, its published articles often undergirding AJC's policy positions.

Since the American Jewish Committee's stated purpose was "to prevent infringement of the civil and religious rights of Jews, and to alleviate the consequences of persecution,"[39] the *Year Book* focused more than ever, under Friedenwald, on the central issues affecting world Jewry: the dis-

---

[36]See Naomi W. Cohen, *Not Free to Desist: The American Jewish Committee, 1906–1966* (Philadelphia, 1972), pp. 33–34.

[37]The above five paragraphs adapted from Sarna, *JPS*, pp. 72–73, where full documentation is provided.

[38]Vol. 46 (1944–45), pp. 47–54.

[39]Cohen, *Not Free to Desist,* p. 17.

crimination and oppression that Jews continued to experience in Russia, the possible curtailment of their free immigration into the United States, and manifestations of anti-Jewish prejudice at home and abroad. In every case, the *Year Book* stressed the American dimension of the situation, and, even more significantly, it displayed an activist tone not previously found in its pages.

In 1909, for example, the *Year Book* published a lead article on "The Passport Question," the campaign to abrogate America's 1832 treaty of commerce with Russia. The Russian treaty, negotiated during the presidency of Andrew Jackson, provided for "reciprocal liberty of commerce and navigation," and promised inhabitants of both countries freedom of entry, residence, and movement, as well as protection on a par with natives, provided only that they submit "to the [domestic] laws and ordinances . . . and particularly to the regulations in force concerning commerce." This proved uncontroversial until Russia, in the late 19th century, issued a series of "laws and ordinances" severely restricting the commercial and residence rights of Jews, and then interpreted this treaty to mean that Jews visiting from America also needed to submit to them. Beginning in 1865, and especially after 1881, Russia selectively denied visas to American Jews on grounds of their religion. Russia was not exactly a popular destination for turn-of-the-century American Jews, and those with wealth could usually obtain visas if they wanted them. Still, the effect of the Russian policy clearly discriminated: while most American citizens easily gained visas to enter Russia, American Jews, as a rule, did not.

The American Jewish Committee, according to Friedenwald's assistant (and later *Year Book* editor) Harry Schneiderman, focused on this issue for a high-minded reason, "the deep conviction that it was fighting not only to end the legalization of discrimination by a foreign power, as between American citizens, on the basis of religion, but also to uphold and safeguard the sanctity of the American principle of equality of all citizens, regardless of ancestry or religious affiliation."[40] We now know, however, that there was an even more compelling, unstated, reason motivating the AJC stand. As the Jewish banker Jacob Schiff admitted in a private letter to *New York Times* editor Adolph S. Ochs, "the moment Russia is compelled to live up to its treaties and admit the foreign Jew into its dominion upon a basis of equality . . . the Russian Government will not be able to maintain the pale of settlement against its own Jews."[41] While officially and in the *Year Book* the battle was fought solely on the

---

[40]Vol. 46 (1944–45), p. 49.
[41]Cyrus Adler, *Jacob H. Schiff: His Life and Letters* (Garden City, N.Y., 1929), pp. 151–52.

basis of the American principle of equality, those on the inside understood that the hidden "Jewish" agenda was to undermine discriminatory Russian laws that barred Jews from major commercial centers and confined them within a prescribed area of settlement.[42]

The *Year Book* played a critical role in the "Passport" campaign. A 1909 article by Friedenwald, expanding on an article from the 1904 volume, included all resolutions passed by Congress on the subject dating back to 1879. The article closed on an upbeat note—"the hope is reasonable that the present administration will accomplish what was unattainable by its predecessors"—but Friedenwald made clear in his preface to the volume that if it did not, American Jews would fight for their rights. Using language that the previous editors would never have permitted, he wrote that "the continued discrimination by the Russian Government against American citizens of the Jewish faith . . . is an infringement upon the equal rights of our people which, as American citizens, they will energetically contend against until this disability is removed."[43]

Two years later, when the American Jewish Committee's faith that President Taft would remedy the situation was shattered, its leaders fulfilled this pledge, and again they utilized the *Year Book* as one of their main platforms. A 110-page brief, written by Friedenwald and published as the lead article in 1911, set forth a full history of the "Passport Question," complete with numerous documents attesting to "hopes [that] have not been realized." Self-confidently and deftly exploiting the sinking political fortunes of President Taft, the *Year Book* appealed directly "to the people of the United States." "We have Petitioned for Redress . . . . Our repeated Petitions have been answered only by repeated injury," it concluded, echoing the Declaration of Independence. In the belief that the "righteousness" of its cause would ultimately triumph, the AJC, through the *Year Book,* submitted its "Facts . . . . to a candid world."[44] As added ammunition (not disclosed in the *Year Book*), AJC, behind the scenes, organized mass demonstrations, newspaper editorials, and petition campaigns, and even dangled discreet political promises. On December 18, 1911, these efforts bore fruit. President Taft, seeking to head off certain congressional action, gave notice of America's intention to terminate the 1832 treaty. The *Year Book,* echoing the sentiments of the American Jewish Committee, exulted. It dubbed the successful conclusion of its long campaign an event of "epochal significance," ranking it hyperbolically

---

[42]Judith Goldstein, *The Politics of Ethnic Pressure: The American Jewish Committee Fight Against Immigration Restriction, 1906–1917* (New York, 1990), pp. 143–44; Cohen, *Not Free to Desist,* p. 59.

[43]Vol. 11 (1909–10), pp. 43, vii.

[44]Vol. 13 (1911–12), pp. 13, 42, 54, 62.

"with such historical events as the emancipation of the Jews in France and the removal of the disabilities of the Jews of England, if it does not surpass them in importance."[45]

As it turned out, the political success achieved in the "Passport" campaign proved disappointingly fleeting. The tactics that succeeded in forcing the president's hand failed to work their magic when circumstances changed, and in their second major political battle of the early 20th century—the effort to keep America's doors open to immigrants—the Jewish community came up short.

Once again, the cause was spearheaded by the American Jewish Committee and played out in the pages of the *Year Book*. In 1908, the *Year Book* reprinted a letter sent by AJC president Mayer Sulzberger to Senator William Dillingham. "We are keenly alive to the right and duty of every government to protect its people," Sulzberger informed the senator—who chaired a new congressional commission investigating the subject of immigration—but "we deprecate most sincerely any nerveless or unmanly timidity about evils which may be coolly and sanely guarded against, without violating our national traditions and the dictates of common humanity, or depriving our country of a natural and healthy means of increasing its population and prosperity." He warned against "persons . . . carried away by passion," and requested permission for the AJC itself to present evidence to the commission, promising, somewhat disingenuously, to supply "facts, without color or prejudice."[46] Actually, AJC leaders were "uptown" Jews, mostly Central European in origin, and sometimes they did display prejudice against their East European brethren. Yet they remained stalwart in their commitment to the idea of America as an immigrant haven. Year in and year out, the *Year Book* monitored congressional action bearing on immigration—in a section entitled "the Government of the United States and affairs of interest to the Jews"—and it carefully documented for the AJC and for Jewish voters not only what legislation had been proposed but also how individual senators and congressmen had responded. Its pro-immigration sentiments were unmistakable.

As the clamor of the restrictionists grew louder, the *Year Book*'s defense of immigrants became more spirited. In 1910 its lead article was "In Defense of the Immigrant," and it devoted some 80 pages to the testimony offered by such Jewish leaders as Simon Wolf, Cyrus L. Sulzberger, Louis Marshall, Abram I. Elkus, and Max Kohler before the House Committee on Immigration and Naturalization, which the *Year Book* considered

---

[45]Vol. 14 (1912–13), p. v.
[46]Vol. 10 (1908–09), pp. 244–45.

"the best collection of information bearing upon the subject of Jewish immigration ever got together." Every charge leveled against East European Jewish immigrants—criminality, economic dependency, aversion to farming, resistance to Americanization, and more—was exhaustively refuted, and the immigrants themselves won extravagant praise for their desire, as one witness put it, "not only to become acquainted with our language and our customs, but to become thoroughly acquainted with the spirit of Americanism and to try their best to become American citizens of the real type."[47]

In 1912, following the publication of the Dillingham Commission's voluminous report on immigration, the *Year Book* warned "the friends of the immigrant," that they "must be prepared for another contest, to prevent him from being shut out of the country." It insisted, against the views of Congress, that the report, issued at the end of 1910, furnished "no justification" for immigration restriction. In fact, it charged (with considerable justification, as historian Oscar Handlin has subsequently shown[48]) that the summary of the report "made hasty generalizations" unsupported by the evidence that the commission itself had collected. The implication was clear, and the report of the American Jewish Committee, published in the *Year Book,* trumpeted the call to action. It urged "all those who favor the maintenance of this country's traditions" to exert their influence "to oppose drastic changes in our immigrant laws."[49] The *Year Book* also published as its main article that year a long study of "Agricultural Activities of the Jews in America," an obvious effort to rebut claims, heard even in Congress, that Jewish immigrants were "unproductive" and crowded into cities. The truth, according to the *Year Book* (which exaggerated) was that Jewish agricultural activity in the United States had displayed "remarkable growth" during the first decade of the century, largely owing to immigration, and that "the movement of the Jews in the United States toward the farm has gone beyond the capacity of any organization or any number of organizations to control."[50]

For all of the *Year Book*'s efforts, however, the battle to thwart immigration restriction was ultimately lost. While Jewish advocacy, chronicled in the *Year Book,* repeatedly delayed the passage of the literacy test for immigrants, and then ensured that victims of religious persecution were exempted from it, the legislation eventually passed over a presidential veto in 1917. Subsequently, in the face of burgeoning anti-Semitism, fervent

---

[47]Vol. 12 (1910–11), pp. vii, 19–98, esp. p. 67.
[48]Oscar Handlin, *Race and Nationality in American Life* (Garden City, N.Y., 1957), pp. 74–101.
[49]Vol. 14 (1912–13), pp. vii, 295.
[50]Ibid., p. 55; cf. Vol. 12 (1910–11), pp. 35, 64–65.

nationalism, and overwhelming anti-immigrant sentiment in the early 1920s, a highly restrictive anti-immigrant quota was imposed that reduced Jewish immigration by more than 80 percent.[51]

In addition to the great campaigns over the passport issue and immigration, the *Year Book,* under Friedenwald, devoted more space than before to battling anti-Jewish prejudice in the United States. The very first volume Friedenwald edited, in 1908, carried a long, somewhat awkwardly titled article on "Sunday Laws of the United States and Leading Judicial Decisions Having Special Reference to the Jews." Since Sunday laws effectively discriminated against those who observed the Sabbath on Saturday, the subject had long been of concern to Jews, affecting them more than any other church-state issue. For Sabbath observers, these "blue laws" served as a weekly reminder that, religious liberty notwithstanding, they paid a stiff price to uphold the tenets of their faith. Rather than complaining outright, however, the *Year Book,* in this instance, made its case indirectly, using the words of a prominent non-Jewish jurist to legitimate its cause. Judge Thomas M. Cooley of Michigan, the distinguished author of *Constitutional Limitations,* was highly critical of American Sunday laws and it was with a powerful quote from him that the *Year Book* article closed:

> But the Jew who is forced to respect the first day of the week, when his conscience requires of him the observance of the seventh also, may plausibly urge that the law discriminates against his religion, and by forcing him to keep a second Sabbath in each week, unjustly, though by indirection, punishes him for his belief.[52]

The *Year Book* also noted, especially in its annual review of the year, a range of anti-Jewish incidents across the country. Yet, whereas in its listing for Eastern Europe, similar incidents were assumed to reflect the pervasive anti-Semitism of the local populations and regimes, in America case after case was presented as an aberration, and the *Year Book* seemed happy to note that the problem had quickly been rectified. So, for example, it reported in 1909 on "the statement of Commissioner of Police Theodore A. Bingham, of New York, that alien Jews make up one-half of our criminals." It then explained that the statement "was completely disproved by statistics, and it was withdrawn." Another potentially explosive report—that a marine in uniform had been barred from synagogue services—was caused, it disclosed, by a "newspaper distortion" that "promised to have unpleasant consequences." Happily, these consequences "were averted by the prompt action of the American Jewish

---

[51]Cohen, *Not Free to Desist,* pp. 37–53.
[52]Vol. 10 (1908–09), p. 189; Also see Jonathan D. Sarna and David G. Dalin, *Religion and State in the American Jewish Experience* (South Bend, Ind., 1997), pp. 139–65.

Committee." In yet a third case that year, in Springfield, Illinois, a "local chief of police attempted to fasten upon the Jews the responsibility for the lynching of negroes." Once again, the evil decree was averted: the Jew involved, "Abraham Raymers . . . was acquitted."[53]

The most infamous case of American anti-Semitism from this period, the 1913 arrest, trial, and subsequent lynching of Leo Frank in Atlanta on charges of murdering a young Christian employee named Mary Phagan, did not, of course, fit this pattern. The *Year Book,* however, totally ignored the case until Frank was dead, and then dismissed it in exactly one sentence: "August 16 [1915]. Leo M. Frank, leading figure in celebrated murder trial, victim of mob near Marietta, Ga." Many Jews, in a private capacity, had tried to help Frank, believing him to have been the innocent victim of anti-Semitic hysteria—which we now know to have been the case. At the same time, however, Jewish leaders feared that any effort to turn the case into a "Jewish issue"—as opposed to a "matter of justice"—would harm the Jewish community and not help Frank at all. The American Jewish Committee, in the end, resolved to take no official action on the case, even though its president, Louis Marshall, vigorously advocated Frank's cause in his private capacity as a lawyer. The *Year Book* apparently took its cue from this policy decision, and its silence gave further evidence of the American Jewish community's unwillingness at that time to confront anti-Semitism openly. The less said publicly about it, Jews thought, the better.[54]

To be sure, the *Year Book* did notice some anti-Jewish manifestations that continued to fester. "Jacques Loeb, biologist Rockefeller Institute," the *Year Book* of 1913 reported, was "excluded from Century Club, New York City."[55] Such social discrimination against Jews was quite the norm by that time—even in the case of the Century Club, which Jews had helped to found—and all the *Year Book* could do was publicize the slight. Worse news, too, was recorded: In Roxbury, Massachusetts, Jews at a mass meeting adopted a resolution "protesting against assaults upon them and demanding more adequate police protection."[56] Nothing came of the meeting, and physical attacks on Jews in Boston continued into the 1930s, protests notwithstanding. Still, the overwhelming impression presented by the *Year Book* of that time was that anti-Jewish prejudice was antithetical to America, and could be combated—America, the *Year Book* insisted, was not Europe.

The same sense of American uniqueness apparently underlay Frieden-

---

[53]Vol. 11 (1909–10), pp. 62–63.
[54]Vol. 18 (1916–17), p. 86; Leonard Dinnerstein, *The Leo Frank Case* (New York, 1968), esp. pp. 74–76.
[55]Vol. 15 (1913–14), p. 246.
[56]Ibid., p. 244.

world's reorganization of the way the *Year Book* presented the "leading events" of the year. American Jewish news now came first and generally occupied more space than the listing of events in any other country. One year, the events were actually divided into two sections, "the United States" and "Other Countries," as if Jews everywhere outside of America—including Palestine—occupied a totally different realm.[57] Later, the division was modified to read "United States" and "Foreign Countries," but the subheadings proved telling. Under United States, the first category of news was "the Government of the United States and Affairs of Interest to the Jews." Under Russia, the parallel category of news was "Persecution and Repression."[58]

The *Year Book*'s most significant paean to America in that era came in 1913–14, when it devoted more than a quarter of the volume to a celebration of the 25th anniversary of the Jewish Publication Society (1888–1913). Since the JPS had founded and continued to publish the *Year Book,* the decision to devote so much space to the anniversary was natural. As the published proceedings reveal, however, the celebration was much more than an institutional birthday party. It also served as a public declaration that American Jewry had arrived and was making significant cultural contributions. "You in America are setting an example," the Anglo-Jewish author and bibliophile Elkan Adler wrote in a letter published in the proceedings; "indeed," he continued, "the eyes of Jewry are nowadays directed westward across the ocean . . . ." The great Yiddish author Isaac Leib Peretz wrote from Warsaw, "How we envy you, our free brethren in a free land!" The Orientalist Nahum Slouschz, writing from Paris, compared American Jewry to the former great Jewish centers of "Jerusalem, Tiberias, Pumbedita, Toledo, and Wilna," and wrote that "the great Jewish metropolis of the United States is preparing for the bright day of the future renaissance."[59] Overall, the anniversary celebration articulated and symbolized the central values that both the Jewish Publication Society and the *Year Book* stood for: the centrality of American Jewry, the unity of American Jews, and the perpetuation of Jewish life and culture. A message published in the *Year Book* from the leaders of Jews' College in London captured both the prevailing mood and the vision of the future that the *Year Book*'s own editors certainly shared:

> We on the other side, in the older country, watch with deepest interest the marvellous [*sic*] strides you have made and are making in this great and glo-

---

[57]Vol. 11 (1909–10), pp. 55, 67.
[58]Vol. 15 (1913–14), pp. 230, 232.
[59]Ibid., pp. 44, 48, 53.

rious land of freedom and independence, where careers and opportunities are open to talent and industry. . . . May you advance by leaps and bounds, and when we celebrate the Jubilee, which may we all live to see, when America will be the centre of Jewry, may this Publication Society be a world-wide organization fostering the Jewish spirit, strengthening the Jewish consciousness, giving adequate expression, and thus helping to do justice, to the Jewish life, the Jewish character, the Jewish soul.[60]

The 1913–14 *Year Book* was the last to be edited by Herbert Friedenwald. He resigned from the American Jewish Committee in 1913, apparently because of ill health, and, while still comparatively young, retired to private life. Replacing him proved to be a most difficult task. The AJC first turned to the Russian-born former *New York Times* journalist Herman Bernstein—the first East European Jew to hold a significant position at the organization—but he lasted only a year before returning to journalism. Joseph Jacobs, who had founded and edited England's *Jewish Year Book,* succeeded him, but he died in 1916 after editing only a single volume. Cyrus Adler, who by then was overwhelmed with administrative responsibilities elsewhere, filled in for a year, and then turned the job over to Samson Oppenheim, like Jacobs an expert in statistics and research. The *Year Book* thus passed through five different editors in five years, 1913–1918. It nevertheless managed to appear dependably every fall, its format largely unaffected by the changes at the helm.

The "Great War" and its Aftermath

This period of instability coincided with the largest war the world had ever seen, known then as the Great War, and later (after an even greater cataclysm) renamed World War I. From the beginning, the *Year Book* carefully chronicled the war's devastating impact on Jewish communities on both sides of the struggle, based on the sources available. In addition to "events affecting Jews," it listed a whole series of Jewish towns as having been "partially or wholly destroyed" by invading armies. The section on Russia, for example, noted the following:

SEPTEMBER 25 [1914]. Kalish: Seven hundred and fifty houses, mostly Jewish, burnt.—Dzevitza (Radom): Jewish quarter and synagogue burnt.—OCTOBER 16. Druskeniki burnt.—. . . [November] 25. Plotzk: Jewish townlet, and Blony and Bakalarzevo reported ruined by invaders. . . .[61]

The news from Austria-Hungary was no better:

---

[60]Ibid., pp. 155–56.
[61]Vol. 17 (1915–16), p. 269.

NOVEMBER 6 [1914]. Podheitze, Husiatyn, and Temboole: Galician Jewish townlets burnt in course of battle. — Halicz: The Jewish quarter burnt by retreating Austrians. — 13. Jewish quarters of Balshevitzi and Bolshabi, Galicia, burnt by Austrians. — 27. Belsitz and Burgatch, Jewish townlets, Galicia, almost completely destroyed. — Brod: Fire set to town; twelve Jews and three hundred houses burnt.[62]

At the same time, the *Year Book* chronicled the heroism of Jewish soldiers on both sides of the struggle, listing their battlefield decorations and promotions, as well as the names of those who gave their lives in battle. Lest anyone miss the point, Cyrus Adler, in 1916, underscored in his preface why the information was so important: "The list of events, if judged alone by the military promotions and the necrology on account of the war, shows conclusively that the Jewish people are taking their equal share in the stupendous conflict."[63]

The *Year Book* repeatedly apologized for its inability to present a full-scale narrative account of how the European war was affecting Jewish interests. It was simply too difficult to obtain full and accurate news from the war zone, it explained. Instead, in 1915, it provided background on one issue that the war was expected "to settle . . . for a long time to come," and that was "the fate of Palestine." An almost book-length article, written by Henrietta Szold, described "Recent Jewish Progress in Palestine," based on her wide reading as well as first-hand observations from her visit of a few years before. Her mood was characteristically upbeat, even concerning Arab-Jewish relations, which she found to be improving ("mutual respect is increasing"[64]). Her tone, moreover, was overtly pro-Zionist, even though she knew that the *Year Book*'s readers and sponsors remained deeply divided over the issue. Now that she was financially independent, she could be much more open about this than when she wrote the "Review of the Year" back in 1900. Her 1915 article was easily the best account of Jewish life in Palestine then available in English. As a guide to the future, however, it proved very wide of the mark. The impact that World War I would have on the Middle East eluded her completely.

America's entry into the war transformed the *Year Book*'s coverage. Eager once again to prove the dedication of American Jews to the war effort,[65] the *Year Book* marshaled statistical evidence compiled by the AJC's "Office of War Records" to demonstrate Jewish patriotism and heroism. A (probably generous) preliminary count, taken before Amer-

---

[62]Ibid., p. 226.
[63]Vol. 18 (1916–17), p. vi.
[64]Vol. 17 (1915–16), p. 95.
[65]See Cohen, *Not Free to Desist*, p. 100.

ica had entered the war, estimated the number of Jews in the United States armed forces at 4,585, or 6 percent of the fighting force—far more than the Jewish percentage of the population as a whole.[66] In the midst of the war (1918), the *Year Book* listed some 1,500 Jewish commissioned officers by name.[67] Julian Leavitt, who oversaw the collection of war records for the AJC, reported four positive, if preliminary, conclusions: (1) "that the Jews of America are acquitting themselves magnificently, as soldiers and citizens, in this war;" (2) "that their contributions of men and means tend to exceed, by a generous margin, their due quotas;" (3) "that the Jewish soldiers at the front fight with no less valor than their comrades;" and (4) "that their losses are as great—and their rewards no less."[68]

Beyond documenting military service, the *Year Book* reported with great pride on the material support that American Jews were supplying to those in need during the war, which was a turning point in the history of American Jewish philanthropy. An article on "Jewish War Relief Work," published before America's own entry into the war, recounted in bountiful detail how American Jews responded to the "beseeching eyes" of their fellow Jews around the world, and united to form a "Joint Distribution Committee" to coordinate war relief.[69] The JDC appropriated over $32 million between 1914 and 1920, according to subsequently published figures in the *Year Book*.[70]

American Jews also generously supported their own soldiers in uniform, through the medium of the Jewish Welfare Board (JWB). The War Department, the *Year Book* revealed, had sparked the creation of the JWB, since it needed a Jewish organization as a counterpart to the YMCA, which met the spiritual and social needs of Protestant soldiers, and the Knights of Columbus, which did the same for Catholics. "It is a commentary upon Jewish life in America," JWB executive director Charles J. Teller observed in an unusual editorial aside, "that with 260 years of history . . . and with literally thousands of organizations, no single agency could be selected as representative of the Jewry of America." The JWB was created to fill this void, with the mandate "to contribute on behalf of the Jews of America to the national work of welfare among the nation's uniformed men." Committed, as were the *Year Book,* the Jewish Publication Society, and the AJC, to the ideal of a unified American Jewry, the JWB proudly reported that it preached "no special –*ism* (ex-

---

[66]Vol. 18 (1916–17), pp. v–vi, 78.
[67]Vol. 20 (1918–19), pp. 173–227.
[68]Ibid., p. 112.
[69]Vol. 19 (1917–18), p. 194.
[70]Vol. 22 (1920–21), p. 343.

cept Judaism), and it permits none to be preached," attempting instead to meet the religious needs of soldiers in their camps "as these needs are there ascertained." It then proceeded to explain to *Year Book* readers *how* the JWB met the religious needs of Jewish soldiers, providing in the process a rare description of American Jewish religious pluralism played out in military life:

> For Jews desiring an orthodox service it promotes orthodox services. For sons of Reform Jews it supplies reform services with the Union Prayer Book. For the preponderating group of soldiers of orthodox Jewish families, whose requirements are best met by what is called Conservative Judaism, appropriate services are conducted accordingly. Without standardizing any doctrine of its own, the Welfare Board endorses all degrees of doctrine, if soldiers of Jewish faith uphold them.[71]

The "Great War" ended in 1918, but it still dominated the *Year Book* a year later. It was "not only fitting but also urgent," the book explained, "to record, while the recollection was still vivid, the salient facts respecting the participation of the Jews of various countries in the struggle."[72] The task fell to a new editor—again—but this time he was a man who had already assisted in the preparation of the *Year Book* for a decade, and would last in his new position for 28 more years: Harry Schneiderman (1885–1975). Born in Saven, Poland, Schneiderman immigrated to the United States in 1890 along with his parents and siblings, including his sister, Rose Schneiderman, later a prominent labor organizer and social reformer. While she was organizing the first female local of the Jewish Socialist United Cloth Hat and Cap Makers' Union,[73] he, upon graduating from the City College of New York in 1908, joined the staff of the anything-but-socialist American Jewish Committee. Almost immediately, he began to assist with the publication of the *Year Book*. Named assistant secretary of the AJC in 1914, in 1919 he undertook to edit the *Year Book* as well. His one-time boss, Morris Waldman, characterized him as "the chronicler par excellence of world Jewish events: detached, impartial, with the historian's perspective."[74]

Bringing these skills to the first volume under his supervision, Schneiderman published lengthy accounts of "The Participation of the Jews of France in the Great War," "The Story of British Jewry in the War," and "The Jewish Battalions and the Palestine Campaign." He also published another article by Julian Leavitt on "American Jews in the World War,"

---

[71]Vol. 20 (1918–19), p. 95.
[72]Vol. 21 (1919–20), p. v.
[73]Nancy Schrom Dye, "Rose Schneiderman," *Notable American Women: The Modern Period,* eds. Barbara Sicherman and Carol Hurd Green (Cambridge, Mass., 1980), p. 631.
[74]Morris D. Waldman, "Harry Schneiderman," *Universal Jewish Encyclopedia* (1943), vol. 9, p. 413.

though it was much shorter than his earlier piece, since a separate volume on the subject was planned. Still, Leavitt was able to confirm all of his earlier conclusions about Jewish heroism, explaining that "the qualities which had enabled the Jew to survive through the centuries—his capacity to endure, without breaking, prolonged and intense nerve strain; his qualities of initiative, his elasticity of mind, his capacity for organization, and above all, his idealism . . . [made] him a worthy fighter in America's cause."[75] Finally, Leavitt pointed to what he optimistically believed to be the lasting legacy of American Jewish participation in the war effort: a new appreciation, on the part of non-Jews, for what the Jewish soldier could accomplish:

> [I]t is no secret that when the regular army officers were, in the early days of mobilization, confronted with the problem of converting the city-bred Jews into what they conceived to be proper soldier material, they were openly sceptical, not to say apprehensive. But it was not long before the ready wit of the Jewish recruits, their cool intelligence, their amenability to discipline, and the deadly seriousness with which they threw themselves into the work, convinced all sceptics of their worth.[76]

As the Jewish soldiers returned from the front and America retreated into isolationism, the *Year Book* too shifted its focus back to domestic affairs. Once again, it sought to present a statistical portrait of American Jewish life based on questionnaires sent to Jewish organizations. Harry Schneiderman understood that "the manner in which the data were collected—almost exclusively through the mails—cannot be expected to yield complete and accurate results." Still, as a firm believer in the dispassionate character of facts and statistics, he presented what data he had. First, he revised the list of Jewish national organizations, and—under a new policy he initiated—added a brief introductory analysis to provide "a clearer interpretation of the facts presented." He pointed out that over one million American Jews were connected with one or another national Jewish organization, more than half of them in 15 fraternal orders and mutual benefit associations.[77]

He also updated the *Year Book*'s Directory of Local Jewish Organizations, last compiled 12 years earlier. In this case he concluded, based on less than fully persuasive evidence, that "two and one-half million of the three and one-third million Jews of the country, or nearly five out of six, come into direct contact with Jewish religious influences sometime during the year."[78] He also provided a tantalizing, if necessarily inadequate portrait of synagogue life in the United States (excluding New York

---

[75]Vol. 21 (1919–20), p. 155.
[76]Ibid., p. 148.
[77]Ibid., pp. 331, vi, 303.
[78]Ibid., p. 331.

City), showing that half of the congregations reporting held services only on Sabbaths and festivals, a little over a third met daily, and the rest far less frequently. Of these synagogues, 60 percent conducted services only in Hebrew; 12 percent only in English, and the rest in both. While the *Year Book* did not officially categorize these congregations by movement—believing, as it did, in Jewish unity, it rarely paid attention to Orthodox, Conservative, and Reform differences—the growing number of dual-language congregations was another sign that the Conservative movement in Judaism was steadily gaining ground.[79]

Finally, Schneiderman found a new way to list "Jewish Periodicals Appearing in the United States." He separated "general newspapers and magazines" from "organs of associations and trade journals," and presented in tabular form a full-scale portrait of the 145 periodicals, in four different languages (English, Yiddish, Hebrew, and Judeo-Spanish), that the postwar American Jewish community produced. Revealingly, not a single American Jewish periodical appeared any longer in German. Most first generation German-Jewish immigrants had passed from the scene by the end of World War I, and given the wave of anti-German hysteria that pervaded the country during the war, German periodicals could not survive.[80]

Getting the Facts

The *Year Book*'s renewed interest in statistics, carrying forward a tradition that went back to Joseph Jacobs and the English *Jewish Year Book,* was reinforced in 1919 by the establishment of an independent Bureau of Jewish Social Research, formed from a merger of the Bureau of Philanthropic Research, the Field Bureau of the National Conference of Jewish Charities, and the Bureau of Jewish Statistics and Research of the American Jewish Committee. According to its assistant executive director, Hyman Kaplan, writing in the *Year Book,* the bureau was designed to be the "social research agency of American Jewry, prepared to study its problems, to advance standards of philanthropic administration, and to serve as a central source of information on matters of sociological interest pertaining to Jewry all over the civilized world."[81] It promised to employ the "best standards in every phase of social endeavor" and to serve "as a guiding hand for executive action." Its "accumulated experience," it believed, could be "applied with redoubled ef-

---

[79]Ibid., p. 332.
[80]Ibid., p. 588.
[81]Vol. 22 (1920–21), pp. 37–38.

fect and economy" to find the "best solution," to the "many problems" of the Jewish community "still awaiting attention." Meanwhile, its surveys, many of which appeared in the *Year Book,* sought to promote efficiency and a greater degree of professionalism in Jewish life—goals similar to those advocated by urban reformers throughout the United States—as well as to provide factual ammunition for use in communal defense.

Lithuanian-born Harry Linfield, a Reform rabbi with a Ph.D. from the University of Chicago and a specialty in statistics, was the moving force behind the Bureau of Jewish Social Research. Later, in 1928, when the AJC ended its arrangement with the bureau, he came to head the statistical bureau of the AJC. Throughout the interwar period, the *Year Book's* most important quantitative studies were produced under his direction. An early study, "Professional Tendencies Among Jewish Students in Colleges, Universities and Professional Schools"—undertaken in 1918–19 just before many of these places initiated anti-Jewish quotas—examined 106 "prominent educational institutions" in order to secure "concrete information" concerning the professional career patterns of Jewish students. The information gathered—little known today even among scholars—sheds fascinating light on college training among postwar Jews. It is especially noteworthy for what it discloses about how Jews differed from their neighbors, and for its findings concerning Jewish women. The conclusions, which the study conveniently summarized, were as follows:

(1)   The Jewish enrolment in the 106 institutions covered is 14,837 or 9.7 per cent of the total registration, 153,085.
(2)   For the institutions in New York City, where comparison could be made on the basis of population, the proportion of Jewish students in the educational institutions is 38.5 per cent compared with a 25 per cent representation in the general population.
(3)   The proportion of Jewish female students to the Jewish registration is one to five, a much lower ratio than in the non-Jewish group where the proportion of females is more than one to three.
(4)   The following five branches of study, in the order mentioned, attract the largest number of Jewish students: Commerce and finance, medicine, engineering, law, and dentistry, representing together 84.5 per cent of the total Jewish enrolment in professional schools.
(5)   Of the total registration of Jewish female students 32.1 per cent are enrolled in departments of commerce and finance, 28.4 per cent in schools of education, and 14 per cent are in law schools, the latter proportion being almost equal to the proportion of Jewish men preparing to enter this field.[82]

---

[82]Ibid., p. 386.

In 1927, in conjunction with the United States Census, which at that time regularly surveyed "Religious Bodies," Linfield collected information on the Jewish population in the United States and on Jewish communal organizations. The most important and sophisticated study of the American Jewish population yet undertaken, it disclosed a raft of important new information that the *Year Book* published in two chart-filled articles occupying more than 250 pages. By 1927, Linfield found, the Jewish population of the United States stood at 4,228,029 (3.58 percent of the population), up from 3,388,951 (3.27 percent) ten years earlier. The Jewish population continued to grow at a faster rate than the general population, but he warned that "this growth is slowing down."[83] He also found Jews "widely distributed within the states," spread over no fewer than 6,420 cities, towns, and villages, as well as 3,292 rural unincorporated districts. Seeking, perhaps, to counter the image that Jews "crowded" into narrow regions of the country, he somewhat downplayed the fact that more than 90 percent of the Jews continued to live in the North, that 87 percent lived in only ten states (New York, Pennsylvania, Illinois, Massachusetts, New Jersey, Ohio, California, Connecticut, Michigan, and Missouri), and that 69 percent lived in but 11 cities—New York, Chicago, Philadelphia, Boston, Cleveland, Detroit, Baltimore, Los Angeles, Newark, Pittsburgh, and St. Louis.[84]

The data concerning Jewish organizations was even more revealing. Linfield found a total of 3,118 Jewish congregations in the United States, an increase of 1,217—more than 64 percent—from ten years before. This was particularly surprising since the Jewish population as a whole had only grown by 24.7 percent in the decade. The reason, he pointed out, was that synagogue growth had not previously kept pace with the growth of the Jewish population: the population increased more than 17 times over between 1877 and 1917, while the number of congregations had multiplied by less than six times. In the postwar period, however, as immigration lagged and Jewish communal wealth increased, new synagogues mushroomed. Linfield, in keeping with past *Year Book* practice, did not disclose how many synagogues followed Orthodox, Conservative, and Reform Judaism, but he did note that only 22 percent of them belonged to any national congregational federation at all; most remained independent. Moreover, only 56 percent of America's synagogues employed their own rabbis, another 5 percent shared rabbinic services, and the other 39 percent, including 112 (small) Jewish communities, had no rabbis at all. Moving beyond the synagogue, Linfield provided a blizzard of data

---

[83]Vol. 30 (1928–29), p. 158.
[84]Ibid., pp. 101–98.

concerning Jewish education, culture, and philanthropy. He counted 1,754 Jewish elementary schools of various kinds (including 12 day schools), 912 Jewish youth organizations, 2,957 "social-philanthropic organizations," another 3,699 that he described as "economic-philanthropic organizations" (loan societies, mutual benefit societies, cemetery societies, etc.), 62 institutions for the promotion of health, 1,019 organizations devoted to the care of dependents, 1,227 Zionist organizations (divided into ten national federations), and much more. He even counted the number of Jewish theaters in the United States—24—and revealed that in any given month they collectively "gave 645 performances of 86 different plays."[85] Never before, the *Year Book* boasted, had the "varied types of organization which have been developed as instruments for performing the multifarious functions required by our many-sided communal life" been so comprehensively described.[86]

Through most of the 1920s, the Bureau of Jewish Social Research's "guiding hand" shaped large sections of the *American Jewish Year Book,* especially as Harry Schneiderman was more than ever taken up with the affairs of the American Jewish Committee. Besides updating the population statistics on the basis of newly released census data, Harry Linfield also wrote the survey of the year till Schneiderman returned to the *Year Book* on a more full-time basis in 1928. Linfield reorganized the survey according to themes rather than by country, thereby making America seem much less distinctive than before. On the other hand, he added and enhanced the lists of appointments, honors, elections, bequests, gifts, and the necrology, all showcasing the achievements of Jews in American society.

Presenting Jews in a Good Light

This sharpened focus on Jewish achievements, while not wholly new, nevertheless reflected a heightened defensiveness on the part of American Jews. Anti-Semitism increased alarmingly in the postwar era as Americans, in Leonard Dinnerstein's words, grew "disillusioned with internationalism, fearful of Bolshevik subversion, and frightened that foreigners would corrupt the nation's values and traditions."[87] Henry Ford's rantings against "The International Jew: The World's Problem," in his widely circulated newspaper, the *Dearborn Independent,* coupled with social discrimination against Jews in many quarters, left the American Jewish com-

---

[85]Vol. 31 (1929–30), pp. 99–254.
[86]Ibid., p. iii.
[87]Leonard Dinnerstein, *Anti-Semitism in America* (New York, 1994), p. 78.

munity feeling uneasy and vulnerable. In subtle ways, the *Year Book* sought both to uplift it and to help it respond to critics. Thus in 1922 it published a list of about 1700 "Jews of Prominence in the United States." The list contained far less information than the biographical sketches printed back in 1903–06, and was described as "preparatory to an exhaustive 'Who's Who,' which is a desideratum" (in fact, after he retired from the *Year Book,* Schneiderman went on to edit *Who's Who in World Jewry*). Its virtue, if not its main aim, as the *Year Book* stated twice, was "to compile a new record of Jews who contribute to the sum of American life," and to serve as "an index to the contribution of Jews to the culture and civilization of America."[88]

The next volume, the 25th (1923–24), may well have been the most apologetic in the *Year Book's* entire history. Five different articles in the volume aimed to respond, in different ways, to anti-Semitic critics who maligned and belittled the Jewish people and its faith. Hannah London's seemingly innocuous article, "Portraits of Early American Jews"—a topic far removed from the *Year Book's* standard fare—underscored, in the words of its author, "the encouragement given to American art by the Jews who first came to these shores and helped to establish the foundations of our Republic." In a tacit response to those who claimed that Jews were interlopers in America who confined themselves to mercantile pursuits, the *Year Book* article underscored "the positions of usefulness occupied by many Jews in the Colonial period," and their role in the "development of the fine arts."[89]

Rabbi Moses Hyamson's article, revealingly entitled "The Jewish Method of Slaying Animals From the Point of View of Humanity," was a more obvious apologetic. An explicit response to calls for "the Jewish method of slaughtering animals [to] be abolished," on grounds of cruelty, the article patiently explained what the Jewish laws of *shehitah* (ritual slaughtering) entailed, and insisted that "the Jewish method of slaughter does not fall below, but, in many respects, is superior to all other methods . . . from the point of view of humanity and kindness to animals." In the best tradition of apologetics, it then proceeded to back up this claim by citing a bevy of great [non-Jewish] professors, surgeons, and physiologists who agreed.[90]

Professor Israel Davidson's article, entitled simply "Kol Nidre," dealt with a prayer that, the *Year Book* explained, "has been the occasion of much misunderstanding and even misrepresentation." Anti-Semites had

---

[88]Vol. 24 (1922–23), pp. iii, 111.
[89]Vol. 25 (1923–24), pp. 161, iii.
[90]Ibid., pp. iii, 174.

long pointed to the prayer, recited at the beginning of the evening service on the Day of Atonement, as evidence that Jewish oaths could not be trusted. Davidson's exceedingly learned article, more appropriate to a scholarly journal than to the *Year Book,* placed the prayer in a different context, explaining that it referred "only to vows in which the votary alone is involved, but not to those which concern other people." Concluding with an adage that might appropriately have been applied to the *Year Book* itself, he advised against indulging "in too many explanations, because friends do not need them and enemies would not believe them."[91]

The article that followed, Benjamin Harrow's "Jews Who Have Received the Nobel Prize," was far less esoteric. Occasioned by the Nobel Prize awarded in 1921 to Albert Einstein, it pointed out that Jews had won nine of the 107 Nobel Prizes distributed since they began, and that one of America's own five Nobel Prize winners was a Jew, Albert A. Michelson. In an era when anti-Semites labeled Jews as the source of major world problems, the article served as a timely reminder to the faithful that they had made important positive contributions to the world that should not be overlooked.

Finally, this volume of the *Year Book* published, in 25 pages of small print, the one and only full-scale rabbinic responsum ever to appear between its covers. Professor Louis Ginzberg's "A Response to the Question: Whether Unfermented Wine May be Used in Jewish Ceremonies," translated from the Hebrew, was, once again, an obvious apologetic, designed to put a stop to widespread rabbinic abuse of the Prohibition Enforcement Act which permitted the manufacture and sale of wine for sacramental or ritual purposes only. The American Jewish Committee, concerned that the image of the Jewish community was being tarnished by the many cases of "so-called Rabbis" who took advantage of the Act "to enable wine to be procured for non-ritual purposes," gleefully trumpeted Ginzberg's "profound and exhaustive study," mischaracterized it as showing "a distinct preference" in Jewish law "in favor of unfermented wine," and ordered it published in the *Year Book* so as to make its recondite learning "readily accessible."[92]

The following year, in a continuation of this defensive posture, the

---

[91]Ibid., p. 192.

[92]Ibid., pp. 377–79, 401–25. David Golinkin, *The Responsa of Professor Louis Ginzberg* (New York, 1996), pp. 111–33 [Eng. Section], 1–77 [Heb. Section], notes that the *Year Book* version "is much more than a translation" from the Hebrew, since it adds one new section and synopsizes much of the original. He also lists several errors (p. 132). See also Hannah Sprecher, "'Let Them Drink and Forget Our Poverty': Orthodox Rabbis React to Prohibition," *American Jewish Archives* 43, Fall–Winter 1991, pp. 134–179; and Baila R. Shargel, "Louis Ginzberg as Apologist," *American Jewish History* 79, Winter 1989–90, pp. 210–20.

Year Book published "The Yiddish Press—An Americanizing Agency," by Mordecai Soltes. The article appeared at the very moment that American nativism stood at its peak and immigration into the United States was being severely restricted by a new quota system based on geography. Opponents of immigration charged that foreigners fomented radicalism and undermined American values. They viewed foreign-language materials, particularly newspapers, with great suspicion; a few years earlier, during World War I, some had sought to ban such newspapers entirely. Soltes's study, originally his Columbia University Teachers College doctoral dissertation and later published separately as a book, responded to these charges. Without questioning the goals of Americanization, he argued that the Yiddish press in fact furthered these goals, creating an "environment which not only does not interfere, but actively coöperates with the civic and patriotic purposes of the school."[93] He admitted that the best-selling Yiddish newspaper, Abraham Cahan's *Forward,* supported socialism, but insisted that it disavowed radicalism and sought to improve working conditions through democratic means. Indeed, by the time he was done with his exhaustive, chart-filled analysis, he had composed a paean to the Yiddish press, crediting it with promoting in its readers every value that supporters of Americanization cherished:

> [I]t exhorts them to become citizens, to exercise their right to vote at the primaries and elections, and not to leave the control of politics entirely in the hands of professional politicians; to take advantage of their power to remedy the defects in our present social and industrial order by means of the ballot, and not to permit themselves to be swayed by agitators who advocate sabotage or terrorism; to adapt themselves to American conditions and standards, to leave the congested city life and to settle upon the farm; to organize and to remain faithful to their union, thereby aiding in maintaining proper American standards of living; in brief, not to remain strangers in this land but to become part and parcel of the American people.[94]

The original German-Jewish leaders of the American Jewish Committee might have balked at such praise of the Yiddish press. Privately, many of them disdained Yiddish as an embarrassing "jargon" of minor cultural significance, and the *Year Book* had not previously paid it much heed. But in the face of xenophobic attacks, and with the emergence of East European Jews (like Harry Schneiderman) into positions of influence, these old cultural battles were beginning to fade. As the *Year Book*'s articles amply demonstrated, American Jews were now much more united, bound together by common fears and a common determination to defend themselves against enemies both foreign and domestic.

93Vol. 26 (1924–25), p. 332.
94Ibid., pp. 328–29.

Years of Pessimism

In fact the old German-Jewish leadership of the American Jewish community was fast passing from the scene. The same issue of the *Year Book* that carried Soltes's article also noted the death of "an unusually large number" of the community's "most active leaders and public workers," including such well-known figures of German birth or descent as Rabbis Emil G. Hirsch, Joseph Krauskopf, and Henry Berkowitz, the lawyer and lobbyist Simon Wolf, and Judge Mayer Sulzberger. Subsequent issues noted other prominent deaths—California congressman Julius Kahn, Hebrew Union College president Kaufmann Kohler, former commerce secretary Oscar Straus, and many more. All of these men received "warm and sympathetic and, at the same time vivid portrayals"[95] in the *Year Book.* Recounting just five of their lives took up 99 pages in volume 26. By volume 50, some 74 prominent American Jews had been memorialized at length. They were selected, Schneiderman explained on one occasion, "because of the profound impress they made upon their generation, and because it is believed that their lives will inspire future generations to live nobly, in consonance with the most exalted teachings of Judaism."[96] He felt that the biographies, most of them chronicling the lives of elite German Jews, constituted "a key to the history of Jewish life in America during the past century."[97] They also served as a tribute to an era that was waning. In its wake, Jewish leadership opened up to a new generation of Jews, many of them East European in origin.

The *Year Book,* like the American Jewish community as a whole, had many doubts about what all this portended. Pessimism, marked by fears about anti-Semitism and the fate of Jews abroad, had replaced the optimism of the century's first two decades. The problems of assimilation and communal decline evoked great concern, as the children of the immigrants seemed to be abandoning the synagogue, and many Jewish organizations suffered financial reversals. As early as 1914, the Jewish educator Julius Greenstone had apprised *Year Book* readers of the challenge that lay ahead. "The problem with which American Jewry is now confronted," he warned, "is nothing less than the problem of self preservation, the problem of preserving the Jewish people in Judaism in the new environment." He estimated that "more than two-thirds" of American Jewish children were growing up "outside the sphere of any religious influence and guidance," and he admonished his fellow Jews to feel "not

---

[95]Vol. 33 (1931–32), p. iii.
[96]Ibid.
[97]Vol. 50 (1948–49), p. 95.

only anxious about our future, but thoroughly ashamed."[98] A subsequent article, published in 1921, warned of the need "to Americanize without dejudaizing the immigrant and his children."[99] Some of these fears concerning the future of Judaism seemed to be coming true by the end of the decade. Reform and Conservative rabbis, according to the *Year Book,* were lamenting that the synagogue was "being invaded by secularism."[100] The decline of the synagogue was so pronounced by the early 1930s that Judge Horace Stern of Pennsylvania wrote an entire article on the subject for the *Year Book,* blaming the problem, among other things, on competition from "automobiles, golf clubs, radios, bridge parties, extension lectures, and the proceedings of various learned and pseudo-learned societies."[101]

Even before the great stock market crash of 1929, a good many synagogues and other Jewish organizations had fallen upon hard times. Cyrus Adler declared in 1920 that "practically every Jewish organization of higher learning or science" in America "was broke."[102] The Jewish Publication Society, copublisher of the *Year Book,* was $120,000 in debt in the early 1920s, and later in the decade the fraternal order B'rith Abraham went bankrupt.[103] The *Year Book* itself was radically downsized for a time: volume 23, published in 1921, was condensed to 300 pages (plus reports), owing to "the greatly increased cost of paper, printing and binding," while volume 30, published in 1928, had to be compressed into just 270 pages (plus reports).

We know, in retrospect, that the problem was not confined to Jews. Historians of American religion now characterize the 1920s and early 1930s as an era of "religious depression" marked by declining church attendance and a deepening "secular" interest in universalism and the "cosmopolitan spirit."[104] Jews and Christians alike lamented, as Judge Stern did in the *Year Book,* that "religion at least in its organized forms, has to an appreciable extent lost its hold upon the present generation."[105] In its place, many young Jews turned to secular movements like socialism, Communism, and Zionism. The *Year Book* took little notice of these developments at the time, perhaps because neither its editors nor its spon-

---

[98]Vol. 16 (1914–15), pp. 92, 121.
[99]Vol. 23 (1921–22), p. 89.
[100]Vol. 32 (1930–31), p. 72.
[101]Vol. 35 (1933–34), pp. 162–63.
[102]As quoted in Sarna, *JPS,* p. 142.
[103]Vol. 30 (1928–29), p. 31.
[104]Robert T. Handy, "The American Religious Depression, 1925–1935," *Church History* 29, 1960, pp. 3–16.
[105]Vol. 35 (1933–34), p. 163.

sors had much contact with the younger generation. Instead, it registered the fears of an older generation.

What the *Year Book* certainly did notice was the Great Depression. It chronicled both the hardships in the Jewish community and Jewish efforts to relieve the suffering. "Every Jewish social service organization in the country," it reported in 1931, saw its facilities and services "in demand as never before, and yet, at the same time, their resources were drastically reduced." It found that "practically every local federation in the country was compelled to reduce its budget," and that some Jewish social service agencies combined forces "as a result of the hard times." Several factors increased Jewish suffering, it observed, including "the failure of banks in which a very large proportion of the depositors and investors were Jews, strikes in trades employing many Jews, and discrimination . . . against Jews seeking employment"—the latter a theme that the *Year Book* had only rarely noted before. Jewish educational agencies were particularly hard hit, "necessitating in many cases the reduction of teaching staffs and the consolidation of classes." Nor were religious institutions "immune from the effects of the business depression." Graduating rabbis could not find jobs, and existing synagogues in several communities were compelled to merge. More broadly, the *Year Book*'s annual listing of national Jewish organizations registered a small decline in 1930, its first since World War I, as three organizations went out of existence. The *Year Book* could not have realized at the time what historian Beth Wenger discovered only in retrospect, that "the Great Depression constituted a defining moment for American Jews, inaugurating alterations in Jewish families, occupational structures, political preferences, and communal organization that changed the face of Jewish life in the twentieth century."[106] What the *Year Book* did proudly record was that Jews not only participated "in all civic efforts to relieve suffering in general, but Jewish organizations also established special agencies to help meet the crisis." The Hebrew Immigrant Aid Society (HIAS) opened its facilities to those needing food and shelter; synagogues welcomed the homeless; Jewish employment bureaus were formed; and special fund-raising campaigns were initiated.[107]

The domestic problems that plagued American Jewry in the wake of the Great Depression diverted the community's attention from the international arena. As the *Year Book* itself admitted in 1931, "the Jews of the United States did not during the past years watch the situation of their overseas co-religionists with the same concentration as in the preceding

---

[106]Beth S. Wenger, *New York Jews and the Great Depression* (New Haven, 1996), p. 9.
[107]Vol. 33 (1931–32), pp. 38–44.

twelve months."[108] Nevertheless, the annual "Review of the Year" did continue to monitor the unsettling developments in Germany, where Adolf Hitler was gaining in popularity.

Chronicling the Nazi Menace

Back in 1928, the *Year Book* had described Hitler as a "notorious agitator" and noted approvingly that "anti-Jewish demonstrations were suppressed whenever their proceedings went beyond legal bounds."[109] Hitler's activities received continuing notice in the ensuing volumes, and in 1931, after his National Socialists became the second largest party in the *Reichstag* (German parliament) by gaining 95 seats in the September 1930 elections, the *Year Book* reported "the same exhibitions of anti-Semitic fury and folly as have come to be universally associated with the Hitler movement—street attacks against Jews, molestation of Jews in cafes and theatres, disturbance of religious services in synagogues and of Jewish meetings of all kinds, desecration of synagogues, and pollution of cemeteries."[110] German-Jewish leaders, who maintained close ties to the American Jewish Committee, played down the Hitler threat at that time, and the *Year Book,* to some extent, echoed their views. It cited Albert Einstein in describing support for the Nazis as "a symptom of despair in the face of depressed economic conditions and unemployment," and described the American Jewish community as being hopeful that the debt moratorium declared by President Herbert Hoover would improve Germany's economic situation and thus deal the National Socialist movement a "serious setback."[111]

These hopes proved illusory, and when Hitler became Germany's chancellor in 1933 the *Year Book* reversed itself. The preface to volume 35 began with the announcement that the year "will stand out in the post-exilic history of the Jewish people as the year in which a country universally regarded as an outpost of civilization and culture permitted itself to be led astray by a malicious race mania onto a path of the most degrading mass persecution." It described the "world-shocking catastrophe which has befallen the Jews of Germany" as a development of "momentous significance to Jews everywhere," and devoted many pages to chronicling the events in Germany in frightening detail.[112] The next year, it chillingly listed "the names of a number of distinguished German Jews who

---

[108]Ibid., p. 23.
[109]Vol. 30 (1928–29), p. 40.
[110]Vol. 33 (1931–32), p. 76.
[111]Ibid., pp. 35, 75.
[112]Vol. 35 (1933–34), pp. iii, 21–39.

died by their own hands" as well as others, "ousted from the laboratories and lecture halls of German colleges and universities," whom, it said (with some exaggeration), were "cordially welcomed" in other countries.[113] By 1935 it was warning of a "deliberate premeditated policy of a ruling clique ruthlessly to exterminate German Jewry—a policy springing from maniacal adherence to a fanatical dogma of race nationalism." Presciently, it also noticed that Nazism was extending beyond Germany's borders and "threatening the welfare of Jews in a number of countries outside of Germany."[114]

The press, even some Jewish newspapers, underreported German atrocities in the 1930s and misinterpreted their significance. The *New York Times,* for example, as Deborah Lipstadt and others have shown, "was anxious not to appear 'too Jewish,' " and therefore paid more attention to the deaths of non-Jewish civilians than to the murder of Jews.[115] Even the Jewish Telegraphic Agency, Haskel Lookstein has shown, had a "tendency . . . to bury atrocity stories rather than to give them prominence."[116] Not so the *American Jewish Year Book.* Throughout the 1930s it documented in graphic detail both the Nazi horrors and the sorry plight of German-Jewish refugees. At the height of its concern, in the annual review of the year covering July 1, 1938–June 30, 1939, it warned of the "speeding up of the continuing process of liquidation of what still remained of Jewish life and interests in Germany." There is "no doubt," it mourned, "that the Nazi Government was bent upon annihilating the last vestiges of the German-Jewish community." It then proceeded to elaborate, revealing "the murder of hundreds of Jews in concentration camps," as well as the "frequent arrests and expulsions of Jews," both native born and immigrants. The dramatic conclusion—tragically prophetic and largely ignored in 1939—was that Germany would "not rest with the annihilation of the Jewish community within her own frontiers, but sought insofar as it was able, to visit the same fate upon Jews all over the world."[117]

More, perhaps, than any other single English-language source in the United States, the *Year Book* chronicled the unfolding tragedy not just of German Jewry but of European Jewry as a whole. Thus, 11 pages of small print in 1939 detailed the decline of Czechoslovak Jewry, particularly following the Munich Pact of September 1938 which, as the *Year*

---

[113]Vol. 36 (1934–35), p. iii.
[114]Vol. 37 (1935–36), p. 135.
[115]Deborah E. Lipstadt, *Beyond Belief: The American Press and the Coming of the Holocaust, 1933–1945* (New York, 1986), pp. 155, 169–71.
[116]Haskel Lookstein, *Were We Our Brothers' Keepers?* (New York, 1985), p. 49.
[117]Vol. 41 (1939–40), pp. 261, 264, 268.

Book put it, "proved to be as disastrous to the Jewish population as to the Czechoslovak State itself." Seven pages chronicled the deteriorating situation of Hungarian Jewry, where anti-Jewish laws undermined Jewish life, and domestic support of Nazism rose precipitously. With tragic accuracy, the *Year Book,* summarizing the situation, expressed "gloomy forebodings regarding the future." Turning to Italy, the *Year Book* reported in six pages on how the " 'Aryanizing' machinery was set into motion" by Mussolini, with the result that Jews were being excluded from political, economic, and social life. Though "the policy failed to win the support of many sections of the Italian population," the *Year Book* reported, this "did little to impede the speedy deterioration of the once great Italian Jewish community." The situation in Poland was no better. Discriminatory legislation, anti-Jewish agitation, the elimination of Jews from economic and professional life, "violence of almost unprecedented proportions," and a policy of forced emigration all were detailed in 15 pages of text—though in this case even the *Year Book* could not envisage the horrors that lay ahead. So the narrative proceeded, country after country, in perhaps the most shattering review of the year in the *Year Book*'s whole history. A concluding section on "the refugee problem" did not mince words either. It described the situation in 1938–39 as "cruel" and "discouraging."[118]

Worse was still to come, of course, and subsequent volumes of the *Year Book* continued the horrific story, setting forth the known facts in excruciating detail. In 1940, for example, it reported the death rate at the Buchenwald concentration camp as 30 percent, and described the condition of Polish Jewry under Hitler as "probably the greatest tragedy in the entire history of Israel." Fourteen pages chronicled the year's events there under such headings as "expulsions," "depredations," "massacres and executions," "mass arrests and forced labor," and "fate of Jewish women."[119] Two years later, the *Year Book* reported that "200,000 Jews have been killed by the Nazis since the occupation of Poland, most of them since March 1942 . . . . . It was also confirmed from underground sources that thousands of Jews were being gassed by the Gestapo."[120] By 1943, when reports of the Final Solution had been publicly confirmed, the *Year Book* understood that its predictions and fears had come true: "the Nazis," it proclaimed, "are endeavoring to exterminate the Jews of Europe by all possible methods in the shortest possible time."[121]

In setting forth this record of contemporary tragedy, the editors of the

---

[118]Ibid., pp. 270, 285, 291, 374.
[119]Vol. 42 (1940–41), pp. 365–74.
[120]Vol. 44 (1942–43), p. 247.
[121]Vol. 45 (1943–44), p. 232.

Year Book believed that the facts spoke for themselves. They therefore spared no effort in collecting and detailing the horrors facing European Jewry, devoting hundreds of pages to this task in the *Year Book,* just as the American Jewish Committee did in the bimonthly *Contemporary Jewish Record,* which it founded in 1938. In 1941 the *Year Book's* annual "Review of the Year" became a collaborative work, with chapters assigned to regional or local experts. The brilliantly crafted reports on events in the British Commonwealth, for example, were written for several years by Theodor H. Gaster, then editorial secretary of London's Institute of Jewish Affairs and later a famous Orientalist. Yet neither Gaster nor anybody else accompanied their report with any call to action — that had not been the *Year Book's* province since the days of the Russian Passport campaign. Moreover, in retrospect, we can surmise that the reviews of the year, graphic as they were, remained all too little read and appreciated by contemporaries. Most Americans, even a great many American Jews, failed to assimilate the magnitude of the unfolding Holocaust until it was practically complete. The problem, as a rereading of the *Year Book* clearly reveals, was not the absence of accurate information — in fact, those who took the trouble to read could learn a great deal about what was going on. The problem instead was a failure to come to terms with the information available. Far too many people dismissed what the *Year Book* and other Jewish periodicals published as being simply, in Deborah Lipstadt's memorable phrase, "beyond belief."

Although the contemporary reader cannot but be impressed by the extent and accuracy of the *Year Book's* coverage of the unfolding tragedy of European Jewry, the annual "Review of the Year" which contained these reports rarely won pride of place in the *Year Book* during this period. The headlined articles in the front of the book, highlighted in gold on the cover, focused almost exclusively on domestic issues. There were the usual panegyrical obituaries, yet another article on American Jews in agriculture ("more Jews are today thinking in terms of the farm than in any other period in the whole of American history," it wishfully proclaimed), various articles on Jewish organizations, a list of Jewish fiction in English (omitting books deemed "unwholesome in content or treatment, or [that] present Jewish life in a distorted way"), and a series of articles on historic Jewish personalities (Maimonides, Rashi, Saadiah Gaon, Jehuda Halevi, Heinrich Graetz, and Nachman Krochmal), whose anniversaries occasioned popular retrospectives on their work and on its relevance for American Jews. Thus the front of the *Year Book* generally projected a message of continuity and normalcy, a sense of "business as usual" that stood in abject tension to the horrific reports found further on. This same tension characterized American Jewish life as a whole at that time, torn between a quest for domestic tranquility and the frightening realization that the world Jews had known would never be the same.

Once the United States entered the war, the *Year Book*'s focus broadened to include Jews in the military, notably "lists of American Jewish men who have been cited for bravery or have lost their lives in the service." The Jewish Welfare Board, the body charged with meeting the needs of American Jews in the armed forces, compiled this information, and its executive director, Louis Kraft, admitted in a *Year Book* article that, as before, the compilation served both patriotic and apologetic purposes: "to continue the story of our historic contribution to the preservation of America and to write in clear, bold letters the facts that bear witness to the willingness of Jews, from the beginning of their history, to fight and die in the struggle for the victory of the ideals of freedom and justice."[122]

More substantial articles on Jews and the American war effort appeared only after Germany's surrender, in the volume issued in time for the High Holy Days of 1945. Pride of place that year went to "Franklin D. Roosevelt and the Jewish Crisis 1933–1945," by Edward N. Saveth, then a young AJC researcher and later a distinguished historian. Roosevelt, of course, had only just died, and Saveth's radiant appreciation of his "sympathetic . . . attitude toward the Jewish people" and his "defense of Jews against their oppressors" amply reflected what most Jews of that day fervently believed. To be sure, Saveth conceded that the administration's efforts to aid Jewish refugees "were not as effective as some had hoped." He insisted, however, that this "was not because the Administration was wanting, but because of the savage and inhuman character of the adversary." Later historians, relying on documents unavailable to Saveth, would disagree. Franklin D. Roosevelt's "steps to aid Europe's Jews were very limited," David Wyman concluded in his 1984 bestseller, *The Abandonment of the Jews.* "If he had wanted to, he could have aroused substantial public backing for a vital rescue effort by speaking out on the issue. . . . But he had little to say about the problem and gave no priority at all to rescue."[123]

Other articles in the 1945 volume included a summary of "Jewish War Records of World War II" by the director of the Bureau of War Records of the National Jewish Welfare Board, and a survey of the work of "Jewish Chaplains in World War II" by the executive director of the Welfare Board's Committee on Army and Navy Religious Activities. By far the

---

[122]Vol. 44 (1942–43), p. vi; Vol. 45 (1943–44), p. 180.
[123]Vol. 47 (1945–46), pp. 40, 45; David Wyman, *The Abandonment of the Jews* (New York, 1984), p. 311.

most important article, however, was by Jacob Kaplan, then acting grand rabbi of France (and later its courageous chief rabbi), who produced a remarkable 48-page detailed account of "French Jewry Under the Occupation," complete with primary documents. Kaplan witnessed many of these events, playing a leading role in some of them, so his account was that of a historically sensitive participant-observer. For years, no better English-language survey of the Holocaust in France existed. The editors' hope that Kaplan's would be "the first of a series of articles on the experiences of the various Jewish communities of Europe during Nazi occupation"[124] however, went unrealized. The *Year Book,* like the American Jewish community generally, soon turned away from the bleak tragedy of European Jewry and focused upon the brighter future that everyone hoped lay ahead.

Postwar Challenges

Even before the war ended, the *Year Book* had been promoting American Jewry as the linchpin of the new postwar Jewish world order. In 1941, for example, editor Harry Schneiderman wrote:

> In the United States, the only important Jewish community of the world left unscathed by the direct effects of the Hitler war, there were indications during the past year as in several preceding years, of a growing awareness of both the challenge and the opportunity presented by the community's unique situation. Although grateful for its immunity from the plague which has virtually destroyed Jewish life in Europe, it would seem that American Jews are realizing that they have been spared for a sacred task—to preserve Judaism and its cultural, social and moral values, to ransom Jewish captives as much as this can be done, to alleviate the sufferings of their brethren and to prepare themselves against the coming of the day when the way will be open for them to succor and rehabilitate the survivors of the unspeakable disaster which has temporarily prostrated them.[125]

In the same volume, Maurice Jacobs, executive director of the Jewish Publication Society, declared bluntly that "America must now assume the full leadership in Jewish life. The day of German Jewry has passed. . . ." Historian Jacob Rader Marcus, in an address on "New Literary Responsibilities" also published in that year's *Year Book,* echoed the same theme: "The burden is solely ours to carry: Jewish culture and civilization and leadership are shifting rapidly to these shores."[126]

As if to prepare American Jewry for its new mission, the *Year Book* began to devote greater attention to religious, educational, and cultural

---

[124]Vol. 47 (1945–46), pp. v–vi.
[125]Vol. 43 (1941–42), p. 28.
[126]Ibid., pp. 780, 789.

activities in the United States, adding sections on these subjects to its annual review of the year. In 1943, it published major articles on "Jewish Book Collections in the United States" and on "American Jewish Scholarship." The latter, produced just before his death by the renowned German-Jewish scholar Ismar Elbogen, then a refugee in New York, symbolized a transfer of power. The Old World scholar offered his blessing to the land where he found refuge, describing it as "a center of Jewish scholarship," indeed, in the wake of the war, "the sole center—with the exception of Palestine." Reminding American Jewry that its intellectual forces had, in the past, been foreign-born immigrants, he challenged the community "to produce native scholars of its own."[127]

Within two years, the *Year Book* reported that "the leading Jewish theological seminaries" had, in effect, responded. Spurred in part "by the catastrophic extinction of Jewish centers of learning abroad" and by the "glaring need of the American community for religious direction and informed leadership" they announced far-reaching programs of expansion. The *Year Book* also reported "increased community interest and support for Jewish education in many cities throughout the United States," and it saw "signs which indicated that American Jewish education was breaking away from its European moorings and becoming rooted in the American Jewish community and psyche." More broadly, it reported in 1945 a surge in Jewish organizational development in the United States, with "a larger number of new organizations . . . formed during the past five years than in any previous five-year period, forty seven new organizations having been established since 1940."[128]

What these noteworthy facts all pointed to was confirmed statistically in the *Year Book* of 1946, when new figures revealed that "the major part of the present world Jewish population—about 5,176,000" were living in the United States and Canada. By contrast, "in Europe only an estimated 3,642,000 remain[ed] of the total Jewish pre-war population of approximately 9,740,000." The two continents had thus "reversed their order of 1939." Where before Europe had been "the greatest center of Jewish population," now, as a consequence of the Holocaust, that designation fell to North America.[129] The news was heralded by historians Oscar and Mary Handlin on the first page of the 50th volume of the *American Jewish Year Book,* published in 1949. "The events of the Second World War," they declared, "left the United States the center of world Judaism. The answers to the most critical questions as to the fu-

---

[127]Ibid., pp. 47–65.
[128]Vol. 47 (1945–46), pp. 215, 234, 242, 559.
[129]Vol. 48 (1946–47), p. 599.

ture of the Jews everywhere will be determined by the attitudes and the position of the five million Jews who are citizens of the American Republic."[130]

The Triumph of Zionism

Yet at the very moment that the *Year Book* trumpeted American Jewry's centrality, highlighting its religious and cultural advances and focusing on its future challenges, the eyes of the Jewish world actually turned eastward, toward Zion. The 1939 British White Paper that severely limited Jewish immigration into Palestine, the refusal of country after country—before, during, and even after the war—to take in Jewish refugees, and the mass murder of millions whose only crime was that they had nowhere to go, persuaded many who had formerly been apathetic of the need for an independent Jewish homeland. In 1942, a celebrated Zionist conference held at New York's Biltmore Hotel demanded that "the gates of Palestine be opened . . . and that Palestine be established as a Jewish Commonwealth integrated in the structure of the new democratic world."[131] A year later, an unprecedented "American Jewish Conference," representing some 64 national Jewish organizations as well as many local communities, reiterated these demands, calling "for the attainment of a Jewish majority and for the re-creation of the Jewish Commonwealth."[132] With the coming of peace, and the urgent need to find a home for hundreds of thousands of Jewish survivors and "displaced persons," the campaign to end the British Mandate and to establish an independent Jewish state in Palestine intensified. As the great Jewish historian Salo Baron noted in a retrospective on the year published in the 1947 *Year Book,* "the Palestine situation . . . has focused the world's attention." "More and more Jews, even among the non-Zionists, became convinced that the creation of some sort of Jewish state in Palestine had become a historic necessity."[133]

Some leaders of the American Jewish Committee, however, remained unconvinced. For decades, AJC members had maintained divergent views on Zionism, and the *Year Book* had followed suit. Only once, in 1922, did it list news of Palestine under the heading, "The National Homeland."

---

[130]Vol. 50 (1948–49), p. 1.

[131]Melvin I. Urofsky, *American Zionism from Herzl to the Holocaust* (Garden City, N.Y., 1975), pp. 424–27; Paul Mendes-Flohr and Jehuda Reinharz, eds., *The Jew in the Modern World,* 2nd ed. (New York, 1995), pp. 617–19.

[132]Vol. 46 (1944–45), p. 169; Alexander S. Kohanski, ed., *The American Jewish Conference: Its Organization and Proceedings of the First Session* (New York, 1944), pp. 178–81.

[133]Vol. 49 (1947–48), pp. 103, 107.

Taking its cue from the U.S. Senate resolution supporting the Balfour Declaration, it quoted AJC president Louis Marshall who dismissed the "small minority" of Jews who opposed the declaration as "erroneous," their fears "groundless."[134] Thereafter, though, the *Year Book* took a more cautious stance, perhaps in deference to the AJC's non-Zionist proclivities. It reviewed events of the year under neutral headings ("Palestine and Zionism"), expressed sympathy toward Jewish settlers, gloried in their economic and cultural achievements, and sought to avoid political controversy by sticking to the facts.

The *Year Book's* challenge became more acute in the 1940s when the Zionist demand for an independent Jewish commonwealth in Palestine—as opposed to international trusteeship or a binational state—hardened the lines of division between Zionism and its opponents. "A bitter controversy raged within the Committee," Naomi Cohen writes in her history of the AJC, "as both sides continued to debate the issues of Jewish statehood, Arab-Jewish relations, and Diaspora Jewry."[135] The reports of the American Jewish Committee, published annually in the back of the *Year Book,* chronicled this controversy, which became more virulent in 1943 with the ascension to the AJC presidency of Judge Joseph M. Proskauer, who considered the creation of a Jewish state in Palestine "a Jewish catastrophe."[136] In 1944, ten percent of the AJC's members, including representatives from ten affiliated organizations, resigned, protesting the AJC's withdrawal from the American Jewish Conference, which had come out in support of Zionism. The AJC, whose leaders favored an international trusteeship over Palestine, labeled the Conference's call for an independent Jewish commonwealth "extreme." In a 1945 address published in the AJC report at the back of the *Year Book,* Proskauer went further, labeling supporters of the resolutions favoring an independent commonwealth in Palestine "ultra-Zionists" and accusing them of marring "the harmony of Jewish collaboration."[137]

Meanwhile, the *Year Book's* annual review of the year, which included "Zionist and Pro-Palestine Activities," continued to chronicle events, sometimes, indeed, from a Zionist perspective. Rabbi Joshua Trachtenberg of Easton, Pennsylvania, who wrote the section on "religious activities" for the *Year Book* in 1943, was a lifelong Zionist and a leader in the League for Labor Palestine. In writing about the Reform opponents of political Zionism who founded the (anti-Zionist) American Council

---

[134]Vol. 24 (1922–23), pp. 66, 68.
[135]Cohen, *Not Free to Desist,* p. 253.
[136]As quoted by Jerold S. Auerbach in *American Jewish History* 61, September 1979, p. 111.
[137]Vol. 47 (1945–46), p. 688.

for Judaism, he barely concealed his contempt. Devoting many sentences to opponents of the new organization, he closed by noting that the Central Conference of American Rabbis, which spoke for the Reform rabbinate, "urged the Council to disband."[138] Samuel Dinin, who wrote the section on "Zionist and Pro-Palestine Activities" a year later, was likewise a committed Zionist. While he displayed determined neutrality in writing about the American Jewish Committee's stance, he felt less inhibited in writing about the American Council for Judaism, which he characterized, quoting others, as "an attempt to sabotage the collective Jewish will . . . by a small body of men speaking for only themselves."[139]

Pro-Zionist sentiments continued to appear in the *Year Book* throughout the Proskauer era, testimony to the AJC's commitment to the *Year Book*'s editorial independence and its continuing tolerance of diverse views. The ordering of subjects within the annual "Review of the Year," however, remained telling. Headings like "religion," "education and culture," "social welfare," "anti-Jewish agitation," and "interfaith activities" always preceded news about "Zionist and pro-Palestine activities" in the United States. In the international section, developments in Palestine also took a back seat, appearing after the review of Jewish events in Latin America, the British Commonwealth, and Europe. Proskauer and the AJC eventually muted their opposition to Zionism, as the plight of Jewish refugees became clearer and American government support for the partition of Palestine into Jewish and Arab states crystallized. Still, in the face of mounting interest in Zion, they remained determinedly America-centered, and so, likewise, did the *Year Book*.

Changes for the Golden Anniversary

The fiftieth anniversary issue of the *American Jewish Year Book*, published in 1949, marked a turning point both in the history of the series and in the history of the Jewish people. The *Year Book* itself announced that the year just passed, 1947–48, had "witnessed the most dramatic and perhaps most significant event in post-exilic Jewish history—the establishment of the first independent Jewish state since the loss of Jewish political independence some 2000 years before." It published the full English text of Israel's "Declaration of Independence" as well as a map of Palestine's "Jewish and Arab held sections." It also published, in English translation, a Jewish Agency survey of "Thirty Years of Jewish Immigration to Palestine," including an attractive graph, especially prepared

---

[138]Vol. 45 (1943–44), p. 141.
[139]Vol. 46 (1944–45), p. 170.

for the *Year Book,* that portrayed the different waves of Zionist immigration, periodized into different "aliyot," from the Hebrew word meaning "ascents" or "pilgrimages."[140]

Still, it was America that occupied center stage in the 50th anniversary volume. The 14 pages devoted to three decades of Jewish immigration to Palestine were dwarfed by a pathbreaking 84-page article reviewing a full century of Jewish immigration to the United States, written by historians Oscar and Mary Handlin. Similarly, the "Review of the Year" section dealing with the United States occupied 149 pages as compared to the 40 pages in the parallel section dealing with "Palestine and the Middle East." With time, Israel would come to occupy more and more space in the *Year Book,* but the focus remained firmly fixed on the American scene. The aim, the editor explained, was to keep American Jews sufficiently informed concerning Israel and world Jewry so as to help "keep alive and to nurture . . . that sense of kinship and common destiny which has inspired our community worthily to fill the role of big brother to our overseas brethren."[141]

The celebration of the *Year Book's* golden anniversary afforded an opportunity for a reflective look back over its first half century. Harry Schneiderman, who had been involved with every issue of the *Year Book* since volume 11 (1909–1910), rose to the occasion with a fact-filled retrospective that described the *Year Book* as a "running contemporary record of the growth of the community as reflected in the development of its institutions and in the outcropping of problems, both those special to the Jewish people and those general world problems that have affected Jews." Back in 1899, when the *Year Book* began, he noted, the American Jewish population numbered about a million; 50 years later it stood at four-and-a-half million. Volume one of the *Year Book* listed 20 national Jewish organizations; volume 50 listed about 270. In 1900, 42 Jewish periodicals were published in the United States; volume 50 listed 175. Finally, as one more indication of how much had changed not just numerically but politically, culturally, and editorially as well, he noted that "the Review of the Year in 1948 covered almost 500 pages, compared with nineteen pages which the equivalent material covered in the first volume."[142]

As it turned out, volume 50 was also Harry Schneiderman's final volume as editor. After 40 years of association with the *Year Book,* 30 as editor, he was ready to retire; he likewise retired at that time from the Amer-

---

[140]Vol. 50 (1948–49), pp. 107, 744.
[141]Ibid., p. 88.
[142]Ibid., pp. 85–104. The quotations are on pp. 85 and 102.

ican Jewish Committee. He was succeeded as editor by his 36-year-old associate, Morris Fine, who had by then already spent 13 years at the AJC, and who would remain on as editor until he retired in 1979.

The first volume of the *Year Book* under Fine's sole editorship, volume 51, published in 1950, was visibly different from any of its predecessors, signaling a new era. Changes began with the cover, where a handsome blue replaced the drab green that had garbed every *Year Book* since 1899. The new *Year Book* also stood an inch taller and half an inch wider than its predecessor, its very appearance suggesting the enlarged stature not only of the *Year Book* but of the community that it represented. Finally, the new cover dropped the Hebrew year that once so visibly placed the volume in Jewish time. Where the spine of volume 50 had read "5709" and only below that "1948–1949," volume 51 listed only "1950" on the spine, cover, and title page; mention of the Hebrew year 5710 was banished to the calendar section beginning on page 529. In fact, the *Year Book* no longer even appeared in time for Rosh Hashanah, the Jewish New Year. The *Year Book's* readers — Jewish and non-Jewish — now almost all marked time according to the Christian calendar, beginning on January 1, and the *Year Book* followed suit.

The "primary function" of the *Year Book* — defined in volume 51 "as a volume of reference summarizing developments in Jewish life and those larger events of Jewish interest,"[143] remained the same under the new format, but the contents, subjected to a "thorough re-examination," changed markedly. The front of the book was now divided geographically, beginning with the United States, and coverage was extended to cover four broad headings: "socio-economic," "civic and political," "communal," and "cultural." A whole series of new subjects appeared under these headings, some of which, like "Civil Rights," anticipated the great themes of the postwar era. Others, like "Films" and "Radio and Television," reflected a growing appreciation for the significance of popular culture. The *Year Book* also promised to devote greater attention to statistical data — volume 51 included more than 100 tables and graphs, along with a special listing making them easy to find. In order to make room for these new features, the necrology section was cut back, and the self-congratulatory listings of institutional anniversaries, "appointments, honors, elections," and large bequests and gifts were eliminated altogether. In addition, for the first time, the volume was fully indexed, making information much easier to locate. Volume 51 also commenced a new arrangement with the Jewish Publication Society, the longtime publisher of the *Year Book*. After somewhat acrimonious negotiations, the AJC be-

---

[143]Vol. 51 (1950), p. v.

came copublisher of the *Year Book* and assumed responsibility for its production and for distribution to non-JPS members. The JPS continued to distribute the *Year Book* to its own members at a substantial discount.

Beyond these surface changes, the new *Year Book* reflected dramatic structural changes that were transforming the American Jewish community as a whole in the postwar period, an era when both American government agencies and secular non-profit organizations also underwent massive restructuring. The professionalization of the organized American Jewish community revolutionized the contents and staffing of the *Year Book* as well as its editorial machinery. Indeed, the *Year Book*'s reorganization into discrete topical sections, each one written by a professional who specialized in his or her area, mirrored the reorganization that had taken place earlier at the American Jewish Committee and the two other major Jewish defense organizations of the period, the American Jewish Congress and the Anti-Defamation League of B'nai B'rith. All alike witnessed significant staff increases, a host of new, highly specialized job titles and divisions, and an influx of young, college-trained experts with professional training who gradually supplanted the once-dominant lay leaders. At the American Jewish Committee, historian Naomi Cohen found that "lay policy-making" gave way during these years to "institutional policy," and professionals, "to a large degree . . . determined policy and strategy."[144] It was these same professionals — members of what came to be known as the "Jewish civil service" — to whom the *Year Book* now turned as contributors; there were 43 of them in 1950 alone.

The second dramatic change reflected in the new *Year Book* was even more fundamental: It moved from its original concern with communal issues and achievements toward a much broader agenda defined by "intergroup relations" and social action. Before World War II, issues like anti-Semitism and the promotion of Jewish rights at home and abroad dominated the *Year Book,* much as they dominated the work of the American Jewish Committee and the other Jewish defense organizations. Now, they all modified their agendas seeking, in historian Stuart Svonkin's words, "to ameliorate interethnic, interracial and interreligious tensions by reducing prejudice and discrimination."[145] The American Jewish Committee explained this change, in its annual report in volume 50 of the *Year Book,* on the grounds "that there is the closest relation between the protection of the civil rights of all citizens and the protection of the civil rights

---

[144]Stuart Svonkin, *Jews Against Prejudice: American Jews and the Fight for Civil Liberties* (New York, 1997), pp. 16–17; Cohen, *Not Free to Desist,* p. 238.
[145]Svonkin, *Jews Against Prejudice,* p. 18.

The Jewish Twentieth Century: Images that highlight the themes of this tumultuous era, its tragedies and its triumphs, from an American Jewish perspective.

Over two million East European Jews arrive in the "golden land" between 1881 and 1919, before restrictive immigration laws effectively close the gates.

Orchard Street, on the Lower East Side of
New York—first home for thousands of
new arrivals . . .

many of whom find
employment in
"sweat shops,"
here, as cigar makers.

To lessen the concentration in the urban ghettos, immigrant Jews are encouraged to settle in rural areas such as this farm colony in Woodbine, New Jersey, established by the Baron de Hirsch Fund (ca. 1900).

Still others strike out for the Midwest and the West. Here, in St. Paul, Minnesota, are the four Rose brothers, fur traders, in 1911, posing with Blackfoot Indians.

The masses of Jews fleeing Europe are propelled by the combined forces of persecution and economic hardship. Here, following the Kishinev pogrom of 1903, wounded Jews wait outside a hospital.

Two famous cases of anti-Semitism: (r.) Mendel Beilis, convicted in Russia in 1913 on a "blood libel" charge but later freed;

(l.) Leo Frank, lynched by a mob near Atlanta in 1915, after being falsely convicted of murdering a young girl.

An American Jewish Committee delegation goes to Washington, D.C., in 1911 to press the U.S. to terminate its 1832 treaty with Russia because of Russia's refusal to grant visas to American Jews. The first three in the front row, from the left, are Louis Marshall, AJC's second president; Judge Mayer Sulzburger, AJC's first president; and Oscar S. Straus, former U.S. secretary of commerce and ambassador to Turkey.

The fire at the Triangle Shirtwaist Co. in New York, in 1911, where 146 workers, mostly young Jewish women, perish, spurs the growth of labor unions and the fight for improved working conditions.

Jewish and Italian garment workers on strike, 1913.

Classes in English and citizenship help "Americanize" the immigrants.

Zionist activity in Palestine gains momentum in the first two decades of the century. Here, Jewish farmers in Zichron Ya'akov, one of the early settlements.

The American Jewish women who establish Hadassah send two visiting nurses (with support from philanthropist Nathan Straus) to Jerusalem in 1913, to provide medical aid to needy Jews.

World War I—Jews on both sides of the conflict fight patriotically alongside their countrymen. Here, German Jewish soldiers . . .

(and) a joint seder for Allied American, British, and French Jewish soldiers, somewhere in Europe.

A meeting of World Zionist Organization leaders in New York in 1915. Seated l. to r., Henrietta Szold, founder of Hadassah; Rabbi Stephen S. Wise, Jacob de Haas, Joseph Kesselman, Louis Lipsky, Charles A. Cowen, Shmarya Levin, and Rabbi Meyer Berlin.

General Edmund Allenby enters Jerusalem on Dec. 11, 1917, after his British troops defeat Turkish forces. The League of Nations would give Britain a mandate over Palestine in 1922.

The ceremonial opening of the Hebrew University on Mt. Scopus, Jerusalem, 1925. Lord Balfour and Chaim Weizmann are among the speakers; an American Reform rabbi, Judah Magnes, is the university's first president.

YIVO

In the postwar years, some Jews seek desperately to leave Europe and come to America. The Warsaw office of the Red Star Shipping Line, ca. 1921.

But throughout the diverse worlds of East European Jews, normal life resumes. A heder in Lublin . . .

YIVO

The Jewish Sports Club of Bialystok, 1923 . . .

A demonstration of the Jewish socialist Bund in Vilna.

1933 in Germany—the start of the Nazi era. One early step is a boycott of Jewish stores. "Germans! Defend yourselves! Don't buy from Jews!" reads the sign.

Nov. 9, 1938, *Kristallnacht*. This synagogue in Wiesbaden, along with hundreds of others, is set aflame and destroyed.

**Throughout the territories conquered by the Third Reich,
Jews are deported to ghettos . . .**

**Or rounded up and slaughtered in mass graves, like this one
in the Ukraine.**

Jewish partisans in Poland fight the Germans.

In the U.S., various Jewish groups try—unsuccessfully—to win government intervention to save Jews in Europe. In 1943 a delegation of the Union of Orthodox Rabbis of the U.S. and Canada marches in Washington to dramatize its appeal for help.

The Warsaw Ghetto

The entrance to the Auschwitz-Birkenau extermination camp

U.S. Jewish soldiers at the Siegfried Line toward the end of World War II, led in prayer by Chaplain Sidney Lefkowitz.

At war's end—survivors. Buchenwald, 1945.

With thousands of "displaced persons" eager to find safe haven in Palestine, the Haganah ship *Exodus* sails in July 1947 with 4,500 refugee passengers—only to be apprehended by the British.

Standing beneath a portrait of Theodor Herzl, David Ben-Gurion proclaims Israel's independence on May 14, 1948.

With the aid of the Jewish Agency and the American Jewish Joint Distribution Committee, orphans of the war are gathered in a children's village in Holland and prepared for settlement in the new Jewish state.

Pres. Harry Truman greets Chaim Weizmann, Israel's first president, in Washington, May 1948.

One of the many temporary *ma'abarot*, transit camps, that house hundreds of thousands of new immigrants to Israel.

Aug. 23, 1950, a historic meeting at Jerusalem's King David Hotel . . . Prime Minister David Ben-Gurion; Jacob Blaustein, president of the American Jewish Committee; Minister of Labor Golda Meir; and Minister of Foreign Affairs Moshe Sharett, at the signing of the "Blaustein–Ben-Gurion agreement" clarifying Israel's relationship to Jews in other countries.

The mammoth enterprise of raising funds for Israel enlists the aid of leading Americans. Here, in Sept. 1961, as an expression of gratitude, Foreign Minister Golda Meir presents a State of Israel Bonds plaque to Eleanor Roosevelt.

The 1961 trial in Jerusalem of former SS officer Adolf Eichmann focuses world attention anew on the Nazi era and the Holocaust.

June 7, 1967, the start of the Six-Day War. At the UN Security Council debate on the fighting in the Middle East, Abba Eban, foreign minister of Israel, addresses the council. To his left at the table are Lord Caradon (U.K.) and U. S. ambassador Arthur J. Goldberg.

UNITED NATIONS

1967: These images inspire pride and jubilation among Israelis and Jews world-wide over the recapture of the Old City of Jerusalem

Gen. Uzi Narkiss, Defense Minister Moshe Dayan, and Chief-of-Staff Yitzhak Rabin enter the Old City through the Lions' Gate.

Rabbi Shlomo Goren, chief chaplain of the Israel Defense Forces, sounds the shofar at the Western Wall, the *kotel.*

Milestones on the road to peace—

With Egypt,
March 26, 1979.
Anwar Sadat,
Jimmy Carter,
Menachem Begin. . .
the Camp David Accords.

With the Palestinians,
Sept. 13, 1993. Yitzhak Rabin,
Bill Clinton, Yasir Arafat. . .
a Declaration of Principles.

With Jordan, Oct. 26, 1994.
Yitzhak Rabin, Bill Clinton,
King Hussein. . . a peace treaty.

Nov. 4, 1995. The peace rally in Tel Aviv at which Prime Minister Yitzhak Rabin is assassinated.

Nov. 6, 1995. World leaders attend Rabin's funeral on Mt. Herzl in Jerusalem.

Images of American Jewish life:

In the 1960s, the civil rights struggle becomes a sacred cause for many American Jews. Among them is Rabbi Abraham Joshua Heschel. In this 1965 demonstration in Selma, Ala., Heschel (2nd from right) marches with Ralph Bunche (3rd from right), Rev. Martin Luther King, Jr. (4th from right), and Ralph Abernathy (5th from right).

In the 1970s, Jewish women create a Jewish feminist movement that presses for equal partici-pation in religious life. In 1978, Sally Jane Priesand is ordained by the Hebrew Union College-Jewish Institute of Religion, becoming the first woman rabbi in the U.S.

In the 1980s, the plight of Jews in the Soviet Union arouses American Jews to action on many fronts. This mass rally in Washington, D.C., on Dec. 6, 1987, demands "freedom now" for Soviet Jews.

Toward the close of the century, the focus turns inward: return to tradition, Jewish education, search for new forms of religious life, outreach to marginalized Jews, an emphasis on "spirituality."

A Shabbat service of the New York Havurah.

A class performance at the Solomon Schechter Day School of Westchester, a Conservative institution.

BILL ARON

A Havdalah service at the Reform movement's
Henry S. Jacobs Camp, Utica, Miss.

Youngsters from the Orthodox Union's National
Jewish Council for the Disabled participate in the
Israel Day Parade in New York City.

UNION OF ORTHODOX JEWISH CONGREGATIONS OF AMERICA

Orthodox Jews celebrate the tenth *Siyyum Hashas*—completion of the *Daf Yomi* cycle of Talmud study—at Madison Square Garden, on September 28, 1997. Simultaneous events are held in the Nassau Coliseum and 35 cities nationwide.

The beginning of the century—and its end.

Confirmation class of the Washington Hebrew Congregation, Washington, D.C., about 1900.

Confirmation class of Temple Emanuel, Birmingham, Ala., 1997.

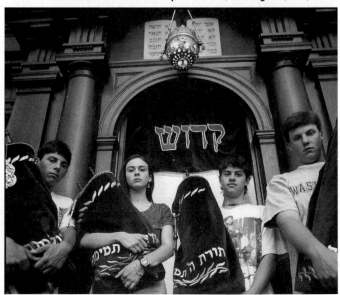

of the members of particular groups." Historian John Higham has dubbed this view, widely held at the time, as "the theory of the unitary character of prejudice."[146] It was self-evident to the many Jews who espoused it that they should "join with other groups in the protection of the civil rights of the members of all groups irrespective of race, religion, color or national origin."[147] Added encouragement may have come from the perceived postwar decline of domestic anti-Semitism that "allowed—and even compelled—Jewish defense organizations to develop a new raison d'être," and from non-Jewish organizations like the National Council of Churches, the National Conference of Christians and Jews, and the American Civil Liberties Union, which had cooperated with Jewish defense organizations during the war, and which now sought to continue to work with them on a common social agenda.[148] Whatever the case, the *American Jewish Year Book,* in its new garb, both documented and furthered the new communal emphases. Throughout the 1950s it published regular articles on civil rights, civil liberties, church-state relations, and, for a time, housing, education, and employment as well. These articles chronicled the battle against hatred and prejudice—no longer just anti-Semitism—in the United States. A few of the articles, like the one on "Civil Rights: The National Scene" in volume 51, did not mention Jews at all.

Finally, the new *Year Book* reflected a heightened Jewish organizational emphasis on social science as a tool for resolving communal problems. Quantitative studies, of course, had appeared before in the *Year Book,* and the American Jewish Committee had, from its beginnings, sought to ground social planning in scientific inquiry. But for the most part, statistical studies published in the *Year Book* during its first 50 years had been descriptive, designed simply to make data available or, in some cases, to rebut critics. This changed in the postwar period as both government agencies and private think tanks demonstrated the broader policymaking implications of the social sciences. The pathbreaking works undertaken in the 1940s and 1950s by German refugee scholars at the Institute of Social Research and Gunnar Myrdal's well-publicized and highly influential 1944 study, *An American Dilemma: The Negro Problem and Modern Democracy,* proved particularly influential in Jewish circles. Dr. John Slawson, the Jewish social worker and Columbia-trained psychologist who became executive vice-president of the American Jewish Committee in 1943, appreciated the potential of social-science research, and greatly encouraged it. The *Year Book* now followed the same path.

---

[146]John Higham, *Send These to Me: Immigrants in Urban America* (Baltimore, 1984), p. 155.

[147]Vol. 50 (1948–49), p. 826.

[148]Svonkin, *Jews Against Prejudice,* pp. 18, 25.

The opening article of volume 51, entitled "The American Jew: Some Demographic Features," set the tone for this new research agenda. "American Jews," it began, "are as yet unable to ascertain with any degree of precision how many persons make up that grouping, where they live, how old they are, where they came from, and how they earn their livelihoods." The periodic United States census of American religious bodies that Harry Linfield's statistical articles in earlier *Year Books* had relied upon did not ask these kinds of questions, and in any case the last such census had been taken 13 years before. In search of better data, Ben Seligman, then of the Council of Jewish Federations and Welfare Boards (and later a professor at the University of Massachusetts and an expert on poverty), turned to local Jewish community population studies. For all of their faults and limitations—the biggest being that they did not exist for the Jews of New York, Chicago, and Philadelphia—the aggregated data offered productive policy-related insights. Seligman discovered, for example, that middle-class Jews, "the largest part of the Jewish population included in these surveys," had restricted their family size during the Great Depression and then experienced a spurt of births as prosperity returned during the war years and beyond. This, of course, was an early sign of what would become known as the "baby boom," and Seligman, who viewed the expansion as "purely a temporary phenomenon," underestimated its significance. In the long run, though, his warning about the "continuous aging of the Jewish population, a process which appears to be more marked than in the general population in this country," was absolutely on target. He was also prescient in noting that "American Jewry is . . . replenishing itself at a rate slow enough to cause concern to community leadership."[149] To be sure, he expressed no concern about intermarriage: It was not an issue in his day and he barely noticed it. His data concerning economic status, education, nativity and citizenship, and internal migration were also unsurprising. But his questions concerning the community's future were precisely those that postwar Jews would focus upon, and they also followed his lead in looking to Jewish population studies to answer them.

The problem of anti-Semitism, formerly a dependable feature of the *Year Book,* played less of a role in the postwar era, largely, as we have seen, because American anti-Semitism markedly declined. The section on "anti-Jewish agitation" in 1950 thus opened with the announcement, unthinkable in earlier days, that "organized anti-Semitic activity . . . continued at a low ebb."[150] Subsequent years painted a gloomier picture, especially as right-wing anti-Semitism rebounded, but through the 1950s

---

[149]Vol. 51 (1950), pp. 7, 9, 23.
[150]Ibid., p. 110.

the section never exceeded ten pages—out of a *Year Book* that usually ran to more than 500 pages. George Kellman, the AJC staff member who wrote the annual article, portrayed organized anti-Semitism as the work of marginal individuals and groups—people, in other words, who required careful monitoring but did not pose a serious threat. Of greatest interest, perhaps, were the themes that he distilled from the anti-Semitic literature he annually perused. He astutely observed in his first article (1950) "that the principal theme exploited by anti-Semitic agitators was the identification of Jews as Communists. . . ."[151]

Communism and the Jewish Community

The spread of Communism, which terrified many Americans in the years immediately following World War I, haunted the country anew from the late 1940s through the 1950s. The Cold War against the Soviet Union, the protracted military conflict in Korea, revelations of damaging Soviet espionage activity in the United States, and domestic tensions combined to create the fear that supporters of the Communist Party were working to subvert the American way of life. Across the United States, and even in courtrooms and in the halls of Congress, Communists, suspected Communists, and former Communists saw their civil liberties curtailed: many lost their jobs, some were jailed.

For Jews, and especially for Jewish defense organizations, this "Red Scare" proved particularly unsettling. Anti-Semites had long insisted that Jews and Communism were linked, and it was no secret that Jews had for decades comprised a disproportionate part of the membership and leadership of the American Communist Party. Even though the overwhelming majority of American Jews were *not* Communists, to defend Jewish victims of the Red Scare—even to speak out for civil liberties at such a highly emotional time—risked the wellbeing of all Jews. The challenge, as the American Jewish Committee defined it, was to formulate a program of action, "having due regard to the problem of national security," that struck a balance "between the danger of Communism on the one hand and the necessity for preserving civil liberties on the other."[152] As a corollary to this challenge, the AJC worked hard to combat the popular stereotype associating Jews with Communism. It set up its own "Committee on Communism" to counter Communist Party propaganda and to help undermine support for Communism in the American Jewish community.

The *American Jewish Year Book* pursued a parallel course. Beginning

---

[151]Ibid.
[152]Svonkin, *Jews Against Prejudice,* p. 165.

in 1951, it highlighted the issue of civil liberties by devoting a special article to this theme and by placing it first in the section devoted to civic and political affairs. It sought to present the year's developments in an unbiased and balanced way, often by giving equal space to both sides. Careful readers may nevertheless have detected where the *Year Book*'s real sympathies lay, as the following example from 1951 shows:

> Considerable attention was given to the investigation of charges by Senator Joseph McCarthy (Rep. – Wis.) that the Department of State was lax in its hiring and retention of Communists, fellow travelers, and sexual perverts. Much criticism was levelled at Senator McCarthy and his supporters for allegedly making wild and irresponsible claims, for refusing to admit errors and exaggerations, and for actually hindering the effective carrying out of the government's own loyalty check on Federal employees.[153]

There was nothing explicitly Jewish about the *Year Book*'s discussions of civil liberties. Indeed, it rarely mentioned by name and never identified as Jews those charged with Communist sympathies, even when these were matters of common knowledge. Such silence echoed the American Jewish Committee's pledge "to be watchful of any and all attempts . . . falsely and viciously to identify Jews and Communists."[154] An italicized heading in the report of the American Jewish Committee, published at the back of the 1954 *Year Book,* made explicit the message that the rest of the book, with somewhat more subtlety, sought to convey: *"Communism: The Enemy of Judaism."*[155] On the other hand, the *Year Book* did identify as Jews those who opposed Communism, and, as we shall see, paid particular attention to ugly manifestations of anti-Semitism behind the Iron Curtain. It placed "American Jews" and "Jewish organizations" at the forefront of those seeking to halt "the further development of the Communist anti-Semitic campaign" abroad, and quoted verbatim from Communists who used "anti-Jewish invective" — as if this demonstrated that Communists could not be Jews themselves.[156]

For all this, it comes as something of a shock to discover that the *American Jewish Year Book,* which advertised itself as "a record of events and trends in American and world Jewish life," paid practically no attention to the central drama involving American Jews and Communism in the early 1950s — the arrest, trial, and execution of Julius and Ethel Rosenberg on charges of spying for the Soviet Union. Astonishingly, the 1953 issue devoted exactly one footnote to this sensational case, and it read as follows:

---

[153]Vol. 52 (1951), p. 25.
[154]Vol. 53 (1952), p. 554.
[155]Vol. 55 (1954), p. 501.
[156]Ibid., p. 146.

In the case of Ethel and Julius Rosenberg (convicted spies), Communist propaganda insistently charged that the fact that the defendants were Jewish had been a factor in their conviction. On May 18, 1952, the National Community Relations Advisory Council denounced as fraudulent the effort of the National Committee to Secure Justice in the Rosenberg Case "to inject the false issue of anti-Semitism."[157]

Subsequent *Year Books* did nothing to fill out this elliptical statement. Indeed, the most thoroughgoing discussion of the Rosenberg Case appeared in a 1954 article in the *Year Book* reviewing Jewish events in France! While Abraham Karlikow of the AJC's Paris office devoted an entire page to the impact of the Rosenbergs' execution on French public opinion and why Jews and Christians there had protested it, the impact of the case on America and American Jewry found nary a mention in the whole volume. One can only assume that, despite the complete editorial independence that *Year Book* editor Morris Fine remembers enjoying, the climate of opinion in AJC circles won out. Rabbi S. Andhil Fineberg, who led the American Jewish Committee's battle against Communism and served as its leading spokesman on the Rosenbergs, sought "to avoid any publicity which would help the Communists attract attention to the case."[158] In keeping with AJC policy on the case—"repudiate the false claim of anti-Semitism raised by the Communists to deceive American Jews" and "protect our country's reputation from the circulation abroad of Communist-inspired slanders"—he wrote a popular article for the *American Legion Magazine,* later reprinted in *Reader's Digest* and expanded into a book, that served as an influential brief against the Rosenbergs.[159] The *Year Book,* meanwhile, committed both to its goal of objective reporting and its responsibility to the needs of the Jewish community, remained guardedly silent.

The *Year Book* contributed much more to the elucidation of Communist attitudes toward Judaism through its detailed articles in the 1950s on Jewish life behind the Iron Curtain. In an era when some American Jews still believed in the myth of the Soviet "paradise," and a noted American Jewish Communist editor could publicly proclaim that Jews were better off in the USSR than in the United States,[160] the *Year Book*'s reports on the purges and liquidations of Jews served as a pungent antidote. In the same way that it reported on Nazi activities in the 1930s, the *Year Book*

---

[157]Vol. 54 (1953), p. 26.

[158]Quoted in Svonkin, *Jews Against Prejudice,* p. 151. After reading an early draft of this article, Mr. Fine commented that AJC management had never sought to influence the *Year Book's* content, and expressed surprise that the Rosenberg case had not been covered.

[159]Vol. 56 (1955), p. 620.

[160]Ibid.

in the 1950s documented, in graphic detail, atrocities that other Jewish publications ignored or swept carelessly under the rug. Thus in 1950—reviewing events that took place from July 1948 to July 1949—it reported on "a drastic purge of a great part of the Soviet Jewish intelligentsia," and "mass deportations of Jews from the Western border regions of the Soviet Union." A year later, it disclosed that discrimination against Soviet Jews had risen sharply and that "the percentage of Jews in high party, state, army, and foreign service positions continued to decline considerably." In 1952, it told how "tens of thousands of Jews" were forced to work as "slave laborers" in Russian "concentration camps" and announced that "there were no Jewish communal or cultural organizations, schools, periodicals, or Jewish institutions of any kind [left] in the Soviet Union except for a few remaining synagogues." Two years after that, it chronicled in harrowing detail the notorious 1953 "Doctors' Plot," the allegation that leading Soviet doctors, most of them Jews, conspired with foreigners in a supposed attempt "to wipe out the leading cadres of the Soviet Union," and it detailed the "orgy of denunciations, demotions and arrests of Jewish citizens in all parts of the Soviet Union" that followed.[161]

In its coverage of the Soviet satellite states, the *Year Book* followed a similar path. It devoted seven pages to the sensational 1952 Slansky Trial—the courtroom drama and "confession" of General Rudolf Slansky, secretary of the Czechoslovak Communist Party, and 13 others, ten of them Jews, on trumped-up charges of conspiring with Zionists and Westerners against the state. Eleven of the defendants were hanged and, in the words of the *Year Book,* "an anti-Jewish campaign slightly masked as an international campaign against 'Zionism'" commenced throughout the country.[162] In Communist Romania, East Germany, and Hungary, similar anti-Jewish campaigns took place, and the *Year Book* carefully documented their propaganda, "designed to show that Jews were apt to be traitors, spies, imperialist agents, embezzlers, and outright murderers." Taken together, all of these events added up to what AJC Soviet-affairs specialist Joseph Gordon, who authored these reports based in part on foreign-language and clandestine sources, described as "an immense cold pogrom." Even after Josef Stalin's death, he found, Communist leaders were dismissing Jews from their jobs, trying them in secret, and condemning them to lengthy terms at forced labor.[163]

In publishing these accounts of Communist atrocities abroad, the *Year*

---

[161]Vol. 51 (1950), pp. 338, 340; Vol. 52 (1951), p. 329; Vol. 53 (1952), p. 317; Vol. 55 (1954), p. 273.

[162]Vol. 55 (1954), p. 292.

[163]Ibid., pp. 264, 266.

Book was also contributing to the battle against Communism at home. The annual report of the American Jewish Committee for 1951, published in the *Year Book,* made this connection explicit, pointing to the *Year Book* accounts, as well as other widely cited "scientific studies" by AJC, as evidence that the organization was fighting Communist propaganda. It boasted that the *Year Book*'s "information on Soviet slave labor camps, as well as the details about the steady liquidation of Jewish life in the Iron Curtain countries" had "precipitated widespread comment in the American press, and references to them appeared in nearly 200 newspapers and periodicals throughout the nation."[164] This fact, however, takes nothing away from the veracity or significance of the *Year Book*'s articles on the Soviet Union and its satellites: History proved them right on all major counts.

The Issues of the '50s

The other European Jewish community that received extensive coverage in the *Year Book*s of the 1950s was Germany. Though its postwar Jewish population was small—the 1955 *Year Book* estimated it at 23,000, fewer than the number of Jews in India—developments in Germany accounted for more pages in the mid-1950s than were allocated to any other foreign country, including Israel. The American Jewish Committee's historically strong interest in Germany partly explains this anomaly. Whereas most other Jewish organizations, according to Shlomo Shafir's careful study, "did not want contact with Germans and did not care much about the future development of Germany and its political culture," the AJC remained vitally interested, partly because so many of its leaders boasted German roots, and partly because it maintained close links to the U.S. State Department, which supported the rebuilding of [West] Germany as a bulwark against Communism and Russian expansionism.[165] As early as 1951, the AJC's executive committee endorsed a democratic Germany as "the best safeguard against the threat of Communism today and Neo-Nazism in the future."[166] More tangibly, the AJC sponsored programs designed to promote democratic values in Germany, especially among the young. The *Year Book,* for its part, carefully monitored German events, paying particular attention to the success of democratization, the progress of "denazification," evidence of "renazifica-

---

[164]Vol. 54 (1953), p. 574.
[165]Shlomo Shafir, *Ambiguous Relations: The American Jewish Community and Germany Since 1945* (Detroit, 1999), p. 105.
[166]Quoted ibid., p. 96.

tion" ("the regaining of influence . . . of those who had supported Nazism, or exploited the conditions it created"[167]), manifestations of anti-Semitism, debates over reparations and restitution, and the gradual reestablishment of Jewish communal life. At its best, the *Year Book* functioned as something akin to Germany's conscience, reminding readers of precisely that legacy of the past that some Germans seemed eager to put behind them.

At the same time, the coverage was pervaded by an underlying sense of anxiety. Several articles on Germany during the 1950s appeared without an accompanying byline—an indication that they were written by "foreign correspondents or native observers"[168] who, probably fearing repercussions, took refuge in anonymity. The review of the year in 1950 found "anti-Semitism still virulent in Germany." An article five years later pointed to Germany's "moral rehabilitation of outstanding Nazis." The last article of the decade, citing German public-opinion polls, indicated "a considerable survival of Nazi attitudes."[169] By then, West Germany was a trusted ally of the United States, an economic and military power, and a full member of NATO. Yet the editors of the *Year Book,* like so many of the Jews who read it, remained profoundly ambivalent toward the country, following developments there with a strong mingling of emotions and a great measure of uncertainty and mistrust.

Israel, by contrast, enjoyed growing support from the *Year Book.* While the AJC remained officially "non-Zionist," and strove, in the words of its historian, "to demonstrate the compatibility of support for Israel with a concern for American affairs,"[170] the *Year Book* demonstrated the extraordinary interest of American Jews in Israel's development and followed news of the country closely. Beginning with volume 51, Israel always rated at least one article of its own in the *Year Book,* and, as if to highlight its special significance, the article (or articles) appeared in the table of contents under a distinct "Israel" heading, rather than, as heretofore, as part of the "Middle East." Most of the reporting was factual, but the *Year Book*'s sympathies were clear. In 1950, for example, the review-of-the-year article on Israel went out of its way to note that Arabs enjoyed "equal voting rights with Jews" under Israeli law, and that in Israel's first general election, January 25, 1949, "Moslem women went to the polls for the first time in history."[171] A year later, it initiated extensive coverage of Israel's flourishing Jewish culture. In 1952, it gushed that "progress" in

---

[167]Vol. 53 (1952), p. 438.
[168]Vol. 55 (1954), p. v.
[169]Vol. 51 (1950), p. 332; Vol. 56 (1955), p. 359; Vol. 60 (1959), p. 188.
[170]Cohen, *Not Free to Desist,* p. 309.
[171]Vol. 51 (1950) p. 395.

Israel was being "made in every field," and that the previous year (Ju. 1950–June 1951) "was marked not only by a remarkable growth of population through immigration, but also by the construction of new roads, houses and factories; the founding of new settlements and towns; the planting of new groves; the development of new skills, machines, and methods; and in some areas by the introduction of new amenities and conveniences."[172]

The 1952 *Year Book* also carried, as an appendix to the AJC annual report, the full text of the historic August 23, 1950, exchange between Israel's prime minister, David Ben-Gurion, and AJC president Jacob Blaustein (later known as the Blaustein–Ben-Gurion agreement) defining the relationship between Israel and American Jewry.[173] Responding to fears lest Israel interfere with the "internal affairs" of the American Jewish community and provoke charges of "dual loyalty" by promoting the "ingathering of [American Jewish] exiles" to the Jewish state, the agreement aimed to ensure the ongoing support of American Jewish leaders for Israel, which both sides understood to be vital to its continued welfare. The AJC summarized the major points of the agreement as follows:

> (1) that Jews of the United States, as a community and as individuals, have only one political attachment, namely, to the United States of America; (2) that the Government and people of Israel respect the integrity of Jewish life in the democratic countries and the right of the Jewish communities to develop their indigenous social, economic and cultural aspirations, in accordance with their own needs and institutions and (3) that Israel fully accepts the fact that the Jews in the United States do not live "in exile," and that America is home for them.[174]

Despite this declaration of independence between Israel and American Jewry, in 1954 the *Year Book* initiated special coverage of the relationship between "The American Jewish Community and Israel," as well as between "the United States and the State of Israel." These were merged into a single article the next year, and for almost a decade its author would be historian Lucy Dawidowicz, then a researcher on the AJC staff. Her annual analyses underscored the importance of America's role in the Middle East and helped American Jewish leaders keep tabs on Israel's friends and critics. She paid particular attention to Russia's growing interests in the Arab world—emphasizing the point that Israel supported the West—and she chronicled some of the failures of America's Middle East policy, something that the *Year Book* had rarely done be-

---

[172]Vol. 53 (1952), p. 407.
[173]Ibid., pp. 564–68.
[174]Ibid., p. 552.

re. Thus in 1958, reporting on the aftermath of Israel's 1956 Suez Campaign, she quoted a series of administration critics, including Eleanor Roosevelt, Prof. Hans Morgenthau, and former secretary of state Dean Acheson, who opposed the American policy demanding an Israeli withdrawal from the Sinai. She noted as well that "many Jewish organizations criticized American policy," including 16 that urged the United States to reappraise the conflict as one "between the Free World and Nasserism [the policy of Egypt's dictator] backed by Moscow."[175] A year later, she criticized America's Middle East policy even more directly:

> America's major objective in the Middle East—to keep Russia out—had manifestly been defeated. America's second objective—to maintain the peace—was not very much nearer attainment. The Baghdad Pact and the Eisenhower Doctrine, the two major American instruments that had been created to help preserve peace and stability in the Middle East, seemed, at the end of this period, to have outlived their effectiveness. None of the problems within the region had been settled . . . .[176]

Not since the early-20th-century debates over the Russian passport issue and immigration restriction had the *Year Book* permitted such direct criticisms of American policy to appear in its pages. The change undoubtedly reflected American Jewry's heightened self-confidence, partly influenced by the existence of the State of Israel, but also related to the decline of American anti-Semitism and the healthier national political atmosphere. The *Year Book* felt far less constrained in challenging American policy on the basis of its own sense of where the country's best interests lay. Like its sponsor, the American Jewish Committee, it "could believe and seek to convince the general public that its goals"—including support for the State of Israel—"were in fact more advantageous to the country than other alternatives."[177]

While references to Israel multiplied in the *Year Book*s of the 1950s, reflecting its increasingly important if not yet fully recognized role in Jewish life, the American Jewish community, its achievements and challenges, continued to dominate the *Year Book*'s pages. In 1952, for example, some 50 percent of the front half of the book dealt with the United States, as well as most of the back half, which consisted of directories, lists, necrology, calendars, and two (AJC and JPS) annual reports. Most of the special articles in the 1950s, "surveys on important subjects of Jewish interest covering longer periods of history . . . [that] fill in the lacunae

---

[175]Vol. 59 (1958), pp. 206–07.
[176]Vol. 60 (1959), p. 109.
[177]Cohen, *Not Free to Desist,* pp. 324–25.

necessarily left in the annual reviews,"[178] also dealt with the United State
The 1952 feature article, for example, was a "popular, yet authoritative
summary" of the American Jewish labor movement, written by the ex-
Communist writer and intellectual, Will Herberg. The *Year Book* had
largely ignored the Jewish labor movement until then, but under the impact of contemporary controversies over the power and influence of
unions, it now discovered the subject. Herberg's article, a comprehensive,
sympathetic, readable, and somewhat apologetic survey that relied heavily on the scholarly insights of Professor Selig Perlman of the University
of Wisconsin, stressed that Jewish unions, for all of their seeming sepa-
ratism, radicalism, and socialism, were actually thoroughly patriotic,
"committed to the responsible conduct of industrial relations under capitalism." Herberg traced at length the battle against Communism in the
Jewish unions—a story he knew firsthand as a former Marxist and one-
time editor of *Workers Age*—and emphasized that, with the exception
of the furriers' union, "the Jewish labor organizations were saved from
Communist control" and took "the initiative in fighting Communism on
many fronts at home and abroad." Finally, in an oft-quoted observation,
he noted that "the Jewish worker in America was typically a man of one
generation: he was 'neither the son nor the father' of a proletarian." By
his count, Jews in 1951 made up less than 40 percent of the membership
of the so-called "Jewish unions," and that number was dropping. "The
day of the old-time Jewish labor movement," he dramatically concluded,
". . . is over."[179]

Three years passed before the *Year Book* published other "special articles" of significance, but in 1955 and 1956, in celebration of the American Jewish Tercentenary, it published a series of four of them, all designed to illuminate "the forces" that shaped the development of the
American Jewish community from its beginnings.[180] Nathan Glazer, a rising star of American Jewish intellectual life, opened the series with a
thought-provoking historical survey, "Social Characteristics of American Jews, 1654–1954," that reconceptualized the nature of American
Jewish life from a postwar, middle-class perspective. "The fundamental
ground-tone of American Jewish life," he announced, harmonized with
Jews' "respectable, prosperous, 'middle-class' existence." Both the occu-

---

[178]Vol. 53 (1952), p. v.

[179]Ibid., pp. 3–74. The American Jewish Historical Society discovered the labor move-
ment at precisely the same time. See Selig Perlman, "Jewish-American Unionism: Its Birth
Pangs and Contribution to the General American Labor Movement," *Publications of the
American Jewish Historical Society* 41, 1952, pp. 297–338.

[180]Vol. 56 (1955), p. v.

ational structure and the values of American Jews, he found, were also decidedly bourgeois, if not in fact then at least in aspiration. The buoyant optimism and spirit of consensus that characterized the America of his day obviously found reflection here, especially as Glazer pointed to the emergence of a unified American Jewish community and to its rapidly rising "social and economic position." His paean to the middle class also scored points against Communists, who invariably glorified the virtues of the working class. But in seeking to account for Jews' extraordinary record of success, Glazer also pointed to a kind of "spirit of capitalism" that he discerned in Jewish culture. He even cited Alfred Kinsey's study of male sexual behavior to buttress this claim—an allusion that loosened the *Year Book*'s traditionally Victorian standard of propriety. In a sense, Glazer discovered in American Judaism a parallel to what sociologist Max Weber had found in his study of Protestantism—a religion, history, and culture that were decidedly middle-class in orientation and that predisposed its members to success.[181]

The other articles in the series—Oscar and Mary Handlin on "The Acquisition of Political and Social Rights by Jews in the United States," Joseph L. Blau on "The Spiritual Life of American Jewry," and Herman Stein on "Jewish Social Work in the United States"—hewed more closely to the official Tercentenary line. Well-grounded historically and carefully researched, the articles also reflected the sense of pride and achievement that swelled the American Jewish heart during the celebration. The Handlins, for example, concluded their survey by promising "that the enormous distance the Jews have already come toward the acquisition of equal rights can leave only optimistic expectations for the future." Blau cited the social-justice ideals of American rabbis and argued that, to the extent they could be realized, "America, too, can be a holy land, not only for American Jews but for all mankind." Stein found that "after 300 years of living in this country, during which every diverse form of Jewish life has been able to appear, participation in social work under Jewish auspices has become the most universally accepted expression of Jewish communal feeling."[182] A thoughtful review of the Tercentenary celebration by its executive director, David Bernstein, published in the 1956 *Year Book,* argued that these articles, along with the many hundreds of publications, ceremonies, exhibits, television and radio shows, and other tercentenary events, offered American Jews "a new degree of self-confidence," encouraging them "to reassess their own place in the American community." A more recent analysis of the Tercentenary, by

---

[181]Ibid., pp. 3–41.
[182]Ibid., pp. 96, 164; Vol. 57 (1956), p. 93.

historian Arthur A. Goren, argues that it "intensified group conscious- ness and pride," and "encouraged the search for self-definition and self- understanding," thereby setting "the terms for the years to come."[183]

The Upheaval of the '60s

The serene 1950s gave way to the turbulent 1960s, the decade of the civil rights movement, the controversy over the Vietnam War, the countercul- ture, and, of great significance for American Jewry, the great migration from inner cities to outer suburbs, and from the chilly Northeast and Mid- west toward the sunbelt. While, as we shall see, the *Year Book* alluded to these great themes, its featured "special articles," highlighted in the pref- ace and awarded pride of place at the front of the book, focused else- where. Some reflected the central Jewish issues of the day, like the Eich- mann trial, the Second Vatican Council, and the Six-Day War. Only a few articles — in retrospect, the most influential and significant that it pub- lished — helped expose and define new trends in Jewish life.

The last *Year Book* volume of the 1950s featured two important changes that affected coverage of the 1960s. First, the volume was more than 150 pages shorter than its predecessor. At Morris Fine's suggestion, the AJC dropped publication of its annual report in the *Year Book* (the annual re- port of the Jewish Publication Society lingered through 1986). At the same time, the editors trimmed back many sections, particularly in the coverage of foreign affairs, dropping articles on smaller overseas Jewish communities. As a result, the Jewish world as reflected in the *Year Book* now seemed narrower, portending a long-term shift in world Jewry: the section entitled "foreign countries" that had covered 39 different coun- tries in 1950, covered only 23 in 1959. By 1999, it would cover a mere 14.

The second change that took place on the eve of the 1960s was the ap- pointment of Milton Himmelfarb to serve, along with Morris Fine, as *Year Book* editor. Himmelfarb had joined the American Jewish Com- mittee in the 1940s, soon after his graduation from the City College of New York and the Jewish Theological Seminary College, and a year of study at the University of Paris. Since 1955 he had been AJC's director of information and research. A brilliant writer, editor, and thinker, he himself wrote nothing for the *Year Book,* publishing most of his provoca- tive essays in *Commentary.*

The highlight of the 1961 *Year Book* was "Jewish Fertility in the United States," written by sociologist Erich Rosenthal, which demonstrated in-

---

[183]Vol. 57 (1956), pp. 101–18; Arthur A. Goren, "A 'Golden Decade' for American Jews: 1945–1955," *Studies in Contemporary Jewry* 8, 1992, pp. 3–20.

controvertibly that Jews gave birth to significantly fewer children than their Protestant and Catholic neighbors—about 20 percent fewer than Protestants and 25 percent fewer than Catholics. Rosenthal's data quoted and supported demographer Donald J. Bogue's conclusion, in his *Population of the United States* (1959), that American Jews were "scarcely reproducing themselves." In keeping with the *Year Book's* ethos, Rosenthal drew no lessons from these findings, but Himmelfarb, who became something of a crusader for increased Jewish fertility (and himself fathered seven children) was far less shy. Summarizing Rosenthal's article in *Commentary*, he suggested that modern Jews, and women in particular, were placing material desires above the demographic needs of their own people.[184]

Low fertility was not the only demographic problem facing American Jews. In the early 1960s, intermarriage began to be seen as a major concern. Earlier studies had found the intermarriage rate among American Jews to be extraordinarily low. Julius Drachsler's study of intermarriages in New York between 1908 and 1912 had pegged the rate in the world's largest Jewish community at 1.17 percent, approximately equivalent to the incidence of interracial marriages at that time. Barnett Brickner's analysis of Jewish-Christian intermarriages in Cincinnati (1916–1918) put the rate there at 4.5 percent. As late as 1950, Ruby Jo Reeves Kennedy's analysis of intermarriages in New Haven found that only 3.9 percent of Jews married out of their faith.[185] The *Year Book* itself, in 1959, cited U.S. census data that placed the intermarriage rate for Jews at 3.7 percent, and argued that the true rate was "somewhere below 7 percent."[186] While all of these studies suffered from methodological flaws—some, for example, relied on "distinctively Jewish names," forgetting that the Jews most likely to intermarry had changed their names—they pointed to what was then a widely recognized truth. Through the 1950s, most Americans married people of their own background and faith. Notwithstanding melting-pot rhetoric, endogamy in America was the rule, and Jews were even more endogamous than their Protestant and Catholic neighbors.

In a pathbreaking 53-page "special article" published amid considerable fanfare in the 1963 *Year Book*, Erich Rosenthal argued that this sit-

---

[184]*Commentary*, September 1961, reprinted in Milton Himmelfarb, *The Jews of Modernity* (New York, 1973), p. 120.

[185]Julius Drachsler, *Intermarriage in New York City* (New York, 1921), p. 43; Jonathan D. Sarna and Nancy Klein, *The Jews of Cincinnati* (Cincinnati, 1989), pp. 9, 20 n.28. Ruby Jo Kennedy, "Single or Triple Melting Pot? Intermarriage Trends in New Haven, 1870–1940," *American Journal of Sociology* 49, 1944, pp. 331–39; idem, "Single or Triple Melting Pot? Intermarriage in New Haven, 1870–1950," ibid. 58, July 1952, pp. 56–59.

[186]Vol. 60 (1959), p. 9.

uation was changing. "Intermarriage," he warned, " is going to be of ever increasing significance in the future demographic balance of the Jewish population in the United States." Analyzing intermarriage data from Washington D.C., he found that the rate there had risen "from about 1 per cent among the first generation—the foreign born immigrants—to 10.2 per cent for the native-born of foreign parentage and to 17.9 per cent for the native-born of native parentage (third and subsequent generations)." College attendance, he found, "doubled the intermarriage rate." Moreover in smaller Jewish communities—the data he analyzed came from Iowa—the rate stood much higher. Between 1953 and 1959 it "fluctuated between 36.3 and 53.6 per cent and averaged 42.2 percent."[187] A follow-up study of intermarriages in Indiana that Rosenthal published in the 1967 *Year Book* placed the intermarriage rate in that state at 49 percent.[188]

The *Year Book*'s pioneering treatment of intermarriage in the 1960s placed the issue on the Jewish communal agenda. Reviewing some of Rosenthal's data, Marshall Sklare, the preeminent Jewish sociologist, writing in *Commentary,* underscored Rosenthal's findings, calling them "a sharp corrective" to prevailing assumptions concerning intermarriage. In memorable prose, he warned that "Jewish complacency" on this issue dare not continue, for the very survival of the American Jewish community was at stake. Himmelfarb's article on Rosenthal's findings was entitled starkly, "The Vanishing Jew."[189] Intermarriage rates continued to soar over the next three decades, but the "Jewish indifference" that Sklare and Himmelfarb so decried soon came to an end. Thanks in considerable part to the *Year Book,* which returned to the issue repeatedly, the intermarriage rate came to be as widely followed, in some circles, as the inflation rate, and it became a subject of discussion and concern throughout the American Jewish community.

At the very moment when American Jewry began to be concerned for its own demographic future, it was powerfully reminded of what had happened to European Jewry less than one generation earlier. In May 1960, Nazi leader Adolf Eichmann was found in Argentina and secretly transported to Israel for trial, an event that captured headlines around the world and stirred considerable controversy. The American Jewish Committee was itself divided over the legality of Israel's actions: Some, according to Peter Novick, "wanted to condemn Israel's 'violations of legal norms' and thus 'uphold our good name among our natural allies,

---

[187]Vol. 64 (1963), pp. 3–53.
[188]Vol. 68 (1967), pp. 243–64.
[189]Marshall Sklare, *Observing America's Jews* (Hanover, N.H., 1993), pp. 234–47; Himmelfarb, *Jews of Modernity,* pp. 120–24.

the liberals of America.' Others worried that such a stand would alienate Jewish opinion."[190] The Committee, in the end, issued no statement. A short *Year Book* article carefully set forth the arguments on both sides of the controversy.[191] A year later, in the wake of Eichmann's well-publicized Jerusalem trial, the *Year Book*'s entire front section was devoted to the case, filling 129 pages (shown off in a beautiful new typeface introduced that very year). Much of this space was taken up with a review of the proceedings, the full text of the indictment, a summary of the judgment, and an analysis of "America's response" to the trial, as exemplified in editorials, radio and television coverage, and opinion polls. The opening article, however, was written by America's preeminent Jewish historian, Salo W. Baron, and it provided a full-scale survey of "European Jewry Before and After Hitler," based "on a memorandum that Professor Baron prepared for himself when he was invited to testify at the Eichmann trial . . . on the Jewish communities destroyed by the Nazis." The fact that Baron's testimony had been widely publicized—he was the opening witness at the trial—lent the article added significance. Though nobody knew it at the time, Israeli prime minister David Ben-Gurion met with Baron before the trial. "I told him," Ben-Gurion wrote in his diary, "that it is important to explain to our younger generation (and also to the rest of the world) how great was the qualitative loss in the destruction of the six million, and therefore, he must describe the spiritual character of the Judaism that was destroyed, illustrated by her great personalities. . . ."[192] Baron, in spite of his well-known aversion to the "lachrymose conception of Jewish history," seems to have heeded the advice. He began by describing the Nazi onslaught as "the greatest catastrophe in Jewish history," and proceeded to spell out the "extraordinary intellectual and artistic fecundity of 20th-century European Jewry." Indeed, he went so far as to describe the "first third of the 20th century" as "the golden age of Ashkenazi Jewry in Europe" (a judgment that even his sympathetic biographer dismisses as "hyperbole"[193]). More soberly, Baron concluded that:

> Through the disappearance of the Jewish communities the European continent has been deprived of an industrious and enterprising population that contributed significantly to economic and cultural progress. Moreover, the Nazis' genocide left behind a permanent precedent and menace for all mankind.[194]

---

[190]Peter Novick, *The Holocaust in American Life* (New York, 1999), p. 132.
[191]Vol. 62 (1961), pp. 199–208.
[192]Ben-Gurion Diary, entry of 10 April 1961, as quoted in Robert Liberles, *Salo Wittmayer Baron: Architect of Jewish History* (New York, 1995), p. 330.
[193]Liberles, *Salo Wittmayer Baron,* p. 329.
[194]Vol. 63 (1962), p. 48. The entire article is on pp. 3–53.

Longtime readers of the *Year Book* should not have been surprised at Baron's presentation, since the story of European Jewry—before, during, and after Hitler—had been extensively covered through the years in its pages. Postwar developments within Germany, as we have seen, were also closely followed. In 1960, the *Year Book* even devoted 17 pages to the activities of the Conference on Jewish Material Claims Against Germany.[195] But never, before Baron's 1962 contribution, had the *Year Book* devoted its lead article to the destruction of European Jewry, nor had it previously stressed so strongly the distinctively *Jewish* aspects of the tragedy. In the wake of the Eichmann trial, the article both reflected, and helped to further, a larger transformation within American culture as a whole: a growing appreciation for the enormity of the "Holocaust"—a term that only came into common usage in the 1960s—as well as its horrific impact on Jews and Jewish life everywhere.

The Holocaust also played a significant role in transforming the postwar relationship between Christian churches and the Jewish community. A whole series of publications appeared in the 1950s and 1960s that called attention to Christian anti-Semitism and sought to change what the French-Jewish scholar Jules Isaac, in a widely read book, called the "teaching of contempt." In response, Protestants and Catholics in the United States scrutinized their religious textbooks in an effort to purge them of anti-Jewish references. The *Year Book* devoted only sporadic coverage to these developments in the 1950s as part of its reviews of "Intergroup Activities." In the mid-1960s, however, it devoted two lengthy "special articles" to a single highly significant chapter in Jewish-Christian relations. The articles were entitled "The Church and the Jews: The Struggle at Vatican Council II."

Vatican Council II, an ecumenical council of cardinals and bishops, was announced by Pope John XXIII in 1959, just 90 days after his election. The new pope sought to promote "*aggiornamento,*" an Italian word meaning modernization or adaptation; his idea was to harmonize tradition "with the new conditions and needs of the time."[196] Meeting from 1962 to 1965, the Council heeded his call, producing 16 documents that brought about *aggiornamento* in everything from liturgy and revelation to religious liberty and the relationship of the Church to the modern world. For Jews, one aspect of Vatican II was of paramount interest—its proposed statement on the Jews, part of its "Declaration on the Relation of the Church to Non-Christian Religions." In her two *Year Book* special articles, Judith Hershcopf (Banki), then the assistant director of the AJC's Department of Interreligious Affairs, described in absorbing

---

[195]Vol. 61 (1960), pp. 110–27.
[196]"Aggiornamento," *Dictionary of Christianity in America* (1990), p. 31.

etail the contentious behind-the-scenes process that took place over the wording of this document.[197] Never before had a high-level internal Catholic debate concerning the Church's relationship with the Jews been so explicitly chronicled.

Hershcopf understood that the debate over the statement on the Jews was part of a larger struggle within the Catholic hierarchy:

> [I]t was from the outset a highly-charged matter which became one of several key issues dramatizing the split between liberal and conservative viewpoints within Roman Catholicism and the fierce struggle for control between forces representing these viewpoints at the council. Like some of the other controversial subjects on which there was sharp division between a majority of the bishops and a small, but powerful and influential minority, it was subjected to various procedural delays and other tactics designed to prevent it from coming to a vote. Furthermore, the statement on the Jews became involved with political considerations never intended by its authors and the object of intensive diplomatic representations and political pressures.[198]

She also set forth the full spectrum of Jewish engagements in this struggle, from those who sought to influence Church teachings, to those who considered the entire matter an internal Catholic affair that Jews should ignore. In the end, she showed, the final text of the Vatican II statement was diluted from what had previously been approved. The admonition "do not teach anything that could give rise to hatred or contempt of Jews in the hearts of Christians" was watered down to "do not teach anything that does not conform to the truth of the Gospel and the spirit of Christ." Similarly, the injunction never to "present the Jewish people as one rejected, cursed, or guilty of deicide" was weakened into "the Jews should not be presented as rejected or accursed by God, as if this followed from the Holy Scriptures." While Hershcopf recognized Jewish disappointment at the new document, especially in its failure to condemn what Abraham Joshua Heschel called "the demonic canard of deicide," she observed that "in the perspective of 2,000 years of Catholic-Jewish history," the declaration still had "profound implications." "In years to come," she predicted, "it may well be seen as a definitive turning point in Jewish history and the beginning of a new era in relations between the Roman Catholic church and Jewry."[199]

With interfaith relations improving, the *Year Book* felt free to edge away from a more traditional area of American Jewish concern, anti-Semitism. The late 1950s and early 1960s witnessed a "precipitous decline of every variety of anti-Semitism," historian John Higham has shown. He cites a

---

[197]Vol. 66 (1965), pp. 99–136; Vol. 67 (1966), pp. 45–77.
[198]Vol. 66 (1965), pp. 100–01.
[199]Vol. 67 (1966), pp. 59, 46.

1962 opinion poll where only "one percent of the respondents . . . named the Jews as a threat to America. Only 3 percent said they would dislike having a Jewish family move in next door."[200] As a result of this and other evidence, the *Year Book* in 1965 dropped its longstanding section on "Anti-Jewish Agitation," and covered the material instead under the headings "Rightist Extremism" and "Civil Rights and Intergroup Tensions." External threats against American Jews, this implied, no longer required the same kind of careful attention that the *Year Book* had historically lavished upon them. As its extended coverage of fertility and intermarriage indicated, the *Year Book* considered the most serious threats facing American Jews to be internal, and of their own making.

Civil Rights, Race Relations, Cold War, and Counterculture

The decision to cover some aspects of "anti-Jewish agitation" in the section on "Civil Rights and Intergroup Tensions" also reflected changes in the Jewish attitude toward the civil rights movement. From 1950 through 1966, lengthy articles on "civil rights" had appeared in the "Civic and Political" section of the *Year Book*'s coverage of the United States, and they often enjoyed pride of place in that section. In 1958, the article on "Civil Rights" was the longest single article in the *Year Book* — 53 pages — even though it scarcely mentioned Jews at all. The *Year Book* even went out of its way to define and defend its commitment to civil rights. The following message was reprinted annually, with slight changes, from 1955 through 1964:

> Civil rights refer to those rights and privileges which are guaranteed by law to each person, regardless of race, religion, color, ancestry, national origin, or place of birth: the right to work, to education, to housing, and to the use of public accommodations, health and welfare services, and facilities; and the right to live in peace and dignity without discrimination or segregation. They are the rights which government in a democratic society has the duty to defend and expand.[201]

Year after year, the *Year Book* traced developments in civil rights in all of the areas set forth in this statement, often with extensive charts that traced desegregation state by state. It especially highlighted progress: "the 'sit-in' movement at lunch counters," "desegregation of public elementary and secondary schools," "the Civil Rights Act of 1960," and "the

---

[200]Higham, *Send These to Me*, p. 172.
[201]Vol. 65 (1964), p. 15. Compare vol. 56 (1955), p. 195, where the "rights and privileges" are "morally the heritage of every human being," instead of being "guaranteed by law." Also, the word "government" appears there without the qualifier, "in a democratic society." Other small stylistic improvements were added to the statement through the years.

inclusion of liberal civil-rights planks in the election platforms of both major political parties." In 1962 it exulted that "more state civil-rights laws were enacted in the United States during the period under review . . . than in any similar period in history." While in 1963 it described the process of desegregation of public schools in the South as "painfully slow" and it balanced its description of "numerous significant activities" by noticing "failures to act," the very next year it gave "especially full coverage to civil rights and the status of the Negro drive for equality, including the March on Washington and the progress of school desegregation."[202]

The 1965 *Year Book* introduced a new theme into the annual civil rights article: For the first time, subsections were devoted to "Negro-Jewish Tensions" and to "Antisemitism Among Negroes." Lucy Dawidowicz, who wrote the article that year, reported on the hundreds of Jewish stores "looted and damaged" during black riots in the North, and addressed tensions between Jews and African Americans in the Crown Heights section of Brooklyn. She warned of the "tragic possibility" that in "resentment" against "antisemitism among Negroes," Jews would "withdraw from the struggle for Negro equality."[203] A year later, the *Year Book* devoted three pages of its "Civil Rights" article to "Negro-Jewish Relations," and described at length the "demonstrably increased expression of anti-Jewish feeling in . . . almost every level of the Negro community."[204] That, in fact, was the last time that the words "Civil Rights" appeared in the *Year Book*'s table of contents. Thereafter the subject was covered only in an omnibus article now retitled "Intergroup Relations and Tensions in the United States." Then, in the 1969 volume, civil rights was placed in a subsection of that article entitled, "The Urban Crisis." Revealingly, the 1969 article's subsection devoted to "Black Antisemitism" was three times as long as the "Civil Rights" subsection.[205]

The *Year Book* handled a parallel tension—between its commitment to civil rights and its concern for the welfare of the Jewish community—somewhat differently in the case of South Africa. For years, the annual review of developments in South Africa, home to more than 100,000 Jews, had been written by Edgar Bernstein of the *South African Jewish Times*. Among other things, he described the government's segregationist policies, known as apartheid, and observed that "both Jews and non-Jews were divided on the government's program, and Jewish organizations refrained from political action except on matters directly affecting Jew-

---

[202]Vol. 62 (1961), p. 67; Vol. 63 (1962), p. 150; Vol. 64 (1963), p. 80; Vol. 65 (1964), p. v.
[203]Vol. 66 (1965), pp. 187–89.
[204]Vol. 67 (1966), p. 124.
[205]Vol. 70 (1969), pp. 76–89.

ish interests."[206] Beginning in 1961, however, the *Year Book* divided its treatment of South Africa into two, with two different authors—something done for no other foreign country. One article, written in New York, dealt with political developments in South Africa. It described apartheid and its ramifications in highly critical terms, blaming them for the country's problems, and attacking white minority rule, segregation, discrimination, and repression.[207] Generally, this article (like the parallel article on civil rights in the United States) made no mention of Jews at all. The second article, written by Bernstein in South Africa, focused only on the Jewish community—its religious and communal activities, incidents of anti-Semitism, cultural activities, and the like. In most cases this article, which had an entirely different tone, made no mention of apartheid at all.

Fear probably motivated this "two-article" policy: In the 1960s, critics of apartheid in South Africa, Jews included, were either exiled, imprisoned, or quarantined. Still, the *Year Book* made it appear as though political developments in South Africa had nothing to do with the internal Jewish community, and vice versa. Only in 1973 did this well-intentioned but utterly misleading policy come to an end, and it was not until 1988 that the *Year Book* finally set the record straight with a long lead article by the South-African-born Hebrew University scholar Gideon Shimoni, entitled "South African Jews and the Apartheid Crisis."[208]

No similar timidity affected the *Year Book*'s coverage of events behind the iron curtain. As before, it carefully documented developments pertaining to Jews in the Soviet Union, relying for some 35 years upon the careful research of the Russian-born scholar, writer, and communal professional, Leon Shapiro. In addition, two articles by Jerry Goodman, in 1965 and 1969, chronicled American responses to Soviet anti-Semitism—the incipient stages of what became known in the United States as "the Soviet Jewry movement." Goodman, then on the staff of the American Jewish Committee and later executive director of the National Conference on Soviet Jewry, reported with satisfaction in 1969 on the efforts to improve the situation of Russia's Jews. He listed public-relations successes, collective demonstrations, new groups that were demanding "even greater efforts on behalf of Soviet Jews," and academic and intellectual appeals on behalf of Soviet Jewry. "No other issue in Jewish community relations," he wrote, "received such steady focus . . . except the Middle East crisis."[209]

---

[206]Vol. 61 (1960), p. 338.
[207]Vol. 62 (1961), p. 362.
[208]Vol. 88 (1988), pp. 3–58.
[209]Vol. 70 (1969), p. 111.

One might have expected that the Vietnam War too would have benefited from such a "steady focus." America's longest and fourth most deadly war, Vietnam involved the American Jewish community in myriad ways. Thousands of Jewish soldiers fought in the war, many (but nobody knows how many) died or were wounded, Jewish chaplains and the National Jewish Welfare Board tried to meet the needs of the Jewish soldiers, and, of course, numerous Jews and Jewish organizations vigorously and publicly protested the war. Yet, between the Tonkin Gulf Resolution of 1964, which authorized the use of American military forces in Vietnam, and the fall of Saigon in 1975 that ended the war, the word "Vietnam" appeared in the *Year Book* index exactly three times, once in 1968 and twice in 1970 (a few other mentions, including a brief but important discussion in the 1967 *Year Book,* did not, for some reason, appear in the index.) Remarkably, the indexed citations all dealt with the relationship between America's Vietnam policy and its Middle East policy. Neither the contributions that American Jews made to the war effort (the kinds of articles that had appeared during the Spanish-American War, World War I, and World War II), nor the contributions that they made to the antiwar effort received any sustained treatment. The *Year Book* did note, in 1967, the "disquiet experienced by American Jews in 1966 . . . as a consequence of President Johnson's criticism of Jewish attitudes toward the war in Vietnam," and his suggestion (later denied) that "American support for Israel would depend on Jewish support of administration policies in Vietnam." Lucy Dawidowicz, reporting on this for the *Year Book,* observed that "the public positions taken by some Jewish organizations on the war in Vietnam remained unaffected by the incident," and she provided evidence, not entirely persuasive, that Jews were as divided over the conflict as other Americans.[210] A year later, Dawidowicz chronicled the debate among liberals, many of them Jews, over support for Israel in the Six-Day War, given their vigorous opposition to the Vietnam War. In a sharply worded analysis that deviated from the *Year Book*'s usual standard, she concluded that "many leftists were too committed to their political ideologies to respond to political realities."[211] Two years after that, the "Middle East and Vietnam" again briefly occupied the *Year Book* when it noted criticism by American Jewish peace activists of a letter seen as supportive of Vietnam policy sent by Israeli prime minister Golda Meir to President Richard Nixon.[212]

Looking back, though, what the *Year Book* failed to report about the

---

[210]Vol. 68 (1967), pp. 79–81.
[211]Vol. 69 (1968), p. 224.
[212]Vol. 71 (1970), pp. 238–39.

American Jewish community and the Vietnam War looms far larger than what it did cover. Internal divisions within the Jewish community (including the American Jewish Committee) about the war, a history of playing down communal controversies, and perhaps a sense that no dispassionate analysis of "American Jewry and the Vietnam War" was even possible, given the mood of the country, resulted in a "record of events and trends" that was wholly inadequate. Twenty-five years later, this painful gap in our knowledge still makes it difficult properly to assess the war's impact on American Jewish life, and the Jewish role both in the war and in the struggle to end it.

The *Year Book*'s coverage of Jewish student activism in the 1960s was only slightly better. Although it was widely known that Jews played a disproportionate role in the riots and demonstrations that overtook college campuses in the late 1960s and early 1970s, and even *Fortune* magazine (January 1969) devoted an article to "The Jewish Role in Student Activism," written by Nathan Glazer, the *Year Book* played down these matters, a reticence that recalls its silence about Jewish Communists a generation earlier. In 1969, "Student Activism" and the "New Left" did receive brief coverage under the heading "Patterns of Antisemitism" in the article on Intergroup Relations. Quoting Glazer, the *Year Book* concluded that at most "3 to 4 per cent" of "committed, identifiable radicals on the most active campuses" were Jews, and, paraphrasing Glazer, it explained their radicalism as being "rooted in the Jewish politico-cultural heritage of liberal and Socialist thought, and the influence of liberal and/or radical parents."[213] A year later, it quoted a similar explanation by sociologist Seymour Martin Lipset, that Jewish student leftists exhibited "familiar forms of Jewish self-hatred."[214] It was not until 1971 that the *Year Book* offered a more sympathetic analysis, citing Rabbi Oscar Groner of B'nai B'rith Hillel, who described "a new breed" of Jewish students, "not Jewish radicals but radical Jews . . . [who] are radical in and about their Jewishness." In conjunction with this, the *Year Book* also noted the explosive growth of Jewish student newspapers "expressing a wide range of opinion: radical Zionist, Jewish nationalist, and religious Orthodox."[215] But though the article alluded to Jewish students' "reawakened sense of Jewishness," it failed to explore, then or later, what this development meant. Indeed, coverage of Jewish student activities (outside of what went on in formal Jewish college organizations like Hillel) remained relegated, along with civil rights and anti-Semitism, to the *Year*

---

[213]Vol. 70 (1969), p. 73.
[214]Vol. 71 (1970), p. 209.
[215]Vol. 72 (1971), p. 142.

Book's section on "Intergroup Relations and Tensions in the United States," as if Jewish student activists were not an integral part of the Jewish community at all.

Seminal Studies of Communal Change

For all that it excluded and missed, however, the *Year Book* under Fine and Himmelfarb provided broad coverage of Jewish communal affairs as well as a series of stunning articles that focused attention on developments in Jewish life that had previously gone unrecognized. In addition to Rosenthal's pieces on fertility and intermarriage, the 1960s saw the publication of such classic special articles as "Orthodoxy in American Jewish Life" and "The Training of American Rabbis," both by Charles Liebman, and "Jewish Studies in American Liberal-Arts Colleges and Universities," by Arnold J. Band. All three of these focused on the United States, and each pinpointed themes that would become increasingly important in coming decades.

"Orthodoxy in American Jewish Life" was the first major sustained treatment of that subject anywhere. Prior to its 1965 publication, the *Year Book* had noted Orthodox Judaism, for the most part, in its annual article on religious developments. In 1956, for example, it cited an American Jewish Committee study of a medium-sized Northeastern Jewish community ("Riverton") that found Orthodoxy on a steep decline, dropping in one generation from 81 percent among "grandparents" to only 16 percent among "parents."[216] Most scholars of the subject believed that Orthodoxy in the United States had no future. In the early 1960s, however, Milton Himmelfarb noticed that Orthodoxy was on the upswing, especially in New York, and felt that the subject deserved in-depth examination. After rejecting one manuscript on the subject, he turned to a young assistant professor of political science at Yeshiva University who had just published a sociological analysis of contemporary Orthodoxy in the journal *Judaism,*[217] and offered him what seemed like an enormous sum at that time, $500, for a full-scale survey. Charles Liebman accepted, and after three drafts and hours of editing Himmelfarb pronounced his long article acceptable. In fact, the article revolutionized the study of Orthodox Judaism in America, and turned a generation of wisdom concerning the subject on its head.

From its opening page, Liebman's article exuded optimism about "the

---

[216]Vol. 57 (1956), p. 189.

[217]Charles S. Liebman, "A Sociological Analysis of Contemporary Orthodoxy," *Judaism* 13, Summer 1964, pp. 285–304.

vitality of American Orthodoxy." He characterized predictions of the movement's demise as "premature, to say the least," and pronounced Orthodoxy to be "on the upsurge," its inner core "growing in numbers and financial strength." Then, in pages filled with provocative insights drawn from the sociological study of religion, he proceeded to describe the full spectrum of Orthodox Jews, from the "uncommitted" to the "sectarians," as well as a wide range of Orthodox institutions. His closing echoed the surprising optimism of his opening paragraph, and set the tone for much of what has been written about Orthodox Judaism, even by many non-Orthodox writers, ever since. Orthodoxy, he concluded, was "the only group which today contains within it a strength and will to live that may yet nourish all the Jewish world."[218]

Liebman's second article, "The Training of American Rabbis," published in 1968, looked critically at the students, faculty, curriculum, and overall environment at the "three American institutions having the largest rabbinical training programs" — Yeshiva University (Orthodox), the Jewish Theological Seminary of America (Conservative), and Hebrew Union College-Jewish Institute of Religion (Reform).[219] The very subject matter of the article, let alone its critical tone, would have been unthinkable in earlier decades. "Any bias in this article is on the side of criticism rather than praise," Liebman warned in his introduction. Reflecting the anti-establishment ethos of the late 1960s, he suggested that "the public-relations department of each seminary can be relied upon to extol its glories."[220] Meanwhile, he himself lashed out at the seminaries, arguing that they "to some extent" had "failed to prepare rabbis adequately for the pulpit," that they were less concerned than their Christian counterparts with "self-evaluation and criticism," that they stressed "tradition and continuity" over "renewal and change," and that they had "little to say about the Jewish community." A "personal conclusion" — another innovation that earlier editors, concerned about objectivity, would have deleted — argued for alternative programs of rabbinic training. The fact that two such programs were founded that very year, the Reconstructionist Rabbinical College in Philadelphia and Havurat Shalom Community Seminary in Boston, shows that Liebman had his finger on the community's pulse, especially since both of the new schools stressed several of the same ideals and values that he called for. Within a generation, not only would the training of rabbis at all the institutions he studied be completely transformed, but all three programs would also face significant new competition.

---

[218]Vol. 66 (1965), pp. 21–92, quote on p. 92.
[219]Vol. 69 (1968), pp. 3–112.
[220]Ibid., p. 4.

Arnold Band's "Jewish Studies in American Liberal-Arts Colleges and Universities" was no less prescient. Charting "the spread of Jewish studies as an accepted academic discipline" in America's colleges and universities—from about 12 positions in 1945 to over 60 full-time positions in 1965—Band concluded, correctly, that "we are on the threshold of a new and promising period in Jewish scholarship in America." Two decades earlier in the *Year Book,* Ismar Elbogen had already described America as "a center of Jewish scholarship," based on the activities of individual scholars, most of whom taught at Jewish institutions. Band, by contrast, excluded Jewish institutions from his survey completely (only Brandeis, as a non-sectarian Jewish-sponsored university was included), and focused on the development of Jewish studies under non-Jewish auspices. Without overlooking problems—he generously estimated, for example, that only 5 percent of Jewish students took these courses, and he found the courses scattered over a wide range of different programs and departments—he nevertheless exuded optimism.[221] In fact, the field burgeoned far more quickly than he could have imagined. By 1969, it was large enough to warrant the creation of a professional organization, the Association for Jewish Studies. In 1974, Charles Berlin, surveying, in the *Year Book,* library resources for Jewish studies, reported that the association's membership had grown "to nearly 600, with more than half engaged in Jewish studies on a full-time basis."[222] By the turn of the century that number would more than double: The "new and promising period" that Band had foreseen had come to pass.

The *Year Book* under Fine and Himmelfarb looked at many other areas of Jewish communal concern in the 1960s as well. Its strategy was to turn to leading scholars and thinkers and help them translate academic prose into language that Jewish communal leaders could understand. Walter Ackerman thus surveyed the state of Jewish education in the United States, and Lou Silberman reported developments in Jewish theology, a subject the *Year Book* had never even considered before.[223] Previously, for 24 years (1942–1965), the *Year Book's* "American Jewish Bibliography" section had carefully listed English-language publications on Jewish themes with only descriptive notes. Now that annotated listing was dropped, replaced by bibliographical essays, one by Daniel J. Elazar analyzing recent literature on Jewish public affairs, and another by Menahem Schmelzer reviewing contemporary offerings in Jewish scholarship.[224] The "steady increase in the number, diversity and specialization of books

---

[221]Vol. 67 (1966), pp. 3–30.
[222]Vol. 75 (1974–75), p. 5.
[223]Vol. 70 (1969), pp. 3–36, 37–58.
[224]Vol. 68 (1967), pp. 178–221; Vol. 71 (1970), pp. 308–24.

in English about themes of . . . Jewish interest"[225] partly explained the change, but a larger transformation, already evident in the *Year Book*'s "special articles," also underlay it. In the 1960s, the *Year Book,* like many American newspapers and magazines, embraced a more personal and passionate style that allowed authors to express more freely their own views and judgments. It now regularly published subjective and even controversial articles—such as those of Charles Liebman—and was no longer satisfied with lists of facts or chronologies of events.

The Six-Day War and its Legacy

"June 1967 marked a watershed in contemporary Jewish public affairs," Daniel Elazar boldly announced in the 1969 *Year Book.* The Temple University professor of political science described Israel's victory in the Six-Day War as "the climax of a generation, the sealing of an era, and the culmination of a 1900-year cycle." The war, he believed, made Jews both old and young "deeply aware of the shared fate of all Jews, and of the way that fate is now bound up with the political entity that is the State of Israel."[226] Scholars have since debated the extent to which the Six-Day War actually transformed contemporary Jewish life. Some of the changes attributed to the war—including a greater focus on Israel and a shift toward emphasizing Jewish issues, as opposed to universal ones—had, at least in the case of the *Year Book,* begun to show themselves earlier, and the changes that did take place in the war's wake were subtle rather than drastic.

Nevertheless, the *Year Book* treated the Six-Day War as an event of supreme significance, worthy of a special 115-page section that included five different articles. The first, contributed by the Israeli journalist and editor Misha Louvish (who wrote the annual article on Israel for the *Year Book* from 1959 to 1983), summarized what he described as "the greatest victory in Jewish military annals," and went on to trace the political and economic developments that followed in its wake. The American Jewish Committee's Abraham S. Karlikow followed with a piece that revealed the war's devastating impact upon Jews in Arab lands, where he painted a tragic portrait of persecution and suffering. In the war's aftermath, he disclosed, "Jewish life in Aden and Libya came to an end"; "the disappearance of the Jewish community in Egypt" became "almost . . . inevitable"; the Jewish community in Lebanon was "melting away"; and conditions for the remaining Jews in Iraq and Syria were grim and getting worse, since Jews could not leave owing to a "ban on Jewish emigration."[227] The next

---

[225]Vol. 68 (1967), p. vi.
[226]Vol. 70 (1969), p. 172.
[227]Vol. 69 (1968), p. 133.

...ece, covering "international politics," was written by George E. Gruen, the American Jewish Committee's resident Middle East specialist and for more than two decades the author of the *Year Book*'s annual article on "The United States, Israel and the Middle East." He provided readers with a masterful synthesis of diplomatic activities surrounding the Six-Day War, especially on the roles of the United States and the United Nations. Following his piece, Leon Shapiro and Jerry Goodman, in a joint article, traced responses to the Six-Day War in the Communist world, paying particular attention to the fate of Jews there. Finally, Lucy Dawidowicz devoted 31 pages to "American Public Opinion" during the war. Her opening paragraphs summarized her findings, and spelled out critical themes that students of the war's impact on America and American Jews would elucidate for years to come:

> For four weeks, beginning May 15, 1967, when Egypt, Syria, Jordan and Iraq began mobilizing their forces against Israel, until June 10, when the six-day war ended, most Americans were caught up in Middle East events. The Israeli-Arab crisis affected Americans more deeply than any foreign conflict—except, of course, the war in Vietnam—partly because it was a microcosm reflecting the larger conflict between the Soviet Union and the United States.
>
> The conflict aroused in American Jews unpredictedly [sic] intense feelings regarding Israel, Jewish survival, and their own sense of Jewish identity. The relatively cool responses from official Catholic and Protestant spokesmen had unforeseen and dramatic consequences for relations between Jews and Christians. Finally, the crisis, especially because of what was called its parallels with the war in Vietnam, created deep and lasting divisions among a wide variety of leftist parties and organizations in the United States.[228]

For all of the intense feelings that it generated, the war soon faded from public discussion, and by 1970 the *Year Book*'s main coverage of Israel had returned to the pattern established in the 1950s with two annual articles, one on "Israel" and the other on "The United States, Israel, and the Middle East." Four years later, the 1973 Yom Kippur War did not even rate a special article, let along a special section, in the *Year Book*; George Gruen and Misha Louvish simply dealt with the war and its aftermath in expanded versions of their regular articles. Nevertheless, Israel did slowly assume a more important position within the *Year Book*'s coverage of events. This was evident in the number of "special articles" concerning Israel, three in the 1970s alone. Whereas before, only the Eichmann Trial and the Six-Day War had brought Israel to the front of the book, articles now appeared concerning "North American Settlers in Israel" (1970), "Religion in Israel" (1976), and "Israel and the United Nations" (1978), as well as a full account of the 1975 United Nations reso-

---

[228]Ibid., p. 198.

lution equating Zionism with "racism and racial discrimination" (1977). The first of these articles was particularly interesting, for it predicted (quite wrongly) that "the post-June war spiral of American *aliyah* [would] continue," and it linked the rise in the number of North American Jews settling in Israel to growing dissatisfaction with life in the United States. After listing a long litany of domestic American problems—a reflection of the times in 1970, and a harbinger of the *Year Book*'s own changing mood—it concluded that "Jews in America . . . feel a sense of frustration and guilt at what happened to their dream of a brave new world." Some of these dissatisfied Jews, it claimed, "make their way to Israel," hoping to find in the Promised Land what they miss in the United States: "like-minded, socially alert human beings."[229]

The article on "Religion in Israel," by Zvi Yaron, then a senior executive at the Jewish Agency, was even more significant since it represented the *Year Book*'s first in-depth effort to help its readers understand an internal Israeli problem that was receiving growing coverage in the United States. The *Year Book* had reported on religious tensions in Israel for years, and back in 1959 it noted that Reform and Conservative rabbis, "emerging from a self-imposed silence," had begun "to criticize more openly the political agreements between the Orthodox parties and the Israel government, and the continued discrimination against non-Orthodox forms of Judaism."[230] The importance of Yaron's article was that it sought to move beyond these issues, eschewing "simplistic interpretations of the problem" in order to place the debate over religion in Israel in historical and conceptual perspective based on the uniqueness of the Israeli situation:

> [W]hat we have in modern Israel is not the classical church-state conflict between secular and religious forces, but a debate between opposing views of the relationship between the Jewish nation and traditional Judaism. . . . To religious Jews the new secularism is an aberration that is not only untrue but also un-Jewish. To secular Jews the traditional religion is an unconscionable burden that depresses the potentialities of man and thwarts the free development of Jewish culture.[231]

While he offered "no shortcut to resolving the religious problem in Israel," his long and copiously footnoted study set a new standard for *Year Book* coverage of such divisive issues. Israeli ambassador Shabtai Rosenne's article two years later on "Israel and the United Nations: Changed Perspectives, 1945–1976" reflected a similar attempt to place an Israeli problem in a broader perspective for American Jewish readers.

---

[229]Vol. 71 (1970), pp. 183–84.
[230]Vol. 60 (1959), p. 63.
[231]Vol. 76 (1976), p. 43.

Beyond representing an expansion of the *Year Book*'s mission, both articles also exemplified an important new development in post-1967 American Jewish life: Increasingly, American Jews were embracing Israel's problems as their own.

The growing importance of Israel in American Jewish life also appeared in the *Year Book* in a more subtle way, through the articles on "Jewish Communal Services: Programs and Finances." Introduced back in 1952, and written for more than two decades by the assistant director of the Council of Jewish Federations and Welfare Funds, S. P. ("Pete") Goldberg, this regular feature analyzed and published the disbursements and the receipts of Jewish communal agencies. While no more interesting than most other budget reports—which may be why the feature disappeared in the 1980s—Goldberg's articles pointed to important trends. In this case, reviewing the figures for the mid-1970s, he noted that more and more communal funds were flowing to Israel:

> Since the six-day war in 1967, Jews in the United States, Canada, and other countries have recognized that the welfare, health, education, and related needs of immigrants in Israel required massive additional voluntary support for services which the people of Israel could no longer help finance because of their other direct responsibilities. The result was a historic outpouring of aid for the Emergency Fund of UJA [United Jewish Appeal] in 1967, with $173 million obtained by the community federations and welfare funds in addition to the proceeds of the 1967 regular campaign. Together, welfare funds raised a record sum of $318 million in 1967. This record was exceeded each year since 1971 and a new peak was reached in 1974 ($660 million) in response to the challenge faced by Israel in meeting human needs after the Yom Kippur war.[232]

All told, according to Goldberg, about 75 percent of amounts budgeted in the early 1970s went to Israel, compared with less than 60 percent a decade earlier.

Finally, Israel's impact on American Jewish life was reflected in the *Year Book* through the appearance of articles dealing with American Jewish life written by scholars who had themselves settled in Israel. In the years following the Six-Day War, a small stream of important American Jewish academics settled there, and several of them—notably Charles Liebman and Daniel Elazar—had contributed to the *Year Book* regularly. Having moved to Israel, these scholars continued to write for the *Year Book,* demonstrating in the process that the study of American Jewry was no longer confined to the United States, and that the bonds linking Jewish scholars in America and Israel were growing stronger.

---

[232]Vol. 78 (1978), p. 175.

The '70s, Decade of Doubt

Nevertheless, after the Six-Day War, as formerly, American issues continued to dominate the *Year Book*. What changed—and rather dramatically—was the *Year Book*'s perception of America. In the face of an unexpected rise in anti-Semitism, negative demographic news, burgeoning religious and political tensions within the Jewish community, and a national atmosphere poisoned by the Vietnam War, the Watergate scandal, and economic woes, the buoyant optimism of the earlier postwar decades collapsed. Against this generally unhappy background, the *Year Book* in the 1970s offered a much more pessimistic assessment of contemporary and future trends in American Jewish life, and it was not alone. For American Jews generally, the 1970s were a decade of doubt.

Earl Raab, executive director of the Jewish Community Relations Council of San Francisco, noticed signs of the new national mood as early as 1970 in his survey for the *Year Book* of "Intergroup Relations and Tensions in the United States." He spoke of a sense of "uneasiness" within the American Jewish community, and wrote that Jews were "developing some insecurities." "There was," he discerned, "a growing sense of the minority status of the Jews in America, as a new administration [that of Richard Nixon] took office and the Middle East crisis became chronic."[233] A year later, Philip Perlmutter, director of the New England region of the American Jewish Committee, confirmed this trend. In his survey of intergroup relations for the *Year Book,* he found that the events of the year "rekindled suspicion, anxiety and fear in Jews about their own security."[234] By America's bicentennial in 1976, historian Henry Feingold was lamenting, in his lead article, that "a year seldom passes without some new gloomy readings of the community's condition." While he pronounced himself "optimistic about American Jewry," he knew that his was a decidedly minority stance.[235] David Dalin, then at the San Francisco Jewish Community Relations Council, reviewed the developments of the decade on the opening page of the 1980 *Year Book*:

[The] "Golden Age" in American Jewish life has come to an end. American Jews have been experiencing a growing anxiety over various developments in the last decade, including the growth of Black Power, the emergence of quotas in employment and education, and the growth of Arab influence in the United States. The political climate of the country is clearly changing;

---

[233]Vol. 71 (1970), p. 191.

[234]Vol. 72 (1971), p. 132.

[235]Vol. 76 (1976), pp. 3, 37. The *Year Book* published one volume covering 1974–75 "so that in future, volume numbers will coincide with years." Vol. 75 (1974–75), p. v.

there appears to be a growing indifference to Jewish concerns. Jews see themselves faced with new threats to their security.[236]

In addition to these external threats, the *Year Book* highlighted internal risks that the American Jewish community faced. Writing from a demographic perspective, Sidney Goldstein of Brown University, in a comprehensive review of available data published in 1971, warned that Jews, already less than 3 percent of the total population, were "undergoing a continuous decline in proportion, as the total population grows at a faster rate." He also found that Jews were aging, becoming "more geographically dispersed," intermarrying more, and coming increasingly to resemble their non-Jewish neighbors in education, occupation, and income. "To what extent," he wondered ominously, "will the diminution in the distinctive population characteristics of Jews and their greater residential integration lead to behavioral convergence?" While he personally advocated the creation of "a meaningful balance between Jewishness and Americanism," his question hung in the air.[237]

By the mid-1970s additional demographic data became available, thanks to the first National Jewish Population Study, sponsored by the Council of Jewish Federations and Welfare Funds, under the scientific direction of Fred Massarik of UCLA. The *Year Book* published articles based on this study every year from 1973 to 1978, and much of the news was disturbing. For example, the study lowered the estimated number of Jews in the United States by 400,000, and acknowledged that Jews had never reached the six-million mark in the United States—contrary to the *Year Book*'s earlier, overly optimistic estimates. In addition, Massarik disclosed that "the proportion of individuals under 5 years of age has been decreasing for the last ten years," and that "the proportion of Jewish persons intermarrying in the period 1966–1972 was 31.7 per cent, much higher than in any comparable earlier period."[238] Reviewing this data in 1981, Sidney Goldstein reported that the concerns expressed in his earlier article had been borne out and "many of the patterns that were then emerging have become further accentuated."[239]

Beyond demography and intergroup relations, the *Year Book*'s downbeat view of American Jewish life was reinforced by a spate of obituary articles. Nine men (no women) received long, loving tributes in the *Year Book*s of the 1970s, compared to only four (Herbert H. Lehman, Felix Frankfurter, Martin Buber, and Max Weinreich) who received such treatment in the 1960s. While all nine were significant figures (Jacob Blaustein,

---

[236]Vol. 80 (1980), p. 3.
[237]Vol. 72 (1971), pp. 3–87.
[238]Vol. 74 (1973), pp. 270, 292; Vol. 75 (1974–75), p. 295.
[239]Vol. 81 (1981), p. 56.

Jacob Glatstein, Abraham Joshua Heschel, Horace M. Kallen, Reinhold Niebuhr, Joseph Proskauer, Maurice Samuel, Leo Strauss, and Harry A. Wolfson), the disproportionate attention paid to them only added to the overall sense of gloom and loss that pervaded the *Year Book,* as if American Jewry's best years lay behind it and its greatest men were passing from the scene. This was even true in the case of Niebuhr, the only non-Jew ever memorialized by the *Year Book,* whose passing seemed to symbolize the end of a transformative era in Jewish-Christian relations. The great Protestant theologian was "a true and tested friend of the Jewish community," Seymour Siegel wrote in his obituary. He then pointed out that Niebuhr's widow, shortly after her husband's death, sought to have his name removed from the masthead of *Christianity and Crisis,* a journal he had founded, because its editorial policy changed and it now "published articles critical of Israel's administration of Jerusalem."[240] This same heavy sense of loss may be seen in YIVO secretary Shmuel Lapin's obituary for the Lublin-born, American Yiddish poet, Jacob Glatstein. Describing how Glatstein came from a world where Jews "lived, thought, and felt as Jews twenty-four hours a day," and where "their heroes and models were drawn from the Jewish tradition," he paused to lament: "How different this is from our condition, in which the young of even the most committed segments of the Jewish community identify with the same sports and television heroes as does the rest of American society."[241]

Indeed, the *Year Book* projected an American Jewry that was literally coming apart during the 1970s, just as racial, ethnic, religious, generational, and gender differences were simultaneously sundering American society at large. Before, the *Year Book* had generally focused on the Jewish community as a whole, and only rarely—in articles like "Roumanian Jews in America" (1901) and "Orthodoxy in American Jewish Life" (1965)—on its component parts. In the 1970s, by contrast, about a third of its special articles dealt with subcommunities or movements within the American Jewish community, including articles on Reconstructionism, Reform Judaism, Sephardic Jews, Jewish academics, and the Jewish women's movement. One article based on the National Jewish Population Study went so far as to divide the community into 11 "socio-ideological types," including the affiliated and unaffiliated members of the three main religious movements, plus "agnostic-atheist Jews," "just-Jewish" Jews, "ex-Jews," "non-Jews" (married or born to Jews), and "miscellaneous Jews."[242] References to the American Jewish community as a whole by no means disappeared during this time, but analyses of its constituent

---

[240]Vol. 73 (1972), pp. 605–10.
[241]Ibid., p. 617.
[242]Vol. 78 (1978), p. 263.

elements attracted far more attention, especially when they gave voice to those who had not been heard from before.

Charles Liebman, in 1970, focused on one of the smallest pieces of the American Jewish religious pie, Reconstructionist Judaism.[243] His article—which was widely discussed and frequently cited—detailed Reconstructionism's ideology, programs, history, institutions, and constituency, and argued that the study of this "numerically and institutionally insignificant" movement was nevertheless "basic to an understanding of American Judaism." Reconstructionism, he explained, embodied, with some minor exceptions, the values and attitudes of the great bulk of American Jews; it encompassed what Jonathan Woocher would later describe as "civil Judaism." While Orthodox, Conservative, and Reform Judaism represented "three *elitist* ideologies of the American Jewish religion," Reconstructionism, Liebman declared, articulated "the folk religion . . . the *popular* religious culture"; indeed, it sought "to formulate the folk religion in elitist terms." In keeping with the downbeat temper of the times, Liebman was pessimistic about Reconstructionism's future; in fact, he was pessimistic about American Judaism as a whole—which may be why, by the time the article appeared, he had settled in Israel.

For related reasons, the *Year Book*'s articles on Reform Judaism and Sephardic Jews also reached pessimistic conclusions. The former, written by historian Sefton Temkin, was timed to mark the centennial of Reform's congregational body, the Union of American Hebrew Congregations, and for the most part it chronicled in a straightforward way the history of Reform Judaism in the United States. But as it turned to the question "what of the future," it changed tone. It warned that in the course of time Reform Judaism's base "may be eroded through intermarriage and assimilation," and quoted a survey of Reform rabbis, who "expressed concern that Reform Judaism was in the midst of a crisis—a situation that will become worse, many felt, before it becomes better." The Union of American Hebrew Congregations, it concluded, "has lost a vision of itself as pioneer, together with the exhilaration of recent success." It was, according to Temkin, "shadowed by the disenchantment that hangs over much of American life."[244] In the same volume, Rabbi Marc Angel's article on "The Sephardim of the United States," while more innovative methodologically and highly significant in terms of placing Jews of Iberian and Levantine descent on the radar screen of the American Jewish community, ended just as pessimistically. "If there is no reversal

---

[243]Vol. 71 (1970), pp. 3–99.
[244]Vol. 74 (1973), pp. 3–75, esp. pp. 71–75.

in the trends indicated by our data, no viable Sephardi communities may be left in the United States in two or three generations from now," it concluded. Unless religious observance strengthened and the "widespread ignorance of Judaism and Sephardi Jewish tradition" reversed, Angel warned, "the Sephardi heritage will be lost."[245]

Year Book articles on "Jewish Academics in the United States" and on "The Movement for Equal Rights for Women in American Jewry" offered a welcome respite from all this pessimism, addressing timely themes that had not been considered before. The "Jewish Academics" article, by Seymour Martin Lipset and Everett Carll Ladd, Jr., looked beyond Arnold Band's focus on Jewish studies and found that Jews generally formed "a heavy proportion of academe"—a far cry from just one generation earlier, when the *Year Book* reported that, owing to anti-Semitism, Jews represented "but an insignificant proportion of the faculties" in America's colleges and universities,[246] and some infamous departments hired no Jews at all. After an exhaustive chart-filled study, Lipset and Ladd, both distinguished sociologists, concluded that Jews had not only found a home in the academy, but "by every criterion of academic accomplishment, Jewish faculty as a group . . . far surpassed their Gentile colleagues." They explained this success, following the economist Thorstein Veblen, on the basis of Jewish academics' marginality, "the impact of their 'hyphenate' status, of having left the traditional Jewish world, but not becoming fully part of Gentile society."[247]

" 'Who Hast Not Made Me a Man': The Movement for Equal Rights for Woman in American Jewry," by Anne Lapidus Lerner, then an instructor in modern Hebrew literature at the Jewish Theological Seminary of America, covered what Lerner described as a "specifically Jewish brand" of feminism, "which, while questioning many traditional Jewish assumptions, was frequently accompanied by growing respect for Judaism and Jewish values." Tracing developments among Orthodox, Conservative, and Reform Jews, as well as in Jewish organizational and family life, she predicted, accurately, that Jewish feminism was "not likely to disappear." To the contrary, she optimistically concluded that "Judaism has always survived by evolution, never painless," and that in the same way Jewish feminism should be "confronted and accommodated to ensure the survival of American Jewry."[248] Twelve years later, Professor Sylvia Barack Fishman of Brandeis University, as part of her larger *Year Book* study of feminism's impact on American Jewish life, found that a

---

[245]Ibid., p. 136.
[246]Vol. 39 (1938), pp. 61–62.
[247]Vol. 72 (1971), p. 125.
[248]Vol. 77 (1977), pp. 37–38.

great deal of accommodation had in fact taken place. "Jewish religious life and Jewish culture have been profoundly transformed by Jewish feminism in all its guises," she wrote. "From birth onward, American Jewish girls today are more likely than ever before in Jewish history to be treated in a manner closely resembling the treatment of boys." Looking back, she pointed to Lerner's article as a "striking piece of evidence for the legitimation of Jewish feminism by the Jewish intellectual and organizational establishments."[249] Like Liebman's article on Orthodoxy, Lerner's piece both recognized a significant trend in American Jewish life and focused communal attention upon it.

Yet the most significant Jewish movement of the 1970s from the *Year Book*'s perspective—the only one that received article-length treatments year after year, and the only one in which the American Jewish Committee actively participated—was the Soviet Jewry movement, the campaign to fight anti-Semitism in the Soviet Union and (increasingly) to promote the right of Jews there to emigrate. In 1971, the *Year Book* reprinted the summary report prepared by the American Jewish Conference on Soviet Jewry covering its activities during 1970. In 1973, it devoted 15 pages to the "American Response to Soviet Anti-Jewish Policies." In 1974/75 and 1976, it chronicled, in 46 surprisingly frank pages, the struggle (at times within the Jewish community itself) over the "Jackson-Vanik amendment," the law sponsored by Senator Henry Jackson and Congressman Charles Vanik that made American "most favored nation" trade benefits and bank credits to the Soviet Union contingent on free emigration, even at the expense of the "détente" policy favored by the Nixon administration. In 1977, it reprinted the declaration of the second Brussels conference ("The Second World Conference of Jewish Communities on Soviet Jewry") and profiled the 11,000 Soviet Jewish immigrants who had recently settled in the United States. In 1979 it offered a retrospect on "Soviet Jewry Since the Death of Stalin," paying special attention to "anti-Jewish policies" and "Jewish dissidence."[250] To be sure, Leon Shapiro, the author, found it "difficult to envision a mass exodus of Soviet Jews." He urged that the emigration issue "not monopolize the attention and efforts of those seeking to help Soviet Jews," and called for parallel efforts "to strengthen Jewish life in the Soviet Union."[251] That, in part, was a slap at the anti-establishment organizations working to free Soviet Jews, notably the Union of Councils for Soviet Jews and the Student Struggle for Soviet Jewry, whose activities (and very existence, in the case of the Union

---

[249]Vol. 89 (1989), p. 11.
[250]Vol. 72 (1971), pp. 165–69; Vol. 74 (1973), pp. 210–23; Vol. 75 (1974–75), pp. 199–234; Vol. 76 (1976), pp. 160–70; Vol. 77 (1977), pp. 153–81; Vol. 79 (1979), pp. 77–103.
[251]Vol. 79 (1979), p. 103.

of Councils), the *Year Book*s of the 1970s largely ignored. As the *Year Book* portrayed it, the Soviet Jewry movement in the United States was basically an establishment movement, directed by recognized leaders who operated through regular organizational channels (closely linked, we now know, to the *Lishka,* the clandestine liaison operation funded by the Israeli government) in order to bring diplomatic pressure to bear on the problem.

In fact, this was only part of the story. Another part, the saga of the "army of housewives" who maintained direct contact with the "refuseniks," employing underground channels to support and free them, has yet to be fully told. Still, by focusing as it did, the *Year Book* helped to nurture and publicize the "established" Soviet Jewry movement. Given the longtime commitment of the *Year Book* (and the American Jewish Committee) to human rights, religious freedom, and anti-Communism, the decision to focus on the movement was a natural one, a reflection of the *Year Book*'s central ethos and values.[252]

Anxieties of the '80s

In 1980, Morris Fine retired as coeditor of the *Year Book*. "For close to forty years now, whatever merit the *Year Book* has had has been very largely Morris Fine's doing," his successors wrote in tribute. In fact, Fine continued on as editor emeritus, and was still helping out in the *Year Book* office two decades later. David Singer now joined Milton Himmelfarb as coeditor of the *Year Book*. Singer became sole editor of the *Year Book* in 1987, when Ruth R. Seldin joined as associate editor.

The watchword of the *Year Book* at the commencement of the 1980s was "anxiety." Summarizing the state of intergroup relations in 1980, Murray Friedman of the American Jewish Committee described "a deepening sense of Jewish anxiety" occasioned by, among other things, the rise of evangelical Protestant missionary activities directed toward Jews, black-Jewish friction, and "a resurgence of Nazi groups."[253] That same year sociologist Steven M. Cohen expressed anxiety over the future of Jewish philanthropy, warning—wrongly as it turned out—that "relatively fewer Jews in the future will amass large fortunes" and—accurately—that younger Jews would be less inclined to contribute to organized Jewish philanthropy than their elders.[254] David Dalin, in the lead article that year, used the same term—"growing anxiety"—to describe

---

[252]See Murray Friedman and Albert D. Chernin, eds., *A Second Exodus: The American Movement to Free Soviet Jews* (Hanover, N.H., 1999).

[253]Vol. 80 (1980), pp. 71, 83, 86.

[254]Ibid., p. 50.

the response to Nazi provocations against Jews in Skokie and San Francisco. In both cities, he reported, Holocaust survivors "viewed the reappearance of the swastika in their midst as a direct threat to both American democracy and Jewish survival."[255]

As a consequence of this "anxiety," the *Year Book* portrayed an American Jewish community that was lurching rightward politically. Friedman noted "a new militancy with regard to the defense of Jewish interests [that] . . . was bound to effect [*sic*] the usually liberal social-political posture of American Jews."[256] Dalin traced growing Jewish disaffection with the American Civil Liberties Union, which had defended the right of Nazis to march, and observed that "whereas in the past most Jews supported liberal causes, including free speech for Nazis, even when they seemed to threaten Jewish interests and security, this is no longer the case."[257] The results of the 1980 election—the so-called Reagan landslide—seemed to confirm that political changes were in the wind. "The GOP candidate made sizeable gains among Jewish voters," the *Year Book* reported. "In 1980, for the first time since 1928, most Jews did not vote for the Democratic candidate." Milton Himmelfarb, however, read the election returns differently. In a symposium quoted in the *Year Book* he warned "that the figures on the decline in the Jewish vote for the Democratic presidential candidate were deceiving." "In local races," he pointed out, "the Jewish Republican vote increased, but not significantly."[258]

Lucy Dawidowicz, in 1982, sought to place the situation of American Jews of the day in broader historical context. In one of the most ambitious special articles ever to appear in the *Year Book*—described by the editors as "comprehensive and magisterial"—she reviewed a full century of historical developments since the onset of mass East European immigration in 1881, examining American Jewry "from the twin perspectives of Jewish history and American history." Her survey, later published as a book entitled *On Equal Terms,* uncovered "cycles of distress and oppression" as well as "cycles of prosperity and tolerance." As for the new era beginning in 1967, she explained, it reflected both cycles at once, its "swinging pendulum" inaugurating "an era of unpredictable crisis and an even more unpredictable Jewish revival." Jews in this era, she reported, "no longer felt at ease, no longer felt quite at home." Young people were taking over and everything was "new"—culture, politics, even anti-Semitism. Internally, Jewish life was also undergoing great changes. She detected, especially among the religiously Orthodox and the

---

[255]Ibid., pp. 3–4.
[256]Ibid., p. 86.
[257]Ibid., p. 5.
[258]Vol. 82 (1982), p. 105.

politically aware, a "new Jewish assertiveness," "openly acknowledged pursuit of Jewish self-interest," and "more intensely felt Jewish commitments."[259] The phenomenon that Dawidowicz discerned became known as bipolarity, the sense that Jewish life was oscillating between the best of times and the worst of times. This theme, expressed in countless ways, characterized much of the *Year Book*'s coverage through the next two decades, as it documented the crises and anxieties that plagued the American Jewish community, as well as its initiatives and achievements.

Some of the bleakest data that appeared in the *Year Book* flowed from surveys: national and local Jewish community surveys, poll data, and random samples designed to quantify demographic and social trends in American Jewish life. The 1980s saw a pronounced rise in the number of articles printed based on survey data — several per year — and for a time the *Year Book* also admitted into its pages specialized methodological studies, such as "Counting Jewish Populations: Methods and Problems."[260] The results, almost invariably, contained bad news, boding even worse for the future. The Israeli demographer, Usiel O. Schmelz, for example, concluded his study of "Jewish Survival: The Demographic Factors," with the grim prediction that "roughly around 1990, the total number of Jews in the world will start to decline. This decline will accelerate as the losses due to insufficient fertility, aging and assimilation in the Diaspora increasingly outweigh the natural growth of Jews in Israel."[261] As it turned out, the prediction was partially correct, partially self-fulfilling, and partially wrong. The very next year, the *Year Book* did register a whopping drop of 1.5 million in the world Jewish population — fully 10 percent — but that was because it abandoned the old overly optimistic estimates of Leon Shapiro in favor of the newer more pessimistic ones produced by Schmelz's own division of Jewish demography and statistics at the Institute of Contemporary Jewry of the Hebrew University in Jerusalem.[262] Schmelz and his associate, Sergio DellaPergola, also calculated a slight decline in the world Jewish population in 1990, just as predicted. But that population, according to their subsequent calculations, began thereafter to rise again, thanks to Israel's prodigious birthrate, and by the end of the 1990s it was still rising. Schmelz did much better with his 1983 prediction concerning Diaspora population trends. He and DellaPergola foresaw that the American Jewish population would decrease at a slower rate than the rest of Diaspora Jewry, and calculated that "the

---

[259]Ibid., pp. 88–97.
[260]Vol. 88 (1988), pp. 204–21.
[261]Vol. 81 (1981), p. 108.
[262]Vol. 82 (1982), pp. 277–90. See vol. 70 (1969), pp. 273–88, for Schmelz's critique of the *Year Book*'s earlier estimates of world Jewish population.

joint share of Jews in the United States and Israel" would consequently increase from two-thirds of world Jewry in 1975 to fully 80 percent in the year 2000. That, in fact, is precisely what happened.[263]

Other social scientists who published in the *Year Book,* while more circumspect in their predictions, were as a group no more optimistic. Steven M. Cohen, reporting on a national survey of American Jews, found that "on all measures of communal activity . . . younger respondents (ages 18–39) score[d] considerably lower than their elders"—a finding that boded ill for the future.[264] Barry Chiswick described American Jews as a successful but "troubled minority." Given the effects of secularization, very low fertility, and increasing intermarriage, he concluded that their numbers would likely decline as Jews fell victim "to their own success."[265] Gary Tobin and Alvin Chenkin ended a survey of "Recent Jewish Community Population Studies" by showing that Jews had a "lower birth rate and a higher average age" than most Americans and that "families consisting of two parents and children" had become "a distinct minority."[266] Eytan Gilboa warned that notwithstanding the "remarkably stable and consistent" pattern of American Jewish support for Israel, "older, less educated, and more religious individuals" displayed more commitment "than those who are younger and better educated, and who cannot remember a time when there was no Israel."[267] Finally, Bruce A. Phillips reported that Los Angeles Jewry had a higher intermarriage rate and a lower rate of communal affiliation than Jews back east. In these and in many other ways, he argued, Los Angeles represented "the new face of American Jewry."[268]

A Bipolar Community?

By the late 1980s, a few social scientists came to believe that what looked and sounded like bad news really reflected, as Phillips implied, a new form of American Jewish community—not decline, but an historic transformation. Nathan Glazer described this development in the *Year Book* as "a substantial and meaningful debate over the future of the American Jewish community" pitting pessimistic "assimilationists" against optimistic "transformationists." In fact, the debate revolved around a pivotal question, in Glazer's words, whether "American Jewry is headed for assimilation or whether it is engaged in transforming the

---

[263]Vol. 83 (1983), p. 185.
[264]Ibid., p. 94.
[265]Vol. 85 (1985), p. 131.
[266]Ibid., p. 177.
[267]Vol. 86 (1986), pp. 124–25.
[268]Ibid., p. 158.

terms in which Jewishness and Judaism are to be understood." Glazer found merit in both positions, though on balance he was more pessimistic than optimistic, and his essay—unadorned by even a single table or chart—helped clarify the debate for *Year Book* readers.[269] What is remarkable, however, is that the *Year Book* itself scarcely opened its pages to the optimistic "transformationists," notwithstanding the academic status of some of the group's scholars and the popularity of their views in the community at large, as reflected in Charles Silberman's 1985 bestseller, *A Certain People: American Jews and their Lives Today*. It was left to Lawrence Grossman in his "Jewish Communal Affairs" article in the 1988 *Year Book* to explain the issue dispassionately, based on an AJC conference (where in fact Glazer had spoken) that brought both sides in the clamorous debate together:

> What emerged was a recognition that the questions were much more complex than simply whether Jewish life in the United States was thriving or declining. It became clear that demographic data were hard to interpret and even harder to project into the future, and that any assessment of the "quality" of Jewish culture was inescapably subjective. One thesis that drew considerable attention was that, while certain parts of American Jewry were indeed deepening their Jewishness, others were on an accelerated assimilatory course out of the Jewish community.[270]

For the most part, however, the *Year Book* continued to challenge the transformationist approach, notably in a 1992 multi-authored article on "Jewish Identity in Conversionary and Mixed Marriages," where the optimistic arguments of transformationists were forcefully rejected. "The chances of a mixed marriage resulting in a single-identity household at any level of Jewish identification," the authors concluded gravely, "are extremely slim." They went on to warn that if "present trends continue, the already low overall level of Jewish identification is likely to fall further, and dual-identity households may eventually rival if not outnumber single-identity households. Unambiguous Jewish identity may become the mark of a minority."[271]

If demographic and social scientific data found in the *Year Book* portended the "worst of times," *Year Book* coverage of Jewish education, religious life, and culture in the 1980s and 1990s painted a brighter picture altogether. Walter Ackerman, in a 1980 article on "Jewish Education Today," highlighted the "continued growth of the day school movement." He reported that about one-fourth of all the children in Jewish elementary schools studied in Jewish all-day schools, and because of this the av-

---

[269]Vol. 87 (1987), pp. 3–19.
[270]Vol. 88 (1988), p. 203.
[271]Vol. 92 (1992), pp. 39–40.

erage number of pupil hours per Jewish school year had increased in just over a decade by 35 percent. He also pointed to "the expansion of educational camping," the "explosive expansion of Jewish Studies programs in American colleges and universities," and to a variety of other new educational initiatives. No Pollyanna, he did take account of many negative trends in American Jewish education, notably the fact that "the vast majority of children who enter a Jewish school terminate their studies long before they can be expected to have attained any recognizable or long-lasting skills and competencies."[272] But if his conclusions were mixed, in keeping with the regnant "bipolar" interpretation of American Jewish life as a whole, an extensive *Year Book* survey of "Jewish Education in the United States" 19 years later, by historian Jack Wertheimer, ended on a much more ebullient note: "the field of Jewish education today, perhaps as never before, is arguably the most dynamic sector of the American Jewish community."[273]

Wertheimer, professor of American Jewish history and later provost of the Jewish Theological Seminary, became the *Year Book*'s foremost interpreter of American Jewish life at the end of the 20th century. Besides his survey of Jewish education, he authored three additional articles: "Jewish Organizational Life in the United States Since 1945" (1995), "Current Trends in American Jewish Philanthropy" (1997), and "Recent Trends in American Judaism" (1989). The latter, by far the most important discussion of Jewish religious life ever published in the *Year Book,* appeared just a year after Lawrence Grossman announced in his review of Jewish communal affairs that "the issue that most worried American Jewish leaders . . . was conflict between the Jewish religious movements."[274] Annual coverage of American Jewish religious life resumed that year, after a quarter-century hiatus, and much of the coverage was given over to "religious polarization" and "tensions within each movement." Wertheimer, however, sought to transcend these "headline-making clashes" in order to shed light on deeper questions of religious observance and the overall condition of Judaism in the United States. His 100-page article, later expanded into a book, offered a balanced portrayal of American Judaism, noting both positive and negative trends, and it concluded, as Dawidowicz and Ackerman had, with a mixed assessment, another warning that the American Jewish community was polarizing:

[I]n the religious sphere, a bipolar model is emerging, with a large population of Jews moving toward religious minimalism and a minority gravitat-

---

[272]Vol. 80 (1980), pp. 130–48.
[273]Vol. 99 (1999), p. 115.
[274]Vol. 88 (1988), p. 188.

ing toward greater participation and deepened concern with religion. The latter include: newly committed Jews and converts to Judaism, whose conscious choice of religious involvement has infused all branches of American Judaism with new energy and passion; rabbinic and lay leaders of the official denominations, who continue to struggle with issues of continuity and change within their respective movements; and groups of Jews who are experimenting with traditional forms in order to reappropriate aspects of the Jewish past. These articulate and vocal Jews have virtually transformed American Judaism during the past two decades. At the same time, an even larger population of American Jews has drifted away from religious participation. Such Jews have not articulated the sources of their discontent but have "voted with their feet," by absenting themselves from synagogues and declining to observe religious rituals that require frequent and ongoing attention. To a great extent, their worrisome patterns of attrition have been obscured by the dynamism of the religiously involved. It remains to be seen, therefore, whether the transformation of American Judaism wrought by the committed minority during the past two decades will sustain its present energy and inspire greater numbers of Jews to commit themselves to a living Judaism.[275]

The one area where the *Year Book* proved less equivocal—indeed, it was refreshingly upbeat—was in its appraisals of Jewish culture. The editors placed new emphasis on culture in the 1990s, just as "cultural studies" in the academy were taking off, and in 1991 two articles appeared: Sylvia Barack Fishman's "American Jewish Fiction Turns Inward," and Ruth R. Seldin's "American Jewish Museums: Trends and Issues." Fishman set out to describe "a remarkable literary trend . . . a new, inward-turning genre of contemporary American Jewish fiction which explores the individual Jew's connection to the Jewish people, to Jewish religion, culture and tradition, and to the chain of Jewish history." She concluded, enthusiastically, that contributors to this genre "articulate[d] the spiritual struggles of their age."[276] Seldin, meanwhile, traced "the proliferation of Jewish museums over the last few decades," which she, following Charles Silberman, related to "a major renewal of Jewish religious and cultural life in the United States . . . on the part of third- and fourth-generation American Jews who are not in flight from their past—as were their second generation parents—but who, on the contrary, are trying to recapture it." She described "the burgeoning of Jewish museums" as "one of the success stories of American Jewish life."[277] A subsequent article on Jewish film, if less evaluative, was similarly upbeat, and so were the annual surveys of American Jewish culture (replete with words like "fertile," "diverse," and "inventive") begun in 1998 by Trinity College professor of

---

[275]Vol. 89 (1989), p. 162.
[276]Vol. 91 (1991), pp. 35, 69.
[277]Ibid., pp. 75, 112.

humanities Berel Lang. The only negative cultural note was sounded by Brandeis University's Alan Mintz, in an article on "Israeli Literature and the American Reader." "Despite favorable notices," he observed, "Israeli novels in translation have not sold very well." Since the literature is so good, he wondered, "why don't people read it?"[278]

By the 1980s, the *Year Book*'s coverage of anti-Semitism reflected the bipolarity of the American Jewish community on this topic as well. Involved members of the American Jewish community knew that anti-Semitism was no longer a serious problem in the United States. While it had not totally disappeared, it had declined to historically low levels. But the majority of American Jews continued to view it as a highly important problem—more important, according to one of Steven M. Cohen's surveys, than assimilation or the quality of Jewish education.[279] The *Year Book,* of course, refused to cater to this popular notion. As we have seen, it had long since dropped its section on "anti-Jewish agitation." In fact, the word "anti-Semitism" (or any variant thereof) did not even appear in its index! The subject was covered to some extent under "intergroup relations," but it rarely occupied more than ten pages, and in 1989 it filled less than two.[280] As a sign of the times, the "anti-Semitism" subsection of "intergroup relations" was merged in 1991 with the section on "extremism," and, beginning in 1996, the whole article on "Intergroup Relations" disappeared, incorporated into an overview of "national affairs." Even then, there was so little news that "anti-Semitism and extremism" together occupied only two pages in 1999, mostly devoted to the aftermath of a riot that took place eight years before. Nevertheless, as the *Year Book* regularly noticed, "both behavioral and attitudinal anti-Semitism were perceived by many Jews to be greater than was reflected in the data collected and assessed by Jewish agencies."[281] The establishment and the masses, in other words, viewed reality very differently.

In 1986, the threat of anti-Semitism seemed momentarily to bring the two sectors of the Jewish community back together. As the *Year Book* noted in retrospect:

> Many of the specters haunting the consciousness of American Jews materialized at some point during 1986. Organized anti-Semitic groups made front-page news, some of them trying to turn economic crisis in the farmlands to their advantage. A Jewish Wall Street financier [Ivan Boesky] was caught in some illicit and profitable deals. There were continuing attempts to "Chris-

---

[278]Vol. 97 (1997), pp. 93–114.
[279]Vol. 83 (1983), p. 100.
[280]Vol. 89 (1989), pp. 179–81.
[281]Vol. 95 (1995), p. 104.

tianize" America. And an American Jewish spy [Jonathan Pollard] was arrested for turning over valuable American secrets to Israel.[282]

In the end, though, the *Year Book* reported that "general empirical measures of anti-Semitism remained historically low," and the issues that seemed so threatening at the time quickly faded away. Only black anti-Semitism continued to be newsworthy; in 1993 it was described as "the major source" of American Jewish anxiety. That same year, the *Year Book* devoted four pages of small type to the August 19, 1991, anti-Semitic riot by African-Americans in Crown Heights, and to the murder, close to the scene, of Yankel Rosenbaum, an Australian Hassid. In a rare admission, it confessed that mainstream Jewish organizations were "noticeably hesitant" both in responding to these incidents and in labeling them anti-Semitic, in part because "mainstream Jewish organizations were generally distant from the Hassidim and ambivalent toward them."[283] By 1999, though, even black anti-Semitism no longer seemed so important an issue, at least from the *Year Book*'s perspective. Indeed, that year it quoted a finding by the Foundation for Ethnic Understanding that "cooperation, rather than conflict, was 'the dominant theme between African-Americans and Jews.'"[284] There was no evidence, however, that popular opinion had yet come around to the same position.

Imperfect Israel and Shrinking Diaspora

As domestic issues polarized the American Jewish community, the State of Israel—which, around the time of the Six-Day War, had been a focal point of communal unity—now became a divisive communal issue as well. Policies toward the Arabs, the peace process, Israel's religious life—these and other Israel-related themes became increasingly controversial during the 1980s and 1990s. Through these years, Israel dominated the agenda of the American Jewish community, especially given the American government's role in the peace process. The *Year Book* provided reliable information concerning these developments, documenting the clamorous debates that filled the press and the airwaves. The surpassing importance of Israel to American Jewish leaders was demonstrated by the large fraction of the *Year Book* that Israel annually occupied. In one extraordinary year, 1990, Israel-related articles occupied more than half the

---

[282]Vol. 88 (1988), p. 143.
[283]Vol. 93 (1993), p. 92.
[284]Vol. 99 (1999), p. 134.

volume! And while its articles reflected a range of perspectives, they aimed to inform public opinion rather than to sway it.

Already in 1980, the *Year Book*, reporting on the events of 1978, discerned "growing concern in Israel and within the American Jewish community that the special relationship between the United States and Israel was being eroded under the impact of new circumstances in the Middle East." It described two camps — "Peace Now" and "Secure Peace" — that held opposite views concerning the policies of Israeli prime minister Menachem Begin, and it observed that criticism by American Jews of the Begin government had attracted substantial press attention.[285] Two years later, George Gruen reported in the *Year Book* that "the American Jewish community found itself increasingly caught in a painful dilemma" concerning Israel. He himself bitterly criticized American policies, describing them as revealing both "a lack of consistency" and a failure to understand Arab motives.[286] The disastrous 1982 war in Lebanon, to which the *Year Book* devoted three special articles in 1984, underscored the divisiveness surrounding Israel's policies. Ralph Mandel opened the volume by describing Israel as "deeply divided" and a "land of extremes, where the middle ground was often inhospitable, when it was not totally inaccessible." George Gruen showed that American Jews, too, were divided. He quoted one rabbi who declared that the invasion "threatens to tear us apart," and devoted seven pages to documenting both the range of American Jewish responses to the war as well as press coverage of these internal communal divisions.[287] The *Year Book* was also highly critical of media coverage of the war, describing some reporters as lacking "essential background information on the complicated situation" and quoting experts who found "distortions and biases," especially in the nightly newscasts.[288]

Meanwhile, the *Year Book*'s own coverage of Israel was in the process of changing. In the early 1980s it referred to the lands Israel won in 1967 as "Judea and Samaria," the traditional biblically rooted term for Jewish settlement preferred by Israel's Likud government. By the late 1980s it spoke instead of "occupied territories" and "administered areas," implying that Israel exercised only temporary oversight over these lands.[289] It also began to display a great deal more sympathy for the Arabs living under Israeli administrative rule, criticizing the Israeli security forces for "stifling at birth any potential emergence of a local Palestinian leadership," and attacking the government's policies of deportation and ad-

---

[285]Vol. 80 (1980), pp. 87, 104–05.
[286]Vol. 82 (1982), pp. 119, 131.
[287]Vol. 84 (1984), pp. 3, 84–90.
[288]Ibid., pp. 79, 121.
[289]Compare vol. 83 (1983), p. 231, and vol. 88 (1988), pp. 364, 388.

ministrative detention.[290] The Arab uprising known as the *Intifada* received extensive coverage in the *Year Book,* and, again, much of it was critical of Israeli policies. Ralph Mandel documented cases of military brutality against Arab civilians and disputed government claims that such abuses were "exceptional." He described what he called a "chasm of mistrust, enmity and sheer hatred that was generated by IDF [Israel Defense Forces] activity in the territories," and quoted sympathetically data critical of government actions provided by B'Tselem, the Israeli Information Center for Human Rights in the Occupied Territories.[291] By 1991 the *Year Book* was speaking openly of "American Jewish disenchantment with Israeli actions."[292] Almost the same words—"the disenchantment of U.S. Jews with Israel"—were repeated seven years later, and the phenomenon was blamed both on "discomfort with the Israeli government's hard-line approach to the peace process" and on proposed legislation that, if passed, would have rendered "Conservative, Reform or other non-Orthodox conversions performed in Israel or abroad invalid under Israeli civil law."[293]

Even as the *Year Book* admitted these criticisms into its pages and gave voice to divisions concerning Israel's policies among both Israeli and American Jews, it also devoted new attention to the cultural life of Israel, which it generally reviewed in upbeat terms, paralleling its positive view of American Jewish culture. "Israel, at the end of the 1980s, was a society with an impressive and dynamic cultural life," the Yale-trained journalist Micha Z. Odenheimer reported in 1991. "In poetry and music, fiction, art and philosophy, Israel maintained a pace of creative achievement and intensity unmatched by many older, larger, and wealthier countries." Two years later, the *Year Book* reported that the same "cultural foment [*sic*] and vitality . . . continued into the early 1990s," and four years after that it found that "the peace process created a sense of hope and liberation that encouraged artistic expression."[294] While it did notice cultural cleavages surrounding both religious and ethnic issues, the *Year Book*'s coverage of culture, in Israeli life as in American Jewish life, emphasized the creative and the vibrant. Culture, the *Year Book* implied, carried with it an almost redemptive quality, articulating and sometimes bridging the sharp divisions in Jewish and Israeli life and pointing the way toward new solutions to problems that political and religious leaders found intractable.

---

[290]Vol. 89 (1989), p. 372.
[291]Vol. 90 (1990), pp. 402, 405–06, 457.
[292]Vol. 91 (1991), p. 178.
[293]Vol. 98 (1998), pp. 443–44.
[294]Vol. 91 (1991), p. 424; Vol. 93 (1993), p. 403; Vol. 97 (1997), p. 497.

The double celebration in 1998 of the 100th anniversary of the Zionist movement and the 50th anniversary of the State of Israel permitted the *Year Book* to reexamine Zionism and Israel from a broader historical perspective. To mark these occasions, it commissioned four different special articles, as well as an eight-page photographic spread—an editorial first. But it stoutly resisted panegyrics. To the contrary, Professor Anita Shapira of Tel Aviv University, in an article that placed Zionism in the context of the "upheavals of the 20th century," observed that "Zionism, like other 'isms,' is suffering the symptoms of aging. Its ideological fervor has been dampened; its recruiting abilities have declined considerably." Journalist Yossi Klein Halevi, while noting Israel's most significant contributions—"ingathering diasporas, psychologically healing the Jews, and re-empowering Judaism"—pointed to "unforeseen dilemmas" that threatened "to undermine those remarkable achievements." Finally, Professor Arnold Eisen of Stanford, offering an American Jewish perspective on "Israel at 50," spoke of a "combination of joy and apprehension, illumination and perplexity, transcendent faith and satisfaction in the everyday" that characterized his own feelings concerning this milestone. At "the heart of the American Jewish response to Israel," he explained, was a "combination of relationship and distancing."[295] The *Year Book,* through the century, had captured and reflected all of these contradictory themes. As in so many other respects, so too in relation to Zionism and Israel, it mirrored, through the eyes of American Jews, the twists and turns of historical development.

The same was true, of course, for the *Year Book*'s coverage of Jewish life outside of Israel and the United States. As already noted, the Diaspora both shrank and consolidated in the postwar era. With the passage of half a century since the close of World War II, some 67.4 percent of Diaspora Jewry lived in the United States, according to Sergio DellaPergola's figures in the *Year Book,* and 95 percent of Diaspora Jews lived in just 14 countries. Only 36 Diaspora countries boasted Jewish populations of 5,000 Jews or more. Most of the 200 or so countries of the world were completely barren of Jews or contained communities so small as to be unsustainable.[296] Against this background, the *Year Book*'s coverage of Jewish life in "other countries" markedly contracted, largely due to the difficulty of finding capable and willing authors. Even significant Jewish communities, like Argentina, no longer received annual coverage, while Brazil, the eighth largest Jewish community in the Diaspora, and Belgium, the 14th largest, received no article-length coverage in the

---

[295]Vol. 98 (1998), pp. 24, 26, 48, 64.
[296]Vol. 99 (1999), p. 578.

1990s. The *Year Book* focused instead on those Diaspora countries that American Jews, and Americans generally, cared most about, English-speaking countries like Canada, Great Britain, Australia, and South Africa; and European countries like Germany, France, Italy, and the former Soviet Union. Meanwhile, occasional special articles filled in some of the gaps. In 1985, for example, the *Year Book* devoted its entire front section to Latin American Jewry, including a survey article by Judith Laikin Elkin and a demographic study by U.O. Schmelz and Sergio DellaPergola. In 1993 the front section was devoted to articles about Europe. Still, whole regions, including the Caribbean, North Africa, and Asia, received minimal *Year Book* attention in the final decade of the century. From the cloudy perspective of the American Jewish community, which the *Year Book,* in this case, did little to clarify, these dwindling Jewish communities had already ceased to exist.

The Year Book *and the Jewish 20th Century*

As the *Year Book* reached its centennial, coinciding with the start of a new century and a new Christian millennium, the American Jewish community stood at a crossroads in its history. Demographically, the community was stagnant. It had not grown appreciably since 1960, comprised a smaller percentage of America's total population than it had in 1920, and seemed likely to witness an actual decline in numbers in the decades ahead. In 1998, for the first time, the *Year Book* reported that (based on 1996 data) Greater New York had fallen from the top spot on the list of "metropolitan areas with the largest Jewish populations." Greater Tel Aviv had overtaken it.[297] Furthermore, Israel seemed poised to overtake the United States as the largest Jewish community in the world; its Jewish population was just under one million less than that of the United States, and growing fast.

Meanwhile, the great issues of the 20th century, including immigration, Zionism, and the battle against anti-Semitism, no longer inspired and united American Jews as once they had. Nor was there any large community of suffering or persecuted Jews anywhere in the world calling upon the American Jewish community for assistance. As a result, Jack Wertheimer noted in the *Year Book,* Jewish organizational life in the United States had entered a "period of introspection and retrenchment." With funds, energy and priorities being reallocated, he heard one message resounding unambiguously: "the future begins at home."[298]

---

[297]Vol. 98 (1998), p. 511.
[298]Vol. 95 (1995), p. 3.

For a century, the *American Jewish Year Book* has been attentive to just such messages as it chronicled events and trends in American and world Jewish life. From its modest, imperfect beginnings, it helped to inform and educate American Jews as they assumed the burden of Jewish leadership, and annually it documented American Jewry's burgeoning and multifaceted role at home and abroad. Its listings, directories, population figures, quantitative studies, annual reviews, and special articles supplied the basic information that Jewish leaders required for their work, and helped to clarify the central issues affecting Jews everywhere.

Through the years, the *Year Book* summarized the leading events of Jewish life, striving for dispassion but often, as we have seen, displaying subtle biases and agendas perhaps more evident in retrospect than to contemporaries. At times, the *Year Book* also assumed a prophetic voice, forecasting events and trends with stunning accuracy. And occasionally, it even served as the community's censor, shaping and withholding information to support the community's "best interests" as it conceived them. Whatever its imperfections, though, the *Year Book* has consistently served as an invaluable guide to Jewish life, and especially American Jewish life, in the 20th century. Its wide-ranging coverage, its emphases, its reliability, and its dependable quality make the *Year Book* an unparalleled resource for those who seek to study the history of American Jewry and for those who seek to shape its future.

Prospecting the Jewish Future: Population Projections, 2000–2080

By Sergio DellaPergola, Uzi Rebhun, and Mark Tolts

T HIS STUDY ARTICULATES different scenarios for the development of Jewish population worldwide up to the year 2080.[1] The results are presented in full awareness that forecasting, in demography as in any other field, tends to underestimate the range of possible developments. Slow and gradual trends occasionally clash with sudden breaking points—geopolitical revolutions, technological innovations, even environmental catastrophes. One intriguing phenomenon in recent decades—whose consequences are still not fully clear—is globalization, the growing political, economic, and technological integration between different regions and levels of the world system that makes local communities increasingly dependent on events and trends that stand at great geographical distance. If world society is becoming more fluid and less stable and predictable, this is even truer of world Jewry, given its wide geographical spread and dependence on external circumstances.

Long-term transformations of Jewish population and society—especially over the course of the 20th century, which witnessed the *Shoah* and

[1]This article reflects prolonged research at the Division of Jewish Demography and Statistics, the Avraham Harman Institute of Contemporary Jewry, and The Hebrew University of Jerusalem. The idea of projecting new population estimates for each of the major Jewish communities worldwide was initiated by the late Professor Uziel O. Schmelz, who actively participated in establishing the conceptual and technical framework. Preparation of the projections was made possible through a grant from the Philanthropy and Education Fund in memory of Jean and Charlotte Abramovici, the Israel Humanitarian Foundation, New York. We gratefully acknowledge the encouragement of Marvin Sirota and Stanley J. Abrams. Most of the population projections presented here were managed by Dalia Sagi, whose assistance in the project was invaluable. Benjamin Anderman, Ester Bassan, and Judith Even helped at various stages of data collection, processing, and editing. Dr. Hania Zlotnik, head of mortality and population statistics, Population Division, Department of Economic and Social Affairs, The United Nations, and Dr. Thomas Buettner of the same division, kindly provided unpublished materials on mortality models. Ari Paltiel, Dorit Tal, and Yifat Klopstock of the Israel Central Bureau of Statistics (CBS) kindly provided unpublished materials relevant to the project. Responsibility for the contents of this article rests solely with the authors.

Israel's independence—defy conventional forecasting. Crisis and resilience, continuity and change, have continually reordered Jewish realities, as centers of Jewish life rose, fell, or were transformed. While such a complex history renders problematic all approaches to figuring out the future, the alternative position—fatalistic indifference to that future—can be dangerous. Population projections, which depend not only on biological-demographic factors but also on the cultural and psychological impact of group identity, provide necessary background for the discussion of critical Jewish policy issues.

Since we cannot predict the full spectrum of future developments, our approach extends over time the path of trends presently observed among Jewish populations, allowing for change within the limits of what currently appears to be a reasonable range of variation. After reviewing the main directions and mechanisms of global Jewish population change since the end of World War II, we will present alternative projections for world Jewry and for each of six major geographic regions over the 21st century.[2] The main focus is the period 2000–2020, since current trends are more likely to provide guidance for the immediate future than for later in the century. Nevertheless, population projections for 2030, 2050, and 2080 are also provided to illustrate, if only roughly, the nature of possible changes in the longer term.

JEWISH POPULATION TRENDS, 1945–2000

Size of Jewish Population and Factors of Change

After the loss of six million in the *Shoah,* world Jewish population was estimated at 11 million in 1945.[3] Over the subsequent 55 years world Jewry grew, but the rate of growth gradually slowed, and the population size attained did not even approach prewar numbers.[4] It took about 13 years to add one million Jews to the post-*Shoah* total, but another 38 years to add a second million. World Jewish population grew by 782,000 during the 1950s, 506,000 in the 1960s, 234,000 in the 1970s, 49,000 in the

---

[2]Previous issues of the AJYB contained detailed overviews of Jewish population trends worldwide. See, for example, Sergio DellaPergola, "World Jewish Population, 1997," AJYB 1999, vol. 99, pp. 543–80. A short summary of the current update appears below, pp. 484–95.

[3]In this study we consider the conventional date of May 1, 1945, as the ending point of World War II and the beginning of the postwar period.

[4]The estimates reported here provide rough orders of magnitude only, and in no way can be considered absolutely accurate or definitive. Several of the estimates revise previous work by us and by other authors.

1980s, and 282,000 in the 1990s (see table 1). The diminished returns (until the 1990s) reflected a progressive decline of the Jewish natural increase—the difference between Jewish births and Jewish deaths—and a generally negative balance of accessions to and secessions from Judaism. Thus world Jewry had average annual growth rates of 0.18 percent in the 1970s, 0.04 percent in the 1980s, and 0.22 percent in the 1990s—hence virtually zero population growth.

One major contributing factor to these demographic trends was an "effectively Jewish" birthrate generally lower than total birthrates in the same locales.[5] One reason was the moderate-to-low fertility level among Jews. This was exacerbated, for European communities, by a significantly distorted age composition resulting from high child mortality and very low birthrates during World War II. Indeed, these postponed effects of the *Shoah* on Jewish population are equal to or greater than those directly generated by genocide.[6] Another factor was the rapid increase of marriages between Jews and non-Jews in Diaspora communities, particularly since the 1960s, and the non-identification as Jews of most of these couples' children.

Jews have constituted a solid majority of the population in the State of Israel since 1948, while being a small minority in the rest of the world. From the outset, sharp demographic differences emerged between these two main typological components of world Jewry. Israel's Jewish population consistently increased, from approximately half a million in 1945[7] and one million in 1950, to nearly 4.9 million in the year 2000. Meanwhile, Diaspora Jewry declined from 10.4 million in 1945, to 10.2 million in 1960, and to an estimated 8.3 million in 2000. This divergence reflected patterns in international migration, vital statistics, and Jewish identity. During the whole 1945–2000 period there was a net migration transfer of over 2.1 million Jews from the Diaspora to Israel. Diaspora Jewry produced an estimated natural increase of 800,000 until about 1970. Since then, however, the balance of Diaspora Jewish births, deaths, and identification changes has been consistently negative, wiping out all of the previously accumulated natural increase. In Israel the natural increase (and, to a minor extent, conversions) significantly added to Jewish population size. Over the 55 years considered here, the total Jewish population growth in Israel of over 4.3 million was split about equally between a positive

---

[5]The "effectively Jewish" birthrate includes all children identified as Jewish according to the "core" Jewish population definition (see below).

[6]Sergio DellaPergola, "Between Science and Fiction: Notes on the Demography of the Holocaust," *Holocaust and Genocide Studies* 10, no. 1, 1996, pp. 34–51.

[7]Palestine Government, Department of Statistics, *Vital Statistics Tables 1922–1945* (Jerusalem, 1947); Roberto Bachi, *The Population of Israel* (Jerusalem, 1977).

TABLE 1. WORLD, DIASPORA, AND ISRAEL JEWISH POPULATION, BY MAIN FACTORS OF CHANGE, 1945–2000 (ROUGH ESTIMATES, THOUSANDS)[a]

Region and Factors of Change	1945–[b] 1950	1950– 1960	1960– 1970	1970– 1980	1980– 1990	1990– 2000	1945– 2000[c]
Total world							
Initial Jewish population	11,000	11,297	12,079	12,585	12,819	12,868	11,000
Final Jewish population	11,297	12,079	12,585	12,819	12,868	13,192	13,192
Difference	297	782	506	234	49	324	2,192
Diaspora							
Initial Jewish population	10,438	10,283	10,220	10,078	9,601	9,151	10,438
Final Jewish population	10,283	10,220	10,078	9,601	9,151	8,310	8,310
Difference	−155	−63	−142	−477	−450	−841	−2,128
Israel migration balance	−389	−513	−280	−218	−39	−677	−2,116
Natural and other change[d]	234	450	138	−259	−411	−164	−17
Israel							
Initial Jewish population	562	1,014	1,859	2,507	3,218	3,717	562
Final Jewish population	1,014	1,859	2,507	3,218	3,717	4,882	4,882
Difference	452	845	648	711	499	1,165	4,320
Diaspora migration balance	389	513	280	218	39	677	2,116
Natural and other change[d]	63	332	368	493	460	488	2,204
Yearly rate of change %							
World	0.57	0.67	0.41	0.18	0.04	0.25	0.33
Diaspora	−0.32	−0.06	−0.14	−0.48	−0.48	−0.96	−0.41
Israel	13.47	6.25	3.04	2.53	1.45	2.76	3.97

[a]Beginning-of-year estimates unless otherwise stated.
[b]May 1.
[c]Provisional estimates based on periodic update of world Jewish population data.
[d]Balance of births, deaths, and Jewish identification change.

migration balance, on the one hand, and natural and other population changes occurring locally, on the other.[8]

Since the beginning of the 1990s the new circumstances emerging from the end of the (former) Soviet Union (FSU) allowed for large-scale Jewish emigration. This also set the stage for return or first-time access to Jewish identification among people whose families had significantly assimilated out of Judaism. Migration to Israel, the adoption there of somewhat higher levels of fertility, and the passage to a more explicit Jewish identification among new immigrants from the FSU—through spontaneous rediscovery or formal conversion—translated into a somewhat higher pace of population growth for Israel and for world Jewry.

Jewish Migration and the World System

International mobility, besides reshaping the geographical map of world Jewry, has changed the environment within which Jewish life has developed. Since 1945 nearly five million Jews, including their non-Jewish family members, moved between countries—mostly between different continents. This amounts to an average yearly mobility rate of nearly 1 percent of the total Jewish population over a period of more than 50 years—a very high rate in international comparison. The general thrust of these changes was the massive movement out of countries and societies where the position of Jews had long been precarious and subject to discrimination, toward societies with a better balance of political freedom and socioeconomic opportunities.

Jewish international migration developed over time in a typical wavelike pattern that was push-dominated, that is, responsive to crisis. Since 1948 there have been several periods of intensive Jewish immigration. The first major wave occurred in the wake of Israel's independence, between May 1948 and 1951, and the last, since the end of 1989, with the great exodus from the FSU. The suddenness and range of yearly variation was greater than commonly observed in other large-scale migrations. Insofar as Jews were granted a possibility to leave, many migrated from predominantly Muslim countries in Asia and Africa, and from Eastern Europe and the Balkans. Migration propensities were lower or very low from western countries and from Israel—the main recipient countries of Jewish migration—but fluctuations over time reflected changing circumstances in each country of origin. Over the period 1948–1996, Israel

---

[8]The estimates reported here slightly revise those for the 1970s quoted in U.O. Schmelz and Sergio DellaPergola, "World Jewish Population," AJYB 1982, vol. 82, pp. 277–90.

TABLE 2. JEWISH POPULATION BY MAJOR REGIONS, ABSOLUTE NUMBERS, AND PERCENT DISTRIBUTION, 1948–2000 (ROUGH ESTIMATES)

Region	Number (thousands)[a]			Percent[a]			Percent change		
	1948[b]	1970[c]	2000[c]	1948[b]	1970[c]	2000[c]	1948[b]–1970	1970–2000	1948–2000
Total world	11,185	12,585	13,192	100.0	100.0	100.0	12.5	4.5	17.9
Diaspora	10,535	10,078	8,310	94.2	80.1	63.0	−4.3	−17.8	−21.1
Israel	650	2,507	4,882	5.8	19.9	37.0	285.7	94.3	651.1
North America[d]	5,100	5,700	6,062	45.6	45.3	46.0	11.8	6.4	18.9
Latin America	520	515	422	4.6	4.1	3.2	−1.0	−18.1	−18.8
Europe[e]	1,700	1,335	1,145	15.2	10.6	8.7	−21.4	−14.2	−32.6
FSU[f]	2,200	2,151	468	19.7	17.1	3.5	−2.2	−78.2	−78.7
Other Asia[g], North Africa[h]	870	183	29	7.8	1.5	0.2	−79.0	−84.2	−96.7
South Africa[i], Oceania[j]	145	194	184	1.3	1.5	1.4	33.8	−5.2	26.9

[a]Revised estimates based on periodic update of world Jewish population data. Figures for 2000 provisional. Minor discrepancies due to rounding.
[b]May 15.
[c]Beginning-of-year estimates.
[d]U.S.A., Canada.
[e]European Union, Rest of West Europe, East Europe other than FSU.
[f]Former Soviet Union, European and Asian parts.
[g]Asian parts of Turkey included in Europe.
[h]Including Ethiopia.
[i]South Africa, Zimbabwe, and other sub-Saharan countries.
[j]Australia, New Zealand.

absorbed 63 percent of total Jewish migrants, varying between a high of 84 percent in 1948–52 and a low of 34 percent in 1983–88.[9]

Primarily as a consequence of international migration, the geographical map of world Jewry changed significantly (see table 2). The Middle East, North Africa, Ethiopia, the FSU, and other parts of Eastern Europe and the Balkans saw most of their Jews moving out. Other Jewish communities that experienced significantly negative long-run migration balances included Latin America and South Africa, and to a lesser extent countries in Western Europe such as the United Kingdom. Major re-

[9]Sergio DellaPergola, "The Global Context of Migration to Israel," in Elazar Leshem and Judith T. Shuval, eds., *Immigration to Israel: Sociological Perspectives* (New Brunswick, 1998), pp. 51–92.

cipients of Jewish migration in the West, besides Israel, were the U.S., France, Canada, Australia, and, more recently, Germany. The overall effect of these changes was a significant concentration of the Jewish presence in more advanced societies: over time, there emerged a significant correlation between, on the one hand, the size of Jewish population, its share of the total population, and its propensity to stay permanently in a country, and, on the other, major indicators of that country's socioeconomic development and quality of life. After many centuries spent in comparatively less developed and peripheral parts of the world system, over the last decades the Jews were increasingly associating with the societal forces of the world system's core countries. As part of this process, Israeli society itself—quite apart from the unique cultural-ideological effects of Zionism—rose during the second half of the 20th century from a small and underdeveloped society to a more serious and stable geopolitical and economic global presence. This strengthened Israel's capacity to attract new immigrants and retain old residents. In the year 2000, 46 percent of world Jewry lived in North America, 37 percent in Israel, and 17 percent in other countries.

Dramatic changes also emerged in the social structure of other Jewish communities at the end of the 20th century. The older dispersed geographical distribution in smaller localities was replaced by a massive tendency to concentrate in major metropolitan areas. Currently over 50 percent of world Jewry live in only six major urban areas: Greater New York, Los Angeles, and Southern Florida in the U.S., and Greater Tel Aviv, Haifa, and Jerusalem in Israel. Two-thirds of all Jews worldwide live in about 20 large metropolitan areas. The total populations of these cities are typically very large, dense, and heterogeneous, and many of the inhabitants have extensive transnational connections. All of these features fit with the changing socioeconomic stratification of Jewish populations. The Jewish populations, with some variation between countries, generally include high percentages of college and university graduates. A massive movement out of the older Jewish occupations in trade and industry has led to growing concentration in management, and even more in academic, liberal, and technical professions. Thus Jews in urban centers all over the world—with due attention to the structural differences inherent in their being a majority in Israel and minorities elsewhere—became more and more similar in social class, and possibly also in cultural outlook and political interests and behaviors.

The Changing Jewish Family

Sweeping changes have affected the family in more developed societies over the last decades. In some respects Jewish communities anticipated the general changes while in others they were slow to catch up. The family has long functioned as the cornerstone of Jewish society. But the conventional roles of marriage and procreation in the family have undergone unprecedented erosion over the last few decades under the impact of individualism. Observed changes included delayed marriages, higher rates of permanent non-marriage, more frequent cohabitation, rising rates of divorce, low birthrates, growing proportions of births out of marriage (the latter still uncommon among Jews), increasing numbers of one-parent households, and accelerating intermarriage. Children of intermarriage have shown comparatively weak Jewish identification, while the propensity of the non-Jewish spouses to convert to Judaism has declined relative to the total number of such marriages.[10]

Wide gaps prevailed between Jewish family trends in Israel and outside it. In Israel, more conservative patterns led to comparatively frequent and younger Jewish marriages, in contrast to higher frequencies of postponed marriage in the Diaspora. Marriage across religious lines occurs only rarely in Israel. Elsewhere around 1990, frequencies of mixed marriage surpassed 70 percent in Russia, Ukraine, and several smaller western Jewish communities, reached 50 percent in the U.S. and (based on older evidence) France, close to 40 percent in the United Kingdom, and probably above 30 percent in Canada and Australia. Divorce rates among Jews were lower than among the total population of the same countries, but the gap has narrowed considerably in recent years, reflecting more Jewish divorce. Jewish divorce was less frequent in Israel than in the largest Jewish communities worldwide. Israel's current Jewish fertility rate of 2.6 children per woman (regardless of marital status) was nearly double that observed for most Diaspora communities (0.9–1.7 children). Significantly, affiliation with Judaism was normally automatic for nearly every Jewish child born in Israel. In other countries, a majority of outmarried Jewish parents preferred another religious or ethnic identity for their children, leading to major percentage losses in the potential size of the new generation.

The Jewish population's current age composition reflects the prolonged effect of these demographic patterns (see table 3). The data on age presented for major geographical areas are based on available sources and, wherever direct information was lacking, hypotheses on similarity or dissimilarity with neighboring Jewish populations.[11] In Israel, and to a lesser extent in the now nearly depleted communities in Asia and Africa, higher

---

[10]See the overview in Sergio DellaPergola, "Recent Trends in Jewish Marriage," in Sergio DellaPergola and Leah Cohen, eds., *World Jewish Population: Trends and Policies* (Jerusalem, 1992), pp. 65–92.

[11]Detailed sources are listed in DellaPergola, "World Jewish Population, 1997."

TABLE 3. JEWISH POPULATION BY AGE GROUPS AND MAJOR REGIONS, 1995[a]

Region	Total[b]	Total %	0–14	15–29	30–44	45–64	65+
Total world	13,020	100.0	20.8	18.8	22.3	22.2	16.1
Diaspora	8,498	100.0	17.6	16.1	23.6	24.2	18.5
Israel	4,522	100.0	26.9	23.8	19.8	18.0	11.5
North America	6,052	100.0	19.2	16.1	24.8	23.2	16.8
Latin America	433	100.0	16.8	21.9	17.7	24.5	19.1
Europe	1,133	100.0	15.6	16.4	23.9	23.8	20.3
FSU	659	100.0	7.1	10.3	17.4	34.3	31.0
Asia, Africa	29	100.0	22.8	18.2	19.3	20.6	19.1
South Africa, Oceania	192	100.0	17.8	19.9	20.6	23.1	18.5
% in Israel[c]		34.7	44.8	44.1	30.8	28.4	24.8
% in North America[c]		46.5	42.8	39.9	51.7	48.9	48.5
% in other countries[c]		19.8	12.4	16.0	17.5	22.7	26.7

[a]Projections baseline. Minor discrepancies due to rounding.
[b]Thousands.
[c]Out of world total in age group.

birthrates generally followed by high rates of retention of Jewish children within the Jewish community resulted in higher percentages of children and youth. However among Jewish communities in Europe, Latin America, South Africa, and Oceania, and — to an extreme extent — in the FSU, lower birthrates and the effects of out-marriage on the Jewish identity of children produced markedly older age compositions. International migration, primarily a movement of younger people, also contributed to the aging of the sending countries and to the stability if not rejuvenation of the receiving countries.

By 1995, Israel included only about 35 percent of the world Jewish population, but it had over 44 percent of all Jews younger than 30. And while North American Jewry constituted over 46 percent of the world Jewish population, it had a smaller percentage of Jewish children and younger adults than Israel. Communities elsewhere, which made up about 20 percent of world Jewry, had only 12–16 percent of the younger age groups. Israel's share of the worldwide pool of Jews aged 65 and over was just 25 percent, versus 48 percent in North America and 27 percent in the aggregate of other communities.

Jewish Identity and Population Boundaries

Defining "Jewish" population is not a simple matter, since Jewish identification has undergone widespread transformation over time. Viewing the process sequentially, many Jews passed from an all-encompassing and exclusive religious community, to voluntary membership in a cohesive ethnic group, to maintaining a loose individual relationship with Jewish culture, to the final loss of even that faint last distinctive residue.[12] These changes reflected increased opportunities for equality, mobility, and interaction with others, and, eventually, greater acceptance of Jews by their non-Jewish counterparts, in a context of secularization. Both a cause and a consequence of these changing circumstances, the already-noted spread of intermarriage led to a growth in the number of families composed of both Jewish and non-Jewish members.

Jewish demography, which is based on the empirical data of population censuses and sociodemographic surveys, has to consider the various criteria for counting and defining the population in Jewish households. The so-called "core" Jewish population includes all those who, when asked, identify themselves as Jews; or, if the respondent is a different person in the same household, are identified by that respondent as Jews. This approach is intentionally comprehensive and pragmatic. Reflecting subjective feelings about identity, it broadly overlaps but does not necessarily coincide with Halakhah (Jewish religious law) or with other normatively binding definitions. Furthermore it does not depend on any measure of a person's Jewish commitment or behavior—in terms of religiosity, beliefs, knowledge, communal affiliation, or otherwise. The core Jewish population includes all those who converted to Judaism by any procedure, or joined the Jewish group informally, and declare themselves to be Jewish. It excludes those of Jewish descent who formally adopted another religion, as well those who did not convert out but currently refuse to acknowledge their Jewish identification.

The "enlarged" Jewish population in these same households includes the sum of (a) the core Jewish population; (b) persons who have themselves adopted another religion, even though they may claim still to be Jews ethnically; (c) other persons with Jewish parentage who claim not to be Jews; and (d) all of the respective further non-Jewish household members (spouses, children, etc.). For both conceptual and practical reasons, this definition does not include any other non-Jewish relatives living elsewhere in exclusively non-Jewish households.

---

[12]Sergio DellaPergola, "Arthur Ruppin Revisited: The Jews of Today, 1904–1994," in Steven M. Cohen and Gabriel Horenczyk, eds., *National Variations in Jewish Identity: Implications for Jewish Education* (Albany, 1999) pp. 53–83.

Israel's distinctive legal framework for the acceptance and absorption of new immigrants—the Law of Return—further widens the possible boundaries for the analysis of Jewish demography and identity. This law extends its provisions to all current Jews, their Jewish or non-Jewish children and grandchildren, as well as to their respective spouses, thus defining a significantly larger population than the core and enlarged Jewish populations defined above.[13] It is difficult to estimate what the total size of the Law-of-Return population might be. Since many non-Jewish descendants of Jews identify only marginally or not at all with anything Jewish, what the Law of Return defines is less a real population than a theoretical concept—though a significant one for Jewish discourse.

The following data provide some notion of the divergent results obtained, in major Jewish population centers, from using different definitions of Jewish identification. In the U.S. in 1990, the core Jewish population was estimated at 5,515,000, as opposed to an enlarged Jewish population of 8,200,000—including households without any core Jews—a difference of 49 percent.[14] In the Russian Federation in 1994, the respective figures for households with at least one core Jew were 409,000 and 720,000—a 76-percent difference.[15] The gap between core and enlarged figures grew rapidly since the 1970s in most world Jewish communities, reflecting the increasing effects of assimilation, although there have been countries, such as Mexico in 1991, where the difference between core and enlarged definitions barely reached 5 percent.

The problem of defining Jewish population will probably become more complex over time, making it increasingly difficult to reach a common understanding about criteria for inclusion or exclusion. Thus while Jewish population estimates for the present, and projections for the future, may create an impression of a clear-cut community, in reality group boundaries are getting more blurred and unstable. In any case, the estimates and projections in this article generally refer to the core Jewish population, unless otherwise specified.[16]

---

[13]For a concise review of the rules of attribution of Jewish personal status in rabbinic and Israeli law, including reference to Jewish sects, isolated communities, and apostates, see Michael Corinaldi, "Jewish Identity," chap. 2 of his *Jewish Identity: The Case of Ethiopian Jewry* (Jerusalem, 1998).

[14]Barry A. Kosmin, Sidney Goldstein, Joseph Waksberg, Nava Lerer, Ariella Keysar, and Jeffrey Scheckner, *Highlights of the CJF 1990 National Jewish Population Survey* (New York, 1991).

[15]Mark Tolts, "Jews in the Russian Federation: A Decade of Demographic Decline," in *Jews in Eastern Europe* 3 (40), Winter 1999, pp. 5–36.

[16]We do not deal here with "lost tribes" or with crypto-Jews, categories that may have some relevance in long-term historical-demographic analysis.

JEWISH POPULATION PROJECTIONS, 2000-2080

Data and Assumptions

Modern population projections seek to illustrate the long-range implications of specific demographic trends for population growth.[17] Projections need to be based on a good understanding of the mechanisms of population change. This in turn requires: (a) explicit or implicit theoretical guidelines for making assumptions about future changes in demographic trends; and (b) a wealth of accumulated data on the demographic composition and on the main factors of change among the studied population. With the improvement in projection methods and a better understanding of demographic processes, good demographic projections have predicted actual developments quite accurately, at least within a 20-30-year range.[18] For example, studies done 20 years ago predicted that continuation of the demographic trends of the 1970s would lead to significant erosion of Jewish population size in the Diaspora.[19] Longer-term projections are shakier, especially since they are subject to broader political, socioeconomic, and cultural developments that stand outside the field of demography proper. The new set of demographic projections

---

[17]Population projections are carried out routinely by the United Nations and numerous other research bodies. See, e.g.: United Nations, Department of Economic and Social Affairs, Population Division, *World Population Projections to 2150* (New York, 1998), and Wolfgang Lutz, ed., *The Future Population of the World: What Can We Assume Today?* (London, 1996). For an evaluation of methods and accuracy performance see two essays in the Lutz volume, Tomas Frejka, "Long-range Global Population Projections: Lessons Learned," pp. 3-13, and Wolfgang Lutz, Joshua R. Goldstein, and Cristopher Prinz, "Alternative Approaches to Population Projection," pp. 14-44.

[18]Henri Leridon, "Six milliards . . . et après?" *Population et sociétés* 352 (Paris, 1999) pp. 1-4.

[19]See U.O. Schmelz, *World Jewish Population Regional Estimates and Projections* (Jerusalem, 1981). This influential study projected the Jewish population as of 1975 through 2010. Regarding the Jewish population in the United States see U.O. Schmelz, "The Demographic Consequences of U.S. Jewish Population Trends," AJYB 1983, vol. 83, pp. 141-87. For a more recent set of global Jewish population projections discussing aggregate change in Diaspora communities, see Sergio DellaPergola, "The Jewish People Toward the Year 2020: Sociodemographic Scenarios," in Anat Gonen and Semadar Fogel, eds., *Israel 2020, Masterplan for Israel in the 21st Century; The Macro Scenarios: Israel and the Jewish People* [Hebrew] (Haifa, 1996), pp. 155-87. See also: Vivian Klaff, "Broken Down by Age and Sex: Projecting the Jewish Population," *Contemporary Jewry,* 1998, pp. 1-37; and, related to our current study, Sergio DellaPergola, Mark Tolts, and Uzi Rebhun, *World and Regional Jewish Population Projections: Russian Republic, 1994-2019 (Interim Report)* (Jerusalem, 1996), and Uzi Rebhun, Sergio DellaPergola, and Mark Tolts, "American Jewry: A Population Projection," in Roberta Rosenberg Farber and Chaim I. Waxman, eds., *Jews in America: A Contemporary Reader* (Hanover, N.H. and London, 1999), pp. 33-50. Projections of the Jewish and total populations in Israel are routinely carried out. See CBS, *Statistical Abstract of Israel,* vol. 50, 1999.

presented here addresses the expected evolution of Jewish population worldwide, and in each of several major regions, over the period 2000–2080.

We projected Jewish population using the demographic cohort-component method. The basic idea is simple. The Jewish population of a given region at a given time reflects the Jewish population at an earlier point of time, plus the number of Jews born in the time interval, Jewish immigrants to the region, and accessions to Judaism, less the number of Jewish deaths, Jewish emigrants from the region, and secessions from Judaism. In the global synthesis, the negative and positive migration balances offset each other.

In the case of a group like the Jews, who operate as a religious or ethnic subpopulation in their countries of residence, change of identification may significantly affect population size. Several studies have shown increasing numbers of people not born Jewish who had converted to Judaism, and of people who were born or raised Jewish but currently preferred another religio-ethnic identification. Most of these accessions to and secessions from Judaism are likely by-products of interreligious marriage, and such marriage may also have a long-term effect on the number of newborn who are identified or raised Jewish. In our projections, the gains or losses arising from intermarriage were all incorporated with the levels of Jewish fertility.[20] The projection's base population was the distribution of Jews in each country and region by sex and by five-year age groups, estimated for the year 1995. All available data on the size and composition of world Jewish population were compiled, and if the data related to base years other than 1995, they were processed to bring them to the common 1995 baseline. The projections were prepared for the Jewish population of Israel and for 19 other major countries, or groups of neighboring countries, in the Diaspora: the United States, Canada, Central America, Argentina, Brazil, Rest of Latin America, France, United Kingdom, Germany, Rest of European Union, Rest of West Europe, Rest of East Europe and the Balkans besides the FSU,[21] Russian Federation, Rest of FSU in Europe, FSU in Asia, Rest of Asia, North Africa, South Africa, and Oceania. For each geographic unit, six alternative projections were

---

[20]This is one of the methodological differences between our projections and those of Schmelz in *World Jewish Population*. In the latter, age-specific assimilation rates were assumed for each age group in the Jewish population. Another difference between the two sets of projections concerns the levels of life expectancy assumed. While Schmelz assumed a constant life expectancy according to the levels of the mid-1970s, we assumed a gradual increase in accordance with the observed trends over the last decades. A further difference involves the levels of international migration expected. In both cases they reflect a possible extension of the situation prevailing in the 1970s and the 1990s, respectively.

[21]Results for Europe outside the European Union and outside the FSU will be presented jointly.

prepared providing lower and upper ranges for the size and composition of the Jewish population over the projection period. Three sets of projections evaluated the influence of different fertility levels in the absence of international migration; three more projections added the assumed effects of international migration to each of those same fertility assumptions. While the data presented cover selected years over a span of 80 years, the results of the projection are also available for five-year intervals.[22]

The projections relied on the following assumptions:

MORTALITY. Jews have been historically at the forefront of the transition to lower mortality. Consistent with the patterns in more developed countries, we assumed continuing health improvements leading to gradual increases in life expectancy—that is, of the average number of years a person is expected to live after reaching a given age. Towards the end of the 1990s, the actual life expectancy at birth among Israeli Jews was about 76 years for men and 80 for women. The steady tendency, observed since the 1970s, has been a regular rise by nearly one year of life every five calendar years. The few studies available about life expectancy among Jewish communities in the Diaspora revealed very similar results. Therefore, we applied the same initial levels of life expectancy to the majority of Diaspora Jews. Extending the same trend over time, by 2080 life expectancies were anticipated to approach 90 years for Jewish men and 93 years for Jewish women worldwide. In the FSU, where life expectancy was recently estimated at 69 years for Jewish men and 73 years for Jewish women, lower survivorship levels were assumed. Assuming improvements at a pace similar to other Jewish communities, by 2080 life expectancy there would reach 78 years for Jewish men and 82 years for Jewish women.[23]

FERTILITY. Jews were among the forerunners in the general transition toward lower and controlled levels of fertility. After a period of recovery following World War II, particularly in North America (the baby boom) and in Western Europe, Jewish fertility in the Diaspora receded to very low levels. According to the projection's medium version, we assumed steady continuation, throughout the projection period, of Total Fertility Rates (TFR) prevailing during the 1990s in each of the 20 geographic units considered.[24]

---

[22]A more detailed publication of the present projections and further scenarios is planned by the authors. The software package used for the projections was *PEOPLE: A User-Friendly Package for Making National and Sub-National Population Projections,* Version 3.0.

[23]Experts on mortality agree on the expected continuing increase in life expectancy, particularly at older ages. There is, however, disagreement about the possible upper boundaries of the length of human life. See James W. Vaupel and Hans Lundström, "The Future of Mortality at Older Ages in Developed Countries," in Lutz, *Future Population of the World,* pp. 278–95.

[24]The TFR is a measure of the average number of children expected to be born per woman, assuming indefinite continuation of current age-specific fertility levels. Current

Higher and lower Jewish TFR levels were also projected, respectively 0.4 children above or below the medium fertility.[25] These rates reflect the "effectively Jewish" fertility and account for possible losses or gains of Jewish children as a consequence of mixed marriage. Average fertility levels are the weighted product of very different modes of family formation that may exist within a Jewish population, along the continuum between the most to the least religiously attached. Fertility increases or decreases over time may reflect changes: (a) in the actual number of children born; (b) in the patterns of religious affiliation of the children of mixed marriage; or (c) in the respective share within a Jewish population of various sectors whose fertility levels are markedly different.[26]

INTERNATIONAL MIGRATION. Since the early 1990s, international migration, primarily the exodus from the FSU to Israel and other western countries, became again a major factor of Jewish demographic change. A first set of projections, focused on the expected buildup of internal Jewish population changes in each region, assumed a zero balance of international migration. A second set of projections, based on mobility trends observed during the late 1990s, allocated Jewish migrants in two stages. For those areas with a negative migration balance—primarily the FSU but also most Jewish communities in Latin America, other countries in East Europe, Asia, North and South Africa, and the U.K.—we calculated detailed measures of the incidence of emigration (net of immigration) for each age and sex. These age- and sex-specific rates were determined principally (but not only) according to the observed number of Jewish emigrants during the 1990s relative to the 1995 base population of each region, and the composition by age and sex of those who went to Israel. These same net emigration rates were applied to the average Jewish population remaining in the region in each five-year span of the projected period. The computed numbers of Jewish migrants reflecting the

---

medium Jewish TFRs for the various geographic regions were determined as follows: Russia, Rest of FSU in Europe, and Germany, 1.1; FSU in Asia, 1.3; U.S., Argentina, Brazil, France, Rest of European Union, Rest of West Europe, Rest of East Europe and the Balkans, 1.5; Canada, Rest of Latin America, U.K., Rest of Asia, South Africa, and Oceania, 1.7; Central America, 2.1; North Africa, 2.3; and Israel, 2.5.

[25]These higher or lower fertility levels were assumed to be attained since the outset of the projection rather than gradually from current levels. Therefore, the projected results should be interpreted as the lowest and highest possible under the given range of assumptions.

[26]The assumption is generally accepted that fertility will remain at current low levels in the total population of more developed countries. See Ron Lesthaeghe, "A Century of Demographic and Cultural Change in Western Europe: An Exploration of Underlying Dimensions," *Population and Development Review* 9, no. 3, 1983, pp. 411–35; Dirk van de Kaa, "Europe's Second Demographic Transition," *Population Bulletin* 42, no. 1, 1987; Wolfgang Lutz, "Future Reproductive Behavior in Industrialized Countries," in Lutz, *Future Population of the World,* pp. 253–77.

assumed Jewish emigration rates in each five-year period were then added up and proportionally divided between the areas with a positive migration balance, in accordance with the trends observed during the late 1990s. The receiving countries include Israel, the U.S., Canada, Germany, Rest of the European Union, and Australia.[27]

It should be noted that fixed emigration rates produced varying absolute numbers of expected migrants because of the changing Jewish population size of sending countries. Three areas—France, Rest of West Europe, and Rest of Asia—were assumed to have a zero migration balance. It should be reiterated that, as the projections concern the core Jewish population, we only considered the potential impact of Jewish migrants. Non-Jewish migrant members of Jewish households were disregarded, though they tend to constitute a growing percentage of all migrants.[28]

In the different sets of projections presented below we assumed similar changes in life expectancy across all regions, uniformity of change in fertility behaviors—whether decline or growth—and a global spread of international migration. Different scenarios may result from recombining the assumptions about fertility and migration in each region in different ways.

World Overview

In the hypothetical absence of international migration, if effectively Jewish fertility rates continue at approximately the current (medium) levels, Jewish population worldwide would increase moderately from 13.1 million in the year 2000 to 13.8 million by 2020.[29] Thereafter, the total

---

[27]The assumed distribution of Jewish migrants among regions with a positive net migration balance was as follows: Israel was first allocated 54 percent of all migrants below the age of 40, and 46 percent of the migrants aged 40 and over. The remaining migrants were subdivided regardless of age as follows: U.S., 63 percent; Germany, 25 percent; Canada, 7 percent; Oceania, 3 percent; European Union, 2 percent.

[28]As our allocation method of projected migrants is based on current net migration balances, it may somewhat underestimate the future volume of emigration. Indeed, emigration from countries with a currently positive migration balance, primarily Israel but also some western countries, may continue even after emigration from the current main suppliers such as the FSU fades away. Projections with further assumptions about possible future developments in Jewish international migration will be presented in a later and more detailed version of this study. For an overview of global trends, see Hania Zlotnik, "Migration to and from Developing Regions: A Review of Trends," in Lutz, *Future Population of the World,* pp. 299–335.

[29]Jewish population estimates for the year 2000 in tables 1–3 derive from periodic updates based on local sources and the assessment of ongoing demographic changes, namely international migration. Projections for the year 2000 in tables 4–8 were independently obtained from the 1995 baseline and the various assumptions mentioned above. There are minor discrepancies between the two sets of data. For the world's total Jewish population the estimates in tables 1 and 2 fall between the medium and high projections listed in table 4 and following.

number of Jews would pass 14 million at the beginning of the 2030s, and 15 million around the year 2080. Thus, by the end of the entire projection period, world Jewry would be 17 percent larger than it is today.

This overall increase masks very different trends in Israel and the Diaspora. Due to its above-replacement-level fertility, the Israeli Jewish population would gradually increase to about 6 million by 2020, slightly less than 8 million by 2050, and over 10 million in 2080 — twice its size today. The picture for the Diaspora is quite different. There, current low fertility levels combined with an already old age composition — despite the ongoing increase in life expectancy — would inevitably lead to shrinkage in Diaspora Jewry as a whole, and in each country and region individually. According to the medium assumption without migration, the Diaspora Jewish population would decline from 8.3 million in 2000, to 7.8 million in 2020, 6.5 million in 2050, and 5.2 million in 2080. A plurality of the total Jewish population would live in Israel before the year 2020, and an absolute majority would live there by the middle of the century.

Projection results incorporating international migration are reported in table 4. Reflecting our conservative assumptions about the continuation of international migration at current levels, we expect such migration to have little impact on Jewish population change. As the major reservoir of the FSU becomes depleted, the volume of migration is expected to decline. Reflecting immigration and the birth of children of immigrants, Israel's population would be 300,000 bigger in 2020, 400,000 bigger in 2050, and 500,000 bigger in 2080, or 5 percent more than without migration. By 2080, the cumulative impact of migration on population size would range between 400,000 at lower fertility levels and 600,000 at higher fertility levels. As against such moderate expected impact of migration, different fertility assumptions generate a significantly wider range of scenarios. In 2020, Israel might have 5.6–6.3 million Jews without migration, versus 5.8–6.6 million with migration.[30] By 2080, the range would be 7.2–13.7 million without migration versus 7.6–14.3 million with migration. In other words, a difference of 0.8 children between the lower and the higher levels of fertility assumed here, would produce double the Israeli Jewish population.

As for Diaspora Jewry as a whole, in the absence of migration and according to lower or higher fertility levels, it would be 7.3–8.3 million in 2020, 5.3–7.8 million in 2050, and 3.4–7.7 million in 2080. The impact of international migration would lower the projected totals to 7.2–8.1 million in 2020, 5.2–7.5 million in 2050, and 3.3–7.3 million in 2080.

---

[30]According to the CBS projections, Israel's Jewish population in 2020 (with migration) will be 6.1–6.5 million. Our projections therefore outline the same trend, but the range of variation is slightly greater.

TABLE 4. JEWISH POPULATION PROJECTIONS ASSUMING MIGRATION RATES AS OF
LATE 1990s AND VARIOUS LEVELS OF FERTILITY, BY MAJOR REGIONS,
2000–2080 (THOUSANDS)[a]

Region	2000	2010	2020	2030	2050	2080
Medium fertility						
Total world	**13,109**	**13,428**	**13,847**	**14,125**	**14,480**	**15,574**
Diaspora	8,235	7,863	7,619	7,250	6,251	5,016
Israel	4,874	5,565	6,228	6,876	8,230	10,558
North America	6,065	6,025	5,980	5,763	5,036	4,094
Latin America	420	394	364	335	277	199
Europe	1,125	1,084	1,030	962	795	609
FSU	413	163	62	22	2	0
Asia, Africa, Oceania	212	196	183	168	141	114
% in Israel[b]	37.2	41.4	45.0	48.7	56.8	67.8
% in North America[b]	46.3	44.9	43.2	40.8	34.8	26.3
% in other countries[b]	16.5	13.7	11.8	11.5	8.4	5.9
Lower fertility						
Total world	**12,944**	**12,935**	**13,002**	**12,825**	**12,026**	**10,887**
Diaspora	8,137	7,586	7,161	6,589	5,153	3,336
Israel	4,807	5,349	5,841	6,236	6,873	7,551
North America	5,991	5,810	5,617	5,234	4,146	2,716
Latin America	414	379	341	303	229	134
Europe	1,112	1,047	971	878	659	409
FSU	410	160	60	22	2	0
Asia, Africa, Oceania	210	189	172	152	116	77
% in Israel[b]	37.1	41.4	44.9	48.6	57.2	69.4
% in North America[b]	46.3	44.9	43.2	40.8	34.5	24.9
% in other countries[b]	16.6	13.7	11.9	10.6	8.3	5.7
Higher fertility						
Total world	**13,273**	**13,916**	**14,698**	**15,498**	**17,286**	**21,653**
Diaspora	8,332	8,140	8,084	7,957	7,544	7,320
Israel	4,940	5,777	6,614	7,541	9,741	14,333
North America	6,138	6,239	6,349	6,328	6,086	5,985
Latin America	425	410	387	369	333	287
Europe	1,138	1,121	1,090	1,052	954	883
FSU	416	166	64	24	3	0
Asia, Africa, Oceania	215	204	194	184	169	165
% in Israel[b]	37.2	41.5	45.0	48.7	56.4	66.2
% in North America[b]	46.2	44.8	43.2	40.8	35.2	27.6
% in other countries[b]	16.5	13.7	11.8	10.5	8.4	6.2

[a]Projection baseline: 1995. Minor discrepancies due to rounding.
[b]Out of world total.

The impact of migration, while surely significant at the regional level, does not affect the leading trends inherent in fertility, mortality, and Jewish identification. The impact of migration may be decisive in the FSU, where by 2080, according to the medium fertility projection without migration, there might be about 100,000 core Jews, whereas continuing at current emigration levels the Jewish population would disappear altogether. In North America, the expected impact of a positive migration balance would raise the projected totals by about 150,000 throughout the period 2000–2080. Elsewhere the impact of migration would range between a few thousands to a few tens of thousands.

In spite of an expected long-term decline in numbers, North American Jewry, with a medium projected population of close to 6 million in 2020, would constitute an even larger share of the Diaspora than it does today, due to the younger age composition of North American Jews as compared to most other Diaspora communities such as those in Europe. Over the last two decades in North America, large baby-boom cohorts were concentrated in the most procreative ages. A second echo effect of the baby boom might be seen around the years 2005–2020, as many of the children of the baby boomers themselves reach reproductive ages.

Therefore, significant demographic erosion would probably affect North American Jewry only after the 2030s. In the absence of migration it would decline to 4.9 million by 2050, and to about 3.9 million by 2080. Migration would raise the Jewish population to about 6 million in 2020, and then it would drop to 5 million in 2050, and 4.1 million in 2080. From mid-century on, the pace of decline in the size of the North American Jewish population will coincide with that of the rest of Diaspora Jewry, and thus its relative share will remain unchanged. The Jewish populations in European countries and in the FSU will diminish more significantly due to their older age composition and lower levels of fertility. Trends among Latin American Jewry and in Asia, Africa, and Oceania point in a similar direction, although at least until the middle of the century Jewish population decline there will be moderate.

Alternative assumptions about decline or increase in Jewish fertility would obviously affect the evolution of the Jewish population. In the lower-fertility version, the number of Jews in the world would remain little changed over the next two decades, after which it is expected to decline gradually to 11.8 million by the year 2050, and to 10.6 million by 2080. This diminution reflects the smaller increase expected in the number of Israeli Jews as compared to the medium version, along with the more rapid decline among Diaspora Jewry. Even in this scenario, however, Israel is expected to be home to the largest Jewish concentration and to have the majority of world Jewry at about the same time as in the medium projection. According to the lower fertility assumption, North

American Jewry will decline to approximately 5 million by the year 2030 and to half that, 2.5 million, by 2080. Latin American Jewry and the Jewish communities in Asia, Africa, and Oceania also would be half their current sizes by the year 2080.

An increase in the levels of Jewish fertility, on the other hand, would result in substantially greater numbers of Jews in the world—14.7 million in the year 2020, 17.2 million in 2050, and up to 21.4 million by 2080. Thus a century after the *Shoah,* the Jewish people might approach its pre-World-War-II size, and later could even rise to higher figures unprecedented in Jewish history.[31] According to this projection, Israel's Jewish population would grow to 6.3 million by 2020, 9.3 million by 2050, and 13.7 million by 2080. North American Jewry would peak at 6.2 million in 2020 and maintain this level for another decade, after which a modest, gradual decline is projected, to 5.8 million in 2080. A similarly modest decline over the next 80 years is also anticipated, according to this assumption, for the Jewish population of Europe. Among Jews in the FSU, even an increase in fertility would still be much below the replacement level, and, given the already distorted age composition of a reversed pyramid shape, the size of FSU Jewry is expected to decline. Latin American communities, as well as those in Asia, Africa, and Oceania, would be expected to grow in the event of a fertility increase. The direction and pace of change in the balance between Israel and the Diaspora in the higher version is very similar to those in the medium and lower versions.

While these scenarios portray different possible paths of demographic evolution for world Jewry, the final outcome depends significantly on possible fluctuations in Jewish fertility which, as noted, reflect among other things the patterns of identification of children born to out-married Jewish parents. International migration, though merely the transfer of people from one place to another, may also marginally affect world Jewish population size. Indeed, the higher fertility levels in Israel mean that the higher the share of world Jewry in Israel, the faster Jewish population would grow.

As for demographic change at the regional level, table 5 specifies ten countries with major Jewish communities and nine other regional Jewish population aggregates. The data refer to the projection with international migration and medium fertility levels. Three main patterns emerge. Israel is the only country where, under the continuation of present circum-

---

[31]Even if this becomes true in absolute numbers, the percentage of Jews in the total world population was irreversibly cut down by the *Shoah.* It was over 8 per 1,000 inhabitants on the eve of World War II, and is currently around 2 per 1,000. See below for future projections.

TABLE 5. JEWISH POPULATION PROJECTIONS ASSUMING MIGRATION RATES AS OF LATE 1990s AND MEDIUM FERTILITY, BY DETAILED REGIONS, 2000–2080 (THOUSANDS)[a]

Region	2000	2010	2020	2030	2050	2080
Total world	13,109	13,428	13,847	14,125	14,480	15,574
Canada	368	375	381	375	348	313
United States	5,697	5,650	5,600	5,388	4,688	3,781
Central America	54	56	56	56	53	47
Argentina	193	171	149	130	96	55
Brazil	98	93	87	80	67	50
Rest of South America	75	75	72	67	61	47
France	520	502	482	455	380	299
United Kingdom	272	253	238	221	183	137
Germany	85	106	108	103	87	65
Rest of European Union	136	131	127	121	105	85
Rest of Europe (non-FSU)	111	92	75	61	39	22
Russia	249	115	49	19	2	0
Rest of FSU in Europe	131	37	10	2	0	0
Rest of FSU in Asia	34	11	3	1	0	0
Israel	4,874	5,565	6,228	6,876	8,230	10,558
Rest of Asia	21	21	21	21	21	19
North Africa	7	5	3	2	1	0
South Africa	86	70	57	44	25	10
Oceania	99	100	101	100	94	85

[a]Projection baseline: 1995. Minor discrepancies due to rounding.

stances, steady Jewish population increase is expected. In four areas—Canada, Central America, Germany, and Oceania—population would increase until 2020, but demographic aging would subsequently generate population decline. In all of the remaining areas, steady decrease is expected after 2000, though at different rates. Regional findings are discussed below in greater detail.

Table 6 provides a synopsis of the changes expected in Jewish population size among world Jewry, in Israel, and in the Diaspora, according to the medium projection with international migration. The small and declining overall expected impact of international migration leaves natural increase and identification changes as the primary factors determining Jewish population change. Such change will continue to be negative for the Diaspora as a whole, and may follow a cyclical pattern due to the alternation of larger and smaller cohorts at reproductive ages (see below).

TABLE 6.   WORLD, DIASPORA, AND ISRAEL JEWISH POPULATION PROJECTIONS, BY
MAIN FACTORS OF CHANGE, ASSUMING MIGRATION RATES AS OF LATE
1990S AND MEDIUM FERTILITY, 2000–2080 (THOUSANDS)[a]

Region and Factors of Change	2000– 2010	2010– 2020	2020– 2030	2030– 2050	2050– 2080
Total world					
Initial Jewish population	13,109	13,428	13,847	14,125	14,480
Final Jewish population	13,428	13,847	14,125	14,480	15,574
Difference	319	419	278	355	1,094
Diaspora					
Initial Jewish population	8,235	7,863	7,619	7,250	6,251
Final Jewish population	7,863	7,619	7,250	6,251	5,016
Difference	−372	−244	−369	−999	−1,235
Israel migration balance	−105	−49	−28	−34	−29
Natural and other change[b]	−267	−195	−341	−965	−1,206
Israel					
Initial Jewish population	4,874	5,565	6,228	6,876	8,230
Final Jewish population	5,565	6,228	6,876	8,230	10,558
Difference	691	663	648	1,354	2,328
Diaspora migration balance	105	49	28	34	29
Natural and other change[b]	586	614	620	1,320	2,299
Yearly rate of change %					
World	0.24	0.31	0.21	0.12	0.24
Diaspora	−0.46	−0.31	−0.50	−0.74	−0.73
Israel	1.33	1.13	0.99	0.90	0.83

[a]Beginning-of-year estimates. Projection baseline: 1995. Minor discrepancies due to rounding.
[b]Balance of births, deaths, and Jewish identification change.

The rate of yearly growth for Israel's Jewish population is expected to diminish, falling below 2 percent after 2000 and below 1 percent after 2020.

Changes in Age Composition

Significant changes are bound to occur in the age composition of Jewish populations (see table 7). In the event of continuing international migration and depending on different fertility assumptions, by the year 2020 the proportion of children under age 15 is expected to be 21–26 percent of the Jewish population in Israel (27 percent in 1995), and 11–16 percent of the total Diaspora communities (18 percent in 1995). The elderly population, aged 65 and over, would make up 14–16 percent in Is-

TABLE 7. JEWISH POPULATION AT AGES 0–14 AND 65+ ASSUMING MIGRATION RATES AS OF LATE 1990S AND VARIOUS LEVELS OF FERTILITY, BY MAJOR REGIONS, 2000–2080 (PERCENTAGES)[a]

Region	2000		2020		2050		2080	
	0–14	65+	0–14	65+	0–14	65+	0–14	65+
Medium fertility								
Total world	**19.5**	**15.7**	**18.2**	**20.7**	**17.5**	**25.8**	**17.6**	**28.8**
Diaspora	16.0	18.2	13.5	25.8	11.6	34.0	10.4	41.2
Israel	25.4	11.5	24.0	14.5	22.1	19.5	21.0	23.0
North America	17.0	16.5	13.7	25.2	11.6	33.6	10.4	41.0
Latin America	15.7	19.6	13.9	24.5	11.7	35.9	10.9	41.4
Europe	14.5	20.6	12.4	27.8	10.9	36.6	9.9	42.8
FSU	5.6	35.3	2.4	59.2	1.0	72.0	-	-
Asia, Africa, Oceania	17.0	17.8	15.0	24.8	13.2	32.2	12.2	37.6
% in Israel[b]	48.4	27.3	59.2	31.5	71.5	43.0	81.0	54.0
% in North America[b]	40.4	48.6	32.6	52.5	23.1	45.3	15.5	37.4
% in other countries[b]	11.3	24.2	8.2	15.9	5.4	11.7	3.5	8.6
Lower fertility								
Total world	**18.5**	**15.9**	**15.4**	**22.1**	**13.7**	**31.0**	**13.6**	**36.0**
Diaspora	15.0	18.4	10.5	27.5	7.5	41.3	6.1	52.6
Israel	24.3	11.7	21.3	15.5	18.3	23.3	16.9	28.6
North America	16.0	16.7	10.7	26.9	7.5	40.8	6.1	52.5
Latin America	14.5	19.8	11.1	26.2	7.9	43.3	7.0	52.0
Europe	13.5	20.9	9.6	29.5	7.0	44.1	5.8	54.3
FSU	4.9	35.6	1.3	60.7	0.2	79.7	-	-
Asia, Africa, Oceania	16.0	18.0	12.1	26.4	9.2	39.0	7.9	47.7
% in Israel[b]	48.9	27.3	62.3	31.5	76.4	43.0	86.2	55.2
% in North America[b]	40.0	48.6	30.0	52.5	19.0	45.3	11.2	36.4
% in other countries[b]	11.0	24.2	7.7	15.9	4.6	11.7	2.6	8.4
Higher fertility								
Total world	**20.5**	**15.5**	**20.8**	**19.5**	**21.2**	**21.6**	**21.3**	**23.4**
Diaspora	17.0	18.0	16.2	24.3	15.6	28.2	14.7	32.5
Israel	26.4	11.4	26.3	13.7	25.5	16.5	24.7	18.7
North America	18.0	16.3	16.5	23.8	15.7	27.8	14.8	32.3
Latin America	16.8	19.3	16.5	23.1	15.4	29.9	14.9	33.2
Europe	15.5	20.4	15.0	26.2	14.9	30.5	14.2	33.9
FSU	6.2	35.1	3.5	57.6	2.2	64.5	-	-
Asia, Africa, Oceania	18.0	17.6	17.6	23.3	17.1	26.8	16.4	29.9
% in Israel[b]	47.9	27.3	57.1	31.5	67.8	43.0	76.7	53.0
% in North America[b]	40.6	48.6	34.3	52.5	26.1	45.3	19.1	38.2
% in other countries[b]	11.5	24.2	8.6	15.9	6.1	11.7	4.2	8.8

[a]Out of Jewish population in each region. Projection baseline: 1995. Minor discrepancies due to rounding.
[b]Out of world total in age group.

rael (11.5 percent in 1995), and 24–27 percent in the Diaspora (18.5 percent in 1995). Low levels of fertility combined with longer life expectancy will age the Diaspora Jewish population, a trend that will accelerate as we move further into the second half of the 21st century. Although the higher fertility levels in Israel will somewhat moderate this process, Israel will also experience a decline in the proportion of children under the age of 15, while the proportion of elderly is expected to grow. According to the medium projection, by the year 2080 more than 40 percent of Diaspora Jews will be 65 and over. According to the medium and lower scenarios, Israel, like all Diaspora communities, will eventually have more Jewish elders than children. A rise in fertility is the only way for Israel to continue having more children than old people.

Another important finding is the changing distribution of different age groups across world Jewry. Already today, approximately 48 percent of all Jews 15 years old or younger live in Israel, a figure expected to rise, depending on fertility behavior, to 57–62 percent of the world total by the year 2020. In other words, within the next two decades Israel will most likely be home to the absolute majority of the world's Jewish children. By 2080, extending present demographic trends, 77–86 percent of all Jews under age 15 will be living in Israel. Since Israel will have a growing overall share of world Jewry, the proportion of Israelis aged 65 and over, out of the total of the world's Jewish elderly, is expected to rise too. Under each of the alternative assumptions, however, Israel will have comparatively fewer elders than its total share of world Jewish population.

The projection's medium version shows a decline in the proportion of children in most Diaspora communities and an overall convergence toward aging. Since this process occurs at the same time that the total size of the Diaspora diminishes, led by declining numbers of Jewish children due to continuing low fertility, the age composition of North American Jewry will change very rapidly. The proportion of children will drop from 17 percent in 2000 to 14 percent by 2020, and the share of the elderly will rise from 17 to 25 percent, largely because baby boomers will be turning 65. By the year 2020, the age compositions of North American and European Jewry are expected to be very similar. Overall, according to the medium-fertility assumption, the relative shares of the two extreme age groups, children and older persons, are expected to converge in the various Diaspora communities. By the year 2020, the group that is 65 and over is projected to be larger than the group that is 15 years or younger in all Diaspora communities. This movement toward an inverted age pyramid will accelerate as we move further into the century. Israel, too, is expected to undergo a process of aging, though much more slowly than in the Diaspora. Thus the proportion of those aged 65 and over among Israel's Jewish population, which was 5–10 percent lower than in Diaspora communities in 2000 (with the exception of the FSU), would be 15–20 percent lower by 2080.

If fertility levels decline, the proportion of children among the North American Jewish population will diminish to 11 percent by the year 2020 and to only 6 percent in 2080. This would be an exceptionally quick decrease in the proportion of Jewish children, though in other communities, such as in Europe, the percentage will be even lower. Nevertheless, because of its large size, the Jewish community of North America would remain the home of the absolute majority of Diaspora Jewish children. Toward the end of the projection period, by 2080, North American Jewry would also host the second largest share of elderly Jews, following European Jewry, which would be more than 50-percent elderly.

Increasing fertility would moderate but not prevent the decline in the proportion of children among North American Jewry, which would drop from 18 percent in 2000, to 16–17 percent in 2020, and 15 percent in 2080, as the proportion of elderly would grow from 16 percent in 2000, to 24 percent by 2020, and over 30 percent by 2080. In other Diaspora communities, too, higher fertility would lead to no more than a slow decrease in the proportion of Jewish children.

In the higher version of our projection, North American Jewry is anticipated to experience the most significant changes in age composition. From initially being the Diaspora region with the highest percentage of children, by 2080 its share of children would resemble the average for Diaspora communities. Similarly, from initially hosting a comparatively low proportion of elderly, North American Jewish communities will have a share of elderly persons similar to the rest of world Jewry, with the exception of Israel.

The United States and Canada

Toward the year 2000, the Jewish population in the U.S.[32] and Canada[33] was moderately increasing thanks more to continuing immigration than to natural increase. The future demographic development of North American Jewry will depend on the present generation's ability to transmit a Jewish identity to the next, and this, in turn, will depend on ongoing patterns of marriage and child-rearing. According to

---

[32]Sidney Goldstein, "Profile of American Jewry: Insights from the 1990 National Jewish Population Survey," AJYB 1992, vol. 92, pp. 77–173.

[33]Jim L. Torczyner and Shari L. Brotman, "The Jews of Canada: A Profile from the Census," AJYB 1995, vol. 95, pp. 227–60.

a follow-up study of the 1990 NJPS, more than 50 percent of born Jews who married during the late 1980s did so with a partner not born Jewish and who did not convert to Judaism. Among all existing mixed marriages with children at home, 18 percent of the children were raised as Jews only, 25 percent as Jews and Christians, 33 percent as Christians only, and 24 percent with no religion.[34] This implies a loss of at least 20 percent in the potential number of children who would have joined the Jewish population at a given level of fertility in the absence of mixed marriage, and a consequent fall in the level of "effectively Jewish fertility." The reported frequency of mixed marriage being lower for Canada than for the U.S., effectively Jewish fertility levels are assumed to be somewhat higher.

The results of the medium projections discussed above for North American Jewry suggest a somewhat different demographic evaluation for Canada than for the U.S. When the two communities are examined separately, the number of Jews in Canada is anticipated to increase, though very modestly, in the next two decades. Thereafter, it will decline to 313,000 in the year 2080, reflecting an overall 15-percent decrease relative to its size in 2000. By contrast, the U.S. Jewish population is expected gradually to decline throughout the projection period. At the beginning, the pace of decrease is likely to be slow—from 5.7 million in 2000 to 5.6 in 2020—but with the fading away of the baby-boom generation it will accelerate, resulting in a Jewish population of 4.7 million at mid-century and 3.8 million in 2080. Over the projection period, the U.S. Jewish population is expected to shrink by a third, more than twice the percentage loss for Canadian Jewry. Thus the relative share of Canada within total North American Jewry will increase slightly.

Around 2010, the size of the Jewish population in the U.S. and Israel is projected to converge. The different demographic trends of the two main centers of world Jewry—decline in the U.S. versus increase in Israel—will then lead to a widening gap in the respective populations. Israel is projected to have a Jewish population almost double the size of the U.S. by 2050, and three times as large by 2080. As for Canadian Jewry, given the modest demographic change anticipated relative to stronger decrease in other Diaspora communities, it is bound to become, by 2080, the third largest Jewish community in the world, or the second within Diaspora Jewry next to the U.S., though significantly smaller.

---

[34]Bruce A. Phillips, *Re-examining Intermarriage: Trends, Textures, Strategies* (Los Angeles-New York, 1997).

CHANGING WEIGHT OF JEWISH RELIGIOUS DENOMINATIONS[35]

The assumptions made in the preceding projections for U.S. Jewry reflect the average of very different behaviors among specific segments of the Jewish community, as defined by religious-ideological orientation. Demographic and sociocultural trends clearly differ between Orthodox, Conservative, Reform, and other and nondenominational Jews. Likewise, many American Jews have shifted their denominational preferences and, accordingly, their lifestyles and demographic characteristics. Thus, an attempt was made to assess separately the future demographic prospects of each of the major denominational groups within U.S. Jewry. According to the 1990 NJPS, the distribution of American Jews aged 18 and over by denominations at birth was 23 percent Orthodox, 34 percent Conservative, 26 percent Reform, and 17 percent other and nondenominational. The distribution of current denominational preferences reported was 6 percent Orthodox, 35 percent Conservative, 38 percent Reform, and 21 percent other and nondenominational. These changes are mostly due to the large number of Jews who switched their ideological preferences — usually from denominations committed to rigorous observance of Jewish tradition to those allowing more personal freedom.

In the past, the group of Jews identifying themselves Orthodox at birth incurred the strongest erosion. The share of those who in 1990 declared they were raised in Orthodox homes was 44 percent among Jews aged 60 and over, 19 percent among those aged 40–59, and 12 percent among those aged 20–39, pointing to a narrowing preferential basis over time. Hence, a plurality of the older age group, whose family roots were usually abroad, was raised in an Orthodox environment. In America, the Conservative movement grew the most among the second generation, attracting many people with an Orthodox background. It became the movement in which the largest share of Jews below age 60 were raised, and the current preference of a plurality of those aged 60 and above. The plurality of Jews younger than 60 years old in 1990 expressed a preference for the Reform movement. At the same time, that part of American Jewry not identifying with any of the three major denominations is quickly growing among the younger generations.

To sharpen the analysis, the two partially overlapping, yet different, notions of *retention* and *resilience* should be clarified. *Retention* is the pro-

---

[35]Parts of this section appeared in somewhat different form in Sergio DellaPergola and Uzi Rebhun, "American Orthodox Jews: Demographic Trends and Scenarios," *Jewish Action* 59, no. 1, Fall 1998, pp. 31–33.

portion of those born or raised within a given Jewish denomination who prefer the same denomination at a later stage in life; *resilience* is the ratio between the number of those who currently identify with a denomination and those born/raised within that denomination. Here, losses due to non-retention of old followers may be partially compensated by gains of new joiners. In 1990, reflecting trends that operated several decades back, both retention and resilience indexes were lowest among the Orthodox, moderate among the Conservative, and highest among the Reform and the aggregate of other and nondenominational. Among the 20–39 age group in 1990, resilience indexes were 51 percent for the Orthodox, 90 percent for the Conservative, 117 percent for the Reform, and 116 percent for the other and nondenominational—the two latter figures indicating actual expansion. Interestingly, both retention and resilience indexes for the Orthodox and Conservative were much higher for younger cohorts than for the older. Apparently these movements are finding ways to keep their children within the fold. (Losses to the Orthodox identification were significant among adults born or raised in Orthodox homes during the 1950s, 1960s, and early 1970s.) Preference shifts across denominations often occur in connection with marriage or residential mobility. In 1990 a significant proportion of Jewish adults below the age of 40 were still unmarried, and many of these were likely to move from locales with strong Jewish infrastructures to places with weaker ones, with possible implications for future denominational preferences.[36]

Looking to the future, assuming no further passages between denominations, existing differences in age composition and fertility behaviors should be considered. The average number of children ever born to Jewish women who were 40–44 years old in 1990 was 1.6.[37] The figures by denomination—adjusted for Jewish identity of the children of mixed marriages—were 3.7 for the Orthodox, 1.6 for the Conservative, 1.5 for the Reform, and 1.0 for the other and nondenominational. Taking these figures as future TFRs would result in the rise of the Orthodox segment (both children and adults) from 7 percent of total U.S. Jewry in 2000 to 10 percent in 2020 and 19 percent in 2050. The Conservative denomination would lose a significant portion of its current share, dropping from 32 percent in 2000, to 29 percent in 2020, and down to 26 percent by mid-century. The proportion of Reform Jews would remain stable up to 2020,

[36]Sidney and Alice Goldstein, *Jews on the Move: Implications for Jewish Identity* (Albany, 1996); Uzi Rebhun, "Changing Patterns of Internal Migration 1970–1990: A Comparative Analysis of Jews and Whites in the United States," *Demography* 34, no. 2, 1997, pp. 213–23.

[37]Sidney Goldstein, "Profile of American Jewry," p. 122. These estimates refer to all Jewish women regardless of marital status.

after which it would modestly decline to 34 percent by 2050. No changes would be expected in the relative share of Jews with other or no denominational preferences up to 2020, which would decline to 22 percent by 2050. The changing share broken down by denomination would be more salient among Jewish children. Orthodox children below the age of 15, who in 2000 accounted for approximately 10 percent of all Jewish children in the U.S., would be expected to reach 22 percent in 2020 and as much as 44 percent in 2050. The concurrent expected decline in the absolute size of U.S. Jewry would mean that Orthodox Jews, who counted about 400,000 persons in 2000, would amount to about 560,000 in 2020 and 890,000 by 2050. All the other denominations would be expected to suffer substantial numerical losses, according to the hypothesis of full denominational resilience.

If, on the other hand, interdenominational passages continue as observed among the NJPS younger adults aged 20–40 in 1990, the share of Orthodox Jews would grow only minimally to 9 percent by mid-century. The share of Conservative Jews would decline somewhat more significantly as compared to the previous scenario, to 28 percent in 2020 and to 25 percent in 2050. By contrast, the Reform movement would increase its share of American Jewry to 39 percent in 2020 and 41 percent in 2050. The proportion of other and nondenominational would remain almost unchanged. Under this scenario of continuing switches in ideological preferences, all denominations would experience absolute quantitative decreases ranging from moderate to very substantial.

The significance of a religiocultural movement need not be related to the size of that movement. For example, the comparative smallness of the Orthodox movement obscures the role it has played as a supplier of Jewish services, such as day-school education, to the entire American Jewish community. Nevertheless, a group's viability is in many respects determined by its underlying demographic trends. The larger or smaller size of a group, coupled with a much younger or older age composition, will have a definite impact on the scope and quality of interactions within the group and on its outside-oriented activities. One decisive factor for the future size of Jewish denominations in the U.S. will be their ability to retain their younger generations.

Israel

As noted, projections of Israel's population indicate continuing substantial growth moderated by an expected decline in immigration. As past Jewish population growth largely depended on large-scale and heterogeneous immigration, Israel's demographic composition and trends initially reflected socioeconomic and cultural diversity that had developed in the Diaspora throughout the centuries. Of particular significance, patterns of cultural and socioeconomic modernization were different among immigrants from different continents. Over time, the main demographic variables for groups with different geographic origins—such as age at marriage and the number of children born—underwent a process of convergence.[38] Groups with higher fertility abroad lowered it in Israel, while those with lower fertility abroad raised it. At a slower rate, Israeli society was reducing educational and economic gaps. On the other hand, demographic variations were and continue to be associated with levels of religiosity within the Jewish population and with socioeconomic and cultural differences between the Jewish, Arab, and other segments of the total Israeli population.

RELIGIOUS, TRADITIONAL, AND SECULAR

It is not easy to categorize the Jewish population in Israel by degree of religious observance, since Jewish ideological-cultural differences tend to operate along a nuanced and multidimensional continuum.[39] One indirect way to estimate the size of different groups is by looking at the number of pupils enrolled in the diverse educational networks that officially operate in Israel—State, State religious, and Independent (*haredi*, sectarian Orthodox).[40] In 1998/99, the distribution of pupils was: State—70 percent; State religious—19.5 percent; Independent—10.5 percent.[41] Considering the larger family size of the more religious population groups, their share of the total population is actually smaller. Indeed in a national survey of religious attitudes in Israel in 1993, 14 percent defined themselves as strictly observant, 24 percent as observant to a great extent, 41 percent as somewhat observant, and 21 percent as totally nonobservant.[42] Another national survey, conducted in 1991/92, revealed a somewhat different picture: 15 percent called themselves religious (including *haredi*), 11 percent traditional-religious, 34 percent

---

[38]U.O. Schmelz, Sergio DellaPergola, and Uri Avner, "Ethnic Differences Among Israeli Jews: A New Look," AJYB 1990, vol. 90, pp. 3–204.

[39]Perry Kedem, "Dimensions of Jewish Religiosity in Israel," in Zvi Sobel and Benjamin Beit-Hallahmi, eds., *Tradition, Innovation, Conflict: Jewishness and Judaism in Contemporary Israel* (Albany, 1991), pp. 251–72.

[40]*Haredim* are generally categorized by their strict interpretation of Jewish law, their rejection of secular culture, and their ambivalent attitude to the present Jewish state—which, in the case of some, is hostile. See Charles S. Liebman, ed., *Religious and Secular* (Jerusalem, 1991).

[41]CBS, *Statistical Abstract of Israel*, vol. 50 (Jerusalem, 1999), pp. 22–28.

[42]Shlomit Levy, Hana Levinsohn, and Elihu Katz, *Beliefs, Observances and Social Interaction Among Israeli Jews* (Jerusalem, 1993).

traditional-not-so-religious, and 40 percent not religious.[43] In light of these data, one can roughly estimate the more religious part of Israel's Jewish population at about 25 percent—about 7 percent *haredi* and 18 percent "national religious"—and the majority, ranging from moderately traditional to very secular, at about 75 percent.

Keeping in mind that these are only estimates, we will attempt to evaluate the prospective demographic growth of the different ideological-cultural segments of Israeli Jewry. One in-depth study of the demography of Jerusalem in 1995 used the average number of children born to the inhabitants of various types of neighborhoods as proxies for the underlying Jewish population segments. The respective TFRs were 6.4 children in areas where 70 percent or more of residents voted for religious parties—a proxy for the *haredi* segment; 4.4 in areas with a religious vote of 40–70 percent—a proxy for the "national religious" segment; and 2.4 in areas with a religious vote below 40 percent—a proxy for the moderately traditional to very secular.[44] The ensuing annual rates of Jewish population growth due to natural increase only were, respectively, 3.6 percent, 2.3 percent, and 1 percent.

If the same rates of growth can be applied to the countrywide distribution of Jewish population segments by religiosity (always keeping in mind that the distribution prevailing in Jerusalem is markedly different from Israel's total) the *haredi* share would grow from 7 percent in 2000 to 11 percent in 2020 and 17 percent in 2050, the "national religious" would grow from 18 percent in 2000 to 21 percent in 2020 and 24 percent in 2050, and the moderately-traditional-to-secular majority would drop from 75 percent in 2000 to 68 percent in 2020 and 59 percent in 2050.

Such estimates operate within the constraints of the grand totals for Israel's medium population projection with migration, already discussed above and obtained without reference to ideological divisions. Since separate projections for each population segment would generate higher totals, this constraint implies a gradual slowing down in the current rates of demographic growth for each segment. Alternatively, the projection implies continuation of the existing trend, but with a net transfer from the more to the less religious segments of Jewish population in Israel.[45] In either case this projection of observed trends would produce a significant—yet not truly revolutionary—change in the relative share of different religio-cultural groups until the middle of the 21st century.

---

[43]CBS, *Time Use in Israel: Time Budget Survey 1991/92* (Jerusalem, 1995).

[44]Sergio DellaPergola and Uzi Rebhun, *Summary of Jerusalem Population Projections 1995–2020* [Hebrew] (Jerusalem, 1999).

[45]Levy, Levinsohn, and Katz, *Beliefs, Observances and Social Interaction,* p. C-1.

JEWS, ARABS, AND OTHERS

Population projections that consider various scenarios for the Arab and other minorities in the State of Israel generally point to a continuation of very rapid demographic growth. The main factor at work here is the continuing fertility gap between Israeli Muslims, whose TFR of 4.6 is significantly lower than in the West Bank and Gaza, though higher than several other Arab countries,[46] versus Jews (and Christians), whose TFR is 2.5–2.7. These traditionalist Muslim family patterns continue in a context of significant modernization, involving improvements in educational attainment, employment status, and standard of living. The question of demographic interest is whether, and when, the higher fertility of Israeli Muslims will converge toward that of the Jews, as has already happened among the Israeli Christian Arabs and Druze. Demographic scenarios will vary according to the timetable for such a possible development.

Assuming gradual convergence to the current levels of Jewish fertility, Israel's non-Jewish population of 1.3 million in the year 2000 would grow to 2.1 million in 2020 and to 3.7 million in 2050. If TFRs continue at present levels, non-Jews would reach 2.3 million in 2020 and 5.3 million in 2050. Adding these figures to the estimated higher and lower Jewish population projections, Israel's total population of 6.2 million in the year 2000 would grow to 7.8–8.9 million in 2020,[47] and 10.4–15 million in 2050.[48]

One further aspect of Israel's demographic future has to do with the absorption of non-Jewish members of households who have recently immigrated under the Law of Return, mostly from the FSU but also from Ethiopia and other countries. These persons are recorded either under their other religious affiliation, or as "unclassified." People in the latter group generally have at least partial Jewish parentage, and an unknown number of them might, in the course of time, formally apply for Jewish identification. The number of "unclassified" approached 150,000 in 1999 and might increase to several hundreds of thousands due to continuing immigration and some natural increase in Israel. Since, in the preceding projections, these persons were not included as Jews, they constitute a further potential source of growth for the Israeli and global Jewish population.

---

[46]The TFRs are currently estimated at 5.7 in the West Bank, 7.4 in Gaza. See Palestinian Central Bureau of Statistics, *The Demographic Survey in the West Bank and Gaza* (Ramallah, 1997). According to UN estimates, the TFR was 4.0 in Syria, 3.4 in Egypt, 2.9 in Kuwait.

[47]CBS projects a total population of 8.2–9 million for Israel in 2020.

[48]Our projections ignore the additional factor of temporary (non-Jewish) foreign workers in Israel, roughly estimated at 200,000 in 1999, including the undocumented. Many of these may become permanent residents, thus further augmenting Israel's total population.

Demographic developments among the total Palestinian population of the West Bank and Gaza—roughly approaching 3 million in 2000—must also be taken into account. If fertility declines gradually to levels similar to those of Israel's Jews, that population would grow to 5.7 million in 2020, and 11.8 million in 2050; if current fertility levels continue, it would grow to 6.6 million in 2020 and to 22 million in 2050. The total number of inhabitants in the whole piece of land extending between the Mediterranean Sea and the Jordan River—including Israel's Jews, Arabs and others, and the Palestinians—would then grow from 9 million in 2000 to a total of 13.5–15.5 million in 2020, and 22.2–37 million in 2050.

Admittedly, some of these figures defy imagination and cannot be taken seriously. Some feedback mechanisms will undoubtedly intervene to modify current trends. The high population densities implicit in these projections, however, unveil a possible course of demographic development with problematic consequences for the land's "carrying capacity" and for the optimal equilibrium between human, economic, and environmental resources.[49] These trends also foreshadow serious social and political challenges for the State of Israel and the Palestinian Authority.

Other World Regions

LATIN AMERICA

The Jewish population in Latin America has been subject to the patterns of frequent economic and political instability typical of most countries in the region. Since the 1960s, more Jews have emigrated out of the region than immigrated into it.[50] Countries where the impact of emigration was particularly high included Cuba, Argentina, Uruguay, and, more recently, Colombia. Greater stability prevailed in Mexico, Brazil, Venezuela, and Chile (aside from the 1970–73 period). Some of the latter communities, as well as the smaller one in Panama, in fact absorbed some of the Jewish emigration from the former group of countries. Continuing security concerns[51] and socioeconomic uncertainty support the assumption that emigration will continue.

Significant variation in Jewish demographic and identification patterns

---

[49]It stands to reason that these concepts imply an upper boundary, which, however, is not easily quantifiable.

[50]U.O. Schmelz and Sergio DellaPergola, "The Demography of Latin American Jewry," AJYB 1985, vol. 85, pp. 51–102.

[51]Both for Jewish individuals and for Jewish institutions, as demonstrated by the terrorist attacks in Buenos Aires against the Israeli embassy in 1992 and the AMIA headquarters in 1994.

prevailed in different communities. Among the factors that enabled particular communities to preserve a strong and, to some extent, isolated pattern of Jewish life were the timing of immigration, and the socioeconomic and ethnocultural characteristics of the majority population. Mexico was an example of a Jewish community still preserving a comparatively young age composition and relatively low rates of out-marriage, though it too was affected by emigration.[52] Argentina stood at the opposite demographic end, with a larger proportion of elderly, higher rates of assimilation, and frequent bouts of increased emigration. Venezuela, Chile, Brazil, and Uruguay represented the whole range of intermediate situations. Hence, future Jewish population prospects are not identical for each country and regional division in Latin America.

According to the projection with continuing emigration and medium fertility (see table 5), Argentina would see its Jewish population shrinking from about 200,000 in the year 2000 to about 150,000 in 2020, 100,000 in 2050, and 55,000 in 2080. Even in the event of no emigration, and according to the lower and higher fertility scenarios respectively, Argentine Jewry would decrease to 171,000–195,000 in 2020, 129,000–192,000 in 2050, and 83,000–188,000 in 2080. The Jewish population in Brazil, whose recent Jewish fertility has rapidly declined,[53] would be reduced, according to the medium fertility scenario, from about 100,000 today to less than 90,000 in 2020, less than 70,000 in 2050, and 50,000 in 2080. Communities in Central America and in the rest of South America look more stable demographically, though they are bound to decrease in the longer run, albeit at a slower pace. To a great extent, the future of these communities, and of Latin American Jewry as a whole, will be determined by the amount of political and socioeconomic stability in the region.

EUROPE

The current process of political and economic integration, including the planned eastward expansion of the European Union, suggests that the continent's various Jewish communities will develop along similar demographic lines. Certain basic differences, though, should be acknowledged. The Jewish population of France grew rapidly during the 1950s and 1960s following immigration from North Africa, and kept a rather stable profile thereafter.[54] The number of Jews in the United Kingdom

[52]Sergio DellaPergola and Susana Lerner, *La población judía de México: Perfil demográfico, social y cultural* (Mexico-Jerusalén, 1995).

[53]René Daniel Decol, "Imigrações urbanas para o Brasil: o caso dos Judeus," Ph.D. diss., Campinas, 1999.

[54]Doris Bensimon and Sergio DellaPergola, *La population juive de France: socio-démographie et identité* (Jerusalem-Paris, 1984).

has steadily decreased since the 1960s due to aging and some emigration.[55] German Jewry grew rapidly through the 1990s thanks to immigration from the FSU, which, however, joined a heavily aged and out-married community.[56] Jewish communities in Belgium, Italy, the Netherlands, Switzerland, Sweden, and some smaller states all received some Jewish immigrants, compensating, to varying extents, for the ongoing internal demographic erosion.[57] In Eastern Europe, primarily Hungary and the Balkans, Jewish demographic trends were especially hurt by the postponed effects of the *Shoah* and by the relatively poor economic and civil-rights situation in the broader society. Emigration and a negative balance of births and deaths also brought a decrease in the Jewish population of Turkey.[58]

With this background, the size of European Jewry is bound to decrease under each of the scenarios considered here, though the profile of different countries may differ substantially. Under the medium-fertility-with-migration assumption, French Jewry would experience slow but steady decline from 520,000 in 2000, to 480,000 in 2020, to 380,000 in 2050, and 300,000 in 2080 (see table 5). Jewish population decrease would be quicker in the United Kingdom, to about 240,000 in 2020, 180,000 in 2050, and 140,000 in 2080. Jews in Germany, on the other hand, would experience continuing growth to a peak of about 110,000 in 2020, followed by a decrease which would reflect exhaustion of the migration reservoir in the FSU and German Jewry's high average age and extremely low fertility. The aggregate of Jewish population in other European Union countries would also slowly decline, to less than 130,000 in 2020, 195,000 in 2050, and 85,000 in 2080. In Eastern Europe and the Balkans, Jewish population is bound to diminish faster.

While international migration, especially from the Mediterranean basin and Eastern Europe, generally meant significant Jewish population increases for communities in Western Europe, the more recent migration balance was negative—with the noted exception of Germany. The future of Jewish life in the region depends on a change in the general migration trends, or on a reversal of the very low fertility patterns prevailing in the general society, neither of which seems likely. In the event of lower or

---

[55]Stephen Miller, Marlena Schmool, and Antony Lerman, *Social and Political Attitudes of British Jews: Some Key Findings of the JPR Survey* (London, 1996); Marlena Schmool and Frances Cohen, *A Profile of British Jewry: Patterns and Trends at the Turn of the Century* (London, 1998).

[56]Zentralwohlfartsstelle der Juden in Deutschland, *Mitgliederstatistik; Der Einzelnen Jüdischen Gemeinden und Landesverbände in Deutschland* (Frankfurt, annual).

[57]Sergio DellaPergola, "Jews in the European Community: Sociodemographic Trends and Challenges," AJYB 1993, vol. 93, pp. 25–82.

[58]Shaul Tuval, "The Jewish Community in Istanbul 1948–1992," Ph.D. diss., Jerusalem, 1999.

higher fertility scenarios, European Jewry outside of the FSU would range between 971,000 and 1,030,000 in 2020, between 659,000 and 954,000 in 2050, and between 409,000 and 883,000 in 2080.

FORMER SOVIET UNION

Mass emigration is the fundamental demographic fact of the Jewish population in the FSU. The size of the FSU core Jewish population diminished from 1.5 million in 1989 to an estimated 440,000 in 2000. The continuing excess of Jewish deaths over Jewish births contributed about 200,000 of the total loss of nearly 1.1 million. These trends were not spread equally across the 15 FSU republics, for various reasons. Assimilation tended to spread earlier in the Russian Federation than in the other Soviet territories, the western parts of the FSU suffered more intensely the direct and postponed consequences of the *Shoah,* and the cultural and socioeconomic conditions of the Jews reflected regional variation within the FSU.[59] The demise of the Soviet Union in 1991 greatly enhanced the effects of different ethnocultural, political-military, and economic realities in different local contexts, significantly affecting the volume and pace of the great exodus. This internal differentiation, as well as the nature of the available data sources for various parts of the FSU, suggest a separate view of Jewish population trends for three major regional divisions: the Russian Federation, the other six European republics of the FSU (Ukraine, Belarus, Moldova, and the three Baltic states), and the eight republics of the Caucasus and Central Asia. The differences between them, however, involve particulars, not the overall demographic picture and its likely consequences.

Jewish population projections concerning the FSU should take into account emigration patterns and internal demographic evolution. Jewish emigration has been highly selective by republics and regions, with much higher propensities to leave from the more peripheral and problematic regions in the FSU and within the Russian Federation, and lesser mobility from the more central and comparatively more attractive regions, particularly the Greater Moscow area.[60] On the other hand, the trends of pervasive low fertility, out-marriage, and an aging population rapidly

---

[59]Mordechai Altshuler, *Soviet Jewry on the Eve of the Holocaust: A Social and Demographic Profile* (Jerusalem, 1998); Mordechai Altshuler, *Soviet Jewry Since the Second World War: Population and Social Structure* (New York-Westport, Conn., 1987).

[60]Mark Tolts, "Demographic Trends of the Jews in the Three Slavic Republics of the Former USSR: A Comparative Analysis," in S. DellaPergola and J. Even, eds., *Papers in Jewish Demography 1993* (Jerusalem, 1997), pp. 147–75; Mark Tolts, "The Interrelationship between Emigration and the Sociodemographic Trends of Russian Jewry," in N. Levin Epstein, Y. Ro'i, and P. Ritterband, eds., *Russian Jews on Three Continents* (London, 1997), pp. 147–76; Tolts, "Jews in the Russian Federation."

spread out from Russia to all the other republics. Looking first at the projected course of Jewish population without considering emigration, depending on lower or higher fertility levels, the FSU total would be reduced to 339,000–377,000 by 2020, 169,000–218,000 by 2050, and 51,000–161,000 by 2080. Regarding the Russian Federation alone, medium fertility levels would have the Jewish population reduced to 188,000 in 2020, 85,000 in 2050, and 45,000 in 2080. The respective figures would be 125,000, 76,000, and 30,000 for the Jewish population of the other FSU republics in Europe, and 45,000, 30,000, and 20,000 for the Jewish population in the Asian republics.[61]

A more realistic projection takes into account continuing emigration at current age-specific rates, relative to the Jewish population in the republics of origin. The assumption is that the current determinants of migratory push will continue to operate in the foreseeable future, and that no administrative or political barriers will intervene to prevent emigration — though in fact there were such barriers until the late 1960s and during the 1980s. For the total of the FSU, this would produce a sharp decline to 160,000–166,000 Jews in 2010, 60,000–64,000 in 2020, 22,000–24,000 in 2030, 2,000–3,000 in 2050, and virtually none by 2080. Examining the three regional components separately, according to the medium assumption Russian Jewry would go down to 115,000 by 2010, 40,000 by 2020, 19,000 by 2030, and would then gradually disappear (see table 5). In the rest of the FSU the process of Jewish extinction would proceed even faster. In the European republics there would remain 37,000 Jews in 2010 and 10,000 in 2020, while in the Asian republics there would remain 11,000 in 2010 and 3,000 in 2020.

While these scenarios unequivocally point to the demise of the once large Jewish presence in the FSU, a final word of caution is in order about the complex question of Jewish identification. As noted, all of the data reported here refer to a core Jewish population whose frame of reference is a concept of ethnic identity (*natsyonalnost* in Russian) and whose documentation relies on official censuses, vital statistics, and passport registrations. Local surveys have shown that Jews may have been recorded under another nationality, thus underreporting the actual Jewish population according to ethnic or religious criteria.[62] It has been consistently assumed, though, that such underreporting involves a relatively minor share of the total Jewish population. The existence of a broader periphery of non-Jews of Jewish origin has also been acknowledged. Incorporation into the Jewish mainstream of some of these peripheral fringes

---

[61]Since the baseline of the population projections is 1995, emigration that occurred between 1995 and 2000 is ignored.

[62]Sidney and Alice Goldstein, *Lithuanian Jewry 1993: A Demographic and Sociocultural Profile* (Jerusalem, 1997).

might, to some extent, expand the future Jewish population size in the FSU and help postpone a demographic decline which, under continuation of the present circumstances, seems headed toward extinction.

ASIA, AFRICA, OCEANIA

Since the end of World War II, Jewish population changes in Asia, North and South Africa, and Oceania (Australia and New Zealand) were determined mainly by international migration. The large historical Jewish presence nearly disappeared from the countries of older settlement, from the Maghreb through Egypt to Ethiopia, while it increased (to a far lesser extent) in Australia and New Zealand. The recent political changes in South Africa stimulated an outflow of Jews, speeding up the numerical decline of that community.[63] Australia was one of the main recipients of that and other Jewish migrations.[64]

Continuation of current trends would bring an end to the Jews in North Africa, a further shrinking of South African Jewry to half its current size, and a moderate increase in the Jewish population of Australia and the Oceania region (see table 5). The latter increase, however, seems bound to peak around 2020, as the low fertility and aging typical of that Jewish community would eventually more than compensate for continuing immigration at current levels. Oceania might have 88,000–108,000 Jews in 2020 and 70,000–113,000 in 2050. As for the projection of a small but comparatively stable Jewish presence in the "Rest of Asia" region, it was assumed that the remnants of the Jewish population in Iran will further shrink, and that the Jewish presence might moderately increase in countries of Southeast Asia that, for a variety of reasons, have attracted significant numbers of Israeli visitors and sojourners. In the course of time, with the expected further economic growth of Japan, China, and other countries in the region, and the possible development of their economic relations with Israel, a Jewish presence in those parts of Asia might become somewhat more permanent.

---

[63]Allie A. Dubb, *The Jewish Population of South Africa; The 1991 Sociodemographic Survey* (Cape Town, 1994); Barry A. Kosmin, Jaqueline Goldberg, Milton Shain, and Shirley Bruk, *Jews in the "New South Africa": Highlights of the 1998 National Survey of South African Jews* (London, 1999).

[64]William D. Rubinstein, "Jews in the 1996 Australian Census," *Australian Jewish Historical Society Journal* 14, no. 3, 1998, pp. 495–507.

IMPLICATIONS FOR WORLD JEWRY

Effects on the Global Jewish Presence

The different Jewish population scenarios presented above carry far-reaching implications for the future of world Jewry. While the significance of Jewish culture and society clearly transcends the quantitative dimensions analyzed in this study, demographic trends deeply impinge on the relationship between Jews and other people, on the internal functioning of the Jewish community system, and, ultimately, on Jewish survival.

The scenario of medium fertility with international migration continuing at present levels shows that a minor increase in world Jewish population may occur, from 13.1–13.2 million in 2000, to 13.9 million in 2020, 14.5 million in 2050, and 15.6 million in 2080.[65] For 2020, the expected variation in Jewish population size ranges between 12.9 million in case of lower fertility without international migration, and 14.7 million in case of higher fertility with international migration. In 2050 the projected variation in world Jewish population under the same conditions ranges between a low of 12.7 million and a high of 17.3 million, and in 2080 the range would be between 10.6 million (lower fertility without migration) and 21.6 million (higher fertility with migration). Although expected stability in Jewish population size is one main finding of our projections, it is not the only possibility. Modest deviations from currently observed levels of Jewish fertility could conceivably bring a global Jewish population decrease, or a significant Jewish population increase. The percentage expected to live in Israel out of total world Jewry, starting from 37 percent in 2000, would increase according to the various scenarios to 43–45 percent in 2020 and would surpass 50 percent after 2030, approaching 54–57 percent in 2050, and 64–69 percent in 2080. The respective share of world Jewry living in North America would change from 46 percent in 2000, to 42–43 percent in 2020, 34–35 percent in 2050, and 24–28 percent in 2080. The overall weight of Jewish communities in other countries would steadily decline.

---

[65]When reading these figures it is interesting to consider the performance of Jewish population projections for the year 2000 based on 1975 data reported by Schmelz, *World Jewish Population.* Based on a Jewish population baseline for 1975 of: World, 13 million; Diaspora, 10 million; Israel, 3 million, Schmelz's projected low-high estimates for 2000 were: World, 11.8–12.9 million; Diaspora, 7.4–8.2 million; Israel, 4.4–4.7 million. Our 2000 Jewish population baseline was: World, 13.15 million; Diaspora, 8.28 million; Israel, 4.87 million (see table 2). In other words, Schmelz's higher assumptions were reasonably close to the target.

Focusing first on the expected effects of these demographic changes on the global Jewish presence, it may be useful to compare Jewish population projections to similar projections for the total population routinely processed by the United Nations.[66] Table 8 illustrates changes expected in the number of Jews per 1,000 inhabitants of the world's major regions. The range of results reflects the lower and higher fertility and migration scenarios discussed above. In the year 2000 the Jewish global presence constituted about 2.2 per 1,000 of a total population just above 6 billion people. By 2020, when the world total population may reach 7.1–7.9 billion, Jews would be 1.8–1.9 per 1,000 inhabitants. By 2050, out of a world total population expected to increase to 7.3–10.7 billion, the Jewish presence would be 1.6 per 1,000 inhabitants.

The relative weight of Jewish population is quite different in specific areas, starting with the major difference between Israel and the Diaspora. In the aggregate of Diaspora communities, the share of Jewish population is expected to diminish by half, from 1.4 per 1,000 population in 2000, to 1.0–1.1 in 2020, to 0.7 per 1,000 in 2050. In North America, where the share of Jews is by far higher than in any other region outside of Israel, it is expected to diminish from 20 per 1,000 in 2000, to 16–17 per 1,000 in 2020, and 12–13 per 1,000 in 2050. In Israel, too, because of the faster growth of the Arab and other communities, the Jewish share of total population is expected to diminish from 787 per 1,000 in 2000 to 725–748 per 1,000 in 2020, and 641–658 per 1,000 in 2050. In Europe outside the FSU, the share of Jews out of total population is expected to remain fairly stable at 2 per 1,000 or slightly less, due to the parallel population shrinkage expected among both Jews and non-Jews in the low scenario. In the FSU, the share of Jews among total population is expected to diminish in any case, and, as noted, it would dwindle to zero were international migration to continue at its present intensity. In the aggregate of Asia and Africa, bound to constitute 75–77 percent of the world's total population in 2020 and 2050, the Jewish presence would be negligible. In Oceania the weight of Jewish population would shrink from the current 3.3 per 1,000 to 2.4–2.7 per 1,000 in 2020, and 1.9–2.2 in 2050.

The common denominator of all projections is a general decline in the expected share of Jews among the total population, as a consequence of a slower growth or diminution of Jewish population at a time of contin-

---

[66]United Nations, Department of Economic and Social Affairs, *World Population Prospects, The 1998 Revision,* vol. I: *Comprehensive Tables* (New York, 1999). See also: Wolfgang Lutz, Warren Sanderson, Sergei Scherbov, and Anne Goujon, "World Population Scenarios," in Lutz, *Future Population of the World,* pp. 361–96; Joop De Beer and Leo Van Wissen, eds., *Europe: One Continent, Different Worlds: Population Scenarios for the 21st Century* (Dordrecht, 1999).

TABLE 8. JEWS PER 1,000 TOTAL POPULATION ACCORDING TO VARIOUS ASSUMPTIONS[a], BY MAJOR REGIONS, 2000–2050

Region	2000	2020				2050			
		Without Jewish migration		With Jewish migration		Without Jewish migration		With Jewish migration	
		Lower	Higher	Lower	Higher	Lower	Higher	Lower	Higher
Total population[b]	**6,055**	**7,095**	**7,904**	**7,095**	**7,904**	**7,343**	**10,674**	**7,343**	**10,674**
Jewish population[c]	**13,150**	**12,931**	**14,648**	**13,002**	**14,698**	**11,847**	**17,159**	**12,026**	**17,286**
Jews per 1,000 of total:									
Total world	**2.2**	**1.8**	**1.9**	**1.8**	**1.9**	**1.6**	**1.6**	**1.6**	**1.6**
Diaspora	1.4	1.0	1.1	1.0	1.0	0.7	0.7	0.7	0.7
Israel	787.3	725.2	739.3	735.2	747.6	640.7	647.8	651.8	657.7
North America	20.3	16.2	16.5	16.7	16.9	12.3	12.7	12.8	13.1
Latin America	0.9	0.6	0.6	0.5	0.5	0.5	0.5	0.4	0.3
Europe	2.0	2.0	2.1	2.0	2.1	1.7	1.9	1.7	1.8
FSU	1.5	1.2	1.2	0.2	0.2	0.6	0.6	0.0	0.0
Asia, Africa	0.0	0.0	0.0	0.0	0.0	0.0	0.0	0.0	0.0
Oceania	3.3	2.4	2.5	2.6	2.7	1.9	2.0	2.1	2.2

[a]Jewish population: Lower and Higher fertility assumptions (see text). Total population: Lower and High projections, United Nations, Department of Economic and Social Affairs, *World Population Prospects, The 1998 Revision*, vol. I: *Comprehensive Tables* (New York, 1999).
[b]Billions.
[c]Millions.

uing substantial growth of population in general. The implications of these changes are obviously different for Israel and for the Diaspora. But in both cases the expected reduction in the weight of Jewish population as a share of the total society portends tougher competition with other groups in the allocation of resources and the defense of group interests. The impact of projected demographic trends, therefore, tends to weaken the standing of Jews locally and globally.

Effects on the Jewish Organizational Framework

Population change carries significant implications for Jewish service delivery locally, nationally, and internationally. Many such services are attuned to specific age groups, each characterized by special needs. The extent of the provision of formal and informal Jewish education is determined, among other factors, by the size of younger age groups. At the opposite end of the age ladder, services for the elderly reflect the changing size of older age cohorts. In between, younger and middle-age adults tend to be interested in the fundamental needs of family and economic activity.

Our population scenarios clearly point to a process of Jewish aging, though the specific extent of this trend may be quite different in particular countries and regions. The growing demand for the allocation of resources to cover the needs of the elderly at a time when the number of Jewish adults at productive ages is declining, can be expected to generate tougher competition with other fundamental services, such as Jewish education. Toward the later stages of the projection, the imbalance of the Jewish age composition in most countries outside of Israel could become so overwhelming as to endanger the effective functioning of Jewish community services.

Demographic trends in Israel different from those in other major Jewish communities imply a shifting global balance of mutual relations and a change in where decisions are made. As part of a stronger global focus on Israeli society, the chief responsibility for ensuring adequate Jewish education and cultural continuity among future generations will gradually pass from the Diaspora to Israel.[67] And, to the extent that a growing share of world Jewry will reside in Israel, Israeli society will be asked increasingly to rely on its own productive and intellectual resources, and less on the material and moral help that has long come from the Diaspora. While the extent or intensity of the Diaspora-Israel relationship

---

[67]Sergio DellaPergola, *World Jewry Beyond 2000: The Demographic Prospects* (Oxford, 1999).

need not be affected by demographic change, the donor-recipient relationship will in all likelihood evolve to reflect the rise or decline of major centers of Jewish life. Israel will increasingly have to take up a supportive role in relation to shrinking and aging Jewish communities elsewhere. And, in the wake of emerging demographic realities, North American Jewry — long the backbone of the world Jewish community system — might find itself more concerned with internal needs and less available to aid other Jewish communities.

A further consequence of demographic trends for Jewish life is that differential population growth may not only reflect but also enhance religious, ideological, and cultural differences within a community, sharpening existing cleavages, especially those of a denominational-ritual nature, and those stemming from the large-scale absorption of immigrants. Thus demographic developments may have much to do with the great challenge of preserving unity while acknowledging diversity, both within the Jewish camp in Israel as well as in the United States and other Diaspora Jewish communities.

For its part, the Jewish population of Israel faces complex problems related to the regional development and geopolitical equilibrium of the Middle East. The Jewish/others demographic balance both within Israel and in relation to its adjacent populations is bound to affect Israeli strategic thinking and decision making.

CONCLUSIONS

Demographic projections are not prophecies. Rather, they reflect changes expected in a population if it develops according to certain assumptions about demographic variables. The projections presented here used "realistic" assumptions; they reflect recent sociodemographic trends among the Jewish populations of different countries and regions, including the expected effects of current levels of international migration and of changes in Jewish identification. Only conditions of stability or moderate change were considered in our alternative scenarios. While substantially expanding the range of scenarios would produce a more lively and provocative overview, learning from the possible implications of present trends is a contribution both for social scientific research interested in the Jewish group in comparative theoretical perspective, and for applied research aimed at Jewish community planning and policy making.

The demographic projections discussed above tend to follow a linear path, though we know for sure that history, and Jewish history in particular has not followed such a straight-line course. In reality the direction of political, socioeconomic, and other processes may suddenly shift, as it has so often in the past—particularly in the 20th century. Based on past experience it is likely that the world system's geopolitical balance will continue to change both globally and within specific regions.[68]

One imponderable of major relevance for world Jewry is the possible outcome of the ongoing political process in the Middle East and its demographic consequences. Peace might generate significant economic benefits for the region that, in turn, might stimulate Jewish migrations of varying magnitude to and from Israel. If peace does not come to the Middle East, on the other hand, there might be heavy long-term economic and social costs for Israeli society, accompanied, perhaps, by large-scale emigration. Similarly, other changes in the world geopolitical equilibrium could happen anywhere, affecting the position of Jews.

Even if no such unexpected shift occurs, one important goal of population projections is to outline undesirable developments that may emerge from the indefinite continuation of present demographic trends, and to stimulate thoughts about possible policy interventions that might prevent the scenarios from becoming reality. The findings presented here hint at enormous challenges—for example, the balance between the young and the elderly within world Jewry, the balance between Israel and Diaspora Jewries, and the balance between Jewish and non-Jewish populations in Israel. Such issues, with their human, cultural, economic, and environmental implications, should elicit serious thinking and sophisticated response.

---

[68]For three different general approaches to the question see: Samuel P. Huntington, *The Clash of Civilizations and the Remaking of World Order* (New York, 1996); Terence K. Hopkins and Immanuel Wallerstein, *The Age of Transition: World-System Trajectory, 1945–2025* (Binghamton, 1996); and Ronald Inglehart, *Modernization and Postmodernization: Cultural, Economic, and Political Change in 43 Societies* (Princeton, 1997).

Review
of
the
Year

UNITED STATES

United States

National Affairs

$\mathbf{W}$ITH THE COUNTDOWN TO A new millennium under way, 1999 began as a year of uncertainty for the United States and for its Jewish community, notwithstanding unprecedented national prosperity and the absence of any imminent threats to national security. Attention focused on the spectacle of a president of the United States facing an impeachment trial in the Senate, and no one knew what impact this would have on the domestic agenda, international concerns, and the next round of elections.

Long before year's end, however, the situation had changed markedly. Following President Clinton's acquittal there was stunningly little discussion of the impeachment, as forces in both major parties sought, for their own reasons, to direct the nation's attention to other matters. And there was, indeed, much else to which to attend, as far as the Jewish community was concerned. A range of domestic congressional initiatives—such as measures affecting religious liberty, immigration, and hate crimes—were on the Jewish agenda, as was the proposal for a substantial foreign-aid package to sustain and promote a reviving Middle East peace process. 1999 was also a year of paradox when, despite the undoubted acceptance of Jews by the larger society, dread news broke time and again of attacks on Jews and other minorities by haters on the fringes of society. And, in a reminder of the darkest days of the Jewish people, it seemed that every day brought further developments in the tortuous negotiations to obtain reparations on behalf of Holocaust survivors and their heirs.

THE POLITICAL ARENA

The Clinton Administration

As 1999 began, the Senate had to deal with the hot potato that had been dumped in its lap when the House of Representatives voted, in December 1998, to impeach President Clinton. Although the most likely eventuality was a Senate trial that could remove the president from office—the first such trial in over 130 years—there were those who sought to forestall it. Among them were leaders of

149

the Reform movement's Central Conference of American Rabbis (CCAR) and the Conservative movement's Rabbinical Assembly (RA), who wrote to the Senate urging that it censure the president but not hold a trial.

As the trial neared with little chance that the necessary two-thirds of the Senate could be mustered to remove the president, many wondered what the entire process portended for the remainder of the 106th Congress. Some Jewish leaders feared a breakdown of bipartisan cooperation after a partisan and contentious trial, preventing progress on a range of issues that many in the Jewish community were promoting. "It's going to be harder to get legislators' attention for the progressive side of our agenda because there's a lot of background noise from impeachment," commented Michael Lieberman, Washington counsel for the Anti-Defamation League (ADL), "there's a lot of ill will and there's a lot of people who almost immediately will begin to think about the 2000 election." Others speculated that the trial might actually encourage compromise and conciliation. "You have two major trends coming together," said Rabbi David Saperstein, director of the Reform movement's Religious Action Center. "The president wants to leave a legacy of significant positive change for America and the world, and the Republican leadership knows the worst thing that can happen is to be perceived as a do-nothing Congress."

When the votes were taken, all ten Jewish Democratic senators stood with their party for acquittal on both the perjury and obstruction-of-justice charges. Nevertheless, earlier in the proceeding Senator Russell Feingold, a Jewish lawmaker from Wisconsin, was the only Democrat to vote with the Republican majority. He did so twice, first in opposing an unsuccessful motion to dismiss the charges without trial, and then in supporting the taking of testimony from three witnesses called by the House impeachment managers. In contrast to the Democrats, several Republicans did break party ranks by voting for acquittal on both charges, including the sole Jewish Republican, Arlen Specter of Pennsylvania. But Senator Specter put his own unique spin on the matter by pronouncing, as he cast his vote, that his verdict was "not proved, therefore not guilty." The senator earlier explained that he would be voting in this fashion in accordance with Scottish judicial practice, which allows this alternative verdict. After acquittal, another Jewish senator, Dianne Feinstein (D., Cal.), sought to bring up a resolution censuring the president, for which she had gathered 38 signatures, only to be forestalled by a parliamentary maneuver by Senator Phil Gramm (R., Tex.).

Once the proceedings were over Jewish lobbyists expressed the hope for bipartisan cooperation on a range of issues. But some Jewish observers could not resist criticizing the nature of the investigation conducted by special prosecutor Kenneth Starr and the impeachment process to which it had led. Rabbi Paul Menitoff, executive vice president of the CCAR, called Starr's methods "McCarthyesque." Rabbi Harold Schulweis of Encino, California, charging that the House managers seemed to have presented their case in a fashion calculated to shame the president, noted that, in Jewish tradition, "to shame somebody in public is considered as if you had shed his blood."

Some two months later, with the impeachment proceedings behind him, President Clinton was the featured speaker as some 700 people, representing the entire religious and political spectrum of Washington, gathered to salute Rabbi Saperstein as he marked 25 years as director of the Religious Action Center. President Clinton praised Saperstein for his dedication to religious liberty and social justice, and for his ability to turn words into action.

Presidential Politics

January 1999 was not too soon for issues relating to the 2000 elections. Responding to the concerns of Jewish communities in western states about plans to schedule eight presidential primaries for the Jewish Sabbath—Saturday, March 11, 2000—Utah governor Michael Leavitt and Montana secretary of state Mike Cooney, the chairs of a task force responsible for organizing these primaries, recommended that they be held a day earlier. Most of the primaries were ultimately rescheduled. While Arizona's Democratic primary remained set to go forward as originally planned, opportunity was provided for early mail-in and Internet voting. Democratic presidential caucuses were scheduled for Michigan and Minnesota on that Saturday.

Issues of historical revisionism of concern to Jews became tied to the upcoming presidential campaign. In September, likely presidential hopeful Patrick Buchanan, at that point still a Republican, suggested, in his new book *A Republic, Not an Empire*, that Nazi Germany had presented no physical threat to the United States. Therefore, he claimed, the U.S. should not have fought Germany. He also repeated earlier criticisms of Jewish and Israeli influence on American foreign policy. Jewish groups and Holocaust historians immediately condemned Buchanan's views. Both the Republican Jewish Coalition and the National Jewish Democratic Council also joined in the condemnation, with RJC executive director Matthew Brooks commenting that Buchanan's views were "way outside the mainstream of the Republican Party." As the prospect of a Buchanan bolt to the Reform Party became more likely, contenders for the Republican nomination reacted in different ways. Texas governor George W. Bush declined to ask Buchanan to leave the party, Buchanan's views on the U.S. role in World War II notwithstanding, because, Bush explained, "I'm going to need every vote I can get among Republicans to win the election." The governor's spokesman, however, stressed that Bush disagreed strongly with Buchanan's "strange ideas" and "believes that World War II was a great and noble cause." Senator John McCain of Arizona, in contrast, called for Buchanan's ejection from the party because of his extreme views, and suggested that, in failing to take a similar position, Bush was "putting politics ahead of principle."

While clearly disappointed with Bush's response to the Buchanan issue, Jewish leaders generally avoided strong criticism of Bush and concentrated on Buchanan himself. ADL national director Abraham Foxman asserted that he was troubled that so many still seemed to regard Buchanan as within the political mainstream, notwithstanding that he was "an anti-Semite, . . . a Hitler apologist, . . . a Nazi war criminal defender, an Israel basher, . . . [and] a racist on so many levels." In October, the American Jewish Congress ran an ad in the *New York Times* calling on American leaders to reject Buchanan's views and accusing Buchanan of becoming "the spokesman for a virulent cadre of extremists and revisionists who insist on ignoring the entire point of the 20th century's greatest challenge to mankind." But beginning October 25, when Buchanan announced his candidacy for the Reform Party nomination, there was little comment from Jewish communal organizations, reflecting the legal prohibitions on nonprofit organizations becoming involved in political campaigns. The next day Buchanan, on a nationally broadcast morning news program, asserted that *New York Times* columnist William Safire "has always put Israel a little ahead of his own country," after a Safire column criticized Buchanan for his views about Jewish influence on American foreign policy.

The first debate of the election season to include all the declared Republican candidates, held in Iowa in December, ignited controversy over the role of religion in politics. Asked to name his favorite political philosopher, George W. Bush replied that it was Jesus. "I don't know if I can explain it," he said when asked to expand on his answer. "When you turn your heart over to Christ, it changes your life." Two other candidates, Sen. Orrin Hatch (R., Utah), and former Family Research Council head Gary Bauer, also named Jesus in response to the same question. On the Democratic side, Vice President Al Gore made explicit reference to his religious convictions, asserting that his guide, when faced with a difficult decision, was to ask, "WWJD—What Would Jesus Do?"

Congressional Elections

In January 1999, in response to David Duke's announcement that he would run in the special spring election to fill the House seat vacated by Rep. Bob Livingston (R., La.), the American Jewish Congress called upon the Republican National Committee to expel the former Klansman. In March, following the RNC's assurance to the AJCongress that steps had been taken to ensure that Duke would receive no assistance from the Republican Party, the Jewish organization pronounced itself satisfied that the party had done all it could to disavow the white supremacist. During the course of his campaign Duke published a new book, *My Awakening*, which the Jewish Telegraphic Agency characterized as "more outspokenly racist" than the positions Duke had previously asserted. Among other things, the book called for a revolution to "free" white people as "justified by the highest laws of Nature and God." Duke was defeated in his bid for the House, coming in third in an open primary.

Throughout much of 1999, as First Lady Hillary Rodham Clinton inched closer to a contemplated run for a U.S. Senate seat from New York, she worked to distance herself from a statement she had made in 1998 that indicated support for a Palestinian state. Clinton now asserted that the matter should be addressed in the final-status negotiations between the Palestinian Authority and Israel. In a July 2 letter to the Union of Orthodox Jewish Congregations (known as the Orthodox Union, or OU), Clinton endorsed moving the U.S. embassy from Tel Aviv to Jerusalem, albeit at a time "sensitive to Israel's interest in achieving a secure peace with her neighbors." She reinforced this message later that month in speeches to Hadassah and the National Jewish Democratic Council.

An unexpected Hillary Clinton connection to the Jewish community surfaced in August when the *Forward* reported that her step-grandfather had been Jewish and that her mother's half-sister—"the feisty wife of a Yiddish-speaking Jewish immigrant"—had converted to Judaism. Reflecting the common wisdom that Jews do not vote on the basis of a candidate's Jewish identity or lack thereof, former New York mayor Ed Koch pronounced the news "much ado about nothing." In fact, a compilation of polls coincidentally released the same week as the story about Jewish relatives indicated that Mrs. Clinton was running slightly behind New York City mayor Rudolph Giuliani, her probable Republican rival, among Jewish voters—hardly the strong Jewish support for a Democratic candidate that one would expect in New York.

Even as she prepared to announce her intention to run for the Senate, Mrs. Clinton had to deal with fallout from her November trip to Israel and the West Bank, in the course of which she sat by while Suha Arafat, wife of Yasir Arafat, accused Israel of using poison gas against Palestinians. Clinton took until the next day to condemn the remarks as "baseless" and "inflammatory." She later defended her initial lack of response on the grounds that she did not want to cause an "international incident" and that the remarks had not sounded as harsh in translation as they were in the original Arabic. While Democratic colleagues defended Clinton as "a strong supporter of a safe and secure Israel at peace with its neighbors," the Republican Jewish Coalition issued a commercial showing Clinton sitting silently as the Palestinian first lady spoke, and criticizing her lack of response that day. However Israeli prime minister Ehud Barak, during a visit to New York soon after the incident, asserted that, as far as he was concerned, "the first lady's visit to Israel contributed to the peace process."

Political-Action Organizations

In May, the National Jewish Coalition announced that it was changing its name to the Republican Jewish Coalition, and at the same time establishing a political action committee (PAC) to direct contributions to Republican congressional and presidential candidates. This restructuring followed in the footsteps of a similar action by the National Jewish Democratic Council, which, in 1995, had created its own PAC to provide support to Democratic candidates.

Terrorism

In October 1999, Senators Frank Lautenberg (D., N.J.) and Connie Mack (R., Fla.) introduced the Justice for Victims of Terrorism Act to help American victims of terrorism enforce court judgments against state sponsors of terrorism. This initiative grew out of the lawsuit brought by Stephen Flatow against the Iranian government for financially supporting the terrorist group that murdered his daughter, Alisa, in a 1995 bus bombing in Israel. Flatow had obtained a $247.5-million judgment against Iran under a 1996 congressional enactment, supported by the administration, allowing such suits to be filed. But the administration later switched its position, concerned that allowing execution of a judgment against diplomatic property would endanger American diplomatic property abroad and possibly prevent the U.S. from using frozen assets as a tool of foreign policy. Consequently, in 1998 the administration blocked Flatow from attaching Iranian assets frozen in the U.S. to satisfy the judgment. Congress responded that year by amending the 1996 law so as to permit frozen assets of countries to be used to satisfy judgments arising from their support of terrorism. The administration, unhappy with this action, invoked an ambiguous "national security" waiver provision authorized by the 1998 amendment so as to continue to protect the frozen assets.

The new Lautenberg-Mack bill of 1999 sought to accommodate administration concerns by permitting the president to waive enforcement of a judgment pursuant to the 1996 law, on an asset-by-asset basis. However it denied the president authority to waive enforcement of such a judgment against the real property of a foreign diplomatic mission or its assets, if the property was being used for non-diplomatic purposes—such as rental property—or if the assets were proceeds of a sale of property. But the administration immediately indicated its opposition, reiterating that, even under this new proposal, blocked assets would no longer be available as leverage in dealing with Iran and similar countries, and that U.S. diplomatic property around the world would be placed at risk.

In December, U.S. customs officials arrested Ahmed Ressam, an Algerian national with ties to Osama Bin-Laden, the wealthy Muslim extremist suspected of masterminding a number of attacks against American facilities around the world. Ressam was caught allegedly attempting to bring into the United States a rental car full of enough explosives to kill hundreds of people. This was a sobering reminder that the horrors of the waning century would not be left behind with the turning of the calendar.

Soviet Jewry, Refugees, and Immigration

On January 15 the Immigration and Naturalization Service (INS) increased the fee for filing an application for U.S. citizenship from $95 to $225. This came at a time when there was a backlog of some 1.8-million people waiting for the INS to deal with their pending applications, including thousands of Jews from the former Soviet Union (FSU). The Council of Jewish Federations (CJF) warned that the higher cost would impose a serious financial burden on Jewish applicants.

In testimony before congressional committees in February and March, David A. Harris, executive director of the American Jewish Committee, Mark Levin, executive director of the National Conference on Soviet Jewry, and Diana Aviv, director of the CJF's Washington Action Office, raised alarm signals about the situation of Jews and other religious minorities in the FSU. For a number of years there had been voices, even within the Jewish community, that had questioned the need for the extension of the Lautenberg Amendment, a provision that relaxed criteria for the refugee admission of Jews, Christian minorities, and some other designated groups from the FSU into the U.S. But the apparent increase of anti-Semitism there led Jewish leaders to call, in 1999, for an unprecedented two-year extension. In the end, the notion of a two-year extension found no traction in Congress. A one-year extension—through the end of September 2000—was included without controversy in appropriations legislation.

In March, Senators Gordon Smith (R., Ore.) and Joseph Biden (D., Del.), chair and ranking member, respectively, of the Senate Foreign Relations Subcommittee on Europe, wrote Vice President Al Gore urging that, in a planned meeting with Russian prime minister Yevgeny Primakov in Washington, he make clear that the U.S. expected "a strong commitment to human rights and religious freedom" in Russia. In Moscow, on the eve of his planned trip to the meeting, the Russian premier met with officials of the ADL and the Russian Jewish Congress, taking the occasion to condemn the rise in anti-Semitic incidents in the country and to call for hate-crimes legislation. At the last moment the trip to the U.S., which was also to have included a meeting with American Jewish leaders, was cancelled, apparently because of the deepening crisis in Kosovo. Later that week the U.S. House of Representatives unanimously approved a nonbinding resolution condemning anti-Semitic statements that had recently been made in the Russian Duma.

Congress weighed in with the Russian leadership again in June—soon after attacks on several Russian synagogues—when 99 out of the 100 U.S. senators signed a letter, circulated by Senators Smith and Biden and addressed to Russian president Boris Yeltsin, warning that if Yeltsin failed to "demonstrate . . . emphatic disagreement with those who espouse anti-Semitism" in his country, American economic and political support might be jeopardized. The American Jewish Committee and the National Conference on Soviet Jewry were particularly active in urging senators to sign the letter, and the AJC later reprinted the text of the letter, along with the names of all the signatories, in full-page advertisements in the *New York Times* and the *Los Angeles Times.*

The ad appeared just as President Clinton rejected Yeltsin's request for outright repeal of the Jackson-Vanik law, which conditioned U.S.-Russia trade relations on the freedom of Jews and others to leave Russia. Although Congress had earlier suspended the Jackson-Vanik sanctions in light of improvement in Russian emigration policies, the administration now stated that "the rise of anti-Semitic statements and rhetoric" in Russia showed the need for the law to remain in place.

In August, President Clinton increased the number of refugees allowed to enter the United States—90,000 for fiscal year 2000, as compared to 78,000 the prior year. Slots for refugees from the FSU were reduced, however, to 20,000, as compared to 23,000 for fiscal year 1999. Jews were expected to fill approximately 6,000 of the new slots. Leonard Glickman, executive vice president of the Hebrew Immigrant Aid Society (HIAS), praised the president's action, but Diana Aviv, now vice president for public policy of the United Jewish Communities (UJC, the reconstituted CJF), expressed disappointment "that the refugee numbers are as low as they are," pointing out that there had been a 40-percent drop in refugees permitted to enter the U.S. over the previous six years.

Meanwhile, HIAS and its affiliated agencies continued to grapple with the consequences of a dramatic downturn in the number of new refugees arriving in this country and requiring resettlement—some 5,000–7,000 in 1999 compared to 47,000 in 1992, the peak year for the arrival of Soviet Jews. Since federal funding for resettlement agencies—a major component of their resources—was calculated on the basis of the number of people served, the reduction in federal funding necessitated reexamination of the entire resettlement operation. HIAS convened a major conference on the subject in New York in November, where Jewish groups concerned with resettlement policy continued to grapple with the question of whether the community should increase service to non-Jewish arrivals, accept the realities of a new, more modest mission, or get out of the resettlement business entirely.

Jewish groups committed to a liberal immigration policy joined other pro-immigrant groups in a campaign that sought to take advantage of a perceived favorable trend in national attitudes toward immigrants and immigration. This "Fix '96" campaign—so called because it advocated rolling back provisions of the 1996 immigration and welfare reform laws—focused on a number of legislative proposals introduced in 1999. Among other things, these bills were intended to restore health and nutritional benefits to legal immigrants, provide for judicial review of decisions of the INS and immigration courts, give the attorney general authority to cancel the mandatory detention and removal requirements in the 1996 law, and limit the application of expedited review procedures for asylum seekers established in 1996. However none of these initiatives moved very far during 1999.

Jewish organizations also participated in the debates over reorganization of the INS, an agency that both advocates and opponents of immigration agreed was long overdue for reform. There were serious differences, however, about what would constitute appropriate reform. The Jewish groups, led by the CJF (and its successor agency, UJC, later in the year), opposed a proposal by Rep. Lamar Smith (R., Tex.), chairman of the House Judiciary Subcommittee on Immigration, to split the INS into separate enforcement and service bureaus. These groups feared that the creation of two separate agencies would lead to a disproportionate allocation of resources on the side of enforcement. They supported, instead, a proposal to separate the two immigration functions but to create a high-level office with clear lines of authority over both. On November 4, 1999, the immigration subcommittee adopted Chairman Smith's approach, leaving resolution of the matter in the House and action in the Senate for the next year.

Foreign Aid

Throughout the debate on federal funding levels for fiscal year 2000, Jewish organizations urged Congress to maintain funding for international programs generally, and, specifically, for Israel and its partners in the Middle East peace process. Particular focus was placed on the $1.9 billion the president requested to help implement the 1998 Wye River peace accords signed by Israel, the Palestinian Authority, and Jordan. Following King Hussein's death in February, $100 million of the $300 million requested for Jordan was funded, but the remainder—$1.2 billion for Israel, $400 million for the Palestinian Authority, and the additional $200 million for Jordan—was not included in the foreign-aid bill that Congress sent the president in October. The bill, which provided $12.6 billion in foreign-aid funding, was also $2 billion short of the president's foreign-aid request, although it did include nearly $3 billion in economic and military aid for Israel.

The foreign-aid legislation narrowly achieved final, post-conference passage (214-211 in the House and 51-49 in the Senate), largely on the basis of Republican votes, and with unprecedented opposition from all Jewish Democrats. Senator Arlen Specter of Pennsylvania and Representative Benjamin Gilman of New York, the only two Jewish Republican lawmakers, voted in favor. The American Israel Public Affairs Committee (AIPAC) nominally favored the bill since it provided aid to Israel. But, according to certain unnamed Capitol Hill aides quoted by the Jewish Telegraphic Agency on October 11, AIPAC did not lobby aggressively for the bill because Wye River funding was not included. Another concern in the Jewish community was that the foreign-aid bill was too heavily weighted toward Israel and its peace partners. "If Israel is going to exist in a stable environment then it is very important for the United States to be engaged as much as possible throughout the region and the world," said Lewis Roth, a spokesman for Americans for Peace Now.

President Clinton vetoed the bill, as expected, and Jewish groups geared up to advocate improving the package. AIPAC took advantage of a previously scheduled Washington meeting to send nearly 200 of its members to Capitol Hill to call for Wye funding. While some in the Republican leadership assured Jewish leaders that the Wye money would indeed be appropriated, if not in this foreign-aid bill then at some future time, other Republican leaders warned that appropriations for Wye would necessitate cuts in domestic spending. In the end, Congress passed a $15.3-billion foreign-aid package that included the Wye funding, plus an additional $800 million for some of the administration's key foreign-policy initiatives, as part of the year-end omnibus spending bill.

Arab Boycott

The U.S. Department of Commerce took action in 1999 to enforce the law prohibiting U.S. businesses from complying with conditions imposed by foreign companies that goods contain no Israeli materials. In June, the New York branch of Deutsche Bank was hit with a $5,000 civil penalty for paying a letter of credit that contained such a prohibited condition, as part of a 1998 transaction with Lebanon.

In September, Arab American and Muslim American groups, joined by the Arab League, called for a boycott of Walt Disney, Inc. Their complaint centered on a special exhibit about Israel at Disney's EPCOT Center in Orlando, Florida, scheduled to open on October 1. These groups asserted that the exhibit—an $8-million project to which Israel was contributing $1.8 million, and which was intended to depict the history of Israel and display cutting-edge Israeli technology—portrayed Jerusalem as Israel's capital. Israel's Foreign Ministry, in response, asserted that the exhibit was designed to depict Jerusalem as a central site for Jews, Christians, and Muslims, although it would also reflect "the position of Jerusalem as the key component to the Israeli pavilion," which "speaks for itself." Disney, for its part, maintained that the pavilion was apolitical, did not portray Jerusalem as Israel's capital, and simply told "the story of the role that Jerusalem has played throughout history."

American Jewish groups criticized the talk of boycott, which followed hard on the heels of an earlier boycott threat by Arab American and Muslim American groups that had, in August, apparently induced Burger King to withdraw a franchise it had granted to an Israeli in the West Bank town of Ma'aleh Adumim. While acknowledging that "there is nothing illegitimate about the Arab community pressing its view of Jerusalem" even as Jewish leaders and Israelis pressed their own, Martin Raffel, director for international concerns at the Jewish Council for Public Affairs (JCPA), said that the actions directed at Burger King and Disney reminded him of "the day when Arabs used a boycott to strangle Israel."

By the end of September both sides in the Disney dispute were declaring victory. Israel's Foreign Ministry issued a statement claiming that visitors to the pavilion "will have no doubt that Jerusalem is and will forever remain Israel's capital," while Arab foreign ministers pointed to a written assurance from Disney that "the Israeli exhibit does not reference Jerusalem as the capital of Israel." American Arab groups too, by and large, also said that Disney had accepted their position. When the exhibit opened, Israeli officials acknowledged that changes had been made in the pavilion in the wake of the protests, but that these were "minor," not "substantive." In his remarks at the opening reception, Eitan Ben-Tsur, director-general of the Israeli Foreign Ministry, referred three times to "Jerusalem, the capital of Israel."

Kosovo and Turkey

In March, when President Clinton decided to participate in the NATO air strikes on Yugoslavia in response to that country's actions in Kosovo, a number of Jewish groups weighed in with their support. The JCPA pronounced the move consonant with "U.S. national interests and moral values," and many Jews concurred with the lessons President Clinton drew from the failure of the appeasement of Hitler before World War II.

Jewish groups mobilized to provide assistance to hundreds of thousands of Kosovar refugees who fled into Albania and Macedonia. Under the leadership of the American Jewish Joint Distribution Committee (JDC), they raised millions of dollars from American Jews and disbursed the funds to provide needed shelter, medicine, food, and clothing for the refugees. A leadership delegation of the American Jewish Committee—which itself, in the course of the year, raised over a million dollars for relief—traveled to Macedonia in April to view firsthand the conditions of the Kosovar Albanians living there. Others made their own distinctive contributions. The ORT joined with Albanian nongovernmental agencies to document Serbian human-rights violations, and worked with the JDC in developing a program to train refugees for jobs. The Simon Wiesenthal Center announced plans to purchase a mobile medical clinic to provide assistance to the refugees. And as it became apparent, after NATO peacekeepers came to Kosovo, that some refugees would not be able to return home, Jewish refugee resettlement organizations, including HIAS, began to focus on providing services for those Kosovar refugees who would be coming to the United States.

Jewish groups also mobilized to provide assistance to victims of an earthquake in Turkey that killed thousands, and injured and left homeless many more. The JDC organized some 40 American Jewish groups to raise relief funds, and its representative in Turkey pledged to carry out JDC's on-site relief work in cooperation with the Turkish Jewish community. The American Jewish Committee, for its part, raised more than $500,000 for earthquake relief in the two months following the calamity. In October, AJC executive director David A. Harris traveled to Adaparazi, Turkey, to inaugurate an AJC-funded school for children left homeless by the earthquake, as part of a ceremony dedicating a prefabricated village erected in less than two months by Israel. American Jewish World Service also raised funds for the village.

U.S.-Israel Relations

A Maryland murder case with international ramifications reached its conclusion in 1999. One of two suspects in the crime, 17-year-old Samuel Sheinbein, fled to Israel in September 1997, where he claimed that his father's Israeli citizenship made him an Israeli citizen as well. Israeli law at that time clearly forbade extradition of its citizens, providing for trial in an Israeli court for crimes committed abroad. The likelihood that Sheinbein would avoid prosecution in the U.S. through this "loophole" angered many Americans, posing a threat to U.S.-Israel relations.

In 1998, however, the Israeli government addressed the problem by interpreting the law so as to allow extradition, a position that was sustained by an Israeli district court that same year. But in February 1999, the Israeli Supreme Court reversed the district court, ruling 3-2 that Sheinbein had legitimately claimed citizenship through his father and that he could not be extradited. Although U.S. officials expressed regret on hearing of this ruling, the decision was not greeted with nearly the vehemence that had accompanied the early stages of the case, when Sheinbein first fled to Israel. Thus Rep. Sonny Callahan (R., Ala.), chair of the House Appropriations Subcommittee on Foreign Appropriations — who two years earlier had threatened to cut aid to Israel if Sheinbein were not extradited — this time commented only that he was "naturally disappointed" but that he trusted "the decision will not prevent due process from taking its course." A number of officials, both American and Israeli, spoke of the need to respect the determination of an independent judiciary, and urged that the case against Sheinbein proceed so that justice could be done.

Not everybody treated the Israeli Supreme Court's decision with equanimity, however. The mother of the murder victim demanded that the United States recall its ambassador to Israel until Sheinbein was extradited, while others held protests outside the Israeli embassy in Washington. In the meantime, Israeli attorney general Elyakim Rubinstein filed a petition with his nation's Supreme Court asking for a reconsideration of its decision. That petition was denied on March 21, opening the door to Sheinbein's trial on murder charges in Israel. The next day, Sheinbein was indicted on charges of first-degree murder. In April, the Knesset enacted its own response to the Supreme Court's decision, passing a law providing that henceforth a citizen of Israel not resident in the Jewish state would be subject to extradition.

In July, Sheinbein pleaded not guilty before a Tel Aviv court, setting the stage for trial. But instead of a trial, the attorney general reached a plea bargain with Sheinbein, who would plead guilty in exchange for a 24-year prison sentence. The deal was immediately criticized by U.S. prosecutors as too lenient (Sheinbein would have been subject to a life sentence had he been convicted in Maryland) and for leaving open the possibility that Sheinbein could be paroled after serving two-thirds of his sentence. A number of Israeli officials also criticized plea bargaining in such a politically charged case. But Rubinstein maintained that the sentence Sheinbein would receive was extremely harsh by Israeli standards, and that it would ultimately be up to the courts, years down the road, to determine — based on "the criminal act and its nature, not only good behavior" — if Sheinbein should be paroled. On October 24, the trial court approved the plea bargain and sentenced Sheinbein to the agreed-upon prison term.

United Nations

In the omnibus spending bill that closed out the 1999 session, Congress included a statement calling for an end to a long-standing inequity in the UN's treatment of Israel—the Jewish state's exclusion from membership in any of the world body's regional groups. In order to be eligible for a seat on the Security Council and on other crucial UN committees, a state must belong to a regional group. Objections from Arab and Muslim states had kept Israel out of the Asian group, where it belonged geographically. Congress called upon the secretary of state to report to it annually on actions taken by U.S. representatives to the UN to gain Israel temporary membership in the Western Europe and Others Group (WEOG, the regional group to which the U.S. belonged).

Even as Jewish organizations urged Congress to take steps to improve the UN's treatment of Israel, they also sought to maintain U.S. involvement in the UN, and to save America's vote in the General Assembly by urging the U.S. to make good on its arrears to the world body. One of the last budget items settled by the administration and congressional negotiators was the authorization of $926 million in back dues to the UN. In December, the U.S. paid $151 million to the UN, $100 million of which constituted the first of three payments of those arrears.

American Jewry's sense of grievance about the UN's treatment of Israel was heightened when the world body set the date for its 1999 opening session on September 20, Yom Kippur. In a letter to UN secretary general Kofi Annan, Representatives Benjamin Gilman (R., N.Y.) and Samuel Gejdenson (D., Conn.), chairman and ranking member, respectively, of the House International Relations Committee, urged the world body—unsuccessfully—to change the opening date, terming the scheduling "insensitive and inappropriate." President Clinton then announced that, because of this scheduling, he would not address the UN at its opening ceremony, a decision that was hailed by Jewish groups.

Jonathan Pollard

1999 began with the expectation of an early administration review of Israel's request, conveyed and agreed to at the Wye River talks the previous October, that convicted spy Jonathan Pollard be granted a commutation of his sentence. Opponents of such a move, including senior members of the U.S. intelligence community and some 60 U.S. Senators—including the two highest-ranking members of the Senate Intelligence Committee—quickly weighed in during January, opposing Pollard's release because, they maintained, he had done enormous harm to American national security. A number of American Jewish leaders, in the meantime, continued to urge Pollard's release, even as others cautioned against taking too high a profile because, in the words of American Jewish Congress executive director Phil Baum, "the more drama that's associated with this, the worse it turns out to be for Pollard." By March, with no action having been taken, the Conference of Presidents of Major American Jewish Organizations requested a meeting with White House counsel Charles Ruff to argue the point that Pollard had been treated more harshly than other spies in a similar situation. Conference leaders were offered, instead, the opportunity to set forth their argument in writing.

As the year ended, the administration was saying that the Pollard matter would not be resolved "imminently." White House spokesman Joe Lockhart stated that the high-level review promised at Wye River had been completed, but that "no recommendation has gone to the president." Earlier in the year, after his election, Prime Minister Ehud Barak had stated during a visit to Washington that he wanted "to see Pollard released," even as he reportedly made clear to the president that Pollard's fate would not be linked to the peace process.

ANTI-SEMITISM AND EXTREMISM

Assessing Anti-Semitism

The Anti-Defamation League's annual audit of anti-Semitic incidents, released in March, indicated a rise in 1998, reversing a three-year decline. In 1998, 1,611 incidents were reported to the ADL, an increase of more than 2 percent from 1997. But not all kinds of offenses increased. Cases of harassment, threat or assault held steady (896 in 1998 as compared to 898 in 1997). However incidents of anti-Semitic vandalism (a category ranging from anti-Semitic graffiti and defacement, to arson, to threatened and attempted bombing) showed a 6-percent increase to a total of 715. The ADL cautioned against reading too much into the higher numbers. "Any increase is disturbing," said Kenneth Jacobson, the organization's assistant national director, "but it's too early to make some definitive judgment that we're heading into a period of constant increase." The report itself pointed out that the total number of incidents was still below the ten-year annual average of 1,741, and substantially below the peak year of 1994, when 2,066 incidents were reported.

Other experts cautioned that the ADL audit did not provide a complete picture of the state of American anti-Semitism. Kenneth Stern, the American Jewish Committee program specialist on anti-Semitism and extremism, stated that "anti-Semitic incidents are only part of the package," and noted that anti-government and hate groups continued to threaten "the security of Jews and the vibrancy of American democracy." Indeed, the ADL and other Jewish organizations viewed with alarm what Rabbi Abraham Cooper, the associate dean of the Simon Wiesenthal Center, described as an "absolute explosion of hate sites on the Internet," which meant that "the potential pool of young people" exposed to these groups was growing.

Jewish organizations took steps later in the year to document and respond to hate on the Internet. In March, the Wiesenthal Center released "Digital Hate 2000," a CD-ROM documenting 1,400 Web sites that targeted religious and ethnic groups. A special version was designed for use by law-enforcement officials and educators.

Acts of Violence

The nation was stunned on April 20 when two heavily armed students went on a shooting spree in Columbine High School in Littleton, Colorado, killing 12 fellow students and a teacher before killing themselves. It soon became known that the killers had been obsessed with Nazi Germany, and that other students had heard them speaking about April 20 as Adolf Hitler's birthday. The killing of one of the students, an African American, was preceded by one perpetrator's comment, "I hate niggers." Attempts to fathom what motivated the killers and whether they had subscribed to anything resembling an extremist ideology were complicated by the revelation that one of the gunmen, Dylan Klebold, was the great-grandson of a prominent Ohio Jewish philanthropist, and that while Klebold was raised as a Lutheran, his mother had been raised in a Jewish home.

Columbine, it turned out, was just the beginning. A note found at Shawnee High School in Medford, New Jersey, in May, announced: "A bomb is in the school to kill Jews." Police quickly arrested several teenagers charged with having written the note. And then, just before dawn on Friday, June 18, there were arson attacks on two Reform synagogues and an Orthodox synagogue in the Sacramento area, one of the worst anti-Semitic crime sprees in decades. Total damage was estimated at $1 million, with one synagogue—B'nai Israel, possibly the oldest synagogue west of the Mississippi River—suffering the bulk of the harm, including the destruction of a 5,000-book library and 300 videotapes on Jewish history. Federal and state law-enforcement authorities swiftly commenced an investigation, proceeding on the assumption that the timing of the attacks— at locations up to ten miles apart, all taking place within 35 minutes—meant that more than one person was involved. The arsonists left notes at two of the sites, one of which denounced the "North Atlantic Terrorist Organization" and asserted that "the fake Albanian refugee crisis was manufactured by the International Jewsmedia to justify the terrorizing, the bestial bombing of our Yugoslavia back into the dark ages."

The affected congregations found alternative sites for their Sabbath services, and their members vowed to persevere. B'nai Israel librarian Poshi Mikalson displayed a charred book at Friday evening services, promising, "from these ashes we will rise again." California governor Gray Davis termed the "despicable hate crimes" an "offense to all decent people," and the Rev. Dobrivoje Milunovic, pastor of Sacramento's Serbian Orthodox Church of the Assumption, denounced "this act of terror, this act of hate." Within days, the California State Assembly passed a resolution condemning the attacks, and public rallies demonstrated community support. Jewish and non-Jewish organizations around the country contributed to restore the synagogues and their lost treasures. The U.S. Department of Housing and Urban Development offered low-interest loans to the synagogues pursuant to the Church Arson Prevention Act, for which many Jewish organizations had successfully advocated a few years before.

Barely two weeks after the arsons Americans were stunned by yet another violent assault, this time a shooting spree that included Jews among the victims. Benjamin Nathaniel Smith, a 21-year-old member of the white supremacist World Church of the Creator, wounded six residents of West Rogers Park, a Chicago suburb and the largest Orthodox Jewish community in the area, while they were walking to and from synagogue on Friday evening, July 2. A local rabbi pronounced it "nothing short of miraculous" that none of the Jewish victims had been killed.

But, in additional shootings by Smith that took place that weekend, other victims were not so lucky. That same evening Smith traveled to Skokie, another Chicago suburb, where he killed an African American man out for a walk with his children. Other shootings in the Chicago area and elsewhere in Illinois—Urbana and Springfield—that evening and the next resulted in an additional injury. Smith's spree culminated in a second murder in Bloomington, Indiana, on Sunday morning, this time of a male Korean American on his way to church. Pursued by police later that day, Smith shot and killed himself.

In the days after the shootings, national attention focused on the World Church of the Creator, which law-enforcement authorities considered one of the fastest growing hate groups in the country. The "church," claiming a membership of 7,000 (observers placed the number closer to 2,000), believed that a "racial holy war" between whites and subhuman "mud people"—Jews and nonwhites—was necessary and inevitable for the survival of the "white race." The group claimed not to condone violence, but Smith's actions were not the first violent attacks associated with it. And, after the attacks in Illinois and Indiana, the ADL reported that World Church fliers had been found at one of the three burned Sacramento synagogues prior to the arsons.

One week later, California authorities arrested two brothers suspected of murdering a gay couple, and found in the brothers' home an apparent "hit list" of 32 Jews who lived in the Sacramento area, mostly officials and members of the synagogues burned the previous month, whose names had appeared in press coverage of the arsons. Investigators also discovered a torn piece of paper that matched another piece of paper found at one of the burned synagogues, as well as a cache of semiautomatic weapons and hate literature, including material produced by the World Church of the Creator. The brothers were later named as suspects in the Sacramento attacks.

What Kenneth Stern of the American Jewish Committee would later call the "summer of hate" still had more surprises in store. On the morning of August 10, a gunman walked into the lobby of the North Valley Jewish Community Center and shot between 20 and 30 rounds from an automatic weapon, wounding two adults and three children, one of whom—five-year-old Benjamin Kadish—was left in extremely critical condition. Police quickly cordoned off the area and evacuated 22 children from the center to a nearby synagogue. The next day, Kadish was said to be in "serious but stable" condition, and within two weeks doctors were hopeful that, after an initial period in a wheelchair and then on crutches, Kadish would be "back 100 percent."

Buford O'Neal Furrow, a suspect in the shootings, turned himself in to FBI officials in Las Vegas the next day, reportedly explaining that he "wanted this to be a wake-up call to America to kill Jews." Furrow was said to have a history of mental problems and criminal assaults, and to be affiliated with a number of racist and anti-Semitic groups, including the Aryan Nations. A van he abandoned after the shooting contained additional weapons as well as a book written by an author associated with the anti-Semitic Christian Identity movement. The following week Furrow was indicted by a federal grand jury for killing a mail carrier, a Filipino American, soon after the shooting at the community center. This indictment was superseded by a later federal indictment, in December, which encompassed the attack at the community center as well. In the wake of the attack, the Jewish Community Centers Association of North America, the umbrella organization for JCCs, urged its 275 affiliates to coordinate plans with local law-enforcement authorities for upgrading security. Other Jewish organizations also took security precautions, and the UJC and the ADL made plans to work together in developing security awareness among Jewish community-relations councils.

Even as the Jewish community, local and national, coped with this latest attack, there were more anti-Semitic incidents. Over the weekend following the community-center shootings, worshipers at a Hollywood synagogue found a swastika and the words, "Jews die," spray painted on an outside wall of their house of worship; a Palo Alto community center received threatening telephone calls praising the most recent shootings; and—at the other end of the country—a synagogue in Hauppage, New York, was damaged in an arson that police investigated as a hate crime. Before the end of August, San Jose police arrested three suspects for throwing a Molotov cocktail at the home of a judge they mistakenly thought to be Jewish, and swastikas and anti-Semitic graffiti were found on the wall of a building in San Francisco that housed the offices of the Jewish Family Children's Services. Then, on November 30, a Molotov cocktail was tossed at a synagogue in Reno, Nevada, but fell to the ground outside when the window that it hit did not break. Police later arrested several white supremacists suspected in the attack.

The shootings at the Jewish community center stimulated renewed calls by many Jewish groups and other Americans for stronger gun-control laws. President Clinton termed the attack "another senseless act of gun violence" that "calls on all of us not only to give our thoughts and prayers to the victims and their families, but to intensify our resolve to make America a safe place." The following Sunday, more than 1,000 people of various faiths and colors gathered at a "Community Unity Rally" in Los Angeles to honor the victims and the rescue workers. Attorney General Janet Reno and Governor Gray Davis were among the speakers. But when Congress returned from its summer recess there was little indication that new gun-control measures were in the offing, even against the background of the summer's violence (which included other incidents besides those described above). The American Jewish Congress held a Capitol Hill press conference in September calling for action, and announced the opening of a petition drive to obtain as many as a million signatures calling on Congress to enact gun-control legislation. Members of Congress in attendance included two Jews, Senator Dianne Feinstein (D., Cal.), and Representative Jerrold Nadler (D., N.Y.), and several rabbis blew shofars outside the Capitol as a call to action.

Holocaust Denial and Hate Speech

In March, Gary Lauck, an American neo-Nazi who had served four years in a German prison for hate crimes, was deported to the U.S. Described by German prosecutors as the largest distributor of Nazi literature and paraphernalia in their country, Lauck had been extradited to Germany on an international arrest warrant after he was arrested in Denmark while attending a neo-Nazi convention. The charges on which he was convicted—inciting racial hatred, distributing anti-Semitic material, and using banned Nazi symbols—would have been protected by the First Amendment in the U.S., but in Germany they carried criminal penalties.

Even as the Jewish community and the nation were reeling from a summer of violent acts, the Washington-area Jewish community mobilized to respond to a march of the neo-Nazi American Nationalist Party along Pennsylvania Avenue, planned for Saturday afternoon, August 7. Local chapters of the American Jewish Committee and the National Conference for Unity and Justice planned a vigil in front of the Lincoln Memorial during the march, while the ADL and other cooperating organizations asked individuals and businesses to pledge a few cents for every minute of the hate demonstration, to benefit victims of hate crimes. Some 300 marchers and 500 counterdemonstrators were expected. When the day arrived, the American Nationalist Party unexpectedly canceled the event, but the counterrally went forward anyway with hundreds appearing at Lincoln Memorial and Lafayette Park, in front of the White House, to take a stand against anti-Semitism and racism. Eleanor Holmes Norton, the District of Columbia delegate to Congress, proclaimed to the crowd: "The difference between them and us is we showed up and they couldn't."

A demonstration in October by members of the Church of the American Knights of the Ku Klux Klan in New York City was no more successful. It went ahead as scheduled when a New York judge ruled that the city was obligated to allow the event, but the marchers were not permitted to wear their hoods and were denied a permit for the use of a sound truck. Only about 15 Klansmen showed up; they were met by an estimated 6,000 counterdemonstrators, seven of whom were arrested when they physically assaulted participants in the rally, giving the Klan what, in the words of one commentator, they "hope[d] for . . . , a real news story."

Legislative Activity

The organized Jewish community continued its efforts to enact the Hate Crimes Prevention Act, a bill that would extend existing hate-crimes law to those victimized because of their gender, sexual orientation or disability, and would remove judicial impediments that sometimes prevented federal authorities from stepping in when local officials were unable or unwilling to investigate and prosecute. Following the bill's introduction in both houses of Congress as a freestanding piece of legislation, the Senate passed the bill in July as an amendment to an appropriations bill. However the House-passed version of that spending bill, which followed in August, did not include the hate-crimes provision. Despite a determined effort by House and Senate supporters to retain the language, conferees dropped hate crimes from the final version. The president vetoed the bill, in part because of this omission.

Following the veto, President Clinton continued to press for inclusion of the hate-crimes provision in the omnibus appropriations bill that would close out the 1999 session. In October, the president told the ADL's national commission meeting: "We need to stand against manifestations of our inhumanity and we need to do more to reaffirm our common humanity." Earlier that month, Republican supporters of the bill, Senators Jim Jeffords (Ver.) and Gordon Smith (Ore.), and Representative Mark Foley (Fla.), held a press conference—joined by the family of a hate-crime victim—at which they issued a similar call for action. But as the year ended, the omnibus bill was enacted without mention of hate crimes.

Claims of Discrimination

In February, federal judge Alan Gold, sitting in Florida, accorded class-action status to a lawsuit alleging that Avis Rent-a-Car had discriminated against Jews. Originally filed in 1997, the suit asserted that Avis employees had been directed to avoid renting to "yeshivas," apparently a code word for corporate applicants calling from areas with heavily Jewish populations, or callers with Jewish-sounding names or accents. In his decision, Judge Gold found that testimony from former Avis employees demonstrated that "Avis employed a 'yeshiva' policy" that turned "thousands of potential customers" away. Avis officials asserted that the company had a strict policy against discrimination, and that the use of the "yeshiva" term was simply a shorthand for identifying students who, the company believed, sought corporate accounts for their yeshivas so as to circumvent age restrictions.

Discrimination was also alleged against the CIA. In April, with negotiations for a settlement at an apparent standstill, Adam Ciralsky, a Jewish attorney on forced leave from the CIA, announced through his lawyer that he planned to sue the agency for discriminating against him on the basis of his religion. In October 1997 he had been placed on leave without pay after he failed a lie-detector test that he was apparently asked to take because his family gave money to the United Jewish Appeal and Israel Bonds, and because he himself had maintained contacts with Israelis. Ciralsky's attorney, Neal Sher, former head of the Justice Department's Office of Special Investigations and former executive director of AIPAC, asserted, "There's a dirty little secret within America's security apparatus. Jews who support Israel are held to a different standard." He pointed to a series of internal CIA documents that focused on Ciralsky's Jewish background and to the problems two other Jewish government employees had experienced in obtaining security clearances. When the matter became public, the CIA denied that there was any anti-Semitism at the agency, with former director John Deutch weighing in to note his own Jewish background. Soon thereafter George Tenet, the current director, acknowledged that agency memos referring to Ciralsky did include "insensitive, unprofessional and highly inappropriate" language but, in a letter to the ADL, Tenet asserted that a panel had found that there was no anti-Semitism at the CIA.

INTERGROUP RELATIONS

African Americans

On January 18—Martin Luther King Day—the New York-based Foundation for Ethnic Understanding, headed by Rabbi Marc Schneier, launched a Web site with links to the sites of other organizations that supported dialogue between African Americans and American Jews. The site also provided access to the foundation's annual reports on the state of black-Jewish relations, and related materials. In October, the foundation joined with the World Jewish Congress to cosponsor its third annual conference on black-Jewish relations, held at Yeshiva University's Wurzweiler School of Social Work. The Rev. Jesse Jackson, the keynoter, pronounced black-Jewish relations to be "better than ever," but he also noted that "we still have unfinished business." The conference focused on the need for greater economic cooperation between the two communities in the 21st century. Jackson's largely positive assessment of black-Jewish relations was supported by the foundation's third annual report, which indicated increased interaction between the two communities at the grassroots level. Rabbi Schneier announced the formation of a black-Jewish task force to identify business and community leaders in the New York area who might assist in the development of mentoring programs, economic initiatives, and peer-support networks for the African American community.

The Jewish community also turned to Jackson for assistance in securing the release of 13 Iranian Jews held by their government on charges of spying for Israel, allegations denied by Israel. Jackson was joined by Ronald Lauder, chairman of the Conference of Presidents of Major American Jewish Organizations, and other Jewish leaders at a New York press conference in June, at which Jackson discussed efforts he had already made on behalf of the captives, as well as the possibility of flying to Tehran himself. The outreach to Jackson and his enthusiastic agreement to take on this mission underlined the improvement in relations between Jackson and the American Jewish community since the late 1970s. But as the year ended, Iran had not yet issued Jackson a visa, and the Iranian Jews were still in prison.

On March 2, a Florida jury convicted the Rev. Henry Lyons, president of the National Baptist Convention, on charges of racketeering and grand theft for his misuse of a $244,500 donation by the ADL in 1996 for the rebuilding of burned black churches. After the matter came to light, the missing money had been returned to the ADL and then redistributed to churches in need.

An "outrageous insult" was what Abraham Foxman, ADL national director, called CNN's use of Nation of Islam head Louis Farrakhan as one of a series of spokesmen against racism. Foxman termed Farrakhan "one of the nation's most notorious racists" and called on CNN to stop using this "outrageously inappropriate segment." Later in the year, as if to prove Foxman right, Farrakhan met with leaders of Neturei Karta, the militantly anti-Zionist ultra-Orthodox sect, joining with them in condemning the "Zionist-controlled media" and the "Zionist lobby."

Arabs and Muslims

Conflicts over particular Arab Americans holding or appointed to sensitive government positions underlined the problematic nature of Arab-Jewish relations in the United States. One conflict arose in April, when the Zionist Organization of America released two letters written in 1998 by Joseph Zogby, son of Arab American Institute president James Zogby, accusing Israel of acting like a "colonizer" and of "genocidal treatment" of the Palestinians. The letters had been written before the younger Zogby came to work as a special assistant to Martin Indyk, assistant secretary of state for Near Eastern affairs. While expressing support for Zogby, Indyk nevertheless asserted that the views expressed in the letters were "distasteful and distressing" and "not acceptable to me or this administration." In May, several weeks after this issue came to light, it was announced that Zogby was leaving the State Department to take a position in the civil rights division of the Justice Department.

Following the announcement of Zogby's decision, 11 Arab American and Muslim American groups launched a campaign to address what they termed an "imbalance" of American Jews working in the State Department, including some half-dozen American Jews in senior foreign-policy positions. Acknowledging that "it is not an issue we feel comfortable in raising," James Zogby nevertheless argued the need to redress an "imbalance that exists" and to respond to a situation "where it appears that Arab Americans are excluded from policy positions in the administration." ADL national director Abraham Foxman termed this effort to base government hiring decisions on ethnic background "crude anti-Semitism" because it was premised on a view of "all Jewish Americans in the State Department as not representative of America but of the Jewish community."

The Zogby controversy paled in comparison to the stir raised in June, when House minority leader Richard Gephardt (D., Mo.) appointed Salam Al-Marayati, head of the Los Angeles-based Muslim Public Affairs Council, to serve on the newly created National Commission on Terrorism. The 1998 legislation that created the ten-member commission, some of whose members would be chosen by the president and others by various leaders of Congress, charged it with making recommendations on national counterterrorism policy. Jewish groups immediately attacked Al-Marayati's nomination, asserting that the Muslim leader had made statements inconsistent with the mission of the commission. He had, they said, justified or condoned terrorism, as in his assertion on his organization's Web site that it was Israel's prime minister who bore "the brunt of responsibility for a Hamas suicide attack." Jewish groups pointed, as well, to Al-Marayati's statements equating the actions of Islamic fundamentalists with America's Revolutionary War, and his support for a renewed Arab economic boycott against Israel. Malcolm Hoenlein, executive vice chairman of the Conference of Presidents, warned that Al-Marayati's presence on the commission would raise questions as to whether "the commission will be able to function, whether people will be able to feel free to talk in his presence, after taking the kinds of positions he has taken." For his part, Al-Marayati rejected the criticism, maintaining that "Islam has no room for terrorism" and that his organization had "been on record as condemning terrorism."

In a move applauded by several Jewish groups, Gephardt withdrew the appointment of Al-Marayati in July, citing the long time it would have taken the nominee to obtain a security clearance. Arab and Muslim leaders responded angrily, describing Al-Marayati as a "moderate" and asserting that American Jewish leaders were engaged in a "witch hunt" to prevent Arabs and Muslims from holding policy-making positions. Khalil Jahshan, president of the National Association of Arab Americans, felt that the opposition to Al-Marayati's appointment had done "significant damage" to Jewish-Arab relations at a time when there was already "very little trust" between the two communities. But David A. Harris, executive director of the American Jewish Committee, rejected any suggestion that the Jewish community's reaction had been cast in "an anti-Muslim, anti-

Arab framework." While reaffirming the Jewish community's commitment to dialogue with Muslims and Arabs, Harris stressed that the battle against terrorism would not be sacrificed for its sake.

But not everyone in the Jewish community agreed. A number of Jewish leaders in Los Angeles, who had worked with Al-Marayati locally and had developed a relationship with him, condemned the steps taken by the national Jewish organizations to keep him off the commission. Leonard Beerman, rabbi emeritus of Leo Baeck Temple in Los Angeles, termed the opposition to Al-Marayati's appointment "an appalling display of ignorance, mindlessness and arrogance."

A further demonstration of the division in the Jewish community came in December, when some two-dozen Muslim and Jewish leaders from the Los Angeles area agreed on a code of ethics denouncing terrorism and hate crimes, promoting civil dialogue, and urging an end to stereotyping and incitement. At a well-covered press conference, the signatories hailed the agreement as the beginning of a new era in intergroup relations. For the most part, however, the national Jewish organizations kept their distance, and some, such as the American Jewish Committee, were openly critical. While noting that the local AJC chapter was engaged in dialogue with Muslim groups, Rabbi Gary Greenebaum, AJC regional director for Los Angeles, said of two of the Muslim leaders who signed the agreement (one was Al-Marayati), "They keep rationalizing terrorism and I have a problem with that, as should all Jews." AJC executive director David Harris criticized the Los Angeles initiative as one "largely borne by naïveté" that ignored the "long-term implications on the national scene."

A modicum of consensus emerged between the Arab American and American Jewish communities, however, with Rep. Gephardt's appointment of Juliette Kayyam to the commission seat that Al-Marayati would have occupied. Kayyam, an Arab American of Lebanese Christian descent, came to the commission from service in the Justice Department's civil rights division, in the course of which she had worked on policy issues relating to antiterrorism. The appointment was hailed by Jewish and Arab groups alike, all sides agreeing with James Zogby's assessment of Kayyam as "a very competent and sensitive civil rights attorney who brings that perspective to her work." Zogby, however, continued to assert that the Jewish community had "behaved very badly."

In September, the ADL reached a final settlement with Arab American and other ethnic groups in a class-action lawsuit that had dragged on for six years. The groups had accused the ADL of illegally obtaining information on them and their members. While continuing to deny any wrongdoing, saying that it had engaged only in lawful monitoring, the ADL agreed to purge certain sensitive information, such as criminal arrest records and social security numbers, from records maintained about the plaintiffs. The settlement also called for the ADL to pay $175,000 to the plaintiff groups to cover their legal fees, and to contribute $25,000 to a community-relations fund.

In June, the American Jewish Congress and a number of Arab American groups joined to denounce an article published in an online Christian magazine in which an aide to the Senate Republican Policy Committee called Islam "a giant Christian-killing machine" and made light of Muslim beliefs about the afterlife.

Imam W. Deen Muhammad, the son of the founder of the Nation of Islam — who long ago rejected his father's black-separatist beliefs — attended Friday night services at Temple Israel of Greater Miami in June. He told the congregation that he felt "very much at home in soul with you," and Rabbi Jeffrey Kahn expressed hope for a continuing and "very special relationship between Jews and Muslims in the community."

Catholics

Pope John Paul II's continuing efforts to reach out to the Jewish community were evident in the program organized for his brief visit to St. Louis at the end of January: Rabbi Robert Jacobs, the 90-year-old executive vice president of the St. Louis Rabbinical Association, read a passage from the Book of Isaiah at a prayer service held by the pontiff. The pope's commitment to Catholic-Jewish relations was further underlined when, on April 13, Holocaust Remembrance Day, a four-foot-tall menorah commemorating the Holocaust was placed, on a permanent basis, in the gardens of a seminary in Rome, located outside of St. Peter's and belonging to the Vatican. Senior Roman Catholic and American Jewish religious leaders attended the event, which Edward Cardinal Cassidy, president of the Pontifical Commission for Religious Dialogue with the Jews, hailed as a "milestone."

To be sure, this ceremony had another subtext. Cardinal Cassidy had stirred controversy with his remarks, delivered at a February conference in Baltimore, that the "aggressive" anti-Church attitudes of some Jewish organizations posed a threat to Jewish-Catholic relations. In his Holocaust Remembrance Day speech in Rome, the Cardinal acknowledged that his earlier remarks had been interpreted by some as angry, but asserted that this was not what he had meant. Rather, he was seeking only to express "concern about anything that takes us backwards, concern at the insensitivity that some organizations have."

Another noteworthy chapter in Jewish-Catholic relations took place in September. With Yom Kippur, the most solemn day in the Jewish calendar, approaching, John Cardinal O'Connor of New York wrote a letter to Jewish friends apologizing for centuries of Catholic anti-Semitism. "I ask this Yom Kippur," he wrote, "that you understand my own abject sorrow for any member of the Catholic Church, high or low, who may have harmed you or your forebears in any way." Nobel laureate and Holocaust survivor Elie Wiesel and other Jewish leaders were so moved by the letter that they published it as a full-page ad in the *New York Times* on Sunday, September 8.

Rapprochement between the Church and the Jewish community continued to be hampered by differences over the role of Pope Pius XII during the Holocaust, especially as the Vatican moved forward with its consideration of Pius XII for sainthood. Jewish groups pointed to recently released documents showing that the Vatican's representative in Washington had cautioned President Franklin Roosevelt against the creation of a homeland for the "Hebrew Race" in Palestine, and contrasted this advocacy in opposition to Jewish interests with the pope's failure to advocate action to stop the Nazi persecution of Jews. "If only he had spoken with such clarity when it came to rescuing European Jewry," said Rabbi Marvin Hier, dean of the Simon Wiesenthal Center.

The controversy escalated with the publication in September of *Hitler's Pope: The Secret History of Pius XII,* by John Cornwell, which claimed that Pius's inaction reflected anti-Semitic attitudes, and that the pope had even helped facilitate Hitler's rise to power. Cornwell, himself a practicing Catholic, asserted that he had begun the work intending to defend Pius's wartime actions but that as he delved into "secret material" in the Vatican archives, he came to the conclusion that the pope's record could not be defended. Catholic scholars and advocates denounced the book as bad scholarship. But Richard Heideman, president of B'nai B'rith International, asserted that the book "reinforces our position that the Vatican needs to open its Holocaust-era archives to independent historians and journalists so that controversy over Pius XII's wartime actions can be dealt with fully." In October, the Rev. Pierre Blet, a senior Vatican historian, held a news conference to reject, on behalf of the Holy See, Cornwell's charges. Pius XII "helped the Jews," said Blet, and his public silence "was the cover for a secret activity through Vatican embassies and bishoprics to try to stop the deportations," which helped to save hundreds of thousands of lives.

In October, the Vatican and Jewish leaders formally agreed that a team of Jewish and Catholic scholars would review published material from Vatican archives relating to the Church's role during World War II. While this did not open the wartime archives themselves to outside researchers as Jewish groups had long demanded, Seymour Reich, chairman of the International Jewish Committee on Interreligious Consultations (IJCIC), termed the agreement "a useful first step in resolving the matter of the Vatican's role during World War II."

As the year ended, in a move applauded by many in the Jewish community, Pope John Paul II recognized the "heroic virtues" of Pope John XXIII, a predecessor hailed by the Jewish community for his role in opening Catholic-Jewish dialogue and setting the stage for Vatican Council II's revolutionary statement on the Jews. This action by the current pope constituted a formal step toward the beatification of Pope John in the year 2000.

Even as the Jewish and Catholic communities concluded a year filled with both positive developments and continuing tensions, the two faith groups found common ground on a pressing political goal. In December, Jewish and Catholic leaders, under the framework of the National Jewish/Catholic Coalition, launched a campaign at the national, state, and local levels to abolish the death penalty.

Evangelical Christians

Several incidents during 1999 illustrated the strains in Jewish-evangelical relations. The first occurred in January, when the Rev. Jerry Falwell shocked Jews—and many others—when he stated that the Antichrist would be a Jewish male who was probably already alive. Jewish organizations immediately denounced his remarks as anti-Semitic, with the potential to set back whatever progress had been made in Jewish-evangelical dialogue. Further, the American Jewish Congress asserted in a statement, Falwell's remarks would "have an inevitably incendiary and degrading effect on Christian attitudes toward Jews." Falwell initially asserted that his statement was not intended to be anti-Semitic, but was grounded in the view that the Antichrist must be Jewish because Jesus himself was a Jew. Later, he apologized for having made the statement at all.

Another flash point occurred in September, when the Southern Baptist International Mission Board distributed a prayer guide calling on Baptists to pray for Jews to convert to Christianity during the upcoming High Holy Days. Rabbi A. James Rudin, director of interreligious affairs for the American Jewish Committee, criticized the timing of this prayer as "particularly offensive" and added, "it's not going to work." Don Kammerdiener, executive vice president of the Mission Board, defended the prayer guide as following the Bible's direction to share "the gospel with the Jews." This response was intensely unsatisfactory to the Jewish community, even to those Jews who were most committed to dialogue with evangelicals. In December, Rabbi Yechiel Eckstein, president of the International Fellowship of Christians and Jews, called for a break in relations with the Mission Board's parent organization, the Southern Baptist Convention. Although his organization had been founded for the express purpose of building bridges between American Jews and evangelical Christians, Eckstein asserted that the prayer guide had "crossed the line."

This tension notwithstanding, evangelical Christians could not simply be dismissed as hostile to Jewish interests. In fact, on the Jewish community's primary concerns, the evangelicals continued to present a mirror image of the positions taken by the mainline Protestant churches. Thus while evangelical Christians generally disagreed with much of the Jewish community on such domestic concerns as church-state separation and social policy, they firmly supported Israel. By one estimate, evangelical Christians donated approximately $10 million to American Jewish philanthropies during 1999 to support Jewish immigration to Israel. The International Fellowship of Christians and Jews, which collected more than $20 million over five years to help resettle Jews in Israel, estimated that 95 percent of its 130,000 donors were Christians.

This strong evangelical support for Israel was evident when Representative Steve Largent (R., Okla.) invited Palestinian Authority chairman Yasir Arafat to the annual national prayer breakfast at the White House on February 4. "It is an ill-informed, bad decision to invite a known terrorist, a murderer of Jews and

Christians, and Americans, to participate in a public exercise of faith here in the nation's capital," said Jeffrey Taylor, director of government relations for the Christian Coalition. Largent, whose record was pro-Israel and whose constituency was heavily evangelical, sought to distance himself from the invitation, saying that he had not been aware of every name on the list. In his remarks at the breakfast, Largent ignored Arafat's presence. Ironically and in striking contrast, President Clinton and Senator Joseph Lieberman (D., Conn.)—also regarded as strong friends of the Jewish state—specifically welcomed the Palestinian leader.

The imminent turn of the millennium highlighted the ambivalent relationship between evangelicals and Jews. Richard Landes, director of Boston University's Center for Millennial Studies, observed that never before in history had so many Christians and Jews worked together—and yet many Jews were uneasy about the future. "During apocalyptic times, Christians have a tendency to be philo-Semitic," Landes commented. "They believe that if they love Jews, they will convert." But if the millennium should come and go without the conversion of the Jews and without the arrival of the apocalypse, he wondered, would there be a new wave of anti-Semitism?

CHURCH-STATE MATTERS

The Courts

The ongoing question of whether it is constitutional to use government-funded vouchers to support student attendance at religious schools remained unresolved in 1999. In April, the Maine Supreme Court upheld a lower court's ruling that parents had no right to compel the state to provide them with vouchers to send their children to a parochial school when the state did provide vouchers, under certain circumstances, for children who attended secular schools. The Orthodox Union asserted that this ruling discriminated "against parents who wish to send their children to religious schools." In October, the U.S. Supreme Court declined to accept the Maine case for review, leaving the decision in place. In December, the Supreme Court declined to take an appeal from a similar decision of the Vermont Supreme Court.

Ohio's high court also weighed in on this issue when, at the end of May, it struck down a Cleveland voucher program on a technicality. The ruling explicitly stated, however, that Cleveland's program providing taxpayer-funded scholarships for low-income students, usable toward private- and parochial-school tuition, did not violate the constitutional principle of separation of church and state. This left the door open for the city of Cleveland—or the state legislature—to try again. David Zwiebel, general counsel and director of government affairs of Agudath Israel of America, hailed the clarification that "this is not unconstitutional." And he suggested that as more courts followed suit (Wisconsin's high court had upheld Milwaukee's voucher programs the year before), "we'll be able to hone in on the public policy issues, which is really the debate that should be taking place." However Marc Stern, codirector of the American Jewish Congress's legal department, termed the Ohio ruling a "disappointment."

Within weeks of the Ohio ruling, the state's legislature reenacted the identical program, but drafted so as to avoid the technical problem that the state high court had found. But the constitutionality of the Cleveland program was placed in question once again in August, when a federal judge issued a preliminary ruling indicating that he was likely to rule that the arrangement violated church-state separation—and therefore no new students would be permitted to enroll in the program, pending his final decision. In November, the U.S. Supreme Court voted 5-4 to stay the lower court's order, thus allowing the program to accept new students. As the year ended, however, the lower court issued a final ruling that the program violated the Constitution, in part because it failed to ensure that state funding went only to secular educational functions. Nevertheless, pursuant to an agreement of the parties, the program would continue operating pending further appellate review.

Opponents of vouchers had at least one other victory as well. Another federal appellate court, declining to follow the path staked out by the Wisconsin and Ohio state high courts, struck down as unconstitutional a Maine program that reimbursed students who attended private or parochial schools because their towns did not have public schools. In line with its actions in respect to other state court rulings, the U.S. Supreme Court declined to review this case.

The ongoing story of Kiryas Joel finally appeared to reach the end of the road in May 1999. New York State's Court of Appeals, the state's highest court, voted 4-3 to strike down as unconstitutional—for the third time—an effort by the state legislature to create a special school district encompassing this suburban village comprised entirely of Satmar Hassidim. The state had sought to enable students residing in Kiryas Joel to receive publicly financed remedial instruction without having to go to schools outside the village. This plan, the court's majority pronounced, had "the primary effect of advancing one religion over others and constitutes an impermissible religious accommodation." The dissenters on the court argued that the state legislature had, at long last, cured the constitutional flaws that had caused the first two plans to be struck down. Marc Stern of the American Jewish Congress—one of the organizations that had challenged the plan—suggested that a 1997 Supreme Court decision allowing public-school teachers to enter religious schools to give certain secular remedial classes provided the means to meet the students' needs without creating a separate school district for the Hassidic community. In June, the U.S. Supreme Court granted a temporary stay of the latest Kiryas Joel decision, which allowed the school district to continue to function while the high court determined whether to hear an appeal. But in October, the high court declined to accept the case for review.

While the Supreme Court declined to address the question of vouchers, it did hear one case that had potential ramifications for the public funding of religious education. In December, the high court heard arguments in a lawsuit challenging the arrangement under which a Catholic school in Louisiana was allowed to receive federally funded computers, software, and library books for use in the secular-studies portion of the school day. The Clinton administration defended the practice, asserting that there were sufficient safeguards to insure that these materials were not used for religious instruction.

Jewish reaction reflected the usual communal divisions. Many of the Jewish organizations argued that the program was unconstitutional because, among other things, it relied on the teachers in religious schools to be "guardians of the separation between church and government." But Orthodox groups argued that the practice was consistent with earlier court precedents. What both sides could agree on was that the applicable law was, at best, muddled. The year ended without a decision by the court. While the case had the potential to open—or close—the door to vouchers, it was just as likely that the court would rule narrowly, dealing only with the issue at hand.

On another church-state matter, the high court agreed in November to consider an appeal from the decision of a federal appellate court that prohibited a Texas public high school from allowing student-led prayers at football games. Observers believed that a decision in this case would probably have implications for the constitutionality of prayers at graduation ceremonies.

The usual alliance between "separationist" Jewish groups and the American Civil Liberties Union came undone in August when the ACLU filed a lawsuit to bar a suburban Cincinnati school district from closing on Yom Kippur. The ACLU, bringing the suit on behalf of Muslim and Hindu parents, asserted that the decision to close was "expressly favoring" Judaism. School officials, however, said that closing on that day was "a simple matter of numbers," based on the expected large number of absences. Joel Ratner, regional director of the ADL, defended the school district's decision, saying that the policy "cannot properly be interpreted as promoting or endorsing religion."

Legislative Activity

In September, Representative Ernest Istook (R., Okla.) once again introduced the so-called "Religious Freedom" Amendment that, on a House vote in 1998, fell well short of the two-thirds majority required for passage. Istook's proposal, among other things, would have opened the way for prayer in classrooms and at graduations, and allowed religious symbols on government property. Most observers agreed that the initiative had virtually no chance of passage by a Congress which, after the 1998 elections, was operating with an even narrower Republican majority than the year before. Nevertheless, Jewish organizations— joined by a wide array of other religious and civil-liberties groups—lost no time in denouncing the amendment as, in the words of Rabbi David Saperstein of the

Religious Action Center of Reform Judaism, "unnecessary, divisive and dangerous." Istook's amendment went nowhere during 1999.

There were a number of congressional initiatives during the year to allow the use of tax dollars to support parochial and other private schools, often through the use of vouchers. The issue generally arose within the context of congressional debate over the nation's education policy, which itself attracted increased public attention both because of the upcoming presidential election and because of the coincidental fact that the omnibus 1965 Elementary and Secondary Education Act (ESEA) was coming up for reauthorization.

Thus on several occasions during House deliberations on Title I of the ESEA, congressional leaders attempted to include "portability" or voucher programs into the bill, which would have allowed states the discretion to move public funding out of general programs for low-income and disadvantaged students and into private or religious education for certain of them. Opponents of vouchers succeeded in defeating these attempts. As a compromise, however, an amendment was adopted to permit those children served by Title I who were victims of violent crime at school or attended schools deemed unsafe by local school authorities, to transfer to alternative public schools.

The House also considered the Academic Achievement for All Act, a bill allowing states to convert education programs into broad block grants. Under the original bill, a state could have used federal funds for any educational purpose permitted by state law, possibly including the expenses of attending private or religious schools. After pressure from House Republican moderates who worried that this would undermine services to Title I students, the House leadership agreed to scale back the plan to a ten-state pilot program. This passed, generally along party lines, 213-208.

While the Senate did not reach either of these education proposals during 1999, it did adopt an amendment to the Bankruptcy Reform Act in November, offered by Senator Orrin Hatch (R., Utah), allowing local education authorities to use federal education funds to send student victims of violent crimes to public, private or religious schools. But the bill itself did not achieve final passage before the end of the year.

All of these voucher initiatives were opposed by much of the organized Jewish community as both inconsistent with church-state separation and as bad public policy. But Orthodox Jewish organizations such as the Orthodox Union and Agudath Israel strongly supported them. By year's end, none of these bills had become law. Nor, given President Clinton's ongoing threat to veto all such legislation, were they likely to be.

If they made little progress at the federal level, advocates of vouchers celebrated a victory when the state legislature of Florida passed a bill in late April providing for the nation's first statewide, government-funded voucher program. Governor Jeb Bush, who had made tuition tax credits a key element of his election campaign the year before, gladly signed the bill into law. The program provided vouchers for at least $4,000 a year for students in Florida's worst public schools to attend private and religious schools, regardless of income or grades. Enactment of the law split the Jewish community once again along Orthodox/non-Orthodox lines. Speaking for the great bulk of the organized Jewish community both in Florida and around the country, Sam Dubbin, chairman of the Jewish community relations council in Miami, asserted that "public funding going to private schools would . . . truly undermine the public school system" and was "an inappropriate encroachment on the separation between church and state." But the Orthodox Union hailed the governor and the legislature for "setting an example of leadership and commitment."

The Jewish community divided along these same lines in dealing with efforts to extend to other government-funded social services the "charitable choice" provisions of the 1996 welfare reform law, which had created a framework for allowing federal funds to go to religious social-service providers. "Separationist" groups opposed the extension of "charitable choice," arguing, among other things, that in the absence of explicit safeguards, religious providers might receive federal funds for programs that discriminate on the basis of religion in hiring, or might require beneficiaries to adhere to the practices of a certain faith as a condition of receiving the service. Supporters of "charitable choice" within the Jewish community—generally the Orthodox and politically conservative organizations—argued that it was simply a nondiscriminatory and beneficial way for religious institutions to be involved in the provision of social services.

"Charitable choice" amendments were proposed for a number of social service initiatives that Congress considered during the year, including the Juvenile Justice bill, which passed both chambers but remained stalled in conference at year's end; the Substance Abuse Mental Health Reauthorization Act, which passed the Senate in early November by unanimous consent; and the Fathers Count Act, which passed the House, 328-93, in November. Rep. Chet Edwards (D., Tex.) sought to amend Fathers Count on the floor so as to remedy the flaws he and others saw in "charitable choice." Though he had the support of a number of Jewish groups—and of Rep. Benjamin Cardin (D., Md.), chief Democratic sponsor of Fathers Count—the amendment went down to defeat. In May, Senator John Ashcroft (R., Mo.) reintroduced the Charitable Choice Expansion Act, which would extend "charitable choice" to all federally funded social-service programs.

"Charitable choice" became an issue in the early stages of the 2000 presidential campaign. Vice President Al Gore endorsed the "charitable choice" concept—already a mainstay of Texas governor George W. Bush's political agenda—during an Atlanta campaign speech in May 1999, stirring criticism from Jewish groups opposed to these programs and applause from those supporting it. While stressing his continued commitment to the separation of church and state, the vice president termed "charitable choice" a "carefully tailored approach to . . . vital services where faith-based organizations can play a role." Mark Pelavin, associate director of the Religious Action Center of Reform Judaism, worried that the vice president's approach would constitute "an alarming alteration to the careful balance between church and state," while the Orthodox Union, in a letter to the vice president, claimed: "There exists an even greater potential for building a better society if faith based institutions are invited into this enterprise [of providing federally funded social services]." The National Jewish Democratic Council, which was on record in opposition to "charitable choice," drew attention to Gore's assurance that any program he would support would have to respect church-state separation, and asserted that this claim should "be taken at face value."

In May, the American Jewish Committee announced that it had received a grant from the Pew Charitable Trusts to pursue—in partnership with the Feinstein Center for American Jewish History at Philadelphia's Temple University—a two-year study of whether proponents of the rival points of view on separation of church and state could build a consensus on the role of religious institutions in the provision of social services.

Church-state issues also came up in connection with the Juvenile Justice bill, even though the shocking series of shootings in public schools and other places— most notably the killings at Columbine High School—focused much of the debate on that bill on the issue of gun control. The Senate-passed bill included an amendment permitting prayer services and the construction of religious memorials on public-school premises for any victim of gun violence on school property. The House-passed bill included amendments allowing the display of the Ten Commandments in public schools, and providing tax dollars to faith-based providers of social services to juveniles, without safeguards to prevent proselytization or religious coercion of beneficiaries. The House bill also denied attorneys' fees to people who might successfully sue a public school for violating church-state separation. The Ten Commandments provision drew particular public attention and stirred considerable debate. Jewish lawmakers and many Jewish organizations challenged both the constitutionality of the measure and its effectiveness in dealing with school violence. "Whose Ten Commandments" will hang on the school walls, asked Rep. Jerrold Nadler (D., N.Y.), "The Catholic version? The Protestant version? Or the Jewish version?" While not addressing the church-state issue, a spokesman for the Orthodox Union stated that "from a sincere religious perspective that takes the Ten Commandments . . . seriously, it's hard to see how posting [them] on a wall has much value." At year's end, the Juvenile Justice bill had not emerged from a House-Senate conference.

"Free-Exercise" Developments

The Jewish community and the U.S. Congress continued to wrestle with the fallout from a pair of Supreme Court decisions, the first, in 1990, that weakened constitutional protections of the free exercise of religion, and the second, in 1997, that struck down a 1993 federal law intended to restore those protections. That law, the Religious Freedom Restoration Act (RFRA), stated that government at all levels—federal, state, and local—had to demonstrate a compelling interest if it enacted a law or regulation that substantially burdened an individual's free exercise of religion. In its 1997 decision, however, the high court ruled that this law infringed on states' prerogatives, thus leaving in place the previous understanding that only a "reasonable" basis was needed for a state to enact legislation requiring individuals to violate their religious beliefs.

Immediately following the Supreme Court's decision, the politically and religiously diverse coalition that had come together in the early 1990s to secure passage of RFRA reconvened to draft and promote new legislation that might survive the high court's scrutiny. The drafting process, which stretched out over several months, resulted in the 1998 Religious Liberty Protection Act (RLPA), a bill drawn more narrowly than RFRA.

Early in 1999, RLPA was reintroduced in the House, and it passed 306-118 in July. But the debate in the House gave evidence of a fissure in the bipartisan support that had earlier mobilized behind RFRA. Most Republicans supported RLPA without exceptions, but most Democrats favoring a failed substitute, introduced by Representative Jerrold Nadler (D., N.Y.), that would have largely excluded state and local civil-rights laws from RLPA's purview. Representative Nadler, an original sponsor of RLPA, proposed this substitute because of claims by civil-rights and gay-rights groups that RLPA might undermine anti-discrimination laws by creating exceptions on religious grounds. All of the Jewish members of the House voted for Nadler's amendment. The vote on final passage, however, found Republicans and Democrats on both sides. Jewish members split on this last vote, with a majority voting "no" because the civil-rights concerns had not been resolved.

The House's division on the Nadler amendment signaled an uphill battle for RLPA in the Senate. Senate Judiciary Committee chairman Orrin Hatch (R, Utah), a one-time sponsor of RFRA, was expected to introduce a Senate version of the bill. But this prospect stalled when some members of the RLPA coalition withdrew their support in the face of opposition from the civil-rights and gay-rights communities, and after Senate Democrats began to voice their own concerns about the initiative. A promise by the Senate Republican leadership to bring the House bill directly to the Senate floor for a vote did not materialize before year's end.

Jewish organizations, which until the summer of 1999 had been united in support of RLPA, now came down on different sides of the issue. The National Council of Jewish Women, the ADL, and the Religious Action Center of Reform Judaism announced that they would no longer work for its enactment as passed by the House, with no civil-rights exception. The American Jewish Congress, B'nai B'rith, Agudath Israel, and the Orthodox Union, however, continued to support the bill. The American Jewish Committee took yet another course, continuing to advocate for RLPA, but insisting upon the inclusion of an amendment that would clarify and limit the extent to which it might be asserted as a defense against a civil-rights claim.

Efforts continued through the year to enact religious freedom restoration laws on the state level, similar to the defunct federal statute. During the year, Arizona and South Carolina joined the handful of states with such laws. Texas passed its own legislation in June, but with limited applicability to civil rights, prisoner, and zoning cases.

Even though the absence of a federal religious-liberty law made it more difficult successfully to assert a free-exercise defense against a government action or court suit, a judicial opinion rendered in June demonstrated that, in certain cases, such a defense remained available. A New Jersey federal court ruled that the issuing of statements based on interpretation of religious doctrine was not subject to a suit for damages in civil court. The court's reasoning was that "inquiry into the methodology of how religious organizations arrive at their conclusions concerning questions of religious doctrine are, like the conclusions themselves, beyond the ken of civil courts." Thus the court dismissed a lawsuit for defamation that a married couple had brought against a rabbinical council in Monsey, New York, which had criticized the husband for his long refusal to provide a Jewish divorce to his first wife, and for refusing to show the council the rabbinic documents he claimed to have obtained in Israel that enabled him to remarry. Rabbi Alfred Cohen, a member of the Monsey rabbinical council, praised the ruling, asserting that it "will give us a certain freedom that we desperately need" not only to speak out on family matters but also to comment publicly about facilities that fell short in adhering to the standards of Jewish dietary law. The American Jewish Congress defended the rabbinical council in the case.

The Workplace Religious Freedom Act, a bill with wide support in the Jewish community that was intended to insure religiously observant employees reasonable accommodation of their religious practices, made little progress during 1999, largely because of concerns raised by businesses and labor unions. The bill was reintroduced in September, following the decision of Senator Sam Brownback (R., Kan.) to sign on as chief Republican sponsor in the Senate, replacing retired Senator Dan Coats (R., Ind.). The chief Democratic sponsor remained Senator John Kerry (D., Mass.), and additional cosponsors included Senators Joseph Lieberman (D., Conn.), Barbara Mikulski (D., Md.), Daniel Patrick Moynihan (D., N.Y.), and Tim Hutchinson (R., Ark.). American Jewish Committee legislative director and counsel Richard Foltin, chair of the coalition dedicated to passage of the legislation, stated, "We all hope it will speed up. But above all, we have to be persistent in moving it forward and educating members of Congress about the need for this initiative." Supporters of WRFA sought additional Senate sponsors and reintroduction of the bill in the House.

Advocates of religious accommodation in the workplace enjoyed a pair of rare judicial victories. In June, a federal appellate court ruled that the mere existence of a seniority system did not exempt the sheriff's office of Carson City, Nevada, from trying to accommodate a Seventh-day Adventist's religious obligation not to work on Saturday. A number of Jewish groups joined with other organizations in a friend-of-the-court brief urging this result. And in October, the U.S. Supreme Court left in place another federal appellate ruling that obligated Newark, New Jersey, to allow two Muslim police officers to continue to wear the beards they said were required by their faith.

Jewish groups, joined by leaders of other religious communities and the American Civil Liberties Union, reacted with outrage in August when Mississippi school officials directed a Jewish high-school student not to wear a Star-of-David pin while in class because it could be construed as a gang symbol. With the threat of a lawsuit by the student and the ACLU looming, the school board changed course, voting that same month to allow 15-year-old Ryan Green to wear the pin. School board president Randy Williams acknowledged that the school's action had "infringed on freedom of religious expression."

In December, the Tanenbaum Center for Interreligious Understanding issued a study indicating that American Jews were less likely to perceive themselves as victims of religious discrimination in the workplace than members of other faiths — Buddhists, Christians, Hindus, Muslims, and practitioners of Shintoism. The Tanenbaum Center suggested a reason: Jewish respondents "have been here longer than a great percentage of the sample, and they tend to be assimilated into the larger culture." But it was not clear to what extent observant Jews, who would be most likely to require accommodation of their religious practices, were included in the survey.

Steps were taken during the year to implement the International Religious Freedom Act, legislation that was enacted in 1998 thanks to an unusual left-right coalition that brought together such groups as the Episcopal Church, the Religious Action Center of Reform Judaism, the National Association of Evangelicals, and the National Jewish Coalition. The administration and congressional leaders named the nine commissioners of the new U.S. Commission on Religious Freedom, established by the act. Among them were two Jews, Rabbi David Saperstein — director of the Religious Action Center of Reform Judaism — who became the commission's first chair, and Elliot Abrams, president of the Ethics and Public Policy Center. Later in the year, Robert Seiple, former head of the World Vision relief agency, was sworn in as ambassador-at-large for religious freedom — another position created by the law — and Steven McFarland, formerly with the Christian Legal Society, became executive director of the commission.

The first U.S. State Department report on religious persecution, mandated by the International Religious Freedom Act, was issued in September. Afghanistan, Burma, Iraq, Iran, and Serbia were singled out for the harshest criticism. Israel was cited for failing to provide Arab residents with the same level of services as the Jewish population.

HOLOCAUST-RELATED MATTERS

Reparations

The year began with word that the German government had begun paying monthly pensions to Holocaust survivors residing in Eastern Europe, pursuant to an agreement with the Conference on Material Claims Against Germany that had been reached in January, 1998. Germany had initially refused to make such direct payments on the ground that its obligation to these individuals was covered by funds it paid to those countries. However, pressure from the American Jewish Committee and other Jewish organizations, coupled with revelations that Germany was paying pensions to former SS officers—including war criminals—ultimately led to the commencement of negotiations. Karl Brozik, director of the Frankfurt office of the Conference on Material Claims, estimated that some 30,000 survivors would be applying for the $150 monthly payments.

Other reparation matters also received attention. Early in the year, AJC executive director David A. Harris praised Germany's efforts to speed up compensation for Nazi-era slave laborers, but suggested that the process of resolving claims might continue past the end of the year. This proved to be an understatement. 1999 was marked by intense and often bitter negotiations over compensation for some 250,000 surviving concentration camp survivors—135,000 of them Jewish—and between 475,000 and 1.2 million non-Jewish forced laborers. Finally, in October, lawyers for the German government and German companies offered $3.3 billion in response to the survivors' demand for $28 billion. The survivors' representatives rejected the German figure as "shameful" and "a pittance," inasmuch as it worked out to a few hundred dollars per victim. Stuart Eizenstat, U.S. deputy secretary of the treasury, acting as a mediator in the negotiations, called on both sides to demonstrate "greater flexibility." An agreement was announced in Berlin on December 17. German industry and the German government agreed to provide 10 billion DM ($5.2 billion) in return for a settlement of all Holocaust-related claims and a "legal peace" that would preclude any future lawsuits. But despite the widely publicized announcement of the agreement, there were still many details to be worked out: defining the categories of recipients and determining the individual payments; setting up a process for claims and payment; resolving what portion of the overall package would be applied to claims against German banks for their role in the "aryanization" of Jewish property; and determining what was to be set aside for a "future fund" to support education and research.

The Conference on Material Claims played the lead role in representing Holocaust victims in the ongoing negotiations. In addition, the Berlin office of the American Jewish Committee was instrumental in researching and publishing a list of more than 250 German companies that had used forced labor. That list, released by AJC in November, played a critical role in marshaling German public opinion in support of an agreement, and drawing more private companies into the initiative.

In a related development in August, California governor Gray Davis signed into law a bill allowing former slave laborers or their heirs to sue companies doing business in California that had exploited their labor during the war—an enactment that was likely to become moot once the global settlement was reached. Also in August, additional evidence emerged that Ford Motor Company's German operation had relied on slave labor. A Nazi-era document found at the Auschwitz

Museum indicated that the Ford plant in Cologne had used slave laborers made available to them at the industrial and commercial complex adjacent to the death camp. Present-day Ford officials maintained that the American company did not control the activities of the German branch during the Nazi era.

There was little progress in settling the many unpaid insurance claims of Holocaust victims and their heirs. The International Commission on Holocaust-Era Insurance Claims, created in 1998 and chaired by former secretary of state Lawrence Eagleburger, faced slow going in its efforts to establish a process for identifying Holocaust-era policies and claimants, and to arrange for valuation of and payment on those policies. Commission members included representatives of Jewish organizations, the Israeli government, U.S. and Israeli insurance commissioners, and five European insurance companies that had insured Holocaust victims. One of the insurance companies, Assicurazioni Generali of Italy, committed itself in January to achieving a resolution, and was reported to have independently begun making payments on outstanding policies from a $12-million fund it had established, using the valuation procedures urged by the Jewish groups. But other insurers—particularly those without subsidiaries in the U.S.—proved reluctant to join, delaying any agreement on a claims-identification process. At year's end, Eagleburger insisted that there would be no further delays, but uncertainty remained as to how the insurance companies would act on claims that were identified. Throughout the year, several state insurance commissioners (including those from California, Florida, and New York) sought to use their regulatory authority as leverage to press insurance companies doing business in their states to settle.

In 1998, Swiss banks, as part of a settlement of Holocaust-era claims, set up a $1.25-billion fund to provide restitution to those who had lost assets during the Holocaust. In June 1999, following the appearance of newspaper ads about the fund, survivors began to make inquiries. In the meantime, however, payments were not expected to begin until the year 2001, since the formal settlement proceedings were still going on. Indeed, protests were heard at those proceedings when lawyers for the roughly half-million survivors they were representing in a federal class action asked New York federal judge Edward Korman for $22.5 million in attorneys' fees, representing 1.8 percent of the settlement. "First, it was the Germans, then it was the Swiss, and then it's the lawyers stealing everything," said Roman Katz, Auschwitz survivor and chair of the American Gathering of Holocaust Survivors. A spokesman for the lawyers retorted that "it's important for lawyers to get remuneration in human-rights cases" if those cases are to be pursued. While a hearing on attorneys' fees was put over to the new year, at a fairness hearing on November 30, Judge Korman heard representatives of the survivors argue that the overwhelming majority of class-action members thought the settlement was appropriate. These issues, and others relating to the distribution of the settlement fund, were still pending at year's end.

In a related development, a panel headed by former U.S. Federal Reserve chairman Paul Volcker reported that a massive research effort had identified nearly 54,000 accounts that may have belonged to victims, but that there were some two million other accounts opened between 1933 and 1945 that lacked sufficient documentation to identify ownership.

In another Swiss banking matter, a humanitarian fund of nearly $200 million created by the banks and others in 1997—an initiative separate from the $1.25 billion intended to settle claims by account holders and their heirs—made first payments to about 60,000 needy Holocaust survivors residing in the United States. Each payment came to about $500. Survivors living in other countries had earlier received money from this fund.

Early in the year, Representatives Jerrold Nadler (D., N.Y.) and David McIntosh (R., Ind.) introduced legislation to exempt settlements paid to Holocaust survivors or their heirs from federal income taxes, following similar legislation introduced in a number of states. This relief was included in the Taxpayer Refund and Relief Act of 1999, passed by both houses of Congress but vetoed by the president in September for reasons unrelated to the Holocaust provisions. Another piece of legislation introduced in Congress at midyear extended through the end of 2000 the life of the Presidential Advisory Commission on Holocaust Assets, chaired by World Jewish Congress president Edgar Bronfman, that was searching for looted assets that had found their way to the U.S. After easy passage in both houses, the bill was signed into law in December.

In November, representatives of that commission met with Library of Congress officials to find out whether there were books that had come to the library after World War II that had been taken from Holocaust victims. The following month, responding to an inquiry from the Jewish Telegraphic Agency, the Library of Congress acknowledged that of some 500,000 "heirless" books received from the Jewish Cultural Foundation, Inc., after the war, 5,708 appeared to have been Holocaust-related loot.

OSI Actions

The Justice Department's Office of Special Investigations continued to seek the deportation of the ever-more-elderly World War II-era war criminals who had found refuge in the U.S. after the war by hiding their involvement in atrocities. In May, 81-year-old Kazys Ciurinskas left Chicago for Lithuania after an immigration judge ordered his departure. After the OSI brought proceedings against him based on his membership in a Nazi-sponsored unit that murdered thousands of Jews and others, Ciurinskas admitted his involvement to the court. But upon his return to Lithuania, Ciurinskas told Lithuanian authorities that though he had been a collaborator, he had not killed any Jews. The Lithuanian Prosecutor General's Office then asserted that it had insufficient information to proceed with criminal prosecution.

In June, 78-year-old Lithuanian-born Vincas Valkavickas left the U.S. for his native country rather than face deportation proceedings arising out of his failure, in his 1950 visa application, to disclose that he had been a member of a Nazi-sponsored battalion during the war. Also in June, the Simon Wiesenthal Center called upon Lithuania to try these deportees along with several others who had recently lost their U.S. citizenship and had been returned to the Baltic nation because of alleged participation in atrocities. The center described Lithuania as Europe's leading haven for Nazi-era war criminals. In September, criticism of Lithuania intensified when a Vilnius court adjourned indefinitely, on grounds of poor health, the war-crimes trial of 92-year-old American deportee Aleksandras Lileikis. Vilnius head of the Nazi-sponsored Lithuanian security police during World War II, Lileikis was accused of having given written orders to kill dozens of Jews in a local labor prison, and of having cooperated with Nazi death squads in the murder of Jews. OSI director Eli Rosenbaum called for the appointment of an independent panel of international experts to assess whether Lileikis was in fact unable to stand trial.

As the summer drew to a close, the OSI began deportation proceedings against 84-year-old Michael Gruber, based on charges that he had served as an SS guard at the Sachsenhausen concentration camp from September 1942 through December 1944.

John Demjanjuk

In May, the OSI filed a complaint in U.S. district court in Cleveland, renewing its efforts to strip Ukrainian-born John Demjanjuk of his U.S. citizenship. This time, the move was based on evidence that the 79-year-old retired auto worker had been a guard at several concentration camps and had served with a Nazi-run SS unit that participated in the mass murder of European Jews. An earlier decades-long effort to deport him, premised on allegations that he was the Nazi war criminal known as Ivan the Terrible, seemed to come to an end in February 1998, when U.S. federal judge Paul Matia restored the American citizenship that had been stripped from Demjanjuk in 1981. Demjanjuk had been extradited to Israel in 1986, where he was convicted of crimes against humanity and sentenced to death two years later, but his conviction had been overturned on appeal when the Israeli Supreme Court ruled, in 1993, that there was no proof beyond a reasonable doubt that Demjanjuk was Ivan the Terrible. The Israeli court at that time decided not to allow further proceedings on the basis of other charges against Demjanjuk. The 1998 U.S. court ruling restoring Demjanjuk's citizenship followed a 1993 decision of the U.S. Court of Appeals for the Sixth Circuit that the Justice Department had knowingly withheld information in 1981 that Demjanjuk could have used to fight extradition. But in restoring his citizenship, the district court left the door open for the Justice Department to file new naturalization and deportation proceedings, an invitation now taken up in 1999. American Jewish groups hailed the OSI's action.

Other Holocaust-Related Matters

At the beginning of the year, President Clinton took steps to implement legislation enacted in 1998 requiring that classified U.S. records relating to Nazi war criminals be made available to the public. He announced the formation of a cabinet-level working group, including Defense Secretary William Cohen and Attorney General Janet Reno, that would review and release classified records, but it was only at the end of the year that the first documents were released.

RICHARD T. FOLTIN

The United States, Israel, and the Middle East

F̲OR ISRAEL AND MUCH OF the Middle East, 1999 was a year of transition, uncertainty, and anticipation. The inevitability of change was underscored by the deaths of King Hussein of Jordan in February and King Hassan II of Morocco in July. From geographically distant parts of the Arab world, these two experienced and pragmatic leaders—both tracing their dynastic lineage to Islam's founder Mohammed—had fought against extremist Islamic tendencies at home and struggled to lead their people into the modern world. They had generally supported good relations with the United States, although sometimes clashing with Washington over specific policies, such as the means to counter Saddam Hussein's invasion of Kuwait, and both had worked vigorously over the years, at first in secret and then in public, to help bring an end to the Arab-Israel conflict and promote Muslim-Jewish reconciliation and regional cooperation. In both countries there was an initially smooth transition to their young, Western-educated sons, although it was too early to tell how well they were prepared to cope with the political and economic problems facing their countries. Both Abdullah II of Jordan, 38, and Mohammed VI of Morocco, 36, pledged to continue their fathers' support of the Arab-Israel peace process and welcomed Israeli leaders to their countries.

Concern in both Washington and Jerusalem for future political stability in the region and continuation of the Arab-Israel peace process was heightened by persistent reports that two other key figures, Palestinian Authority chairman Yasir Arafat, 70, and Syrian president Hafez al-Assad, 68, were not only aging, but were also in increasingly frail health. Arafat, who appeared unsteady on his feet and displayed the tremors of what was believed to be Parkinson's disease, had not designated a successor. There was much speculation as to what would happen should the forceful and wily leader of the Palestine Liberation Organization (PLO) no longer be in charge. While increasingly criticized by the younger generation of Palestinians for his autocratic rule and the corruption among his bureaucratic cadres, Arafat was venerated as the indispensable leader who had managed to dominate the fragmented and diverse elements within the Palestinian national movement. He had maneuvered to transform the PLO from a revolutionary group of refugees dedicated to elimination of Israel through armed struggle to the administrators of a nascent Palestinian state formally committed to negotiating peaceful coexistence with Israel. But this process was by no means complete and Arafat still faced determined opposition both from Islamic fundamentalist and secular rejectionist elements within the Palestinian movement, some of whom were actively supported by Syria and Iran. Both Washington and Jerusalem were pressing Arafat to fulfill his commitments under the Oslo agreements to crush the terrorist elements. In the past Arafat had vacillated between efforts to co-opt Hamas and other dissident elements, and arresting their armed gangs.

A Sense of Urgency

A realization of his own mortality and fear that the Palestinian movement would splinter after his death added a sense of urgency to Arafat's repeated vow to proclaim an independent Palestinian state, with Jerusalem as its capital, on May 5, 1999. This date was to have marked the end of the five-year interim period and the completion of the final-status negotiations, as specified in the Oslo agreements. But since the permanent-status talks had not yet even begun, and further implementation of the Wye River agreements of the previous October had been stalled following Prime Minister Benjamin Netanyahu's call for new Israeli elections, the Clinton administration sought to dissuade Arafat from declaring independence and intensified its efforts to invigorate the Palestinian-Israeli talks.

On the Syrian front, questions were increasingly raised by knowledgeable Middle East observers both in the United States and Israel over the stability of the regime in Damascus, which had been under the iron rule of Hafez al-Assad since his successful coup in 1970. Visitors to Damascus said that Assad, who was known to have survived a massive heart attack in 1983 and also to suffer from diabetes, had exhibited signs of physical weakness and a diminution of his mental acuity and the legendary stamina that had enabled him to engage in lengthy negotiating sessions with foreign diplomats. Assad had been grooming his son Bashar to succeed him, giving him increasing responsibilities, including the important "Lebanon file." But since Bashar lacked the military credentials and long political experience of his wily father, the Syrian president had an incentive to try to complete the negotiations with Israel and obtain the return of the Golan Heights while he could still maintain firm control of the country. There had reportedly already been clashes between supporters of President Assad and of his exiled brother Rifaat, as well as purges of some military and intelligence officers. It was impossible to predict the outcome of a power struggle among the various intelligence chiefs and other groups among the Sunni majority, unhappy with the long dominance of Assad and his fellow Alawites, who represented only some 12 percent of the population. Were the conflict with Israel ended and Syria to shift its priorities from war to meeting the domestic needs of its people, Bashar, 35, a London-trained ophthalmologist and the head of Syria's nascent Internet community, might be a suitable candidate to open up the economy and the society.

In television and newspaper interviews in mid-September, newly elected Israeli prime minister Barak also cited the declining health of Assad and Arafat among the reasons he was eager to complete the peace process as quickly as possible. Rejecting the idea that he would be better off waiting for their successors, Barak said he preferred negotiating with established leaders who can make big decisions. "Assad is the symbol of the [Arab national] revolution," Barak said, and Arafat is "the one who molded his people" (AP report from Jerusalem, September 23). American and Israeli analysts concluded that the time was ripe for negotiation. Assad's sense that his time was running out, compounded by a worsening of the Syrian economic situation and the diminished ability of Russia to play a role in the Middle East, all raised expectations during 1999 that the aging Syrian leader was eager to improve relations with the United States. Since the Clinton administration made it abundantly clear that ending Syria's conflict with Israel was a precondition for American assistance, Assad was prepared to reach a peace agreement with Israel, brokered by the Americans, if his terms for complete Israeli withdrawal from the Golan Heights were met.

American Efforts Behind the Scenes

While there were some in the U.S. and Israel who saw in the uncertainty about Syria's political future a reason for caution, the prevailing view was well summarized by Itamar Rabinovich, the former Israeli ambassador in Washington and an academic authority on Syria who headed the Israeli negotiating team in the last round of talks with the Syrians during 1992–96. Asked whether it was better to wait until the succession in Syria was clear, Rabinovich, who in June 1999 was appointed president of Tel Aviv University, conceded that Syrian domestic politics is "totally in the realm of the unknown." But, he added, "We can make one general assumption: it is better to deal with Assad because he is authoritative, he can make an agreement, and he can implement it." The Clinton administration and officials in Jerusalem shared this view, and made persistent efforts during 1999 to resume the Syrian-Israeli talks that had broken off early in 1996.

In fact, it was revealed in November 1999 that Prime Minister Netanyahu had engaged in extensive secret back-channel contacts with the Syrian leader beginning in 1997. Uzi Arad, who had been Netanyahu's senior foreign-policy adviser, disclosed that a trusted American intermediary, industrialist and cosmetics heir Ronald S. Lauder, a personal friend of the prime minister and a Likud campaign supporter, had shuttled 12 times between Jerusalem and Damascus. (Lauder was also president of the Jewish National Fund and in 1999 became chairman of the Conference of Presidents of Major American Jewish Organizations.) According to Arad, in an interview with Amir Rappaport published in *Yediot Aharonot* (November 26), Netanyahu had gotten Assad to agree to the continuation of the ground monitoring station on Mt. Hermon, with Israel obtaining continuous access to real-time data through American auspices even after a peace agreement. Netanyahu agreed to the principle of Israeli withdrawal, but refused to agree to return to the pre-1967 lines, which would have given the Syrians access to the Sea of Galilee. The talks were suspended when Assad asked Lauder to bring a map showing precisely where Israel was prepared to withdraw to, but, Arad explained, "We wanted to buy time and not give Assad the map he demanded."

Assad's decision personally to attend King Hussein's funeral, even though he had been furious over Jordan's decision to make a separate peace with Israel in 1994, was seen as symbolic of the shift in Syria's approach to peace with Israel. King Abdullah II of Jordan seized the opening and worked hard to improve the chilly relations between Amman and Damascus, eagerly serving as another channel for Israeli-Syrian contacts. The young Jordanian monarch reported to the Americans on his first official visit to the United States as king at the end of May that he was convinced that Assad had made a "strategic decision" to achieve a deal with Israel. As evidence of Assad's intention to prepare the Syrian people for the shift from war to peace, he noted that he had seen large-size banners unfurled all over Damascus, proclaiming: "We fought with honor; we will negotiate with honor; we will have peace with honor." European Union envoy Miguel Angel Moratinos made a similarly positive assessment after visiting Damascus toward the end of May. He found Syria "extremely ready and anxious" to resume talks with Israel following Ehud Barak's decisive defeat of Netanyahu in the May election, which the Syrians welcomed.

Clash Over PA Compliance

Aside from the biological clock ticking for aging Middle East leaders, there was also a political timetable to focus the attention of the potential peacemakers as the year began. Israeli elections were coming up. Prime Minister Netanyahu had suspended further scheduled Israeli troop withdrawals from additional territory on the West Bank under the Wye agreements, after the first phase of withdrawal, ostensibly because of the failure of the Palestinian Authority to fulfill its security-related obligations toward Israel. United States and other observers, however, attributed the renewed stalemate in the peace process primarily to the defection of Netanyahu's right-wing supporters and the unraveling of the coalition, resulting in the prime minister's decision to call for early elections in the hope of obtaining a broader mandate for his policies.

The Americans faced the dilemma of how to express their criticism of the Netanyahu freeze on territorial withdrawal without appearing to intervene in Israeli politics. In mid-January State Department spokesman James Rubin asserted that the Palestinians "have been making a good faith effort to implement a number of the commitments in the Wye agreement, including the commitment to amend the charter of the Palestine National Council and the fight against terrorism." In contrast, he said, "it is the Israelis who have not fulfilled any of their Phase Two obligations" by postponing indefinitely the required West Bank redeployments. This public criticism was mild compared to the reported fury of the administration's Middle East peace-process team at an op-ed in the *Washington Times* by Israeli ambassador Zalman Shoval that shifted all the blame for the stalled talks onto the Palestinians. But the Clinton administration resisted Palestinian demands that Washington openly pressure the Netanyahu government. Doing so, it believed, would produce a backlash in Israel that would give the embattled prime minister a powerful weapon in his bid for reelection. An Israeli Foreign Ministry memorandum of February 1 asserted that "despite recent internal political developments in Israel, the Government of Israel has reiterated its commitment to the Wye Memorandum in all its aspects" and pledged to "continue to negotiate all outstanding issues and implement its obligations on the basis of reciprocity." The memorandum said that Israel was pleased to note that the PNC had adopted a resolution amending its charter, as required by Wye and earlier undertakings, but then listed a long series of unfulfilled PA commitments.

The growing feelings of mistrust and mutual recrimination between Arafat and Netanyahu, following the brief rapprochement and commitment to cooperation that Clinton had elicited from them at Wye, also caused United States officials to reexamine their role in the process. In connection with the 1998 Wye agreements the United States had, reluctantly, been increasingly drawn into the minutiae of the process, with even the CIA given an unaccustomed role of verifying and judging details of compliance on security matters. Addressing the annual seminar of the Peres Center for Peace in mid-January, Dennis Ross, the U.S. special peace-process envoy, suggested that the administration would play a much less intrusive role in the final-status negotiations, if and when they actually started. "The key here is not that you have anybody mediate," he said. "For them to be able to do it in the end," he stressed, "they have to approach it from the standpoint of partnership. If there is not going to be partnership, then there is not going to be a permanent-status agreement."

New York Times foreign affairs analyst Thomas L. Friedman, in a scathing column on January 12, pointed to the disastrous consequences of Netanyahu's "constant wavering" in response to the conflicting pressures from the international community and his far-right supporters. The result of this "total absence of strategy," Friedman declared, "has left Israel's relations with the Arabs in tatters and produced the most intimate relationship between America and the Palestinians in the history of this conflict." If Netanyahu continued on this track, he would give up 50 percent of the West Bank, as opposed to the 60 percent that Labor would give up, Friedman predicted, but "he will end up with no partnership with the Palestinians and a crisis of confidence with the U.S."

The U.S.-Israeli dispute regarding Palestinian Authority compliance with its antiterrorism promises flared up again at the end of February during a public meeting in Washington. After Lenny Ben-David, the deputy chief of mission of the Israeli embassy, declared that the PA had freed "known terrorists, murderers," without consultation with the Israelis or the Americans, Assistant Secretary of State for Near Eastern Affairs Martin Indyk rose to challenge Ben-David's assertion. After checking all the Israeli, Palestinian, and U.S. sources, the U.S. had concluded that the charge "is simply not true. . . . The fundamental point is they did not release terrorists or murderers." Indyk, a former ambassador to Israel, elaborated that the PA had arrested "a lot of Hamas people" and had released those for whom no grounds for detention existed, just as Israel released some suspects it arrested. He conceded that the PA did not always consult with Israel and the U.S. Netanyahu spokesman Aviv Bushinsky responded that Indyk may have been technically correct that those released "had not pulled a trigger or blown themselves up," but Israel had evidence that they conspired to commit terrorism.

Evidence for the benefits of closer Israeli-Palestinian security cooperation was soon available. At the end of February Israeli intelligence sources warned the Palestinian Preventive Security Service (PPSS) that Hamas terrorists had infiltrated the country and planned new suicide attacks. Numerous Hamas militants were arrested. In March, when Mohammed Dahlan, the PPSS director in Gaza, learned of new terrorist plans, he alerted CIA director George Tenet, who urged Dahlan to intensify direct cooperation with Israel's Shin Bet. This resulted in the uncovering of several terrorist cells in Gaza and the foiling of bomb attacks planned in crowded locations in Tel Aviv. Prime Minister Netanyahu telephoned Arafat from Moscow on March 23 and warmly thanked him for the PA's cooperation in preventing "a major disaster in Israel." Arafat, who was in London at the time, received a similar congratulatory call from President Clinton.

Benefits for Deferring Statehood

As it became clear that the Netanyahu government was not going to carry out the additional withdrawals by the target date agreed to at Wye Plantation, Chairman Arafat turned increasingly to President Clinton for signs of American support to counter the complaints of his restive PLO followers that diplomacy was producing no practical results. Another Arafat tactic to maintain their allegiance was his increasingly strident declarations that he would unilaterally proclaim the independent State of Palestine on May 4, 1999, if there was no agreement with Israel by then.

The Clinton administration adopted a two-pronged approach to deal with the problem. On the one hand it reiterated its opposition to a unilateral Palestinian declaration of statehood, while on the other it signaled support for Arafat through the increasingly frequent and warm receptions he received from the White House as well as renewed U.S. efforts to reinvigorate the frozen peace process. The clearest authoritative statement of the American position was contained in a mid-January interview that President Clinton gave the London-based Saudi newspaper *Al-Sharq al-Awsat* (January 16). Since the United States had always maintained that "an acceptable solution can only be found through negotiations, not through unilateral actions," he explained, "we would oppose any unilateral declaration of statehood" or other unilateral actions that "prejudge or predetermine the outcome of those negotiations." (On the same grounds the administration had opposed controversial new Israeli housing projects around the Arab sections of Jerusalem and the expansion of settlements in the West Bank.)

In his comments to the Saudi paper, Clinton added: "For the present, we are doing all we can to promote permanent-status negotiations on an accelerated basis and we are stressing that those who believe they can declare unilateral psitions or take unilateral acts when the interim period ends [on May 4] are courting disaster." Congress powerfully endorsed his position in mid-March, when bipartisan and overwhelming majorities in the House of Representatives (380-24) and the Senate (98-1) passed identical resolutions warning that the declaration of a Palestinian state "would introduce a dramatically destabilizing element into the Middle East." And, both houses added, "any attempt to establish Palestinian statehood outside the negotiating process will invoke the strongest congressional opposition." During the debate in the House, Rep. Mark Foley (R., Fla.) addressed Arafat directly, expressing skepticism about the PLO leader's commitment to peace with Israel, and warning that "the U.S. is putting you on notice; declare statehood on May 4, and we will declare your financial support from the U.S. null and void."

At the same time, the administration sought to reassure the Palestinian leader. On February 4, Arafat came to Washington as an invited guest to attend the 47th annual National Prayer Breakfast, after which he was received by President Clinton at the White House. Arafat was again an honored guest when he was hosted by the secretary of state for dinner at her home on March 22, and the following day he had a one-on-one meeting with the president at the White House. While reiterating U.S. opposition to a unilateral declaration of statehood, the president reportedly emphasized that Israel and the Palestinian Authority should resume talks on permanent status as soon as possible, on an accelerated basis. At a summit conference in Berlin on March 25 the European Union took a similar position, counseling Arafat to defer the declaration of independence and calling for early resumption of final-status talks, with negotiations to be completed within one year. But it went farther than the U.S. in support of Palestinian national rights when it backed "the continuing and unqualified Palestinian right to self-determination, including the option of a State, and look[ed] forward to the early fulfillment of this right." State Department spokesman James Rubin said that the Clinton administration did not share the EU position, adding: "We believe Oslo is based on the principle that all permanent-status issues can only be resolved through negotiations. We are thus opposed to a unilateral declaration of a Palestinian state."

In a further effort to defuse the impending crisis, President Clinton sent a lengthy and highly significant letter to Chairman Arafat on April 26. (Although not made public either by the White House or the Palestinian Authority, the full text was obtained by the Israeli newspaper, *Yediot Aharonot*, and it was published in the *Near East Report* of May 17.) Clinton began by praising the Palestinian leader for having made "historic decisions for peace" and declared it was critical that he maintain "the courage and vision" to help achieve that goal. The president declared that the United States "is a full partner with Palestinians and Israelis" and stressed how important it was that "you and I work closely in the period ahead." In a scarcely veiled criticism of Netanyahu, Clinton bemoaned the

.ct that "the Palestinian-Israeli partnership—so essential to peacemaking—has been badly shaken" and that "much time has been wasted and many opportunities have been lost." Pledging to work actively for Israel's implementation of the second and third phases of the Wye agreement, Clinton expressed appreciation for Arafat's efforts to implement many of the Palestinian commitments for the second phase, "particularly in the security area where Palestinians are engaged in a serious effort to fight terror."

Acknowledging that the approach of May 4 presented Arafat with "enormous pressures and challenges" to achieve Palestinian aspirations and also keep the hopes for peace alive, President Clinton urged him to remove the May 4 deadline and to continue to rely on the negotiating process. In this context and "in the spirit of my remarks in Gaza" (see AJYB 1999, p. 161), the president declared: "We support the aspirations of the Palestinian people to determine their own future on their own land." This was the clearest American statement of support for Palestinian statehood, and was actually a bit more explicit than his comment in Gaza, which he reiterated in the letter, that "I believe Palestinians should live free today, tomorrow and forever."

Clinton then outlined the steps the United States was taking to reenergize the peace process. Washington, he said, had called on both parties, even after May 4, to continue to adhere to the terms of reference of the peace process as defined in Madrid and Oslo, which was to implement "UN Security Council Resolutions 242 and 338, *including land for peace*, and all other agreements under the Oslo process."(Italics added.) The U.S. was urging both sides to implement "without further delay" the interim agreement and the Wye River memorandum. He added that, "the United States further believes that the Oslo process was never intended to be open-ended." Therefore, Clinton was calling on both parties to engage in "accelerated permanent-status negotiations" with the goal of reaching an agreement within one year. Clinton promised that as soon as the Israeli elections were over and a new government was formed, the U.S. was "ready to help launch those negotiations," to review and monitor their progress, and to bring the parties together within six months.

As a further inducement for the Palestinians to extend the negotiating deadline beyond May 4, Clinton expressed his support for some key Palestinian demands. Declaring that "the United States knows how destructive settlement activities, land confiscations, and house demolitions are to the pursuit of Palestinian-Israeli peace," he pledged that the U.S. "will continue to exercise maximum efforts to have both parties avoid unilateral steps or actions designed to change the status of the West Bank and Gaza or to prejudge or preempt issues reserved for permanent-status negotiations." And Clinton assured Arafat that he was personally "committed to continuing to enhance the U.S.-Palestinian partnership," and pledged: "I will do everything possible to strengthen that partnership and through the U.S.-Palestinian Bilateral Committee to remove impediments to our relationship."

As Israeli observers noted (*Ha'aretz*, May 5), the term "partnership" had previously been reserved for the U.S.-Israel relationship. (The routinization of high-level official Palestinian contacts in Washington was noted by departing guests at the gala White House dinner in July for newly elected Israeli prime minister Ehud Barak, when the loudspeaker blared insistently: "Ambassador from the PLO, your car is ready! Ambassador from the PLO, your car is ready!")

The timing of President Clinton's April 26 letter was designed to influence the deliberations of the Palestine Central Council (PCC), which Arafat convened in Gaza the following day. After two days of debate, the PCC decided to heed the advice offered "by the overwhelming majority of brotherly [i.e. Arab] and friendly states" to postpone actions affirming Palestinian independence. Aside from the Berlin statement of the EU, the primary statement of a "friendly state" was President Clinton's letter. As the mid-May issue of the *Monthly Bulletin of the Permanent Observer Mission of Palestine to the United Nations* noted, "That letter and its content represented an important development, moving the American position to a new level." Explaining the postponement of a formal declaration of independence, the PCC affirmed that "the Palestinian State already exists on the basis of the natural rights of the Palestinian people, [UN] General Assembly Resolution 181(II) of 1947 [the so-called Palestine Partition Plan], and the Declaration of Independence by the Palestine National Council in [Algiers in] 1988."

The U.S. and the Revival of the Partition Resolution

The repeated references by Arafat and other Palestinian spokesmen to Resolution 181 raised alarm bells in Washington and Jerusalem. This was the November 1947 UN General Assembly resolution which proposed partition of Mandatory Palestine into two sovereign states, one "Jewish" and one "Arab," with an enlarged Jerusalem area under international administration. It was ironic that the leader of the Palestine Liberation Organization was now citing as a legal basis for his Palestinian state the very resolution that the Arabs states had not only voted against and denounced, but the one the Palestinians and neighboring Arab states had sought to nullify through war against the Jewish state at its birth. In fact, the PLO-controlled Palestine National Council had declared in its founding covenant in 1964 that the resolution was "illegal." Thus the position of the Netanyahu government was that the hostile Palestinian and Arab actions had made the 1947 resolution "null and void."

In response, Ambassador Mohammed Al-Kidwa, the permanent observer of Palestine at the UN, sent a letter on March 25 to UN secretary general Kofi Annan denouncing the Israeli rejection as "pathetic statements involving illegal positions." He explained the evolution in the PLO position as follows: "For the Palestinian side, and since the strategic decision to forge a peace on the basis of coexistence, resolution 181 (II) has become acceptable." He pointed out that the resolution "provides the legal basis for the existence of both the Jewish and the

Arab States in Mandated Palestine." Had he ended his letter there, it would not have aroused much concern in Washington and Jerusalem. But the Palestinian representative added: "According to the resolution, Jerusalem should become a *corpus separatum*, which the Palestinian side is willing to take into consideration and to reconcile with the Palestinian position that East Jerusalem is part of the Palestinian territory and the capital of the Palestinian State." Even more disturbing was the conclusion of the letter: "Moreover, we believe that Israel must still explain to the international community the measures it took illegally to extend its laws and regulations to the territory it occupied in the war of 1948, beyond the territory allocated to the Jewish State in resolution 181 (II)."

The Clinton administration hastened to reassure Israel's American supporters that the U.S. rejected the Palestinian attempt to revive the 1947 resolution. Addressing the AIPAC Policy Conference in Washington on May 23, Vice President Al Gore declared that the outcome of the peace process "must be determined by negotiation alone, and the only basis for Israeli-Palestinian negotiation are the terms of reference defined in Madrid and the Oslo agreement: UN Security Council Resolutions 242 and 338, and the principle of land for peace." Assistant Secretary of State Indyk told the Center for Policy Analysis on Palestine, on June 3, "I think it's a big mistake" for the Palestinians to try to utilize the 1947 resolution as a basis for negotiations, because this raises "a very real concern on the Israeli side" about the ultimate intentions of the Palestinians. "To change the terms of reference in midstream is to really undermine the negotiations," he added.

The United States also strongly opposed another Palestinian anti-Israeli maneuver at the UN. In February the Palestinians had succeeded in getting the General Assembly to approve, by a vote of 115-2 (the U.S. and Israel), a special conference of the High Contracting Parties to the Fourth Geneva Convention, on July 15, to "enforce the Convention in the Occupied Palestinian territory, including Jerusalem." The UN had adopted this convention on the rights of civilians in occupied territories in 1949, in the aftermath of the Holocaust, to prevent the repetition of Nazi policies, which included the forced relocation and murder of millions of civilians. The Palestinians' UN supporters intended the July 15 review conference to score points against Israeli settlement policies. As William Korey, a veteran human-rights authority, pointed out (*Near East Report*, August 9), in its 50-year history the convention "has never been invoked to deal with the most egregious examples of violence and mass murder," including Saddam Hussein's brutalization of Kuwaiti civilians in 1990 or Slobodan Milosevic's "ethnic cleansing" in Bosnia and Kosovo.

The Clinton administration worked behind the scenes to derail the proposed meeting. Assistant Secretary of State Indyk declared that the timing was counterproductive to peace since the meeting would take place just as a new postelection Israeli government was being formed, and, in any case, the "settlements issue is an issue to be dealt with in the permanent-status negotiations." Not only would the U.S. not attend, he declared on June 29, but "we will do everything we can to urge the parties involved in this exercise not to have the meeting." The meeting was held as scheduled, but the American arguments and the new hopes for revival of the peace process apparently had their effect. When 103 contracting parties (out of a total of 188) assembled in Geneva, the session lasted just ten minutes. Korey noted that "after deciding, rather arbitrarily, that the Fourth Geneva Convention was relevant to the situation in the 'Occupied Territory,' the delegates promptly adjourned without setting a date for the next meeting."

Elections in Israel

The Knesset had set May 17, 1999, as election day. Voters would cast two separate ballots, one for prime minister and the other for the new Knesset. A variety of new parties and personalities emerged during the hotly contested campaign, which also witnessed the increasing use of American media consultants and pollsters by the major parties to project their messages in television commercials and on billboards. Among the most prominent were Clinton advisor James Carville and pollster Stanley Greenberg, who led the American team helping Ehud Barak, the candidate of One Israel (the expanded Labor Party). Heading the American advisers for Netanyahu and the Likud Party was Arthur Finkelstein, who had worked for a number of Republican candidates in the U.S. and had been instrumental in Netanyahu's victory in the last election. Various Israeli parties sought and received indirect financial and political support from American backers, despite Israeli election rules which bar contributions from overseas. Since Israel does not permit absentee ballots, supporters of the major parties also arranged reduced-fare flights to Israel to help Israeli citizens living in the U.S. to vote in the Israeli elections.

The result was an unexpectedly decisive first-ballot victory for One Israel (Labor) and its leader, the new prime minister, Ehud Barak. Netanyahu announced his decision to resign from politics within hours of his stunning defeat. Upon his victory, Barak promised that he would rapidly implement the Wye River memorandum, enter into permanent-status talks with the Palestinians, and vigorously pursue resumption of peace talks with Syria and Lebanon, which had been suspended in February 1996. Barak also managed by early July to put together a broad-based coalition that gave him a comfortable initial majority of 75 in the 120-member Knesset.

Syrian Conundrum

Most of the leaders of the Arab world welcomed Barak's victory, most notably President Assad of Syria, young King Abdullah of Jordan, President Hosni Mubarak of Egypt, and PLO leader Arafat. King Hassan's funeral in Rabat on July 25 provided an opportunity for Barak to meet with some formerly hostile

Arab leaders. Not only was the funeral the scene of the first three-way meeting between Barak, Clinton, and Arafat, but it also provided an opportunity for the new Israeli premier to be seen having a friendly chat and a warm handshake with Abdelaziz Bouteflika, the recently elected president of Algeria, a country that was still nominally at war with Israel. President Assad, who had been expected to attend, decided against it at the last minute, reportedly because he had heard that Clinton hoped to use the occasion to arrange an impromptu summit meeting between Assad and Barak. *New York Times* reporter Douglas Jehl reported, "The Syrian leader knew what the other guests were plotting, and he had no intention of allowing himself to be cajoled or even bumped into a first-ever encounter with an Israeli leader." (The organizers of the funeral for King Hussein in Amman had made sure that the Israeli and Syrian delegations were kept at a discrete distance from one another.)

Assad maintained this standoffish Syrian posture throughout the year, refusing Israeli offers to meet Barak either in Jerusalem or elsewhere. Even in December, after Clinton succeeded in organizing Syria-Israel meetings in Washington, Assad send Foreign Minister Farouk al-Shara to head the Syrian delegation, and neither Clinton nor the expectant photographers could induce the Syrian foreign minister to shake the hand of the Israeli prime minister. The significance of the Syrian stance was more than just a missed photo opportunity. Since Barak had pledged to submit any agreement with Syria to a national referendum, he and the Americans were hoping for some positive gestures from Assad to reassure and win over the skeptical Israeli public. They recalled that Anwar Sadat had grasped the psychological aspect of the conflict and had managed to turn around Israeli public opinion through his dramatic visit to Jerusalem in November 1977 and his declaration to the Knesset that Egypt welcomed Israel as a recognized neighbor in the Middle East. But Assad was no Sadat. Throughout the year Syria, and its client state Lebanon, continued their boycott of the multilateral working groups that had been set up to deal with regional aspects of the Arab-Israel conflict.

After the Israeli elections Netanyahu briefed Barak on the points that had been agreed to in the earlier Syrian talks, which Netanyahu adviser Uzi Arad said would provide a useful basis for Barak to pursue his own negotiations. Arad's revelations confirmed that despite Likud rhetoric that Israel would never give up the Golan, Netanyahu had in fact been willing to consider a significant Israeli withdrawal on that front. The Syrians indicated that they were prepared to resume talks with Israel from the point where they had been broken off in 1996. A key sticking point was what commitments Israel had made to the Americans in 1996. The Syrians claimed that Yitzhak Rabin, who was then prime minister, had told U.S. secretary of state Warren Christopher that Israel was prepared to withdraw fully to the lines of June 4, 1967, as demanded by Syria, so long as Israel's security concerns were fully met. But that would give the Syrians access to the Sea of Galilee as well as a strip of the Jordan River. As noted above, not only Netanyahu but also most Labor supporters wanted to retain Israeli control over its vital water resources, which were considered vital to Israel's national security. They therefore argued for withdrawal to, at most, the international border established in 1923. That had been set in negotiations conducted by Britain and France, which held the mandates over Palestine and Syria, respectively. That left all of the Sea of Galilee and the Jordan River within the borders of Palestine/ Israel. Barak was also to take the position that the proposal made by his mentor, Rabin, to the American secretary of state was not intended as a binding commitment but only as a hypothetical statement designed to help Christopher elicit a Syrian response. United States officials tended to agree with Barak's interpretation.

Impending U.S. Elections Add Urgency

The political timetable in the United States was also very much on the mind of the new Israeli premier when he declared his intention to achieve a final and comprehensive peace not only with the Palestinians but also with Syria and Lebanon within 15 months, that is, by September 2000. This self-imposed deadline took into account the reality that by then the American presidential election campaign would be in its final months. Not only would domestic politics dominate public attention, but President Clinton would be approaching the end of his final year in office. Although the Republican-led impeachment of the president had failed to win the two-thirds majority in the Senate necessary to convict and remove him from office, the bitterness of the partisan debate continued to impede Clinton's ability to win bipartisan support for his initiatives, compounding the standard problems faced by lame-duck presidents.

Clinton's desire to redeem his reputation and to leave his mark on history by presiding over the conclusion of a comprehensive Arab-Israeli peace agreement, dovetailed well with Barak's own passionate desire to bring an end to the decades of warfare and bloodshed that he had witnessed in a long and distinguished military career. Not only did the Clinton administration and Barak's One Israel share similar approaches to solving the Arab-Israel conflict, but the two relatively youthful leaders developed a sense of mutual trust and a warm personal chemistry. This contrasted with the prickly relations, distrust, and scarcely disguised personal animosity that had developed between Clinton and Netanyahu.

Yet this point should not be carried too far, since U.S.-Israeli strategic and defense cooperation had continued to broaden under the Netanyahu administration, and there would surely be some policy disagreements even under a Barak regime, as there had been under earlier Labor governments. A minor complication in U.S.-Israeli relations was to be introduced during 1999 by another election, namely, First Lady Hillary Rodham Clinton's exploration of the option of running for the senate seat from New York being vacated by the retirement of Senator Daniel Patrick Moynihan. There was occasionally confusion as to whether

Mrs. Clinton was speaking as first lady or as political candidate when she made comments on Middle East issues that were not consistent with those of the administration.

When Barak met with Clinton in Washington on July 15 and told him of his plans to achieve agreements both with Syria and the Palestinians within 15 months, he found that the president shared his "sense of urgency," according to a senior White House aide. One of Barak's goals during this trip, Israeli officials explained, was to establish a rapport with President Clinton so that they could deal with each other person-to-person and not through their staffs. The two leaders spent an extraordinary eight hours together, most of the time alone, and the remainder with their wives. Both gave effusive positive assessments of their interaction, which went beyond a basic agreement on how to pursue the peace process. An aide to the prime minister attributed the apparent bonding to several factors. Not only were they of the same generation—Barak was 57 and Clinton 52—but both apparently had the patience to delve into multiple subjects at length. Yitzhak Rabin, Barak's mentor, said the aide, would not have had the patience to stay one-on-one with Clinton for so long.

In remarks to the press before their White House meeting, Barak emphasized that restarting the dialogue between Israel and the Palestinians, and with Syria and Lebanon, would require "American leadership and support all along the way." However he indicated that he would prefer a less prominent and intrusive American role in the negotiations. Barak emphasized the importance of direct talks with the Arabs and did not want the United States to serve as "policeman, judge and arbitrator." President Clinton publicly agreed that the U.S. had become overly enmeshed in the details of the Arab-Israeli dialogue. He said Washington should have served merely as a "facilitator" of the talks and not as an active participant. "We took a more active role, in effect as a mediator, when the bonds of trust and the lines of communication had become so frayed that we were in danger of losing the peace process," the president said.

Arab capitals had responded positively to Barak's declaration on July 6, in his inaugural speech to the Knesset: "I call on all regional leaders to take our outstretched hands and build a peace of the brave." But it was soon apparent that the United States would continue to play a crucial role in bringing the opposing sides together and revitalizing the Palestinian-Israeli and Syrian-Israeli talks. The U.S. also had the burden of trying to defuse escalating tensions in southern Lebanon. The experience and negotiating skills of U.S. peace envoy Dennis Ross were instrumental in crafting detailed language bridging the Israeli and Arab positions on a new Palestinian-Israeli agreement. Frequent phone calls from President Clinton to Arafat and Barak, as well as new letters of assurances from the president delivered to Chairman Arafat by Secretary of State Madeleine Albright, helped prod the two sides to overcome their final differences. After meeting with Barak for three-and-a-half hours, Albright announced an agreement in Gaza City, with Arafat standing by her side, late on September 3. The agreement was officially consummated on May 5 at the Egyptian resort of Sharm el-Sheik with President Mubarak of Egypt and King Abdullah of Jordan signing as witnesses. Mrs. Albright stressed that she was not a mediator, perhaps not even a facilitator. "Maybe I was just the handmaiden," she said.

The agreement spelled out the implementation process for the Wye River agreements. Referring to Barak as "my new partner in the peace process," Arafat pledged to carry out the Palestinian obligations promptly. Barak declared, "Today we are paving the way toward the end of a century-old conflict between us and the Palestinians." Prime Minister Barak, who was also serving as Israel's minister of defense, said, "I am committed to Israel's security." But he immediately added: "I also want the Palestinians to feel secure." After the signing Mrs. Albright embraced Barak and Arafat, and noted that the two sides had begun to rebuild their partnership, "a partnership that is vital to the region's future." King Abdullah recalled his late father's efforts for regional peace, adding, "I hope and pray we do not let him down."

The new agreement provided a three-stage process for Israel's withdrawal from an additional 11 percent of West Bank territory, with the process to be completed by January 20, 2000. Other details dealt with the release of Palestinian prisoners held by Israel, the construction of a Palestinian port in Gaza to complement the airport that had already been put into service, and the arrangements for opening two "safe-passage" routes connecting Gaza to the West Bank. The southern route was to be completed before the end of the year. The agreement also included a commitment to begin final-status talks immediately, with a statement of principles to be drafted by February 15 and the definitive Palestinian-Israeli agreement covering all the outstanding issues to be completed by mid-September 2000. Many veteran observers were skeptical that all the difficult issues, including the status of Jerusalem, final borders, settlements, water rights, and the claims of the Palestinian refugees, could be resolved so quickly, even with the newfound spirit of cooperation between the leaders of the two sides.

The first sign of trouble soon became evident as Secretary Albright arrived in Damascus on the next leg of her Middle East journey. This was her first visit to the Syrian capital in two years, and it followed President Clinton's exchange of letters with Assad in July, in which Clinton offered to act as a facilitator to resumed Israeli-Syrian talks. Although President Assad told Mrs. Albright that he regarded Prime Minister Barak as a "serious and honorable man," there was no apparent change in the Syrian position that the talks must resume at the point where they broke off in 1996, which the Syrians insisted meant an Israeli commitment to withdraw to the lines of June 4, 1967, so that Syria's border would go to the shore of the Sea of Galilee. Denying that Rabin had made any such commitment, Barak insisted that the talks begin with discussions of security issues and the extent to which Syria was prepared to normalize relations with Israel. There was some progress on another important matter. Mrs. Albright reminded Foreign Minister Shara that Syria remained on the State Department's list of

...ates supporting terrorism, and was therefore barred from American aid. Shara confirmed that Damascus, in apparent preparation for making peace with Israel, had told Palestinian groups in Syria to stop their anti-Israel military actions and limit themselves to political activities. Mrs. Albright also visited Beirut, the first American secretary of state to go there since George Shultz in 1983. Prime Minister Selim Hoss reassured her that he welcomed U.S. efforts to resume Lebanese-Israeli talks. Assad similarly assured her that he also favored a Lebanese-Israeli agreement, but only if this was part of a comprehensive peace in which Syrian-Israeli issues were resolved. Assad had been furious when Netanyahu had proclaimed a "Lebanon first" policy. And despite his official endorsement of a Lebanese-Israeli agreement, Assad was troubled by Barak's announcement that Israel intended to pull out of Lebanon by July 2000, whether there was a broader agreement or not.

As noted above, the United State finally managed to bring the Israeli and Syrian delegations together for talks in Washington in December, with the participation of President Clinton. The Syria-Israel impasse over whether to first discuss borders or security was finessed by an agreement that the talks would begin at the point where they had broken off in 1996, allowing each side to stick to its own interpretation of what had transpired then. No substantive agreement was reached between Barak and Shara, who headed the Syrian delegation and maintained a frosty demeanor toward Barak, despite the best efforts of Clinton to bring the two together. They did agree to resume their deliberations in January 2000 at a secluded conference center in Shepherdstown, West Virginia, a historic U.S. Civil War battle site, which Clinton hoped would impress upon the Syrians and Israelis the tragic futility of fraternal conflict. Another reason for this choice, after Assad had rejected Camp David because of its association with the Egyptian-Israeli agreement, was that Shepherdstown was sufficiently close to Washington that President Clinton could quickly fly in from the White House by helicopter when needed.

Congress Approves Aid

Despite their continuing disputes over the substantive aspects of the peace process, the Arab parties and Israel shared a common desire to obtain tangible American economic support. The total cost of a Syrian-Israeli agreement—including new security arrangements, monitoring of the agreement, redeployment of armed forces, compensation to Israeli settlers evacuated from the Golan Heights, and aid to Syria for economic reconstruction—was estimated at around $17 billion. There were serious questions as to how much of this vast sum the U.S. Congress was prepared to authorize. But this was a problem for the future, since there were no signs during 1999 of an imminent breakthrough in the talks.

The immediate issue was to obtain the $1.9 billion that the Clinton administration had already pledged to fund implementation of the Wye agreements over a three-year period. In appealing for the money Clinton commented: "the costliest peace is far cheaper than the cheapest war." Washington observers noted that the six-week Gulf War in 1991 had cost an estimated $61 billion. The Wye package included $1.2 billion for Israel, $400 million for the Palestinians, and $200 million for Jordan, which was suffering serious economic difficulties compounded by a severe drought ($100 million had already been sent to Jordan as an American goodwill gesture following the death of King Hussein). By mid-September Congress had not yet acted. The general mood in Congress was to cut foreign aid wherever possible, and the Wye package was tied to the broader debate over federal funding, tax cuts, and Social Security. Moreover, the Republicans, who controlled both houses and were looking toward the election of 2000, were not about to make the president's task any easier.

The good news was that Israel continued to enjoy widespread bipartisan support and the Clinton administration hoped that some of this could be transferred to the Palestinians and other Arab states that demonstrated a commitment to peace. However the congressional debate was complicated by the Capitol Hill activities of Israeli and American groups that shared the skepticism of Benjamin Netanyahu, Ariel Sharon, and many other Israelis over the sincerity of Arafat's commitment to lasting peace, and that opposed Israeli withdrawal from the Golan Heights. The House of Representatives passed the Wye aid package on November 5 by 351-58, evidence of the bipartisan support the peace process enjoyed. This margin was considerably greater than that for the foreign aid bill as a whole, approved by 316-100. Later in November Congress approved an omnibus appropriation bill that also included the regular U.S. aid to Israel and Egypt. (The vote in the House, on November 18, was 296-135, and in the Senate the following day the vote was 74-24.) The bill included $1.92 billion in military assistance and $960 million in economic assistance for Israel (both figures in line with Israel's commitment gradually to reduce the level of economic aid it receives), plus $60 million for refugee assistance. To help free up money for the Wye aid and an additional $799 million for other international aid programs, Israel agreed to waive the early disbursement of about one-third of U.S. military aid for the coming year.

U.S.-Israeli strategic cooperation was also further developed during the year. Additional funding was provided for important joint defense projects, including the Arrow antimissile defense system and Tactical High Energy Laser, as well as for the improvement of the Israeli-designed Hunter Unmanned Aerial Vehicle, which was used effectively by NATO forces for surveillance in their campaign against Yugoslav forces in Kosovo. During Barak's July 1999 visit to Washington an agreement was concluded to broaden cooperation between NASA and the Israeli Space Agency. As part of a broader program to develop strategic cooperation among America's allies in the region, the United States Sixth Fleet participated with Israeli and Turkish naval units in a joint maneuver to rescue survivors of disasters at sea. Jordanian officers were present as observers.

Personnel Shifts

On November 10 the Senate confirmed Martin Indyk as U.S. ambassador to Israel and Ned Walker, then the U.S. ambassador in Tel Aviv, as assistant secretary of state for Near East affairs. Washington explained this unusual trading of places by the two experienced Middle East diplomats as designed to promote the peace process and U.S. policy in the Middle East. In view of the intensive negotiations that were anticipated to bring the Arab-Israeli negotiations to a successful conclusion, Clinton believed that Indyk would be the best man to be on the ground in the region. Indyk, who had previously served as U.S. ambassador to Israel (1995–97), knew all the key players and had over the years worked tirelessly behind the scenes to broker Israeli-Palestinian compromises that made the Wye and other agreements possible. Walker was a career diplomat with more than 30 years of service in the Middle East. Prior to his current assignment in Israel he had served in senior positions at the U.S. embassies in Syria and Saudi Arabia, and as U.S. ambassador to Egypt and the United Arab Emirates. Back in Washington as assistant secretary of state, Walker would have the opportunity to deal with the broader regional issues, such as formulating effective policies for containing Iraq and Iran.

Indeed, in the Persian Gulf region the United States had experienced nothing but failure and frustration in its dealings with both Tehran and Baghdad. Iranian leaders had rebuffed Secretary of State Albright's efforts to resume a dialogue, and despite the popular groundswell within Iran for liberalization and reform, hardliners still controlled the country's foreign policy. During 1999 Tehran stepped up its shipment of arms to Hezballah guerrillas in southern Lebanon, denounced the Arab-Israeli peace process, imprisoned 13 Iranian Jews on espionage charges, and also continued its efforts to obtain nuclear and long-range missile technology from Russia and North Korea. The United States barred several Russian companies from doing business in the United States after they were found to have been sending sensitive equipment to Iran.

With regard to Iraq, concern was mounting in both the United States and Israel over the failure of the UN Security Council to reach agreement on a new comprehensive system of inspection of Iraq's suspected continuing efforts to develop chemical and biological as well as nuclear arms. Baghdad's uncooperative attitude was compounded by the refusal of Russia, China, and France to support the firm measures demanded by the United States and the United Kingdom. The U.S. suspected that it was these recalcitrant countries' hope for future commercial benefits, rather than their professed concern for the Iraqi civilian population, that motivated their calls for easing the sanctions. For much of the year the Security Council was in disarray, and Baghdad rejected even the new and less intrusive inspection scheme that it finally approved. The anti-Saddam Iraqi opposition was in no better shape. Although Congress had appropriated over $70 million to finance efforts to strengthen Iraqi efforts to remove Saddam Hussein, the disparate Iraqi opposition groups continued to squabble among themselves. A U.S.-sponsored gathering of the major opposition groups in New York in September broke up without achieving agreement on an effective plan for replacing the dictator in Baghdad. Clearly, Secretary of State Albright could well benefit from the experience in the Gulf that assistant secretary of state Walker was bringing back to Washington.

GEORGE E. GRUEN

Jewish Communal Affairs

SUMMING UP THE LAST thousand years, the *New York Times* magazine devoted its entire October 17 issue to "The Me Millennium." "We put the self at the center of the universe," the cover announced. "Now, for better or for worse, we are on our own." In 1999, Jews, like so many other Americans, faced a new millennium in search of personal meaning in their lives. No one knew where this would lead or whether it would ultimately strengthen or weaken American Jewry. Was the absorption with the self just a fin-de-siècle fad, or did it portend a new kind of American Judaism? In 1999 the search for personal Jewish meaning even overshadowed the security of Israel on the agenda of Jewish concerns.

Jewish Identity

There were Jews who were becoming more Jewish, such as free-agent baseball slugger Shawn Green, who announced that he would only sign to play in a city with a large Jewish community. Raised with minimal exposure to his Jewish heritage, Green said he had been so moved by the cheers of Jewish fans around the league that he wanted to learn more about, and to contribute to, the Jewish people. (He signed with the Los Angeles Dodgers.) Evidence that it was "in" to be Jewish came from non-Jews as well: Pop star Michael Jackson, for example, attended Sabbath services at the Carlebach Synagogue in New York City and said it was one of the most moving experiences of his life. Perhaps it was a sign of the times that 15 of the 100 most influential people of the 20th century, according to *Time* magazine, were Jews, including the single most influential person, Albert Einstein.

But there were many Jews who were not finding personal meaning in Judaism. According to a Gallup Poll released in October, American Jews were only half as likely as other Americans to consider religion "very important in their daily lives." Every other religious group scored higher than the Jews on this question; the only group with a lower affirmative response was the category with "no religion." Despite the objection of some social scientists that the findings were misleading because many Jews with little or no religious conviction strongly identified as Jews on a cultural or ethnic basis, the survey was scarcely heartening news for those optimistic about a Jewish renaissance.

MATTERS OF THE SPIRIT

Many had high hopes that more emphasis on "spirituality" could make Judaism more compelling. This notion was most prevalent on the West Coast. "Who am

I? What am I all about?" declared Rabbi Daniel Gordis, dean of the Ziegler School of the University of Judaism, the Conservative rabbinical seminary in Los Angeles. And he went on, "I don't feel that most people feel that, walking into the typical American synagogue, which is very stodgy, is not particularly experimental." The popular vogue of Kabbalah, Jewish mysticism, intensified, and to judge by the media, it seemed to hold a special fascination for Jewish and non-Jewish Hollywood celebrities. Actress Roseanne Barr, a regular at the Kabbalah Learning Center in Los Angeles, explained that "fragmentations and divisions of my mind have come together." Roseanne was only one of many Hollywood personalities to attend a kabbalistic Rosh Hashanah service where the rabbi blew the shofar and "for the next three hours, everyone stood in utter silence in intense spiritual concentration to remove chaos, pain, and suffering from the world. (*Jewish Telegraphic Agency Daily Bulletin*, September 14). The cover of the October issue of *Psychology Today,* devoted to "Spirituality: Why We Need It," featured a picture of Madonna, a non-Jew, who found her "spiritual light" in Kabbalah, which, she told the magazine, "is about wonderment."

By 1999 Jewish spirituality was thriving on the East Coast as well. In April, Congregation Anshe Chesed in New York hosted a three-day "Exploration of Meditation in Jewish Life." There were speakers, workshop sessions, and guided meditations. Many of the 900 participants took and kept a vow of silence over Shabbat. Then in November, it was standing room only at the Park East Synagogue, another New York congregation, for a discussion by Rabbi Shmuel Boteach, the charismatic author of *Kosher Sex,* and Deepak Chopra, the Hindu mystic, about relations between Jewish and other forms of spirituality.

Not everyone was enamoured of the turn to spirituality. For one thing, there was the suspicion that much of the material presented as Jewish spiritual teachings was nothing but pop psychology. Rabbi Adin Steinsaltz, the Israeli scholar and author of books on Jewish mysticism, complained: "I'm not averse to popularization. I'm averse to prostitution" (*New York Jewish Week*, November 19). Others had fundamental objections to the reinterpretation of Judaism in personalist terms. Bar-Ilan University political scientist Charles Liebman, for one, blamed this focus on the self for declines in Jewish philanthropy, Jewish organizational involvement, Jewish political mobilization, and the sense of Jewish peoplehood. And he warned that many of the newly "spiritual" Jews were all too likely to take their quest for personal meaning outside the bounds of Judaism and end up following other religious traditions. Liebman, in collaboration with his colleague, Bernard Susser, elaborated this thesis in a book, *Choosing Survival: Strategies for a Jewish Future.*

The convention of the (Conservative) Rabbinical Assembly in April hosted a public debate over the spirituality phenomenon in a session that featured two non-rabbis. Elliot Abrams, president of the Ethics and Policy Center, called the new trend "baloney," denied that the term "spirituality" had any concrete meaning, and charged that those promoting it were using a feel-good approach to rationalize laxity in the fulfillment of Jewish responsibilities. Countering Abrams was Rodger Kamenetz, author of *The Jew in the Lotus*. Kamenetz felt that spirituality was deeply rooted in classical Jewish tradition and wondered whether Abrams would prefer a "feel-bad" Judaism. "God forbid the synagogue becomes hostile to people with spiritual questions," he said (*New York Jewish Week,* April 30).

A number of Jewish federations, recognizing that their traditional focus on "secular" social-services failed to excite many younger Jews, moved to reconcile the new spiritual strivings with the more mundane needs of their communities. At the annual meeting of New York UJA-Federation, Executive Vice President John Ruskay, noting "the growing hunger of Jews for community and intellectual and spiritual engagement," declared that it was time for "ongoing structured partnership with our synagogues." The Jewish Federation of Greater Kansas City went so far as to reinvent itself. After an extensive series of task force meetings encompassing all the synagogues and Jewish social-service agencies, the federation, now calling itself a *kehillah*—the Hebrew term for the premodern local Jewish community—published the task force recommendations as *Covenant for a Sacred Community.*

Across the country federations that for years had stayed out of synagogue matters were now conducting consultations with local synagogues to assess their needs, and then allocating money for their programs. Several federations contributed to local congregations that were part of Synagogue 2000, a joint Reform-Conservative-Reconstructionist initiative, launched with the aid of foundation grants, that worked to revitalize the experience of worship. In November, at the General Assembly of the United Jewish Communities—the new entity that included what had been the Council of Jewish Federations, the United Jewish Appeal, and the United Israel Appeal—"Jewish Renaissance and Renewal" was named one of the organization's four "pillars," and a task force was authorized "to provide a bold and vigorous leadership for building a Jewish community permeated by Torah, *chesed* (loving-kindness), and *tsedek* (justice)."

Interest in revamping the American synagogue to address the spiritual needs of a new generation went beyond the federations. In December philanthropists Charles Bronfman, Charles Schusterman, and Michael Steinhardt announced that they were contributing considerable sums toward the formation of Synagogue Transformation and Renewal (STAR), and they hoped to attract other donors as well. The purpose of this project was, in consultation with a wide spectrum of leading rabbis, to develop and disseminate innovative ideas to make the synagogue an exciting and inspiring place.

EDUCATION, FORMAL AND INFORMAL

The debate over what priority to give Jewish day schools in the struggle for the Jewish future intensified. At the February plenum of the Jewish Council for Public Affairs—the public-policy umbrella organization that included the major na-

tional organizations and the local Jewish community-relations councils—a re
olution urging enhanced federation support for day schools was overwhelmingly
defeated. This occurred despite backing for the proposal from the Orthodox, Conservative, and Reform organizations, as well as several of the secular national Jewish bodies. The reason stated by opponents of the resolution was reluctance to
dictate allocation priorities to the federations.

In June, however, the Jewish Educational Service of North America (JESNA),
the educational arm of the federation world, announced that "No Jewish family
that desires to send its children to a Jewish day school should be prevented from
doing so due to financial reasons." While calling on federations to increase support for all forms of Jewish education, it singled out day schools for special mention. Leaders of the major federations praised the report and noted that they had
already moved substantial new sums of money into local day schools. But the
leading national force behind the drive for day-school education, George Hanus,
a Chicago businessman and founder of the National Jewish Day School Scholarship Committee, had lost patience with the federations and was targeting his
appeal directly to the Jewish grass roots. Hanus traveled across the country urging day schools to set up endowment funds and asking all Jews to leave 5 percent
of their estates to these funds. This, he argued, would provide $11 billion and
make day-school education—which he considered the only effective means of in-
culcating Jewish commitment—affordable for every Jewish child. Though skep-
tics pointed out that finances were rarely the only reason for the failure to pa-
tronize day schools, by year's end Hanus's organization was about to open offices
in five large cities, and had already contacted every rabbi in the country. The
American Jewish Committee, as well, mobilized support. At its December board
meeting AJC passed a resolution calling for a Jewish education endowment fund,
with priority to go toward the tuition of the children of Jewish communal professionals.

In the spring, results of the New York State Standard Achievement Tests, a new
and more demanding set of exams for elementary schools, were brought into the
debate over day schools. While the day-school students did better, on average, than
their counterparts in public school, there were great variations among the day
schools, and in many of them substantial percentages of students did not meet
state standards—more than half of the fourth-graders, for example, failed the
reading test. Embarrassed day-school educators explained, first of all, that in the
absence of appropriate preparation, any new kind of test was likely to yield dis-
appointing results. Also, the day schools pointed out that they were committed
to accommodating all Jewish children, including those with learning disabilities
and academic deficiencies, and therefore could not compete with the elite private
schools when it came to test scores.

But the test results had no effect on the bigger picture: Jewish day schools were
multiplying and attracting more students, while supplementary afternoon and
Sunday morning programs were in decline. A study released at the end of the year,

sponsored by the Avi Chai Foundation, found that some 185,000 students were enrolled in day schools, an increase of 25,000 since 1990. And now, in addition to the hundreds of Orthodox schools, the 70 Solomon Schechter schools (Conservative), and the 22 Reform-sponsored schools, a growing number of communities were creating nondenominational Jewish day schools. A sign of the day school's popularity was the harsh attack on it that appeared in the *Atlantic Monthly,* the prestigious magazine of culture and public affairs that had rarely, if ever, addressed Jewish communal concerns before. Writing in the October issue, Peter Beinart worried that the growing popularity of Jewish day schools could threaten the public school system (the proportion of Jewish children in the public schools, he noted, had declined to 65 percent from 90 percent in 1962) because it might lead Jewish organizations to support government vouchers for private education. And he darkly suggested that Jewish unwillingness to make use of the public schools might be taken by Christians as a reluctance to integrate into American society. But Professor Jack Wertheimer, provost of the Jewish Theological Seminary, countered in *Commentary* (December) that "the real danger is of a precisely opposite sort: not that American Jews will stand too much apart but that they will disappear," and to this problem, "dual-curriculum day schools offer a unique solution." Rejecting Beinart's fear of how non-Jews might react, Wertheimer harshly criticized the JCPA's continuing opposition, in the name of the Jewish community, to government vouchers for nonpublic education.

Another widely touted strategy for Jewish continuity was the promotion of trips to Israel for young American Jews. In November 1998 a small group of philanthropists led by Michael Steinhardt and Charles Bronfman had launched Birthright Israel, aimed at ensuring that every Jew between the ages of 15 and 26 would have, as a "birthright" and at no personal expense, a round-trip ticket and ten days in Israel. The philanthropists entered into negotiations with the Israeli government and with American federations to get their cooperation in securing the $60 million the program would need each year. Critics contended that such a short stay in Israel, with no set program and no preparation or follow-up, would have little effect, and would, indeed, divert money that could be better used by the day schools. But proponents of Birthright Israel argued that the ten-day trip would whet the appetite of marginally affiliated young Jews for longer and more intense Israel experiences. The government of Israel pledged to match the contributions of the American philanthropists, though the federations remained reluctant to commit themselves to a project conceived and planned by others.

By the summer of 1999 Birthright Israel had narrowed its immediate focus to sending some 6,000 college students to Israel during the coming winter break, through existing programs for young people run by Hillel and other organizations. To qualify, students must never have been to Israel on an organized tour before. Despite fears of a lack of interest that stimulated Birthright Israel to launch a $3-million media campaign in college newspapers, the response was overwhelming, far greater than anticipated, and many had to be turned away. On some campuses

Hillel held lotteries to choose who would go. "American Jewry will not be the same in February after the participants return home," predicted Richard Joel, president and international director of Hillel.

"Informal" Jewish education—Jewish programming of a recreational nature in the U.S.—was also touted as an aid to Jewish identity. Thus the Jewish Community Centers Association of North America issued a press release on July 2 announcing: "JCC Teens Ahead of Peers in Avoiding the Pitfalls of Assimilation." This claim was based on a survey of 940 American Jewish participants in the 1998 JCC Maccabi Games in Israel, which showed that the rates of synagogue membership, youth-group involvement, and Jewish identification were far higher for these young JCC athletes than for Jews the same age who were not JCC members. Jewish summer camps, attended by some 30,000 young Jews each year, were now being helped by the Foundation for Jewish Camping, which distributed its initial $200,000 in grants in 1999. Part of the money went toward planning new camps near growing Jewish communities, and the rest toward enhancing the offerings of existing camps. The foundation also funded a study of Jewish camping, in conjunction with the Institute for Jewish and Communal Research, that found a strong relationship between camp attendance as a child and subsequent Jewish affiliation and observance as an adult.

Offering an entirely different approach to developing the Jewish consciousness of young people was Makor, which opened in October on New York City's West Side. This project, sponsored by the Partnership for Jewish Life, was funded by an $11-million gift from philanthropist Michael Steinhardt. Makor sought to attract secular, unaffiliated "Generation Xers" with avant-garde educational, social, recreational, artistic, and musical programs. While some who attended certain Makor activities reported that there was nothing recognizably Jewish about them—and that a good many non-Jews attended the events, unaware that this was a Jewish operation—Makor also housed a kosher cafeteria with Sabbath dinners, and offered lectures and films on Jewish topics. The challenge facing Makor was somehow to get those who came to enjoy a jazz concert to develop a similar enjoyment of things Jewish.

INTERMARRIAGE AND THE NUMBERS GAME

Anxieties about intermarriage abounded. Still reeling from the 52-percent rate found in the 1990 National Jewish Population Survey and unsure whether the phenomenon had peaked or accelerated since, American Jewish leaders wondered whether the community was about to experience massive demographic erosion. New evidence that such erosion was likely came in a study, "Children of Intermarriage: How 'Jewish'?" by Professor Bruce Phillips of Hebrew Union College, which appeared in *Studies in Contemporary Jewry*. Phillips found that 34 percent of the children of intermarriage were being raised as Christians and only 18 percent as Jews, while 25 percent were being raised in both faiths. Furthermore, over two-thirds of the offspring of intermarriage who had married, had non-Jewish spouses. It was, then, hardly a surprise to read on the front page of the *New York Times* (December 7) that greeting-card companies were now producing millions of syncretistic "interfaith" cards for the holiday season that melded Christmas, Hanukkah, and even Kwanzaa symbols. A sample accompanied the article: a picture of a reindeer whose eight-branched antlers contained lit candles.

Many synagogues, especially those affiliated with Reform and Reconstructionism, had for some time been conducting aggressive outreach to intermarried families, hoping that making them feel at home and giving them spiritual sustenance would induce the parents to raise their children in Judaism even in the absence of conversion. In April, Hillel of Greater Philadelphia, with the support of several foundations, hosted 20 college-age children of such families for a conference at Haverford College. At least for these participants, who considered themselves Jewish, the outreach policy was working. But the overall national trend toward loss of Jewish identity in such families indicated that the old methods were inadequate.

The Jewish Outreach Institute, which had long argued for a far more aggressive strategy to win over the intermarried to Judaism, released a study by Israeli demographers Sergio DellaPergola and Uzi Rebhun indicating that low birth rates and assimilation were likely to shrink the size of American Jewry over the next century even if all intermarriage ceased. On the other hand, the community would grow even with a high intermarriage rate, if a large percentage of the intermarried identified Jewishly. According to the institute's interpretation of the data, lingering communal opposition to intermarriage should be replaced by outreach on a massive scale.

More far-reaching was the thesis of demographer Gary Tobin, whose book, *Opening the Gates: How Proactive Conversion Can Revitalize the Jewish Community*, dismissed the angst over intermarriage as irrelevant and called for a campaign to triple the number of American Jews by converting non-Jews to Judaism. The plan, which Tobin estimated would cost billions of dollars, would also have another benefit, he said. By bringing in many blacks, Hispanics, and Asian Americans, it would make the Jewish community more ethnically diverse and therefore more integrated into American society. (Filmmaker Steven Spielberg, it appeared, was already funding a study of non-white American Jews). In a separate study, Tobin buttressed his argument with the charge that current synagogue outreach efforts had failed. On the basis of in-depth interviews with 30 rabbis, Tobin concluded that rabbis felt overwhelmed by, and unable to cope with, the challenge of intermarriage. Critics, however, faulted Tobin for seeking to expend resources on bringing outsiders into Judaism at a time when so many Jews were at risk to leave. Dr. Steven Bayme of the American Jewish Committee told the *Forward* (May 14): "You won't be able to make up for current losses by bringing in a new crew."

Meanwhile, demographers—allocated $3.5 million by private donors and local federations—were preparing the questions for the next National Jewish Population Survey, scheduled for the year 2000. A March 5 draft of the proposed questions, leaked to the press, showed the impact of the high intermarriage rate found in 1990. Many of the items probed issues of Jewish identity—for example, whether the respondent read Jewish books, went to Jewish movies, or had been involved in outreach programs—questions clearly geared to gauging whether the Jewish continuity programs launched in the 1990s had had any effect. This emphasis, in turn, meant fewer questions about traditional priorities such as social-service needs and perceptions of anti-Semitism. Trouble surfaced, however, from two sources. The Orthodox, who suspected that they had been undercounted in 1990, insisted that no telephone interviews be conducted for the 2000 study on Sabbaths and Jewish holidays, since Orthodox Jews would not answer the phone on these days. While this would add to both the time and the cost of the survey, top UJC officials acceded to the Orthodox request in October. More ominous was a ten-page letter from five well-known demographers and sociologists to the UJC leadership charging that the proposed survey was a waste of money because it would collect a lot of useless information without providing answers to questions the community needed to know to plan for the future. The letter was sent in August but did not become public till late September. It was not clear what role personal and professional jealousies played in this contretemps. On December 7 the UJC announced that the population survey, scheduled to begin phone interviews in January, would be postponed "in order to ensure full consideration by its recently appointed top leadership." (See below, pp. 244–45.)

HOLOCAUST AS SYMBOL

The memory of the Holocaust, which had become an increasingly central component of American Jewish identity even as the event itself faded into historical memory, took on, in 1999, a political and cultural significance that evoked controversy within the Jewish community and beyond.

By 1999 the international uproar and consequent hardball negotiations over what was owed survivors by numerous European governments, banks, insurance companies, and businesses had resulted in several monetary settlements yielding billions of dollars, with the prospect of more to come. Indeed, a 20-member U.S. presidential commission, chaired by World Jewish Congress president Edgar Bronfman, charged with the task of tracking down the assets of Holocaust victims that had ended up in the possession of American state governments, held its first meeting in March. But the Jewish community itself was roiled by conflicts over how the money should be divided, whether primarily as cash payments to individual survivors and their heirs, or with substantial sums set aside in the form of pooled funds to provide health care for elderly survivors and/or Holocaust educational projects. Most controversial was the question of compensation for the lawyers who had initiated the class-action lawsuits that had ultimately led to the payments. Many of those involved, most notably the World Jewish Congress, which had led the negotiations with the foreign governments and institutions, felt that the standard practice of lawyers charging a set percentage of the settlement amount was unconscionable in this instance since it would deprive the survivors of needed funds. They suggested instead that the lawyers charge a reasonable hourly rate, and only for the time actually spent on the litigation. But in the settlement of the case of the Swiss banks in December before a U.S. district judge in Brooklyn, the class-action lawyers resisted submitting their time sheets for examination on the grounds that the defendants—the banks—might use the information to challenge the decision.

In a televised address to the nation on March 24, President Clinton explained why the planes of the U.S. and its NATO allies were bombing Serb targets in Kosovo. Forcing a halt to attacks on ethnic Albanians, he said, was an application of the lessons of World War II: "Just imagine if leaders back then had acted wisely and early enough, how many lives could have been saved?" Using the same rationale, Jewish groups enthusiastically endorsed the bombings, their full-page newspaper ads soliciting aid for the refugees evoking memories of the Hitler years. American Jewish World Service announced, "Once again, there's a reason to remember" (*Forward,* April 16), while the Anti-Defamation League urged: "Respond as you wish the world had responded the last time" (*New York Jewish Week,* April 16). Both appended pictures of Kosovar refugees packed into trains. And a month later (May 13), with Serb forces still not defeated, several prominent Jewish leaders signed on to a *New York Times* ad calling for the use of ground troops and the indictment of the president of Yugoslavia for war crimes. The most distinguished Jewish proponent of NATO action was author Elie Wiesel, winner of the Nobel Peace Prize and identified in the *New York Times* (June 2) as "a Holocaust survivor and moral philosopher." Delivering a lecture at the White House on April 12, Wiesel backed the policy of the administration, saying, "This time the world was not silent. This time we did respond." Supporting the air strikes as part of a "moral war" even while acknowledging that Serb policies were not on the scale of Hitler's, Wiesel went on a highly publicized three-day tour of refugee camps in Macedonia and Albania at the beginning of June, at the president's request.

Yet there were nagging doubts—outside the Jewish organizational and Holocaust-survivor networks—over the use of Holocaust metaphors to seek to foreclose debate over the administration's policy in the Balkans. Historian Tony Judt worried, in the *New Republic,* that "The Holocaust is now ubiquitous in American pedagogy and conversation. . . . It is sufficient to name the reference to have made the case." And Henry Kissinger expressed his distaste for "the appalling, oozing self-righteousness."

The conflict over what constituted legitimate use of Holocaust imagery, in fact, went beyond the specific case of Kosovo. In recent years the Holocaust had been subjected to analysis from the standpoints of various contemporary social causes, among them feminism, gay rights, environmentalism, and even scientology. One professor, for example, published an article in 1999 arguing that, had Anne Frank lived, she would have been a lesbian. Gabriel Schoenfeld, a senior editor at *Commentary,* was himself accused of Holocaust denial when he took the lead in publicizing and criticizing such uses of the Holocaust.

Another phenomenon that many found disturbing was the film industry's recent tendency to portray the Holocaust through the lens of comedy. If *the* Holocaust movie of 1998 was the Oscar-winning Italian film "Life is Beautiful," in which a father convinces his son that life in a concentration camp is all a game, its counterpart in 1999 was Columbia Pictures' "Jakob the Liar," starring famed comic actor Robin Williams, in which the residents of a Polish ghetto under Nazi rule have their morale buoyed by the optimistic lies of Jakob, who claims to know about the progress of the war from a nonexistent radio.

How the very consciousness of a "Holocaust" had developed in the U.S. was subjected to searching analysis by historian Peter Novick in *The Holocaust in American Life,* which appeared in 1999. Novick argued that at least since the 1970s Jewish leaders had invoked the memory of the Holocaust as a way of shutting off criticism of Israeli policies and maintaining Jewish identity among the young. That, he noted, was why so many Jews insisted that the Nazi destruction of European Jewry was a unique event and the Jews a distinctively "victimized" people. Critics generally praised the book's painstaking research and accepted its thesis that "Holocaust consciousness" had been socially constructed. But many also pointed out that Novick's own evident distaste for the idea of Jewish distinctiveness and his commitment to a universalistic political agenda gave the book a polemical edge that diminished its value as history.

The institution most clearly and officially associated with America's consciousness of the Holocaust was the U.S. Holocaust Memorial Museum. Dogged by controversy in 1998, it continued to encounter problems in 1999. In February, Sara Bloomfield, the acting executive director, was named to the permanent post, which had been vacant for almost a year. A primary reason for the delay in the appointment, and, indeed, a major cause of the museum's difficulties for some time, was the question of whether the Holocaust would be presented primarily as an experience undergone by the Jewish people, or, in keeping with the institution's government sponsorship, its message would be more universalistic, stressing the evil inherent in all bigotry and hate.

August was a bad month for the museum. At a book signing and forum it held for the authors of a new book, *Crimes of War: What the Public Should Know,* some who perused the volume noticed that it accused the State of Israel of serious war crimes including "ethnic cleansing." The museum then disavowed its own press release that had called the book "of landmark importance," and Miles Lerman, chairman of the museum's governing council, said that he had not read the book before the event. But worse was soon to come: A congressionally mandated report prepared by outside management experts severely criticized the museum.

While acknowledging that it had achieved great success in drawing more than 12 million visitors in its six years of existence, the report found "a lack of professionalism" in the governance of the museum, the result of excessive control wielded by a tiny group of lay leaders. "They're running the place like a Jewish organization," commented the chairman of the panel issuing the report—himself a former commissioner of the Internal Revenue Service. While the museum's leadership acknowledged the criticism and said that plans were already in place to rectify the administrative problems, one comment in the report once again raised the Jewish-universalistic tension inherent in a federally sponsored Holocaust museum: There was, according to the investigators, "inadequate representation of non-Jews in general and of African-Americans and Latinos in particular" on the governing council.

In the area of Holocaust education, filmmaker Steven Spielberg announced that his Shoah Visual History Foundation had achieved its goal of recording the personal testimonies of over 50,000 Holocaust survivors. The next step was to index and digitize the multimedia collection so that it could be accessed on line at major Holocaust museums in the U.S. and Israel, and, later on, at universities. A CD-ROM using material from four of the interviews was already a popular teaching tool at many high schools.

Denominational Developments

REFORM JUDAISM

Reform expanded institutionally in 1999 with the announcement on February 15 that Hebrew Union College's Los Angeles school would start offering a full rabbinical program, culminating in ordination. Like the similar step taken by the Conservative movement in 1995, the initiation of a full-blown Reform seminary in Los Angeles signaled the emergence of the West Coast as a major center of Jewish life. It was also expected to help alleviate the drastic shortage of rabbis in the Reform movement. Plans for expansion overseas were announced in December, when the Union of American Hebrew Congregations (UAHC) launched a $50 million fund-raising drive to strengthen the Reform presence in Israel and the former Soviet Union.

Internally, the Reform movement continued to be buffeted by two forces that often seemed contradictory: the impulse to nonjudgmental openness, on the one hand, and greater interest in tradition and ritual, on the other.

Reform openness was on display at a three-day UAHC symposium in April on "Expanding the Covenant: Fulfilling the Mitzvah of Keruv." This event celebrated 20 years since Reform launched its programs to reach out to the religiously unaffiliated—essentially, the non-Jewish spouses in intermarriages. In his keynote address, UAHC president Rabbi Eric Yoffie acknowledged that the two decades of Reform outreach, while a "triumph," had fallen short of expectations: non-Jewish spouses of Jews were rarely asked to convert; Reform nursery schools provided meager Jewish content; and there was no consensus on the degree to which non-Jewish spouses might participate in synagogue services. He urged the movement to address these shortcomings through reinvigorated outreach. While Yoffie did not want "a lowest-common-denominator/no-one-must-ever-be-hurt Judaism," he insisted that setting up barriers—as, he charged, the Conservative movement had done in barring intermarried Jews from leadership positions—was counterproductive. And Yoffie firmly restated Reform's commitment to the controversial patrilineal position, which, contrary to classical Jewish law, held that the child of one Jewish parent, mother or father, might be considered Jewish.

At the same time, ritual practice was on the upswing within Reform, partly due to greater interest in spirituality among younger Reform Jews but also because of the heavy influx into the movement of Jews raised in the traditional branches of Judaism, who felt comfortable with ritual. Not only were such practices as praying in Hebrew with a head covering and prayer shawl, and celebrating Rosh Hashanah for two days, on the rise, but the kosher laws were also being taken more seriously than ever, and not just in private homes. In planning a new Reform summer camp in Ontario, Canada, which would be patronized by many campers from the U.S., the UAHC decided it would serve only kosher food. This was the first time that any Reform camp in North America had ever gone kosher.

But Reform interest in ritual was far from universal. The proposed new platform for Reform Judaism, whose first draft, prepared by Central Conference of American Rabbis (CCAR) president Richard Levy, was circulated in 1998, came under heavy criticism that continued into 1999. Seeking to reorient the movement toward greater Jewish traditionalism, the original version of the platform not only asserted that "the mitzvot (commandments) of the Torah"—not modern values—were at the center of Judaism, but actually spelled out some of those mitzvot as viable options for Reform Jews, including the kosher laws, Sabbath observance, and immersion in the *mikveh* (ritual bath). For those raised in the tradition of Classical Reform, which stressed ethics rather than ritual, it seemed as if their religion was being swept out from under them, replaced by another sort of Judaism that seemed to differ little from Conservatism. For many younger Reform rabbis, however, who tended to be more traditional than their older colleagues and their own congregations, the new manifesto struck a welcome note.

Inevitably, Levy's draft went through numerous revisions that moderated its radicalism. By May 26, 1999, the sixth version of the text was ready for consideration by the CCAR at its annual convention in Pittsburgh (the same city where, in 1885, that body had officially repudiated Jewish law and ritual). By now, however, the references to mitzvot that had so upset many Reform Jews in the original platform were restricted to Sabbath and the holidays, and even these did not mention any specific practices.

The platform that passed by 324-68 asserted "God, Torah and Israel" as the central tenets of Judaism, balancing this affirmation with an acknowledgement of "the diversity of Reform Jewish beliefs and practices." Torah, identified as "the foundation of Jewish life," called on Jews to study the mitzvot, "the means by which we make our lives holy." Some of those mitzvot, the platform continued, "demand renewed attention": the Sabbath brings holiness and rest to the end of the work week, the High Holy Days "call us to account for our deeds," the festivals give Jews the opportunity "to celebrate with joy" the Jewish "religious journey," and days of remembrance "remind us of the tragedies and the triumphs" of the Jewish historical experience. The platform went on to address the traditional Reform concern with ethics, social action, and world peace. In the context of "love for the Jewish people," it endorsed "religious and cultural pluralism" in Jewish communal life, and welcomed converts, the intermarried, and those of any sexual orientation. Endorsing "a vision" of a State of Israel that gave equal rights to all and sought peace with its neighbors, the platform urged American Jews to learn Hebrew and visit Israel, even as Israeli Jews should "learn from the religious life of Diaspora Jewish communities."

When the overwhelmingly affirmative vote was announced the platform's proponents cheered and sang, while Rabbi Levy got the last pro and con speakers to stand together at the rostrum in a show of unity. But observers differed over the broader meaning of the vote. The reporters who covered the convention for the *New York Times* (May 27) portrayed the statement of principles as a turning point for encouraging the observance of rituals that Reform's founders had discarded. Similarly, *Time* magazine (June 7) headlined its story "Back to the Yarmulke," and a *New York* magazine headline (June 21) cynically quipped that "attendance at Woody Allen films no longer qualifies as religious observance." But the Jewish media, with far greater accuracy, stressed just how much the platform had had to be watered down to gain passage. In fact the reporter for the *New York Jewish Week* (May 28) judged the situation just the opposite from the *New York Times*, calling the platform "a victory for the classical wing of the movement, which rejected attempts by Reform leaders to inject more tradition and observance into daily practice." In the same spirit, Rabbi Yoffie, president of the UAHC, the lay arm of the movement, sent letters to Reform lay leaders urging them to ignore the exaggerated media reports about a revolution in their movement and to read the actual text of the new principles instead.

Among the rabbis themselves there turned out to be little enthusiasm for a compromise platform that many called pareve—the Yiddish word for food that is neither milk nor meat. None could say with any degree of assurance what would follow for the movement. Speculation ran the gamut from assertions that the platform would be ignored, to Rabbi Lance Sussman's suggestion that it might generate a "neoclassical counter-movement" (*Congress Monthly*, July–August), to Rabbi Arnold Jacob Wolf's declaration that "the old Reform Judaism is dead: a new post-Reform is struggling to be born" (*Judaism*, Summer).

The biennial convention of the UAHC, held in December, focused on the renewal of prayer in the Reform movement. In his Sabbath sermon, Rabbi Yoffie used the word "revolution" to describe what was necessary. Charging that prayer had become little more than a "tedious, predictable and dull" spectator sport in many Reform temples, Yoffie urged the laity to study the meaning and theology of the liturgy, improve Hebrew literacy, and participate in a movement-wide dialogue to make prayer an expression of joy and enthusiasm. In stressing the reinvigoration of worship, Yoffie was tapping into the widespread search for spirituality in his movement. Yoffie's address was repeatedly interrupted by applause, and his initiative was endorsed by acclamation. In addition, small workshop sessions at the convention on the topic of prayer, as well as the prayer services themselves, drew overflow crowds, in contrast to workshops on public-policy matters, such as social action and Israel. In line with the new thrust of the movement, plans were announced for a revamped Reform prayer book, projected for release in 2005, that would incorporate many of the traditional prayers that Classical Reform had discarded, but would, at the same time, reflect the concerns of contemporary feminism.

CONSERVATIVE JUDAISM

Conservative Judaism, like Reform, continued to be buffeted by the conflicting forces of tradition and openness. But the Conservative commitment to the discipline of Jewish law—however liberally interpreted—made its struggle to maintain a balance considerably more difficult.

The relatively low levels of religious observance among the Conservative laity—bemoaned for years by movement leaders—came into even sharper relief when contrasted with the steadily rising observance patterns of the younger Conservative rabbis. So religiously estranged had these rabbis become from the movement's congregations that, in 1999, more than half of the new Conservative rabbinical graduates were not interested in taking pulpits, fearing that the typical Conservative synagogue would not provide them with a congenially observant community. They preferred, instead, to go into teaching or counseling.

In 1998, seeking to raise religious standards, the Committee on Law and Standards of Conservative Judaism had declared that intermarried Jews should not hold professional positions that might make them religious role models, such as Hebrew-school principals and teachers, and youth-group leaders. In 1999 the United Synagogue of Conservative Judaism, the movement's congregational body, sought to elevate the standards for lay leaders as well. Rabbi Jerome Epstein, executive vice president of the United Synagogue, explained: "The synagogue is not simply a Jewish organization. It is not merely a club to which people belong for Jewish identification. The synagogue is mandated to challenge its members toward Jewish growth" (*Forward,* March 12). In September the United Synagogue issued a pamphlet setting forth "eight behavioral expectations" for those wishing to serve on its governing boards. While no specific rituals were required, the "expectations" included praying, if at all possible, with a minyan, studying Torah at least one hour a week, deciding to be guided by Jewish tradition even in opposition to one's personal inclination, adding the performance of three new mitzvot each year, helping to repair the world through charitable activity, strengthening ties with Israel, and learning Hebrew.

But the drive for greater traditionalism aroused a storm of protest since the reality in many Conservative synagogues was far removed from the suggested standards, especially outside the New York area. From the perspective of nonobservant and intermarried families belonging to Conservative congregations, "higher standards" could very well send signals of exclusion and rejection.

A nonexclusionary, and therefore uncontroversial, initiative to upgrade the Judaic competence of the Conservative laity was the United Synagogue's *Perek Yomi* (chapter a day) program, inspired by the success of *Daf Yomi* (page a day) of Talmud study in the Orthodox community. Beginning on the holiday of Simhat Torah in October, participants—either individuals or synagogue groups—studied one chapter of the Bible per day, beginning with the Book of Joshua. The goal was to cover all of the Prophets and the Writings by early 2001. The United Synagogue provided study guides and set up a Web site to facilitate the project.

If greater observance and Jewish knowledge was the battle cry of Conservative traditionalists, whose power base lay in the leadership of the United Synagogue, gay rights was the leading cause of those advocating inclusion. These advocates, ironically, were primarily rabbinical students, who combined high levels of ritual practice with a commitment to the elimination of barriers to gays and lesbians. In January, 25 students at the Jewish Theological Seminary, the Conservative rabbinical school in New York, petitioned Chancellor Ismar Schorsch for an end to the policy of not admitting known gays and lesbians to the rabbinical program. This JTS regulation had been instituted to enforce the movement's 1992 decision against the ordination of homosexual rabbis. At a discussion forum with students on March 23 that the students described as "heated," Schorsch argued that homosexuality was explicitly prohibited in the Torah, that ordaining gay rabbis would make it harder to gain recognition for the Conservative movement in Israel, and that there was little demand within the Conservative rabbinate for a change in policy. Some rabbis sympathetic to gay rights did seek to raise the matter at the April meeting of the movement's Rabbinical Assembly, but the meeting adjourned without addressing the issue. In May JTS students—many wearing gay-pride symbols—conducted a lunchtime study session dedicated to a fundamental reconsideration of gay and lesbian rights in Judaism. A few faculty members also participated.

Signs of another potential conflict between traditional and innovative forces developed at the November convention of the United Synagogue where a preliminary draft of a new Conservative Torah commentary—the final version of which would be published in 2001—was unveiled. In contrast to the classic Hertz commentary of the 1930s that it was intended to replace, the new one would incorporate the findings of contemporary Bible scholarship even when at odds with the traditional understanding of the text, interpret Scripture from a strongly feminist perspective, and note instances where the Conservative movement had altered biblical law in accordance with modern sensibilities.

RECONSTRUCTIONIST JUDAISM

Though still much smaller than the three major Jewish denominations, in 1999 Reconstructionism could boast 98 congregations and some 50,000 adherents in the United States, roughly 2 percent of religiously affiliated American Jews.

In August, in time for Rosh Hashanah, the Jewish Reconstructionist Federation released a prayer book for the High Holy Days. This was the sixth and final volume in a new series of Reconstructionist prayer books, called *Kol Haneshama* (Voice of the Soul), that covered the cycle of the Jewish year, replacing earlier versions written a half-century before. Like the others in this series, the volume for the High Holy Days reflected Reconstructionism's interest in pluralism, active participation, experimentation, and contemporary relevance. The English translation was gender-neutral. Three separate versions of the services were presented, one relatively traditional, a second designed to be innovative, and a third heavily oriented to English readings. Those readings included not only translations from the classical Hebrew texts but also selections from modern Jewish and non-Jewish writers. Such inclusiveness did not make for convenience: The book was 1,275 pages long and weighed 2.75 pounds.

ORTHODOX JUDAISM

The changeover in the leadership of Agudath Israel that occurred in 1998 marked a significant shift in the evolution of separatist Orthodoxy in the U.S. Rabbi Yaakov Perlow, the new head of the organization, explained his approach at the annual convention of Agudath Israel in November 1999. There would be no surrender on matters of religious principle, such as the insistence that Orthodoxy, as interpreted by sectarian rabbis, was the only valid form of Judaism. Yet, Rabbi Perlow went on, Orthodoxy, "no longer poor and shaky," was now secure enough to relax its fortress mentality and project "love and friendship" toward those outside the group. Thus earlier in the year, when the Reform movement issued its new, more traditional, platform, Rabbi Perlow publicly rejected the impulse to treat the principles with "cynicism." On the contrary, wrote Perlow, the Reform principles should be seen as "a new stirring in the hearts of Jews that deserves our attention and reflection" (*Jewish Observer*, Summer).

Agudath Israel also demonstrated a new willingness to recognize problems within the sectarian community that had previously been ignored or minimized on the assumption that its members were insulated from the temptations of the open society. At an Agudath Israel-sponsored conference in April in New York

City on "The Interface of Ethics and Halakhah in the Business and Professional World," a number of speakers, including Rabbi Perlow, called on Orthodoxy to face up to—and not rationalize or excuse—incidents of financial dishonesty and outright crime committed by Orthodox Jews. Also, rabbis and educators began to speak openly of teenage yeshivah "dropouts" who, like their counterparts outside Orthodoxy, were falling into delinquency, rejecting religion, and joining the drug culture. As investigative reports about the situation in Baltimore and New York were appearing in the Anglo-Jewish press (*Baltimore Jewish Times,* November 12, *New York Jewish Week,* December 10), Agudath Israel devoted the entire November issue of the *Jewish Observer,* its monthly magazine, to the problem. A number of the articles recommended changes in Orthodox attitudes, such as a greater willingness to consult professional counselors and therapists, allowing more leeway for the individual child's particular talents and emotional needs, eliminating corporal punishment, and reconsidering the prevalent assumption that a year of study in an Israeli yeshivah would cure behavioral problems.

If sectarian Orthodoxy was starting to see that limiting contact with contemporary culture did not necessarily protect the faithful, modern Orthodox Jews, who were, on principle, committed to combining tradition and modernity, faced a different problem. These Jews—described in a front-page *New York Times* story (September 16) as having their business lunches at "haute cuisine restaurants," and praying, on the Sabbath, in their Orthodox synagogues while their children played with Pokémon cards in the lobby—lacked clear guidelines as to which elements of American culture were compatible with Orthodoxy and which were not.

Nothing better illustrated the tensions of participating simultaneously in these two worlds than the well-publicized odyssey of 17-year-old Tamir Goodman. A basketball sensation at the tiny Talmudical Academy of Baltimore where he was a high-school junior, Goodman reached a verbal agreement in January with the University of Maryland that upon graduation he would receive an athletic scholarship and join the basketball team, which was ranked fourth in the nation. To accommodate Goodman's religious needs, the university said it would seek to avoid scheduling games on the Jewish Sabbath. But what seemed at the time to be a modern Orthodox success story proving that you could "have it all," disintegrated in September. First, Goodman, seeking more serious competition, left the academy and transferred to a Seventh Day Adventist school (where he could keep the Sabbath) for his senior year. Then Maryland backed away from its verbal agreement—according to Goodman's parents, because of the Sabbath issue. It was now unlikely that the young man would fulfill the modern Orthodox dream of a skullcap-wearing basketball star on a major college team.

For years the growth of sectarian Orthodoxy had put the modernists on the defensive, making many modern Orthodox Jews suspect that their own religious behavior was inconsistent and even inauthentic. The influence of sectarian teachers in the Orthodox day schools on youngsters from modern Orthodox homes reinforced the challenge to these families' religious morale. As historian Jack Wertheimer noted: "Modern Orthodox parents have come to expect that their children will reject at least certain aspects of their own outlook on life, and cannot even be certain that they will choose to attend a secular university, or pursue careers requiring advanced study" (*Commentary*, February).

It was to combat this malaise that Edah—an organization founded in 1996 under the slogan, "The courage to be modern and Orthodox"—sponsored a major conference entitled "Orthodoxy Confronts a Changing World," on February 14–15 in New York City. Some 1,500 gathered for the event, twice as many as expected. Especially noteworthy was the presence of over 200 college students, an indication that the sectarian impact on modern Orthodox education had not completely extinguished the modernist impulse.

In his keynote address, Rabbi Saul Berman, director of Edah, argued that Orthodox engagement with the contemporary world benefited both the general society and Orthodoxy. Values inherent in Jewish religious texts, he said, could improve society, and, conversely, the insights of contemporary culture could help Orthodox Jews see their own tradition in a new light—as, for example, in enhancing the role of women. In fact, the place of women in Orthodox life was the single most pervasive topic discussed at the sessions, and in that sense the conference could be seen as a follow-up to the two conferences on Orthodoxy and feminism that took place in 1997 and 1998. But the Edah conference also included sessions devoted to the other issues confronting Orthodox Jews who sought to remain open to outside cultural influences, such as the religious significance of the State of Israel, modern critical study of Scripture, the conflict between personal autonomy and rabbinical authority, relations with non-Orthodox movements, the compatibility of democracy and Orthodoxy, and maintaining the modern Orthodox approach in day-school education.

Although the Edah conference marked the first time in many years that modern Orthodoxy had asserted itself intellectually, the organizations and leaders of modern Orthodoxy—sensitive to the inevitable criticism from sectarians and concerned over institutional prerogatives—reacted with discomfort. Rabbi Berman and a few of the other speakers at the conference taught at Yeshiva University (YU), the flagship modern Orthodox educational institution, but no member of the Yeshiva rabbinical school faculty would have anything to do with the conference. One YU Talmud professor, Rabbi Moses Tendler, declared the participants "outside the pale of Judaism" and said that any rabbi attending was committing a sin. YU president Dr. Norman Lamm, who for years had been the most articulate voice in the modern Orthodox camp, publicly disassociated his institution from Tendler's remark. Yet while he said that he had no "major objection to the substance of the conference," Lamm stayed away because he felt that Edah threatened to splinter the Orthodox community (*New York Jewish Week*, February 12). He arranged, however, for his writings to be distributed at the conference. Dr. Mandell Ganchrow, president of the Union of Orthodox Jewish Congregations of America (Orthodox Union), echoed Lamm in charging Edah with promoting Orthodox fragmentation. And the Rabbinical Council of America, the body representing modern Orthodox rabbis, advised young rabbis asking for guidance not to attend the Edah event.

In the immediate aftermath of the conference sociologist Samuel Heilman, one of the presenters, warned that if it "was only a one-time feel-good gathering it will at best be a small footnote to contemporary Jewish life, the bright blast before the light burns out" (*New York Jewish Week*, February 26). The conference announced the formation of two task forces—one on alleviating the plight of women whose husbands refused to give them Jewish divorces, the other on modern Orthodox education—and there was some talk of convening regional conferences in other parts of the country.

One of Edah's priorities—promoting a distinctively modern Orthodox system of day-school education—was quickly co-opted by YU. In May, Yeshiva University announced the establishment of an Association for Modern Orthodox Day Schools in North America, and it held its founding conference October 31–November 1. In contrast to Torah Umesorah, the leading existing Orthodox day-school organization, which had become increasingly sectarian, the new group hoped to attract schools espousing a positive approach to secular knowledge, a devotion to religious Zionism, and a commitment to the serious Jewish education of both boys and girls.

In December Rabbi Saul Berman, the Edah director, and Rabbi Avi Weiss announced plans to open a new modern Orthodox rabbinical seminary in September 2000 at a synagogue near Columbia University. This move, a clear challenge to YU's monopoly on modern Orthodox rabbinical training, was another signal of growing dissatisfaction in modern Orthodox circles with Yeshiva's perceived abandonment of its old openness to modernity.

CHABAD-LUBAVITCH

June 17 marked the fifth anniversary of the death of Rabbi Menachem M. Schneerson, the leader of the Lubavitch Hassidic sect, who, from his headquarters in Brooklyn, New York, had guided the movement for 44 years and made it a prominent force in Jewish life around the world. Thousands commemorated the day with visits to his grave. The childless rabbi had not named a successor, and there was still no candidate on the horizon. Yet despite predictions by outsiders that the movement would wither without a charismatic leader, Lubavitch outreach efforts continued to grow—roughly 100 new institutions were opened each year—thanks to the efforts of a small central bureaucracy in Brooklyn and some 2,000 dedicated emissaries posted in 107 countries. For them, the religious discourses of their late leader, available in writing and on videotape, were sufficient inspiration. Epitomizing the health of the movement were the opening of a $2 million center in Washington, D.C., to coordinate Lubavitch's diplomatic and legislative operations, and a $19.5 million Jewish Children's Museum—the first ever in the U.S.—in Brooklyn.

Yet ongoing friction over messianic elements within Lubavitch cast a pall over the movement's future. An unknown number of adherents continued to deny that their leader had actually died, and expected his imminent reappearance as the messiah. Some went so far as to pray to him as God. Mainstream Lubavitch leaders tended to downplay the significance of the messianists and predicted that they would gradually moderate their views. But some scholars outside Lubavitch, citing early Christianity and the 17th-century messianic movement of Sabbetai Zvi as precedents, suggested that, over time, the messianists could very well split off entirely from Judaism.

DENOMINATIONAL RELATIONS

Only once during 1999 did the heads of rabbinical seminaries of all the movements sign on to a joint statement, and, significantly, it dealt with an external threat to Judaism. In a letter dated November 8, Presidents Norman Lamm of Yeshiva University, Sheldon Zimmerman of Hebrew Union College, and David Teutsch of the Reconstructionist Rabbinical College, and Chancellor Ismar Schorsch of the Jewish Theological Seminary, denounced the "deceptive tactics" used by the Southern Baptist Convention to seek to make Jews believe that one can be both a Jew and a Christian.

Some steps were taken during the year to improve relations between the Jewish religious movements. The North American Boards of Rabbis (NABOR), which first convened in 1998, held a national meeting in Washington in February. Representing 25 local boards of rabbis around the country, and led by its president, Rabbi Marc Schneier, NABOR was intended to take the place of the Synagogue Council of America, the interdenominational body that, weakened by the reluctance of Orthodox rabbis to participate, had disbanded in 1995 due to lack of funds. Schneier, himself Orthodox, emphasized that "in light of the current state of divisiveness and polarization within the Jewish community, boards of rabbis can play a significant role in finding common ground." Jewish philanthropists had contributed enough money to keep NABOR operating for two more years. The existing rabbinical organizations of the Orthodox, Conservative, and Reform movements, however, considered NABOR unnecessary and possibly harmful because it might be viewed, inaccurately, as speaking for all American rabbis. In September, in time for Rosh Hashanah, NABOR issued its second annual report on the state of Jewish interdenominational cooperation in the U.S., detailing instances of joint holiday celebrations and study groups.

A number of Jewish family foundations sponsored an interdenominational retreat, February 7–9, at a retreat center north of New York City, to discuss rabbinic education. Nineteen leading administrators and professors from eight rabbinical schools gathered to address common concerns—how to inculcate religion in a secular society, how to educate students who enter with varying levels of textual skills, how to deal with issues of spirituality—but there was no Orthodox representation.

In early November, building on a precedent set in 1996 by the Sapirstein-Stone-Weiss Foundation, 11 Jewish philanthropic foundations announced that they "look with disfavor upon institutions, or individuals representing institutions" that engaged in "irresponsible rhetoric" that "negatively impacts the unity of the Jewish people." Funding request from such sources, they warned, "will be viewed with a predisposition toward a negative response."

THE PLURALISM BATTLE

Once again, denominational bickering in the U.S. tended to focus on the struggles in Israel over relations between religion and state. The year began with the Israeli Knesset considering bills sponsored by the Orthodox parties that would effectively circumvent Supreme Court decisions that had weakened the power of the Orthodox religious establishment. Reform and Conservative leaders in the U.S. held a joint news conference in New York on January 5 to announce a public campaign against the legislation. Rabbi Eric Yoffie, UAHC president, speaking for Reform, called the proposed bills an Orthodox attempt to "thumb their noses in the face of our Judaism"; Stephen Wolnek, president of the United Synagogue of Conservative Judaism, used the metaphor of "spit[ting] in our eye." With Israeli elections coming up in May, both movements urged constituents to express their sense of outrage to Israeli officials and members of the Knesset, and to withhold financial support from "any person or organization that cannot state to your satisfaction that they support pluralism." That same day the Reform movement placed an ad in the *New York Times* charging that "religious fundamentalists" in Israel threatened Jewish unity. Seeking to head off any damage to the campaign, officials of the UJA Federations of America (not yet renamed the UJC), urged Knesset members against taking any steps that might alienate American Jews. This, in turn, evoked criticism from Dr. Mandell Ganchrow, president of the Orthodox Union, who suggested that the federations stick to fund-raising and stay out of Israeli politics.

On January 26 the Knesset passed one of the Orthodox-sponsored bills, requiring all members of local religious councils—bodies that provide religious services such as maintaining synagogues and handling kosher supervision—to pledge to accept the authority of the (Orthodox) Chief Rabbinate of Israel. This was intended to keep Reform and Conservative representatives off the councils, despite a Supreme Court ruling that they be allowed to serve. Orthodox leaders in the U.S. backed the law, with the Orthodox Union's Ganchrow wondering: "How can the Reform be entitled to decide the religious life of Israel and impose their non-halakhic way?"

Leaders of the non-Orthodox movements expressed disappointment and anger, and warned of dire consequences for the State of Israel. The law drove another wedge, they claimed, between Israel and the overwhelmingly non-Orthodox American Jewish community. Not only might this translate into a weakening of emotional support and political solidarity, but it could also hurt fund-raising. "We'll never say don't give," said Rabbi Ammiel Hirsch, the executive director of ARZA, the Reform Zionist organization. "But we are sounding a warning about our inability to hold the fort." Indeed, even as New York UJA-Federation quickly initiated an ad campaign stressing how much money it had contributed toward religious pluralism in Israel, its executive vice president, Stephen Solender, echoing the nation's chief executive, told the non-Orthodox groups, "we feel your pain." But, Solender went on, "we are not going to become involved in the political process" (*Jerusalem Report,* March 1). Further inflaming the situation, a delegation of 33 Reform rabbis, praying near the Western Wall in Jerusalem on February 1, was jostled and heckled by yeshivah students who objected to men and women praying together. Am Echad (One Nation), the American Orthodox group set up by Agudath Israel to rally support for the Orthodox establishment in Israel, charged that the rabbis had deliberately provoked the confrontation. Meanwhile, the legislation on religious councils as well as the Supreme Court decision that provoked it proved meaningless, at least for the time being, since the Conservative and Reform Jews elected to the councils pledged to accept the Chief Rabbinate's authority, and the Orthodox members proceeded to boycott council meetings if non-Orthodox members were there.

In 1999, for the first time, the annual February leadership mission to Israel of the Conference of Presidents of Major American Jewish Organizations put religious pluralism high on its agenda—to the chagrin of Orthodox participants—quizzing leading Israeli politicians about where they stood on the rights of Reform and Conservative Jews. And, while on the mission, representatives of close to 20 American Jewish organizations—those affiliated with the non-Orthodox movements, along with some secular groups—announced the creation of the North American Coalition for the Advancement of Religious Freedom in Israel. Basing itself on the guarantee of religious freedom in the Israeli Declaration of Independence, the new body committed itself to breaking the Orthodox hold on Israeli Judaism.

At the same time that religious pluralism was occupying the attention of the Conference of Presidents mission, it was also bedeviling the plenum of the Jewish Council for Public Affairs (JCPA), the umbrella organization for local Jewish community-relations councils and the national defense organizations that was meeting Washington. Rabbi Harold Schulweis, the scholar in residence, charged in a February 21 address that the religious and political right wing of the Jewish community was made up of "contemporary cave dwellers" who "find solace and security and the promise of salvation in the insulation of an exclusive enclave." The Orthodox were outraged. David Luchins of the Orthodox Union commented: "In the name of pluralism he preached hatred."

The conflict over the religious situation in Israel continued to simmer in the American Jewish community. In a massive show of solidarity with *haredi* Orthodoxy in Israel, tens of thousands of American Orthodox Jews braved a heavy rain on February 28 to participate in a prayer vigil in Manhattan. This was intended to protest the Israeli Supreme Court's moves to introduce religious pluralism in the Jewish state. In early March, Natan Sharansky, Israel's minister of industry and trade and a hero of the movement to free Soviet Jewry, was subjected to verbal abuse while addressing 250 Reform rabbis in Jerusalem, when he sought to explain why his party had voted with the Orthodox parties in the Knesset against religious pluralism.

The election of Ehud Barak as prime minister on May 17 was greeted with joy in pro-pluralism circles since Barak was on record against "any legislation that divides the Jewish people." And the transfer of two key cabinet portfolios out of Orthodox hands to secular parties—education and the interior—also appeared to signal progress. Yet the inclusion of three Orthodox parties in the new governing coalition, and the clear sense that pluralism was subordinate in Barak's mind to his priority of making peace, prevented any sense of euphoria from developing among Reform and Conservative leaders. Indeed, with Barak's attention apparently taken up by foreign affairs, the government's approach to the American Jewish interest in pluralism seemed to fall into a "bad cop-good cop" pattern. In September Haim Ramon, minister of Jerusalem affairs and a close confidant of Barak, angered those who attended a closed-door meeting in New York sponsored by Americans for Peace Now, when he told them that placating the Orthodox parties was the price required to maintain a coalition that would bring peace. "Don't give me this social justice business," he snapped. "I'm a politician. I know what this is about. This is about power." In contrast, Rabbi Michael Melchior, the Danish-born minister for Diaspora affairs and leader of the moderate Orthodox Meimad faction, was far more conciliatory, seeking dialogue between Israel and the Diaspora and examining a variety of scenarios that, if enacted, might open the way for some recognition of non-Orthodox religious streams in Israel.

American Jews and Israeli Politics

The Israeli election on May 17 drew less interest from American Jews than any election there in years. While some suggested that this was a positive signal of American Jewry's recognition that Israel's security was no longer in danger, others viewed it as a worrisome symptom of the increasing cultural and psychological distance between the American and Israeli Jewish communities.

To be sure, the minority of American Jews who held strong views about Israeli politics considered the election vital. This was especially evident among the American Jewish supporters of Ehud Barak, the Labor candidate running at the head of the One Israel slate, who was seeking to unseat Likud prime minister Benjamin

Netanyahu. The barely concealed desire of the American administration to see the defeat of Netanyahu, who appeared to be dragging his heels in implementing the peace process, energized American Jewish groups opposed to the incumbent. Vice President Al Gore addressed the annual dinner of the dovish Israel Policy Forum (IPF) in January, and both the IPF and the New Israel Fund, which gave money to organizations in Israel promoting civil rights and Jewish-Arab cooperation, reported significant increases in support.

Attitudes in the broader Jewish community, however, were unclear. The American Jewish Committee's annual poll, released just before the election, indicated that 44 percent of American Jews supported Palestinian statehood and 39 percent felt that Israel should accept a unilateral Palestinian declaration of independence. Yet according to that same poll, 66 percent suspected that the Palestinians still intended to destroy Israel, and 91 percent believed that the Palestinian Authority was not doing enough to control terrorism against Israel. Perhaps the most telling statistic was that only 25 percent of American Jews said they felt "very close" to Israel.

Although Israeli law barred direct campaign contributions from non-Israelis, American Jews donated millions of dollars to allegedly nonpartisan Israeli "causes" whose links to political parties were transparent. Even national Jewish organizations that were on record in opposition to such funneling of money into Israeli politics could not prevent visiting candidates from using meetings convened by these groups to establish contacts for fund-raising. In addition, every major political party in Israel employed American political consultants, whose fees were suspected to be coming from Jews outside Israel. And since Israel had no provision for absentee ballots for civilians, two new organizations sprang up overnight, funded by American Jews, offering Israeli citizens in the U.S. cut-rate airline tickets so they could get to Israel to vote. One of them targeted secular Israelis who would presumably vote Labor, while the other appealed to the Orthodox, who were likely to support Likud.

Despite the presence in the race till a few days before the election of centrist candidate Yitzhak Mordechai, who, some thought, would create the need for a runoff by preventing either of the two leading contenders from achieving a majority, Barak won by a landslide. But the strong showing of the smaller parties in the separate Knesset balloting indicated that Barak might find it difficult to control whatever coalition he managed to put together, since it was certain to be ideologically diverse. American Jewish organizations that had opposed Netanyahu's policies were jubilant over Barak's victory, some suggesting that the election results would help renew waning American Jewish enthusiasm for the Jewish state. Likud supporters—especially among the Orthodox, who tended to back the West Bank settlements that were likely to be dismantled in a peace deal—expressed their chagrin. The mainstream Jewish bodies congratulated Barak and cited the election as a shining example of Israeli democracy in action. Yet they felt some anxiety: Barak, till now, had had little contact with American

Jewry, and there was no indication that he considered Israel's relations with American Jews a priority.

Barak's victory created an embarrassing situation for the American Israel Public Affairs Committee (AIPAC), the preeminent pro-Israel lobbying organization. As opposition leader at the time of the Netanyahu government, Barak had castigated AIPAC for what he considered its hard-line stance on the peace process and its uncritical deference to Netanyahu's policies. AIPAC, for its part, had taken the position that its mandate was to interpret and support the stance of Israel's government, no matter which party was in power. But AIPAC committed a serious faux pas by inviting Netanyahu, and not Barak, to address its 1999 annual policy conference in Washington, scheduled for May. When AIPAC had issued the invitation, long before the election, it had assumed that the April balloting would not produce a winner and, pending an expected June 1 runoff, Netanyahu would still be a functioning prime minister—and AIPAC's consistent policy was to host the prime minister, not the opposition leader. But Barak's April victory meant that Netanyahu was a lame duck in May—in fact he resigned as leader of his party following the vote—and Barak was the overwhelming choice of the Israeli people. AIPAC swiftly reversed gears, uninviting Netanyahu and inviting Barak, who politely turned the invitation down.

A NEW ISRAELI GOVERNMENT

The AIPAC policy conference moved to readjust to the new Israeli government. AIPAC dropped its previous opposition to a Palestinian state, declaring that it now would back a negotiated "Palestinian self-government" that did not endanger Israeli security. Also, deferring to Barak, AIPAC sent word to its friends in Congress that it did not want a showdown with President Clinton over his expected use of the "national security" waiver to avoid meeting the May 31 deadline for moving the U.S. embassy from Tel Aviv to Jerusalem. "Mr. Barak," declared AIPAC executive director Howard Kohr, "we look forward to working with you in your most awesome task of all: the pursuit of peace."

AIPAC's about-face did little to silence speculation that the organization was likely to lose influence with Barak in power, and that more dovish American Jewish groups would benefit. (Indeed, *Fortune* magazine, in its November issue ranking lobbying groups, would drop AIPAC from second place to fourth.) Perhaps suggestive of things to come was the May 22 reception in New York for King Abdullah of Jordan, sponsored by the Center for Middle East Peace and Development, a strong backer of the peace process. Though held while the AIPAC conference was going on in Washington, it attracted a large and distinguished audience of politicians and Jewish leaders. In light of the power shift in Israel, Jack Bendheim, president of the Israel Policy Forum, went so far as to suggest a new definition of "pro-Israel." It was now, he wrote, pro-Israel to speak out for the peace process, to provide Palestinians with a demilitarized "national entity," to support financial aid for the Palestinian Authority, and to argue for "some sort" of withdrawal from the Golan Heights as part of an Israeli-Syrian settlement (*Forward*, June 18).

But neither Bendheim's version of pro-Israelism nor AIPAC's newfound enthusiasm for the Barak approach to peace made any impact on the Zionist Organization of America (ZOA) or on Morton Klein, its president, who continued to insist that the Palestinian Authority could not be trusted. The ZOA's charges put AIPAC in a quandary since, on the one hand, they raised valid questions about the peace process that resonated in the Jewish community, but, on the other, their placement on the public agenda could only complicate the new Israeli government's peace-process diplomacy. It was largely through Klein's influence that a bill was proposed in Congress in June that would make aid to the Palestinian Authority dependent on compensation to the families of 13 Americans killed in terror attacks inside Israel, and on the investigation and prosecution of those responsible. (AIPAC said it was "not opposed" to such legislation.) And despite the reluctance of the new Israeli government and of AIPAC to press the issue, Klein mobilized congressional opposition against President Clinton's failure to move the American embassy to Jerusalem.

On July 14 Barak landed in Washington for a visit to the U.S., his first as prime minister. In contrast to the strained atmosphere of President Clinton's meetings with Barak's predecessor, Netanyahu, the new prime minister was treated with great cordiality. There were two formal meetings between the two men, plus an overnight trip to Camp David (Barak was only the third foreign leader to be hosted there since Clinton took office) and the largest formal White House dinner of the Clinton presidency. Barak announced that he hoped to conclude all Middle East peace negotiations within 15 months and Clinton assured him that he would ask Congress to increase military aid for Israel, as well as to pass the aid to the Palestinians and Jordanians that had been promised as part of the Wye River agreement. When appearing in public, Clinton and Barak seemed eager to demonstrate that their views on the Middle East coincided—despite an apparently careless comment by the American president before Barak's arrival, quickly retracted, that Palestinian refugees had the right to return to their old homes.

Despite the release of an Israel Policy Forum survey indicating that 88 percent of American Jews backed the peace process, Barak had a more difficult time with the American Jewish community than with the administration. Leaders of the Conference of Presidents of Major American Jewish Organizations—the umbrella group that traditionally represented the consensus of American Jewry on Israel and the Middle East—were miffed at the news that Barak planned to meet with only some of its constituent organizations. Adding insult to injury, Barak wanted the meeting to be held jointly with the IPF, the pro-peace-process group that was not a member of the Conference of Presidents. Barak, some observers suggested, seemed eager to elevate the significance of the IPF, with which he was ideologically compatible, at the expense of the broader-based Conference of Presidents. In the end, Barak held two separate meetings, one with all the constituents of the conference, the other with the IPF. His message to both audiences of American Jews was to stop the political infighting, accept the results of the Israeli election, and unify behind the peace process. And at a closed-door meeting with AIPAC in Washington, Barak reportedly requested an end to all pressure for the relocation of the American embassy to Jerusalem, since this issue, he felt, unnecessarily complicated the peace talks. As a result, AIPAC reiterated the position that, while it wanted the embassy moved, it would not back any initiative that threatened the peace process. Members of Congress who had hoped to try to force the president's hand on the embassy issue also got the message, and abandoned their plans. Thus in December, the next time the president would exercise the "national security" waiver so as not to move the embassy (he was required to reassess the situation every six months), there was virtually no complaint from Congress or the Jewish community.

No sooner was Barak back in Israel in August than Morton Klein and the ZOA launched a new attack on the conduct of the peace process. Klein convinced 42 members of Congress to sign a letter to President Clinton that argued for holding back aid to Jordan till it arrested and extradited Abu Daoud, who had admitted to planning the 1972 killings of 11 Israeli athletes at the Munich Olympics. But Jordan denied that it knew his whereabouts. AIPAC, in its role as defender of the peace process, denounced Klein's initiative as detrimental to the best interests of Israel, and Congress voted the aid for Jordan.

UNEXPECTED COMPLICATIONS

In September the organized Jewish community became increasingly concerned about a pattern of economic pressure launched by Arab and Muslim states against Israel's presence in the territories, a campaign that seemed eerily reminiscent of the old Arab boycott of the Jewish state. The companies targeted all succumbed: Burger King withdrew the franchise of the store on the West Bank it had authorized, Ben and Jerry's halted its use of water from the Golan Heights, and Sprint stopped using a picture of the Dome of the Rock in its ads. More ominous, since the initiative came not from overseas but from a coalition of seven American Muslim groups, was a threat to boycott all Walt Disney companies because a planned exhibit about Israel at EPCOT Center in Florida allegedly portrayed Jerusalem as the capital of Israel. Disney, which had already made changes in the exhibit to avoid offending Muslims, denied the charge.

The effective mobilization of Arab Americans against Israeli interests, a new phenomenon on the American scene, reflected the group's growing numbers and political sophistication, and presented a serious challenge to American Jewry. And there were other indications, beside the Disney affair, that Arab Americans were emerging as a political force to reckon with. For the first time, they were being appointed to government positions that had some relationship to Middle East issues, and in 1999 Jews raised their voices to complain about two of them.

In April, the ZOA disclosed that Joseph Zogby, an Arab American serving as special assistant to the U.S. assistant secretary of state for Near Eastern affairs, Martin Indyk, had, before being hired, published two letters that compared Israeli behavior toward West Bank Palestinians to South African apartheid, and criticized the U.S. for supporting Israel. This, argued ZOA president Morton Klein, should disqualify Zogby from any role in Middle East policy. Indyk responded by expressing his own disagreement with Zogby's opinions, and offered Zogby a promotion that would remove him from involvement with the Israel-Arab dispute. Zogby instead accepted an offer to work in the Justice Department.

Then in July, House Minority Leader Richard Gephardt felt compelled to withdraw the nomination of Salam Al-Marayati, an Arab American leader from Los Angeles, to a position on the National Commission on Terrorism. Though the reason stated for the withdrawal was the length of time it would take to get the nominee a security clearance, the decision was made soon after Jewish groups pointed to statements Al-Marayati had made that appeared to condone Palestinian terrorism. This time, however, unlike the Zogby case, the Jewish community was split. A number of Jewish leaders in Los Angeles who had worked with Al-Marayati praised him as a moderate and thoughtful man, and denounced the campaign launched against him by national Jewish organizations.

It was clear to everyone, however, that the growing Muslim and Arab American presence in the political system was likely to make such confrontations more frequent. A first step in seeking to contain the problem came on December 6, when 20 Muslim and Jewish leaders in Los Angeles (one of the Muslims was Al-Marayati, and most of the Jews were rabbis) endorsed a pledge to repudiate violence and avoid stereotyping. Most of the mainstream Jewish organizations, however, distanced themselves from the agreement on the grounds that some of the Muslim signers had endorsed violence. The issue of the Muslim role in politics, however, clearly transcended local community relations. On December 21, at the first-ever State Department break-the-Ramadan-fast dinner for American Muslim leaders, Secretary of State Madeleine Albright pledged to recruit American Arabs for positions in the department, and assured her guests that the views of Arab and Muslim Americans on foreign policy would be taken into account.

1999 was also the first time that American Jewish support for Israel became entangled with the political ambitions of the first lady of the United States. Considering a run for the Senate from New York in the year 2000 and recognizing the importance of the Jewish vote there, Hillary Rodham Clinton met at the White House with 25 rabbis in February to clarify her stand on a Palestinian state. Although in 1998 she had publicly favored such a state, Mrs. Clinton now told the rabbis that this was an issue to be decided through negotiations between Israelis and Palestinians. The contradiction was somewhat neutralized, however, by the election victory of Barak, who himself had tacitly accepted the inevitability of such a state.

Mrs. Clinton's position on the status of Jerusalem now took center stage. In response to a June letter from the Orthodox Union asking for a statement of her views, the first lady responded on July 2 that in her personal opinion Jerusalem was "the eternal and indivisible capital of Israel" and the appropriate location for the U.S. embassy. This seemed to place her at odds with her husband the president, even though her statement did condition the timing of the movement of the embassy on the need to "be sensitive to Israel's interest in achieving a secure and lasting peace with its neighbors."

For her work on behalf of women and children, Mrs. Clinton was scheduled to receive the prestigious Henrietta Szold Award on July 26 from Hadassah, the 300,000-member women's Zionist organization. On July 14, 25 people picketed Hadassah headquarters in New York in protest and burned an enlarged replica of a Hadassah membership card. The demonstration was organized by Americans for a Safe Israel, an organization deeply skeptical of the peace process, which took the position that the first lady was no friend of Israel and that honoring her as a potential candidate was tantamount to an endorsement. Hadassah president Marlene Post shrugged off the protest and said that, despite the demonstration, her group had received few complaints from members. In her address to the Hadassah convention, Mrs. Clinton received enthusiastic applause when she reaffirmed her view that Jerusalem should be Israel's capital and expressed strong support for the peace process.

Mrs. Clinton's delicate courting of the New York Jewish vote—presumably buttressed in August by the revelation that her grandmother's second husband had been Jewish ("OY VEY! Hillary's ALMOST Jewish" was the headline in the *New York Post*)—ran into trouble on a November visit to Israel and the Palestinian self-rule areas. She managed to extricate herself from one potential disaster when, at the last minute, she changed her itinerary so as to include the Western Wall, the holiest site of Judaism, which she had originally intended to avoid in deference to Arab sensibilities. But in the West Bank town of Ramallah, on November 11, the first lady sat by silently as Suha Arafat, wife of Palestinian Authority chairman Yasir Arafat, charged that Israel used poison gas against the Palestinians and deliberately contaminated their water. Even worse, since a picture is worth a thousand words, she was photographed kissing Mrs. Arafat after the event. Not till the next day, in Jordan, did Mrs. Clinton declare that "inflammatory rhetoric and baseless accusations" were harmful to the cause of peace. Asked why she had not challenged Mrs. Arafat immediately, Mrs. Clinton said that the English translation she had been given at the time did not sound as extreme as the Arabic had apparently been.

On December 14 Mrs. Clinton met for over an hour with the Orthodox Union at its headquarters. Questioned about her views on issues of Jewish concern, she reiterated her explanation for not challenging Mrs. Arafat right away, repeated her support for moving the U.S. embassy to Jerusalem so long as this did not jeopardize chances for peace, and went so far as to suggest conditioning aid for the Palestinian Authority on its cessation of anti-Israel propaganda and action against terrorism—a position that went beyond that of the Israeli government. The Orthodox leaders came away impressed by her knowledge and poise, and gratified, on the whole, by her stand on Jewish issues. Nonetheless, they expressed some uneasiness about whether the first lady was emotionally committed to their priorities.

When Congress began consideration of the administration's foreign-aid package in the fall, the $1.9 billion for Israel, Jordan, and the Palestinian Authority promised a year earlier as part of the Wye package attracted controversy. In addition to opposition from Republicans in Congress who feared that the expenditure might endanger the solvency of the social-security system, Israeli lobbyists in Washington affiliated with the Likud opposition and American Jewish groups distrustful of Wye told congressmen that the Palestinians should not get the $400 million due them under Wye because they had not complied with their pledge to halt anti-Israel incitement. Wye supporters, however, strongly suspected that the Jewish opposition to aid for the Palestinians was nothing more than a tactic to scuttle the entire peace process, and, in essence, reverse the result of the Israeli election. Prime Minister Barak, in a November 20 address before the Israel Policy Forum in New York, argued that to wait for the Arabs to stop their anti-Israel rhetoric before implementing Wye meant postponing the chance for peace indefinitely. And AIPAC proceeded to use all of its considerable political leverage to win congressional approval for the entire Wye aid package.

The spectacle of different factions of Israelis and American Jews lobbying Congress for and against legislation that Israel's government wanted was nothing new—it had gone on under both Likud and Labor governments. But the wrangle over Wye aid was so divisive that many observers feared it could permanently cripple Israel's standing in Washington and the political clout of American Jewry. In November, addressing the General Assembly of the United Jewish Communities, Ariel Sharon, Netanyahu's successor as Likud leader, called for an end to all lobbying of the U.S. government by the Israeli opposition.

The suggestion received a warm welcome on all sides, at least in theory. But the initiation of Israel-Syria peace talks in Washington in December (after a few fruitless sessions they were postponed till January) meant that Sharon's proposal would soon be put to the test. An agreement entailing Israeli withdrawal from the Golan Heights in return for an end to the state of war between Israel and Syria would probably require billions of American dollars for implementation, money that Congress would have to appropriate. Were Israeli and American Jewish opponents of a Golan withdrawal likely to refrain from making their feelings known in Washington?

The Organizational World

CONFERENCE OF PRESIDENTS

In early January the nominating committee of the Conference of Presidents of Major American Jewish Organizations unanimously nominated Ronald Lauder, president of the Jewish National Fund, to be the next chairman of the conference, the umbrella organization generally recognized as American Jewry's voice on international affairs. Lauder was heir to a cosmetics fortune, an international businessman, a generous philanthropist who supported the revival of Jewish life in Eastern Europe, and a political activist—for the Republican Party in the U.S. and for the Likud in Israel. Even though Lauder told the nominating committee that there was no truth to rumors he had contributed large sums of money to the Netanyahu campaign in 1996, his identification with the policies of the Likud government made the more dovish groups in the 55-member conference wonder whether he would be able to overcome his personal political proclivities and act as a consensus-builder. Another reason for anxiety was the antipathy between Lauder and the Clinton administration.

With the entire conference membership due to vote on the Lauder nomination in a few days, the January 29 issue of the *New York Jewish Week* ran a cover story questioning whether Lauder had been altogether candid when he denied contributing to the Netanyahu campaign. The day before, January 28, when the story broke, some 20 member organizations of the conference met and decided to ask for a postponement of the vote pending an investigation of whether Lauder had indirectly funneled money into Likud coffers. Instead, Lauder met with the nominating committee again on February 2 to respond to the new allegations. His answers were apparently satisfactory, and the next day the full conference elected him chairman with 41 affirmative votes; none voted against him and four organizations abstained. He was slated to take office in June. In his acceptance speech Lauder said: "Unity does not require conformity, but rather a recognition that we are one people bound together by faith, history, and commitment." But even in the wake of the overwhelming vote in Lauder's favor, questions lingered over the selection process: Lauder, it turned out, had, over the years, contributed to some of the organizations that voted in his favor, and also to the Conference of Presidents itself. A few weeks later it was reported that Lauder had negotiated in August 1998 with the government of Yugoslavia to provide long-distance telephone service, possibly violating the U.S. administration's ban on investment in Serbia. But since no deal had been signed and no law broken the story soon disappeared from the headlines.

UNITING THE JEWISH COMMUNITIES

The long (over five years) and contentious process of bringing together the United Jewish Appeal (UJA), the United Israel Appeal (UIA), and the Council of Jewish Federations (CJF) under one organizational banner to handle fundraising and allocation for North American Jewry and help bring a renaissance of Jewish life, was finally completed in 1999. In February, at the CJF executive committee meeting in Miami, merger documents were drawn up and sent out to the 189 local federations for approval. But the inchoate new entity was still searching for a name and for lay and professional leaders.

The easiest decision, it turned out, was the choice of a chairman of the board— 67-year-old Charles R. Bronfman, approved unanimously by a 25-person nominating committee in February. Bronfman was a billionaire philanthropist from Canada, where he cochaired the Seagram Company. The other decisions were still not finalized as federation representatives convened in Washington for the first meeting of the Founders Forum, the name given to the new body's first meeting, in April. Unable to reach consensus on a professional head after a painstaking six-month search, the new entity chose 61-year-old Stephen Solender, the executive vice president of New York UJA-Federation, as part-time interim president for six months, giving the search committee more time to recommend someone for the position. Market research was used to help pick the name of the merged organization. Much to the chagrin of federation activists, proposed names that included the word "federation" did not do well, especially among younger Jews. Nevertheless the Founders Forum might have overruled the market researchers and included the controversial word had it not been for the plea of Charles Bronfman, who pointed out that while "federation" had heroic connotations for members of the older generation, it only conjured up "Star Trek" for their children and grandchildren. The new name, "United Jewish Communities "(UJC), passed by a close 73-59 vote, defeating "United Jewish Federations."

The proposed makeup of the UJC's policymaking bodies aroused controversy in the broader Jewish community. The idea of federation "ownership" of the UJC was put into practice, with a vengeance. There was to be a 580-member delegate assembly of which 550 would be federation representatives, with one delegate each from the American Jewish Joint Distribution Committee (JDC), the Jewish Agency, some of the major beneficiary organizations, and the Orthodox, Conservative, Reform, and Reconstructionist synagogue bodies. A 120-member board of trustees was to have 68 percent of its members selected by federations. Of great significance, federation representatives would hold a comfortable majority on the Overseas Needs Assessment and Distribution Committee (ONAD), which decided how much money would go to the JDC to help overseas Jewish communities and to the Jewish Agency for aid to Israel. The religious bodies complained of what they saw as their token representation in UJC deliberations, and the rabbinical organizations were appalled at apparently having none at all. Zionist groups were upset that federation leaders, with their domestic priorities, would determine how much money would go to Israel.

More problematic for the fledgling UJC was the rebellion of a major federation, the Combined Jewish Philanthropies of Boston. In July the Boston group decided to withhold the money it was to have forwarded to the UJC for distribution to the JDC and the Jewish Agency for overseas relief, and instead give $1 million directly to the JDC, and other funds to specific, targeted programs in Israel and the former Soviet Union. While some UJC officials called this an abandonment of a federation commitment to maintain the existing level of overseas aid for at least two years, Barry Shrage, president of the Boston body, noted that the level was being maintained but the recipients were being shifted to reflect changing needs. Shrage was particularly harsh on the Jewish Agency, which he considered too inefficient and politicized to serve as an effective conduit for American giving to Israel.

The Boston decision became public in August, just as the UJC was collectively beginning to address the question of overseas funding. The first meeting of the ONAD took place in New York on August 11. A report that emerged suggested dividing overseas needs into two categories, rescue, to which all federations would be obliged to contribute, and less immediate needs, which would be optional. The report raised the possibility that federations might funnel overseas aid through organizations other than the JDC and the Jewish Agency, which was what Boston was already doing without authorization, and also called for saving money by slashing subsidies for federation missions to Israel. At the end of August the UJC endorsed the ONAD report and announced several new moves regarding the four "pillars" of its work. ONAD, dealing with overseas aid, would be based in Jerusalem, and the office dealing with the domestic services and policy pillar would be headquartered in Washington. One-third of the committee in charge of the third pillar, Jewish renaissance and renewal, would come from the synagogue bodies, in this way addressing the complaints of underrepresentation that had been coming from the religious denominations. The fourth pillar would deal with campaign and fund-raising.

On October 5 Charles Bronfman announced that Stephen Solender, the interim president for the last six months, was to be the new UJC president on a permanent basis. Chosen as executive vice president and chief operating officer was Louise Stoll, who had held managerial positions in the Clinton administration and in private industry. David Altschuler, the founding director of New York's Museum of Jewish Heritage-A Living Memorial to the Holocaust, was to head a semiautonomous UJC foundation that would seek to secure funds from large corporations and "mega-donors," many of whom had forsaken the federation system to set up their own family foundations, which, in 1998, had probably disbursed more charity, in the aggregate, than the federations.

The November General Assembly, held this year in Atlanta, was the first conducted under the aegis of the new UJC, instead of the defunct CJF. The 5,000 participants attended sessions organized around the four "pillars." Of the four, Jewish renaissance and renewal drew the largest audiences, by far. (The single major "draw," however, was a speech by Vice President Gore.) As for the process of ratifying the organization of the new entity, things did not go according to plan only with regard to Altschuler; questions from federation leaders about the degree of autonomy his "mega-donor" foundation would enjoy led to a postponement of his appointment. The UJC's top leaders repeatedly reassured the participants that this new enterprise remained open to new suggestions. "Rome was not built in a day," said Charles Bronfman, "but we are going to build Rome."

CONFLICT OVER JCPA

In the panoply of national Jewish organizations the one most closely associated with the liberal social-action causes of the 1960s was the Jewish Council on Public Affairs (JCPA), formerly known as the National Jewish Community Relations Advisory Council (NJCRAC), an umbrella organization for local Jewish community-relations councils and the major national organizations. On June 30 James Tisch, president of New York UJA-Federation, and Stephen Solender, its executive vice president, sent a letter to the JCPA suggesting that its agenda no longer reflected the concerns of the Jews of New York. Specifically, the letter mentioned the JCPA's support for more government services, affirmative action, and universal health care, and its opposition to tax reductions and school vouchers. "There is a portion of our community," they went on, "who questions if it is even appropriate for an organization to speak on behalf of the Jewish community on some of these issues." The letter urged a clearer focus on issues of direct concern to Jews. On August 6 Steven Nasatir, president of the Jewish Federation of Metropolitan Chicago, sent the JCPA a similar letter. Both letters included reminders that these two federations together footed a large part of the bill (30 percent) for the JCPA's activities. The letters evoked praise from the ranks of Jewish political conservatives, who had long complained that the social-action agenda was an anachronism. Old-line liberals, however, defended the JCPA on the ground that issues of broad concern to the American people were Jewish issues too, not only because Jewish tradition mandated a just society, but also because only such a society could guarantee the security of American Jews.

LAWRENCE GROSSMAN

/Jewish Population in the United States, 1999

$\mathbf{B}$ASED ON LOCAL COMMUNITY counts—the method for identifying and enumerating Jewish population that serves as the basis of this report—the estimated size of the American Jewish community in 1999 was approximately 6.0 million, half a million more than the 5.5 million "core" Jewish population estimated in the Council of Jewish Federations' 1990 National Jewish Population Survey (NJPS).[1] The NJPS 2000, to be conducted in the second half of 2000, will provide a new national estimate (see below).

The difference between the national figure and the aggregated local figures may be explained by varying definitions of "Jewish," disparate sample sources (outdated lists, distinctive Jewish names, random digit dialing, etc.), the passage of time, and the lack of a uniform methodology for local demographic research.

Analysis of the 1990 NJPS and other sources suggested that the population grew slightly during the late 1980s as the number of Jewish births exceeded the number of Jewish deaths. Extrapolation from the age structure, however, suggests that births and deaths were in balance by the late 1990s, creating a situation of zero population growth. It was only Jewish immigration into the U.S.—particularly from the former Soviet Union—that provided some growth in numbers.

The NJPS used a scientifically selected sample to project a total number for the United States as a whole, but could not provide accurate information on the state and local levels. Therefore, as in past years, this article contains local population estimates provided by knowledgeable local informants, and these serve as the basis for calculations of state and regional population counts.

Leaders at the approximately 200 Jewish federations that are part of the new philanthropic entity, United Jewish Communities (comprised of the Council of Jewish Federations, United Jewish Appeal, and United Israel Appeal), provided estimates of the largest Jewish population centers. However, their service areas vary in size and thus may represent quite different geographic divisions: several towns, one county, or an aggregate of several counties. In some cases we have subdivided federation areas to reflect more natural geographic boundaries.

Local rabbis and other informed Jewish communal leaders provided estimates from small communities without federations. A form requesting the current population estimate was mailed to leaders of 108 such communities that had not pro-

---

[1] See Barry A. Kosmin et al., *Highlights of the CJF 1990 National Jewish Population Survey* (New York, Council of Jewish Federations, 1991).

vided an update in more than five years, and 59 replied. About 20 other requests were returned with indications that the synagogue whose leader had previously provided an estimate had either closed in recent years, had moved without leaving a forwarding address, or could otherwise not be found. For communities that did not provide a current estimate, figures have either been retained from past years or extrapolations made from the older data. The estimates requested from informants were for the resident Jewish population, including those in private households and in institutional settings. Non-Jewish family members were excluded from the total.

The state and regional totals shown in Appendix tables 1 and 2 are derived by summing the local estimates shown in table 3, including communities of less than 100, and then rounding to the nearest hundred or thousand, depending on the size of the estimate.

Because population estimation is not an exact science, the reader should be aware that in cases where a figure differs from last year's, the increase or decrease did not occur suddenly, but occurred over a period of time and has just now been substantiated. The primary sources for altering previously reported Jewish population figures in larger communities are recently completed local demographic studies. The results of such studies should be understood as either an updated calculation of gradual demographic change or as the correction of faulty older estimates.

In determining Jewish population, communities count both affiliated and non-affiliated residents who are "core" Jews, as defined in NJPS 1990. This definition includes born Jews who report adherence to Judaism, Jews by choice, and born Jews without a current religion ("secular Jews"). A common method for estimating the population is to multiply the number of households containing at least one self-defined Jew by the average number of self-defined Jewish persons per household. As stated above, non-Jews living in Jewish households — primarily the non-Jewish spouses and non-Jewish children — are not included in the 1999 estimates presented below.

Only persons residing in a community for the majority of the year are included in local counts. In many Sunbelt and resort communities, the population increases during the winter months, but these part-year residents are not included in these estimates. However, demographer Ira Sheskin notes that if we were to include residents who are present for at least three months per year, four Southeast Florida communities would increase as follows: Boca Raton-Delray Beach, 30,000 (32 percent); Broward County, 21,000 (10 percent); Miami-Dade County, 11,000 (8 percent); and Palm Beach County (excluding Boca Raton-Delray Beach), 11,000 (15 percent). Many other Sunbelt communities, resort areas throughout the country, college towns, and communities with seasonally affected industries also become home to more Jews for part of the year, but there are no accurate data for such communities.

Local Population Changes

The community reporting the largest population gain in 1999 was Portland, Oregon, up 7,500 to 25,000. Though no survey was conducted, the 43-percent increase reported by the Portland Federation reflects protracted growth over time. Five other communities experienced large growth, four in Florida and one in South Carolina. Boca Raton-Delray Beach, at the southern end of Palm Beach County, increased by 6,000 (7 percent). Growth in the rest of Palm Beach County, documented in a recent study, was 7,000 (9 percent). The adjacent community to the north, Stuart-Port St. Lucie (Martin and St. Lucie counties) took part in that same Palm Beach study and showed a growth of 1,300 (43 percent). Tampa reported a population increase of 5,000 (33 percent). The increase in Charleston, South Carolina, was 1,000, up from 3,500 to 4,500 (a 29-percent increase).

Other places showing more modest growth included Naples and Sarasota, Florida; Bloomington, Illinois; Baton Rouge, Louisiana; Annapolis, Maryland; Portsmouth, New Hampshire; Saratoga Springs and Utica, New York; Salem, Oregon; and Stroudsburg-Monroe County and York, Pennsylvania. York's growth was documented in a recent population study, while Utica's growth was mainly due to the expansion of the Utica Federation list, which now includes many previously unknown households.

The community with the largest loss was Broward County, Florida (7,000, a 3-percent decrease). This decline, documented in a new study, reflects patterns established in the 1980s by Dade County, its neighbor to the south. Newcomers to Florida chose to locate further north on the coast, particularly in Palm Beach County. Rochester, New York, completed a study that showed a loss of 1,500 since its previous study in 1986. Smaller losses were reported in Waukegan, Illinois, Altoona, Pennsylvania, and Williamsport, Pennsylvania.

Progress on NJPS 2000

Recognizing the need for current data, United Jewish Communities is sponsoring a new National Jewish Population Survey in 2000. The questionnaire and overall study design were developed by the Research Department of United Jewish Communities in close collaboration with its National Technical Advisory Committee (NTAC), a distinguished group of academicians and federation professionals with expertise in demography, sociology, religion, geography, economics, education, and other relevant disciplines.

In addition, the UJC Research Department worked closely with local federation planning, campaign, marketing, and other departments, as well as with the four newly formed UJC "pillars": Israel/Overseas, Human Services and Social Policy, Jewish Renaissance and Renewal, and Financial Resource Development. In fact, the interviewing for NJPS 2000, which was to have begun in January 2000, was postponed till the second half of the year in order to give the four pillars sufficient input. Meetings were held with these groups and with Jewish religious denominations, other major Jewish organizations, UJC regions, and other constituencies. The NJPS Board of Trustees has provided the financial resources for conducting this effort, and a federation Professional Advisory Committee has provided guidance on issues relevant to the federation system. The NJPS Steering Committee, comprised of the chairs of all the committees involved in NJPS, sets policy for the study. All of the aforementioned groups have provided significant input toward questionnaire development. Focus groups were conducted to improve the introductory part of the interview and cognitively test the phrasing of questions. The questionnaire has been extensively pretested for length, the most appropriate language, and correct skip patterns.

NJPS 2000 is being administered by telephone using random-digit-dialing techniques, with a sample of approximately 5,000 adults, age 18 and older, residing in the 50 United States. The sample will be stratified by census region, metropolitan/nonmetropolitan area, and then by zip code within each region. Areas of high incidence and density of Jewish settlement will be sampled at a higher rate than other areas so as to speed up execution of the study and cut costs. Results will be weighted to ensure accurate projectability to the Jewish population at different geographic levels.

When the data are released, NJPS 2000 will become the definitive source of data on the Jewish community for the first decade of the 21st century. The information will help UJC, Jewish federations, synagogues, and other elements of the Jewish community conduct communal planning, policy-making, resource development, Jewish education, scholarly research, and many other necessary functions. The results will be comparable, as much as possible, to the 1990 NJPS and the 2000 U.S. Census, facilitating trend analyses, projections, and segmentation of the population.

Among the multitude of topics being explored in NJPS 2000 are population size, geographic distribution, socioeconomic characteristics, family structure, fertility, marital history, intermarriage, Jewish identification, religious practices, Jewish education, synagogue affiliation, philanthropic behavior, and relationship to Israel. UJC and others will underwrite a broad range of analyses based on the NJPS results to help drive informed decision-making within the Jewish community.

JIM SCHWARTZ
JEFFREY SCHECKNER

APPENDIX

TABLE 1. JEWISH POPULATION IN THE UNITED STATES, 1999

State	Estimated Jewish Population	Total Population*	Estimated Jewish Percent of Total
Alabama	9,200	4,369,000	0.2
Alaska	3,500	620,000	0.6
Arizona	81,500	4,778,000	1.7
Arkansas	1,600	2,551,000	0.1
California	967,000	33,145,000	2.9
Colorado	68,000	4,056,000	1.7
Connecticut	101,000	3,282,000	3.1
Delaware	13,500	753,000	1.8
Dist. of Columbia	25,500	519,000	4.9
Florida	637,000	15,111,000	4.2
Georgia	87,500	7,788,000	1.1
Hawaii	7,000	1,185,000	0.6
Idaho	1,000	1,252,000	0.1
Illinois	270,000	12,128,000	2.2
Indiana	18,000	5,943,000	0.3
Iowa	6,500	2,869,000	0.2
Kansas	14,500	2,654,000	0.5
Kentucky	11,000	3,961,000	0.3
Louisiana	16,500	4,372,000	0.4
Maine	7,500	1,253,000	0.6
Maryland	216,000	5,172,000	4.1
Massachusetts	274,000	6,175,000	4.4
Michigan	107,000	9,864,000	1.1
Minnesota	42,000	4,776,000	0.9
Mississippi	1,400	2,769,000	(z)
Missouri	62,500	5,468,000	1.1
Montana	800	882,000	0.1
Nebraska	7,000	1,666,000	0.4
Nevada	57,500	1,809,000	3.2
New Hampshire	9,900	1,201,000	0.8
New Jersey	465,000	8,143,000	5.7
New Mexico	10,500	1,740,000	0.6
New York	1,651,000	18,197,000	9.1
North Carolina	25,000	7,651,000	0.3

State	Estimated Jewish Population	Total Population*	Estimated Jewish Percent of Total
North Dakota	700	634,000	0.1
Ohio	144,000	11,257,000	1.3
Oklahoma	5,000	3,358,000	0.1
Oregon	30,500	3,316,000	0.9
Pennsylvania	282,000	11,994,000	2.4
Rhode Island	16,000	991,000	1.6
South Carolina	10,500	3,886,000	0.3
South Dakota	350	733,000	(z)
Tennessee	18,000	5,484,000	0.3
Texas	124,000	20,044,000	0.6
Utah	4,500	2,130,000	0.2
Vermont	5,700	594,000	1.0
Virginia	76,000	6,873,000	1.1
Washington	35,500	5,756,000	0.6
West Virginia	2,400	1,807,000	0.1
Wisconsin	28,500	5,250,000	0.5
Wyoming	400	480,000	0.1
U.S. TOTAL	**6,061,000	272,690,000	2.2

N.B. Details may not add to totals because of rounding.
* Resident population, July 1, 1999 (*Source:* U.S. Bureau of the Census, *Population Estimates Program, Population Division, Report, #ST-99-2.*)
** Exclusive of Puerto Rico and the Virgin Islands which previously reported Jewish populations of 1,500 and 350, respectively.
(z) Figure is less than 0.1 and rounds to 0.

TABLE 2. DISTRIBUTION OF U.S. JEWISH POPULATION BY REGIONS, 1999

Region	Total Population	Percent Distribution	Estimated Jewish Population	Percent Distribution
Midwest	63,242,000	23.2	700,000	11.6
East North Central . .	44,442,000	16.3	567,000	9.4
West North Central .	18,800,000	6.9	133,000	2.2
Northeast	51,830,000	19.0	2,812,000	46.4
Middle Atlantic	38,334,000	14.1	2,398,000	39.6
New England	13,496,000	4.9	414,000	6.8
South	96,468,000	35.4	1,280,000	21.1
East South Central . .	16,582,000	6.1	40,000	0.7
South Atlantic	49,560,000	18.2	1,093,000	18.0
West South Central . .	30,325,000	11.1	147,000	2.4
West	61,150,000	22.4	1,268,000	20.9
Mountain	17,127,000	6.2	224,000	3.7
Pacific	44,023,000	16.1	1,044,000	17.2
TOTALS	272,690,000	100.0	6,061,000	100.0

N.B. Details may not add to totals because of rounding.

TABLE 3. COMMUNITIES WITH JEWISH POPULATIONS OF 100 OR MORE, 1999 (ESTIMATED)

State and City	Jewish Population	State and City	Jewish Population	State and City	Jewish Population
ALABAMA		**Little Rock	1,100	*Napa County	1,000
*Birmingham	5,300	Other places	200	Oakland (incl. in	
Decatur (incl. in				Alameda County,	
Florence)		CALIFORNIA		under S.F. Bay Area)	
Dothan	100	***Antelope Valley		Ontario (incl. in	
Florence	100		700	Pomona Valley)	
Huntsville	750	Aptos (incl. in Santa		Orange County[N]	
**Mobile	1,100	Cruz)			60,000
**Montgomery	1,300	Bakersfield-Kern		Palm Springs[N]	14,000
Tuscaloosa	300	County	1,600	Palmdale (incl. in	
Other places	300	Berkeley (incl. in		Antelope Valley)	
		Contra Costa County,		Palo Alto (incl. in	
ALASKA		under S.F. Bay Area)		South Peninsula,	
*Anchorage	2,300	Carmel (incl. in		under S.F. Bay Area)	
*Fairbanks	540	Monterey Peninsula)		Pasadena (incl. in L.A.	
Juneau	285	*Chico	500	area)	
Kenai Peninsula	200	Corona (incl. in		Petaluma (incl. in	
Ketchikan (incl. in		Riverside area)		Sonoma County,	
Juneau)		*Eureka	1,000	under S.F. Bay	
Other places	200	Fairfield	800	Area)	
		Fontana (incl. in San		Pomona Valley[N]	6,750
ARIZONA		Bernardino)		*Redding area	150
Cochise County	350	*Fresno	2,300	Redwood Valley (incl.	
*Flagstaff	500	Lancaster (incl. in		in Mendocino	
Lake Havasu City		Antelope Valley)		County)	
	200	Long Beach[N]	15,000	Riverside area	2,000
*Phoenix	60,000	Los Angeles area[N]		Sacramento[N]	21,300
Prescott	300		519,000	Salinas	1,000
Sierra Vista (incl. in		Mendocino County	600	San Bernardino area	
Cochise County)		*Merced County	190		3,000
*Tucson	20,000	*Modesto	500	*San Diego	70,000
Yuma	125	Monterey Peninsula		San Francisco Bay	
Other places	200		2,300	Area[N]	210,000
		Moreno Valley (incl. in		Alameda County	
ARKANSAS		Riverside)			32,500
***Fayetteville	150	Murrieta Hot Springs		Contra Costa County	
Hot Springs	150		550		22,000

[N]See Notes below. *Includes entire county. **Includes all of two counties. ***Figure not updated for at least five years.

| | Jewish | | Jewish | | Jewish |
State and City	Population	State and City	Population	State and City	Population

Marin County
.... 18,500
N. Peninsula . . 24,500
San Francisco
.... 49,500
San Jose...... 33,000
Sonoma County
.... 9,000
S. Peninsula . . . 21,000
*San Jose (listed under
S.F. Bay Area)
*San Luis Obispo
.... 1,700
*Santa Barbara . . . 7,000
*Santa Cruz 6,000
Santa Maria...... 700
Santa Monica (incl. in
Los Angeles area)
Santa Rosa (incl. in
Sonoma County,
under S.F. Bay Area)
Sonoma County (listed
under S.F. Bay Area)
South Lake Tahoe
.... 150
*Stockton........ 850
***Sun City...... 200
Tulare and Kings
counties 300
Ukiah (incl. in
Mendocino Co.)
Vallejo area 900
*Ventura County[N]
.... 15,000
Visalia (incl. in Tulare
and Kings counties)
Other places...... 200

COLORADO
Aspen........... 750
Boulder (incl. in
Denver)
Breckenridge (incl. in
Vail)

Colorado Springs
.... 1,500
Denver[N]....... 63,000
Eagle (incl. in Vail)
Evergreen (incl. in
Denver)
*Fort Collins..... 1,000
*Grand Junction . . . 320
Greeley (incl. in Fort
Collins)
Loveland (incl. in Fort
Collins)
Pueblo 425
Steamboat Springs . 160
Telluride........ 125
**Vail........... 650
Other places..... 200

CONNECTICUT
Bridgeport[N].... 13,000
Bristol (incl. in
Hartford)
Cheshire (incl. in
Waterbury)
Colchester 300
Danbury[N] 3,200
Danielson........ 100
Darien (incl. in
Stamford)
Greenwich...... 3,900
Hartford[N] 25,200
Hebron (incl. in
Colchester)
Lebanon (incl. in
Colchester)
Lower Middlesex
County[N]....... 1,600
Manchester (incl. in
Hartford)
Meriden (incl. in New
Haven)
Middletown..... 1,200
New Britain (incl. in
Hartford)

New Canaan (incl. in
Stamford)
New Haven[N] . . . 24,300
New London[N] . . . 3,800
New Milford (incl. in
Waterbury)
Newtown (incl. in
Danbury)
Norwalk[N] 9,100
Norwich (incl. in New
London)
Rockville (incl. in
Hartford)
Shelton (incl. in
Bridgeport)
Southington (incl. in
Hartford)
Stamford....... 9,200
Storrs (incl. in
Willimantic)
Torrington area . . . 580
Wallingford (incl. in
New Haven)
Waterbury[N] 4,500
Westport (incl. in
Norwalk)
Willimantic area. . . 700
Other places...... 200

DELAWARE
Dover (incl. in Kent
and Sussex County)
Kent and Sussex
counties....... 1,600
Newark area 4,300
Wilmington area . 7,600

DISTRICT OF COLUMBIA
Washington D.C.[N]
.... 25,500

FLORIDA
Arcadia (incl. in Fort
Myers)

State and City	Jewish Population
Boca Raton-Delray Beach (listed under Southeast Fla.)	
Brevard County. .	5,000
***Crystal River . . .	100
**Daytona Beach	2,500
Fort Lauderdale (incl. in Broward County, under Southeast Fla.)	
**Fort Myers	7,500
Fort Pierce.	1,060
Gainesville	2,200
Hollywood-S. Broward County (incl in Broward County, under Southeast Fla.)	
**Jacksonville. . . .	7,300
Key West	650
Lakeland.	1,000
*Miami-Dade County (listed under Southeast Fla.)	
Naples-Collier County	3,800
New Port Richey (incl. in Pasco County)	
Ocala-Marion County	500
Orlando[N]	21,000
Palm Beach County (listed under Southeast Fla.)	
Pasco County . . .	1,000
**Pensacola	900
Pinellas County .	24,200
Port Charlotte-Punta Gorda (incl. in Fort Myers	
**Sarasota	17,500
Southeast Florida	514,000
Boca Raton-Delray Beach	93,000

State and City	Jewish Population
Broward County	213,000
Miami-Dade County	134,000
Palm Beach County (excl. Boca Raton-Delray Beach)	74,000
*St. Petersburg-Clearwater (incl. in Pinellas County)	
Stuart-Port St. Lucie[N]	4,300
Tallahassee	2,200
*Tampa	20,000
Venice (incl. in Sarasota)	
*Vero Beach.	400
Winter Haven.	300
Other places.	100
GEORGIA	
Albany area	200
Athens	400
Atlanta Metro Area	80,000
Augusta[N]	1,300
Brunswick	100
**Columbus	1,100
**Dalton	140
Macon.	1,000
*Savannah.	2,800
**Valdosta	100
Other places.	250
HAWAII	
Hilo	280
Honolulu (incl. all of Oahu)	6,400
Kauai.	100
Maui	210
IDAHO	
**Boise	800

State and City	Jewish Population
Lewiston (incl. in Moscow)	
Moscow	100
Other places.	150
ILLINOIS	
Aurora area	500
Bloomington-Normal	500
Carbondale (incl. in S. Ill.)	
*Champaign-Urbana	1,400
Chicago Metro Area[N]	261,000
**Danville	100
*Decatur	130
DeKalb	180
East St. Louis (incl. in S. Ill.)	
Elgin[N].	500
Freeport (incl. in Rockford)	
*Joliet.	450
Kankakee.	100
Moline (incl. in Quad Cities)	
*Peoria.	850
Quad Cities-Ill. portion	550
Rock Island (incl. in Quad Cities)	
Rockford[N]	1,100
Southern Illinois[N] .	600
*Springfield.	1,090
Waukegan	300
Other places.	250
INDIANA	
Bloomington. . . .	1,000
Elkhart (incl. in S. Bend)	
Evansville.	400
**Fort Wayne.	950

| | Jewish |
| State and City | Population |

**Gary-Northwest
Indiana 2,000
**Indianapolis . . 10,000
**Lafayette 600
*Michigan City 300
Muncie. 120
South Bend[N] 1,950
*Terre Haute 250
Other places 200

IOWA
Ames (incl. in Des
Moines)
Cedar Rapids 420
Council Bluffs 150
*Davenport (incl. in
Quad Cities)
*Des Moines 2,800
*Iowa City 1,300
Postville 100
Quad Cities-Iowa
portion 650
**Sioux City 500
*Waterloo 170
Other places 300

KANSAS
Kansas City area-
Kansas portion[N]
. . . . 12,000
Lawrence 100
Manhattan 425
*Topeka 400
Wichita[N] 1,300
Other places 100

KENTUCKY
Covington-Newport
area 500
Lexington[N] 1,850
*Louisville 8,700
Other places 150

LOUISIANA
Alexandria[N] 350

| | Jewish |
| State and City | Population |

Baton Rouge[N] . . . 1,600
Lafayette (incl. in S.
Central La.)
Lake Charles area
. . . . 200
Monroe (incl. in
Shreveport)
**New Orleans . . 13,000
**Shreveport 815
***South Central La.[N]
. . . . 250
Other places 150

MAINE
Augusta 140
Bangor 1,000
Biddeford-Saco (incl. in
S. Maine)
Brunswick-Bath (incl.
in S. Maine)
Lewiston-Auburn . . 500
Portland (incl. in S.
Maine)
Rockland area 180
Southern Maine[N]
. . . . 5,500
*Waterville 200
Other places 150

MARYLAND
Annapolis area . . 3,000
**Baltimore 94,500
Columbia (incl. in
Howard County)
Cumberland 275
*Frederick 1,200
*Hagerstown 325
*Harford County
. . . . 1,200
*Howard County
. . . . 10,000
Montgomery and
Prince Georges
counties 104,500

| | Jewish |
| State and City | Population |

Ocean City 100
Salisbury 400
Silver Spring (incl. in
Montgomery County)
Other places 250

MASSACHUSETTS
Amherst area 1,300
Andover[N] 2,850
Athol area (incl. in N.
Worcester County)
Attleboro area 200
Beverly (incl. in North
Shore, under Boston
Metro Region)
Boston Metro Region[N]
. . . . 227,300
Boston 21,000
Brockton-South
Central 31,500
Brookline 20,300
Framingham . . . 19,700
Near West 35,800
Newton 27,700
North Central . . 22,900
North Shore . . . 18,600
Northeast 7,700
Northwest 13,600
Southeast 8,500
Brockton (listed under
Boston Metro Region)
Brookline (listed under
Boston Metro Region)
Cape Cod-Barnstable
County 3,250
Clinton (incl. in
Worcester-Central
Worcester County)
Fall River area . . 1,100
Falmouth (incl. in Cape
Cod)
Fitchburg (incl. in N.
Worcester County)
Framingham (listed

State and City	Jewish Population	State and City	Jewish Population	State and City	Jewish Population
under Boston Metro Region)		Salem (incl. in N. Shore, listed under Boston Metro Region)		MISSISSIPPI	
Gardner (incl. in N. Worcester County)				Biloxi-Gulfport	250
Gloucester (incl. N. Shore, listed under Boston Metro Region)		South Worcester County	500	**Greenville	120
				**Hattiesburg	130
		Southbridge (incl. in S. Worcester County)		**Jackson	550
Great Barrington (incl. in Pittsfield)		Springfield[N]	10,000	Other places	300
*Greenfield	1,100	Taunton area	1,300	MISSOURI	
Haverhill	800	Webster (incl. in S. Worcester County)		Columbia	400
Holyoke	600			Joplin	100
*Hyannis (incl. in Cape Cod)		Worcester-Central Worcester County	11,000	Kansas City area-Missouri portion[N]	7,100
Lawrence (incl. in Andover)		Other places	150	Springfield	300
Leominster (incl. in N. Worcester County)		MICHIGAN		*St. Joseph	265
Lowell area	2,000	*Ann Arbor	5,000	**St. Louis	54,000
Lynn (incl. in N. Shore, listed under Boston Metro Region)		Bay City	150	Other places	150
		Benton Harbor area	240	MONTANA	
*Martha's Vineyard	300	**Detroit Metro Area	94,000	*Billings	300
New Bedford[N]	2,600	*Flint	1,800	Butte	100
Newburyport	280	*Grand Rapids	1,600	Helena (incl. in Butte)	
Newton (listed under Boston Metro Region)		**Jackson	200	*Kalispell	150
		*Kalamazoo	1,100	Missoula	200
North Adams (incl. in N. Berkshire County)		Lansing area	2,100	Other places	100
North Berkshire County	400	Midland	120	NEBRASKA	
		Mt. Clemens (incl. in Detroit)		Grand Island-Hastings (incl. in Lincoln)	
North Worcester County	1,500	Mt. Pleasant[N]	130	Lincoln	700
Northampton	1,200	*Muskegon	210	**Omaha	6,350
Peabody (incl. in N. Shore, listed under Boston Metro Region)		*Saginaw	115	Other places	50
		Traverse City	200	NEVADA	
		Other places	400	Carson City (incl. in Reno)	
Pittsfield-Berkshire County	3,500	MINNESOTA		*Las Vegas	55,600
Plymouth area	500	**Duluth	485	**Reno	2,100
Provincetown (incl. in Cape Cod)		*Minneapolis	31,500	Sparks (incl. in Reno)	
		Rochester	550	NEW HAMPSHIRE	
		**St. Paul	9,200	Bethlehem	200
		Other places	150	Concord	500
				Dover area	600

State and City	Jewish Population	State and City	Jewish Population	State and City	Jewish Population
Exeter (incl. in Portsmouth)		incl. in Northeastern N.J.)[N]	76,200	Middlesex County)	
Franconia (incl. in Bethlehem)		East Essex	10,800	Newark (incl. in Essex County)	
Hanover-Lebanon	500	Livingston	12,600	Northeastern N.J.[N]	386,000
*Keene	300	North Essex	15,600	Ocean County (also	
**Laconia	270	South Essex	20,300	incl. in Northeastern	
Littleton (incl. in Bethlehem)		West Orange-Orange	16,900	N.J.)	11,500
Manchester area	4,000	*Flemington	1,500	Passaic County (also incl. in Northeastern	
Nashua area	2,000	Freehold (incl. in Monmouth County)		N.J.)	17,000
Portsmouth area	1,250	Gloucester (incl. in Cherry Hill-S. N.J.)		Passaic-Clifton (incl. in Passaic County)	
Rochester (incl. in Dover)		Hoboken (listed under Hudson County)		Paterson (incl. in Passaic County)	
Salem	150	Hudson County (also incl. in Northeastern		Perth Amboy (incl. in Middlesex County)	
Other places	150	N.J.)	12,200	Phillipsburg (incl. in Warren County)	
		Bayonne	1,600	Plainfield (incl. in Union County)	
NEW JERSEY		Hoboken	1,100	Princeton area	3,000
Asbury Park (incl. in Monmouth County)		Jersey City	6,000	Somerset County (also incl. in Northeastern	
**Atlantic City (incl. Atlantic and Cape May counties)	15,800	North Hudson County[N]	3,500	N.J.)	11,000
Bayonne (listed under Hudson County)		Jersey City (listed under Hudson County)		Somerville (incl. in Somerset County)	
Bergen County (also incl. in Northeastern		Lakewood (incl. in Ocean County)		Sussex County (also incl. in Northeastern N.J.)	4,100
N.J.)	83,700	Livingston (listed under Essex County)		Toms River (incl. in Ocean County)	
Bridgeton	200	Middlesex County (also incl. in Northeastern		Trenton[N]	6,000
Bridgewater (incl. in Somerset County)		N.J.)[N]	45,000	Union County (also incl. in Northeastern	
Camden (incl. in Cherry Hill-S. N.J.)		Monmouth County (also incl. in Northeastern		N.J.)	30,000
Cherry Hill-Southern N.J.[N]	49,000	N.J.)	63,000	Vineland[N]	1,890
Edison (incl. in Middlesex County)		Morris County (also incl. in Northeastern		Warren County	400
Elizabeth (incl. in Union County)		N.J.)	33,500	Wayne (incl. in Passaic County)	
Englewood (incl. in Bergen County)		Morristown (incl. in Morris County)		Wildwood	330
Essex County (also		Mt. Holly (incl. in Cherry Hill-S. N.J.)		Willingboro (incl. in Cherry Hill-S. N.J.)	
		New Brunswick (incl. in		Other places	170

State and City	Jewish Population	State and City	Jewish Population	State and City	Jewish Population

NEW MEXICO
*Albuquerque.... 7,500
Las Cruces....... 600
Los Alamos...... 250
Rio Rancho (incl. in
  Albuquerque)
Santa Fe....... 1,500
Taos............ 300
Other places...... 150

NEW YORK
*Albany........ 12,000
Amenia (incl. in
  Poughkeepsie-
  Dutchess County)
Amsterdam...... 150
*Auburn.......... 115
Beacon (incl. in
  Poughkeepsie-
  Dutchess County)
*Binghamton (incl. all
  Broome County)
  2,600
Brewster (incl. in
  Putnam County)
*Buffalo....... 26,000
Canandaigua (incl. in
  Geneva)
Catskill.......... 200
Corning (incl. in
  Elmira)
*Cortland........ 150
Ellenville....... 1,600
Elmira[N]......... 950
Fleischmanns..... 100
Fredonia (incl. in
  Dunkirk)
Geneva area...... 300
Glens Falls[N]..... 800
*Gloversville...... 300
*Herkimer........ 130
Highland Falls (incl. in
  Orange County)

*Hudson......... 500
*Ithaca area..... 2,000
Jamestown....... 100
Kingston[N]...... 4,300
Kiryas Joel (incl. in
  Orange County)
Lake George (incl. in
  Glens Falls)
Liberty (incl. in
  Sullivan County)
Middletown (incl. in
  Orange County)
Monroe (incl. in
  Orange County)
Monticello (incl. in
  Sullivan County)
New Paltz (incl. in
  Kingston)
New York Metro Area[N]
  1,450,000
Bronx........ 83,700
Brooklyn.... 379,000
Manhattan... 314,500
Nassau County
  207,000
Queens...... 238,000
Staten Island.. 33,700
Suffolk County
  100,000
Westchester County
  94,000
Newark (incl. in
  Geneva total)
Newburgh (incl. in
  Orange County)
Niagara Falls..... 150
Olean........... 100
**Oneonta........ 300
Orange County. 15,000
Pawling (incl. in
  Poughkeepsie-
  Dutchess County)
Plattsburg........ 250

Port Jervis (incl. in
  Orange County)
Potsdam......... 200
*Poughkeepsie-Dutchess
  County....... 3,600
Putnam County.. 1,000
**Rochester..... 21,000
Rockland County
  83,100
Rome........... 150
Saratoga Springs.. 700
**Schenectady.... 5,200
Seneca Falls (incl. in
  Geneva)
South Fallsburg (incl.
  in Sullivan County)
***Sullivan County
  7,425
Syracuse[N]...... 7,500
Troy area........ 800
Utica[N]......... 1,300
Walden (incl. in Orange
  County)
Watertown....... 100
Woodstock (incl. in
  Kingston)
Other places...... 490

NORTH CAROLINA
Asheville[N]...... 1,300
**Chapel Hill-Durham
  4,000
Charlotte[N]...... 7,800
Elizabethtown (incl. in
  Wilmington)
*Fayetteville....... 300
Gastonia........ 210
*Greensboro..... 2,500
Greenville........ 240
*Hendersonville.... 250
**Hickory........ 110
High Point (incl. in
  Greensboro)

State and City	Jewish Population	State and City	Jewish Population	State and City	Jewish Population
Jacksonville (incl. in Wilmington)		Oxford (incl. in Butler County)		Bethlehem (incl. in Lehigh Valley)	
Raleigh-Wake County	6,000	**Sandusky	105	Bucks County (listed under Philadelphia area)	
Whiteville (incl. in Wilmington)		Springfield	200		
Wilmington area	1,200	*Steubenville	125	*Butler	250
Winston-Salem	485	Toledo[N]	5,900	**Chambersburg	150
Other places	450	Warren (incl. in Youngstown)		Chester (incl. in Delaware County, listed under Phila. area)	
		Wooster	175		
NORTH DAKOTA		Youngstown[N]	3,600	Chester County (listed under Phila. area)	
Fargo	500	*Zanesville	100		
Grand Forks	130	Other places	350	Coatesville (incl. in Chester County, listed under Phila. area)	
Other places	100				
		OKLAHOMA		Easton (incl. in Lehigh Valley)	
OHIO		Norman (incl. in Oklahoma City)			
**Akron	5,500	**Oklahoma City	2,300	*Erie	850
Athens	100			Farrell (incl. in Sharon)	
Bowling Green (incl. in Toledo)		*Tulsa	2,650	Greensburg (incl. in Pittsburgh)	
Butler County	900	Other places	100	**Harrisburg	7,000
**Canton	1,550			Hazleton area	300
Cincinnati[N]	22,500	OREGON		Honesdale (incl. in Wayne County)	
Cleveland[N]	81,000	Ashland (incl. in Medford)			
*Columbus	15,600	Bend	175	Jeannette (incl. in Pittsburgh)	
**Dayton	5,500	Corvallis	175	**Johnstown	275
Elyria	155	Eugene	3,000	Lancaster area	2,600
Fremont (incl. in Sandusky)		Grants Pass (incl. in Medford)		*Lebanon	350
Hamilton (incl. in Butler County)		**Medford	1,000	Lehigh Valley	8,500
Kent (incl. in Akron)		Portland[N]	25,000	Lewisburg (incl. in Sunbury)	
*Lima	180	**Salem	1,000	Lock Haven (incl. in Williamsport)	
Lorain	600	Other places	200	McKeesport (incl. in Pittsburgh)	
Mansfield	150			New Castle	200
Marion[N]	125	PENNSYLVANIA		Norristown (incl. in Montgomery County, listed under Phila. area)	
Middletown (incl. in Butler County)		Allentown (incl. in Lehigh Valley)			
New Philadelphia (incl. in Canton)		*Altoona	300		
Norwalk (incl. in Sandusky)		Ambridge (incl. in Pittsburgh)			
Oberlin (incl. in Elyria)		Beaver Falls (incl. in Upper Beaver County)			

State and City	Jewish Population	State and City	Jewish Population	State and City	Jewish Population
**Oil City 100		Chester County, listed		Chattanooga 1,350	
Oxford-Kennett Square		under Phila. area)		Kingsport (incl. in	
(incl. in Chester		Wilkes-Barre[N] . . . 3,200		Johnson City)	
County, listed under		**Williamsport 225		Knoxville. 1,650	
Phila. area)		York 1,800		Memphis 8,500	
Philadelphia area[N]		Other places 800		Nashville 6,000	
. . . . 206,000				Oak Ridge 250	
Bucks County		RHODE ISLAND		Other places 250	
. . . . 34,800		Cranston (incl. in			
Chester County		Providence)		TEXAS	
. . . . 10,100		Kingston (incl. in		Amarillo[N] 200	
Delaware County		Washington County)		*Austin 10,000	
. . . . 15,700		Newport-Middletown		Bay City (incl. in	
Montgomery County		 700		Wharton)	
. . . . 58,900		Providence area . 14,200		***Baytown 300	
Philadelphia . . 86,600		Washington County		Beaumont. 500	
Phoenixville (incl. in		 1,200		*Brownsville 450	
Chester County, listed		Westerly (incl. in		***College Station-	
under Phila. area)		Washington County)		Bryan 400	
***Pike County 300				*Corpus Christi . . 1,400	
Pittsburgh[N] 40,000		SOUTH CAROLINA		**Dallas 45,000	
Pottstown. 650		*Charleston. 4,500		El Paso 4,900	
Pottsville 225		**Columbia 2,750		*Fort Worth 5,000	
*Reading. 2,200		Florence area 220		Galveston. 800	
*Scranton 3,100		Georgetown (incl. in		Harlingen (incl. in	
Shamokin (incl. in		Myrtle Beach)		Brownsville)	
Sunbury)		Greenville 1,200		**Houston[N]. 42,000	
Sharon 300		Kingstree (incl. in		Kilgore (incl. in	
State College 700		Sumter)		Longview)	
Stroudsburg-Monroe		**Myrtle Beach 425		Laredo 130	
County 600		Rock Hill 100		Longview 100	
Sunbury[N] 200		*Spartanburg 500		*Lubbock. 230	
Tamaqua (incl. in		Sumter[N] 140		Lufkin (incl. in	
Hazleton)		York (incl. in Rock		Longview)	
Uniontown area . . . 150		Hill)		Marshall (incl. in	
Upper Beaver County		Other places 450		Longview)	
. . . . 180				*McAllen[N] 500	
Washington (incl. in		SOUTH DAKOTA		Midland-Odessa. . . 200	
Pittsburgh)		Sioux Falls 180		Port Arthur 100	
***Wayne County		Other places 150		*San Antonio . . . 10,000	
. . . . 500				South Padre Island	
Waynesburg (incl. in		TENNESSEE		(incl. in Brownsville)	
Pittsburgh)		Bristol (incl. in Johnson		Tyler. 400	
West Chester (incl. in		City)		Waco[N] 300	

State and City	Jewish Population	State and City	Jewish Population	State and City	Jewish Population
Wichita Falls	260	Harrisonburg (incl. in Staunton)		WEST VIRGINIA	
Other places	550	Lexington (incl. in Staunton)		Bluefield-Princeton	200
UTAH		Lynchburg area	275	*Charleston	975
Ogden	150	**Martinsville	100	Clarksburg	110
*Salt Lake City	4,200	Newport News-Hampton[N]	2,400	Fairmont (incl. in Clarksburg)	
Other places	100	Norfolk-Virginia Beach	19,000	Huntington[N]	250
VERMONT		Northern Virginia	35,100	Morgantown	200
Bennington area	300	Petersburg area	350	Parkersburg	110
*Brattleboro	350	Portsmouth-Suffolk (incl. in Norfolk)		**Wheeling	275
**Burlington	3,000	Radford (incl. in Blacksburg)		Other places	300
Manchester area	325	Richmond[N]	15,000	WISCONSIN	
Montpelier-Barre	550	Roanoke	900	Appleton area	300
Newport (incl. in St. Johnsbury)		Staunton[N]	370	Beloit	120
Rutland	550	Williamsburg (incl. in Newport News)		Fond du Lac (incl. in Oshkosh)	
**St. Johnsbury	140	Winchester[N]	270	Green Bay	500
Stowe	150	Other places	100	Janesville (incl. in Beloit)	
Woodstock	270			*Kenosha	300
Other places	100	WASHINGTON		La Crosse	100
VIRGINIA		Bellingham	500	*Madison	4,500
Alexandria (incl. in N. Virginia)		Ellensburg (incl. in Yakima)		Milwaukee[N]	21,300
Arlington (incl. in N. Virginia)		Longview-Kelso (incl. in Vancouver)		Oshkosh area	170
Blacksburg	175	*Olympia	560	*Racine	375
Charlottesville	1,500	***Port Angeles	100	Sheboygan	140
Chesapeake (incl. in Portsmouth)		*Seattle[N]	29,300	Waukesha (incl. in Milwaukee)	
Colonial Heights (incl. in Petersburg)		Spokane	1,500	Wausau[N]	300
Danville area	100	*Tacoma	2,000	Other places	300
Fairfax County (incl. in N. Virginia)		Tri Cities[N]	300	WYOMING	
Fredericksburg[N]	500	Vancouver	600	Casper	100
Hampton (incl. in Newport News)		**Yakima	150	Cheyenne	230
		Other places	350	Laramie (incl. in Cheyenne)	
				Other places	100

Notes

CALIFORNIA
Long Beach—includes in L.A. County: Long Beach, Signal Hill, Cerritos, Lakewood, Rossmoor, and Hawaiian Gardens. Also includes in Orange County: Los Alamitos, Cypress, Seal Beach, and Huntington Harbor.

Los Angeles—includes most of Los Angeles County, but excludes the eastern portion as well as those places listed above which are part of the Long Beach area. Also includes eastern edge of Ventura County.

Orange County—includes most of Orange County, but excludes towns in northern portion that are included in Long Beach.

Palm Springs—includes Palm Springs, Desert Hot Springs, Cathedral City, Palm Desert, and Rancho Mirage.

Pomona Valley—includes Alta Loma, Chino, Claremont, Cucamonga, La Verne, Montclair, Ontario, Pomona, San Dimas, and Upland.

Sacramento—includes Yolo, Placer, El Dorado, and Sacramento counties.

San Francisco Bay area—North Peninsula includes northern San Mateo County. South Peninsula includes southern San Mateo County and towns of Palo Alto and Los Altos in Santa Clara County. San Jose includes remainder of Santa Clara County.

COLORADO
Denver—includes Adams, Arapahoe, Boulder, Denver, and Jefferson counties.

Pueblo—includes all of Pueblo County east to Lamar, west and south to Trinidad.

CONNECTICUT
Bridgeport—includes Monroe, Easton, Trumbull, Fairfield, Bridgeport, Shelton, and Stratford.

Danbury—includes Danbury, Bethel, New Fairfield, Brookfield, Sherman, Newtown, Redding, and Ridgefield.

Hartford—includes most of Hartford County and Vernon, Rockville, Ellington, and Tolland in Tolland County.

Lower Middlesex County—includes Branford, Guilford, Madison, Clinton, Westbrook, Old Saybrook, Old Lyme, Durham, and Killingworth.

New Haven—includes New Haven, East Haven, Guilford, Branford, Madison, North Haven, Hamden, West Haven, Milford, Orange, Woodbridge, Bethany, Derby, Ansonia, Quinnipiac, Meriden, Seymour, and Wallingford.

New London—includes central and southern New London County. Also includes part of Middlesex County and part of Windham County.

Norwalk—includes Norwalk, Weston, Westport, East Norwalk, Wilton, and Georgetown.

Waterbury—includes Bethlehem, Cheshire, Litchfield, Morris, Middlebury, Southbury, Naugatuck, Prospect, Plymouth, Roxbury, Southbury, Southington, Thomaston, Torrington, Washington, Watertown, Waterbury, Oakville, Woodbury, Wolcott, Oxford, and other towns in Litchfield County and northern New Haven County.

DISTRICT OF COLUMBIA

Washington, D.C.—For a total of the Washington, D.C., metropolitan area, include Montgomery and Prince Georges counties in Maryland, and northern Virginia.

FLORIDA

Orlando—includes all of Orange and Seminole counties, southern Volusia County, and northern Osceola County.

Stuart-Port St. Lucie—includes all of Martin County and southern St. Lucie County.

GEORGIA

Augusta—includes Burke, Columbia, and Richmond counties.

ILLINOIS

Chicago—includes all of Cook and DuPage counties and a portion of Lake County.

Elgin—includes northern Kane County and southern McHenry County.

Rockford—includes Winnebago, Boone, and Stephenson counties.

Southern Illinois—includes lower portion of Illinois below Carlinville.

INDIANA

South Bend—includes St. Joseph and Elkhart counties.

KANSAS

Kansas City—includes Johnson and Wyandotte counties. For a total of the Kansas City metropolitan area, include Missouri portion.

Wichita—includes Sedgwick County and towns of Salina, Dodge City, Great Bend, Liberal, Russell, and Hays.

KENTUCKY
Lexington—includes Fayette, Bourbon, Scott, Clark, Woodford, Madison, Pulaski, and Jessamine counties.

LOUISIANA
Alexandria—includes towns in Allen, Grant, Rapides, and Vernon parishes.
Baton Rouge—includes E. Baton Rouge, Ascension, Livingston, St. Landry, Iberville, Pointe Coupee, and W. Baton Rouge parishes.
South Central—includes Abbeville, Lafayette, New Iberia, Crowley, Opelousas, Houma, Morgan City, Thibodaux, and Franklin.

MAINE
Southern Maine—includes York, Cumberland, and Sagadahoc counties.

MASSACHUSETTS
Andover—includes Andover, N. Andover, Boxford, Lawrence, Methuen, Tewksbury, and Dracut.
Boston Metropolitan region—Brockton-South Central includes Avon, Bridgewater, Brockton, Canton, East Bridgewater, Easton. Foxborough, Halifax, Randolph, Sharon, Stoughton, West Bridgewater, Whitman, and Wrentham. Framingham area includes—Acton, Bellingham, Boxborough, Framingham, Franklin, Holliston, Hopkinton, Hudson, Marlborough, Maynard, Medfield, Medway, Milford, Millis, Southborough, and Stow. Northeast includes—Chelsea, Everett, Malden, Medford, Revere, and Winthrop. North Central includes—Arlington, Belmont, Cambridge, Somerville, Waltham, and Watertown. Northwest includes—Bedford, Burlington, Carlisle, Concord, Lexington, Lincoln, Melrose, North Reading, Reading, Stoneham, Wakefield, Wilmington, Winchester, and Woburn. North Shore includes—Lynn, Saugus, Nahant, Swampscott, Lynnfield, Peabody, Salem, Marblehead, Beverly, Danvers, Middleton, Wenham, Topsfield, Hamilton, Manchester, Ipswich, Essex, Gloucester, and Rockport. Near West includes—Ashland, Dedham, Dover, Natick, Needham, Norfolk, Norwood, Sherborn, Sudbury, Walpole, Wayland, Wellesley, Weston, and Westwood. Southeast includes—Abington, Braintree, Cohasset, Duxbury, Hanover, Hanson, Hingham, Holbrook, Hull, Kingston, Marshfield, Milton, Norwell, Pembroke, Quincy, Rockland, Scituate, and Weymouth.
New Bedford—includes New Bedford, Dartmouth, Fairhaven, and Mattapoisett.

Springfield—includes Springfield, Longmeadow, E. Longmeadow, Hampden, Wilbraham, Agawam, and W. Springfield.

MICHIGAN

Mt. Pleasant—includes towns in Isabella, Mecosta, Gladwin, and Gratiot counties.

MISSOURI

Kansas City—For a total of the Kansas City metropolitan area, include the Kansas portion.

NEW HAMPSHIRE

Laconia—includes Laconia, Plymouth, Meredith, Conway, and Franklin.

NEW JERSEY

Cherry Hill-Southern N.J.—includes Camden, Burlington, and Gloucester counties.

Essex County-East Essex—includes Belleville, Bloomfield, East Orange, Irvington, Newark, and Nutley in Essex County, and Kearney in Hudson County. North Essex—includes Caldwell, Cedar Grove, Essex Fells, Fairfield, Glen Ridge, Montclair, North Caldwell, Roseland, Verona, and West Caldwell. South Essex—includes Maplewood, Millburn, Short Hills, and South Orange in Essex County, and Springfield in Union County.

Middlesex County—includes in Somerset County: Kendall Park, Somerset, and Franklin; in Mercer County: Hightstown; and all of Middlesex County.

Northeastern N.J.—includes Bergen, Essex, Hudson, Middlesex, Morris, Passaic, Somerset, Union, Hunterdon, Sussex, Monmouth, and Ocean counties.

North Hudson County—includes Guttenberg, Hudson Heights, North Bergen, North Hudson, Seacaucus, Union City, Weehawken, West New York, and Woodcliff.

Somerset County—includes most of Somerset County and a portion of Hunterdon County.

Trenton—includes most of Mercer County.

Union County—includes all of Union County except Springfield. Also includes a few towns in adjacent areas of Somerset and Middlesex counties.

Vineland—includes most of Cumberland County and towns in neighboring counties adjacent to Vineland.

NEW YORK

Elmira — includes Chemung, Tioga, and Schuyler counties.

Glens Falls — includes Warren and Washington counties, lower Essex County, and upper Saratoga County.

Kingston — includes eastern half of Ulster County.

New York Metropolitan area — includes the five boroughs of New York City, Westchester, Nassau, and Suffolk counties. For a total Jewish population of the New York metropolitan region, include Fairfield County, Connecticut; Rockland, Putnam, and Orange counties, New York; and Northeastern New Jersey.

Syracuse — includes Onondaga County, western Madison County and most of Oswego County.

Utica — southeastern third of Oneida County.

NORTH CAROLINA

Asheville — includes Buncombe, Haywood, and Madison counties.

Charlotte — includes Mecklenburg County. For a total of the Charlotte area, include Rock Hill, South Carolina.

OHIO

Cincinnati — includes Hamilton and Butler counties. For a total of the Cincinnati area, include the Covington-Newport area of Kentucky.

Cleveland — includes all of Cuyahoga County and portions of Lake, Geauga, Portage, and Summit counties. For a metropolitan total, please include Elyria, Lorain, and Akron.

Toledo — includes Fulton, Lucas, and Wood counties.

Youngstown — includes Mahoning and Trumbull counties.

PENNSYLVANIA

Philadelphia — For total Jewish population of the Philadelphia metropolitan region, include the Cherry Hill-Southern N.J., Princeton, and Trenton areas of New Jersey, and the Wilmington and Newark areas of Delaware.

Pittsburgh — includes all of Allegheny County and adjacent portions of Washington, Westmoreland, and Beaver counties.

Sunbury — includes Shamokin, Lewisburg, Milton, Selinsgrove, and Sunbury.

Wilkes-Barre — includes all of Luzerne County except southern portion, which is included in the Hazleton total.

SOUTH CAROLINA
Sumter—includes towns in Sumter, Lee, Clarendon, and Williamsburg counties.

TEXAS
Amarillo—includes Canyon, Childress, Borger, Dumas, Memphis, Pampa, Vega, and Hereford in Texas, and Portales, New Mexico.
Houston—includes Harris, Montgomery, and Fort Bend counties, and parts of Brazoria and Galveston counties.
McAllen—includes Edinburg, Harlingen, McAllen, Mission, Pharr, Rio Grande City, San Juan, and Weslaco.
Waco—includes McLennan, Coryell, Bell, Falls, Hamilton, and Hill counties.

VIRGINIA
Fredericksburg—includes towns in Spotsylvania, Stafford, King George, and Orange counties
Newport News—includes Newport News, Hampton, Williamsburg, James City, York County and Poquoson City.
Richmond—includes Richmond City, Henrico County, and Chesterfield County.
Staunton—includes towns in Augusta, Page, Shenandoah, Rockingham, Bath, and Highland counties.
Winchester—includes towns in Winchester, Frederick, Clarke, and Warren counties.

WASHINGTON
Seattle—includes King County and adjacent portions of Snohomish and Kitsap counties.
Tri Cities—includes Pasco, Richland, and Kennewick.

WISCONSIN
Milwaukee—includes Milwaukee County, Eastern Waukesha County, and Southern Ozaukee County.
Wausau—includes Stevens Point, Marshfield, Antigo, and Rhinelander.

Review
of
the
Year

OTHER COUNTRIES

Canada

National Affairs

CANADA ENJOYED A RELATIVELY calm and prosperous 1999. Inflation remained in check, economic growth was good, unemployment declined to the lowest levels in years, and the dollar recovered from its record lows of 1998, as the country shared in the strong economy south of the border. Politically, the specter of Quebec secession receded as the provincial government was mired in efforts to balance its budget while maintaining a reasonable level of services. Prime Minister Jean Chrétien's Liberals dominated federal politics, with the opposition ineffectively divided among four parties.

The government, whose earlier attempts to prosecute Nazi war criminals had been undermined by an adverse court decision, proposed legislation to the House of Commons in December providing for the prosecution and trial of anyone accused of genocide, crimes against humanity, or war crimes. The draft legislation explicitly barred the defense of "following orders." Introducing the bill, Justice Minister Anne McLellan asserted that "Canada is not, and will not be, a safe haven for war criminals."

At the Ontario election in June the Progressive Conservative government of Premier Mike Harris won reelection with a majority. David Young for the Tories and David Caplan and Monte Kwinter for the Liberals were elected in Toronto-area constituencies. Young was named parliamentary secretary to the minister of education.

Manitoba went to the polls in September and replaced the Conservative government with one led by the New Democrats. All three Jewish candidates who ran were defeated.

Sheila Finestone, who had represented a suburban Montreal district with a significant Jewish population for 15 years, resigned from the House of Commons in August upon being appointed to the Senate. That immediately set off a scramble to succeed her in the November by-election. McGill University law professor and former Canadian Jewish Congress (CJC) president Irwin Cotler, the Liberal nominee, won handily. With his background as an international human-rights advocate, Cotler promised to pursue that agenda and also announced his support for increased social spending.

In August Elinor Caplan, an MP from the Toronto area, was appointed to the sensitive post of minister of immigration. Very soon she had to contend with some

600 illegal immigrants from China caught trying to enter the country. In explaining her decision to admit them pending resolution of their refugee claims, Caplan cited the Talmudic principle that "if you save one life, you've saved the entire world." Caplan, indeed, proclaimed her commitment to continued immigration, specifying goals for the year 2000 of 200,000 immigrants and 25,000 refugees.

Israel and the Middle East

In January Canada began a two-year term on the UN Security Council. Although welcoming the development, Brian Morris, national chair of the Canada-Israel Committee (CIC), pointed out the inconsistency of Canada's UN record on Israel. While it had opposed efforts to expel or suspend Israel from the international body, it had supported resolutions that declared all Israeli actions in eastern Jerusalem and the occupied territories, especially settlement activity, illegal and even punishable. As the new term started, Morris called upon the government to withstand the pervasive anti-Israel bias in the UN system.

Less than a month later Canada antagonized pro-Israel groups by supporting a General Assembly resolution that called for an international conference to discuss the situation in the "occupied Palestinian territory" and the application of the Geneva conventions to the civilian population there. Subsequently the government reversed itself and worked to have the conference postponed. That effort failed, but when the conference convened in Geneva on July 15 Canada did not attend because, in the words of a foreign affairs spokesman, "it was unhelpful to the peace process."

Prime Minister Chrétien's remarks during Yasir Arafat's March visit to Ottawa raised hackles among many supporters of Israel. While rejecting Arafat's attempt to garner support for a unilateral declaration of Palestinian independence, Chrétien suggested that the outcome of Middle East negotiations should be a Palestinian state. Jewish leaders criticized him for the inconsistency of calling for negotiations while specifying the result in advance. Also in March, representatives of several key Jewish organizations met with Foreign Affairs Minister Lloyd Axworthy. They urged that negotiations between Israel and the Palestinians proceed without external intervention, argued against a unilateral Palestinian declaration of independence, and reminded the minister of continuing concerns about Canada's voting record in the UN.

On another front, Syrian foreign minister Farouk al-Shara, visiting Ottawa in June, requested Canada to take a central role in any peacekeeping operation that might become necessary on the Golan Heights in the event of an Israeli-Syrian peace agreement. He also opened Syria's first embassy in Canada.

After an investigation, the government announced in September that it had found no evidence that Israel was still using Canadian passports for clandestine purposes. A Canadian living in Israel had claimed in 1998 that he had been asked by Israeli officials to turn over his Canadian passport.

In October Canada and Israel signed a treaty pledging mutual legal assistance, designed to facilitate cooperation between the two states on criminal matters such as evidence, records, fugitives, and witnesses. Justice Minister Yossi Beilin of Israel visited Ottawa for the signing.

In May the Canada Customs and Revenue Agency revoked the charity status of the Press Foundation in Toronto because it was raising funds for the council of settlers in the occupied territories. Charities may not send money to bodies which further causes that are inconsistent with Canadian foreign policy, and the government considered Israeli settlements beyond the Green Line illegal hindrances to the peace process. The foundation appealed the decision.

In July rallies were held in several cities in support of 13 Iranian Jews who were arrested and awaiting trial on espionage charges. Jewish organizations asked the government to intervene with Iranian authorities to obtain their release.

Sergio Marchi, the minister of international trade, brought a group of Canadian businesspeople to the Middle East, including Israel, in March. Praising the success of the Canada-Israel free trade agreement, Marchi lauded the Israeli economy, singling out the trade opportunities made available by Israeli high tech. Marchi also used the opportunity to sign a trade agreement with the Palestinian Authority.

A major irritant in Canada-Israel relations concerned airline flights between the two countries. El Al, the Israeli national airline, had had a monopoly on the route until 1998, but was now rapidly losing its North American market share to Air Canada, which utilized its partner relationships to funnel U.S. passengers through Toronto on their way to Israel. Air Canada, allowed four weekly flights to Israel in the winter and seven in the summer, wanted more weekly flights, especially in the winter, than Israel was prepared to allow. When Israel threatened to terminate the air agreement, which would effectively have barred Air Canada from flying to Israel, Canada reportedly reminded Israel that its U.S. flights go over Canadian territory, and that if such overflights were barred, El Al would incur significant additional fuel costs and longer flight times. This led to a breakdown of the bilateral airline agreement and a crisis that threatened to terminate service between the two countries. Israel, however, backed down and allowed Air Canada daily flights throughout the winter. Then, at a meeting in November, El Al sought the right to transport passengers originating in the United States to Israel via Canada, but was turned down by Canada. Stanley Morais, El Al's Canadian sales director, declared that Canada's stance was "definitely not a fair competition" and the Israeli airline announced that it would terminate its nonstop service between Montreal and Tel Aviv at the end of the year, leaving that route to Air Canada. In the meantime El Al inaugurated twice-weekly nonstop service from Toronto. (In the past all flights from Toronto had stopped in Montreal.) In December the two countries finally hammered out a temporary agreement, good only until April 1, 2000. It allowed Air Canada to continue with its daily flights and authorized El Al to increase its service from five to seven flights per week, though it only planned to operate a maximum of three during the winter. And El Al was now allowed, for the first time, to transport U.S. passengers via Canada.

Palestinian terrorist Mahmoud Mohammad Issa Mohammad, who lived in Brantford, Ontario, faced deportation after an immigration adjudicator cited him, in April, for an attack against an El Al plane in Athens in 1968. At that time, as a member of the Popular Front for the Liberation of Palestine, Mohammad and an accomplice shot at the plane, killing an Israeli passenger. Mohammad, who had been imprisoned in Greece for less than a year of a 17-year sentence, was released in response to a terrorist hijacking of a Greek airliner, and immigrated to Canada by lying about his past in 1987. Authorities had tried to deport him for over ten years but his application for refugee status tied up the deportation in procedural difficulties. Mohammad planned to appeal the deportation decision to the Immigration and Refugee Board.

A murder in Toronto complicated Canada-Israel relations. Dmitri Matti Baranovski, a 15-year-old Russian immigrant, was beaten to death in November. Police charged 19-year-old Daniel Weiz with second-degree murder, along with three younger teenagers whose identities were not revealed because of their age. Weiz was an Israeli citizen and had the status of a permanent resident of Canada. At the time of the murder he was visiting Toronto, though before being charged with the crime he returned to Israel, where he was on active duty in the army. He was arrested in Israel in December at Canada's request, but denied any involvement in the killing. When a formal extradition request is filed Israel will have to decide what to do, in light of a recent Israeli statute that, for the first time, allows Israelis to be sent abroad for criminal trials.

The number of Israelis granted refugee status in Canada continued to decline in 1998, with only 24 accepted and 625 rejected. This was in sharp contrast to the situation four years earlier when some 50 percent of applications were approved, a development that harmed the Canada-Israel relationship. Israel had put considerable effort into persuading Canadian authorities that, in the words of the Israeli embassy, "In a democratic and law-based society such as Israel, there can be no justification for refugees, as there are sufficient judicial avenues for persons suffering grievances." Many of the claimants had come to Israel from what had been the Soviet Union, and Israel believed that they had used the Law of Return as a device to pave the way for eventual immigration to Canada.

Minister of National Defense Art Eggleton visited Israel in September where he conferred with Prime Minister and Defense Minister Barak. One of the issues discussed was the possible use of Canadian troops as peacekeepers on the Golan Heights in the event of an Israel-Syria peace treaty. While in Israel Eggleton commented that "we will continue to make our contribution. Israel has a good friend in Canada."

In remarks to Jewish community leaders in June, Louis Beaudoin, Quebec's minister of international relations, said that the province—which pursues its own foreign policy—sought to enhance its economic, cultural, and technological relations with Israel. A concrete manifestation of that interest was the visit to Israel in November of Deputy Premier and Finance Minister Bernard Landry, accompanied by the chair of the Quebec-Israel Committee, Thomas Hecht. Other participants included key industrial and financial leaders from the private and public sectors. The delegation met with Regional Cooperation Minister Shimon Peres and explored a number of possible avenues for commercial collaboration with Israeli counterparts. Earlier in the year a group of Quebec University rectors had visited Israel to discuss cooperative projects with Israeli universities.

In October it was revealed that Canada, through its embassy in Havana and with the implicit blessing of Cuban president Fidel Castro, had been instrumental in enabling some 400 Cuban Jews to immigrate to Israel since 1995. The immigrants entered Israel with Canadian travel documents.

Anti-Semitism and Racism

Holocaust denier and Nazi sympathizer Ernst Zundel had sued the major political parties and their leaders in 1998 for banning him from the Parliament buildings where he wanted to hold a press conference. Douglas Christie, his lawyer, was also banned early in 1999. In January, Justice James Chadwick dismissed Zundel's case because there was no actionable legal issue raised and because the dignity and integrity of Parliament had to be preserved. In another case involving Zundel—his hearing before a human-rights tribunal in connection with his racist and anti-Semitic Web site—the publisher succeeded in forcing one member of the tribunal, Rita Devins, off the panel on the grounds of bias. Devins had been a member of the Ontario Human Rights Commission in 1988 when it issued a press release commending a guilty verdict in Zundel's criminal trial for spreading "false news" (i.e., Holocaust denial).

The Human Rights Tribunal of British Columbia, acting on the complaint of a local businessman, ruled in January that journalist Doug Collins had published articles in the *North Shore News* that promoted hatred of Jews. He was ordered to pay a fine of $2,000, apologize publicly, and refrain from publishing further anti-Semitic material. The tribunal concluded that several articles in 1994 "collectively and through repetition of anti-Semitic themes, take on a vicious tone that taps into a centuries-old pattern of persecution and slander of Jews." Collins's lawyer appealed, contending that the province's law against the promotion of hatred was unconstitutional. In September, when Collins and his lawyer held a "free speech" meeting at the main branch of the Vancouver Public Library to raise funds for the appeal, some 100 protesters demonstrated against them. In December the appeal was rejected.

In October George Burdi, a promoter of racist music who operated in the Windsor and Detroit areas, pleaded guilty to the charge of willfully promoting hatred and was given a conditional one-year jail sentence.

A frightening anti-Semitic incident in August shook the Toronto Jewish community. Two elderly men walking to synagogue for Friday evening services were accosted by two strangers and badly beaten with a crowbar. One of the victims was a Holocaust survivor. Also in Toronto, a Jewish cemetery was vandalized in October: six monuments and a Holocaust memorial were spray painted with anti-Semitic graffiti. Overall, Toronto police reported that out of the 110 hate crimes reported during the first half of the year, 11 were anti-Semitic.

Winnipeg Jews experienced the worst synagogue desecration in memory in August, when over 200 headstones were knocked over or uprooted at the Hebrew Sick Benefit Association Cemetery. The damage was estimated at $100,000. Five young men between the ages of 15 and 21 were arrested and charged with mischief. The incident appeared to have grown out of a rowdy party at a home near the cemetery, and it was unclear whether the motive was anti-Semitism.

In March Jewish students protested against an anti-Israel and anti-Jewish campaign by pro-Palestinian students at Montreal's Concordia University. The Arab group was partially funded by the university, and the president of Montreal Hillel charged Concordia with "giving money to something that is blatantly anti-Semitic." In June anti-Semitic graffiti were repeatedly sprayed on the walls of a kosher food store in Montreal.

How to deal with racist propaganda on the Internet presented a challenge to law enforcement authorities. The Web site of the Nationalistes Québecois Aryens attacked Jews and other minorities. After the Canadian representative of the Simon Wiesenthal Center notified the Internet service provider, in January, the provider responded that it had a policy of zero tolerance toward threatening or harassing material, and shut the site down. The Wiesenthal Center also identified another racist Web site that was being disseminated through CadVision, an Internet service provider in Calgary. When notified of the content of the site maintained by the Society for the Segregation of the Races, the provider removed it. The Canadian representative of the Wiesenthal Center claimed to have shut down a total of some 50 such racist Web sites in Canada by intervening with the service providers. The Canadian government itself refused to take steps against extremist Internet sites despite calls from Jewish organizations for action either by the Canadian Radio and Television Commission or by the Human Rights Commission.

In January a Polish-language newspaper in Toronto, *Gazeta,* ran an anti-Semitic article by Father Jan Kurdybelski that accused Jews of treachery, greed, Bolshevism, and collaboration with the Nazis, and claimed that the Jewish nation is "perfidious and hated by God." CJC Ontario Region chair Keith Landy described this as "unbridled anti-Semitism of the worst kind" and the paper published a retraction in March.

CJC in Quebec complained to the provincial press council about an article in the French daily *La Presse* in February that used the word "*juiverie,*" which the CJC considered highly offensive. The press council rejected the complaint in December, noting that the author had issued a clarification. The CJC's additional claim that other pieces by this journalist about Israel and Jews were also marred by anti-Semitic stereotypes was also rejected.

Quinn McFarlane, an Ontario white supremacist with a long history of racist and criminal activity, had been given a conditional one-year sentence in 1998 for punching a reporter outside a Toronto court during the trial of a skinhead. In 1999 the Ontario Court of Appeal changed the conditional sentence into a mandatory year in jail because of the man's previous record and the danger that he posed to the community.

The role of the CJC in Canadian life was dragged into a trial, in April, of seven skinheads charged with racist protests against Roma (Gypsy) refugees. The skinheads' defense attorney subpoenaed Bernie Farber, executive director of CJC's Ontario Region. The questioning of Farber was designed to suggest that the CJC had inordinate influence over politicians and law-enforcement authorities, leading to the allegedly selective prosecution of people such as the defendants.

Journalist and McGill University chancellor Gretta Chambers addressed a conference in Montreal in April about relations between Jews and Quebecois. Endeavoring to explain the identification of Montreal Jews with the anglophone community, which had subjected Jews to genteel anti-Semitism for so many decades, she suggested that Jews felt the need to be closely tied to English-speaking Jewish communities throughout North America. And she noted the irony that, over the last 20 years, Jews had assumed a leadership role in the life of English-speaking Montreal. She said that "the contribution of the Jewish component of the anglophone minority of Quebec has become an essential part of its vitality, of its institutional power, of its cultural roots and of its modern relevance."

When British New Age writer David Icke spoke at the University of Toronto in October Jews and members of the Green Party protested outside. Bernie Farber of the CJC described his writings as "the worst anti-Semitic garbage I have ever read." Police and immigration officials monitored his marathon speech for possible legal offenses.

Nazi War Criminals

Since the Supreme Court barred the criminal prosecution of people accused of Nazi-era crimes in Europe, the government sought, instead, to denaturalize and deport such individuals. This, however, took a very long time and did not always succeed.

In January the Federal Court of Canada found that Vladimir Katriuk had misrepresented his life history when applying to immigrate to Canada in 1951. The decision made it possible for the federal cabinet to strip him of his citizenship, leaving him vulnerable to deportation to his native Ukraine. Judge Marc Nadon held that Katriuk had voluntarily participated in the activities of Battalion 118, a unit that operated as part of the Waffen-SS in what is now Belarus, and had been implicated in numerous atrocities between 1941 and 1944. Katriuk concealed his involvement and used a false name when he applied for admission to Canada. CJC national executive director Jack Silverstone welcomed the ruling, adding, "I personally believe the government is going in the right direction." Katriuk appealed to the Federal Court of Appeal, despite a provision of the Citizenship Act that does not allow appeals in cases of fraudulent entry into Canada. The appeal was denied, clearing the way for his deportation in 2000.

Prosecutors achieved another victory in the case of Serge Kisluk, who had been a police officer in Ukraine during the war. In June Allan Lufty, a judge of the Federal Court, ruled that Kisluk had lied to immigration authorities about his collaboration with the Nazis. Contrary to Kisluk's testimony the judge found that he had participated in the shooting of an innocent Jewish woman and the beating of a Jewish man: "Simply put, I do not believe the respondent's testimony on any contentious issue." Lufty's decision was based on testimony that Kisluk must have been asked certain questions when he sought to enter the country in 1948, which, if answered truthfully, would have disqualified him. Jack Silverstone hailed the decision, noting that it was at variance with the finding in the 1998 Dueck case, which had found that there had been no uniform procedure for interrogating prospective immigrants. The decision was expected to lead to Kisluk's deportation.

Eduards Podins, on the other hand, successfully defended himself against deportation by convincing a Federal Court judge that he had not been asked about his wartime experience when he applied to enter Canada from Britain in 1958. He was accused of having worked as a guard at a Nazi camp in Latvia, but the judge concluded that he had worked as a shopkeeper, despite being on the payroll of an auxiliary police unit.

Court proceedings against Michael Baumgartner, begun in February, had not been concluded by the end of the year. The government contended that he had joined the SS voluntarily in 1942, subsequently served in two concentration camps, and then lied about his associations when he applied to immigrate to Canada.

The case of Ukrainian labor-camp guard and alleged Nazi collaborator Wasyl Odynsky went to trial in March. He was accused of having served as a guard at the Trawniki and Poniatowa labor camps in Poland during 1943 and 1944, and then lying about his record when he applied to enter Canada in 1948. After historical testimony was presented about the mass killings of remaining camp inmates after the SS had liquidated most of them in the fall of 1943, Odynsky denied any involvement in the murders.

The government initiated a case against Jacob Fast, who was originally from Ukraine. It alleged that he had concealed his German citizenship, collaboration with the Nazi occupiers in Ukraine, and association with the SD. Fast's was the 16th and latest such case brought by the government.

Holocaust-Related Matters

Prime Minister Chrétien visited the Auschwitz-Birkenau extermination complex in January, accompanied by CJC president Moshe Ronen, Ronen's father — a survivor of Auschwitz — and Jack Silverstone. In ceremonies at the camp Chrétien stressed the need for tolerance and affirmed a "collective responsibility to make sure such things do not happen again." It was the first visit to the site by a Canadian head of government. The trip was marred by criticism from the Canadian-Polish Congress for not being invited to participate.

Controversy about a proposed Holocaust museum in Ottawa continued to swirl. The Ukrainian-Canadian Civil Liberties Association brought together some 20 groups to form Canadians for a Genocide Museum (CFAGM), which would commemorate victims of all 20th-century genocides. Jewish groups declined to join this effort, fearing that such a genocide museum would lead to the abandonment of the Holocaust museum project. CJC president Ronen, pointing out that the idea for a genocide museum was being promoted primarily by Eastern European ethnic groups, charged that it was motivated by opposition to official recognition of the Holocaust's uniqueness. In addition, Palestine Heritage Canada was among the supporters of the more general genocide approach, and one of its members was secretary of CFAGM. Ronen claimed that Prime Minister Chrétien had assured him, when they visited Auschwitz, that a suitable site for a Holocaust museum would be found.

While contending that humanitarian intervention was necessary in Kosovo, human-rights advocate Irwin Cotler rejected the relevance of Holocaust analogies. Writing in the *Canadian Jewish News* in May, Cotler drew a distinction between the Holocaust and contemporary events in the former Yugoslavia. As he put it, "to suggest that Kosovo is another Holocaust, runs the risk of trivializing the Holocaust, while minimizing the evil of Kosovo."

Michael Marrus, the noted historian and dean of graduate studies at the University of Toronto, was appointed in November to a panel of experts that will review published Vatican archival material from the World War II period. Marrus is one of three Jewish historians on the six-member panel.

JEWISH COMMUNITY

Demography

Greater Toronto, already the country's largest Jewish community, was expected to grow rapidly in the coming years. A study by Jay Brodbar, the Toronto federation's planning specialist, suggested that the 2001 census may show a population in excess of 200,000, which would likely mean that over half of Canada's Jews lived in and around Toronto. Brodbar found that the fastest growth was occurring in the suburban area known as the York Region, containing the towns of Markham, Vaughan, and Richmond Hill, where about 60,000 Jews, primarily young families, lived in a number of heavily Jewish neighborhoods.

The Canadian Jewish community continued to receive immigrants, primarily from the former Soviet Union, but also from Latin America, the Middle East, and Europe. Jewish Immigrant Aid Services reported that it helped resettle over 3,000 newcomers during the 1998–99 fiscal year.

Poverty continued to be a problem for the community. Carleton University professor Allan Moscovitch estimated that 17 percent of Canada's Jews lived below the poverty line, a figure comparable to that for the general population. Moscovitch estimated that more than a quarter of the Jewish poor had arrived in Canada within the past five or six years. In a presentation to a conference on Jewish poverty in Winnipeg in November, he contended that "there's a reluctance in the Jewish community to acknowledge poverty." And Mark Zarecki, executive director of the Jewish family services agency in Ottawa, called upon the community to insure equal treatment for poorer Jews.

Communal Affairs

There was considerable excitement among Montreal's Jews over the construction of the new community campus, achieved by expanding and renovating existing facilities. Some $12 million was spent to remodel the Cummings House—the site of agency offices—the Jewish Public Library, and the Montreal Holocaust Museum, as well as to build a new conference center. Another $18 million was spent on the YM-YWHA across the street. The dedication took place in November even though the work was not yet complete. The federal, provincial, and local governments had each contributed $1.3 million to the project, and their representatives were in attendance: Deputy Prime Minister Herb Gray, Quebec premier Lucien Bouchard, and Montreal mayor Pierre Bourque. Outgoing Federation CJA president Stan Plotnick, the driving force behind the new campus, remarked that "I believe today the Montreal Jewish community stands a bit more proudly, is more secure, more understood, more recognized, more appreciated, and more encouraged about its future." No funds from the regular federation campaign were used for this privately funded undertaking. Indeed, after several years of budgetary restraint, increased campaign receipts in 1998 enabled the federation to boost agency budgets by 2.7 percent for 1999.

One of the changes connected with the new campus was the move of the Quebec regional office of CJC from its old downtown location to the new campus. As part of a reorganization, CJC also moved most of its national departments and personnel from Montreal to Ottawa, and then donated the Samuel Bronfman House, its national headquarters for over a quarter of a century, to Concordia University. Only the administrative offices and the archives remained in the Montreal building. Since the CJC has tended to focus increasingly on political advocacy, the move to Ottawa would put it in closer proximity to the federal government. "That should have been done years ago," said National Executive Director Jack Silverstone. He added that the move had nothing to do with political developments in Quebec and was not meant to reflect on the status of the Montreal Jewish community.

Controversy over the circumstances surrounding the death of Herman Krausz at the Jewish General Hospital in Montreal in 1998 led to a coroner's inquest in February 1999. Krausz died after physicians removed him from life support in the intensive care unit despite moral and religious objections raised by his two sons. The doctors testified that, despite the opposition from the family, they had followed hospital policy. In addition, there was some dispute over what the dying man wanted done. In August, summarizing the family's case, lawyer Peter Kalichman argued that the doctors had erred "morally, ethically, and legally." He also criticized the hospital's ethics committee, alleging that it "completely failed in its responsibility to resolve the conflict" between the family and the physicians.

Canadian Jews took up the cause of 13 of their brethren who were imprisoned in Iran, facing espionage trials and possible death sentences. At a June rally in Toronto, religious leaders from several faith communities joined Jewish leaders in condemning the arrests and calling for the speedy release of the captives. CJC regional chair Keith Landy proclaimed that "when one of us is threatened, all of us are threatened," while Ontario UJA Federation president Alan Sandler added, "we are here because for us, silence itself would be criminal." MP Jim Peterson assured the demonstrators that the government had expressed its concerns to Iran and was monitoring the situation closely. Rallies were also held in Montreal, Vancouver, Ottawa, Calgary, and Winnipeg.

The Communauté Sépharade du Québec (CSQ) held a memorial service in August for King Hassan II of Morocco, who died in July. Speakers praised the late king for maintaining good relations between Muslims and Jews. CSQ president Moise Amsellem declared that the king was part of the "providential force that kept us at peace with our Muslim compatriots and sealed, as never before, the bonds of friendship and affection, of neighborliness, and tolerance."

Charles R. Bronfman, the longtime Canadian Jewish community leader, became the first board chairman of the newly formed United Jewish Communities of North America (UJC), an amalgamation of the United Jewish Appeal (UJA), the United Israel Appeal (UIA), and the Council of Jewish Federations (CJF). Steve Ain, a senior executive with CJF Canada, became the interim CEO of the UJC. In another major undertaking, Bronfman and Michael Steinhardt launched Birthright Israel, a project designed to insure a free trip to Israel for every young Jew.

Maxyne Finkelstein, the new executive director of UIA Federations Canada, was named to succeed Ain as the executive vice president of the organization when Ain moves to New York in 2000. She said that, in her view, the merger of CJF Canada and UIA Canada simply gave recognition to the way that the Canadian community had already been operating. Finkelstein will be the first woman to hold the top professional position in any Jewish federation on the continent.

In a new edition of his book, *Coat of Many Colors,* historian and former CJC president Irving Abella expressed optimism about the community. He explained that the "sense of insecurity and marginality that has dominated the Canadian Jewish community for too much of this century" had been due to the country's small population and immense size. Canadian Jews, he argued, had internalized many of the "hang ups" of Canadians in general in addition to those common to Jews. But Abella found the situation vastly improved from a half-century before, when Canada was a "benighted, xenophobic, and anti-Semitic country."

Montreal's Mount Sinai Hospital won a court case in June against a Quebec government effort to eliminate its short-term beds as part of a health care reorganization scheme. After a favorable ruling from the Quebec Court of Appeal, the hospital will be able to maintain both its short-term and long-term beds. Had the change been implemented, Mount Sinai would have lost a significant portion of its funding.

Stanley Diamond of Montreal established Jewish Records Indexing-Poland, to provide a comprehensive source of information about individual 19th-century Polish Jews. The listing is expected to become an invaluable tool for genealogical research.

The *Canadian Jewish News* won several Simon Rockower Awards for excellence in Jewish journalism from the American Jewish Press Association, as well as an award from the Quebec Community Newspaper Association.

Israel-Related Matters

In January Toronto's UJA Federation asked the Israeli Knesset to drop two bills that were before it that would have cemented the Orthodox domination over the Jewish religion. One bill would have recognized only those conversions performed in Israel that were under Orthodox auspices, while the other would have required all members of local religious councils to pledge loyalty to the Chief Rabbinate.

Religion

In May, after the Central Conference of American Rabbis, meeting in Pittsburgh, adopted a new statement of principles emphasizing religious observance, Canadian rabbis in attendance did not anticipate any radical change in Canadian Reform congregations, since Reform in Canada had long been more traditional than in the U.S. The Canadian Reform movement opened its first summer camp, Camp George, north of Toronto, in 1999. A Jewish educational component formed an integral part of the program.

A rift developed in the Winnipeg community over the performance of marriages. Rabbi Michael Levenson, who assumed the pulpit of Temple Shalom, a Reform synagogue, in 1998, obtained his board's approval to perform same-sex marriages as well as mixed marriages, and announced his intention to do so in January 1999. The Winnipeg Council of Rabbis condemned the move in February, five of the eight members signing a statement to the effect that "this step is fraught with danger to the Jewish community," and arguing that mixed marriages meant "communal suicide." Levenson, however, the only Reform rabbi in Winnipeg, insisted that his policy "will strengthen the community by bringing in more people than we lose."

In an action that created considerable publicity, the Vaad Harabonim (Orthodox rabbinical council) of Toronto, in June, barred the burial in a Jewish cemetery of a man who had become an ordained Christian minister. According to Rabbi Moshe Stern, head of the Vaad, Malvern Jacobs had accepted Jesus as the messiah, become a deacon of a Christian church, and worked to convert Jews to Christianity, facts that the Vaad discovered only after his death. The funeral service was held at a Jewish chapel, followed by a procession to the cemetery where Jacobs had owned a plot, but the gates were locked. After two hours of waiting on the street outside the cemetery, the hearse returned to the chapel. Jacobs was interred in a non-Jewish cemetery the next day. CJC Ontario Region chair Keith Landy, speaking on behalf of Pardes Shalom cemetery, said that Jacobs's actions had "clearly left him outside the Jewish community."

In Montreal, a 1998 court decision denying a condominium owner the right to build a sukkah on his balcony was appealed to Quebec's highest court in March 1999. The League of Human Rights of B'nai Brith Canada intervened in the case on behalf of the aggrieved condominium residents, filing papers that argued that the judge had erred in accepting one of two conflicting expert opinions on what Jewish law required.

Levitts Kosher Foods, Inc., a Montreal meat producer, became involved in a dispute with the Council of Orthodox Rabbis (COR) in Toronto, which supervises kashrut in that city. The COR announced that it would withdraw certification from any store or restaurant that sold or used fresh meat from Levitts, even though the company had kashrut certification from Montreal's Vaad Ha'ir as well as from a respected U.S. body. The reasons for this action were two policies that the COR had adopted during the 1980s, one barring ritually slaughtered meat from outside the community, and the other requiring that the principals in kosher firms be Sabbath observers. Levitts failed to meet either standard. Levitts took the case to court, but in July Madam Justice Mary Lou Benotto granted a stay to the three COR rabbis named as respondents in the case, essentially telling the parties to resolve their differences in a bet din, a court of Jewish law.

In April, in another court case, Rabbi Joseph Ben-David won a $130,000 judgment from his former employer, Congregation B'nai Israel in St. Catharines, Ontario, for wrongful dismissal. After serving the synagogue in several capacities for

25 years, his contract was terminated in 1994. Justice William Festeryga of the Ontario Court, general division, found that the congregation had acted in a "cruel, abusive, insolent, and hurtful manner."

Rabbi Allan Nadler, appointed by the Orthodox Congregation Chevra Kadisha B'nai Jacob in Montreal to officiate for the High Holy Days, dramatically walked out of the congregation after delivering his sermon at the beginning of the Kol Nidre service on Yom Kippur eve and did not return. At issue was the participation of non-Jews in the synagogue choir assembled for the holidays, in contravention of Orthodox practice. When the makeup of the choir became known after Rosh Hashanah, Nadler's rabbinical colleagues protested, and when the synagogue board denied his request to have only Jewish choir members for Yom Kippur, he decided to deliver his Kol Nidre sermon and leave.

Education

For some time the Ontario Jewish community had been trying to secure public funding for its Jewish day schools. Even though the provincial government funded Catholic schools, officials steadfastly refused to treat Jewish schools equally. Ontario, the province with the largest Jewish population by far, was the only province that discriminated in this way. CJC leadership met with Premier Mike Harris in February, but he refused even to discuss school funding. The most he would agree to was that the government should make health-support services available in Jewish schools.

During the spring election campaign Harris again dashed any hopes for a breakthrough by proclaiming his commitment to the public schools. Jewish leaders strongly criticized him for seeming to make the matter a Jewish issue when the fact was that other religious groups were also asking for school aid. Just before the election Harris sent a letter to the CJC saying that he would consider the Jewish community's request for $6.5 million for health services in Jewish schools, which included funds for the education of the handicapped. At an October meeting with the executive of CJC's Ontario Region, Minister of Education Janet Ecker listened sympathetically but gave no encouragement. No action was expected before mid-2000.

Later in October, in response to a complaint from a Toronto Jewish parent, the UN Human Rights Commission found that Ontario discriminated against non-Catholics in school funding, in violation of a 1976 human-rights covenant. In response, Ecker reiterated her government's determination to fund only the public and Catholic schools. Although the UN decision did not have the force of law, it did have the effect of embarrassing Canada, which claimed a leadership role in the international struggle for human rights and was a signatory to the covenant in question. The Ontario Region of CJC called upon the federal government to put pressure on the provincial government, since "in order for Canada not to be named a human rights violator, our country must remedy the situation quickly."

However even though the federal government was legally the respondent in this human-rights case, education was purely a provincial responsibility in the Canadian federal system, placing limits on what the federal government could do. In December Canada was given three months to comply, but Ecker vowed that under no circumstances would Ontario extend funding to private and non-Catholic religious schools: "Period. End of story." With the CJC insisting that "we are going to battle for justice," the situation was unresolved as the year ended.

Montreal's Jewish People's Schools and Peretz Schools were the surprise beneficiaries of an anonymous bequest from someone in South America. The $3.4 million will be used to set up a foundation in memory of long-time principal Shloime Wiseman. The four main emphases of the foundation will be the study and use of Yiddish language and culture, the love and appreciation of Israel, a pluralistic approach to Judaism, and study of the Holocaust.

Yeshiva Beit Yizchak in Hamilton announced plans to open Maimonides College in 2000. The college, expected to attract some 30 students, will be the first institution in Canada to ordain rabbis.

In an unusual collaboration, the Torah and Vocational Institute (TAV), with ties to Chabad, established a relationship with the Université du Québec à Montréal that will enable TAV to offer bachelor's degree programs in computer science and business administration. The courses, offered in the TAV facility in the western part of Montreal and taught by the university faculty, began in September.

An 11-person delegation from Israel's Ministry of Education visited several Canadian cities during May to study Jewish educational practices and to foster exchanges and other relationships between students and educators in the two countries.

Concordia University in Montreal established an Institute for Canadian Jewish Studies. In August the university announced that the first holder of the chair in Quebec and Canadian Jewish Studies would be Norman Ravvin, a specialist in Canadian Jewish literature.

Community and Intergroup Relations

The question of prayer in the public schools was a major community-relations issue. In 1993, Unitarian, Muslim, and Jewish parents in Saskatchewan challenged the common practice of reciting the Lord's Prayer daily, contending that it had the effect of discriminating against non-Christians even though they were allowed to leave the classroom or remain without participating in the exercise. The case went to a provincial human-rights tribunal, which finally completed hearing testimony in July 1999.

Both the local Jewish community in Saskatoon and B'nai Brith Canada intervened in the case. Rabbi Roger Pavey, the retired leader of a local congregation, testified that the manner in which the prayer was used was in fact coercive, and since real prayer was by definition voluntary, this religious exercise was meaningless. He also objected to the practice of singling out those who wished not to recite the prayer, which amounted, he said, to labeling them as "deviant." Dr. Karen Mock, a psychologist and director of B'nai Brith Canada's League of Human Rights, testified that the self-esteem of the non-Christian children was jeopardized. Late in July the tribunal issued a decision banning the Lord's Prayer from classrooms in the province. Retired judge Ken Halvorson, who chaired the tribunal, found that mandatory prayers denied children their religious freedom. He urged the school board to "shed its image as a backwater of religious intolerance" and condemned the practice of leaving it to individual teachers to decide whether or not to have the class recite the prayer.

In another Lord's Prayer case the Ontario Court of Appeal overturned a lower-court decision and banned recitation of the prayer at town council meetings in Penetanguishene. In affirming town resident Henry Freitag's complaint, the court found that the purpose of the exercise was to "impose a Christian moral tone on the deliberations of council."

In the Montreal suburb of Outremont there were strained relations between Hassidim, on the one hand, and their neighbors and the city government, on the other. For a decade a woman had complained that Vishnitzer Hassidim had established a synagogue in her building without obtaining a permit. With the support of the Outremont Residents' Association, Celine Forget sued the congregation in 1997. The Hassidim claimed that they had asked the city several times to rezone the property from residential to public use, but each time had been rebuffed by the city council. They also claimed that since the property had once been zoned commercial, they had acquired rights to use it for a synagogue. The case was scheduled to go to court in June 1999, but just before the court date the congregation announced that it had found new premises a short distance away, making the matter moot.

In October Outremont Hassidim were again in the news, complaining that they were being harassed by numerous complaints lodged against them, primarily by the same Ms. Forget. A spokesperson claimed that members of the community were being bothered by verbal abuse and the petty enforcement of municipal regulations. Alex Werzberger, head of the Hassidic community council, added that his constituents perceived the police to be biased against them, since their own complaints were not taken seriously.

Forget ran for the city council in November and won, thereby raising apprehensions that she would use her position of power against the interests of the Hassidim. Forget claimed that all she wanted was to have the laws applied and enforced evenly, implying that the Hassidim were getting special treatment. She contended that Hassidim had insulted her and spat on her for objecting to the location of the synagogue in her building and organizing a petition to oppose the rezoning. She claimed to have received some 60 intimidating or threatening phone calls over an 18-month period.

In another Montreal suburb there was also tension between a Hassidic group, this time Lubavitch, and the neighboring community, in this case Jewish. The city of Côte Saint-Luc is predominantly Jewish, as are the mayor and most of the city councilors. When a French Chabad group asked for a rezoning in order to establish Beit Chabad, a community center and synagogue, there were numerous objections. When the city offered to sell the necessary plot of land for the $3-million project ($800,000 of it contributed by the Quebec government) residents of the area protested, expressing concerns about increased traffic, noise, parking, encroachment on a senior citizens' garden, and lowered property values. The proposed site was the third considered, since protests had blocked the first two. The dispute carried negative communal implications, as it publicly pitted one group of Jews against another. There were those who blamed the opposition on dislike of Orthodox Jews, of Hassidim, or specifically of the Lubavitch movement. But there may have been another reason: the clientele of the new center was expected to be made up mostly of francophone Sephardim, whereas most of the opponents were anglophone Ashkenazim. Rabbi Mendel Raskin, head of Beit Chabad, expressed puzzlement about the opposition, calling it a shame that there should be such a reaction in a Jewish neighborhood. A number of raucous public meetings only exacerbated the situation and intensified the bad feelings. After months of public posturing, matters came to a head in September when the city council finally voted the necessary rezoning. The eight councilors split evenly, and Mayor Robert Libman cast the tie-breaking vote in favor of the project. He praised Chabad for its extraordinary work: "The city should be proud to have it in its midst." Final approval was granted in October. However residents quickly collected sufficient signatures on petitions to force a referendum on the zoning change. But then, instead of putting the matter to a referendum, the city council reconsidered the issue in early November and reversed itself, effectively terminating the project at that location. A deeply disappointed Rabbi Raskin said that Chabad would continue to search for a suitable site in Côte Saint-Luc.

A school supervisor in Thornhill, a Toronto suburb, formally reprimanded a Jewish teacher for taking off the day before Passover in order to prepare for the seder. The teacher claimed that her absence was for a religious purpose, even though not on a religious holiday. Several months later the superintendent of the York Region Board of Education reversed the decision and excised the reprimand from her file.

After a long struggle, Jewish teachers in the Fort Garry School District in Winnipeg were given the right to take three days off with pay for religious holidays, instead of two. This was the first time that any Manitoba school board had enabled teachers to observe both Rosh Hashanah and Yom Kippur without penalty.

The relationship between Jews and French Quebecois continued to be a subject of concern. A conference on the topic was held in April at Temple Emanu-El–Beth Shalom in Montreal, sponsored by the Jewish Public Library, Dialogue St.-Urbain, and a population-research institute. Gerard Bouchard, head of the institute, asked why Jews were not more sympathetic to Quebec nationalism and more sensitive to Quebecois fears about survival, and why they were quicker to criticize anti-Semitism in Quebec than in the rest of Canada. David Bensoussan responded by comparing the relative openness of English Canada to the "cultural exclusivity" of Quebec. He argued that excessive nationalism, especially the language laws, were symptoms of a lack of tolerance in Quebec, which adversely affected Jews and other minorities. Professor Ira Robinson of Concordia University lamented the failure to achieve real dialogue between Jewish and Quebecois intellectuals.

A young Jewish businessman, Mordechai Quezada, ran afoul of the Quebec language laws in June by publishing an advertising circular primarily in English, with some copy in Hebrew and Yiddish. He was cited by the Commission de Protection de la Langue Française for not publishing in French. The circular was directed primarily to Hassidic homes in Outremont. After reviewing the facts, officials found that his publication might indeed qualify for an exemption.

Quebec Liberal leader Jean Charest addressed the board of the Communauté Sépharade du Québec in October, praising the contributions of Sephardim to Quebec life as evidence of "exemplary citizenship."

A controversial M.A. thesis at Quebec City's Université Laval, which soft-pedaled certain aspects of the Nazi treatment of the Jews, provoked an angry reaction from the Quebec Region CJC. After meeting with CJC officials in February, François Tavenas, the rector, acknowledged that the thesis had not been evaluated properly and undertook to insure that future research would not misrepresent historical facts. Dorothy Zalcman Howard, regional CJC chair, declared that the case "clearly illustrates the increasingly insidious nature of Holocaust revisionism and our ongoing, unconditional obligation to vigorously oppose, attack, and curtail this trend."

Controversial political scientist Esther Delisle claimed that she was the victim of a conspiracy to keep her off a panel on the subject of anti-Semitism in Quebec that was held in Los Angeles in February and sponsored by the Canadian Consulate General and the Simon Wiesenthal Center. Delisle, a leading authority on the subject, was very unpopular in Quebec intellectual circles because of her view that Quebec nationalism has been historically anti-Semitic. An official of the consulate admitted that Delisle had been dropped after an invitation was already issued because the sponsors wanted to avoid the appearance of an unbalanced program.

Rabbi Eli Gottesman of Montreal, who served as chaplain at an upstate New York penitentiary, pleaded guilty in U.S. District Court in Albany in September to a charge of conspiracy to defraud the government in connection with accusations that he had smuggled drugs into the prison. He admitted bringing sundry items to prisoners, but denied knowingly bringing in drugs, even though marijuana and cocaine were found in a large shampoo bottle that he was bringing into the prison on the day he was arrested. In January 2000 he was sentenced to six months of home detention, two years of probation, and 500 hours of community service.

Culture

Miriam Schneid-Ofseyer, widow of the painter Otto Schneid, donated his art collection to the University of Toronto in November. The collection consisted of photographs, letters, and catalogs that chronicled the lives of European Jewish artists. Barry Walfish, the university's Judaica specialist, described the gift as "an important archive of Jewish art in the first half of the 20th century."

Two films produced by Niv Fichman, "The Red Violin" and "Last Night," won a total of 11 Genie Awards from the Academy of Canadian Cinema and Television in February. Two of his other films won Emmy Awards in the United States.

Lea Pool's new film, "Emporte Moi," was an autobiographical story set in Montreal in 1963, when the filmmaker was 13. It related the experience of a young Quebec girl who is the product of a Catholic-Jewish marriage.

Among the Israeli films exhibited at the Toronto International Film Festival in September were Amos Gitai's "Kadosh," Jonathan Sagall's "Urban Feel," Arik Kaplun's "Yana's Friends," and Eyal Sivan and Ron Brauman's "The Specialist." The last of these was a documentary that utilized actual films of the Eichmann trial. The Toronto Jewish Film Festival in April and May featured some 60 films. "Shylock," a documentary by the National Film Board that traced the impact of Shakespeare's character, was one of the films featured at the Montreal Jewish Film Festival in May.

The Ashkenaz Festival of New Yiddish Culture was held at Toronto's Harbourfront Centre in August and September. It featured dozens of programs including music, theatre, dance, film, visual arts, and literature, as well as lectures and workshops.

One of the highlights of the celebration of Jewish Book Month in Montreal was an evening of tribute to poet Irving Layton. Some 20 speakers recounted their experiences with Layton, and Prime Minister Chrétien sent a message characterizing him as "one of Canada's most gifted poets, who has made a lasting and unparalleled contribution to Canadian literature."

Radio Shalom, the continent's first 24-hour Jewish radio station, began broadcasting in Montreal in August. However it was on a frequency that is not carried by ordinary radios, and this severely limited the number of its listeners. Programming was half in English and half in French.

Publications

In *Fugitives of the Forest*, Allan Levine examined the Jewish partisan movement during World War II in great detail. Using interviews with over 60 former partisan fighters as well as documentary material, Levine showed how Jews from rural areas succeeded as partisans to a much greater extent than their urban counterparts. He also described the relationship the Jewish partisans had with the Soviet army and the peasantry.

Harold Troper's *The Ransomed of God* was a tribute to the work of Jewish community leader Judy Feld Carr on behalf of Syrian Jewry, which, between 1970 and 1995, resulted in freedom for some 3,000 people.

The life of a consummate Montreal community professional was recounted by Joel Yanofsky in *Architect of a Community: The Manny Batshaw Story*.

Other nonfiction works included David Bensoussan's three-volume cultural and analytical study of the Bible, *La Bible prise au Berceau; Surpassing Wonder: The Invention of the Bible and the Talmuds* by Donald Harman Akenson; *Politique et Religion* by Julien Bauer; Clara Balinsky's autobiographical *Clara's Clock;* Michael Brown and Bernard Lightman's edited volume, *Creating the Jewish Future; Voicing the Void: Muteness and Memory in Holocaust Fiction* by Sara Horowitz; show-business personality and actor Al Waxman's autobiography, *That's What I Am;* Gitel Donath's Holocaust memoir, *My Bones Do Not Rest in Auschwitz: A Lonely Battle to Survive German Tyranny;* and Arthur Lermer's *Toward A Brighter Dawn*.

The River Midnight by Lillian Nattel was a novel set in a late-19th century Polish shtetl. The focus was on four women and their families, but the beautifully described context of Jewish life during that period created a remarkable backdrop to their stories. *Katifa* by Peter Ginsberg was a futuristic speculation about Israeli-Palestinian relations. Chava Rosenfarb published two novels, *Bociany* and *Of Lodz and Love*. Other works of fiction included Nora Gold's collection, *Marrow and Other Stories;* a reissue of A.M. Klein's *The Second Scroll; The Secret of Gabi's Dresser* by Kathy Kacer; *Then Again* by Elyse Friedman; *Tell You All* by David Brown; *Sulha* by Malka Maron; *Get on Top* by David Homel; and *Felix Roth* by Cary Fagan.

Books of poetry included *A Rich Garland* by Seymour Mayne and Glenn Rotchin, and *Kaddish for My Father: New and Selected Poems* by Libby Scheier.

Two members of the community received the prestigious Governor-General's Literary Award. Sheila Fischman won in 1998 for her translation of a Michel Tremblay novel, *Bambi and Me*. In 1999 Matt Cohen received the award for his novel *Elizabeth and After*.

Jewish Book Awards were presented in Toronto in June to Lillian Nattel, Nora Gold, Gerald Tulchinsky, Kenneth Sherman, N.N. Schneidman, Allan Levine, Elizabeth Raab, Rabbi Elyse Goldstein, and Irene Watts.

Personalia

A number of Jews were appointed to the Order of Canada. Officers: Howard Alper, Irving Pink, Frederick Lowy, Barry Posner, and Bernard Shapiro. Members: Sheldon Godfrey, Marnie Paikin, Gerald Rose, Paul Godfrey, Nathan Saul Mendelsohn, Rose Wolfe, and Herschel Victor. Sheila Kussner, Henry Mintzberg, and David Azrieli were named to the Ordre National du Québec while Susan Charness, Victor Feldbrill, and Maxwell Goldhar joined the Order of Ontario.

The prime minister named Robert Rabinovitch president of the Canadian Broadcasting Corporation. He had earlier been appointed chair of the board of McGill University. Ed Fitch was promoted to brigadier general and given command of Land Force Western Area. Dr. Lucien Abenhaim was appointed director-general for health in France while journalist Ghila Sroka received the gold medal of La Renaissance Française. Jack Grossman was appointed to the Ontario Court of Justice.

Dalhousie University named Thomas Donald Traves president while Harvey Secter was appointed dean of law at the University of Manitoba. Victor Goldbloom retired as commissioner of official languages and was named head of the Jules and Paul-Émile Leger Foundation. Irving Abella was elected president of the Canadian Historical Association. A. Earl Kimmel became president of the Canadian Federation of Law Societies while Lynne Kassie was elected batonnier of the Montreal Bar.

Within the community Alan Sandler was elected president of UJA Federation in Toronto and Marilyn Blumer president of Federation CJA in Montreal. David Goldstein became president of UIA Federations Canada while Joseph Wilder assumed the chair of the Canada-Israel Committee. Manuel Prutschi was appointed national director of community relations for the Canadian Jewish Congress and David Birnbaum became the Quebec regional director. Seymour Epstein was appointed director of the Toronto Bureau of Jewish Education and vice president of UJA Federation. Erez Anzel and Frank Guttman became copresidents of Canadian Friends of Peace Now. Doreen Green was elected president of the YM-YWHA in Montreal. Hy Goldman won the Dr. Hirsh and Dvora Rosenfeld Prize in the Yiddish achievement category.

Members of the community who died this year included lawyer and war-crimes prosecutor Arnold Fradkin, in January, aged 56; music teacher, composer and choir leader Yehuda David Weinberg, in January, aged 75; major community fund-raiser and organizational leader Lewis Moses, in February, aged 79; Alex Koenigsberg, longtime Toronto synagogue sexton, in March, aged 80; social activist and Hillel benefactor Ann Bailey, in April, aged 95; intensive-care physician Dr. Allen Spanier, in April, aged 52; community leader Gerald Rose, in April, aged 78; Ruth Kelman, rebbetzin and educator, in June, aged 65; Lorry Greenberg, former mayor of Ottawa, in July, aged 65; organizational leader Jules Sundin, in September, aged 79; Agudah leader Moshe Nussbaum, in September, aged 88; former professional football player George Klein, in October, aged 67; Rabbi Leib Kramer, founder and longtime head of Lubavitch's Rabbinical College of Canada, in November, aged 80; distinguished novelist Matt Cohen, in December, aged 56; Holocaust educator and community volunteer Robert Engel, in December, aged 76; Lawrence Greenberg, former president of Ottawa's Jewish Community Council, in December, aged 54; and Florence Kirshner, founding director of Montreal's Golden Age Association, in December, aged 84.

HAROLD M. WALLER

Western Europe

Great Britain

National Affairs

P RIME MINISTER TONY BLAIR'S Labor government retained its popularity, as opinion polls gave the government a 10-to-25-percent lead over the
Conservative opposition through the course of the year. While Labor's strength
was undoubtedly due, in part, to the weakness and occasional ineptitude of the
opposition, the government could boast a number of substantial achievements.
Most important was an apparent resolution to the Northern Ireland impasse, at
least for the moment. With the Ulster Unionists prepared to trust the judgement
of their leader, David Trimble, that the IRA would disarm, on November 29 a
power-sharing executive was inaugurated in Belfast embracing both Unionists
and Republicans. A former terrorist, Martin McGuinness, became minister of education in the devolved executive. In June two other forms of devolved government emerged following elections for a Scottish Parliament and a Welsh Assembly. The system of proportional representation kept Labor from securing a clear
majority in either body. The elections themselves were uninspiring affairs, and the
first act of each set of representatives was to argue over their perquisites and their
pay. Another constitutional innovation was the virtual abolition of the upper
house of Parliament, the House of Lords, largely dominated by hereditary peers.
It remained uncertain how a revised upper house will be constituted.

On the economic front the year went well. Unemployment continued to fall,
and inflation, at 2.2 percent, remained lower than the government's 2.5-percent
target. Rises of .25 percent in the minimum lending rate in September and again
in October seemed to moderate any inflationary tendencies. Prices in many sectors were static or even declined, although rising costs for services constituted a
worrying counter-symptom. The chancellor's budget statement in March and his
November preview of next year's budget combined redistribution to the working
poor with incentives to entrepreneurs. The chancellor was also successful in keeping discussion of possible entry into the unpopular European Monetary System
out of the limelight. This tactic was politically wise because the Tories' more explicitly negative view on joining the single-currency system was the one issue on

which the public agreed with them rather than with Labor. The lack of interest in Europe was shown by the very low 23-percent turnout in the June elections to the European Parliament.

In light of the government's popularity, the Tory opposition, led by William Hague, made little impact. The party did enjoy some minor successes. In the local elections held in May, for example, the Tories won a total of about 1,300 seats with 33 percent of the vote, just three points behind Labor nationwide and neck-and-neck in England. But these successes could not compensate for some self-inflicted wounds toward the end of the year. The party's candidate for the elected mayoralty of London had to resign suddenly when it was disclosed that he had encouraged a friend to commit perjury on his behalf; the Tory treasurer was the subject of damaging financial allegations; a leading MP, sacked from the Tory front bench over his support for gay rights, defected to Labor; and Hague's policies came under attack from senior members of his own party who claimed that he had neglected the middle ground by "lurching to the right," especially on the single-currency issue.

On the eve of the millennium celebrations Dr. George Carey, the archbishop of Canterbury, joined with representatives of virtually all other Christian churches in apologizing for "falling short" of Christian standards, and for the wars, acts of racism, and other sins committed in the name of Christianity over the last two millennia.

Israel and the Middle East

Early in the year British relations with Israel were problematic. In February a Foreign Office statement seemed to put the onus for ending violence in Lebanon solely on Israel. In April Derek Fatchett, Foreign Office minister responsible for Middle East affairs, voiced "deep concern" over Israel's decision to close three Palestinian Authority offices at Orient House, East Jerusalem. Britain, he said, would ask the European Union to look into the issue. And in May Prime Minister Blair told the *Jewish Chronicle* that he was "very concerned" about the deadlock in negotiations between Israel and the Palestinians and about the "failure to implement" the Wye River agreement whereby Israel was to cede further land on the West Bank in exchange for security guarantees.

Although in April Foreign Office minister Tony Lloyd stressed Britain's opposition to any unilateral Palestinian declaration of independence when the period envisaged in the Oslo accord expired in May, more than 60 MPs from all parties, including Liberal Democrat foreign affairs spokesman Menzies Campbell, signed a parliamentary motion in the House of Commons favoring the European Union's backing for the creation of a Palestinian state, and in May the British Friends of Peace Now organized a petition, signed by some 300 Anglo-Jewish personalities and published in the *Jewish Chronicle,* calling for the creation of a Palestinian state.

The election of Ehud Barak as Israeli prime minister marked a new phase in relations between Britain and Israel. On his first official visit to London, in July, Barak received "101 percent support" from Prime Minister Blair for his peace efforts. Describing Blair as not only a friend but "a partner in international support of the Middle East peace process," Barak outlined Britain's potential leading role in helping unite the European Union behind the peace process and in providing "both political and financial support, especially to the Palestinians." At the Labor Party conference in Bournemouth in October Blair praised Barak's "courage and leadership" and pronounced Britain "ready and willing" to encourage peace talks. Peter Hain was named the new Foreign Office minister in charge of Middle East policy in August. Disavowing his anti-Zionist past, Hain promised to work toward a "peace settlement that was lasting, secure and rooted in absolute concrete." Michael Abraham, the Lord Levy — Labor peer, businessman, and communal personality — was described as the "prime minister's special envoy in the Middle East." In December Hain said Levy's three informal visits to Damascus in 1999 helped bring about talks between Israel and Syria.

In June Foreign Office minister Geoff Hoon summoned the Iranian ambassador to the Foreign Office to make clear his concern about 13 Iranian Jews held in an Iranian prison on a charge of spying for Israel. The following month, as the Board of Deputies of British Jews staged a protest vigil outside the Iranian embassy in London, Foreign Secretary Robin Cook warned Iran that Britain took the fate of the 13 extremely seriously. In September Cook met with Iran's foreign minister about the case. At the Labor Party conference in October, Poale Zion, the socialist Zionist group, moved a resolution voicing concern about the prisoners, which passed unanimously. In December a Hanukkah demonstration was held outside London's Syrian embassy in support of the release of four missing Israeli servicemen.

Also in December, lack of funds forced the Britain-Israel Public Affairs Center (BIPAC) to close. For 23 years it had provided an information service on all aspects of Israel and Middle East policy.

Anti-Semitism and Racism

The government's dream, said Home Secretary Jack Straw in October, was to celebrate "the rich diversity of a multi-racial Britain." Throughout the year the government introduced measures against racism and worked to promote ethnic harmony.

In February Straw told Board of Deputies president Eldred Tabachnik that he fully understood the Jewish community's concern about the threat of terrorism and that police would continue to provide enhanced protection for Israeli and Jewish institutions. In April nail-bombs exploded in Brick Lane (East London) and Brixton (South London), and the neo-Nazi group White Wolves claimed responsibility. In response, an unprecedented security operation was mounted in Jewish neighborhoods, including surveillance by MI5 (the national security services) and by Scotland Yard's new antiracist task force. A similar security alert was ordered after threats were received from Islamic extremists in September, just prior to the High Holy Days.

In March and May the antiracist task force staged major operations against far-right extremist organizations suspected of planning violence—such as Combat 18—seizing weapons, ammunition, racist literature, and computer disks, and making arrests. Following the March action the Ministry of Defense emphasized its determination to root out racism from the armed forces.

In April, in the run-up to the June elections to the European Parliament, the Union of Jewish Students and the Oxford University Jewish Society persuaded the Oxford Union to withdraw a speaking invitation to John Tyndall, leader of the far-right British National Party (BNP). The next month groups opposed to racism tried to persuade the BBC not to transmit BNP political broadcasts, and asked the attorney general to examine the BNP's election manifesto for incitements to racial hatred. Postal workers, backed by the Communication Workers' Union, refused to handle BNP campaign leaflets, and the Board of Deputies urged Jews to turn out on election day to prevent British extremists from winning a foothold in the European Parliament. Although it contested all 82 seats in England and Scotland, the BNP made little impact, securing only 102,647 votes, 1.11 percent of the total. Following the elections, 86 MPs signed a parliamentary motion charging that the BNP breached the Representation of the People Act by providing false addresses on nomination papers for some candidates.

In January Assistant Commissioner John Grieve, the head of Scotland Yard's antiracist task force, promised a massive campaign against racism. In July he told a meeting of the Indian-Jewish Association in London that arrests for racial crimes had increased threefold, and that much more was now known about the activities of racist organizations. The next month Grieve sought to involve religious institutions in a campaign to increase the reporting of racial offences. The Board of Deputies Community Security Trust was to play a leading role, training volunteers to collect information. Already in April the London metropolitan police had launched a program to recruit more officers from ethnic minorities, including Jews. At that time there were 75 known Jews on a force of 26,000.

In August Home Secretary Straw renewed the 1986 exclusion order against Louis Farrakhan, leader of the U.S.-based black nationalist Nation of Islam. This followed a campaign by MPs, peers, and Jewish representatives to keep him out of the country. Straw said that continuing the ban was conducive to good race relations and the maintenance of public order. In September an invitation to anti-Zionist Holocaust revisionist Roger Garaudy to address a conference at London University's School of Oriental and African Studies was canceled due to protests by the Board of Deputies. Then in October, public protest surrounded the visit to London by Austrian far-right leader Jörg Haider. And that same month communal leaders urged Straw to deport Germar Rudolf, a neo-Nazi who had fled from Germany to Britain in order to escape a prison term for breaching Germany's Holocaust-denial laws.

In November communal leaders welcomed government plans, announced in the queen's speech at the opening of Parliament, to strengthen the laws against racial discrimination to cover the acts of public bodies, including the police. In fact the

Board of Deputies wanted the new legislation to go even further and outlaw discrimination on grounds of religion. Also that month the Immigration and Asylum Act received royal assent and became law despite efforts by the Board of Deputies, the Jewish Council for Racial Equality (JCore), and the Labor Zionist organization Poale Zion to eliminate from it the withdrawal of benefit rights to asylum seekers, plans to disperse refugees around the country, and the replacement of cash awards by vouchers for the purchase of essentials.

Holocaust-Related Matters

In February the Board of Deputies, which had been allocated some £220,000 from a Swiss humanitarian fund for needy Holocaust victims, set up a mechanism to distribute the money to survivors. In July the British Foreign Office hosted the first annual meeting of the International Fund for Needy Victims of Nazi Persecution. One-third of Britain's contribution to the fund is earmarked for needy survivors in the UK; the remainder, which goes to survivors in Eastern Europe, is distributed by the American Jewish Joint Distribution Committee.

After months of discussion, in February the Department of Trade and Industry set up a secretariat for restitution payments for assets seized by the Custodian of Enemy Property during World War II under the Trading with the Enemy Act. The next month the department published the names of thousands of people whose bank accounts and assets had been seized; by July more than 200 applications had been received and ten approved. The money will come from a fund set up by the government.

In October the government released a proposal, backed by the prime minister, for the establishment of a national day of Holocaust remembrance.

NAZI WAR CRIMINALS

Britain's second war crimes trial ended in April when Anthony Sawoniuk received a life sentence. The Old Bailey jury, which in February had visited Domachevo in western Belarus where the crimes took place, found Sawoniuk guilty on two counts of murder under the 1991 War Crimes Act: the shooting of two Jewish men and a woman; and the machine-gunning of 15 Jewish women who were forced to strip and stand at the edge of an open grave. The killings were carried out when Sawoniuk was a member of a Nazi-recruited local police force. He denied all charges.

In October Scotland Yard detectives referred to the Crown Prosecution Service the case of a 78-year-old Georgian-born man living in Wales, whose name was not disclosed, suspected of involvement in an operation by an SS extermination squad.

Considerable anger greeted the decision at the end of the year to allow Konrad Kalejs, aged 86, an alleged Nazi death-squad officer, to leave Britain voluntarily for Australia. Kalejs, who had been deported from the U.S. in 1994 and from

Canada in 1997, had lived in Leicestershire since September. He was accused of involvement in the killing of 30,000 people, mainly Jews, in Latvia, but according to the Home Office there was insufficient evidence to justify his prosecution. Home Secretary Straw, who earlier had said that he was minded to deport Kalejs because his presence "was not conducive to the public good," met with Board of Deputies leaders to explain his change of mind. Many disagreed with the decision on the ground that the case had not been sufficiently investigated. Foreign Secretary Cook promised Lord Janner, the chairman of the Holocaust Education Trust, that British diplomats would pass on any new information about Kalejs to relevant overseas authorities.

JEWISH COMMUNITY

Demography

After rising for the previous two years, the number of marriages conducted under Jewish religious auspices fell from 986 in 1997 to 921 in 1998, a drop of 6.6 percent, according to statistics published by the Board of Deputies of British Jews Community Research Unit. Only marriages performed under the Union of Orthodox Hebrew Congregations significantly increased in number, accounting for 21 percent of the total. The number of gittin (religious divorces) completed in 1998 remained constant at 233. Burials and cremations under Jewish auspices fell to 3,910 in 1998 from 4,070 the year before. The estimated number of births, based on figures for circumcision, was 2,663 in 1997 compared with 2,897 in 1996.

A profile of an aging provincial community emerged from a population survey of Glasgow Jewry released in October, which identified 5,500 Jews from the membership lists of synagogues and cultural and recreational groups. Commissioned by five local Jewish welfare organizations, the survey found that only 15 percent of the total were 18 years old or younger, while 28 percent were 60 and above and 17 percent over 70.

Communal Affairs

Norwood-Ravenswood, the Jewish community's largest child-and-family-services organization, announced in January that it was cutting 16 jobs and closing one of its North-West London administrative offices due to lack of funds, though in October it opened a new center in Redbridge. In May a major welfare organization, Jewish Care, announced the closing of its only seaside resort residential home, in Bournemouth, Hampshire.

In July the Central Council for Jewish Community Services, the umbrella organization for some 50 Jewish welfare bodies, announced that it would close. Asher Corren, the director, said that it had "fulfilled its original purpose in the light of changing community needs." Founded in 1972 to coordinate the work of the Jewish social-care organizations, it had been the prime mover in bringing about partnerships betweeen hitherto independent welfare organizations.

British Jews raised over £100m in 1997 for Jewish causes, according to a survey by the Institute for Jewish Policy Research. The survey, based on a representative sample taken from more than 2,300 listed Jewish organizations, also showed that Jewish communal groups spent a total of over £419m, more that 43 percent of which went for staff salaries.

Religion

A vigorous campaign kept alive the plight of *agunot,* "chained" wives whose husbands refuse to give them a religious divorce. Activists organized a fast on their behalf on International Women's Day in March, and conducted a vigil outside the chief rabbi's office in October. Chief Rabbi Jonathan Sacks, accused by the protesters of "moral blindness" for his alleged inaction in the face of Judaism's "discriminatory" divorce laws, insisted that he identified totally with the plight of the *agunot* and pledged to do his utmost "to make firm and sustainable progress" in the matter. In June he met with Rabbi Moshe Morgenstern of New York, who had developed a controversial annulment procedure to free such women. But Rabbi Sacks found the Morgenstern method "a breach of Halakhah" (Jewish religious law). Instead, he announced that he would set up a special post at the London Bet Din (religious court) dedicated to solving the problem "within the framework of Halakhah." Yet Dayan (Judge) Ehrentreu, the head of the Bet Din, told representatives of the campaign for *agunot:* "If there was a loop-hole, we would have found it by now." Meanwhile, religious courts of the Orthodox mainstream United Synagogue (US), the Orthodox right-of-center Federation of Synagogues, and the Sephardi religious community invalidated a wedding, conducted secretly by Morgenstern, of an erstwhile *agunah* whose first marriage Morgenstern claimed to have annulled.

By the end of the year a combination of communal sanctions against recalcitrant husbands and rabbinic mediation had been successfully employed in individual cases. Rabbi Sacks himself mediated in one instance, after pro-*agunah* campaigners joined by US leaders staged nightly protests in November outside a North-West London kosher restaurant owned by the husband's family. In October Rabbi Yitzhak Schochet of the Mill Hill Synagogue and Rabbi Pini Dunner of the Saatchi Synagogue announced that they would name and shame uncooperative husbands over the Internet. Hope of help for *agunot* from the British legal system diminished in June when the Lord Chancellor's Office announced a delay in implementing the Family Law Act of 1996, which enabled judges to withhold a civil divorce until the completion of religious procedures. And in July a family-court judge ruled that the prenuptial agreement drafted by the Chief Rabbi's Office, whereby both parties pledge to follow Jewish divorce law should the marriage break up, was unenforceable in British law.

Sacks also came under fire from Orthodox elements over implementation of "communal peace" meetings between the US and Reform, Liberal, and Masorti (Conservative) movement leaders. Although the US sent no rabbis to the meetings, the Union of Orthodox Hebrew Congregations (Adath) rabbinical council in March expressed "anguish and bewilderment" that Sacks and US leaders were showing respect for those aiming "to lead Jews away from the paths of the Torah and uproot basic beliefs of Judaism." The Federation of Synagogues and the leaders of British Agudath Israel also voiced disapproval. In June the Chief Rabbi's Office launched a newsletter, *Renewal,* as part of a program to make the chief rabbi more accessible. In November Chief Rabbi Sacks expanded and reshuffled his "cabinet," bringing in ten new rabbis and creating eight additional portfolios, including one for the Internet and another for the electronic media.

The US, Britain's largest synagogue grouping, experienced mixed fortunes. A report by independent accountants, commissioned in September 1998, was published in March 1999. It found no evidence of dishonesty or deliberate omission of data, but it criticized specific individuals for lax management and control. Among the problems described were the burial society scandal at Waltham Abbey cemetery, Essex, which lost the US at least £750,000; by October, 12 people had been arrested. The report also dealt with the theft of books from the London Bet Din by Dayan Casriel Kaplin, which was resolved in February when US honorary officers ratified a "full and final settlement" whereby Kaplin paid £280,000 toward the cost of the books and the US's expenses. Kaplin was stripped of his title and barred from communal honors within the US.

The US did its utmost to put its affairs in order. In April it ended a seven-year dispute by paying £2.5m to settle legal claims against it by its own pension fund. In June a New York auction of 150 manuscripts and rare books from the Bet Din library fetched a record $4 million, part of which would replenish the depleted pension fund. A further boost to the fund was projected in November when the US announced plans to sell 30 valuable silver items through Sotheby's, Tel Aviv. In June co-treasurer Jeremy Jacobs reported a rise in US membership from 33,811 in 1997 to 34,006 in 1998. This was coupled with a healthier financial position: total income had risen from £16m to £17.1m. The deficits, Jacobs said, had largely disappeared through the sale of property and cost-cutting measures, such as making the heder (elementary Hebrew school) system and the *mikveh* (ritual bath) operations self-supporting.

In September the US appointed Katherine McDermott, a Catholic, as its first head of fund-raising. It also mediated successfully to end a dispute with an alternative minyan, aiming for a more informal and participatory service, at Golders Green Synagogue, North-West London. The minyan, temporarily housed in the premises of the Jewish Vegetarian Society, voted to return to the synagogue when Golders Green voted in a team of honorary officers pledged to reunite the community. In April the US embarked on a series of open meetings designed to make it more responsive to members' needs, while the US's rabbinical council appointed its first-ever executive. The US launched a mentoring program for young rabbis in September. Business consultant Peter Sheldon was elected US president in October. The vote had been postponed several times when competing candidate Malcolm Cohen challenged Sheldon's eligibility. Cohen finally decided to withdraw.

The police received complaints in May about the management of the L'Chaim Society, the organization run by Shmuel Boteach, the maverick American-born rabbi. The charity commissioner launched an inquiry in August and ordered L'Chaim's bank accounts frozen.

Edgware Masorti, one of the largest synagogues in the Masorti group, was rocked by discord which began when some members objected to women wearing the *tallit* (prayer shawl) and *kippah* (skullcap). The introduction of separate egalitarian services to run parallel with the main service did not heal the breach, and in December the synagogue's officers resigned en bloc.

In response to an offer from the Council of Christians and Jews to choose a second Jewish officer in addition to the chief rabbi, who served as vice president, the Liberal and Reform movements agreed in October to name as associate president Rabbi Dr. Albert Friedlander, emeritus minister of the independent progressive Westminster Synagogue and dean of Leo Baeck College. In November Reform leaders launched a £4m appeal over five years to promote the 40,000-member movement as "the most dynamic force in Anglo-Jewry."

Education

In 1999 approximately 45 percent of Jewish primary-age pupils and 33 percent of secondary-age pupils attended Jewish schools. The government continued its support of Jewish educational institutions: in May two more Orthodox elementary schools were awarded voluntary-aided status, one in North-West London, the other in Gateshead. Some 30 Jewish schools will be state-aided by the end of 2000. In December the Jewish Community Day School Advisory Board, formed in May by members of the Reform, Liberal, and Masorti movements, opened the Clore Shalom school in Shenley, Hertfordshire, with five classes and a total of 120 pupils drawn from across the Jewish religious spectrum.

In March the London School of Jewish Studies (LSJS), the former Jews' College, appointed its first full-time woman lecturer, Shani Berrin, and a month later Rabbi Dr. Sasha Stern was named Leon and Freda Schaller senior lecturer in Jewish studies. In June LSJS signed an agreement for academic cooperation with London University's School of Oriental and African Studies. London's first modern Orthodox yeshivah, Ohr Torah, launched in 1998 by Rabbi Chaim Brovender, announced in July that it was merging with LSJS since it had become clear that there was not sufficient demand for an institution like Ohr Torah. LSJS director David-Hillel Ruben resigned in August to establish a London campus for New York University. He was replaced in December by Dr. Ian Rabinowitz, who had been director of the Department of Medicine at University College, London.

Pursuing its policy of fostering Jewish renewal, the United Jewish Israel Appeal (UJIA) launched a magazine in March aimed at raising the profile and enhancing the self-esteem of Jewish educators. In April it established two lectureships "to encourage professional excellence" in Jewish education, one (Orthodox) at LSJS, the other (progressive) at Leo Baeck College. In October, in the absence of suitable applicants, Jewish educator Clive Lawton, former chief executive of Jewish Continuity, the erstwhile national fund-raising program for education, was appointed consultant to help the LSJS set up a program in Jewish education. Chief executive Jonathan Kestenbaum told UJIA's annual general meeting in October that the organization was blending its two roles of rescue and renewal into a single mission to embrace young Jews worldwide. He reported a 12-percent increase in the number of donors from the previous year, but a fall in income from £19.1m in 1997 to £12.8m in 1998. In December UJIA launched its Ashdown Fellowships program to train prospective Jewish teachers and youth leaders. The same month UJIA's Makor educational resource center merged with the Association of Jewish Youth to create a single agency serving over 20,000 young Jews.

Historian Bernard Wasserstein, the controversial president of the Oxford Centre for Hebrew and Jewish Studies (OCHJS), announced in April that he would leave the post in January 2000. Peter Oppenheimer, an Oxford economist, was appointed the new president in October, with specific responsibility for OCHJS funding; Hebrew literature specialist Dr. Glenda Abramson was named to the new position of academic director.

In January Sussex University's Centre for German-Jewish Studies received a grant from the Anne Frank Foundation to fund the post of director of research; in July historian Tony Kushner became the third professor in the Department of Jewish Studies at Southampton University; and in October Girton College, Cambridge, launched a scholarship for postgraduates studying modern Hebrew.

Overseas Aid

British Jewry reacted promptly throughout the year to a number of threats to overseas Jewish communities, and enlisted British government intervention when possible. British Jews also aided non-Jewish victims of hostilities abroad.

Concern over rising anti-Semitism in Russia caused more than 40 MPs from all parties to sign a motion in January sponsored by Labor Friends of Israel (LFI) chairman Stephen Twigg. It called on the government to put pressure on Russia to crack down on anti-Semitic statements by opposition members of its parliament. Redeeming a promise to the "35s" — the Women's Campaign for Jews in the Former Soviet Union — Foreign Secretary Cook, on a visit to Russia in March, relayed to the Russian leadership Britain's concern about anti-Jewish propaganda, reinforcing a similar message already conveyed by the UK's ambassador to Moscow.

Jewish organizations launched projects to help Jews in the former Soviet Union.

World Jewish Relief (WJR) focused on Ukraine. In January it sent tape recorders to blind and elderly Jews in Odessa, and in July it dispatched to the western Ukraine two mobile "welfare centers" called "Chesedmobiles" (*chesed* = act of kindness) to help Jews living in remote areas. The WJR also announced plans to set up ten community centers in western Ukraine over the next three years. In February and November the 35s made two separate appeals for unwanted fur coats for pensioners in Belarus.

In April British Jewry donated almost £250,000 to an emergency appeal fund, launched and later coordinated by United Kingdom Jewish Aid and International Development (UKJ Aid), to help victims of ethnic cleansing in Serbia. The Jewish Emergency Aid Coalition (JEAC) convened a meeting of Jewish groups to collect money for Kosovo refugees. Part of the money raised was used in May by the Jewish Council for Racial Equality (JCore). Backed by the Board of Deputies and all the major Jewish religious bodies, JCore joined forces with the Refugee Council, assigned by the government to coordinate contingency planning for the possible arrival in Britain of 1,000 refugees weekly. JEAC, in partnership with the Albanian Educational Development Project, used some of the money to erect mobile schools for Kosovar refugee children in Albania. In October the final allocation from the fund went to reopen the first school in the devastated Gjakova district in Kosovo. UJIA raised funds to take 500 Jews from former Yugoslavia to Israel.

Publications

The 1999 annual *Jewish Quarterly*-Wingate literary award for fiction went to Israeli-born Dorit Rabinyan for her novel *Persian Brides;* the nonfiction prize went to Edith Velmans for *Edith's Book,* an account of her wartime years in hiding in Holland. The controversy which erupted over the authenticity of the 1997 nonfiction winner, *Fragments, Memories of a Childhood, 1939–1948* by Binjamin Wilkomirski, was the subject of a television program.

The *Jewish Quarterly,* founded in 1953 and with a current circulation of 2,000, announced plans to merge with *Jewish Book News and Reviews,* launched in 1986, published three times a year, and selling 700 copies. The new journal would incorporate all the elements of *Book News,* including its bibliography of Jewish books available in Britain.

Books on anti-Semitism published during the year included *Demonizing the Other: Antisemitism, Racism and Xenophobia* edited by Robert Wistrich; *Remembering Cable Street: Facism and Anti-Fascism in British Society* by Tony Kushner and Nadia Valman; and *Patriotism Perverted: Captain Ramsay,the Right Club and British Anti-Semitism 1939–40* by Richard Griffiths.

Works dealing with Israeli-Arab affairs were *Acting Up* by David Hare, his diary of producing the play "Via Dolorosa" that deals with Israeli-Arab relations; *Israel in Search of a War: The Sinai Campaign, 1955–56* by Motti Golani; *Gideon's*

Spies: Mossad's Secret Warriors by Gordon Thomas; *Drinking the Sea at Gaza* by Amira Hass; and *Touching Peace: From the Oslo Accord to a Final Agreement* by Yossi Beilin.

The large and varied body of biographies and autobiographies included *Sir Sidney Hamburger and Manchester Jewry* by Bill Williams; *Stranger than Fiction*, an autobiography by Mark Braham; *Are You Still Circumcised? A Collection of Autobiographical Stories* by Harold Rosen; *World's End for Sir Oswald* by Alf Goldberg; *Lord Goodman* by Brian Brivati; *Rembrandt's Eyes* by Simon Schama; *Lip Reading* by Maureen Lipman; *Rodinsky's Room* by Rachel Lichtenstein with Iain Sinclair; *The Writing Game* by Rosemary Friedman; *They Called Him Mr. Brighton*, David Winner's biography of Lewis Cohen, who revolutionized the building-society movement and ended up a millionaire socialist; *The Arithmetic of Memory* by Anthony Rudolf; *On Life and Death: The Tale of a Lucky Man* by Zvi Aharoni; *God Made Blind: Isaac Rosenberg, His Life and Poetry* by Deborah Maccoby; *Roses from the Earth: The Biography of Anne Frank* by Carol Ann Lee; *Eyes Wide Open*, Frederic Raphael's memoir of his collaboration with Stanley Kubrick on the film "Eyes Wide Shut"; and *Football Memories* by Brian Glanville.

Books on Anglo-Jewish and local history were *Scotland's Jews* by Kenneth Collins; *Care in the Jewish Community*, a history of the Jewish Welfare Board and Leeds Jewish Housing Association by Heinz Skyte; *Anglo-Jewry in Changing Times* by Israel Finestein; and *The Lost Jews of Cornwall* edited by Godfrey Simmons, Keith Pearce, and Helen Fry.

Holocaust studies were *The Cap* by Roman Frister; *To See You Again: The Betty Schimmel Story* by Betty Schimmel with Joyce Gabriel; *Studying the Holocaust* by Ronnie S. Landau; *Facing the Extreme: Moral Life in the Concentration Camps* by Tzvetan Todorov; *My Mother's Diamonds: In Search of Holocaust Assets* by James Kirby; *Images of the Holocaust: The Myth of the "Shoah Business"* by Tim Cole; *Just One More Dance* by Ernest Levy; *One Young Man and Total War: From Normandy to Concentration Camp: A Doctor's Letters Home* by Robert Barer; *Resisting the Holocaust* edited by Ruby Rohrlich; *In the Shadow of the Swastika* edited by Donald Kenrick; *I Have Lived a Thousand Years* by Livia Bitton-Jackson; *Spectator in Hell* by Colin Rushton; *Shake Heaven and Earth: Peter Bergson and the Struggle to Rescue the Jews of Europe* by Louis Rapoport; *Refugees in an Age of Genocide* by Katharine Knox and Tony Kushner; *From Anschluss to Albion: Memoirs of a Refugee Girl, 1939–40* by Elisabeth M. Orsten; and *My Darling Diary* by Ingrid Jacoby.

Books on history were *Ploughing Sand: British Rule in Palestine, 1917–1948* by Naomi Shepherd; *The Jewish Brigade: An Army with Two Masters, 1944–45* by Morris Beckman; *A People Apart: The Jews in Europe, 1789–1939* by David Vital; *Israeli-Soviet Relations, 1953–1967* by Yosef Govrin; and *The World's Banker: The History of the House of Rothschild* by Niall Ferguson.

Among works on Judaism were *Ritual and Morality: The Ritual Purity System and Its Place in Judaism* by Hyam Maccoby; *The Twilight of Jewish Philosophy:*

Emmanuel Levinas's Ethical Hermeneutics by Tamra Wright; *Must a Jew Believe Anything?* by Menachem Kellner; *The Explorer's Guide to Judaism* by Jonathan Magonet; and *Jewish Religious Law: A Progressive Perspective* by John D. Rayner.

Notable fiction included *The Oxford Book of Jewish Stories* edited by Ilan Stavans; *For the Relief of Unbearable Urges* by Nathan Englander; *The Mighty Walzer* by Howard Jacobson; *Foreign Brides* by Elena Lappin; *Children of the Rainbow* by Moris Farhi; *Erotic Stories* by Arnold Wesker; *Gravity* by Erica Wagner; *Live Bodies* by Maurice Gee; and *High on a Cliff* by Colin Shindler.

Books of verse included *Testament without Breath,* Jon Silkin's last volume; *A Moon at the Door* by Wanda Barford; and *Poet to Poet* edited by Richard McKane.

Two books on Yiddish were *Yiddish Proletarian Theatre: The Art and Politics of the ARTEF, 1925–1940* edited by Edna Nahshon; and *When Joseph Met Molly: a Reader on Yiddish Film* by Joseph McBride.

Personalia

Vivien Stern, secretary-general of the Penal Reform International Centre for Prison Studies, received a life peerage, while knighthoods went to industrialist Maurice Hatter, vice-president of World ORT, for his contribution to public services; to ORT's British president, David Sieff, for services to the National Lottery Charities Board; to Arthur Gilbert, an American multimillionaire but a British citizen, who donated a £75m art collection to Britain; to Tate Gallery director Nicholas Serota for services to the visual arts; to Professor John Krebs, chief executive of the Natural Environment Research Council, for his contribution to behavioral ecology; to Victor Blank, chairman of the Mirror Group; and to international-law expert Nigel Rodley for his contributions to human rights and international law.

Prominent British Jews who died in 1999 included Rabbi Jonah Indech, emeritus rabbi of the Bournemouth Hebrew Congregation, in Bournemouth, in January, aged 90; George Nador, Talmudist, in London, in January, aged 78; Sir Emmanuel Kaye, engineering magnate, in Hampshire, in February, aged 84; Alec (Al) Phillips, former boxing champion, in London, in February, aged 79; Gerry Dickson, driving force of the Union of Liberal and Progressive Synagogues outreach program, in Watford, in February, aged 56; Salmond S. Levin, scholar, educator, and president of the United Synagogue, 1977–81, in London, in February, aged 93; Minna Keal, composer, in London, in March, aged 90; Rabbi Bernard Hooker, first executive president of the Union of Liberal and Progressive Synagogues, in Ledbury, Herefordshire, in March, aged 77; Rosalie Gassman-Sherr, general secretary of the Federation of Women Zionists, 1940–1972, in Hemel Hempstead, in March, aged 87; Yehudi Lord Menuhin, internationally renowned violinist, in March, aged 82; Max, Lord Beloff, Oxford historian, in London, in March, aged 85; Gladys Dimson, social worker for Jewish and national projects, in London, in March, aged 83; Lionel Bart, composer, in April, aged 69; Charles Rappaport, communal civil servant, in London, in April, aged 85; Flora Leipman, artist and author, in London, in April, aged 81; David Englander, social historian, in Milton Keynes, in April, aged 49; Norman Williams, philatelist, in London, in April, aged 85; Arthur Levin, medical pioneer, in London, in April, aged 86; Bert Firman, band leader, in London, in April, aged 93; Monty Henig, pillar of the Leicester Hebrew Congregation, in Hove, Sussex, in May, aged 84; Corinne Bellow, art historian, in London, in May, aged 71; Harry Blech, musician, in London, in May, aged 89; Mollie Fishberg, WIZO stalwart, in London, in May, aged 87; Adam Raphael, journalist and broadcaster, in London, in May, aged 61; Henry Grunfeld, chairman and president of S.G. Warburg merchant bank, in London, in June, aged 95; Joseph Vandernoot, musician, in London, in June, aged 84; Harry Blacker, cartoonist, in London, in June, aged 89; Sir John Wolf, television producer, in London, in June, aged 86; Joe Hyman, textile magnate, in Surrey, in July, aged 77; Manfred Altmann, academic philanthropist, in London, in July, aged 87; Max Pianka, organic chemist and Zionist, in London, in August, aged 83; Prof. Percy Cohen, anthropologist, in London, in September, aged 71; Frankie Vaughan (Frank Abelson), leading entertainer, in Oxford, in September, aged 71; David Baum, pediatrician, in Norfolk, in September, aged 59; Tony Crombie, jazz drummer, in London, in October, aged 74; Ralph Sallon, cartoonist, in London, in October, aged 99; Allan Burke, one-time general secretary of the Anglo-Israel Chamber of Commerce, in London, in October, aged 84; Mitzi Lorenz, milliner, in London, in October, aged 88; David Kessler, for 50 years chairman and managing director of the *Jewish Chronicle,* in Stoke Hammond, Buckinghamshire, in November, aged 93; Emanuel (Meyer) Freilich, for 38 years cantor at Hampstead Garden Suburb synagogue, North London, in London, in November, aged 85; Rabbi Lord Immanuel Jakobovits, honored and respected chief rabbi of the United Hebrew Congregations of the British Commonwealth, 1967–91, in London, in November, aged 78; Alexander Baron, novelist and film writer, in London, in December, aged 82; Ralph Finn, writer, in Middlesex, in December, aged 87.

MIRIAM & LIONEL KOCHAN

France

National Affairs

THE TWO KEY FACTS of French public life during 1999 were political cooperation between the right and the left, and economic growth.

Political "cohabitation," as the French called it, involved sharing executive power between the two rival blocs. On the one side was Jacques Chirac, head of the leading right-wing party, who had been elected president in 1995 for a seven-year term; on the other side was Prime Minister Lionel Jospin, head of the leading left-wing party, which had won the 1997 legislative election.

Under Prime Minister Jospin, the parliamentary majority, made up primarily of Socialists, Communists, and Greens, passed a number of laws that furthered the agenda of the political left, instituting a maximum 35-hour work week, recognizing a nonmarital contractual partnership for couples (including same-sex couples), and requiring political parties to run an equal number of male and female candidates in elections. Against the advice of his own allies in the right-wing parliamentary opposition, President Chirac supported some of these laws. Chirac and Jospin planned to run against each other in the next presidential election, expected to come in 2002.

Jospin hoped to advance his popularity on the basis of his economic policies, and the statistics were indeed impressive. France's Gross Domestic Product grew by 2.7 percent in 1999 (compared to approximately 2 percent in the euro-currency area and 1.4 percent in Germany). With an extremely low inflation rate of 0.5 percent and a 3.6-percent increase in exports, business exuded optimism and created new jobs. Almost three million people were unemployed in France at the beginning of 1999, but by the end of the year that number had fallen by 330,000. Nevertheless, the unemployment rate at year's end, 10.6 percent, was slightly higher than the EU average.

The new European currency unit, the euro, was introduced on January 1, 1999. Eleven countries created a zone, nicknamed "Euroland," inside which they adopted fixed exchange rates and will eventually have a common currency. The euro will not replace the national currencies (including the franc) until January 1, 2002. Before then, prices will be listed in both currencies, but payment will be made solely with the national currency. In 1999, then, this currency revolution remained purely symbolic. But the major publicity campaign surrounding the impending changes strengthened consciousness among the French of their membership in the European community. Even though the euro had a rough ride in the world of international finance (it lost 16 percent of its value against the

American dollar in the course of 1999), the simple fact of its existence represented, for the French, the prospect of a stable and prosperous Europe.

In June 1999, France—along with the other EU countries—elected representatives to the European Parliament. These elections, in which seats are divided proportionally, generally offer a good indication of the state of public opinion in France, even though the stakes are much lower than in French national politics. Fewer than half the voters turned out, a very low percentage for France. The parties of the left won more than 38 percent of the vote, compared to slightly more than 32 percent for the parties of the right. The Socialists, the main left-wing party, had 22 percent, far outpacing the Communists, who came in at 7 percent. The biggest surprise came from the Greens, who, under the leadership of Daniel Cohn-Bendit—one of the leaders of the French student revolt of May 1968—won almost 10 percent of the vote.

On the right, the surprise was the success of a dissident group, the "sovereignists," who opposed what they considered the excessive power held by European authorities in Brussels. They received a little more than 13 percent of the vote, placing the new faction first among the right-wing parties, just ahead of President Chirac's own party. Charles Pasqua, an old friend of Chirac, and Philippe de Villiers, representing the most conservative (although not racist or anti-Semitic) strain of the French right, led the new party.

THE NATIONAL-FRONT CHALLENGE

The National Front—the extreme right-wing party led by Jean-Marie Le Pen that obtained 15 percent of the vote in the presidential election of 1995 and again in the legislative election of 1997—suffered a harsh blow when Bruno Mégret and his followers broke away. Disagreement between Le Pen and Mégret, who until then had been the number-two figure in the party, became public in late 1998. Their argument was not ideological, although Mégret claimed to have a more modern approach (not necessarily a more democratic one) to the shared principles of the far right.

The split became final on January 23, 1999, during a conference organized by Mégret's faction. Following a fierce legal battle, Le Pen won the right to keep most of the National Front's assets, consisting primarily of the party's bank accounts and some properties owned by the party. The party's moral assets were also at stake: On May 11, 1999, a Paris court decided that only Jean-Marie Le Pen could use the name "National Front" and its insignia (a tricolored flame). This enabled Le Pen to strengthen his image as the legitimate leader, at the expense of the "traitors" led by Mégret.

Nevertheless, the post-split National Front—undermined by internecine fighting and diminished in the public eye—no longer resembled the one that appeared to be a threat to French democracy in the second half of the 1990s. In the European elections in June, Le Pen's list received 5.7 percent of the vote (less than the party representing hunters and fishers), while the group led by Mégret obtained 3.3 percent (less than a small Trotskyist party). Even combining the votes of the two factions, the tally added up to less than 9 percent.

Although kept below the symbolically significant 10-percent mark, the far right continued to pose a danger. Confusion unleashed by socioeconomic changes, and fear that immigration and globalization could erode national identity still left the door open to demagogues. But the threat that Le Pen's theories would become accepted and commonplace, which loomed large for at least a decade, now appeared remote. A survey conducted in April 1999 by SOFRES, France's leading market- and opinion-research organization, indicated that 11 percent of the French population "completely agreed with or mostly agreed with" Le Pen's ideas, while 86 percent "mostly disagreed with or completely disagreed with" them. This was the worst showing for the National Front in the 15 years that SOFRES polls had included this question.

Le Pen also faced legal problems. In 1999, courts in both Germany and France found him guilty for repeating, at a public meeting in Bavaria on December 5, 1997, his remark that the gas chambers constituted a "detail" in the history of World War II (a French civil court had previously required him to pay damages). He was also convicted for shoving a Socialist candidate during an election campaign, and was declared removed from elective office, although this was not to take effect until the year 2000.

In October 1999, the rupture in the ranks of the far right became complete when the camp led by Bruno Mégret took the name National Republican Movement (MNR). Some activists were shocked by the use of the term "republican," which is not part of the French far right's tradition. But an internal movement document clarified that "using our adversary's terms does not mean that we are using the same content," and that the "republic" according to the MNR was not the republic of the French Revolution of 1789.

Israel and the Middle East

On January 24, 1999, France introduced a new stamp commemorating the 50th anniversary of France's recognition of the State of Israel. The stamp, on which the flags of the two countries framed the words *"Relations diplomatiques France-Israël"* (France-Israel diplomatic relations), was covered extensively in the press. It was later boycotted by the Lebanese post office.

Counseil Représentatif des Institutions Juives de France (CRIF, the Representative Council of Jewish Institutions of France) engaged in intense diplomatic activity early in 1999. After meeting with Israeli foreign minister Ariel Sharon and Egyptian president Hosni Mubarak in Paris, CRIF's president, Henri Hajdenberg, traveled to Tunis where he met Tunisian president Zine El Abidine Ben Ali. He then attended the funeral of King Hussein in Jordan, where he met Hussein's son and successor, King Abdullah.

CRIF also sent a delegation to the Middle East, March 7–10, which met with President Mubarak, Yasir Arafat, King Abdullah, and Israeli president Ezer Weizman (a planned meeting with Israeli prime minister Benjamin Netanyahu had to be canceled at the last minute). This initiative by CRIF elicited some criticism, most notably from France's chief rabbi, Joseph Sitruk, who called it "a form of pressure exerted on the cabinet in Jerusalem."

An odd event concerning French-Israeli relations occurred on May 3, when Mohammed Daoud Odeh, a Palestinian better known as Abu Daoud, was refused entry into France, where he had hoped to promote the autobiography he had written in collaboration with a French journalist. Abu Daoud had been responsible for the hostage-taking incident at the 1972 Olympic games in Munich, during which 11 members of the Israeli contingent were killed. In 1999, however, Daoud sat as a member of the Palestinian National Council, and moved freely between Gaza and Ramallah without being disturbed by Israeli authorities. France treated him more harshly than the Israeli government. This was because Abu Daoud had been arrested in France in 1977, and the government of the day, not wanting to turn him over to the German justice system for fear of unleashing a wave of terrorist attacks, chose instead to expel him from French territory. This expulsion order, never annulled, was still in place when Abu Daoud tried to cross the border in 1999.

France followed the Israeli election of May 1999 with great interest, and public opinion across the political spectrum favored Ehud Barak. Thus the editor of the right-wing daily newspaper *Le Figaro* wrote the day after the election, "Israel had to find in Ehud Barak an heir worthy of Yitzhak Rabin, so that the parenthesis of the Netanyahu era could be closed so authoritatively."

For his part, the new Israeli prime minister promised Europe—France in particular—a role to play in renewed diplomatic efforts to find peace in the Middle East, and the French were quite receptive to this prospect. Both President Chirac and Prime Minister Jospin applauded Barak's visit to France in September, followed a few days later by a visit from Yasir Arafat, as the beginning of a new era for French involvement in Middle East diplomacy.

Anti-Semitism and Racism

In January 1999, the International League against Racism and Anti-Semitism (LICRA)—which was, despite its name, a French organization—elected Patrick Gaubert as its new president. A dentist by profession, Gaubert has been an adviser to right-wing politician Charles Pasqua when the latter had been minister of the interior, and in this capacity Gaubert had done much to combat racist activities. This record—plus the fact that he was Jewish—earned Gaubert vicious personal attacks from the far right, including death threats.

The National Consultative Commission on Human Rights, a body under the aegis of the prime minister's office (though the prime minister is not obligated to follow its advice), published the results of its annual survey, conducted by the CSA

Institute, on the state of racism and xenophobia in France. The commission reported that 38 percent of the French population described themselves as "rather" or "a bit" racist, compared to 24 percent who were "not very" racist, and 36 percent who said they were "not racist at all." Compared to the findings of previous years, this marked a slight decline in the proportion of self-declared racists.

The findings on attitudes toward immigrants showed some contradictions. Thus 79 percent agreed with the statement, deliberately phrased to identify latent as well as overt anti-immigrant feeling, that "the behavior of certain people can sometimes justify racist reactions," and 50 percent agreed with the statement, "Today, in France, one no longer feels at home as in the past." But at the same time, 67 percent accepted the idea that one of the criteria for judging a democracy was "its ability to integrate foreigners," 69 percent believed that "immigrant laborers should be regarded as being at home here because they contribute to the economy," and 60 percent endorsed the statement that "immigrants in France offer a source of cultural enrichment."

The survey also asked respondents to rate different minority groups: 62 percent found North Africans "nice" (*"sympathique"*), a figure that rose to 74 percent for black Africans, 75 percent for Jews, 78 percent for Asians, and 85 percent for those from the French West Indies (Martinique and Guadeloupe, which are part of the French republic). On the other hand, 51 percent declared that there were too many Arabs in France (down from 70 percent in 1990), 30 percent that there were too many blacks (46 percent in 1991), 24 percent that there were too many Asians (35 percent in 1991), and 14 percent that there were too many Jews (21 percent in 1991).

In May 1999, France witnessed an unprecedented event: the official opening of legal proceedings against one of the top judges in the land for "racial insults." The case was brought against Alain Terrail, who was, until quite recently, general counsel to the Appeals Court, one of the highest positions in the French judicial hierarchy. In 1998 Terrail had written an article for the newsletter of a small judges' association with a distinctly right-wing political stance. In the article, he had attacked a judge named Albert Lévy in such a way that Lévy's name was strangely linked with the word "oven." Terrail denied that he was suggesting a connection with the Nazi crematoria, and asserted that no anti-Semitic slur was intended. But the minister of justice, Élisabeth Guigou, reacted immediately. Terrail was forced to resign, and charges were laid against him. Another judge, Georges Fenech, who was publisher of the newsletter at the time the article attacking Lévy appeared, was also charged.

In September, Jean d'Ormesson published a book, *Le Rapport Gabriel*, which recounted a conversation he had had with François Mitterrand shortly before the end of Mitterrand's presidential term in 1995 (he died a year later). D'Ormesson raised the issue of the criticism Mitterrand had received for maintaining his friendship with René Bousquet, chief of police under the Vichy government and organizer of the roundup of Jews bound for Auschwitz at the Germans' request. In response, Mitterrand had brought up "the powerful and noxious influence of the Jewish lobby." Publication of this comment by Mitterrand—which d'Ormesson quoted but did not endorse—brought impassioned reactions. Some were certain that it was false, that Mitterrand could never have said such a thing; others declared that even if he said it, that did not make him an anti-Semite; still others agreed with the remark. In France, the word "lobby" carried a decidedly negative connotation. The very idea that a group could organize itself to protect its interests separate and apart from the general political will was considered intolerable, no matter how legitimate those interests might be. What's more, the concept of a "Jewish lobby" harked back to the rhetoric of France's far-right tradition—from Philippe Pétain to Jean-Marie Le Pen—against "the Jews and the freemasons."

HOLOCAUST DENIAL

In the portrait gallery of Holocaust deniers, 1999 saw the arrival of a new character. He was Jean Plantin, 35 years old, who lived in Lyons with his 75-year-old mother—with no officially declared income. On May 27 Plantin was given a six-month suspended sentence and a 10,000-franc fine for having "advertised for a publication that is dangerous to young people" in the third issue of a small magazine he published, *Akribeia*. The publication in question denied the reality of the Holocaust. This did not discourage Plantin, however, and in the next issue he published material that earned him yet another conviction on October 7. This time the charge was "contesting the existence of crimes against humanity," and he got a six-month suspended sentence and a 30,000-franc fine.

A decade or so earlier, Plantin had studied history in his home town of Lyons, and in 1990 he submitted a master's thesis dedicated to Paul Rassinier, the founder of Holocaust revisionism in France. The next year he published a thesis for his advanced diploma (under the French university system, this is between a master's degree and a doctorate) on the typhus epidemics in the concentration camps, which, he argued, were what killed most of the Jews who died during World War II. These two revisionist theses were approved at the time by two professors at the university. Plantin's recent revisionist activities attracted attention to those earlier writings, and criticism came from the press and from within the university, since, in France, Holocaust denial constitutes a crime. The two professors who had approved the theses affirmed that they rejected Holocaust denial, but in late April both announced that they would no longer direct postgraduate research projects at the university.

Other Holocaust-Related Matters

According to a poll conducted by the CSA Institute and published on December 20, 1999, in the daily *Le Parisien*, a plurality of the French considered the fall of the Berlin Wall "the political event of the century" (47 percent, with up to three responses allowed). The Holocaust took second place (26 percent), followed by the French student revolt of May 1968 (23 percent), World War I (22 percent), and the assassination of John F. Kennedy (20 percent). That more people chose the Holocaust than World War I—during which France lost a million and a half killed, and which was, despite the passage of time, still commemorated by monuments to the dead in even the tiniest village—was astonishing.

In the collective consciousness of contemporary France, the Shoah (this Hebrew term had entered fully into current usage, as the word *Holocauste* had practically disappeared, and the word *génocide* had a much broader application) had come to symbolize the inability of people in the 20th century to control the forces of evil. Actually, French historians had not studied the ghettos of Eastern Europe, the mass executions in Russia or the extermination camps, and the French public was not particularly well informed about the details of any of these. Rather, people were fascinated by the French dimension: the roundups of Jews (usually by the local police chief under orders from the occupying German commander) and their transport to Auschwitz (handled directly by the Germans).

PAPON

The year 1999 saw the conclusion of the jury trial of Maurice Papon, which had begun two years earlier in the city of Bordeaux. From 1942 to 1944 Papon had served as a young bureaucrat in the collaborationist Vichy government led by Philippe Pétain. Papon was accused of having organized, under orders from the occupying Germans, four convoys of Jews from Bordeaux to a camp called Drancy, from which the Germans then took them to Auschwitz. After a six-month trial, he had been sentenced on April 21, 1998, to ten years in prison for "complicity in crimes against humanity."

Much about the case was symbolic. Papon had been quite low in the French administrative hierarchy when the crimes took place. Furthermore, he was not considered a Nazi collaborator or even an anti-Semite. In a profound sense, the verdict was a judgment against the Vichy government's participation—often passive, but nevertheless real—in the persecution of the Jews. In 1995 President Chirac had publicly acknowledged the responsibility of *"l'État français"*—an ambiguous term that could mean either the French state as an abstraction, or, specifically, the Vichy state of World War II—for the events of that time. The Papon trial translated that principle to the legal arena—a translation all the more stunning since Papon, who joined the Gaullist movement at the end of the war, went on to a brilliant administrative and political career.

The trial's end turned out to be heavy with symbolism as well. Papon, who appealed his conviction, remained free until the appeal could be heard and decided by France's highest court. But on October 19 it was discovered that Papon had fled. For ten days, all of France focused on this incredible episode, as the police launched a manhunt for an 89-year-old former police chief and minister. Some imagined him already in Latin America, in a country that had no extradition treaty with France. Finally, he was traced to Switzerland, where he had been hiding since October 11 under a false identity. On October 22, Papon was returned to France, where, his appeal rejected, he began to serve his prison term. But his lawyer had already launched another appeal, this time to the European Court of Justice. Meanwhile, some of his friends asked that he be pardoned because of heart problems (President Chirac denied the request a few months later).

NAZI WAR CRIMINALS

During 1999, the French judicial system completed the procedural steps to try Alois Brunner for crimes against humanity. This would mean a trial in absentia, since the Nazi criminal was last seen in Syria, where he found refuge during the 1950s. If alive, he would be 87 years old. Right-hand man to his fellow Austrian Adolf Eichmann, Brunner supervised the deportation of 130,000 Jews—Austrians, Germans, Greeks, French, and Slovaks. Based in France in 1943 and 1944, he was best known for running the Drancy camp from which French Jews were deported to Auschwitz.

In 1954, Brunner was condemned to death in absentia for war crimes by courts in both Paris and Marseilles. But he was beyond the reach of French justice, having taken refuge in Damascus under the name Georg Fischer. Since then, there had been news about Brunner: He had been wounded by a parcel bomb addressed to him, and there was the text of an interview he gave in 1985 to a German magazine. But the Syrian government consistently refused to respond to questions about Brunner. According to the official line in Damascus, no one had ever heard of him.

The two lawyers who initiated the legal proceedings, Serge Klarsfeld and Charles Libman, focused on elements that were not considered in the two earlier cases. The most important of these was Brunner's removal from Drancy of 352 children, of whom 345 were deported either to Auschwitz-Birkenau or Bergen-Belsen, and 284 of whom were later murdered. This fell under the category of crimes against humanity, and according to a French law passed in 1964, such crimes were subject to no statute of limitations.

RESTITUTION

On February 2, 1999, the commission charged with reviewing the archives on property stolen during World War II, headed by Jean Mattéoli, submitted its second interim report to the prime minister. The final report was expected early in 2000.

On March 24, the French Banking Association solemnly promised to restore "all the heirless property held in banks that belonged to victims of the Shoah." This promise, though late, was met with satisfaction. According to Professor Ady

Steg, former president of CRIF and vice president of the Mattéoli Commission, "When we started, the banks were very reticent. They told us the records could not be found, there had been mergers since the liberation, etc. Then they went to work. Little by little, the truth became apparent. To me, their cooperation is now 100 percent. The banks are walking the walk."

In 1998, the Mattéoli Commission (whose mandate was limited to fact-finding) had proposed the creation of a special commission to review individual restitution requests. Prime Minister Jospin had agreed in principle in November 1998, and Justice Minister Élisabeth Guigou announced in July 1999 that such a commission would be established. This happened at the end of the year, and it was scheduled to begin its work in earnest early in 2000. Presided over by Pierre Drai—an Algerian Jew who, as first president of the Court of Appeals, held the highest position in the French judicial system—the new commission is to have broad powers to examine individual claims, even beyond those the law normally allows, and trustees will be required to accept its rulings.

JEWISH COMMUNITY

Demography

Little was known about the Jewish population of France, either in terms of demographic trends, religious practices, perceptions of Jewish identity, or incidence of mixed marriage. Religious or ethnic identity was not recorded in any official document or in the national census, and any such mention would have been against French law. Responses to public-opinion polls taken in the last few years indicated that Jews made up about 1 percent of the French population, approximately 700,000 people. Membership in Jewish communal institutions was low—but a reluctance to affiliate with nongovernmental organizations, including labor unions, was a characteristic of French society generally. Jewish organizations jealously guarded their membership records. Paradoxically, while Jews had become more visible in French society and culture, they remained statistically elusive.

Education

Jewish schools remained the strongest institutions in French Jewish life. According to the department of education of the Fonds Social Juif Unifié (FSJU, United Jewish Philanthropic Fund), 23,104 students were registered with Jewish schools in 1999 in classes "under contract" with the national Ministry of Education. This "contract" meant that the students received an education based on the official programs used in the public schools, and that the state paid the teachers' salaries for those subjects. The schools had the option of offering additional subjects, the fees for which were paid by parents or by associations supporting the schools. In addition, there were Jewish schools "without contracts," and hence not subject to direct state control, and they had slightly over 2,000 students. Thus approximately 25,000 children, some 20 percent of Jewish school-age children (6–18 years old) attended a full-time Jewish day school.

This was a remarkable phenomenon in historical terms. Just after World War II, France had only three Jewish schools, and in 1999 it had 220. In the last ten years the number of students attending Jewish schools had increased by 40 percent. Previously, the schools had welcomed younger students, but steered the older ones toward public schools. Recently, however, schools had been adding classes for the older grades.

While the "contract" system, with its state funding, provided a financial boost for the growth of day schools, and a decline in the reputation of the public schools led many families to send their children to private schools, the new popularity of Jewish day schools also indicated parental interest in transmitting Jewish identity. Almost all of the schools had a religious orientation, with the Orthodox tendency heavily represented.

Communal Affairs

On April 18, the closing concert of one of the most important popular-music festivals in France, the Printemps de Bourges, was dedicated to Judeo-Arab music. The main performer was Enrico Macias, who had achieved fame performing songs with melodies inspired by Arab-Andalusian folklore and lyrics that told the stories of the *pieds noirs* — the million French people who had to leave Algeria when it became independent in 1962, after a long and bloody war.

Macias, born Gaston Ghrénassia, was the son of a Jewish Algerian musician. He had made his debut alongside his father in the band led by Raymond Leyris, which, in the Algerian city of Constantine, was a symbol of Jewish-Arab cultural symbiosis. Leyris ("Sheikh Raymond"), son of a Jewish Algerian and a non-Jewish Frenchwoman, was Macias's teacher and father-in-law. His assassination in 1961 by Muslims fighting for independence marked the end of an era for the Jews in the region. Now, in 1999, the concert at Bourges in tribute to Sheikh Raymond brought Macias together with the Algerian band of Taoufik Bestandji. This collaboration between a Jewish singer and an Algerian band seemed to hint at the beginning of a historic reconciliation between Algerian Jews, forced to leave a country where they had lived for centuries, and the Algerian people of today, and, in a broader sense, between the Jewish world and the Muslim Arab world.

On July 29, 1999, Odette Abadi committed suicide in her Paris apartment at the age of 85. Born Odette Rosenstock, she had studied medicine, and at a very young age had joined the ranks of the antifascists in the Spanish Civil War. While in Nice in 1942 she became reacquainted with Moussa Abadi, whom she had known before, a young Jew from Syria who had come to France to study literature. When the Italian army, which had occupied Nice since 1940, handed it over to the Germans, the two started "the Marcel network," an underground operation to hide Jewish children, with help from Archbishop Rémond of Nice. They saved 527 children this way. In April 1944, the French police arrested Odette and handed her over to the Germans, who sent her to Auschwitz. There, and in Bergen-Belsen, she survived by working as a doctor. On returning to France, she found Moussa Abadi, who had escaped the Nazis, and they married. They remained very discreet about their role in the Resistance, and only the loyalty of the "Abadi children" caused the story to come to public attention. Moussa Abadi died in 1997, and apparently Odette, who had no children, decided to follow him, after leaving good-bye letters to her friends.

Two Jewish social-service organizations merged in 1999—CASIP (Comité d'Action Sociale Israélite de Paris, the Israelite Social Action Committee of Paris), and COJASOR (Comité Juif d'Action Sociale et de Reconstruction, the Jewish Committee of Social Action and Reconstruction). CASIP, founded 190 years ago and headed by Éric de Rothschild, helped Jewish families in and around Paris, the majority of which were of North African origin. COJASOR, led by Jean-Claude Picard, was established soon after the Holocaust to care for refugees, and in recent years it had primarily run social-service programs and retreat centers. The organization born of the merger, Fondation CASIP-COJASOR, will have Éric de Rothschild as president, Jean-Claude Picard as vice president, and Gabriel Vadnai as director general, the same post he held in CASIP.

Religion

The French republic did not recognize any "religion," since religion was regarded as belonging to the private sphere. Instead, the republic recognized what it called *"cultes"*: institutional manifestations that benefited from tax advantages and were eligible to receive donations and bequests. To be recognized as a *culte*, an institution was legally required to meet three criteria: universality, respectability, and respect for public order. In addition to Christian denominations, Judaism, Islam, and Buddhism were recognized as *cultes*.

The traditional framework for administering the Jewish *culte* in France was the consistory system. Established by Napoleon I in the early 19th century, the consistories were religious institutions made up of directors elected at a local or regional level by synagogue members. With typically French logic, this structure was crowned by a Central Consistory of France, whose rabbi was the chief rabbi of France, just as the rabbi of the Paris Consistory was the chief rabbi of Paris.

However, the consistories were not guaranteed protection from competing organizations, and they had no legal power (except in the three eastern departments that were part of Germany when France separated religion from state in the early-20th century). Thus they could not claim any special legitimacy relative to the "nonconsistorial" communities that developed over the years. In fact, the consistories labored under burdens not shared by their competitors. In light of their central position in the tradition of French Jewry, the consistories were required to assume certain tasks in the public interest (maintenance of synagogues, social functions), which absorbed a large part of their budget. The non-consistorial communities, however, could choose their spheres of activity. One consequence of this imbalance was the dominant position of independent ultra-Orthodox communities—Chabad-Lubavitch in particular—in education, where the consistories played only a marginal role.

In recent years considerable conflict had arisen between the Central Consistory and the Paris Consistory, to a great extent rooted in disagreements over the central body's demands for assessment payments that would have had to come out of the money the Paris body received for certifying kosher products. Relations between Central Consistory president Jean Kahn and Paris Consistory president Moïse Cohen had deteriorated, a situation made more difficult by Kahn's serious health problems. Tensions increased during 1999, and although not all the incidents reached the public ear, by the end of the year the cohesion of the consistorial system appeared seriously compromised. Complicating matters even further, Chief Rabbi Joseph Sitruk, who was formally responsible to the Central Consistory, expressed his autonomy by continuing to maintain his own network of followers and donors. On October 31, he organized a large public rally near Paris called Yom HaTorah (Torah Day).

Jewish-Christian Relations

On February 7, 1999, Paul Thibaud was elected president of the AJCF (l'Amitié Judéo-Chrétienne de France), France's Jewish-Christian friendship organization. He succeeded historian Pierre Pierrard, president since 1985. Thibaud, former publisher of the magazine *Esprit*, was one of France's most eminent Catholic intellectuals. At the same time, four people were elected to the AJCF board: Shmuel Trigano, sociologist and head of the Collège des Études Juives, the Jewish-studies college at the Alliance Israélite Universelle; Paul Bernard, a 22-year-old student and member of the Mouvement Juif Libéral de France (Liberal Jewish Movement of France); Guy Petitdemange, a Jesuit and philosophy professor; and Jean-Claude Eslin of *Esprit*.

Culture

For 22 years, the port of Douarnenez in Brittany had hosted an annual festival devoted to "the cinema of minority and minoritized cultures." The theme of the 1999 festival was "Yiddishland." From July 10 to 17, visitors could see a large selection of Yiddish-language and other Jewish films. There were also concerts of Yiddish songs and klezmer music, lectures on Ashkenazi Jewish culture, and a display on the Yiddish press, as well as exhibitions of paintings and photographs, debates on Jewish culture and human rights, and Jewish books for sale.

Some of the visitors were Jews from various regions of France (there were very few Jews in Brittany), but many were French non-Jews who viewed Jewish culture as a minority expression deserving of protection. This event was organized by Jean-François Malthête, grandson of Georges Méliès, one of the founders of French cinema. Malthête, though not Jewish, had devoted years to learning and teaching Yiddish and Hebrew.

A noteworthy event in the world of film was the release of Emmanuel Finkiel's *Voyages*, shot partially in Yiddish, which dealt with three women's memories of the Holocaust. Praised unanimously by the critics, this was Finkiel's first full-length feature. Also worth noting was *Un spécialiste*, a film by Rony Brauman and Eyal Sivan about the Jerusalem trial of Nazi war criminal Adolf Eichmann, which consisted entirely of documentary footage.

Also in 1999, the library of the Alliance Israélite Universelle, the main Jewish library in France, celebrated the tenth anniversary of its renovation. Located in Paris, it had a large collection of documents and historical works. The anniversary was celebrated with a number of public events, and leading French personalities participated.

In theatre, the Molière prize for best play was awarded to Jean-Claude Grumberg's *L'Atelier* (The Workshop), a play about the Jews in France just after the Holocaust that had been performed periodically by various French theatres over the last several years.

Finally, there were two exhibitions, in Aix-en-Provence and Marseilles, devoted to Varian Fry, an American who saved thousands of people during World War II, including many Jews. Fry had to work against the opposition of the Vichy government and his own consulate. The exhibitions, which received considerable attention in the press, presented the works of artists whom he helped to escape from France. Fry, who died in 1967, wrote a memoir of the period, *Assignment: Rescue,* which appeared in French as *La liste noire.*

Publications

A number of significant nonfiction works on Jewish themes appeared in 1999: Georges-Elia Sarfati's *Discours ordinaire et identités juives* (Ordinary Discourse and Jewish Identities); Maurice-Ruben Hayoun's *Le Zohar — Aux origines de la mystique juive* (The Zohar: The Origins of Jewish Mysticism); Claude Klein's *Israël, un État en quête d'identité* (Israel: A State in Search of an Identity); *Jésus dans la littérature arabe et hébraïque contemporaine* (Jesus in Contemporary Arabic and Hebraic Literature) by Jean-Marie Delmaire and Najib Zakka; Philippe Landau's *Les Juifs et la Grande Guerre* (The Jews and the Great War, referring to World War I); Annette Wieviorka's *Auschwitz expliqué à ma fille* (Auschwitz Explained to My Daughter); *Le Mal et l'Exil* (Evil and Exile) by Elie Wiesel and Michaël de Saint Cheron; *Yiddishland* by Gérard Silvain and Henri Minczeles (an album of period postcards with commentary); *Enseigner le judaïsme à l'univer-*

sité (Teaching Judaism in the University) by Jean-Christophe Attias and Pierre Gisel; Gérard Nahon's *La Terre sainte au temps des kabbalistes* (The Holy Land at the Time of the Kabbalists); Shmuel Trigano's *L'idéal démocratique à l'épreuve de la Shoah* (The Democratic Ideal Confronts the Holocaust); Gérard Israël's *La question chrétienne* (The Christian Question, about how Jews have viewed Christianity); *La loi juive à l'aube du XXIe siècle* (Jewish Law at the Dawn of the Twenty-first Century) by Rivon Krygier, a French Conservative rabbi; Delphine Deroo's *Les enfants de la Martellière* (Children of the Martellière, about a group of children who were hidden during World War II, most of whom were eventually deported by the Nazis); Nadine Fresco's *Fabrication d'un antisémite* (a biography of Paul Rassinier, one of France's first Holocaust deniers); Stéphane Mosès's *L'Éros et la loi* (Eros and Law, a biblical study); *Le judaïsme libéral* (Liberal Judaism) by Pauline Bebe, a French Reform rabbi; Mireille Hadas-Lebel's *Hillel;* Marek Halter's *Le judaïsme raconté à mes filleuls* (Judaism Told to My Godchildren); *La parole et l'écrit* (The Spoken and Written Word) by the late Orthodox rabbi Léon Askénazi.

Works of fiction included Emmanuel Mosès's *La danse de la poussière dans les rayons du soleil* (Dance of the Dust in the Sun's Rays); Michèle Kahn's *Savannah;* Maya Nahum's *Les gestes* (Deeds); Cyrille Fleischman's *Un slow des années 50* (A Fifties Slow Dance); Laurent Seksik's *Les mauvaises pensées* (Bad Thoughts); Robert Bober's *Berg et Beck* (Berg and Beck).

Personalia

Henry Bulawko, president of the Amicale des Anciens Déportés d'Auschwitz (Society of Former Auschwitz Deportees) and vice president of CRIF, was named a commander of the Legion of Honor. Théo Klein, a lawyer and former president of CRIF, was named an officer of the Legion of Honor. Rabbi Paul Roitman, an activist for religious Zionism in France and, more recently, in Israel, was made an honorary citizen of the city of Jerusalem.

The following prominent Jews died in 1999: Yves Jouffa, former president of the Ligue des Droits de l'Homme (Human Rights League), 78, on January 13; Elie Kagan, news photographer, 70, on January 25; Jean Pierre-Bloch, former president of LICRA, 93, on March 17; Loleh Bellon, actor and playwright, 74, on May 22; Nathalie Sarraute, writer, 99, on October 19.

MEIR WAINTRATER

Italy

National Affairs

I<small>N</small> M<small>ARCH</small>, <small>FORMER</small> I<small>TALIAN</small> prime minister Romano Prodi was named president of the European Commission. Carlo Azeglio Ciampi became president of Italy in May, succeeding Oscar Luigi Scalfaro. Throughout the spring, Italy was a key staging point for NATO air strikes against Yugoslavia. The left-wing government of Prime Minister Massimo D'Alema was strained by squabbling among coalition partners and fell briefly in December, but D'Alema managed to put together a new government—Italy's 57th since World War II—within a few days. The Kosovo bombings and general instability in the Balkans, which spurred thousands to seek asylum in Italy, made immigration and refugee issues major themes throughout the year.

On a visit to the synagogue in Turin in January, President Scalfaro praised ethnic diversity. Turin had been the scene of recent tensions between native Italians and Muslim immigrants. Although Scalfaro had had numerous previous contacts with Jewish leaders, the visit was believed to be his first to an Italian synagogue as president.

Italy's commitment to diverse ways of life came into question in the summer over a child-custody case. A family court in Genoa separated two Israeli girls from their mother, who had become Orthodox, and placed them in the custody of their non-observant father, who was living in Italy. The court dismissed the claim of the mother, Tali Pikan, to her daughters because, it said, she belonged to a "religious cult"—fervently Orthodox Judaism. The court strictly limited her contact with the children and even barred her from speaking Hebrew to them. Instead, it ordered the father, Moshe Dulberg, to wean the girls from Orthodoxy so that they might "gradually reenter alternative cultural and behavioral models." Agudath Israel, the Union of Orthodox Jewish Congregations of America, the European Council of Rabbis, and other international groups protested that the decision showed bias against the Jewish religion. In December, a Genoa appeals court threw out the ruling and set a new custody hearing for April 2000.

In February, Gianfranco Fini, the leader of the right-wing Alleanza Nazionale, made a brief visit to Auschwitz. Many Jewish commentators viewed the trip as part of Fini's continuing effort to prove that his party was a "normal" democratic right-wing party despite its neo-fascist roots.

During the summer, Jews protested an attempt by Italy's Radical Party to forge an alliance in the European Parliament with France's far-right Front National.

The alliance—which was to be purely administrative, with no ideological or programmatic implications—was part of a broader Radical plan to link up with a number of other small European parties that operated outside the major political blocs in the European Parliament. One of the most vocal protests came from Bruno Zevi, a prominent Jewish architect who was honorary president of the Radicals. In December Zevi announced he was quitting the party over this issue.

Attempts to affix plaques or to name streets in honor of supporters of the fascist regime created controversy. In November the local government of Palermo decided to reconsider a decision to name a street after Giuseppe Maggiore, a former rector of the University of Palermo, after a newspaper pointed out that he had strongly supported the fascist-era anti-Semitic laws. In September, after years of debate, the University of Pisa decided to commemorate an illustrious alumnus and professor, Giovanni Gentile, who was Mussolini's education minister before being killed by partisans in 1944. A plaque would be affixed that honored Gentile as a philosopher, but condemned his involvement in the fascist regime.

Israel and the Middle East

There was considerable contact between Israel and Italy of a political, commercial, cultural, scholarly, and touristic nature. Italy was Israel's third largest trading partner, after the U.S. and Germany, and the Israeli embassy's cultural section promoted concerts, performances, and exhibits by Israeli actors, artists, writers, and filmmakers.

Israeli foreign minister Ariel Sharon visited Italy in April. In July the small town of Scanzano Jonico, in southern Italy, became a sister city with Ashkelon. On a state visit in October, President Ciampi planted an olive tree in the Forest of Peace in Jerusalem in memory of his longtime friend, scientist Elvio Sadun. Also in October, when soccer star Roberto Baggio went to Israel to promote soccer contacts among young people, Prime Minister Barak received him. In October, too, in Rome, the Hebrew University of Jerusalem held its 18th European Conference for Peace, on the theme "Jerusalem, cradle of three religions, in the coming millennium." Jews, Christians, and Muslims took part. Prime Minister D'Alema celebrated Christmas in Bethlehem at the invitation of Palestinian president Yasir Arafat. At the beginning of December, D'Alema paid a landmark visit to Libya where he and Libyan head of state Col. Muammar Qaddafi issued a joint statement pledging to fight terrorism.

Vatican-Mideast Relations

After months of speculation, the Vatican announced in November that the pope would make a pilgrimage to the Holy Land in March 2000 to mark the start of the third millennium of Christianity.

There was talk that the pope might go to Iraq, since it was known that he wanted to visit Ur, the traditional birthplace of Abraham, as part of his millennial pilgrimage. Opposition came from the U.S., Britain, and Jewish groups, as well as from Iraqi exiles hostile to Saddam Hussein's regime. Vatican officials traveled to Iraq in November to discuss plans for the trip. But in December, a Vatican spokesman announced that it would not take place, citing Iraqi complaints about UN sanctions, as well as security concerns.

Throughout the year the Vatican maintained an interest in the peace process and other events in the Middle East. In April Israeli foreign minister Sharon met for more than two hours at the Vatican with top church officials, including a half-hour private audience with the pope. According to a Vatican statement the talks centered on "the tormented peace process in the Middle East, on the conditions of the presence and activity of the Catholic Church in the country, as well as on the necessary cooperation in view of the celebration" of the millennium. Sharon told reporters that he had underscored that "Jerusalem has been the capital of the Jewish people for 3,000 years and the capital of the state of Israel for 51. It will never be divided. It will always be the only and indivisible capital of Israel." The Vatican had long maintained that Jerusalem should be either internationalized as a holy city, or made the capital of both Israel and an eventual Palestinian state. Vatican officials had called the Israeli occupation of eastern Jerusalem illegal.

In June the Vatican sent a letter to the World Jewish Congress calling the arrest of 13 Iranian Jews a "matter of concern" to all those committed to human rights. In September the pope met with King Abdullah, Jordan's new monarch. The pope discussed with him his own desire to visit biblical sites as well as the "new positive climate" for peace in the Middle East. That same month, in a message written to three teenagers from the Israel-based Peres Center for Peace, the pope urged Israeli and Palestinian youth to maintain the momentum of the Middle East peace process so that it "will grow ever stronger and lead to an effective and lasting peace."

Israel's attempt to defuse a Christian-Muslim conflict in Nazareth soured relations with the Vatican and called into question whether the pope would visit the town during his March 2000 millennium pilgrimage. The conflict centered on plans to construct a mosque in Nazareth near the Basilica of the Annunciation, believed by Christians to be the spot where the Archangel Gabriel announced to Mary that she would bear the son of God. Israel granted the go-ahead for the mosque after two years of mounting tension and violent clashes between local Christians and Muslims. Muslims laid the cornerstone at a ceremony on November 23. In protest, churches throughout Israel shut their doors for two days, November 22–23, and the Vatican lashed out at Israel for fomenting division among religions. Israeli foreign minister David Levy told Israel Radio that the Vatican statement was "very grave" and that "we reject it."

Holocaust-Related Developments

A commission set up by the government at the end of 1998 examined hundreds of documents relating to the confiscation of Jewish possessions under the fascist regime before and during World War II. The material confiscated, it turned out, had included not only valuables but also household objects such as brooms, bathroom fixtures, nightgowns, books, and shower caps.

Senior government officials, including President Scalfaro, took part in commemorative ceremonies in Rome on January 27 and 28 marking the liberation of Auschwitz. On January 27, the actual anniversary of the liberation, there was a ceremony marking the establishment of the Children of the Shoah Association. Several speakers renewed calls for the government to declare the day a national "Day of Memory." That same day, in a downtown Rome piazza, there was a separate, open-air "Day of Memory" commemoration sponsored by the Jewish community, a Roma (Gypsy) study center, and other private organizations. On January 28, Luciano Violante, president of the Chamber of Deputies (who is himself of Jewish origin) launched a book, published by the chamber, *La persecuzione degli ebrei durante il fascismo — Le leggi del 1938* (The Persecution of the Jews During Fascism—The Laws of 1938). The book was made available free to schools around the country. Also at the end of January, Rome's mayor Francesco Rutelli led a delegation of 400 Roman students and various dignitaries on a commemorative visit to Auschwitz.

In March, Scalfaro, Rutelli and other top government officials marked another anniversary, that of the March 24, 1944, massacre of 335 Roman men and boys, 75 of them Jews, at the Ardeatine Caves south of Rome. The massacre, the worst Nazi atrocity in Italy, was ordered in retaliation for a partisan attack that killed 33 German soldiers. Elio Toaff, chief rabbi of Rome, and a Roman Catholic priest presided at the memorial ceremony. Some Jewish and partisan groups, however, protested posters put up by the Rome municipal government to advertise the ceremony, which read: "Rome, city of peace, confirms its support for those who fought and died for democracy, and expresses respect and mercy for the defeated." The protestors complained that this seemed to pay respect to the Nazis.

Indeed, there were right-wing Italians who blamed the Ardeatine Caves massacre on the partisans, arguing that the massacre would not have taken place had those who killed the German soldiers turned themselves in. Surviving members of the partisan squad were sued by two right-wing Italian parties for having provoked the massacre, but in March Italy's highest court threw out the suit, ruling that the partisan attack was a legitimate act of war.

On October 16, the 56th anniversary of the Nazi deportation of Roman Jews, the San Egidio community, a Catholic group that advocates human rights, joined the Rome Jewish community in sponsoring a memorial march through the center of the city. Marchers carried a banner reading: "Those who don't remember the past are condemned to repeat it."

A case involving stolen artwork was resolved in October. In 1997 Italian authorities had confiscated five paintings from a gallery in Florence—on loan from a New Zealand museum—because a Florentine Jewish family claimed the paintings had been taken from their home during World War II. The case was settled by compromise: three of the paintings went back to New Zealand and two to the family.

In November a survey carried out for the magazine *Liberal* asked which event Italians thought was the most important of the century. The largest number of respondents—37 percent—cited the landing on the moon, while the second largest, 32 percent, said the Holocaust. A similar year-end poll by the daily *Corriere della Sera* put the Holocaust in first place.

Nazi War Criminals

The trial of former Nazi officer Theodor Saevecke, accused of killing 15 antifascist Italians in Milan's piazza Loreto on August 10, 1944, continued before a military court in Turin. In mid-December, 87-year-old Erich Priebke, the former SS captain who was sentenced to life in prison in March 1998 for his role in the Ardeatine Caves massacre, was hospitalized after suffering a heart attack. Priebke had been serving his sentence under house arrest.

Anti-Semitism and Racism

There was concern throughout the year over skinhead and other extreme right-wing activity. As in several other countries, particular attention was focused on the behavior of extremist soccer fans who often waved anti-Semitic banners. For years Jewish leaders had been trying to get soccer authorities to do something about the problem. In March there was a conference on the issue at the Rome Jewish Center, with the participation of journalists, soccer personalities, and even Rome's mayor. In September, Enzo Foschi, a member of Rome's Municipal Council, warned that skinhead fans were turning whole sections of stadiums into "a megaphone for the xenophobic and racist extreme right" and driving out other fans. He criticized the authorities for not taking action.

There were two disturbing incidents in November. A rudimentary bomb damaged the entrance to Rome's Liberation Museum in downtown via Tasso, an institution dedicated to commemorating the anti-fascist resistance. Three days later police defused a similar homemade bomb at the entrance to a Rome movie theater that had presented a special screening of a documentary on Adolf Eichmann. Anonymous callers saying they represented the "anti-Zionist movement" claimed responsibility for both bombs (police, however, were inclined to believe that the second was a copycat crime). Authorities stepped up security at other possible targets, and the government vowed once again to clamp down on racist and anti-Semitic behavior in the soccer stands. On November 28, in an important match in Rome, players took the field in overshirts bearing the slogan "No to Anti-Semitism, Violence and Racism." On December 8, the Rome Jewish community, in cooperation with other organizations, sponsored a daylong program of concerts, debates, and discussions at the Liberation Museum to promote tolerance and protest racism.

Earlier in the year, a multimedia kit, *Antisemitismo Perche?* (Why Anti-Semitism?), was prepared as a project by students at a Rome high school and made available to the public. It included interviews with skinheads and other right-wingers, as well as historical documents.

JEWISH COMMUNITY

Demography

About 26,000 people were registered as members of Italian Jewish communities. Since many others did not formally affiliate, the total number of Jews was estimated at 30,000 to 40,000. Three-quarters of Italy's Jews lived in two cities: Rome, with about 15,000, and Milan, with about 10,000. The rest were scattered in a score of other towns and cities, mostly in northern and central Italy.

About half of Italy's Jews were born in the country, and most of the others had arrived in the past few decades. Somewhere between a third and a half of Rome's Jews were Libyan Jews, or their offspring, who fled after bloody anti-Jewish riots following the 1967 Six-Day War. The Milan Jewish community included recent arrivals from more than two dozen countries. The largest contingent was from Iran, with many Jews hailing from other Middle Eastern countries.

How to maintain Jewish life and Jewish identity in small, scattered communities was an ongoing problem. At the national congress of Italy's Jewish communities in 1998, representatives of small communities—some with only a few score or a few hundred members—complained that the two big communities, Rome and Milan, ignored their interests. This year, on March 14, representatives of small and medium-sized communities—Casale, Genoa, Bologna, Padova, Venice, Mantua, Pisa, Turin, and Florence—met in Florence to discuss common challenges. This was the first such meeting ever held.

Communal Affairs

Italy's Jews are nominally Orthodox—there are no Reform or Conservative movements. Those converted by non-Orthodox rabbis abroad are not permitted membership in Italian Jewish communities, and adult conversions, even of the Orthodox variety, are discouraged. Three types of rites are celebrated: Sephardi, Ashkenazi, and Italian—a local rite that evolved from the Jewish community that lived in Italy before the destruction of the Temple.

Chabad-Lubavitch was also a growing presence in Italy. In Venice, a Chabad House as well as a Chabad yeshivah, almost all of whose students were foreigners, operated in the historic ghetto, and there was also a Chabad-operated kosher restaurant and a Chabad Venice Web site. But Chabad had little contact with the established Venice Jewish community, and its presence was resented by some. Chabad also sponsored giant Hanukkah menorahs in several cities and erected a sukkah in a Milan public square for the holiday of Sukkot that attracted as many as 500 people a day.

Most Italian Jews, however, were not strictly observant, and even observant Jews tended to be highly acculturated, with a strong Italian identity. The rate of intermarriage was estimated at 50 percent or more. In recent years, however, there had been a move toward stricter observance in several communities, including Rome and Milan, and this created friction between increasingly militant traditionalists, on the one hand, and nonobservant and "cultural" (secular) Jews — many of them married to non-Jews — on the other.

In Milan the large number of Jews from Muslim countries who maintained their own rites and meticulously Orthodox lifestyles complicated the situation, setting the stage for emotional religious-secular debates. The Milan Jewish community organized several open meetings to discuss such topics as "Why and How to Remain Together in One Community." The role of Jewish schools was a particularly touchy matter. An announcement for one public meeting, held in March, summed up the pressing issues: "The Jewish world is going through many tensions: between 'secular' Jews and 'religious' Jews; between different conceptions of being Jewish. The Jewish Community of Milan must decide who has the right to enroll in its schools, what attitude to take toward children of mothers who are not Jewish and intend to become involved in Judaism."

In the spring, the board of the Milan Jewish community formally recognized and granted funding to Shorashim, an organization that had for ten years been teaching Jewish topics and promoting Jewish identity among children of mixed marriages, outside the auspices of the community. For three years Shorashim had been receiving financial support from the Province of Milan.

In Rome religious and political tensions exacerbated by personal animosities led to the dissolution of the Jewish community board in the fall. The Rome community, whose schools and other institutions were beset by budgetary problems, was also shaken during the summer by the suicide of a Jewish couple who were being squeezed by loan sharks. In his Rosh Hashanah sermon, Chief Rabbi Elio Toaff said such tragedies occurred because "we are too assimilated into the worst part of the people among whom we live. With the drugs, violence, immorality, marital infidelity, and slander." But the suicides were also taken as a sign of the failure of the Jewish community: How could Jews have been driven to such desperate straits without the community knowing anything about it? In his Rosh Hashanah message, community president Sandro Di Castro called for more communal solidarity in the coming year. On October 16, at the Pitigliani Jewish community center, there was a soul-searching roundtable discussion about the future of the Rome Jewish community.

Jewish communities, Jewish centers, and other Jewish organizations throughout Italy made increasing use of the Internet. Jewish publications such as *Shalom*, the monthly put out by the Rome community, ran regular columns advising readers about Jewish sites on the World Wide Web. Among the most important Italian Jewish Web sites was www.menorah.it.

Despite the difficulties they faced, the larger Jewish communities continued to maintain a wide range of activities. In Milan alone, for instance, there were three Jewish choirs. In November, in collaboration with the European Council of Jewish Communities, the Rome Jewish community hosted "Yachad," a singles weekend for young Jewish adults from all over Europe, and there were a number of other large social and educational get-togethers over the course of the year. In May a large delegation of Italian Jews attended the general assembly of the European Council of Jewish Communities, held in Nice. In Rome, a small new synagogue in a residential neighborhood was opened with joyous ceremony in December.

Jewish-Catholic Relations

Formal relations between Catholics and Jews had their ups and downs during the year. There were a number of positive developments. The pope met with Jewish representatives in the U.S. in January, and on Holocaust Memorial Day, April 13, a huge menorah donated by American Jews was dedicated in a courtyard of the North American College, a Roman Catholic seminary just outside the Vatican. Jews took part in a major interfaith meeting at the Vatican in October. And throughout the year a number of leading Catholic figures expressed public apology for anti-Semitism committed by Catholics, in line with the pope's call to Catholics to ask forgiveness for sins as part of the run-up to the Holy Year of 2000. On September 29, Cardinal Carlo Maria Martini of Milan joined the city's mayor and chief rabbi for a visit to the Chabad sukkah.

Nevertheless, early in the year, Cardinal Edward I. Cassidy, president of the Vatican's Commission for Relations with the Jews, expressed concern about the course of Catholic-Jewish dialogue. He criticized the "aggressive" anti-Church attitudes of some Jewish organizations. "Jewish responses to what we seek to do to improve our relationship are often so negative," Cassidy said, "that some now hesitate to do anything at all for fear of making the situation worse." And he suggested that the International Jewish Committee for Interreligious Consultations (IJCIC), the official Jewish partner for dialogue with the Holy See, had essentially ceased functioning.

What Cassidy had in mind included the controversy over the wartime role of Pope Pius XII: Plans were going ahead to beatify him despite criticism by Jews and others that he had not done enough to prevent the Shoah. In May, Rabbi

Marvin Hier of the Simon Wiesenthal Center in the U.S. described Pius as "the pope of the Holocaust" who "sat on the throne of St. Peter in stony silence, without ever lifting a finger, as each day thousands of Jews were sent to the gas chambers with his full knowledge." Hier and others called on the Vatican to open its secret wartime archives to uncover the truth. In the fall, British author John Cornwell, himself a Catholic, further inflamed the controversy with his highly publicized book, *Hitler's Pope*. Claiming to base his findings on previously unavailable documents, Cornwell accused Pius of anti-Semitism and of having fostered the rise of Hitler. The Vatican rejected the accusations and said that Cornwell had not had the access to secret archives that he claimed.

In response to Cassidy's warnings of a possible crisis in Catholic-Jewish relations, Jewish organizations involved in interfaith dialogue held a "summit" in April in New York. The meeting took place less than a week after the death at the age of 76 of Israeli scholar Geoffrey Wigoder, the chairman of IJCIC. During the summer Seymour Reich was named to replace him. Representatives of IJCIC, including Reich, met with Cardinal Cassidy at the Vatican on October 18. As a first step toward clarifying the Church's role during the Holocaust, a six-member group of scholars — three Jews and three Catholics — was charged to review the Vatican documents that had already been published. They held their first meeting in December, in New York.

Also in December, Pope John Paul II cleared the way for the beatification of two other former popes by signing decrees recognizing the "heroic virtues" of John XXIII and a miracle attributed to Pius IX. John XXIII, who reigned from 1958 to 1963, had worked to save Jews during World War II when he served as apostolic delegate to Turkey. Then, as pope, he had called the Second Vatican Council in 1962 that produced the Nostra Aetate decree repudiating the collective responsibility of the Jewish people for the death of Christ, thus opening the way to formal Catholic-Jewish dialogue.

The possible beatification of Pius IX, however, who reigned from 1846 to 1878, was viewed by some Jewish commentators as highly problematic. The last pope with temporal power, Pius IX was also the last pope to confine Jews to a ghetto: The Jewish ghetto in Rome was not abolished until 1870, when he lost his temporal power. And in 1858 he was behind the notorious kidnapping of seven-year-old Edgardo Mortara from his home in Bologna, after a servant told a priest that she had secretly baptized the boy when he was a baby. That incident sparked a public outcry and a wave of international protests, but Pius refused to yield, and the boy grew up to be a priest. In a statement released to the Italian media, Amos Luzzatto, president of the Union of Italian Jewish Communities, expressed "embarrassment and displeasure" at the news of the impending beatification. The Mortara case, he said, had left a wound "that has never been closed, and, whatever the theological reasons for beatifying Pius IX might be, represents for the Jewish community a tragic memory that has never been overcome."

Culture

Throughout the year Jewish cultural associations and other organizations in cities around Italy sponsored a wide variety of exhibits, debates, lectures, concerts, courses, workshops, sports activities, film series, Jewish studies encounters, festivals, and other events. The Pitigliani Jewish Center in Rome was particularly active, as was the Rome Jewish Culture Center, which was celebrating its 25th year of operation.

Many of these events were sponsored jointly with municipal bodies or non-Jewish private organizations. The Israeli embassy was very active in sponsoring cultural events. Another indication of rising interest in things Jewish within the general population were the numerous articles, broadcasts, and cultural events on Jewish themes not organized under any Jewish auspices but rather sponsored commercially or by non-Jewish institutions.

A few examples illustrate the variety of Italian Jewish or Jewish-themed cultural life. A Jewish Film Festival took place in Milan from October 9 to November 7. In Turin there was a photographic exhibition on Jewish wedding practices in June. In November the Venice Jewish community sponsored a daylong seminar on the Sephardi experience, ranging from history to music to culinary traditions. Also in November a multimedia presentation on "The Legend of the Dybbuk" was held under the patronage of the presidency of the Lazio region, and was sponsored by several radio stations and the Hungarian and Polish cultural institutes in Rome, among others. And the November issue of *Gulliver,* a popular travel magazine, had a special 65-page section devoted to "Yiddishland"—Jewish-theme tourism in a number of countries.

At the end of March, after Purim, RAI—Italian government television—broadcast a new feature film on the Purim story, the 16th episode in a series of feature-length television movies on biblical themes. Before it was aired there was a special showing for Chief Rabbi Toaff of Rome, other community leaders, and 400 pupils from Rome's Jewish school. Roberto Benigni's controversial Holocaust film "Life Is Beautiful" won three Academy Awards—for best actor (Benigni himself), best foreign-language film, and best music. A festival of Jewish film and culture, focusing on the image of Jewish women, took place in the Tuscan village of Pitigliano, once a thriving Jewish community, October 30–November 1.

Several institutions of higher learning had Jewish studies programs or offered courses in Jewish studies. From January through March the philosophy department of Milan University sponsored the second semester of a special seminar for scholars, artists, and writers on the question of whether there is such a thing as a Jewish aesthetic. In the spring, the Giorgio Perlasca Study Center in Pignataro Maggiore held a conference on "The State of Israel, fifty years of history, millennia of hope."

The theme of the prestigious Ravenna Music Festival in June and July was "Toward Jerusalem," and the inaugural concert featured 13 cantors from Jerusalem representing diverse cantorial traditions. In July the fourth annual Klezmer Music Festival took place in Ancona. In August, Moni Ovadia, Italy's leading Jewish performer, produced the opera by Rossini, "Adina, or the Calif of Baghdad," at the annual Rossini Opera Festival. A sprawling festival of Jewish culture called "Zachor" took place in July and August in Senigallia, home to but a few dozen Jews. A festival of Jewish music took place in Pisa in December. In August members of the Israeli Philharmonic, conducted by Zubin Mehta, shocked concert-goers in Sardinia when they took off their black tuxedo jackets and performed the second half of their concert in shirtsleeves because of the heat.

There were a number of activities relating to Jewish sites. At the end of August a number of synagogues and other historic Jewish buildings were part of the international "Open Doors" initiative promoting the Jewish cultural heritage and tourism in Europe. In October the 600-year-old Jewish cemetery of Venice was rededicated and opened to the public after more than a year of restoration, funded by a long list of public, private, and international donors. All the tombstones were photographed and cataloged, and, during the restoration, more than 130 tombstones were found buried. In November there was a conference on "Jewish Cultural Heritage" at the Gallery of Modern Art in Turin, which included the premiere of a film on the synagogues of Piedmont by Daniele Segre.

In May a new Jewish museum in Bologna opened its doors, sponsored by the city and region of Emilia Romagna. Conceived as a "virtual museum," it displayed few actual objects, but instead functioned primarily as an information center, which served as an educational base linked to other Jewish museums in Emilia Romagna, such as those in Soragna and Ferrara, where collections of ritual objects and other material were displayed. The Bologna museum also organized concerts, lectures, and tours. In July the Jewish community of Milan announced that it would open a Jewish museum in the building complex that housed the main synagogue. The regional government of Sicily announced that it would sponsor a Jewish museum in Palermo.

Publications

The main Jewish community periodicals were the monthlies *Shalom* in Rome and *Bolletino* in Milan. Several smaller communities, including Turin, Florence, and Genoa, issued newsletters. Other publications included the intellectual journal, *Rassegna Mensile d'Israel*. In addition to the growing number of Jewish Internet sites, there was a regular Jewish slot on state-run television and a regular Jewish music program on state-run radio.

Scores if not hundreds of books by Jewish authors or on Jewish themes were published in Italy, including histories, biographies, memoirs, essays, religious works, and fiction, as well as "how-to" books, Jewish travel guides, and cookbooks, some written originally in Italian and others translated. A well-stocked Jewish bookstore, Menorah, operated in Rome and maintained its own Web site, while the Claudiana and Tikkun bookstores in Milan specialized in Jewish themes. The first Jewish book fair in Rome was held March 6–7, while the third annual Jewish book fair in Milan was held in May.

The mainstream press gave books of Jewish interest broad exposure. There were also numerous public book signings and book launches, as well as lectures, interviews, and public appearances by authors. In September, for example, Israeli author A. B. Yehoshua, who is very popular in Italy, made a number of personal appearances and conducted a four-day seminar on writing for 25 aspiring authors in Turin.

Personalia

In March, Radu Mihaileanu, the Romanian-French Jewish director of the Holocaust comedy "Train de Vie," received the silver ribbon for best European film, awarded by the Italian Union of Cinema Journalists. Also in March, Maria Luisa Moscati, author of a Jewish guidebook to the Marche region, was given an award by that regional government for her work in promoting Jewish heritage and culture. Rita Levi-Montalcini, who won the Nobel Prize for Medicine in 1986, turned 90, an occasion marked by an international scientific symposium. President Carlo Azeglio Ciampi received the International Primo Levi award, in Genoa, for his contribution to "the promotion of a society founded on peace, justice, and freedom." In May, Cobi Benatoff, past president of the Milan Jewish community, was elected president of the European Council of Jewish Communities. In July, Gad Lerner, who wrote for leading publications and also hosted television programs, received the Alfio Russo journalism prize. In October, the Friends of the Hebrew University presented the Scopus Award to Giancarlo Elia Valori, president of Italy's Autostradas.

Award-winning writer, poet, and editor Alberto Vigevani died in February at the age of 80. Aldo Sonnino, a writer, editor, teacher, and leading figure in the Rome Jewish community for decades, died in the spring at the age of 88. In June, Shulamit Kaczyne-Reale, the daughter of Polish photographer and Yiddish writer Alter Kaczyne, died in Rome at the age of 80. The widow of an Italian diplomat and parliament member, she worked tirelessly to bring her father's work to public attention. Leo Valiani, a Jewish hero of the resistance and senator-for-life, died in September at the age of 90. Many Jews were indignant that his official funeral, attended by the highest government officials, was held on Yom Kippur. Noted Trieste-based author and intellectual Giorgio Voghera also died at the age of 90.

RUTH ELLEN GRUBER

Switzerland

National Affairs

IN 1999 THE ROTATING one-year presidency of the Swiss Confederation, a position more of honor than of power, was held by Ruth Dreifuss, a Social Democrat who became the first woman and the first Jew to be president of Switzerland. During her year in office, and to some extent because of her urging, the government addressed a number of sensitive issues such as the Kosovo war and its refugees, the need for a better health-care system, and the debate over Switzerland's role during World War II.

The same broad-based coalition that had controlled the Swiss government for 40 years continued in power, and the seven members of the Federal Council, reelected in December, continued the so-called "magic formula": two Christian Democrats (Catholics), two Radicals (right-wing Protestants), two Social Democrats, and one representative of the Swiss People's Party.

At the parliamentary elections in October, the big winner was the Swiss People's Party (SVP/UDC), a nationalist populist party that received 22.5 percent of the vote. The SVP/UDC ran many extreme-right candidates for local office and focused its campaign on nationalistic themes: severe limitations on refugees seeking asylum; fewer naturalizations; staying out of the European Union, the UN, and NATO; and opposing the establishment of a Swiss Solidarity Foundation to fight bigotry and youth violence. Many speeches by party leaders—most notably Christoph Blocher, head of the Zurich branch—contained explicit xenophobic and anti-Semitic statements.

The Kosovo war sent thousands of refugees streaming into Switzerland, stimulating a major debate over asylum policy. About two-thirds of the 45,000 refugees admitted to Switzerland in 1999 came from the former Yugoslavia. After the war the Swiss government provided financial inducements for the refugees to go home, an opportunity seized by more than 16,000 of them. Former Yugoslavs now numbered 160,000 in Switzerland, and they represented the second largest foreign community, after those who came from Italy. The Kosovar refugees elicited a mixed reaction in Swiss society. There were racist and populist speeches, but also generous donations of food, clothing, and other material support.

The Swiss economy was the last in Europe to emerge from recession, and 1999 was a year of growth, especially in the service sector (banks, insurance companies) and high-value-added industries (chemicals, watches, technological research). The unemployment rate decreased from 3.9 percent to 2.4 percent, though some disparities between cantons remained. The Swiss people voted against maternity insurance, making their country one of the last in Europe with an incomplete welfare system. At the same time, to the growing dissatisfaction of the population, health insurance premiums had steadily gone up. Such anomalies reflected deep dichotomies in Switzerland's identity. It was a European country outside the European Union, a centuries-old democratic system sometimes paralyzed by its own democratic institutions, and a rich country with a growing number of people on welfare.

Israel and the Middle East

Relations between Switzerland and Israel were somewhat tense in 1999. The Swiss government and people expressed their annoyance after the Knesset awarded prizes to Edgar Bronfman, president of the World Jewish Congress, and Alfonse D'Amato, then senator from New York, in 1998, for their fight to retrieve dormant accounts from Swiss banks. Following the Swiss uproar, Israeli prime minister Benjamin Netanyahu canceled an official visit to Switzerland at the last minute. This left a residue of resentment in Switzerland, even after both D'Amato and Netanyahu were voted out of office.

In July 1999 Geneva agreed to host an unprecedented meeting of the 188 states that had signed the Fourth Geneva Convention, in order to examine Israel's record on the treatment of Palestinians in the Occupied Territories. The conference was called in response to an Arab request at the UN General Assembly. It took place in Geneva because Switzerland is depositary of the 50-year-old conventions extending protection to sick, wounded, and captured combatants and civilians. Not once in the previous 50 years had the Fourth Convention—the one that applies to treatment of civilians—been invoked against a state, and its use against Israel was clearly intended to make a political statement. In the end, however, the Swiss-chaired meeting took only a few minutes. Israel was never mentioned in the text of the statement adopted and there was no finding that Israel had committed grave breaches of the Fourth Convention.

The Swiss Agency for Development and Cooperation (SDC), a branch of the Ministry of Foreign Affairs, repeatedly funded publications libeling Israel and lauding Palestinian achievements. The Israeli embassy and local Jewish organizations vigorously protested the use of federal funds for a purpose that violated Switzerland's legendary neutrality.

In addition, the press often blurred the distinction between Jews and Israelis. Much of this seemed deliberate, and anti-Semitism often lurked behind criticism of Israel. One could often hear comparisons between the Holocaust and Israel's treatment of the Palestinians, and criticism of Switzerland's past was sometimes countered with: "Let Israel face its own behavior towards the Palestinians before accusing Switzerland of wrongdoings."

Holocaust-Related Issues

What started in 1995 as the "dormant accounts controversy" grew into a major debate about Switzerland's role during World War II, encompassing Holocaust victims' accounts, high-ranking Nazi officers' accounts, Nazi gold laundered by the Swiss National Bank, looted art, unpaid insurance policies, and the closure of borders to Jewish refugees.

The controversy over Switzerland's role during World War II was exacerbated in 1999 by the publication of the Volcker report on dormant accounts and the Independent Experts' Commission report on Switzerland's asylum policy before and during the war. In August 1998 a global settlement had been reached between Jewish organizations, lawyers representing class actions, and the two major Swiss banks, Union Bank of Switzerland and Crédit Suisse. According to the agreement, $1.25 billion would be distributed to Holocaust survivors who held bank accounts or other assets in Switzerland during the war, or to their heirs.

Judge Edward Korman of Brooklyn Federal Court in the United States, authorized to examine thousands of claims of Holocaust survivors or their heirs, was expected to release a list of valid claims in the spring of 2000. Money from the fund is then to be distributed among the plaintiffs. Judge Korman's research will be facilitated by the report of the International Committee of Eminent Persons (ICEP), chaired by Paul Volcker, the former head of the U.S. Federal Reserve. This seven-member committee (three appointed by Swiss banks, three by Jewish organizations, and Volcker) was commissioned to audit most of the Swiss banks that were active before and during wartime. The Federal Council voted a unique lifting of banking secrecy laws to allow auditors to examine the accounts. After careful review of the relevant documentation still available for some 4.1 million accounts that were open in the 1933–1945 period, 54,000 dormant accounts were judged to be "probably or possibly related to victims." These accounts represented $20 million for that period, which, with interest, came to an estimated $150–270 million in 1999. The Federal Banking Commission had yet to authorize the publication of the 25,000 names of account holders for further identification.

This gigantic audit was not well received by a number of banks, some of which denied archival access to the audit teams. Overall, the Volcker report, released in early December in Zurich, did not receive much attention from the Swiss press. There was a broad consensus that the research had been conducted seriously, and everyone seemed satisfied by the results. Swiss banks were relieved that the amount found in dormant accounts was not higher, while Jewish organizations felt that their claims had been confirmed. The Swiss government also expressed satisfaction.

BERGIER REPORT

That very same week in December came another report, from the Independent Experts' Commission headed by Swiss historian Jean-François Bergier. Following up on its 1998 report about gold transactions made by the Swiss National Bank during the war, the commission now released a study of Switzerland's asylum policy before and during wartime.

While the findings were hardly new to scholars, media coverage was intense because this was the first time that a report commissioned by the Swiss government was so critical of Swiss politicians during World War II. The study clearly showed that anti-Semitism motivated many political decisions even before the war. For instance, Swiss leaders pressed Nazi Germany to find a way to identify Jewish refugees arriving at Switzerland's borders, and in 1938 the Nazis agreed to stamp the letter "J" in the passports of German and Austrian Jews. From then on Swiss customs officers could easily deny access to Jewish refugees. The J stamp also prevented German Jews from entering other countries.

The report also proved that Swiss authorities knew, by 1942, that the Nazis had decided to exterminate all European Jews. Nevertheless the Swiss closed the borders to Jewish refugees in August of that year. The report concluded that Switzerland could have taken in many more Jewish refugees than it did (22,000 were admitted and many thousands turned back). It also stressed that while government officials were motivated by anti-Semitic feelings, the Swiss population as a whole could not be considered anti-Semitic, nor were all Swiss collectively responsible for the official policy at the time. Many individuals, in fact, took great risks to organize the illegal entry of refugees into Switzerland, or to shelter and feed them.

It was too soon to assess the political and educational impact of this remarkable study. It was well received by the media, but less so by the prewar generation and nationalist circles. The Federal Council issued a lukewarm statement that repeated old apologies for the J stamp and focused on Switzerland's defense of human rights after World War II. The final report of the commission is due in 2001.

The Volcker and Bergier reports refocused public attention on the Holocaust at a crucial time, when the issue had begun to recede from Swiss consciousness. The Switzerland-World War II task force set up in 1996 to defend the official view had been dissolved, reflecting the government's desire to bury the debate. The special fund for Holocaust victims, created in 1997 by major banks, the Swiss National Bank, and some industries, had almost finished distributing its $180 million to needy Holocaust survivors around the world. The beneficiaries, mostly Jews, but also Gypsies and handicapped people, had each received about $500 from this humanitarian fund.

The last pending Holocaust-related project was the Swiss Solidarity Foundation, proposed in 1997 but not yet approved. The idea was to use almost $4.5 billion of gold reserves to fight poverty and violence both domestically and internationally, especially among young people. But the goals of the foundation were never well defined, and the expenditure elicited loud criticism, especially at a time of economic crisis. One of the strongest critics of the project was Christoph Blocher of the Swiss People's Party who wanted to use this gold to fund social security. The topic was expected to be addressed by the parliament in 2000.

Four more Swiss citizens who helped Jews during the war were granted the title "Righteous among the Nations" by the Yad Vashem Institute in Jerusalem, bringing the number of Swiss recipients of the title to 35.

Other issues related to the Holocaust included the escape into Switzerland of Maurice Papon, the 89-year-old French war criminal convicted to ten years in prison for his role in deporting Jews from Bordeaux. He was arrested by the Swiss police and handed over to French authorities. A few months earlier a local Jewish newspaper discovered that Josef Mengele, the notorious Nazi doctor, had often vacationed in Switzerland after the war. One day the Swiss police came to arrest him, but he had fled.

SWITZERLAND FACING THE HOLOCAUST

In spite of the challenges to the old myths about Switzerland's role during World War II, no serious political step had been taken to assimilate the lessons of the past. The Federal Commission against Racism, appointed in 1995 by the Federal Council, issued an important report about anti-Semitism in late 1998, but few of its recommendations had been implemented. Nothing had been done in the areas of education, culture, religion, or general information.

Since each canton (state) was responsible for its own school system, there were no national textbooks or curricular guidelines. The choice of topics, books, and approach was made by each school individually, and often by each teacher. Some teachers and schools espoused recent findings about Switzerland's not-so-glorious past while others refused to break with the myths. And the recommendation for the establishment of a museum for tolerance went nowhere.

There was as yet no serious attempt to make the general public sensitive to issues of racism, anti-Semitism, tolerance, and remembrance. So far, all projects had relied on the ideas of individuals, funded privately by nongovernmental organizations, religious communities, teachers or intellectuals. The Jewish community of Switzerland was often solicited for the financial support of such projects.

Anti-Semitism and Racism

The wave of anti-Semitism that greeted the World War II debate did not abate. Anti-Jewish feelings were regularly expressed publicly and privately. Even many people with no previous history of anti-Semitism tended to associate Jews with stereotypes of money and power. As for racism and xenophobia, shelters for refugees were set on fire, and, depending on their nationality, foreigners could have great difficulty acquiring Swiss citizenship. Some right-wing politicians sought to limit the number of foreigners in residential buildings and to separate native speakers from immigrants in public schools.

MAINSTREAM POLITICS

In July 1998, weeks before the global settlement between banks and Jewish organizations was reached, a representative of Basel in the Federal Assembly, Rudolf Keller—head of the far-right Swiss Democrats—issued a press release calling for a boycott of "all American and Jewish stores, restaurants and travel offers." The Federal Assembly voted to lift his immunity so that he could be tried for violating the antiracism law. But in June 1999 the Council of States, the upper house of parliament, refused to follow suit, and Keller did not have to stand trial. The Keller case, which dragged on for almost a year, touched off intense debate in Switzerland. Antiracist associations across the country joined forces in an attempt to make the public sensitive to the expression of anti-Semitism in mainstream politics. Two organizations collected thousands of signatures from citizens of various backgrounds and religions asking the upper house of parliament to agree to lift Keller's immunity. Prominent Jewish and non-Jewish personalities added their voices to the protest. Despite the failure to bring Keller to account, this national mobilization against racism made a deep impression on a country not accustomed to popular demonstrations.

Anti-Semitism reappeared before the federal elections of October 1999. According to media reports, at least five candidates on the Swiss People's Party (SVP/UDC) lists were notorious far-right activists, and some of them had been convicted under the antiracism law. Roger Etter, from Ticino, was a Waffen-SS sympathizer. Michael Mathys, from Argau, contributed racist comments to an Internet forum. Jean-Jacques Kottelat, from the Jura, had been convicted for racist slurs against refugees. Pascal Junod, a Geneva lawyer, had close ties to Holocaust deniers, skinheads, and neo-Nazis. On the same Geneva list stood Pierre Schifferli and Henri Rappaz, both of whom had been active in a defunct xenophobic party. None of these candidates, however, was elected.

The SVP/UDC leadership did not oppose any of these candidates on the party's lists, nor did it distance the party from their views. Thus extreme-right militants—Holocaust deniers, anti-Semites, and racists—found respectability by entering mainstream politics with the SVP/UDC. In fact, two weeks before the election, a Zurich court convicted Christoph Blocher, head of SVP/UDC's Zurich chapter, for a 1997 speech aggressively attacking Jewish organizations that demanded the restitution of dormant accounts. For using anti-Semitic stereotypes associating Jews with money, Blocher was fined $7,000. He has since appealed. A week later, a newspaper disclosed a 1997 letter signed by Blocher lauding a pamphlet written by Switzerland's most notorious Holocaust denier, Jürgen Graf.

Blocher responded that he had not read the 18-page pamphlet but liked the title, *The Downfall of Swiss Freedom.*

Outside mainstream politics there was no evidence that far-right groups were growing in numbers, though they had become more active. The World War II and asylum debates reinvigorated their notions of a Jewish plot to milk Swiss banks, of the Holocaust as a hoax made up by Jews to gain financial compensation, and of the "white race" being threatened by immigration. Far-right groups seemed to be well organized both within the country and internationally, exchanging mailing lists and advertising, and importing propaganda from abroad. Skinheads, who probably numbered only about 500, increased the frequency of their "private concerts" that attracted hundreds of people from outside the skinhead movement itself. (The "private" label avoided prosecution under the antiracism law, which applied only to public events.) The police seized neo-Nazi propaganda (music, publications, and clothing) worth many thousands of francs. Hooligans yelled racist slurs at soccer games.

Holocaust deniers continued to hold secret lectures in various cities. The New Right, with close links to deniers and skinheads, held an increasing number of them. At these meetings of Thulé, Proudhon Circle, European Synergies, or Friends of Robert Brasillach, propaganda was distributed. Other anti-Semitic organizations included a group of Catholic fundamentalists based in Ecône, in the Valais canton, esoteric cults like the Universal Church, and the far-left Parti National-Communautaire Européen.

Popular anti-Semitism was inflamed by the World War II debate. Though not as numerous in 1999 as in the two previous years, anti-Semitic letters were still sent to newspaper editors (and sometimes published), to Jewish leaders, and to antiracist organizations. Anti-Semitic, racist or xenophobic statements were regularly heard in public places such as restaurants, streets, and offices. Anti-Semitic graffiti, posters, and flyers were common. An Israeli tourist was stabbed in downtown Zurich because his skullcap identified him as a Jew. The assailant turned himself in to the police but had not yet been tried as the year ended.

FIGHTING ANTI-SEMITISM

Under the antiracism law passed in 1994, a few hundred cases had been tried in the courts and many led to convictions. In an atmosphere already tense over asylum policy and Holocaust victims' assets, far-right parties attempted to have the law suppressed, but three national attempts failed.

In the meantime, the Federal Court issued a major decision in 1999 affirming that anyone distributing or selling racist propaganda was just as culpable as the author or publisher. This resolved an ambiguity in the original law and was expected to help in a number of pending trials, including one involving veteran neo-Nazi Gaston-Armand Amaudruz, scheduled for April 2000. Holocaust deniers convicted for their writings, such as René-Louis Berclaz, Jürgen Graf, and Arthur

Vogt, lost their appeals. The implementation of this law presumably discouraged many far-right activists from writing, publishing or distributing materials that could send them to jail.

Beside the Geneva-based CICAD (Committee against Anti-Semitism and Defamation), another Jewish organization with a similar purpose was founded, this one in Zurich. Called DAVID, the Center against anti-Semitism and Defamation, it reacted vigorously, in the media and other public forums, against anti-Semitism. The Swiss Federation of Jewish Communities continued to be a leading voice in the expression of Jewish opinions and concerns, and individual members of the Jewish community became more forthright in their public denunciations of anti-Semitism.

Non-Jewish reactions to anti-Semitism tended to come from individual teachers or priests who organized special classes or lectures, people who sent letters to newspaper editors, and antiracist organizations that held public events.

JEWISH COMMUNITY

Demography

The number of Jews in Switzerland remained at about 18,000. The ethnic background of the Jewish community was diverse: old Swiss families of German and East European background lived in the German-speaking part, while Jews of Middle Eastern origin outnumbered Ashkenazim in the French-speaking part (especially Geneva). Some small communities, like the one in La Chaux-de-Fonds, were declining, since younger people were moving to larger cities.

Communal Affairs

The umbrella organization of Swiss Jews, the Swiss Federation of Jewish Communities, renewed efforts to modernize and improve the efficiency of its operations. The impetus for this was the World War II controversy, which put Swiss Jewry under an unaccustomed spotlight. The federation was both a political and a religious body, though it still refused to allow in the two Reform communities in Geneva and Zurich, which had a combined membership of 2,000. The keynote speaker at the annual meeting in St. Gallen was the president of the Swiss Confederation, Ruth Dreifuss. Since the incumbent, Rolf Bloch, was not seeking a new term, the federation would elect a new president in June 2000.

Culture

A number of books about Switzerland and World War II were published in 1999, and some were very critical of the government's asylum policy, such as

Hans-Ulrich Jost's *Politik und Wirtschaft im Krieg* and Anne Weill's *Suisse: Essai sur un racisme d'Etat.* Other books of Jewish interest included *Chroniques du Désastre,* an anthology of testimonies from Polish ghettos, *Zwischen Ausgrenzung und Integration,* a textbook about Swiss Jewry, and *Chronologie der rassistischen Vorfällen in der Schweiz,* an analysis of racist events in 1998–99. Franz Ricken-bach filmed a documentary about the practically extinct community of Delémont. A traveling exhibition about Jews in Switzerland was shown in the German-speaking part of the country.

Personalia

Ruth Dreifuss was the most prominent Jew, thanks to her position as president. But she was not primarily identified as a Jew in the public mind because she actually personifed, for many, several minorities: a woman, a social democrat, a native French speaker, as well as a Jew.

Dr. Branco Weiss, a successful high-tech entrepreneur and generous patron of educational projects, emerged as an outspoken voice against anti-Semitism in Switzerland. He personally stood against the political decision not to lift the immunity of the anti-Semitic parliament member Rudolf Keller, and resigned from various national boards in protest. Weiss also initiated DAVID, the Zurich-based center that combats anti-Semitism.

Edmond Safra died in a mysterious fire in his Monaco apartment on December 3. The successful Lebanese-born banker had recently sold his Republic National Bank to HSBC. He considered Geneva his second home and was a generous benefactor of many institutions, among them the Jewish school, the restored Ashkenazi synagogue — now named Beit Yaacov in his father's memory — and numerous other Jewish charities.

BRIGITTE SION

Central and Eastern Europe

Federal Republic of Germany

National Affairs

T HE ADOPTION OF A NEW capital city was only one transition among many that transformed the Bonn Republic into the Berlin Republic in 1999. In the spring, usually vocal intellectuals of the left watched in stunned silence as Chancellor Gerhard Schröder of the Social Democratic Party (SPD), and Foreign Minister Joschka Fischer, the leader of the Greens, led Germany into its first military engagement since World War II. For decades, pacifism had been the lesson drawn by the German left from Auschwitz, yet Fischer justified his support for the NATO bombing campaign in the Balkans by comparing Serbian crimes in Kosovo to the Holocaust. For his part, the "war chancellor" believed that the military engagement marked the dawn of a new age in which the German role on the world stage would reflect its economic strength.

Finance Minister Oskar Lafontaine shocked his loyal followers in the SPD in March when he resigned from both his government post and the chairmanship of the party. His retreat ended months of conflict within the government over economic policy. In addition to appointing a minister of finance more amenable to neoliberal thinking, the chancellor reluctantly assumed the chairmanship of the SPD. Then, when the government announced plans in the summer to tighten the reins on government spending, the left wing of the SPD revolted, and Schröder needed months to silence traditionalists within his own party.

This crisis within the SPD and the disillusionment of rank-and-file Greens with the performance of their party in the coalition translated into dismal returns for the governing parties in state elections throughout the year. The first victory for the opposition Christian Democratic Union (CDU) came in Hesse on the heels of a petition drive against Red-Green plans to introduce dual citizenship into German law. This election altered the makeup of the Bundesrat, the second house of the federal parliament, so that the government no longer held a majority. Dual citizenship was, for the time being, dead. Nevertheless, even the watered-down version of the reform, which was to take effect on January 1, 2000, granted citizenship for the first time to children of non-ethnic Germans born in Germany.

By the last state election of the year, in Berlin, several patterns had become clear. The SPD had suffered significant losses to its working-class base, while the CDU had achieved a majority in the Bundesrat on the strength of an anti-Schröder campaign. The realities of governance had torn the Greens asunder, and the liberal Free Democratic Party (FDP), which had played a critical role for decades as a small party in a system based on coalition government, faced the prospect of extinction. The postcommunist Party of Democratic Socialism (PDS), meanwhile, was maneuvering itself into the social democratic void to the left of the SPD, which occupied the "new middle." Aside from Brandenburg, where the German People's Union (GPU) secured seats in the parliament, extreme right-wing parties proved more successful in local races than in state or national elections.

On November 9, with the seat of government firmly established in Berlin, Germany celebrated the tenth anniversary of the fall of the Berlin Wall. One day prior to the festivities the highest court in the land rejected appeals from two former members of the politburo of the German Democratic Republic (GDR), ordering them to serve their prison sentences. Unemployment in the new federal states (the former GDR) was close to 18 percent.

As the year came to a close, a scandal broke that threatened to shake the CDU to its core. Among other embarrassing revelations, former chancellor Helmut Kohl acknowledged in a television interview that he had accepted suitcases of cash donations totaling at least DM 2 million ($1.2 million) over a period of five years without reporting it. Government attorneys considered indicting the "chancellor of unity." Nevertheless, Kohl found support among the many in his party who owed their rise to his favor.

Chancellor Schröder, buoyed both by the turmoil within the CDU and by the popularity of a tax-reduction plan he introduced just before Christmas, ended the year on a confident note. His New Year's Eve address to the nation called on German citizens to take greater responsibility for themselves in the century to come, making clear that he intended to continue reducing the role of the state.

Israel and the Middle East

After a few awkward moments in German-Israeli relations in the early part of the year, Schröder and Prime Minister Ehud Barak of Israel, the first members of the so-called second generation to be elected head of state in their respective countries, developed what they called a friendly relationship. A series of events in February highlighted the tensions between the countries under Barak's predecessor, Benjamin Netanyahu. First, Netanyahu's foreign minister, Ariel Sharon, called Avi Primor, Israel's ambassador to Germany, back to Israel after hearing of an interview with Primor published in the German daily *Die Welt*. Primor, widely respected in Germany, had called into question the democratic convictions of Shas, a religious party in Netanyahu's government. Although the German government remained silent about the recall, the German press backed Primor and harshly criticized the Israeli government's action.

Less than two weeks later, on February 11, Foreign Minister Fischer arrived in Jerusalem for his first official visit. Because Germany held the presidency of the European Union Council of Ministers at the time, he represented the EU as well. The 15 member states of the EU, meanwhile, had voted two days earlier, together with 100 other states in the UN, to condemn the settlement policy of the Netanyahu government. Sharon canceled his meeting with Fischer, citing a foot injury; Netanyahu met with Fischer some eight hours later than planned. Neither Israeli officials nor Fischer attached political significance to these moves, but German headlines spoke of "diplomatic irritations." Germany did, however, make good on its pledge to promote closer cooperation between Israel and the EU via Israeli participation in EU research and technology programs.

Back in Berlin, two Israeli guards shot and killed three of 50 Kurdish radicals attempting to occupy the Israeli consulate on February 17. Both the Israeli press and representatives of the Berlin SPD accused the police of failing to take the necessary measures to deter the protestors from entering the building. The German press, in turn, asked why no one in Israel had questioned whether or not the guards, who enjoyed diplomatic immunity and were recalled to Israel within days, had been justified in firing their weapons. The motive for the attack was said to lay in the cooperation of Israeli intelligence agents with Turkey in the capture of Kurd leader Abdullah Ocalan in Nairobi.

At his last press conference as Israeli ambassador, Primor announced that his embassy's move from Bonn to Berlin on August 6 would inaugurate a new chapter in German-Israeli relations. Although Primor's successor did not take office in 1999, the symbolism of Prime Minister Barak's September trip to Germany lent credence to Primor's assertion. Disregarding criticism back home, Barak accepted Schröder's invitation to be the first foreign leader to visit the Berlin Republic in its new capital. Survivors of the Sachsenhausen concentration camp and their grandchildren accompanied Schröder and Barak to the memorial at the site of the camp just north of Berlin. After the German chancellor reassured his Israeli guests with the phrase "Never again Sachsenhausen," the Israeli prime minister wrote in the guest book that it is "a strong and secure Israel that guarantees that there will never again be a Sachsenhausen or an Auschwitz."

Beyond the political realm, the legacy of the Holocaust continued to define the German-Israeli relationship. In March, Yad Vashem granted seven women from Berlin the title "Righteous among the Nations," the highest honor given by Israel to non-Jews. The women, four of whom were decorated posthumously, had risked their lives during the Second World War to save Jews. There are now 400 Germans among the approximately 16,000 Europeans so decorated.

An April production in Tel Aviv of a much-debated German play attracted a good deal of German press, but little controversy. Because a character named "the Rich Jew" embodied anti-Semitic stereotypes reminiscent of the Nazi era, Jews in Germany had refused, in 1985 and again in 1998, to allow the play, Werner Fassbinder's "Garbage, the City, and Death," to be performed (see AJYB 1999, pp. 352–53). In contrast, the Israeli artists involved in the Israeli production understood the work as a confrontation with racism and hatred that could be applied just as easily to Tel Aviv as to any other setting. Nonetheless, the director of the production, Avi Malka, declined an invitation to perform the play in Berlin. Well aware of the controversy surrounding the play in Germany, he said that he had no desire to put a "kosher stamp" on Fassbinder's work.

In spite of the persistent ambivalence underlying much of the German-Israeli dialogue, cultural institutions continued to pursue cooperative projects in 1999. For the first time in the history of the Federal Republic, Israel provided financial assistance to the Jewish community in Germany, in the form of grants from the Pinkus Foundation for youth projects. The University of Haifa established its first office in Germany in April with the goal of developing student exchange programs, visiting professorships, and a lecture series with partner institutions across Germany. On September 2, the Cologne-based Society for Jewish Information and Services (SJIS) sent its first group of high-school students to Israel for a year as part of a Europe-wide program called "Amichai." The SJIS hoped the students would return from Israel able and willing to breathe new life into the Jewish community of Germany.

Right-Wing Extremism

While the number of crimes attributed to right-wing extremists fell by 9.2 percent in 1999, the number of violent crimes committed by skinheads and neo-Nazis rose from 708 in 1998 to 746 in 1999. The Federal Office for the Protection of the Constitution (FOPC) counted fewer individual activists in 1999 than in 1998, but Interior Minister Otto Schilly (SPD) nevertheless expressed concern about the greater visibility of their organizations and an increase in their willingness to resort to violence. Almost half of the recorded cases of right-wing violence were perpetrated in the new federal states of the former GDR, where just over a fifth of the German population lived.

According to FOPC vice president Klaus-Dieter Fritsche (CSU), neo-Nazis viewed the public debate over liberalizing the citizenship law as a call to action. Recruitment and communication within the radical right milieu followed trends established in previous years. The number of Internet sites maintained by German extremists rose from 130 to 330, and the FOPC estimated the worldwide total at 600. In the first half of 1999 alone, skinhead bands played at some 50 "birthday parties," the time and place of which were generally announced only hours beforehand over the Internet or via mobile phones. The fashion, music, and camaraderie of the skinhead scene, if not its politics, had gained in popularity among German youth. Over half of the young people involved lived in the former GDR.

Skinheads in Brandenburg were especially aggressive. The number of violent hate crimes there in the first half of 1999 was 50 percent higher than in the first half of 1998. The death of a 28-year-old Algerian asylum seeker in the town of Guben caught the nation's attention. On February 13, after allegedly being injured in a fight with a "dark-skinned man," a group of skinheads in three cars decided to "hunt down dark-skinned Africans." They spotted Omar Ben Noui with a couple of friends at a gas station. The skinheads chased Ben Noui until he ran through the glass door of an apartment house and bled to death. The next day the Brandenburg SPD hosted a conference in Potsdam on xenophobia and rightist extremism. Government representatives explained that violence against foreigners had receded in 1998 because of the creation of special police units. Minister President Manfred Stolpe urged the public not to prejudge the youth of Brandenburg. Meanwhile, surveys revealed that almost one-fifth of young people over the age of 14 agreed to some degree with right-wing extremist rhetoric, and the police identified five different towns as centers of violence-prone gangs. The following Tuesday, February 16, an unknown vandal painted a swastika on the site where Ben Noui bled to death. Fearful of attracting more undesired attention, residents of the apartment house resisted efforts to erect an antiracist memorial at the site. Over the next several weeks German journalists flocked to Guben, a town of 28,000 that had also been the site of antiforeigner violence in the early 1990s. Now, hundreds of residents filed down the streets to protest against xenophobia and violence. A local social worker insisted that no more than 15 men constituted the hard core of the haters; their followers, numbering at least 150, were simply in search of belonging and recognition. The Greens and the PDS demanded that the CDU/CSU discontinue its petition drive against dual citizenship, which, they felt, had fueled the flames of xenophobia.

Echoing the views of many other observers, the minister for education in Brandenburg announced that changes were needed in the classroom. Teams would be sent to all state schools to instruct teachers—who had not been systematically replaced after the demise of the GDR—how to deal with rightist youth. The state also would increase the number of social workers in the educational system by 25 percent. Stolpe, who had originally suggested that the problem was one of violent individuals, now began speaking of a troubling "milieu" in his state.

Local residents, especially asylum seekers and immigrants, greeted the attention of politicians and reporters with cynicism, sure that Guben would return to its anti-foreigner status quo once the national wave of indignation wore off. Indeed, on February 22 an employee at the local youth club was fired for attending a demonstration in honor of Omar Ben Noui, and thereby jeopardizing the "foundation of trust with a portion of our young clientele." The town made headlines again in March, when the director of a home for refugees lambasted the Guben police for ignoring his calls for protection against skinhead intimidation.

According to experts, though, skinheads had more influence in Saxony than in Brandenburg or any other German state. In several towns of less than 20,000 residents, as few as 60 neo-Nazis could effectively close off sections of town to foreigners and leftists. The threat of violence combined with the silent complicity of the majority to enforce these "no-go areas" without the need for repeated physical attacks. Because they did not actually witness acts of violence or intimidation, local politicians and proprietors of youth hangouts rejected the notion that their towns had become the "nationally liberated zones" that neo-Nazi propaganda advocated.

In spite of the occasional crimes committed by their followers, leaders of the extreme right discouraged violence. Instead, they attempted to win the hearts and minds of citizens on the local level by speaking to their concerns. First infiltrating youth clubs, then neighborhood associations, then the city council, right-wing extremists hoped to make their nationalistic, xenophobic worldview part of the communal cultural fabric. Championing order, discipline, and cleanliness, the National Democratic Party won seats on six different city councils in Saxony in 1999. Government programs even subsidized efforts of NPD activists to start businesses and clean out long-neglected houses in small towns. In Berlin, it was the Republicans rather than the NPD who gained a foothold in local politics. While neither extreme rightist party made it into the municipal senate of the German capital, the Republicans did win seats on several district councils in October elections.

Opponents confronted these right-wing extremists at the local level with varying degrees of success. Coalitions of socialists, anarchists, unionists, and independent concerned citizens countered virtually every public march of skinheads with a demonstration of their own. In late February, after the courts lifted a municipal prohibition against their rally, skinheads roused by the NPD cry "No German Passports for Foreigners" faced off in Magdeburg with the Coalition against Rightists. Days later, in the wake of a similar court struggle over the right to demonstrate, 400 NPD supporters and 600 antifascists rallied in different parts of Angermünde. In March, residents of the Berlin district of Pankow protested the establishment of a Republican party office in a house formerly owned by a Jewish factory owner. Export-dependent business leaders recognized the damage that right-wing extremism could do to their international interests. In July, the EKO Steel Corporation held a "Festival against Xenophobia, Rightist Extremism and Violence" at its factory in the Brandenburg town of Eisenhüttenstadt. After another legal battle, local NPD activists held a counterdemonstration in mid-August for "Freedom of Opinion for Nationalists—Arguments instead of Prohibition."

In contrast to the grassroots approach of the NPD, the German People's Union (GPU) was little more than a troupe of disaffected loners following the orders of Munich-based publisher Gerhard Frey. In February 1999, a failed mutiny split the party caucus in parliament, and four members left the GPU to become independents. The GPU's parliamentary tactics consisted of asking provocative questions—faxed from Munich—of the governing parties about the relation between foreigners and criminality. The party had no concrete policy proposals of its own. Several GPU members of parliament hired family members to receive salaries from the public treasury.

Despite this state of affairs, the GPU had great success in the 1999 state elections in Brandenburg. Following the same strategy that brought him success in Saxony-Anhalt (see AJYB 1998, pp. 338–39), Frey financed a direct-mail campaign in mid-August that placed GPU flyers in every Brandenburg household just weeks before the September 5 election. In response, the minister of justice in Brandenburg, Hans Otto Bräutigam, an independent, called on all democratic parties to distance themselves from right-wing tendencies generally and the GPU in particular. The SPD and the PDS, drawing on the experience of their colleagues in Saxony-Anhalt, launched a public-education campaign. The CDU, in contrast, did not want to alienate GPU voters. Jörg Schönbohm, the leader of the Brandenburg CDU, agreed that the presence of the GPU in parliament would damage the state's reputation, but complained that the SPD-led state government had ignored the problem of left-wing extremism. Schönbohm, who himself had stirred controversy in 1998 with his comments about the Turkish minority in Berlin, had granted an interview to the skinhead publication *Young Freedom* in March, arguing that some CDU positions could appeal to a segment of the rightist crowd.

The campaign turned ugly in the last week of August. Vandals tore down signs and posters of the CDU, SPD, and PDS. In the Brandenburg town of Lauchhammer street fights broke out between rightists and leftists, who had been tearing down GPU materials. When the votes were counted on September 5, the GPU had just cleared the 5-percent hurdle necessary to win representation in the Brandenburg parliament.

In Mecklenburg-Pomerania, meanwhile, the NPD splintered in the aftermath of its poor showing in the September 1998 elections. On April 1, 1999, disgruntled members left the party to establish the Socialist People's Party (SPP) and pursue an agenda based on the socialist model of the former GDR. State authorities considered the new party far more radical than the NPD.

Anti-Semitism

While rightist violence almost exclusively targeted foreigners and leftists, there were still 991 anti-Semitic crimes reported in 1998. This came to just about 9 percent of all "right-wing extremist" crimes, but the number becomes more significant in light of the fact that Jews made up only one-tenth of 1 percent of the German population.

On March 9, 1999, the same day that a bomb exploded outside the Wehrmacht exhibit in Saarbrücken, vandals desecrated a memorial in Berlin that marked the former site of a synagogue. On August 17 Berlin police arrested 26 men and women who were planning to commemorate the anniversary of Nazi party leader Rudolf Hess's death; the same night, vandals desecrated another synagogue memorial. Two weeks later, on August 31, arsonists in Berlin destroyed a subway car in which Miphgasch/Begegnung, an association dedicated to interfaith and German-Israeli reconciliation, had installed an exhibit on the gradual social exclusion of Jews from everyday life in Nazi Germany. The next day marked the 60th anniversary of the German invasion of Poland.

Neo-Nazis also mobilized for the "Day of German Unity" on October 3. Tombstones in the Weissensee cemetery of the Berlin Jewish community were uprooted, and swastikas were painted on both a Berthold Brecht monument and a memorial to Jews deported from Berlin. Several local masons, outraged by the vandalism, offered to clean up the mess in Weissensee free of charge. The workshop of one of these masons was ransacked in November. His willingness to help the Jewish community had translated into DM 80,000 ($48,000) in damages.

Jewish public figures repeatedly complained of the standard German dismissal of anti-Semitic acts as isolated incidents. Author Jürgen Elsässer argued that the German authorities had the responsibility to repudiate the vandals' October 3 message that Jews did not belong to the nation. Whereas Eberhard Diepgen (CDU), the mayor of Berlin, could find no time to attend a demonstration against hate the week following the "Day of German Unity," Elsässer recalled the words of French president François Mitterand in response to the desecration of graves in Carpentras in 1992: "The Jews are part of the nation. We celebrate together — and we mourn together." Mitterand, Elsässer noted, then walked at the head of a protest march in Carpentras.

Holocaust-Related Matters

CONTESTED MEMORY

The so-called Walser-Bubis debate, in which German novelist Martin Walser offended Ignatz Bubis, president of the Central Council of Jews in Germany (CCJG), by speaking against the "hollow rituals" associated with Holocaust remembrance in Germany, dominated the German press in the last weeks of 1998 (see AJYB 1999, p. 345). The central actors in the dispute achieved a cold peace in December, and January 1999 brought a reassertion of the German commitment to memory. On January 27, German schoolchildren, politicians, and scholars participated in a variety of events to mark the fourth annual Memorial Day for the Victims of National Socialism, observed on the anniversary of the liberation of Auschwitz. Representatives of several victim groups, including Jews, Roma (Gypsies), and homosexuals, held ceremonies to commemorate those who died at the hands of the Nazis. Over the course of the year, however, aftershocks of the Walser-Bubis debate would provide the subtext for an ongoing struggle over how to define the political culture of the Berlin Republic.

In what experts believed would be the last such trial in Germany, an 80-year-old ethnic German from Ukraine was sentenced to ten years in prison for his role in the so-called Harvest Festival Action, in which the SS shot an estimated 40,000 Jews within 48 hours in Lublin, Poland. He was not required to serve his sentence, however, because he had already spent more than ten years in a Soviet labor camp.

German authorities agreed in 1999 that once the Central Office for the Clarification of National Socialist Crimes, which had the responsibility for pursuing such criminals, wrapped up its pending cases, it would be transformed into an archive on Nazi crimes. To date, of the 106,000 Nazi war criminals brought to trial before German courts, only 6,500 had been convicted.

In another act designed less to serve justice than to facilitate future historical research, state authorities in Bavaria were ordered in April to transfer all information related to the "treatment of the racially persecuted" to state archives. These papers included tax records that would shed light on the aryanization of Jewish property. The Bavarian authorities had denied the existence of such records for years. In accordance with the laws protecting the secrecy of tax records, the documents would not be made available to researchers for 80 years.

In October, Professor Micha Brumlik, the Green politician and leader of the progressive Jewish movement in Germany, published a provocative editorial in a Jewish newspaper suggesting that novelist Günter Grass, recipient of the 1999 Nobel Prize for Literature, and Martin Walser represented two alternative views of the German future. Whereas Grass felt that the history of National Socialism placed a serious responsibility on the nation, Walser viewed it as a liability weighing down the nation. Brumlik believed the young Berlin Republic to be in the midst of a struggle between a "democratic culture" of responsibility and "an un-culture of forgetting built on national pride."

The events of November 9 seemed to bear out Brumlik's analysis. For the first time, on the tenth anniversary of the fall of the Berlin Wall, the celebration of national unity overshadowed the commemoration of Kristallnacht. To be sure, in his speech at the Brandenburg Gate, Chancellor Schröder also mentioned the "other" anniversary that November 9 marked. What spoke volumes, however, was his absence from the central Jewish commemoration of Kristallnacht.

DEATH OF IGNATZ BUBIS

As a final act in a life devoted to raising public awareness of the relationship between the Nazi past and the German future, Ignatz Bubis provoked one last controversy. In late July, in an interview in the German weekly *Stern,* the CCJG president said that he had accomplished little to bridge the chasm between Jewish and non-Jewish Germans. He criticized the Jewish minority for segregating itself too much from the rest of the nation, and the non-Jewish majority for seeking, all too often, to cast off the historical burden of the Holocaust. Bubis also told the interviewer that in spite of his German patriotism, he would prefer to be buried in Israel. After vandals bombed the tombstone of Heinz Galinski, his predecessor, in December 1998, Bubis saw too high a risk that "the dignity of the dead would be injured" in Germany. Bubis died on August 13, 1999, and was buried on August 15 in Tel Aviv. Jewish communities across Germany held memorial services. His successor as head of the CCJG was to be elected in January 2000.

A CENTRAL MEMORIAL

As 1998 came to a close, State Minister for Culture Michael Naumann appeared poised to bring the decade-long public debate over a central Holocaust memorial to an end (see AJYB 1999, pp. 342–44). As it turned out, however, it would take another year of controversy before a firm date could be set for the groundbreaking.

In January 1999, Naumann attempted to garner support for the construction of a "house of memory" on the designated site for the memorial in the center of Berlin. According to a compromise worked out with American architect Peter Eisenmann, the building would border a reduced version of Eisenmann's design—large stone columns reminiscent of a graveyard. But critics charged that Naumann had spent too much time seeking advice and affirmation abroad and not enough familiarizing himself with the needs and concerns of cultural institutions in Berlin. It was, in fact, true that the original impulse for his idea had come from Bruce Ramer, president of the American Jewish Committee. Furthermore, Naumann and Chancellor Schröder met with Steven Spielberg in early January to discuss the incorporation of Spielberg's Shoah Foundation video archives into the proposed Berlin educational center. Schröder acknowledged that he could live without a memorial, yet he also asserted that, in the aftermath of the Walser-Bubis debate, political pragmatism made opposition to the project untenable. By the middle of January, Schröder, other government figures, and representatives of the Jewish community had signaled their satisfaction with the Naumann-Eisenmann compromise.

The struggle was far from over, as critics continued to challenge Naumann's methods and ideas. Other finalists in the competition for the design of the memorial objected to the Naumann-Eisenmann behind-the-scenes deal before a winner had been officially determined. Furthermore, both architect Daniel Libeskind and conceptual artist Jochen Gerz complained that Eisenmann had incorporated elements from their work into his design. And the directors of other memorial sites in Berlin objected to the prospect of watching DM 100–180 million ($60–108 million) flow to the construction of a "house of memory" on a site with no relation to the Nazi past, at a time when their own institutions, situated where Nazi history was made, had to compete with one another for scant public resources. It also remained unclear what purpose this new center could serve that was not already being served by existing institutions. In mid-March Berlin mayor Eberhard Diepgen (CDU) withdrew the support of the Berlin municipal government for the undertaking.

By then opponents were rallying around yet another proposal, that of theologian and politician Richard Schröder (SPD). Instead of conjuring an image of a cemetery for the murdered, he maintained, the memorial should speak directly to the perpetrators and their descendants. Schröder suggested that the memorial bear the commandment, "Thou shalt not murder," in Hebrew as well as in the languages of all the victim groups, so as to include the non-Jewish victims and to emphasize the connection between Jewish law and Christian civilization. Jewish public figures objected that the proposal lacked specific historical reference to the Holocaust. They also considered the use of Hebrew in a message to Germans to be problematic. Within weeks, Schröder's contribution had nonetheless won support among prominent conservatives, including Mayor Diepgen, the chairman of the Council of Evangelical Churches in Germany, the president of the Central Committee of German Catholics, the Catholic Bishops' Conference, and Minister President Edmund Stoiber of Bavaria (CSU).

A diverse coalition of Naumann's opponents dominated both committee hearings that the Bundestag held on the subject, and 63 members of the German parliament announced their opposition to any form of central monument on May 5. Naumann managed nonetheless to win over many of his earlier critics by mid-June, when the committee voted along party lines to limit the Bundestag debate to the proposals of Naumann and Richard Schröder. Finally, on June 25, the German parliament capped ten years of debate by voting to build a central German Holocaust memorial, to restrict it to the commemoration of the murdered Jews of Europe, and to build it according to the Naumann-Eisenmann concept. In the fall, the Bundestag passed a law establishing a memorial foundation to oversee construction. The foundation's board of trustees met for the first time on December 17. The projected groundbreaking date, January 27, 2000, would mark the 55th anniversary of the liberation of Auschwitz.

As critics had feared, several other victim groups petitioned for their own memorials in Berlin. The municipal government said that it would carefully review proposals on behalf of Roma and Sinti (Gypsies), homosexuals, victims of the Nazi euthanasia program, deserters from the German army, women, and the Dutch Communist blamed for the Reichstag fire of 1933. The memorial foundation created by the Bundestag was charged with reconciling their interests.

WEHRMACHT EXHIBIT

Few issues over the last several years have brought into such clear relief the connections between academic debate, mainstream party politics, and right-wing extremism as the so-called Wehrmacht exhibit. Devoted to the photo-documentation of the crimes of the German army on the Eastern Front, this exhibit first attracted public controversy in March 1997, two years after its opening, when conservative politicians complained that it defamed the German army. Since then there had been demonstrations in the streets of Munich, Kiel, and other cities where the exhibit was shown. In February 1999 the dispute flared up in Saarbrücken. Two days before the February 22 opening, 300 skinheads demonstrated with signs declaring that "Our fathers were no criminals." Days later local CDU politicians Gerd Bauer and Manfred Hayo placed an ad in the city newspaper insisting that they would not allow the organizers of the exhibit to defame their fathers "and with them the millions of dead, who can no longer defend themselves." The newspaper received many letters attacking the exhibit, among them a good number of form letters distributed by neo-Nazis in other cities.

On March 9 the building housing the exhibit exploded, causing an estimated DM 500,000 ($300,000) worth of damage. Police believed it to be the work of right-wing extremists. But Jan Philipp Reemtsma, director of the Hamburg Institute for Social Research that organized the exhibit, saw a direct connection to the rhetoric of mainstream politicians: "Wherever party politicians failed to distance themselves clearly from the far right, extremists have felt encouraged to use violence." For his part, Bauer refused to acknowledge any connection between the bombing and his ad, which he continued to defend.

Opponents of the exhibit who preferred the methodical evaluation of documents over rhetorical appeals to nationalist sentiments ultimately forced Reemtsma and his colleagues to acknowledge inaccuracies in their exhibit. In detailed critiques issued in January, two East European historians asserted that some of the photographs in question documented crimes committed not by the German army, but by the Red Army, the Soviet secret police, and Hungarian soldiers. By October these critiques had found the support of a broad spectrum of the German press.

On November 4 the Institute for Social Research announced a moratorium on the display of the Wehrmacht exhibit. To ensure the project's scholarly integrity, a panel of leading historians was charged with a thorough review of its content. Scheduled openings in Braunschweig and New York were postponed indefinitely. The panel convened for the first time on November 20.

RESTITUTION

After a year of tense negotiations, U.S. and German government representatives, class-action lawyers, Jewish organizations, and German industry officials reached agreement in mid-December on compensation for surviving victims of the National Socialist forced-labor system. Only after victim groups filed class-action suits in the U.S. in 1998 did a small number of export-driven German corporations agree to consider participating in a central compensation fund. On their behalf, Chancellor Schröder resolved to achieve an agreement that would protect German industry from any future legal action (see AJYB 1999, pp. 340–42).

Over the course of 1999 the nature of the discussion shifted dramatically. In January Alan Hevesi, the New York City controller, announced that he would approve the merger of Deutsche Bank with Bankers Trust only if the former made a concrete compensation offer to Holocaust survivors. With Deutsche Bank then taking the lead, a handful of German corporations offered less than two billion marks. Headlines announced that Bonn and Washington had all but reached agreement, and that representatives of the two countries would soon meet to work out a way to insulate German industry from future legal claims. The Jewish organizations had agreed that German industry would establish two funds, one of which would be dedicated to the direct financial restitution of former forced laborers, while the other, a "memory fund," would promote research and the preservation of the memory of the Holocaust. The payments were to begin on September 1, 1999, the 60th anniversary of the German invasion of Poland. Bilateral negotiations with Israel and with East European states were expected to follow the successful conclusion of the German-American talks.

In late January, however, lawyers Mel Weiss and Michael Hausfeld filed new class-action suits in American courts against a number of German corporations on behalf of non-Jewish Polish victims. The lawyers insisted that there should be only one fund, which would compensate victims, and they called into question the granting of immunity to German industry from future lawsuits.

On February 15 Chancellor Schröder announced that 12 German corporations would voluntarily establish a compensation fund for former forced laborers, conditioned on immunity from future litigation. Although the federal government did not plan to contribute to this fund, it would set up a foundation to compensate forced labor in agriculture, communal work, and other sectors not covered by the industry initiative.

Public discussion, meanwhile, indicated that a final settlement was not going to be easy. Non-Jewish victim groups—Roma and Sinti, Ukrainians, Poles, and Russians—demanded to be represented in the negotiations. Historians of forced labor in the Third Reich, whose work was not yet widely known, announced at press conferences and in opinion pieces that forced labor during the war was far more extensive than previously assumed. New historical research detailed the involvement of Dresdner Bank, Bertelsmann Publishing, and the Deutsche Bank, which helped finance the construction of Auschwitz-Birkenau.

Within days of the establishment of the industry fund, lawyers in America filed a class-action suit against Bayer, which had been part of the I.G. Farben chemical combine during the war, on behalf of 112 surviving victims of Josef Mengele's infamous medical experiments. At the end of March, days after three survivors of Auschwitz filed a lawsuit against the I. G. Farben consortium, stockholders voted to create a foundation through which it would compensate former forced laborers. The following week, Stefan Zdzislaw Kozlowski, chairman of the Polish Association of Former Political Prisoners in Nazi Prisons and Concentration Camps, announced that more than 22,000 members of his association had filed suit against the German government. California governor Gray Davis also took to the courts, suing five German and two American companies to compel them to compensate surviving forced laborers living in his state. Not only did German leaders from all points on the political spectrum express resentment at the multiplying number of lawsuits, but Ignatz Bubis and World Jewish Congress president Israel Singer also criticized the lawyers, who were seeking, in their opinion, to profit from the suffering of Holocaust victims.

The prominent role played by Jewish organizations up to that point had contributed to the misperception that Jews had made up the majority of forced laborers exploited in the Nazi economy. Once the victims' lawyers were incorporated into the U.S.-German negotiations in May, Jews made up no more than 10 percent of the potential recipients of restitution payments. The entry of the victims' lawyers into the discussion also escalated the financial stakes enormously, and the consideration of boycotts of German companies by the legislatures of 12 U.S. states added to the urgency of the matter. During the summer, the number of lawsuits grew.

Hardball negotiations began in earnest on August 19. Claiming to represent some 2.3 million forced laborers, Michael Hausfeld insisted on a total exceeding $20 billion. Industry representatives had been speaking of less than $2 billion for an estimated 600,000 legitimate recipients, with guaranteed immunity from future claims. The result was stalemate. To move the negotiations forward, Chancellor Schröder announced in October that his government would contribute to the industry fund after all. Because the combined public-private compensation offer of DM 4 billion ($2.4 billion) still remained well below the plaintiffs' demands, the two sides spent the subsequent several weeks doing little more than throwing numbers around and trading accusations in the press.

By early fall, only 16 German companies had joined the industry initiative. In September, an appeal from the Berlin office of the American Jewish Committee to 117 additional German companies to contribute to the fund fell on deaf ears. Then, on December 7, the AJC office released a list of 255 German companies that, according to widely accessible sources, had ties to firms that used forced laborers during the war. The release of the list thus helped turn an issue concerning a handful of huge corporations into a multitude of stories about local complicity in National Socialist crimes. Within one week, 23 of the companies joined the industry initiative.

The list also contributed to a breakthrough in the negotiations. On December 17, agreement was reached on a figure of DM 10 billion ($6 billion) in compensation for forced labor. German taxpayers stood to shoulder the lion's share of that figure, through tax deductions for industry and direct contributions from federal and state treasuries. At a ceremony announcing the agreement, Federal President Johannes Rau sought to smooth over the ill will generated over the course of the negotiations by asking for forgiveness from the victims of National Socialism on behalf of the German nation.

The foundation to be created by the German government would have representation from all states where surviving forced laborers lived, and forced labor of all kinds would be compensated. The claims of those who died after the creation of the industry initiative on February 16 were passed on to their heirs. German officials acknowledged that there would not be enough money to compensate all eligible recipients. It thus remained unclear how much money would be available for the "Future Fund" dedicated to the preservation of the memory of the Holocaust. By year's end, more than 90 companies had joined the industry initiative. Officials said that the first payments would be delivered in the summer of 2000, but Munich-based lawyer Michael Witti made headlines on December 31 by threatening not to withdraw his clients' lawsuits. He complained of a proposed ceiling on compensation for aryanized property and the disqualification of former slave laborers who had previously received payments from the Federal Republic.

JEWISH COMMUNITY

Demography

Immigration from the former Soviet Union (FSU) gained momentum in 1999, reaching its highest level to date. Almost 9,000 Russian-speaking newcomers contributed to an increase in the total membership of communities represented by the CCJG from 74,289 to 81,730 over the course of the year. Almost half of the immigrants settled in the five new federal states of the former GDR. The numbers of affiliated Jews in the largest communities for 1999 were as follows, with 1998 figures as the basis for comparison: Berlin, 11,190 (up from 11,008); Frankfurt, 6,602 (down from 6,618); Munich, 7,219 (up from 6,595); Hamburg, 4,270 (up from 3,993); Cologne, 3,654 (up from 3,408).

Communal Affairs

A number of special programs facilitated the integration of Jewish immigrants from the FSU in 1999. Early in the year, the Central Welfare Administration of Jews in Germany (CWA) sponsored an exhibit of art created by Russian-speaking Jews. A series of chess tournaments in the federal state of Hesse fostered a spirit of belonging among the old and new members of the seven participating communities. Close to 200 young Jews traveled to Düsseldorf in March for the national Jewish Youth Congress sponsored by the CCJG and the CWA. The delegates, many of whom were native Russian-speakers, participated in social events and German-language discussions of current affairs.

In spite of these signs of cohesion, communal leaders also recognized and sought to address the problems generated by immigration. In an editorial entitled "We were all strangers," Rabbi Henry Brandt asked the readers of the Passover edition of the national Jewish newspaper to show more understanding toward their brothers and sisters from the FSU. "The lack of Jewish education and a familiarity with Jewish religious customs is all too often a premise," Brandt charged, "to treat them as second-rate members of the community." In the same forum, Andreas Nachama, president of the Berlin Jewish community, recalled the successful integration of the 2,500 Russian-speaking immigrants who had settled in Berlin between the mid-1970s and 1989. He drew on this positive example to urge representatives of established communal institutions to avoid paternalism and not to expect complete assimilation.

Jewish institutions followed the hundreds of government offices, nonprofit organizations, and media outlets that relocated to Berlin, the new capital, in 1999. On April 19, the same day the Bundestag convened its first session in the Reichstag, the CCJG installed a mezuzah on the door of its new home. The building, which was named the Leo Baeck House in memory of the late German Jewish leader, stood on the same spot where Baeck presided over the College for the Study of Judaism until 1942. The CCJG-sponsored national Jewish newspaper, the *Allgemeine Jüdische Wochenblatt* (AJW), also relocated there.

Jewish communities throughout Germany, experiencing remarkable growth, either opened or planned to build new facilities in 1999. In Cologne, for example, a century-old synagogue housing a community center—the only one of the city's seven synagogues to have been restored after the Holocaust—could no longer accommodate the growing membership. The community announced plans in January for the construction of a second community center. In Bavaria, the Würzburg community sought to build on its reputation as a pillar of Orthodoxy with the construction of a Jewish community and cultural center that would train teachers of religion and serve as a gathering place for Jewish youth. The Jewish community of Munich also had plans for a new community center. On May 30, both the Delmenhorst and the Mülheim-Duisburg-Oberhausen communities celebrated the opening of substantial new community centers that housed synagogues, classrooms, administrative facilities, and more. Chemnitz had seen its membership rise from 11 to 290 during the 1990s. Reflecting the difficulties faced by many communities in the new federal states, its members discussed plans for a new synagogue despite the fact that they had no full-time rabbi.

Other communities had to deal with crises borne of corruption and avarice. Four years after being elected, the new board of the Hannover Jewish community finally took office on March 25. Rejecting the election as invalid and fighting every legal measure taken against him, former president Leo Kohn had refused to grant the new board access to the community center (see AJYB 1999, p. 347). Because neglect and a leaking roof had taken a serious toll on the building during the stalemate, the new board inherited an estimated bill of DM 900,000 ($540,000) to repair the center in addition to an existing communal debt of DM 1 million ($600,000). Eli Meir Gampel's successor as president of the Halle community also inherited a troubled legacy. A new board was elected in March to replace Peter Fischer, who had been given interim authority over the community by the CCJG to restore order in the wake of Gampel's alleged mismanagement.

Religion

A peculiar constellation of German law, historical legacies, and idiosyncratic personalities contributed to several religious conflicts within the Jewish communities of Germany in 1999. All religious communities in Germany are corporate entities under public law; the state collects fees for religious affiliation from taxpayers and passes them on to the institutions representing each confession. Based on a centuries-old system, Jewish communities in Germany are *Einheitsgemeinden,* meaning in theory that liberal and Orthodox congregations function under a single communal administration. Until this year Berlin had been the only community to maintain peaceful coexistence between the denominations.

The CCJG resolved at a meeting of its governing body on May 16 to provide financial support for the establishment of a central Orthodox religious court, a move favored by the European Conference of Rabbis. Such a body would provide, for the first time, national regulation of Orthodox conversions and resolve "who is a Jew" cases among the thousands of immigrants from the FSU, who would no longer have to prove their Jewishness over again when moving to a new community. This would not, of course, help immigrants or converts recognized as Jews by liberal rabbis.

Earlier that month, Eli Meir Gampel, the former chairman of the Halle Jewish community, established a new association designed to unite Orthodox Jewish communities. Gampel's enterprise planned to recruit among recently arrived immigrants from the FSU. Peter Sichrovsky, an Austrian Jewish politician in the right-wing Freedom Party of Jörg Haider, voiced his support for the initiative. With an eye to Gampel's scandal-ridden tenure in Halle and allegations of his association with the Church of Scientology, CCJG president Bubis dismissed Gampel's Association of Law-Abiding Communities as "law-abiding according to neither Jewish nor civil law."

More threatening to the unity of Jewish communities in Germany were ongoing disputes between Orthodox and Liberal congregations, and within Liberal Judaism itself. Over 100 women from all over the continent attended the first "European Conference of Women Rabbis, Cantors, Scholars and all Spiritually Interested Women and Men—Bet Debora," held May 13–16 in Berlin. The dialogue focused on egalitarian Judaism and the promotion of positive Jewish identity in East and Central Europe.

Despite the engagement of these women, the notion of females leading services remained anathema in most German Jewish communities. Marian Offmann, a member of the governing board of the Munich community, explained that "the overwhelming majority of community members do not live as Orthodox Jews, but they respect the Orthodox leadership because they know that such is the only way to ensure the survival of our community." In the eyes of many Orthodox leaders and their supporters, the inclusion of liberal and/or egalitarian congregations in communal structures would precipitate a schism, whereas liberals blamed the conflict on the refusal of the *Einheitsgemeinden* to accommodate their needs. One ray of hope for pluralism was the incorporation of an "egalitarian minyan," which had existed independently for years, into the official Jewish communal structure of Frankfurt.

Friction within the Berlin *Einheitsgemeinde* in 1999 demonstrated the difficulties of "unity in diversity." Early in the year, the World Union for Progressive Judaism sent letters to the CCJG and to various government offices complaining of discrimination against progressive congregations in Germany. Because the state only recognized communities represented by the CCJG, the letter stated, progressive Jews preferring to organize their religious lives outside of Orthodox communal institutions had no access to tax money or state subsidies. At an October meeting of communal representatives, Moishe Waks, a member of the governing board of the CCJG, responded by proposing that the Berlin community resign from the World Union. The suggestion provoked heated debate because of the historical and personal connections between the World Union and the Berlin community. Jews from Berlin had been among the founders of the World Union in the 1920s. Both the community as a whole and the Pestalozzistrasse Synagogue held memberships. Andreas Nachama, president of the community and lifelong member of the congregation, sat on its board of governors.

Rabbi Walter Homolka played a prominent role in the controversy. In 1997 Homolka cofounded the Union of Progressive Jews in Germany, Austria, and Switzerland (UPJGAS) as a branch of the World Union, in which Homolka also played a leading role. In previous years, his conversion to Judaism and Protestant theological training had raised doubts among progressive and Orthodox observers alike. In its first years of existence, the UPJGAS granted membership to 12 congregations that had been established outside of their cities' *Einheitsgemeinden* and, therefore, outside of the CCJG. Supporters of the already existing institutional framework in Germany interpreted Homolka's activities as an attempt to build the UPJGAS into a competitor with the CCJG for tax money and for the right to represent Jews in Germany. Waks demanded that the World Union distance itself from Homolka as a condition of the Berlin community's continued membership. He thereby shifted the focus of the dispute from the general issue of progressive efforts to undermine Orthodox control of *Einheitsgemeinden* to Homolka, a specific problem for progressives opposed to schism, like Nachama.

Together with Walter Jacob, former vice president of the World Union and a rabbi in Munich, Homolka planned to establish an Abraham Geiger Theological Seminary in Potsdam. The seminary would be the first educational center for progressive rabbis in postwar Germany. The announcement of their intentions infuriated leaders of the Berlin Jewish community. Just as the CCJG had resented the World Union effort to undermine the *Einheitsgemeinden*, Nachama and his colleagues insisted that any seminary established without the cooperation of communal institutions would be doomed to failure. The only show of support for Homolka came in the form of an editorial by Julius Schoeps, director of the

Moses Mendelssohn Center of Potsdam University, welcoming the Abraham Geiger Seminary to town. In spite of these initial words of welcome, Schoeps declared at a November 4 meeting of the Berlin Assembly of Representatives that the Mendelssohn Center had no plans to cooperate with Homolka's seminary. A letter from Rabbi Richard Block, the president of the World Union, was read aloud at the same meeting. It made clear that the World Union also had nothing to do with the seminary and that Homolka was acting only with the support of the UPJGAS. Nachama convinced a majority of the assembled representatives to postpone any action on Waks's resolution until its meeting on January 19, 2000, when Rabbi Block would be invited to explain his position on the tensions between the Berlin community and his organization.

A new year did not promise an end to these intracommunal struggles. Julius Schoeps planned to call for a vote of no confidence in Waks, the vice president of the Berlin community, at the January 19 meeting. Waks's proposal to withdraw the communal membership in the World Union, Schoeps argued, was an obvious effort to discredit Nachama and to roll back the religious pluralism that had defined the Berlin community for generations. Nachama endured a setback in December when he failed to win a seat on the governing board of the CCJG. He attributed his loss in part to Orthodox hostility to his activities in the Progressive movement, but also to the jealousy of other communities toward the vibrant and populous Berlin community.

In the synagogues of Berlin, meanwhile, liberal Rabbi Walter Rothschild attempted to address the needs of a diverse community. Rothschild arrived in Berlin in the fall of 1998 to fill a position that had been vacant for years. Trained in England, where he also began his rabbinic career, Rothschild had to adjust to the unique legal framework and social milieu of the Berlin Jewish community. Although more than 10,000 of the 11,500 members of the community considered themselves liberal, their definition of liberal Judaism did not always extend as far as Rothschild's progressive religious views. Indeed, disagreements over the structure and content of services in the Pestalozzistrasse, one of the four liberal congregations under his jurisdiction, reached such a boiling point that Nachama attacked Rothschild in the December community newsletter. Under the title "Polarization," Nachama declared it to be the "job of a rabbi to bring the community together and not to allow it to become polarized. Especially for a rabbi who comes in from the outside, it is imperative to develop an understanding of the needs, the religious sensibilities and the accepted practices of the synagogue." Nachama also demonstrated his commitment to the religious pluralism of the community by hiring Rabbi Yizhak Ehrenberg to serve the religious needs of the Orthodox Jews of Berlin.

Interfaith Relations

At the annual meeting of Evangelical Churches in Germany (ECG), held in Stuttgart in the fall, the Working Group of Jews and Christians condemned

Christian efforts to convert Jewish immigrants from the FSU. Manfred Kock, president of the ECG, chose to boycott the meeting, which he dismissed as "one-sided in its fixation on a rejection of a mission to the Jews."

The Society for Christian-Jewish Cooperation (SCJC) in Oldenburg helped finance the construction of a new local Jewish community center by selling a valuable piece of art. The German-Jewish artist Felix Nussbaum painted "Jew at the Window" in 1943 while in Belgian exile. The SCJC sold it to the Felix Nussbaum Collection in Osnabrück for DM 250,000 ($150,000). Viewing the "memory of the Shoah as a living responsibility for the present," the association donated all of the proceeds, which will cover almost a third of the center's construction costs, to the Jewish community.

The theme of the SCJC's Brotherhood Week in March was Poland. Henryk Josef Muszynski, archbishop of Gniezno, received the Buber-Rosenzweig Medal in Potsdam for his contribution to Polish-Jewish and Catholic-Jewish understanding.

Academic institutions also sought to further the Jewish-Christian dialogue. In August the Center for Christian-Jewish Studies of the Humboldt University in Berlin hosted the seventh annual Christian-Jewish Summer University. Professors from Israel, Germany, and the United States came together with students to explore the theme of "State and Religion in Jewish and Christian Perspective." In October, scholars analyzed the troubled relationship between "Judaism and Protestantism: Historical Patterns of a Religious, Political, and Philosophical Confrontation." Conference panels ran concurrently in Halle and Wittenberg, the locations of the sponsoring institutions, the Leopold Zunz Center for the Research of European Jewry and the Center for the History of the Reformation and Lutheran Orthodoxy.

Education

Jewish communities in Germany still lacked enough rabbis and teachers of Judaism to meet the needs of their burgeoning memberships. To remedy the situation the Lauder Jüdisches Lehrhaus, established by the Ronald S. Lauder Foundation (see AJYB 1999, pp. 349–50), offered its first courses in the summer of 1999. The school sought to prepare future teachers of Hebrew and religion, and to help active teachers and communal workers deepen their understanding of the Hebrew language, as well as Jewish history and religion. Joel Levy, founding director of the Lehrhaus, envisioned it as a "third Jewish center" in the new German capital alongside the Centrum Judaicum and the community center in western Berlin.

The College for Jewish Studies in Heidelberg also announced plans to expand its training program for educators. The college had been criticized for not achieving more along these lines over the previous 20 years. Indeed, non-Jews constituted a large majority of the 432 students to have enrolled since the CCJG founded the college in 1979. Of the 20 Jewish students who received the M.A.

from the college, two went on to pursue rabbinical training elsewhere, nine went to work in Jewish institutions, and another became professor of Jewish history and culture at a German university. In light of the dearth of rabbis in Germany, Rabbi Nathan Peter Levinson publicly called for closing the Heidelberg college and its replacement with a rabbinical seminary in Berlin. Notwithstanding this controversy, German politicians were unanimous in their praise of the college at a ceremony marking its 20th anniversary.

In November, youth leaders, teachers, and social workers from Switzerland, Vienna, Amsterdam, Berlin, Munich, Düsseldorf, and Cologne traveled to Zurich to discuss religious education and youth programs. To redress the shortage of German-language educational materials, they agreed to support the work of the Pedagogical Center of the Zurich Jewish community. With the opening of the Jüdisches Lehrhaus in Munich, meanwhile, founding director Rabbi Moshe Dick planned to build on the tradition of Franz Rosenzweig's interwar efforts to cultivate Jewish knowledge among adults via lectures and discussion groups.

Finally, on the university level, Leipzig University opened the Simon Dubnow Institute for Jewish History and Culture on July 1, 1999. Historian Dan Diner was named director of the institute, which would focus its research on the cultural exchange between the Jewish communities of Eastern Europe and those of Central and Western Europe from the Middle Ages to the present. Named after the great historian of Jewry murdered by the Nazis in Riga in 1941, the institute also sought "to strengthen awareness of the uniqueness of the Holocaust."

Culture

Once again in 1999, German anti-Semitism before, during, and after the Holocaust took to the stage, the silver screen, and the television screen. An "alternative" cabaret in Cologne, renowned for provoking controversy with its taboo-breaking satires, offended many in the local Jewish community with its production "Hey Jude 2000." Taking aim at the cynical foot-dragging of German industry in restitution negotiations, the troupe portrayed the efforts of the advertising agency "Sit and Watch" to develop a "pro-Jewish image campaign." Jewish members of the audience did not appreciate the humor of the campaign slogan, "Taste the feeling of Jewish culture, or, it also works without smoke." The affair made headlines in the local press before Jewish representatives sat down with members of the cabaret to express their concerns. The president of the Cologne Jewish community did not question the intent of the piece, but had qualms about the impact of the language on the sensibilities of Holocaust survivors.

From September 1943 till September 1944, before most of them were deported to Auschwitz, children in Theresienstadt performed a fairy-tale opera, Brundibár, more than 50 times. While the production provided both performers and audience with some degree of hope, the Nazis used it as propaganda to demonstrate the normality of life in the concentration camp. On January 27, 1999, the day designated in Germany to commemorate victims of the Holocaust, children from across Berlin participated in the premiere of a new interpretation of the opera. On the night of the premiere, a surviving member of the Theresienstadt cast joined the children on stage for the final scene.

Later in the year, the State Theater of Stuttgart returned the tragic historical figure of Jud Süss Oppenheim to the stage. The portrayal of the 18th-century judicial lynching of a Jewish financier in Stuttgart played to full houses every night. Critics understood the pedagogical intent of the play as a protest against the Holocaust fatigue of the German public.

The Berlinale film festival offered another response to German Holocaust fatigue, devoting the documentary portion of its program to the theme, "Looking more closely at the turning away." Israeli filmmaker Eyal Sivan showed his film "The Specialist," which consisted exclusively of filmed excerpts from the testimony of Adolf Eichmann at his 1961 trial in Jerusalem. Other documentaries featured in this series included Kaspar Kasic's "Closed Country," an exploration of Swiss policy toward Jewish refugees from Nazi Germany, and Ilona Ziok's "Kurt Gerron's Carousel," about the Jewish film star of Weimar Germany. Outside the documentary series, the Holocaust figured in many other festival entries. In "Aimée and Jaguar," director Max Förberbock dramatized the love affair between Felice Schargenheim and Lissy Wust. Wust, whom Yad Vashem honored in 1999 as one of the Righteous among the Nations, helped Schargenheim survive for years in the Berlin underground. The Berlinale chose the life work of Otto Preminger, the Austrian-born director of "Exodus," for its annual retrospective.

Of the many films to deal with the Holocaust at the Munich Film Festival, Israeli director Dan Setton's documentary "Kapo" proved the most provocative. For obvious reasons, the collaboration of Jewish inmates as police in ghettos and concentrations camps has not received the attention in Germany that it has in Israel, where a number of Jewish collaborators were tried and sentenced to prison terms. Jewish participants in the discussion in Munich criticized the narrow focus of Setton's film. They argued that Germans were responsible for the construction of the twisted world that created Kapos in the first place, that most Kapos were not Jewish, that Jews had no opportunity to affect the course of events, and that expectations of Jewish solidarity were historically unrealistic. These criticisms took on added urgency in view of the interest shown by a German television station in broadcasting an abbreviated version of the film.

The star power of its leading man contributed to the hype generated by the September release of "Nothing but the Truth." In this fictional portrayal of Josef Mengele as an elderly Nazi living in exile, Götz George played the doctor responsible for carrying out medical experiments on concentration camp inmates. Suffering from cancer, Mengele voluntarily turns himself in to stand trial and justify his actions. Whatever the intentions of the filmmaker, critics judged the film harshly for giving the Mengele character a charismatic and sympathetic presence, allowing him to dominate both the trial and the film as a whole.

Similar hype surrounded the television miniseries "Klemperer: A Life in Germany," based on the best-selling diaries of the sociolinguist and victim of Nazi persecution Victor Klemperer. The series set itself apart from other German-made dramatizations of the Nazi era by portraying the gradual and seamless transformation of "normal" Germans into Nazis. Whether because of German Holocaust fatigue or because the series did not accommodate the traditional hero/villain formula for successful television, the ratings of its October broadcast did not live up to expectations.

Seeking to focus on Jewish life rather than on Nazi crimes, an exhibit at the Nassau Art Association in Wiesbaden showcased the work of 13 Israeli artists. The German past, though, exerted an impact on the German stopover of the exhibit, which was originally scheduled only for London and Athens. Moshe Kupfermann chose to withdraw his work from the Wiesbaden presentation. The show nonetheless represented an unusually comprehensive overview of three generations of Israeli art. One of the artists, Yigal Azeri, even traveled to Wiesbaden for the opening.

The building erected to house the Berlin Jewish museum was opened to the public in August. The structure, built according to architect Daniel Libeskind's innovative design, represented a Holocaust memorial in itself and attracted hundreds of thousands of visitors within months. Director Michael Blumenthal announced in December that the permanent exhibit would not open until summer or fall of 2001. In Munich, scholars and museum curators met in July and again in November to discuss both the general question of how to treat Jewish history in Germany and the specific challenge of constructing a Jewish museum in the former "capital of the movement."

Publications

A number of books published in 1999 either documented or contributed to public discussion of the meaning of Auschwitz in the Berlin Republic. Political scientist Helmut Dubiel provided historical perspective on the topic with his *Niemand ist frei von der Geschichte* (No One is Free From History), an edited collection of the most important Bundestag debates concerning the Nazi era since 1945. Andy Markovits and Jürgen Elsässer explored the application of the lessons of history to current affairs in *Die Fratze der eigenen Geschichte. Von der Goldhagen Debatte zum Jugoslavien-Krieg* (The Ugly Face of One's Own History. From the Goldhagen Debate to the War in Yugoslavia). Considering German participation in the NATO bombing campaign in Kosovo, Elsässer questioned whether a similar intervention in Israel might not be a logical consequence in *Nie wieder Krieg ohne uns. Das Kosovo und die neue deutsche Geopolitik* (Never Again War Without Us. Kosovo and the New German Geopolitics).

Die Walser-Bubis-Debatte (The Walser-Bubis Debate), edited by Frank Schirmacher, provided one-stop shopping for readers interested in sorting out who wrote what amidst the dizzying rhetorical crossfire that characterized the affair. An otherwise underrepresented constituency in the debate expressed its views in *Was bleibt von der Vergangenheit? Die junge Generation im Dialog über den Holocaust* (What Remains of the Past? The Young Generation in Dialogue About the Holocaust), which was published by the Foundation for the Rights of Future Generations, with a foreword by Roman Herzog, the former federal president.

Reflecting on her ten years of experience as the leading advocate of a central Holocaust Memorial, Lea Rosh released *Ein deutsches Mahnmal. Der Streit um das Denkmal für die ermordeten Juden Europas* (A German Memorial. The Debate over the Monument for the Murdered Jews of Europe). Several collections of previously published essays also documented the debate.

The Wehrmacht exhibit was also immortalized in print in 1999. Its organizers at the Hamburg Institute for Social Research released *Eine Ausstellung und ihre Folgen. Zur Rezeption der Ausstellung "Vernichtungskrieg. Verbrechen der Wehrmacht 1941 bis 1944"* (An Exhibit and its Consequences. On the Reception of the Exhibit "War of Destruction. Crimes of the Wehrmacht 1941–1944"). Albert Lichtblau and others offered portraits of one city's reaction to the exhibit in the volume of essays, *Umkämpfte Errinnerung. Die Wehrmachtsausstellung in Salzburg* (Contested Memory. The Wehrmacht Exhibit in Salzburg).

The complicity of historians in the Nazi regime also remained a focus of debate in 1999 (see AJYB 1999, pp. 344–45). In the spring and summer three history students at the Humboldt University questioned 17 historians born between 1922 and 1942 about their experiences as graduate students, their views on the complicity of historians in the Third Reich, and the political dimension of historical writing. The results were published, under the title *Fragen, die nicht gestellt wurden* (Questions That Were Not Asked), on the homepage of the Internet magazine H-Soz-u-Kult.

Three prominent public figures published memoirs of their persecution at the hands of the Nazis. Michael Blumenthal, director of the Jewish Museum, recounted his family's 300-year history in *Die unsichtbare Mauer* (The Invisible Wall). The popular German stage actor Michael Degen paid homage to the Germans who saved his life in wartime Berlin in *Nicht alle waren Mörder. Eine Kindheit in Berlin* (Not all were Murderers. A Childhood in Berlin). Literary critic Marcel Reich-Ranicki entitled his own memoir *Mein Leben* (My Life).

The Berlin-based group Meshulash sought in 1999 to generate a Jewish culture independent of the much larger and more assertive communities in Israel and North America. In November the group published a catalog to its museum exhibit, *Davka. Jüdisches Leben in Berlin-Traditionen und Visionen* (Davka. Jewish Life in Berlin-Traditions and Visions). With the establishment of the magazine *Golem-Europäisch-jüdisches Magazin* (Golem-European-Jewish Magazine), the first issue of which appeared in December, Meshulash broadened its vision beyond Berlin and Germany. Contributors from all over Europe, including novelist Albert Memmi, poet Esther Discherheit, and historian Diana Pinto contemplated the familiar question of how to define being Jewish in the specific context of post-Auschwitz, post-Cold-War Europe.

Walter Homolka, the controversial rabbi intent on reinvigorating Jewish life in Germany, issued three books in 1999. These were *Progressives Judentum. Leben und Lehre* (Progressive Judaism. Life and Teachings), *Das Judentum hat viele Gesichter. Die religiösen Strömungen der Gegenwart* (Judaism Has Many Faces. Religious Currents of the Present), and *Die Weisheit des Judentums. Gedanken für jeden Tag des Jahres* (The Wisdom of Judaism. Thoughts for Every Day of the Year). Homolka also edited the late Shalom Ben-Chorin's *Ein Leben für den Dialog* (A Life for Dialogue), on Jewish-Christian reconciliation.

Personalia

In accepting the 1999 Peace Prize of the German Book Trade, Fritz Stern, the eminent Columbia University professor, expressed his confidence in the democratic foundations of the Berlin Republic and reflected on the vulnerability of democracy in times of social upheaval. The 73-year-old Breslau native emigrated with his family in 1938 to the U.S., where he went on to become one of the world's most respected historians of modern Germany. In light of the fact that the recipient of the 1998 Peace Prize, Martin Walser, had used his acceptance speech to ignite a controversy about historical memory in the Berlin Republic, the selection of Stern took on added significance. It was announced in December that Stern would return to Germany in 2000 as the first Gutenburg Foundation Visiting Professor at the University of Mainz to teach a seminar on "National Socialism as a Temptation."

Three Jewish Berliners who were also forced to flee their hometown in the 1930s were honored in 1999 for their commitment to cultural life in postwar Germany. Meinhard Tennéfeld fled to Switzerland with his father in 1938; his mother and sister were killed in Auschwitz. After settling in Stuttgart in 1970, Tennéfeld occupied key positions in the local Jewish community, the German-Israeli Society, the CCJG, and the SCJC. The city of Stuttgart awarded him the Otto Hirsch Medal in January for his contribution to Christian-Jewish understanding and to the integration of Jewish immigrants from the FSU.

After leaving Berlin in 1936, Heinz Berggruen returned to Germany in 1944 as an American soldier. In 1995, he decided to bring his priceless collection of expressionist paintings to the city in which he first learned to appreciate art in the 1920s. The Berggruen Collection, with its impressive array of Picassos and Paul Klees, immediately became a fixture in the cultural landscape of the new Berlin. In recognition, Berggruen received the National Prize in June 1999.

Michael Blumenthal left Berlin with his family for Shanghai when he was 13. In 1997 the former secretary of the treasury of the U.S. became the director of the Jewish Museum in Berlin. In June, Berlin mayor Eberhard Diepgen conferred the Officer's Cross of the Order of Merit of the Federal Republic of Germany on Blumenthal. In his acceptance speech Blumenthal praised the German "willingness to confront, recognize and learn from the past."

Contributions of the second generation to Jewish life in Germany were also celebrated in 1999. Rachel Salamander was born in 1949 in a Bavarian DP camp. In recognition of the role her Jewish bookstores have played in the spread of Jewish knowledge in Germany, the city of Munich granted her its cultural prize. The historian Michael Brenner was singled out by the World Zionist Organization for his service to the Zionist idea. In November, the National Architecture Prize went to Daniel Libeskind for his Jewish Museum in Berlin.

Several important figures in the reconstruction of Jewish life in postwar Germany passed away in 1999. On February 11, the lifelong Zionist Maximilian Tauchner died in Munich after a long illness. After living and studying in Vienna, Kraków, and Lemberg, Tauchner established a legal practice in Munich in the 1950s to represent Holocaust survivors seeking restitution. Walter Feuchtwanger, nephew of the novelist Lion Feuchtwanger, also returned to Munich after World War II. Among his many services to the Jewish community, he played a central role in restitution negotiations and founded the German branch of the Maccabi sports association. He died at the age of 83. Like Bubis, Feuchtwanger wished to be buried in Israel.

In the 1950s, Rabbi Hans Isaak Grünewald left Israel, where he had studied with Martin Buber and Gershom Scholem, to pursue rabbinical studies in London in order to serve Jewish communities in Germany. From 1963 until 1988 he devoted himself to the religious and communal life of Jews in Munich. He died in Jerusalem on November 28. Hanna Herzberg, a leader in the Women's International Zionist Organization and active participant in Jewish-Christian dialogue, died on July 23 in Esslingen outside of Stuttgart. Another key player in that postwar dialogue, the novelist Shalom Ben-Chorin, died in Jerusalem at the age of 85. Born in Munich as Fritz Rosenthal in 1913, he took on the Hebrew name meaning "Peace, Son of Freedom" after emigrating to Palestine in 1935. His German-language writings earned him honors in his native country.

GREG CAPLAN

EDITOR'S NOTE

The reference to Prof. Dr. Michael Wolffsohn that appeared in the 1997 AJYB stated that he was "labeled positively" as "nationally oriented" by the neo-Nazi publication *Wer ist wer im Judentum?* In fact the neo-Nazi publication says that Prof. Dr. Wolffsohn is "hostile to the National Right in Germany."

Austria

National Affairs

Nothing short of a political volcano erupted at the national elections on October 3 when the far-right Freedom Party (FPÖ) emerged as the second strongest political party, edging out the mainstream conservative People's Party. The Social Democratic Party, which finished first with 33.4 percent of the vote, garnered 65 seats in parliament. In scoring an unprecedented 27.2 percent of the vote, the Freedom Party upped its representation from 41 to 53 seats. The People's Party fell to third place in the polling with 26.9 percent, retaining the 52 seats it had held in the outgoing parliament. The Greens won 7.1 percent of the vote, increasing their representation from 9 to 13 seats. The Liberal Forum, with only 3.4 percent, was no longer represented in parliament, having failed to pass the requisite 4-percent threshold.

After the election, President Thomas Klestil ignored the electoral gains of the FPÖ and invited Chancellor Viktor Klima, the leader of the Social Democrats, and Foreign Minister Wolfgang Schüssel, head of the People's Party, to form another government and extend their longstanding coalition. The left-of-center Social Democrats had been ruling the country for the previous 13 years with the support of the People's Party.

Following three months of sporadic and sometimes acrimonious negotiations the two sides proved unable to form a new government as the year ended. A seeming sticking point was Schüssel's insistence that the Social Democrats give up control of the powerful Finance Ministry, and Klima's refusal to do so. It was widely rumored at the time that the People's Party deliberately created an impasse in the talks, leaving President Klestil no other choice but to turn to it and the Freedom Party to form a government. These two parties controlled 105 out of the 183 seats in parliament, more than enough to win a vote of confidence. It was assumed that, in such an arrangement, Schüssel would become chancellor and the Freedom Party would play a junior role. Under this scenario, Jörg Haider, the head of the Freedom Party, would remain out of the federal government and continue to serve as governor of the province of Carinthia. For some time it had been common knowledge that a powerful element in the People's Party wanted to join with the Freedom Party in forming a government. Chancellor Klima, in contrast, had unequivocally opposed a coalition with Haider's party on the ground that its racist and anti-immigrant proclivities placed it outside the bounds of acceptable political discourse.

The Freedom Party's success placed Haider front and center in Austrian politics. A charismatic politician, Haider had taken over the party in 1985 when it polled a mere 5 percent of the vote. In strident tones he inveighed against the numerous foreigners and immigrants who were living in Austria, insisting that they took away jobs from Austrians and were the source of much of the country's crime. In one speech Haider blamed Africans residing in Austria for the sale of illegal drugs. Sometimes Haider maintained that he was not against all foreigners, only those working in the country illegally. Partially in response to the popularity of Haider's views, the government had slowed immigration to a trickle and had tightened the criteria for people seeking political asylum. To many observers, it was actually somewhat surprising that Haider had managed to fan the flames of xenophobia with his talk of job loss and crime. Not only was the rate of unemployment in Austria a mere 4.3 percent—well below the average for European Union countries—but, by all objective standards, the incidence of crime was low.

What fueled the growing fear at home and abroad of a coalition that included the FPÖ was that never, since the end of World War II, had any politician widely considered to have Nazi sympathies and antecedents come so close to power in a German-speaking country. To be sure, he had disavowed earlier pro-Nazi statements and had characterized Hitler's rule "a cruel and bloody dictatorship." Nevertheless people found it hard to forget his praise for Hitler's "employment policies" and his appearance at a meeting of Austrian Waffen-SS veterans whom he described as "decent fellows." His father had been a Nazi and served in the German army during the war, while his mother had been a member of Hitler's League of German Maidens. The large estate Haider owned was aryanized property that had belonged to Jews.

The Freedom Party's growing popularity was not just due to the appeal of xenophobia. It was also rooted in its positions on other, more conventional, issues. Many people were fed up with 13 years of the same "Red-Black" (socialist and conservative) government, and almost 30 years under Social Democratic chancellors. Also, the party opposed the time-honored but widely unpopular system whereby the two main parties carved up most of the public-sector jobs, from ambassadors to secretaries. Another winning issue was the party's complaint about the stifling hand of government regulation over the economy. A right-wing alliance between the People's Party and the Freedom Party, it was thought, would presumably hasten the pace of economic privatization and deregulation.

Foreign policy also played a role in Haider's rise. He and his party had opposed Austria's entry into the European Union, warning that it would bring in its wake a new flood of foreigners. Bowing to reality, however, Haider accepted the irreversibility of membership. But he sounded hostile to the idea of the EU's expansion eastward, a step that would confer membership on Hungary, the Czech Republic, and Poland. The Freedom Party leader played on the fears of blue-collar workers that immigrants from these countries would steal jobs from Austrians. A coalition between the Freedom Party and the People's Party could also lead to a break in Austria's tradition of "perpetual neutrality" since, unlike the Social Democrats, both rightist parties were strongly in favor of Austrian membership in NATO. In fact, opposition to NATO membership may very well have cost the Social Democrats support among voters who wished to see Austria move closer to Europe's security system.

The election results provoked a sharp reaction. On November 12 some 75,000 people gathered in the center of Vienna to hear speaker after speaker denounce the Freedom Party and its leader, and warn against the inclusion of the party in any coalition. Ariel Muzicant, the president of the Israelitische Kultusgemeinde (IKG), the nation's Jewish community organization, also came out strongly against allowing the Freedom Party into the government, warning that such a step would seriously threaten all freedom-loving people.

OTHER ELECTIONS

Indications that the Freedom Party would make striking electoral gains nationally had been evident in regional elections held earlier in the year. In the March elections in Carinthia—the poor, unemployment-ridden, and conservative southern province which was Haider's political base—the Freedom Party received 42 percent of the vote, an 8-percent gain since the last election, pushing the Social Democrats into second place and the People's Party into third place. As a result, Haider once again became governor of the province, a post he had been forced to resign in 1991 after he praised the employment policies of Adolf Hitler. In Voralberg, the country's westernmost province, the party increased its popularity by more than a third in the September elections, its vote shooting up to over 27 percent from 18 percent in the last Voralberg election held five years earlier. In both provincial elections, Freedom Party posters exploited suspicion of foreigners by promising to stop "overforeignization" and "misuse of asylum," a pledge that was widely understood as calling for a ban on immigration.

Paradoxically, however, the ascendancy of Haider and his party could not have been foretold from the outcome of the elections to the European Parliament that took place in May. The campaign to fill the 21 Austrian seats in the 626-member Strasbourg parliament centered largely on the issue of the country's neutrality. The Social Democrats favored maintaining Austria's status as a neutral, while their conservative coalition partners had gone on record in favor of joining NATO. Chancellor Klima's anti-NATO views helped his party during the election campaign because most Austrians abhorred the NATO bombing of Serbia even more, it seemed, than they deplored the actions of Yugoslav president Slobodan Milosevic in Kosovo. (The Austrian government refused to grant NATO warplanes permission to fly over Austrian territory for bombing missions against Serbian targets.) The Social Democrats won 31.74 percent of the vote while the People's Party came in second with 30.64 percent, a reversal of the result of the previous election for the European Parliament in 1996. Haider's Freedom Party finished third with 23.4 percent. Some 5.8 million people were eligible to vote, but apathy cut turnout to 49 percent, as opposed to the 68 percent who had voted in the 1996 elections.

Israel and the Middle East

Relations between Austria and Israel remained friendly, still benefiting from the aftereffects of the 1998 visit of Chancellor Klima to the Jewish state. At the diplomatic level, Austria supported Israel's efforts to gain membership in the Western Europe and Others Group (WEOG), the regional grouping of western-style democracies at the UN. Israel remained the only country in the world organization that was not a member of a regional group, and the support of such a group is necessary for a country to be elected to one of the UN's permanent bodies such as the Security Council or the Economic and Social Council.

Since both countries were busy with national elections, there were no new diplomatic initiatives between Israel and Austria until the Austrian election in October. When it became clear how well Haider's party had done, the real possibility that the Freedom Party could enter the government provoked a strong reaction in Israel. Foreign Minister David Levy warned that if this were to happen, Israel might withdraw its ambassador from Vienna. Following the election, the Knesset Diaspora Committee invited the Austrian ambassador, Wolfgang Paul, to discuss the results, and the ambassador was also invited to appear on the Gideon Levi TV talk show. Both the Austrian and the Israeli media gave extensive coverage to Israel's reaction to the election and to Ambassador Paul's view that the results would not change Austria's friendly attitude toward Israel.

Low-level diplomatic exchanges continued following the Austrian elections. Israeli justice minister Yossi Beilin received a delegation of Austrian judges in October and, in December, the presidents of the Vienna and Upper Austria school boards held a meeting with Education Minister Yossi Sarid. Under an agreement signed by Sarid and the school-board presidents, Austrian teachers were invited to visit the Yad Vashem Holocaust Memorial. In the cultural sphere, the Israeli Philharmonic Orchestra performed twice in August at the Salzburg Festival, and the Batsheva dance troupe gave a performance in Austria in September.

Holocaust-Related Developments

WAR CRIMINALS

Justice Minister Gerhard Litzka announced that a former Nazi doctor, 84-year-old Dr. Heinrich Gross, would be tried in March 2000 for the murder of five of the estimated 700 disabled children killed at the Spiegelgrund Children's Clinic in Vienna. This was the first such prosecution to be brought in Austria in 20 years. In March 1950 Dr. Gross had been convicted of a single charge of "inciting homicide," but a higher court overturned the verdict. Although a retrial was ordered, it was never held, and the case was subsequently abandoned. Permitted to return to his work, Dr. Gross became a well-known neurologist and forensic psychiatrist. The case was reopened in 1998 after fresh evidence, including thousands of documents from the archives of the former East German secret police, surfaced. In an interview, Dr. Gross admitted referring children to a euthanasia board but denied ever having killed anyone.

COMPENSATION

The Austrian government created the Historiker Kommission (Historical Commission) in September 1998 to examine instances of property confiscation during the Nazi period and to determine what had been done after the war to restore such property to the rightful owners or heirs, or to compensate them. It was also charged with investigating the use of slave labor in Austrian factories and farms during the war (see AJYB 1999, pp. 361–62). The nine-member commission, created on the initiative of IKG president Ariel Muzicant and chaired by Clemens Jabloner, president of the Austrian Administrative Court, engaged a professional staff of historians and archivists, and in August 1999 it issued a document setting forth the main lines of the work it intended to pursue.

In July the Federation of Jewish Communities in Austria established a Claims Office for Jewish Holocaust Survivors in and of Austria and their Heirs. Located in Vienna with a professional staff of nine, the office will conduct research to document individual compensation claims filed by Austrian and former Austrian Jewish victims and their heirs, whether or not they now lived in the country. By retracing the mechanism of Nazi expropriation and identifying those institutions that seized Jewish assets, the office was expected to develop the groundwork for future restoration of, or compensation for, looted Jewish assets, should the Austrian parliament vote to authorize such restitution or compensation.

The Nationalfond was the special fund established by the Austrian government in June 1995 "for the victims of national socialism." It was to help compensate anyone, Jew or non-Jew, who had been persecuted because of political beliefs, religion, nationality, sexual orientation, physical or mental disability, or whom the Nazis considered "asocial," as well as anyone forced to flee Austria to escape persecution. By 1999 it had contacted 31,000 people considered eligible to receive payments under terms of the fund. By September 1999, payments had been made to 27,000 of those people in 65 countries. The largest number lived in the United States (9,863), followed by Austria (5,736), Israel (3,611), the United Kingdom (3,024), and Australia (1,356). Of the recipients, 228 had been born between 1891 and 1900. Originally, a certification of Austrian nationality and proof of residence in the country as of March 13, 1938, were needed to qualify, but the cut-off date had been moved back to July 12, 1936 (the date of a new German-Austrian treaty), thus making several hundred more people eligible.

The amount paid to each beneficiary was fixed at 70,000 shillings ($5,800), though in special cases this could be tripled. In 1999 the Ministry of Finance allocated 150 million shillings (approximately $11.5 million) to the fund. The steep decline from the 1998 allocation, which had been 500 million shillings, was explained by the fact that the fund had by now already paid out money to most of those qualified. Since the establishment of the fund in 1995, the government had allocated a total of 1.95 billion shillings (approximately $155 million) to it. In addition, the government allocated to the fund the $8.5 million in gold it received at the Tripartite Gold Conference that was held in London in December 1997 (see AJYB 1999, p. 360). This additional money went to needy survivors who did not meet the fund's criteria for eligibility, to so-called "double victims" who had suffered under both Nazism and Communism, and for special projects.

Two noteworthy amendments were made to the law in 1999. The first, adopted in January, established a center that would provide information on the restitution issue. The second, in July, allowed the fund to accept money from any legal entity. Under it own authority, the fund changed the composition of the Kuratorium, its policy-making body. Heretofore only government representatives could serve. Now the Kuratorium could also include a single new member from each of several victims' organizations: those representing the Roma and Sinti (Gypsies), Jews, and victims of political persecution.

"The Presence of the Absence: International Holocaust Conference for Eyewitnesses and Descendants of Both Sides," was held September 1–3 at the University of Vienna. The sessions focused on interdisciplinary approaches to the Holocaust from the perspectives of the descendants of the victims and of the perpetrators.

JEWISH BANK ASSETS

The shareholders of the Bank of Austria voted to approve the settlement of class-action lawsuits filed in the United States by survivors of the Holocaust and their families. The settlement, which called for the bank and its Credit Anstalt subsidiary to provide $45 million to set up a fund for the claimants, was to be presented to the Federal District Court in Manhattan for approval. Of this sum, $30 million was to be distributed by a committee chaired by Simon Wiesenthal to survivors who held accounts in the bank or their heirs; $10 million was to be allocated for administrative expenses, legal fees, and the work of a historical commission that will examine the relationship of the bank to its German sister bank during the Nazi period; and the other $5 million was to go to the Conference on Jewish Material Claims.

LOOTED JEWISH ARTWORK

The Jewish community of Austria issued a final report on the so-called Mauerbach Fund, established in 1996 from the proceeds of a sale of artworks plundered from Jews by the Nazis (see AJYB 1999, p. 362). The auction of some 8,000 works yielded $14.5 million, of which 12 percent was set aside for needy non-Jewish Holocaust victims and the balance went to needy Jewish victims of Austrian origin living in Israel, Austria, and other countries.

On November 5, 1998, the Austrian Parliament approved legislation allowing works of art seized by the Nazis and later incorporated into federal and state museums to be returned to their rightful owners. Valuable artworks belonging to hundreds of Austrian Jews had been confiscated during the Nazi rule of Austria between 1938 and 1945, and much of it was still held in Austrian museums. Following World War II, the government had imposed what amounted to an "art tax" on the survivors of Nazism when they sought to take their recovered artworks to their new homelands. This tax was now abolished.

One of the more prominent people to benefit from the new legislation was the widow of Alphonse de Rothschild, younger brother of Louis de Rothschild, head of the Austrian branch of the family. Following the war, Mrs. Rothschild had left behind 170 works of art—5 percent of the family's holdings—in Vienna, including three paintings by Frans Hals that she donated to the famed Kunsthistorisches Museum. In July 1999 the trove of artwork returned to the family was sold at auction by Christie's in London. The sale of the collection, which included Old Master paintings, medieval manuscripts, and antiques of every variety, brought in $89.9 million, more than twice the amount expected. Lord Hindlip, chairman of Christie's, said: "It was one of the most successful sales in the history of auctions in Europe. Never before has such a cross section of the arts fetched such extraordinary sums of money in one evening."

The Austrian government also agreed to the restitution to the heirs of Ferdinand Bloch-Bauer of certain items from his art collection. Seized by the Nazis in 1939, this collection came into the possession of the Austrian government after the war, and, like other paintings and drawings from other collections held by the government, many of the pieces had been hanging in Austrian museums without the knowledge or permission of the owners or their heirs. The government, acting under the new law, agreed to return to Ferdinand Bloch-Bauer's heirs 19 porcelain settings and 16 Klimt drawings, but only one of the six Klimt paintings from the collection. Some of the heirs served notice that they will sue the government to recover the other five Klimt paintings, whose estimated market value was $100 million.

In January 1998 Manhattan district attorney Robert M. Morgenthau had obtained a subpoena ordering the Museum of Modern Art in New York to hold on to two Egon Schiele paintings pending a criminal inquiry into their ownership. The paintings, "Portrait of Wally" and "Dead City," had been exhibited at the museum beginning in late 1997 as part of a 150-piece collection owned by the Austrian-government-financed Leopold Foundation. Just hours before they were to be returned to Austria, Morgenthau, in response to complaints from relatives of the former Jewish owners that the paintings had been stolen by the Nazis, impaneled a grand jury to determine the truth of the allegations. Pending the outcome of these judicial proceedings, the museum was ordered to retain custody of the paintings (see AJYB 1999, p. 363). The museum filed suit, challenging the seizure on the grounds that a 1968 law prohibited such action. The New York Supreme Court found for the museum in May 1998, but the Appellate Division reversed that ruling in March 1999. In a unanimous decision, the four-member tribunal ruled that the state law was intended to apply to civil matters, not criminal proceedings. The court declared that "the public interest is not served by permitting the free flow of stolen art into and out of the state." But the Court of Appeals, the highest court in the state, handed down a ruling in September 1999 that once again reversed the decision and allowed the paintings to go back to the Leopold Foundation. Shortly after this latest decision, however, the United States attorney in New York filed a complaint in federal court alleging that the "Portrait of Wally" painting was stolen property when brought into the United States, and therefore should be impounded. Pending a ruling on the complaint, the museum was to retain custody of the painting.

JEWISH COMMUNITY

Demography

About 6,500 Jews were registered with the Israelitische Kultusgemeinde (IKG), but knowledgeable observers claimed that the actual number of Jews was twice as large. In recent years, to encourage affiliation, the IKG had been offering financial incentives to parents to register newborn children with the community. Continuing a long-established pattern, the overwhelming majority of Jews were concentrated in Vienna, with only about 500 making their homes elsewhere, primarily in the large provincial cities of Salzburg, Innsbruck, Graz, and Linz.

For the first time in some years, the Jewish community was shrinking in size, between 300 and 400 people leaving the country during 1999. Many of the Jews emigrating had originally come from the former Soviet republic of Georgia. These Georgians, and other Sephardi Jews as well, were concentrated in the garment and shoe trades, which were undergoing a severe depression, and so they left to seek better economic opportunities in Eastern Europe. The IKG requested the government to waive certain provisions of Austria's highly restrictive immigration laws so as to allow in the same number of Jews as had left. Reflecting a trend in all European Union countries, immigration to Austria had slowed to a trickle—only 9,000 immigrants were allowed into the country in 1999.

Communal Affairs

The IKG celebrated its 150th anniversary on June 20—the first representative delegation of Austrian Jewry had met with the young Kaiser Franz Joseph in 1849. The historic anniversary event, held at the famed Burg Theater in Vienna, was attended by over 1,000 guests, including leading members of the government and of the Jewish community, representatives of the Catholic and Evangelical Churches, and foreign ambassadors. Among Austrian government leaders present were President Klestil, Chancellor Klima, cabinet members, the president of the national parliament, and the mayor of Vienna. Presiding was Dr. Ariel Muzicant, president of the IKG.

The European regional office of the Anti-Defamation League (ADL), located in Vienna, which opened in August 1997 under the direction of journalist Marta Halpert, broke new ground in the development of training programs for leaders of the Hungarian and Polish Jewish communities, who were taught techniques of combating anti-Semitism and xenophobia in their countries.

A new monthly journal, *Jewish Austria: Past and Present,* made its first appearance in November 1998. The journal featured articles about anti-Semitism in Austria, the Holocaust, and Jewish contributions to Austria's culture, history, and economy. Published by the Institute for the History of Jews in Austria, it will also provide information about new research projects and data about public attitudes on topics of interest to Jews.

Among the several exhibitions mounted by the Jewish Museum of Vienna in 1999, one attracted special attention. This was "Eden*Zion* Utopia: The History of the Future In Judaism," which opened on November 24, 1999, and was scheduled to run through February 20, 2000. Taking the new millennium as its theme, the exhibition focused on strategies that Jews have historically used for dealing with the problems associated with approaching momentous dates or other kinds of uncertainty, strategies ranging from fatalism, to messianic speculation, to plans for utopian Jewish societies. George Segal's installation, "The Expulsion from Paradise," started off the exhibition, followed by Avraham Ofek's sculpture, "The Bird of Choice," which examined how 20th-century painters have depicted prophets and others who claim to be in contact with the future.

Robert S. Wistrich, professor of modern European history at Hebrew University, made an official presentation of his recent publication, *Österreich und das Vermächtnis des Holocausts* (Austria and the Legacy of the Holocaust), at IKG headquarters in Vienna on June 21. This study, published by the American Jewish Committee and released in both English and German, traced in detail the development of Austrian attitudes and government policies toward the legacy of the Holocaust in the country since the end of World War II.

MURRAY GORDON

East-Central Europe

THE YEAR 1999 MARKED the tenth anniversary of the fall of Communism in Europe, an appropriate time to take stock of a decade of astonishing change both for the states involved and for their Jews. In March three of these states—Poland, the Czech Republic, and Hungary—joined the North Atlantic Treaty Organization (NATO), once the sworn enemy of the Soviet bloc. That same month the Kosovo crisis flared up and the NATO bombing campaign against Yugoslavia began. Several Jewish communities in the region were directly involved, and Israel and international Jewish organizations were among those providing humanitarian aid. In December the European Union (EU) agreed to invite five former Communist states—Slovakia, Latvia, Lithuania, Bulgaria, and Romania—as well as Malta, to begin talks aimed at achieving their membership in the EU. Hungary, the Czech Republic, and Poland were already negotiating entry terms.

The Jewish communities in these postcommunist countries continued their transformation into "normal" communities, sharing the same issues and concerns as long-established communities in the west. Continuing evidence for this was their participation in international Jewish conferences, including a February meeting in Brussels with delegates from the Conference of Presidents of Major American Jewish Organizations, and the landmark General Assembly of the European Council of Jewish Communities, which drew some 600 delegates from more than 30 countries to Nice in May. Key issues for the postcommunist communities were compensation for elderly Holocaust survivors and the restitution of Jewish property, as well as education, social welfare, and the development of a new generation of lay leaders. Religious tensions between secular and Reform streams, on the one hand, and Orthodox official structures, on the other, also emerged in some communities, often centering on the question of "who is a Jew."

Albania

Albania was sorely tested during the NATO bombardment of Yugoslavia as hundreds of thousands of ethnic Albanians sought refuge there. Jewish and Israeli organizations sent teams of relief workers to help. The first Jewish Agency relief mission arrived in early April. Only a handful of Jews were known to be living in Albania, where the political and economic situation remained anarchic.

Bosnia-Herzegovina

In November, at a luncheon in New York hosted by the American Jewish Committee and the Conference of Presidents of Major American Jewish Organizations, Bosnia's three presidents thanked the American Jewish community for the support that enabled La Benevolencija, the Sarajevo Jewish humanitarian aid organization, to operate during the Bosnian war. That same month New York's Shearith Israel (Spanish and Portuguese) Synagogue said it would donate four-dozen prayer books to La Benevolencija.

In early December there was an emotional ceremony in the Jewish cemetery of Mostar to dedicate a Holocaust memorial bearing the names of 138 Mostar Jews killed in the Shoah. Both the Muslim and ethnic Croatian mayors of the divided city attended the ceremony, as well as leading Orthodox, Catholic, and Muslim clergy. Following the ceremony there was a screening of "Mandlbaum's Mission," a Dutch-made film that detailed how Mostar Jewish community leader Zorin Mandlbaum saved several people and carried out other humanitarian acts during the recent war in Bosnia.

Bulgaria

Despite some strong domestic opposition, the Bulgarian government not only publicly supported the NATO air campaign against Yugoslavia but also provided logistical support and allowed NATO the use of Bulgarian airspace. This paved the way for a 35-hour visit to Bulgaria in November by President Clinton, the first-ever official visit to Bulgaria by a U.S. president. Bulgaria paid a high economic price for the bombing, however. By the end of the year, vital trade routes across Yugoslavia—including the Danube River, a major shipping route—remained closed. Over the first eight months of 1999 Bulgaria ran a deficit of $426.4 million, as compared to a $53.5-million surplus in the same period in 1998. Exports dropped by 16 percent and it was predicted that the growth rate for the year would be zero. In December two rapporteurs for the Council of Europe expressed concern over "widespread corruption" in the country, but praised some human-rights developments, including Bulgaria's abolition of the death penalty.

In April an Anti-Defamation League delegation visited Sofia and met with President Petar Stoyanov and other officials to express appreciation to Bulgaria for saving the Jewish population of Bulgaria during World War II, despite the country's alliance with Germany and despite the fact that it deported 14,000 Jews of Bulgarian-occupied Macedonia and Thrace to their deaths. The ADL funded a Bulgarian translation of *Beyond Hitler's Grasp: The Heroic Rescue of Bulgaria's Jews,* by Israeli author Michael Bar-Zohar, and pledged to distribute 30,000 copies to Bulgarian educational institutions.

About 4,000 Jews lived in Bulgaria, most of them in Sofia; more than 1,000 Bulgarian Jews had left for Israel since the sharp downturn in the economy that began in early 1997. Still, about 400 Jewish children attended the Jewish elementary school in Sofia, and there was also a Jewish summer camp.

At the end of November, B'nai B'rith International held a ceremony in Sofia to commemorate 100 years of the organization's activity in Bulgaria and the 90th anniversary of its Carmel Lodge in Sofia. Seymour Saideman, just elected president of B'nai B'rith Europe, headed a delegation that met with President Stoyanov, other high government officials, and members of the National Assembly. The Bulgarian leaders pledged restitution for Jewish property expropriated by Bulgarian authorities during World War II and retained by the Communist regime.

Croatia

President Franjo Tudjman, the Communist partisan general in World War II who became Croatia's founding father, died in December at the age of 77, leaving a mixed legacy. Throughout his tenure Tudjman was accused of trying to whitewash Croatia's past by rehabilitating the homegrown fascist Ustasha regime that ruled Croatia as a Nazi puppet state during World War II. Ignoring the record of Ustasha atrocities, he incorporated symbols and personalities of the fascist state into Croatia's political fabric. Streets and squares were renamed, and antifascist monuments were destroyed. His autobiography included statements that were interpreted as anti-Semitic, and Tudjman attempted to turn the memorial to scores of thousands of Jews and Serbs slaughtered during World War II at the Ustasha's infamous Jasenovac concentration camp into a memorial to victims of Communism and the 1991 Serbo-Croat war as well. All this drew sharp protests from Jews, former anti-fascist partisans, and others inside Croatia, as well as condemnation from Israel, which did not establish diplomatic relations with Croatia until September 1997.

Yet Tudjman openly courted Jewish support. Local Jewish leaders met regularly with him and other senior officials, and several high-ranking members of the government were Jews or of Jewish origin. These included Nenad Porges, a former president of the Jewish community, who was commerce minister at the time of Tudjman's death, and Slobodan Lang, a top adviser on humanitarian affairs.

In February Croatian defense minister Paval Miljavac visited Israel and the two countries signed a multimillion dollar arms and defense pact. Under the deal, Israel agreed to upgrade Croatia's fleet of aging MIG-21 jets at a cost of about $100 million. The agreement drew criticism from the Labor opposition in Israel.

Croatia was home to about 2,000 Jews, the majority living in the capital of Zagreb. Most community members were secular and assimilated into the mainstream community; indeed, most of the children were from mixed marriages. Rabbi Kotel Dadon, who was officially installed as chief rabbi in November 1998, served the community's religious needs. Croatian Jews took part in a meeting of Jews from all parts of the former Yugoslavia, which was held in September on the Adriatic coast.

The Jewish community in the historic Adriatic town of Dubrovnik celebrated the return, in late 1998, of three centuries-old Torah scrolls and other precious ritual objects that had been taken to the U.S. several years earlier by Michael Papo, a former president of the tiny Dubrovnik Jewish community, when he moved to the United States. Papo had argued that the objects would not be safe in Dubrovnik given the continuing Balkan conflicts. Backed by the Croatian government, the Dubrovnik Jewish community won a long legal battle in Zagreb and New York courts to get the objects returned.

Croatian Jews reported little overt anti-Semitism, though they worried about the open sale this year of *Mein Kampf* and the *Protocols of the Elders of Zion.* Jews were also concerned about the officially sanctioned historical revisionism that had emerged during the Tudjman era and the potential danger that the state might exploit the Jewish community for its own political ends.

Against this background, a Zagreb court's guilty verdict pronounced in October against Dinko Sakic, the former commander of the Jasenovac camp, was hailed as a landmark of justice. Sakic had been extradited to Croatia from Argentina in 1998 after he gave an interview there on local television. The subsequent six-month trial forced Croatians to confront their country's history as an ally of the Nazis and a participant in the Holocaust. Sakic, who expressed no remorse and dismissed the testimony of survivors as "anti-Croat propaganda," was found guilty of crimes against humanity and received the maximum sentence—20 years in prison. This was the first time that a postcommunist regime in Europe had convicted one of its nationals for such crimes. "We hope that this sentence, made 55 years after the events, will be a warning that all those who committed crimes in the near or distant past will not escape justice," said the chief justice.

Czech Republic

Along with Hungary and Poland, the Czech Republic joined NATO in March. Xenophobia and racism, particularly against Roma (Gypsies), continued to raise considerable concern throughout the year. There were also manifestations of anti-Semitism from the far right. In December photographs of President Vaclav Havel, Premier Milos Zeman, Civic Democratic Party chairman Vaclav Klaus, and Freedom Union chairman Jan Ruml, all labeled "Jewish Free Masons and Murderers of the Czech Nation," were displayed in the town of Decin, in an exhibit organized by the extraparliamentary far-right Republican Party. The display also included a list of hundreds of names identified as a "partial list of Jews and Jewish half-breeds in politics since 1989." The list was quickly removed from the exhibit, and party leaders disassociated themselves from it. The chairman of the local Jewish community lodged a complaint against the exhibit's organizers, and on December 28 local police charged a party member with racial defamation and incitement to ethnic hatred.

Skinheads were active around the country throughout the year. In February police detained 12 leading skinheads and seized lists of skinhead supporters as well as racist and neo-Nazi magazines, CDs, cassettes, and badges, in an unprecedented operation that followed a nine-month investigation. In another operation, Czech riot police detained more than a score of anarchists and neo-Nazi skinheads after the two groups clashed during demonstrations in downtown Prague on May Day. Police separated the two groups, but later some 300 skinheads wearing fascist insignia marched through the city chanting anti-Semitic slogans and giving Nazi salutes. In November, 23 skinheads were charged with violent behavior, hooliganism, and causing damage to property after attacking a group of Roma (Gypsies) in a restaurant in Ceske Budejovice. A survey carried out for the American Jewish Committee in late August and early September showed that 81 percent of Czechs "prefer not" to have Gypsies as neighbors, and 76 percent believed that Gypsies "behave in a manner which provokes hostility in our country."

The most highly publicized anti-Gypsy action took place in the northern town of Usti nad Labem where, in October, a fence-like concrete wall two meters high was erected separating Roma living in a low-income housing project from private homeowners across the street who complained about noise and other disturbance. Construction of the wall evoked protests from politicians and human-rights groups in the Czech Republic and abroad, including the European Union. Under pressure from the Czech government, the Usti nad Labem city council pulled down the wall in November.

The American Jewish Committee survey of Czech opinion also examined knowledge about the Holocaust, feelings about Holocaust remembrance, attitudes toward Jews and other minorities, and awareness of the role of Jews in the Czech historical experience. The survey showed that 74 percent of respondents felt that "we should keep the remembrance of the Nazi extermination of the Jews strong even after the passage of time," while 17 percent maintained that "50 years after the end of World War II, it is time to put the memory of the Nazi extermination of the Jews behind us." Some 57 percent answered "yes" when asked whether "teaching about the Nazi extermination of the Jews during the Second World War should be required in Czech schools."

In the survey, 92 percent could correctly identify Auschwitz, Dachau, and Treblinka as concentration camps, and 67 percent cited the yellow star or a variant as the symbol that Jews were forced to wear during the Second World War. But only 31 percent, in a multiple-choice format, selected six million as the approximate number of Jews killed by the Nazis during the Second World War, 40 percent chose much lower figures, and 20 percent answered "don't know." Both knowledge of the Holocaust and recognition of the importance of remembering it tended to correlate with education, as university-trained Czechs scored considerably higher on both measures. According to the survey, a large majority of Czechs supported some form of property restitution to Jews: 36 percent maintained that "all property [Jews were deprived of during World War II] should be returned to Jews," while 35 percent felt that "only buildings serving religious purposes should be returned to Jews." Just 18 percent opposed the return of any property to Jews.

Current attitudes to Jews were mixed. Only 4 percent believed that Jews "behave in a manner which provokes hostility in our country" and 8 percent thought that Jews have "too much influence in our society." But 34 percent (9 percent "strongly") subscribed to the idea that, "as in the past, Jews exert too much influence on world events." Similarly, 23 percent (6 percent "strongly") agreed that "Jews are exploiting the memory of the Nazi extermination of the Jews for their own purposes." Only 34 percent said they knew someone who was Jewish, 41 percent had visited the Jewish ghetto memorial in Terezin, and only 16 percent had been to the Jewish Museum in Prague.

In October President Havel hosted "Phenomenon Holocaust," a conference held at Prague Castle and at the Terezin ghetto concentration camp. The conference, aimed at continuing the Czech Republic's examination of Holocaust issues that had been ignored under Communism, was part of Havel's two-year-old initiative to engage the country in a dialogue about its own history. Participants included representatives of the United States Holocaust Memorial Museum, Israel's Yad Vashem, and Poland's State Museum at Auschwitz, as well as other academics, teachers, and Holocaust specialists. The Czech cabinet allocated the equivalent of more than $14,000 to support publications based on the conference, and the ministry of education was instructed to develop Holocaust curricula for the schools.

Early in the year German prosecutors said that there was not enough evidence to try Anton Malloth, a Terezin guard who had been convicted of war crimes and sentenced to death in absentia by a Czechoslovak court in 1948, and had been discovered in Munich in 1987. But in November the Czech state attorney sent new evidence implicating Malloth to German authorities.

In other developments, new tourist maps showing Jewish heritage sites in Moravia and Czech Silesia were published in the spring. Jewish journalist and intellectual Daniel Kumermann was named Czech ambassador to Israel in May. In June, Austrian Nazi-hunter Simon Wiesenthal received the Czech Republic's highest honor, the Order of the White Lion, from President Havel, who described Wiesenthal as a "physical symbol of human memory." In July the government completed an investigation of the collections of the National Gallery to identify works stolen from Jews by the Nazis, or from the Jewish Museum by the Communists. The government then ordered the minister of culture to prepare legislation that would transfer stolen works from the National Gallery to the Jewish Museum.

JEWISH COMMUNITY

There were ten official Jewish communities in the Czech Republic, with a total of approximately 3,000 registered members. About half lived in Prague. But Jewish leaders estimated that there were many more—perhaps as many as 10,000–15,000—unaffiliated Jews in the country. The official communities and a number of secular Jewish institutions came under the aegis of the Federation of Jewish Communities. Among the secular organizations were Beit Praha, a non-Orthodox congregation in Prague that attracted mostly expatriate Americans and other foreigners, the Union of Jewish Youth, the Maccabi and Hakoach sports clubs, the Women's Zionist Organization (WIZO), and the Terezin Initiative, a group of Czech Holocaust survivors. In addition, there was the independent group Bejt Simcha, which maintained links with Progressive Judaism, and Chabad-Lubavitch. Three synagogues functioned regularly in Prague: the Old-New Synagogue (Orthodox), the High Synagogue (modern Orthodox) and the Jubilee Synagogue (Neolog/Conservative). Beit Praha held regular services in the Jewish Town Hall on Friday nights and the High Holy Days, and sponsored lectures and other events. Bejt Simcha held Friday night services and other gatherings, which often featured rabbis and other guest lecturers from abroad. The Jewish community in Prague operated a kosher restaurant and a home for the elderly, as well as a Jewish kindergarten, day school, and high school with a combined student body of about 100.

Simmering religious tensions within the nominally Orthodox official Jewish community were highlighted by a dispute over a wedding ceremony in Pilsen in the fall. Chief Rabbi Karol Sidon refused to send a rabbi to officiate at the ceremony, the first in the Pilsen synagogue in 50 years, since the bride had converted to Judaism under the auspices of the American Reform movement. A rabbi flew in from the United States to perform the wedding.

Many Jewish groups visited Prague during the year. One of them, a ten-member delegation from the North American Boards of Rabbis (NABOR), made a two-day visit in March. They met with senior government officials and said they found no signs of serious anti-Semitism in the Czech Republic.

Construction continued on a new synagogue in Liberec, in the Sudetenland near the border with Germany. It will be part of a complex on the site of the prewar synagogue that was burned down on Kristallnacht in 1938. Beside the synagogue the complex will include a municipal library housing a large collection about the Sudetenland, and a Jewish community center. As a so-called "building of reconciliation," the complex qualified for funding from Germany. The Sudentenland, historic home to many ethnic Germans, was ceded to Hitler's Reich in 1938, and the Czechoslovak government, regaining the territory after World War II, expelled several million ethnic Germans.

A newly discovered medieval Jewish cemetery in Prague became the center of controversy. Dating to the 13th century and voluntarily relinquished by Prague's Jewish community in the 15th century, the cemetery had been built over ever since. It came to light in 1999 when a Czech insurance company began preparations for the construction of a high-rise apartment block and underground garage on the site. Before construction began, archaeologists brought in by Prague city authorities confirmed the cemetery's existence and estimated that the site contained some 400 graves. The building project infuriated Jewish groups around the world who believed that the cemetery had been desecrated. Many, however, were reacting to false information relayed over the Internet that the famous old Jewish cemetery in Prague's medieval ghetto was threatened. On September 28, after some 100 gravesites had been removed and transferred to another cemetery, Prague Jews led a protest demonstration at the site, and the next day the minister of culture called for a halt to the archaeological work. In November Chief Rabbi Karol Sidon reached a compromise with the insurance company. It called for excavating ground beneath the existing level of burial remains, encasing the remains in concrete, and then sinking these remains to a deeper level, which would be undisturbed by any future development on the site. This solution, however, was decisively rejected by many Orthodox groups around the world, and at year's end the situation remained unresolved.

As in past years, there were numerous Jewish cultural events in 1999. In March a new concert series, "Music in the Spanish Synagogue," was launched with a concert by Cantor Joseph Malovany of New York. All concerts took place in the magnificent, newly restored Spanish Synagogue, which is part of the Jewish Museum. The museum's Education Center sponsored regular lecture series on a variety of topics, as well as concerts and film screenings. It also held teacher-training seminars, including one in the spring on the history of the State of Israel, done in collaboration with the Institute of World History at Prague's Charles University. The center also prepared study programs for university students and younger pupils on Jewish topics, among them one on the history of Jewish settlement in various parts of the country and another on Jewish holidays, customs, and traditions. The center also sponsored a project to teach tolerance to kindergarten pupils. With the support of the Ronald S. Lauder Foundation, the center brought to the stage "Jonah and the Others," written and directed by Vida Neuwirthova, a play that acquaints preschool children with Jewish history and traditions. Its premier took place in January at the Theater Minor.

Early in the year Jewish Museum director Leo Pavlat and other Czech Jewish leaders became embroiled in a controversy over a new edition of Itamar Levin's book, *The Last Chapter of the Holocaust?* Published at the end of 1998 by the Jewish Agency for Israel in cooperation with the World Jewish Restitution Organization (and including a foreword by Jewish Agency chairman Avraham Burg), it detailed the looting, dispersal, and destruction of Jewish property after the Holocaust in various European countries. It also sharply criticized the Prague Museum and called for its collection to be transferred to Israel. Pavlat prepared a 60-page rebuttal.

In September Czech Radio ran a series of programs, "Days of Jewish Culture," which culminated on September 16 with the live broadcast of a memorial service at the Pinkas Synagogue, now a Holocaust memorial, for the Czech and Moravian Jews who died in the Holocaust. From six until ten P.M., 300 invited guests read out the names, one by one, of 3,000 victims. The readers including President

Havel, U.S. secretary of state Madeleine Albright, writer Ivan Klima, members of the Czech government, Holocaust survivors, and celebrities.

This year marked the 100th anniversary of the infamous Hilsner case, in which Leopold Hilsner, a Czech Jew from the small town of Polna, was sentenced to death for involvement in the alleged ritual murder of a Christian woman. The case, which was compared to the Dreyfus affair in France, sparked a wave of anti-Semitism, and only a few intellectuals, led by Tomas Garrigue Masaryk, the future president of Czechoslovakia, spoke out against the ritual murder accusation. Although an appeals court confirmed the verdict, the emperor commuted it to life imprisonment, and Hilsner was eventually released in 1918. A number of events were held to mark the anniversary. The Prague Museum presented an exhibition, "Murder in Polna," stressing the anti-Semitic atmosphere that surrounded the Hilsner trial. A conference of historians and philosophers that discussed the Hilsner case at the end of November decided to send a letter to Austrian president Thomas Klestil asking for Hilsner's full rehabilitation.

Hungary

Hungary had one of the fastest growing economies in Central Europe, with an estimated GDP of over 4 percent in 1999. It entered NATO in March and, as the only NATO country to border on Yugoslavia, immediately found itself on the front lines of the conflict there. While stressing its loyalty to NATO, the government also had to be sensitive to the 300,000 ethnic Hungarians living in Yugoslavia. In July the European Jewish Congress, the Conference of European Rabbis, and the European Council of Synagogue Organizations sponsored a conference in Budapest for Jewish, Christian, and Muslim leaders from the former Yugoslavia and other Balkan countries to discuss how religious leaders could work to overcome hate in the region. The group set up a permanent interreligious committee to instill a spiritual dimension into reconstruction efforts for the war-torn region.

Jews were concerned throughout the year about anti-Semitism and xenophobia. In January chess legend Bobby Fischer launched into an anti-Semitic tirade during a live interview on Hungarian public radio. Fischer, 55, ignored questions about chess and claimed that Jews had invented the Holocaust to make money. When the interviewer asked why he was saying such things, since Fischer was himself Jewish, the former chess champion responded, "Shall we go to the toilets and prove it?" In the studio, he began waving around photocopies of checks and said, "Those damn Jews are persecuting me. They are ripping me off all the time." When a tape of the interview was later rebroadcast, Fischer's anti-Semitic comments were cut out. (It was reported in September that Laszlo and Klara Polgar, the parents of three Hungarian chess masters, were planning to live in Israel for half the year because of the rise of anti-Semitism in Hungary. One of their daughters already lived in Israel, and another was married to an Israeli.)

More worrying was the evident growth of political anti-Semitism expressed not just by skinheads and extremists, but by elements of the government and by mainstream parties and politicians. In February at least 600 neo-Nazis, including more than two dozen from outside Hungary, marched in Budapest, brandishing swastikas and giving the Nazi salute. In July police arrested two neo-Nazi skinheads in connection with the desecration of the Jewish cemetery in Szombathely, where swastikas and anti-Semitic slogans were scrawled on 15 graves. President Arpad Goncz denounced the incident. In October right-wing politicians unveiled a plaque honoring the Hungarian royal police who died during the two world wars. They did not mention that it was mainly these police who, after the German occupation in March 1944, carried out orders to round up Jews from the countryside and, in seven weeks, herded 437,000 Jews into ghettos and then deported them to death camps. In October Hungary was showcased at the Frankfurt Book Fair with a series of events, exhibits, and book presentations. Many Hungarian Jewish authors were represented, and the Hungarian Jewish Museum mounted an exhibition. Right-wing extremist politician Istvan Csurka attacked the event, claiming that Jewish writers were "overrepresented" in the exhibit and "only Hungary's Holocaust literature" was on display.

Also in October, the Hungarian government had to drop plans to revamp its exhibit at Auschwitz. To be sure, no one denied that the original needed revamping, since it had been mounted in the Soviet era and exalted Communism. Prime Minister Viktor Orban, who had pledged to modernize the exhibit if elected, allocated the equivalent of $230,000 for the task. In late summer a 73-page draft of the exhibition proposal was sent to the Jewish Museum, Jewish officials, and historians for feedback. A copy of the draft was leaked to a leading newspaper, which warned that implementation of the proposal would spark "a scandal from Washington to Tel Aviv" since it laid the blame for the Holocaust in Hungary on Germany's shoulders, ignoring the involvement of Hungarian fascists. Jewish leaders publicly charged the government with doctoring the historical record. In response to the furor, Orban dropped the Auschwitz project.

In August an obscure publisher released the first Hungarian edition of the *Protocols of the Elders of Zion* since the Holocaust, and two more editions were published during the year. Jewish leaders and antiracist civic organizations protested, accusing the publisher of inciting hatred against Jews. The publicity caused book sales to soar, reportedly from an initial press run of 3,000 into the tens of thousands. The Office of the Chief Prosecutor ruled that the book was intended to incite hatred, and in November police raided bookstores in Budapest and two provincial towns and confiscated copies. (In October a Hungarian edition appeared of *The Lie That Wouldn't Die*, by the Israeli jurist Hadassa Ben-Itto, debunking the *Protocols*.)

In September the Council of Europe branded two of the six parties in Hungary's National Assembly as "extremist." On October 15 alarmed Jewish leaders forwarded to the prime minister's office a legislative proposal, based on German and Austrian models, that would make fomenting intercommunal hatred a crime.

In November the Alliance of Jewish Communities in Hungary asked the government to take action against "fascist, racist, and anti-Semitic" outbreaks that were causing concern among the public. It specifically noted the planned rehabilitation of Laszlo Bardossy, Hungary's World War II prime minister, the desecration of Jewish cemeteries, and the publication of anti-Semitic books. It noted that Maria Schmidt, an adviser to Prime Minister Orban, had described the Holocaust as a marginal issue of the war. In December the Anti-Defamation League issued a report citing "increasingly virulent expressions of anti-Semitism, xenophobia and racism in Hungary, especially among extreme national and far-right politicians," and faulted Hungary's political leaders for not protesting. Government officials rejected the ADL analysis and maintained that extremism was a marginal phenomenon.

There was, to be sure, evidence of more positive developments. Three Hungarian-born British Jews raised £20,000 to restore the Jewish cemetery in their hometown of Kapuvar, and about 500 people attended the dedication ceremony in August. Restoration of the Orthodox community's large main synagogue in downtown Budapest neared completion, and other projects were under way.

In April a memorial to Raoul Wallenberg was unveiled in the Budapest neighborhood where the Swedish diplomat saved thousands of Jews during the Holocaust. In attendance were Budapest's mayor, the Hungarian chief rabbi, politicians, and many Jews, including survivors saved by Wallenberg. The monument was to have been unveiled 50 years earlier, in 1949, but Communist secret police confiscated it two days before the scheduled event. Since the early 1950s the monument, depicting a man wrestling with a snake, stood outside a pharmaceutical plant in the eastern city of Debrecen, which was bought by an Israeli firm in 1995. Istvan Csurka and other right-wing politicians questioned the need to erect the monument, the third in Budapest to honor Wallenberg. Then in June President Arpad Goncz attended the opening of an exhibition, supported by the Simon Wiesenthal Center, on diplomats who saved Jews from deportation. In December Hungary announced plans to renovate a disused Budapest synagogue and make it a Holocaust museum. The government will also finance the renovation of the synagogue, located on Pava Street, which was designed by Lipot Baumhorn and is owned by the Jewish community.

JEWISH COMMUNITY

Estimates of the number of Jews in Hungary ranged from 54,000 to 130,000. The latter figure would make the community the third largest in Europe (after France and Great Britain) outside the former Soviet Union. About 90 percent of Hungary's Jews lived in Budapest, the vast majority of them unaffiliated or secular. Only 6,000 or so were formally registered with the Jewish community and about 20,000 had some sort of affiliation with Jewish organizations or institutions. According to lists of contributions and other records—such as orders for matzo for Passover—at most about 8,000 families (many of which consisted of just one person) led an active religious life. The dominant religious affiliation was Neolog, similar to America's Conservative Judaism. There was a small Orthodox community made up of both modern Orthodox and Hassidim. Neolog communities were grouped in the Alliance of Jewish Communities in Hungary, while the Orthodox operated as the Autonomous Orthodox Community.

Sim Shalom, a 50-family Reform congregation established in Budapest in 1992, functioned outside these official umbrella structures. It was associated with the World Union of Progressive Judaism. This year Katalin Kelemen was ordained and took up her post as Hungary's first progressive rabbi. There was also an active Chabad-Lubavitch presence, which this year included the opening of a Chabad yeshivah with an enrollment of 25 students, most of them from abroad. In December the Chabad synagogue in Budapest was robbed of ritual objects worth tens of thousands of dollars, and the next day some of the objects turned up in an auction of Judaica.

At the end of the year research was completed on an in-depth survey of Hungary's Jewish community. It aimed to provide the first full-scale postwar demographic portrait of the community, and probe social, political, and religious attitudes, as well as lifestyle, identity, and behavioral patterns. Preliminary analysis of the results was expected in early 2000.

The Neolog community elected new officers early in the year. Businessman Peter Tordai was elected president of the Alliance of Hungarian Jewish Communities, and Tibor Lancz, also a businessman, was elected president of the Budapest Jewish Communities. Gusztav Zoltai was elected to a third, four-year term as executive director of both groups. Tordai introduced a seven-point "short-term executive program" to supervise and modernize the management of the community and inventory its real estate and other property. He stressed the importance of outreach to the unaffiliated, especially young people, and said that he would try to improve education and bolster communal institutions. A seven-member advisory board of experts and public figures was chosen to aid him.

In June, in a ceremony at Budapest's main Dohany Street synagogue, two new rabbis were ordained after graduating from Budapest's rabbinical seminary. These were the first ordinations in Hungary since the fall of Communism. One of the new rabbis, Tamas Vero, assumed the position of rabbi of the Ronald S. Lauder-Joint Distribution Committee International Jewish Camp at Szarvas in southern Hungary. This is where, each summer, some 2,000 Jewish young people from Hungary and neighboring countries spend two-week sessions participating in standard camping activities combined with Jewish education.

In addition to the rabbinical seminary, there were three Jewish day schools, a teachers college, and kindergartens operating in Budapest, with a total enrollment of 1,800 students. The day schools were the Scheiber Sandor community high school, the secular Ronald S. Lauder Javne School, and a downtown Orthodox school. Chabad also ran a kindergarten that extended into elementary grades. Budapest was the site of a conference on Jewish education in November, which drew teachers and Jewish school principals from all over Europe.

When NATO began bombing Yugoslavia in March, several hundred Yugoslav Jews took refuge in Budapest to sit out the war, at the invitation of Hungary's Jewish leaders. The offer was part of an unprecedented contingency plan worked out months before the bombing by Yugoslav and Hungarian Jewish leaders. The Budapest community conducted a seder for the earliest arrivals, about 140 Yugoslav Jews who came on the eve of Passover.

On the cultural front, the Balint Jewish Community Center, the site of many important cultural events, celebrated its fifth anniversary in 1999. The Budapest Jewish Museum mounted a major exhibition on the work of Lipot Baumhorn, Europe's most prolific prewar synagogue architect, and another exhibit on Hungarian Jews in Hollywood. The second annual festival of Jewish culture took place at the end of August.

Central European University in Budapest—founded in 1990 by philanthropist George Soros to serve the needs of a student body coming mainly from the former Communist states—actively promoted Jewish studies. In 1999 it sponsored regular public lectures on Jewish topics and a summer course in Jewish studies. At the beginning of the academic year Israeli scholar Yehuda Elkana, a Yugoslav-born survivor of Auschwitz, took up his post as the CEU's new rector. The press of the university released a major work, *Jewish Budapest: Monuments, Rites, History*, edited by Geza Komoroczy, the director of the Center of Jewish Studies at the Hungarian Academy of Sciences. The book was an English-language translation of the two-volume Hungarian edition, which came out in 1992 and 1994.

Restitution and compensation issues remained high priorities throughout the year. In December 1998, as part of the state budget, the National Assembly had allocated the equivalent of $120 for each parent killed in the Holocaust, and half that for each sibling. Jewish leaders made it clear to Prime Minister Orban that they considered such sums "shameful," "discriminatory," and "insulting," since they amounted to far less than the $4,500 that had been given to relatives of people killed or executed under Communism. In October evidence emerged that U.S. servicemen looted a train filled with the stolen property of Hungarian Jews toward the end of World War II. Hungarian Jewish leaders met in Budapest with U.S. officials to request return of this property.

Macedonia

Macedonia, with a population of two million, hosted more than 200,000 Kosovar refugees during the bombing of Kosovo. In April Israel set up a field hospital for refugees that operated for two weeks near the Macedonian capital, Skopje. It also contributed $100,000 worth of medicine to Macedonian relief, and took in a number of refugees. Macedonia itself was deeply affected by the conflict since 70 percent of its trade was with Yugoslavia, and the destruction of bridges over the Danube River effectively cut Macedonia off from the rest of Europe. In presidential elections on December 5, Boris Trajkovski of the center-right Internal Macedonian Revolutionary Organization defeated Social Democrat Tito Petkovski. Trajkovski's party was the senior partner in the governing coalition that emerged, which also included the Democratic Alternative and the Democratic Party of the Albanians. One-third of the population was ethnic Albanian.

The Macedonian Jewish community consisted of some 190 registered members from 52 families. Most lived in Skopje, but community leaders estimated that there were 200 to 300 unaffiliated Jews elsewhere in the country. Macedonian Jews had excellent relations with local authorities, but, like the Jews of Yugoslavia, they walked a diplomatic tightrope during the Kosovo conflict since every statement could be construed as a political gesture. Jewish community president Viktor Mizrahi joined Yugoslav Jewish leaders in denouncing the NATO bombings. At the end of June Mizrahi helped Eli Eliezri, a representative of the American Jewish Joint Distribution Committee (JDC), enter Kosovo and evacuate the leader of Pristina's Jewish community and his family to Skopje.

Despite the conflict, community members attempted to maintain normal lives. The rabbi from Belgrade visited once a month. Work began to build a synagogue on the top floor of the recently renovated Jewish center in Skopje. Classes in Jewish folk dancing were held regularly. Still, community leaders worried about the negative consequences of the ongoing instability in the region.

La Benevolencija Skopje, a Jewish social-service organization dedicated to non-sectarian humanitarian aid, was established at the end of June. It was modeled on La Benevolencija of Sarajevo, which provided nonsectarian aid in the besieged city during the war in Bosnia. The Skopje body dedicated itself to furnishing help to refugees from Kosovo who were still in camps or in private housing in Macedonia, as well as to Macedonian institutions that needed financial aid because of the conflict. Pledges to help fund the organization came from the JDC, the American Jewish Committee, the European Council of Jewish Communities, the Coordinating Committee of Belgian Jews, and the Union of Swiss Jews.

Poland

Though Poland's GDP dropped from 4.8 percent in 1998 to 4.1 percent in 1999, this was still one of the highest rates in Europe. Like Hungary and the Czech Republic, Poland entered NATO in March.

President Aleksander Kwasniewski made a state visit to Israel in January where he said that Poland was ready for a "new chapter" in its relations with the Jewish people.

Also in January, Poland marked its second annual Day of Judaism, a Catholic initiative designed to foster interfaith dialogue and education. A number of Polish churches included the theme in their services, and a million postcards bearing a photograph of Pope John Paul II together with Rome's chief rabbi, Elio loaff, were distributed in all the country's parishes. Leaders of Poland's Jewish community attended a Roman Catholic mass in Wroclaw celebrated by Bishop Stanislaw Gadecki, head of the Polish Church Commission for Interreligious Dialogue, and Gadecki and scores of other Catholic faithful attended Jewish services there.

These ceremonies, however, took place amid continuing tension over the hundreds of crosses that militant Catholics, led by the outspoken Kazimierz Switon, had erected at the site of the Auschwitz death camp in defiance of both the Catholic hierarchy and the Polish government. In addition, these militants had sometimes issued anti-Semitic statements. In May, with Pope John Paul II due to visit his native Poland the next month, the Polish government removed all but one of the crosses. The fate of the last cross, erected a decade earlier in honor of the pope, remained the subject of delicate negotiations. Switon was charged with inciting racial hatred.

In March the Polish government named Malgorzata Dzieduszycka, a former theater critic and Polish consul in Montreal, as its new roving ambassador to the Jewish Diaspora. She replaced Krzystof Sliwinski, who was the first person appointed to the unprecedented post that had been created in 1995 to improve the country's often-troubled relations with the world Jewish community.

Also in March a controversy over a planned housing complex on the site where 300,000 Jews were deported during the Holocaust was resolved. Warsaw's mayor agreed to turn over a different plot of land for the proposed complex, leaving the area around the Umschlagplatz free for the possible construction of a memorial. A monument stood at the Umschlagplatz since the late 1980s, but the site as a whole had not been maintained. In June the Pope stopped at the Umschlagplatz monument during his visit to Warsaw, part of his 13-day trip to his homeland. Visibly moved, he prayed in silence for at least five minutes, and then said, "Lord, hear our prayer for the Jewish nation, because its ancestry is very dear to you. Support it so that it receives respect and love from those who still do not understand the magnitude of its suffering."

There were some instances of vandalism at Jewish sites. On Rosh Hashanah, for example, several tombs of rabbis in Warsaw's historic Jewish cemetery were damaged.

Legislation came into effect in January that made Holocaust denial a crime in Poland. In the spring Dariusz Ratajczak, a 37-year-old historian from Opole, was suspended from his teaching post after issuing 320 copies of his book, *Dangerous Topics*, which presented the opinions of historians who deny that Zyklon B gas was used to kill Jews in Nazi death camps. In November Ratajczak went on trial before the Opole district court on charges of disseminating Holocaust denial. Ratajczak said he was not guilty since he had merely summarized the opinions of others without necessarily agreeing with them. The Ratajczak affair, considered the first real legal case involving Holocaust denial in Poland, became a rallying point for the extreme right. Ratajczak was accompanied in court by Kazimierz Switon, the leader of the movement to erect crosses at Auschwitz, and Leszek Bubel, a Switon associate who edited a revised edition of Ratajczak's book. On December 7 the court confirmed that Ratajczak had supported revisionist views about the Holocaust in his book, but said that this did not warrant punishment since the "social threat" was of a "low degree." The court noted that in the revised edition and in public appearances, Ratajczak had criticized revisionist views.

Prime Minister Jerzy Buzek made an official visit to Israel in December, where he and his Israeli counterpart, Ehud Barak, discussed the possibility of a joint defense project, and the deputy defense ministers of the two countries discussed Poland's cancellation, in 1998, of an $800-million arms purchase from Israel. An immediate result of the meetings was an agreement to end visa requirements between the two countries. During his stay Buzek met with Holocaust survivors on an Israeli kibbutz. He acknowledged lingering anti-Semitism in Poland, but pledged to fight it. He told the Polish News Agency PAP that the Israeli side had assured him it would oppose attempts to blame Poles for the Holocaust.

JEWISH COMMUNITY

This was a tumultuous year for Poland's emerging Jewish community. Estimates of the number of Jews in Poland ranged widely, from the 7,000–8,000 officially registered with the community or receiving aid from the JDC, to the 10,000–15,000 people of Jewish ancestry who had shown interest in rediscovering their heritage, to as many as 30,000–40,000 people with some Jewish ancestry.

The Lauder Foundation ran the country's most extensive Jewish educational programs. Each week 16 Jewish organizations used the premises of the Lauder Community Center in Warsaw for Jewish education. The foundation itself sponsored five youth clubs and education centers around Poland, including schools in Warsaw and Wroclaw, and supported the glossy monthly Jewish magazine *Midrasz*. In October it sponsored Poland's second postwar Jewish book fair. In that month, too, the Lauder Morasha School's state-of-the-art new campus opened in Warsaw, serving 165 pupils from kindergarten through 12th grade. Ronald Lauder and senior Polish government officials took part in the opening ceremonies. Hillary Rodham Clinton had already visited the school during a trip to Warsaw a week before the official opening.

The Jewish community had difficulty grappling with the gap left by the departure in 1998 of Rabbi Michael Schudrich, a charismatic American who, for over a decade, had been the director of the Lauder Foundation in Poland and a key catalyst for Jewish renewal. In March the Warsaw Jewish community hired its own rabbi, the Orthodox 25-year-old Baruch Rabinowicz. He was the first rabbi hired by the community in at least four decades, and the move was hailed as an important symbol of Jewish revival. Since the late 1980s Poland had been served by an elderly chief rabbi, Menachem Joskowicz, in addition to Schudrich. A Polish-born Hassid and an Auschwitz survivor, Joskowicz spent much of his time in Israel and was criticized for being out of touch with Polish Jewry. His Orthodoxy put him in conflict with the younger, more liberal Jewish leadership, and he demonstrated little sympathy for assimilated young Poles seeking to recover their Jewish roots, many of whom were the products of mixed marriages.

Joskowicz retired from his post in June, shortly after angering and embarrassing Poland's Jewish leaders by what they saw as the clumsy and disrespectful way he appealed to the visiting Pope John Paul to remove the one remaining cross standing outside Auschwitz. The Union of Jewish Communities in Poland issued a statement declaring that Joskowicz had spoken in a strictly personal capacity, not in the name of the Jewish community. Their complaint was not with what was said but the manner in which he said it. The incident reflected the deep changes, including generational changes, which had occurred in Polish Jewry in the past decade. It spotlighted the question of who should speak for Polish Jewry as well as the insistence of Poland's baby-boom generation of Jewish leaders on managing communal affairs on their own. This underlying ferment in the community was evident in intense, sometimes public, debates on Jewish identity. Local Jewish leaders also engaged in at-times heated negotiations with the World Jewish Restitution Organization on how restituted property or income from such property should be distributed.

Several other problems also demonstrated the growing pains of the emerging community. There was a financial scandal that forced the Union of Jewish Communities to fire its treasurer, Jakub Szadaj, who was also chairman of the Gdansk Jewish community, and downgrade the status of the Jewish communities in Gdansk and Poznan. The union's board cited "very serious financial irregularities" committed by Szadaj, as well as a "slanderous campaign" by Szadaj in the mainstream media against the board and other Jewish organizations. The problem had not been fully resolved by the end of the year.

Problems also arose regarding Rabbi Rabinowicz. In November, six months into his two-year contract, Rabinowicz resigned as rabbi of Warsaw. Community leaders greeted his departure with relief, as tensions regarding both style and substance had been mounting since his arrival. Most of the younger members of the Warsaw community, including its lay leaders—Jews with a secular or liberal orientation—were put off by Rabinowicz's Orthodoxy, as well as by his apparent timidity. Rabinowicz, on the other hand, complained that the community was fragmented and factionalized, and seemed unprepared to support a rabbi and other religious professionals in the traditional fashion. He had also been the target of taunts by local children, and on one or two occasions had had tomatoes thrown at him.

There were, as usual, cultural events, seminars, conferences, and exhibits on Jewish themes throughout the year. Some were sponsored by the Jewish community or Jewish institutions and directed toward the Jewish public. Others were sponsored by the Israeli embassy and other organizations, such as the Jewish Culture Center in Kraków, and directed to the public at large as well as Jews.

Kraków again held its annual summer festival of Jewish culture. In September, to mark the 60th anniversary of the outbreak of World War II, Yad Vashem held a conference in Warsaw, sponsored jointly with the Jewish Historical Institute in the city, on Europe under Nazi rule and the Holocaust. This was the first time that Yad Vashem had ever held a conference outside Israel. Also in September, the town of Plonsk, where David Ben-Gurion was born, held a Jewish culture week at which prizes were awarded in the international essay competition that Plonsk authorities had sponsored on the topic of Polish Jewish remembrance. On November 25 the University of Humanities in Pultusk, in cooperation with the Israeli embassy, celebrated "Israel Day" with lectures about Israeli history, society, culture, and Jewish traditions, displays of books and photographs, and Israeli dancing. There was an Israeli film festival in Warsaw in early December.

The formal groundbreaking for the restoration and expansion of the only surviving synagogue in Auschwitz, the town in southern Poland near the death camp, and the creation there of an information center as well as a place for prayer and Jewish study, occurred in early November. The old synagogue, used for years as a carpet warehouse, had been returned to the community in 1998. Participants — including local bishop Tadeusz Rakoczy, former speaker of the Knesset and Holocaust survivor Shevach Weiss, and visiting American Jews — donned souvenir hardhats and buried stones from Jerusalem in a corner of the sanctuary. The $10-million project was conceived and sponsored by the New York-based Auschwitz Jewish Center Foundation, founded in 1995 by businessman and philanthropist Fred Schwartz. A Torah scroll donated by a Long Island congregation was placed in the synagogue during the summer in a joyous celebration.

Romania

Romania continued to suffer economic, social, and political problems. The average wage was only $80 a month, the 1999 inflation rate was 55 percent, and workers staged numerous protests and strikes over working conditions and living standards. Polls taken in the fall, as the country prepared to mark the tenth anniversary of the overthrow and execution of dictator Nicolae Ceauşescu, indicated that many Romanians were nostalgic for the Ceauşescu era: As many as two-thirds felt they were better off under Communism. Nonetheless, on December 10 the European Union invited Romania, along with five other states, to talks about joining the EU. On December 13 President Emil Constantinescu dismissed Radu Vasile from his post as prime minister. Under the constitution, however, the president does not have the authority to dismiss the prime minister, and Vasile refused to resign for several days. Constantinescu justified the dismissal on the grounds that the government had become paralyzed after most of its ministers resigned. Vasile was eventually forced to step down, and Mugur Isarescu, governor of the National Bank, was named prime minister.

Some Romanians were nostalgic not just for the Ceauşescu regime, but for the

World War II fascists, including pro-Nazi leader Ion Antonescu, and the Iron Guard, the fascist organization that terrorized Romanians and Jews before and during World War II. On November 30 about 100 people, most of them elderly, held a ceremony in a forest near Bucharest to mark the anniversary of the death of Corneliu Zelea Codreanu, the first head of the Iron Guard. The ceremony took place at the spot where Codreanu was shot dead in 1938 on orders of King Carol II. Some wept openly as the group sang fascist songs, some gave the Nazi salute, and an Orthodox priest led a brief service.

On December 2, B'nai B'rith International president Richard D. Heideman sent a letter to President Constantinescu calling on him to combat the continuing campaign to honor Antonescu. He noted that, after 11 unsuccessful attempts, the mayor and city council of Cluj had cleared the way for the erection of a statue of Antonescu on public land. This followed the decision of Timisoara, another Romanian city, to name a main street for Antonescu. Heideman wrote that his organization was "particularly disturbed" that two of Constantinescu's coalition partners, the National Peasant Christian and Democratic Party and the National Liberal Party, voted with the far-right Romania Mare Party to permit Cluj to erect the statue.

JEWISH COMMUNITY

About 12,000 Jews were known to live in Romania, most of them elderly. About half lived in the capital, Bucharest, and the rest were scattered in more than 40 communities around the country. Fewer than 700 Romanian Jews were under the age of 35 and fewer still were middle-aged adults. Two rabbis served the country, an elderly rabbi in Timisoara and a chief rabbi in Bucharest, Menachem Hakohen, who spent most of his time in Israel and visited Romania every month or so. Educational, religious, and welfare programs were carried out by the Federation of Romanian Jewish Communities (FEDROM), funded by the JDC. The economic problems in the country had induced hundreds of elderly Jews who never had contact with the community to step forward and join in order to be eligible for welfare benefits and emigration to Israel. Non-Jews, too, attempted to join the Jewish community for the same reasons, compelling Rabbi Hakohen to tape a sign to his door: "We do not convert people to Judaism."

The Lauder Foundation ran the Lauder Re'ut Kindergarten and Lower School in Bucharest. It was considered one of the best schools in the city, and many non-Jews sent their children there. The Jewish publishing house HaSefer issued books on Jewish themes, and a biweekly Jewish newspaper, *Realitatea Evreiasca*, included pages in Hebrew and English as well as Romanian. In October, the Moshe Carmilly Institute for Hebrew and Jewish History at Babes-Bolyai University in Cluj held its annual conference on Jewish studies. An institute for Jewish studies also operated in Craiova.

For decades the pattern of Jewish life in Romania had been to encourage aliyah among young people and, with the support of the JDC, to make sure that the elderly who wanted to stay lived out their lives in dignity. At the end of October, however, Romanian Jewish leaders sought to reverse this pattern and approved plans for an ambitious and unprecedented program of outreach and leadership development. This entailed revamping the educational system, developing clubs and cultural and recreational activities for children, teenagers, and university students, and reaching out to unaffiliated adults.

There were episodes of vandalism against Jewish cemeteries during the year. Tombstones were smashed in Alba Iulia in February and in Satu Mare and Resita in November.

Slovakia

In May, Rudolf Schuster, the popular mayor of the eastern city of Kosice and the candidate of Slovakia's pro-Western government, was elected to a five-year term as president in the country's first direct presidential election. He soundly defeated Vladimir Meciar, the authoritarian former prime minister who was voted out of office in 1998. Slovakia had been without a president since Michal Kovac's term expired in March 1998. Parliament, which had the responsibility of appointing a president, had been unable to agree on a successor to Kovac, and the choice was put to a direct vote. Schuster's election was seen as strengthening the new democratic image of Slovakia that had come with the 1998 election of Mikulas Dzurinda as prime minister. A further step in this process occurred in December, when Slovakia was one of six countries invited by the European Union to begin talks about joining.

Nonetheless, racism and xenophobia, directed particularly against Roma (Gypsies), was a constant concern. In December, meeting at a human-rights conference in Bratislava, representatives of Poland, the Czech Republic, Slovakia, and Hungary asked the European Union to help them resolve the social problems of the region's Romany population since this was an issue "of European dimensions." An opinion poll conducted by the TNS polling institute and published in December showed that 60.4 percent of Slovaks said they favored separating the country's Romany minority from the majority population, including separate schools. Earlier in December Slovakia's deputy prime minister for minorities, human rights, and regional development met with journalists to announce the publication of the first textbook on Roma history to be used in Slovak schools.

A survey gauging knowledge about the Holocaust, feelings about Holocaust remembrance, attitudes toward Jews and other minorities, and awareness of the Slovak Jewish experience was conducted for the American Jewish Committee at the beginning of September. More than three-fifths of the respondents favored keeping the remembrance of the Holocaust alive. The great majority of Slovaks knew some of the basic facts of the Holocaust, 81 percent correctly identifying Auschwitz, Dachau, and Treblinka as concentration camps and 78 percent citing the yellow star or a variant as the symbol that Jews were forced to wear. But only

24 percent, in a multiple-choice format, selected "six million" as the approximate number of Jews killed by the Nazis during the Second World War; 42 percent chose much lower figures.

Slovaks demonstrated mixed attitudes toward Jews. Only 9 percent believed that Jews "behave in a manner which provokes hostility" in Slovakia and 15 percent thought that Jews have too much influence in the country. But 53 percent believed (23 percent "strongly") that "Jews exert too much influence on world events" and 25 percent (7 percent "strongly") that Jews were exploiting the memory of the Holocaust for their own purposes. As for Slovak involvement in the Holocaust, 49 percent agreed (19 percent "strongly") that Slovak leaders bore a share of the responsibility, 19 percent disagreed (5 percent "strongly"), and fully 30 percent said they did not know—a breakdown almost identical to the responses given to the same question in a 1993 survey. As was the case in the AJC survey of the Czech Republic, those with more education tended to know more about the Holocaust and cared more about keeping its memory alive.

Slovakia and Israel kept up their extensive diplomatic and commercial contacts, and tourism between the two countries remained at a high level. In the fall an Israeli-run fertility and assisted-conception clinic opened in the capital city of Bratislava.

JEWISH COMMUNITY

Fewer than 4,000 Jews were known to live in Slovakia, though there were surely other nonaffiliated or nonidentifying Jews. The two largest communities were in Bratislava, home to 500–800 Jews, and in the eastern city of Kosice, which had about 700. Both had a rabbi and a kosher restaurant, Jewish classes, clubs, and other activities. The Ohel David old-age home, which opened at the end of 1998, functioned in Bratislava, where there was also a new Holocaust documentation center. Smaller Jewish communities functioned in about a dozen other towns. All came under the umbrella of the Union of Jewish Religious Communities head-quartered in Bratislava. There were Jewish museums in Bratislava and Presov, and an Institute of Jewish Studies in Bratislava. Restoration work was under way at several Jewish cemeteries and synagogues around the country. In July a landmark agreement was reached between the Bratislava Jewish community, the Bratislava municipality, and the New York-based International Committee for the Preservation of the Gravesites of Geonai Pressburg, for the reconstruction of the tombs of the revered 19th-century rabbinic scholar Hatam Sofer and other sages. The tombs are located underground, and the project entails rerouting a major city tramline and building a prayer house. The reconstruction was to be completed in 2001. On a brief visit to Bratislava in October, Hillary Rodham Clinton visited both the old-age home and Hatam Sofer's tomb. In November the government passed legislation to compensate World War II victims.

In Bratislava, American-born Chabad rabbi Baruch Myers published a newsletter, *Keser,* in Slovak and English. He ran adult classes ranging from basic prayers to the Kabbalah, as well as seminars, including a two-day seminar in June on Jewish feminism and the role of women in Jewish law. There was a Sunday school for children aged 6–11 and a kindergarten cosponsored with the Lauder Foundation and taught by Myers's wife. Holidays were celebrated with communal activities, and some 30 children attended a two-week summer camp in July. More than 100 people attended a Purim party on March 2, which featured the local Pressburger Klezmer band and "all you can drink" beer donated by the Stein brewery. On Passover more than 100 people attended communal seders, at a local hotel on the first night and at the Myers home on the second night. There was also a model matzo bakery for children. On the holiday of Lag b'Omer, in May, more than 150 people attended a bonfire party that coincided with the *opsherenish*, or first haircutting ceremony, for the Myers's 3-year-old son.

Yugoslavia

Thanks to an arrangement made by Yugoslav and Hungarian Jewish leaders, as many as 500 of Yugoslavia's 3,500 Jews, most of them elderly people, women, and children, were able to leave Yugoslavia for neighboring Hungary during the four-month NATO bombing campaign, which began in March. About 200 of these people then went on to Israel.

Those who remained in Yugoslavia shared the same fears, hardships, and concerns as their Serbian neighbors during the bombing. Electric power and water were cut, bombs and missiles destroyed buildings, roads, and bridges, air-raid sirens sent people running for shelters, and food and other consumer goods were either rationed or in short supply. Throughout the NATO campaign, however, Yugoslav Jewry's strong central organization helped sustain a semblance of normality for community members, two-thirds of whom lived in Belgrade. Contingency measures had been adopted months before, including stockpiling medicine and other essentials and providing for the temporary housing of people unable or afraid to stay in their homes. Regular communal activities that ceased for the first month of the bombings resumed thereafter, though only during daylight hours: the Maccabi sports club met, the Jewish choir held rehearsals, and the monthly community newsletter, *Bilten,* did not miss an issue. Community leaders in Belgrade maintained daily phone contact with the eight smaller communities in the provinces, including the tiny Jewish community of Pristina, the capital of Kosovo.

Most of Yugoslavia's Jews, though not strong supporters of the Milosevic regime, tended to share the Serbian view of the bombing, and thus felt quite isolated from the rest of the Jewish world. They complained about "one-sided" support by foreign Jews and Jewish organizations for the Kosovar refugees and the NATO bombing. Some Belgrade Jews expressed disappointment that the Israeli ambassador left Yugoslavia shortly after the beginning of the air strikes.

At the end of May, Misa David, a leader of the Belgrade Jewish community, and Aca Singer, president of the Federation of Jewish Communities in Yugoslavia, got permission from Yugoslav military authorities to attend the General Assembly of the European Council of Jewish Communities, held in Nice. At the meeting, attended by 600 Jewish representatives from all over Europe, they issued an appeal for an end to the bombing.

Once peace was restored, the JDC and other Jewish aid organizations tried to help the community face its uncertain future. The first priority was bringing home the Jews who had sat out the war in Budapest. Other necessary tasks were arranging emergency cash relief for the elderly, including as many as 800 destitute Holocaust survivors; arranging shipments of medicine to replenish the pharmacy in Belgrade, which was set up long before the conflict and was maintained by World Jewish Relief; refurbishing the kitchen in the Belgrade community and opening soup kitchens there and in Novi Sad; and expanding non-sectarian medical aid for the sick and wounded in the Pristina hospital and for autistic children in Belgrade.

Before the bombing some 40 Jews were known to be living in the Kosovo capital of Pristina. At the end of June only seven were there. The leader of Pristina's Jewish community, Chedar Prlincevic, and his family had been evacuated to Skopje, Macedonia, after armed men — apparently rogue paramilitaries operating on their own — entered their home and ordered them to leave town, presumably because they identified the Serbian-speaking Prlincevic family as Serb. In the aftermath of the bombing, a small group of Albanian-speaking Jews was identified in the Kosovo town of Prizren.

When the conflict was over Jews shared with fellow Yugoslavs the hardships brought on by the devastated economy. In Belgrade a Jewish business club met every two weeks in the hope of developing a coordinated plan for small-business owners to provide jobs to the unemployed. In November and December JDC-supported soup kitchens began operating in the three largest Jewish communities of Belgrade, Novi Sad, and Subotica. Problems were reported in finding vehicles that could distribute meals to the homebound sick and elderly. In December, at the annual assembly of the Federation of Jewish Communities in Yugoslavia, President Aca Singer described the situation of Jewish refugees from Kosovo as still "very difficult and uncertain."

RUTH ELLEN GRUBER

Former Soviet Union

National Affairs

Boris Yeltsin, president of the Russian Federation, chose the last day of the year, the century, and the millennium to make one of his characteristically surprising announcements—he was resigning. Prime Minister Vladimir Putin, in office only since August, became acting president, instantly gaining the leading position in the race for the presidency, with the election to be held on March 26, 2000.

Yeltsin had been Communist Party secretary in his native Sverdlovsk region before joining the central leadership in Moscow. A major rival of the last Soviet leader, Mikhail Gorbachev, he had weathered many political storms, including an armed confrontation with a recalcitrant parliament in 1993, a presidential election, a two-year war in Chechnya, and continuous economic crisis and political upheaval. As the economy spiraled downward and Yeltsin was often incapacitated by health problems, his popularity plummeted. Whereas in the late 1980s many Russians were fascinated and energized by new freedoms and political opportunities, a decade later the mood had turned apathetic, cynical, and despairing.

A nationwide survey taken in July 1999 showed only 3 percent of the population expressing confidence in Yeltsin. When Putin succeeded Sergei Stepashin as prime minister in August, 56 percent of a nationwide sample said they "felt nothing in particular" about the latest leadership change. Indeed, the Russian people had seen four prime ministers come and go within 14 months. Back in May, Stepashin had replaced Yevgeny Primakov, one of the most popular politicians in the Russian Federation. The next day the Duma (lower house of the parliament) began debating the impeachment of Yeltsin on five counts—conspiring to break up the USSR, overthrowing the constitutional order in 1993, launching war against Chechnya, undermining the defense of the country, and committing genocide against the Russian people through harmful economic reforms. None of the five charges got the necessary 300 affirmative votes, and Yeltsin, like his American counterpart earlier in the year, survived impeachment.

Three key problems shook confidence in Yeltsin's ability to govern and undermined his hold on power: economic crisis, which profoundly affected the lives of the Russian people; corruption, which ranged from petty schemes to scandals reaching into his own family; and Islamic terrorism and militancy, which spread from Chechnya into Dagestan, and even to Moscow and other Russian cities.

In 1998 the Gross Domestic Product of Russia had fallen by 5 percent, and it continued to decline in 1999. Inflation was calculated at 55 percent. The number of people officially categorized as living in poverty rose from 33 million in 1998 to 55 million in 1999. The newspaper *Argumenty i fakty* (No. 21) calculated that if one pegged the amount of goods and services consumed by an "average" American at 100, the average consumption in Russia would be 17.7, in Latvia 16, in Belarus 14.3, in Ukraine 10.3, and in Moldova 7.7. The average wage in Russia was $50 a month—and millions of employees were not being paid on time—while the average monthly pension was $17. The Communist-dominated Duma continued to block legislation that would permit the buying and selling of land, protect foreign investments, and overhaul a distorted and inefficient tax system.

One consequence of the economic crisis was a continuing population decline. From 1992 till 1998 the population of the Russian Federation dropped by two million. In the year 1998 alone it declined by 600,000, and in the first half of 1999 by another 406,000 to a total of 146 million. If not for migration into Russia by people from other successor states of the USSR, the decline would have been even sharper. There were twice as many abortions as births; one of every five families had only one parent; and a quarter of all births were out of wedlock. Drug use was increasing among the young, and their health was declining.

One study found that there were 950 single-industry towns in Russia, and these were home to 25 million people, nearly a fifth of the population. Those towns had very high unemployment, leading many of the inhabitants to resort to subsistence farming. It was also in these places that Vladimir Zhirinovsky, leader of the anti-Semitic, extreme nationalist Liberal Democratic Party, and Viktor Anpilov, head of the Stalin Bloc for the USSR, received very high levels of support.

Widespread economic despair was compounded by the cynicism of the economic and political elites. For example, money that the International Monetary Fund had loaned Russia was transferred by the Russian Central Bank to a secret offshore financial firm. Yeltsin's immediate family was said to have received huge economic favors from Swiss companies doing business in Russia, and one of Putin's first decisions as acting president was to grant Yeltsin and his family immunity from prosecution. The Bank of New York was exposed as being heavily involved in laundering millions of dollars coming out of Russia, not only from criminal elements, but, presumably, from businessmen and high government officials as well. Several employees of the bank, Jewish émigrés from the former Soviet Union (FSU), were dismissed for their involvement in these schemes, though it was later shown that some of them were innocent.

A two-year war in Chechnya had ended in 1996, but in 1999 Islamic forces from that region infiltrated into bordering Dagestan, a multinational region in the northern Caucasus with many Muslims. Under the leadership of Shamil Basayev, a Chechen, and "Khattab," a Chechen reputed to have been born in Jordan, these forces seized several villages in Dagestan in the late summer till they were chased out by federal troops. In September, within less than three weeks, five apartment houses in Moscow and other cities were blown up, killing over 300 people and injuring many more. It was widely assumed that this was the work of Islamic militants. The Russian air force began massive bombardment of Chechnya in late September, causing hundreds to flee to neighboring Ingushetia. When Russian troops proceeded to capture major Chechen towns and close in on the capital of Grozny in December, Prime Minister Putin's popularity, as measured in the opinion polls, soared, propelling him from obscurity into the forefront of the candidates to succeed Boris Yeltsin as president.

In the political jockeying that preceded the elections to the Duma in December, former prime minister Yevgeny Primakov allied himself with Yuri Luzhkov, mayor of Moscow, in a "Fatherland-All Russia" coalition. Three other former prime ministers—Sergei Stepashin, Viktor Chernomyrdin, and Sergei Kirienko—also formed a joint electoral bloc. Zhirinovsky's xenophobic Liberal Democratic Party was disqualified because too many of the candidates on its list were either convicted criminals or under police investigation; rumor had it that he had sold places on his list to those seeking parliamentary immunity from criminal prosecution. Zhirinovsky himself managed to maintain his candidacy for president. With 28 parties and movements running in the election, the Communist Party once again emerged as the most popular, garnering 24 percent of the vote. In a big surprise, a list hastily put together and backed by Putin managed to get 23 percent, signaling significant public approval of Putin and his aggressive handling of Chechnya. Fatherland-All Russia got only 13 percent, and Kirienko's Union of Right Wing Forces only 9 percent.

In other former Soviet states with significant Jewish populations, President Leonid Kuchma was reelected president of Ukraine after four rivals, who had united to oppose him, split up the following day. In Belarus, President Aleksandr Lukashenka stepped up his repression of political opponents. Some disappeared without a trace, others were jailed, and still others took refuge in neighboring countries or in the United States. Police suppressed mass demonstrations against the government.

Israel and the Middle East

Israeli foreign minister Ariel Sharon visited Moscow in January in the hope of persuading his hosts to end Russia's cooperation with Iran on dual-use technologies. In March, Prime Minister Benjamin Netanyahu made a whirlwind tour of Kiev, Tbilisi, and Moscow in what many interpreted as an attempt to win the votes of Soviet immigrants in Israel. (As it turned out, the victorious Ehud Barak won more of that immigrant vote in the May 17 election than Netanyahu.) While in Moscow, Netanyahu reiterated Israel's worries about the supply of Russian technology and expertise to Iran. In August, Ehud Barak, now the Israeli prime minister, arrived in Moscow, where President Yeltsin greeted him warmly. Barak said that Russia could play a leading role in the Middle East peace process, and Yeltsin promised to "fight anti-Semitism together." Like the other visiting Israeli officials before him, Barak asked Yeltsin to reconsider plans to transfer nuclear and missile technology to Iran, and also requested that he intervene on behalf of 13 Iranian Jews arrested in April. There were rumors in Moscow that the wealthy and politically well-connected Vladimir Gusinsky had contributed heavily to Barak's election campaign, and that Barak had asked Yeltsin to persuade the Russian government to ease its "attacks" on Gusinsky's Most bank. Journalist Zakhar Gelman claimed that Israel supported Russia's attacks on Chechnya and had contributed funds and medical aid to the refugees fleeing the republic, thus helping relieve the burden on the Russian government and, by encouraging the population to flee, depriving the Chechen fighters of logistical support and hiding places.

Anti-Semitism

There were several attacks on Jewish institutions over the course of the year. In May a large unexploded bomb was found at Moscow's Bol'shaya Bronnaya Synagogue. Bombs did go off near two Moscow synagogues on May 1, and the synagogue in Birobidzhan in the Jewish Autonomous Oblast in Siberia was vandalized twice in five days. Ten swastikas were formed out of stones in the yard, and windows and a menorah were smashed. Also in Siberia, the synagogue in Novosibirsk was vandalized and symbols of the neo-Nazi Russian National Union (RNU) daubed on its walls. The RNU organized a march in Moscow in January and was active in Belarus and Latvia as well. On February 5 the prosecutor of Moscow's northern administrative district dropped proceedings that had been initiated against RNU leader Aleksandr Barkashov. In July, outside the Choral Synagogue in Moscow, a student stabbed and seriously wounded 52-year-old Leopold Kaimovsky, commercial director of a Jewish arts center. According to one report, the assailant, Nikita Krivchun, was wearing a swastika on his chest. Anti-Semitic pamphlets were disseminated in the Kirov region and in Krasnodar, southern Russia.

General Albert Makashov, a Communist deputy in the Duma who had caused a sensation by making public anti-Semitic statements in late 1998, caused a stir once again in February 1999 by stating that "The reason Jews are so insolent . . . is that none of us has yet knocked on their door, none of us has yet pissed on their windows." Of his "Movement to Support the Army" he defiantly said: "We will be anti-Semites and we will triumph." Communist Party leader Gennady Zyuganov refused to condemn Makashov's sentiments. The prosecutor of the Rostov region said that Makashov's remarks contained "nothing prejudicial," and the federal Duma refused, in March, to put a resolution on its agenda condemning the statements. Instead, the Duma adopted a resolution asserting that those responsible for "political extremism" were "a number of television channels, certain press publications, and the forces behind them." Nevertheless, Yuri Skuratov, the prosecutor general of Russia (dismissed from office the next month for unrelated reasons), initiated criminal proceedings against Makashov under

Article 282 of the Criminal Code of Russia, which categorizes the incitement of ethnic, racial, or religious hostility as a crime. Then in August, "Civil Control," a watchdog organization in St. Petersburg, asked the prosecutor's office to initiate criminal proceedings against a local television station which, it charged, had an "overt anti-Semitic orientation" and had invited viewers to take part in polls asking whether "ethnic purges should be carried out in St. Petersburg."

The U.S.-based Anti-Defamation League commissioned a Russian polling firm to survey attitudes on anti-Semitism in the country, and over 1,500 people were interviewed in May and June. The survey concluded that 44 percent of the respondents held views "that would be considered anti-Semitic by most analysts," as compared to 12 percent of an American sample that were asked the same questions in 1998. The report noted that anti-Semitic attitudes were spread more widely through the population of the Russian Federation than in the United States, where anti-Semitism tended to be concentrated within specific groups. Russian respondents were most critical of what they saw as Jewish clannishness, power, and unethical behavior. Men over 45, Communist Party members, and men with no higher education tended to be more anti-Semitic than other Russians. Many observers, however, questioned the value of the survey, since the questions seemed based on American conceptions of anti-Semitism that were not necessarily applicable to Russia. For example the notion that "Jews, more than other groups, support each other," which may have had anti-Jewish connotations in the U.S., could have been interpreted as a positive attribute in Russia.

Holocaust-Related Developments

The government of Lithuania continued to avoid prosecuting Nazi war criminals who had been deported from the United States to the land of their birth. Though the government did bring legal action against Vincas Valkavickas, who had left the United States before he could be deported for complicity in Nazi war crimes and returned to Lithuania, it delayed the trials of several others. Kazys Ciurinskas, who had led a battalion involved in the mass killings of Jews and others, was deported by the American authorities in May. The Lithuanian prosecutor's office said it had been collecting information on Ciurinskas for two years but had "insufficient evidence to launch proceedings against him." Kazys Gimzauskas, a 90-year-old accused of handing Jews over to execution squads when he was deputy police chief in Vilnius, did not attend the opening of his trial since, his lawyer said, he was too old to do so. No trial had taken place by the end of the year. Similarly, the trial of Aleksandras Lileikis, Gimzauskas's superior, was suspended pending medical tests to determine whether he was fit to stand trial.

On a visit to Vilnius on January 14, Dan Tichon, the speaker of the Israeli Knesset, said that Lithuania should be "more vigorous" in prosecuting Nazi war criminals. The U.S. Department of Justice also criticized the continuing postponements of these trials. At an official event in Vilnius on June 21, Oded Ben-Hur, Israel's ambassador to Lithuania, charged that the country had become a paradise for war criminals, and criticized the commission established by President Valdas Adamkus to investigate both Nazi and Soviet war crimes. Lithuanian politicians protested and suggested that Israel replace Ben-Hur. In September, President Adamkus claimed that Lithuania "firmly supports the further prosecution of those who participated in Nazi war crimes" and insisted that the postponement of trials "should not be interpreted in any way as a weakening of the Lithuanian government's resolve to bring those who are guilty of such crimes to justice."

In March the Latvian Parliament voted to retain the celebration of March 16 as Latvian Soldiers Day, even though veterans of the Latvian Waffen-SS marked the occasion as commemorating the day they first went into combat against the Soviet army. Jewish leaders said they would boycott the celebrations and defy the law requiring all buildings to display the Latvian flag on that day.

JEWISH COMMUNITY

Emigration

There was a dramatic rise in Jewish emigration from the FSU in 1999, probably due to the deepening economic crisis and to the anti-Semitic outbursts of Albert Makashov that began in late 1998. 72,372 Jews (and their non-Jewish first-degree relatives) left in 1999, an increase of about a third over 1998, when 53,720 emigrated. Of the 1999 total, 66,190 went to Israel and only 6,182 to the United States (7,347 came to the U.S. in 1998). Some claimed that the decline in immigration to the U.S. was due to the expense and difficulty of getting to Moscow for the required personal interview. Of all the Jewish emigration from the FSU, the Russian Federation showed the largest percentage increase, more than doubling from 13,019 in 1998 to 29,534 in 1999. Within the Russian Federation, Jewish emigration was especially large from the areas hardest hit economically—the Russian Far East, the Urals, and northern Russia.

Among the immigrants arriving in Israel, only 11 percent were over 65 years old and nearly a quarter were younger than 24. For the first time since 1995, Russia accounted for nearly half the immigrants from the FSU to Israel. The proportion of non-Jews among the immigrants—according to the criteria of Israel's Ministry of the Interior—reached about half in 1999. In November, 18 veteran Soviet immigrants in Israel, several of them prominent former "refuseniks," issued a statement asking the Israeli government to limit the number of non-Jews allowed to settle in Israel. And on the floor of the Knesset, Shas deputy Shlomo

Benizri not only attacked the non-Jewish immigrants but went so far as to criticize the post-Soviet immigration as a whole as being full of "prostitutes, criminals and goyim."

Communal Affairs

In April Vadim Rabinovich, a leading businessman in Ukraine, convened over 1,600 delegates in Kiev to found the United Jewish Communities of Ukraine, which was intended to serve as an umbrella organization and national representative for Ukraine's nearly 300,000 Jews. Popular singer Iosif Kobzon was elected honorary chairman of the organization. Rabinovich, who owned a four-story building in central Kiev that housed the offices of many Jewish organizations, claimed to have succeeded in gaining back for the Jewish community the building of the famed Brodsky Synagogue, which had been confiscated decades earlier by the Soviet government and was being used to house a puppet theater. However in June, Ukraine's State Security Service (SBU) barred Rabinovich from entering Ukraine for five years because of his supposed ties to organized crime, especially to Leonid Wolf, a Ukrainian immigrant to Israel. The U.S. had previously refused to issue Rabinovich a visitor's visa for the same reason. Rabinovich retorted that he was being framed by Volodymyr Horbulin, chairman of the National Security and Defense Council and a politician close to President Kuchma. Three prominent Ukrainian Jewish leaders—Iosif Zissels of the Va'ad, Chief Rabbi Yaacov Bleich, and Ilya Levitas—set up an alternative umbrella organization, which they called the Jewish Confederation of Ukraine.

In Russia, the Russian Jewish Congress (RJC) was clearly the most powerful national Jewish organization. Backed by some of Russia's "oligarchs"—wealthy and politically connected businessmen and bankers—it had a 1999 budget of $2.6 million. The RJC had representation in 45 cities and was said to have distributed $5.2 million outside of Moscow over the previous three years. Vladimir Gusinsky and Boris Khait, two "oligarchs," were said to be contributing 60 percent of the RJC's budget. In the late 1980s Gusinsky had become close to Yuri Luzhkov, then deputy chairman of the Moscow city soviet, and was put in charge of the burgeoning cooperative movement in that city. After winning contracts to restore some municipal buildings, in 1989 he founded the Most bank, which did a lot of business with the city of Moscow. Gusinsky controlled the Media-Most conglomerate that owned the NTV television network, the *Ekho Moskvy* radio station, the daily newspaper *Segodnya*, and other holdings.

Gusinsky's chief rival was Boris Berezovsky, a confidant and strong supporter of President Yeltsin. Berezovsky had started his career as an academic mathematician, but had become perhaps Russia's wealthiest businessman. At one point he took out Israeli citizenship but was forced to give it up when he became secretary general of the Commonwealth of Independent States. Yeltsin dismissed him from this post in March. Though Berezovsky was rumored to have converted to Russian Orthodoxy, he was still widely perceived as Jewish. Berezovsky controlled a television network (ORT), three newspapers (*Komersant, Nezavisemaya gazeta,* and *Noviye izvestiia*), a major oil company (Sibneft), and a net of automobile distributorships (Avtovaz). He also had a controlling interest in Aeroflot, a major airline. While Evgeny Primakov was prime minister, charges of embezzlement and other criminal activities were lodged against Berezovsky and a warrant was issued for his arrest. Berezovsky left the country for a while and returned to announce that he would run for the Duma from one of the national regions of the Russian Federation.

In November a new national organization came into being. Calling itself the Federation of Jewish Communities and apparently dominated by Chabad-Lubavitch, it quickly arranged for a meeting with Vladimir Putin.

In December, the Russian Va'ad (Federation of Jewish Organizations and Communities in Russia) held its third congress in Moscow, with 117 delegates from 57 localities. They represented religious, cultural, welfare, educational, and social organizations said to encompass 23,000 active members, and to reach about 52,000 others who occasionally participated in their activities.

On the local level, the American Jewish Joint Distribution Committee (JDC) continued to play a major role in funding and organizing educational, cultural and welfare activities, with the staffing increasingly being taken over by local people. The network of organizations providing assistance to the elderly, poor, and disabled grew apace, and their personnel were becoming more professional.

To cite one example, Penza, a city southeast of Moscow, was a typical small Jewish community. In the late 1980s a couple from Penza visited Moscow and contacted one of the first Jewish organizations that had emerged there during perestroika. Upon their return to Penza they founded a Jewish cultural club, Hatikvah. Then they struggled, successfully, to have the local synagogue, built at the turn of the century and sequestered by the Soviet government in 1931, returned to the local Jews. It now serves as headquarters for local Jewish organizations, including a choir, a handicrafts club, a Yiddish study circle, and a welfare organization, Hesed Mordechai. The latter, operating with 50 volunteers servicing 590 clients, provides medicines and serves meals to needy people five times a week. A supplementary school that meets five days a week has 48 pupils who study Jewish history and traditions, and the Hebrew language. Among the other organizations in the community are a Hillel group, a club for war veterans, and youth groups. Several holidays are celebrated communally. There is a Hebrew *ulpan* (intensive language program) and a "distance learning" arrangement with the Open University of Israel.

Education and Culture

The Institute for Jewish Education of the Petersburg Jewish University surveyed Jewish education in the FSU in 1997–98. It found 51 Jewish day schools—

19 in Russia and 16 in Ukraine—with a total of 10,700 students and nearly 1,600 teachers, including teachers of general studies. In 1992–93 there had been only 28 schools. The survey found 213 Sunday schools with a total of 10,000 students and a thousand teachers. Altogether, there were 296 schools, nearly 22,000 students and over 2,800 teachers. Despite the fact that 77 percent of the schools were supplementary, nearly half the students were in day schools. The number of schools and students had leveled off since 1996, probably due to ongoing emigration.

The Institute of Jewish Studies in Kiev, Ukraine, sponsored lectures, symposia, and exhibits, as well as several historical research projects, including the collection of oral histories, documents, and photographs of Jewish life in Ukraine. Several projects focused on contemporary affairs, including the development of a demographic data bank and the documentation of the revival of public Jewish life since 1988.

The Hillel movement, which was established in Russia in 1994, expanded to 22 centers and over 60 affiliates in six former Soviet republics. In each of seven cities Hillel established a "lehrhaus," where knowledgeable students taught basic Judaism to their peers. In many localities Hillels came under pressure from local representatives of Jewish denominations to affiliate with them, but Hillel sought to maintain its nondenominational character.

The Jewish Agency for Israel, whose main mission was the promotion of immigration to Israel, employed 67 emissaries in the former FSU and administered 22 stations that provided direct flights to Israel. It also sponsored nearly 300 *ulpanim,* in which, it claimed, over 21,000 students were enrolled.

Judaic higher education was available at the Jewish universities of Moscow and St. Petersburg, and at "Project Judaica" at the Russian State University for the Humanities. The Hebrew University of Jerusalem joined with Moscow State University's Institute of African and Asian Studies to mount a Judaica program in cooperation with Moscow's Jewish university. There were also a number of less formal institutions for adult Jewish education in several of the major FSU cities.

ZVI GITELMAN

Australia

National Affairs

$\mathbf{A}$T THE BEGINNING OF 1999, the Liberal-National coalition government led by Prime Minister John Howard was starting its second term in office, rejuvenated by its election victory the previous October. Key items on the government's agenda were tax reform and, later in the year, a promised referendum on changing Australia from a constitutional monarchy to a republic.

Tax reform, incorporating a goods-and-services tax, was passed in amended form, and the voters defeated the proposal for a republic because of division over how to select a president. But the major public-policy issue of the year was one that could not have been predicted: The tumultuous events in East Timor and the crisis they created for Australia's relationship with its closest neighbor, Indonesia, dramatically tested the nation.

Australia took a prominent role in the lead-up to the UN-sponsored referendum of the East Timorese on their future, providing political and logistical support for the vote. Confronted by the shocking violence of the pro-Indonesian militias and their Indonesian army sponsors against the East Timorese after the vote, Australia persuaded both Indonesian president B. J. Habibie and the international community to agree to the introduction of an Australia-led international peacekeeping force. While earning the gratitude of the East Timorese, Australia's actions were greeted coolly by some Asian nations like Malaysia, and with outright hostility by many Indonesians. The diplomatic fallout from the intervention took a high toll on the carefully cultivated Jakarta-Canberra relationship, and Australia's ongoing commitment to the rebuilding of the newly independent East Timor required it to reassess its defense and foreign-aid priorities.

After three years of divisive and acrimonious debate, far-right populist Pauline Hanson and her controversy-riddled party, One Nation, faded into the political background during 1999. With Hanson herself no longer a member of Parliament, her party was beset by lack of direction, internal upheavals, disaffection, and humiliating losses in legal cases brought against it.

The Australian Electoral Commission found that One Nation's senator-elect for Queensland, Heather Hill, had not undertaken proper steps to relinquish her British citizenship, and disqualified her from taking her seat. Also in Queensland, the state where the party was strongest, the 11 One Nation state representatives elected in June 1998 were reduced to just five by April 1999, after internecine feuds led five to quit the party and another to leave the state parliament altogether. Then, a court upheld the challenge of a disaffected former One Nation candidate to the validity of the party's registration in Queensland (the party's appeal of the ruling subsequently failed). In the ensuing chaos, the five remaining MPs defected from the party at the end of the year, expressing dissatisfaction with the management of the party's finances. Widespread closings of local One Nation branches added to the sense that this party had entered terminal free-fall.

The country's National Multicultural Advisory Council, which included Dr. Colin Rubenstein, executive director of the Australia/Israel & Jewish Affairs Council (AIJAC), prepared a report for the government that recommended continuing and strengthening Australia's successful policies on multiculturalism. Prime Minister Howard endorsed the report on May 5. Subsequently, in December, the federal government cited this report when it released *A New Agenda for Multicultural Australia,* which announced the government's commitment to make multiculturalism relevant to all Australians, and to ensure that the social, cultural, and economic benefits of Australia's diversity were fully maximized in the national interest. The government also pledged to establish a broad-based Council for Multicultural Australia to advance the practical implementation of multicultural policy.

On September 9, in the midst of the appalling outbreak of violence against the East Timorese, the chairman and executive director of AIJAC wrote to Foreign Minister Alexander Downer imploring Australia to do everything possible to restore peace in East Timor. The American Jewish Committee, with encouragement from AIJAC—its Australian associate—wrote President Clinton to persuade Indonesia to allow the deployment of an international force.

Israel and the Middle East

The Australian government continued to maintain warm relations with Israel, expressing full support for a continuation of the Middle East peace process regardless of any change in the Israeli government. The opposition Australian Labor Party largely shared the same view. For some years that had been an Australia-Israel Parliamentary Friendship group consisting of MPS of all the major parties. This group coordinated a visit of selected Australian MPs to Israel in January 1999, led by its chairman, MP Christopher Pyne (Liberal). The year also saw the establishment of the Australian Parliamentary Friends of Palestine (a similar group had started earlier among New South Wales state MPs), the first Australian parliamentary friendship group created for a non-state.

Following the arrest in March of 13 Iranian Jews on spying charges, AIJAC and other Jewish organizations brought the issue to the attention of the foreign minister in the hope that strong Australian representations to the Iranian government might help secure their release. The Australian government joined other

Western countries in urging the Iranians to release the prisoners, and on nine occasions raised the issue in bilateral talks with the Iranian government. In September, Liberal MPs Christopher Pyne and Petro Georgiou, and Labor MPs Bernie Ripoll and Laurie Ferguson delivered speeches in the national Parliament in support of the Iranian Jews. The organized Jewish community also rallied to the cause of the Iranian Jews. On June 24, Dr. Rubenstein addressed a rally organized by Jewish high-school students on the steps of the Victorian Parliament House, and on July 1 the Jewish Community Council of Victoria held a solidarity rally at the Werdiger Hall, Melbourne, that was addressed by federal MPs Peter Nugent and Michael Danby.

Australia's record in the UN on Middle East issues was essentially positive, albeit somewhat tempered by its membership in the Western European and Others Group (WEOG), which occasionally obliged it to support General Assembly resolutions unsympathetic to Israel. Australia refused to support or to attend a UN conference convened in Geneva in July to discuss and recommend action regarding Israel's alleged noncompliance with the Fourth Geneva Convention. Along with the U.S., Australia was one of the first nations to express its reservations. The issue of Israel's continuing exclusion from UN regional groups, and hence from the Security Council and other UN bodies, had concerned Australian Jewry for some time. On November 6 a joint AIJAC-American Jewish Committee leadership delegation met with Prime Minister Howard and received his assurance that Australia would back Israel's admission into WEOG, and thus make it eligible to participate in all UN activities.

A number of prominent Australians visited the Middle East during the year. Upon his return from a trip to Iran in March, Deputy Prime Minister and Trade Minister Tim Fischer said that he wanted to end "unfair stereotyping" of Iran, a country that, he claimed, was making "real progress" on terrorism and human rights. Mr. Fischer further stated Australia's opposition to continued economic sanctions against Iran. His remarks alarmed Jewish observers, who felt that Iran's recent record on international terrorism, human rights, and Israel did not justify such a favorable assessment. Mr. Fischer left the ministry later in the year.

Senator Aden Ridgeway (Democrat)—the second indigenous Australian ever elected to the federal Parliament—visited Israel in January as a member of the Australia-Israel Parliamentary Friendship delegation. He had long been interested in how Israel dealt with its social and cultural conflicts. On his return, Ridgeway pointed out similarities between Israel and Australia—the "deep spiritual connection to the land, the feeling of being exiled or dispossessed"—and expressed regret at the existing state of "cold peace" in the Middle East. Another MP to visit Israel was Con Sciacca, the parliamentary opposition's spokesman on immigration. He took inspiration from Israel's approach to immigration policy, saying: "They're using it in a way that is building the country enormously."

Responding to Ehud Barak's decisive election victory over Benjamin Netanyahu, leaders of the Australian Jewish community were quick to offer support to Israel's new prime minister. In Canberra, Foreign Minister Downer congratulated Barak on his victory.

Anti-Semitism and Extremism

In 1999, with bipartisan support, the Australian government launched an aggressive educational campaign to undo the damage done by the public debate over racism that had been going on since 1996. Nevertheless, the continuing high number of reports of racial harassment in the workplace and in educational institutions showed that the situation was still volatile.

For the 12 months ending September 30, 1999, the database of anti-Semitic activities compiled by the Executive Council of Australian Jewry (ECAJ) recorded 280 incidents. While lower than the record-high number of 327 incidents over the previous 12 months, this was still the second highest number on record, and 23 percent more than the annual average over the previous nine years. In fact the combined number of incidents involving physical assault, property damage, and direct face-to-face harassment were at the highest level ever. The incidence of hate mail was at a rate almost 50 percent above the nine-year average, but the rate of threatening telephone calls was the lowest for any 12-month period. Reports were received of graffiti on Jewish institutions in areas frequented by Jewish community members, as well as specifically anti-Semitic graffiti in locations with no evident Jewish connections. Most disturbing were the graffiti that defaced the homes of Australian Jews.

During the year, hostile commentators continued their use of anti-Jewish stereotypes to justify their opposition to Israel in the Middle East debate. This often took the form of alleging analogies between Nazi treatment of the Jews and Israeli policies toward the Palestinians. There were no overtly anti-Semitic newspapers, radio stations, or television broadcasters in the mainstream Australian media. Nevertheless, there were occasional hostile statements by some commentators, and prejudiced remarks in letters-to-the-editor and on some call-in shows. Of particular concern was the anti-Israel bias of the government-funded ethnic SBS (Special Broadcasting Service) television, which carried a number of stories during the year that suggested that a Jewish state could not be democratic.

Anti-Semitic individuals and organizations greatly increased their presence on the Internet in 1999 through Australia-based newsgroups. Whenever issues related to Jews arose on these newsgroups—developments in the Middle East, matters concerning the xenophobic One Nation, or concerns about the continuity of the Jewish community—anti-Semites intervened with derogatory comments about Jews. There was a similar problem with Internet newsletters, which are sent to individuals with an interest in a specific subject. Since many of these were produced by people unable to judge the appropriateness of material submitted by others, anti-Semitic comments often found their way in.

As more and more members of the Jewish community, including Holocaust survivors, established e-mail accounts, reports of anti-Semitic and threatening e-mail—sent to individuals and to communal offices, or left in Internet guest books of Jewish organizations—escalated, making this form of communication a major method of harassing and threatening Jewish Australians. Anonymous re-mailing services allowed persons sending such e-mail to disguise their identities, and existing laws were not enforced against those who sent traceable messages.

An Internet site of particular concern was that of the Adelaide Institute, a small organization devoted to Holocaust denial run by Frederick Toben. Linked to other Holocaust-denial sites around the world, it put out material designed to in-fluence media opinion, and sent unsolicited e-mail to Jews as a form of hate mail. (When the site was launched in 1996, Jeremy Jones, executive vice president of the ECAJ, had lodged a complaint with the Human Rights and Equal Opportu-nity Commission alleging that the site breached the Racial Hatred Act.) In Feb-ruary 1999, Toben commenced an overseas trip, which he described to a regional newspaper as a mission to challenge the German laws against Holocaust denial. While traveling, Toben continued to distribute anti-Semitic material through his Web site and to write letters to public officials denying the Holocaust. He and his supporters also mailed offensive material to a number of recipients, includ-ing Holocaust survivors. In Germany, Toben was arrested under the laws that he was planning to challenge. Despite his best efforts and those of his supporters, his arrest got little media attention and he did not become a martyr in the eyes of the Australian public, receiving support only from his associates at the Ade-laide Institute and from English writer David Irving.

Sections of the Arabic media also produced anti-Semitic material. *Nida'ul Islam*, available both as a magazine and on the Internet, published the extreme anti-Zionist and anti-Semitic views of several members of Australia's Islamic community, as well as similar sentiments from overseas commentators, such as assertions that any peace accord with Zionists was a violation of "Allah's Code," and that "Jihad against the Jews" was an "Islamic tradition." Similarly, the weekly Internet magazine *Al-Moharer Al-Australi* attacked international "Zionist con-trol" and denied the Holocaust.

EXTREMIST GROUPS

While the better-known Australian extremist groups tended to avoid open anti-Semitism, they maintained links with foreign extremist groups such as militia movements in the U.S., Christian Identity churches, the Lyndon LaRouche or-ganization, various groups of conspiracy theorists, the Australian League of Rights, and others that promoted anti-Jewish mythology.

The Australian League of Rights—described by Australia's Human Rights and Equal Opportunity Commission as "undoubtedly the most influential and ef-fective, as well as the best organized and most substantially financed, racist or-ganization in Australia"—received occasional and largely negative publicity, as the more mainstream parties were well aware that any hint of a link to the league was a political kiss of death. Though it claimed to stand apart from party politics and did not put forward candidates, the league had a "great white hope," former MP Graeme Campbell—who had addressed a series of league functions—and his Australia First Party. The league itself continued its program of lectures and seminars aimed at equipping "actionists" around Australia with information to combat their Zionist, socialist, and humanist enemies, and league material was regularly included in anti-Jewish mailings.

The Citizens Electoral Councils (CEC), based in a well-staffed office in suburban Melbourne, sent out mass mailings reflecting the views of Lyndon LaRouche—including bizarre anti-Semitic conspiracy theories—and particularly targeted Jewish and other antiracist organizations in Australia. The scale and impact of the CEC's operations, however, had declined since the publication of an extensive exposé in the *Australia/Israel Review* in 1996 that was then reported on national television. Nevertheless the CEC's annual report, lodged with the Australian Electoral Commission, indicated that, despite its negligible political profile, the group's high-pressure fund-raising techniques had brought in a remarkable amount of money.

Small neo-Nazi groups such as the Southern Cross Hammer Skinheads, the Australian National Socialist Movement, and White Australian Revolutionaries operated in all the major Australian cities, distributing racist pamphlets, placing abusive e-mail and phone calls, and engaging in intimidation, graffiti, and vandalism. The largest neo-Nazi group, National Action, based in Adelaide with a substantial cell in Melbourne, distributed a newsletter, maintained an Internet site, and, during the year, harassed the antiracist activists in Melbourne who forced the closure of the National Action store.

The deceptively named Australian Civil Liberties Union (ACLU) continued to advocate Holocaust denial. Virtually every public announcement from this "letterhead" organization was directed at protecting the "rights" of Holocaust deniers or others racists. John Bennett, its moving force, sat on the editorial advisory committee of the *Journal of Historical Review,* published by the Institute for Historical Review in California, the world's most famous Holocaust-denial organization. *Your Rights 1999* was the 25th annual edition of the handbook published by John Bennett for the ACLU. Through the years, the book had attacked multiculturalism and Asian immigration, promoted xenophobes and anti-Semites, and strongly criticized behavior attributed to the Jewish community. A particular campaign of the ACLU during 1999 was the portrayal of Holocaust denier Frederick Toben as a victim of suppression of free speech.

The reversals suffered by Australian imitators of the U.S. "militias" over the course of the previous three years continued during 1999. The militia subculture was hard hit by new, more restrictive gun-ownership legislation, the changeover in government from the socialists—who could easily be demonized by right-wing extremists—to a conservative coalition, and the rise of Pauline Hanson's

One Nation, which seemed to offer the militias' constituency a more mainstream way of "rescuing" Australia. Thus the violently extremist gun magazine *Lock, Stock & Barrel* was not published during 1999, although some copies of 1996 editions appeared on newsstands and at political meetings. Instead, under the continued editorship of the notorious Ron Owen, *Lock, Stock & Barrel* established an Internet site that carried the full address as well as a photograph of the home of Education Minister David Kemp. The resulting public outrage forced the temporary closing of the site and removal of the offending page.

Holocaust-Related Matters

War crimes remained an exceptionally emotional issue, both because the Australian Jewish community had the highest proportion of Holocaust survivors in any Jewish community outside Israel, and because Australia had considerable experience with similar tragedies, having taken in many refugees from such killing fields as Cambodia and the former Yugoslavia.

In April, the Swiss Fund for Needy Victims of the Holocaust was launched in Australia. Originally established and funded by Swiss corporations and the Swiss National Bank in 1997 as a humanitarian gesture to aid needy survivors of the Holocaust worldwide, the fund allocated US$2.5 million to Jewish survivors in Australia, to be distributed by a communal committee under the auspices of the ECAJ. Nina Bassat, ECAJ president, described the fund as "a welcome initiative for those who suffered under the Nazis and are today still bearing the repercussions of those years. It may help to alleviate some of the pain felt by survivors, especially those living in situations of need."

The issue of Nazi war criminals living in Australia remained on the public stage during 1999. Especially concerned about revelations that Nazi scientists had been allowed into Australia after World War II with the full knowledge and approval of the government, Jewish groups argued for a revived Special Investigations Unit (SIU) to look into such cases, and suggested that war criminals be deprived of citizenship and deported.

In July, the Lithuanian government submitted an official request for Australian assistance in its investigation of alleged Nazi war criminal Antanas Gudelis, who was living in Adelaide. Evidence, including new material unearthed by the Lithuanians and by the Simon Wiesenthal Center in Jerusalem, placed Gudelis in command of a Nazi auxiliary unit that operated in and around Kaunas and Kupiskis. Like two other accused war criminals living in Australia—Karlis Ozols and Konrad Kalejs (declared a war criminal by United States courts)—Gudelis had emigrated to Australia after World War II and had taken out citizenship. Because of an anomaly in the Citizenship Act that set a ten-year time limit for challenging a person's citizenship, none of the three could be stripped of citizenship even if there were proof that citizenship had been obtained by fraud. A change in the law in 1997 eliminated this limitation, but it was not made retroactive. In 1999

AIJAC submitted a proposal to the Australian Citizenship Council to denaturalize citizens implicated in war crimes, but the council's report reaffirmed the government's position against retrospectively lifting the ten-year limitation.

The continuing presence of Nazi war criminals in Australia received international publicity in November when the ABC television network in the United States ran a major story about it on its popular "20/20" program. The show helped revive interest in the continuing war-crimes debate in Australia, and the atrocities in East Timor also contributed to a greater public willingness to address the subject. In December, the War Crimes Act of 1945 was amended to eliminate exceptional evidentiary hurdles in war-crimes cases, where general extradition requirements had been met. This was expected to facilitate prosecution of the Gudelis case and others like it.

JEWISH COMMUNITY

Demography

The Australian Jewish community continued to grow through immigration, particularly from South Africa and the former Soviet Union. Estimates of the total number of Jews in the country ranged from 100,000 to 125,000, out of a total population of some 19 million. There were probably hundreds of thousands of other Australians who had some ancestral relationship with the Jewish community, largely due to the predominantly male Jewish immigration to Australia in the first century of colonization. More than half of all Jews in Australia were born overseas: South African-born Jews were the largest group, followed by natives of Poland, Russia, Hungary, and Germany. The losses attributable to aliyah and a low birthrate were more than made up by immigration. The Jewish community was still heavily concentrated in Melbourne and Sydney, with the Brisbane-Gold Coast area showing the fastest growth.

Census figures — which were approximate, since it was not compulsory to answer questions on religion — indicated that 15–20 percent of married Jewish women and men had non-Jewish partners in 1999, though anecdotal evidence suggested a considerably higher figure. Compared to members of other religions, Jewish Australians were more likely to marry and to do so at a later age, and they were less likely to cohabit without marriage. The Jewish community included an exceptionally high percentage of elderly members, placing a considerable burden on the community's welfare and service agencies.

There were 14,000–20,000 Jews from the former Soviet Union in Australia, most of them living in Sydney and Melbourne. Australia's Jewish community had received, per capita, more immigrants from the FSU than even Israel, at least double the proportion received by the U.S., and seven times the number that went to Canada. Integrating this community continued to be a major challenge, especially since many of the new arrivals lacked Jewish literacy. Despite the assistance provided by the local communities, particularly on the arrival of these Jews in the country, communal leadership remained concerned that these newcomers were finding it easier to assimilate into Australian society than to integrate into its Jewish community.

Communal Affairs

The Executive Council of Australian Jewry (ECAJ), continued under the presidency of Nina Bassat, while Ron Weiser remained as president of the Zionist Federation of Australia (ZFA). Mark Leibler was national chairman of the Australia/Israel and Jewish Affairs Council (AIJAC) (he also headed the United Israel Appeal), and Dr. Colin Rubenstein was AIJAC's executive director. In August 1999, the Australian Institute of Jewish Affairs (AIJA) became a division of AIJAC, and in that same month Adam Indikt, the editor of AIJAC's monthly journal, the *Review*, resigned after one year at the helm and five years as a senior researcher. Doctoral student and former contributing editor Tzvi Fleischer was appointed in his place. AIJAC continued its association with the American Jewish Committee, and, together with the AJC's Asia and Pacific Rim Institute, issued *Islam In Asia: Changing Political Realities*, which was launched at the Park Hyatt Hotel in Melbourne in November, and in Washington in December.

David Bernstein resigned as editor of the *Australian Jewish News* after the publishers removed a column he wrote in support of a cartoon that many readers found offensive. Deborah Stone was appointed editor of the Melbourne edition of the *Australian Jewish News*, while Vic Alhadeff remained the editor of the Sydney edition.

MACCABIAH TRAGEDY

Nearly three years after the tragedy at the 15th Maccabiah Games in Israel, when a bridge collapsed killing four Australian athletes and injuring more than 70 others, the victims still had not been paid compensation. While the Israeli government's agreement to stand as the insurer of last resort was a welcome development, the question of compensation could not be finalized until the extent of the insurance companies' liability was established. The Israeli Knesset reestablished a committee of inquiry into the tragedy, and, by order of an Israeli court, a team of doctors was to visit Australia to examine those who suffered injuries. But Maccabi Australia resolved not to participate in the next Maccabiah unless all victims were compensated, safety procedures were professionally assured, and the entire organization of the Maccabiah underwent review. Maccabi Australia, which worked together with the ECAJ and the ZFA on these issues, also called for the resignations of the president and chairman of the Maccabi World Union, but did not make these preconditions for attending the next Maccabiah.

Interreligious Dialogue

Jewish-Christian dialogue continued. In New South Wales, the Association of Jewish Jurists and the St. Thomas More Centre cosponsored a seminar on the Catholic Church and the Shoah, which was addressed by Cardinal Edward Cassidy, the author of the Vatican document on this subject published in 1998. Papers were also presented by Rabbi Raymond Apple and Professor Colin Tatz. Governor-General Sir William Deane and a number of other dignitaries attended. A second major interreligious event was a seminar convened by the Australian Catholic Bishops' Committee on Ecumenism. It was designed to discuss, with other faith communities, the Catholic Church's plans for the year 2000. Rabbi Selwyn Franklin of Central Synagogue Sydney presented a paper there.

Education

More than half of all Jewish children aged 4–18—close to 70 percent of those aged 4–12—received full-time Jewish education in the 19 Jewish day schools in Australia. Spanning the religious spectrum, these schools continued to rank at the highest level for academic achievement. This reflected the community's major investment in the schools as a means of preserving Jewish continuity. Day-school enrollments continued to expand, despite ongoing concerns over high costs and the challenge to the community to find new sources of funding. In Melbourne alone there were over 5,500 children in Jewish day schools, and in Sydney one school had a waiting list of over 300.

Prime Minister Howard reassured the Jewish community that day schools had "an absolute guarantee that their right to exist and receive a reasonable level of government support, will continue," adding that tuition fees would be exempt from the new goods-and-services tax, as would the cost of any other activity included as part of the normal curriculum.

There was an increased emphasis on adult education via the Melton Program, which had nearly 500 students in Sydney and Melbourne. Short-term courses utilizing guest lecturers also proved popular. Top priorities for the future, according to Australian Jewish educators, were Jewish studies on the university level, and teacher education to provide quality faculty for the day schools.

Culture

Australian Jews played a significant role in the artistic and cultural life of the Australian community, with writers, artists, performers, and directors in every sphere of cultural endeavor. Examples in 1999 included: Jack Feldstein's play "A Small Suburban Crisis"; Neer Korn's book *Shades of Belonging: Conversations with Australian Jews;* Lily Brett's novel *Too Many Men;* Yossi Berger's *A Kind of Violence;* and Gabriel Kune's biography of John Saunders, *Nothing Is Impossi-*

ble (which was launched by Prime Minister Howard). Inge Clendinnen (not Jewish) won the NSW Premier's Prize for her book, *Reading the Holocaust*.

Apart from the extremely valuable contributions to Jewish cultural life made by the Jewish Museum of Australia in Melbourne and the Sydney Jewish Museum—both of which were world-class institutions—the various Australian Jewish film festivals (Melbourne, Sydney, and now Canberra) and Jewish theater groups added immeasurably to the cultural life of the community. A rock extravaganza with a Holocaust theme, called "Kaddish," was featured at the 1999 Melbourne International Festival of the Arts.

Personalia

The following members of the Jewish community received national honors: Brian Gaensler, astrophysicist, Young Australian of the Year; Harry Triguboff, businessman and communal benefactor, AO; Rodney Adler, insurance industry leader, AM; Lynne Davies, past president of the National Council of Jewish Women, AM; Dr. Gerhart Lowenthal, nuclear scientist and teacher, AM; Bernard Gold, sportsman and Maccabi life member, OAM; Alwynne Beryl Jona, communal worker, OAM; Harry Sebel, architect, OAM; and Professor A. G. Klein, scientist.

Australia and the Jewish community mourned the untimely death of Ron Castan AM QC, a brilliant lawyer, activist, and philanthropist, who passed away in Melbourne on October 21 at the age of 59 due to complications from an operation. Castan, widely recognized as one of the best legal minds in Australia, worked tirelessly on behalf of human rights, civil liberties, and communal tolerance both in Australia and abroad. A former director and editorial board member at AIJAC, Castan was best known to the wider community for his pioneering work on behalf of aboriginal rights. He helped establish the Victorian Aboriginal Legal Service in 1972 and was a leading member of the legal team that, in the 1992 Mabo case, overturned the legal fiction that Australia had been *terra nullius* (unoccupied land) before white settlement. He also contributed significantly to drafting the proposed constitution of a newly independent East Timor.

Other notable members of the Jewish community to pass away during 1999 included: businessmen/industrialists Eric Smorgon and Sir Peter Abeles; David Aronson, labor lawyer; George Molnar, philosopher; Joe Rose, artist; Sam Goldbloom, political activist; and Sidney Sinclair, former president of the Australian Jewish Welfare Society.

COLIN L. RUBENSTEIN

South Africa

National Affairs

THE YEAR 1999 SAW the retirement of President Nelson Mandela, the country's first democratically elected leader. South Africa's second democratic elections, held in June, demonstrated overwhelming support for the ruling African National Congress (ANC), in alliance with its junior partner, the South African Communist Party (SACP). The ANC increased its share of the national vote to 66.3 percent from 62.6 percent in 1994, and formed a coalition government with the mainly Zulu Inkatha Freedom Party (IFP), which obtained 8.5 percent.

In addition the ANC gained exclusive control of seven of the nine provincial legislatures. The Democratic Party (DP), with 9.5 percent of the national vote, replaced the New National Party (NNP), which won 6.8 percent, as the official opposition. In the Western Cape legislature the NNP formed a ruling coalition with the DP, and in KwaZulu-Natal the IFP and ANC shared control of the legislature.

The performance of the Pan Africanist Congress (PAC) on the left, with 0.7 percent of the national vote, and the Freedom Front on the right, with 0.8 percent, demonstrated the weakness of the extremist parties.

The atmosphere surrounding the elections was more sober than in 1994, perhaps because there was a greater appreciation of the enormous social and economic problems facing the government. "Among Jewish South Africans", noted the *SA Jewish Report* on the eve of the elections (May 28), "there has been a significant degree of withdrawal from involvement in the country's burning issues. Many feel that their electoral power has shrunk so much from the old days of apartheid, when only five million people were enfranchised, that their vote will make little difference. The result is a disturbingly high degree of voter apathy." The newspaper urged the community "to dispel such feelings, to get involved and to vote for their future in this country which nourished them. A vote for a more prosperous, happier South Africa is also a vote for the future of the Jewish community. Whining about the problems from the sidelines does no one any good."

Notwithstanding this alleged apathy, South African Jewish leaders expressed optimism about the new government under its new president, Thabo Mbeki. Marlene Bethlehem, national chairperson of the South African Jewish Board of Deputies (SAJBOD) was confident "because, based on the experience of the SAJBOD with Mbeki, I think we will see strong leadership from him." Russell

Gaddin, chairman of the Gauteng Council of the SAJBOD, considered Mbeki "a born leader" able to deal with the issues in South Africa (*SA Jewish Report*, June 6).

South African Jewry was well represented at Mbeki's inauguration in June. Chief Rabbi Cyril Harris was one of five religious leaders to offer a prayer, and Justice Arthur Chaskalson, president of the Constitutional Court, administered the formal oath as prescribed by the constitution. Ambassador Uri Oren represented Israel, and SAJBOD leaders Mervyn Smith, national president, Marlene Bethlehem, national chairperson, and Seymour Kopelowitz, national director, represented the Jewish community.

In July the SAJBOD lobbied the South African government to intervene on behalf of 13 Jews accused of spying in Iran. It was hoped that the government would use its relationship with Iran to request that the 13 be given a fair trial.

The ANC-led government under President Mbeki continued to pursue a conservative monetary policy. After two years of stagnation, real economic growth began, and inflation fell to approximately 8 percent. Addressing a group of young Jewish businessmen, Gill Marcus, deputy governor of the Reserve Bank, contended that the environment for operating a business in South Africa had never been as favorable.

The government continued to seek a balance between the interests of the investment community and those of the labor unions. Despite wage strikes by public-sector unions, the government did not waver from its GEAR (Growth, Employment and Redistribution) policy. The Basic Conditions of Employment Act, enacted in December, contained worker-friendly provisions. Affirmative-action programs continued. However, after an initial surge of black business activity on the Johannesburg Stock Exchange, the market capitalization of black-controlled companies dipped.

Violent crime, fueled by the unemployment of about one-third of the workforce, remained a major source of concern, as did the rampant spread of AIDS. According to a report by the UN Development Program, the infection rate, estimated at about 20 percent, will climb to 25 percent by 2010. Employers, who are only gradually realizing the importance of a healthy workforce, are beginning to introduce educational programs about AIDS.

Of particular concern for those living in the Western Cape Province was the ongoing campaign of urban terror sponsored primarily by the largely Muslim vigilante group People Against Gangsterism and Drugs (PAGAD). Not only had there been no convictions, but in December there were disturbing accusations of police involvement in the terrorism.

Israel-Related Activity

In January, Nobel Peace Prize laureate Archbishop Desmond Tutu told Jerusalem's Yakar Institute for Social Concerns that Israel and the Palestinians could achieve reconciliation if their leaders were prepared to take risks (*Citizen,* January 8).

Yehuda Duvdevani, head of youth programs at Israel's Ministry of Defense, visited South Africa, where he met with youth leaders and educators with a view to enhancing Jewish and Zionist education in South Africa.

Chana Glustron, Ulpan director at Ben-Gurion University, visited South Africa to set up an Ulpan for pupils in grades 11 and 12.

Mendel Kaplan, industrialist and international Jewish leader, officially launched the Israel United Appeal-United Communal Fund (IUA-UCF) Welfare Campaign in Cape Town. In his address he looked at common challenges facing Israel and South Africa.

Speaking at the 24th annual meeting of the South Africa/Israel Chamber of Commerce in Johannesburg, Gauteng premier Mbhazima Shilowa noted that trade between South Africa and Israel had contributed to the economic expansion of both countries. South Africa exports more goods to Israel than to any other country in the Middle East.

The South African press gave extensive coverage to the Israeli elections, generally welcoming the election of Prime Minister Ehud Barak as someone who could get the peace process moving. Interviewed in Pretoria on the eve of President Mbeki's inauguration, Yasir Arafat said the Israeli electorate had "sent an important signal because the majority of Israelis voted for peace" (*Business Day,* June 17). In August the first Palestinian ambassador to South Africa, Salman El'Herfi, addressed a Jewish gathering where he spoke of his people's desire for peace with Israel.

Nelson Mandela, the former president of South Africa, visited Israel in October, hoping to act as a political intermediary between Israel and her Arab neighbors. At a special dinner in his honor Mandela explained that "One of the reasons I am so pleased to be in Israel is as a tribute to the enormous contribution of the Jewish community of South Africa [to South Africa]. I am so proud of them" (*SA Jewish Report,* October 22). At Yad Vashem he spoke of being "deeply pained and enriched" by the visit and emphasized how important it was for the world not to forget the Holocaust. Mandela also visited the grave of Yitzhak Rabin. The visit received wide coverage in the South African media. "There is extensive speculation in international diplomatic circles," wrote the editor of the *Sunday Independent,* John Battersby (October 24), "that Mandela could head or play a key advisory role" in an international commission that might conceivably be formed to oversee a comprehensive Middle East peace.

The only sour note of the trip, which also included visits to Iran, Syria, and the Palestinian Authority, was a quarrel with Israeli foreign minister David Levy that found its way into the press. Levy strenuously contested Mandela's assumption that Iran and Syria were interested in peace with Israel.

The president of the South African Union of Progressive Judaism (SAUPJ), Simon Jocum, expressed concern at Orthodoxy's preferential position in the religious life of Israel. "The Orthodox dominate and this has led to a feeling that they should separate religion from the state. There's too much discrimination against the non-Orthodox. The political parties are virtually blackmailed by the Orthodox" (*SA Jewish Report*, June 18).

Anti-Semitism

Although anti-Semitism was of marginal significance in South African public life during the period under review, a number of troubling incidents occurred. There were anti-Semitic letters in the press, accusations of Jewish power and influence over the government (mainly in *Die Afrikaner*, a far-right newspaper), vulgar comments about Jews by individuals, and Holocaust denial. In August a Jewish cemetery in Kempton Park, outside Johannesburg, was vandalized.

The SAJBOD condemned the visit to South Africa of conspiracy theorist David Icke, who claimed that he believed in the *Protocols of the Elders of Zion* and was certain that a global Jewish conspiracy had started the two world wars and the Russian Revolution.

In October, Jani Allan, a host on "Cape Talk Radio," interviewed Keith Johnson, leader of an American militia group, on her show. In addition to diatribes against Israel, "race mixing," and homosexuals, Johnson called the Holocaust a hoax and claimed that rabbinical teachings promoted pedophilia. Jani Allan distanced herself from Johnson's views. Though unwilling to acknowledge that it was a mistake to have conducted the interview, she did apologize for the offense to Jewish listeners. The matter was then brought to the Broadcasting Complaints Commission of South Africa (BCC), which ordered the show to broadcast an apology to members of the Jewish community because it had contravened the broadcasting code. The show complied.

The SAJBOD's position was that hate speech should be made a criminal offence punishable by law.

JEWISH COMMUNITY

Demography

In 1999 it was estimated that the South African Jewish population had declined to approximately 70,000, an assessment made on the basis of preliminary results of the 1996 census. Further analysis demonstrated substantial errors in the census, and it is now estimated that the Jewish population is between 80,000 and 90,000.

A major study conducted jointly by the Kaplan Centre for Jewish Studies and Research at the University of Cape Town and the London-based Institute for Jewish Policy Research was reported in *Jews of the "New South Africa": Highlights of the 1998 National Survey of South African Jews*. It found that South African Jewry remained remarkably cohesive, with relatively high levels of religious observance and Jewish and general education, a positive sense of Jewishness, and a very strong attachment to Israel and Zionism. The vast majority of Jews did not seriously contemplate leaving the country, although as many as one in four in the 20–30-year-old age bracket anticipated emigrating over the next five years because of concern about crime and personal safety. There was certainly no indication, however, that the Jewish minority was fearful about its future in the new South Africa. Citing statistics derived from the survey, Rabbi Cyril Harris spoke of an "air of optimism." He said: "It would appear that although we are a diminishing community in quantity due to emigration, we have much to be proud of regarding our quality of Yiddishkeit" (*SA Jewish Report*, September 17).

Demographic shifts within Johannesburg led to the closing of a number of Jewish institutions and the opening of others. The Sandton Beth Hamedrash Hagadol was consecrated in January, the Berea Hebrew Congregation was closed in February, and the Adas Yeshurun Congregation moved from Yeoville to Percelia in June. In January the Jewish Women's Benevolent Society and Jewish Community Services in Johannesburg moved from Yeoville to Sandringham Gardens.

Communal Affairs

The diminishing size of the community necessitated a reassessment of the needs of Johannesburg Jewry, a process that the Cape Town community had already undergone. Isaac Joffe, coordinator of the Johannesburg reassessment, explained: "The priorities of the community are changing and besides our normal concerns, we need to focus more on caring for the aged and educating our youth. Security is also a concern that demands increasing resources" (*SA Jewish Report,* April 15). Moves to integrate Jewish organizations and to share personnel costs were set in motion, though there was no intention of blurring the individual identities of the SAJBOD, the Israel United Appeal-United Communal Fund (IUA-UCF), and the South African Zionist Federation (SAZF).

A cut in government subsidies resulted in a serious financial crisis for the Sandringham Gardens Home for the Aged, a Jewish institution in Johannesburg.

Jewish Community Services (JCS) reported that there was a problem of child abuse in the Jewish community, though it did not usually involve physical violence. Most of the cases of suspected abuse or neglect were discovered through the reports of teachers who noticed marked behavioral changes in students.

The Union of Jewish Women of South Africa (UJW) contributed to a number of clinics in Gauteng to support the rehabilitation of rape victims. In August the Coordinating Council of Jewish Women in the Western Cape, comprising the UJW, Bnoth Zion Association, representatives of synagogue women's guilds, and the sisterhood of Temple Israel, organized a National Women's Day rally to protest against the increasing incidence of crime and violence. A cross section of prominent Cape Town religious and civic leaders attended.

Security concerns were high on the communal agenda. In February, Russell

Gaddin, chairman of the Gauteng Council of the SAJBOD, spoke of the enc mous physical and mental battering that crime imposed on the Jewish community. "But the Jewish community is not being singled out as such. It so happens that the majority of Jews in Johannesburg tend to live in the more affluent suburbs which is where crimes such as burglary and hijackings are prevalent." Marlene Bethlehem, chairperson of the SAJBOD, considered crime the major reason for emigration (*SA Jewish Report,* February 12).

In August, Mark Notelowitz, head of the Community Services Organizations (CSO), reported on the question of security at the SAJBOD's 40th national congress. Despite high levels of general crime, as well as incidents involving rightwing and neo-Nazi anti-Semites and Islamic extremists, he believed that the CSO was serving as an effective deterrent. In November the SAJBOD initiated a community crime coalition to combat car hijacking.

Russell Gaddin was elected chairman of the SAJBOD at the 40th national congress. He called on the community to avoid insularity and engage with the wider society.

An editorial in the Rosh Hashanah edition of the *SA Jewish Report* was devoted to the low morale of the community. Crime, it said, had eroded optimism and weakened institutions. Though South African Jewry was described as a community in crisis, the editorial claimed that the community's own efforts could improve the situation: "Top of our agenda in this regard must be striving to attain unity. There has been far too much divisiveness based on religious observance and groupings, organizational disputes and petty squabbles among individuals." The editorial called for younger people to volunteer for positions of leadership and for greater transparency in communal institutions. "In order to extricate ourselves from the quagmire of despair, South African Jewry needs to re-examine itself collectively from the inside and keep abreast with the rest of the country's populace on the outside."

A number of prominent visitors addressed the community. Rabbi Adin Steinsaltz, the noted Talmudist, addressed the 40th SAJBOD national congress, Canadian deputy prime minister Herb Gray met with the Gauteng Council of the SAJBOD, and Evelyn Sommer, Women's International Zionist Organization representative at the UN and chair of the North American section of the World Jewish Congress, addressed the 30th conference of the World Zionist Organization of South Africa.

The refurbished Albow Jewish Cultural Centre opened in Cape Town in August, housing the new Gitlin Library, the Gardens Synagogue offices and sukkah, and the newly established Cape Town Holocaust Centre..

Community Relations

In February, Deputy President Thabo Mbeki addressed a gala dinner of the Union of Orthodox Synagogues (UOS) in Cape Town. He stressed the need to manage our multi-ethnic, multi-cultural and multi-faith society to ensure that none among us uses the diversity of our society to engulf all of us in unacceptable confrontation and conflict. In this regard it is important that we deal firmly with the abuse of any religious fundamentalism to pursue objectives that threaten any of our communities. Among others, we cannot allow that unacceptable views of anti-Semitism become a platform to justify the launching of a campaign of terror against the Jewish citizens of our country." In thanking Mbeki, Chief Rabbi Cyril Harris stressed how fortunate South Africans were to have a leader of such courage and inspiring vision. On behalf of the Jewish community he endorsed the need to eliminate poverty and pledged that Jews would bring their Jewish skills to bear in helping alleviate current problems.

A storm erupted in February over an essay written by Layla Cassim, a high-school student in Johannesburg, which articulated a pro-Palestinian view of the Middle East. A shadowy Jewish organization calling itself the Jewish Defense League (JDL) somehow found out about her essay and sent the young woman hostile mail. Following intervention by the SAJBOD, the JDL's senior spokesperson apologized to the Cassim family and admitted to having not been in possession of all the facts.

Chief Rabbi Cyril Harris delivered his Passover message on television from Robben Island, which he referred to as a "political symbol of captivity and freedom. . . . There is almost an exact parallel between the slavery of the Israelites in Egypt and the eventual exodus and the incarceration of Nelson Mandela on Robben Island and his eventual release to begin the new South Africa."

President Mandela praised the speech as "an indication of the rabbi's strong bond with the efforts for freedom and democracy in South Africa." Mandela's spokesman said that the president always drew strength from the teachings of the chief rabbi. "He has noted the important role that Rabbi Harris is playing in encouraging participation in reconstruction and development in South Africa, especially within the Jewish community" (*SA Jewish Report,* March 26).

In a speech to the Gauteng Province chapter of the World Conference on Religion and Peace prior to the elections, Rabbi Harris called on privileged whites to move from "a protective myopia" and to become aware of the plight of the millions of people living close to them. Ninety percent of the country's wealth, he noted, was held by 10 percent of the population. "I pray that people will not be selfish when they vote, but consider which party advances this key issue of eradicating poverty and making a better life for all" (*SA Jewish Report,* May 14).

The Jewish community continued to involve itself in outreach projects, particularly under the auspices of Tikkun, an umbrella organization for Jewish groups working to help the disadvantaged. One project involved the adoption of a small rural elementary school in Rietfontein with 120 pupils. The school, according to Tikkun CEO Herby Rosenberg, "has experienced difficulties which fortunately have been overcome. Tikkun is determined to make a success of the country and of this school" (*SA Jewish Report*, May 7). Nelson Mandela praised another Tikkun project, the Phakamani agricultural and training settlement, describing it as a "miracle" (*SA Jewish Report*, November 19). Also under the umbrella of Tikkun, and with a grant of R500,000 (nearly $85,000) from the Ministry of Welfare for this and other projects, Temple Israel in Johannesburg ran a program for the children of the inner-city neighborhood of Hillbrow.

The Jewish National Fund, the South African Department of Water Affairs and Forestry, the ABSA banking group, and the residents of Mangondi village in Venda sponsored a project to make water more readily available to this remote village. Thus the local women would not need to walk miles, as they previously had to do, to fetch water.

The SAJBOD and King David Primary School, Linksfield, established an adult education program for the disadvantaged, while ORT continued to involve itself in training disadvantaged adults to improve their employment possibilities.

A "one-man show" by Craig Hummel, head boy (elected by fellow students) of Yeshivah High in Johannesburg, attracted the attention of the *SA Jewish Report* (July 23). Hummel dedicated his spare time to raising money, collecting used clothing, and securing old benches for the use of poor children in Diepkloof, Johannesburg.

Shortly after his election as president, Thabo Mbeki sent a letter of goodwill to the readers of the *SA Jewish Report*. He wrote: "In particular I would like to make mention of the manifold projects undertaken by the Jewish community, which since the new dispensation of 1994, became official under the umbrella of the Tikkun organization" (*SA Jewish Report*, June 6). In his first address to the Jewish community as president, at the SAJBOD's 40th national congress in August, President Mbeki once again paid tribute to the role of South African Jewry and called on it to continue helping to build a new South Africa.

Religion

Over the previous 20 years many small synagogues had proliferated in Johannesburg. The phenomenon was not universally welcomed. Chief Rabbi Harris expressed ambivalence, noting that while he admired the intensity of the prayers and the high level of observance, he feared negative consequences from the decentralization of worship.

A 1998 law requiring new medical graduates to serve for one year in a rural area before they can be registered aroused concern among observant medical students who feared that they would find it difficult to practice Judaism during that year away from any organized Jewish community. There was some apprehension that many of these young Jewish doctors might emigrate.

Addressing the 19th biennial conference of the UOS in Johannesburg, Rabbi Abner Weiss, formerly of South Africa and now living in the U.S., declared that, as far as he could tell, Jewish consciousness in South Africa was stronger than ever.

Cape Town Jewry was shocked and bewildered in June when Rabbi Dr. E. J. Steinhorn, spiritual leader of the Green and Sea Point Hebrew Congregation, was declared persona non grata by Chief Rabbi Harris, the Cape Town Bet Din (religious court), and other rabbis of Cape Town. Members of Rabbi Steinhorn's congregation, the largest in the Western Cape, received a letter informing them of the situation. Accusations against Rabbi Steinhorn included matters of halakhic interpretation (such as who may be invited to speak in the synagogue and whether women might wear slacks at the cemetery), the alleged inclusion in certain religious ceremonies of people who were not Jews according to Halakhah, and complaints about his personal conduct.

At the annual meeting of his synagogue, the close-to-700 congregants gave Rabbi Steinhorn a standing ovation. The two sides in the dispute met with a mediator, Justice Dennis Davis. Commenting in the wake of the meeting, Chief Rabbi Harris explained that the issue had nothing to so with the popularity of Rabbi Steinhorn. "It is about his rabbinic function in relation to the Chief Rabbinate, the Bet Din and his Cape Town colleagues" (*Sunday Independent*, June 27). Following negotiations, Rabbi Steinhorn's status as persona non grata was withdrawn. The rabbi, in turn, agreed to abide by rulings of the Bet Din and accept the jurisdiction of the Chief Rabbinate.

In Durban there was a row between two rabbis over whether a *kohen* (descendant of the ancient priestly family) might marry a convert. The dispute, which included harsh personal attacks, raged in the Durban communal newspaper, *Hashalom,* through June and July. Jack Notelovitz, director of the Council of KwaZulu-Natal Jewry, described the rift as a dangerous threat to communal unity (*SA Jewish Report,* July 9).

The 50,000 Lemba, who live in northern South Africa and southern Zimbabwe and claim Jewish ancestry, were once again the focus of attention. A study undertaken by the Centre for Genetic Anthropology at University College, London, found that certain DNA mutations were more common among *kohanim* than lay Jews, and that DNA samples from the Lemba exhibited a high proportion of the Lemba men carrying the *kohen* genetic signature. Because that *kohen* genetic signature is extremely rare in all non-Jewish populations tested hitherto, the scientists believed their findings support the Lemba tradition of Jewish ancestry. In traditional Judaism the matrilineal line determines who is a Jew, whereas the status of *kohen* is passed from father to son. This particular gene was found on the Y, or male, chromosome. Furthermore, Dr. Tudor Parfitt of the School of Oriental and African Studies, University of London, claimed to have discovered the route to southern Africa taken by the Lemba about a thousand years ago from Senna in Yemen. Up to now South African rabbis had treated Lemba claims of Jewish ancestry with skepticism (*SA Jewish Report*, August 29).

In December the Parliament of World Religions convened in Cape Town. Seven thousand people from around the world registered, making it the largest gathe. ing of its kind ever to take place on the continent. Chief Rabbi Harris and a number of other Jewish scholars and theologians participated.

Education

The Cape Town Holocaust Centre (CTHC), under the directorship of Myra Osrin, opened in August at a ceremony that drew 500 Jewish and non-Jewish dignitaries and well-wishers. Stephen Smith, founder and director of Beth Shalom Holocaust Memorial Centre in England and the inspiration behind the establishment of the CTHC, stressed the role of Holocaust memory in providing a beacon of hope in an inhumane and violent world. Messages of goodwill came from Nelson Mandela, Archbishop Desmond Tutu (a patron of the CTHC), and Minister of Education Kadar Asmal. Speaking on behalf of the patrons, Justice Richard Goldstone said that the new institution could help teach the disastrous consequences of racial ideology in a South Africa that still contained a "huge pool of intolerance."

From its inception the CTHC was involved in outreach programs. Many school groups visited, and a seminar for 250 Western Cape teachers was held in August. Marlene Silbert, the education director, told the teachers "to teach young people in South Africa, many of whom have their own history of discrimination and prejudice, what happens when discrimination goes unchecked. . . . We are committed to the struggle against prejudice, racism, discrimination and promoting tolerance and respect for diversity" (*SA Jewish Report*, November 12).

Culture

Suzanna Belling and Geoff Sifrin were appointed, respectively, managing editor and opinion-and-feature editor of the *SA Jewish Report*. The Jewish weekly continued to struggle for financial support.

Shalom TV, the longest running locally produced Jewish television program on a community channel, closed because of the lack of subscribers.

Renowned photographer David Goldblatt held an exhibition, "Structures," at the Johannesburg Art Gallery.

Publications

Some noteworthy new publications of Jewish interest were *Memory Against Forgetting* by Lionel Bernstein, one of the accused at the Rivonia trial; *The Jewish Community of Graaff Reinet—A Brief History* by South African Friends of Beth Hatefutsoth; *Jews of the "New South Africa": Highlights of the 1998 National Survey of South African Jews* by Barry A. Kosmin, Jacqueline Goldberg, Milton Shain, and Shirley Bruk; and *Rivonia's Children* by Glenn Frankel. Five of the 12 chapters in *Jewries at the Frontier: Accommodation, Identity and Conflict,* edited by Sander L. Gilman and Milton Shain, were about the Jews of South Africa.

Personalia

Seymour Kopelowitz, national director of the SAJBOD, took up a Jewish communal position in Cleveland, Ohio, U.S.A.; Ronnie Kasrils was appointed minister of water affairs and forestry in President Mbeki's new cabinet; Gill Marcus was appointed deputy governor of the Reserve Bank; Tony Leon, leader of the Democratic Party, became the first Jew to lead the official opposition; Leon Medalie, Hanns Saenger, and Cyril Goldstein were honored by the United Hebrew Congregation in Johannesburg for their communal contributions; Nadine Gordimer, Nobel Laureate, and Phillip Tobias, professor emeritus of anatomy and human biology at the University of the Witwatersrand, were awarded the Order of the Southern Cross (Silver); Judith Harrisberg, president and honorary life vice-president of the Union of Jewish Women of South Africa, was made an honorary life member of the International Council of Jewish Women; Taffy Adler, historian, activist, and housing specialist, was named Gauteng Housing Person of the Year by the Institute of Housing in South Africa, for his initiatives to provide low-income rental accommodations; and the SAJBOD awarded Arthur Chaskalson, president of the Constitutional Court, its Humanitarian Award.

Among prominent South African Jews who died in 1999 were Percy Baneshik, playwright and art critic, Geoffrey Levenson, judge and founding member of Lawyers for Human Rights, and Gerald Lubner, international businessman.

MILTON SHAIN

Israel

THE MOST DRAMATIC EVENT OF 1999 was Ehud Barak's landslide victory over Prime Minister Benjamin Netanyahu in the May 17 election. While few had given Barak much chance of beating Netanyahu when the Knesset voted for early elections on January 4, the One Israel leader ran a focused and disciplined campaign. Ultimately, the coalition of "outsider" groups that had brought Netanyahu to power in 1996 imploded as Barak won by 56-44 percent.

The other dramatic election result was the huge success of the ultra-Orthodox Sephardi Shas party, which catapulted from ten seats to 17. Part of the explanation for the party's popularity was the March 17 conviction of Shas leader Arye Deri for corruption—a verdict that many Sephardim viewed as ethnically tainted.

After cobbling together a broad-based 75-member coalition that included secular and religious parties as well as parties on the left and the right, Barak set about reigniting the stalled peace process. After some hard bargaining he signed the Sharm el-Sheikh agreement with the Palestinians in early September which stipulated a further 11 percent Israeli withdrawal from the West Bank. Then, after U.S. president Bill Clinton announced the renewal of the Israeli-Syrian negotiating track in December, Barak traveled to Washington for talks with Syrian foreign minister Farouk al-Shara.

New momentum on the peace front did not immunize Barak from growing social discontent. Barak's promises of social reform during the elections—including his pledge to create 300,000 jobs—raised expectations among the poor and the unemployed, and there was growing pressure on him to deliver, especially after he presented a budget that seemed to hold out little salvation for the lower classes.

Barak also faced a series of coalition crises. The first came soon after he took office when the ultra-Orthodox parties took exception to the transport of a huge electric turbine on the Sabbath, threatening to leave the coalition if it went ahead. And there was an ongoing coalition squabble with Shas over funding for the party's debt-ridden educational network.

The economic slowdown continued through 1999 with unemployment crossing the 9-percent mark. Even the low rise in the cost-of-living index for the year was seen as a sign of the ongoing recession. In the second half of the year, though, there were some signs that the protracted economic slowdown might be coming to an end.

Battles over religion and state as well as over religious pluralism continued, as did the ultra-Orthodox attacks on the Supreme Court, which culminated in a huge demonstration in Jerusalem in February.

POLITICAL DEVELOPMENTS

Barak Wins in a Landslide

NETANYAHU TAKES AN EARLY LEAD

Despite the collapse of his ruling coalition and the Knesset decision on January 4 to approve early elections—more than a year ahead of schedule—the conventional wisdom was that Prime Minister Benjamin Netanyahu could not be counted out of the race. While opinion polls in early January showed Netanyahu and opposition Labor leader Ehud Barak running neck-and-neck, these surveys were at a time when Netanyahu appeared to be at an all-time political low. Furthermore, such polls had traditionally underestimated the power of the right. And the surveys also revealed that, whatever their personal preferences, a clear majority believed that Netanyahu would win a second term.

Especially on the left there were few who believed Barak could oust Netanyahu, who was seen as the consummate campaigner. When, toward the beginning of the campaign, a Likud supporter was beaten to the ground and passed out after anxious bodyguards tried to keep him from reaching Netanyahu to shake his hand, the prime minister quickly got water to the man, and, after the fracas, appeared smiling with him for the cameras. Even potential disaster, one pundit pointed out, was transformed into media points by Netanyahu. By the end of January, a poll in the daily *Yediot Aharonot* showed Netanyahu with a slim 46-43–percent lead over Barak.

By contrast, Barak's campaign started disastrously. When Addisu Messele, an Ethiopian member of Knesset, was replaced on the Labor Knesset slate by Russian-born Sofa Landver at the party primaries on February 15, he reacted bitterly. With Barak about to announce Labor's Knesset slate live on national television, Messele and his supporters burst into the room, screaming that they had been cheated. Ultimately, Barak allowed Messele a chance at the microphone where he lambasted the Labor Party, accusing it of being racist and patronizing—an image of the party Barak had been trying hard to alter. As the fiasco ended and long-faced Labor leaders traipsed out of the hall, one was reportedly heard saying that the election had already been lost.

Barak also drew criticism for not sounding a clear message on policy issues. An oft-repeated gripe was that "Barak is not taking off," and that seemed to be born out by his stationary position in the polls. Many in his party also wondered how their candidate, whose television appearances were often awkward and stiff, would be able to counter the TV-savvy Netanyahu.

One ominous sign for Netanyahu, however—reflecting the deep dissatisfaction with him inside the Likud—was the January 11 announcement by the prime minister's mentor and former Likud defense minister, Moshe Arens, that he would challenge Netanyahu in the party primaries. Arens insisted that "if we do nc manage to cure the present crisis in the Likud and stop the hemorrhaging of our top people from the party, our chances for winning the elections are not good." But when Netanyahu easily won the internal election on January 25 with 82 percent of the vote Arens agreed to stay on and replace Yitzhak Mordechai as defense minister. (Netanyahu had dismissed Mordechai on January 23 after the latter began talks with the leaders of a new party.)

BARAK STARTS TO TAKE OFF

To help his campaign Barak hired James Carville, Stanley Greenberg, and Robert Shrum, American experts who had all worked for U.S. president Bill Clinton. The impact of the three was already evident in January as Barak looked much more feisty and focused on television, if not necessarily smooth and slick.

Together with his advisers Barak built a campaign strategy based on the assumption that, to beat Netanyahu, Barak would have to win at least twice as many votes in the race for prime minister as his party would win in the separate Knesset elections. Hence he had to form a broad coalition of parties and groups — some even former rivals of Labor—which would support him, even without identifying with the Labor Party. A key strategic goal of such a coalition, to be called "One Israel," was to erode Labor's elitist Ashkenazi and, at times, anticlerical image so as to draw in Sephardi and religious elements traditionally allied with the right. Also, Barak, who had visited England to study the successful campaign model of Tony Blair, would adopt a social democratic message. By late January, Barak was already harping on social issues like education, health care, and jobs for the unemployed. He attacked Netanyahu incessantly, describing patients lying in beds in hospital corridors because of insufficient space, the need for free education from kindergarten on, and the current government's inability to deal with growing unemployment. While some criticized Barak for losing sight of the peace and security issues that had always decided Israeli elections, the Labor candidate stuck to his message, believing that Israelis were ready to vote on social issues as well.

The Barak campaign portrayed Netanyahu as a divisive force, in contrast to Barak, who could unify the country. And Barak's military past was emphasized — he was a former chief of staff and Israel's most decorated soldier — in an effort to convince undecided voters that Labor was not soft on security. "Every time I'm in a meeting, I can't take my eyes off his hands, thinking how many people he shot to death," James Carville told the *Jerusalem Report* in a January interview. "This is a guy who went into Beirut dressed as a woman, knocked the door down and killed four terrorists. Then he gunned down two jeeps full of Palestinian soldiers, got back on the mother ship and went back to Israel. Goddam! For somebody who looks like my daughter's uncle, he's one tough mother."

Barak was also boosted by the support of some high-profile public figures. For-

...er deputy-chief-of-staff Matan Vilnai joined Labor on January 19 despite reports that Netanyahu had sounded him out as a possible defense minister. The fact that leading Labor politicians such as Shlomo Ben-Ami and Haim Ramon remained in the party and did not follow ex-defense minister Yitzhak Mordechai and ex-chief-of-staff Amnon Lipkin-Shahak into the newly-formed Center Party also helped stabilize Barak's campaign.

CHALLENGE FROM THE CENTER

Nevertheless it did appear, early in the campaign, that the Center Party might smash the traditional left-right tie that had characterized Israeli politics for so long. The strategy was simple: Supporters of the new centrist venture believed that Israel's system of direct election for prime minister would enable them to conquer the country's highest office even if they didn't win the most Knesset seats, by tapping into the public's perceived disillusionment with Labor and Likud. They banked on taking some support from the right while at the same time convincing left-wing voters that a Labor candidate had no hope of toppling Netanyahu.

Several candidates saw themselves as potential centrist leaders. Already back in mid-1998 then Tel Aviv mayor Roni Milo had announced his intention to run for prime minister as a centrist. But the real centrist hope was former chief-of-staff Amnon Lipkin-Shahak, who had turned down requests by his ex-army buddy Barak to join him. With his military past and fresh, Mr. Clean image, Shahak was seen by many as a legitimate alternative to the big-party candidates. Initial polls showed him way ahead of Netanyahu by 48 percent to 33.

But no sooner did Shahak hold a much-heralded press conference on January 5 announcing his plans to run for prime minister than his popularity began to ebb. First, he told reporters that Prime Minister Netanyahu was "dangerous to Israel"—a comment that did not go down well among right-wing voters from whom Shahak hoped to draw support. He then made an unplanned visit on January 7 to South Tel Aviv's Hatikvah Quarter—a Likud bastion. An angry mob, still smarting over Shahak's comments about Netanyahu, hurled fruit, vegetables, and verbal abuse at the new candidate. Three days later market vendors who had shouted at Shahak brought fruit to his home as an offering of apology. But some political commentators charged that his unannounced walkabout in the Hatikvah market reflected the judgement of a political novice, and in a matter of days his popularity was seriously dented. But Shahak was also hurt by his inability to articulate a clear position on the country's most pressing issues. He spent most of the time during TV interviews talking vaguely about the need for national unity.

The Center's hopes were also undermined by disagreement between Shahak and another would-be prime minister, Dan Meridor, a former finance minister under Likud, who also hoped to lead the new party. As the two bickered the hopes of an effective centrist challenge receded.

Ultimately it was neither Meridor nor Shahak who ended up leading the party, but Yitzhak Mordechai, the defense minister in Netanyahu's government and one of the key drawing cards in Netanyahu's 1996 electoral victory. Aware that his defense minister was holding talks with Meridor, Shahak, and Milo, and that Mordechai had missed the deadline to register as a candidate for the January 22 Likud primaries, the prime minister ascended the podium at a Likud convention the next day, TV cameras rolling, and fired his defense minister live on the air. Reading out the letter of dismissal, he accused Mordechai of "personal ambition." The defense minister, he charged, had deserted Likud because he had not been promised the same post in the next government, and so had gone shopping for a better offer elsewhere.

An incensed Mordechai, who had watched his dismissal at his home near Jerusalem where he was meeting with Center Party leaders, came outside and told reporters: "The only thing I asked of Prime Minister Netanyahu was that he fulfill the diplomatic, security, and social policies that we had championed together." A few days later Mordechai attended his final cabinet meeting, angering the ministers present by reading aloud to them from Psalm 120: "Too long have I had my dwelling among those who hate peace, I am for peace but when I speak, they are for war."

The decision to place the Kurdistan-born Mordechai, an ex-general, at the head of the party was taken with the help of opinion polls the party commissioned to see who had the best chance of winning. Mordechai, a very popular figure viewed by the left as a moderate voice in the Netanyahu government, edged out Shahak by a fraction of a percent. In addition to the polls, the decision was also based on Mordechai's ethnic background, which would presumably enable him to draw Sephardi voters who traditionally supported the right. Mordechai was the country's first candidate for prime minister to hail from the "other Israel," the Sephardi lower classes.

While the centrists argued that only they could bring together left and right to move the peace process forward, internal tensions within the party weakened its chances. The stridently secular Milo, for instance, clashed with the traditional-leaning Mordechai. One of Mordechai's first visits after announcing his candidacy was with Rabbi Ovadia Yosef, the spiritual head of the ultra-Orthodox Shas party. For Mordechai, keen to draw Sephardi votes, it was a natural stop on the campaign trail. But it could not have pleased Milo, who feared such moves would alienate secular voters who looked to a centrist option as a way of ending the pivotal role of the religious parties in the country's coalition politics. The two were at loggerheads again after Mordechai supported a late-January Knesset vote in favor of Orthodox control over religious councils.

The four party heads bickered over the Knesset slate, with each pushing their own candidates. Ultimately, Uri Savir, one of the architects of the Oslo accords with the Palestinians and former director general of the Foreign Ministry, filled the number five slot, while Dalia Rabin Pelossof, daughter of the assassinated prime minister Yizhak Rabin, was number six. But the popular Alex Lubotzky, a Meridor man and former Knesset member for the centrist Third Way, was relegated to the unrealistic 12th spot.

The polls showed Mordechai trouncing Netanyahu in a two-way race, while Barak was only marginally ahead of Netanyahu. But they also revealed that Mordechai wouldn't make it into the second round to face Netanyahu. In a first-round Netanyahu-Mordechai-Barak race, the polls had Mordechai trailing far behind the other two candidates. Undeterred, the Center Party predicted that the polls would shift dramatically in the final weeks before the election when the public would opt for a "strategic vote." By this they meant that voters on the left would understand that Mordechai had the best chance of beating Netanyahu. This strategy was summed up by their slogan: "A vote for Barak is a vote for Bibi."

At the party's glitzy launch in Tel Aviv on March 10, Mordechai lashed out at the other two candidates. "He is incapable of understanding the mentality of the East and of Arab leaders," Mordechai said of Barak. He then attacked Netanyahu's credibility: "Neither his ministers nor world leaders believe him," he declared.

BARAK SCENTS VICTORY

Some of Barak's campaign strategists felt that Mordechai's running might actually help their candidate by wrenching traditional Likud voters away from Netanyahu. Having contemplated voting for Mordechai, or having actually done so in the first round, explained Stanley Greenberg, Likud voters might find it easier, psychologically, to move over to supporting Barak in the second.

In early March, Barak seized control of the campaign agenda with a carefully crafted electoral move. If elected, he declared, he would withdraw Israeli forces from Lebanon within a year of taking office. Netanyahu initially denounced Barak's pledge as a danger to the country's security. But soon after, seeking to counter Barak's move, Foreign Minister Ariel Sharon proposed that the elections be cancelled and that a government of national unity be formed with the express purpose of withdrawing Israeli forces from Lebanon.

Barak received another boost on March 15 when the state comptroller released a report determining that the ex-chief of staff had not abandoned wounded soldiers during a training accident at the Tze'elim base in 1992, where an elite unit had reportedly been rehearsing for a mission to assassinate Iraqi president Saddam Hussein. In an investigative report in the daily *Yediot Aharonot* some time after the accident, Barak had been accused of leaving the scene before the wounded were attended to. (Five soldiers of an elite reconnaissance unit died in the accident.) Justice Minister Tsachi Hanegbi, a close Netanyahu ally, had latched onto the report, holding it up during a 1997 Knesset debate in an effort to blacken Barak's name. Hanegbi continued to attack Barak on this issue even after the exonerating report was published, but this only hurt the Likud and Netanyahu — especially when other Likud politicians quickly dissociated themselves from Hanegbi's remarks.

Barak's plan to form a "One Israel" coalition gathered steam. First he man aged to quell opposition to the idea from Labor backbenchers who feared that incorporating groups representing constituencies traditionally outside of Labor would push veteran Laborites down the Knesset list into unrealistic slots. Undaunted, Barak engineered the inclusion of both David Levy's Gesher Party as well as the moderate Orthodox Meimad movement in the "One Israel" alliance announced on March 22. Barak hoped that the Moroccan-born Levy, a former Likudnik who had risen from being a construction worker and who had resigned as foreign minister in the Netanyahu government, would help attract voters among the Sephardi masses. Levy was promised the number three spot on the One Israel list behind Barak and Shimon Peres, and he was also promised a senior cabinet post if Barak won the election. The inclusion of Meimad, Barak hoped, would soften the party's perceived antireligious image. Meimad was also promised a ministerial post.

Barak received some potentially troubling news on March 25 when Azmi Bishara, an Arab MK from the National Democratic Alliance, announced that he was joining the race for prime minister. While Bishara conceded that he had no chance of winning, he said he hoped his candidacy would serve "to draw attention to Israel's Arab citizens, 20 percent of the electorate, whose inequality is not mentioned in the campaign." Bishara, who acknowledged he would take most of his votes from Barak, said it did not concern him that this might undermine the Labor candidate's chances and ultimately help Mordechai reach the second round against Netanyahu. In his eyes, he said, there was "no difference between Barak and Mordechai." "I am doing this," he said, "because I want empowerment of the Arab minority. That's the key issue."

One question on everyone's mind was whether Mordechai—as well as Bishara and Benny Begin, the son of former prime minister Menachem Begin who had announced his far-right bid for prime minister earlier in the campaign—would pull out before the first round and make it a two-horse race. Journalists repeatedly asked Mordechai whether he would stay the course. His progressively more agitated response was always the same: "Yes!"

While Barak's campaign was gaining momentum, many of his supporters were uneasy about a second round. One fear was that Arab voters—the vast majority of whom were Barak supporters—having cast their ballots for their own parties in the first round as well as for Barak, would not turn out in similarly high numbers for a second round in which the only race was for prime minister. By contrast, Netanyahu could most likely count on ultra-Orthodox voters—the vast majority of whom supported him—coming out in droves a second time. Labor's Yossi Beilin, fearful that Mordechai's insistence on running even though he had almost no chance of making it into the second round could doom Barak, suggested in April that if Mordechai wanted "to achieve his main goal—getting rid of Netanyahu—now's the time to join Barak." Beilin was basing his assertion on internal Labor polls conducted in late March that showed Barak demolishing Netanyahu—55 percent to 38 percent—if Mordechai withdrew and backed him.

ɔut despite the poll numbers showing him languishing at around 15 percent, Mordechai refused to quit.

The March 17 conviction of Shas leader Arye Deri for bribery, fraud, and breach of public trust ultimately played into Barak's hands. Initially the three leading candidates remained largely silent on the matter, fearful that criticism of the Shas leader would lose them votes in his constituency. Even after Deri received a four-year sentence on April 15, only Benny Begin announced that he would not engage in coalition negotiations with a convicted felon. But after Attorney General Elyakim Rubinstein accused the three leading candidates of being guilty of "the silence of the lambs," Barak added his voice to that of Begin's, saying that if he were elected he would refuse to negotiate with Deri. Barak surely calculated that he would win few votes in the Shas constituency anyway, and the announcement did not harm him among other swing voters, such as the Russians and middle class right-wingers. Netanyahu, who needed the support of Shas voters, refused to commit himself.

Netanyahu suffered a major blow on April 13 in one of the most dramatic events of the campaign—a live television debate between himself and Mordechai. Barak, who was not comfortable appearing on television, took the advice of his aides and stayed away. While most of the public expected the prime minister, a consummate TV performer, to overwhelm the often stiff and labored Mordechai, by the time the debate was over it was evident that Mordechai had delivered a telling setback to Netanyahu's reelection bid. Mordechai, surprisingly, was the more relaxed of the two, and on orders from his advisers he often flashed a derisory smile which seemed to unnerve the prime minister. Netanyahu's original plan to address his questions to an absent Barak and to ignore Mordechai failed dismally, as the Center Party leader launched a blistering assault on the prime minister's character and credibility. When, for instance, Netanyahu declared that he would never make any territorial compromises on the Golan Heights, Mordechai sneered at him, challenging Netanyahu to "look me in the eye." Then, when Netanyahu spoke of how he had reduced terror, Mordechai suggested that the prime minister had not had the patience to listen to security briefings at cabinet meetings. "Bibi," Mordechai said witheringly, "you know that your best friends don't believe you. . . . You're bankrupt. You're a personal failure."

The most embarrassing moment for Netanyahu, though, came when talk-show host Nissim Mishal threatened to end the debate if the prime minister did not put away a Likud statistical chart on economic performance, on the grounds that it was a violation of election propaganda restrictions. Resting his chin on the chart—like a naughty schoolboy, as some commentators later described it—Netanyahu refused to put it away, but was ultimately forced to back down by Mishal. One post-debate poll gave Mordechai a stunning 56-24 victory. While Mordechai had clearly humiliated Netanyahu, he had not really boosted his own chances since he failed, when challenged by Netanyahu, to outline a clear program for the Center Party. "You're a party of losers," Netanyahu chided Mordechai.

By refusing to join the bitter, often personal confrontation, Barak had clearly made a wise decision. He was perceived as being above the fray while the other two candidates had damaged one another. Barak commented: "As entertainment, it wasn't bad." During the campaign Barak cleverly turned his problem with TV to his own advantage, tacitly accepting Netanyahu's superiority with the medium but at the same time pointing out that this was exactly the prime minister's problem: He was great on TV, but had failed miserably at governing.

Polls toward the end of April showed Barak with a bigger lead over Netanyahu than that enjoyed by Mordechai. An April 23 poll in the daily *Ma'ariv*, for instance, showed Barak beating the prime minister by 46-40, whereas Mordechai held a much slimmer 42-39 lead. When the TV commercials got underway on April 28, Barak's ads were far more effective than those of Netanyahu. It had been Netanyahu, in 1996, who had introduced an American-style campaign with short messages repeated incessantly, and the Barak campaign followed suit in 1999. Barak's commercials chipped away at Netanyahu on the economic front. "If you've lost your job," one commercial went, "then why should he (Netanyahu) keep his?" Barak's slogan, "Israel Wants Change – Ehud Barak," seemed to capture the national mood.

To beef up his image among Russian voters — Barak trailed Netanyahu 70-20 in this sector at the start of the campaign — the opposition leader played up his military past. His ads ran a famous picture of himself in white overalls, standing over the body of a dead terrorist on the wing of a Sabena plane in 1972, after his reconnaissance unit had foiled a hijacking by storming the plane at Ben-Gurion Airport. Barak's commercials also portrayed Netanyahu as devious and untrustworthy: One ad showed a slow motion picture of the prime minister winking conspiratorially.

The Netanyahu ads, in contrast, appeared to lack a clear message or strategy. While Netanyahu did effectively highlight the drop in terror attacks since he had taken office, his TV campaign appeared to be a rerun of 1996. He attacked the "left," saying it would be soft in negotiations with the Arabs and would ultimately divide Jerusalem — a charge that had worked against Shimon Peres in 1996. But Barak's security credentials — as well as some assistance from Jerusalem's Likud mayor, Ehud Olmert — undermined these claims. Olmert announced that he did not believe that Barak would divide Jerusalem, and Barak's campaign chiefs cleverly wove Olmert's statement into one of their election ads.

As the elections drew closer Netanyahu seemed to become increasingly desperate. Against the advice of his Likud colleagues, in what appeared to be a last-ditch effort to swing the tide in his direction, he used footage of the 1996 Hamas suicide bus bombings. But instead of winning back those who had supported him in 1996, the decision seemed to signal panic. And when Netanyahu began copying one of Barak's ads by running slow motion footage of the Labor leader flashing a knowing wink, it was clear that Barak had the upper hand.

The fact that so many important Likud members — Dan Meridor, David Levy, Benny Begin, Yitzhak Mordechai — had all abandoned the prime minister, severely dented his credibility. If so many senior party members had left ministerial posts, many voters reasoned, the problem must lie with the prime minister. Netanyahu's reputation was further sullied by two other developments in late April. Yossi Peled, the former head of the IDF's Northern Command who had supported Netanyahu in 1996, announced he was thoroughly disillusioned with the prime minister and was shifting his support to Barak. This boosted Barak's credentials among right-wing voters. Then, with only weeks to go to the election, a personal letter Peled had written to Netanyahu 18 months earlier, which included a stinging personal indictment of the prime minister, was published in the press. "You are a tremendous disappointment," Peled wrote. "You broadcast panic, a lack of leadership, a lack of private and public honesty."

Netanyahu sustained yet another serious blow with the highly publicized April 25 resignation of Ya'akov Kedmi, the head of Nativ, a semisecret organization dealing with Jewish emigration from the former Soviet Union. Kedmi resigned after the contents of a harshly critical letter he sent to the prime minister accusing him of "deserting" Soviet Jews was broadcast on Israel TV. Kedmi held legendary status among many Russian voters because of his efforts on the emigration front and the fact that he had been, under his original name of Yasha Kazakov, a prisoner of Zion. Netanyahu hit back, declaring that he had planned to fire Kedmi anyway because a state comptroller's report had found irregularities in Nativ. But the dispute damaged the prime minister's image among the immigrant voters. And Kedmi, who had been part of Barak's tank crew in the 1973 Yom Kippur War, publicly lauded his former commander.

Barak made another shrewd move in late April when he effectively promised the Ministry of the Interior—a Shas stronghold for 15 years—to the Yisrael B'Aliyah Party, headed by former dissident Natan Sharansky. This was a clear sop to Russian voters who despised the ministry that had subjected some of them to the humiliation of having to prove their Jewishness. While not making an outright promise to Sharansky, Barak said he would give the post to someone who would give citizenship to all those people who were eligible under the Law of Return. Netanyahu, however, was in a Catch-22: he needed Russian support, but he couldn't afford to abandon Shas, most of whose voters supported him.

In an effort to win back right-wing voters, especially the settlers whom he had disappointed when he signed the Wye River accord in October 1998, Netanyahu turned a blind eye to settlement activity, specifically the establishment of several dozen West Bank hilltop outposts aimed at blocking future territorial concessions to the Palestinians. It seemed to pay off, belatedly, when the settler leadership announced on April 28 that it was backing Netanyahu over the more hard-line Benny Begin.

But by the end of April Barak had built a substantial lead over Netanyahu. One poll showed him ahead by 47 to 42 and another by 48 to 41. But Barak supporters remained skeptical, as polls had traditionally underestimated the power of the right. And they feared that Netanyahu might pull one last preelection rabbit from his hat.

Barak did experience a potentially disastrous setback only two-and-a-half weeks before the election. With Barak present at a rally in support of him, actress Tiki Dayan got up on stage and belittled Netanyahu voters. "We are talking about a different nation," said Dayan mockingly. "Don't you understand? We're talking about people of the shuk, the riffraff." Even though Dayan was herself Sephardi, the comments smacked of the ethnic condescension that many Sephardi voters associated with the Labor Party and its leaders. The Likud was quick to make political capital out of the ethnic slur: Bumper stickers announcing, "I Am Proud Riffraff," soon began appearing on the cars of Netanyahu supporters, and Likud politicians attacked Barak for not having immediately denounced Dayan.

But the incident failed to derail the Barak campaign, thanks in no small measure to Netanyahu. Desperate to turn the electoral tide by exploiting Dayan's comments, he headed for the Hatikvah Market—a Likud stronghold—to ignite his lethargic supporters. But the prime minister was caught live on camera telling a crowd that Barak and the left "hate the Sephardim, hate the Russians . . . Ethiopians . . . everybody." Netanyahu's somewhat irresponsible rhetoric served to neutralize Dayan's remarks. Netanyahu's market whisper, Barak campaign strategist Robert Shrum remarked after the election, "proved our claim that he really was divisive." By early May Barak's lead had grown. Polls in both *Yediot Aharonot* and *Ma'ariv* showed him ahead by eight percentage points.

By this time Netanyahu was also criticized by some in his own Likud for sacrificing the party. Not only was the party being ignored in the campaign, they charged, but Netanyahu, desperate to get Shas votes, was willingly surrendering Likud voters to the Sephardi party as long as they voted for him for prime minister. When police served orders on May 10 to close down three departments at Orient House, the Palestinian headquarters in East Jerusalem, there were fears that Netanyahu might try to force a showdown in one final desperate effort to turn the electoral tide. Netanyahu insisted that the three offices were engaging in illegal activity, but the Palestinians threatened bloodshed if the police entered the building. The issue was defused when the Supreme Court issued an injunction that forestalled closure of the offices until a date that was after the elections.

As election day drew closer and the polls showed Barak pulling away, Netanyahu increasingly clashed with Likud campaign chief Limor Livnat, until he finally took over the running of the campaign himself. Arthur Finkelstein, Netanyahu's campaign guru who had engineered his 1996 electoral success, also clashed with Netanyahu, leaving the country a few days before the election.

On election day Netanyahu arranged to be interviewed on pirate Shas radio stations to appeal to Sephardi voters for their support. He knew that his action was a clear violation of the law—not only because he was appearing on a pirate station, but also because of legislation barring the broadcasting of campaign propaganda on election day.

The contrast to the Barak campaign was stark. Extremely well organized, with many of Barak's ex-army buddies in charge rather than politicians, Barak supporters carrying placards and banners took control of the streets and major intersections around the country, helping to create momentum for their candidate. In a stunning visual display, fields around the country were "plowed" with hundreds of Barak posters as far as the eye could see. During the campaign Barak had some 18,000 volunteers working for him; that number rose to 50,000 on election day. Many on the left, still traumatized by the Rabin assassination, Netanyahu's 1996 victory, and the disintegration of the peace process, needed little coaxing to get involved. (On the day of the election Barak's campaign even had special squads combing the ultra-Orthodox areas to deter suspected electoral fraud.) The Likud's Michael Eitan, however, complained that Barak's extensive organization was being funded in violation of the law, through the channeling of money to campaign needs via a series of nonprofit organizations. Later in the year the state comptroller began to investigate these allegations.

BARAK'S VICTORY

With the polls giving Barak a substantial lead, pressure mounted on the minor candidates to pull out and enable the winner to be determined in the first round. The Arab candidate, Azmi Bishara, set a chain reaction in motion on Saturday evening, May 15, when he announced that he was withdrawing and that Barak had promised him improved treatment for Arab citizens—a claim denied by the Barak camp but quickly seized on by the Likud. The next day, with less than 24 hours to go, Mordechai called a dramatic press conference where he announced that he was withdrawing, and he issued a lukewarm endorsement of Barak. Hours later Benny Begin also withdrew, leaving Barak and Netanyahu to conduct a two-horse race. For Netanyahu, who knew that he could only win if there were a second round, this was the final nail in his electoral coffin.

When the voting booths closed, straw polls conducted by TV stations confirmed what the pollsters had been saying. Channel Two gave Barak a 57-43 victory, while Channel One's projection was 58.5-41.5. When the votes were ultimately counted Barak ended up with a little over 56 percent and Netanyahu a little under 44 percent. The result was stunning, considering that for 20 years Israeli elections had been decided by the slimmest of margins.

Within 35 minutes of the announcement of the exit polls, the prime minister entered a room at the Tel Aviv Hilton filled with party faithful and announced, in remarks broadcast live around the world, that he was stepping down as leader of the Likud. Stunned activists, some crying, listened as Netanyahu announced that he wanted "a time-out to be with my family and to decide my future." Political commentators suggested that by bowing out immediately, Netanyahu spared himself the feeding frenzy he would have endured at the hands of his embittered Likud colleagues had he decided to stay on. (Ten days later Netanyahu announced at a Likud Central Committee meeting that he was also quitting the

Knesset. "We'll be back," he vowed, as the crowd cheered him and beseeched him not to leave. At the convention Sharon was named temporary party leader until the September primaries.)

As it became clear that Barak had won a landslide victory, tens of thousands of his supporters began streaming to Rabin Square in Tel Aviv to celebrate. They danced into the night and cracked open champagne. In the early hours of the morning Barak arrived with his wife, Navah, and Rabin's widow, Leah. "I came here, to Rabin Square, to this place where our hearts were broken," Barak told the jubilant crowd. "I came to swear to you . . . that this indeed is the dawn of a new day." Leah Rabin declared: "We have been walking in the fog for three years. Now the sky is clearing."

Barak emphasized the unity theme that had characterized his campaign. "I respect the hundreds of thousands of voters who exercised their democratic right and did not vote for me," he declared. "But from this moment on, we're together, we're one nation. I intend to be the prime minister of all the people. Whatever our differences, we are brothers, and brothers go forward together." Barak's first visit after his victory was to the Western Wall where he recited psalms and placed a piece of paper with a prayer between the stones. From there he headed for Rabin's grave on Mt. Herzl. He had thus signified his respect for Jewish values and at the same time acknowledged the anguish of the left.

How They Voted

A shift in the Russian immigrant vote was key to Barak's success. Three months before the election, polls showed Netanyahu with more than 50 percent of the vote and Barak with less than 20 percent—a trend that appeared certain to return Netanyahu to power. Netanyahu visited Russia in late March to boost his support even further in the immigrant sector. At one point Ariel Sharon confidently announced that Likud polls showed Netanyahu winning 67 percent of the Russian vote.

But Barak refused to give up on the immigrants and he launched a highly effective campaign to reverse the trend. Barak had his biography translated into Russian and distributed thousands of copies among the immigrants. He also wrote regularly in the usually right-leaning Russian press. Barak's strategists played up his military past among the immigrants, and the public falling-out between Netanyahu and Nativ head Ya'akov Kedmi also enhanced Barak's popularity among the Russians.

While Sharansky had quietly helped Netanyahu in the 1996 elections, this time he repeatedly asserted that his party was "not in anybody's pocket." One reason was that Avigdor Lieberman, the ex-director general of the Prime Minister's Office under Netanyahu, had set up a new immigrant party in what many saw as a bid to secure votes for his former boss among the Russians. In Sharansky's eyes this was a direct threat to his party, and it caused tension between him and the prime minister. In some areas around the country local Yisrael B'Aliyah activists even teamed up with One Israel supporters to work for Barak's election—a reversal of what had happened in 1996.

One feature of the campaign that had a defining influence on the race for prime minister was the showdown between the ultra-Orthodox Sephardi Shas Party and Yisrael B'Aliyah. Socioeconomic and cultural tensions between Sephardim and immigrants from the former Soviet Union—many of whom lived in the same development towns—had been growing for some time. They were brought to the surface by a Yisrael B'Aliyah campaign commercial signaling the party's intention to wrest the Ministry of Interior from Shas. The slogan in the Yisrael B'Aliyah ad became a highlight of the campaign. In English the slogan translated as, "The Interior Ministry in Shas Control? No. The Interior Ministry in Our Control." In response, incensed Shas leaders threatened to run TV campaign ads showing Russian prostitutes and immigrant shops selling pork. One Shas radio ad in fact described the Russian immigrants as prostitutes, churchgoers, and pork-eaters.

While the Yisrael B'Aliyah commercial increased support for Shas, it also boosted Russian immigrant support for Ehud Barak in the prime ministerial race, since Shas had strongly embraced Netanyahu. The result: Many of the Russian immigrants who at the start of the campaign had expressed a preference for Netanyahu switched their support to Barak, who had also publicly hinted that if elected he would give the interior portfolio to Yisrael B'Aliyah. When the votes were counted it emerged that Barak had turned the tables on Netanyahu and had won 58 percent of the immigrant vote. Political analysts suggested that many Russians had opted for Barak because they viewed Shas and the other ultra-Orthodox parties with whom Netanyahu was so closely identified as proponents of religious coercion and threats to their secular culture.

But it wasn't only the Russians who swung the election to Barak. Netanyahu lost votes in all his traditional constituencies. In the Likud stronghold of Beersheba, for instance, party activists literally crossed the lines in droves to work for Barak. The disillusionment with Netanyahu in this southern Negev city that had helped propel him to power in 1996 was palpable. "Bibi promised so many things," said one bitter ex-Likudnik. "Factories, investors. Not to open a national garbage dump here. He didn't keep any promise, not one."

Even on the Golan Heights Barak won 58.5 percent of the vote. This was despite his statement during the campaign that he planned to restart talks with the Syrians, and the fact that he had gone up to the Golan while opposition leader and told the residents at a public gathering that "painful compromises" would have to be made for peace with Syria, a deal that would require Israeli withdrawal. Even among the West Bank settlers Netanyahu didn't fare as well as in 1996, with some preferring to place a blank slip in the ballot box to register their protest over his signing of the Wye accords.

The two constituencies that repeated their 1996 voting patterns were the Arabs,

94 percent of whom voted for Barak, and the ultra-Orthodox, of whom well over 90 percent supported Netanyahu.

A New Government

BATTLE FOR THE KNESSET

The Likud chose its Knesset slate at primaries on February 8 in an atmosphere of acrimony among the top contenders. When the votes were counted Science Minister Silvan Shalom placed first, followed by Communications Minister Limor Livnat, Tourism Minister Moshe Katsav, and coalition chairman Meir Shitreet, who had recently been appointed finance minister. There were also a number of surprises, especially the fact that Foreign Minister Ariel Sharon only managed to place eighth and Justice Minister Tsachi Hanegbi 12th. Defense Minister Moshe Arens placed a humiliating 26th.

Shlomo Ben-Ami, the Algerian-born history professor and ex-ambassador to Spain, placed first in the Labor primaries held on February 15, followed by Yossi Beilin and Matan Vilnai, the former deputy-chief-of-staff and a new face in politics. (Shimon Peres had already been automatically guaranteed the second slot behind Barak.)

The National Religious Party chose a list made up mostly of moderate Orthodox candidates, while settler ideologue Hanan Porat was demoted to the unrealistic 11th spot. Angered by this and by his party's apparent shift toward pragmatism on the peace process, Porat abandoned the NRP together with another settler representative, MK Zvi Hendel, and formed the Emunim (Believers) faction. On March 12 Porat joined up with Rehavam Ze'evi's far-right Moledet and Benny Begin's Herut to form the National Union, headed by Begin and supported largely by the settlers. Now fearing that their list might seem too moderate and that they would lose voters to the National Union, the NRP parachuted former MK Haim Druckman—a settler rabbi who had once signed a letter calling on Orthodox soldiers to refuse any order to evacuate settlements—into the number two spot behind party leader Yitzhak Levy. In the primaries of the left-wing secular Meretz party, four women got into the top ten slots, with the tenth filled by Hussnia Jabara, an Israeli Arab woman.

When registration for parties ended at midnight on March 30, 33 lists were set to run. Among the new parties was the immigrant list Yisrael Beiteinu (Israel Our Home), set up by Avigdor Lieberman, the former director general of the Prime Minister's Office under Netanyahu. At the press conference launching his party Lieberman, who had been the subject of several police investigations, blasted the legal establishment and the police. "The president of the Supreme Court has more power today than does the prime minister," he railed. "We cannot agree to what is happening in the police and the public prosecution. We have become a police state." Lieberman said his party would support fundamental change in the electoral system, with the presidential-style model being the most preferable. But many saw Lieberman's new party as an attempt by the man who had been Netanyahu's closest ally to draw immigrant votes for his former boss in the race for prime minister. Asked whether Lieberman posed a threat to Yisrael B'Aliyah, senior party member Roman Bronfman demurred: While Lieberman "offers breaking down the Israeli establishment" to newcomers from the former Soviet Union, he argued, "we offer a share in its success."

The centrist Shinui Party broke away from the Meretz bloc (which had been a coalition of Ratz, Shinui, and Mapam) and decided to run separately. In what was to prove a stroke of genius, party leader Avraham Poraz stepped back into second spot and invited veteran firebrand journalist Yosef "Tommy" Lapid to head the stridently secular ticket. Lapid, violently opposed to religious coercion, immediately drew attention to himself and the party as he launched a verbal barrage against the ultra-Orthodox.

A new Arab nationalist party called Balad and headed by MK Azmi Bishara, also announced it would run. At the party's convention Bishara said that Balad would work to do away with the definition of Israel as a Jewish state and to have the Law of Return revoked.

Histadrut union leader Amir Peretz left Labor to set up his own One Nation Party, which aimed to represent workers' interests, while Nehama Ronen, the director general of the Environment Ministry, left her post early in the year to form the Voice of the Environment Party. (Ultimately the party was disbanded when Ronen linked up with the Center Party and ran in the seventh slot, narrowly missing out on a Knesset seat.) Cosmetics tycoon Pnina Rosenblum set up her own party and vowed to work for women's rights.

Some of the more curious electoral bids included a Casino Party, which pushed for the legalization of gambling; a party promoting transcendental meditation; and the Green Leaf Party which supported the legalization of marijuana.

RESULTS OF THE KNESSET VOTE

While the exit polls' prediction of a stunning victory for Barak drew immediate attention, the focus of the evening soon shifted to the remarkable electoral success of Shas, which moved from ten seats to 17. After Shas leader Arye Deri had been convicted in March and then sentenced to four years for bribery a month before the election, he had refused to stand down. Instead, he launched himself into the party campaign and boasted that Shas would get 18 seats; if it failed to retain its present ten seats, he pledged to take personal responsibility.

Deri turned his trial into the centerpiece of the Shas campaign, as party activists played up the charge that he had been persecuted and unfairly treated because of his Sephardi ethnic background and religious beliefs. Deri instigated the production of a video titled "I Accuse" in which the judicial system was portrayed as biased against Sephardim. Thousands of copies were distributed to potential

Shas supporters and, according to a postelection poll in the daily *Yediot Aharnot*, the ploy appeared to have paid off: 29 percent of those who voted for Shas pointed to the Deri trial as one of the cardinal reasons. (The battle between Yisrael B'Aliyah and Shas also served to boost the party's support.)

The gains made by Shas came largely at the expense of the Likud, which plummeted from 32 seats to 19. Many lower-class Sephardim who had voted Likud for much of their lives as a protest against the establishment, which they viewed as Ashkenazi-dominated and represented by Labor, shifted to Shas, which they felt had become a much more authentic representative of their ethnic and social interests. In the Likud stronghold of Tiberias, Shas went from 17.5 percent of the vote to 24.1 percent. In towns like Safed, Kiryat Shmonah, Akko, and Migdal Ha'Emek, the trend was similar. Overall, Shas became the biggest party in 30 different locations around the country. These included the major cities of Jerusalem (17.3 percent of the vote) and Beersheba (22.7 percent), and the development towns of Netivot (43.5 percent) and Beth She'an (40.6 percent).

While the Likud's support had been almost halved, Labor also suffered, falling from 34 seats to 26. Once again the hybrid electoral system introduced in 1996, which allowed voters to place one ballot for prime minister and another for a party, further fractionalized the political map, resulting in the election of no fewer than 15 parties. Immediately after the election there were renewed calls from politicians in Labor and Likud for a change in a system that had created a situation where, together, the two largest parties did not command a majority in the Knesset.

While Shas provided the electoral shock with 17 mandates, its secular rival Shinui also surprised by winning six seats. Two months before the election the avowedly secular and free-market party looked like it had little hope of crossing the electoral threshold of 1.5 percent (or close to 50,000 votes). But, led by Yosef "Tommy" Lapid, known for his fiery rhetoric and sharp tongue—a reputation he earned as a panelist on Israel TV's boisterous "Popolitika" talk show—the party focused on a single issue: ultra-Orthodox power and the need to curb it. The ultra-Orthodox, he railed, were trying to impose their religious lifestyle on secular Israel, lived parasitically off the tax money paid by non-ultra-Orthodox Israelis, and didn't serve in the army. Lapid's TV ads portrayed this message crudely: Rows of black fedoras were used to represent the ultra-Orthodox, and in one commercial he appeared with boxes of dog food and deodorant, all with a kosher stamp, and pointed out to viewers that they were paying bloated prices for "absurd" rabbinic stamps of approval. Lapid's at times brutal assault on the ultra-Orthodox—at one point he referred to them as "the sickness" and himself as "the doctor"—paid off: Secular voters, fed up with ultra-Orthodox political power, gave the party a stunning six seats. For its part, the ultra-Orthodox press began spelling Lapid's name "La Pid," in an effort to evoke the name of far-right French politician Jean Marie Le Pen. And in the weeks after the election Lapid was given a bodyguard detail as a result of a slew of telephone death threats.

The fact that Benny Begin's National Union—the party that most vociferously ampioned the Greater Israel cause—won only four Knesset seats, was taken as a sign that the settler ideology had been dealt a major blow. But many settlers adopted a fatalistic approach, pointing out that there was not a huge ideological chasm between Barak and Netanyahu. In fact, almost 20 percent of the settlers voted for Barak, while others placed a blank slip in the ballot box. Many settlers felt that the dismantling of settlements was inevitable. They hoped to persuade Barak to limit the damage and preserve as many settlements as possible.

The great disappointment of the election was the Center Party, which ended up with only six seats after polls had given it as many as 15 early in the campaign. Sharansky's Yisrael B'Aliyah maintained its six seats, while Lieberman's Yisrael Beiteinu did well, garnering four seats, with support coming not only from immigrants but also from disgruntled Likudniks. The Ashkenazi ultra-Orthodox United Torah Judaism (UTJ) increased its Knesset share from four to five seats. Despite Shinui's good showing, Meretz still managed to win ten seats, with Hussnia Jabara, number ten on the list, becoming the first-ever Arab woman in the Knesset. Amir Peretz's One Nation won two seats. The Arab parties won a total of ten seats, with the United Arab list winning five, Hadash (Communist) taking three, and Balad two.

Some parties faded into oblivion, failing to pass the electoral threshold. These included the centrist Third Way, which was headed by Internal Security Minister Avigdor Kahalani, and which had, with its four seats, been part of the Netanyahu coalition. Another party that disappeared was Tzomet, headed by former chief-of-staff Rafael Eitan, who had been agriculture and environment minister in Netanyahu's government.

BUILDING A COALITION

Barak's coalition-building task was highly intricate. He had inherited a fragmented political system, and while his One Israel was the biggest party, it only had 26 seats. To be true to his plan to build a broad-based coalition Barak would have to bring together parties with diametrically opposed worldviews, like the stridently secular Meretz and the ultra-Orthodox. Intent on keeping Labor politicians out of the talks, Barak chose a group of lawyers to conduct the coalition negotiations. (Barak was probably influenced by Yitzhak Rabin's failure to build a broad-based coalition in 1992, partly because politicians from his own party, often driven by their own interests, had conducted the negotiations.)

The big question facing Barak was whether to include Shas or the Likud. Barak's preference was clearly Shas, which he believed would make a more amenable peace partner than the Likud, even though a deal with Shas would mean at least a temporary postponement of internal reforms such as drawing up a constitution and addressing issues of religion and state.

There was, however, strong opposition among many of Barak's secular voters to having Shas in the coalition. They demonstrated outside the Herzliyah hotel where the coalition talks were taking place, holding up placards pleading with the prime minister-elect, "Just not Shas." For these people Shas was anathema because it stood, in their eyes, for religious fundamentalism and disregard for the rule of law, as embodied in the claim that Arye Deri was innocent, irrespective of what the court had ruled. "Read my lips," declared Meretz leader Yossi Sarid. "Meretz won't sit in a cabinet with Shas." But some of Labor's top leaders like Haim Ramon and Shlomo Ben-Ami came out in support of bringing Shas into the coalition on the grounds that the party represented over 400,000 Israelis, many of whom felt marginalized. Keeping them out, the argument went, would alienate them even further from the left.

Toward the end of June, though, Barak suddenly began talks with Likud leader Ariel Sharon, triggering speculation that he may have made a strategic switch, preferring the Likud to Shas. But when the talks with Sharon broke down it was widely believed that Barak had simply used the Likud leader to lower Shas's price for entry into the coalition. "The behavior of One Israel was unworthy and dishonorable," an angry Sharon charged.

Barak refused to back down on his preelection pledge not to negotiate with Shas as long as Deri remained at the helm. Hoping to appease Barak, Deri resigned from the Knesset. But a short while later at a postelection rally he gave the impression that he had no intention of leaving politics. He shouted into the microphone: "I am not retiring. I am not retiring. I am not retiring." But Barak stood firm, and Shas leaders, anxious to be in the coalition in order to ensure a steady flow of funds to their education system, which was in heavy debt, searched for a way around the Deri dilemma. A battle of nerves ensued with Barak hinting that, if necessary, he was prepared to set up a narrow coalition and even a minority government. Ultimately it was Deri and Shas who blinked first. With Barak announcing that he was getting ready to seal coalition deals, Deri made a dramatic announcement on June 15: He was resigning as head of Shas. The next day Shas's Council of Torah Sages — the party's supreme spiritual body which was headed by Rabbi Ovadia Yosef — accepted Deri's resignation and two days later coalition negotiations between Barak and Shas began, ultimately leading to Shas joining the government. Despite Sarid's initial proclamations, Meretz also finally agreed to join.

During the coalition negotiations Barak came under fire from Arab politicians who charged that despite their support for him the prime minister-elect had discounted them as possible coalition partners and had not even invited them to a preliminary discussion. "Ninety-five percent of our people backed Barak," complained Mohammed Baraka, leader of Hadash, "and we are not considered legitimate partners even for coalition talks, never mind membership in the coalition. You can't call that anything but racism." (Adding to the friction, several Arab demonstrators, including Azmi Bishara, were injured when police fired rubber bullets at a crowd of some 200 protesting the demolition of an illegally built house in the city of Lod near Tel Aviv. The police claimed that they had only opened fire after they were pelted with rocks.)

Finally, with the 45 days afforded him by law to build a coalition almost up,

Barak announced on July 6 that he had a government. The 75-member coalition included seven parties: One Israel (26 seats); Shas (17); Meretz (10); Yisrael B'Aliyah (6); the Center Party (6); the National Religious Party (5); and United Torah Judaism (5). "We have been able to set up a coalition that is both wide and stable," Barak said in an interview. "It represents an amalgam of the entire Israeli political spectrum from left to right, and I am convinced it will be able to meet all the challenges facing Israel today."

While a broad coalition would presumably ensure that no single party could make excessive demands, Barak's inclusive approach produced a coalition riddled with internal contradictions, a sure recipe for regular crises. One potential minefield was the peace process. Could Barak deal with peacemaking in a way that satisfied both the left-wing Meretz and the right-wing NRP? And as for religion and state, how would Barak deal with the thorny subject of religious pluralism and find a way out of the conversion showdown, and at the same time satisfy the secular Meretz, the moderate Orthodox Meimad, and the ultra-Orthodox Shas and United Torah Judaism?

To deal with settlements, Barak negotiated a coalition agreement calling for a ministerial committee, including representatives from all the coalition parties. Each party would have veto power, but in the event of a deadlock Barak would have the final say. On the thorny issue of drafting yeshivah students, Barak backtracked on his original pledge to push through legislation that would conscript almost all of them—estimated at some 30,000—and agreed in coalition talks with UTJ that only a small number would do full army service, while the majority would be exempted after a month of basic training at age 24 or 25. Most importantly the agreement meant that for the first time yeshivah students—barred from working until they had served in the army—could enter the workforce in their mid-20s, a move that would lessen the economic hardship in the ultra-Orthodox community.

Barak believed that the existence of multiple options to reshape the coalition if necessary reinforced the government's stability. If, for example, the NRP and Shas were to leave over the peace process or religious-secular issues, Barak knew he had a backup option in the form of Shinui, One Nation, the Arab parties, and possibly the Likud. Some commentators even suggested that Barak had a two-stage plan: First, to forge ahead on the peace front while sidestepping a showdown over religion and state, then, once agreements had been achieved with the Palestinians and the Syrians, to reconstitute the coalition with the Likud and Shinui but without Shas and UTJ, so as to move forward on domestic issues like religion and state. "This is a peace coalition," Barak announced on forming his government. "It is not a coalition of peaceniks, but it is a coalition committed to depart from the policies of the Netanyahu government, which were policies of confrontation and paralysis."

Meanwhile, Labor Party leaders had been anxiously waiting to see who would be rewarded with ministerial posts. Many of them were already irritated with

Barak at having been kept out of the coalition negotiations, and when he announced the list of Labor ministers disillusionment deepened. Some were peeved at not receiving senior portfolios, while others were placed in ministries for which they had no particular enthusiasm. Yossi Beilin, who had hoped for the Foreign Ministry, had to settle for the Ministry of Justice, while Shlomo Ben-Ami, who had his eye on the treasury portfolio, was shoved into the Ministry of Internal Security. Barak also overlooked two senior Laborites completely: ex-Jewish Agency chief Avraham Burg and Uzi Baram, a minister in the previous Labor government. Barak, some Laborites griped, had gone for loyalty over ability.

The discontent escalated into dissension when, in an internal Labor Party ballot on July 6, angry Laborites voted in Burg as speaker of the Knesset over Barak's candidate, Shalom Simhon. At a party meeting to announce the results Burg was caught on camera mouthing the words "let him choke" to Haim Ramon, as Barak spoke from the podium. There was also tension between Barak and Peres over which ministry would be allotted to the former party leader. When Barak offered Peres the undefined portfolio of regional cooperation minister, which was to be made up of various pieces taken from other ministries, many in the party saw it as a slap in the face for Peres. Political commentators suggested that Barak's intention was to keep Peres as far as possible from the decision-making process, especially on peace matters.

GOVERNMENT MINISTERS

Prime Minister and Defense Minister: Ehud Barak, 57, Labor-One Israel
Foreign Minister: David Levy, 61, Gesher
Finance Minister: Avraham Shochat, 63, Labor-One Israel
Internal Security Minister: Shlomo Ben-Ami, 56, Labor-One Israel
Justice Minister: Yossi Beilin, 51, Labor-One Israel
Minister for Jerusalem Affairs: Haim Ramon, 49, Labor-One Israel
Communications Minister: Binyamin Ben-Eliezer, 63, Labor-One Israel
Regional Cooperation Minister: Shimon Peres, 75, Labor-One Israel
Environment Minister: Dalia Itzik, 46, Labor-One Israel
Interior Minister: Natan Sharansky, 51, Yisrael B'Aliyah
Labor and Social Affairs Minister: Eli Yishai, 36, Shas
Infrastructure Minister: Eli Suissa, 43, Shas
Health Minister: Shlomo Benizri, 38, Shas
Religious Affairs Minister: Yitzhak Cohen, 47, Shas
Transport Minister: Yitzhak Mordechai, 54, Center Party
Education Minister: Yossi Sarid, 58, Meretz
Industry and Trade Minister: Ran Cohen, 60, Meretz
Housing Minister: Yitzhak Levy, 52, NRP

Barak drew fire from the opposition as well as from his own party over his plan to expand the number of ministers from 18 to 24. Opponents argued that the move as not only costly but would also set a dangerous precedent, since a Basic Law had to be changed in order to accommodate the enlarged cabinet. Barak, however, argued that an increase in the number of ministers was vital to produce a broad, inclusive coalition that would unify as many different parts of the nation as possible. In the end the legislation passed, and five additional ministers were sworn in on August 5, leaving one slot still open:

Culture, Science and Sports Minister: Matan Vilnai, 55, Labor-One Israel
Minister in the Prime Minister's Office, responsible for Jewish communities: Rabbi Michael Melchior, 46, Meimad
Tourism Minister: Amnon Lipkin-Shahak, 56, Center Party
Absorption Minister: Yuli Tamir, 45, Labor (not a Knesset member)
Agriculture Minister: Haim Oron, 60, Meretz

Barak had come under heavy attack from women's groups for not fulfilling his campaign pledge to appoint at least three women to the cabinet; only one, Dalia Itzik, was in the original cabinet. The appointment of Tamir, a professor at Tel Aviv University, to the expanded cabinet now brought that number up to two. But Barak was still criticized in his own party for overlooking Labor veteran Yael Dayan in favor of Tamir, who had placed lower down the party slate in the primaries and had not made it into the Knesset. And Dayan, the daughter of the legendary general, Moshe Dayan, made her anger known from the Knesset podium the day Tamir was sworn in.

To mollify another disgruntled sector, the Arabs, Barak appointed Labor MK Nawaf Massalhe as deputy minister of foreign affairs on August 5—the most significant political post ever held by an Arab politician. But Massalhe and other Arab leaders insisted that Barak should have gone further and appointed the first-ever Arab minister. (Just before Massalhe's appointment Hashem Mahmeed had become the first-ever Arab Knesset member to sit on the prestigious Knesset Foreign Affairs and Defense Committee, whose membership until then had been confined to Jews.)

EARLY TEETHING PROBLEMS

The first coalition crisis emerged in early August over Sabbath observance: the decision by the police and relevant road authorities to transport parts for a huge electricity turbine on a Friday night south from Ramat Hasharon near Tel Aviv, to Ashkelon. It was decided that the Sabbath was the best time to carry out the 12-hour trip since this was when traffic was lightest and the turbine transport would not create massive traffic jams in the center of the country. But Infrastructure Minister Eli Suissa, a Shas member, warned that if the turbine moved on the Sabbath the coalition could well unravel. Suissa's decision to raise the turbine issue—in the past such transports had taken place on the Sabbath—was also connected to the leadership battle raging inside Shas. Suissa was an ally of deposed leader Arye Deri and appeared intent on embarrassing Deri's successor,

Eli Yishai. By precipitating a coalition crisis, some political commentators suggested, Suissa was trying to force Shas out of the coalition and create a situation where Deri would be asked to return as party savior.

Suissa's threats rapidly escalated into a full-blown crisis, with the UTJ adding its voice to that of Shas. But Barak refused to buckle and on Friday evening, August 13, the first 250-ton, three-lane-wide transport set out. (In an attempt to defuse the crisis it was agreed that the loading of the turbine would take place before the Sabbath and the unloading once the Sabbath had ended, while the workers involved in the transport, except for a handful, would not be Jewish.)

While no one immediately left the coalition, Shas and the UTJ made it clear that they would do so if a further five planned transports were carried out on the Sabbath. In the end, all five transports went ahead and the government did not fall, although the five-man UTJ did finally leave the coalition in protest on September 5.

The turbine showdown became a litmus test for Barak in the eyes of his secular supporters, and, in a rather amusing scene, some of them lined the road to cheer on the turbine as it set out on August 13. Threats by some of the ultra-Orthodox to sprinkle nails on the road to impede progress of the turbine never materialized. "Science and technology triumphed over religious extremism and fundamentalism," announced Meretz MK Anat Maor. But the turbine crisis indicated that Barak would have his work cut out to keep his disparate coalition together.

Barak also had problems with Natan Sharansky and his Yisrael B'Aliyah Party. On several occasions Sharansky opposed key government decisions, like the September 4 Sharm el-Sheikh agreement with the Palestinians and the budget vote in the cabinet. Sharansky also publicly opposed any peace settlement with Syria that would include a withdrawal from the Golan Heights, though Barak had made it clear that a settlement with Syria, including "painful" territorial compromises, was at the top of his agenda. Yisrael B'Aliyah also abstained in a Knesset no-confidence vote over expanding the size of the government.

Relations between One Israel and Yisrael B'Aliyah had begun to sour shortly after the elections when two members of the immigrant party bolted. Leading the way was Roman Bronfman, angered when it became clear that he would not get the party's second cabinet post—the Ministry of Absorption—since Sharansky preferred Yuli Edelstein, who had served in the post under Netanyahu. For his part, Bronfman said he was leaving because the party had neglected issues pertinent to secular immigrant voters. Yisrael B'Aliyah members were quick to blame One Israel, saying that it had lured Bronfman and Alexander Zinker away. The fact that Barak then refused to give Yisrael B'Aliyah a second ministry because the party no longer had enough Knesset members to merit it, further damaged relations. In what appeared to be a warning to Barak that he had other options, Sharansky met publicly with Yisrael Beiteinu leader and one-time sworn political foe Avigdor Lieberman.

The public, anxious to see quick results after the paralysis of the Netanyahu years and the many election promises made by Barak, cut the new prime minister little slack. With the economic recession deepening and unemployment growing, the public was especially anxious to see Barak move on the economic front. He came in for serious criticism even in his own party when he presented a budget in August that seemed reminiscent of the cost-cutting, belt-tightening years of Netanyahu, and held out little hope for economic growth.

In October, disabled protesters gathered outside Barak's office demanding increased subsidies. The Treasury Ministry took a tough stance, allowing the negotiations to drag on for several weeks. But ultimately, with public support squarely behind the disabled and Barak facing a major public-relations fiasco, he acceded to their demands. But the original stubbornness and Barak's comment that nothing would be achieved through "tears" portrayed the government as insensitive to social distress.

Despite renewed momentum on the peace front, social issues remained high on the agenda. Toward the end of the year unemployment crossed the 9-percent mark. When talk emerged of hunger in Israel, Barak ordered social workers to go out and find the hungry. The result: The Union of Local Authorities came up with the figure of 135,000 hungry Israelis—a number that was roundly disputed. Barak's response: "I don't know one citizen in the country who wouldn't take [food] from his refrigerator or table to help a truly hungry person." Then, in mid-December, the National Insurance Institute published figures revealing that over one million Israelis, about 40 percent of them children, were living below the poverty line. Figures were also published indicating that the income gap in Israel was expanding. Barak's view was that movement toward peace would boost the economy.

But Barak had little to fear from the opposition, especially with the Likud still in disarray after its rout in the election. Likud held a primary for the party leadership on September 2. Many saw it as a mere warm-up for the real event, to take place two years down the line, when party members would once again go to the polls to choose a candidate for prime minister. This time Sharon easily beat off Jerusalem mayor Ehud Olmert and former finance minister Meir Shitreet. Needing 40 percent to win in the first round, Sharon ended up with 53 percent. Olmert placed second with 24 percent and Shitreet third with 22 percent.

As the end-of-year budget vote drew closer, Shas began threatening to leave the coalition if funds were not allocated to its debt-ridden educational system. Getting the government to help Shas with its educational network's 100-million-shekel debt was one of the reasons Shas had joined the coalition. In fact, in the months after the election, there had been reports of widespread financial irregularities in the network and police had begun investigating Ya'akov Hemed, its director general. On September 15, Attorney General Elyakim Rubinstein had ordered funding to the network stopped until Hemed was suspended.

Shas leaders had also been asked to sign a letter committing themselves to a comprehensive recovery plan for their educational network. But the issue con-

tinued to trouble the coalition. With Education Minister Yossi Sarid hold⸱
back the funds Shas needed to pay its teachers, Shas MKs began voting agains
the government in Knesset committees. The danger to the coalition became all
the more glaring as the budget vote approached. Rabbi Ovadia Yosef ordered his
disciples to "go all the way" if their demands for funding were not met—a clear
threat to bolt the coalition. Then, on the morning of December 27, with the budget vote only four days away, Shas leader Yishai announced that his party was
indeed leaving the coalition. Barak asked the Shas ministers to delay handing in
their letters of resignation for 24 hours so as to give him time to find a compromise. In the end the Shas schools received their funding, and the budget passed.

DIPLOMATIC DEVELOPMENTS

Palestinian Statehood

The peace process, which had limped along during Netanyahu's term, went into
deep freeze during the election campaign. Netanyahu had essentially put the
process on hold in December 1998 when he refused to implement the Wye Plantation deal he had signed two months earlier, arguing that the Palestinians were
not complying with their obligations. Any movement on the diplomatic front, Netanyahu feared, would lose him the support of the right wing—especially the settlers—which had helped propel him to power in 1996. Indeed, the fact that he
had signed the Wye deal had already placed a question mark over their support.

While terror had dropped significantly under Netanyahu, it had not disappeared altogether, and on January 5 two women were injured, one seriously, when
a Palestinian gunman opened fire on a van carrying passengers from the West
Bank town of Kiryat Arba to Hebron. The next day Israeli soldiers shot and killed
a 20-year-old mentally disabled Palestinian man in Hebron, who ran toward them
brandishing what turned out to be a toy pistol. A week later, on January 13, a
member of the border police undercover antiterror unit, 24-year-old Sgt.
Yehoshua Gideon, was killed during a shootout with two Hamas gunmen near
Hebron. One of the Palestinians was wounded and captured; the other escaped.

The early months of 1999 were dominated by the question of whether Arafat
would unilaterally declare an independent state on May 4, the end of the five-
year interim Oslo agreement and the date by which a final settlement was supposed to have been reached. Foreign Minister Ariel Sharon wrote to European
foreign ministers in mid-March, informing them that if they recognized such a
Palestinian state they would be guilty of "complicity in violation of peace agreements." A war of words between Palestinian and Israeli officials ensued as the
two sides issued threats and counterthreats over the statehood issue. Arafat, for
instance, warned in late March that the Palestinians had "conducted the greatest Intifada in history"—a veiled threat as to what would ensue if Israel moved

block the declaration of a Palestinian state on May 4 with Jerusalem as its capital. "They must know that we can start it again if they prevent us from exercising our rights." An incensed Netanyahu, who had consistently warned that a unilateral declaration of statehood would undermine the entire peace process, countered: "They shouldn't dare to unilaterally declare an independent Palestinian state on the territories given over to them." (Netanyahu had hinted in the past that if the Palestinians unilaterally declared a state, Israel might respond by annexing those parts of the West Bank still under its control.)

Meanwhile, Arafat visited capitals around the world in an effort to drum up support for a Palestinian state. But international pressure to postpone the declaration, especially with Israeli elections only months away, mounted. Arafat met Clinton in Washington on March 23, and the president reportedly tried to persuade the Palestinian leader to desist from a unilateral declaration of statehood. The meeting came a week after the U.S. House of Representatives voted 380-24 to call on Clinton to oppose any unilateral Palestinian declaration of independence. By contrast, European Union leaders supported Palestinian statehood, if not an immediate declaration, in a meeting in Berlin on March 26. Calling on Israel to conclude negotiations with the Palestinians within a year, the EU countries reaffirmed "the continuing unqualified Palestinian right to self-determination including the option of a state."

Finally, on April 29, Palestinian leaders voted to delay a declaration of statehood. Arafat, some suggested, feared that such a declaration would play into Netanyahu's hands on the eve of the election by giving credence to his skeptical view of the Palestinians and the peace process. Others believed that Arafat had never intended to declare a state, but only to use this contrived "crisis" to elicit pro-statehood sentiment in Europe—and he had succeeded brilliantly.

Expectations Rise

With Barak's election, expectations were high in Israel and the entire Middle East that the new prime minister would move rapidly to reinvigorate the stalled peace process. A key question was which track Barak would choose to move on first, the Syrian or the Palestinian. His campaign pledge to withdraw the army from Lebanon within a year of taking office appeared to necessitate a deal with Syria, Lebanon's patron. But the Palestinians were also champing at the bit, their threat of a unilateral declaration of statehood still hanging in the air. In early July Barak announced plans to move forward on both tracks simultaneously.

Immediately after taking office on July 6 Barak began a whirlwind diplomatic tour, taking in neighboring states as well as the U.S., in an effort to break the diplomatic impasse of the Netanyahu years and restore relations with the Arab world and the Americans. In his first days in office he met with Egyptian president Hosni Mubarak, Arafat, Jordan's king Abdullah, Turkey's president

Suleiman Demirel, and President Clinton. In his first meeting with Arafat on July 11, Barak reiterated his commitment to carrying out the Wye accords.

Barak made his first visit to the U.S. from July 14 to 20 and immediately generated an optimism that had been lacking during the Netanyahu years, when U.S.-Israel relations were often chilly. In meetings with Clinton and Secretary of State Albright, Barak focused on implementing the remainder of the Wye accords and restarting peace talks with Syria. During his visit Barak made an ambitious announcement: Within 15 months he hoped to conclude a comprehensive framework for peace with Syria, Lebanon, and the Palestinians.

One sign of the changing atmosphere in the Middle East was the warm reception that the Israeli delegation—including Barak, Foreign Minister David Levy, and President Ezer Weizman—received at the funeral for King Hassan II of Morocco in Rabat on July 25. During the funeral an impromptu meeting took place between Barak and Algerian president Abd al-Aziz Bouteflika. The two men shook hands and exchanged words in front of the TV cameras.

Another signal of the changing atmosphere was a July 26 private visit by Abu Ala (Ahmed Qurei), speaker of the Palestinian Legislative Council, to the Knesset, at the invitation of its speaker, Avraham Burg. While right-wingers criticized the visit, Jerusalem's Likud mayor Ehud Olmert said it was a sign of Palestinian recognition of Israel's sovereignty over the city. Burg, who said he hoped he would soon be able to host both Syrian president Assad and Arafat, said it was unacceptable "that the government is dealing with peace and people below are dealing with peace and the Knesset does nothing related to peace." Abu Ala, though, made it clear that his visit in no way indicated Palestinian recognition of Israeli control of Jerusalem. In July there was also talk that Naif Hawatmeh, the head of the Democratic Front for the Liberation of Palestine—responsible for the 1974 Ma'alot massacre of 20 Israeli schoolchildren—might move to the Palestinian Authority-controlled areas. (Receiving Israel's approval to enter the Palestinian areas in late October, Hawatmeh announced in an interview on an Arabic news station that armed struggle was still legitimate so long as Jewish settlers remained on Arab lands, and Barak reversed his decision to allow him into the PA areas.)

Optimism grew for renewed Israel-Syria talks, especially after Danny Yatom, a senior security adviser to Barak, announced in late July that negotiations between the two sides could be renewed at the point they had broken off three years earlier—a Syrian precondition for restarting talks. Yatom did admit, however, that the two sides still differed over what exactly Israel and Syria had agreed on before negotiations broke down in 1996, when Shimon Peres was prime minister. Yatom's solution: Restart the talks and each side could bring its version to the table.

According to the Syrians, Prime Minister Yitzhak Rabin had agreed to a full withdrawal from the Golan Heights, an assertion consistently denied by Israel.

Barak did not make any public commitment to withdraw from the strategic mountain range in exchange for a comprehensive peace treaty with Syria, but he did say on more than one occasion that Israel was ready to make the "painful compromises" necessary to reach a deal with Syria. This was widely interpreted as a readiness to withdraw from most, if not all, of the Golan.

A late-July poll published in the daily *Yediot Aharonot* showed for the first time a majority supporting withdrawal from most or all of the Golan in exchange for full peace with Syria. While 48 percent said they would support such an agreement, 46 percent opposed it. A similar poll conducted five months earlier had shown 41 percent of Israelis supporting such a deal and 56 percent opposing it.

Speculation grew over whether Assad was truly ready to make the compromises on his side that would be needed for a deal. There were suggestions that the deaths of King Hussein of Jordan and King Hassan of Morocco had made him aware of his advancing years. By finally sealing a deal with Israel and getting back the Golan Heights, some said, the Syrian leader hoped to hand over a stable regime to his son, Bashar. Assad also knew that a deal with Israel meant a lucrative U.S. aid package.

The Sharm el-Sheikh Agreement

Instead of implementing the stalled Wye Plantation land-for-security deal immediately after taking office, Barak began by trying to convince the Palestinians to delay part of the remaining Wye-stipulated Israeli troop redeployments in the West Bank till final-status negotiations. Barak suggested this to Arafat on July 27 when they met at the Erez checkpoint, but the PA chairman displayed no enthusiasm.

Barak, concerned about security, feared that the withdrawals would leave around 15 Jewish settlements in the West Bank isolated within Palestinian-controlled territory, and thus exposed to attack by Palestinians bent on derailing the peace process. But the Palestinians insisted that the prime minister carry out Wye to the letter. "With all our willingness to listen to Barak's proposals," said Palestinian negotiator Nabil Sha'ath in late July, "there is not much chance that he will manage to convince us." The Palestinians insisted on a detailed timetable for implementation of the two remaining Israeli troop withdrawals in the West Bank that were stipulated in Wye. (Netanyahu had carried out the first of three redeployments before freezing the deal. Under Wye, a further 13.1 percent of the West Bank was to be handed over to the Palestinians, leaving them in full or partial control of around 40 percent of the West Bank.) The Palestinians also wanted set dates for the release of Palestinian security prisoners in Israeli jails—another Wye provision that had only been partially implemented.

The Palestinians had several reasons for pushing a quick and full implementation of Wye, beside their impatience over the three years of foot-dragging they

had experienced at the hands of Netanyahu. Speedy implementation of
would help Arafat shore up his support among his own people. What's more,
Palestinian leader was eager to gain land that would put him in a stronger posi
tion going into final-status talks with the Israelis that would deal, among other
things, with the borders of the new Palestinian entity. Finally, Arafat wanted to
move fast because he feared that Barak planned to veer sharply onto the Syrian
track, leaving the Palestinians on the backburner until the business with Damascus was completed.

At a press conference after their July 27 meeting, Barak said the two leaders
had agreed to a two-week timeout during which the Palestinians would consider
his ideas. But Arafat was less upbeat, insisting on "the precise, accurate implementation of agreements signed on the basis of reciprocity." On August 1, though,
a Barak aide announced that Israel aimed to begin implementation of Wye by
October 1, and a joint Israeli-Palestinian committee set up to discuss implementation of Wye began meeting in early August. Meanwhile, the Americans urged
Barak to carry out the agreement, but at the same time they asked Arafat to hear
out the Israeli prime minister before rejecting his proposals.

According to media reports Barak was prepared to offer the Palestinians several enticements to defer part of Wye to final-status talks. These included a rapid
release of Palestinian security prisoners and the speedy opening of "safe-passage"
corridors that would enable Palestinians to travel between the Gaza Strip and the
West Bank. Barak repeatedly made it clear, however, that if the Palestinians
turned down his suggestions, he would insist that Wye be implemented to the letter. Barak seemed to be telling the Palestinians that if they refused to alter Wye,
he would revert to Netanyahu's hyperstrict implementation of every Palestinian
obligation, such as the confiscation of all illegal weapons in Palestinian Authority areas, the reduction of the Palestinian police force, and the jailing of Islamic
militants.

As time dragged on and the joint committee appeared mired in disagreement,
the initial euphoria over a renewal of the peace process began to wane. "There is
an attempt to evade the accurate and complete implementation of the agreements," Arafat declared in early August. In response, Israeli foreign minister
David Levy accused the Palestinians of generating a crisis rather than seriously
dealing with Israel's proposals. Barak's office released a statement intimating
that the problem was the Palestinian lack of flexibility, while "Israel is proposing real progress."

Barak faced criticism from within his own party. Some ministers asserted—
anonymously—that Barak would have had a greater chance of convincing Arafat
to delay part of Wye had he made his suggestions privately rather than in the
media. Uzi Baram, a senior Labor member whom Barak had not appointed to
the cabinet, publicly argued that the prime minister would have been better off
implementing Wye immediately so as to rebuild confidence with the Palestinians.

..heduled early-August visit by U.S. secretary of state Madeleine Albright to .e region was delayed as the two sides failed to reach agreement over the implementation of Wye.

There were fears of widespread Palestinian demonstrations after the prime minister ordered the police to seal an opening in the southern wall of the Temple Mount in early August. The opening, which was small and had been enlarged to door size by the *waqf* (Muslim religious trust), was seen by Israel as an effort to change the Temple Mount status quo by enlarging the Al-Aqsa Mosque. Sealing the opening, though, did not result in widespread protests, unlike the opening of an archaeological tunnel adjacent to the Temple Mount by Netanyahu in 1996 that had led to bloody clashes.

Early August saw two separate terror attacks. First, two Jewish residents were shot and injured while driving in the Israeli-controlled section of Hebron on the West Bank. Then, on August 10, a Palestinian rammed his car twice into a hitchhiking post at the Nahshon junction about 25 minutes from Jerusalem, injuring nine people. The driver was shot dead by police and soldiers at the scene.

With the talks over the implementation of Wye still dragging on, signs of growing impatience with the new prime minister emerged in the Arab world and on the Israeli left. Both the Syrians and the Palestinians complained that Barak, despite his oft-stated claim to be Yitzhak Rabin's successor, was not continuing his legacy. In the Arabic press he was compared to Netanyahu, and a nickname for him soon appeared, "Barakyahu." Left-wing supporters of Barak expressed concern that he was not immediately implementing the Wye accords and that doves like Yossi Beilin and Shimon Peres were excluded from his inner circle.

Finally, after several weeks of tough negotiations, the two sides announced that they had reached agreement over the implementation of Wye. The rehashed deal was signed by Barak and Arafat at Sharm El-Sheikh in the Sinai desert on the evening of September 4. The Sharm agreement included several key provisions: Israel would withdraw from a further 11 percent of the West Bank; 350 Palestinian security prisoners in Israeli jails would be released; "safe-passage" routes between the Gaza Strip and the West Bank would be opened; and a seaport would be built in Gaza. Crucially, the deal also included a timetable for permanent-status talks which would deal with the most sensitive of issues between the two sides: the future of Jerusalem, the final borders of the Palestinian entity, the Palestinian refugee problem, and the future of the Jewish settlements in the West Bank. A framework agreement on permanent status (FAPS) was to be reached by February 2000, and a comprehensive final deal by September—exactly seven years after Oslo. The Israeli right was quick to criticize the deal, accusing Barak of having given up on the principle of "reciprocity," whereby not only Israel, they argued, but also the Palestinians, would have to implement the agreement in full.

Given that the previous deadlines in the Oslo process had almost never been met, the Barak-instigated timetable outlined in the Sharm deal appeared overly optimistic. There were those who suggested that Israel and the Palestinians would not be able to agree on all the final-status issues and that some would have to be put off to a later date, thus giving birth to another interim agreement.

Final-Status Talks Begin

The day after the signing the upbeat atmosphere was marred by bomb attacks in Haifa and Tiberias. Miraculously, the booby-trapped cars detonated prematurely, killing the three bombers; one female pedestrian was seriously injured. While suspicion immediately fell on the fundamentalist Hamas organization, it soon emerged that the three bombers were not Palestinians from the territories but Israeli Arabs. That revelation set off warning bells for security officials who feared that they might be facing a new type of Israeli Islamic terrorism. Israeli Arab leaders, though, quickly condemned the acts. Around the same time police announced that Abdallah Agbrallah, 20, from an Arab village in Wadi Ara in northern Israel, had confessed to the August 30 murder of two Orthodox students—Yehiel Shai Finchter, 26, and Sharon Steinitz, 21—in the Megiddo nature reserve. "It would be a terrible mistake," warned Internal Security Minister Shlomo Ben-Ami, "to start relating now to Israeli Arabs as an intelligence target."

On September 9, 199 Palestinian prisoners were released from Israeli jails as part of the Sharm agreement; all signed an oath to refrain from terror. In order to fill the quota stipulated in the agreement, the government changed the criteria for the release of Palestinian security prisoners. For the first time, those who had wounded Israelis, killed Palestinian collaborators or had been indirectly involved in terror acts were included. This decision sparked strong criticism on the right. Those freed did not, however, include Palestinians who had been jailed for killing Israelis, those the Israelis defined as having "blood on their hands." The next day, September 10, Israel began to hand over some 400 sq. km of the West Bank to Palestinian civilian control.

On September 13 Foreign Minister David Levy and Palestinian chief negotiator Abu Mazen met at the Erez checkpoint for the formal opening of final-status talks on a permanent Israeli-Palestinian settlement. Levy outlined Israel's red lines: "No return to the '67 borders; united Jerusalem under Israel's sovereignty will forever remain Israel's capital—period; settlement blocks will remain under Israeli sovereignty; and no foreign army will be found west of the Jordan River." Abu Mazen spelled out the Palestinian opening position: an independent state with Jerusalem as its capital.

In line with his concept of large settlement blocks remaining in place after a final-status deal, Barak visited the 25,000-strong settlement of Ma'aleh Adumim near Jerusalem in mid-September and declared that the West Bank city would always remain part of Israel. "Every tree planted here, every house and every stone here is part of the State of Israel forever," Barak pledged. Irritated by the remarks,

Faisal Husseini, the PLO executive committee member with responsibility for Jerusalem, countered that Ma'aleh Adumim would ultimately have to be evacuated under a final deal. Any permanent peace, added Abu Mazen, would require a "complete evacuation" of all the settlements in the West Bank and Gaza Strip. On September 17 it was reported that Barak and Arafat had held a secret meeting the previous evening, but the final-status talks did not get underway, as Barak procrastinated over who should head the Israeli delegation.

Barak and Clinton faced a problem at the end of September when the Republican-controlled Congress balked at giving the green light to the $1.9 billion pledged in 1998 for the implementation of the Wye Plantation agreement. This aid package was meant to cover the relocation of Israeli army bases in the West Bank and to compensate Israel—with helicopters and state-of-the-art intelligence-gathering equipment—for the strategic depth it was foregoing as a result of the agreement. (Israel's share of the package was $1.2 billion, while $400 million was earmarked for the Palestinians and $300 million for Jordan.)

As part of the Sharm agreement, Israel released another 151 Palestinian security prisoners on October 15. The fact that some of them were affiliated with radical Palestinian groups caused an outcry on the right. Ten days earlier Israeli minister of internal security Shlomo Ben-Ami and Palestinian civil affairs minister Jamil Tarifi had reached agreement for the opening of a safe-passage route. This southern route was the first of two corridors between the West Bank and the Gaza Strip stipulated in the Sharm agreement. The second was to be opened by January 2000.

According to the agreement Israel was to have the final say on who could travel along the 44-kilometer route linking the Erez checkpoint at the northern tip of Gaza, via regular Israeli roads, to the Tarkumiya junction near Hebron in the West Bank. A Palestinian wanting to use the route had to first apply to the PA for a magnetic passage card, and the PA then had to hand over a list of applicants to Israel for approval. After several delays the safe-passage finally opened on October 25. Now large numbers of Palestinians could finally travel between the Gaza Strip and the West Bank, either in private cars or by bus, for business purposes or for visits. While the Israeli government insisted that there were strict security arrangements, including checkpoints at both departure points, politicians on the right attacked the safe-passage opening as a threat to Israel's security. "The mere fact that Palestinian vehicles will be on this road," warned Likud MK Danny Naveh, "presents a serious challenge to the security forces, which will have to ensure that these vehicles don't slip away into other parts of Israel."

Palestinian terrorists struck again on October 30 when gunmen opened fire on an Israeli bus traveling near Hebron. Five of the passengers on the bus, which was carrying Ramat Gan residents back home after spending a solidarity Shabbat in Hebron, were wounded.

Barak, Arafat, and Clinton met in Oslo on November 1 and 2 to discuss plans for the final-status talks. The three also attended a memorial ceremony for Yitzhak Rabin. After vacillating for weeks, Barak decided that Israel's ambassador to Jordan, Oded Eran, would head the Israeli team. On November 8, Eran sat down with Yasir Abd Rabbo, the head of the Palestinian team, at Ramallah's Grand Park Hotel, and both sides outlined their opening positions. At the outset they appeared far apart. The Palestinians demanded that Israel evacuate all the territory it had conquered in 1967, while Israel said it would never return to the Green Line and would maintain Israeli sovereignty over most of the settlements; the Palestinians demanded half of Jerusalem as their capital, while Israel insisted that Jerusalem would remain undivided and under its sovereignty; the Palestinians insisted on the right of return for refugees who had fled or had been expelled in 1948, but Barak made it clear Israel would never allow refugees back in. But after the meeting both Eran and Abd Rabbo sounded upbeat. (Labor MK Yossi Katz caused a stir in early December when he declared that Israel had "to ensure that at least a certain number, maybe 100,000 refugees, return to their homes." Katz was roundly criticized in his party.)

Both Barak and Arafat made it clear that, in addition to the formal talks, they planned to meet regularly face-to-face to accelerate the negotiations. Clinton also announced that he would be prepared to host a summit in January 2000 in an effort to reach agreement.

The threat posed by Palestinian extremism was starkly illustrated on November 7 when three pipe bombs exploded in a busy shopping area in the coastal town of Netanyah, injuring 33 Israelis. While there was no immediate claim of responsibility, police suspected Palestinian fundamentalists bent on destroying the peace process.

Settlement Showdown

The issue of Jewish settlements was back on the agenda in October. Barak reached an agreement with the settler leaders that 12 out of the 42 outposts set up on the West Bank in the final months of Netanyahu's term—intended to block any further territorial concessions—would be dismantled by the settlers themselves. Barak had initially declared that 15 of the outposts, many consisting of a water tower and a few mobile homes, were illegal and would be dismantled. Another eight, he had said, were legal, while 16 were to be frozen and permits for a final three would be completed retroactively.

Well aware of the bitter relations that had existed between Rabin and the settlers, Barak tried to avoid confrontation and seek compromise. "I am nearer to the position of [NRP leader] Yitzhak Levy on the settlement question than to that of [Meretz leader] Yossi Sarid," he declared in a TV interview. "Beit El and Ofrah will be ours forever, just as Ramallah will be Palestinian forever." By removing some of the outposts, though, Barak was also able to illustrate to many on the left that he would not balk at dismantling settlements.

The deal with Barak divided the settler community, as radical leaders opposed any deal that required the dismantling of even a single outpost. Several thousand demonstrators gathered outside Barak's official Jerusalem residence on October

17 to protest the evacuation, but unlike what happened in the Rabin era, most of the speakers emphasized nonviolent opposition. A new group calling itself "Dor Hemshekh" (Next Generation), which included many young settlers, emerged as an opposition to the established settler leadership and sought to block the evacuations. There was, however, some rhetoric that brought back memories of the preassassination period when Rabin became the target of wild incitement by elements on the right. "No entity has the authority to remove and cancel the right of the Jewish nation from any area in Israel," declared Rabbi Dov Lior of Kiryat Arba. At the same time, though, 54 rabbis, including five from West Bank settlements, signed a statement excommunicating Rabin's assassin Yigal Amir and forbidding contact with him until he expressed regret for what he had done.

By November 10, all but one of the 12 settlement outposts had been voluntarily dismantled. At the remaining outpost of Havat Maon (Maon Ranch) near Hebron, hundreds of settlers gathered and refused to budge. The prime minister rejected the advice of cabinet ministers Yitzhak Levy and Natan Sharansky that he hold off on a deadline he had set for the evacuation of Maon. In the early morning hours of November 10 he ordered troops in to evict the settlers. As hundreds of troops fanned out over the largely barren hilltop—which contained a few huts and tents—settlers barricaded themselves in shacks, climbed onto roofs of makeshift structures, and clung to doors in what turned out to be largely a show of passive resistance. Some settlers shouted at soldiers to refuse orders. "You are removing Jews from the Land of Israel," screamed others. For his part, Barak insisted that he would not allow a small militant minority to dictate policy.

The same day as the evacuation of Havat Maon the cabinet voted 17-1 to carry out the next Israeli troop withdrawal in the West Bank as outlined in the Sharm agreement. Thus a further 5 percent of the West Bank would come under full or partial Palestinian control. But the withdrawal, scheduled for mid-November, was delayed after Arafat refused to accept the territory being offered on the grounds that it was too sparsely populated with Palestinians. But Israel insisted that, under the agreement, it had sole right to determine which parts of the West Bank would be transferred.

November 21 brought good news for Barak when Congress approved the 2000 foreign-aid package, including the special allocation for Wye that had been held up. On December 7 Barak ordered a freeze on all new settlement building until February, but said construction already in progress would continue. At the end of the year, the Israelis and Palestinians were still at loggerheads over the second Sharm withdrawal.

Assad Decides To Talk

There was no movement on the Syrian front in the first half of the year. In fact, the Knesset passed legislation on January 26 stipulating that any government decision to give up territory subject to Israeli law, such as the Golan Heights and

East Jerusalem, would require an absolute Knesset majority of 61 and not a simple majority of those present.

But Barak's election renewed speculation about the possible resumption of talks between Israel and Syria, stalled since early 1996. One positive sign was the June visit to Israel by Patrick Seale, the British biographer of Syrian president Hafez al-Assad. Seale had a meeting with Barak. "I am very heartened," Seale said when asked about the chances of an Israeli-Syrian peace deal. "For the first time, for many years, I think there is a real chance for peace, for many reasons. I was deeply impressed by prime minister-elect Barak, I think he is a very clear-minded, strong man with a great personal mandate, and I think he knows that hard decisions will have to be taken."

In an effort to thaw the chill between the two countries, Assad and Barak engaged in a round of mutual praise. Assad referred to Barak as "a strong and honest man." Barak declared that Assad "has given Syria its present formula: strength, independence and self-confidence. I think," Barak added, "Syria is the most important [factor] for stability in the Middle East."

As another sign of Assad's intentions to move forward in the peace process, it emerged in July that Syrian officials had informed Palestinian rejectionist groups based in Damascus to cease the armed struggle against Israel and become political bodies, or face expulsion. Assad also hoped with this move to improve ties with the U.S., so as to be removed from the State Department's list of states encouraging terrorism.

By early August, though, the Syrians were expressing disappointment with Barak, and after Albright and U.S. Middle East envoy Dennis Ross met with Assad in Damascus on September 4, Syrian officials were reported to have expressed disappointment with the message Barak had delivered via the secretary of state. Syrian foreign minister Farouk al-Shara was in Washington twice in late September to meet with Albright and Clinton, but there were no real signs of movement. In a message aimed at the Syrians, Barak announced, at the start of the Knesset winter session on October 4, that the "door of opportunity is open today — but no one can know until when."

Till early December the Israel-Syria track appeared to be going nowhere. But on December 8 President Clinton issued a dramatic announcement: Israel and Syria would be renewing talks, and Prime Minister Barak and Foreign Minister al-Shara would meet in Washington in mid-December to kick off the negotiations. Middle East analysts suggested that Assad's surprise decision to restart talks almost four years after they had broken off was spurred by his fear of being left behind as Israel and the Palestinians moved toward a final settlement. Also, it was suggested, Assad was worried that Barak would make good on his pledge to pull the Israeli army out of south Lebanon by July, and thus rob the Syrian leader of one of his major bargaining cards.

Amid great anticipation, Barak and al-Shara met in Washington in mid-December for a two-day summit, but the opening was anything but encouraging as the Syrian refused to shake Barak's hand and then engaged in an anti-Israel diatribe in his opening address. According to reports, though, the atmosphere inside the meetings was far less frosty. At the end of the summit, which dealt with many of the procedural issues, Clinton announced that the two leaders would be back on January 3, 2000, for a second round. Al-Shara later told journalists he was encouraged by the talks and that Barak was serious about making peace. Barak was a little less upbeat, saying that tough negotiations still lay ahead. But Barak's cautious approach was seen by some as a tactic to convince the Israeli public that he would not make irresponsible, hasty decisions that could endanger Israel's security. There was also some speculation over whether Barak had agreed to the initial Syrian precondition for the restart of talks—an Israeli withdrawal to the lines of June 4, 1967. While the right wing accused Barak of capitulating even before the start of negotiations, Barak said he had given no such commitment.

The key issues on the table included an Israeli withdrawal, security arrangements, normalization, water rights, and a timetable for implementation. It was generally assumed that any accord would most likely mean an Israeli withdrawal from virtually all of the Golan. The key border dispute was likely to be over whether Israel would withdraw to the 1923 international boundary or to the de facto line that existed on June 4, 1967, on the eve of the Six-Day War during which Israel conquered the Golan.

Soon after Clinton's announcement, reports emerged that secret diplomacy had led to the restart of the talks. Uri Saguy, a former head of military intelligence—and the man Barak chose to head the Israeli delegation to the talks—had been meeting with American and Syrian representatives abroad in the months before Clinton made his announcement. According to some reports, however, it was Clinton who had played the crucial role, making phone calls to Assad and sending him messages, culminating in a mid-November cable to the Syrian leader saying that the U.S. would back an Israeli withdrawal from the Golan and give both parties aid as part of a peace treaty. But Clinton had added a rider: If Assad failed to bite, he would be left empty-handed: No Golan—no aid.

No sooner had the announcement been made about the renewal of talks than the opponents of a withdrawal from the Golan began organizing, led by many of the 18,000 Jewish settlers living there. Their aim was to block a withdrawal by persuading a majority of Israelis to vote "no" in the referendum Barak had promised if he reached an agreement with Syria.

Opponents of withdrawal argued that relinquishing the strategic mountain range posed an existential threat to Israel, robbing it both of strategic depth and its elevation over Syria, which provided an early-warning capacity. Opponents of withdrawal also argued that Assad was sick and that Israel was taking a grave risk signing an agreement with him because he could be replaced at any time. Some on the right demanded that Israel's Arab citizens not be allowed to vote in the referendum, saying this was a matter for the Jews to determine. In a thinly veiled effort at excluding Arab voters, some right-wing politicians began pushing for a super-majority, arguing that a deal with Syria should require a majority of 60 percent, or a majority of all Israelis of voting age.

The balance of forces in the Knesset looked unclear. Barak, it seemed, co. probably count on 57 or 58 definite votes, leaving him dependent on Shas. The price for Shas's support, many suggested, would be funding for its educational network. An early indicator of the troubles Barak was expected to face in the Knesset was the December 13 vote, which decided 47-31 to support the resumption of negotiations. With thousands of Golan residents and antiwithdrawal protesters demonstrating outside, Shas abstained and the NRP voted against. "The agreement with Syria," said Barak during his Knesset address, "will be the price our generation pays . . . for an end to wars, an end to the spilling of blood, and for peace. I am convinced the citizens of Israel will see the agreement and say 'yes.' " In response, opposition leader Ariel Sharon referred to Assad as a "cruel dictator, near the end of his days. No one knows," warned Sharon, "who will rule in Syria. . . . We are likely to end up without the Golan and without peace."

For his part Barak argued that an agreement with Syria would bring an end to the conflict in the Middle East and open the way for ties with countries like Saudi Arabia, Kuwait, and Qatar. A deal, he said, would also put an end to the Lebanese nightmare and spur economic growth through foreign investment. Barak was reported to have told the cabinet that if a deal with Syria were rejected, the result could be war. Proponents of a deal also argued that adequate security arrangements, such as deep demilitarized zones on the Syrian side of the border, could compensate for the loss of the Golan.

Labor minister Haim Ramon produced a document in mid-December that suggested that Netanyahu had been ready to agree to a substantial withdrawal from the Golan in exchange for a deal with Syria. The document had been the product of meetings which American cosmetics tycoon Ronald Lauder had held with Assad on behalf of Netanyahu. Earlier in the year, after his election loss, Netanyahu had said that in these indirect talks the Syrians had agreed to an Israeli early-warning station on the Hermon—known in Israel as "the eyes of the country." He rebuffed Ramon's assertions, insisting he had talked only of a withdrawal on the Golan, not from all of it.

At the end of the year polls showed just over 50 percent of Israelis opposing full withdrawal in exchange for peace with Syria, and around 45 percent in favor. But some political commentators argued that these polls had little meaning since the referendum would take place in a different atmosphere, following extensive negotiations and, possibly, a series of confidence-building measures.

RELATIONS WITH OTHER ARAB STATES

Lebanon

The deaths of six Israeli soldiers and of Kol Yisrael radio reporter Ilan Roeh in the south Lebanon security zone during the last week in February once again sparked debate over Israel's presence there. One of the dead was 38-year-old ıg. Gen. Erez Gerstein, the chief liaison officer between Israel and its proxy south Lebanon Army (SLA) militia. He was the most senior Israeli officer to be killed since the IDF invasion of Lebanon in 1982. He, two soldiers, and Roeh were all killed in a Hezballah roadside bombing. Gerstein's death raised speculation about improved Hezballah intelligence capacity. Israel responded by bombing suspected guerilla targets in the south and in the Bekaa Valley. Netanyahu also threatened massive retaliation, and IDF artillery and troops were moved up to the northern border in early March. But a possible major Israeli offensive into Lebanon—the subject of considerable speculation—never materialized, perhaps, some suggested, because the U.S. had signaled its disapproval.

In what was seen as an attempt by the government to cut down on casualties in south Lebanon, Israel announced on April 9 that it was reducing the number of soldiers stationed there. Netanyahu insisted, though, that this was not the beginning of a unilateral withdrawal.

One of the most strident prowithdrawal voices was that of Labor politician Yossi Beilin, who had argued for some time that Israel should instead deploy its forces massively along its northern border. That way, he reasoned, Israel would no longer be criticized for occupying part of Lebanon, and so would be free to respond with massive force if the Iranian-backed Shi'ite fundamentalist Hezballah movement continued its attacks after an IDF pullback. Opponents of a quick withdrawal, however, insisted that Hezballah would not stop its operations, and that Israel, having withdrawn, would have to respond with ever greater force, ultimately leaving the army no other option than another invasion of south Lebanon.

Withdrawal from the security zone became an election issue when Barak announced, following Gerstein's death, that, if elected, he would withdraw the army from Lebanon within a year. A poll conducted by Tel Aviv University's Jaffee Center for Strategic Studies and released in late March, revealed that 55 percent of Israelis supported an immediate withdrawal from Lebanon. In a similar poll the previous year, only 44 percent had backed a pullout.

In March, Lebanese prime minister Selim al-Hoss seemed to hint in a BBC interview that if the IDF withdrew from southern Lebanon, Hezballah would be stopped from acting against Israel. "An Israeli withdrawal," said Hoss, "would revive the armistice agreement, and according to the agreement there can be no military actions across the border." But after having most likely been rapped on the knuckles by his Syrian patrons, Hoss said he had been misunderstood.

The IDF moved into the village of Arnun just north of the security zone in April, and sealed it off. Hezballah guerilas, the army contended, had been operating out of the village, and the roadside bomb that killed 21-year-old Staff-Sgt. Noam Barnea on April 12, officials said, had been planted by Hezballah militants hiding out in Arnun. The Lebanese government complained, and international monitors criticized the Israeli move. Two weeks later, on May 3, 23-year-old Sgt. Mollo Nagato was killed by another Hezballah roadside bomb in the security zone.

Lebanon was back in the news on election night, May 17, when residents in towns on Israel's northern border were forced to spend the night in air-raid shelters after Hezballah fired Katyusha rockets across the border. No one was injured, and Hezballah claimed the attack was in retaliation for the killing of two Lebanese civilians by an Israeli-launched rocket on May 16.

In early June, Israel's South Lebanon Army (SLA) militia began unilaterally pulling out of the Jezzine enclave just north of the security zone. A Christian town, Jezzine had been under the control of the SLA for 14 years, during which it had been subject to ongoing Hezballah attacks. Israel chose not to send in its firepower to bolster the SLA in Jezzine since the enclave held no major strategic value. Yet observers asked how Israel's passivity would impact on the local population in the zone, who were already jittery about talk of a unilateral withdrawal. If the retreat from Jezzine were seen as a sign of an impending Israeli withdrawal from south Lebanon, some warned, it could spark desertions from the SLA to Hezballah as locals tried to protect themselves and their families ahead of such a pullback.

On June 10, Lt. Ro'i Keller, 21, was killed in the security zone. Keller was a member of the elite Sayeret Egoz reconnaissance unit. Two Israeli civilians — 38-year-old Tony Zana and 47-year-old Shimon Almaliah — were killed when Hezballah fired Katyusha rockets into the northern city of Kiryat Shmona on June 24. In retaliation, the outgoing Netanyahu government ordered a strike deep inside Lebanon, with Israeli planes hitting power plants and relay systems in and around Beirut. Nine Lebanese civilians were reported killed. Prime Minister-elect Barak, it emerged, was told of the government's decision to strike.

Three more Israeli soldiers were killed when Hezballah attacked an Israeli military position on the edge of the security zone on August 17. Hezballah claimed the attack was in retaliation for the death of one of its commanders, Ali Hassan Deeb, who had been killed the day before when two roadside bombs exploded on the outskirts of the port city of Sidon. Hezballah blamed Israel for Deeb's death; Israel denied any responsibility, blaming it on a rival Lebanese group. Israel responded with aerial and artillery bombardments.

It emerged in November that for several months the army had been employing new tactics in Lebanon, increasing air strikes and reducing ground operations to cut down on casualties. The change began with the Netanyahu-ordered June 24 bombing of Lebanese infrastructure targets in response to the rocket attack on Kiryat Shmona. The switch appeared to be effective: While ten Israeli soldiers were killed and 32 wounded in the period between January and June, the army suffered three dead and 21 wounded between late June and early November.

Lebanon was on the agenda when Barak met French president Jacques Chirac during a visit to Paris in September. The French leader reiterated his country's willingness to send troops to south Lebanon as part of an international peacekeeping force, but only within the framework of a peace agreement between Israel and Syria, not following a unilateral Israeli withdrawal. The U.S. expressed a similar position.

Lebanon was on the agenda again when Israel-Syria talks resumed in mid-December. On the day of the Washington summit, Hezballah guerillas launched a massive artillery bombardment of IDF and SLA positions in south Lebanon. But after an SLA shell landed in a school, wounding several Lebanese children, Hezballah did not respond by firing Katyusha rockets into northern Israel and there were reports that the Syrians had restrained it. In the days after the summit there were reports that Syria and Israel had agreed that negotiations with the Lebanese would begin after the second round of talks in early 2000.

Egypt

While Egypt welcomed Barak's election, President Hosni Mubarak was quick to criticize some of the prime minister-elect's early statements. On May 22, only five days after the election, for instance, Mubarak said that Barak's comment that he was not prepared to withdraw from all of the West Bank was "damaging" and could create a "bad atmosphere among the Arab and Egyptian public." But Mubarak also said he believed Barak would push the peace process forward, and the official Egyptian newspaper *Al-Ahram* wrote that if Barak remained true to his declared intentions to move on the peace front, he was likely "to open a new path in the relations between Israel and the Arab states."

After meeting Arafat in Cairo on May 24 to discuss the change of government in Israel, Mubarak called on Barak "to adopt a positive approach so as to bring about a historic rapprochement between Jews and Arabs, based on mutual respect." Barak traveled to Cairo on July 29 seeking Egyptian backing in his efforts to convince the Palestinians to accept alterations in the Wye accords. "All I can say is that we reached an understanding," Mubarak declared.

While Barak's election changed the atmosphere between Jerusalem and Cairo, relations seemed to revert to the pattern of the Rabin-Peres days, with Mubarak acting as the "good cop" helping to push forward talks with the Palestinians, while his foreign minister, Amre Moussa, played the "bad cop," leading the diplomatic battle to block Israel's full absorption into the region and demanding that Israel dismantle its nuclear capability.

In early October the renewal of multilateral talks — on issues like regional economic development, water, arms control, and environment — which had been frozen for a long time, was on the table. Israel wanted the negotiations to restart as a sign of the revival of the peace process, but the Egyptians said the talks could only resume once multilateral talks had begun with Syria and Lebanon. According to the daily *Ha'aretz*, another stumbling block was the Egyptian demand that a multilateral committee be set up on the future of Jerusalem, a demand that Israel flatly rejected.

Jordan

A large Israeli delegation, including Prime Minister Netanyahu, President Weizman, Shimon Peres, Foreign Minister Sharon, and opposition leader Barak, attended King Hussein's funeral on February 8 in Amman. After filing past the coffin of the deceased king, the Israelis offered their condolences to his successor—his eldest son, Abdullah, aged 37. (While many had assumed that Hussein's successor would be his brother, Crown Prince Hassan, with whom Israel had excellent relations, in the days before his death King Hussein had named his son instead.)

During the funeral President Ezer Weizman shook hands with Naif Hawatmeh, head of the Democratic Front for the Liberation of Palestine and the man who had been responsible for the Ma'alot massacre. When criticized by right-wingers back home, Weizman retorted: "What was Arafat a few years ago, an angel?"

Relations between the Jordanians and Netanyahu—soured in 1997 by a botched Mossad assassination attempt on a Hamas official in Amman—remained problematic. Ahead of a February 28 trip to Amman, Netanyahu again angered the Jordanians when he asked, during an address at Bar-Ilan University, "What happened the last time Saddam Hussein was very strong? Who joined him? Jordan, under King Hussein. . . ."

In March there was tension between Israel and Jordan over water allocations. As a result of the drought, Israel announced to Jordan that it would be unable to fulfill its fixed annual water quota to Amman, which was part of the peace treaty signed between the two countries in 1994. On March 15 Jordan said it would not accept Israel's position and it asked the U.S. to intervene. "We are not engaging in negotiations with Israel and we are demanding that we receive our full and legitimate quota of water," announced Jordanian prime minister Abd a-Rauf Ruabdeh.

While King Abdullah moved to improve ties between Jordan and Syria, he also began to play a role in the peace process. When Arafat visited Amman on April 4 seeking support for a declaration of a Palestinian state, Abdullah tried to convince him to hold off until after the May 17 Israeli elections, reportedly telling the Palestinian leader that such a move would play into the hands of the Israeli far right. Abdullah also tried mediating between Syria and Israel. In early May he announced that there was a real desire on the part of Damascus to talk peace with Israel after the elections, and, once Barak came to power, Abdullah continued to pass messages between the two sides. After Abdullah returned from a meeting with Assad in late July, he immediately spoke to Barak to update him.

While in the U.S. in late May, Abdullah told Jewish leaders that the Middle East peace process had to be swiftly renewed by Barak. "There is a feeling of euphoria and excitement in the Middle East," Abdullah told his guests in New York, "and I fear that if within three, four months there won't be any results, then that will have severe consequences."

Israel watched with interest as Abdullah took on the Hamas movement in Jordan. Several leading figures of the fundamentalist organization were arrested and then expelled to Qatar on November 21. One of them was the movement's political bureau head, Khaled Mashaal, who had been the target of the unsuccessful Israeli assassination attempt in September 1997.

Relations with Other Countries

IRAN

In March it emerged that 13 Jews were in custody in Iran facing charges of spying for Israel. The 13, including a rabbi, a ritual slaughterer, and a 16-year-old boy, were from the cities of Shiraz and Isfahan. While there was much speculation over why they had originally been arrested, the case soon took on international proportions as Iranian judicial officials hinted that they might face the death penalty. Fearful that any public meddling on its part would worsen the plight of the 13, Israel left much of the diplomatic activity to American Jewish leaders, who waged an intensive campaign for their release. Iran watchers suggested that the jailed Jews had become pawns in the domestic battle in Iran between the moderates, led by President Mohammad Khatami, and the conservatives, led by supreme spiritual leader Ali Khamenei. The arrests, they suggested, were an effort to embarrass Khatami and undermine his reformist approach. By the end of the year the 13 were still languishing in jail and no date had been set for a trial.

TURKEY

When a massive earthquake struck Turkey in August, Israel dispatched rescue and medical teams to the stricken areas where they worked round the clock to extricate survivors. On the morning of August 21, Israeli viewers were gripped by the televised scenes of an IDF rescue team extracting 9-year-old (Israeli) Shiran Franco from the ruins of a holiday apartment in Cinarcik, in northwest Turkey, where she had been trapped for almost 100 hours. The remarkable footage of the head of the rescue team holding Shiran in his arms and wiping water on her parched lips was played over and over. At its peak the Israeli rescue effort in Turkey included some 300 people.

Ehud Barak visited Turkey in late October for talks with government officials about the growing strategic ties between the two countries. Up for discussion was the sale to Ankara of weaponry, including intelligence drones, attack helicopters, and Popeye air-to-ground missiles, as well as the upgrading of hundreds of Turkish tanks, and the conduct of joint naval maneuvers and air force training exercises in one another's air space.

MAURITANIA

On October 28, Mauritania became the third Arab country, after Egypt and Jordan, to establish full diplomatic ties with Israel. The event was marked by a ceremony in Washington attended by Foreign Minister David Levy.

AUSTRIA

Israel's ties with Austria became somewhat strained after Jörg Haider's far-right Freedom Party performed well in elections there. Israeli foreign minister David Levy made it clear that Israel would have to reevaluate its relations with Austria if Haider were included in a ruling coalition.

RUSSIA

Barak was in Moscow in early August where he met with President Boris Yeltsin. In their Kremlin meeting the two discussed the stalled Israel-Syria track and Russia's desire to play a more central role in the Middle East peace process. Also on the agenda was Israel's concern over the continued flow of hi-tech nuclear expertise and materials, as well as Russian missile technology, from Russia to Iran.

ECONOMIC DEVELOPMENTS

The recession continued in 1999, although there were some indications of renewed growth in the second half of the year. Overall, economic growth for the year was 2.2 percent. Inflation was only 0.3 percent — though commentators attributed this to the recession — while unemployment was high at 9 percent. Tourism was up, as over 2.5 million people visited Israel in the course of 1999, a 15-percent increase over 1998.

Figures released by the Central Bureau of Statistics toward the end of the year seemed to indicate an upturn in the economy and raised hopes that Israel might be emerging from the extended economic slowdown. The annualized GDP growth rate, for instance, rose from 0.9 percent in the first six months of the year to 3.3 percent in the second six months. Business sector GDP rose from zero percent to 4 percent.

The consumer price index (CPI) stayed low, especially during the first half of the year, symptomatic of the economic slowdown. In January, for instance, the index dropped by 0.5 percent. The next month, the CPI declined by 0.8 percent, the biggest drop in 13 years. With inflation low, officials in the Ministry of Finance called for a lowering of interest rates by the Bank of Israel in order to spur growth, but the bank's governor, Jacob Frenkel, who had kept interest rates high in a bid to cut inflation, refused. Overall, in the first seven months of 1999, the CPI rose by only 0.1 percent—the lowest figure in 32 years.

Some 400,000 public workers went on strike in late March over demands for a wage increase that would compensate for inflation. The Histadrut Labor Federation demanded an 8.1-percent increase while the government offered 3.8 percent. The strike finally ended on March 29 with the Histadrut accepting 4.8 percent.

Unemployment continued to rise through 1999. In April, for instance, the number of unemployed reached 201,600, according to the Central Bureau of Statistics. By the end of November the number had ballooned to over 213,000—almost 9 percent. While unemployment at the end of 1999 remained at around 9 percent, in many of the country's poor development towns and Arab villages the figure was as high as 12, 13, and even 14 percent. This led to growing pressure on Barak, especially since one of his main electoral promises had been to generate 300,000 new jobs during his four-year term. Barak's view was that movement in the peace process would spur economic growth, which meant that the unemployed would have to wait for real progress on the diplomatic front.

In a preliminary vote on October 27, the Knesset voted 53-32 in favor of the 2000 budget, which totaled 227 billion shekels ($44 billion). But the budget was criticized for ignoring pressing social concerns like unemployment, and not allocating sufficient funding for infrastructure development. Barak knew, though, that the real test would come at the end of the year when the budget would have to pass a second and a third reading.

One of the most dramatic developments of 1999 was the sudden resignation of Bank of Israel governor Jacob Frenkel, who announced on November 14 that he would not complete his second five-year term and would leave the central bank at the end of the year. While there was speculation that Frenkel's decision was sparked by an ongoing disagreement with Finance Minister Avraham Shochat over the governor's tight monetary policies, Frenkel insisted that the decision was personal. The announcement was met with satisfaction among industrialists who had regularly criticized Frenkel for keeping interest rates high in an effort to keep inflation down—a policy they said was to blame for the recession. Frenkel's supporters, however, argued that his policies had lowered inflation significantly and thus boosted Israel's reputation for economic stability in the international community. His successor had not yet been appointed as the year ended.

DEMOGRAPHIC DEVELOPMENTS

The Central Bureau of Statistics (CBS) reported that Israel's population stood at 6.2 million at the end of 1999. According to figures released in the CBS's annual abstract on November 8, Jews comprised 79 percent of Israel's population at the end of 1998; Muslims 14.9 percent; Christians 2.1 percent; and Druse 1.6

percent. According to CBS projections, non-Jews would constitute a quarter of Israel's population by 2020.

The total number of immigrants in 1999 was 77,921, up significantly from 58,200 the previous year. The vast majority of the new arrivals—some 67,704—were from Eastern Europe. There were 2,628 who came from Western Europe, 2,279 from North America, 1,799 from South America, 2,715 from Africa, and 686 from Asia.

In mid-September it emerged that a secret operation to bring Cuban Jews to Israel had been underway for several years. According to London's *Jewish Chronicle,* which first reported the news, around 400 Cuban refugees had arrived in Israel over the past three years.

When it emerged in November that a little over 50 percent of the immigrants from the former Soviet Union (FSU) who had arrived in 1999 were not Jewish according to Halakhah, ultra-Orthodox politicians began pressing for a review of the Law of Return. They wanted to do away with the "grandparent clause" that granted automatic citizenship to anyone with a Jewish grandparent. "Herzl must be turning in his grave," declared Health Minister Shlomo Benizri (Shas) during a cabinet meeting. "He envisioned a Jewish state and not a country where 50 percent of its immigrants are non-Jewish."

Barak, however, made it clear that he would not entertain any discussion about altering the law. He was strongly backed by Absorption Minister Yuli Tamir, who pointed out that when the immigrants arrived from the FSU they underwent "a kind of secular conversion, joining our culture, language and traditions. American Jewry," she said, "long ago realized that it had to expand the criteria beyond Halakhah for admitting non-Jews into the Jewish people. The Law of Return is the Israeli response to that same problem of ensuring that we don't exclude people who want to join us."

RELIGION

Religion and State

The secular-religious battle continued to make headlines throughout 1999, as did the battle over religious pluralism. In a precedent-setting decision in January, the Jerusalem District Court ruled that 23 people who had undergone Reform and Conservative conversions in Israel and abroad should be registered as Jews in the population registry. (In Israel the Orthodox had a de facto monopoly on conversions, and had always refused to recognize Reform and Conservative conversions.) At the time of the court ruling, ultra-Orthodox parties were pressing for the passage of a bill that would make their monopoly on conversion the law in Israel. "The court asked for a war," railed Shas's Shlomo Benizri, "and it's going to get it."

In the early part of the year the pluralism battle was waged around the issue of non-Orthodox representation on the country's state-funded religious councils, which were responsible for supplying services like kashrut and ritual baths. Aside from their bitter dispute with non-Orthodox Judaism, the Orthodox were keen on maintaining their monopoly on the religious councils because they served as a major source of patronage—especially for Shas and the National Religious Party—in the form of money and jobs, such as kashrut supervisors and ritual-bath attendants.

On January 26 the Knesset approved a law by the narrowest of margins—50 to 49—requiring all members of the state-run religious councils to swear an oath accepting the authority of the Chief Rabbinate regarding all matters in the councils' authority. The legislation was an effort by the Orthodox to circumvent a Supreme Court ruling requiring that non-Orthodox members be allowed to sit on the councils. The oath, religious legislators hoped, would be impossible for the Reform and Conservative members to take since they did not recognize the authority of the Chief Rabbinate. But much to the chagrin of the religious politicians, some of the non-Orthodox leaders announced that they would take the oath. The actual act of signing, said Rabbi Ehud Bandel, the head of the Masorti (Conservative) movement in Israel who had been elected to the Jerusalem religious council but had yet to take his seat, did not change the fact that he was a Conservative rabbi. "I don't plan to change my beliefs," he said.

Ultra-Orthodox politicians went on the attack. "They are prepared to sign, yet they claim that they are not subject to Halakhah," fumed Avraham Yosef Lazerzon, a Knesset member of United Torah Judaism. "Separate councils for Reform and Conservative can be set up," added Shas MK David Tal, "just like the Christians and Muslims have bodies that deal with their religious services."

After the court fined the Jerusalem religious council for not convening (not convening was a ploy to block non-Orthodox members from participating) the head of the council called a meeting in February. Bandel and the Reform representative turned up, but then sat in a boardroom with the press and waited in vain for the Orthodox members to arrive. After an hour, when only one had appeared, and with the council head closeted in his office, they departed. Two weeks before this Jerusalem council meeting, the Haifa religious council had convened with its non-Orthodox members, but was adjourned straight away at the request of the Orthodox members. In Tel Aviv the scene was similar, with the council meeting adjourned after only the Reform and Likud representatives turned up.

In February, Israel's Sephardi chief rabbi, Eliyahu Bakshi-Doron, added fuel to the fire when he pinned responsibility on the Reform movement for the disappearance of more Jews than those killed in the Holocaust. Shortly afterward Bakshi-Doron asserted that the rabbinate was in possession of data that revealed that for every 100 Reform Jews, "only 50 Jews are left by the fourth generation."

The nature of Barak's coalition, which included the ultra-Orthodox parties, was a clear signal that the prime minister would not push forward on issues of religion and state and religious pluralism. Nevertheless, Barak did set up a ministerial committee headed by Rabbi Michael Melchior, the leader of the moderate Orthodox Meimad faction and minister responsible for relations with Jewish communities overseas. The committee was meant to complete the work of the Ne'eman Commission, whose compromise recommendations on conversion and marriage had been rejected by the ultra-Orthodox parties and the Chief Rabbinate.

Shortly after the committee assembled for the first time, Melchior angered the ultra-Orthodox when he boldly suggested, in a November *Jerusalem Report* interview, that the state should recognize non-Orthodox conversions performed in Israel for the purpose of turning non-Jews into Israeli citizens, even though Orthodox Jews like himself would not consider such conversions religiously valid. Furthermore, he declared that Israel should recognize civil marriage and give equal funding to Orthodox, Conservative, and Reform institutions.

The Ultra-Orthodox Versus the Courts

The focus of the religious-secular battle in the first months of the year was the Supreme Court, which the ultra-Orthodox saw as a direct threat to the Jewishness of the state, but which secular Israelis viewed as a bastion of democracy and civil liberties and a bulwark against religious coercion. Attacks by the ultra-Orthodox on the Supreme Court were frequent. Rulings that particularly upset them were one stipulating that exemption from military service for yeshivah students was illegal, and another decreeing that shops located on kibbutzim could remain open on the Sabbath. They also strongly opposed petitions submitted to the court by the Reform movement demanding recognition for non-Orthodox conversions.

In February, Shas spiritual leader Rabbi Ovadia Yosef called the Supreme Court judges "unworthy" and blamed "everything suffered by Israel" on "these evil men." After considering indicting Yosef for his comments, Attorney General Elyakim Rubinstein decided not to prosecute. "His comments outraged me as a Jew, an Israeli and a jurist," explained Rubinstein. But, he added, "criminal law cannot be the solution to all Israeli society's ills."

The atmosphere was further soured by a comment by Oded Alyagon, a Beersheba judge, who reportedly described the ultra-Orthodox as "human-sized lice trying to take over the judicial system via brutal and relentless attacks and blood libels." The religious parties called for his dismissal.

Tensions peaked on February 14 when the ultra-Orthodox held a massive rally in Jerusalem against the Supreme Court. Estimates put the number of protesters at the rally at around a quarter of a million. A short distance away, in Jerusalem's Sacher Park—located just below the Supreme Court building—tens of thousands of mainly secular demonstrators turned out for a counterrally in support of the court.

Chief Justice Aharon Barak hit back in December, advising the ultra-Orthodox that it was actually in their long-term interest to support constitutional legislation. The ultra-Orthodox, he said, referring to their political power, "are a minority that act like a majority. . . . The day will come when they can no longer act like a majority, and so it's the ultra-Orthodox who should work towards a constitution for civil rights. [They] must demand that freedom of religion be anchored in law, but they oppose this because they don't believe in the courts."

Nazareth Showdown

Religious battles were not confined to the Jews. In Nazareth tensions festered between Christians and Muslims over the insistence by the Muslim majority (of at least 65 percent) that they be allowed to build a mosque adjacent to the Basilica of the Annunciation where, according to tradition, the Angel Gabriel visited Mary, and which was to have been turned into a huge piazza for the pilgrims expected to throng the church for the millennium. The Muslims argued that the plot contained a tomb of a 12th-century Islamic hero who perished in a battle against the Crusaders, and they insisted on building a mosque there.

With the millennium drawing closer and the city preparing for a possible visit by the pope, the battle heated up again in October. A tent erected by the Muslims as a temporary mosque quickly became the site of Friday prayers.

Although the Nazareth District Court ruled against the Muslim claim, a government committee headed by Minister of Internal Security Shlomo Ben-Ami came up with a compromise in early November. A mosque would be built on part of the land near the church, but it would be smaller than the one the Muslims originally demanded. Following the compromise deal, the government, which feared that the 2000 celebrations would be sabotaged, removed the tent, and a cornerstone for the mosque was laid. As part of the compromise it was agreed that work would only begin in the year 2001. Both Muslims and Christians reluctantly accepted the compromise so as not to deter tourism.

The Vatican, however, did not go along. In a strongly worded statement it blamed Israel for fomenting religious divisions and it called on all churches to close for two days in late November in protest. "We want the whole world to hear that the State of Israel ignored Christian interests," railed Michel Sabah, the Latin patriarch of Jerusalem. "Israel is inciting a civil war between Muslims and Christians in Nazareth."

Israel faced another tricky diplomatic situation toward the end of the year over the need to build an additional door, for safety reasons, at the Church of the Holy Sepulcher in Jerusalem. The problem was how to reach agreement between the several different churches that controlled the Holy Sepulchre on where exactly to build the door. Large numbers of pilgrims were expected to visit in the millennium year, with the peak expected on Holy Saturday, April 29 — the day before the Greek Orthodox Easter — when up to 20,000 people carrying lighted torches would try to cram into the church. Much of the interior of the church was made from wood and there was only one exit. Thus the church was not only a firetrap, but it was impossible to access with ambulances or helicopters. Israel turned to the pope for assistance, but that move itself was problematic. "There's an ongoing conflict between the various churches who control the Holy Sepulchre," explained Yitzhak Minerbi, an expert on Israel-Vatican relations. "By going to the pope, you're going to one of the sides in the conflict and asking them to settle it."

The Vatican finally confirmed in December that Pope John Paul II would in fact visit Israel in the millennium year. Date of arrival: March 21, 2000.

Millennium Madness

With the millennium approaching, the police and security services began taking a closer look at Christian groups and individuals in the Holy Land who might threaten public safety. A task force was set up with the specific purpose of monitoring extremists among the millions of tourists and pilgrims expected to arrive. On January 3, police arrested 14 members of an American group called the Concerned Christians, and deported them a week later. The Denver-based group's leader, Monte Kim Miller, who was not among those detained, had apparently prophesied his death in Jerusalem, and the group had allegedly planned to instigate violence in the final days before the millennium so as to trigger the second coming of Jesus.

In October, authorities deported 26 Irish and Romanian members of the Irish-based Pilgrim Foundation Community, which cared for the handicapped. Later that month 21 more Christian pilgrims, many of whom had rented homes on the Mount of Olives, were arrested and deported. Some criticized the police for what seemed to be a heavy-handed approach of deporting first and asking questions later.

OTHER DOMESTIC MATTERS

Violence

A series of family and wife murders, and attacks on women by a serial rapist, thrust the issue of violence, especially domestic violence, into the spotlight. In May, for instance, 31-year-old Erez Tivoni murdered his two children, aged two and four, then doused their bodies in flammable liquid, and set them on fire. He later confessed he had also planned to kill the children's mother, from whom he was divorced just a week. Then on July 24, Amnon Cohen, a Tel Aviv taxi driver, was taken into custody for killing his wife and two children and burning their bodies. Cohen reportedly thought his wife was conducting an affair via the Internet.

The spate of family killings continued in late September when a 56-year-old East Jerusalem man, Musa Damri, shot his three daughters and then took his own life. On October 1, 31-year-old Gad Carmi killed his nine-month-old daughter by slitting her throat, and then seriously injured a nine-year-old boy who was passing outside his apartment. Three days later a 45-year-old father of seven from the West Bank settlement of Ma'aleh Adumim stabbed his wife to death and then handed himself over to the police. In late October, Uri Gershuni stabbed his wife Doli to death at their home in the northern moshav of She'ar Yashuv.

Police figures showed an alarming 15-percent rise in domestic abuse in the first half of the year. While police, prosecutors, and social services blamed each other, experts searched for deeper reasons. Some pointed to the stresses of immigration and the macho culture in Israel. Others suggested the patriarchal nature of large sectors of Israeli society, in which women were viewed as possessions.

During the course of the year the police undertook a nationwide manhunt for a serial rapist who terrorized women, carrying out most of his assaults in the center of the country. The police finally got their man on December 14. He was Beni Sela, a 28-year-old plumber. While Sela initially refused to cooperate with his interrogators, police said they had clear DNA proof from ten of the rape sites.

Two teen murders in the space of a week in early June thrust youth violence into the spotlight. First, five schoolmates of 15-year-old immigrant Yevgeny Yakobovich stabbed and beat him to death on June 3. A week later, 15-year-old Gilad Raviv was stabbed to death in Jerusalem's East Talpiot neighborhood by 19-year-old Shlomo Gabai. The police responded by doubling the number of youth officers. They were also said to be considering the use of undercover agents and surprise weapons searches at schools.

The Deri Verdict

In early March it was announced that the verdict in the seemingly interminable corruption trial of Arye Deri—leader of the Sephardi ultra-Orthodox Shas Party and mastermind of the Sephardi religious revolution it had spawned—would be handed down on the 17th of the month. As the day approached there were fears that a guilty verdict would spark violent outbursts among Shas supporters. Some Shas leaders played up the trial's ethnic overtones, declaring that all of Sephardi Jewry was in the dock with Deri.

On the day of the verdict, Shas supporters gathered behind police barriers set up a few hundred meters from the Jerusalem District Court building in East Jerusalem. The Deri supporters stood in clusters, listening to the live radio broadcast in disbelief as the judge read the verdict: Arye Deri was guilty of bribery, fraud, and breach of trust. Deri had been convicted of taking a total of $155,000 in bribes from three former associates—they had also been found guilty—over a five-year period in which he served as director general and then minister of the Interior Ministry. In their verdict the judges castigated Deri for seeking "to derail the investigation and obstruct police efforts to get to the truth."

While many in Israel's mainstream Ashkenazi bastions perceived the guilty verdict as a victory for the rule of law, Shas supporters in the poor inner-city neighborhoods and development towns saw it as another case of ethnic and religious discrimination. In their eyes, Deri's conviction confirmed that the secular Ashkenazi elite was trying to destroy the man who had challenged its hegemony.

On April 15, Deri was sentenced to four years imprisonment and a 250,000-shekel ($60,000) fine. In sentencing Deri the judges noted that he had received dozens of gifts over several years while in public office. "They were interwoven and intertwined with his economic advancement," the judges wrote. "They increased as he climbed the rungs of power. . . . What makes this affair even more grave is the fact that Deri was a minister. He began receiving bribes in his previous public positions and continued to accept them as a cabinet minister. . . . This has never happened before." Deri announced he would appeal, and the court ruled that the sentence would only go into effect after the appeal had been heard.

The "Amedi Affair"

An investigative article in the daily *Yediot Aharonot* in September alleged that Benjamin and Sara Netanyahu had taken bribes and misused public funds while Netanyahu was in office. The report sparked a high-profile police investigation that ran for weeks and was still not over at the end of the year.

According to the allegations, a private contractor named Avner Amedi had carried out numerous services free of charge for the Netanyahus, including removing furniture and polishing the floors of their private apartment. Toward the end of Netanyahu's term, however, Amedi suddenly submitted a whopping bill for 440,000 shekels, and efforts had allegedly been made to pay the bill out of state funds. The newspaper also charged that the Netanyahus had kept hundreds of presents given to the prime minister during his term of office, which by law belonged to the state.

On October 20 police searched the Netanyahus' home and office and seized boxes of presents from a government warehouse—an event witnessed by journalists who had been tipped off earlier. For weeks the Netanyahus, along with other senior officials who had served under the prime minister, underwent intensive interrogations. Likud members and Netanyahu associates launched an all-out attack on the police, accusing them of leaking information about the case to the media and of launching a witch-hunt against the former prime minister.

Netanyahu rehired Ya'akov Weinroth, who had represented him during a 1997 influence-peddling scandal. "If the prime minister was going to steal $100,000, would he steal it from a lowly moving contractor?" asked Weinroth during a TV interview. "And would he steal it so clumsily, knowing he was being carefully watched? No, he'd take a bribe from General Motors or some foreign arms company."

The "Nimrodi Affair"

In early October it emerged that Ofer Nimrodi, the owner and publisher of *Ma'ariv*, Israel's second largest daily, was being investigated by the police for conspiracy to commit murder. The targets allegedly included the chief witness in a 1998 trial in which Nimrodi had been convicted of wiretapping, as well as the owners of two rival newspapers. The stunning revelations came a little over six months after Nimrodi had been released from jail after serving eight months for bugging his main competitor and Israel's largest daily, *Yediot Aharonot*, back in 1993. Two *Yediot Aharonot* editors had also been tried for their involvement in the wiretapping of *Ma'ariv*.

In a bizarre twist, both papers had employed the same private investigator, Rafi Pridan, to do the wiretapping, and Nimrodi's conviction had been largely the result of the fact that Pridan's partner, Ya'akov Tzur, had turned state's evidence. With Pridan about to begin a four-year jail term in the fall of 1999 for his role in the wiretapping scandal, he told prosecutors that he had remarkable information for them about Nimrodi. The *Ma'ariv* boss, Pridan alleged, had put out a contract on Tzur and had also expressed a desire to do away with *Yediot* owner Arnon Mozes and *Ha'aretz* publisher Amos Schocken.

As the story unfolded, one serving and two former police officers were arrested on suspicion of taking bribes from Nimrodi to supply him with information about the investigation. Nimrodi suspended himself as editor in chief and publisher of *Ma'ariv* as well as managing director of the Israel Land Development Corporation, *Ma'ariv*'s holding company. Nimrodi's defense was that Pridan had tried to blackmail him and he had refused to pay up, and that Pridan was now trying to get even.

In late November police arrested Nimrodi. In a dramatic court appearance, the head of the investigating team, Brig. Gen. Moshe Mizrahi, described Nimrodi's efforts to sabotage the investigation as the most serious attempt to undermine justice he had ever encountered. The press baron, said Mizrahi, had almost succeeded in "stealing" his whole International Serious Crimes Investigation Unit by offering hundreds of thousands of dollars in bribes.

The investigation began to branch out. In late December allegations emerged that two senior officers in the Prisons Authority had helped Nimrodi while he was in custody. Also, two other senior police officers had met with Nimrodi when the investigation was still secret, and he had asked them how he could find out if he was the target of an investigation. While the two officers had no knowledge of the investigation at the time, they failed to report the fact that Nimrodi suspected the secret probe against him.

On December 26, Nimrodi was formally charged on eight different counts, including conspiring to either murder Tzur, or to have him arrested on drug charges in Thailand. (The charge sheet did not include any reference to Mozes and Schocken.)

The Rabin Assassination

The Rabin assassination continued to make waves in 1999 as a former Shin Bet informer went on trial for failing to prevent the 1995 murder. There were also calls from across the political spectrum to reopen the investigation into the killing. On April 25, Avishai Raviv, the Shin Bet informer known as "Champagne" who had been a member of the extreme right-wing Eyal group and knew Yigal Amir, was indicted for failing to prevent the assassination and for inciting terror. Meanwhile, Margalit Har-Shefi, a law student at Bar-Ilan University who had been convicted and sentenced to nine months for failing to report that Amir was planning to kill Rabin, lost her appeal in the Tel Aviv District Court. Har-Shefi said she would appeal to the Supreme Court. When Raviv's trial began on October 3, he pled not guilty.

In early November Attorney General Elyakim Rubinstein slapped a gag order on the minutes of a 1996 Ministry of Justice meeting about whether to prosecute Raviv for not preventing the assassination. Right-wing politicians charged that the minutes proved an attempt to cover up Raviv's role. On November 11, however, the Supreme Court lifted the gag order and the minutes were publicized. They quoted a Shin Bet agent asserting that the murder of Rabin could have been prevented had Raviv been better supervised. They also appeared to intimate that Dorit Beinish, then the state's attorney but who had subsequently moved to the Supreme Court bench, had been prepared to accept the framing of a certain individual in order to beef up Raviv's cover. The Ministry of Justice denied the assertions, insisting that the minutes were not an accurate record of the meeting.

In early November tens of thousands attended a memorial rally in Rabin Square. This year the event did not have the bitterness of previous years, when it had been as much a protest against Netanyahu—whom many on the left held partly responsible for the climate of incitement around the time of the assassination—as a memorial ceremony. The Shin Bet, fearing for Ehud Barak's safety, advised the prime minister not to address the crowd. Barak attended the rally, sitting in a specially constructed "sterile" structure at the edge of the square, while his address was relayed on large screens to the crowd. Toward the end of the evening, however, Barak did emerge. Ascending the podium to briefly address the crowd, he reiterated, "We are not afraid; We are not afraid; We are not afraid."

Around the time of the memorial, Dalya Rabin Pelossof, the daughter of the assassinated prime minister and a Center Party member of the Knesset, told an interviewer that there were still unanswered questions about the assassination that needed to be investigated. Why, for example, had someone called out, "Blank, blank," as Amir fired the shots that killed her father?

A plaque placed at the site of the assassination in November generated controversy by referring to a "*kippah*-wearing" assassin. When Tel Aviv mayor Ron Huldai ordered removal of the reference following complaints that it defamed the entire Orthodox community, Leah Rabin remarked angrily that what Huldai had done was "an act of violence. A distortion of history has been committed," she said.

Sports

Israel's swimmers continued to impress. At the European championships in Turkey in early August, Miki Halikah, 21, took the silver medal in the 400-meter medley after being edged out in the final meters of the race. In the process, Halikah shaved four seconds off the Israeli record. Eitan Orbach, 22, took the bronze medal in the 100-meter backstroke.

The Israeli national soccer team continued to disappoint its supporters when it failed to reach the Euro 2000 soccer championships. After Israel placed second in its qualifying group, the national team faced Denmark for a place in the finals, scheduled for June 2000. But in front of a capacity crowd at the Ramat Gan National Stadium on November 13, Israel was trounced 5-0 by the Danes. Four days later Denmark won the return leg 3-0, handing Israel a humiliating overall 8-0 aggregate loss.

But the soccer was overshadowed by a report that appeared after the first game in the daily *Ma'ariv*. Allegedly, some of the national team players had been up most of the night before the game in their hotel rooms with prostitutes. The players denied the charge and, banding together, they refused to cooperate with private investigators hired by the Israel Soccer Federation. The findings of the investigation proved inconclusive, but Sports Minister Matan Vilnai said the matter should not be allowed to rest.

Other Developments

Two Mossad agents, known as Yigal Damary and Udi Hargov, were sentenced in a Cyprus court on February 1 to three years in prison for having trespassed in an illegal area and for being in possession of illegal telecommunications devices. The two had been arrested in November 1998 in the vicinity of a military base in the Cypriot town of Zigy. The court dismissed the far more serious charges of espionage and conspiracy. On August 12, after serving several months of their term, the two were released and flown back to Israel.

Surveys released on March 8, International Women's Day, revealed that Israeli women lived longer than Israeli men did — 79.9 years versus 76.3. The survey also showed that women were paid less than men; in senior executive posts the difference came to about $850 per month.

Samuel Sheinbein was indicted in Tel Aviv District Court on March 22 for the murder of a teenager in Maryland in 1997. Sheinbein, 18, was indicted after the Supreme Court ruled that he was protected by a law which exempted Israeli citizens from extradition for trial abroad. Sheinbein, whose father was Israeli, had never lived in Israel, but had fled there after the murder to avoid prosecution. The loophole exploited by Sheinbein was closed on April 19 when the Knesset enacted legislation allowing for the extradition of someone resident in Israel who had committed crimes abroad. The law, though, was not retroactive, and so Sheinbein remained in Israel to stand trial. As part of a plea bargain, Sheinbein pleaded guilty on September 2, and on October 24 the court sentenced him to 24 years, with the possibility of parole after 14. Already angry that Israel had refused to extradite Sheinbein for trial in a U.S. court, Maryland prosecutors called the plea bargain an "outrage."

On March 9, Rana Raslan became the first Israeli Arab to win the Miss Israel competition. Raslan, 22, was raised in a working-class neighborhood in Haifa.

The Supreme Court ruled on March 21 that 600 members of the al-Azazmeh Bedouin tribe, who had crossed the border into Israel illegally after feuding with another tribe, had to return to Egypt.

In late March the Supreme Court ruled that Brig. Gen. Nir Galili should be barred from promotion to the position of major general because he had harassed an 18-year-old female soldier under his command. Galili, a 47-year-old married officer, had argued that the affair was consensual and that the two-year freeze on his promotion that he had already received was sufficient punishment. The court, though, left open the question of Galili's future in the army, and women's groups threatened to take to the streets were he given a senior post. Chief-of-Staff Shaul Mofaz decided not to promote Galili to the position of corps commander.

Three men serving life sentences for the gruesome 1983 murder of Danny Katz, a Haifa schoolboy, were freed on bail on April 4 after being granted a retrial by Chief Justice Aharon Barak. Two other men, also convicted of the Katz murder, remained behind bars because of another murder conviction. The five, all Arab Israelis, had been convicted almost entirely on the basis of their confessions, which, they claimed, were extracted under duress.

In mid-February it emerged that Foreign Minister Ariel Sharon was under police investigation for allegedly offering business favors involving energy deals with Russia to Avigdor Ben-Gal, an ex-general. The favors, it was charged, were in exchange for Ben-Gal changing his testimony in Sharon's libel suit against the daily Ha'aretz over the paper's accusation that Sharon had deceived Prime Minister Menachem Begin about plans for the IDF invasion of Lebanon in 1982. On June 24, Attorney General Elyakim Rubinstein closed the investigation on grounds of insufficient evidence.

Thirty-one years after the Dakar submarine had mysteriously disappeared with its crew of 69, it was discovered on the Mediterranean seafloor between Crete and Cyprus in late May. The navy had launched countless searches over the years but said it had not had the technology required to search at the three-kilometer depth where the Dakar had settled. The Dakar was reported missing while on its maiden voyage from Portsmouth, England, to Haifa in January 1968. The evidence indicated that the submarine had gone down as a result of an accident.

In a bizarre episode in late July, a shocked Knesset stood for a moment of silence in memory of Amnon Rubinstein after a caller to the parliament announced that the Meretz Knesset member, recovering in a hospital after suffering a mild stroke, had died. Speaker Avraham Burg, who had rushed to make the announcement to the Knesset, eulogized Rubinstein as stunned members looked on, some of them crying. Half an hour later, though, after someone bothered to check with the hospital, it emerged that Rubinstein was alive and well and that the call had been a hoax. Police soon announced that they suspected an elderly couple, who were taken in for questioning and exposed to the TV cameras. But the police were left red-faced when it emerged that the culprit was a well-known transvestite, Zalman Shoshi. The police formally apologized to the couple.

In a September 6 ruling, a nine-judge Supreme Court panel banned the use of force in Shin Bet interrogations of prisoners. The landmark decision reversed a 1987 ruling allowing the use of "moderate physical pressure." The judges now barred the use of sleep deprivation, loud music, violent shaking, and the covering of prisoners' heads with hoods for long periods. Prime Minister Barak and others expressed concern that the ruling might make it difficult to fight terror, but Israeli human-rights groups hailed the decision as one of the most important ever by the Supreme Court. A short while later the Likud drafted a bill that would allow the use of force in interrogations of suspected terrorists where it was fairly certain that a suspect had information that could save lives and where all other methods had been exhausted.

Nur Shlomo, a Milan travel agent, was found guilty by the Tel Aviv District Court on October 6 of raping Israel's Miss World, Linor Abargil. Nur, an Egyptian who had converted to Judaism and become an Israeli citizen, was found guilty of raping and assaulting Abargil when she was in Italy for a modeling interview in late 1998, a few weeks before the Miss World pageant. On December 30 Shlomo was sentenced to 16 years behind bars.

Sixteen people died in a horrific October 9 crash in the Galilee when a bus carrying a group of singles veered off the road. In total, 469 people died on Israel's roads in 1999 (down 15.5 percent from 1998), 3,091 were seriously injured (down 8 percent), and 40,570 were lightly injured (down 10.3 percent).

Partial transcripts of the 1988 trial of Mordechai Vanunu, sentenced to 18 years for revealing the country's nuclear secrets, were released in November. "I wanted things to be properly supervised," said Vanunu in one extract. "Now Peres can't lie to Reagan and tell him we don't have nuclear weapons."

Personalia

Dr. Yosef Burg (1909–1999), founder and former head of the National Religious Party. Burg served as a cabinet minister for 35 years under eight different prime ministers. He resigned from the cabinet and the NRP leadership in 1986 after serving in almost every government since 1951.

Shlomo Baum, 70, right-wing activist and one of the founders of the legendary

Commando 101 Unit which carried out reprisal raids across the Jordanian border in the 1950s; Haim Stoessel, 69, former chairman of the Tel Aviv Stock Exchange and later chairman of Avner Insurance; Rabbi David Povarsky, 98, head of Bnei Brak's Ponevezh Yeshivah; Nahum Stelmach, 63, Israeli soccer legend and longtime coaching consultant, died of a heart attack at Barcelona airport; Geoffrey Wigoder, 77, British-born editor-in-chief of the *Encyclopedia Judaica* and of the English edition of the *Encyclopedia of the Holocaust;* Baroness Batsheva de Rothschild, 84, established the Batsheva Dance Company and later was a co-founder of the Bat Dor Company; Rafael Recanati, 75, former chairman of the Israel Discount Bank and IDB group, in New York; Meir Ariel, 57, popular Israeli singer; Yitzhak Raphael, 85, former leader of the National Religious Party and religious affairs minister from 1974–1977; Shulamith Katznelson, 80, founder of the famous Ulpan Akiva in Netanyah in 1951, where Jews studied Arabic and Arabs learned Hebrew, winner of the Israel Prize for life achievement in 1986; Zohara Schatz, 83, sculptor of Yad Vashem's emblematic menorah representing the six million Jews killed in the Holocaust, and the first woman to win the Israel Prize, in 1954; Hanoch Levin, 56, Israeli playwright and director, many of whose 50 controversial plays challenged national myths, of cancer; Shimon Finkel, 94, actor and director, winner of the Israel Prize in 1969, veteran of the Habimah National Theater.

PETER HIRSCHBERG

World Jewish Population, 2000

T HE WORLD'S JEWISH POPULATION was estimated at 13.2 million at the beginning of the year 2000, an increase of nearly 100,000 over the previous two-year period.

The present volume of the AJYB carries a detailed article about contemporary demographic trends among world Jewry and population projections for the period 2000–2080.[1] Therefore instead of the customary detailed overview of current Jewish population developments only a brief summary is given here. The following tables provide an update of the data available about the size of Jewish population and its share of the total population in each country. While the population estimates presented in previous volumes of the *American Jewish Year Book* referred to December 31 of the year preceding by two the date of publication,[2] the current estimates refer to January 1 of the current year of publication. Since this attempt to present the most recent possible picture entails a shorter span of time for evaluation and correction of the available information, the margin of inaccuracy is somewhat greater than in previous years. As in the past, we provide revised estimates for the previous date so as to ensure a better base for comparisons with the more recent figures. Corrections of the latest estimates, if needed, will be presented in future volumes of the AJYB. It should be emphasized, in any case, that the elaboration of a worldwide set of estimates for the Jewish populations of the various countries is beset with difficulties and uncertainties, all the more so at a time of enhanced international migration. Thus the analyst has to come to terms with the paradox of the *permanently provisional* character of Jewish population estimates.

Definitions

A major problem with Jewish population estimates periodically circulated is a lack of coherence and uniformity in the definition of "Jewish." Often, the problem of defining the Jewish population is not even addressed. The following estimates of Jewish population distribution in each continent and country (tables 1–7 below) consistently aim at the concept of *core* Jewish population.

We define as the *core Jewish population* all those who, when asked, identify

---

[1]Sergio DellaPergola, Uzi Rebhun, Mark Tolts, "Prospecting the Jewish Future: Population Projections, 2000–2080," above, pp. 103–46.

[2]The previous estimates as of December 31, 1997 (or January 1, 1998) were published in AJYB 1999, vol. 99, pp. 543–80.

themselves as Jews; or, if the respondent is a different person in the same household, are identified by him/her as Jews. This is an intentionally comprehensive and pragmatic approach. Such definition of a person as a Jew, reflecting *subjective* feelings, broadly overlaps but does not necessarily coincide with Halakhah (rabbinic law) or other normatively binding definitions. It does *not* depend on any measure of that person's Jewish commitment or behavior — in terms of religiosity, beliefs, knowledge, communal affiliation, or otherwise. The *core* Jewish population includes all those who converted to Judaism by any procedure, or joined the Jewish group informally, and declare themselves to be Jewish. It excludes those of Jewish descent who formally adopted another religion, as well as other individuals who did not convert out but currently refuse to acknowledge their Jewish identification.

Two additional operative concepts must be considered in the study of Jewish population. The *extended Jewish population* includes the sum of (a) the *core* Jewish population and (b) all other persons of Jewish parentage who are *not* Jews currently (or at the time of investigation). These non-Jews with Jewish background, as far as they can be ascertained, include: (a) persons who have themselves adopted another religion, even though they may claim still to be Jews ethnically; (b) other persons with Jewish parentage who disclaim to be Jews. It is customary in sociodemographic surveys to consider the religioethnic identification of parents. Some censuses, however, do ask about more distant ancestry. The *enlarged Jewish population*, in addition to all those who belong in the *extended* Jewish population, also includes all of the respective further non-Jewish household members (spouses, children, etc.). For both conceptual and practical reasons, this definition does not include any other non-Jewish relatives living elsewhere in exclusively non-Jewish households.

The Law of Return, Israel's distinctive legal framework for the acceptance and absorption of new immigrants, awards Jewish new immigrants immediate citizenship and other civil rights. According to the current, amended version of the Law of Return, a Jew is any person born to a Jewish mother, or converted to Judaism (regardless of denomination). By decision of Israel's Supreme Court, conversion from Judaism, as in the case of some ethnic Jews who currently identify with another religion, entails loss of eligibility for Law of Return purposes. The law extends its provisions to all current Jews and to their Jewish or non-Jewish spouses, children, and grandchildren, as well as to the spouses of such children and grandchildren. As a result of its three-generation time perspective and lateral extension, the Law of Return applies to a population significantly wider than *core, extended,* and *enlarged* Jewish populations as defined above. It is actually quite difficult to estimate what the total size of the *Law of Return* population could be.

Accuracy Rating

We provide separate figures for each country with approximately 100 or more resident *core* Jews. Residual estimates of Jews living in other smaller communities supplement some of the continental totals. For each of the reported countries, the four columns in tables 2–6 provide an estimate of mid-year 2000 total population,[3] the estimated January 1, 2000, Jewish population, the proportion of Jews per 1,000 of total population, and a rating of the accuracy of the Jewish population estimate.

There is wide variation in the quality of the Jewish population estimates for different countries. For many Diaspora countries it would be best to indicate a range (minimum-maximum) rather than a definite figure for the number of Jews. It would be confusing, however, for the reader to be confronted with a long list of ranges; this would also complicate the regional and world totals. The figures actually indicated for most of the Diaspora communities should be understood as being the central value of the plausible range of the respective core Jewish populations. The relative magnitude of this range varies inversely to the accuracy of the estimate.

The three main elements that affect the accuracy of each estimate are the nature and quality of the base data, the recency of the base data, and the method of updating. A simple code combining these elements is used to provide a general evaluation of the reliability of the Jewish population figures reported in the detailed tables below. The code indicates different quality levels of the reported estimates: (A) Base figure derived from countrywide census or relatively reliable Jewish population survey; updated on the basis of full or partial information on Jewish population movements in the respective country during the intervening period. (B) Base figure derived from less accurate but recent countrywide Jewish population investigation; partial information on population movements in the intervening period. (C) Base figure derived from less recent sources, and/or unsatisfactory or partial coverage of Jewish population in the particular country; updating according to demographic information illustrative of regional demographic trends. (D) Base figure essentially speculative; no reliable updating procedure. In categories (A), (B), and (C), the year in which the country's base figure or important partial updates were obtained is also stated. For countries whose Jewish population estimate of end 1997-beginning 1998 was not only updated but also revised in the light of improved information, the sign "X" is appended to the accuracy rating.

One additional tool for updating Jewish population estimates is provided by a new set of demographic projections developed at the Hebrew University of Jerusalem.[4] Such projections extrapolate the most likely observed or expected trends out of a Jewish population baseline assessed by sex and detailed age-groups as of end-year 1995. Even where detailed information on the dynamics of

---

[3]For general population data see United Nations, Department of Economic and Social Affairs, *World Population Prospects, The 1998 Revision,* Vol. I: *Comprehensive Tables* (New York, 1999).

[4]See note 1 above.

Jewish population change is not immediately available, the powerful connection that generally exists between age composition of a population and the respective vital and migration movements helps to provide plausible scenarios of the developments bound to occur in the short term. In the absence of better data, we used indications from these projections to refine the estimates for 2000 as against previous years. On the other hand, projections are clearly limited by a definite and comparatively limited set of assumptions and need to be periodically updated in the light of actual demographic developments.

World Jewish Population Size

Table 1 gives an overall picture of Jewish population for January 1, 2000, as compared to January 1, 1998. For 1998 the originally published estimates are presented along with somewhat revised figures that take into account, retrospectively, the corrections made for certain countries in the light of improved information. These corrections resulted in a net increase of the 1998 world Jewry's estimated size by 3,400. This change resulted from upward corrections for Belarus (+10,500), Moldova (+1,500), India (+2,100), Australia (+500), and New Zealand (+300); and downward corrections for Venezuela (-1,000) and South Africa (-10,500).

The size of world Jewry at the beginning of 2000 is estimated at 13,191,500, or about 2.2 per 1,000 of the world's total population of 6.055 billions in 2000. According to the revised figures, between 1998 and 2000 the Jewish population grew by an estimated 93,800 people, or about +0.4 percent per year. Despite all the imperfections in the estimates, world Jewry continued to be close to "zero population growth," with the natural increase in Israel overcompensating for demographic decline in the Diaspora. Another factor affecting Jewish population size in recent years is the renewed interest in Judaism among persons who had not previously revealed their Jewish identification, as well as an increased number of conversions to Judaism among new immigrants in Israel.

The number of Jews in Israel rose from 4,701,600 at the beginning of 1998 to 4,882,000 in 2000, an increase of 180,400 people, or a 1.9-percent yearly average. In contrast, the estimated Jewish population in the Diaspora declined from 8,394,600 (according to the revised figures) to 8,309,500—a decrease of 85,100 people, or -0.5 percent per year. These changes primarily reflect the continuing Jewish emigration from the former USSR (FSU). In 1998, the estimated Israel-Diaspora net migratory balance amounted to a gain of about 29,200 Jews for Israel,[5] and a higher net migration gain was estimated for 1999 following increased immigration from Russia and other parts of the FSU. Internal demographic evo-

---

[5]Israel, Central Bureau of Statistics, *Statistical Abstract of Israel 1999*, vol. 50 (Jerusalem, 1999), and unpublished data.

lution (births, deaths, and conversions) produced a further two-year growth of over 110,000 among the Jewish population in Israel, and a further loss of about 20,000 in the Diaspora. The latter estimates allow for cases of accession or "return" to Judaism observed in connection with migration from Eastern Europe and Ethiopia made possible by comprehensive provisions of the Israeli Law of Return (see above).

About half of the world's Jews reside in the Americas, with 46 percent in North America. Over 37 percent live in Asia, including the Asian republics of the former USSR (but not the Asian parts of the Russian Federation and Turkey)— most of them in Israel. Europe, including the Asian territories of the Russian Federation and Turkey, accounts for 12 percent of the total. Less than 2 percent of the world's Jews live in Africa and Oceania. Among the major geographical regions listed in table 1, the number of Jews in Israel—and, consequently, in total Asia—increased between 1998 and 2000. Moderate Jewish population gains were also estimated for the 15-country European Union (mostly reflecting migration from the FSU to Germany), and Oceania. The number of Jews in North America was estimated to be stable, pending the reassessment expected from the new National Jewish Population Survey. Central and South America, Eastern Europe, Asian countries outside of Israel, and Africa (particularly South Africa) sustained visible decreases in Jewish population size.

SERGIO DELLAPERGOLA

TABLE 1.   ESTIMATED JEWISH POPULATION, BY CONTINENTS AND MAJOR GEO-
GRAPHICAL REGIONS, 1998 AND 2000

Region	1998[a] Original Abs. N.	Revised Abs. N.	Percent[c]	2000[b] Abs. N.	Percent[c]	Yearly % Change 1998–2000[d]
World	13,092,800	13,096,200	100.0	13,191,500	100.0	0.4
Diaspora	8,391,200	8,394,600	64.1	8,309,500	63.0	−0.5
Israel	4,701,600	4,701,600	35.9	4,882,000	37.0	1.9
America, Total	6,490,400	6,489,400	49.5	6,483,900	49.2	−0.1
North[e]	6,062,000	6,062,000	46.3	6,062,000	46.0	0.0
Central	52,900	52,900	0.4	52,800	0.4	−0.1
South	375,500	374,500	2.9	369,100	2.8	−0.9
Europe, Total	1,637,400	1,649,400	12.6	1,583,000	12.0	−2.0
European Union	1,018,300	1,018,300	7.8	1,026,700	7.8	0.4
Other West	19,900	19,900	0.2	19,900	0.2	0.0
Former USSR[f]	499,200	511,200	3.9	438,100	3.3	−7.5
Other East and Balkans[f]	100,000	100,000	0.8	98,300	0.7	−0.9
Asia, Total	4,762,500	4,764,600	36.4	4,932,900	37.4	1.8
Israel	4,701,600	4,701,600	35.3	4,882,6000	37.0	1.9
Former USSR[f]	41,100	41,100	0.3	30,000	0.2	−14.6
Other[f]	19,800	21,900	0.2	20,900	0.2	−2.3
Africa, Total	102,400	91,900	0.7	89,800	0.7	−1.1
North[g]	7,800	7,800	0.1	7,700	0.1	−0.6
South[h]	94,600	84,100	0.6	82,100	0.6	−1.2
Oceania[i]	100,100	100,900	0.8	101,900	0.8	0.5

[a]January 1. The data were originally published as of December 31, 1997.
[b]January 1.
[c]Minor discrepancies due to rounding.
[d]Two-year period.
[e]U.S.A. and Canada.
[f]The Asian regions of Russia and Turkey are included in Europe.
[g]Including Ethiopia.
[h]South Africa, Zimbabwe, and other sub-Saharan countries.
[i]Australia, New Zealand and the Pacific.

TABLE 2. ESTIMATED JEWISH POPULATION DISTRIBUTION IN THE AMERICAS, 1/1/2000

Country	Total Population	Jewish Population	Jews per 1,000 Population	Accuracy Rating
Canada	31,147,000	362,000	11.6	B 1996
United States	278,357,000	5,700,000	20.5	B 1990
Total North America[a]	309,631,000	6,062,000	19.6	
Bahamas	307,000	300	1.0	D
Costa Rica	4,023,000	2,500	0.6	C 1993
Cuba	11,201,000	600	0.1	C 1990
Dominican Republic	8,495,000	100	0.0	D
El Salvador	6,276,000	100	0.0	C 1993
Guatemala	11,385,000	1,000	0.1	B 1993
Jamaica	2,583,000	300	0.1	A 1995
Mexico	98,881,000	40,500	0.4	B 1991
Netherlands Antilles	320,000	300	0.9	B 1995
Panama	2,856,000	5,000	1.8	C 1990
Puerto Rico	3,869,000	1,500	0.4	C 1990
Virgin Islands	114,000	300	2.6	C 1986
Other	23,051,000	300	0.0	D
Total Central America	173,361,000	52,800	0.3	
Argentina	37,032,000	200,000	5.4	C 1990
Bolivia	8,239,000	700	0.1	B 1990
Brazil	170,115,000	98,000	0.6	B 1991
Chile	15,211,000	21,000	1.4	A 1995
Colombia	42,321,000	3,800	0.1	C 1996
Ecuador	12,646,000	900	0.1	C 1985
Paraguay	5,496,000	900	0.2	B 1997
Peru	25,662,000	2,800	0.1	C 1993
Suriname	417,000	200	0.5	B 1986
Uruguay	3,337,000	22,800	6.8	C 1993
Venezuela	24,170,000	18,000	0.7	B 1999X
Total South America[a]	345,782,000	369,100	1.1	
Total	828,774,000	6,483,900	7.8	

[a]Including countries not listed separately.

TABLE 3. ESTIMATED JEWISH POPULATION DISTRIBUTION IN EUROPE, 1/1/2000

Country	Total Population	Jewish Population	Jews per 1,000 Population	Accuracy Rating
Austria	8,211,000	9,000	1.1	C 1995
Belgium	10,161,000	31,700	3.1	C 1987
Denmark	5,293,000	6,400	1.2	C 1990
Finland	5,176,000	1,100	0.2	B 1999
France[a]	59,114,000	521,000	8.8	C 1990
Germany	82,220,000	92,000	1.1	B 1999
Greece	10,645,000	4,500	0.4	B 1995
Ireland	3,730,000	1,000	0.3	B 1993
Italy	57,298,000	29,600	0.5	B 1995
Luxembourg	431,000	600	1.4	B 1990
Netherlands	15,786,000	26,500	1.7	C 1995
Portugal	9,875,000	300	0.0	C 1999
Spain	39,630,000	12,000	0.3	D
Sweden	8,910,000	15,000	1.7	C 1990
United Kingdom	59,062,000	276,000	4.7	B 1995
Total European Union	375,542,000	1,026,700	2.7	
Gibraltar	25,000	600	24.0	B 1991
Norway	4,465,000	1,200	0.3	B 1995
Switzerland	7,386,000	18,000	2.4	A 1990
Other	852,000	100	0.1	D
Total other West Europe	12,728,000	19,900	1.6	
Belarus	10,236,000	26,600	2.6	B 1999 X
Estonia	1,327,000	2,000	1.5	C 1997
Latvia	2,357,000	8,600	3.6	C 1997
Lithuania	3,670,000	4,400	1.2	C 1997
Moldova	4,380,000	6,500	1.5	B 1999 X
Russia[b]	146,934,000	290,000	2.0	B 1997
Ukraine	50,456,000	100,000	2.0	C 1997
Total former USSR in Europe	219,360,000	438,100	2.0	

TABLE 3.—*(Continued)*

Country	Total Population	Jewish Population	Jews per 1,000 Population	Accuracy Rating
Bosnia-Herzegovina	3,972,000	300	0.1	C 1996
Bulgaria	8,225,000	2,600	0.3	B 1992
Croatia	4,473,000	1,300	0.3	C 1996
Czech Republic	10,244,000	2,800	0.3	B 1998
Hungary	10,036,000	52,000	5.2	D
Macedonia (FYR)	2,024,000	100	0.0	C 1996
Poland	38,765,000	3,500	0.1	D
Romania	22,327,000	11,500	0.5	B 1997
Slovakia	5,387,000	3,300	0.6	D
Slovenia	1,986,000	100	0.1	C 1996
Turkey[b]	66,591,000	19,000	0.3	C 1996
Yugoslavia[c]	10,600,000	1,800	0.2	C 1996
Total other East Europe and Balkans[d]	187,743,000	98,300	0.5	
Total	795,373,000	1,583,000	2.0	

[a]Including Monaco.
[b]Including Asian regions.
[c]Serbia and Montenegro.
[d]Including Albania.

TABLE 4. ESTIMATED JEWISH POPULATION DISTRIBUTION IN ASIA, 1/1/2000

Country	Total Population	Jewish Population	Jews per 1,000 Population	Accuracy Rating
Israel[a]	6,201,000	4,882,000	787.3	A 2000
Azerbaijan	7,734,000	6,000	0.8	C 1997
Georgia	4,968,000	6,000	1.2	C 1997
Kazakhstan	16,223,000	7,000	0.4	C 1997
Kyrgyzstan	4,699,000	2,000	0.4	C 1997
Tajikistan	6,188,000	1,200	0.2	C 1997
Turkmenistan	4,459,000	800	0.2	C 1997
Uzbekistan	24,318,000	7,000	0.3	C 1997
Total former USSR in Asia[b]	72,109,000	30,000	0.4	
China[c]	1,284,485,000	1,000	0.0	D
India	1,013,662,000	5,500	0.0	B 1996 X
Iran	67,702,000	12,000	0.2	C 1986
Iraq	23,115,000	100	0.0	C 1997
Japan	126,714,000	1,000	0.0	C 1993
Korea, South	46,844,000	100	0.0	C 1988
Philippines	75,967,000	100	0.0	C
Singapore	3,567,000	300	0.1	B 1990
Syria	16,125,000	100	0.0	C 1995
Thailand	61,399,000	200	0.0	C 1988
Yemen	18,112,000	200	0.0	B 1995
Other	799,957,000	300	0.0	D
Total other Asia	3,537,649,000	20,900	0.0	
Total	3,615,959,000	4,932,900	1.4	

[a]Total population of Israel: end 1999.
[b]Including Armenia. Not including Turkey and Asian regions of Russian Federation.
[c]Including Hong Kong.

TABLE 5. ESTIMATED JEWISH POPULATION DISTRIBUTION IN AFRICA, 1/1/2000

Country	Total Population	Jewish Population	Jews per 1,000 Population	Accuracy Rating
Egypt	68,470,000	200	0.0	C 1993
Ethiopia	62,565,000	100	0.0	C 1998
Morocco	28,351,000	5,800	0.2	B 1995
Tunisia	9,586,000	1,500	0.2	B 1995
Other	67,158,000	100	0.0	D
Total North Africa	236,130,000	7,700	0.0	
Botswana	1,622,000	100	0.1	B 1993
Congo D.R.	51,654,000	300	0.0	B 1993
Kenya	30,080,000	400	0.0	B 1990
Namibia	1,726,000	100	0.1	B 1993
Nigeria	111,606,000	100	0.0	D
South Africa	40,377,000	80,000	2.0	B 1999 X
Zimbabwe	11,669,000	800	0.1	B 1993
Other	299,581,000	300	0.0	D
Total other Africa	548,315,000	82,100	0.1	
Total	784,445,000	89,800	0.1	

TABLE 6. ESTIMATED JEWISH POPULATION DISTRIBUTION IN OCEANIA, 1/1/2000

Country	Total Population	Jewish Population	Jews per 1,000 Population	Accuracy Rating
Australia	18,886,000	97,000	5.1	B 1996 X
New Zealand	3,862,000	4,800	1.2	A 1996 X
Other	7,645,000	100	0.0	D
Total	30,393,000	101,900	3.4	

TABLE 7. COUNTRIES WITH LARGEST JEWISH POPULATIONS, 1/1/2000

| | | | | % of Total Jewish Population | | |
| | | Jewish | | In the World | | In the Diaspora |
Rank	Country	Population	%	Cumulative %	%	Cumulative %
1	United States	5,700,000	43.2	43.2	68.6	68.6
2	Israel	4,882,000	37.0	80.2	=	=
3	France	521,000	3.9	84.1	6.3	74.8
4	Canada	362,000	2.7	86.9	4.4	79.2
5	Russia	290,000	2.2	89.1	3.5	82.7
6	United Kingdom	276,000	2.1	91.2	3.3	86.0
7	Argentina	200,000	1.5	92.7	2.4	88.4
8	Ukraine	100,000	0.8	93.4	1.2	89.6
9	Brazil	98,000	0.7	94.2	1.2	90.8
10	Australia	97,000	0.7	94.9	1.2	91.9
11	Germany	92,000	0.7	95.6	1.1	93.1
12	South Africa	80,000	0.6	96.3	1.0	94.1
13	Hungary	52,000	0.4	96.7	0.6	94.7
14	Mexico	40,500	0.3	97.0	0.5	95.2
15	Belgium	31,700	0.2	97.2	0.4	95.6

Directories
Lists
Obituaries

National Jewish Organizations*

UNITED STATES

Organizations are listed according to functions as follows:

Community Relations	499
Cultural	504
Israel-Related	512
Overseas Aid	524
Religious, Educational	
Organizations	526
Schools, Institutions	538
Social, Mutual Benefit	549
Social Welfare	551

Note also cross-references under these headings:

Professional Associations	555
Women's Organizations	556
Youth and Student	
Organizations	557
Canada	557

COMMUNITY RELATIONS

AMERICAN COUNCIL FOR JUDAISM (1943). PO Box 9009, Alexandria, VA 22304. (703)836-2546. Pres. Alan V. Stone; Exec. Dir. Allan C. Brownfeld. Seeks to advance the universal principles of a Judaism free of nationalism, and the national, civic, cultural, and social integration into American institutions of Americans of Jewish faith. *Issues of the American Council for Judaism; Special Interest Report.* (WWW.ACJNA.ORG)

AMERICAN JEWISH COMMITTEE (1906). The Jacob Blaustein Building, 165 E. 56 St., NYC 10022. (212)751-4000. FAX: (212) 750-0326. Pres. Bruce M. Ramer; Exec. Dir. David A. Harris. Protects the rights and freedoms of Jews the world over; combats bigotry and anti-Semitism and promotes democracy and human rights for all; works for the security of Israel and deepened understanding between Americans and Israelis; advocates public-policy positions rooted in American democratic values and the perspectives of

*The information in this directory is based on replies to questionnaires circulated by the editors. Web site addresses, where provided, appear at end of entries.

Jewish heritage; and enhances the creative vitality of the Jewish people. Includes Jacob and Hilda Blaustein Center for Human Relations, Project Interchange, William Petschek National Jewish Family Center, Jacob Blaustein Institute for the Advancement of Human Rights, Institute on American Jewish-Israeli Relations. *American Jewish Year Book; Commentary; CommonQuest; AJC Journal.* (www. AJC.ORG)

AMERICAN JEWISH CONGRESS (1918). Stephen Wise Congress House, 15 E. 84 St., NYC 10028. (212)879-4500. FAX: (212)249-3672. E-mail: pr@ajcongress. org. Pres. Jack Rosen; Exec. Dir. Phil Baum. Works to foster the creative survival of the Jewish people; to help Israel develop in peace, freedom, and security; to eliminate all forms of racial and religious bigotry; to advance civil rights, protect civil liberties, defend religious freedom, and safeguard the separation of church and state; "The Attorney General for the Jewish Community." *Congress Monthly; Judaism; Inside Israel; Radical Islamic Fundamentalism Update.* (www. AJCONGRESS.ORG)

ANTI-DEFAMATION LEAGUE OF B'NAI B'RITH (1913). 823 United Nations Plaza, NYC 10017. (212)885-7700. FAX: (212) 867-0779. E-mail: webmaster@adl.org. Natl. Chmn. Howard Berkowitz; Natl. Dir. Abraham H. Foxman. Seeks to combat anti-Semitism and to secure justice and fair treatment for all citizens through law, education, and community relations. *ADL on the Frontline; Law Enforcement Bulletin; Dimensions:A Journal of Holocaust Studies; Hidden Child Newsletter; International Reports; Civil Rights Reports.* (WWW.ADL.ORG)

ASSOCIATION OF JEWISH COMMUNITY RELATIONS WORKERS (1950). 7800 Northaven Road, Dallas, TX 75230. (214) 369-3313. FAX: (214)373-3186. Pres. Marlene Gorin. Aims to stimulate higher standards of professional practice in Jewish community relations; encourages research and training toward that end; conducts educational programs and seminars; aims to encourage cooperation between community-relations workers and those working in other areas of Jewish communal service.

CENTER FOR JEWISH COMMUNITY STUDIES (1970). Temple University, Center City

Campus, 1515 Locust St., Suite 703, Philadelphia, PA 19102. (215)772-0564. FAX: (215)772-0566. E-mail: CJCS. dElazar@worldnet.att.net. Jerusalem office:Jerusalem Center for Public Affairs. Dir. Gen. Zvi Marom; Chmn. Bd. of Overseers Michael Rukin. Worldwide policy-studies institute devoted to the study of Jewish community organization, political thought, and public affairs, past and present, in Israel and throughout the world. Publishes original articles, essays, and monographs; maintains library, archives, and reprint series. *Jerusalem Letter/Viewpoints; Jewish Political Studies Review.*

CENTER FOR RUSSIAN JEWRY WITH STUDENT STRUGGLE FOR SOVIET JEWRY/SSSJ (1964). 240 Cabrini Blvd., #5B, NYC 10033. (212)928-7451. FAX: (212)795-8867. Dir./Founder Jacob Birnbaum; Chmn. Dr. Ernest Bloch; Student Coord. Glenn Richter. Campaigns for the human rights of the Jews of the former USSR, with emphasis on emigration and Jewish identity; supports programs for needy Jews there and for newcomers in Israel and USA, stressing employment and Jewish education. As the originator of the grassroots movement for Soviet Jewry in the early 1960s, possesses unique archives.

COALITION ON THE ENVIRONMENT & JEWISH LIFE (1993). 443 Park Ave. S., 11th fl., NYC 10016-7322. (212)684-6950, ext. 210. FAX: (212)686-1353. E-mail: coejl@ aol.com. Dir. Mark X. Jacobs. Promotes environmental education, advocacy, and action in the American Jewish community. Sponsored by a broad coalition of Jewish organizations; member of the National Religious Partnership for the Environment. *Bi-annual newsletter.* (www. COEJL.ORG)

COMMISSION ON SOCIAL ACTION OF REFORM JUDAISM (1953, joint instrumentality of the Union of American Hebrew Congregations and the Central Conference of American Rabbis). 633 Third Ave., 7th fl., NYC 10017. (212)650-4160. FAX: (212)650-4199. E-mail: csarj@ uahc.org. Wash. Office:2027 Massachusetts Ave., NW, Washington, DC 20036. Chmn. Judge David Davidson; Dir. Leonard Fein; Dir. Religious Action Center of Reform Judaism, Rabbi David Saperstein. Policy-making body that relates ethical and spiritual principles of Judaism to social-justice issues; implements resolutions through the Religious Action Center in Washington, DC, via advocacy, development of educational materials, and congregational programs. *Tzedek V'Shalom (social action newsletter); Chai Impact (legislative update).*

CONFERENCE OF PRESIDENTS OF MAJOR AMERICAN JEWISH ORGANIZATIONS (1955). 633 Third Ave., NYC 10017. (212) 318-6111. FAX: (212)644-4135. Chmn. Ronald S. Lauder; Exec. V.-Chmn. Malcolm Hoenlein. Seeks to strengthen the U.S.-Israel alliance and to protect and enhance the security and dignity of Jews abroad. Toward this end, the Conference of Presidents speaks and acts on the basis of consensus of its 54 member agencies on issues of national and international Jewish concern.

CONSULTATIVE COUNCIL OF JEWISH ORGANIZATIONS-CCJO (1946). 420 Lexington Ave., Suite 1731, NYC 10170. (212)808-5437. Chmn. Ady Steg & Clemens N. Nathan; Sec.-Gen. Warren Green. A nongovernmental organization in consultative status with the UN, UNESCO, ILO, UNICEF, and the Council of Europe; cooperates and consults with, advises, and renders assistance to the Economic and Social Council of the UN on all problems relating to human rights and economic, social, cultural, educational, and related matters pertaining to Jews.

COORDINATING BOARD OF JEWISH ORGANIZATIONS (1947). 823 United Nations Plaza, NYC 10017. (212)557-9008. FAX: (212)687-3429. Ch. Cheryl Halpern; Exec. Dir. Dr. Harris O. Schoenberg. To promote the purposes and principles for which the UN was created.

COUNCIL OF JEWISH ORGANIZATIONS IN CIVIL SERVICE, INC. (1948). 45 E. 33 St., Rm. 310, NYC 10016. (212)689-2015. FAX: (212)684-7694. Pres. Louis Weiser; 1st V.-Pres. Melvyn Birnbaum. Supports merit system; encourages recruitment of Jewish youth to government service; member of Coalition to Free Soviet Jews, NY Jewish Community Relations Council, NY Metropolitan Coordinating Council on Jewish Poverty, Jewish Labor Committee, America-Israel Friendship League. *Council Digest.*

INSTITUTE FOR PUBLIC AFFAIRS (*see* UNION OF ORTHODOX JEWISH CONGREGATIONS OF AMERICA)

INTERNATIONAL LEAGUE FOR THE REPATRIATION OF RUSSIAN JEWS, INC. (1963). 2 Fountain Lane, Suite 2J, Scarsdale, NY 10583. (914)683-3225. FAX: (914)683-3221. Pres. Morris Brafman; Chmn. James H. Rapp. Helped to bring the situation of Soviet Jews to world attention; catalyst for advocacy efforts, educational projects, and programs on behalf of Russian Jews in the former USSR, Israel, and U.S. Provides funds to help Russian Jewry in Israel and the former Soviet Union.

JEWISH COUNCIL FOR PUBLIC AFFAIRS (formerly NATIONAL JEWISH COMMUNITY RELATIONS ADVISORY COUNCIL) (1944). 443 Park Ave. S., 11th fl., NYC 10016-7322. (212)684-6950. FAX: (212)686-1353. E-mail: contactus@jcpa.org. Chmn. Steven Schwarz; Sec. Dr. Steven Stone. National coordinating body for the field of Jewish community relations, comprising 13 national and 122 local Jewish community-relations agencies. Promotes understanding of Israel and the Middle East; supports Jewish communities around the world; advocates for equality and pluralism, and against discrimination, in American society. Through the Council's work, its constituent organizations seek agreement on policies, strategies, and programs for effective utilization of their resources for common ends. *JCPA Agenda for Public Affairs.* (WWW.JEWISHPUBLICAFFAIRS.ORG)

JEWISH LABOR COMMITTEE (1934). Atran Center for Jewish Culture, 25 E. 21 St., NYC 10010. (212)477-0707. FAX: (212) 477-1918. Pres. Morton Bahr; Exec. Dir. Avram B. Lyon. Serves as liaison between the Jewish community and the trade union movement; works with the U.S. and international labor movement to combat anti-Semitism, promote intergroup relations, and engender support for the State of Israel and Jews in and from the former Soviet Union; promotes teaching in public schools about the Holocaust and Jewish resistance; strengthens support within the Jewish community for the social goals and programs of the labor movement; supports Yiddish-language and cultural institutions. *Jewish Labor Committee Review; Issues Alert; Alumni Newsletter.*

———, NATIONAL TRADE UNION COUNCIL FOR HUMAN RIGHTS (1956). Atran Center for Jewish Culture, 25 E. 21 St., NYC 10010. (212)477-0707. FAX: (212)477-1918. Exec. Dir. Avram Lyon. Works with the American labor movement in advancing the struggle for social justice and equal opportunity, and assists unions in every issue affecting human rights. Fights discrimination on all levels and helps to promote labor's broad social and economic goals.

JEWISH PEACE FELLOWSHIP (1941). Box 271, Nyack, NY 10960. (914)358-4601. FAX: (914)358-4924. E-mail: jpf@forusa.org. Hon. Pres. Rabbi Philip Bentley; Co-Ch. Carolyn Toll-Oppenheim & Murray Polner. Unites those who believe that Jewish ideals and experience provide inspiration for a nonviolent philosophy and way of life; offers draft counseling, especially for conscientious objection based on Jewish "religious training and belief"; encourages Jewish community to become more knowledgeable, concerned, and active in regard to the war/peace problem. *Shalom/Jewish Peace Letter.* (WWW.JEWISHPEACEFELLOWSHIP.ORG)

JEWISH WAR VETERANS OF THE UNITED STATES OF AMERICA (1896). 1811 R St., NW, Washington, DC 20009. (202)265-6280. FAX: (202)234-5662. E-mail: jwv@erols.com. Natl. Exec. Dir. Herb Rosenbleeth; Natl. Commander Monroe E. Mayer. Seeks to foster true allegiance to the United States; to combat bigotry and prevent defamation of Jews; to encourage the doctrine of universal liberty, equal rights, and full justice for all; to cooperate with and support existing educational institutions and establish new ones; to foster the education of ex-servicemen, ex-servicewomen, and members in the ideals and principles of Americanism. *Jewish Veteran.*

———, NATIONAL MUSEUM OF AMERICAN JEWISH MILITARY HISTORY (1958). 1811 R St., NW, Washington, DC 20009. E-mail: jwv@erols.com. (202)265-6280. FAX: (202)462-3192. Pres. Neil Goldman; Asst. Dir./Archivist Sandor B. Cohen. Documents and preserves the contributions of Jewish Americans to the peace and freedom of the United States; educates the public concerning the courage, heroism, and sacrifices made by Jewish Americans who served in the armed forces; and

works to combat anti-Semitism. *Museum News (quarterly newsletter).*

NATIONAL ASSOCIATION OF JEWISH LEGISLATORS (1976). 65 Oakwood St., Albany, NY 12208. (518)527-3353. FAX: (518)458-8512. E-mail: najl01@aol.com. Exec. Dir. Marc Hiller; Pres. Sen. Richard Cohen, Minn. state senator. A nonpartisan Jewish state legislative network focusing on domestic issues and publishing newsletters. Maintains close ties with the Knesset and Israeli leaders.

NATIONAL CONFERENCE ON SOVIET JEWRY (formerly AMERICAN JEWISH CONFERENCE ON SOVIET JEWRY) (1964; reorg. 1971). 1640 Rhode Island Ave., NW, Suite 501, Washington, DC 20036-3278. (202)898-2500. FAX: (202)898-0822. E-mail: ncsj@access.digex.net. N.Y. office:823 United Nations Plaza, NYC 10017. (212)808-0295. Chmn. Denis C. Braham; Pres. Howard E. Sachs. Coordinating agency for major national Jewish organizations and local community groups in the U.S., acting on behalf of Jews in the former Soviet Union (FSU); provides information about Jews in the FSU through public education and social action; reports and special pamphlets, special programs and projects, public meetings and forums. *Newswatch; annual report; action and program kits; Tekuma.* (WWW.NCSJ.ORG)

———, SOVIET JEWRY RESEARCH BUREAU. Chmn. Denis C. Braham; Pres. Howard E. Sachs. Organized by NCSJ to monitor emigration trends. Primary task is the accumulation, evaluation, and processing of information regarding Jews in the FSU, especially those who apply for emigration.

NATIONAL JEWISH COMMISSION ON LAW AND PUBLIC AFFAIRS (COLPA) (1965). 135 W. 50 St., 6th fl., NYC 10020. (212)641-8992. FAX: (212)641-8197. Pres. Allen L. Rothenberg; Exec. Dir. Dennis Rapps. Voluntary association of attorneys whose purpose is to represent the observant Jewish community on legal, legislative, and public-affairs matters.

NATIONAL JEWISH COMMUNITY RELATIONS ADVISORY COUNCIL (*see* JEWISH COUNCIL FOR PUBLIC AFFAIRS)

NATIONAL JEWISH DEMOCRATIC COUNCIL (1990). 777 N. Capital St., NE, Suite 305, Washington, DC 20002. (202)216-9060.

FAX: (202)216-9061. E-mail: njdconline@aol.com. Chmn. Monte Friedkin; Founding Chmn. Morton Mandel; Exec. Dir. Ira N. Forman. An independent organization committed to strengthening Jewish participation in the Democratic party primarily through grassroots activism. The national voice of Jewish Democrats, NJDC is dedicated to fighting the radical right and promoting Jewish values and interests in the Democratic party. *Capital Communiqué; Extremist Watch.* (WWW.NJDC.ORG)

REPUBLICAN JEWISH COALITION (1985). 415 2nd St., NE, Suite 100, Washington, DC 20002. (202)547-7701. FAX: (202)544-2434. E-mail: rjc@rjchq.org. Natl. Chmn. Cheryl Halpern; Hon. Chmn. Max M. Fisher, Richard J. Fox, Sam Fox, Lawrence Kadish, George Klein, and Amb. Mel Sembler; Exec. Dir. Matt Brooks. Promotes involvement in Republican politics among its members; sensitizes Republican leaders to the concerns of the American Jewish community; promotes principles of free enterprise, a strong national defense, and an internationalist foreign policy. *RJC Bulletin.* (WWW.RJCHQ.ORG)

SHALEM CENTER (1994). 1140 Connecticut Ave., NW, Suite 801, Washington, DC 20036. (202)887-1270. FAX: (202)887-1277. E-mail: patrick@shalemcenter.org. Pres. Yoram Hazony (Israel); US Office Mng. Patrick Hussey. The purposes and activities of the Shalem Center are to increase public understanding and conduct educational and research activities on the improvement of Jewish national public life, and to develop a community of intellectual leaders to shape the state of Israel into a secure, free, and prosperous society. *Azure.* (WWW.SHALEMCENTER.ORG)

SHALOM CENTER (1983). 6711 Lincoln Dr., Philadelphia, PA 19119. (215)844-8494. E-mail: shalomctr@aol.com. (Part of Aleph Alliance for Jewish Renewal.) Exec. Dir. Arthur Waskow. National resource and organizing center for Jewish perspectives on dealing with environmental dangers, unrestrained technology, and corporate irresponsibility. Initiated A.J. Heschel 25th Yahrzeit observance. Trains next generation of *tikkun olam* activists. Holds colloquia on issues like environmental causes of cancer. *New Menorah.* (WWW.SHALOMCTR.ORG)

STUDENT STRUGGLE FOR SOVIET JEWRY (*see* CENTER FOR RUSSIAN JEWRY)

UN WATCH (1993). 1, rue de Varembé, PO Box 191, 1211 Geneva 20, Switzerland. (41-22)734.14.72/3. FAX: (41-22)734.16.13. E-mail: unwatch@unwatch.org. Pres. David A. Harris; Exec. Dir. Michael D. Colson. An affiliate of the AJC and World Jewish Congress, UN Watch measures UN performance by the yardstick of the UN's Charter; advocates the non-discriminatory application of the Charter; opposes the use of UN fora to attack Israel and promote anti-Semitism; and seeks to institutionalize at the UN the fight against worldwide anti-Semitism. *The Wednesday Watch.* (WWW.UNWATCH. ORG)

UNION OF COUNCILS (formerly UNION OF COUNCILS FOR SOVIET JEWS) (1970). 1819 H St., NW, Suite 230, Washington, DC 20005. (202)775-9770. FAX: (202)775-9776. E-mail: ucsj@ucsj.com. Pres. Yosef I. Abramowitz; Natl. Dir. Micah H. Naftalin. Devoted to promoting religious liberty, freedom of emigration, and security for Jews in the FSU (former Soviet Union) through advocacy and monitoring of anti-Semitism, neo-facism, human rights, rule of law, and democracy. Offers educational, cultural, medical, and humanitarian aid through the Yad L'Yad partnership program pairing Jewish communities in the US and the FSU; advocates for refuseniks and political prisoner. (WWW.FSUMONITOR.COM)

WORLD CONGRESS OF GAY, LESBIAN, & BISEXUAL JEWISH ORGANIZATIONS (1980). 8 Letitia St., Philadelphia, PA 19106-3050. (609)396-1972. FAX: (215)873-0108. E-mail: rjh@waxmanpartners.com. Pres. Scott R. Gansl (Philadelphia, PA); V.-Pres. Francois Spiero (Paris, France). Supports, strengthens, and represents over 67 Jewish gay and lesbian organizations across the globe and the needs of gay and lesbian Jews generally. Challenges homophobia and sexism within the Jewish community and responds to anti-Semitism at large. Sponsors regional and international conferences. *The Digest.* (WWW.WCGLJO.ORG/WCGLJO/)

WORLD JEWISH CONGRESS (1936; org. in U.S. 1939). 501 Madison Ave., 17th fl., NYC 10022. (212) 755-5770. FAX: (212) 755-5883. Pres. Edgar M. Bronfman; Co-

Chmn. N. Amer. Branch Prof. Irwin Cotler (Montreal) & Evelyn Sommer; Sec.-Gen. Israel Singer; Exec. Dir. Elan Steinberg. Seeks to intensify bonds of world Jewry with Israel; to strengthen solidarity among Jews everywhere and secure their rights, status, and interests as individuals and communities; to encourage Jewish social, religious, and cultural life throughout the world and coordinate efforts by Jewish communities and organizations to cope with any Jewish problem; to work for human rights generally. Represents its affiliated organizations-most representative bodies of Jewish communities in more than 80 countries and 35 national organizations in American section-at UN, OAS, UNESCO, Council of Europe, ILO, UNICEF, and other governmental, intergovernmental, and international authorities. *WJC Report; Bolet'n Informativo OJI; Christian-Jewish Relations; Dateline: World Jewry; Coloquio; Batfutsot; Gesher.*

CULTURAL

AMERICAN ACADEMY FOR JEWISH RESEARCH (1929). 53 Washington Sq., NYC 10012. (212)998-3550. FAX: (212)995-4178. Pres. Robert Chazan. Encourages Jewish learning and research; holds annual or semiannual meeting; awards grants for the publication of scholarly works. *Proceedings of the American Academy for Jewish Research; Texts and Studies; Monograph Series.*

AMERICAN GATHERING OF JEWISH HOLOCAUST SURVIVORS. 122 W. 30 St., #205. NYC 10001. (212)239-4230. FAX: (212) 279-2926. E-mail: mail@americangathering.org. Pres. Benjamin Meed. Dedicated to documenting the past and passing on a legacy of remembrance. Compiles the National Registry of Jewish Holocaust Survivors-to date, the records of more than 165,000 survivors and their families-housed at the U.S. Holocaust Memorial Museum in Washington, DC; holds an annual Yom Hashoah commemoration and occasional international gatherings; sponsors an intensive summer program for U.S. teachers in Poland and Israel to prepare them to teach about the Holocaust. *Together (newspaper).* (WWW. AMERICANGATHERING.ORG)

AMERICAN GUILD OF JUDAIC ART (1991). 15 Greenspring Valley Rd., Owings Mills, MD 21117. (410)902-0411. FAX: (410)581-0108. E-mail: lbarch@erols. com. Pres. Mark D. Levin; 1st V.-Pres. Richard McBee. A not-for-profit membership organization for those with interests in the Judaic arts, including artists, galleries, collectors & retailers of Judaica, writers, educators, appraisers, museum curators, conservators, lecturers, and others personally or professionally involved in the field. Helps to promote members' art. *Hiddur (quarterly); Update (members' networking newsletter).* (WWW.JEW-ISHART.ORG)

AMERICAN JEWISH HISTORICAL SOCIETY (1892). 15 W. 16 St., NYC 10011. (212) 294-6160. FAX: (212)294-6161. E-mail: ajhs@ajhs.org. Pres. Kenneth J. Bialkin; Dir. Dr. Michael Feldberg. Collects, catalogues, publishes, and displays material on the history of the Jews in America; serves as an information center for inquiries on American Jewish history; maintains archives of original source material on American Jewish history; sponsors lectures and exhibitions; makes available audiovisual material. *American Jewish History; Heritage.* (WWW.AJHS. ORG)

AMERICAN JEWISH PRESS ASSOCIATION (1944). Natl. Admin. Off.: 1828 L St. NW, Suite 720, Washington, DC 20036. (202)785-2282. FAX: (202)785-2307. E-mail: toby@dershowitz.com. Pres. Marc Klein; Exec. Dir. Toby Dershowitz. Seeks the advancement of Jewish journalism and the maintenance of a strong Jewish press in the U.S. and Canada; encourages the attainment of the highest editorial and business standards; sponsors workshops, services for members; sponsors annual competition for Simon Rockower Awards for excellence in Jewish journalism. *Membership bulletin newsletter.*

AMERICAN SEPHARDI FEDERATION (1973). 15 W. 16 St., NYC 10011. (212)294-8350. FAX: (212)294-6161. E-mail: asf@am-sephfed.org. Natl. Pres. Leon Levy; Exec. Dir. Elizabeth Mizrahi. The central voice of the American Sephardic community, representing a broad spectrum of Sephardic organizations, congregations, and educational institutions. Seeks to strengthen and unify the community through education, communication, advocacy, and leadership development, creating greater awareness and appreciation of its rich and unique history and culture. *ASF Update Newsletter.* (WWW.AMSEPHFED.ORG)

AMERICAN SOCIETY FOR JEWISH MUSIC (1974). c/o The Center for Jewish History, 15 W. 16 St., NYC 10011. (212)294-8328. FAX: (212)294-6161. Pres. Hadassah B. Markson; V.-Pres. Judith Tischler & Martha Novick; Sec. Fortuna Calvo Roth; Bd. Chmn. Rabbi Henry D. Michelman; Treas. Michael Leavitt. Promotes the knowledge, appreciation, and development of Jewish music, past and present, for professional and lay audiences; seeks to raise the standards of composition and performance in Jewish music, to encourage research, and to sponsor performances of new and rarely heard works. *Musica Judaica Journal.*

ASSOCIATION OF JEWISH BOOK PUBLISHERS (1962). c/o Jewish Lights Publishing, PO Box 237, Woodstock, VT 05091. (802) 457-4000. FAX: (802)457-4004. Pres. Stuart M. Matlins. As a nonprofit group, provides a forum for discussion of mutual areas of interest among Jewish publishers, and promotes cooperative exhibits and promotional opportunities for members. Membership fee is $85 annually per publishing house.

ASSOCIATION OF JEWISH LIBRARIES (1965). 15 E. 26 St.,10th fl, NYC 10010. (212)725-5359. FAX: (212)481-4174. E-mail: ajl@jewishbooks.org. Pres. David T. Gilner; V.-Pres. Toby Rossner. Seeks to promote and improve services and professional standards in Jewish libraries; disseminates Jewish library information and guidance; promotes publication of literature in the field; encourages the establishment of Jewish libraries and collections of Judaica and the choice of Judaica librarianship as a profession; cocertifies Jewish libraries (with Jewish Book Council). *AJL Newsletter; Judaica Librarianship.*

B'NAI B'RITH KLUTZNICK NATIONAL JEWISH MUSEUM (1957). 1640 Rhode Island Ave., NW, Washington, DC 20036. (202)857-6583. FAX: (202)857-1099. A center of Jewish art and history in the nation's capital, maintains temporary and permanent exhibition galleries, permanent collection of Jewish ceremonial objects, folk art, and contemporary fine art, outdoor sculpture garden and museum shop, as well as the American Jewish

Sports Hall of Fame. Provides exhibitions, tours, educational programs, research assistance, and tourist information. *Quarterly newsletter; permanent collection catalogue; temporary exhibit catalogues.*

CENTRAL YIDDISH CULTURE ORGANIZATION (CYCO), INC. (1943). 25 E. 21 St., 3rd fl., NYC 10010. (212)505-8305. FAX: (212) 505-8044. Mng. David Kirszencwejg. Promotes, publishes, and distributes Yiddish books; publishes catalogues.

CONFERENCE ON JEWISH SOCIAL STUDIES, INC. (formerly CONFERENCE ON JEWISH RELATIONS, INC.) (1939). Bldg. 240, Rm. 103. Program in Jewish Studies, Stanford University, Stanford, CA 94305-2190. (650)725-0829. FAX:(650)725-2920. E-mail: jss@leland.stanford.edu. Pres. Steven J. Zipperstein; V.-Pres. Aron Rodrigue. *Jewish Social Studies.*

CONGREGATION BINA (1981). 600 W. End Ave., Suite 1-C, NYC 10024. (212)873-4261. E-mail: ernasam@yahoo.com. Pres. Joseph Moses; Exec. V.-Pres. Moses Samson; Hon. Pres. Samuel M. Daniel; Sec. Gen. Elijah E. Jhirad. Serves the religious, cultural, charitable, and philanthropic needs of the Children of Israel who originated in India and now reside in the U.S. Works to foster and preserve the ancient traditions, customs, liturgy, music, and folklore of Indian Jewry and to maintain needed institutions. *Kol Bina.*

CONGRESS FOR JEWISH CULTURE (1948). 25 E. 21 St., NYC 10010. (212)505-8040. FAX: (212)505-8044. Co-Pres. Prof. Yonia Fain & Dr. Barnett Zumoff. Congress for Jewish Culture administers the book store CYCO and publishes the world's oldest Yiddish journal, *The Zukunft.* Currently producing a two volume anthology of Yiddish literature in America. Activities include yearly memorials for the Warsaw ghetto uprising and the murdered Soviet Yiddish writers, also readings and literary afternoons. *The Zukunft; Bulletin: In the World of Yiddish.*

ELAINE KAUFMAN CULTURAL CENTER (1952). 129 W. 67 St., NYC 10023. (212) 501-3303. FAX: (212)874-7865. Chmn. Leonard Goodman; Pres. Elaine Kaufman; Exec. Dir. Lydia Kontos. Offers instruction in its Lucy Moses School for Music and Dance in music, dance, art, and theater to children and adults, in Western culture and Jewish traditions. Presents frequent performances of Jewish and general music by leading artists and ensembles in its Merkin Concert Hall and Ann Goodman Recital Hall. The Birnbaum Music Library houses Jewish music scores and reference books. *Kaufman Cultural Center News; bimonthly concert calendars; catalogues and brochures.* (WWW.ELAINEKAUFMANCENTER.ORG)

HISTADRUTH IVRITH OF AMERICA (1916; reorg. 1922). 426 W. 58 St., NYC 10019. (212)957-6659. Fax: (212)957-5811. E-mail: general@hist-ivrit.org. Pres. Miriam Ostow; Exec. V.-Pres. Rabbi Abraham Kupchik. Emphasizes the primacy of Hebrew in Jewish life, culture, and education; aims to disseminate knowledge of written and spoken Hebrew in N. America, thus building a cultural bridge between the State of Israel and Jewish communities throughout N. America. *Hadoar; Lamishpacha; Tov Lichtov; Sulam Yaakov; Hebrew Week; Ulpan.* (WWW.HIST-IVRIT.ORG)

HOLOCAUST CENTER OF THE UNITED JEWISH FEDERATION OF GREATER PITTSBURGH (1980). 5738 Darlington Rd., Pittsburgh, PA 15217. (412)421-1500. FAX: (412)422-1996. E-mail: lhurwitz@ujf.net. Pres. Holocaust Comm. Edgar Snyder; Bd. Ch. Karen Shapira; Dir. Linda F. Hurwitz. Develops programs and provides resources to further understanding of the Holocaust and its impact on civilization. Maintains a library, archive; provides speakers, educational materials; organizes community programs. Published collection of survivor and liberator stories.

HOLOCAUST MEMORIAL CENTER (1984). 6602 West Maple Rd., West Bloomfield, MI 48322. (248)661-0840. FAX: (248) 661-4204. E-mail: info@holocaustcenter.org. Founder & Exec. V.-Pres. Rabbi Charles Rosenzveig. America's first free-standing Holocaust center comprising a museum, library-archive, oral history collection, garden of the righteous, research institute and academic advisory committee. Provides tours, lecture series, teacher training, Yom Hashoah commemorations, exhibits, educational outreach programs, speakers' bureau, computer database on 1,200 destroyed Jewish communities, guided travel tours to concentration camps and Israel, and museum

shop. Published *World Reacts to the Holocaust; Newsletter.*

HOLOCAUST MEMORIAL RESOURCE & EDUCATION CENTER OF CENTRAL FLORIDA (1982). 851 N. Maitland Ave., Maitland, FL 32751. (407)628-0555. FAX: (407)628-1079. E-mail: execdir@holocaustedu.org. Pres. Stan Sujka, MD; Bd. Chmn. Tess Wise. An interfaith educational center devoted to teaching the lessons of the Holocaust. Houses permanent multimedia educational exhibit; maintains library of books, videotapes, films, and other visuals to serve the entire educational establishment; offers lectures, teacher training, and other activities. *Newsletter; Bibliography; "Holocaust-Lessons for Tomorrow"; elementary and middle school curriculum.*

THE HOLOCAUST MUSEUM AND LEARNING CENTER IN MEMORY OF GLORIA GOLDSTEIN (1995) (formerly ST. LOUIS CENTER FOR HOLOCAUST STUDIES) (1977). 12 Millstone Campus Dr., St. Louis, MO 63146. (314)432-0020. FAX: (314)432-1277. E-mail: dreich@jfedstl.org. Chmn. Richard W. Stein; Dir. Dan A. Reich; Asst. Dir. Brian Bray. Develops programs and provides resources and educational materials to further an understanding of the Holocaust and its impact on civilization; has a 5,000 sq. ft. museum containing photographs, artifacts, and audiovisual displays. *Newsletter.*

INTERNATIONAL ASSOCIATION OF JEWISH GENEALOGICAL SOCIETIES (1988). 4430 Mt. Paran Pkwy NW, Atlanta, GA 30327-3747. (404)261-8662. Fax: (404) 228-7125. E-mail: homargol@aol.com. Pres. Howard Margol. Umbrella organization of more than 70 Jewish Genealogical Societies (JGS) worldwide. Represents organized Jewish genealogy, encourages Jews to research their family history, promotes new JGSs, supports existing societies, implements projects of interest to individuals researching their Jewish family histories. Holds annual conference where members learn and exchange ideas. (WWW.IAJGS.ORG)

INTERNATIONAL JEWISH MEDIA ASSOCIATION (1987). U.S.: c/o St. Louis Jewish Light, 12 Millstone Campus Dr., St. Louis, MO 63146. (314)432-3353. FAX: (314)432-0515. E-mail: stlouislgt@aol. com and ajpamr@aol.com. Israel:PO Box 92, Jerusalem 91920. 02-202-222. FAX:

02-513-642. Pres. Robert A. Cohn (c/o St. Louis Jewish Light); Exec. Dir. Toby Dershowitz. 1828 L St. NW, Suite 402, Washington, DC 20036. (202)785-2282. FAX: (202)785-2307. E-mail: toby@dershowitz. com. Israel Liaisons Jacob Gispan & Lifsha Ben-Shach, WZO Dept. of Info. A worldwide network of Jewish journalists, publications and other media in the Jewish and general media, which seeks to provide a forum for the exchange of materials and ideas and to enhance the status of Jewish media and journalists throughout the world. *IJMA Newsletter; Proceedings of the International Conference on Jewish Media.*

INTERNATIONAL NETWORK OF CHILDREN OF JEWISH HOLOCAUST SURVIVORS, INC. (1981). 3000 NE 151 St., N. Miami, FL 33181. (305)919-5690. FAX: (305)919-5691. E-mail: xholocau@fiu.edu. Pres. Rositta E. Kenigsberg; Founding Chmn. Menachem Z. Rosensaft. Links Second Generation groups and individuals throughout the world. Represents the shared interests of children of Holocaust survivors; aims to perpetuate the authentic memory of the Holocaust and prevent its recurrence, to strengthen and preserve the Jewish spiritual, ideological, and cultural heritage, to fight anti-Semitism and all forms of discrimination, persecution, and oppression anywhere in the world.

JACOB RADER MARCUS CENTER OF THE AMERICAN JEWISH ARCHIVES (1947). 3101 Clifton Ave., Cincinnati, OH 45220. (513) 221-1875 ext. 403. FAX: (513)221-7812. E-mail: aja@cn.huc.edu. Dir. Dr. Gary P. Zola. Promotes the study and preservation of the Western Hemisphere Jewish experience through research, publications, collection of important source materials, and a vigorous public-outreach program. *American Jewish Archives; monographs, publications, and pamphlets.*

JEWISH BOOK COUNCIL (1946; reorg. 1993). 15 E. 26 St., NYC 10010. (212)532-4949, ext. 297. E-mail: jbc@jewishbooks.org. Pres. Moshe Dworkin; Bd. Chmn. Henry Everett; Exec. Dir. Carolyn Starman Hessel. Serves as literary arm of the American Jewish community and clearinghouse for Jewish-content literature; assists readers, writers, publishers, and those who market and sell products. Provides bibliographies, list of publishers, bookstores, book fairs. Sponsors National Jewish Book Awards, Jewish Book Month, Jewish Book Fair Network. *Jewish Book Annual; Jewish Book World.* (WWW.JEWISHBOOKCOUNCIL.ORG)

THE JEWISH FEDERATION'S LOS ANGELES MUSEUM OF THE HOLOCAUST (MARTYRS MEMORIAL) (org. mid-1960s; opened 1978). 6006 Wilshire Blvd., Los Angeles, CA 90036. (323)761-8170. FAX: (323)761-8174. E-mail: kjosephy@ earthlink.net. Chmn. Osias G. Goren; Dir./Curator Marcia Reines Josephy. A photo-narrative museum and resource center dedicated to Holocaust history, issues of genocide and prejudice, curriculum development, teacher training, research and exhibitions. *Educational guides; Those Who Dared; Rescuers and Rescued; Guide to Schindler's List; Modular Curriculum.*

JEWISH HERITAGE PROJECT (1981). 150 Franklin St., #1W, NYC 10013. (212)925-9067. E-mail: jhpffh@jps.net. Exec. Dir. Alan Adelson. Strives to bring to the broadest possible audience authentic works of literary and historical value relating to Jewish history and culture. With funding from the National Endowment of the Arts, Jewish Heritage runs the National Initiative in the Literature of the Holocaust. Not a grant giving organization. Distributor of the film *Lodz Ghetto,* which it developed, as well as its companion volume *Lodz Ghetto: Inside a Community Under Siege; Better Than Gold: An Immigrant Family's First Years in Brooklyn.*

JEWISH MUSEUM (1904, under auspices of Jewish Theological Seminary). 1109 Fifth Ave., NYC 10128. (212)423-3200. FAX: (212)423-3232. Dir. Joan H. Rosenbaum; Bd. Chmn. Robert J. Hurst. Expanded museum features permanent exhibition on the Jewish experience. Repository of the largest collection of Judaica-paintings, prints, photographs, sculpture, coins, medals, antiquities, textiles, and other decorative arts-in the Western Hemisphere. Includes the National Jewish Archive of Broadcasting. Tours, lectures, film showings, and concerts; special programs for children; cafe; shop. *Special exhibition catalogues; annual report.* (WWW.THEJEWISHMUSEUM.ORG)

JEWISH PUBLICATION SOCIETY (1888). 2100 Arch St., 2nd fl., Philadelphia, PA 19103.

(215)832-0600. FAX: (215)568-2017. E-mail: jewishbook@aol.com. Pres. Judge Norma L. Shapiro; CEO/Ed.-in-Chief Dr. Ellen Frankel. Publishes and disseminates books of Jewish interest for adults and children; titles include TANAKH, religious studies and practices, life cycle, folklore, classics, art, history, belles-lettres. *The Bookmark; JPS Catalogue.* (WWW.JEWISHPUB.ORG)

JUDAH L. MAGNES MUSEUM-JEWISH MUSEUM OF THE WEST (1962). 2911 Russell St., Berkeley, CA 94705. (510)549-6950. FAX: (510)849-3673. E-mail: magnesadmin@eb.jfed.org. Pres. Fred Weiss; Dir. Susan Morris. Collects, preserves, and makes available Jewish art, culture, history, and literature from throughout the world. Permanent collections of fine and ceremonial art; rare Judaica library, Western Jewish History Center (archives), Jewish-American Hall of Fame. Changing exhibits, traveling exhibits, docent tours, lectures, numismatics series, poetry and video awards, museum shop. *Magnes News; special exhibition catalogues; scholarly books.*

JUDAICA CAPTIONED FILM CENTER, INC. (1983). PO Box 21439, Baltimore, MD 21208-0439. Voice Relay Service (1-800)735-2258; TDD (410)655-6767. E-mail: lweiner@jhucep.org. Pres. Lois Lilienfeld Weiner. Developing a comprehensive library of captioned and subtitled films and tapes on Jewish subjects; distributes them to organizations serving the hearing-impaired, including mainstream classes and senior adult groups, on a free-loan, handling/shipping-charge-only basis. *Newsletter.*

LEAGUE FOR YIDDISH, INC. (1979). 200 W. 72 St., Suite 40, NYC 10023. (212)787-6675. E-mail: mschaecht@aol.com. Pres. Dr. Zuni Zelitch; Exec. Dir. Dr. Mordkhe Schaechter. Encourages the development and use of Yiddish as a living language; promotes its modernization and standardization; publisher of Yiddish textbooks and English-Yiddish dictionaries; most recent book publication: *Yiddish Two: An Intermediate and Advanced Textbook, 3rd ed.,* 1995. Afn Shvel (quarterly).

LEO BAECK INSTITUTE, INC. (1955). 129 E. 73 St., NYC 10021. (212)744-6400. FAX: (212)988-1305. E-mail: lbi1@lbi.com.

Pres. Ismar Schorsch; Exec. Dir. Carol Kahn Strauss. A research, study, and lecture center, museum, library, and archive relating to the history of German-speaking Jewry. Offers lectures, exhibits, faculty seminars; publishes a series of monographs, yearbooks, and journals. *LBI News; LBI Yearbook; LBI Memorial Lecture; LBI Library & Archives News; occasional papers.*

LIVING TRADITIONS (1994). 430 W. 14 St., #409, NYC 10014. (212)691-1272. FAX: (212)691-1657. E-mail: livetrads@aol.com. Pres. Henry Sapoznik; V.-Pres. Lorin Sklamberg. Nonprofit membership organization dedicated to the study, preservation, and innovative continuity of traditional folk and popular culture through workshops, concerts, recordings, radio and film documentaries; clearinghouse for research in klezmer and other traditional music; sponsors yearly weeklong international cultural event, "Yiddish Folk Arts Program/'KlezKamp.'" *Living Traditions (newsletter).* (www. LIVINGTRADITIONS.ORG)

MEMORIAL FOUNDATION FOR JEWISH CULTURE, INC. (1964). 15 E. 26 St., Suite 1703, NYC 10010. (212)679-4074. FAX: (212)889-9080. Pres. Rabbi Alexander Schindler; Exec. V.-Pres. Jerry Hochbaum. Through the grants that it awards, encourages Jewish scholarship, culture, and education; supports communities that are struggling to maintain Jewish life; assists professional training for careers in communal service in Jewishly deprived communities; and stimulates the documentation, commemoration, and teaching of the Holocaust.

MUSEUM OF JEWISH HERITAGE—A LIVING MEMORIAL TO THE HOLOCAUST (1984). One Battery Park Plaza, NYC 10004-1484. (212)968-1800. FAX: (212)968-1368. Bd. Chmn. Robert M. Morgenthau; Museum Dir. David Altshuler. New York tri-state's principal institution for educating people of all ages and backgrounds about 20th-century Jewish history and the Holocaust. Repository of Steven Spielberg's Survivors of the Shoah Visual History Foundation videotaped testimonies. Core and special exhibitions. *18 First Place (newsletter); Holocaust bibliography; educational materials.* (WWW.MJH-NYC.ORG)

MUSEUM OF TOLERANCE OF THE SIMON WIESENTHAL CENTER (1993). 9786 W. Pico Blvd., Los Angeles, CA 90035-4792. (310)553-8403. FAX: (310)553-4521. E-mail: avra@wiesenthal.com. Dean-Founder Rabbi Marvin Hier; Assoc. Dean Rabbi Abraham Cooper; Exec. Dir. Rabbi Meyer May. A unique experiential museum focusing on personal prejudice, group intolerance, struggle for civil rights, and 20th-century genocides, culminating in a major exhibition on the Holocaust. Archives, Multimedia Learning Center designed for individualized research, 6,700-square-foot temporary exhibit space, 324-seat theater, 150-seat auditorium, and outdoor memorial plaza. *Response Magazine.*

NATIONAL CENTER FOR THE HEBREW LANGUAGE (1996). 633 Third Ave., 21ˢᵗ Fl., NYC 10017. (212)339-6023. FAX: (212)318-6193. E-mail: ivritnow@aol.com. Pres. Dr. Alvin I. Schiff; Exec. Dir. Dr. Joseph Lowin. The NCHL advocates for Hebrew language and culture; serves as a Hebrew resource center; and is a catalyst for networking in Hebrew language and culture. It coordinates a Mini-Ulpan at the GA, publishes "Directory of Hebrew Classes,"organizes "Lunch & Hebrew Lit"nationwide, and runs a Conference of Hebrew Teacher Trainers. *Ivrit-Now/IvritAkhshav.* (WWW.IVRIT.ORG)

NATIONAL FOUNDATION FOR JEWISH CULTURE (1960). 330 Seventh Ave., 21st fl., NYC 10001. (212)629-0500. FAX: (212)629-0508. E-mail: nfjc@jewishculture.org. Pres. Lynn Korda Kroll; Exec. Dir. Richard A. Siegel. The leading Jewish organization devoted to promoting Jewish culture in the U.S. Manages the Jewish Endowment for the Arts and Humanities; administers the Council of American Jewish Museums and Council of Archives and Research Libraries in Jewish Studies; offers doctoral dissertation fellowships and grants for documentary films, new plays, and music; coordinates community cultural residencies, local cultural commissions, and regional cultural consortia; organizes conferences, symposia, and festivals in the arts and humanities. *Jewish Culture News; Culture Currents (electronic).*

NATIONAL MUSEUM OF AMERICAN JEWISH MILITARY HISTORY (*see* JEWISH WAR VETERANS OF THE U.S.A.)

NATIONAL YIDDISH BOOK CENTER (1980). 1021 West St., Amherst, MA 01002. (413)256-4900. FAX: (413)256-4700. E-mail: yiddish@bikher.org. Pres. Aaron Lansky; V.-Pres. Nancy Sherman. Since 1980 the center has collected 1.5 million Yiddish books for distribution to libraries and readers worldwide; offers innovative English-language programs and produces a magazine. New permanent home in Amherst, open to the public, includes a book repository, exhibits, a bookstore, and a theater. *The Pakn Treger (English language magazine).*

ORTHODOX JEWISH ARCHIVES (1978). 84 William St., NYC 10038. (212)797-9000, ext. 73. FAX: (212)269-2843. Exec. V-Pres. Rabbi Shmuel Bloom & Shlomo Gertzullin; Dir. Rabbi Moshe Kolodny. Founded by Agudath Israel of America; houses historical documents, photographs, periodicals, and other publications relating to the growth of Orthodox Jewry in the U.S. and related communities in Europe, Israel, and elsewhere. Particularly noteworthy are its holdings relating to rescue activities organized during the Holocaust and its traveling exhibits available to schools and other institutions.

RESEARCH FOUNDATION FOR JEWISH IMMIGRATION, INC. (1971). 570 Seventh Ave., NYC 10018. (212)921-3871. FAX: (212) 575-1918. Pres. Curt C. Silberman; Sec./Coord. of Research Herbert A. Strauss; Archivist Dennis E. Rohrbaugh. Studies and records the history of the migration and acculturation of Central European German-speaking Jewish and non-Jewish Nazi persecutees in various resettlement countries worldwide, with special emphasis on the American experience. *International Biographical Dictionary of Central European Emigrés, 1933-1945; Jewish Immigrants of the Nazi Period in the USA.*

SEPHARDIC EDUCATIONAL CENTER (1979). 10808 Santa Monica Blvd., Los Angeles, CA 90025. (310)441-9361. FAX: (310)441-9561. E-mail: secforever@aol.com. Founder & Chmn. Jose A. Nessim, M.D. Has chapters in the U.S., North, Central, and South America, Europe, and Asia, a spiritual and educational center in the Old City of Jerusalem, and executive office in Los Angeles. Serves as a meeting ground for Sephardim from many nations; sponsors the first worldwide movement for Sephardic youth and young adults. Disseminates information about Sephardic Jewry in the form of motion pictures, pamphlets, and books, which it produces. *Hamerkaz (quarterly bulletin in English).* (WWW.SECWORLDWIDE.ORG)

SEPHARDIC HOUSE (1978). 2112 Broadway, Suite 200A, NYC 10023. (212)496-2173. FAX: (212)496-2264. E-mail: sephardichouse@juno.com. Pres. Morrie R.Yohai; Exec. Dir. Dr. Janice E. Ovadiah. A cultural organization dedicated to fostering Sephardic history and culture; sponsors a wide variety of classes and public programs, film festivals, including summer program in France for high-school students; publication program disseminates materials of Sephardic value; outreach program to communities outside of the New York area; program bureau provides program ideas, speakers, and entertainers; International Sephardic Film Festival every two years. *Sephardic House Newsletter; Publication Catalogue.* (WWW. SEPHARDIM.ORG/SEPHARDICHOUSE)

SIMON WIESENTHAL CENTER (1977). 9760 W. Pico Blvd., Los Angeles, CA 90035-4701. (310)553-9036. FAX: (310)553-2709. Dean-Founder Rabbi Marvin Hier; Assoc. Dean Rabbi Abraham Cooper; Exec. Dir. Rabbi Meyer May. Regional offices in New York, Miami, Toronto, Paris, Jerusalem, Buenos Aires. The largest institution of its kind in N. America, dedicated to the study of the Holocaust, its contemporary implications, and related human-rights issues through education and awareness. Incorporates 185,000-sq.-ft. Museum of Tolerance, library, media department, archives, "Testimony to the Truth"oral histories, educational outreach, research department, international social action, "Page One"(syndicated weekly radio news magazine presenting contemporary Jewish issues). *Response Magazine.*

SKIRBALL CULTURAL CENTER (1996), an affiliate of Hebrew Union College. 2701 N. Sepulveda Blvd., Los Angeles, CA 90049. (310)440-4500. FAX: (310)440-4595. Pres. & CEO Uri D. Herscher; Bd. Chmn. Howard Friedman. Seeks to interpret the Jewish experience and to strengthen American society through a range of cultural programs, including museum exhibitions, children's Discovery Center, concerts, lectures, performances, readings,

symposia, film, and educational offerings for adults and children of all ages and backgrounds, through interpretive museum exhibits and programming; museum shop and café. *Oasis magazine; catalogues of exhibits and collections.* (WWW.SKIRBALL.ORG)

SOCIETY FOR THE HISTORY OF CZECHOSLOVAK JEWS, INC. (1961). 760 Pompton Ave., Cedar Grove, NJ 07009. (973)239-2333. FAX: (973)239-7935. Pres. Rabbi Norman Patz; V.-Pres. Prof. Fred Hahn; Sec. Anita Grosz. Studies the history of Czechoslovak Jews; collects material and disseminates information through the publication of books and pamphlets; conducts annual memorial service for Czech Holocaust victims. *The Jews of Czechoslovakia (3 vols.); Review I-VI.*

THE SOCIETY OF FRIENDS OF TOURO SYNAGOGUE NATIONAL HISTORIC SITE, INC. (1948). 85 Touro St., Newport, RI 02840. (401)847-4794. FAX: (401)847-8121. E-mail: sof@tourosynagogue.org. Pres. Andrew M. Teitz; Exec. Dir. B. Schlessinger Ross. Helps maintain Touro Synagogue as a national historic site, opening and interpreting it for visitors; promotes public awareness of its preeminent role in the tradition of American religious liberty; annually commemorates George Washington's letter of 1790 to the Hebrew Congregation of Newport. *Society Update.*

——, TOURO NATIONAL HERITAGE TRUST (1984). 85 Touro St., Newport, RI 02840. (401)847-0810. FAX (401)847-8121. Pres. Bernard Bell; Chmn. Benjamin D. Holloway. Works to establish national education center within Touro compound; sponsors Touro Fellow through John Carter Brown Library; presents seminars and other educational programs; promotes knowledge of the early Jewish experience in this country.

SPERTUS MUSEUM, SPERTUS INSTITUTE OF JEWISH STUDIES (1968). 618 S. Michigan Ave., Chicago, IL 60605. (312)322-1747. FAX: (312)922-6406. Pres. Spertus Institute of Jewish Studies, Dr. Howard A. Sulkin. The largest, most comprehensive Judaic museum in the Midwest with 12,000 square feet of exhibit space and a permanent collection of some 10,000 works reflecting 5,000 years of Jewish history and culture. Also includes the redesigned Zell Holocaust Memorial, permanent collection, changing visual arts and special exhibits, and the children's ARTIFACT Center for a hands-on archaeological adventure. Plus, traveling exhibits for Jewish educators, life-cycle workshops, ADA accessible. *Exhibition catalogues; educational pamphlets.*

SURVIVORS OF THE SHOAH VISUAL HISTORY FOUNDATION (1994). PO Box 3168, Los Angeles, CA 90078-3168. (818)777-7802. FAX: (818)866-0312. Exec. Dir. Ari C. Zev. A nonprofit organization, founded and chaired by Steven Spielberg, dedicated to videotaping and preserving interviews with Holocaust survivors throughout the world. The archive of testimonies will be used as a tool for global education about the Holocaust and to teach racial, ethnic, and cultural tolerance.

UNITED STATES HOLOCAUST MEMORIAL MUSEUM (1980; opened Apr. 1993). 100 Raoul Wallenberg Place, SW, Washington, DC 20024. (202)488-0400. FAX: (202)488-2690. Chmn. Rabbi Irving Greenberg. Federally chartered and privately built, its mission is to teach about the Nazi persecution and murder of six million Jews and millions of others from 1933 to 1945 and to inspire visitors to contemplate their moral responsibilities as citizens of a democratic nation. Opened in April 1993 near the national Mall in Washington, DC, the museum's permanent exhibition tells the story of the Holocaust through authentic artifacts, videotaped oral testimonies, documentary film, and historical photographs. Offers educational programs for students and adults, an interactive computerized learning center, and special exhibitions and community programs. *United States Holocaust Memorial Museum Update (bimonthly); Directory of Holocaust Institutions; Journal of Holocaust and Genocide Studies (quarterly).* (WWW.USHMM.ORG)

THE WILSTEIN (SUSAN & DAVID) INSTITUTE OF JEWISH POLICY STUDIES (1988). 43 Hawes St., Brookline, MA 02146. (617)278-4974. FAX: (617)264-9264. E-mail: wilstein@hebrewcollege.edu. Dir. Dr. David M. Gordis; Assoc. Dir. Rabbi Zachary I. Heller; Chmn. Howard I. Friedman. The Wilstein Institute's West Coast Center in Los Angeles and East Coast Center at Hebrew College in Boston provide a bridge between acade-

mics, community leaders, professionals, and the organizations and institutions of Jewish life. The institute serves as an international research and development resource for American Jewry. *Bulletins, various newsletters, monographs, research reports, and books.*

YESHIVA UNIVERSITY MUSEUM (1973). Center for Jewish History, 15 W. 16 St., NYC 10011-6301. (212)294-8550. E-mail: glickber@ymail.yu.edu. Dir. Sylvia A. Herskowitz; Chmn. Erica Jesselson. Collects, preserves, and interprets Jewish life and culture through changing exhibitions of ceremonial objects, paintings, rare books and documents, synagogue architecture, textiles, contemporary art, and photographs. Oral history archive. Special events, holiday workshops, live performances, lectures, etc. for adults and children. Guided tours and workshops are offered. Exhibitions and children's art education programs also at branch galleries on Yeshiva University's Main Campus, 2520 Amsterdam Ave., NYC 10033-3201. *Seasonal calendars; special exhibition catalogues; newsletters.*

YIDDISHER KULTUR FARBAND-YKUF (1937). 1133 Broadway, Rm. 820, NYC 10010. (212)243-1304. FAX: (212)243-1305. E-mail: mahosu@amc.one. Pres./Ed. Itche Goldberg. Publishes a bimonthly magazine and books by contemporary and classical Jewish writers; conducts cultural forums; exhibits works by contemporary Jewish artists and materials of Jewish historical value; organizes reading circles. *Yiddishe Kultur.*

YIVO INSTITUTE FOR JEWISH RESEARCH (1925). 15 W. 16 St., NYC 10011. (212)246-6080. FAX: (212)292-1892. E-mail: yivo@yivo.cjh.org. Chmn. Bruce Slovin; Exec. Dir. Dr. Carl J. Rheins. Engages in social and cultural research and education pertaining to East European Jewish life; maintains library and archives which provide a major international, national, and New York resource used by institutions, individual scholars, and the public; trains graduate students in Yiddish, East European, and American Jewish studies; offers continuing education classes in Yiddish language, exhibits, conferences, public programs; publishes books. *Yedies-YIVO News; YIVO Bleter; Yidishe Shprakh.*

———, MAX WEINREICH CENTER FOR AD-VANCED JEWISH STUDIES/YIVO INSTITUTE (1968). 15 W. 16 St., NYC 10011. (212)246-6080. FAX: (212)292-1892. E-mail: mweinreich@yivo.cjh.org. Provides advanced-level training in Yiddish language and literature, ethnography, folklore, linguistics, and history; offers guidance on dissertation or independent research; post-doctoral fellowships available.

YUGNTRUF-YOUTH FOR YIDDISH (1964). 200 W. 72 St., Suite 40, NYC 10023. (212)787-6675. FAX: (718)231-7905. E-mail: yugntruf@yugntruf.org. Chmn. Dr. Paul Glasser; V.-Chmn. Marc Caplan; Coord. Brukhe Caplan. A worldwide, nonpolitical organization for young people with a knowledge of, or interest in, Yiddish; fosters Yiddish as a living language and culture. Sponsors all activities in Yiddish:reading, conversation, and creative writing groups; annual weeklong retreat in Berkshires; children's Yiddish play group. *Yugntruf Journal.*

ISRAEL-RELATED

THE ABRAHAM FUND (1989). 477 Madison Ave., 4th fl., NYC 10022. (212)303-9421. FAX: (212)935-1834. E-mail: INFO@ AbrahamFund.org. Chmn. & Co-founder Alan B. Slifka; Co-founder Dr. Eugene Weiner. Seeks to enhance coexistence between Israel's Jewish and Arab citizens. Since 1993, has granted $5.5 million to grassroots coexistence projects in a wide array of fields, including education, social services, economic development, and arts and culture. Publishes *The Handbook of Interethnic Coexistence. The Abraham Fund Quarterly.* (WWW.COEXISTENCE.ORG)

AMERICA-ISRAEL CULTURAL FOUNDATION, INC. (1939). 51 E. 42nd St., Suite 400, NYC 10017. (212)557-1600. FAX: (212)557-1611. E-mail: USA AICF@aol.com. Chmn. Emer. Isaac Stern; Pres. Vera Stern. Supports and encourages the growth of cultural excellence in Israel through grants to cultural institutions; scholarships to gifted young artists and musicians. *Newsletter.*

AMERICA-ISRAEL FRIENDSHIP LEAGUE, INC. (1971). 134 E. 39 St., NYC 10016. (212)213-8630. FAX: (212)683-3475. E-mail: aifl@nyworld.com. Hon. Chmn. Mortimer B. Zuckerman; Bd. Chmn. Kenneth J. Bialkin; Exec.V.-Pres. Ilana Artman. A nonsectarian, nonpartisan organization which seeks to broaden the base of support for Israel among Americans of all faiths and backgrounds. Activities include educational exchanges, tours of Israel for American leadership groups, symposia and public-education activities, and the dissemination of printed information. *Newsletter.*

AMERICAN ASSOCIATES, BEN-GURION UNIVERSITY OF THE NEGEV (1973). 342 Madison Ave., Suite 1224, NYC 10173. (212) 687-7721. FAX: (212)370-0686. E-mail: info@aabgu.org. Pres. Jules I. Whitman; Exec. V-Pres. Bernard C. Moscovitz. Raises funds for Israel's youngest university, an institution dedicated to providing a world-class higher education and fulfilling David Ben-Gurion's vision to develop the Negev and make Israel a 'light unto the nations' through education, research, and projects that fight hunger, disease, and poverty in nearly 50 countries world-wide. *IMPACT Newsletter; videos and brochures.*

AMERICAN COMMITTEE FOR SHAARE ZEDEK JERUSALEM MEDICAL CENTER (1949). 49 W. 45 St., Suite 1100, NYC 10036. (212)354-8801. FAX: (212)391-2674. E-mail: pr@szmc.org.il. Natl. Pres. & Chmn. Intl. Bd. of Gov. Menno Ratzker; Chmn. Erica Jesselson; Exec. Dir. Dr. Stuart Tauber. Increases awareness and raises funds for the various needs of this 100-year old hospital, including new medical centers of excellence, equipment, medical supplies, school of nursing and research; supports exchange program between Shaare Zedek Jerusalem Medical Center and Albert Einstein College of Medicine, NY. *Heartbeat Magazine.*

AMERICAN COMMITTEE FOR SHENKAR COLLEGE IN ISRAEL, INC. (1971). 855 Ave. of the Americas, #531, NYC 10001. (212) 947-1597. FAX: (212)643-9887. E-mail: acfsc@worldnet.att.net. Pres. Nahum G. (Sonny) Shar; Exec. Dir. Charlotte A. Fainblatt. Raises funds for capital improvement, research and development projects, laboratory equipment, scholarships, lectureships, fellowships, and library/archives of fashion and textile design at Shenkar College in Israel, Israel's only fashion and textile technology college. New departments of computer science and jewelry design. Accredited by the Council of Higher Education, the college is the chief source of personnel for Israel's fashion and apparel industry. *Shenkar News.*

AMERICAN COMMITTEE FOR THE BEER-SHEVA FOUNDATION (1988). PO Box 179, NYC 10028. (212)534-3715. FAX: (973) 992-8651. Pres. Ronald Slevin; Sr. V.-Pres. Joanna Slevin; Bd. Chmn. Sidney Cooperman. U.S. fundraising arm of the Beer-Sheva Foundation, which funds vital projects to improve the quality of life in the city of Beer-Sheva: nursery schools for pre-K toddlers, residential and day centers for needy seniors, educational programs, facilities and scholarships (especially for new olim, the physically and mentally challenged), parks, playgrounds, and other important projects. Also offers special services for immigrants—such as heaters, blankets, clothing, school supplies, etc. *Brochures.*

AMERICAN COMMITTEE FOR THE WEIZMANN INSTITUTE OF SCIENCE (1944). 130 E. 59 St., NYC 10022. (212)779-2500. FAX: (212)779-3209. E-mail: info@acwis.org. Chmn. Robert Asher; Pres. Albert Willner, M.D.; Exec. V.-Pres. Martin Kraar. Through 12 regional offices in the U.S. raises funds, disseminates information, and does American purchasing for the Weizmann Institute in Rehovot, Israel, a world-renowned center of scientific research and graduate study. The institute conducts research in disease, energy, the environment, and other areas; runs an international summer science program for gifted high-school students. *Interface; Weizmann Now; annual report.* (WWW.WEIZMANN-USA.ORG)

AMERICAN FRIENDS OF ALYN HOSPITAL (1932). 19 W. 44 St., Suite 1418, NYC 10036. (212)869-8085. FAX: (212)768-0979. E-mail: friendsofalyn@mindspring.com. Pres. Minette Halpern Brown; Exec. Dir. Cathy M Lanyard. Supports the Woldenberg Family Orthopedic Hospital and Pediatric Rehabilitation Center in Jerusalem. Treats children suffering from birth defects (such as muscular dystrophy and spina bifida) and traumas (car accidents, cancer, and fire), enables patients and their families to achieve independence and a better quality of life. (WWW.ALYN.ORG)

AMERICAN FRIENDS OF ASSAF HAROFEH MEDICAL CENTER (1975). PO Box 21051, NYC 10129. (212)481-5653. FAX: (212)481-5672. Chmn. Kenneth Kronen; Exec. Dir. Rhoda Levental; Treas. Robert Kastin. Support group for Assaf Harofeh, Israel's third-largest government hospital, serving a poor population of over 400,000 in the area between Tel Aviv and Jerusalem. Raises funds for medical equipment, medical training for immigrants, hospital expansion, school of nursing, and school of physiotherapy. *Newsletter.*

AMERICAN FRIENDS OF BAR-ILAN UNIVERSITY (1955). 235 Park Ave. So., NYC 10003. (212)673-3460. FAX: (212)673-4856. Chancellor Rabbi Emanuel Rackman; Chmn. Global Bd. Aharon Dahan; Pres. Amer. Bd. Melvin Stein; Exec. V.-Pres. Gen. Yehuda Halevy. Supports Bar-Ilan University, an institution that integrates the highest standards of contemporary scholarship in liberal arts and sciences with a Judaic studies program as a requirement. Located in Ramat-Gan, Israel, and chartered by the Board of Regents of the State of NY. *Bar-Ilan News; Bar-Ilan University Scholar.*

AMERICAN FRIENDS OF BETH HATEFUTSOTH (1976). 633 Third Ave., 21st fl., NYC 10017. (212)339-6034. FAX: (212)318-6176. E-mail: afbhusa@aol.com. Pres. Stephen Greenberg; Chmn. Sam E. Bloch; Exec. Dir. Gloria Golan. Supports the maintenance and development of Beth Hatefutsoth, the Nahum Goldmann Museum of the Jewish Diaspora in Tel Aviv, and its cultural and educational programs for youth and adults. Circulates its traveling exhibitions and provides various cultural programs to local Jewish communities. Includes Jewish genealogy center (DOROT), the center for Jewish music, and photodocumentation center. *Beth Hatefutsoth (quarterly newsletter).*

AMERICAN FRIENDS OF HAIFA UNIVERSITY (*see* AMERICAN SOCIETY OF THE UNIVERSITY OF HAIFA)

AMERICAN FRIENDS OF HERZOG HOSPITAL/EZRATH NASHIM-JERUSALEM (1895). 800 Second Ave., 8th fl., NYC 10017. (212)499-9092. FAX:(212)499-9085. E-mail: herzogpr@hotmail.com. Pres. Rabbi Gilbert Epstein; Exec. Dir. Stephen Schwartz. Israel's foremost center for geriatric and psychiatric health care. It is Jerusalem's third largest hospital with 330 beds. It is a major teaching hospital and maintains a leading research center in the fields of genetics, alzheimer's and schizophrenia. Geriatric specialization in neurogeriatrics; physical rehabilitation; and complex nursing care. Community Mental Health Center treats 16,000 people annually with expertise in treating children with ADHD. *Update newsletter.*

AMERICAN FRIENDS OF LIKUD. 11 W. 34 St., 4th fl., NYC 10001. (212)760-1425. FAX: (212)760-2297. E-mail: Thelikud@aol. com. Pres. Jack B. Dweck; Exec. Dir. Sharon Tzur.

AMERICAN FRIENDS OF NEVE SHALOM/ WAHAT AL-SALAM (1988). 121 Sixth Ave., Suite #507, NYC 10013. (212) 226-9246. FAX: (212) 226-6817. E-mail: afnswas@compuserve.com. Pres. Adeeb Fadil; V.-Pres. Deborah First; Exec. Dir. Deanna Armbruster. Supports and publicizes the projects of the community of Neve Shalom/Wahat Al-Salam, the "Oasis of Peace."For more than twenty years, Jewish and Palestinian citizens of Israel have lived and worked together as equals. The community teaches tolerance, understanding and mutual respect well beyond its own borders by being a model for peace and reaching out through its educational institutions. A bilingual, bicultural Primary School serves the village and the surrounding communities. Encounter workshops conducted by the School for Peace, both in the community and beyond, have reached tens of thousands of Jewish and Palestinian youth and adults.

AMERICAN FRIENDS OF RABIN MEDICAL CENTER (1994). 1328 Broadway, Suite 826, NYC 10001-2121. (212) 279-2522. Fax: (212)279-0179. E-mail: afrmc826@ aol.com. Pres. Woody Goldberg; Exec. Dir. Burton Lazarow. Supports the maintenance and development of this medical, research, and teaching institution in central Israel, which unites the Golda and Beilinson hospitals, providing 12% of all hospitalization in Israel. Department of Organ Transplantation performs 80% of all kidney and 60% of all liver transplants in Israel. Affiliated with Tel Aviv University's Sackler School of Medicine. *New DirectionsQuarterly.*

AMERICAN FRIENDS OF RAMBAM MEDICAL CENTER (1969). 850 Seventh Ave., Suite 305, NYC 10019. (212)397-1123. FAX: (212)397-1132. E-mail: rambam@earthlink.net. Pres. Michael R. Stoler. Represents and raises funds for Rambam Medical Center (Haifa), an 887-bed hospital serving approx. one-third of Israel's population, incl. the entire population of northern Israel (and south Lebanon), the U.S. Sixth Fleet, and the UN Peacekeeping Forces in the region. Rambam is the teaching hospital for the Technion's medical school.

AMERICAN FRIENDS OF TEL AVIV UNIVERSITY, INC. (1955). 360 Lexington Ave., NYC 10017. (212)687-5651. FAX: (212) 687-4085. Bd. Chmn. Alan L. Aufzien; Pres. Robert J. Topchik; Exec. V.-Pres. Stephen Lecker. Promotes higher education at Tel Aviv University, Israel's largest and most comprehensive institution of higher learning. Included in its nine faculties are the Sackler School of Medicine with its fully accredited NY State English-language program, the Rubin Academy of Music, and 70 research institutes, including the Moshe Dayan Center for Middle East & African Studies and the Jaffe Center for Strategic Studies. *Tel Aviv University News; FAX Flash.*

AMERICAN FRIENDS OF THE HEBREW UNIVERSITY (1925; inc. 1931). 11 E. 69 St., NYC 10021. (212)472-9800. FAX: (212) 744-2324. E-mail: info@afhu.org. Pres. Ira Lee Sorkin; Bd. Chmn. Keith L. Sachs; Exec. V.-Pres. Adam Kahan. Fosters the growth, development, and maintenance of the Hebrew University of Jerusalem; collects funds and conducts informational programs throughout the U.S., highlighting the university's achievements and its significance. *Wisdom; Scopus Magazine.* (WWW.AFHU.ORG)

AMERICAN FRIENDS OF THE ISRAEL MUSEUM (1972). 500 Fifth Ave., Suite 2540, NYC 10110. (212)997-5611. FAX: (212) 997-5536. Pres. Barbara Lane; Exec. Dir. Carolyn Cohen. Raises funds for special projects of the Israel Museum in Jerusalem; solicits works of art for permanent collection, exhibitions, and educational purposes. *Newsletter.*

AMERICAN FRIENDS OF THE ISRAEL PHILHARMONIC ORCHESTRA (AFIPO) (1972). 122 E. 42 St., Suite 4507, NYC 10168. (212)697-2949. FAX: (212)697-2943. Pres. Herman Sandler; Exec. Dir. Suzanne K.

Ponsot. Works to secure the financial future of the orchestra so that it may continue to travel throughout the world bringing its message of peace and cultural understanding through music. Supports the orchestra's international touring program, educational projects, and a wide array of musical activities in Israel. *Passport to Music (newsletter)*.

AMERICAN FRIENDS OF THE OPEN UNIVERSITY OF ISRAEL. 180 W. 80 St., NYC 10024. (212)712-1800. FAX: (212)496-3296. E-mail: afoui@aol.com. Natl. Chmn. Irving M. Rosenbaum; Exec.V.-Pres. Eric G. Heffler. *Open Letter*.

AMERICAN FRIENDS OF THE SHALOM HARTMAN INSTITUTE (1976). 42 E. 69 St., Suite 401, NYC 10021. (212)772-9711. FAX: (212)772-9720. E-mail: afshi@banet.net. Pres. Richard F. Kaufman; Exec. V.-Pres. Staci Light; Admin. Dorothy Minchin. Supports the Shalom Hartman Institute in Jerusalem, an international center for pluralist Jewish education and research, serving Israel and world Jewry. Founded in 1976 by David Hartman, the Institute includes:the Institute for Advanced Judaic Studies, with research centers for contemporary halakha, religious pluralism, political thought and peace and reconciliation; the Institute for Teacher and Leadership Training, educating Israeli principals, teachers, graduate students and leaders; and the Institute for Diaspora Education, which offers seminars and sabbaticals to rabbis, educators and lay leaders of diverse ideological commitments. WWW.HARTMANINSTITUTE.COM)

AMERICAN FRIENDS OF THE TEL AVIV MUSEUM OF ART (1974). 545 Madison Ave. (55 St.), NYC 10022. (212)319-0555. FAX: (212)754-2987. Chmn. Stanley I. Batkin; Exec. Dir. Dorey Neilinger. Raises funds for the Tel Aviv Museum of Art for special projects, art acquisitions, and exhibitions; seeks contributions of art to expand the museum's collection; encourages art loans and traveling exhibitions; creates an awareness of the museum in the USA; makes available exhibition catalogues, monthly calendars, and posters published by the museum.

AMERICAN-ISRAEL ENVIRONMENTAL COUNCIL (formerly COUNCIL FOR A BEAUTIFUL ISRAEL ENVIRONMENTAL EDUCATION FOUNDATION) (1973). c/o Perry Davis Assoc., 25 W. 45 St., Suite 1405, NYC 10036. (212)575-7530. Fax: (212)840-1514. Co-Pres. Mel Atlas & Edythe Roland Grodnick. A support group for the Israeli body, whose activities include education, town planning, lobbying for legislation to protect and enhance the environment, preservation of historical sites, the improvement and beautification of industrial and commercial areas, and sponsoring the CBI Center for Environmental Studies located in Yarkon Park, Tel Aviv. *Yearly newsletter; yearly theme oriented calendars in color.*

AMERICAN ISRAEL PUBLIC AFFAIRS COMMITTEE (AIPAC) (1954). 440 First St., NW, Washington, DC 20001. (202)639-5200. FAX: (202)347-4889. Pres. Lonny Kaplan; Exec. Dir. Howard A. Kohr. Registered to lobby on behalf of legislation affecting U.S.-Israel relations; represents Americans who believe support for a secure Israel is in U.S. interest. Works for a strong U.S.-Israel relationship. *Near East Report*. (WWW.AIPAC.ORG)

AMERICAN-ISRAELI LIGHTHOUSE, INC. (1928; reorg. 1955). 276 Fifth Ave., Suite 713, NYC 10001. (212)686-7110. Pres. Mrs. Leonard F. Dank; Sec. Mrs. Ida Rhein. Provides a vast network for blind and physically handicapped persons throughout Israel, to effect their social and vocational integration into the mainstream of their communities. Center of Services for the blind; built and maintains Rehabilitation Center for blind and handicapped persons (Migdal Or) in Haifa.

AMERICAN JEWISH LEAGUE FOR ISRAEL (1957). 130 E. 59 St., NYC 10022. (212) 371-1583. FAX: (212)371-3265. E-mail: AJLImlk@aol.com. Pres. Dr. Martin L. Kalmanson. Seeks to unite all those who, notwithstanding differing philosophies of Jewish life, are committed to the historical ideals of Zionism; works independently of class, party, or religious affiliation for the welfare of Israel as a whole. Not identified with any political parties in Israel. Member of World Jewish Congress, World Zionist Organization, American Zionist Movement. *Newsletter.*

AMERICAN PHYSICIANS FELLOWSHIP FOR MEDICINE IN ISRAEL (1950). 2001 Beacon St., Suite 210, Brighton, MA 02135-7771. (617)232-5382. FAX: (617) 739-2616. E-mail: apf@apfmed.org. Pres. Sherwood

L. Gorbach, M.D.; Exec. Dir. Donald J. Perlstein. Supports projects that advance medical education, research, and care in Israel and builds links between the medical communities of Israel and N. Amer.; provides fellowships for Israeli physicians training in N. Amer. and arranges lectureships in Israel by prominent N. Amer. physicians; sponsors CME seminars in Israel and N. Amer.; coordinates U.S./Canadian medical emergency volunteers for Israel. *APF News.*

AMERICAN RED MAGEN DAVID FOR ISRAEL, INC. (1940) (a/k/a ARMDI & Red Magen David). 888 Seventh Ave., Suite 403, NYC 10106. (212)757-1627. FAX: (212)757-4662. E-mail: armdi@att.net. Natl. Pres. Robert L. Sadoff, M.D.; Exec. V.-Pres. Benjamin Saxe. An authorized tax-exempt organization; the sole support arm in the U.S. of Magen David Adom (MDA), Israel's equivalent to a Red Cross Society; raises funds for the MDA emergency medical, ambulance, blood, and disaster services which help Israel's defense forces and civilian population. Helps to supply and equip ambulances, bloodmobiles, and cardiac rescue ambulances as well as 45 pre-hospital MDA Emergency Medical Clinics and the MDA National Blood Service Center and MDA Fractionation Institute in Ramat Gan, Israel. *Lifeline.*

AMERICAN SOCIETY FOR TECHNION-ISRAEL INSTITUTE OF TECHNOLOGY (1940). 810 Seventh Ave., 24th fl., NYC 10019. (212) 262-6200. FAX: (212)262-6155. Pres. Lawrence Jackier; Chmn. Irving A. Shepard; Exec. V.-Pres. Melvyn H. Bloom. Supports the work of the Technion-Israel Institute of Technology in Haifa, which trains over 13,000 students in 19 faculties and a medical school, and conducts research across a broad spectrum of science and technology. *Technion USA.*

AMERICAN SOCIETY FOR THE PROTECTION OF NATURE IN ISRAEL, INC. (1986). 28 Arrandale Ave., Great Neck, NY 11024. (212) 398-6750. FAX: (212) 398-1665. E-mail: aspni@aol.com. Co-Chmn. Edward I. Geffner & Russell Rothman. A nonprofit organization supporting the work of SPNI, an Israeli organization devoted to environmental protection and nature education. SPNI runs 26 Field Study Centers and has 45 municipal offices throughout Israel; offers education programs, organized hikes, and other activities; seeks ways to address the needs of an expanding society while preserving precious natural resources. *SPNI News.*

AMERICAN SOCIETY FOR YAD VASHEM (1981). 500 Fifth Ave., Suite 1600, NYC 10110-1699. (212)220-4304. FAX: (212) 220-4308. E-mail: yadvashem@aol.com. Chmn. Eli Zborowski; Exec. Dir. Selma Schiffer; Dev. Dir. Shraga Y. Mekel; Ed. Dir. Marlene Warshawski Yahalom, Ph.D. Development arm of Yad Vashem, Jerusalem, the central international authority created by the Knesset in 1953 for the purposes of commemoration and education in connection with the Holocaust. *Martyrdom and Resistance (newsletter).* (WWW.YADVASHEM.ORG)

AMERICAN SOCIETY OF THE UNIVERSITY OF HAIFA (formerly AMERICAN FRIENDS OF HAIFA UNIVERSITY) (1972). c/oRubinbaum, LLP, 30 Rockefeller Center, NYC 10112. (212)698-7700. 220 Fifth Ave., Suite 1301, NYC 10001. (212)685-7880. FAX: (212)267-5916. Pres. Paul Amir; Sec./ Treas. Robert Jay Benowitz. Promotes, encourages, and aids higher and secondary education, research, and training in all branches of knowledge in Israel and elsewhere; aids in the maintenance and development of Haifa University; raises and allocates funds for the above purposes; provides scholarships; promotes exchanges of teachers and students.

AMERICAN ZIONIST MOVEMENT (formerly AMERICAN ZIONIST FEDERATION) (1939; reorg. 1949, 1970, 1993). 110 E. 59 St., NYC 10022. (212)318-6100. FAX: (212) 935-3578. E-mail: info@azm.com. Pres. Melvin Salberg; Exec. Dir. Karen J. Rubinstein. Umbrella organization for 20 American Zionist organizations and the voice of unified Zionism in the U.S. Conducts advocacy for Israel; strengthens Jewish identity; promotes the Israel experience; prepares the next generation of Zionist leadership. Regional offices in Chicago and Dallas. Groups in Detroit, Pittsburgh, Washington, DC. *The Zionist Advocate.* (WWW.AZM.ORG)

AMERICANS FOR A SAFE ISRAEL (AFSI) (1971). 1623 Third Ave., Suite 205, NYC 10128. (212)828-2424. FAX: (212)828-1717. E-mail: afsi@interport.net. Chmn. Herbert Zweibon; Exec. Dir. Helen

Freedman. Seeks to educate Americans in Congress, the media, and the public about Israel's role as a strategic asset for the West; through meetings with legislators and the media, in press releases and publications AFSI promotes Jewish rights to Judea and Samaria, the Golan, Gaza, an indivisible Jerusalem, and to all of Israel. AFSI believes in the concept of "peace for peace"and rejects the concept of "territory for peace." *The Outpost (monthly).* (WWW.AFSI.ORG.AFSI)

AMERICANS FOR PEACE NOW (1984). 1815 H St., NW, 9ᵗʰ fl., Washington, DC 20006. (212)728-1893. FAX: (212)728-1895. E-mail: apndc@peacenow.org. Pres. & CEO Debra DeLee; Chmn. Pat Barr. Conducts educational programs and raises funds to support the Israeli peace movement, Shalom Achshav (Peace Now), and coordinates U.S. advocacy efforts through APN's Washington-based Center for Israeli Peace and Security. *Jerusalem Watch; Peace Now News; Settlement Watch; Fax Facts; Middle East Update (on-line); Benefits of Peace.* (WWW.PEACENOW.ORG)

AMIT (1925). 817 Broadway, NYC 10003. (212)477-4720. FAX: (212)353-2312. E-mail: amitchldrn@aol.com. Pres. Sondra Sokal; Exec. Dir. Marvin Leff. The State of Israel's official reshet (network) for religious secondary technological education; maintains innovative children's homes and youth villages in Israel in an environment of traditional Judaism; promotes cultural activities for the purpose of disseminating Zionist ideals and strengthening traditional Judaism in America. *AMIT Magazine.*

AMPAL-AMERICAN ISRAEL CORPORATION (1942). 1177 Avenue of the Americas, NYC 10036. (212)782-2100. FAX: (212) 782-2114. E-mail: ampal@aol.com. Bd. Chmn. Daniel Steinmetz; CEO Shuki Gleitman. Acquires interests in businesses located in the State of Israel or that are Israel-related. Interests include leisure-time, real estate, finance, energy distribution, basic industry, high technology, and communications. *Annual report; quarterly reports.*

ARZA/WORLD UNION, NORTH AMERICA (1977). 633 Third Ave., 6th fl., NYC 10017-6778. (212)650-4280. FAX: (212)650-4289. E-mail: arza/wupjna@ uahc.org. Pres. Philip Meltzer; Exec. Dir. Rabbi Ammiel Hirsch. Membership organization dedicated to furthering the development of Progressive Judaism in Israel, the FSU, and throughout the world. Encourages Jewish solidarity, promoting religious pluralism and furthering Zionism. Works to strengthen the relationship of N. American Reform Jews with Progressive Jewish communities worldwide and to educate and inform them on relevant issues. *Quarterly newsletter.* (WWW.RJ.ORG/ARZAWUNA)

BETAR ZIONIST YOUTH ORGANIZATION (1935). 625 Broadway, NYC 10012. (212)254-8090. FAX: (212)254-8036. E-mail: betarorg@mail.idt.net. North American Central Shlicha Sharon Tzur. Organizes youth groups across North America to teach Zionism, Jewish identity, and love of Israel; sponsors summer programs in Israel for Jewish youth ages 14-22; sponsors Tagar Zionist Student Activist Movement on college campuses.

BOYS TOWN JERUSALEM FOUNDATION OF AMERICA INC. (1948). 12 W. 31 St., Suite 300, NYC 10001. (212)244-2766. (800) 469-2697. FAX: (212)244-2052. E-mail: btjny@compuserve.com. Pres. Michael J. Scharf; Chmn. Josh S. Weston; V.-Chmn. Moshe Linchner; Exec. V.-Pres. Rabbi Ronald L. Gray. Raises funds for Boys Town Jerusalem, which was established in 1948 to offer a comprehensive academic, religious, and technological education to disadvantaged Israeli and immigrant boys from over 45 different countries, including Ethiopia, the former Soviet Union, and Iran. Enrollment:over 1,000 students in jr. high school, academic and technical high school, and a college of applied engineering. *BTJ Newsbriefs.*

CAMERA-COMMITTEE FOR ACCURACY IN MIDDLE EAST REPORTING IN AMERICA (1983). PO Box 428, Boston, MA 02456. (617)789-3672. FAX: (617)787-7853. E-mail: media@camera.org. Pres./Exec. Dir. Andrea Levin; Chmn. Leonard Wisse. Monitors and responds to media distortion in order to promote better understanding of Middle East; urges members to alert the public and the media to errors, omissions, and distortions. *CAMERA Media Report (quarterly); CAMERA on Campus; Action Alerts; Media Directories; Monographs.* (WWW.CAMERA.ORG)

COUNCIL FOR A BEAUTIFUL ISRAEL ENVIRONMENTAL EDUCATION FOUNDATION (*see* AMERICAN-ISRAEL ENVIRONMENTAL COUNCIL)

EMUNAH OF AMERICA (formerly HAPOEL HAMIZRACHI WOMEN'S ORGANIZATION) (1948). 7 Penn Plaza, NYC 10001. (212)564-9045, (800)368-6440. FAX: (212)643-9731. E-mail: info@emunah. org. Natl. Pres. Dr. Sylvia Schonfeld; Exec. V.-Pres. Shirley Singer. Maintains and supports 200 educational and social-welfare institutions in Israel within a religious framework, including day-care centers, kindergartens, children's residential homes, vocational schools for the underprivileged, senior-citizen centers, a college complex, and Holocaust study center. Also involved in absorption of Soviet and Ethiopian immigrants (recognized by Israeli government as an official absorption agency). *Emunah Magazine; Lest We Forget.* (WWW.EMUNAH.ORG)

FEDERATED COUNCIL OF ISRAEL INSTITUTIONS—FCII (1940). 4702 15th Ave., Brooklyn, NY 11219. (718)972-5530. Bd. Chmn. Z. Shapiro; Exec. V.-Pres. Rabbi Julius Novack. Central fund-raising organization for over 100 affiliated institutions; handles and executes estates, wills, and bequests for the traditional institutions in Israel; clearinghouse for information on budget, size, functions, etc. of traditional educational, welfare, and philanthropic institutions in Israel, working cooperatively with the Israeli government and the overseas department of the Council of Jewish Federations. *Annual financial reports and statistics on affiliates.*

FRIENDS OF THE ISRAEL DEFENSE FORCES (1981). 21 W. 38 St., 5th fl., NYC 10018. (212)575-5030. FAX: (212)575-7815. E-mail: fidf@fidf.com. Chmn. Marvin Josephson; Pres. Jay Zises; Natl. Dir. Brig. Gen. Eliezer Hemeli. Supports the Agudah Lema'an Hahayal, Israel's Assoc. for the Well-Being of Soldiers, founded in the early 1940s, which provides social, recreational, and educational programs for soldiers, special services for the sick and wounded, and summer programs for widows and children of fallen soldiers. (WWW.FIDF.COM)

GESHER FOUNDATION (1969). 25 W. 45 St Suite 1405, NYC 10036. (212)840-1166. FAX: (212)840-1514. E-mail: gesher@

aol.com. Pres./Founder Daniel Tropper; Chmn. Philip Schatten. Seeks to bridge the gap between Jews of various backgrounds in Israel by stressing the interdependence of all Jews. Runs encounter seminars for Israeli youth; distributes curricular materials in public schools; offers Jewish identity classes for Russian youth, and a video series in Russian and English on famous Jewish personalities.

GIVAT HAVIVA EDUCATIONAL FOUNDATION, INC. (1966). 114 W. 26 St., Suite 1001, NYC 10001. (212)989-9272. FAX: (212) 989-9840. E-mail: mail@givathaviva.org. Chmn. Henry Ostberg. Supports programs at the Givat Haviva Institute, Israel's leading organization dedicated to promoting coexistence between Arabs and Jews, with 40,000 people participating each year in programs teaching conflict resolution, Middle East studies and languages, and Holocaust studies. Publishes research papers on Arab-Jewish relations, Holocaust studies, kibbutz life. In the U.S., GHEF sponsors public-education programs and lectures by Israeli speakers. *Givat Haviva News; special reports.* (WWW.GIVATHAVIVA.ORG)

HABONIM-DROR NORTH AMERICA (1935). 114 W. 26 St., Suite 1004, NYC 10001-6812. (212)255-1796. FAX: (212)929-3459. E-mail: programs@habonimdror. org. Mazkir Tnua Jared Matas; Shaliach Dani Lamdan. Fosters identification with progressive, cooperative living in Israel; stimulates study of Jewish and Zionist culture, history, and contemporary society; sponsors summer and year programs in Israel and on kibbutz, 7 summer camps in N. America modeled after kibbutzim, and aliyah frameworks. *Batnua (on-line and print newsletter).* (WWW.HABONIM-DROR.ORG)

HADASSAH, THE WOMEN'S ZIONIST ORGANIZATION OF AMERICA. (1912). 50 W. 58 St., NYC 10019. (212)355-7900. FAX: (212)303-8282. Pres. Bonnie Lipton; Exec. Dir. Dr. Laura S. Schor. Largest women's, largest Jewish, and largest Zionist membership organization in U.S. In Israel: Founded and funds Hadassah Medical Organization, Hadassah College of Technology, Hadassah Career Counseling Institute, Young Judea summer and year-course programs, as well as providing support for Youth Aliyah and JNF. U.S. programs: Jewish and women's health education; advocacy on Israel, Zionism and women's issues; Young Judaea youth movement, including six camps; Hadassah Leadership Academy; Hadassah Research Institute on Jewish Women; Hadassah Foundation. *Hadassah Magazine; Heart & Soul; Update; Hadassah International Newsletter; Medical Update; American Scene.* (WWW.HADASSAH.ORG)

————, YOUNG JUDAEA (1909; reorg. 1967). 50 W. 58 St., NYC 10019. (212)303-8014. FAX: (212)303-4572. E-mail: info@ youngjudea.org. Natl. Dir. Doron Krakow. Religiously pluralist, politically nonpartisan Zionist youth movement sponsored by Hadassah; seeks to educate Jewish youth aged 8-25 toward Jewish and Zionist values, active commitment to and participation in the American and Israeli Jewish communities; maintains six summer camps in the U.S.; runs both summer and year programs in Israel, and a jr. year program in connection with both Hebrew University in Jerusalem and Ben Gurion University of Negev. College-age arm, Hamagshimim, supports Zionist activity on campuses. *Kol Hat'nua; The Young Judaean; Ad Kahn.* (WWW.YOUNGJUDEA. ORG)

HASHOMER HATZAIR, SOCIALIST ZIONIST YOUTH MOVEMENT (1923). 114 W. 26 St., Suite 1001, NYC 10001. (212)627-2830. FAX: (212)989-9840. E-mail: mail@ hashomerhatzair.org. Dir. Giora Salz; Natl. Sec. Ben Zviti & Minna Dubin; Dir. Amnon Ophir. Seeks to educate Jewish youth to an understanding of Zionism as the national liberation movement of the Jewish people. Promotes aliyah to kibbutzim. Affiliated with Kibbutz Artzi Federation. Espouses socialist-Zionist ideals of peace, justice, democracy, and intergroup harmony. *Young Guard.* (WWW.HASHOMERHAZAIR.ORG)

INTERNS FOR PEACE (NITZANEI SHALOM/ BARA'EM AS'SALAAM/BUDS OF PEACE) (1976). 475 Riverside Dr., 16th fl., NYC 10115. (212)870-2226. FAX: (212)870-2119. Intl. Dir. Rabbi Bruce M. Cohen; Intl. Coord. Karen Wald Cohen. An independent, nonprofit, nonpolitical educational program training professional community peace workers. In Israel, initiated and operated jointly by Jews and Arabs; over 190 interns trained in 35 cities; over 80,000 Israeli citizens partici-

pating in joint programs in education, sports, culture, business, women's affairs, and community development; since the peace accord, Palestinians from West Bank and Gaza training as interns. Martin Luther King Project for Black/Jewish relations. *IFP Reports Quarterly; Guidebooks for Ethnic Conflict Resolution.* (WWW.INTERNSFORPEACE.ORG)

ISRAEL CANCER RESEARCH FUND (1975). 1290 Avenue of the Americas, NYC 10104. (212)969-9800. FAX: (212)969-9822. E-mail: icrf-hq-ny@worldnet. att.net. Pres. Yashar Hirshaut, M.D.; Chmn. Leah Susskind; Exec. V.-Pres. Gerald S. Nagel, Ed.D. The largest single source of private funds for cancer research in Israel. Has a threefold mission: To encourage innovative cancer research by Israeli scientists; to harness Israel's vast intellectual and creative resources to establish a world-class center for cancer study; to broaden research opportunities within Israel to stop the exodus of talented Israeli cancer researchers. *Annual Report; Research Awards; ICRF Brochure; Newsletter.*

ISRAEL HISTADRUT FOUNDATION (*see* ISRAEL HUMANITARIAN FOUNDATION)

ISRAEL HUMANITARIAN FOUNDATION (IHF) (1960). 276 Fifth Ave., Suite 901, NYC 10001. (212)683-5676, (800)443-5699. FAX: (212)213-9233. E-mail: info@ihf. net. Pres. Marvin M. Sirota; Exec.V.-Pres. Stanley J. Abrams. Nonprofit American philanthropic organization that supports humanitarian needs in Israel; strives to improve the standard of living of Israel's population in need through its support of education, general health and neonatal care, medical and cancer research, the elderly, disabled and youth-in-need. *Impact.*

ISRAEL POLICY FORUM (1993). 666 Fifth Ave., 21st fl., NYC 10103. (212)245-4227. FAX: (212)245-0517. E-mail: ipforum@ aol.com. 1030 15 St., NW, Suite 850, Washington, DC 20005. (202)842-1700. FAX:(202)842-1722. E-mail: mail@ipforum.org. Chmn. Michael W. Sonnenfeldt; Pres. Jack Bendheim; Exec. Dir. Debra Wasserman. An independent leadership institution whose mission is to create greater awareness of the security and economic benefits of the Middle East peace process and to support an active U.S. role in resolving the Arab-Israeli conflict. IPF generates this support by involving leaders from the business, political, entertainment, academic, and philanthropic communitites in the peace effort, and by fostering a deeper understanding of the peace process among the American public. *Policy Paper; Security Watch.* (www.IPFORUM.ORG)

THE JERUSALEM FOUNDATION, INC. (1966). 60 E. 42 St., Suite 1936, NYC 10165. (212) 697-4188. FAX: (212) 697-4022. E-mail: srubin@jfoundation.com. Chmn. William Ackman; Exec. Dir. Sandra Rubin. A nonprofit organization devoted to improving the quality of life for all Jerusalemites, regardless of ethnic, religious, or socioeconomic background; has initiated and implemented more than 1,500 projects that span education, culture, community services, beautification, and preservation of the city's historic heritage and religious sites.

JEWISH INSTITUTE FOR NATIONAL SECURITY AFFAIRS (JINSA) (1976). 1717 K St., NW, Suite 800, Washington, DC 20006. (202) 833-0020. FAX: (202)296-6452. E-mail: info@jinsa.org. Pres. Norman Hascoe; Exec. Dir. Tom Neumann. A nonprofit, nonpartisan educational organization working within the American Jewish community to explain the link between American defense policy and the security of the State of Israel; and within the national security establishment to explain the key role Israel plays in bolstering American interests. (www.JINSA.ORG)

JEWISH INSTITUTE FOR THE BLIND-JERUSALEM, INC. (1902, Jerusalem). 15 E. 26 St., NYC 10010. (212) 532-4155. FAX: (212) 447-7683. Pres. Rabbi David E. Lapp; Admin. Eric L. Loeb. Supports a dormitory and school for the Israeli blind and handicapped in Jerusalem. *INsight.*

JEWISH NATIONAL FUND OF AMERICA (1901). 42 E. 69 St., NYC 10021. (212)879-9300. (1-800-542-TREE). FAX: (212)517-3293. E-mail: jnfcomm@aol. com. Pres. Ronald S. Lauder; Exec. V.-Pres. Russell F. Robinson. The American fund-raising arm of Keren Kayemeth LeYisrael, the official land agency in Israel; supports KKL in reclamation of land for planting and forestry; environmental concerns; water conservation; recreation and agriculture; employment of new immigrants; tourism; and research and development. (www.JNF.ORG)

JEWISH PEACE LOBBY (1989). 8604 Second Ave., Suite 317, Silver Spring, MD 20910. (301)589-8764. FAX: (301)589-2722. Pres. Jerome M. Segal. A legally registered lobby promoting changes in U.S. policy vis-a-vis the Israeli-Palestinian conflict. Supports Israel's right to peace within secure borders; a political settlement based on mutual recognition of the right of self-determination of both peoples; a two-state solution as the most likely means to a stable peace. *Washington Action Alerts.*

KEREN OR, INC. JERUSALEM CENTER FOR MULTI-HANDICAPPED BLIND CHILDREN (1956). 350 Seventh Ave., Suite 200, NYC 10001. (212)279-4070. FAX: (212) 279-4043. E-mail: kerenorinc@aol.com. Chmn. Dr. Edward L. Steinberg; Pres. Dr. Albert Hornblass; Exec. Dir. Rochelle B. Silberman. Funds the Keren-Or Center for Multi-Handicapped Blind Children at 3 Abba Hillel Silver St., Ramot, Jerusalem, housing and caring for over 70 resident and day students who in addition to blindness or very low vision suffer from other severe physical and/or mental disabilities. Students range in age from 1 1/2 through young adulthood. Provides training in daily living skills, as well as therapy, rehabilitation, and education to the optimum level of the individual. *Insights Newsletter.*

LABOR ZIONIST ALLIANCE (formerly FARBAND LABOR ZIONIST ORDER) (1913). 275 Seventh Ave., NYC 10001. (212)366-1194. FAX: (212)675-7685. E-mail: labzionA@ aol.com. Pres. Jeffry Mallow; Exec. Dir. Stephane Acel. Seeks to enhance Jewish life, culture, and education in U.S.; aids in building State of Israel as a cooperative commonwealth and its Labor movement organized in the Histadrut; supports efforts toward a more democratic society throughout the world; furthers the democratization of the Jewish community in America and the welfare of Jews everywhere; works with labor and liberal forces in America; sponsors Habonim-Dror labor Zionist youth movement. *Jewish Frontier; Yiddisher Kempfer.* (www.JEWISHFRONTIER.ORG)

MACCABI USA/SPORTS FOR ISRAEL (formerly UNITED STATES COMMITTEE SPORTS FOR ISRAEL) (1948). 1926 Arch St., 4R,

Philadelphia, PA 19103. (215)561-6900. Fax: (215)561-5470. E-mail: maccabi@ maccabiusa.com. Pres. Robert E. Spivak; Exec. Dir. Barbara G. Lissy. Sponsors U.S. team for World Maccabiah Games in Israel every four years; seeks to enrich the lives of Jewish youth in the U.S., Israel, and the Diaspora through athletic, cultural, and educational programs; develops, promotes, and supports international, national, and regional athletic-based activities and facilities. *Sportscene Newsletter; Commemorative Maccabiah Games Journal; financial report.* (www. MACCABIUSA.COM)

MERCAZ USA (1979). 155 Fifth Ave., NYC 10010. (212)533-7800, ext. 2016. FAX: (212)533-2601. E-mail: mercaz@compuserve.com. Pres. Evelyn Seelig; Exec. Dir. Rabbi Robert R. Golub. The U.S. Zionist organization for Conservative/ Masorti Judaism; works for religious pluralism in Israel, defending and promoting Conservative/Masorti institutions and individuals; fosters Zionist education and *aliyah* and develops young leadership. *Mercaz News & Views.* (www.MERCAZUSA.ORG)

MERETZ USA FOR ISRAELI CIVIL RIGHTS AND PEACE (1991). 114 W. 26 St., Suite 1002, NYC 10001. (212)242-4500. FAX: (212)242-5718. E-mail: meretzusa@aol.com. Pres. Harold M. Shapiro; Exec. Dir. Charney V. Bromberg. A forum for addressing the issues of social justice and peace in Israel. Educates about issues related to democracy, human and civil rights, religious pluralism, and equality for women and ethnic minorities; promotes the resolution of Israel's conflict with the Palestinians on the basis of mutual recognition, self-determination, and peaceful coexistence. *Israel Horizons.*

NA'AMAT USA, THE WOMEN'S LABOR ZIONIST ORGANIZATION OF AMERICA, INC. (formerly PIONEER WOMEN/NA'AMAT) (1925). 350 Fifth Ave., Suite 4700, NYC 10118-4799. (212)239-2828. FAX: (212)239-2833. E-mail: naamat@naamat.org. Natl. Pres. Dina Spector; Exec. Dir. Sheila Guston. Part of the World Movement of Na'amat (movement of working women and volunteers), the largest Jewish women's organization in the world, Na'amat USA helps provide social, educational, and legal services for women, teenagers, and children in Israel. It also advocates legislation for women's rights and child welfare in Israel and the U.S., furthers Jewish education, and supports Habonim Dror, the Labor Zionist youth movement. *Na'amat Woman magazine.* (www.NAAMAT.ORG)

NATIONAL COMMITTEE FOR LABOR ISRAEL (1923). 275 Seventh Ave., NYC 10001. (212)647-0300. FAX: (212)647-0308. E-mail: ncli@laborisrael.org. Pres. Jay Mazur; Exec. Dir. Jerry Goodman; Chmn. Trade Union Council Morton Bahr. Brings together diverse groups-Jews and non-Jews-to build support for Israel and advance closer Arab-Israel ties. Conducts educational and communal activities in the Jewish community and among labor groups to promote better relations with labor Israel. Raises funds for youth, educational, health, social, and cultural projects. *Occasional background papers* (www.LABORISRAEL.ORG)

NEW ISRAEL FUND (1979). 1101 14th St., NW, 6th fl., Washington, DC 20005-5639. (202)842-0900. FAX: (202)842-0991. E-mail: info@nif.org. New York office:165 E. 56 St., NYC 10022. (212)750-2333. FAX: (212)750-8043. Pres. Yoram Peri; Exec. Dir. Norman S. Rosenberg. A partnership of Israelis and North Americans dedicated to promoting social justice, co-existence, and pluralism in Israel, the New Israel Fund helps strengthen Israeli democracy by providing grants and technical assistance to the public-interest sector, cultivating a new generation of social activists, and educating citizens in Israel and the Diaspora about the challenges to Israeli democracy. *Quarterly newsletter; annual report.* (www.NIF.ORG)

PEC ISRAEL ECONOMIC CORPORATION (formerly PALESTINE ECONOMIC CORPORATION) (1926). 511 Fifth Ave., NYC 10017. (212)687-2400. Chmn. O. Recanati; Pres. Frank J. Klein; Exec. V.-Pres. James I. Edelson; Treas. William Gold. Primarily engaged in the business of organizing, acquiring interest in, financing, and participating in the management of companies located in the State of Israel or Israel-related.

PEF ISRAEL ENDOWMENT FUNDS, INC. (1922). 317 Madison Ave., Suite 607, NYC 10017. (212)599-1260. Chmn. Sidney A. Luria; Pres. B. Harrison Frankel; Sec. Mark Bane. A totally volunteer organization that makes grants to educational, scientific, social, religious, health, and other philanthropic institutions in Israel. *Annual report.*

PIONEER WOMEN/NA'AMAT (*see* NA'AMAT USA)

POALE AGUDATH ISRAEL OF AMERICA, INC. (1948). 2920 Avenue J, Brooklyn, NY 11210. (718)258-2228. FAX: (718)258-2288. Pres. Rabbi Fabian Schonfeld. Aims to educate American Jews to the values of Orthodoxy and aliyah; supports kibbutzim, trade schools, yeshivot, moshavim, kollelim, research centers, and children's homes in Israel. *PAI News; She'arim; Hamayan.*

———, WOMEN'S DIVISION OF (1948). Pres. Miriam Lubling; Presidium: Sarah Ivanisky, Tili Stark, Peppi Petzenbaum. Assists Poale Agudath Israel to build and support children's homes, kindergartens, and trade schools in Israel. *Yediot PAI.*

PRO ISRAEL (1990). 1328 Broadway, Suite 1043, NYC. (212)594-8996. FAX: (212) 594-8986. E-mail: proisrael@aol. com. Pres. Dr. Ernest Bloch. Educates the public about Israel and the Middle East; provides support for community development throughout the Land of Israel, particularly in Judea, Samaria, Gaza, and the Golan Heights. Projects include the Ariel Center for Policy Research and Professors for a Strong Israel.

PROJECT NISHMA (*see* ISRAEL POLICY FORUM)

RELIGIOUS ZIONISTS OF AMERICA. 25 W. 26 ST., NYC 10010. (212)689-1414. FAX: (212)779-3043.

———, BNEI AKIVA OF THE U.S. & CANADA (1934). 25 W. 26 St., NYC 10010. (212)889-5260. FAX: (212)213-3053. Exec. Dir. Judi Srebro; Natl. Dir. Ari Schuchman. The only religious Zionist youth movement in North America, serving over 10,000 young people from grade school through graduate school in 16 active regions across the United States and Canada, six summer camps, seven established summer, winter, and year programs in Israel. Stresses communal involvement, social activism, leadership training, and substantive programming to educate young people toward a commitment to Judaism and Israel. *Akivon; Pinkas Lamadrich; Daf Rayonot; Me'Ohalai Torah; Zraim.*

———, MIZRACHI-HAPOEL HAMIZRACHI (1909; merged 1957). 25 W. 26 St., NYC 10010. (212)689-1414. FAX: (212)779-3043. Pres.Rabbi Simcha Krauss; Exec. V.-Pres. Israel Friedman. Disseminates ideals of religious Zionism; conducts cultural work, educational program, public relations; raises funds for religious educational institutions in Israel, including yeshivot hesder and Bnei Akiva. *Newsletters; Kolenu.*

———, NATIONAL COUNCIL FOR TORAH EDUCATION OF MIZRACHI-HAPOEL HAMIZRACHI (1939). 25 W. 26 St., NYC 10010. Pres. Rabbi Israel Schorr. Organizes and supervises yeshivot and Talmud Torahs; prepares and trains teachers; publishes textbooks and educational materials; organizes summer seminars for Hebrew educators in cooperation with Torah Department of Jewish Agency; conducts ulpan. *Hazarkor; Chemed.*

SCHNEIDER CHILDREN'S MEDICAL CENTER OF ISRAEL (1982). 130 E. 59 St., Suite 1203, NYC 10022. (212)759-3370. FAX: (212)759-0120. E-mail: mdiscmci@aol. com. Bd. Chmn. H. Irwin Levy; Exec. Dir. Shlomit Manson. Its primary goal is to provide the best medical care to children in the Middle East. *UPDATE Newsletter*

SOCIETY OF ISRAEL PHILATELISTS (1949). 24355 Tunbridge Lane, Beachwood, OH 44122. (216)292-3843. Pres Michael Kaltman; Journal Ed. Dr. Oscar Stadtler. Promotes interest in, and knowledge of, all phases of Israel philately through sponsorship of chapters and research groups, maintenance of a philatelic library, and support of public and private exhibitions. *The Israel Philatelist; monographs; books.*

STATE OF ISRAEL BONDS (1951). 575 Lexington Ave., Suite 600, NYC 10022. (212)644-2663; (800)229-9650. FAX: (212)644-3887. E-mail: raphaelrothstein@israelbonds.com. Bd. Chmn. Burton P. Resnick; Pres./CEO Gideon Patt. An international organization offering securities issued by the government of Israel. Since its inception in 1951 has secured $20 billion in investment capital for the development of every aspect of Israel's economic infrastructure, including agriculture, commerce, and industry, and for absorption of immigrants. *Israel "Hadashot-News".* W.ISRAELBONDS.COM)

THEODOR HERZL FOUNDATION (1954). 633 Third Ave., 21st fl., NYC 10017. (212)339-6000. FAX: (212)318-6176. Chmn. Kalman Sultanik; Sec. Sam E. Bloch. Offers cultural activities, lectures, conferences, courses in modern Hebrew and Jewish subjects, Israel, Zionism, and Jewish history. *Midstream.*

———, HERZL PRESS. Chmn. Kalman Sultanik; Dir. of Pub. Sam E. Bloch. Serves as "the Zionist Press of record,"publishing books that are important for the light they shed on Zionist philosophy, Israeli history, contemporary Israel and the Diaspora and the relationship between them. They are important as contributions to Zionist letters and history. *Midstream.*

TSOMET-TECHIYA USA (1978). 185 Montague St., 3rd fl., Brooklyn, NY 11201. (718)596-2119. FAX: (718)858-4074. E-mail: eliahu@aol.com. Chmn. Howard B. Weber. Supports the activities of the Israeli Tsomet party, which advocates Israeli control over the entire Land of Israel.

UNITED CHARITY INSTITUTIONS OF JERUSALEM, INC. (1903). 1467 48 St., Brooklyn, NY 11219. (718)633-8469. FAX: (718)633-8478. Chmn. Rabbi Charlop; Exec. Dir. Rabbi Pollak. Raises funds for the maintenance of schools, kitchens, clinics, and dispensaries in Israel; free loan foundations in Israel.

UNITED ISRAEL APPEAL, INC. (1925). 111 Eighth Ave., Suite 11E, NYC 10011. (212)284-6900. FAX: (212)284-6988. Chmn. Bennett L. Aaron; Exec. V.-Chmn. Daniel R. Allen. Provides funds raised by UJA/Federation campaigns in the U.S. to aid the people of Israel through the programs of the Jewish Agency for Israel, UIA's operating agent. Serves as link between American Jewish community and Jewish Agency for Israel; assists in resettlement and absorption of refugees in Israel, and supervises flow and expenditure of funds for this purpose. *Annual report; newsletters; brochures.*

UNITED STATES COMMITTEE SPORTS FOR ISRAEL (*see* MACCABI USA/SPORTS FOR ISRAEL)

US/ISRAEL WOMEN TO WOMEN (1979). 275 Seventh Ave., 8th fl., NYC 10001. (212) 206-8057. FAX: (212) 206-7031. E-mail: usisrw2w@aol.com. Ch. Jewel Bellush; Exec. Dir. Joan Gordon. Provides critical seed money for grassroots efforts advocating equal status and fair treatment for women in all spheres of Israeli life; targets small, innovative, Israeli-run programs that seek to bring about social change in health, education, civil rights, domestic violence, family planning, and other spheres of Israeli life. *Newsletters.*

VOLUNTEERS FOR ISRAEL (1982). 330 W. 42 St., Suite 1618, NYC 10036-6902. (212) 643-4848. FAX: (212)643-4855. E-mail: vol4israel@aol.com. Pres. Rickey Cherner; Exec. Dir. Edie Silberstein. Provides aid to Israel through volunteer work, building lasting relationships between Israelis and Americans. Affords persons aged 18 and over the opportunity to participate in various duties currently performed by overburdened Israelis on IDF bases and in other settings, enabling them to meet and work closely with Israelis and to gain an inside view of Israeli life and culture. *Quarterly newsletter; information documents.*

WOMEN'S LEAGUE FOR ISRAEL, INC. (1928). 160 E. 56 St., NYC 10022. (212)838-1997. FAX: (212)888-5972. Pres. Harriet Lainer; Exec. Dir. Dorothy Leffler. Maintains centers in Haifa, Tel Aviv, Jerusalem, Natanya. Projects include Family Therapy and Training Center, Centers for the Prevention of Domestic Violence, Meeting Places (supervised centers for noncustodial parents and their children), DROR (supporting families at risk), Yachdav-"Together"(long-term therapy for parents and children), Central School for Training Social Service Counselors, the National Library for Social Work, and the Hebrew University Blind Students' Unit.

WORLD CONFEDERATION OF UNITED ZIONISTS (1946; reorg.1958). 130 E. 59 St., NYC 10022. (212)371-1452. FAX: (212) 371-3265. Co-Pres. Marlene Post & Kalman Sultanik. Promotes Zionist education, sponsors nonparty youth movements in the Diaspora, and strives for an Israel-oriented creative Jewish survival in the Diaspora. *Zionist Information Views (in English and Spanish).*

WORLD ZIONIST ORGANIZATION-AMERICAN SECTION (1971). 633 Third Ave., 21st fl., NYC 10017. (212)688-3197. Chmn.

Kalman Sultanik. As the American section of the overall Zionist body throughout the world, it operates primarily in the field of aliyah from the free countries, education in the Diaspora, youth and Hechalutz, organization and information, cultural institutions, publications; conducts a worldwide Hebrew cultural program including special seminars and pedagogic manuals; disperses information and assists in research projects concerning Israel; promotes, publishes, and distributes books, periodicals, and pamphlets concerning developments in Israel, Zionism, and Jewish history. *Midstream.*

———, DEPARTMENT OF EDUCATION AND CULTURE (1948). 633 Third Ave., 21st fl., NYC 10017. (212)339-6001. FAX: (212)826-8959. Renders educational services to boards and schools: study programs, books, AV aids, instruction, teacher-in-training service. Judaic and Hebrew subjects. Annual National Bible Contest; Israel summer and winter programs for teachers and students.

———, ISRAEL ALIYAH CENTER (1993). 633 Third Ave., 21st fl., NYC 10017. (212)339-6060. FAX: (212)832-2597. Exec. Dir. N. Amer. Aliyah Delegation, Kalman Grossman. Through 26 offices throughout N. Amer., staffed by *shlichim* (emissaries), works with potential immigrants to plan their future in Israel and processes immigration documents. Through Israel Aliyah Program Center provides support, information, and programming for olim and their families; promotes long-term programs and fact-finding trips to Israel. Cooperates with Tnuat Aliyah in Jerusalem and serves as American contact with Association of Americans and Canadians in Israel.

YOUTH RENEWAL FUND. 488 MADISON AVE., 10TH fl., NYC 10022. (212)207-3195. FAX: (212)207-8379. E-mail: info@youthrenewalfund.org. Pres. Samuel L. Katz; Exec. Dir. Karen B. Korn. Provides underprivileged Israeli youth with supplemental educational programs in core subjects including math, science, English, Hebrew, and computers. Since 1989, YRF has raised over $6 million, which has benefited more than 12,500 Israeli children. *YRF Review.* (WWW.YOUTHRENEWALFUND.ORG)

ZIONIST ORGANIZATION OF AMERICA (1897). ZOA House, 4 E. 34 St., NYC 10016. (212)481-1500. FAX: (212)481-1515. E-mail: email@zoa.com. Natl. Pres. Morton A. Klein; Exec. Dir. Dr. Janice J. Sokolovsky. Strengthens the relationship between Israel and the U.S. through Zionist educational activities that explain Israel's importance to the U.S. and the dangers that Israel faces. Works on behalf of pro-Israel legislation; combats anti-Israel bias in the media, textbooks, travel guides, and on campuses; promotes *aliyah.* Maintains the ZOA House in Tel Aviv, a cultural center, and the Kfar Silver Agricultural and Technical High School in Ashkelon, which provides vocational training for new immigrants. *ZOAReport; Israel and the Middle East:Behind the Headlines.* (WWW.ZOA. ORG)

OVERSEAS AID

AMERICAN FRIENDS OF THE ALLIANCE ISRAÉLITE UNIVERSELLE, INC. (1946). 420 Lexington Ave., Suite 1731, NYC 10170. (212)808-5437. FAX: (212)983-0094. E-mail: afaiu@onsiteaccess.com. Pres. Albert Sibony; Exec. Dir. Warren Green. Participates in educational and humanrights activities of the AIU and supports the Alliance system of Jewish schools, teachers' colleges, and remedial programs in Israel, North Africa, the Middle East, Europe, and Canada. *Alliance Review.*

AMERICAN JEWISH JOINT DISTRIBUTION COMMITTEE, INC.—JDC (1914). 711 Third Ave., NYC 10017-4014. (212)687-6200. FAX: (212)370-5467. E-mail: newyork@jdcny.org. Pres. Jonathan W. Kolker; Exec. V.-Pres. Michael Schneider. Provides assistance to Jewish communities in Europe, Asia, Africa, and the Mideast, including welfare programs for Jews in need. Current concerns include rescuing Jews from areas of distress, facilitating community development in the former Soviet Union; helping to meet Israel's social service needs by developing innovative programs that create new opportunities for the country's most vulnerable populations; youth activities in Eastern Europe and nonsectarian development and disaster assistance. *Annual Report; Snapshots: JDC's Activities in the Former Soviet Union; JDC: One People, One Heart.* (WWW.JDC.ORG).

AMERICAN JEWISH PHILANTHROPIC FUND (1955). 122 E. 42 St., 12th fl., NYC 10168-

1289. (212)755-5640. FAX: (212)644-0979. Pres. Charles J. Tanenbaum. Provides college scholarship assistance to Jewish refugees through pilot programs being administered by the Jewish Family Service in Los Angeles and NYANA in New York.

AMERICAN JEWISH WORLD SERVICE (1985). 989 Sixth Ave., 10th Fl., NYC 10018. (212)736-2597. FAX: (212) 736-3463. E-mail:jws@jws.org. Chmn. Don Abramson; Pres. Ruth W. Messinger. Provides nonsectarian, humanitarian assistance and emergency relief to people in need in Africa, Asia, Latin America, Russia, Ukraine, and the Middle East; works in partnership with local nongovernmental organizations to support and implement self-sustaining grassroots development projects; serves as a vehicle through which the Jewish community can act as global citizens. *AJWS Reports (newsletter).* (WWW.AJWS.ORG)

AMERICAN ORT, INC. (1922). 817 Broadway, NYC 10003. (212)353-5800/(800)364-9678. FAX: (212)353-5888. E-mail: info@aort.org. Pres. Michael R. Stoler; Exec. V.-Pres. Brian J. Strum. American ORT coordinates all ORT operations in the U.S., in cooperation with Women's American ORT; promotes and raises funds for ORT, the world's largest non-governmental education and training organization, with a global network teaching over 262,000 students in more than 60 countries. In Israel, 100,000 students attend 140 schools and training centers; there are 22 ORT schools and centers in the former Soviet Union; and in the U.S., over 15,000 students are served by ORT's Technical Institutes in Chicago, Los Angeles, and New York, and in Jewish day school programs in Atlanta, Chicago, Cleveland, Detroit, Florida, Los Angeles, and the National Capital Area (Washington, D.C.). *American ORT News; American ORT Annual Report; Monthly Report to the Board of Directors; President's Letter; American ORT Planned Giving Annual Report.* (WWW.AORT.ORG)

————, WOMEN'S AMERICAN ORT (1927). 315 Park Ave. S., NYC 10010-3677. (212)505-7700; (800)51-WAORT. FAX: (212)674-3057. E-mail: waort@waort.org. Pres. Pepi Dunay; Natl. Exec. Dir. Alice Herman. Strengthens the worldwide Jewish community by empowering people to achieve economic self-sufficiency through technological and vocational training; educates 262,000 students in 60 countries including the United States, Israel and the former Soviet Union; supports ORT programs through membership, fundraising and leadership development; domestic agenda promotes quality public education, women's rights and literacy. *Women's American ORT Reporter; Women's American ORT Annual Report.* (WWW.WAORT.ORG)

CONFERENCE ON JEWISH MATERIAL CLAIMS AGAINST GERMANY, INC. (1951). 15 E. 26 St., Rm. 906, NYC 10010. (212)696-4944. FAX: (212)679-2126. E-mail: info@claimscon.org. Pres. Dr. Israel Miller; Exec. V.-Pres. Gideon Taylor. Represents Jewish survivors in negotiations for compensation from the German government and other entities once controlled by the Nazis. Also an operating agency that administers compensation funds, recovers Jewish property and allocates funds to institutions that serve Holocaust survivors. The Claims Conference—made up of the conference on Jewish Material Claims Against Germany and the Committee for Jewish Claims on Austria—is one of the founders of the World Jewish Restitution Organization, Memorial Foundation for Jewish Culture and the United Restitution Organization. *Newsletter; Annual Report; Guide to Restitution and Compensation; Special Update.* (WWW.CLAIMSCON.ORG)

HIAS, INC. (HEBREW IMMIGRANT AID SOCIETY) (1880; reorg. 1954). 333 Seventh Ave., NYC 10001-5004. (212)967-4100. FAX: (212)967-4442. E-mail:info@hias.org. Pres. Neil Greenbaum; Exec. V.-Pres. Leonard Glickman. The oldest international migration and refugee resettlement agency in the United States, dedicated to assisting persecuted and oppressed people worldwide and delivering them to countries of safe haven. As the migration arm of the American Jewish community, it also advocates for fair and just policies affecting refugees and immigrants. Since its founding in 1880, the agency has rescued more than four and a half million people. *Annual report.*

THE JEWISH FOUNDATION FOR THE RIGHTEOUS (1986). 305 Seventh Ave., 19th fl., NYC 10001. (212)727-9955. FAX: (212) 727-9956. E-mail: jfr@jfr.org. Chmn.

Paul Goldberger; Exec. Dir. Stanlee J. Stahl. Provides monthly support to 1,600 aged and needy Righteous Gentiles living in 28 countries who risked their lives to save Jews during the Holocaust. The Foundation's education program focuses on educating teachers and their students about the history of the Holocaust and the significance of altruistic behavior for our society. *Newsletter (3 times a year)*. (WWW.JFR.ORG)

NORTH AMERICAN CONFERENCE ON ETHIOPIAN JEWRY (NACOEJ) (1982). 132 Nassau St., Suite 412, NYC 10038. (212) 233-5200. FAX: (212)233-5243. E-mail: nacoej@aol.com. Pres. Kenneth Kaiserman; Exec. Dir. Barbara Ribakove Gordon. Provides programming for Ethiopian Jews in Israel in the areas of education (elementary school, high school and college) and cultural preservation. Assists Ethiopian Jews remaining in Ethiopia. National speakers bureau offers programs to synagogues, schools, and Jewish and non-Jewish organizations. Exhibits of Ethiopian Jewish artifacts, photos, handicrafts, etc. available. *Lifeline (newsletter)*. (WWW.CIRCUS.ORG/NACOEJ)

RE'UTH WOMEN'S SOCIAL SERVICE, INC. (1937). 130 E. 59 St., Suite 1200, NYC 10022. (212)836-1570. FAX: (212)836-1114. Chmn. Ursula Merkin; Pres. Rosa Strygler. Maintains, in Israel, subsidized housing for self-reliant elderly; old-age homes for more dependent elderly; Lichtenstadter Hospital for chronically ill and young accident victims not accepted by other hospitals; subsidized meals; Golden Age clubs. *Annual dinner journal*.

THANKS TO SCANDINAVIA, INC. (1963). 745 Fifth Ave., Rm. 603, NYC 10151. (212)486-8600. FAX: (212)486-5735. Natl. Chmn. Victor Borge; Pres. Richard Netter. Provides scholarships and fellowships at American universities and medical centers to students and doctors from Denmark, Finland, Norway, and Sweden in appreciation of the rescue of Jews from the Holocaust. Informs Americans and Scandinavians of these singular examples of humanity and bravery. Speakers available on rescue in Scandinavia; also books, videos, and tapes. *Annual report*.

UJA FEDERATION OF NORTH AMERICA. (1939). (*see* UNITED JEWISH COMMUNITIES)

UNITED JEWISH COMMUNITIES (1999). 111 Eighth Ave., 11th fl., NYC 10011-5201. (212)284-6500. FAX: (212)284-6873. Bd. Chmn. Charles R. Bronfman; Pres./CEO Stephen D. Solender. Formed by a merger of the United Jewish Appeal with the Council of Jewish Federations and United Israel Appeal; represents N. American Jewry's primary fund-raising and service-providing agencies.

RELIGIOUS AND EDUCATIONAL ORGANIZATIONS

AGUDATH ISRAEL OF AMERICA (1922). 84 William St., NYC 10038. (212)797-9000. FAX: (212)269-2843. Exec. V.-Pres. Rabbi Samuel Bloom; Exec. Dir. Rabbi Boruch B. Borchardt. Mobilizes Orthodox Jews to cope with Jewish problems in the spirit of the Torah; speaks out on contemporary issues from an Orthodox viewpoint; sponsors a broad range of projects aimed at enhancing religious living, education, children's welfare, protection of Jewish religious rights, outreach to the assimilated and to arrivals from the former Soviet Union, and social services. *Jewish Observer; Dos Yiddishe Vort; Coalition.*

————, AGUDAH WOMEN OF AMERICA-N'SHEI AGUDATH ISRAEL (1940). 84 William St., NYC 10038. (212)363-8940. FAX: (212)747-8763. Presidium Aliza Grund & Rose Isbee; Dir. Hannah Kalish, Esq. Organizes Jewish women for philanthropic work in the U.S. and Israel and for intensive Torah education. Its new division, N'shei C.A.R.E.S., (Community, Awareness, Responsibility, Education, & Support), conducts seminars and support groups promoting the health and well-being of Jewish women and their families.

————, BOYS' DIVISION-PIRCHEI AGUDATH ISRAEL (1925). 84 William St., NYC 10038 (212)797-9000. Natl. Coord. Rabbi Shimon Grama. Educates Orthodox Jewish children in Torah; encourages sense of communal responsibility. Branches sponsor weekly youth groups and Jewish welfare projects. National Mishnah contests, rallies, and conventions foster unity on a national level. *Leaders Guides.*

————, GIRLS' DIVISION—BNOS AGUDATH ISRAEL (1921). 84 William St., NYC 10038. (212)797-9000. Natl. Dir. Leah Zagelbaum. Sponsors regular weekly programs on the local level and unites girls from throughout the Torah world with extensive regional and national activities. *Kol Bnos.*

———, YOUNG MEN'S DIVISION—ZEIREI AGUDATH ISRAEL (1921). 84 William St., NYC 10038. (212)797-9000, ext. 57. Dir. Rabbi Labish Becker. Educates youth to see Torah as source of guidance for all issues facing Jews as individuals and as a people. Inculcates a spirit of activism through projects in religious, Torah-educational, and community-welfare fields. *Am Hatorah; Daf Chizuk.*

AGUDATH ISRAEL WORLD ORGANIZATION (1912). 84 William St., NYC 10038. (212) 797-9000. FAX: (212)269-2843. Chmn. Rabbi Yehudah Meir Abramowitz; U.N. Rep. Prof. Harry Reicher, Esq. Represents the interests of Orthodox Jewry on the national and international scenes. Sponsors projects to strengthen Torah life worldwide.

ALEPH: ALLIANCE FOR JEWISH RENEWAL (1963; reorg. 1993). 7318 Germantown Ave., Philadelphia, PA 19119-1720. (215) 247-9700. FAX: (215)247-9703. Bd. Chmn. Dr. Sheldon Isenberg; Exec. Dir. R. Daniel Siegel. A multifaceted international organization serving the movement for Jewish renewal. Activities include creation and dissemination of publications, liturgy, curricula, audio and video tapes; a biennial Kallah of about 900 adults; lay and professional leadership training; spiritual activism on social and environmental issues; Ohalah, the Association of Rabbis for Jewish Renewal; and a network of local Jewish renewal communities. *New Menorah (quarterly journal); Or HaDor (newsletter of congregations and havurot affiliated with ALEPH through the Network of Jewish Renewal Communities).*

AM KOLEL JUDAIC RESOURCE CENTER (1990). 15 W. Montgomery Ave., Rockville, MD 20850. (301)309-2310. FAX: (301)309-2328. E-mail: amkolel@aol.com. Pres. David Shneyer. An independent Jewish resource center, providing a progressive Jewish voice in the community. Activities include:religion, educational and cultural programs; classes, workshops and seminars; interfaith workshops and programs; tikkun olam (social action) opportunities. The staff provides training and resources to emerging and independent communities throughout N.

America. *Directory of Independent Jewish Communities and Havurot in Maryland, DC and Virginia; Rock Creek Haggadah.*

AMERICAN ASSOCIATION OF RABBIS (1978). 350 Fifth Ave., Suite 3304, NYC 10118. (212)244-3350, (516)244-7113. FAX: (516)344-0779. E-mail: tefu@aol.com. Pres. Rabbi Jeffrey Wartenberg; Exec. Dir. Rabbi David L. Dunn. An organization of rabbis serving in pulpits, in areas of education, and in social work. *Quarterly bulletin; monthly newsletter.*

AMERICAN STUDENTS TO ACTIVATE PRIDE (ASAP/OU COLLEGE AFFAIRS) (1993). 11 Broadway, 14th fl., NYC 10004. (212) 563-4000. FAX: (212)564-9058. E-mail: davidfel@ix.netcom.com. Pres. Zelda Goldsmith; Natl. Dir. Rabbi David Felsenthal; Chmn. Bernard Falk. A spiritual fitness movement of Jewish college students promoting Torah learning and discussion. Supports 100 learning groups at over 65 campuses as well as regional and national seminars and shabbatonim. *Good Shabbos (weekly); Rimon Discussion Guide (monthly); Jewish Student College Survival Guide (yearly).*

ASSOCIATION FOR JEWISH STUDIES (1969). MB 0001, Brandeis University, PO Box 549110, Waltham, MA 02454-9110. (781) 736-2981. FAX: (781)736-2982. E-mail: ajs@brandeis.edu. Pres. David Berger; Exec. Dir. Aaron L. Katchen. Seeks to promote, maintain, and improve the teaching of Jewish studies in colleges and universities by sponsoring meetings and conferences, publishing a newsletter and other scholarly materials, aiding in the placement of teachers, coordinating research, and cooperating with other scholarly organizations. *AJS Review;AJS Perspectives.*

ASSOCIATION FOR THE SOCIAL SCIENTIFIC STUDY OF JEWRY (1971). c/o Dr. Rela M. Geffen, Gratz College, 7605 Old York Rd., Melrose Park, PA 19027. (215)635-7300. FAX: (215)635-7320. E-mail: aglicksman@aol.com; rela1@aol.com. Pres. Allen Glicksman; V.-Pres. Riv-Ellen Prell; Sec.-Treas. Bruce Phillips. Journal Ed. Rela Geffen; Mng. Ed. Egon Mayer; Newsletter Ed. Gail Glicksman. Arranges academic sessions and facilitates communication among social scientists studying Jewry through meetings, journal, newsletter and related materials and activities. *Contemporary Jewry; ASSJ Newsletter.*

ASSOCIATION OF HILLEL/JEWISH CAMPUS PROFESSIONALS (*see* TEKIAH: ASSOCIATION OF HILLEL/JEWISH CAMPUS PROFESSIONALS)

ASSOCIATION OF ORTHODOX JEWISH SCIENTISTS (1948). 25 W. 45 St., Suite 1405, NYC 10036. (212)840-1166. FAX: (212) 840-1514. E-mail: aojs@jerusalemail. com. Pres. Allen J. Bennett, M.D.; Bd. Chmn. Rabbi Nachman Cohen. Seeks to contribute to the development of science within the framework of Orthodox Jewish tradition; to obtain and disseminate information relating to the interaction between the Jewish traditional way of life and scientific developments—on both an ideological and practical level; to assist in the solution of problems pertaining to Orthodox Jews engaged in scientific teaching or research. Two main conventions are held each year. *Intercom; Proceedings; Halacha Bulletin; newsletter.*

B'NAI B'RITH HILLEL FOUNDATIONS (*see* HILLEL)

B'NAI B'RITH YOUTH ORGANIZATION (1924). 1640 Rhode Island Ave., NW, Washington, DC 20036. (202)857-6633. FAX: (212)857-6568. Chmn. Youth Comm. Audrey Y. Brooks; Dir. Sam Fisher. Helps Jewish teenagers achieve self-fulfillment and make a maximum contribution to the Jewish community and their country's culture; helps members acquire a greater knowledge and appreciation of Jewish religion and culture. *Shofar; Monday Morning; BBYO Parents' Line; Hakol; Kesher; The Connector.*

CANTORS ASSEMBLY (1947). 3080 Broadway, Suite 613, NYC 10027. (212)678-8834. FAX: (212)662-8989. E-mail: caoffice@ jtsa.edu. Pres. Chaim Najman; Exec. V.-Pres. Stephen J. Stein. Seeks to unite all cantors who adhere to traditional Judaism and who serve as full-time cantors in bona fide congregations to conserve and promote the musical traditions of the Jews and to elevate the status of the cantorial profession. *Annual Proceedings; Journal of Synagogue Music.* (WWW.JTSA. EDU/ORG/CANTOR)

CENTER FOR CHRISTIAN-JEWISH UNDERSTANDING OF SACRED HEART UNIVERSITY (1992). 5151 Park Ave., Fairfield, CT 06432. (203)365-7592. FAX: (203)365-4815. Pres. Dr. Anthony J. Cernera; Exec. Dir. Rabbi Joseph H. Ehrenkranz. An educational and research division of Sacred Heart University; brings together clergy, laity, scholars, theologians, and educators with the purpose of promoting interreligious research, education, and dialogue, with particular focus on current religious thinking within Christianity and Judaism. *CCJU Perspective.*

CENTRAL CONFERENCE OF AMERICAN RABBIS (1889). 355 Lexington Ave., NYC 10017. (212)972-3636. FAX: (212)692-0819. E-mail: info@ccarnet.org. Pres. Rabbi Charles A. Kroloff; Exec. V.-Pres. Rabbi Paul J. Menitoff. Seeks to conserve and promote Judaism and to disseminate its teachings in a liberal spirit. The CCAR Press provides liturgy and prayerbooks to the worldwide Reform Jewish community. *CCAR Journal: A Reform Jewish Quarterly; CCAR Yearbook.* (WWW.CCARNET. ORG)

CLAL—NATIONAL JEWISH CENTER FOR LEARNING AND LEADERSHIP (1974). 440 Park Ave. S., 4th fl., NYC 10016-8012. (212)779-3300. FAX: (212)779-1009. E-mail: info@clal.org. Pres. Rabbi Irwin Kula; Chmn. Barbara B. Friedman; Exec. V.-Chmn. Donna M. Rosenthal. Provides leadership training for lay leaders, rabbis, educators, and communal professionals. A faculty of rabbis and scholars representing all the denominations of Judaism make Judaism come alive, applying the wisdom of the Jewish heritage to help shape tomorrow's Jewish communities. Offers seminars and courses, retreats, symposia and conferences, lecture bureau and the latest on-line information through CLAL web site. *Sacred Days calendar; monographs; holiday brochures; CLAL Update.* (WWW.CLAL.ORG)

COALITION FOR THE ADVANCEMENT OF JEWISH EDUCATION (CAJE) (1977). 261 W. 35 St., #12A, NYC 10001. (212)268-4210. FAX: (212)268-4214. E-mail: cajeny@ caje.org. Chmn. Sylvia Abrams; Exec. Dir. Dr. Eliot G. Spack. Brings together Jews from all ideologies who are involved in every facet of Jewish education and are committed to transmitting the Jewish heritage. Sponsors annual Conference on Alternatives in Jewish Education and Curriculum Bank; publishes a wide variety of publications; organizes shared-interest networks; offers mini-grants for special projects; sponsors Mini-CAJEs (one- or two-day in-service programs) around the country; maintains a website for Jewish educators. *Jewish Education News; CAJE Page; timely curricular publications; Hanukat CAJE series.* (WWW.CAJE.ORG)

CONGRESS OF SECULAR JEWISH ORGANIZATIONS (1970). 19657 Villa Dr. N., Southfield, MI 48076. (248)569-8127. FAX: (248)569-5222. E-mail: rifke@earthlink.net. Chmn. Jeff Zolitor; V.-Chmn. Julie Gales; Exec. Dir. Roberta E. Feinstein. An umbrella organization of schools and adult clubs; facilitates exchange of curricula and educational programs for children and adults stressing the Jewish historical and cultural heritage and the continuity of the Jewish people. *New Yorkish (Yiddish literature translations); Haggadah; The Hanuka Festival; Mame-Loshn.*

CONVERSION TO JUDAISM RESOURCE CENTER (1997). 74 Hauppauge Rd., Rm. 53, Commack, NY 11725. (516) 462-5826. E-mail: inform@convert.org. Pres. Dr. Lawrence J. Epstein; Exec. Dir. Susan Lustig. Provides information and advice for people who wish to convert to Judaism or who have converted. Puts potential converts in touch with rabbis from all branches of Judaism.

COUNCIL FOR JEWISH EDUCATION (1926) 426 W. 58 St., NYC 10019. (914)368-8657. Pres. Dr. Morton J. Summer; Journal Ed. Dr. Bernard Ducoff. Fellowship of Jewish education professionals-administrators, supervisors, and teachers in Hebrew high schools and Jewish teachers colleges-of all ideological groupings; conducts national and regional conferences; represents the Jewish education profession before the Jewish community; co-sponsors, with the Jewish Education Service of North America, a personnel committee and other projects; cooperates with Jewish Agency Department of Education in promoting Hebrew culture and studies. *Journal of Jewish Education.*

EDAH (1996) 47 W. 34 St., Suite 700, NYC 10001. (212) 244-7501. FAX: (212)244-7855. Pres. Dr. Michael Hammer; Dir. Rabbi Saul J. Berman. Gives voice to the ideology and values of modern Orthodoxy, valuing open intellectual inquiry and expression in both secular and religious arenas, engagement with the social, political, and technological realities of the modern world, the religious significance of the State of Israel, and the unity of Clal Yisrael. *Monograph series.*

FEDERATION OF JEWISH MEN'S CLUBS (1929). 475 Riverside Dr., Suite 450, NYC 10115. (212)749-8100; (800)288-FJMC. FAX: (212)316-4271. E-mail: fjmc@jtsa. edu. Intl. Pres. Leonard Gimb; Exec. Dir. Rabbi Charles E. Simon. Promotes principles of Conservative Judaism; develops family education and leadership training programs; offers the Art of Jewish Living series and Yom HaShoah Home Commemoration; sponsors Hebrew literacy adult-education program; presents awards for service to American Jewry. Latest innovation-"The Ties that Bind,"a motivational and instructional video about Tefillin. *Torchlight; Hearing Men's Voices.* (WWW.FJMC.ORG)

FEDERATION OF RECONSTRUCTIONIST CONGREGATIONS AND HAVUROT (*see* JEWISH RECONSTRUCTIONIST FEDERATION)

HILLEL: THE FOUNDATION FOR JEWISH CAMPUS LIFE (formerly B'NAI B'RITH HILLEL FOUNDATIONS) (1923). 1640 Rhode Island Ave., NW, Washington, DC 20036. (202)857-6576. FAX: (202)857-6693. E-mail: info@hillel.org. Chmn. Intl. Bd. Govs. Edgar M. Bronfman; Chmn. Foundation for Jewish Campus Life Chuck Newman; Chmn. B'nai B'rith Hillel Comm. Robert B. Spitzer; Pres. & Intl. Dir. Richard M. Joel. The largest Jewish campus organization in the world, its network of 500 regional centers, campus-based foundations, and affiliates serves as a catalyst for creating a celebratory community and a rich, diverse Jewish life on the campus. *The Hillel Annual Report; On Campus newsletter; Hillel Now newsletter; The Hillel Guide to Jewish Life on Campus (published with Princeton Review).* (WWW. HILLEL.ORG)

INSTITUTE FOR COMPUTERS IN JEWISH LIFE (1978). 7074 N. Western Ave., Chicago, IL 60645. (773)262-9200. FAX: (773)262-9298. E-mail: rosirv@aol.com. Pres. Thomas Klutznick; Exec. V.-Pres. Dr. Irving J. Rosenbaum. Explores, develops, and disseminates applications of computer technology to appropriate areas of Jewish life, with special emphasis on Jewish education; creates educational software for use in Jewish schools; provides consulting service and assistance for national Jewish organizations, seminaries, and synagogues.

INTERNATIONAL FEDERATION OF SECULAR HUMANISTIC JEWS (1983). 28611 West Twelve Mile Rd., Farmington Hills, MI 48334. (248)476-9532. FAX: (248)476-8509. E-mail: iishj@speedlink.net. Co-Ch. Yair Tzaban (Israel) & Sherwin Wine (USA). Consists of national organizations in Israel, the United States, Canada, Britain, France, Belgium, Australia, Mexico, Argentina, Uruguay and the countries of the former Soviet Union, involving some 50,000 Jews. The Honorary Co-Chairs are Albert Memmi, well-known French writer and professor of sociology at the University of Paris, and Yehuda Bauer, noted historian and Holocaust scholar at the Hebrew University in Jerusalem. *Newsletter.*

INTERNATIONAL INSTITUTE FOR SECULAR HUMANISTIC JUDAISM (1985). 28611 West Twelve Mile Rd., Farmington Hills, MI 48334. (248)476-9532. FAX: (248)476-8509. E-mail: iishj@speedlink.net. Chmn. Rabbi Sherwin T. Wine. Established in 1985 in Jerusalem to serve the needs of a growing movement, its two primary purposes are to commission and publish educational materials and to train rabbis, leaders, teachers, and spokespersons for the movement. The Institute has two offices-one in Israel (Jerusalem) and one in N. America and offers educational and training programs in Israel, N. America, and the countries of the former Soviet Union. The N. American office, located in a suburb of Detroit, offers the Rabbinic Program, the Leadership Program, and the Adult Education Program. *Brochure, educational papers, and projects.*

JEWISH CHAUTAUQUA SOCIETY, INC. (SPONSORED BY NORTH AMERICAN FEDERATION OF TEMPLE BROTHERHOODS) (1893). 633 Third Ave., NYC 10017. (212)650-4100/ (800)765-6200. FAX: (212)650-4189. E-mail: jcs@uahc.org. Pres. Irving B. Shnaider; Chancellor Stuart J. Aaronson; Exec. Dir. Douglas E. Barden. Works to promote interfaith understanding by sponsoring accredited college courses and one-day lectures on Judaic topics, providing book grants to educational institutions, producing educational videotapes on interfaith topics, and convening inter-

faith institutes. A founding sponsor of the National Black/Jewish Relations Center at Dillard University. *ACHIM Magazine.*

JEWISH EDUCATION IN MEDIA (1978). PO Box 180, Riverdale Sta., NYC 10471. (212)362-7633. FAX: (203)359-1381. Pres. Ken Asher; Exec. Dir. Rabbi Mark S. Golub. Devoted to producing television, film, and videocassettes for a popular Jewish audience, in order to inform, entertain, and inspire a greater sense of Jewish identity and Jewish commitment. "L'Chayim,"JEM's weekly half-hour program, which is seen nationally on NJT/National Jewish Television, features outstanding figures in the Jewish world addressing issues and events of importance to the Jewish community. (WWW.LCHAYIM.COM)

JEWISH EDUCATION SERVICE OF NORTH AMERICA (JESNA) (1981). 111 Eighth Ave., 11th fl., NYC 10011. (212)284-6950. FAX: (212)284-6951. E-mail: info@jesna. org. Pres. Jonathan S. Woocher; Bd. Ch. Joseph Kanfer. The Jewish Federation system's educational coordinating, planning, and development agency. Promotes excellence in Jewish education by initiating exchange of ideas, programs, and materials; providing information, consultation, educational resources, and policy guidance; and collaborating with partners in N. America and Israel to develop educational programs. *Agenda:Jewish Education; planning guides on Jewish Renaissance; research reports; Jewish Educators Electronic Toolkit.* (WWW.JESNA.ORG)

JEWISH RECONSTRUCTIONIST FEDERATION (formerly FEDERATION OF RECONSTRUCTIONIST CONGREGATIONS AND HAVUROT) (1954). 7804 Montgomery Ave., Suite 9, Elkins Park, PA 19027-2649. (215)782-8500. Fax: (215)782-8805. E-mail: info@ jrf.org. Pres. Richard Haimowitz; Exec. V.-Pres. Mark Seal. Provides educational and consulting services to affiliated congregations and havurot; fosters the establishment of new Reconstructionist communities. Publishes *Kol Haneshamah,* an innovative series of prayer books, including a new mahzor and haggadah; provides programmatic materials. Regional offices in NewYork, Los Angeles, and Chicago. *Reconstructionism Today.* (WWW.JRF.ORG)

———, RECONSTRUCTIONIST RABBINICAL ASSOCIATION (1974). 1299 Church Rd.,

Wyncote, PA 19095. (215)576-5210. FAX: (215)576-8051. E-mail: rraassoc@aol. com. Pres. Rabbi Dan Ehrenkrantz; Exec. Dir. Rabbi Richard Hirsh. Professional organization for graduates of the Reconstructionist Rabbinical College and other rabbis who identify with Reconstructionist Judaism; cooperates with Jewish Reconstructionist Federation in furthering Reconstructionism in the world. *Newsletters; position papers.*

———, RECONSTRUCTIONIST RABBINICAL COLLEGE (*see* p. 544)

JEWISH TEACHERS ASSOCIATION—MORIM (1931). 45 E. 33 St., Suite 310, NYC 10016-5336. (212)684-0556. Pres. Phyllis L. Pullman; V.-Pres. Ronni David; Sec. Helen Parnes; Treas. Mildred Safar. Protects teachers from abuse of seniority rights; fights the encroachment of anti-Semitism in education; offers scholarships to qualified students; encourages teachers to assume active roles in Jewish communal and religious affairs. *Morim JTA Newsletter.*

KULANU, INC. (formerly AMISHAV USA) (1993). 11603 Gilsan St., Silver Spring, MD 20902. (301)681-5679. FAX: (301) 681-5679. Pres. Jack Zeller; Sec. Karen Primack. Engages in outreach to dispersed Jewish communities around the world who wish to return to their Jewish roots. Current projects include the formal conversion of Shinlung-Menashe tribesmen in India currently practicing Judaism, and supplying materials and rabbis for conversos/marranos in Mexico and Brazil. *Newsletter.*

NATIONAL COMMITTEE FOR FURTHERANCE OF JEWISH EDUCATION (1941). 824 Eastern Pkwy., Brooklyn, NY 11213. (718)735-0200; (800)33-NCFJE. FAX: (718)735-4455. Pres. Dr. Steven Rubel; Bd. Chmn. Rabbi Shea Hecht; Chmn. Exec. Com. Rabbi Sholem Ber Hecht. Seeks to disseminate the ideals of Torah-true education among the youth of America; provides education and compassionate care for the poor, sick, and needy in U.S. and Israel; provides aid to Iranian Jewish youth; sponsors camps and educational functions, family and vocational counseling services, family and early intervention, after-school and preschool programs, drug and alcohol education and prevention; maintains schools in Brooklyn and Queens. *Panorama; Cultbusters; Intermarriage; Brimstone & Fire; Focus; A Life Full of Giving.*

NATIONAL COUNCIL OF YOUNG ISRAEL (1912). 3 W. 16 St., NYC 10011. (212)929-1525. FAX: (212)727-9526. E-mail: ncyi@ youngisrael.org. Pres. Shlomo Mostofsky; Exec. V.-Pres. Rabbi Pesach Lerner. Through its network of member synagogues in N. America and Israel maintains a program of spiritual, cultural, social, and communal activity aimed at the advancement and perpetuation of traditional, Torah-true Judaism; seeks to instill in American youth an understanding and appreciation of the ethical and spiritual values of Judaism. Sponsors rabbinic and lay leadership conferences, synagogue services, rabbinic services, rabbinic and lay leader training, rabbinic placement, women's division, kosher dining clubs, and youth programs. *Viewpoint Magazine; Divrei Torah Bulletin; NCYI Suggestion Box; The Rabbi's Letter.* (WWW.YOUNGISRAEL.ORG)

———, AMERICAN FRIENDS OF YOUNG ISRAEL IN ISRAEL—YISRAEL HATZA'IR (1926). 3 W. 16 St., NYC 10011. (212)929-1525. FAX: (212)727-9526. E-mail: ncyi@ youngisrael.org. Pres. Meir Mishkoff. Promotes Young Israel synagogues and youth work in Israel; works to help absorb Russian and Ethiopian immigrants.

———, YOUNG ISRAEL DEPARTMENT OF YOUTH AND YOUNG ADULTS ACTIVITIES (reorg. 1981). 3 W. 16 St., NYC 10011. (212)929-1525; (800)617-NCYI. FAX: (212)243-1222. Email:youth@youngisrael.org. Chmn. Kenneth Block; Dir. Richard Stareshefsky. Fosters varied program of activities for the advancement and perpetuation of traditional Torah-true Judaism; instills ethical and spiritual values and appreciation for compatibility of ancient faith of Israel with good Americanism. Runs leadership training programs and youth shabbatonim; support programs for synagogue youth programs; annual national conference of youth directors; ACHVA summer programs for teens IN Israel and U.S.; Nachala summer program in Israel for Yeshiva H.S. girls and Natzach summer program for Yeshiva H.S. boys. *Torah Kidbits; Shabbat Youth Manual; Y.I. Can Assist You; Synagogue Youth Director Handbook.*

NATIONAL HAVURAH COMMITTEE (1979). 7135 Germantown Ave., Philadelphia, PA 19119-1720. (215)248-1335. FAX: (215) 248-9760. E-mail: institute@havurah.org. Ch. Solomon Mowshowitz. A center for Jewish renewal devoted to spreading Jewish ideas, ethics, and religious practices through havurot, participatory and inclusive religious mini-communities. Maintains a directory of N. American havurot and sponsors a weeklong summer institute, regional weekend retreats. *Havurah! (newsletter).* (WWW.HAVURAH.ORG)

NATIONAL JEWISH CENTER FOR LEARNING AND LEADERSHIP (*see* CLAL)

NATIONAL JEWISH COMMITTEE ON SCOUTING (BOY SCOUTS OF AMERICA) (1926). 1325 West Walnut Hill Lane, PO Box 152079, Irving, TX 75015-2079. (972)580-2000. FAX: (972)580-7870. Chmn. Jerrold Lockshin. Assists Jewish institutions in meeting their needs and concerns through use of the resources of scouting. Works through local Jewish committees on scouting to establish Tiger Cub groups (1st grade), Cub Scout packs, Boy Scout troops, and coed Explorer posts in synagogues, Jewish community centers, day schools, and other Jewish organizations wishing to draw Jewish youth. Support materials and resources on request.

NATIONAL JEWISH GIRL SCOUT COMMITTEE (1972). 33 Central Dr., Bronxville, NY 10708. (914)738-3986, (718)252-6072. FAX: (914)738-6752. E-mail: njgsc@aol.com. Chmn. Rabbi Herbert W. Bomzer; Field Chmn. Adele Wasko. Serves to further Jewish education by promoting Jewish award programs, encouraging religious services, promoting cultural exchanges with the Israel Boy and Girl Scouts Federation, and extending membership in the Jewish community by assisting councils in organizing Girl Scout troops and local Jewish Girl Scout committees. *Newsletter.*

NATIONAL JEWISH HOSPITALITY COMMITTEE (1973; reorg. 1993). PO Box 53691, Philadelphia, PA 19105. (800)745-0301. Pres. Rabbi Allen S. Maller; Exec. Dir. Steven S. Jacobs. Assists persons interested in Judaism-for intermarriage, conversion, general information, or to respond to missionaries. *Special reports.*

OZAR HATORAH, INC. (1946). 1350 Sixth Ave., 32nd fl., NYC 10019. (212)582-2050. FAX: (212) 307-0044. Pres. Joseph Shalom; Sec. Sam Sutton; Exec. Dir. Rabbi Biniamine Amoyelle. An international educational network which builds Sephardic communities worldwide through Jewish education.

PARDES PROGRESSIVE ASSOCIATION OF REFORM DAY SCHOOLS (1990). 633 Third Ave., NYC 10017-6778. (212)650-4000. FAX: (480)951-0829. E-mail: educate@uahc.org. Pres. Zita Gardner; Chmn. Carol Nemo. An affiliate of the Union of American Hebrew Congregations; brings together day schools and professional and lay leaders committed to advancing the cause of full-time Reform Jewish education; advocates for the continuing development of day schools within the Reform movement as a means to foster Jewish identity, literacy, and continuity; promotes cooperation among our member schools and with other Jewish organizations that share similar goals. *Visions of Excellence (manual).*

P'EYLIM-LEV L'ACHIM (1951). 1034 E. 12 St. Brooklyn, NY 11230. (718)258-7760. FAX: (718)258-4672. E-mail: joskarmel @aol.com. Natl. Dir. Rabbi Joseph C. Karmel; Exec. V.-Pres. Rabbi Nachum Barnetsky. Seeks to bring irreligious Jews in Israel back to their heritage. Conducts outreach through 12 major divisions consisting of thousands of volunteers and hundreds of professionals across the country; conducts anti-missionary and assimilation programs; operates shelters for abused women and children; recruits children for Torah schools.

RABBINICAL ALLIANCE OF AMERICA (IGUD HARABONIM) (1942). 3 W. 16 St., 4th fl., NYC 10011. (212)242-6420. FAX: (212)255-8313. Pres. Rabbi Abraham B. Hecht; Admin. Judge of Beth Din (Rabbinical Court) Rabbi Herschel Kurzrock. Seeks to promulgate the cause of Torah-true Judaism through an organized rabbinate that is consistently Orthodox; seeks to elevate the position of Orthodox rabbis nationally and to defend the welfare of Jews the world over. Also has Beth Din Rabbinical Court for Jewish divorces, litigation, marriage counseling, and family problems. *Perspective; Nahalim; Torah Message of the Week; Registry.*

RABBINICAL ASSEMBLY (1901). 3080 Broadway, NYC 10027. (212)280-6000. FAX:

(212)749-9166. Pres. Rabbi Vernon H. Kurtz; Exec. V.-Pres. Rabbi Joel H. Meyers. The international association of Conservative rabbis; actively promotes the cause of Conservative Judaism and works to benefit *klal yisrael;* publishes learned texts, prayer books, and works of Jewish interest; administers the work of the Committee on Jewish Law and Standards for the Conservative movement; serves the professional and personal needs of its members through publications, conferences, and benefit programs and administers the movement's Joint Placement Commission. *Conservative Judaism; Proceedings of the Rabbinical Assembly; Rabbinical Assembly Newsletter.*

RABBINICAL COUNCIL OF AMERICA, INC. (1923; reorg. 1935). 305 Seventh Ave., Suite 1200, NYC 10001. (212)807-7888. FAX: (212)727-8452. Pres. Rabbi Kenneth Hain; Exec. V.-Pres. Rabbi Steven M. Dworken. Promotes Orthodox Judaism in the community; supports institutions for study of Torah; stimulates creation of new traditional agencies. *Hadorom; RCA Record; Sermon Manual; Tradition; Resource Magazine.* (www.RABBIS.ORG)

SOCIETY FOR HUMANISTIC JUDAISM (1969). 28611 W. Twelve Mile Rd., Farmington Hills, MI 48334. (248)478-7610. FAX: (248)478-3159. E-mail: info@shj.org. Pres. Bert Steinberg; Exec. Dir. M. Bonnie Cousens. Serves as a voice for Jews who value their Jewish identity and who seek an alternative to conventional Judaism, who reject supernatural authority and affirm the right of individuals to be the masters of their own lives. Publishes educational and ceremonial materials; organizes congregations and groups. *Humanistic Judaism (quarterly journal); Humanorah (quarterly newsletter).* (www.SHJ.ORG)

TEKIAH: ASSOCIATION OF HILLEL/JEWISH CAMPUS PROFESSIONALS (1949). c/o Hillel Foundation of New Orleans, 912 Broadway, New Orleans, LA 70118. (504)866-7060. FAX: (504)861-8909. E-mail: president@tekiah.org. Pres. Rabbi Jeffrey Kurtz-Lendner. Seeks to promote professional relationships and exchanges of experience, develop personnel standards and qualifications, safeguard integrity of Hillel profession; represents and advocates before the Foundation for Jewish Campus Life, Council of Jewish Federations. *Handbook for Hillel Professionals; Guide to Hillel Personnel Practices.* (WWW.TEKIAH.ORG)

TEVA LEARNING CENTER/SHOMREI ADAMAH (1988). 307 Seventh Ave., #900, NYC 10001. (212)807-6376. FAX: (212)924-5112. E-mail: tevacenter@aol.com. Co-Dir. Nili Simhai (Dir. of Ed. & Prog.) & Amy Bram (Dir. of Admin.) Exists to renew the ecological wisdom inherent in Judaism. Runs Jewish environmental education programs for Jewish day schools, synagogues, community centers, camps and other organized groups. *A Garden of Choice Fruit; Let the Earth Teach You Torah.*

TORAH SCHOOLS FOR ISRAEL–CHINUCH ATZMAI (1953). 40 Exchange Pl., NYC 10005. (212)248-6200. FAX: (212)248-6202. Pres. Rabbi Abraham Pam; Exec. Dir. Rabbi Henach Cohen. Conducts information programs for the American Jewish community on activities of the independent Torah schools educational network in Israel; coordinates role of American members of international board of governors; funds special programs of Mercaz Hachinuch Ha-Atzmai B'Eretz Yisroel; funds religous education programs in America and abroad.

TORAH UMESORAH–NATIONAL SOCIETY FOR HEBREW DAY SCHOOLS (1944). 160 Broadway, NYC 10038. (212)227-1000. FAX: (212)406-6934. E-mail: umesorah@aol.com. Chmn. David Singer; Pres. Yaakov Rajchenbach; Exec. V.-Pres. Rabbi Joshua Fishman. Establishes Hebrew day schools and Yeshivas in U.S. and Canada and provides a full gamut of services, including placement, curriculum guidance, and teacher training. Parent Enrichment Program provides enhanced educational experience for students from less Jewishly educated and marginally affiliated homes through parent-education programs and Partners in Torah, a one-on-one learning program. Publishes textbooks; runs shabbatonim, extracurricular activities; national PTA groups; national and regional teacher conventions. *Olomeinu-Our World.*

———, NATIONAL ASSOCIATION OF HEBREW DAY SCHOOL PARENT-TEACHER ASSOCIATIONS (1948). 160 Broadway, NYC 10038. (212)227-1000. FAX: (212)406-

6934. Natl. PTA Coord. Bernice Brand. Acts as a clearinghouse and service agency to PTAs of Hebrew day schools; organizes parent education courses and sets up programs for individual PTAs. *Fundraising with a Flair; PTA with a Purpose for the Hebrew Day School.*

———, NATIONAL CONFERENCE OF YESHIVA PRINCIPALS (1956). 160 Broadway, NYC 10038. (212)227-1000. FAX: (212)406-6934. E-mail: umesorah@aol.com. Pres. Rabbi Rabbi Schneur Aisenstark; Bd. Chmn. Rabbi Dov Leibenstein; Exec. V.-Pres. Rabbi A. Moshe Possick. Professional organization of elementary and secondary yeshivah/day school principals providing yeshivah/day schools with school evaluation and guidance, teacher and principal conferences-including a Mid-Winter Conference and a National Educators Convention; offers placement service for principals and teachers in yeshivah/day schools. *Directory of Elementary Schools and High Schools.*

———, NATIONAL YESHIVA TEACHERS BOARD OF LICENSE (1953). 160 Broadway, NYC 10038. (212)227-1000. Exec. V.-Pres. Rabbi Joshua Fishman; Dir. Rabbi Yitzchock Merkin. Issues licenses to qualified instructors for all grades of the Hebrew day school and the general field of Torah education.

UNION FOR TRADITIONAL JUDAISM (1984). 241 Cedar Lane, Teaneck, NJ 07666. (201)801-0707. FAX: (201)801-0449. Pres. Burton G. Greenblatt; Exec. V.-Pres. Rabbi Ronald D. Price. Through innovative outreach programs, seeks to bring the greatest possible number of Jews closer to an open-minded observant Jewish lifestyle. Activities include Kashrut Initiative, Operation Pesah, the Panel of Halakhic Inquiry, Speakers Bureau, adult and youth conferences, and congregational services. Includes, since 1992, the MORASHAH rabbinic fellowship. *Hagahelet (quarterly newsletter); Cornerstone (journal); Tomeikh Kahalakhah (Jewish legal responsa).*

UNION OF AMERICAN HEBREW CONGREGATIONS (1873). 633 Third Ave., NYC 10017-6778. (212)650-4000. FAX: (212) 650-4169. E-mail: uahc@uahc.org. Pres. Rabbi Eric H. Yoffie; V.-Pres. Rabbi Lennard R. Thal; Bd. Chmn. Russell Sil-

verman. Serves as the central congregational body of Reform Judaism in the Western Hemisphere; serves its approximately 895 affiliated temples and membership with religious, educational, cultural, and administrative programs. *Reform Judaism.* (WWW.UAHC.ORG)

———, AMERICAN CONFERENCE OF CANTORS (1953). 140 Central Ave., Lawrence, NY 11559. (516)239-3650. FAX: (516)239-4318. E-mail: accantors@aol.com. Pres. David M. Goldstein; Exec. V.-Pres. Scott E. Colbert; Dir. of Placement Debra Stein-Davidson; Admin. Asst. Jacqueline A. Maron. Members receive investiture and commissioning as cantors at recognized seminaries, i.e., Hebrew Union College-Jewish Institute of Religion, School of Sacred Music, as well as full certification through HUC-JIR-SSM. Through the Joint Cantorial Placement Commission, the ACC serves Reform congregations seeking cantors. Dedicated to creative Judaism, preserving the best of the past, and encouraging new and vital approaches to religious ritual, music, and ceremonies. *Koleinu.*

———, COMMISSION ON SOCIAL ACTION OF REFORM JUDAISM *(see p. 500)*

———, COMMISSION ON SYNAGOGUE MANAGEMENT (UAHC-CCAR) (1962). 633 Third Ave., NYC 10017-6778. (212)650-4040. FAX: (212)650-4239. Chmn. Marshall Krolick; Dir. Dale A. Glasser. Assists congregations in management, finance, building maintenance, design, construction, and art aspects of synagogues; maintains the Synagogue Architectural Library.

———, NATA (NATIONAL ASSOCIATION OF TEMPLE ADMINISTRATORS) (1941). 6114 La Salle Ave., Box 731, Oakland, CA 94611. (800)966-6282. FAX: (925)283-7713. E-mail: nataorg@hotmail.com. Pres. Fern M. Kamen. Professional organization for UAHC synagogue administrators. Sponsors graduate training in synagogue management with Hebrew Union College; offers in-service training, workshops, and conferences leading to certification; provides NATA Consulting Service, NATA Placement Service for synagogues seeking advice or professional administrators; establishes professional standards. *NATA Journal; Temple Management Manual.*

———, NATIONAL ASSOCIATION OF TEMPLE EDUCATORS (NATE) (1955). 633 Third Ave., 7th fl., NYC 10017-6778. (212)452-6510. FAX: (212)452-6512. E-mail: nateoff@aol.com. Pres. Sharon S. Morton; Exec. Dir. Rabbi Stanley T. Schickler. Represents the temple educator within the general body of Reform Judaism; fosters the full-time profession of the temple educator; encourages the growth and development of Jewish religious education consistent with the aims of Reform Judaism; stimulates communal interest in and responsibility for Jewish religious education. *NATE NEWS.* (WWW.RJ.ORG/NATE)

———, NORTH AMERICAN FEDERATION OF TEMPLE BROTHERHOODS (1923). 633 Third Ave., NYC 10017. (212)650-4100. FAX: (212)650-4189. E-mail: nftb@uahc.org. Pres.Irving B. Shnaider; JCS Chancellor Stuart Y. Aaronson; Exec. Dir. Douglas Barden. Dedicated to enhancing the world through the ideal of brotherhood, NFTB and its 300 affiliated clubs are actively involved in education, social action, youth activities, and other programs that contribute to temple and community life. Supports the Jewish Chautauqua Society, an interfaith educational project. *ACHIM (formerly Brotherhood magazine)* (WWW.RJ.ORG/NFTB)

———, UAHC DEPARTMENT OF JEWISH EDUCATION (1923). 633 Third Ave., 7th fl., NYC 10017. (212)650-4112. FAX: (212)650-4229. E-mail: jkatzew@uahc.org. Chmn. Robin L. Eisenberg; Dir. Rabbi Jan Katzew. Long-range planning and policy development for congregational programs of lifelong education; materials concerning Reform Jewish Outreach, Teacher Development and Reform Day Schools; activities administered by the UAHC Department of Education. *V'Shinantam; Torah at the Center.*

———, WOMEN OF REFORM JUDAISM— THE FEDERATION OF TEMPLE SISTERHOODS (1913). 633 Third Ave., NYC 10017. (212)650-4050. FAX: (212)650-4059. E-mail: wrj@uahc.org. Pres. Judith Silverman; Exec. Dir. Ellen Y. Rosenberg. Serves more than 600 sisterhoods of Reform Judaism; promotes interreligious understanding and social justice; provides funding for scholarships for rabbinic students; founded the Jewish Braille Institute, which provides braille and large-type

Judaic materials for Jewish blind; supports projects for Israel; is the women's agency of Reform Judaism, an affiliate of the UAHC; works in behalf of the Hebrew Union College-Jewish Institute of Religion and the World Union for Progressive Judaism. *Notes for Now; Art Calendar; Windows on WRJ.* (WWW.RJ.ORG/WRJ)

———, YOUTH DIVISION AND NORTH AMERICAN FEDERATION OF TEMPLE YOUTH (1939). 633 Third Ave, NYC 10017-6778. (212)650-4070. FAX: (212)650-4199. E-mail: youthdivision@uahc.org. Dir. UAHC Youth Div. Rabbi Allan L. Smith; Assoc. Dir. UAHC Youth Div. Rabbi Andrew Davids. Dedicated to Jewishly enhancing the lives of the young people of North America's Reform congregations through a program of informal education carried out in UAHC Camp-Institutes (11 camps for grades 2 and up), UAHC/NFTY Israel Programs (summer and semester), NFTY/Junior & Senior High School Programs (youth groups), and Kesher/College Education Department (Reform havurot on campuses).

UNION OF ORTHODOX JEWISH CONGREGATIONS OF AMERICA (1898). 11 Broadway, 14th fl., NYC 10004. (212)563-4000. FAX: (212)564-9058. E-mail: ou@ou.org. Pres. Mandell I. Ganchrow, M.D.; Exec. V.-Pres. Rabbi Raphael Butler. Serves as the national central body of Orthodox synagogues; national OU kashrut supervision and certification service; sponsors Institute for Public Affairs; National Conference of Synagogue Youth; National Jewish Council for the Disabled; Israel Center in Jerusalem; Torah Center in the Ukraine; New Young Leadership Division; Pardes; provides educational, religious, and organization programs, events, and guidance to synagogues and groups; represents the Orthodox Jewish community to governmental and civic bodies and the general Jewish community. *Jewish Action magazine; OU Kosher Directory; OU Passover Directory; OU News Reporter; Synagogue Trends; Our Way magazine; Yachad magazine; Luach & Limud Personal Torah Study.* (WWW.OU.ORG)

———, INSTITUTE FOR PUBLIC AFFAIRS (1989). 11 Broadway, 14th fl., NYC 10004. (212)613-8123. FAX: (212)613-0724. E-mail: ipa@ou.org. Pres. Mandell I.

Ganchrow, M.D.; Chmn. Richard Stone; Dir. Nathan Diament; Dir. Intl. Affairs & Comm. Rel. Betty Ehrenberg. Serves as the policy analysis, advocacy, mobilization, and programming department responsible for representing Orthodox/traditional American Jewry. *IPA Currents (quarterly newsletter)*.

————, NATIONAL CONFERENCE OF SYNAGOGUE YOUTH (1954). 11 Broadway, 14th fl., NYC 10004. (212)563-4000. E-mail: ncsy@ou.org. Dir. Rabbi David Kaminetsky; Exec. Dir. Paul Glasser. Central body for youth groups of Orthodox congregations; provides educational guidance, Torah study groups, community service, program consultation, Torah library, Torah fund scholarships, Ben Zakkai Honor Society, Friends of NCSY, weeklong seminars, Israel Summer Experience for teens and Camp NCSY East Summer Kollel & Michlelet, Teen Torah Center. Divisions include Senior NCSY, Junior NCSY for preteens, Our Way for the Jewish deaf, Yachad for the developmentally disabled, Israel Center in Jerusalem, and NCSY in Israel. *Keeping Posted with NCSY; Darchei Da'at.*

————, WOMEN'S BRANCH (1923). 156 Fifth Ave., NYC 10010. (212)929-8857. Pres. Sophie Ebert. Umbrella organization of Orthodox sisterhoods in U.S. and Canada, educating women in Jewish learning and observance; provides programming, leadership, and organizational guidance, conferences, conventions, Marriage Committee and projects concerning mikvah, Shalom Task Force, and Welcoming Guests. Works with Orthodox Union Commissions and outreach; supports Stern and Touro College scholarships and Jewish braille publications; supplies Shabbat candelabra for hospital patients; NGO representative at UN. *Hachodesh; Hakol.*

UNION OF ORTHODOX RABBIS OF THE UNITED STATES AND CANADA (1902). 235 E. Broadway, NYC 10002. (212)964-6337(8). Dir. Rabbi Hersh M. Ginsberg. Seeks to foster and promote Torah-true Judaism in the U.S. and Canada; assists in the establishment and maintenance of yeshivot in the U.S.; maintains committee on marriage and divorce and aids individuals with marital difficulties; disseminates knowledge of traditional Jewish rites and practices and publishes regula-

tions on synagogal structure; maintains rabbinical court for resolving individual and communal conflicts. *HaPardes.*

UNION OF SEPHARDIC CONGREGATIONS, INC. (1929). 8 W. 70 St., NYC 10023. (212)873-0300. FAX: (212)724-6165. Pres. Rabbi Marc D. Angel; Bd. Chmn. Alvin Deutsch. Promotes the religious interests of Sephardic Jews; prints and distributes Sephardic prayer books. *Annual International Directory of Sephardic Congregations.*

UNITED LUBAVITCHER YESHIVOTH (1940). 841-853 Ocean Pkwy., Brooklyn, NY 11230. (718)859-7600. FAX: (718)434-1519. Supports and organizes Jewish day schools and rabbinical seminaries in the U.S. and abroad.

UNITED SYNAGOGUE OF CONSERVATIVE JUDAISM (1913). 155 Fifth Ave., NYC 10010-6802. (212)533-7800. FAX: (212) 353-9439. E-mail: info@uscj.org. Pres. Stephen S. Wolnek; Exec. V.-Pres. Rabbi Jerome M. Epstein. International organization of 760 Conservative congregations. Maintains 12 departments and 19 regional offices to assist its affiliates with religious, educational, youth, community, and administrative programming and guidance; aims to enhance the cause of Conservative Judaism, further religious observance, encourage establishment of Jewish religious schools, draw youth closer to Jewish tradition. Extensive Israel programs. *United Synagogue Review; Art/Engagement Calendar; Program Suggestions; Directory & Resource Guide; Book Service Catalogue of Publications.* (WWW.USCJ.ORG)

————, COMMISSION ON JEWISH EDUCATION (1930). 155 Fifth Ave., NYC 10010. (212)533-7800. FAX: (212)353-9439. E-mail: education@uscj.org. Chmn. Temma Kingsley; Dir. Rabbi Robert Abramson. Develops educational policy for the United Synagogue of Conservative Judaism and sets the educational direction for Conservative congregations, their schools, and the Solomon Schechter Day Schools. Seeks to enhance the educational effectiveness of congregations through the publication of materials and in-service programs. *Tov L'Horot; Your Child; Shiboley Schechter; Advisories.*

————, COMMISSION ON SOCIAL ACTION AND PUBLIC POLICY (1958). 155 Fifth

Ave., NYC 10010. (212)533-7800. FAX: (212)353-9439. Chmn. J.B. Mazer; Dir. Sarrae G. Crane. Develops and implements positions and programs on issues of social action and public policy for the United Synagogue of Conservative Judaism; represents these positions to other Jewish and civic organizations, the media, and government; and provides guidance, both informational and programmatic, to its affiliated congregations in these areas. *HaMa'aseh.*

———, JEWISH EDUCATORS ASSEMBLY (1951). 426 W. 58 St., NYC 10019. (212)765-3303. FAX: (212)765-3310. Pres. Dr. Mark S. Silk; Exec. Dir. Susan Mitrani Knapp. The Jewish Educators Assembly is the professional organization for the Jewish educators within the Conservative movement. The JEA provides a forum to discuss the trends and challenges within Conservative Jewish education as well as provides professional development and a sense of community for educational directors. Services offered: annual conference, placement service, career services, research grants, personal benefits and *V'Aleh Ha-Chadashot* newsletter.

———, KADIMA (formerly Pre-usy; reorg. 1968). 155 Fifth Ave., NYC 10010-6802. (212)533-7800. FAX: (212)353-9439. E-mail: kadima@uscj.org. Dir. Karen L. Stein; Dir. of Youth Activities Jules A Gutin. Involves Jewish preteens in a meaningful religious, educational, and social environment; fosters a sense of identity and commitment to the Jewish community and the Conservative movement; conducts synagogue-based chapter programs and regional Kadima days and weekends. *Mitzvah of the Month; Kadima Kesher; Chagim; Advisors Aid; Games;* quarterly *Kol Kadima* magazine.

———, NORTH AMERICAN ASSOCIATION OF SYNAGOGUE EXECUTIVES (1948). 155 Fifth Ave., NYC 10010. (212)533-7800, ext 2609. FAX: (631)732-9461. E-mail: hauser@unix.asb.com. Pres. Amir Pilch, FSA; Hon. Pres. Jan Baron, FSA; Exec. Dir. Harry Hauser. Aids congregations affiliated with the United Synagogue of Conservative Judaism to further the aims of Conservative Judaism through more effective administration (Program for Assistance by Liaisons to Synagogues—PALS); advances professional standards

and promotes new methods in administration; cooperates in United Synagogue placement services and administrative surveys. *NAASE Connections Newsletter; NAASE Journal.*

———, UNITED SYNAGOGUE YOUTH (1951). 155 Fifth Ave., NYC 10010. (212)533-7800. FAX: (212)353-9439. E-mail: youth@uscj.org. Pres. Aviva Kieffer; Exec. Dir. Jules A. Gutin. Seeks to strengthen identification with Conservative Judaism, based on the personality, development, needs, and interests of the adolescent, in a mitzvah framework. *Achshav; Tikun Olam; A.J. Heschel Honor Society Newsletter; SATO Newsletter; USY Program Bank; Hakesher Newsletter for Advisors.*

VAAD MISHMERETH STAM (1976). 4907 16th Ave., Brooklyn, NYC 11204. (718)438-4980. FAX: (718)438-9343. Pres. Rabbi David L. Greenfield. A nonprofit consumer-protection agency dedicated to preserving and protecting the halakhic integrity of Torah scrolls, tefillin, phylacteries, and mezuzot. Publishes material for laymen and scholars in the field of scribal arts; makes presentations and conducts examination campaigns in schools and synagogues; created an optical software system to detect possible textual errors in stam. Teaching and certifying sofrim worldwide. Offices in Israel, Strasbourg, Chicago, London, Manchester, Montreal, and Zurich. Publishes *Guide to Mezuzah* and *Encyclopedia of the Secret Aleph Beth. The Jewish Quill; and many other publications.*

WASHINGTON INSTITUTE FOR JEWISH LEADERSHIP & VALUES (1988). 6101 Montrose Road, Suite 200, Rockville, MD 20852. (301) 770-5070. FAX: (301) 770-6365. E-mail: wijlv@wijlv.org. Founder/Pres. Rabbi Sidney Schwarz; Bd. Chmn. Ellen Kagen Waghelstein. An educational organization advancing *tikkun olam,* activism, and civic engagement by American Jews, grounded in Torah and Jewish values. Its flagship program is *Panim el Panim:* High School in Washington. Also sponsors the Jewish Civics Initiative for community and day schools; *E Pluribus Unum,* an interfaith project on religion, social justice and the common good; and a 15 credit program on "Judaism, Advocacy and Social Change"through American University. *Jewish Civics: A Tikkun*

Olam/World Repair Manual; Jews, Judaism and Civic Responsibility.

WOMEN'S LEAGUE FOR CONSERVATIVE JUDAISM (1918). 48 E. 74 St., NYC 10021. (212)628-1600. FAX: (212)772-3507. Pres. Janet Tobin; Exec. Dir. Bernice Balter. Parent body of Conservative (Masorti) women's synagogue groups in U.S., Canada, Puerto Rico, Mexico, and Israel; provides programs and resources in Jewish education, social action, Israel affairs, American and Canadian public affairs, leadership training, community service programs for persons with disabilities, conferences on world affairs, study institutes, publicity techniques; publishes books of Jewish interest; contributes to support of Jewish Theological Seminary of America. *Women's League Outlook magazine; Ba'Olam world affairs newsletter.*

WORLD COUNCIL OF CONSERVATIVE/MASORTI SYNAGOGUES (1957). 155 Fifth Ave., NYC 10010. (212)533-7800, ext. 2014, 2018. FAX: (212)533-9439. E-mail: world council@compuserve.com. Pres. Rabbi Alan Silverstein; Rabbi of Council, Rabbi Benjamin Z. Kreitman. International representative of Conservative organizations and congregations; promotes the growth and development of the Conservative movement in Israel and throughout the world; supports educational institutions overseas; holds biennial international conventions; represents the world Conservative movement on the Executive Committee of the World Zionist Organization. *World Spectrum.*

SCHOOLS, INSTITUTIONS

ACADEMY FOR JEWISH RELIGION (1956). 15 W. 86 St., NYC 10024. (212)875-0540. FAX: (212)875-0541. E-mail: seminary@erols.com. Pres. Rabbi Shohama Wiener; Dean Rabbi Samuel Barth. The only rabbinic and cantorial seminary in the U.S. at which students explore the full range of Jewish spiritual learning and practice. Graduates serve in Conservative, Reform, Reconstructionist, and Orthodox congregations, chaplaincies, and educational institutions. Programs include rabbinic and cantorial studies in NYC and LA, and on/off-campus nonmatriculated studies. Evening classes in Jewish spirituality open to the general public.

ANNENBERG RESEARCH INSTITUTE (*see* CENTER FOR JUDAIC STUDIES)

BALTIMORE HEBREW UNIVERSITY (1919). 5800 Park Heights Ave., Baltimore, MD 21215. (410)578-6900; (888)248-7420. FAX: (410)578-6940. E-mail: bhu@bhu .edu. Pres. Dr. Robert O. Freedman; Bd. Chmn. Michael Hettleman. Offers PhD, MA, BA, and AA programs in Jewish studies, Jewish education, biblical and Near Eastern archaeology, philosophy, literature, history, Hebrew language, literature, and contemporary Jewish civilization; School of Continuing Education; Joseph Meyerhoff Library; community lectures, film series, seminars. *BHU Today.* (WWW.BHU.EDU)

——, BALTIMORE INSTITUTE FOR JEWISH COMMUNAL SERVICE. (410)578-6932. FAX: (410)578-1803. Dir. Karen S. Bernstein; Co-Dir. Cindy Goldstein. Trains Jewish communal professionals; offers a joint degree program: an MA from BHU and an MAJE from BHU, an MSW from U. of Maryland School of Social Work, or an MPS in policy sciences from UMBC; MA with Meyerhoff Graduate School and Johns Hopkins U. in nonprofit management.

——, BERNARD MANEKIN SCHOOL OF UNDERGRADUATE STUDIES. Dean Dr. George Berlin. BA program; interinstitutional program with Johns Hopkins University; interdisciplinary concentrations: contemporary Middle East, American Jewish culture, and the humanities; Russian/English program for new Americans; assoc. of arts (AA) degree in Jewish studies.

——, LEONARD AND HELEN R. STULMAN SCHOOL OF CONTINUING EDUCATION. Dean Dr. George Berlin. Noncredit program open to the community, offering a variety of courses, trips, and events covering a range of Jewish subjects. *Elderhostel, Ulpan Modern Hebrew Department.*

——, PEGGY MEYERHOFF PEARLSTONE SCHOOL OF GRADUATE STUDIES. Dean Dr. Barry M. Gittlen. PhD and MA programs; MA in Jewish studies; MAJE in Jewish education; PhD in Jewish studies; a double master's degree with an MA from BHU and an MAJE from BHU, an MSW from the University of Maryland

School of Social Work, or an MPS in policy sciences from UMBC; MA with Baltimore Institute and Johns Hopkins U. in nonprofit management.

BRAMSON ORT COLLEGE (1977). 69-30 Austin St., Forest Hills, NY 11375. (718)261-5800. Dean of Academic Services Barry Glotzer. A two-year Jewish technical college offering certificates and associate degrees in technology and business fields, including accounting, computer programming, electronics technology, business management, office technology. Additional locations in Brooklyn.

BRANDEIS-BARDIN INSTITUTE (1941). 1101 Peppertree Lane, Brandeis, CA 93064. (805)582-4450. FAX: (805)526-1398. E-mail: info@brandeis-bardin.org. Pres. Helen Zukin. A Jewish pluralistic, nondenominational educational institution providing programs for people of all ages:BCI (Brandeis Collegiate Institute), a summer leadership program for college-age adults from around the world; Camp Alonim, a summer Jewish experience for children 8-16; Gan Alonim Day Camp for children in kindergarten to 6th grade; weekend retreats for adults with leading contemporary Jewish scholars-in-residence; Jewish music concerts; Family Days and Weekends, Grandparents Weekends, Elderhostel, Young Adult programs, dance weekends, institute for newly marrieds. *Monthly Updates; BBI Newsletter; BCI Alumni News.*

BRANDEIS UNIVERSITY (1948). 415 South St., Waltham, MA 02454. (781)736-2000. Pres. Jehuda Reinharz; Provost Irving Epstein; Exec. V.-Pres./CEO Peter B. French; Sr. V.-Pres. of Devel. Nancy Winship. Founded under Jewish sponsorship as a nonsectarian institution offering undergraduate and graduate education. The Lown School is the center for all programs of teaching and research in Judaic studies, ancient Near Eastern studies, and Islamic and modern Middle Eastern studies. The school includes the Department of Near Eastern and Judaic Studies; the Hornstein Program in Jewish Communal Service, a professional training program; the Cohen Center for Modern Jewish Studies, which conducts research and teaching in contemporary Jewish studies, primarily in American Jewish studies; and

the Tauber Institute for the study of European Jewry. *Various newsletters, scholarly publications.*

CENTER FOR JUDAIC STUDIES, School of Arts and Sciences, University of Pennsylvania. 420 Walnut St., Philadelphia, PA 19106. (215)238-1290. FAX: (215) 238-1540. Dir. David B. Ruderman. *Jewish Quarterly Review.*

CLEVELAND COLLEGE OF JEWISH STUDIES (1964). 26500 Shaker Blvd., Beachwood, OH 44122. (216)464-4050. FAX: (216) 464-5827. Pres. David S. Ariel; Dir. of Student Services Diane M. Kleinman. Provides courses in all areas of Judaic and Hebrew studies to adults and college-age students; offers continuing education for Jewish educators and administrators; serves as a center for Jewish life and culture; expands the availability of courses in Judaic studies by exchanging faculty, students, and credits with neighboring academic institutions; grants bachelor's and master's degrees.

DROPSIE COLLEGE FOR HEBREW AND COGNATE LEARNING (*see* CENTER FOR JUDAIC STUDIES)

FEINBERG GRADUATE SCHOOL OF THE WEIZMANN INSTITUTE OF SCIENCE (1958). 51 Madison Ave. NYC 10010. (212)779-2500. FAX: (212)779-3209. Chmn. Melvin Schwartz; Pres. Robert Asher; Dean Prof. Shmuel Safran. Situated on the Weizmann campus in Rehovot, Israel, provides the school's faculty and research facilities. Accredited by the Council for Higher Education of Israel and the NY State Board of Regents for the study of natural sciences, leading to MSc and PhD degrees.

GRATZ COLLEGE (1895). 7605 Old York Rd., Melrose Park, PA 19027. (215)635-7300. FAX: (215)635-7320. Bd. Chmn. Alan Gordon, Esq.; Pres. Dr. Jonathan Rosenbaum. Offers a wide variety of undergraduate and graduate degrees and continuing education programs in Judaic, Hebraic, and Middle Eastern studies. Grants BA and MA in Jewish studies, MA in Jewish education (joint program in special needs education with La Salle U.), MA in Jewish music, MA in Jewish liberal studies, MA in Jewish communal studies, certificates in Jewish communal studies (joint program with U. of Penna. School of Social Work), Jewish education, Israel studies, Judaica librarianship (joint program with Drexel U.), and Jewish music. Joint graduate program with Reconstructionist Rabbinical College in Jewish education and Jewish music. Netzky Division of Continuing Education and Jewish Community High School. *Various newsletters, annual academic bulletin, scholarly publications, centennial volume, and occasional papers.*

HEBREW COLLEGE (1921). 43 Hawes St., Brookline, MA 02446. (617)232-8710. FAX: (617)264-9264. Pres. Dr. David M. Gordis; Ch. Bd. Dir. Mickey Cail; Ch. Bd. Trustees Ted Benard-Cutler. Through training in Jewish texts, history, literature, ethics, and Hebrew language, prepares students to become literate participants in the global Jewish community. Offers graduate and undergraduate degrees and certificates in all aspects of Jewish education, Jewish studies, and Jewish music; serves students of all ages through its Prozdor High School, Camp Yavneh, Ulpan Center for Adult Jewish Learning, and Me'ah–One Hundred Hours of Adult Jewish Learning. *Hebrew College Today; Likut.* (WWW.HEBREWCOLLEGE.EDU)

HEBREW SEMINARY OF THE DEAF (1992). 4435 W. Oakton, Skokie, IL 60076. (847) 677-3330. FAX: (847)677-7945. E-mail: hebrewsemdeaf@juno.com. Pres. Rabbi Douglas Goldhamer; Bd. Co-Chmn. Rabbi William Frankel & Alan Crane. Trains deaf and hearing men and women to become rabbis and teachers for Jewish deaf communities across America. All classes in the 5-year program are interpreted in Sign Language. Rabbis teaching in the seminary are Reform, Conservative, and Reconstructionist.

HEBREW THEOLOGICAL COLLEGE (1922). 7135 N. Carpenter Rd., Skokie, IL 60077. (847)982-2500. FAX: (847)674-6381. E-mail: htc@htcnet.edu. Chancellor Rabbi Dr. Jerold Isenberg. An accredited institution of higher Jewish learning which includes a rabbinical school; Fasman Yeshiva High School; Anne M. Blitstein Teachers Institute for Women; Wm. and Lillian Kanter School of Liberal Arts & Sciences; Max Bressler School of Advanced Hebrew Studies. *Or Shmuel; Torah Journal; Likutei P'shatim; Turrets of Silver.*

HEBREW UNION COLLEGE–JEWISH INSTITUTE OF RELIGION (1875). 3101 Clifton Ave., Cincinnati, OH 45220. (513)221-1875. FAX: (513)221-1847. Pres. Rabbi Sheldon Zimmerman; Chancellor Dr. Alfred Gottschalk; V.-Pres. Admin. & Finance Arthur R. Grant; V.-Pres. Devel. Erica S. Frederick; Chmn. Bd. Govs. Burton Lehman; Provost Dr. Norman J. Cohen. Academic centers: 3101 Clifton Ave., Cincinnati, OH 45220 (1875), Dean Rabbi Kenneth Ehrlich. 1 W. 4 St., NYC 10012 (1922), Dean Rabbi Aaron Panken. FAX: (212) 388-1720. 3077 University Ave., Los Angeles, CA 90007 (1954), Dean Rabbi Lewis Barth; FAX: (213)747-6128. 13 King David St., Jerusalem, Israel 94101 (1963), Dean Rabbi Michael Marmur; FAX: (972-2)6251478. Prepares students for Reform rabbinate, cantorate, Jewish education and educational administration, communal service, academic careers; promotes Jewish studies; maintains libraries, archives, and museums; offers master's and doctoral degrees; engages in archaeological excavations; publishes scholarly works through Hebrew Union College Press. *American Jewish Archives; Bibliographica Judaica; HUC-JIR Catalogue; Hebrew Union College Annual; Studies in Bibliography and Booklore; The Chronicle; Kesher.* (WWW.HUC.EDU)

——, AMERICAN JEWISH PERIODICAL CENTER (1957). 3101 Clifton Ave., Cincinnati, OH 45220. (513)221-1875, ext. 396. FAX: (513)221-0519. Dir. Herbert C. Zafren. Maintains microfilms of all American Jewish periodicals 1823-1925, selected periodicals since 1925. *Jewish Periodicals and Newspapers on Microfilm* (1957); First Supplement (1960); Augmented Edition (1984).

——, EDGAR F. MAGNIN SCHOOL OF GRADUATE STUDIES (1956). 3077 University Ave., Los Angeles, CA 90007. (213)749-3424. FAX: (213)747-6128. E-mail: magnin@huc.edu. Dir. Dr. Reuven Firestone. Supervises programs leading to DHS, DHL, and MA degrees; participates in cooperative PhD programs with U. of S. Calif.

——, GRADUATE STUDIES PROGRAM. 1 W. 4 St. NYC 10012. (212)824-2252. FAX: (212)388-1720. E-mail: nysgrad@huc. edu. Dir. Dr. Carol Ochs. Offers the DHL (doctor of Hebrew letters) degree in a variety of fields; the MAJS (master of arts in Judaic studies), a multidisciplinary degree; and is the only Jewish seminary to offer the DMin (doctor of ministry) degree in pastoral care and counseling.

———, IRWIN DANIELS SCHOOL OF JEWISH COMMUNAL SERVICE (1968). 3077 University Ave., Los Angeles, CA 90007. (800)899-0925. FAX: (213)747-6128. E-mail: swindmueller@huc.edu. Dir. Dr. Steven F. Windmueller. Offers certificate and master's degree to those employed in Jewish communal services, or preparing for such work; offers joint MA in Jewish education and communal service with Rhea Hirsch School; offers dual degrees with the School of Social Work, the School of Public Administration, the Annenberg School for Communication, Marshall School of Business and the School of Gerontology of the U. of S. Calif. and with other institutions. Single master's degrees can be completed in 15 months and certificates are awarded for the completion of two full-time summer sessions. (WWW.HUC.EDU)

———, JACOB RADER MARCUS CENTER OF THE AMERICAN JEWISH ARCHIVES (see p. 507)

———, JEROME H. LOUCHHEIM SCHOOL OF JUDAIC STUDIES (1969). 3077 University Ave., Los Angeles, CA 90007. (213)749-3424. FAX: (213)747-6128. Dir. Dr. Reuven Firestone. Offers programs leading to MA, BS, BA, and AA degrees; offers courses as part of the undergraduate program of the U. of S. Calif.

———, NELSON GLUECK SCHOOL OF BIBLICAL ARCHAEOLOGY (1963). 13 King David St., Jerusalem, Israel 94101. (972)2-6203333. FAX: (972)2-6251478. Dir. Avraham Biran. Offers graduate-level research programs in Bible and archaeology. Summer excavations are carried out by scholars and students. University credit may be earned by participants in excavations. Consortium of colleges, universities, and seminaries is affiliated with the school. Skirball Museum of Biblical Archaeology (artifacts from Tel Dan, Tel Gezer, and Aroer).

———, RHEA HIRSCH SCHOOL OF EDUCATION (1967). 3077 University Ave., Los Angeles, CA 90007. (213)749-3424. FAX: (213)747-6128. Dir. Sara Lee. Offers PhD and MA programs in Jewish and Hebrew education; conducts joint degree programs with U. of S. Calif.; offers courses for Jewish teachers, librarians, and early educators on a nonmatriculating basis; conducts summer institutes for professional Jewish educators.

———, SCHOOL OF EDUCATION (1947). 1 W. 4 St., NYC 10012. (212)824-2213. FAX: (212)388-1720. E-mail: nysed@huc.edu. Dir. Jo Kay. Trains teachers and principals for Reform religious schools; offers MA degree with specialization in religious education.

———, SCHOOL OF GRADUATE STUDIES (1949). 3101 Clifton Ave., Cincinnati, OH 45220. (513)221-1875, ext. 230. FAX: (513)221-0321. E-mail: gradschool@huc.edu. Dir. Dr. Adam Kamesar. Offers programs leading to MA and PhD degrees; offers program leading to DHL degree for rabbinic graduates of the college.

———, SCHOOL OF JEWISH STUDIES (1963). 13 King David St., Jerusalem, Israel 94101. (972)2-6203333. FAX: (972)2-6251478. E-mail: jerusalem@huc.edu. Pres. Sheldon Zimmerman; Dean Rabbi Michael Marmur; Assoc. Dean Rabbi Shaul R. Feinberg. Offers first year of graduate rabbinic, cantorial, and Jewish education studies (required) for North American students; graduate program leading to ordination for Israeli rabbinic students; non-degree Beit Midrash/Liberal Yeshivah program of Jewish studies (English language); in-service educational programming for teachers and educators (Hebrew language); Hebrew Ulpan for immigrants and visitors; Abramov Library of Judaica, Hebraica, Ancient Near East and American Jewish Experience; Skirball Museum of Biblical Archaeology; public outreach programs (lectures, courses, concerts, exhibits).

———, SCHOOL OF SACRED MUSIC (1947). 1 W. 4 St., NYC 10012. (212)824-2225. FAX: (212)388-1720. Dir. Cantor Israel Goldstein. Trains cantors for congregations; offers MSM degree. *Sacred Music Press.*

———, SKIRBALL CULTURAL CENTER (see p. 510)

INSTITUTE OF TRADITIONAL JUDAISM (1990). 811 Palisade Ave., Teaneck, NJ 07666. (201)801-0707. FAX: (201)801-0449. Rector (Reish Metivta) Rabbi David Weiss Halivni; Dean Rabbi Ronald

D. Price. A nondenominational halakhic rabbinical school dedicated to genuine faith combined with intellectual honesty and the love of Israel. Graduates receive "yoreh yoreh"smikhah.

JEWISH THEOLOGICAL SEMINARY (1886; reorg. 1902). 3080 Broadway, NYC 10027-4649. (212)678-8000. FAX: (212) 678-8947. Chancellor Dr. Ismar Schorsch; Bd. Chmn. Gershon Kekst. Operates undergraduate and graduate programs in Judaic studies; professional schools for training Conservative rabbis, educators and cantors; the JTS Library; the Ratner Center for the Study of Conservative Judaism; Melton Research Center for Jewish Education; the Jewish Museum; Ramah Camps and the Ivry Prozdor high-school honors program. Other outreach activities include the Distance Learning Project, the Finkelstein Institute for Religious and Social Studies, the Havruta Program, and the Wagner Institute lay leadership program. *Academic Bulletin; JTS Magazine; Gleanings; JTS News*. (WWW.JTSA.EDU)

———, ALBERT A. LIST COLLEGE OF JEWISH STUDIES (formerly SEMINARY COLLEGE OF JEWISH STUDIES—TEACHERS INSTITUTE) (1909). 3080 Broadway, NYC 10027. (212)678-8826. Dean Dr. Shuly Rubin Schwartz. Offers complete undergraduate program in Judaica leading to BA degree; conducts joint programs with Columbia University and Barnard College enabling students to receive two BA degrees.

———, DEPARTMENT OF RADIO AND TELEVISION (1944). 3080 Broadway, NYC 10027. (212)678-8020. Produces radio and TV programs expressing the Jewish tradition in its broadest sense, including hour-long documentaries on NBC and ABC. Distributes cassettes of programs at minimum charge.

———, GRADUATE SCHOOL OF JTS (formerly INSTITUTE FOR ADVANCED STUDY IN THE HUMANITIES) (1968). 3080 Broadway, NYC 10027-4649. (212)678-8024. FAX: (212)678-8947. E-mail: gradschool@jtsa.edu. Dean Dr. Stephen P. Garfinkel; Asst. Dean Dr. Bruce E. Nielsen. Programs leading to MA, DHL, and PhD degrees in Judaic studies; specializations include Ancient Judaism, Bible and Ancient Semitic Languages, Interdepartmental Studies, Jewish Art and Material Culture, Jewish Education, Jewish History, Jewish Literature, Jewish Philosophy, Jewish Women's Studies, Liturgy, Medieval Jewish Studies, Midrash, Modern Jewish Studies, Talmud and Rabbinics, and Dual Degree Program with Columbia University School of Social Work.

———, H.L. MILLER CANTORIAL SCHOOL AND COLLEGE OF JEWISH MUSIC (1952). 3080 Broadway, NYC 10027. (212)678-8036. FAX: (212)678-8947. Dean Cantor Henry Rosenblum. Trains cantors, music teachers, and choral directors for congregations. Offers full-time programs in sacred music leading to degree of MSM, and diploma of *Hazzan*.

———, JEWISH MUSEUM (*see* p. 507)

———, LIBRARY OF THE JEWISH THEOLOGICAL SEMINARY. 3080 Broadway, NYC 10027. (212)678-8075. FAX: (212)678-8998. E-mail: library@jtsa.edu. Librarian Dr. Mayer E. Rabinowitz. Contains one of the largest collections of Hebraica and Judaica in the world, including manuscripts, incunabula, rare books, and Cairo Geniza material. The 320,000-item collection includes books, manuscripts, periodicals, sound recordings, prints, broadsides, photographs, postcards, microform, videos and CD-ROM. Exhibition of items from the collection are ongoing. Exhibition catalogs are available for sale. The Library is open to the public for on-site use (photo identification required). *Between the Lines*. (www.jtsa.edu/library)

———, LOUIS FINKELSTEIN INSTITUTE FOR RELIGIOUS AND SOCIAL STUDIES (1938). 3080 Broadway, NYC 10027. (212)870-3180. FAX: (212)678-8947. E-mail: finkelstein@jtsa.edu. Dir. Rabbi Gerald Wolpe. Since 1938 has maintained an innovative interfaith and intergroup relations program, pioneering new approaches to dialogue across religious lines. Through scholarly and practical fellowship, highlights the relevance of Judaism and other contemporary religions to current theological, ethical, and scientific issues, including the emerging challenge of bioethics.

———, MELTON RESEARCH CENTER FOR JEWISH EDUCATION (1960). 3080 Broadway, NYC 10027. (212)678-8031. E-mail:

stbrown@jtsa.edu. Dir. Dr. Steven M. Brown; Admin. Lisa Siberstein-Weber. Develops new curricula and materials for Jewish education; prepares educators through seminars and in-service programs; maintains consultant and supervisory relationships with a limited number of pilot schools; develops and implements research initiatives; sponsors "renewal"retreats. *Gleanings; Courtyard: A Journal of Research and Reflection on Jewish Education.*

————, NATIONAL RAMAH COMMISSION (1947). 3080 Broadway, NYC 10027. (212)678-8881. FAX: (212)749-8251. Pres. Alan H. Silberman; Natl. Dir. Sheldon Dorph. Sponsors an international network of 16 summer camps located in the US, Canada, S. America, Russia, and Israel, emphasizing Jewish education, living, and culture; offers opportunities for qualified college students and older to serve as counselors, administrators, specialists, etc., and programs for children with special needs (Tikvah program); offers special programs in U.S. and Israel, including National Ramah Staff Training Institute, Ramah Israel Seminar, Ulpan Ramah Plus, and Tichon Ramah Yerushalayim. Family and synagogue tours to Israel and summer day camp in Israel for Americans.

————, RABBINICAL SCHOOL (1886). 3080 Broadway, NYC 10027. (212)678-8817. Dean Allan Kensky. Offers a program of graduate and professional studies leading to the degree of Master of Arts and ordination; includes one year of study in Jerusalem and an extensive field-work program.

————, REBECCA AND ISRAEL IVRY PROZDOR (1951). 3080 Broadway, NYC 10027. (212)678-8824. E-mail: prozdor@ jtsa.edu. Principal Rhonda Rosenheck; Community Advisory Board Chmn. Michael Katz. The Hebrew high school of JTS, offers a program of Jewish studies for day school and congregational school graduates in classical texts, Hebrew, interdisciplinary seminars, training in educational leadership, and classes for college credit. Classes meet one evening a week and on Sundays in Manhattan and at affiliated programs. *High School Curricula.*

————, SAUL LIEBERMAN INSTITUTE FOR TALMUDIC RESEARCH (1985). 3080 Broadway, NYC 10027. (212)678-8994. FAX: (212)678D8947. E-mail: liebinst @jtsa.edu. Dir. Shamma Friedman; Coord. Jonathan Milgram. Engaged in preparing for publication a series of scholarly editions of selected chapters of the Talmud. The following projects support and help disseminate the research:Talmud Text Database; Bibliography of Talmudic Literature; Catalogue of Geniza Fragments.

————, SCHOCKEN INSTITUTE FOR JEWISH RESEARCH (1961). 6 Balfour St., Jerusalem, Israel 92102. (972)2-5631288. FAX: (972)2-5636857. E-mail: sjssg@ vms.huji.ac.il. Dir. Dr. Shmuel Glick. Comprises the Schocken collection of rare books and manuscripts and a research institute dedicated to the exploration of Hebrew religious poetry *(piyyut)*. *Schocken Institute Yearbook (P'raqim).*

————, WILLIAM DAVIDSON GRADUATE SCHOOL OF JEWISH EDUCATION (1996). 3080 Broadway, NYC 10027. (212) 678-8030. E-mail: edschool@jtsa.edu. Dean Dr. Aryeh Davidson. Offers master's and doctoral degrees in Jewish education; continuing education courses for Jewish educators and Jewish communal professionals; and programs that take advantage of the latest technology, including distance learning and interactive video classrooms.

MAALOT–A SEMINARY FOR CANTORS AND JUDAISTS (1987). 15 W. Montgomery Ave., Suite 204, Rockville, MD 20850. (301)309-2310. FAX: (301)309-2328. Pres./Exec. Off. David Shneyer. An educational program established to train individuals in Jewish music, the liturgical arts, and the use, design, and application of Jewish customs and ceremonies. Offers classes, seminars, and an independent study program.

MESIVTA YESHIVA RABBI CHAIM BERLIN RABBINICAL ACADEMY (1905). 1605 Coney Island Ave., Brooklyn, NY 11230. (718)377-0777. Exec. Dir. Y. Mayer Lasker. Maintains fully accredited elementary and high schools; collegiate and postgraduate school for advanced Jewish studies, both in America and Israel; Camp Morris, a summer study retreat; Prof. Nathan Isaacs Memorial Library; Gur Aryeh Publications.

NER ISRAEL RABBINICAL COLLEGE (1933). 400 Mt. Wilson Lane, Baltimore, MD

21208. (410)484-7200. FAX: (410)484-3060. Rosh Hayeshiva Rabbi Yaakov M. Kulefsky; Pres. Rabbi Herman N. Neuberger. Trains rabbis and educators for Jewish communities in America and worldwide. Offers bachelor's, master's, and doctoral degrees in talmudic law, as well as teacher's diploma. College has four divisions: Israel Henry Beren High School, Rabbinical College, Teachers Training Institute, Graduate School. Maintains an active community-service division. Operates special programs for Iranian and Russian Jewish students. *Ner Israel Update; Alumni Bulletin; Ohr Hanair Talmudic Journal; Iranian B'nei Torah Bulletin.*

RABBINICAL COLLEGE OF TELSHE, INC. (1941). 28400 Euclid Ave., Wickliffe, OH 44092. (216)943-5300. Pres. Rabbi Mordecai Gifter; V.-Pres. Rabbi Abba Zalka Gewirtz; Rosh Hayeshiva Pres. Rabbi Mordechai Gifter. College for higher Jewish learning specializing in talmudic studies and rabbinics; maintains a preparatory academy including a secular high school, postgraduate department, teacher-training school, and teachers' seminary for women. *Pri Etz Chaim; Peer Mordechai; Alumni Bulletin.*

RECONSTRUCTIONIST RABBINICAL COLLEGE (1968). 1299 Church Rd., Wyncote, PA 19095. (215)576-0800. FAX: (215)576-6143. E-mail: rrcinfo@rrc.edu. Pres. David Teutsch; Bd. Chmn. Donald L. Shapiro; Genl. Chmn. Aaron Ziegelman. Coeducational. Trains rabbis and cantors for all areas of Jewish communal life:synagogues, academic and educational positions, Hillel centers, federation agencies, and chaplaincy for hospitals, hospices, and geriatric centers; confers title of rabbi and cantor and grants degrees of Master and Doctor of Hebrew Letters and Master of Arts in Jewish Studies. *RRC Report; Reconstructionist.*

SPERTUS INSTITUTE OF JEWISH STUDIES (1924). 618 S. Michigan Ave., Chicago, IL 60605. (312)922-9012. FAX: (312)922-6406. Pres. Howard A. Sulkin; Bd. Chmn. Franklin Nitikman; V.-Pres. for Academic Affairs Byron L. Sherwin. An accredited institution of higher learning offering one doctor of Jewish studies degree; master's degree programs in Jewish studies, Jewish education, Jewish communal service, and human-services ad-

ministration; plus an extensive program of continuing education. Major resources of the college encompass Spertus Museum, Asher Library, Chicago Jewish Archives, and Spertus College of Judaica Press.

TOURO COLLEGE (1970). Executive Offices: 50 W. 23 St., NYC 10010. (212)643-0700. FAX: (212)714-9048. Pres. Dr. Bernard Lander; Bd. Chmn. Mark Hasten. Chartered by NY State Board of Regents as a nonprofit four-year college with Judaic studies, health sciences, business, and liberal arts programs leading to BA, BS, and MA, MS degrees; emphasizes relevance of Jewish heritage to general culture of Western civilization. Also offers JD degree and a biomedical program leading to the MD degree from Technion-Israel Institute of Technology, Haifa.

———, COLLEGE OF LIBERAL ARTS AND SCIENCES. 27-33 W. 23 St., NYC 10010. (212)463-0400. FAX: (212)627-9144. Exec. Dean Stanley Boylan. Offers comprehensive Jewish studies along with studies in the arts, sciences, humanities, and preprofessional studies in health sciences, law, accounting, business, computer science, education, and finance. Women's Division, 160 Lexington Ave., NYC 10016. (212)213-2230. FAX: (212)683-3281. Dean Sara E. Freifeld.

———, INSTITUTE OF JEWISH LAW. (631) 421-2244, ext. 335. A constituent of Touro College Jacob D. Fuchsberg Law Center, the Institute of Jewish Law provides an intellectual framework for the study and teaching of Jewish law. Coedits *Dinei Israel* (Jewish Law Journal) with Tel Aviv University Law School.

———, JACOB D. FUCHSBERG LAW CENTER (1980). Long Island Campus, 300 Nassau Rd., Huntington, NY 11743. (516) 421-2244. Dean Howard A. Glickstein. Offers studies leading to JD degree.

———, MOSCOW BRANCH. OZTOZHENKA #38, Moscow, Russia 119837. Offers BS program in business and BA program in Jewish studies.

———, SCHOOL OF GENERAL STUDIES. Midtown Main Campus, 27 W. 23 St., NYC 10010. (212)463-0400; Harlem Main Campus, 240 E. 123 St., NYC 10035; Sunset Park extension, 475 53RD St., Brooklyn, NY 11220; Flushing Extension, 133-35 Roosevelt Ave., Queens, NY 11374. Dean Stephen Adolphus. Associate and bachelor degree programs in human services, education N-6, computing, business and liberal arts; special emphasis on service to non-traditional students.

———, TOURO COLLEGE FLATBUSH CENTER (1979). 1602 Ave. J, Brooklyn, NY 11230. (718)252-7800. Dean Robert Goldschmidt. A division of the College of Liberal Arts and Sciences; options offered in accounting and business, education, mathematics, political science, psychology, special education and speech. Classes are given on weeknights and during the day on Sunday.

———, TOURO COLLEGE ISRAEL. 20 Pierre Koenig St., Jerusalem, Israel. (02) 6796666. FAX: (02)6796688. V-Pres., Israel, Matityahu Adler; Dean of Faculty, Israel, Prof. Moshe Lieberman. Touro College Israel offers both undergraduate and graduate degrees in management, marketing, economics, finance, and accounting. Touro College also offers a graduate degree in Jewish Studies. Courses in both these programs are given in Hebrew. In addition undergraduate courses in our one year program are offered in English. (www.touro.ac.il)

———, TOURO COLLEGE SCHOOL OF HEALTH SCIENCES (1986). 1700 Union Blvd, Bay Shore, NY 11706. (516)665-1600. FAX: (516)665-6902. E-mail: edwarda@touro.edu. Pres. Dr. Bernard Lander; Dean Dr. Joseph Weisberg. Offers the following programs:MS/MD with Faculty of Medicine, Technion Institute, Israel; BS/MS Occupational Therapy; BS/MS Physical Therapy; MS Public Health; Advanced MS Orthopedic Physical Therapy; MS Forensic Examination; MS Clinical Engineering; MS Early Intervention; MS Gerontology; BS Physician Assistant; AAS Occupational Therapy Assistant; AAS Physical Therapists Assistant.

———, TOURO GRADUATE SCHOOL OF JEWISH STUDIES (1981). 160 Lexington Ave., NYC 10016. (212)213-2230. FAX: (212) 683-3281. E-mail: moshesh@touro.edu. Pres. Bernard Lander; Dean Michael A. Shmidman. Offers courses leading to an MA in Jewish studies, with concentrations in Jewish history or Jewish educa-

tion. Students may complete part of their program in Israel through MA courses offered by Touro faculty at Touro's Jerusalem center.

UNIVERSITY OF JUDAISM (1947). 15600 Mulholland Dr., Los Angeles, CA 90077. (310)440-1210. FAX: (310)476-0347. E-mail: jblumberg@uj.edu. Pres. Dr. Robert D. Wexler; Acting Provost John R. Lutzker. The College of Arts and Sciences is an accredited liberal arts college for undergraduates offering a core curriculum of Jewish, Western, and non-Western studies, with majors including bioethics (a premedical track in partnership with Cedars-Sinai Medical Center), business, English, Jewish studies, journalism, literature & politics, political science, psychology, and U.S. public policy. Accredited graduate programs in nonprofit business administration (MBA), Jewish education, and psychology with an emphasis on developmental disabilities. The Ziegler School of Rabbinic Studies provides an intensive four-year program with Conservative ordination. Home of the Center for Policy Options, conducting public policy research in areas of concern to the Jewish community, and the Whizin Center for the Jewish Future, a research and programming institute. Offers the largest adult Jewish education program in the U.S., cultural-arts programs, and a variety of outreach services for West Coast Jewish communities. *The Vision.*

WEST COAST TALMUDICAL SEMINARY (Yeshiva Ohr Elchonon Chabad) (1953). 7215 Waring Ave., Los Angeles, CA 90046. (323)937-3763. FAX: (323)937-9456. Dean Rabbi Ezra Schochet. Provides facilities for intensive Torah education as well as Orthodox rabbinical training on the West Coast; conducts an accredited college preparatory high school combined with a full program of Torah-talmudic training and a graduate talmudical division on the college level. *Torah Quiz; Kovetz Migdal Ohr; Kovetz Ohr HaMigdal.*

YESHIVA TORAH VODAATH AND MESIVTA TORAH VODAATH RABBINICAL SEMINARY (1918). 425 E. 9 St., Brooklyn, NY 11218. (718)941-8000. Bd. Chmn. Chaim Leshkowitz. Offers Hebrew and secular education from elementary level through rabbinical ordination and postgraduate work; maintains a teachers institute and community-service bureau; maintains a dormitory and a nonprofit camp program for boys. *Chronicle; Mesivta Vanguard; Thought of the Week; Torah Vodaath News; Ha'Mesifta.*

———, YESHIVA TORAH VODAATH ALUMNI ASSOCIATION (1941). 425 E. 9 St., Brooklyn, NY 11218. (718)941-8000. Pres. George Weinberger. Promotes social and cultural ties between the alumni and the schools through classes and lectures and fund-raising; offers vocational guidance to students; operates Camp Ohr Shraga; sponsors research fellowship program for boys. *Annual Journal; Hamesivta Torah periodical.*

YESHIVA UNIVERSITY (1886). Main Campus, 500 W. 185 St., NYC 10033-3201. (212)960-5400. FAX: (212)960-0055. Pres. Dr. Norman Lamm; Chmn. Bd. of Trustees David S. Gottesman. In its second century, the nation's oldest and most comprehensive independent university founded under Jewish auspices, with 18 undergraduate and graduate schools, divisions, and affiliates; widespread programs of research and community outreach; publications; and a museum. A broad range of curricula lead to bachelor's, master's, doctoral, and professional degrees. Undergraduate schools provide general studies curricula supplemented by courses in Jewish learning; graduate schools prepare for careers in medicine, law, social work, Jewish education, psychology, Jewish studies, and other fields. It has seven undergraduate schools, seven graduate and professional schools, and four affiliates. *Yeshiva University Review; Yeshiva University Today.* (WWW.YU.EDU)

Yeshiva University has four campuses in Manhattan and the Bronx: Main Campus, 500 W. 185 St., NYC 10033-3201; Midtown Campus, 245 Lexington Ave., NYC 10016-4699; Brookdale Center, 55 Fifth Ave., NYC 10003-4391; Jack and Pearl Resnick Campus, Eastchester Rd. & Morris Pk. Ave., Bronx, NY 10461-1602.

Undergraduate schools for men at Main Campus (212)960-5400: Yeshiva College (Bd. Chmn. Jay Schottenstein; Dean Dr. Norman T. Adler) provides liberal arts and sciences curricula; grants BA degree. Isaac Breuer College of Hebraic Studies (Dean Dr. Michael D. Shmidman) awards Hebrew teacher's diploma, AA, BA, and BS. James Striar School of

General Jewish Studies (Dean Dr. Michael D. Shmidman) grants AA degree. Yeshiva Program/Mazer School of Talmudic Studies (Max and Marion Grill Dean Rabbi Zevulun Charlop) offers advanced course of study in Talmudic texts and commentaries. Irving I. Stone Beit Midrash Program (Dean Dr. Michael D. Shmidman) offers diversified curriculum combining Talmud with Jewish studies.

Undergraduate school for women at Midtown Campus (212)340-7700: Stern College for Women (Bd. Chmn. Marjorie Diener Blenden; Dean Dr. Karen Bacon) offers liberal arts and sciences curricula supplemented by Jewish studies programs; awards BA, AA, and Hebrew teacher's diploma.

Sy Syms School of Business at Main Campus and Midtown Campus (Bd. Chmn. Josh S. Weston; Dean Dr. Harold Nierenberg) offers undergraduate business curricula in conjunction with study at Yeshiva College or Stern College; grants BS degree.

———, ALBERT EINSTEIN COLLEGE OF MEDICINE (1955). Eastchester Rd. & Morris Pk. Ave., Bronx, NY 10461-1602. (718)430-2000. Pres. Dr. Norman Lamm; Ch. Bd. of Overseers Burton P. Resnick; Marilyn and Stanley M. Katz Dean Dr. Dominick P. Purpura. Prepares physicians and conducts research in the health sciences; awards MD degree; includes Sue Golding Graduate Division of Medical Sciences (Dir. Dr. Anne M. Etgen), which grants PhD degree. Einstein's clinical facilities and affiliates encompass Jack D. Weiler Hospital of Albert Einstein College of Medicine, Jacobi Medical Center, Montefiore Medical Center, Long Island Jewish Medical Center, Beth Israel Medical Center, Catholic Medical Center of Brooklyn and Queens, Bronx-Lebanon Hospital Center, and Rose F. Kennedy Center for Research in Mental Retardation and Developmental Disabilities. *Einstein; Einstein Today; Einstein Quarterly Journal of Biology and Medicine.*

———, ALUMNI OFFICE, 500 W. 185 St., NYC 10033-3201. (212)960-5373. E-mail: alumdesk@ymail.yu.edu. University Dir. Alumni Affairs Robert R. Saltzman; Dir. Undergraduate Alumni Relations Toby Hilsenrad Weiss. Seeks to foster a close allegiance of alumni to their alma mater by maintaining ties with all alumni and servicing the following associations: Yeshiva College Alumni (Pres. Stuart Verstandig); Stern College for Women Alumnae (Pres. Yonina Langer); Sy Syms School of Business Alumni (Co-Pres. Judah Kaplan & Stephen Wallach); Albert Einstein College of Medicine Alumni (Pres. Dr. Harriette Mogul); Ferkauf Graduate School of Psychology Alumni (Pres. Dr. Nancy Dallek); Wurzweiler School of Social Work Alumni (Co-Pres. Joel Katz & Annette Praeger); Rabbinic Alumni (Pres. Rabbi Gershon C. Gewirtz); Benjamin N. Cardozo School of Law Alumni (Co-Pres. Jonathan & Pamela Henes). *Yeshiva University Review; AECOM Alumni News; Ferkauf Progress Notes; Wurzweiler Update; Jewish Social Work Forum.*

———, AZRIELI GRADUATE SCHOOL OF JEWISH EDUCATION AND ADMINISTRATION (1945). 245 Lexington Ave., NYC 10016-4699. (212)340-7705. FAX: (212) 340-7787. Dir. Dr. Yitzchak S. Handel. Offers MS degree in Jewish elementary and secondary education; specialist's certificate and EdD in administration and supervision of Jewish education. Block Education Program, subsidized by a grant from the Jewish Agency's Joint Program for Jewish Education, provides summer course work to complement year-round field instruction in local communities.

———, BELFER INSTITUTE FOR ADVANCED BIOMEDICAL STUDIES (1978). Eastchester Rd. & Morris Pk. Ave., Bronx, NY 10461-1602. (718)430-3306. Dir. Dr. Dennis Shields. Integrates and coordinates the Albert Einstein College of Medicine's postdoctoral research and training-grant programs in the basic and clinical biomedical sciences. Awards certificate as research fellow or research associate on completion of training.

———, BENJAMIN N. CARDOZO SCHOOL OF LAW (1976). 55 Fifth Ave., NYC 10003-4391. (212)790-0200. E-mail:lawinfo@ ymail.yu.edu. Pres. Dr. Norman Lamm; Bd. Chmn. Earle I. Mack; Dean Paul R. Verkuil. Offers a rigorous and enriched legal education leading to juris doctor (JD) degree and two LLM programs—in intellectual property law and in general studies—for those interested in specialized training and for international students. Programs and services include Jacob Burns Institute for Advanced Legal

Studies; Jacob Burns Center for Ethics in the Practice of Law; Bet Tzedek Legal Services Clinic, including the Herman J. Stich Program for the Aged and Disabled; Cardozo International/Uri and Caroline Bauer Israel Program; Leonard and Bea Diener Institute of Jewish Law; Ford Foundation Program in International Law and Human Rights; Samuel and Ronnie Heyman Center on Corporate Governance; Kukin Program for Conflict Resolution; Romie Shapiro Program in International Law and Human Rights; Stephen B. Siegel Program in Real Estate Law; Sol S. Singer Research Program in Real Property Law; Howard M. Squadron Program in Law, Media, and Society; Center for Professional Development. *Cardozo Life; Cardozo Law Review; Cardozo Arts and Entertainment Law Journal; Cardozo Women's Law Journal; Cardozo Journal of International and Comparative Law; Cardozo Studies in Law and Literature; Post-Soviet Media Law and Policy Newsletter; New York Real Estate Reporter.*

———, BERNARD REVEL GRADUATE SCHOOL (1935). 500 W. 185 St., NYC 10033-3201. (212)960-5253. Pres. Dr. Norman Lamm; Bd. Chmn. Mordecai D. Katz; Dean Dr. Arthur Hyman. Offers graduate programs in Bible, Talmudic studies, Jewish history, and Jewish philosophy; confers MA and PhD degrees. Harry Fischel School for Higher Jewish Studies offers the Revel program during the summer.

———, FERKAUF GRADUATE SCHOOL OF PSYCHOLOGY (1957). 1300 Morris Pk. Ave., Bronx, NY 10461-1602. (718)430-3941. FAX: (718)430-3960. E-mail: gill@aecom.yu.edu. Pres. Dr. Norman Lamm; Ch. Bd. of Govs. Dr. Jayne G. Beker; Dean Dr. Lawrence J. Siegel. Offers MA in applied psychology; PsyD in clinical and school-clinical child psychology; and PhD in developmental and clinical health psychology. Programs and services include the Leonard and Muriel Marcus Family Project for the Study of the Disturbed Adolescent; Max and Celia Parnes Family Psychological and Psychoeducational Services Clinic.

———, PHILIP AND SARAH BELZ SCHOOL OF JEWISH MUSIC (1954). 560 W. 185 St., NYC 10033-3201. (212)960-5353. Dir. Cantor Bernard Beer. Provides professional training of cantors and courses in Jewish liturgical music; conducts outreach; publishes *Journal of Jewish Music and Literature;* awards associate cantor's certificate and cantorial diploma.

———, (affiliate) RABBI ISAAC ELCHANAN THEOLOGICAL SEMINARY (1896). 2540 Amsterdam Ave., NYC 10033-9986. (212)960-5344. Chmn. Bd. of Trustees Judah Feinerman; V.-Pres. for Admin. & Prof. Ed. Rabbi Robert S. Hirt; Max and Marion Grill Dean Rabbi Zevulun Charlop. Leading center in the Western Hemisphere for Torah study and rabbinic training. RIETS complex encompasses 15 educational entities and a major service and outreach center with some 20 programs. Grants semikhah (ordination) and the degrees of master of religious education, master of Hebrew literature, doctor of religious education, and doctor of Hebrew literature. Includes Rabbi Joseph B. Soloveitchik Center of Rabbinic Studies; Gabriel Levine Post-Graduate School for Rabbinic Studies; Morris and Nellie L. Kawaler Rabbinic Training Program; Irving I. Stone Rabbinic Internship Program; Aaron, Martha, Isidore N., and Blanche Rosansky Foundation Contemporary Halakhah Program.

Kollelim include Marcos and Adina Katz Kollel (Institute for Advanced Research in Rabbinics) (Dir. Rabbi Hershel Schachter); Kollel l'Horaah (Yadin Yadin) and External Yadin Yadin (Dir. Rabbi J. David Bleich); Israel Henry Beren Institute for Higher Talmudic Studies (HaMachon HaGavohah L'Talmud) (Dir. Rabbi Michael Rosensweig); Bella and Harry Wexner Kollel Elyon and Semikhah Honors Program (Dir. Rabbi Mordechai Willig); Ludwig Jesselson Kollel Chaverim (Dir. Rabbi J. David Bleich); Caroline and Joseph S. Gruss Institute in Jerusalem (Dir. Rabbi Aharon Lichtenstein).

RIETS sponsors one high school for boys (Manhattan) and one for girls (Queens).

The Max Stern Division of Communal Services (V.-Pres. Rabbi Robert S. Hirt), provides personal and professional service to the rabbinate and related fields, as well as educational, consultative, organizational, and placement services to congregations, schools, and communal organizations around the world; coordinates a broad spectrum of outreach programs, including Association of Modern Orthodox Day Schools and Yeshiva High Schools, Stone-Sapirstein Center for Jewish Education, Gertrude and Morris Bienenfeld Department for Rabbinic Services, Gindi Program for the Enhancement of Professional Rabbinics, Continuing Rabbinic Education Initiatives, Leadership Education and Development Program (LEAD), Kiruv College Outreach Program, Community Kollel and Beit Midrash and Boardroom Learning Programs, Project Kehillah, Torah Umadda Project, Orthodox Forum, Myer and Pauline Senders Off-Campus Lecture Series, Jewish Medical Ethics Consultation Service, National Commission on Torah Education.

Sephardic components are Jacob E. Safra Institute of Sephardic Studies and the Institute of Yemenite Studies; Sephardic Community Program; Dr. Joseph and Rachel Ades Sephardic Outreach Program; Maybaum Sephardic Fellowship Program.

———, SIMON WIESENTHAL CENTER (*see* p. 510)

———, WOMEN'S ORGANIZATION (1928). 500 W. 185 St., NYC 10033-3201. (212) 960-0855. Chmn. Natl. Bd. Dinah Pinczower. Supports Yeshiva University's national scholarship program for students training in education, community service, law, medicine, and other professions. Its Torah Chesed Fund provides monthly stipends to needy undergraduate students.

———, WURZWEILER SCHOOL OF SOCIAL WORK (1957). 500 W. 185 St., NYC 10033-3201. (212)960-0800. Pres. Norman Lamm; Ch. Bd. of Govs. David I. Schachne; Dorothy and David I. Schachne Dean Dr. Sheldon R. Gelman. Offers graduate programs in social work and Jewish communal service; grants MSW and DSW degrees and certificate in Jewish communal service. MSW programs are: Concurrent Plan, 2-year, full-time track, combining classroom study and supervised field instruction; Plan for Employed Persons (PEP), for people working in social agencies; Block Education Plan (Dir. Dr. Adele Weiner), which combines summer course work with regular-year field placement in local agencies; Clergy Plan, training in counseling for clergy of all denominations; Silvia and Irwin Leiferman Center for Professional

Training in the Care of the Elderly. *Jewish Social Work Forum.*

———, (AFFILIATE) YESHIVA OF LOS ANGELES (1977). 9760 W. Pico Blvd., Los Angeles, CA 90035-4701. (310)772-2424. FAX: (310)772-7661. E-mail: mhmay@wiesenthal.com. Dean Rabbi Marvin Hier; Bd. Chmn. Samuel Belzberg; Dir. Academic Programs Rabbi Sholom Tendler. Affiliates are Yeshiva University High Schools of Los Angeles, Jewish Studies Institute and Kollel Torah MiTzion.

———, YESHIVA UNIVERSITY MUSEUM (*see* p. 511)

SOCIAL, MUTUAL BENEFIT

ALPHA EPSILON PI FRATERNITY (1913). 8815 Wesleyan Rd., Indianapolis, IN 46268-1171. (317)876-1913. FAX: (317) 876-1057. E-mail: office@aepi.org. Internatl. Pres. Andrew P. Fradkin; Exec. V.-Pres. Sidney N. Dunn. International Jewish fraternity active on over 100 campuses in the U.S. and Canada; encourages Jewish students to remain loyal to their heritage and to assume leadership roles in the community; active in behalf of Soviet Jewry, the State of Israel, the United States Holocaust Memorial Museum, Tay Sachs Disease, Mazon:A Jewish Response to Hunger, and other causes. *The Lion of Alpha Epsilon Pi (quarterly magazine).*

AMERICAN ASSOCIATION OF JEWS FROM THE FORMER USSR, INC. (AAJFSU) (1989). 119 Fulton St., 5th fl., rm.3, NYC 10038. (212) (212) 964-1946. FAX: (212)964-1946. E-mail: AAJFSU@yahoo.com. Pres. Yury Zilberman; Bd. Chmn. Semyon Torgovnik. National not-for-profit, grassroots mutual assistance and refugee advocacy organization, which unites and represents interests of over 500,000 Russian speaking Jewish refugees and legal immigrants from the former Soviet Union. Has chapters in 6 states, including New York, Ohio, Colorado, New Jersey, Massachusetts and Maryland. The national organization is a member of the National Immigration Forum and it is affiliated with the United Jewish Communities, Washington Action Office. New York Chapter is a member of the Jewish Community Relations Couincil of New York and the New York Immigration Coalition. The AAJFSU assists newcomers in their resettlement and vocational and cultural adjustment, fosters their Jewish identity and involvement in civic and social affairs, fights anti-Semitism and violation of human rights in the FSU and the U.S. through cooperation with other human rights organizations and advocacy, provides advocacy in cases of political asylum for victims of anti-Semitism in the FSU and naturalization, provides assistance in social safety net and naturalization of the elderly and disabled. *Chronicles of Anti-Semitism and Nationalism in Republics of the Former USSR (in English, annually); Information Bulletin (in Russian, bimonthly).*

AMERICAN FEDERATION OF JEWS FROM CENTRAL EUROPE, INC. (1938). 570 Seventh Ave., NYC 10018. (212)921-3871. FAX: (212) 575-1918. Pres. Fritz Weinschenk; Bd. Chmn. Curt C. Silberman; Exec. Asst. Dennis E. Rohrbaugh. Seeks to safeguard the rights and interests of American Jews of German-speaking Central European descent, especially in reference to restitution and indemnification; through its affiliate Research Foundation for Jewish Immigration sponsors research and publications on the history, immigration, and acculturation of Central European émigrés in the U.S. and worldwide; through its affiliate Jewish Philanthropic Fund of 1933 supports social programs for needy Nazi victims in the U.S.; undertakes cultural activities, annual conferences, publications; member, Council of Jews from Germany, London.

AMERICAN VETERANS OF ISRAEL (1951). 136 E. 39 St., NYC 10016. E-mail: sklausne@ mail.sas.upenn.edu. Pres. Samuel Z. Klausner; V-Pres. David Kaplan. Maintains contact with American and Canadian volunteers who served in Aliyah Bet and/or Israel's War of Independence; promotes Israel's welfare; holds memorial services at grave of Col. David Marcus; is affiliated with World Mahal. *Newsletter.*

ASSOCIATION OF YUGOSLAV JEWS IN THE UNITED STATES, INC. (1941). 130 E. 59 St., Suite 1202, NYC 10022. (212)371-6891. V.-Pres. & Chmn. Emanuel Salom; Sec. Dr. Joseph Stock. Assistance to all Jews originally from Yugoslavia—Bosnia, Serbia, Croatia—and new settlers in Israel. *Bulletins.*

BNAI ZION–THE AMERICAN FRATERNAL ZIONIST ORGANIZATION (1908). 136 E. 39

St., NYC 10016. (212)725-1211. FAX: (212)684-6327. Pres. Hon. Alan G. Hevesi; Exec. V.-Pres. Mel Parness. Fosters principles of Americanism, fraternalism, and Zionism. The Bnai Zion Foundation supports various humanitarian projects in Israel and the USA, chiefly the Bnai Zion Medical Center in Haifa and homes for retarded children-Maon Bnai Zion in Rosh Ha'ayin and the Herman Z. Quittman Center in Jerusalem. Also supports building of new central library in Ma'aleh Adumim. In U.S. sponsors program of awards for excellence in Hebrew for high school and college students. Chapters all over U.S. *Bnai Zion Voice* (quarterly).

BRITH ABRAHAM (1859; reorg. 1887). 136 E. 39 St., NYC 10016. (212)725-1211. FAX: (212)684-6327. Grand Master Robert Freeman. Protects Jewish rights and combats anti-Semitism; supports Soviet and Ethiopian emigration and the safety and dignity of Jews worldwide; helps to support Bnai Zion Medical Center in Haifa and other Israeli institutions; aids and supports various programs and projects in the U.S.: Hebrew Excellence Program-Gold Medal presentation in high schools and colleges; Camp Loyaltown; Brith Abraham and Bnai Zion Foundations. *Voice.*

BRITH SHOLOM (1905). 3939 Conshohocken Ave., Philadelphia, PA 19131. (215)878-5696. FAX: (215) 878-5699. Pres. Howard P. Rovner; Exec. Dir. Louis Mason. Fraternal organization devoted to community welfare, protection of rights of Jewish people, and activities that foster Jewish identity and provide support for Israel. Through its philanthropic arm, the Brith Sholom Foundation (1962), sponsors Brith Sholom House in Philadelphia, nonprofit senior-citizen apartments; and Brith Sholom Beit Halochem in Haifa, Israel, rehabilitation, social, and sports center for disabled Israeli veterans, operated by Zahal. Chmn. Bennett Goldstein; Exec. Dir. Saundra Laub. *Brith Sholom Digest; monthly news bulletin.*

FREE SONS OF ISRAEL (1849). 250 Fifth Ave., Suite 201, NYC 10001. (212)725-3690. FAX: (212)725-5874. Grand Master Arlene Hoberman Kyler; Grand Sec. Ronald J. Laszlo. Oldest Jewish fraternal-benefit society in U.S. Affordable membership men & women (18+). Supports Israel,

UJA projects, non-sectarian toy drives/philanthropies. Social Action fights anti-Semitism, supports human rights. Member benefits-IBM Metro Credit Union, scholarships, cemetery, discounted Long Term Care Insurance, educational and social functions, Free Model Seder. *Free Sons Reporter.* (www. FREESONS.ORG)

JEWISH LABOR BUND (Directed by WORLD COORDINATING COMMITTEE OF THE BUND) (1897; reorg. 1947). 25 E. 21 St., NYC 10010. (212)475-0059. FAX: (212) 473-5102. Sec. Gen. Benjamin Nadel. Coordinates activities of Bund organizations throughout the world and represents them in the Socialist International; spreads the ideas of socialism as formulated by the Jewish Labor Bund; publishes books and periodicals on world problems, Jewish life, socialist theory and policy, and on the history, activities, and ideology of the Jewish Labor Bund. *Unser Tsait* (U.S.); *Lebns-Fragn* (Israel); *Unser Gedank* (Australia).

SEPHARDIC JEWISH BROTHERHOOD OF AMERICA, INC. (1915). 97-45 Queens Blvd., Rm. 610, Rego Park, NY 11374. (718)459-1600. Pres. Bernard Ouziel; Sec. Irving Barocas. A benevolent fraternal organization seeking to promote the industrial, social, educational, and religious welfare of its members. *Sephardic Brother.*

THE WORKMEN'S CIRCLE/ARBETER RING (1900). 45 E. 33 St., NYC 10016. (212)889-6800. FAX: (212)532-7518. E-mail: member@circle.org. Pres. Mark Mlotek; Exec. Dir. Robert Kestenbaum. Fosters Jewish identity and participation in Jewish life through Jewish, especially Yiddish, culture and education, friendship, mutual aid, and the pursuit of social and economic justice. Offices are located throughout the U.S. and Canada. Member services include:Jewish cultural seminars, concerts, theater, Jewish schools, children's camp and adult resort, fraternal and singles activities, a Jewish Book Center, public affairs/social action, health insurance plans, medical/dental/legal services, life insurance plans, cemetery/ funeral benefits, social services, geriatric homes and centers, and travel services. *The Call.* (WWW.CIRCLE.ORG)

ZETA BETA TAU FRATERNITY (1898). 3905 Vincennes Rd., Suite 101, Indianapolis,

IN 46268. (317)334-1898. FAX: (317)334-1899. E-mail: zbt@zbtnational.org. Pres. Ronald J. Taylor, M.D.; Exec. Dir. Jonathan I. Yulish. Oldest and historically largest Jewish fraternity; promotes intellectual awareness, social responsibility, integrity, and brotherhood among over 5,000 undergrads and 110,000 alumni in the U.S. and Canada. Encourages leadership and diversity through mutual respect of all heritages; nonsectarian since 1954. A brotherhood of Kappa Nu, Phi Alpha, Phi Epsilon Pi, Phi Sigma Delta, Zeta Beta Tau. *The Deltan (quarterly)*. (WWW.ZBT.ORG)

SOCIAL WELFARE

AMC CANCER RESEARCH CENTER (formerly JEWISH CONSUMPTIVES' RELIEF SOCIETY, 1904; incorporated as American Medical Center at Denver, 1954). 1600 Pierce St., Denver, CO 80214. (303)233-6501. FAX: (303)239-3400. E-mail: edelmanj@amc.org. Pres./CEO Bob R. Baker; Exec. V-Pres. Research Dr. Tom Slaga. A nationally recognized leader in the fight against cancer; employs a three-pronged, interdisciplinary approach that combines laboratory, clinical, and community cancer-control research to advance the prevention, early detection, diagnosis, and treatment of the disease. The exclusive scientific focus of our work is the prevention and control of cancer and other major diseases. *The Quest for Answers; Annual Report. (www.amc.org)*

AMCHA FOR TSEDAKAH (1990). 9800 Cherry Hill Rd., College Park, MD 20740. (301)937-2600. Pres. Rabbi Bruce E. Kahn. Solicits and distributes contributions to Jewish charitable organizations in the U.S. and Israel; accredits organizations which serve an important tsedakah purpose, demonstrate efficiency and fiscal integrity, and also support pluralism. Contributors are encouraged to earmark contributions for specific organizations; all contributions to General Fund are forwarded to the charitable institutions, as operating expenses are covered by a separate fund. *Newspaper supplement.*

AMERICAN JEWISH CORRECTIONAL CHAPLAINS ASSOCIATION, INC. (formerly NATIONAL COUNCIL OF JEWISH PRISON CHAPLAINS) (1937). 10 E. 73 St., NYC 10021-4194. (212)879-8415. FAX: (212) 772-3977. (Cooperates with the New York Board of Rabbis.) Pres. Rabbi Irving Koslowe. Supports spiritual, moral, and social services for Jewish men and women in corrections; stimulates support of correctional chaplaincy; provides spiritual and professional fellowship for Jewish correctional chaplains; promotes sound standards for correctional chaplaincy; schedules workshops and research to aid chaplains in counseling and with religious services for Jewish inmates. Constituent, American Correctional Chaplains Association. *Chaplains Manual.*

AMERICAN JEWISH SOCIETY FOR SERVICE, INC. (1950). 15 E. 26 St., Rm. 1029, NYC 10010. (212)683-6178. Founder/Chmn. Henry Kohn; Pres. Lawrence G. Green; Exec. Dirs. Carl & Audrey Brenner. Conducts voluntary work-service camps each summer to enable high school juniors and seniors to perform humanitarian service.

ASSOCIATION OF JEWISH AGING SERVICES (formerly NORTH AMERICAN ASSOCIATION OF JEWISH HOMES AND HOUSING FOR THE AGING) (1960). 316 Pennsylvania Ave., SE, Suite 402, Washington, DC 20003. (202) 543-7500. FAX: (202)543-4090. E-mail: ajas@ajas.org. Pres. Lawrence M. Zippin; Chmn. Ms. Nita Corré. Represents nearly all the not-for-profit charitable homes and housing for the Jewish aging; promotes excellence in performance and quality of service through fostering communication and education and encouraging advocacy for the aging; conducts annual conferences and institutes. *Directory; The Scribe (quarterly newsletter).*

ASSOCIATION OF JEWISH CENTER PROFESSIONALS (1918). 15 E. 26 St., NYC 10010-1579. (212)532-4949. FAX: (212) 481-4174. E-mail: ajcp@jcca.org. Pres. Karen Stern; V-Pres. Susan Bender & David Jacobs; Exec. Dir. Joe Harris. Seeks to enhance the standards, techniques, practices, scope, and public understanding of Jewish community center professionals and kindred agency work. *Kesher.*

ASSOCIATION OF JEWISH COMMUNITY ORGANIZATION PERSONNEL (AJCOP) (1969). 14619 Horseshoe Trace, Wellington, FL 33414. (561)795-4853. FAX: (561)798-0358. E-mail: marlene@ajcop.org. Pres. Richard Jacobs; Exec. Dir. Louis B. Solomon. An organization of professionals engaged in areas of fund-raising, endowments, budgeting, social planning, financing, administration, and coordination of services. Objectives are to develop and enhance professional practices in Jewish communal work; to maintain and improve standards, practices, scope, and public understanding of the field of community organization, as practiced through local federations, national agencies, other organizations, settings, and private practitioners. *Prolog (quarterly newspaper); Proceedings (annual record of papers and speeches).* (WWW.AJCOP.ORG)

ASSOCIATION OF JEWISH FAMILY AND CHILDREN'S AGENCIES (1972). 557 Cranbury Rd., Suite 2, E. Brunswick, NJ 08816-5419. (800) 634-7346. FAX: (732)432-7127. E-mail: ajfca@ajfca.org. Pres. Richard K. Blankstein; Exec. V.-Pres. Bert J. Goldberg. The national service organization for Jewish family and children's agencies in the U.S. and Canada. Reinforces member agencies in their efforts to sustain and enhance the quality of Jewish family and communal life. Operates the Elder Support Network for the national Jewish community. *Tachlis (quarterly); Professional Opportunities Bulletin; Executive Digest (monthly).* (WWW.AJFCA.ORG)

BARON DE HIRSCH FUND (1891). 130 E. 59 St., 12th fl., NYC 10022. (212)836-1358. FAX: (212)453-6512. Pres. Seymour W. Zises; Mng. Dir. Lauren Katzowitz. Aids Jewish immigrants in the U.S. and Israel by giving grants to agencies active in educational and vocational fields.

B'NAI B'RITH (1843). 1640 Rhode Island Ave., NW, Washington, DC 20036. (202)857-6600. FAX: (202)857-1099. Pres. Richard D. Heideman; Exec. V.-Pres. Daniel S. Manaschin. International Jewish organization, with affiliates in 58countries. Offers programs designed to ensure the preservation of Jewry and Judaism: Jewish education, community volunteer service, expansion of human rights, assistance to Israel, housing for the elderly, leadership training, rights of Jews in all countries to study their heritage. *International Jewish Monthly.*

———, ANTI-DEFAMATION LEAGUE OF (*see* p. 500)

———, HILLEL (*see* p. 529)

———, KLUTZNICK MUSEUM (*see* p. 505)

———, YOUTH ORGANIZATION (*see* p. 528)

CITY OF HOPE NATIONAL MEDICAL CENTER AND BECKMAN RESEARCH INSTITUTE (1913). 1500 E. Duarte Rd., Duarte, CA 91010. (626)359-8111. FAX: (626) 301-8115. E-mail: dhalper@coh.org. Pres./CEO Gil N. Schwartzberg. Offers care to those with cancer and other catastrophic diseases, medical consultation service for second opinions, and research programs in genetics, immunology, and the basic life process. *City of Hope Cancer Research Center Report.*

CONFERENCE OF JEWISH COMMUNAL SERVICE (*see* JEWISH COMMUNAL SERVICE ASSOCIATION OF N. AMERICA)

COUNCIL OF JEWISH FEDERATIONS (*see* UNITED JEWISH COMMUNITIES)

INTERNATIONAL ASSOCIATION OF JEWISH VOCATIONAL SERVICES (FORMERLY JEWISH OCCUPATIONAL COUNCIL) (1939). 1845 Walnut St., Suite 640, Philadelphia, PA 19103. (215) 854-0233. FAX: (215) 854-0212. E-mail: iajvs@jevs.org. Pres. Donald Simons; Exec. Dir. Genie Cohen. Not-for-profit trade association of Jewish-sponsored social service agencies in the U.S., Canada, and Israel. Provides member agencies with technical, informational, and communications support; researches funding opportunities, develops collaborative program models, and represents Jewish vocational network nationally and internationally. Sponsors annual conference for members. Member agencies provide a wide range of educational, vocational, and rehabilitation services to both the Jewish and non-Jewish communities. (WWW.IAJVS.ORG)

INTERNATIONAL COUNCIL ON JEWISH SOCIAL AND WELFARE SERVICES (1961). c/o American Jewish Joint Distribution Committee, 711 Third Ave., NYC 10017. (NY liaison office with UN headquarters.) (212)687-6200. FAX: (212)370-5467. E-mail: steve@jdcny.org. Chmn. David Cope-Thompson; Exec. Sec. Eli Benson. Provides for exchange of views and information among member agencies on problems of Jewish social and welfare services, including medical care, old age, welfare, child care, rehabilitation, technical assistance, vocational training, agricultural and other resettlement, economic assistance, refugees, migration, integration, and related problems; representation of views to governments and international organizations. Members:six national and international organizations.

JEWISH BRAILLE INSTITUTE OF AMERICA, INC. (1931). 110 E. 30 St., NYC 10016. (212)889-2525. FAX: (212)689-3692. Pres. Barbara B. Friedman; Exec. V.-Pres. Gerald M. Kass. Provides Judaic materials in braille, talking books, and large print for blind, visually impaired, and reading-disabled; offers counseling for full integration into the life of the Jewish community. International program serves clients in more than 50 countries; sponsors special programs in Israel and Eastern Europe to assist the elderly as well as students. *Jewish Braille Review; JBI Voice; Likutim, Hebrew-language magazine on blindness issues.* (WWW.JEWISH BRAILLE.ORG)

JEWISH CHILDREN'S ADOPTION NETWORK (1990). PO Box 16544, Denver, CO 80216-0544. (303)573-8113. FAX: (303) 893-1447. E-mail: jcan@uswest.net. Pres. Stephen Krausz; Exec. Dir. Vicki Krausz. An adoption exchange founded for the primary purpose of locating adoptive families for Jewish infants and children. Works with some 200 children a year, throughout N. Amer., 85-90% of whom have special needs. No fees charged for services, which include birth-parent and adoptive-parent counseling. *Quarterly newsletter.* (WWW.USERS.USWEST.NET/jcan)

JEWISH COMMUNAL SERVICE ASSOCIATION OF N. AMERICA (1899; formerly Conference of Jewish Communal Service). 3084 State Hwy. 27, Suite 9, Kendall Park, NJ 08824-1657. (732)821-1871. FAX: (732) 821-5335. E-mail: jcsana@aol.com. Pres. Max L. Kleinman; Exec. Dir. Joel Ollander. Serves as forum for all professional philosophies in community service, for testing new experiences, proposing new ideas, and questioning or reaffirming old concepts; umbrella organization for 7 major Jewish communal service groups. Concerned with advancement of professional personnel practices and standards. *Journal of Jewish Communal Service; Concurrents.*

JEWISH COMMUNITY CENTERS ASSOCIATION OF NORTH AMERICA (FORMERLY JWB) (1917). 15 E. 26 St., NYC 10010-1579. (212)532-4949. FAX: (212)481-4174. E-mail: info@jcca.org. Pres. Jerome Makowsky; Exec. V.-Pres. Allan Finkelstein. The leadership network of, and central agency for, the Jewish Community Center movement, comprising more than 275 JCCs, YM-YWHAs, and camps in the U.S. and Canada, serving over one million members and a million nonmember users. Offers a wide range of services and resources to help affiliates provide educational, cultural, social, Jewish identity-building, and recreational programs. Fosters and strengthens ties between N. American Jews and Israel and with world Jewry. U.S. government-accredited agency for serving the religious and social needs of Jewish military personnel, their families, and patients in VA hospitals through JWB Chaplains Council. *JCC Circle; Chaplines; othernewsletters for JCC profession* als. (WWW.JCCA.ORG)

————, JEWISH WELFARE BOARD JEWISH CHAPLAINS COUNCIL (FORMERLY COMMISSION ON JEWISH CHAPLAINCY) (1940). 15 E. 26 St., NYC 10010-1579. (212)532-4949. FAX: (212)481-4174. E-mail: nathanlandman@jcca.com. Chmn. Rabbi Jacob J. Greenberg; Dir. Rabbi David Lapp; Dep. Dir. Rabbi Nathan M. Landman. Recruits, endorses, and serves Jewish military and Veterans Administration chaplains on behalf of the American Jewish community and the major rabbinic bodies; trains and assists Jewish lay leaders where there are no chaplains, for service to Jewish military personnel, their families, and hospitalized veterans. *CHAPLINES newsletter.*

JEWISH FAMILY AND CHILDREN'S PROFESSIONALS ASSOCIATION (*see* JEWISH SOCIAL SERVICES PROFESSIONALS ASSOCIATION)

JEWISH FUND FOR JUSTICE (1984). 260 Fifth Ave., Suite 701, NYC 10001. (212) 213-2113. FAX: (212)213-2233. E-mail: justiceusa@aol.com. Bd. Chmn. Ronna Stamm; Exec. Dir. Marlene Provizer. A national grant-making foundation supporting efforts to combat the causes and consequences of poverty in the U.S. Provides diverse opportunities for giving, including family and youth endowment funds and the Purim Fund for Women in Poverty; develops educational materials linking Jewish teachings and rituals with contemporary social justice issues; supports Jewish involvement in community-based anti-poverty efforts; and works cooperatively with other denominational and social change philanthropies. *Annual report, newsletter.* (WWW.JFJUSTICE.ORG)

JEWISH FUNDERS NETWORK (1990). 15 E. 26 St., Suite 1038, NYC 10010. (212) 726-0177. FAX: (212) 726-0195. E-mail: jfn@jfunders.org. Exec. Dir. Evan Mendelson. A national membership organization dedicated to advancing the growth and quality of Jewish philanthropy through more effective grant making to Jewish and secular causes. Individual philanthropists, foundation trustees, and foundation staff discuss emerging issues, gain expertise in operational aspects of grant making, explore intergenerational/family dynamics of family foundations, and exchange information among peers. *Quarterly Newsletter; Special Reports on Philanthropy.* (WWW.JFUNDERS.ORG)

JEWISH SOCIAL SERVICES PROFESSIONALS ASSOCIATION (JSSPA) (1965). c/o AJFCA, 557 Cranbury Rd., Suite 2, E. Brunswick, NJ 08816-0549. (800) 634-7346. FAX: (732)432-7127. E-mail: ajfca@ajfca.org. Chmn. Linda Kislowicz. Brings together executives, supervisors, managers, caseworkers, and related professionals in Jewish Family Service and related agencies. Seeks to enhance professional skills, improve personnel standards, further Jewish continuity and identity, and strengthen Jewish family life. Provides a national and regional forum for professional discussion and learning; functions under the auspices of the Association of Jewish Family and Children's Agencies. *Newsletter.* (WWW.AJFCA.ORG)

JEWISH WOMEN INTERNATIONAL (1897). 1828 L St., NW, Suite 250, Washington, DC 20036. (202)857-1300. FAX: (202) 857-1380. E-mail: jwi@jwi.org. Pres. Barbara Rabkin; Exec. Dir. Gail Rubinson. Jewish Women International breaks the cycle of violence by developing emotionally healthy adults, empowering women and strengthening families. Jewish Women International accomplishes its goals through direct service programs, education, advocacy and the promotion of "best practice" models. Offers programs in the United States, Canada, and Israel. *Jewish Woman Magazine (quarterly).* (WWW.JEWISHWOMEN.ORG)

JWB (*see* JEWISH COMMUNITY CENTERS ASSOCIATION OF NORTH AMERICA)

LEVI HOSPITAL (SPONSORED BY B'NAI B'RITH) (1914). 300 Prospect Ave., Hot Springs, AR 71901. (501)624-1281. FAX: (501) 622-3500. E-mail: levihospital@hsnp.com. Pres. Dr. Hal Koppel; Admin. Patrick G. McCabe. Offers outpatient rehab, including therapy sessions in large thermal heated pool. Other programs:adult/geriatric inpatient and outpatient psychiatric program, child/adolescent psychiatric clinic, hospice care, home health care, osteoporosis clinic, Levi Rehabilitation Unit, a cooperative effort of Levi and St. Joseph's hospitals (inpatient rehab). *The Progress Chart; The Legacy.*

MAZON: A JEWISH RESPONSE TO HUNGER (1985). 12401 Wilshire Blvd., Suite 303, Los Angeles, CA 90025. (310)442-0020. FAX: (310)442-0030. E-mail: mazonmail@aol.com. Bd. Chmn. Daniel Levenson; Exec. Dir. Susan Cramer. A grant-making and fund-raising organization that raises funds in the Jewish community and provides grants to nonprofit 501(c)(3) organizations which aim to prevent and alleviate hunger in the United States and abroad. Grantees include food pantries, food banks, multi-service organizations, advocacy, education and research projects, and international relief and development organizations. 1998 grants totaled $2.3 million. *Mazon Newsletter.*

NATIONAL ASSOCIATION OF JEWISH CHAPLAINS (1988). 901 Route 10, Whippany, NJ 07981. (973)884-4800 ext. 287. FAX: (973) 736-9193. E-mail: cecille3@juno.com. Pres. Rabbi Solomon Schiff; Natl. Coord. Cecille Allman Asekoff. A professional organization for people functioning as Jewish chaplains in hospitals, nursing homes, geriatric, psychiatric, correctional, and military facilities. Provides collegial support, continuing education, professional certification, and resources for the Jewish community on issues of pastoral and spiritual care. *The Jewish Chaplain.*

NATIONAL COUNCIL OF JEWISH PRISON CHAPLAINS, INC. (*see* AMERICAN JEWISH CORRECTIONAL CHAPLAINS ASSOCIATION, INC.)

NATIONAL COUNCIL OF JEWISH WOMEN (1893). 53 W. 23 St., NYC 10010. (212) 645-4048. FAX: (212)645-7466. E-mail:

actionline@ncjw.org. Pres. Jan Schneiderman; Exec. Dir. Susan Katz. Works to improve the lives of women, children, and families in the United States and Israel; strives to insure individual rights and freedoms for all. NCJW volunteers deliver vital services in 500 U.S. communities and carry out NCJW's advocacy agenda through a powerful grassroots network. *NCJW Journal; Washington Newsletter.* (WWW.NCJW.ORG)

NATIONAL INSTITUTE FOR JEWISH HOSPICE (1985). PO Box 48025, Los Angeles, CA 90048. (800)446-4448. 330 Broad Ave., Englewood, NJ 07631. (201)816-7324. FAX: (201)816-7321. Pres. Rabbi Maurice Lamm; Exec. Dir. Shirley Lamm. Serves as a national Jewish hospice resource center. Through conferences, research, publications, referrals, and counseling services offers guidance, training, and information to patients, family members, clergy of all faiths, professional caregivers, and volunteers who work with the Jewish terminally ill. *Jewish Hospice Times.*

NATIONAL JEWISH CHILDREN'S LEUKEMIA FOUNDATION (1990). 233 Broadway, Suite 818, NYC 10279. (212)587-7474. FAX: (212)587-7476. E-mail: leukemia@erols.com. Pres./Founder Zvi Shor. Dedicated to saving the lives of children. Programs:Bone Marrow Donor Search, Stem Cell Banking-freezing cells from babies' umbilical cords for long-term storage, in case of need for bone marrow; Make-A-Dream-Come True-granting wishes for terminally ill children; Referral Service; Patient Advocacy. (WWW.LEUKEMIAFOUNDATION.ORG)

NATIONAL JEWISH MEDICAL AND RESEARCH CENTER (formerly NATIONAL JEWISH HOSPITAL/NATIONAL ASTHMA CENTER) (1899). 1400 Jackson St., Denver, CO 80206. (800)222-LUNG. Pres./CEO Lynn M. Taussig, MD; Bd. Chmn. Meyer Saltzman. The only medical and research center in the United States devoted entirely to respiratory, allergic, and immune system diseases, including asthma, tuberculosis, emphysema, severe allergies, AIDS, and cancer, and autoimmune diseases such as lupus. Dedicated to enhancing prevention, treatment, and cures through research, and to developing and providing innovative clinical programs for treating patients regardless of age, religion, race, or ability to pay. *New Directions; Medical Scientific Update.*

NORTH AMERICAN ASSOCIATION OF JEWISH HOMES AND HOUSING FOR THE AGING (*see* ASSOCIATION OF JEWISH AGING SERVICES)

UNITED ORDER TRUE SISTERS, INC. (UOTS) (1846). 100 State St., Albany, NY 12207. (518)436-1670. Pres. Rita Lipkin; Fin. Sec. Betty Peyser; Treas. Rose Goldberg. Charitable, community service, especially home supplies, etc., for indigent cancer victims; supports camps for children with cancer. *Inside UotS.*

WORLD COUNCIL OF JEWISH COMMUNAL SERVICE (1966; reorg. 1994). 711 Third Ave., 10th fl., NYC 10017. (212)687-6200. FAX: (212)370-5467. Pres. Howard Charish; Assoc. Pres. Dr. Jack Habib; Exec. V.-Pres. Theodore Comet. Seeks to build Jewish community worldwide by enhancing professional-to-professional connections, improving professional practice through interchange of experience and sharing of expertise, fostering professional training programs, and stimulating research. Conducts quadrennial conferences in Jerusalem and periodic regional meetings. *Proceedings of international conferences; newsletters.*

PROFESSIONAL ASSOCIATIONS*

AMERICAN ASSOCIATION OF RABBIS (RELIGIOUS, EDUCATIONAL)

AMERICAN CONFERENCE OF CANTORS, UNION OF AMERICAN HEBREW CONGREGATIONS (RELIGIOUS, EDUCATIONAL)

AMERICAN JEWISH CORRECTIONAL CHAPLAINS ASSOCIATION, INC. (SOCIAL WELFARE)

AMERICAN JEWISH PRESS ASSOCIATION (CULTURAL)

AMERICAN JEWISH PUBLIC RELATIONS SOCIETY (1957). 575 Lexington Ave., Suite 600, NYC 10022. (212)644-2663. FAX: (212)644-3887. Pres. Diane J. Ehrlich; V-

---

*For fuller listing see under categories in parentheses.

Pres., membership, Lauren R. Marcus. Advances professional status of public-relations practitioners employed by Jewish organizations and institutions or who represent Jewish-related clients, services, or products; upholds a professional code of ethics and standards; provides continuing education and networking opportunities at monthly meetings; serves as a clearinghouse for employment opportunities. *AJPRS Reporter; AJPRS Membership Directory.*

ASSOCIATION OF HILLEL/JEWISH CAMPUS PROFESSIONALS (RELIGIOUS, EDUCATIONAL)

ASSOCIATION OF JEWISH CENTER PROFESSIONALS (SOCIAL WELFARE)

ASSOCIATION OF JEWISH COMMUNITY ORGANIZATION PERSONNEL (SOCIAL WELFARE)

ASSOCIATION OF JEWISH COMMUNITY RELATIONS WORKERS (COMMUNITY RELATIONS)

CANTORS ASSEMBLY (RELIGIOUS, EDUCATIONAL)

CENTRAL CONFERENCE OF AMERICAN RABBIS (RELIGIOUS, EDUCATIONAL)

COUNCIL OF JEWISH ORGANIZATIONS IN CIVIL SERVICE (COMMUNITY RELATIONS)

INTERNATIONAL JEWISH MEDIA ASSOCIATION (CULTURAL)

JEWISH CHAPLAINS COUNCIL, JWB (SOCIAL WELFARE)

JEWISH COMMUNAL SERVICE ASSOCIATION OF N. AMERICA (SOCIAL WELFARE)

JEWISH EDUCATORS ASSEMBLY, UNITED SYNAGOGUE OF CONSERVATIVE JUDAISM (RELIGIOUS, EDUCATIONAL)

JEWISH SOCIAL SERVICES PROFESSIONALS ASSOCIATION (SOCIAL WELFARE)

JEWISH TEACHERS ASSOCIATION–MORIM (RELIGIOUS, EDUCATIONAL)

NATIONAL ASSOCIATION OF HEBREW DAY SCHOOL ADMINISTRATORS, TORAH UMESORAH (RELIGIOUS, EDUCATIONAL)

NATIONAL ASSOCIATION OF JEWISH CHAPLAINS (SOCIAL WELFARE)

NATIONAL ASSOCIATION OF TEMPLE ADMINISTRATORS, UNION OF AMERICAN HEBREW CONGREGATIONS (RELIGIOUS, EDUCATIONAL)

NATIONAL ASSOCIATION OF TEMPLE EDUCATORS, UNION OF AMERICAN HEBREW CONGREGATIONS (RELIGIOUS, EDUCATIONAL)

NATIONAL CONFERENCE OF YESHIVA PRINCIPALS, TORAH UMESORAH (RELIGIOUS, EDUCATIONAL)

NORTH AMERICAN ASSOCIATION OF SYNAGOGUE EXECUTIVES, UNITED SYNAGOGUE OF CONSERVATIVE JUDAISM (RELIGIOUS, EDUCATIONAL)

RABBINICAL ALLIANCE OF AMERICA (RELIGIOUS, EDUCATIONAL)

RABBINICAL ASSEMBLY (RELIGIOUS, EDUCATIONAL)

RABBINICAL COUNCIL OF AMERICA (RELIGIOUS, EDUCATIONAL)

RECONSTRUCTIONIST RABBINICAL ASSOCIATION (RELIGIOUS, EDUCATIONAL)

UNION OF ORTHODOX RABBIS OF THE U.S. AND CANADA (RELIGIOUS, EDUCATIONAL)

WORLD CONFERENCE OF JEWISH COMMUNAL SERVICE (COMMUNITY RELATIONS)

WOMEN'S ORGANIZATIONS*

AMIT WOMEN (ISRAEL-RELATED)

BRANDEIS UNIVERSITY NATIONAL WOMEN'S COMMITTEE (1948). MS 132, Waltham, MA 02454-9110. (781) 736-4160. FAX: (781)736-4183. E-mail: bunwc@brandeis.edu. Pres. Marcia F. Levy; Exec. Dir. Joan C. Bowen. A friends-of-the-library organization whose mission is to provide financial support for the Brandeis Libraries; works to enhance the image of Brandeis, a Jewish-sponsored, nonsectarian university. Offers its members opportunity for intellectual pursuit, continuing education, community service, social interaction, personal enrichment, and leadership development. Open to all, regardless of race, religion, nationality, or gender. *Connecting.*

EMUNAH WOMEN OF AMERICA (ISRAEL-RELATED)

*For fuller listing see under categories in parentheses.

HADASSAH, THE WOMEN'S ZIONIST ORGA-
NIZATION OF AMERICA (ISRAEL-RELATED)

JEWISH WOMEN INTERNATIONAL (SOCIAL
WELFARE)

NA'AMAT USA, THE WOMEN'S LABOR ZION-
IST ORGANIZATION OF AMERICA (ISRAEL-
RELATED)

NATIONAL COUNCIL OF JEWISH WOMEN (SO-
CIAL WELFARE)

UOTS (SOCIAL WELFARE)

WOMEN OF REFORM JUDAISM—FEDERA-
TION OF TEMPLE SISTERHOODS, UNION OF
AMERICAN HEBREW CONGREGATIONS
(RELIGIOUS, EDUCATIONAL)

WOMEN'S AMERICAN ORT, AMERICAN ORT
FEDERATION (OVERSEAS AID)

WOMEN'S BRANCH OF THE UNION OF OR-
THODOX JEWISH CONGREGATIONS OF
AMERICA (RELIGIOUS, EDUCATIONAL)

WOMEN'S DIVISION OF POALE AGUDATH IS-
RAEL OF AMERICA (ISRAEL-RELATED)

WOMEN'S LEAGUE FOR CONSERVATIVE JU-
DAISM (RELIGIOUS, EDUCATIONAL)

WOMEN'S LEAGUE FOR ISRAEL, INC.
(ISRAEL-RELATED)

WOMEN'S ORGANIZATION, YESHIVA UNI-
VERSITY (RELIGIOUS, EDUCATIONAL)

YOUTH AND STUDENT
ORGANIZATIONS*

AGUDATH ISRAEL OF AMERICA (RELIGIOUS,
EDUCATIONAL)

B'NAI B'RITH YOUTH ORGANIZATION (RE-
LIGIOUS, EDUCATIONAL)

BNEI AKIVA OF NORTH AMERICA, RELI-
GIOUS ZIONISTS OF AMERICA (ISRAEL-
RELATED)

HABONIM—DROR NORTH AMERICA
(ISRAEL-RELATED)

HASHOMER HATZAIR, SOCIALIST ZIONIST
YOUTH MOVEMENT (ISRAEL-RELATED)

HILLEL (RELIGIOUS, EDUCATIONAL)

KADIMA, UNITED SYNAGOGUE OF CONSER-
VATIVE JUDAISM (RELIGIOUS, EDUCA-
TIONAL)

NATIONAL CONFERENCE OF SYNAGOGUE
YOUTH, UNION OF ORTHODOX JEWISH

CONGREGATIONS OF AMERICA (RELI-
GIOUS, EDUCATIONAL)

NATIONAL JEWISH COMMITTEE ON SCOUT-
ING (RELIGIOUS, EDUCATIONAL)

NATIONAL JEWISH GIRL SCOUT COMMITTEE
(RELIGIOUS, EDUCATIONAL) (ISRAEL-
RELATED)

NORTH AMERICAN ALLIANCE FOR JEWISH
YOUTH (1996). 50 W. 58 St., NYC 10019.
(212)303-8014. FAX: (212)303-4572. E-
mail: dkrakow@aol.com. Chmn. Doron
Krakow; Dir. Heather Kibel. Serves the
cause of informal Jewish and Zionist education in America; provides a forum for
the professional leaders of the major N.
American youth movements, camps, Israel
programs, and university programs to address common issues and concerns, and to
represent those issues with a single voice
to the wider Jewish and Zionist community. Sponsors annual Conference on Informal Jewish Education for Jewish youth
professionals from across the continent.

NORTH AMERICAN FEDERATION OF TEMPLE
YOUTH, UNION OF AMERICAN HEBREW
CONGREGATIONS (RELIGIOUS, EDUCA-
TIONAL)

STUDENT STRUGGLE FOR SOVIET JEWRY—
see CENTER FOR RUSSIAN JEWRY (Community Relations)

YOUNG JUDAEA/HASHACHAR, HADASSAH (-
ISRAEL-RELATED)

YUGNTRUF–YOUTH FOR YIDDISH (CUL-
TURAL)

CANADA

AISH HATORAH (1981). 949 Clark Ave., W.,
Thornhill, ONT L4J8G6. (905)764-1818.
FAX: (905)764-1606. E-mail: toronto@
aish.edu. Pres. Harold Nashman; Edu.
Dir. Rabbi Ahron Hoch. An educational
center, a community center, and a network of synagogues throughout Toronto;
seeks to reawaken Jewish values, ignite
Jewish pride and promote Jewish unity
through education; reaches out to Jews
from all backgrounds in a friendly, warm
and non-judgmental environment. *Shabbat Shalom Fax.* (WWW.AISH.EDU)

B'NAI BRITH CANADA (1875). 15 Hove St.,
Downsview, ONT M3H 4Y8. (416) 633-
6224. FAX: (416)630-2159. E-mail: fdi-

---

*For fuller listing, see under categories in parentheses.

mant@bnaibrith.ca. Pres. Dr. Lawrence Hart; Exec. V.-Pres. Frank Dimant. Canadian Jewry's major advocacy and service organization; maintains an office of Government Relations in Ottawa and co-sponsors the Canada Israel Committee; makes representations to all levels of government on matters of Jewish concern; promotes humanitarian causes and educational programs, community projects, adult Jewish education, and leadership development; dedicated to the preservation and unity of the Jewish community in Canada and to human rights. *The Jewish Tribune.*

———, INSTITUTE FOR INTERNATIONAL AFFAIRS (1987). E-mail: institute@bnaibrith.ca. Ch. Rochelle Wilner; Natl. Dir. Ruth Klein. Identifies and protests the abuse of human rights worldwide. Advocates on behalf of Israel and Jewish communities in distress. Monitors national and international legislation dealing with war crimes. Activities include briefs and consultations with governmental and non-governmental organizations, research and public education, advocacy and community mobilization, media monitoring, and international conferences and fact-finding missions. *Ad hoc publications on human rights issues.*

———, LEAGUE FOR HUMAN RIGHTS (1964). Co-Chmn. Marvin Kurz & Dr Harriet Morris. National volunteer association dedicated to combating racism, bigotry, and anti-Semitism. Educational programs include multicultural antiracist workshops, public speakers, Holocaust education, Media Human Rights Awards; legal and legislative activity includes government submissions, court interventions, monitoring hate-group activity, responding to incidents of racism and anti-Semitism; community liaison includes intergroup dialogue and support for aggrieved vulnerable communities and groups. Canadian distributor of ADL material. *Heritage Front Report: 1994; Anti-Semitism on Campus; Skinheads in Canada; Annual Audit of Anti-Semitic Incidents; Holocaust and Hope Educators' Newsletter; Combatting Hate: Guidelines for Community Action.*

———, NATIONAL FIELD SERVICES DEPARTMENT. Natl. Dir. Pearl Gladman. Services community affordable housing projects, sports leagues, food baskets for the needy; coordinates hands-on national volunteer programming, Tel-Aide Distress Line; responsible for lodge membership; direct-mail campaigns, annual convention and foundation dinners.

CANADIAN FRIENDS OF CALI & AMAL (1944). 7005 Kildare Rd., Suite 14, Côte St. Luc, Quebec, H4W 1C1. (514)484-9430. FAX: (514)484-0968. Pres. Harry J.F. Bloomfield, QC; Exec. Dir. Fran Kula. Incorporates Canadian Association for Labour Israel (Histadrut) and Canadian Friends of Amal; supports comprehensive health care and education in Israel. Helps to provide modern medical and surgical facilities and the finest vocational, technical education to the Israeli people of all ages.

CANADIAN FRIENDS OF THE HEBREW UNIVERSITY OF JERUSALEM (1944). 3080 Yonge St., Suite 5024, Toronto, ONT M4N 3N1. (416) 485-8000. FAX: (416)485-8565. E-mail: mgoldman@cfhu.org. Pres. Dr. Charles C. Gold; Exec. Dir. Mark Gryfe. Represents the Hebrew University of Jerusalem in Canada; serves as fund-raising arm for the university in Canada; recruits Canadian students and promotes study programs for foreign students at the university; sponsors social and educational events across Canada.

CANADIAN JEWISH CONGRESS (1919; reorg. 1934). 1590 Dr. Penfield Ave., Montreal, PQ H3G 1C5. (514)931-7531. FAX: (514) 931-0548. E-mail: canadianjewishcongress@cjc.ca. Pres. Goldie Hershon; Natl. Exec. Dir./Genl. Counsel Jack Silverstone. The official voice of Canadian Jewish communities at home and abroad; acts on all matters affecting the status, rights, concerns, and welfare of Canadian Jewry; internationally active on behalf of world Jewry, Holocaust remembrance and restitution; largest Jewish archives in Canada. *National Small Communities Newsletter; DAIS; National Archives Newsletter; regional newsletters.*

CANADIAN YOUNG JUDAEA (1917). 788 Marlee Ave., Suite 205, Toronto, ONT M6B 3K1. (416)781-5156. FAX: (416) 787-3100. E-mail: cyj@idirect.com Natl. Shaliach Ryan Hass; Eastern Region Shaliach Yossi Cadan; Natl. Exec. Dir. Risa Epstein. Strives to attract Jewish youth to Zionism, with goal of aliyah; educates youth about Jewish history and

Zionism; prepares them to provide leadership in Young Judaea camps in Canada and Israel and to be concerned Jews. *Judaean L'Madrich; Young Judaean.*

CANADIAN ZIONIST FEDERATION (1967). 5151 Côte St. Catherine Rd., #206, Montreal, PQ H3W 1M6. (514)739-7300. FAX: (514)739-9412. Pres. Kurt Rothschild; Natl. Sec. Florence Simon. Umbrella organization of distinct constituent member Zionist organizations in Canada; carries on major activities in all areas of Jewish life through its departments of education and culture, aliyah, youth and students, public affairs, and small Jewish communities, for the purpose of strengthening the State of Israel and the Canadian Jewish community. *Canadian Zionist.*

————, BUREAU OF EDUCATION AND CULTURE (1972). Pres. Kurt Rothschild. Provides counseling by pedagogic experts, in-service teacher-training courses and seminars in Canada and Israel; national pedagogic council and research center; distributes educational material and teaching aids; supports annual Bible contest and Hebrew-language courses for adults; awards scholarships to Canadian high-school graduates studying for one year in Israel.

FRIENDS OF PIONEERING ISRAEL (1950s). 1111 Finch Ave. W., Suite 456, Downsview, ONT M3J 2E5. (416)736-1339. FAX: (416)736-1405. Pres. Joseph Podemski. Acts as a voice of Socialist-Democratic and Zionist points of view within the Jewish community and a focal point for progressive Zionist elements in Canada; Canadian representative of Meretz; affiliated with Hashomer Hatzair and the Givat Haviva Educational Center.

HADASSAH–WIZO ORGANIZATION OF CANADA (1917). 1310 Greene Ave., Suite 900, Montreal, PQ H3Z 2B8. (514) 937-9431. FAX: (514)933-6483. E-mail: natoff @canadian-hadassah-wizo.org. Natl. Pres. Marion Mayman; Natl. Exec. V.-Pres. Lily Frank. Largest women's volunteer Zionist organization in Canada, located in 43 Canadian cities; dedicated to advancing the quality of life of the women and children in Israel through financial assistance and support of its many projects, day-care centers, schools, institutions, and hospitals. In Canada, the organization promotes Canadian ideals of democracy and is a stalwart advocate of women's issues. *Orah Magazine.*

HASHOMER HATZAIR (1913). 1111 Finch Ave. W., #456, Downsview, ONT M3J 2E5. (416)736-1339. FAX: (416)736-1405. E-mail: mail@givathaviva.com. Shaliach Noam Massad; Exec. Off. Mintzy Clement. Zionist youth movement associated with the Kibbutz Artzi Federation in Israel. Educational activities emphasize Jewish culture and identity as well as the kibbutz lifestyle and values; runs winter and summer camps as well as programs in Israel.

INTERNATIONAL JEWISH CORRESPONDENCE (IJC) (1978). c/o Canadian Jewish Congress, 1590 Dr. Penfield Ave., Montreal, PQ H3G 1C5.9 (514)931-7531. FAX: (514)931-0548. E-mail: barrys@cjc.ca. Founder/Dir. Barry Simon. Aims to encourage contact between Jews of all ages and backgrounds, in all countries, through pen-pal correspondence. Send autobiographical data and stamped self-addressed envelope or its equivalent (to cover cost of Canadian postage) to receive addresses.

JEWISH IMMIGRANT AID SERVICES OF MONTREAL (JIAS) (1922). Decarie Square, 6900 Decarie, Suite 217A, Côte St Luc, Quebec, H3X 2T8. (514)342-9351. FAX: (514)342-8452. E-mail: jias@pobox.com. Pres. Barry Silverman; Exec. Dir. Bob Luck. Agency for immigration and immigrant welfare and integration. *JIAS News for Clients.*

JEWISH NATIONAL FUND OF CANADA (KEREN KAYEMETH LE'ISRAEL, INC.) (1901). 1980 Sherbrooke St. W., Suite 500, Montreal, PQ H3H 1E8. (514)934-0313. FAX: (514)934-0382. Natl. Pres. Naomi Frankenburg; Exec. V.-Pres. Avner Regev. Fund-raising organization affiliated with the World Zionist Organization; involved in afforestation, soil reclamation, and development of the land of Israel, including the construction of roads and preparation of sites for new settlements; provides educational materials and programs to Jewish schools across Canada.

LABOUR ZIONIST ALLIANCE OF CANADA (1909). 272 Codsell Ave., Downsview, ONT M3H 3X2. (416)630-9444. FAX: (416)630-9451. Pres. Josef Krystal; City Committee Chmn. Montreal-Harry

Froimovitch. Associated with the World Labor Zionist movement and allied with the Israel Labor party. Provides recreational and cultural programs, mutual aid, and fraternal care to enhance the social welfare of its membership; actively promotes Zionist education, cultural projects, and forums on aspects of Jewish and Canadian concern.

MIZRACHI ORGANIZATION OF CANADA (1941). 296 Wilson Ave., North York, ONT M3H 1S8. (416)630-9266. FAX: (416)630-2305. Pres. Jack Kahn. Promotes religious Zionism, aimed at making Israel a state based on Torah; maintains Bnei Akiva, a summer camp, adult education program, and touring department; supports Mizrachi-Hapoel Hamizrachi and other religious Zionist institutions in Israel which strengthen traditional Judaism. *Mizrachi Newsletter.*

NATIONAL COMMUNITY RELATIONS COMMITTEE OF CANADIAN JEWISH CONGRESS (1936). 4600 Bathurst St., Willowdale, Toronto, ONT M2R 3V2. (416)631-5673. FAX: (416)635-1408. E-mail: mprutschi @ujafed.org. Chmn. Mark S. Weintraub; Pres. Moshe Ronen; Dir. Manuel Prutschi. Seeks to safeguard the status, rights, and welfare of Jews in Canada; to combat anti-Semitism, and promote understanding and goodwill among all ethnic and religious groups.

NATIONAL COUNCIL OF JEWISH WOMEN OF CANADA (1897). 118-1588 Main St., Winnipeg, MAN R2V 1Y3. (204)339-9700. FAX: (204)334-3779. E-mail: info@ ncjwc.org. Chmn. Carol Slater; Natl. V.-Pres. Roz Fine & Brenlee Gurvey Gales. Dedicated to furthering human welfare in the Jewish and general communities, locally, nationally, and internationally; through an integrated program of education, service, and social action seeks to fulfill unmet needs and to serve the individual and the community. *National ByLines.*

ORT CANADA (1948). 3101 Bathurst St., Suite 604, Toronto, ONT M6A 2A6. (416)787-0339. FAX: (416) 787-9420. E-mail: ortcan@pathcom.com. Pres. Kathleen Crook; Exec. Dir. Joel Shapiro; Admin. Beverley Schneider. Chapters in 11 Canadian cities raise funds for ORT's nonprofit global network of schools where Jewish students learn a wide range of marketable skills, including the most advanced high-tech professions. *Focus Magazine.*

STATE OF ISRAEL BONDS (CANADA-ISRAEL SECURITIES, LTD.) (1953). 970 Lawrence Ave. W., Suite 502, Toronto, ONT M6A 3B6. (416)789-3351. FAX: (416)789-9436. Pres. Norman Spector; Bd. Chmn. George A. Cohon. An international securities organization offering interest-bearing instruments issued by the government of Israel. Invests in every aspect of Israel's economy, including agriculture, commerce, and industry. Israel Bonds are RRSP-approved.

Jewish Federations, Welfare Funds, Community Councils

UNITED STATES

ALABAMA

BIRMINGHAM

THE BIRMINGHAM JEWISH FEDERATION (1936; reorg. 1971); 3966 Montclair Rd. (35213-0219); (205)879-0416. FAX: (205) 803-1526. E-mail: federation@bjf.org. Pres. Edward Goldberg; Exec. Dir. Richard Friedman.

MOBILE

MOBILE JEWISH WELFARE FUND, INC. (inc. 1966); One Office Park, Suite 219 (36609); (334)343-7197. FAX: (334)343-7197. E-mail: mjwf123@aol.com. Pres. Eileen Susman.

MONTGOMERY

JEWISH FEDERATION OF MONTGOMERY, INC. (1930); 2820 Fairlane Dr. (36120-0058); (334)277-5820. FAX: (334)277-8383. E-mail: jfedmgm@aol.com. Pres. Alan Weil; Admin. Dir. Susan Mayer Bruchis.

ARIZONA

PHOENIX

JEWISH FEDERATION OF GREATER PHOENIX (1940); 32 W. Coolidge, Suite 200 (85013); (602)274-1800. FAX: (602)266-7875. E-mail: info@jewishphoenix.org. res. Neil Hiller; Exec. Dir. Arthur Paikowsky.

TUCSON

JEWISH FEDERATION OF SOUTHERN ARIZONA (1946); 3822 East River Rd., Suite 100 (85718); (520)577-9393. FAX: (520)577-0734. E-mail: jfink@jfsa.org. Pres. Linda Tumarkin; Exec. Dir. Stuart Mellan.

ARKANSAS

LITTLE ROCK

JEWISH FEDERATION OF ARKANSAS (1911); 425 N. University (72205); (501)663-3571. FAX: (501)663-7286. E-mail: jflar@aristotle.net. Pres. Doris Krain; Exec. Dir. Harvey David Luber.

CALIFORNIA

EAST BAY

JEWISH FEDERATION OF THE GREATER EAST BAY (INCLUDING ALAMEDA & CONTRA COSTA COUNTIES) (1917); 401 Grand Ave., Oakland (94610-5022); (510)839-2900. FAX: (510)839-3996. E-mail: admin@jfed. org. Pres. Jerry Yanowitz; Exec. V.-Pres. Ami Nahshon.

FRESNO

JEWISH FEDERATION OF FRESNO; 1340 W. HERNDON AVE., SUITE 103 (93711-0431); (559)432-2162. FAX: (559)432-0425.

LONG BEACH

JEWISH FEDERATION OF GREATER LONG BEACH AND W. ORANGE COUNTY (1937; inc. 1946); 3801 E. Willow St. (90815); (562)426-7601. FAX: (562)424-3915. E-mail: kgibbs@ jewishlongbeach.org. Pres. Richard Lipeles; Exec. Dir. Michael S. Rassler.

LOS ANGELES

JEWISH FEDERATION COUNCIL OF GREATER LOS ANGELES (1912; reorg. 1959); 5700 Wilshire Blvd., 2nd fl. (90036); (323)761-8000. FAX: (323)761-8235. E-mail: webcoordinator@jewishla.org. Pres. Lionel Bell; Exec. V.-Pres. John Fishel.

ORANGE COUNTY

JEWISH FEDERATION OF ORANGE COUNTY (1964; inc. 1965); 250 Baker St., Suite A, Costa Mesa (92626); (714)755-5555. FAX: (714)755-0307. E-mail: info@jfoc.org. Pres. Charles Karp; Exec. Dir. Bunnie Mauldin.

PALM SPRINGS

JEWISH FEDERATION OF PALM SPRINGS AND DESERT AREA (1971); 255 N. El Cielo, Suite 430 (92262-6990); (760)325-7281. FAX: (760)325-2188. E-mail: msjfedps@gte.net. Pres. Larry Pitts; Exec. Dir. Mitzi Schafer.

SACRAMENTO

JEWISH FEDERATION OF THE SACRAMENTO REGION (1948); 2351 Wyda Way (95825); (916)486-0906. FAX: (916)486-0816. E-mail: jfed2@juno.com. Pres. Bill Slaton; Exec. Dir. Beryl Michaels.

SAN DIEGO

UNITED JEWISH FEDERATION OF SAN DIEGO COUNTY (1936); 4797 Mercury St. (92111-2102); (858)571-3444. FAX: (858)571-0701. E-mail: fedujf@ujfsd.org. Pres. Dr. Richard Katz; Exec. V.-Pres. Stephen M. Abramson.

SAN FRANCISCO

JEWISH COMMUNITY FEDERATION OF SAN FRANCISCO, THE PENINSULA, MARIN, AND SONOMA COUNTIES (1910; reorg. 1955); 121 Steuart St. (94105); (415)777-0411. FAX: (415)495-6635. Pres. Harold Zlot; Exec. V.-Pres. Wayne Feinstein.

SAN GABRIEL AND POMONA VALLEY

JEWISH FEDERATION OF THE GREATER SAN GABRIEL AND POMONA VALLEY; 258 W. Badillo St. (91723-1906); (626)967-3656. FAX: (626)967-5135. E-mail: sgpvfed@aol.com.

SAN JOSE

JEWISH FEDERATION OF GREATER SAN JOSE (incl. Santa Clara County except Palo Alto and Los Altos) (1930; reorg. 1950); 14855 Oka Rd., Suite 2, Los Gatos (95030); (408)358-3033. FAX: (408)356-0733. E-mail: federation@JFGSJ.org. Pres. Judy Levin; Exec. Dir. Jon Friedenberg.

SANTA BARBARA

SANTA BARBARA JEWISH FEDERATION (1974); 524 Chapala St., PO Box 90110

(93190); (805)957-1115. FAX: (805)957-9230. E-mail: sbjfed@silcom.com. Pres. Jeri Eigner; Exec. Dir. Shelly Katz.

VENTURA COUNTY

JEWISH FEDERATION OF VENTURA COUNTY; PO Box 6368 (93006); (805)647-7800. FAX: (805)647-0482. E-mail: ujavtacty@aol.com.

COLORADO

DENVER/BOULDER

ALLIED JEWISH FEDERATION OF COLORADO (1936); 300 S. Dahlia St., Denver (80222); (303)321-3399. FAX: (303)322-8328. E-mail: ajfcolo@aol.com. Chmn. Edward A. Robinson; Pres. & CEO:Steve Gelfand.

CONNECTICUT

BRIDGEPORT

JEWISH FEDERATION OF EASTERN FAIRFIELD COUNTY. (1936; reorg. 1981); 4200 Park Ave. (06604-1092); (203)372-6567. FAX: (203)374-0770. E-mail: jccs@snet.net. Chmn. Stanley Strouch; Pres. & CEO Daniel P. Baker.

DANBURY

THE JEWISH FEDERATION OF GREATER DANBURY, INC. (1945); 105 Newton Rd. (06810); (203)792-6353. FAX: (203)748-5099. Pres. Daniel Wolinsky; Exec. Dir. Rhonda Cohen.

EASTERN CONNECTICUT

JEWISH FEDERATION OF EASTERN CONNECTICUT, INC. (1950; inc. 1970); 28 Channing St., PO Box 1468, New London (06320); (860)442-8062. FAX: (860)443-4175. E-mail: jfec@worldnet.att.net. Pres. Myron Hendel; Exec. Dir. Jerome E. Fischer.

GREENWICH

UJA/FEDERATION OF GREENWICH (1956); One Holly Hill Lane (06830-6080); (203)622-1434. FAX: (203)622-1237. E-mail: pezmom3@aol.com. Pres. Jonathan Nelson; Exec. Dir. Pam Zur.

HARTFORD

JEWISH FEDERATION OF GREATER HARTFORD (1945); 333 Bloomfield Ave., W. Hartford (06117); (860)232-4483. FAX: (860)232-5221. E-mail: msilverman@jewishhartford.org. Pres. Henry M. Zachs; Acting Exec. Dir. Steven Bayer.

NEW HAVEN

JEWISH FEDERATION OF GREATER NEW HAVEN (1928); 360 Amity Rd., Woodbridge (06525); (203)387-2424. FAX: (203)387-1818. E-mail: marinak@megahits.com Pres. David Schaefer; Exec. Dir. Howard Bloom.

NORWALK

(See Westport)

STAMFORD

UNITED JEWISH FEDERATION (inc. 1973); 1035 Newfield Ave., PO Box 3038 (06905); (203)321-1373. FAX: (203)322-3277. E-mail: office@ujf.org. Pres. Corrine Lotstein; Dir. of Dev. Edith Samers.

WATERBURY

JEWISH FEDERATION—JEWISH COMMUNITIES OF WESTERN CONNECTICUT, INC. (1938); 73 Main St. S., Box F, Woodbury (06798-3404); (203)263-5121. FAX: (203) 263-5143. E-mail: jfedwtby@aol.com. Pres. Linda Herrmann; Exec. Dir. Rob Zwang.

WESTPORT-WESTON-WILTON-NORWALK

UJA/FEDERATION OF WESTPORT—WESTON—WILTON—NORWALK (inc. 1980); 431 Post Road E., Suite 22, Westport (06880); (203)226-8197. FAX: (203)226-5051. E-mail: rkessler@ujafederation.org. Pres. Sandra Lefkowitz; Exec. Dir. Robert Kessler.

DELAWARE

WILMINGTON

JEWISH FEDERATION OF DELAWARE, INC. (1934); 100 W. 10th St., Suite 301 (19801-1628); (302)427-2100. FAX: (302)427-2438. Pres. Barbara H. Schoenberg; Exec. V. Pres. Judy Wortman.

DISTRICT OF COLUMBIA

WASHINGTON

THE JEWISH FEDERATION OF GREATER WASHINGTON, INC. (1935); 6101 Montrose Rd., Rockville, MD (20852); (301)230-7200. FAX: (301)230-7265. E-mail: info@jewishfedwash.org. Pres. Dede Feinberg; Exec. V.-Pres. Ted B. Farber.

FLORIDA

BREVARD COUNTY

JEWISH FEDERATION OF BREVARD (1974); 108-A Barton Ave., Rockledge (32955); (407)636-1824. FAX: (407)636-0614. E-mail: jfbrevard@aol.com. Pres. Gary Singer; Exec. Dir. Joanne Bishins.

BROWARD COUNTY

JEWISH FEDERATION OF BROWARD COUNTY (1943; 1968); 8358 W. Oakland Park Blvd., #200, Ft. Lauderdale (33351-7319); (954) 748-8400. FAX: (954)748-6332. E-mail: jewishfed@aol.com. Pres. David B. Schulman; Exec. Dir. Gary N. Rubin.

COLLIER COUNTY

JEWISH FEDERATION OF COLLIER COUNTY (1974); 1250 Tamiami Trail N., Suite 202, Naples (33940); (941) 263-4205. FAX: (941) 263-3813. E-mail: jfccfl@aol.com. Pres. Ann Jacobson.

DAYTONA BEACH

(See Volusia & Flagler Counties)

FT. LAUDERDALE

(See Broward County)

GAINESVILLE

GAINESVILLE JEWISH APPEAL, INC.; 1816 NW 21 Street (32604); (352)371-3846. E-mail: oberger@gnv.fdt.net.

JACKSONVILLE

JACKSONVILLE JEWISH FEDERATION, INC. (1935); 8505 San Jose Blvd. (32217); (904)448-5000. FAX: (904)448-5715. Pres. Dr. Kenneth Sekine; Exec. V.-Pres. Alan Margolies.

LEE COUNTY

JEWISH FEDERATION OF LEE AND CHARLOTTE COUNTIES (1974); 6237-E Presidential Court, Ft. Myers (33919-3568); (941)481-4449. FAX: (941)481-0139. Pres. Dr. David Heligman; Exec. Dir. Annette Goodman.

MIAMI

GREATER MIAMI JEWISH FEDERATION, INC. (1938); 4200 Biscayne Blvd. (33137); (305) 576-4000. FAX: (305)573-4584. Pres. Michael Scheck; Exec. V.-Pres. Jacob Solomon.

ORLANDO

JEWISH FEDERATION OF GREATER ORLANDO (1949); 851 N. Maitland Ave.; PO Box 941508, Maitland (32794-1508); (407)645-5933. FAX: (407)645-1172. Pres. James S. Grodin; Exec. Dir. Eric Geboff.

PALM BEACH COUNTY

JEWISH FEDERATION OF PALM BEACH COUNTY, INC. (1962); 4601 Community Dr.,

W. Palm Beach (33417-2760); (561)478-0700. FAX: (561)478-9696. E-mail: info@jfedpbco.org. Pres. Helen G. Hoffman; Exec. V.-Pres. Jeffrey L. Klein.
JEWISH FEDERATION OF SOUTH PALM BEACH COUNTY, INC. (1979); 9901 Donna Klein Blvd. Boca Raton (33428-1788); (561)852-3105. FAX: (561)852-3136. E-mail: dstern@jewishboca.org.

PENSACOLA
PENSACOLA JEWISH FEDERATION; 800 No. Palafox (32501); (850)434-7992.

PINELLAS COUNTY
JEWISH FEDERATION OF PINELLAS COUNTY, INC. (incl. Clearwater and St. Petersburg) (1950; reincorp. 1974); 13191 Starkey Rd., #8, Largo (33773-1438); (727) 530-3223. FAX: (727)531-0221. E-mail: pinellas@jfed-pinellas.org. Pres. David Abelson; Interim Exec. Dir. Bonnie Friedman.

SARASOTA-MANATEE
SARASOTA-MANATEE JEWISH FEDERATION (1959); 580 S. McIntosh Rd. (34232-1959); (941)371-4546. FAX: (941)378-2947. E-mail: jlederman@smjf.org. Pres. Scott Gordon; Exec. Dir. Jan C. Lederman.

TALLAHASSEE
APALACHEE FEDERATION OF JEWISH CHARITIES; PO Box 14825 (32317-4825); (850) 877-3989; FAX: (850)877-7989.

TAMPA
TAMPA JEWISH FEDERATION (1941); 13009 Community Campus Dr. (33625-4000); (813)264-9000. FAX: (813)265-8450. E-mail: jjfjcc@aol.com. Pres. Lili Kaufman; Exec. V.-Pres. Howard Borer.

VOLUSIA & FLAGLER COUNTIES
JEWISH FEDERATION OF VOLUSIA & FLAGLER COUNTIES, INC. (1980); 733 S. Nova Rd., Ormond Beach (32174); (904)672-0294. FAX: (904)673-1316. Pres. Steven I. Unatin; Exec. Dir. Gloria Max.

GEORGIA

ATLANTA
JEWISH FEDERATION OF GREATER ATLANTA, INC. (1905; reorg. 1967); 1440 Spring St., NW (30309-2837); (404)873-1661. FAX: (404)874-7043/881-4027. E-mail: kkaplan@jfga.org. Pres. Arnold Rubenstein; Exec. Dir. David I. Sarnat.

AUGUSTA
AUGUSTA JEWISH FEDERATION (1937); 898

Weinberger Way, Evans (30809-3636), (706)228-3636. FAX: (706)868-1660/823-3960. E-mail: mpousman@hotmail.com. Pres. Dr. Louis Scharff; Exec. Dir. Michael Pousman.

COLUMBUS
JEWISH FEDERATION OF COLUMBUS, INC. (1944); PO Box 6313 (31906); (706)568-6668. Pres. Murray Solomon; Sec. Irene Rainbow.

SAVANNAH
SAVANNAH JEWISH FEDERATION (1943); 5111 Abercorn St. (31403); (912)355-8111. FAX: (912)355-8116. E-mail: jrgreen4@juno.com. Pres. Dr. Paul Kulbersh; Exec. Dir. Sharon Gal.

ILLINOIS

CHAMPAIGN-URBANA
CHAMPAIGN-URBANA JEWISH FEDERATION (1929); 503 E. John St., Champaign (61820); (217)367-9872. FAX: (217)367-0077. E-mail: cujf@shalomcu.org. Pres. Anthony E. Novak; Exec. Dir. (Ms.) L. Lee Melhado.

CHICAGO
JEWISH FEDERATION OF METROPOLITAN CHICAGO/JEWISH UNITED FUND OF METROPOLITAN CHICAGO (1900); Ben Gurion Way, 1 S. Franklin St. (60606-4694); (312)444-2800. FAX: (312)444-2806. E-mail: iepstein@juf.org. Chmn. Manfred Steinfeld; Pres. Steven B. Nasatir.

JOLIET
JOLIET JEWISH WELFARE CHEST (1938); 250 N. Midland Ave. at Campbell St. (60435); (815)741-4600.

PEORIA
JEWISH FEDERATION OF PEORIA (1933; inc. 1947); 2000 W. Pioneer Pwky., Suite 10B (61615-1835); (309)689-0063. FAX: (309) 689-0575. Pres. Jennifer Dolin; Exec. Dir. Eunice Galsky.

QUAD CITIES
JEWISH FEDERATION OF QUAD CITIES (1938; comb. 1973); 1705 2nd Ave., Suite 405, Rock Island (61201); (309)793-1300. FAX: (309) 793-1345. E-mail: qcfederation@juno.com. Pres. Paul Light; Exec. Dir. Ida Kramer.

ROCKFORD
JEWISH FEDERATION OF GREATER ROCKFORD (1937); 1500 Parkview Ave. (61107);

(815)399-5497. FAX: (815)399-9835. E-mail: rockfordfederation@juno.com. Pres. Sterne Roufa; Exec. Dir. Marilyn Youman.

SOUTHERN ILLINOIS

JEWISH FEDERATION OF SOUTHERN ILLINOIS, SOUTHEASTERN MISSOURI, AND WESTERN KENTUCKY (1941); 6464 W. Main, Suite 7A, Belleville (62223); (618)398-6100. FAX: (618)398-0539. E-mail: silfed@aol.com. Co-Pres. Harvey Cohen & Carol Rudman; Exec. Dir. Steven C. Low.

SPRINGFIELD

SPRINGFIELD JEWISH FEDERATION (1941); 730 E. Vine St. (62703); (217)528-3446. FAX: (217)528-3409. E-mail: sjf@spring net1.com. Pres. Rita Victor; Exec. Dir. Gloria Schwartz.

INDIANA

FORT WAYNE

FORT WAYNE JEWISH FEDERATION (1921); 227 E. Washington Blvd. (46802-3121); (219)422-8566. FAX: (219)422-8567. E-mail: fwjewfed@aol.com. Pres. Scott Salon; Exec. Dir. Jeff Gubitz.

INDIANAPOLIS

JEWISH FEDERATION OF GREATER INDIANAPOLIS, INC. (1905); 6705 Hoover Rd. (46260-4120); (317)726-5450. FAX: (317) 205-0307. E-mail controljfg@aol.com. Pres. Claudette Einhorn; Exec. V.-Pres. Harry Nadler.

LAFAYETTE

JEWISH FEDERATION OF GREATER LAFAYETTE (1924); PO Box 3802, W. Lafayette (47906); (765)426-4724. E-mail: jfgl1@aol.com. Pres.Earl Prohofsky; Finan. Sec. Laura Starr; Admin. Judy Upton.

NORTHWEST INDIANA

JEWISH FEDERATION OF NORTHWEST INDIANA (1941; reorg. 1959); 2939 Jewett St., Highland (46322); (219)972-2250. FAX: (219)972-4779. E-mail: defwej@aol.com. Pres. Carol Karol; Exec. Dir. David Tein.

ST. JOSEPH VALLEY

JEWISH FEDERATION OF ST. JOSEPH VALLEY (1946); 105 Jefferson Centre, Suite 804, South Bend (46601-1156); (219)233-1164. FAX: (219)288-4103. E-mail: jfedofnwi@aol.com. Pres. Dr. Douglas H. Barton; Exec. V.-Pres. Marilyn Gardner.

IOWA

DES MOINES

JEWISH FEDERATION OF GREATER DES MOINES (1914); 910 Polk Blvd. (50312); (515)277-6321. FAX: (515)277-4069. E-mail: jcrcia@aol.com. Pres. Robert M. Pomerantz; Exec. Dir. Elaine Steinger.

SIOUX CITY

JEWISH FEDERATION OF SIOUX CITY (1921); 815 38th St. (51104-1417); (712)258-0618. FAX: (712)258-0619. Pres. Michele Ivener; Admin. Dir. Doris Rosenthal.

KANSAS

KANSAS CITY

See listing under Missouri

WICHITA

MID-KANSAS JEWISH FEDERATION, INC. (serving South Central Kansas) (1935); 400 N. Woodlawn, Suite 8 (67208); (316)686-4741. FAX: (316)686-6008. Pres. Marie Levy; Exec. Dir. Judy Press.

KENTUCKY

CENTRAL KENTUCKY

CENTRAL KENTUCKY JEWISH FEDERATION (1976); 340 Romany Rd., Lexington (40502-2400); (606)268-0672. FAX: (606)268-0775. Pres.Martin Barr; Exec. Dir. Daniel Chejfec.

LOUISVILLE

JEWISH COMMUNITY FEDERATION OF LOUISVILLE, INC. (1934); 3630 Dutchmans Lane (40205); (502)451-8840. FAX: (502) 458-0702. E-mail: jfed@iglou.com. Pres. Gerald D. Temes MD; Exec. Dir. Alan S. Engel.

LOUISIANA

BATON ROUGE

JEWISH FEDERATION OF GREATER BATON ROUGE (1971); 3354 Kleinert Ave. (70806); (504) 387-9744. FAX: (504)387-9487. E-mail: jfedofbr@postoffice.att.net. Pres. Harvey Hoffman.

NEW ORLEANS

JEWISH FEDERATION OF GREATER NEW ORLEANS (1913; reorg. 1977); 3500 N. Causeway Blvd., Suite 1240, Metairie (70002-3524); (504)828-2125. FAX: (504)828-2827. E-mail: jewishnews@jewishnola.com. Pres. Hugo Kahn; Exec. Dir. Eli Skora.

SHREVEPORT

NORTHERN LOUISIANA JEWISH FEDERATION (1941; inc. 1967); 4700 Line Ave., Suite 117 (71106-1533); (318)868-1200. FAX: (318) 868-1272. E-mail: sjfed@juno.com. Pres. Rick Murov; Exec. Dir. Howard L. Ross.

MAINE

LEWISTON-AUBURN

LEWISTON-AUBURN JEWISH FEDERATION (1947); 74 Bradman St., Auburn (04210); (207)786-4201. FAX: (207)783-1000. Pres. Scott Nussinow.

PORTLAND

JEWISH FEDERATION COMMUNITY AL-LIANCE OF SOUTHERN MAINE (1942); 57 Ashmont St. (04103); (207)773-7254. FAX: (207)772-2234. E-mail: info@mainejewish. org. Pres. Michael Peisner; Exec. Dir. David Unger.

MARYLAND

BALTIMORE

THE ASSOCIATED: JEWISH COMMUNITY FED-ERATION OF BALTIMORE (1920; reorg. 1969); 101 W. Mt. Royal Ave. (21201-5728); (410) 727-4828. FAX: (410)752-1177. E-mail: information@associated.org. Chmn. Barbara L. Himmelrich; Pres. Darrell D. Friedman.

COLUMBIA

JEWISH FEDERATION OF HOWARD COUNTY; 8950 Rte. 108, Suite 115, Columbia (21045); (410)730-4976; FAX: (410)730-9393. E-mail: jfohc@starpower.net.

MASSACHUSETTS

BERKSHIRE COUNTY

JEWISH FEDERATION OF THE BERKSHIRES (1940); 235 East St., Pittsfield (01201); (413) 442-4360. FAX: (413)443-6070. Pres. Ellen Silverstein; Exec. Dir. Robert N. Kerbel.

BOSTON

COMBINED JEWISH PHILANTHROPIES OF GREATER BOSTON, INC. (1895; inc. 1961); 126 High St. (02110-2700); (617)457-8500. FAX: (617)988-6262. E-mail: info@cjp.org. Chmn. Cynthia B. Shulman; Pres. Barry Shrage.

MERRIMACK VALLEY

MERRIMACK VALLEY JEWISH FEDERATION (Serves Andover, Haverhill, Lawrence, Lowell, Newburyport, and 22 surrounding communities) (1988); 805 Turnpike St., N. Andover (01845-6182); (978)688-0466. FAX: (978)688-1097. E-mail: jan@mvjf.org. Pres. James H. Shainker; Exec. Dir. Jan Steven Brodie.

NEW BEDFORD

JEWISH FEDERATION OF GREATER NEW BEDFORD, INC. (1938; inc. 1954); 467 Hawthorn St., N. Dartmouth (02747); (508) 997-7471. FAX: (508)997-7730. Co-Pres. Harriet Philips, Patricia Rosenfield; Exec. Dir. Wil Herrup.

NORTH SHORE

JEWISH FEDERATION OF THE NORTH SHORE, INC. (1938); 21 Front St., Salem (01970-3707); (978)598-1810. FAX: (978)741-7507. E-mail: mail@jfns.org. Pres. Shepard M. Remis; Exec. Dir. Neil A. Cooper.

SPRINGFIELD

JEWISH FEDERATION OF GREATER SPRING-FIELD, INC. (1925); 1160 Dickinson St. (01108); (413)737-4313. FAX: (413)737-4348. E-mail: cfschwartz@jewishspringfield.org. Pres. Jeffrey Mandell; Exec. Dir. Joel Weiss.

WORCESTER

JEWISH FEDERATION OF CENTRAL MASSA-CHUSETTS (1947; inc. 1957); 633 Salisbury St. (01609); (508)756-1543. FAX: (508)798-0962. E-mail: meyerb@aol.com. Pres. Dr. Robert Honig; Exec. Dir. Meyer L. Bodoff.

MICHIGAN

ANN ARBOR

JEWISH FEDERATION OF WASHTENAW COUNTY/UJA (1986); 2939 Birch Hollow Dr. (48108); (734)677-0100. FAX: (734)677-0109. E-mail: jccfed@aol.com. Pres. Morley Witus; Exec. Dir. Nancy N. Margolis.

DETROIT

JEWISH FEDERATION OF METROPOLITAN DE-TROIT (1899); 6735 Telegraph Rd., Suite 30, PO Box 2030, Bloomfield Hills (48301-2030); (248)642-4260. FAX: (248)642-4941. E-mail: jfmd@jfmd.org. Pres. Penny Blumenstein; Exec. V.-Pres. Robert P. Aronson.

FLINT

FLINT JEWISH FEDERATION (1936); 619 Wallenberg St. (48502); (810)767-5922. FAX: (810)767-9024. E-mail: fjf@gfn.org. Pres. Dr. Steve Burton; Exec. Dir. Joel B. Kaplan.

GRAND RAPIDS

JEWISH COMMUNITY FUND OF GRAND

RAPIDS (1930); 330 Fuller NE (49503); (616)456-5553. FAX: (616)456-5780. E-mail: jcfgr@iserv.net. Pres. Richard Stevens; Admin. Dir. Rosalie Stein; V.P. Maxine Shapiro.

MINNESOTA

DULUTH-SUPERIOR

NORTHLAND JEWISH FUND (1937); 1602 E. Second St., Duluth (55812); (218)724-8857. FAX: (218)724-2560. E-mail: sstevens@computerpro.com. Pres. Neil Glazman.

MINNEAPOLIS

MINNEAPOLIS JEWISH FEDERATION (1929; inc. 1930); 13100 Wayzota Blvd. (55305); (612)593-2600. FAX: (612)593-2544. E-mail: sfreeman@mplsfed.org. Pres. Neil N. Lapidus; Exec. Dir. Joshua Fogelson.

ST. PAUL

UNITED JEWISH FUND AND COUNCIL (1935); 790 S. Cleveland, Suite 201 (55116); (651)690-1707. FAX: (651)690-0228. Pres. James Stein; Exec. Dir. Samuel Asher.

MISSOURI

KANSAS CITY

JEWISH FEDERATION OF GREATER KANSAS CITY MO/KS (1933); 5801 W. 115 St., Overland Park, KS (66211-1824); (913)327-8100. FAX: (913)327-8110. E-mail: cherylm@jewishkc.org. Pres. John Wuhlmann; Exec. Dir. Todd Stettner.

ST. JOSEPH

UNITED JEWISH FUND OF ST. JOSEPH (1915); 1816 Walnut (64503); (816)233-1186. FAX: (816)233-9399. Elliot Zidell; Exec. Sec. Sherri Ott.

ST. LOUIS

JEWISH FEDERATION OF ST. LOUIS (incl. St. Louis County) (1901); 12 Millstone Campus Dr. (63146-9812); (314)432-0020. FAX: (314)432-1277. Pres. Mont S. Levy; Exec. V.-Pres. Barry Rosenberg.

NEBRASKA

LINCOLN

JEWISH FEDERATION OF LINCOLN, INC. (1931; inc. 1961); PO Box 67218 (68506); (402)489-1015. FAX: (402)489-1015. Pres. Herb Friedman; Exec. Dir. Karen Sommer.

OMAHA

JEWISH FEDERATION OF OMAHA (1903); 333 S. 132nd St. (68154-2198); (402)334-8200.

FAX: (402)334-1330. E-mail: pmonsk@top.net. Pres. Howard Kooper; Exec. Dir. Jan Perelman.

NEVADA

LAS VEGAS

JEWISH FEDERATION OF LAS VEGAS (1973); 3909 S. Maryland Pkwy. (89119-7520); (702) 732-0556. FAX: (702)732-3228. Pres. David Dahan; Exec. Dir. Ronni Epstein.

NEW HAMPSHIRE

MANCHESTER

JEWISH FEDERATION OF GREATER MANCHESTER (1974); 698 Beech St. (03104-3626); (603)627-7679. FAX: (603) 627-7963. Pres. Martin Jacobs; Exec. Dir. Richard Friedman.

NEW JERSEY

ATLANTIC AND CAPE MAY COUNTIES

JEWISH FEDERATION OF ATLANTIC AND CAPE MAY COUNTIES (1924); 3393 Bargaintown Rd., Box 617, Northfield (08225-0196); (609)653-3030. FAX: (609)653-8881. E-mail: jfedacm@cyberenet.net. Pres. Joseph Rodgers; Exec. V.-Pres. Bernard Cohen.

BERGEN COUNTY

UJA FEDERATION OF BERGEN COUNTY AND NORTH HUDSON (inc. 1978); 111 Kinderkamack Rd., PO Box 4176, N. Hackensack Station, River Edge (07661); (201)488-6800. FAX: (201)488-3962. E-mail: contact@jewishbergen.org. Pres. Eva Lynn Gans; Exec. V.-Pres. Ron B. Meier.

CENTRAL NEW JERSEY

JEWISH FEDERATION OF CENTRAL NEW JERSEY (1940; merged 1973); 1391 Martine Ave., Scotch Plains (07076); (908)889-5335. FAX: (908)889-5370. Pres. Zygmunt Wilf; Exec. V.-Pres. Stanley Stone.

CLIFTON-PASSAIC

JEWISH FEDERATION OF GREATER CLIFTON-PASSAIC (1933); 199 Scoles Ave., Clifton (07012-1125). (973)777-7031. FAX: (973) 777-6701. E-mail: yymuskin@jfedclifton-passaic.com. Pres. George Kramer; Exec. V.-Pres. Yosef Y. Muskin.

CUMBERLAND COUNTY

JEWISH FEDERATION OF CUMBERLAND COUNTY (inc. 1971); 1063 E. Landis Ave.

Suite B, Vineland (08360-3752); (609)696-4445. FAX: (609)696-3428. E-mail: jfedcc@aol.com. Pres. James Potter; Exec. Dir. Ann Lynn Lipton.

METROWEST NEW JERSEY

UNITED JEWISH FEDERATION OF METRO-WEST (1923); 901 Route 10, Whippany (07981-1156); (973)884-4800. FAX: (973) 884-7361. E-mail: dlarris@ujfmetrowest. org. Pres. Murray Laulicht; Exec. V.-Pres. Max L. Kleinman.

MIDDLESEX COUNTY

JEWISH FEDERATION OF GREATER MIDDLE-SEX COUNTY (org. 1948; reorg. 1985); 230 Old Bridge Tpk., S. River (08882-2000); (732)432-7711. FAX: (732)432-0292. E-mail: jfednj@aol.com. Pres. Roy Tanzman; Exec. V.-Pres. Michael Shapiro.

MONMOUTH COUNTY

JEWISH FEDERATION OF GREATER MON-MOUTH COUNTY (1971); 100 Grant Ave., PO Box 210, Deal (07723-0210); (732)531-6200-1. FAX: (732)531-9518. E-mail: pfdnuss@msn.com. Pres. David Portman; Chmn. William A. Schwartz; Exec. Dir. David A. Nussbaum.

NORTH JERSEY

JEWISH FEDERATION OF NORTH JERSEY (1933); One Pike Dr., Wayne (07470-2498); (973)595-0555. FAX: (973)595-1532. Branch Office: 17-10 River Rd., Fair Lawn (07410-1250); (973)794-1111. E-mail: jfnj@aol.com. Pres. George Liss; Exec. Dir. Martin Greenberg.

OCEAN COUNTY

OCEAN COUNTY JEWISH FEDERATION (1977); 301 Madison Ave., Lakewood (08701); (732)363-0530. FAX: (732)363-2097. Pres. David Rosen; Exec. Dir. Alan Nydick.

PRINCETON MERCER BUCKS

UNITED JEWISH FEDERATION OF PRINCETON MERCER BUCKS (merged 1996); 3131 Princeton Pike, Bldg. 2A, Lawrenceville (08648-2207); (609)219-0555. FAX: (609)219-9040. E-mail: ujfpmb@bellatlantic.net. Pres. Eliot Freeman; Exec. Dir. Andrew Frank.

SOMERSET COUNTY

JEWISH FEDERATION OF SOMERSET, HUN-TERDON & WARREN COUNTIES (1960); 775 Talamini Rd., Bridgewater (08807); (908) 725-6994. FAX: (908)725-9753. E-mail:

somerset@mindpulse.com. Pres. Martin Siegal; Exec. Dir. Daniel A. Nadelman.

SOUTHERN NEW JERSEY

JEWISH FEDERATION OF SOUTHERN NEW JERSEY (incl. Camden, Burlington, and Gloucester counties) (1922); 1301 Springdale Rd., Suite 200, Cherry Hill (08003-2769); (856)751-9500. FAX: (856)751-1697. Pres. Dr. Robert Belafsky; Exec. V.-Pres. Stuart Alperin.

NEW MEXICO

ALBUQUERQUE

JEWISH FEDERATION OF GREATER ALBU-QUERQUE (1938); 5520 Wyoming Blvd., NE (87109-3167); (505)821-3214. FAX: (505) 821-3351. Pres. Dr. Larry Lubar; Exec. Dir. Andrew Lipman.

NEW YORK

ALBANY
(See Northeastern New York)

BROOME COUNTY

JEWISH FEDERATION OF BROOME COUNTY; 500 Clubhouse Rd., Vestal (13850); (607) 724-2332; FAX: (607)724-2311.

BUFFALO (INCL. NIAGARA FALLS)

JEWISH FEDERATION OF GREATER BUFFALO, INC. (1903); 787 Delaware Ave. (14209); (716)886-7750. FAX: (716)886-1367. Pres. Irving M. Shuman; Exec. Dir. James M. Lodge.

DUTCHESS COUNTY

JEWISH FEDERATION OF DUTCHESS COUNTY; 110 Grand Ave., Poughkeepsie (12603); (914)471-9811. FAX: (914) 471-0659. E-mail: jfeddutchess@mindspring.com. Pres. Tomasina Schneider; Exec. Dir. Bonnie Meadow.

ELMIRA-CORNING

JEWISH CENTER AND FEDERATION OF THE TWIN TIERS (1942); PO Box 3087, Elmira (14905-0087); (607)734-8122. FAX: (607) 734-8123. Pres. John Spiegler; Admin. Diane Huglies.

NEW YORK

UJA-FEDERATION OF JEWISH PHILAN-THROPIES OF NEW YORK, INC. (incl. Greater NY, Westchester, Nassau, and Suffolk counties) (Fed. org. 1917; UJA 1939; merged 1986); 130 E. 59 St. (10022-1302); (212)980-1000. FAX: (212)888-7538. E-mail: info@

ujafedny.org. Pres. James S. Tisch; Chmn. Judith Stern Peck; Exec. V.-Pres. John Ruskay.

NORTHEASTERN NEW YORK

UNITED JEWISH FEDERATION OF NORTH-EASTERN NEW YORK (1986); Latham Circle Mall, 800 New Loudon Rd., Latham (12110); (518)783-7800. FAX: (518)783-1557. E-mail: info@jewishfedny.org. Pres. Dr. Lewis Morrison; Exec. Dir. Jerry S. Neimand.

ORANGE COUNTY

JEWISH FEDERATION OF GREATER ORANGE COUNTY (1977); 68 Stewart Ave., Newburgh (12550); (914)562-7860. FAX: (914)562-5114. E-mail: jfogoc@aol.com. Pres. Mona Rieger; Admin. Dir. Joyce Waschitz.

ROCHESTER

JEWISH COMMUNITY FEDERATION OF GREATER ROCHESTER, NY, INC. (1939); 441 East Ave. (14607-1932); (716)461-0490. FAX: (716)461-0912. E-mail: info@jewishrochester.org. Pres. Eileen Grossman; Exec. Dir. Lawrence W. Fine.

ROCKLAND COUNTY

JEWISH FEDERATION OF ROCKLAND COUNTY (1985); 900 Route 45, Suite 1, New City (10956-1140); (914)362-4200. Fax: (914)362-4282.

SCHENECTADY

(See Northeastern New York)

SYRACUSE

SYRACUSE JEWISH FEDERATION, INC. (1918); 5655 Thompson Rd. So., DeWitt (13214-0511); (315)445-2040. FAX: (315)445-1559. Pres. Linda Alexander; Exec. V.-Pres. Mary Ann Oppenheimer.

TROY

(See Northeastern New York)

ULSTER COUNTY

JEWISH FEDERATION OF ULSTER COUNTY (1951); 159 Green St., Kingston (12401); (914)338-8131. FAX: (914)338-8131. E-mail: ucjf@ulster.net. Pres. Michelle Tuchman; Exec. Dir. Joan Plotsky.

UTICA

JEWISH COMMUNITY FEDERATION AND CENTER OF UTICA (1950; reorg. 1994); 2310 Oneida St. (13501-6009); (315)733-2343. FAX: (315)733-2346. Pres. Ann Siegel; Exec. Dir. Barbara Ratner-gantshar.

NORTH CAROLINA

ASHEVILLE

WESTERN NORTH CAROLINA JEWISH FEDERATION (1935); 236 Charlotte St. (28801-1434); (828)253-0701. FAX: (828)254-7666. Pres. Stan Greenberg; Exec. Dir. Marlene Berger-Joyce.

CHARLOTTE

THE JEWISH FEDERATION OF GREATER CHARLOTTE (1938); 5007 Providence Rd. (28226-5849); (704)366-5007. FAX: (704)944-6766. E-mail: magman@shalomcharlotte.org. Pres. William Gorelick; Exec. Dir. Marvin Goldberg.

DURHAM-CHAPEL HILL

DURHAM-CHAPEL HILL JEWISH FEDERATION & COMMUNITY COUNCIL (1979); 3700 Lyckan Pkwy., Suite B, Durham (27707-2541); (919)489-5335. FAX: (919)489-5788. E-mail: jfeddch@mindspring.com. Pres. Elaine Marcus; Exec. Dir. Lew Borman.

GREENSBORO

GREENSBORO JEWISH FEDERATION (1940); 5509C W. Friendly Ave. (27410-4211); (336)852-5433. FAX: (336)852-4346. E-mail: andrewrose@shalomgreensboro.com. Pres. Ronald Green; Exec. Dir. Marilyn Forman-Chandler.

RALEIGH

WAKE COUNTY JEWISH FEDERATION (includes Cary, Apex, Garner, Knightdale, Zebulon, Wake Forest and Smithfield) (1987); 8210 Creedmoor Rd., Suite 104 (27613); (919)676-2200. FAX: (919)676-2122. E-mail: ritaslattery@wcjf.org. Pres. Jim Maass; Exec. Dir. Judah Segal.

OHIO

AKRON

AKRON JEWISH COMMUNITY FEDERATION (1935); 750 White Pond Dr. (44320-1128); (330)869-CHAI (2424). FAX: (330)867-8498. Pres. David Kock; Exec. Dir. Michael Wise.

CANTON

CANTON JEWISH COMMUNITY FEDERATION (1935; reorg. 1955); 2631 Harvard Ave., NW (44709-3147); (330)452-6444. FAX: (330)452-4487. E-mail: cantonjcf@aol.com. Pres. Edward Buxbaum; Exec. Dir. Neil Berro.

CINCINNATI

JEWISH FEDERATION OF CINCINNATI (1896; reorg. 1967); 4380 Malsbary Rd., Suite 200

(45242-5644); (513) 985-1500. FAX: (513)985-1503. E-mail: jfed@jfedcin.org. Pres. Harry B. Davidow; Exec. V.-Pres. Aubrey Herman.

CLEVELAND

JEWISH COMMUNITY FEDERATION OF CLEVELAND (1903); 1750 Euclid Ave. (44115-2106); (216)566-9200. FAX: (216) 861-1230. E-mail: info@jcfcleve.org. Pres. Robert Goldberg; Exec. V.-Pres. Stephen H. Hoffman.

COLUMBUS

COLUMBUS JEWISH FEDERATION (1926); 1175 College Ave. (43209); (614)237-7686. FAX: (614)237-2221. E-mail: cjf@beol.net. Pres. Gordon Zacks; Exec. Dir. Mitchel Orlik.

DAYTON

JEWISH FEDERATION OF GREATER DAYTON (1910); 4501 Denlinger Rd. (45426-2395); (937)854-4150. FAX: (937)854-2850. Pres. Joseph Bettman; Exec. V.-Pres. Peter H. Wells.

STEUBENVILLE

JEWISH COMMUNITY COUNCIL (1938); 300 Lovers Lane (43952); (614)264-5514. FAX:: (740)264-7190. Pres. Curtis L. Greenberg; Exec. Sec. Jennie Bernstein.

TOLEDO

JEWISH FEDERATION OF GREATER TOLEDO (1907; reorg. 1960); 6505 Sylvania Ave., Sylvania (43560-3918); (419)885-4461. FAX: (419)885-3207. E-mail: jftoledo@cjfny.org. Pres. Joel Beren; Exec. Dir. Alix Greenblatt.

YOUNGSTOWN

YOUNGSTOWN AREA JEWISH FEDERATION (1935); 505 Gypsy Lane (44504-1314); (330)746-3251. FAX: (330)746-7926. E-mail: samkoopl@juno.com. Pres. Dr. Ronald Roth; Exec. V.-Pres. Sam Kooperman.

OKLAHOMA

OKLAHOMA CITY

JEWISH FEDERATION OF GREATER OKLAHOMA CITY (1941); 710 W. Wilshire, Suite C (73116-7736). (405)848-3132. FAX: (405) 848-3180. E-mail: okcfed@flash.net. Pres. Harriet Carson; Exec. Dir. Edie S. Roodman.

TULSA

JEWISH FEDERATION OF TULSA (1938); 2021

E. 71 ST. (74136); (918)495-1100. FAX: (918)495-1220. Pres. Andrew M. Wolov; Exec. Dir. David Bernstein.

OREGON

PORTLAND

JEWISH FEDERATION OF PORTLAND (incl. Northwest Oregon and Southwest Washington communities) (1920; reorg. 1956); 6651 SW Capitol Hwy. (97219); (503)245-6219. FAX: (503)245-6603. E-mail: charlie@jewishportland.org. Pres. Gayle Romain; Exec. Dir. Charles Schiffman.

PENNSYLVANIA

BUCKS COUNTY

(See Jewish Federation of Greater Philadelphia)

ERIE

JEWISH COMMUNITY COUNCIL OF ERIE (1946); 1611 Peach St., Suite 405 (16501-2123); (814)455-4474. FAX: (814)455-4475. E-mail: jcceri@erie.net. Pres. Robert Cohen; Admin. Dir. Cynthia Penman; Dir. of Soc. Srvcs. Barbara Singer.

HARRISBURG

UNITED JEWISH COMMUNITY OF GREATER HARRISBURG (1941); 3301 N. Front St. (17110-1436); (717)236-9555. FAX: (717) 236-8104. E-mail: communityreview@desupernet.net. Pres. Raphael Aronson; Exec. Dir. Jordan Harburger.

LEHIGH VALLEY

JEWISH FEDERATION OF THE LEHIGH VALLEY (1948); 702 N. 22nd St., Allentown (18104); (610)821-5500. FAX: (610)821-8946. E-mail: ivfed@enter.net.

PHILADELPHIA

JEWISH FEDERATION OF GREATER PHILADELPHIA (incl. Bucks, Chester, Delaware, Montgomery, and Philadelphia counties) (1901; reorg. 1956); 2100 Arch St. (19103); (215)832-0500. FAX: (215)832-1510. E-mail: lyouman@!philjnet.org. Pres. Michael R. Belman; Exec. V.-Pres. Howard E. Charish.

PITTSBURGH

UNITED JEWISH FEDERATION OF GREATER PITTSBURGH (1912; reorg. 1955); 234 McKee Pl. (15213-3916); (412)681-8000. FAX: (412) 681-3980. E-mail: information@ujf.net. Chmn. David Burstin; Pres. Howard M. Rieger.

READING

JEWISH FEDERATION OF READING, PA., INC. (1935; reorg. 1972); 1700 City Line St. (19604); (610)921-2766. FAX: (610)929-0886. E-mail: stahr@epix.net. Pres. Sheila Lattin; Exec. Dir. Stanley Ramati.

SCRANTON

SCRANTON-LACKAWANNA JEWISH FEDERATION (1945); 601 Jefferson Ave. (18510); (570)961-2300. FAX: (570)346-6147. Pres. Louis Nivert; Exec. Dir. Seymour Brotman.

WILKES-BARRE

JEWISH FEDERATION OF GREATER WILKES-BARRE (1950); 60 S. River St. (18702-2493); (717)822-4146. FAX: (717)824-5966. E-mail: wbreport@aol.com. Pres. Murray Ufberg; Exec. Dir. Don Cooper.

RHODE ISLAND

PROVIDENCE

JEWISH FEDERATION OF RHODE ISLAND (1945); 130 Sessions St. (02906); (401)421-4111. FAX: (401)331-7961. E-mail: shalom @jfri.org. Pres. Edward D. Feldstein; Exec. Dir. Steven A. Rakitt.

SOUTH CAROLINA

CHARLESTON

CHARLESTON JEWISH FEDERATION (1949); 1645 Raoul Wallenberg Blvd., PO Box 31298 (29407); (843)571-6565. FAX: (843)852-3547. E-mail: ejkatzman@aol.com. Pres. Anita Zucker; Exec. Dir. Ellen J. Katzman.

COLUMBIA

COLUMBIA JEWISH FEDERATION (1960); 4540 Trenholm Rd., PO Box 6968 (29206-4462); (803)787-2023. FAX: (803)787-0475. E-mail: ternercjf@hotmail.com. Pres. Stephen Serbin; Exec. Dir. Steven Terner.

SOUTH DAKOTA

SIOUX FALLS

JEWISH WELFARE FUND (1938); 510 S. First Ave. (57102-1003); (605)332-3335. FAX: (605)334-2298. E-mail: asnh94@prodigy. com. Pres. Laurence Bierman; Exec. Sec. Stephen Rosenthal.

TENNESSEE

CHATTANOOGA

JEWISH COMMUNITY FEDERATION OF GREATER CHATTANOOGA (1931); 3601 Ringgold Rd. (37412); PO Box 8947 (37412);

(423)493-0270. FAX: (423)493-9997. E-mail: dlevine@jcfgc.com. Pres. Claire Binder; Exec. Dir. Debra Levine.

KNOXVILLE

KNOXVILLE JEWISH FEDERATION, INC. (1939); 7800 Deane Hill Dr. (37919); (423)693-5837. FAX: (423)694-4861. E-mail: ajcckjf@aol.com. Pres. Mary Linda Schwartzbart; Exec. Dir. Dr. Bernard Rosenblatt.

MEMPHIS

MEMPHIS JEWISH FEDERATION (incl. Shelby County) (1935); 6560 Poplar Ave. (38138-3614); (901)767-7100. FAX: (901)767-7128. E-mail: jfeld@bigriver.net. Pres. Louise Sklar; Exec. Dir. Jeffrey Feld.

NASHVILLE

JEWISH FEDERATION OF NASHVILLE & MIDDLE TENNESSEE (1936); 801 Percy Warner Blvd. (37205-4009); (615)356-3242. FAX: (615)352-0056. E-mail: jnashjfed@aol.com. Pres. Peter Haas.

TEXAS

AUSTIN

JEWISH COMMUNTY ASSOCIATION OF AUSTIN (1939; reorg. 1956); 7300 Hart Lane (78731); (512)735-8000. FAX: (512)735-8001. E-mail: austinjfed@jfaustin.org. Pres. Linda Millstone; Exec. Dir. Sandy Sack.

BEAUMONT

BEAUMONT JEWISH FEDERATION; PO Box 1891 (77704-1981); (409)832-2881.

CORPUS CHRISTI

COMBINED JEWISH APPEAL OF CORPUS CHRISTI; 750 Everhart Rd. (78411-1906; (512)855-6239. FAX: (512)853-9040.

DALLAS

JEWISH FEDERATION OF GREATER DALLAS (1911); 7800 Northaven Rd. (75230-3226); (214)369-3313. FAX: (214)369-8943. Pres. Donald Schaffer; Exec. Dir. Gary Weinstein.

EL PASO

JEWISH FEDERATION OF EL PASO, INC. (1937); 405 Wallenberg Dr. (79912-5605); (915)584-4437. FAX: (915)584-0243. Pres. Gary Weiser; Exec. Dir. Larry Harris.

FORT WORTH

JEWISH FEDERATION OF FORT WORTH AND TARRANT COUNTY (1936); 4801-B Briarhaven Rd. (76109); (817)569-0892. FAX: (817)569-0896. E-mail: jfedfwtc@aol.com. Pres. Harold Gernsbacher; Exec. Dir. Naomi Rosenfield.

HOUSTON
JEWISH FEDERATION OF GREATER HOUSTON (1936); 5603 S. Braeswood Blvd. (77096-3907); (713)729-7000. FAX: (713)721-6232. E-mail: lwunsch@houstonjewish.org. Pres. Marvin Woskow; Exec. V.-Pres. Lee Wunsch.

SAN ANTONIO
JEWISH FEDERATION OF SAN ANTONIO (incl. Bexar County) (1922); 12500 NW Military Hwy., Suite 200 (78231); (210)302-6960. FAX: (210)408-2332. E-mail: markjfsa@aol.com. Pres. Meyer Lifschitz; Exec. Dir. Mark Freedman.

WACO
JEWISH FEDERATION OF WACO & CENTRAL TEXAS (1949); PO Box 8031 (76714-8031); (817)776-3740. E-MAIL: DEBHERSH@AOL.COM. Pres. Abbye M. Silver; Exec. Sec. Debbie Hersh-Levy.

UTAH

SALT LAKE CITY
UNITED JEWISH FEDERATION OF UTAH (1936); 2416 E. 1700 South (84108); (801) 581-0102. FAX: (801) 581-1334. Pres. Robert Wolff; Exec. Dir. Donald Gartman.

VIRGINIA

RICHMOND
JEWISH COMMUNITY FEDERATION OF RICHMOND (1935); 5403 Monument Ave., PO Box 17128 (23226-7128); (804)288-0045. FAX: (804)282-7507. E-mail: executivedirector@jewishrich.com. Pres. Richard J. November; Exec. Dir. Marsha F. Hurwitz.

TIDEWATER
UNITED JEWISH FEDERATION OF TIDEWATER (incl. Norfolk, Portsmouth, and Virginia

Beach) (1937); 5029 Corporate Woods Dr., Suite 225, Virginia Beach (23462-4370); (757)671-1600. FAX: (757)671-7613. E-mail: ujft@ujft.org. Pres. David Brand; Exec. V.-Pres. Mark L. Goldstein.

VIRGINIA PENINSULA
UNITED JEWISH COMMUNITY OF THE VIRGINIA PENINSULA, INC. (1942); 2700 Spring Rd., Newport News (23606); (757)930-1422. FAX: (757)930-3762. E-mail: unitedjc@erols.com. Pres. Roy H. Lasris; Exec. Dir. Rodney J. Margolis.

WASHINGTON

SEATTLE
JEWISH FEDERATION OF GREATER SEATTLE (incl. King County, Everett, and Bremerton) (1926); 2031 Third Ave. (98121); (206)443-5400. FAX: (206)443-0306. E-mail: wnedyj@jewishinseattle.org. Pres. Lucy Pruzan; Exec. V.-Pres. Michael Novick.

WEST VIRGINIA

CHARLESTON
FEDERATED JEWISH CHARITIES OF CHARLESTON, INC. (1937); PO Box 1613 (25326); (304)345-2320. FAX: (304)345-2325. E-mail: mzltov@aol.com. Pres. Stuart May; Exec. Sec. Lee Diznoff.

WISCONSIN

MADISON
MADISON JEWISH COMMUNITY COUNCIL, INC. (1940); 6434 Enterprise Lane (53719-1117. (608)278-1808. FAX:(608)278-7814. E-mail: morrison@mjcc.net. Pres. Joel Minkoff; Exec. Dir. Steven H. Morrison.

MILWAUKEE
MILWAUKEE JEWISH FEDERATION, INC. (1902); 1360 N. Prospect Ave. (53202); (414) 390-5700. FAX: (414)390-5782. Pres. Stephen L. Chernof; Exec. V.-Pres. Richard H. Meyer.

CANADA

ALBERTA

CALGARY
CALGARY JEWISH COMMUNITY COUNCIL (1962); 1607 90th Ave. SW (T2V 4V7); (403)253-8600. FAX: (403)253-7915. E-

mail: cjcc@jewish-calgary.com. Pres. Nate Feldman; Exec. Dir. Joel R. Miller.

EDMONTON
JEWISH FEDERATION OF EDMONTON (1954; reorg. 1982); 7200-156th St. (T5R 1X3);

(780)487-5120. FAX: (780)481-1854. E-mail: edjfed@net.com.ca. Pres. Stephen Mandel; Exec. Dir. Lesley A. Jacobson.

BRITISH COLUMBIA

VANCOUVER

JEWISH FEDERATION OF GREATER VANCOUVER (1932; reorg. 1987); 950 W. 41st Ave., Suite 200 (V5Z 2N7); (604)257-5100. FAX: (604)257-5110. E-mail: jfed@jfgv.com. Pres. Bob Wielmot; Exec. Dir. Drew Staffenberg.

MANITOBA

WINNIPEG

JEWISH FEDERATION OF WINNIPEG/COMBINED JEWISH APPEAL (1938; reorg. 1973); 123 Doncaster St., Suite C300 (R3N 2B2); (204)477-7400. FAX: (204)477-7405. E-mail: bfreedman@aspercampus.mb.ca. Pres. Larry Hurtig; Exec. V.-Pres. Robert Freedman.

ONTARIO

HAMILTON

UJA/JEWISH FEDERATION OF HAMILTON/WENTWORTH & AREA (1932; merged 1971); PO Box 7258, 1030 Lower Lions Club Rd., Ancaster (L9G 3N6); (905)648-0605 #305. FAX: (905)648-8350. E-mail: hamujajf@interlynx.net. Pres. Cheryl Greenbaum; Exec. Dir. Patricia Tolkin Eppel.

LONDON

LONDON JEWISH FEDERATION (1932); 536 Huron St. (N5Y 4J5); (519)673-3310. FAX: (519)673-1161. Pres. Ron Wolf; Off. Mgr. Debra Chatterley.

OTTAWA

UNITED JEWISH APPEAL OF OTTAWA (1934); 1780 Kerr Ave. (K2A 1R9); (613)798-4696. FAX: (613)798-4695. E-mail: hcoleman @ujaottawa.com. Pres. Barbara Farber; Exec. Dir. Mitchell Bellman.

TORONTO

UJA FEDERATION OF GREATER TORONTO (1917); 4600 Bathurst St. (M2R 3V2); (416)635-2883. FAX: (416)631-5715. E-mail: wcbmaven@feduja.org. Pres. Joseph Steiner; Exec. V.-Pres. Allan Reitzes.

WINDSOR

JEWISH COMMUNITY FEDERATION (1938); 1641 Ouellette Ave. (N8X 1K9); (519)973-1772. FAX: (519)973-1774. Pres. Dr. Michael Malowitz; Exec. Dir. Steven Brownstein.

QUEBEC

MONTREAL

FEDERATION CJA (formerly Allied Jewish Community Services) (1965); 1 Carrie Cummings Square (H3W 1M6); (514)735-3541. FAX: (514)735-8972. E-mail: dcantor@federationcja.org. Pres. Stanley Plotnick; Exec. V.-Pres. Danyael Cantor.

Jewish Periodicals*

UNITED STATES

ALABAMA

DEEP SOUTH JEWISH VOICE (1990) (formerly THE SOUTHERN SHOFAR). PO Box 130052, Birmingham, 35213. (205) 595-9255. FAX: (205)595-9256. E-mail: dsjvoice@aol.com. Lawrence M. Brook. Monthly.

ARIZONA

ARIZONA JEWISH POST (1946). 2601 N. Campbell Ave., #205, Tucson, 85719. (520)319-1112. FAX: (520)319-1118. E-mail: edsatpost@aol.com. Sandra R. Heiman. Fortnightly. Jewish Federation of Southern Arizona.

JEWISH NEWS OF GREATER PHOENIX (1948). 1625 E. Northern Ave., Suite 106, Phoenix, 85020. (602)870-9470. FAX: (602)870-0426. E-mail: editor@jewishaz.com. Ed./Pub. Florence Eckstein. Weekly. (www.jewishaz.com)

CALIFORNIA

THE AMERICAN RABBI (1968). 22711 Cass Ave., Woodland Hills, 91364. (818)225-9631. FAX: (818)225-8354. E-mail: david @inpubco.com. Ed.-in-Ch./Pub. David Epstein; Ed. Harry Essrig. Quarterly.

CENTRAL CALIFORNIA JEWISH HERITAGE (1914). 20201 Sherman Way, Winnetka, 91306. (818) 576-9000. FAX: (818) 576-9910. E-mail: heritagepub@earthlink.net. Dan Brin. Six times a year. Heritage Group.

HERITAGE-SOUTHWEST JEWISH PRESS (1914). 20201 Sherman Way, Suite 204,
Winnetka, 91306. (818) 576-9000. FAX: (818) 576-9910. E-mail: heritagepub @earthlink.net. Dan Brin. Weekly. Heritage Group.

JEWISH BULLETIN OF NORTHERN CALIFORNIA (1896). 225 Bush St., Suite 1480, San Francisco, 94104-4281. (415)263-7200. FAX: (415)263-7223. E-mail: sanfranbul@aol.com. Marc S. Klein. Weekly. San Francisco Jewish Community Publications, Inc.

JEWISH COMMUNITY CHRONICLE (1947). 3801 E. Willow St., Long Beach, 90815. (562)426-7601, ext. 1021. FAX: (562)595-5543. E-mail: jchron@surfside.net. Harriette Ellis; Bus. Mng./Prod. Chris Berry. Fortnightly. Jewish Federation of Greater Long Beach & West Orange County.

JEWISH COMMUNITY NEWS (1976). 14855 Oka Rd., Suite 2, Los Gatos, 95030. (408)358-3033, ext. 31. FAX: (408)356-0733. E-mail: jcn@jfgsj.org. Eileen Goss; Adv. Lindsay Greensweig (408)286-6669. Monthly. Jewish Federation of Greater San Jose.

JEWISH JOURNAL OF GREATER LOS ANGELES (1986). 3660 Wilshire Blvd., Suite 204, Los Angeles, 90010. (213)368-1661. FAX: (213)368-1684. E-mail:jjla@aol. com. Gene Lichtenstein. Weekly.

JEWISH NEWS (1973). 11071 Ventura Blvd., Studio City, 91604. (818)786-4000. FAX: (818)760-4648. Phil Blazer. Monthly. (Also weekly Sunday TV and radio broadcasts in LA, NY, and Miami.)

---

*The information in this directory is based on replies to questionnaires circulated by the editors. For organization bulletins, see the directory of Jewish organizations.

JEWISH SOCIAL STUDIES: HISTORY, CULTURE, AND SOCIETY (1939). c/o Program in Jewish Studies, Bldg. 240, Rm. 103, Stanford University, Stanford, 94305-2190. (650)725-0829. FAX: (650)725-2920. E-mail: jss@leland.stanford.edu. Steven J. Zipperstein, Aron Rodrigue. Three times a year. Conference on Jewish Social Studies, Inc.

JEWISH SPORTS REVIEW. 1800 S. Robertson Blvd., #174, Los Angeles, 90035. (800) 510-9003. E-mail: gwallman@igc.org. Shel Wallman/Ephraim Moxson. Bimonthly. www.jewishsportsreview.com)

LOS ANGELES JEWISH TIMES (formerly B'NAI B'RITH MESSENGER) (1897). 5455 Wilshire Blvd., Suite 903, Los Angeles, 90036. (323)933-0131. FAX: (323)933-7928. E-mail: lajtart@aol.com. Ed.-in-Chief Joe Bobker; Mng. Ed. Jane Fried. Weekly.

ORANGE COUNTY JEWISH HERITAGE. 24331 Muirlands Blvd., Suite D-347, Lake Forest, 92630. Phone/FAX: (949)362-4446. E-mail: ocnews@hotmail.com. Stan Brin. Bi-weekly.

SAN DIEGO JEWISH PRESS HERITAGE (1914). 3615 Kearny Villa Rd., #111, San Diego, 92123. (858)560-0992. FAX: (858)560-0993. E-mail: sdheritage@aol.com. Aaron Hoskins. Weekly.

SAN DIEGO JEWISH TIMES (1979). 4731 Palm Ave., La Mesa, 91941. (619)463-5515. FAX: (900) 370-1190. E-mail: jewish times@msn.com. Colleen Silea. Fortnightly.

SHALOM L.A. (1988). 16027 Ventura Blvd., #400, Encino, 91436. (818)783-3090. FAX: (818)783-1104. Gal Shor. Weekly. Hebrew.

TIKKUN MAGAZINE (1986). 2107 Van Ness Ave., Suite 302, San Francisco, 94109. (415)575-1200. FAX: (415)575-1434. E-mail: magazine@tikkun.org. Michael Lerner. Bimonthly. Institute for Labor & Mental Health. (www.tikkun.org)

WESTERN STATES JEWISH HISTORY (1968). 22711 Cass Ave., Woodland Hills, 91364. (818)225-9631. FAX: (818)225-8354. E-mail: david@inpubco.com. Ed.-in-Ch. Gladys Sturman; Ed. David Epstein. Quarterly. Western States Jewish History Association.

COLORADO

INTERMOUNTAIN JEWISH NEWS (1913). 1275 Sherman St., Suite 214, Denver, 80203-2299. (303)861-2234. FAX: (303)832-6942. E-mail: ijn@rmii.com. Exec. Ed. Rabbi Hillel Goldberg; Pub. Miriam Goldberg. Weekly.

CONNECTICUT

CONNECTICUT JEWISH LEDGER (1929). 740 N. Main St., W. Hartford, 06117. (860)231-2424. FAX: (860)231-2428. E-mail: ctjledger@aol.com. Lisa Lenkiewicz. Weekly.

JEWISH LEADER (1974). 28 Channing St., PO Box 1468, New London, 06320. (860)442-7395. FAX: (860)443-4175. E-mail: perlsum4@aol.com. Ed. Mimi Perl; Mng. Henry Savin. Biweekly. Jewish Federation of Eastern Connecticut.

DELAWARE

JEWISH VOICE. 100 W. 10th St., Suite 301, Wilmington, 19801. (302) 427-2100. FAX: (302) 427-2438. E-mail: jewishvoic @aol.com. Lynn Edelman. 22 times per year. Jewish Federation of Delaware.

DISTRICT OF COLUMBIA

AZURE (1996). 1140 Connecticut Ave., NW, Suite 801, Washington, 20036. (202)887-1270. FAX: (202)887-1277. E-mail: patrick@shalemcenter.org. Dan Polisar. Quarterly. Hebrew/English. The Shalem Center.

B'NAI B'RITH INTERNATIONAL JEWISH MONTHLY (1886, under the name Menorah). 1640 Rhode Island Ave., NW, Washington, 20036. (202)857-6646. FAX: (202)296-1092. E-mail: erozenman@ bnaibrith.org. Eric Rozenman. Bimonthly. B'nai B'rith International.

CAPITAL COMMUNIQUÉ (1991). 777 N. Capital St., NE, Suite 305, Washington, 20002. (202)216-9060. FAX: (202)216-9061. Jason Silberberg. Bi-annually. National Jewish Democratic Council.

THE JEWISH VETERAN (1896). 1811 R St., NW, Washington, 20009-1659. (202)265-6280. FAX: (202)234-5662. E-mail: the-jewishveteran@bigfoot.com. Ian Lipner. 5 times per year. Jewish War Veterans of the U.S.A.

MOMENT (1975). 4710 41 St., NW, Washington, 20016. (202)364-3300. FAX:

(202)364-2636. E-mail: editor@moment-mag.com. Hershel Shanks. Bimonthly. Jewish Educational Ventures, Inc.

MONITOR (1990). 1819 H Street, NW, Suite 230, Washington, 20006. (202)775-9770. FAX: (202)775-9776. E-mail: ucsj@ucsj. com. Lindsey Paige Taxman. Quarterly. Union of Councils for Soviet Jews.

NEAR EAST REPORT (1957). 440 First St., NW, Suite 607, Washington, 20001. (202)639-5254. FAX: (202) 347-4916. Dr. Raphael Danziger. Fortnightly. Near East Research, Inc.

SECURITY AFFAIRS (1976). 1717 K St., NW, Suite 800, Washington, 20006. (202)833-0020. FAX: (202)296-6452. E-mail: info@ jinsa.org. Jim Colbert. Quarterly. Jewish Institute for National Security Affairs.

WASHINGTON JEWISH WEEK. *See under* MARYLAND

FLORIDA

THE CHRONICLE (1971). 580 S. McIntosh Rd., Sarasota, 34232. (941)371-4546. FAX: (941)378-2947. Barry Millman. Fortnightly. Sarasota-Manatee Jewish Federation.

HERITAGE FLORIDA JEWISH NEWS (1976). PO Box 300742, Fern Park, 32730. (407)834-8787. FAX: (407)831-0507. E-mail: heritagefl@aol.com. Pub. Jeffrey Gaeser; Assoc. Ed. Chris Allen. Weekly.

JACKSONVILLE JEWISH NEWS (1988). 8505 San Jose Blvd., Jacksonville, 32217. (904)448-5000, (904)262-1971. FAX: (904)448-5715. E-mail: srgnews@aol. com. Susan R. Goetz. Monthly. Jacksonville Jewish Federation.

JEWISH JOURNAL (PALM BEACH-BROWARD-DADE) (1977). 601 Fairway Dr., Deerfield Beach, 33441. (954)698-6397. FAX: (954)429-1207. Alan Gosh. Weekly. South Florida Newspaper Network.

JEWISH PRESS OF PINELLAS COUNTY (CLEARWATER-ST.PETERSBURG) (1985). PO Box 6970, Clearwater, 33758-6970; 13191 Starkey Rd., Crownpointe #8, Largo, 33773-1438. (727)535-4400. FAX:(727) 530-3039. E-mail: jptb@aol.com. Karen Wolfson Dawkins. Biweekly. Jewish Press Group of Tampa Bay (FL), Inc. in cooperation with the Jewish Federation of Pinellas County.

JEWISH PRESS OF TAMPA (1987). PO Box 6970, Clearwater 33758-6970; 13191 Starkey Rd., Crownpointe #8, Largo 33773-1438. (727)535-4400. FAX: (727) 530-3039. E-mail: jptb@aol.com. Karen Wolfson Dawkins. Biweekly. Jewish Press Group of Tampa Bay (FL), Inc.

SHALOM (1994). 8358 W. Oakland Park Blvd., Suite 305, Ft. Lauderdale, 33351. (954)748-8400. FAX: (954) 748-4509. Ed.-in-Chief Rhonda Roseman-Seriani; Mng. Ed. Elliot Goldenberg. Biweekly. Jewish Federation of Broward County.

GEORGIA

JEWISH CIVIC PRESS (1972). 500 Sugar Mill Rd., Suite B-210, Atlanta, 30350. (404)231-2194. Abner L. Tritt. Monthly.

ILLINOIS

CHICAGO JEWISH NEWS (1994). 2501 W. Peterson, Chicago, 60659. (773)728-3636. FAX: (773)728-3734. E-mail: chijew-nes@aol.com. Joseph Aaron. Weekly.

CHICAGO JEWISH STAR (1991). PO Box 268, Skokie, 60076-0268. (847)674-7827. FAX: (847)674-0014. E-mail: chicago-jewish-star@mcimail.com. Ed. Douglas Wertheimer; Assoc. Ed. Gila Wertheimer. Fortnightly.

JEWISH COMMUNITY NEWS (1941). 6464 W. Main, Suite 7A, Belleville, 62223. (618) 398-6100/ (314)567-6955. FAX: (618)398-0539. Steve Low. Quarterly. Jewish Federation of Southern Illinois.

JUF NEWS & GUIDE TO JEWISH LIVING IN CHICAGO (1972). One S. Franklin St., Rm. 701G, Chicago, 60606. (312)357-4848. FAX: (312)855-2470. E-mail: jufnews@ juf.org. Aaron B. Cohen. Monthly (Guide, annually). Jewish United Fund/ Jewish Federation of Metropolitan Chicago.

INDIANA

ILLIANA NEWS (1976). 2939 Jewett St., Highland, 46322. (219)972-2250. FAX: (219)972-4779. E-mail: jfedofnwi@aol. com. Monthly (except July/Aug.). Jewish Federation of Northwest Indiana, Inc.

INDIANA JEWISH POST AND OPINION (1935). 238 S. Meridian St., #502, Indianapolis, 46225. (317)972-7800. FAX: (317)972-7807. E-mail: jpost@surf-ici.com. Ed Stattmann. Weekly.

NATIONAL JEWISH POST AND OPINION (1932). 238 S. Meridian St., Indianapolis, 46225. (317)972-7800. FAX: (317)972-7807. Gabriel Cohen. Weekly.

PROOFTEXTS: A JOURNAL OF JEWISH LITERARY HISTORY (1980). Indiana University Press, 601 N. Morton St., Bloomington, 47404. (812)855-9449. FAX: (812)855-8507. E-mail: journals@indiana.edu. Editorial address (for contributors):NEJS Dept., Brandeis U., Waltham, MA 02254. Alan Mintz, David G. Roskies. Three times a year.

KANSAS

KANSAS CITY JEWISH CHRONICLE (1920). 7373 W. 107 St., Overland Park, 66212. (913)648-4620. FAX: (913)381-1402. E-mail: chronicle@sunpublications.com. Rick Hellman. Weekly. Sun Publications.

KENTUCKY

COMMUNITY (1975). 3630 Dutchmans Lane, Louisville, 40205-3200. (502) 451-8840. FAX: (502) 458-0702. E-mail: jfed@iglou.com. Shiela Steinman Wallace. Biweekly. Jewish Community Federation of Louisville.

KENTUCKY JEWISH POST AND OPINION (1931). 1701 Bardstown Rd., Louisville, 40205. (502)459-1914. Ed Stattman. Weekly.

LOUISIANA

JEWISH CIVIC PRESS (1965). 924 Valmont St., New Orleans, 70115. (504)895-8784. Claire & Abner Tritt, eds. and pubs. Monthly.

JEWISH NEWS (1995). 3500 N. Causeway Blvd., Suite 1240, Metairie, 70002. (504) 828-2125. FAX: (504)828-2827. E-mail: jfedrb@aol.com. Gail Naron Chalew. Fortnightly. Jewish Federation of Greater New Orleans.

MARYLAND

BALTIMORE JEWISH TIMES (1919). 2104 N. Charles St., Baltimore, 21218. (410)752-3504. FAX: (410)752-2375. Phil Jacobs. Weekly.

WASHINGTON JEWISH WEEK (1930, as the National Jewish Ledger). 1500 East Jefferson St., Rockville, 20852. (301) 230-2222. FAX: (301)881-6362. E-mail: wjweek@aol.com. Debra Rubin. Weekly.

MASSACHUSETTS

AMERICAN JEWISH HISTORY (1893). Two Thornton Rd., Waltham, 02453. (781) 891-8110. FAX: (781)899-9208. E-mail: ajhs@ajhs.org. Marc Lee Raphael. Quarterly. American Jewish Historical Society.

JEWISH ADVOCATE (1902). 15 School St., Boston, 02108. (617)367-9100. FAX: (617)367-9310. E-mail: thejewadv@aol.com. Steven Rosenberg. Weekly.

THE JEWISH CHRONICLE (1927). 131 Lincoln St., Worcester, 01605. (508)752-2512. E-mail: jchronicle@aol.com. Pub. Sondra Shapiro; Ed. Ellen Weingart. Bimonthly.

JEWISH GUIDE TO BOSTON & NEW ENGLAND (1972). 15 School St., Boston, 02108. (617)367-9100. FAX: (617)367-9310. Rosie Rosenzweig. Irregularly. The Jewish Advocate.

THE JEWISH JOURNAL/NORTH OF BOSTON (1976). 201 Washington St., PO Box 555, Salem, 01970. (978)745-4111. FAX: (978) 745-5333. E-mail: editorial@jewishjournal.org. Judith Klein. Biweekly. Russian section. North Shore Jewish Press Ltd.

THE JEWISH NEWS OF WESTERN MASSACHUSETTS (see Jewish Advocate)

METROWEST JEWISH REPORTER (1970). 76 Salem End Rd., Framingham, 01702. (508)872-4808. FAX: (508)879-5856. Marcia T. Rivin. Monthly. Combined Jewish Philanthropies of Greater Boston.

PAKN-TREGER (1980). 1021 West St., Amherst, 01002. (413)256-4900. FAX: (413)256-4700. E-mail: pt@bikher.org. Nancy Sherman. Three times a year. National Yiddish Book Center.

SH'MA (1970). 56 Kearney Rd., Needham, 02494. (781)449-9894. FAX: (781)449-9825. E-mail: susanb@jflmedia.com. Susan Berrin. Monthly. Jewish Family & Life.

MICHIGAN

DETROIT JEWISH NEWS (1942). 27676 Franklin Rd., Southfield, 48034. (248) 354-6060. FAX: (248)354-6069. E-mail: smanello@thejewishnews.com. Robert Sklar. Weekly.

HUMANISTIC JUDAISM (1968). 28611 W. Twelve Mile Rd., Farmington Hills, 48334. (248)478-7610. FAX: (248)478-3159. E-mail: info@shj.org. M. Bonnie

Cousens, Ruth D. Feldman. Quarterly. Society for Humanistic Judaism.

WASHTENAW JEWISH NEWS (1978). 2935 Birch Hollow Dr., Ann Arbor, 48108. (734)971-1800. FAX: (734)971-1801. E-mail: wjna2@aol.com. Susan Kravitz Ayer. Monthly.

MINNESOTA

AMERICAN JEWISH WORLD (1912). 4509 Minnetonka Blvd., Minneapolis, 55416. (612)920-7000. FAX: (612)920-6205. E-mail: amjewish@isd.net. Marshall Hoffman. Weekly.

MISSOURI

KANSAS CITY JEWISH CHRONICLE. See under KANSAS

ST. LOUIS JEWISH LIGHT (1947; reorg. 1963). 12 Millstone Campus Dr., St. Louis, 63146. (314)432-3353. FAX: (314)432-0515. E-mail: stlouislgt@aol.com. Robert A. Cohn. Weekly. St. Louis Jewish Light.

NEBRASKA

JEWISH PRESS (1920). 333 S. 132 St., Omaha, 68154. (402)334-6450. FAX: (402)334-5422. E-mail: jshpress@aol.com. Carol Katzman. Weekly. Jewish Federation of Omaha.

NEVADA

JEWISH REPORTER (1996). 3909 S. Maryland Pkwy., Suite 400, Las Vegas, 89119-7520. (702)732-0556. FAX: (702)732-3228. E-mail: Rhjewrprtr@aol.com. Rebecca Herren. Bimonthly. Jewish Federation of Las Vegas.

LAS VEGAS ISRAELITE (1965). PO Box 14096, Las Vegas, 89114. (702)876-1255. FAX: (702)364-1009. Michael Tell. Bimonthly.

NEW HAMPSHIRE

JEWISH SPECTATOR (1935). P.O. Box 267, New London, 03257. (603)526-2513. FAX: (603)526-2514. E-mail: jsisrael@netmedia.net.il. Rabbi Mark Bleiweiss. Quarterly. Friends of Jewish Spectator, Inc.

NEW JERSEY

AVOTAYNU (1985). 155 N. Washington Ave., Bergenfield, 07621. (201)387-7200. FAX: (201)387-2855. E-mail: info@avotaynu.com. Sallyann Amdur Sack. Quarterly.

JEWISH CHRONICLE (1982). 1063 East Landis Ave., Suite B, Vineland, 08360. (856) 696-4445. FAX: (856)696-3428. E-mail: jfedcc@aol.com. Ann Lynn Lipton. Bimonthly. The Jewish Federation of Cumberland County.

JEWISH COMMUNITY NEWS. 1086 Teaneck Rd., Teaneck, 07666. (201) 837-8818. FAX: (201) 833-4959. E-mail: jewishstd2 @aol.com. Rebecca Kaplan Boroson. Fortnightly. Jewish Federation of North Jersey and Jewish Federation of Greater Clifton-Passaic.

JEWISH COMMUNITY VOICE (1941). 1301 Springdale Rd., Suite 250, Cherry Hill, 08003-2762. (856)751-9500, ext. 217. FAX: (856)489-8253. E-mail: jvcheditor@aol.com. Harriet Kessler. Biweekly. Jewish Federation of Southern NJ.

THE JEWISH JOURNAL (1999). 320 Raritan Ave., Suite 203, Highland Park, 08904. (732)393-0023. FAX: (732)393-0026. E-mail: jewish@castle.net. Ron Ostroff. Monthly. Published in cooperation with the Ocean County Jewish Federation.

JEWISH STANDARD (1931). 1086 Teaneck Rd., Teaneck, 07666. (201)837-8818. FAX: (201)833-4959. Rebecca Kaplan Boroson. Weekly.

JEWISH STAR (1985). 230 Old Bridge Turnpike, South River, 08882-2000. (732)432-7711. FAX: (732)432-0292. E-mail: jfgmc @aol.com. Marlene A. Heller. Fortnightly. Jewish Federation of Greater Middlesex County.

THE JEWISH STATE (1996). 320 Raritan Ave., Suite 203, Highland Park, 08904. (732) 393-0023. FAX: (732)393-0026. E-mail: jewish@castle.net. Ron Ostroff. Weekly.

JEWISH VOICE & OPINION (1987). 73 Dana Place, Englewood, 07631. (201) 569-2845. FAX: (201)569-1739. Susan L. Rosenbluth. Monthly.

JEWISH VOICE OF GREATER MONMOUTH COUNTY (1971). 100 Grant Ave., Deal Park, 07723. (732)531-6200. FAX: (732)531-9518. E-mail: pfdnuss@msn.com. Lauren Silver. Monthly. Jewish Federation of Greater Monmouth County and Ocean County Jewish Federation.

JOURNAL OF JEWISH COMMUNAL SERVICE (1899). 3084 State Hwy. 27, Suite 9, Kendall Pk., 08824-1657. (732)821-1871. FAX: (732)821-5335. E-mail: jcsana@

aol.com. Gail Naron Chalew. Quarterly. Jewish Communal Service Association of North America.

NEW JERSEY JEWISH NEWS (1947). 901 Route 10, Whippany, 07981-1157. (973) 887-3900. FAX: (973)887-5999. E-mail: 6853202@mcimail.com. David Twersky. Weekly. United Jewish Federation of MetroWest.

THE SPEAKER (1999). 320 Raritan Ave., Suite 203, Highland Park, 08904. (732) 393-0023. FAX: (732)393-0026. E-mail: jewish@castle.net. Ron Ostroff. Monthly. Published in cooperation with the Jewish Federation of Somerset, Hunterdon & Warren Counties.

NEW MEXICO

NEW MEXICO JEWISH LINK (1971). 5520 Wyoming NE, Albuquerque, 87109. (505)821-3214. FAX: (505)821-3351. E-mail: nmjlink@aol.com. Tema Milstein. Monthly. Jewish Federation of Greater Albuquerque.

NEW YORK

AFN SHVEL (1941). 200 W. 72 St., Suite 40, NYC, 10023. (212)787-6675. E-mail: yidleague@aol.com. Mordkhe Schaechter. Quarterly. Yiddish. League for Yiddish, Inc.

AGENDA: JEWISH EDUCATION (1949; formerly Pedagogic Reporter). JESNA, 111 Eighth Ave., Suite 11E, NYC, 10011-5201. (212)284-6950. FAX: (212)284-6951. E-mail: info@jesna.org. Rabbi Arthur Vernon. Twice a year. Jewish Education Service of North America, Inc.

ALGEMEINER JOURNAL (1972). 225 E. Broadway, NYC, 10002. (212)267-5561. FAX: (212)267-5624. E-mail: Algemeiner @aol.com. Gershon Jacobson. Weekly. Yiddish-English.

AMERICAN JEWISH YEAR BOOK (1899). 165 E. 56 St., NYC, 10022. (212)751-4000. FAX: (212)751-4017. E-mail: research@ ajc.org. David Singer, Lawrence Grossman. Annually. American Jewish Committee.

AMIT (1925). 817 Broadway, NYC, 10003. (212)477-4720. FAX: (212)353-2312. E-mail: amitmag@aol.com. Rita Schwalb. Quarterly. AMIT (formerly American Mizrachi Women).

AUFBAU (1934). 2121 Broadway, NYC, 10023. (212)873-7400. Voice mail: (212) 579-6578. FAX: (212)496-5736. E-mail: aufbau2000@aol.com. Monika Ziegler/ Andreas Mirk/Irene Armbruster. Fortnightly. German-English. New World Club, Inc.

BUFFALO JEWISH REVIEW (1918). 15 E. Mohawk St., Buffalo, 14203. (716)854-2192. FAX: (716)854-2198. E-mail: buffjewrev @aoc.com. Harlan C. Abbey. Weekly. Kahaal Nahalot Israel.

THE CALL (1933). 45 E. 33 St., NYC, 10016. (212)889-6800, ext. 225. FAX: (212)532-7518. E-mail: ericas@circle.org. Erica Sigmon. Quarterly. The Workmen's Circle/Arbeter Ring.

CCAR JOURNAL: A REFORM JEWISH QUARTERLY (formerly JOURNAL OF REFORM JUDAISM) (1953). 355 Lexington Ave., NYC, 10017. (212)972-3636. FAX: (212)692-0819. Ed. Rifat Sonsino. Mng. Ed. Elliot Stevens. Quarterly. Central Conference of American Rabbis.

CIRCLE (1943). 15 E. 26 St., NYC, 10010-1579. (212)532-4949. FAX: (212)481-4174. E-mail: jason@jcca.org. Jason Black. Quarterly. Jewish Community Centers Association of North America (formerly JWB).

COMMENTARY (1945). 165 E. 56 St., NYC, 10022. (212)751-4000. FAX: (212)751-1174. E-mail: commentary@compuserve. com. Ed. Neal Kozodoy; Ed.-at-Large Norman Podhoretz. Monthly. American Jewish Committee.

CONGRESS MONTHLY (1933). 15 E. 84 St., NYC, 10028. (212)879-4500. Jack Fischel. Six times a year. American Jewish Congress.

CONSERVATIVE JUDAISM (1945). 3080 Broadway, NYC, 10027. (212)280-6065. FAX: (212)749-9166. E-mail: rapubs@jtsa.edu. Rabbi Benjamin Edidin Scolnic. Quarterly. Rabbinical Assembly and Jewish Theological Seminary of America.

FORVERTS (YIDDISH FORWARD) (1897). 45 E. 33 St., NYC, 10016. (212)889-8200. FAX: (212)684-3949. Boris Sandler. Weekly. Yiddish. Forward Association, Inc.

FORWARD (1897). 45 E. 33 St., NYC, 10016. (212)889-8200. FAX: (212)447-6406. E-mail: newsdesk@forward.com. J. J. Goldberg. Weekly. Forward Newspaper, L.L.C.

HADAROM (1957). 305 Seventh Ave., NYC, 10001. (212)807-7888. FAX: (212)727-8452. Rabbi Gedalia Dov Schwartz. Annual. Hebrew. Rabbinical Council of America.

HADASSAH MAGAZINE (1914). 50 W. 58 St., NYC, 10019. (212)688-0227. FAX: (212) 446-9521. Alan M. Tigay. Monthly (except for combined issues of June-July and Aug.-Sept.). Hadassah, the Women's Zionist Organization of America.

HADOAR (1921). 426 W. 58 St., NYC, 10019. (212)957-6659. FAX: (212)957-5811. E-mail: general@hist-ivrit.org. Ed. Shlomo Shamir; Lit. Ed. Dr. Yael Feldman. Biweekly. Hebrew. Hadoar Association, Inc., Organ of the Histadruth of America.

I.A.J.E. NEWSLETTER (1999). (718)339-0337. E-mail: sanuav@stjohns.edu. Victor D. Sanua. International Association of Jews from Egypt.

JBI VOICE (1978). 110 E. 30 St., NYC, 10016. (212)889-2525, (800)433-1531. Dr. Jacob Freid. Ten times a year in U.S. (audiocassettes). English. Jewish Braille Institute of America.

JEWISH ACTION (1950). 11 Broadway, NYC, 10004. (212)613-8146. FAX: (212)613-0646. E-mail: friedland@ou.org. Charlotte Friedland. Quarterly. Orthodox Union.

JEWISH BOOK ANNUAL (1942). 15 E. 26 St., 10th fl., NYC, 10010. (212)532-4949, ext. 297. E-mail: jbc@jewishbooks.org. Dr. Stephen H. Garrin. Hebrew & English with bibliography in Yiddish. Jewish Book Council.

JEWISH BOOK WORLD (1945). 15 E. 26 St., NYC, 10010. (212)532-4949, ext. 297. FAX: (212)481-4174. E-mail: jbc@jewishbooks.org. Esther Nussbaum. Three times annually. Jewish Book Council.

JEWISH BRAILLE REVIEW (1931). 110 E. 30 St., NYC, 10016. (212)889-2525, (800)433-1531. Dr. Jacob Freid. 10 times a year in U.S. (braille). English. Jewish Braille Institute of America.

JEWISH CURRENTS (1946). 22 E. 17 St., Suite 601, NYC, 10003-1919. (212)924-5740. FAX: (212)924-5740. Morris U. Schappes. Monthly (July/Aug. combined). Association for Promotion of Jewish Secularism.

JEWISH EDUCATION NEWS (1980). 261 W. 35 St., Fl. 12A, NYC 10001. (212) 268-4210. FAX: (212)268-4214. E-mail: publications @caje.org. Mng. Ed. Roselyn Bell. Triannually. Coalition for the Advancement of Jewish Education.

JEWISH FRONTIER (1934). 275 Seventh Ave., 17th fl., NYC, 10001. (212)229-2280. FAX: (212)675-7685. Nahum Guttman. Bimonthly. Labor Zionist Letters, Inc.

JEWISH HERALD (1984). 1689 46 St., Brooklyn, 11204. (718)972-4000. E-mail: nyjherald@aol.com. Leon J. Sternheim. Weekly.

JEWISH JOURNAL (1969). 11 Sunrise Plaza, Valley Stream, 11580. (516)561-6900. FAX: (516)561-6971. Ed. Paul Rubens; Pub. Harold Singer. Weekly.

JEWISH LEDGER (1924). 2535 Brighton-Henrietta Town Line Rd., Rochester, 14623. (716)427-2434. FAX: (716)427-8521. Barbara Morgenstern. Weekly.

JEWISH OBSERVER (1963). 84 William St., NYC, 10038. (212)797-9000. FAX: (212) 269-2843. E-mail: aiamail@aol.com. Rabbi Nisson Wolpin. Monthly (except July and Aug.). Agudath Israel of America.

JEWISH OBSERVER OF CENTRAL NEW YORK (1978). PO Box 510, DeWitt, 13214. (315) 445-2040. FAX: (315)445-1559. E-mail: jocny@aol.com. Judith Huober. Biweekly. Syracuse Jewish Federation, Inc.

JEWISH POST OF NY (1993). 130 W. 29 St., 10th fl., NYC, 10001-5312. (212) 967-7313. FAX: (212)967-8321. E-mail: jpost@nais.com. Ed. Gad Nahshon; Pub. & Ed.-in-Chief Henry J. Levy. Monthly. Link Marketing & Promotion, Inc.

JEWISH PRESS (1950). 338 Third Ave., Brooklyn, 11215. (718)330-1100. FAX: (718)935-1215. E-mail: jpeditor@aol. com. Jerry Greenwald. Weekly.

JEWISH TELEGRAPHIC AGENCY COMMUNITY NEWS REPORTER (1962). 330 Seventh Ave., 11th fl., NYC, 10001-5010. (212) 643-1890. FAX: (212)643-8498. Lisa Hostein. Monthly.

JEWISH TELEGRAPHIC AGENCY DAILY NEWS BULLETIN (1917). 330 Seventh Ave., 11th fl., NYC, 10001-5010. (212)643-1890. FAX: (212)643-8498. Exec. Ed. Mark Joffe; Ed. Lisa Hostein. Daily.

JEWISH TELEGRAPHIC AGENCY WEEKLY NEWS DIGEST (1933). 330 Seventh Ave.,

11th fl., NYC, 10001-5010. (212)643-1890. FAX: (212)643-8498. Exec. Ed. Mark Joffe; Ed. Lisa Hostein. Weekly.

JEWISH TRIBUNE. PMB #372, 169 South Main St., New City, 10956; Exec. off. (mailing address): 115 Middle Neck Rd., Great Neck, 11021. (914)352-5151. FAX: (516)829-4776. E-mail: lijeworld@aol.com. Jerome W. Lippman. Weekly.

JEWISH WEEK (1876; reorg. 1970). 1501 Broadway, NYC, 10036-5503. (212)921-7822. FAX: (212)921-8420. E-mail: editor@jewishweek.org. Gary Rosenblatt. Weekly.

JEWISH WORLD (1965). 1104 Central Ave., Albany, 12205. (518)459-8455. FAX: (518)459-5289. E-mail: 6859675@mcimail.com. Laurie J. Clevenson. Weekly.

JOURNAL OF JEWISH EDUCATION-CJE (formerly JEWISH EDUCATION) (1929). 426 W. 58 St., Suite 329, NYC, 10019. (914)368-8657. FAX: (212)284-6951. Dr. Bernard Ducoff. Three times a year. Council for Jewish Education.

JOURNAL OF REFORM JUDAISM. See CCAR Journal

JTS MAGAZINE (FORMERLY MASORET) (1991). 3080 Broadway, NYC, 10027. (212)678-8950. FAX: (212)864-0109. E-mail: joginsberg@jtsa.edu. Johanna R. Ginsberg. Three times a year. Jewish Theological Seminary.

JUDAISM (1952). 15 E. 84 St., NYC, 10028. (212)360-1500. FAX: (212)249-3672. Editor's address: Kresge Col., U. of California, Santa Cruz, CA, 95064. (408)459-2566. FAX: (408)459-4872. Subscription address: 15 E. 84 St., NYC 10028. (212)360-1500. E-mail: judaism@cats.ucsc.edu. Prof. Murray Baumgarten. Quarterly. American Jewish Congress.

KASHRUS FAXLETTER-THE MONTHLY KOSHER UPDATE (1990). PO Box 204, Brooklyn, 11204. (718)336-8544. Rabbi Yosef Wikler. Monthly. Kashrus Institute. (www.kosherinfo.com)

KASHRUS MAGAZINE-THE PERIODICAL FOR THE KOSHER CONSUMER (1980). PO Box 204, Brooklyn, 11204. (718)336-8544. Rabbi Yosef Wikler. Five times per year (February), April, June, September, December). Kashrus Institute. (www.kosherinfo.com)

KOL HAT'NUA (VOICE OF THE MOVEMENT) (1975). c/o Young Judaea, 50 W. 58 St., NYC, 10019. (212)303-4576. FAX: (212)303-4572. E-mail: meat345@aol.com. Dov Wilker. Quarterly. Hadassah Zionist Youth Commission-Young Judaea.

KULTUR UN LEBN-CULTURE AND LIFE (1960). 45 E. 33 St., NYC, 10016. (212)889-6800. FAX: (212)532-7518. E-mail: wcfriends@aol.com. Joseph Mlotek. Quarterly. Yiddish. The Workmen's Circle.

LAMISHPAHA (1963). 426 W. 58 St., NYC, 10019. (212)957-6659. FAX: (212)957-5811. E-mail: general@hist-ivrit.org. Dr. Vered Cohen-Raphaeli. Illustrated. Monthly (except July and Aug.). Hebrew. Histadruth Ivrith of America.

LIKUTIM (1981). 110 E. 30 St., NYC, 10016. (212)889-2525. Joanne Jahr. Two times a year in Israel (print and audiocassettes). Hebrew. Jewish Braille Institute of America.

LILITH-THE INDEPENDENT JEWISH WOMEN'S MAGAZINE (1976). 250 W. 57 St., #2432, NYC, 10107. (212)757-0818. FAX: (212)757-5705. E-mail: lilithmag@aol.com. Susan Weidman Schneider. Quarterly. (www.lilithmag.com)

LONG ISLAND JEWISH WORLD (1971). 115 Middle Neck Rd., Great Neck, 11021. (516)829-4000. FAX: (516)829-4776. E-mail: lijeworld@aol.com. Jerome W. Lippman. Weekly.

MANHATTAN JEWISH SENTINEL (1993). 115 Middle Neck Rd., Great Neck, 11021. (212)244-4949. FAX: (212)244-2257. E-mail: lijeworld@aol.com. Jerome W. Lippman. Weekly.

MARTYRDOM AND RESISTANCE (1974). 500 Fifth Ave., Suite 1600, NYC, 10110-1699. (212)220-4304. FAX: (212)220-4308. E-mail: yadvashem@aol.com. Ed. Dr. Harvey Rosenfeld; Ed.-in-Chief Eli Zborowski. Bimonthly. International Society for Yad Vashem.

MIDSTREAM (1954). 633 Third Ave., 21st fl., NYC, 10017. (212)339-6020. FAX: (212)318-6176. E-mail: midstreamthf@aol.com. Joel Carmichael. Eight times a year. World Zionist Organization (Theodor Herzl Foundation, Inc.).

NA'AMAT WOMAN (1925). 350 Fifth Ave., Suite 4700, NYC, 10118-4799. (212)239-

2828. FAX: (212)239-2833. Judith A. Sokoloff. Quarterly. English-Yiddish-Hebrew. NA'AMAT USA, the Women's Labor Zionist Organization of America.

OLOMEINU-OUR WORLD (1945). 5723 18th Ave., Brooklyn, 11204. (718)259-1223. FAX: (718)259-1795. Rabbi Yaakov Fruchter, Rabbi Nosson Scherman. Monthly. English-Hebrew. Torah Umesorah-National Society for Hebrew Day Schools.

PASSOVER DIRECTORY (1923). 11 Broadway, NYC, 10004. (212)563-4000. FAX: (212) 564-9058. Deborah Lieber. Annually. Union of Orthodox Jewish Congregations of America.

PROCEEDINGS OF THE AMERICAN ACADEMY FOR JEWISH RESEARCH (1920). 51 Washington Sq. South, NYC, 10012-1075. (212)998-3550. FAX: (212)995-4178. Dr. Nahum Sarna. Annually. English-Hebrew-French-Arabic-Persian-Greek. American Academy for Jewish Research.

RCA RECORD (1953). 305 Seventh Ave. NYC, 10001. (212)807-7888. FAX: (212) 727-8452. Rabbi Mark Dratch. Quarterly. Rabbinical Council of America.

REFORM JUDAISM (1972; formerly Dimensions in American Judaism). 633 Third Ave., 6th fl., NYC, 10017. (212)650-4240. Aron Hirt-Manheimer. Quarterly. Union of American Hebrew Congregations.

THE REPORTER (1971). 500 Clubhouse Rd., Vestal, 13850. (607)724-2360. FAX: (607)724-2311. E-mail: TReporter@aol. com. Marc S. Goldberg. Weekly. Jewish Federation of Broome County, Inc.

THE REPORTER (1966). 315 Park Ave. S., NYC 10010. (212)505-7700, ext. 265. FAX: (212)674-3057. E-mail; rhayman@ waort.org. Randy Hayman. Quarterly. Women's American ORT, Inc.

RESPONSE: A CONTEMPORARY JEWISH REVIEW (1967). Columbia University Post Office, PO Box 250892, NYC, 10025. E-mail: response@panix.com. Chanita Baumhaft. Annual.

RUSSIAN FORWARD (1995). 45 E. 33 St., NYC, 10016. (212)576-0866. FAX: (212)448-9124. E-mail: elenaleikind@ sprintmail.com. Vladimir Yedidovich. Weekly. Russian.

SYNAGOGUE LIGHT AND KOSHER LIFE (1933). 47 Beekman St., NYC, 10038.

(212)227-7800. Rabbi Meyer Hager. Quarterly. The Kosher Food Institute.

TRADITION (1958). 305 Seventh Ave., NYC, 10001. (212)807-7888. FAX: (212)727-8452. Rabbi Emanuel Feldman. Quarterly. Rabbinical Council of America.

UNITED SYNAGOGUE REVIEW (1943). 155 Fifth Ave., NYC, 10010. (212)533-7800. FAX: (212)353-9439. E-mail: info@uscj. org. Lois Goldrich. Semiannually. United Synagogue of Conservative Judaism.

UNSER TSAIT (1941). 25 E. 21 St., 3rd fl., NYC, 10010. (212)475-0055. Bimonthly. Yiddish. Jewish Labor Bund.

VIEWPOINT MAGAZINE (1952). 3 W. 16 St., NYC, 10011. (212)929-1525, ext. 131. E-mail: ncyi@youngisrael.org. Esther Altman. Quarterly. National Council of Young Israel.

VOICE OF THE DUTCHESS JEWISH COMMUNITY (1989). 110 Grand Ave., Poughkeepsie, 12603. (914)471-9811. FAX: (914)471-0659. E-mail: jfeddutchess@ mindspring.com. Business off.:500 Clubhouse Rd., Vestal, 13850. (607)724-2360. FAX: (607)724-2311. Marc S. Goldberg, Sandy Gardner. Monthly. Jewish Federation of Dutchess County, Inc.

WOMEN'S LEAGUE OUTLOOK MAGAZINE (1930). 48 E. 74 St., New York, 10021. (212)628-1600. FAX: (212)772-3507. E-mail: wleague74@aol.com. Marjorie Saulson. Quarterly. Women's League for Conservative Judaism.

WORKMEN'S CIRCLE CALL. See The Call

WYOMING VALLEY JEWISH REPORTER (formerly WE ARE ONE) (1995). 500 Clubhouse Rd., Vestal, 13850. (607)724-2360. FA X: (607)724-2311. E-mail: TReporter @aol.com. Marc S. Goldberg. Every other week. Wilkes-Barre Jewish Community Board.

YEARBOOK OF THE CENTRAL CONFERENCE OF AMERICAN RABBIS (1890). 355 Lexington Ave., NYC, 10017. (212)972-3636. FAX: (212)692-0819. Rabbi Elliot L. Stevens. Annually. Central Conference of American Rabbis.

YIDDISH (1973). Queens College, NSF 350, 65-30 Kissena Blvd., Flushing, 11367. (718)997-3622. Joseph C. Landis. Quarterly. Queens College Press.

DI YIDDISHE HEIM (1958). 770 Eastern Pkwy., Brooklyn, 11213. (718)735-0458.

Rachel Altein, Tema Gurary. Twice a year. English-Yiddish. Neshei Ub'nos Chabad-Lubavitch Women's Organization.

YIDDISHE KULTUR (1938). 1133 Broadway, Rm. 820, NYC, 10010. (212)243-1304. FAX: (212)243-1305. E-mail: mahosu@ aol.com. Itche Goldberg. Bimonthly. Yiddish. Yiddisher Kultur Farband, Inc.— YKUF.

DOS YIDDISHE VORT (1953). 84 William St., NYC, 10038. (212)797-9000. Joseph Friedenson. Bimonthly, (November-December monthly). Yiddish. Agudath Israel of America.

YIDDISHER KEMFER (1900). 275 Seventh Ave., NYC, 10001. (212)675-7808. FAX: (212) 675-7685. Dr. Jacob Weitzney. Bimonthly. Yiddish. Labor Zionist Alliance.

YIDISHE SHPRAKH (1941). 15 W. 16 St., NYC, 10011. (212)246-6080, ext. 6139. FAX: (212) 292-1892. Dr. Mordkhe Schaechter. Irregularly. Yiddish. YIVO Institute for Jewish Research.

YIVO BLETER (1931). 15 W. 16 St., NYC, 10011. (212)246-6080. FAX: (212)292-1892.E-mail: yivomail@yivo.cjh.org. Dr. David E. Fishman. Biannually. Yiddish. YIVO Institute for Jewish Research.

THE YOUNG JUDAEAN (1909). 50 W. 58 St., NYC, 10019. (212)303-4575. FAX: (212) 303-4572. Vanessa Stark. Quarterly. Young Judaea/Hadassah.

YUGNTRUF: YIDDISH YOUTH MAGAZINE (1964). 200 W. 72 St., Suite 40, NYC, 10023. (212)787-6675. FAX: (212)799-1517. E-mail: mschaecht@aol.com. Elinor Robinson. Two to four times a year. Yiddish. Yugntruf Youth for Yiddish.

ZUKUNFT (THE FUTURE) (1892). 25 E 21 St., NYC, 10010. (212)505-8040. FAX: (212)505-8044. Chaim Beider & Yonia Fain. Quarterly. Yiddish. Congress for Jewish Culture.

NORTH CAROLINA

AMERICAN JEWISH TIMES OUTLOOK (1934; reorg. 1950). PO Box 33218, Charlotte, 28233-3218. (704)372-3296. FAX: (704) 377-9237. E-mail: geri@pop.vnet.net. GeriZhiss. Monthly. The Blumenthal Foundation.

CHARLOTTE JEWISH NEWS (1978). 5007 Providence Rd., Charlotte, 28226. (704)944-6765. FAX: (704) 365-4507.

E-mail: amontoni@shalomcharlotte.org. Amy Krakovitz. Monthly (except July). Jewish Federation of Greater Charlotte.

JEWISH FEDERATION NEWS (1986). 8210 Creedmoor Rd., Suite 104, Raleigh, 27613. (919)676-2200. FAX: (919)676-2122. Sarah Falk. Monthly. Wake County Jewish Federation.

MODERN JUDAISM (1980). Oxford University Press, 2001 Evans Rd., Cary, 27513. (919)677-0977. FAX: (919)677-1714. E-mail: jnlorders@oup-usa.org. (Editorial address:Center for Judaic Studies, Boston University, 745 Commonwealth Ave., Boston, 02215. (617)353-8096. FAX: (617)353-5441.) Steven T. Katz. Three times a year.

OHIO

AKRON JEWISH NEWS (1929). 750 White Pond Drive, Akron, 44320. (330) 869-2424. FAX: (330)867-8498. E-mail: Toby-Liberman@jewishakron.org. Toby Liberman. Fortnightly. Jewish Community Board of Akron.

AMERICAN ISRAELITE (1854). 906 Main St., Rm. 508, Cincinnati, 45202-1371. (513) 621-3145. FAX: (513)621-3744. E-mail: amisralite@aol.com. John Guip. Weekly.

AMERICAN JEWISH ARCHIVES JOURNAL (1948). 3101 Clifton Ave., Cincinnati, 45220-2488. (513)221-1875. FAX: (513) 221-7812. E-mail: aja@cn.huc.edu. Ed. Dr. Gary P. Zola; Mng. Ed. Dr. Frederic Krome. Twice a year. Jacob Rader Marcus Center, American Jewish Archives, HUC-JIR.

CLEVELAND JEWISH NEWS (1964). 3645 Warrensville Center Rd., Suite 230, Cleveland, 44122. (216)991-8300. FAX: (216)991-2088. E-mail: clevjewnew@aol. com. Cynthia Dettelbach. Weekly. Cleveland Jewish News Publication Co.

INDEX TO JEWISH PERIODICALS (1963). PO Box 18525, Cleveland Hts., 44118. (216)381-4846. FAX: (216)381-4321. E-mail: index@jewishperiodicals.com. Lenore Pfeffer Koppel. Annually. Available in book and CD-ROM form. (www. jewishperiodicals.com)

JEWISH JOURNAL (1987). 505 Gypsy Lane, Youngstown, 44504-1314. (330)744-7902. FAX: (330)746-7926. Sherry Weinblatt. Biweekly (except July/Aug.). Youngstown Area Jewish Federation.

OHIO JEWISH CHRONICLE (1922). 2862 Johnstown Rd., Columbus, 43219. (614)337-2055. FAX: (614)337-2059. Roberta Keck. Weekly.

STARK JEWISH NEWS (1920). 2631 Harvard Ave. NW, Canton, 44709. (330)452-6444. FAX: (330)452-4487. E-mail: cantonjcf @aol.com. Linda Sirak. Monthly. Canton Jewish Community Federation.

STUDIES IN BIBLIOGRAPHY AND BOOKLORE (1953). 3101 Clifton Ave., Cincinnati, 45220. (513)221-1875. FAX: (513)221-0519. E-mail: lwolfson@huc.edu. Herbert C. Zafren. Irregularly. English-Hebrewetc. Library of Hebrew Union College-Jewish Institute of Religion.

TOLEDO JEWISH NEWS (1951). 6505 Sylvania Ave., Sylvania, 43560. (419)885-4461. FAX: (419)724-0423. E-mail: Toljewnew @aol.com. Laurie Cohen. Monthly. Jewish Federation of Greater Toledo.

OKLAHOMA

TULSA JEWISH REVIEW (1930). 2021 E. 71 St., Tulsa, 74136. (918)495-1100. FAX: (918)495-1220. Ed Ulrich. Monthly. Jewish Federation of Tulsa.

OREGON

BRIDGES: A JOURNAL FOR JEWISH FEMINISTS AND OUR FRIENDS (1990). PO Box 24839, Eugene, 97402. (541)343-7617. FAX: (541)343-7617. E-mail: ckinberg @pond.net. Mng. Ed. Clare Kinberg. Semiannually.

JEWISH REVIEW (1959). 506 SW Sixth Ave., Suite 606, Portland, 97204. Edit.:(503) 227-7464. FAX: (503) 227-7438. Adv.: 503) 670-2883. FAX: (503) 620-3433. E-mail: editorial@jewishreview.org. Paul Haist. Regular column in Russian. Fortnightly. Jewish Federation of Portland. (www.jewishreview.org)

PENNSYLVANIA

COMMUNITY REVIEW (1925). 3301 N. Front St. Annex, Harrisburg, 17110. (717)236-9555, ext.3402. FAX:(717)236-2552. E-mail: communityreview@desupernet.net. Carol L. Cohen. Fortnightly. United Jewish Community of Greater Harrisburg.

CONTEMPORARY JEWRY (1974, under the name Jewish Sociology and Social Research). Gratz College, 7605 Old York Rd., Melrose Park, 19027. (215)635-7300. FAX:(215)635-7320. E-mail:rela1@aol.

com. Ed. Rela Mintz Geffen; Mng. Ed. Egon Mayer. Annually. Association for the Social Scientific Study of Jewry.

JERUSALEM LETTER/VIEWPOINTS (1978). 1515 Locust St., Suite 703, Philadelphia, 19102. (215)772-0564. FAX: (215)772-0566. Zvi R. Marom. Fortnightly. Jerusalem Center for Public Affairs.

JEWISH CHRONICLE OF PITTSBURGH (1962). 5600 Baum Blvd., Pittsburgh, 15206. (412)687-1000. FAX: (412)687-5119. E-mail: pittjewchr@aol.com. Joel Roteman. Weekly. Pittsburgh Jewish Publication and Education Foundation.

JEWISH EXPONENT (1887). 2100 Arch St., Philadelphia, 19103. (215)832-0740. FAX: (215)569-3389. E-mail: jexponent@ aol.com. Jonathan S. Tobin. Weekly. Jewish Federation of Greater Philadelphia.

JEWISH POLITICAL STUDIES REVIEW (1989). 1515 Locust St., Suite 703, Philadelphia, 19102. (215)772-0564. FAX: (215)772-0566. Mark Ami-El. Twice a year. Jerusalem Center for Public Affairs.

JEWISH QUARTERLY REVIEW (1910). 420 Walnut St., Philadelphia, 19106. (215) 238-1290. FAX: (215)238-1540. E-mail: jqr@mail.cjs.upenn.edu. Ed. David M. Goldenberg; Mng. Ed. Bonnie L. Blankenship. Quarterly. Center for Judaic Studies, University of Pennsylvania.

NEW MENORAH (1978). 7318 Germantown Ave., Philadelphia, 19119-1793. (215)247-9700. FAX: (215)247-9703. Rabbi Arthur Waskow, PhD. Quarterly. Aleph: Alliance for Jewish Renewal.

RECONSTRUCTIONISM TODAY (1993). Beit Devora, 7804 Montgomery Ave., Suite 9, Elkins Park, 19027-2649. (215)782-8500. FAX: (215)782-8805. E-mail: jrfnatl@aol. com. Lawrence Bush. Quarterly. Jewish Reconstructionist Federation.

THE RECONSTRUCTIONIST (1935). 1299 Church Rd., Wyncote, 19095-1898. (215) 576-5210. FAX: (215)576-8051. E-mail: rraassoc@aol.com. Rabbi Richard Hirsh. Semiannually. Reconstructionist Rabbinical College.

SCRANTON FEDERATION REPORTER (1994). 500 Clubhouse Rd., Vestal, NY, 13850. (607)724-2360. FAX: (607)724-2311. E-mail: TReporter@aol.com. Marc S. Goldberg. Biweekly. Scranton-Lackawanna Jewish Federation.

RHODE ISLAND

JEWISH VOICE OF RHODE ISLAND (1973). 130 Sessions St., Providence, 02906. (401)421-4111. FAX: (401)331-7961. E-mail: jvoice @aol.com. Jane S. Sprague. Monthly. Jewish Federation of Rhode Island.

RHODE ISLAND JEWISH HERALD (1930). 99 Webster St., Pawtucket, 02860. (401)724-0200. FAX: (401)726-5820. Kimberly Ann Orlandi. Weekly. Herald Press Publishing Company.

RHODE ISLAND JEWISH HISTORICAL NOTES (1951). 130 Sessions St., Providence, 02906. (401)331-1360. FAX: (401)272-6729. E-mail: rjhist@aol.com. Leonard Moss. Annually. Rhode Island Jewish Historical Association.

SOUTH CAROLINA

CHARLESTON JEWISH JOURNAL. 1645 WAL-LENBERG BLVD., CHARLESTON, 29407. (843)571-6565. FAX: (843)556-6206. ELLEN KATMAN. MONTHLY. CHARLESTON JEWISH FEDERATION.

TENNESSEE

HEBREW WATCHMAN (1925). 4646 Poplar Ave., Suite 232, Memphis, 38117. (901) 763-2215. FAX: (901)763-2216. Herman I. Goldberger. Weekly.

OBSERVER (1934). 801 Percy Warner Blvd., Suite 102, Nashville, 37205. (615)356-3242, ext. 237. FAX: (615)352-0056. E-mail: nashobserv@aol.com. Judith A. Saks. Biweekly (except July). Jewish Federation of Nashville.

SHOFAR. PO Box 8947, Chattanooga, 37414. (423)493-0270, Ext. 12. FAX: (423) 493-9997. E-mail: shofar@jcfgc.com. Rachel Schulson. Ten times a year. Jewish Federation of Greater Chattanooga.

TEXAS

JEWISH HERALD-VOICE (1908). PO Box 153, Houston, 77001-0153. (713)630-0391. FAX: (713)630-0404. E-mail: joexhk@ aol.com. Jeanne Samuels. Weekly.

JEWISH JOURNAL OF SAN ANTONIO (1973). 8434 Ahern, San Antonio, 78213. (210) 828-9511. FAX: (210)342-8098. Barbara Richmond. Monthly (11 issues). Jewish Federation of San Antonio.

TEXAS JEWISH POST (1947). 3120 S. Freeway, Fort Worth, 76110. (817)927-2831. FAX: (817)429-0840. 11333 N. Central

Expressway, Suite 213, Dallas, 75243. (214)692-7283. FAX: (214)692-7285. Jimmy Wisch. Weekly.

VIRGINIA

RENEWAL MAGAZINE (1984). 5029 Corporate World Dr., Suite 225, Virginia Beach, 23462. (757)671-1600. FAX: (757)671-7613. E-mail: news@ujft.org. Reba Karp. Quarterly. United Jewish Federation of Tidewater.

SOUTHEASTERN VIRGINIA JEWISH NEWS (1959). 5029 Corporate World Dr., Suite 225, Virginia Beach, 23462. (757)671-1600. FAX: (757)671-7613. E-mail: news @ujft.org. Reba Karp. 22 issues yearly. United Jewish Federation of Tidewater.

WASHINGTON

JEWISH TRANSCRIPT (1924). 2041 Third Ave., Seattle, 98121. (206)441-4553. FAX: (206)441-2736. E-mail: jewishtran@aol. com. Donna Gordon Blankinship. Fortnightly. Jewish Federation of Greater Seattle.

WISCONSIN

WISCONSIN JEWISH CHRONICLE (1921). 1360 N. Prospect Ave., Milwaukee, 53202. (414)390-5888. FAX: (414)271-0487. E-mail: milwaukeej@aol.com. Vivian M. Rothschild. Weekly. Milwaukee Jewish Federation.

INDEXES

INDEX TO JEWISH PERIODICALS (1963). PO Box 18525, Cleveland Hts., OH 44118. (216)381-4846. FAX: (216)381-4321. E-mail: index@jewishperiodicals.com. Lenore Pfeffer Koppel. Annually. Available in book and CD-ROM form. (www.jewishperiodicals.com)

NEWS SYNDICATES

JEWISH TELEGRAPHIC AGENCY, INC. (1917). 330 Seventh Ave., 11th fl., NYC., 10001-5010. (212)643-1890. FAX: (212) 643-8498. Mark J. Joffe, Lisa Hostein. Daily.

CANADA

CANADIAN JEWISH HERALD (1977). 17 Anselme Lavigne, Dollard des Ormeaux, PQ H9A 1N3. (514)684-7667. FAX: (514) 684-7667. Ed./Pub. Dan Nimrod. Irregularly. Dawn Publishing Co., Ltd.

THE CANADIAN JEWISH NEWS (1971). 1500 Don Mills Rd., Suite 205, North York, ONT M3B 3K4. (416)391-1836. FAX: (416)391-0829 (Adv.); (416)391-1836. FAX: (416)391-0829. Mordechai Ben-Dat. 50 issues a year. Some French.

CANADIAN JEWISH OUTLOOK (1963). #3-6184 Ash St., Vancouver, BC V5Z 3G9. (604)324-5101. FAX: (604)325-2470. E-mail: hjberson@axionet.com. Carl Rosenberg. Six times per year. Canadian Jewish Outlook Society.

DAIS (1985) (formerly Intercom). 100 Sparks St., #650, Ottawa, ONT KIP 5B7. (613)233-8703. FAX: (613)233-8748. E-mail: canadianjewishcongress@cjc.ca. Jack Silverstone. Three times a year. Canadian Jewish Congress.

DIRECTIONS (1998) (formerly Dialogue (1988)). 1 Carré Cummings, Suite 202, Montreal, Quebec H3W 1M6. (514)345-64111. FAX: (514)345-6412. E-mail: etay@cjc.ca. Eta Yudin. Quarterly. French-English. Canadian Jewish Congress, Quebec Region.

JEWISH FREE PRESS (1990). 8411 Elbow Dr., SW Calgary, AB. T2V 1K8. (403)252-9423. FAX: (403)255-5640. E-mail: jewishfp@cadvision.com. Judy Shapiro. Fortnightly.

JEWISH POST & NEWS (1987). 113 Hutchings St., Winnipeg, MAN R2X 2V4. (204)694-3332. FAX: (204)694-3916. E-mail: jewishp@pangea.ca. Matt Bellan. Weekly.

JEWISH STANDARD (1928). 77 Mowat Ave., Suite 016, Toronto, ONT M6K 3E3. (416)537-2696. FAX: (416)789-3872. Ed./Pub. Michael Hayman. Fortnightly.

THE JEWISH TRIBUNE (1950). 15 Hove St., Toronto, ONT M3H 4Y8. (416)633-6224.

FAX: (416)633-6299. E-mail: dantrib@interlog.com. Daniel Horowitz. Bi-weekly.

JEWISH WESTERN BULLETIN (1930). 301, 68 E. Second Ave., Vancouver, BC V5T 1B1. (604)689-1520. FAX: (604)689-1525. E-mail: jbeditor@istar.ca. Baila Lazarus. Weekly. 57786 BC Ltd.

JOURNAL OF PSYCHOLOGY AND JUDAISM (1976). 1747 Featherston Dr., Ottawa, ONT K1H 6P4. (613)731-9119. Reuven P. Bulka. Quarterly. Center for the Study of Psychology and Judaism.

OTTAWA JEWISH BULLETIN (1954). 1780 Kerr Ave., Ottawa, ONT K2A 1R9. (613)798-4696. FAX: (613)798-4730. E-mail: bulletin@jccottawa.com. Myra Aronson. Nineteen times a year. Ottawa Jewish Bulletin Publishing Co. Ltd.

SHALOM (1975). 5675 Spring Garden Rd., Suite 800, Halifax, NS, B3J 1H1. (902)422-7491. FAX: (902)425-3722. E-mail: jgoldberg@theajc.ns.ca. Jon M. Goldberg. Quarterly. Atlantic Jewish Council.

LA VOIX SÉPHARADE (1966). 1 Carré Cummings, Montreal, PQ H3W 1M6. (514)733-4998, (514)733-8696. FAX: (514)733-3158. E-mail: csq@csq.qc.ca. Ed. James Dahan; Pub. Elie Benchitrit. Bimonthly (five times a year). French and occasional Spanish and English. Communauté Sépharade du Québec.

NEWS AND VIEWS (1942) (formerly Windsor Jewish Federation. 1641 Ouellette Ave., Windsor, ONT N8X 1K9. (519)973-1772. FAX: (519)973-1774. Exec. Dir. Harvey Kessler. Quarterly. Windsor Jewish Federation.

THE WORLD OF LUBAVITCH (1980). 770 Chabad Gate, Thornhill, ONT L4J 3V9. (905)731-7000. FAX: (905)731-7005. Rabbi Moshe Spalter. Bimonthly. English-Hebrew. Chabad Lubavitch of Southern Ont.

Obituaries: United States*

AGRONSKY, MARTIN, broadcast journalist; b. Philadelphia, Pa., Jan. 12, 1915; d. Washington, D.C., July 25, 1999. Educ.: Rutgers U. Reporter, *Palestine Post*, 1936–37; freelance journalist, 1937–40; NBC radio war correspondent, 1940–43; ABC Washington correspondent, 1943–64; CBS bureau chief, 1964–73; host, "Agronsky and Company," PBS television, 1969–87 (initiated "talking-heads" format for political news shows). Recipient: Peabody award for distinguished reporting (coverage of Sen. McCarthy); Heywood Broun award for radio reporting; Alfred DuPont award for distinguished TV reporting and commentary (coverage of Eichmann trial); Venice Film Festival award for documentary *Polaris Submarine — Journal Undersea Voyage*; Emmy for documentary *Justice Black and the Constitution*.

ANCELL NATHAN S., business executive, philanthropist; b. NYC, Aug. 22, 1908; d. New Rochelle, N.Y., May 31, 1999. Educ.: Columbia U. (BS, LLB). Established Ethan Allen Furniture Co., 1939, pioneering colonial-style furniture and displays in room-like settings; succeeded brother-in-law as chmn., 1970; sold Ethan Allen to Interco Inc., 1980, becoming Interco v.-pres. as well as dir. and chmn. of Ethan Allen subsidiary; advisor to Ethan Allen since 1985. Active on behalf of many causes and orgs.; hon. officer, N.Y. UJA-Fed.; hon. chmn., Mid-Westchester YM-YWHA; assoc. chmn., Associated YM-YWHAs of Greater N.Y.; mem.: bd., Brandeis U.; bd. overseers, Albert Einstein Coll. of Medicine, Yeshiva U.; chmn, home furnishings campaign, Israel Bonds.

BELIN, DAVID W., lawyer, communal worker; b. Washington, D.C., June 20, 1928; d. Rochester, Minn., Jan. 17, 1999. Educ.: U. Mich. (BA, MBA, JD). Served U.S. Army in Korea and Japan. Practiced law, Des Moines, Ia., and NYC, 1954–, ultimately as sr. partner, Belin Lamson McCormick Zumbach Flynn. Co-owner, *The Tribune* (Ames, Ia.); trustee, Kemper Mutual Funds; dir., Outdoor Technologies Group; counsel, Pres.'s Comm. on Assassination of Pres. Kennedy (Warren Comm.), 1964, which found that Lee Harvey Oswald was sole gunman; exec. dir., comm. on CIA activities within the U.S. (Rockefeller Comm.). Hon. v.-pres. and bd. mem., Union of Amer. Hebrew Congs.; bd. mem., Amer. Jewish Com. Proponent of outreach to intermarried and of rabbinic officiation at mixed marriages; founder, Jewish Outreach Inst., 1987. Au.: *November 22, 1963: You Are the Jury* (1973); *Final Disclosure: The Full*

---

*Including American Jews who died between January 1 and December 31, 1999.

Truth About the Assassination of President Kennedy (1988); *Leaving Money Wisely* (1990).

BERGER, GRAENUM, social worker, communal professional; b. Gloversville, N.Y., Apr. 21, 1908; d. New Rochelle, N.Y., Mar. 31, 1999. Educ.: U. Mo. (BA), Graduate School of Jewish Social Work (MS). Exec. dir., Jewish Community Center, Staten Island, N.Y., 1932–38; head worker, Bronx House, 1939–49; consultant on community center programming to N.Y. Fed. of Jewish Philanthropies, 1949–74. Founder and exec. v-pres., Amer. Assoc. for Ethiopian Jews, 1969–83, which raised public consciousness about the situation of Ethiopian Jews, leading to their airlift to Israel (Operations Moses in 1984–85 and Solomon in 1991. Faculty, N.Y School of Social Work; Yeshiva U.; City Coll. of N.Y. Pres., Natl. Assoc. of Jewish Center Workers. Au.: *The Jewish Community Center* (1966); *Rescue the Ethiopian Jews! A Memoir, 1955–1995* (1996), and other works.

BERNSTEIN, ZALMAN C. (Sanford), investment manager, philanthropist; b. NYC, Apr. 29, 1926; d. NYC, Jan. 6, 1999. Educ.: NYU, Harvard Business School. Served U.S. Navy, WWII. After employment as economist for U.S. govt. and partner at several securities firms, founded and became CEO of Sanford C. Bernstein & Co., 1967–93 (mem., bd. of dirs., 1993–), building it into one of the largest privately held investment firms in the world, with assets of over $8 billion. Major contributor to Jewish causes; founding chmn., Avi Chai Foundation, 1984–, to foster understanding between Jews of different religious backgrounds; founder, with Ronald Lauder, the Shalem Foundation, 1994, to strengthen and enrich Jewish life in Israel. Relocated to Jerusalem, 1989.

CHENKIN, ALVIN, communal professional; b. NYC, October 1, 1918; d. Media, Pa., June 6, 1999. Educ.: City Coll. of N.Y. Government statistician; director of research and statistics, Council of Jewish Feds. and Welfare Funds, 1947–85. Mem., Young People's Socialist League; president, union local 107 of District Council 1707. Au.: AJYB articles on U.S. Jewish demography, 1954–86.

CHERNE, LEO, business consultant, refugee activist; b. NYC, Sept. 8, 1912; d. NYC, Jan. 12, 1999. Educ.: NYU, N.Y. Law School. Founder and exec. dir., Research Institute of America, 1936–85, consultants on the impact of world events on business. Faculty, School of Foreign Service, Georgetown U., 1939–41, New School for Social Research, 1945–52; participated in planning industrial mobilization for the armed forces, WWII; adviser to Gen. MacArthur on economic recovery of Japan, 1946; chmn, Internatl. Rescue Com. (succeeding Reinhold Niebuhr), 1951–91, now the largest refugee-relief organization in the world, helping hundreds of thousands of people worldwide; mem., Pres.'s Foreign Intelligence Adv. Bd., 1973–91 and chmn., 1976–77. Au.: *Adjusting Your Business to War* (1939); *M-Day and What It Means to You* (1940); *Your Business Goes to War* (1942); *The Rest of Your Life* (1944). Recipient: Commander's Cross of Order of Merit, Federal Republic of Germany; Chevalier, French Legion of Honor; U.S. Medal of Freedom.

COHEN, SAMUEL, communal professional; b. Asbury Park, N.J., Apr. 17, 1933; d. NYC, Sep. 10, 1999. Educ.: Brooklyn Coll. (BA), Mesivta Rabbi Chaim Berlin Rabbinical Acad.(ordination), Yeshiva U. (EdD). Exec. dir., Long Island Zionist Youth Comm., 1957–61; Long Island regional dir., B'nai B'rith, 1961–66, and dir., membership dept., N.Y. and New England, 1966–72; dir. of org., Amer. Jewish Cong., 1972–74; exec. dir., Amer. Zionist Fed., 1974–77; exec. v.-pres., Jewish Natl. Fund, 1977–97, where he raised annual income from $6 million to $32 million and initiated the Internatl. Arid Lands Consortium.

DAUBE, DAVID, legal scholar; b. Freiburg, Germany, Feb. 8, 1909; d. Pleasant Hill, Cal., Feb. 24, 1999; in U.S. since 1970. Educ.: Göttingen U. (DJur), Cambridge U. (PhD), Oxford U. (DCL). Fellow, Caius Coll. and lect. in law, Cambridge U., 1938–51; prof., U. Aberdeen, 1951–55; Regius prof. of civil law, fellow, All Souls Coll., Oxford U., 1955–1970; prof.-in-residence and dir., Robbins Hebraic and Roman Law Collections, Boalt Hall, U. Cal. at Berkeley, 1970–81. Au.: *The Aramaic Gospels* (1945); *Studies in Biblical Law* (1947); *The New Testament* and *Rabbinic Judaism* (1956); *Forms of Roman Legislation* (1956); *The Exodus Pattern in the Bible* (1963); *The Sudden in the Scriptures* (1964); *Collaboration with Tyranny in Rabbinic Law* (1969).

ELAZAR, DANIEL J., political scientist; b. Minneapolis, Minn., Aug. 25, 1934; d. Jerusalem, Dec. 2, 1999. Educ.: Wayne State U. (BA), U. Chicago (PhD). Asst. prof., govt. and public affairs, U. Ill., 1959–63; visiting asst. prof., political science, U. Minn., 1963–64; prof., 1964–, and dir., Center for the Study of Federalism, 1967–, Temple U.; Senator N. M. Paterson prof., and head, Inst. for Local Govt., Bar-Ilan U., 1976–; founder and pres., Jerusalem Center for Public Affairs, 1976–. Public mem., U.S. Adv. Comm. on Intergovernmental Relations, 1986–93. Au. or ed. of over 70 books, incl. *American Federalism* (1966); *The Politics of American Federalism* (1968); *Cities of the Prairie* (1970); *Community and Polity: the Organizational Dynamics of American Jewry* (1976); *Kinship and Consent* (1983); *Covenant and Polity in Biblical Israel: Biblical Foundations and Jewish Expressions* (1998). Ed.: *Publius: The Journal of Federalism; Jewish Political Studies Review.* Recipient: Guggenheim fellowship (twice); Fulbright senior lecturership.

FADIMAN, CLIFTON, editor, critic; b. NYC (Brooklyn), May 15, 1904; d. Sanibel Island, Fla., June 20, 1999. Educ.: Columbia U. Editor, Simon and Schuster, 1929–35; book editor, *New Yorker*, 1933–43; editorial com., Book-of-the-Month Club, 1944–; bd. of editors, *Encyclopedia Britannica*, 1959–; editorial consultant., Encyclopedia Britannica Educ. Corp., 1963–70; master of ceremonies, "Information Please," 1938–48, and other radio and television programs. Au.: *Party of One* (1955); *Any Number Can Play* (1957); *The Lifetime Reading Plan* (1959, rev. ed. 1988). Ed.: *Reading I've Liked* (1941); *The American Treasury* (1955); *Fantasia Mathematica* (1958); *World Treasury of Children's Literature* (1984–85); *The World of the Short Story* (1986); *Great Books of the Western World* (1988–); *Treasury of the Encyclopedia Britannica* (1992). Recipient: National Book Foundation medal for distinguished contribution to American letters.

FREUND-ROSENTHAL, MIRIAM, communal worker; b. NYC (Brooklyn), Feb. 17, 1906; d. Miami Beach, Fla., Jan. 16, 1999. Educ.: Hunter Coll., NYU (Ph.D.). Longtime Hadassah leader: mem. Hadassah national bd., 1940–; delegate to Amer. Jewish Conf., 1942; natl. chmn.: Amer. Zionist youth activities, 1943–48, vocational educ. comm., 1948–53, natl. Youth Aliyah comm., 1953–56; natl. president, 1956–60, overseeing creation of a new Hadassah hospital in Jerusalem (to replace the then inaccessible Mt. Scopus facility) and arranging for the Chagall windows there. Founder, charter mem., Brandeis Youth Found., 1948; v.-pres., natl. bd. mem., Brandeis U., 1949–50. Au.: *Jewish Merchants in Colonial America* (1936); *Jewels for a Crown — the Chagall Windows* (1963).

GALIMIR, FELIX, violinist; b. Vienna, Austria, May 12, 1910; d. NYC, Nov. 10, 1999; in U.S. since 1938. Educ.: Vienna Conservatory of Music. Founded Galimir String Quartet, which performed throughout Europe, 1929–36, championing music of Schoenberg, Berg, Webern; hired by Vienna Philharmonic, 1936, dismissed the next year for being Jewish; reorganized and led Galimir String Quartet in NYC, 1938–93. Performed with NBC Symphony Orchestra, Philomusica, and on radio station WQXR, and produced numerous recordings. Taught at Marlboro Festival; City Coll. of N.Y.; Juilliard School of Music; Mannes College of Music; Curtis Inst.; N.Y. String Orchestra seminar.

GOULD, MILTON, lawyer; b. NYC, Oct. 8, 1909; d. NYC, Mar. 22, 1999. Educ.: Cornell U. (BA, LLB). Special attorney for violations of immigration and naturalization laws, U.S. Justice Dept., 1935–37; partner: Kaufman & Cronan and successor firms, 1938–48; Gallop, Climenko & Gould, 1948–64; sr. partner, Shea, Gould, Climenko & Kramer, 1964–94; LeBoeuf, Lamb, Greene & McRae, 1994–. Legendary litigator who successfully represented many big-name corporations — such as Twentieth Century Fox, Columbia Pictures, Curtis Publishing — in major lawsuits, and won Ariel Sharon's libel suit against *Time* magazine. Bd. chmn., Elgin Natl. Industries; dir., genl. counsel, Citizens Utilities Co.; dir., Friendly Frost, Tex. Oil & Gas Corp., Madison Square Garden Corp.; chmn., lawyers div., Anti-Defamation League.

GRILICHES, ZVI, economist; b. Kaunas, Lithuania, Sept. 12, 1930; d. Cambridge, Mass., Nov. 4, 1999; in U.S. since 1951. Educ.: Hebrew U., Jerusalem; U. Cal. at Berkeley; U. Chicago (PhD). Served Israeli Army, 1948–49. Asst. prof., economics, U. Chicago, 1956–59, assoc. prof., 1960–64, prof., 1964–69; Paul M. Warburg prof., Harvard U., 1969–. Consultant: Rand Corp., Brookings Inst. Mem.: Pres.'s Scientific Adv. Council Panel on Youth, 1970–73, bd. of govs. Federal Reserve System, Ford Found., Natl. Science Found. Pres.: Amer. Economic Assoc., 1993; Econometric Soc., 1974–. Au.: *Price Indexes and Quality Change* (1971); *Economies of Scale and the Form of the Production Function* (1971). Recipient: J.B. Clark medal of the Amer. Economic Assoc. for best economist under age 40; award of merit, Amer. Farm Economics Assoc. (four times).

HELLER, JOSEPH, novelist; b. NYC (Brooklyn), May 1, 1923; d. East Hampton, N.Y., Dec. 14, 1999. Educ.: NYU; Columbia U. (MA); Fulbright scholar, Oxford U. Served as bombardier, U.S. Air Force, WWII. Instr. of English, Penn. State U., 1950–52; advertising writer: *Time* magazine, 1952–56, *Look* magazine, 1956–58; promotion manager, *McCall's*, 1958–61. Taught writing at Yale U. and City Coll. of N.Y. and wrote for television and movies. Au: *Catch-22* (1961); *Something Happened* (1974); *Good as Gold* (1979); *God Knows* (1984); *Closing Time* (1994). Recipient: Natl. Inst. of Arts and Letters grantee in literature, 1963.

HESKES, IRENE, music educator; b. NYC (Brooklyn), June 15, 1923; d. New Hyde Park, N.Y., Oct. 14, 1999. Educ.: NYU; Cantors Inst. of the Jewish Theol. Sem.; Juilliard School of Music; Eastman School of Music; Harvard U.; School of Sacred Music at Heb. Union Coll. Music consultant, Theodor Herzl Inst., 1964–76; dir., Natl. Jewish Music Council, 1968–80; founder and dir., Amer. Yiddish Theatre Music Restoration and Revival Project. Mem.: Amer. Musicological Soc.; Internatl. Musical Soc.; Music Library Assoc.; Women Cantors' Network. Au.: *The Cantorial Art* (1966); *Ernest Bloch: Creative Spirit* (1976); *Jewish Music Programs and How to Commission New Works* (1978); *The Resource Book of Jewish Music* (1985); *The Music of Abraham Goldfaden: Father of the Jewish Yiddish Theatre* (1990); *Yiddish American Popular Songs, 1895–1950* (1992); *Passport to Jewish Music: Its History, Traditions and Culture* (1996).

HESS, LEON, business executive, philanthropist; b. Asbury Park, N.J., March 14, 1914; d. NYC, May 7, 1999. Served U.S. Army, WWII, as petroleum-supply officer for Gen. George Patton, reaching rank of major. Entered and reorganized his father's fuel-delivery business, 1933; created Hess Oil and Chemical Corp., 1946: pres., 1962–65, chmn. and CEO, 1965–69; chmn. Amerada Hess, 1971–95, CEO, 1971–82, 1986–95; co-owner, then sole owner, chmn., N.Y. Jets Football Team, 1963–. Major contributor to Jewish and civic causes.

HOFFBERGER, JEROLD C., business executive, philanthropist; b. Baltimore, Md., Apr. 7, 1919; d. Baltimore, Md., Apr. 16, 1999. Educ.: U. Virginia. Served U.S. Army, WWII (purple heart). Pres., chmn., Natl. Brewery Co., 1947–75; pres., chmn., CEO, Carling Natl. Breweries, 1975–78; chmn., pres., Baltimore Orioles Baseball Team, 1965–79, pres., 1979–83; owner, Sunset Hill Farm, 1980–92; chmn., Diversified Resource Mgmt., 1978–90. Pres., Council of Jewish Feds. and Welfare Funds, 1975–78; chmn., United Israel Appeal, 1978–83, hon. chmn., 1983–; chmn., Jewish Agency, 1983–87. Major contributor to Jewish and civic causes.

JACOBSON, GAYNOR, communal professional; b. Buffalo, N.Y., May 17, 1912; d. Sun City West, Ariz., June 6, 1999. Educ.: U. Buffalo (BA, MSW). Exec. sec., Jewish Community Council, Rochester, N.Y., 1937–40; exec. dir.: Jewish Family and Child Care, Rochester, 1938–44, Jewish Child Care Assn., Philadelphia, 1950–51, Amer. Technion Soc., 1951–53; country dir., Amer. Jewish Joint Distrib. Com.: Italy, 1944–45, Greece, 1945–46, Czechoslovakia, 1946–47, Hungary, 1947–50; dir., European and North African operations, HIAS, 1953–54, 1961–66, dir., Latin Amer. operations, 1955–61, exec. dir., 1966–68, exec. v.-pres., 1968–81, hon. exec. v.-pres., 1981–. Recipient: State of Israel independence citation; National Order of the Southern Cross, Brazil; Cross of Merit, Hungary.

JACOBSON, NATHAN, mathematician; b. Warsaw, Poland, Sept. 8, 1910; d. Hamden, Conn., Dec. 5, 1999; in U.S. since 1918. Educ.: U. Alabama; Princeton U. (PhD). Served U.S. Navy, WWII. Asst., Inst. for Advanced Studies, 1933–34; lect., Bryn Mawr Coll., 1935–36; Natl. Research Fellow, U. Chicago, 1936–37; instr., asst. prof., assoc. prof., U. No. Carolina, 1937–42; assoc. instr., Navy Pre-Flight School, 1942–43; assoc. prof., Johns Hopkins U., 1943–47; assoc. prof., mathematics, Yale U., 1947–49, prof., 1949–81, Henry Ford II prof., 1963–81. Expert in "ring" theory, responsible for Jacobson density theorum, Jacobson radical. Pres., Amer. Mathematical Soc., 1971–73; v.-pres., Internatl. Mathematical Union, 1972–74 (fought for right of Soviet Jewish mathematicians to attend conferences). Recipient: Leroy P. Steele prize for lifetime achievement, Amer. Mathematical Soc.

KAMINER, PHYLLIS, educator; b. NYC, Nov. 13, 1932; d. Tenafly, N.J., Oct. 27, 1999. Educ.: Brooklyn Coll.; NYU (MA); Columbia U. (MBA). Founder and pres., Instructional Systems, Inc., developer and marketer of educational technology that pioneered use of personal computers in the classroom. Founder, 1997, Online Learning Project, Jewish Theol. Sem., first "distance learning" program in U.S. enabling Judaica courses to be taken over Internet. Mem., bd. overseers, William Davidson Graduate School of Jewish Educ., JTS.

KAMINETSKY, JOSEPH, rabbi, educational executive; b. NYC (Brooklyn), Nov. 15, 1911; d. Jerusalem, Mar. 17, 1999. Educ.: Yeshiva Coll.; Teachers Coll., Columbia U. (EdD). Educ. dir., The Jewish Center, NYC, 1934–46; natl. dir., Torah Umesorah-Natl. Soc. for Hebrew Day Schools, 1946–82, largely responsible for the proliferation of Orthodox Jewish day schools in U.S. Recipient: Mordecai Ben David award, Dr. Bernard Revel award, both from Yeshiva U.

KELLMAN, JOSEPH A. G., lawyer, communal professional; b. NYC, Dec. 7, 1906; d. Los Angeles, Cal., June 24, 1999. Educ.: St. Johns U. (LLB). Served U.S. Army, WWII. Dir., fact-finding div., legal div., Amer. Jewish Com, 1944–71. Au.: AJYB articles on anti-Semitism and extremism, 1950–64.

KESTENBERG, JUDITH S., psychoanalyst; b. Tarnow, Poland, Mar. 17, 1910; d. Sands Point., N.Y., Jan. 16, 1999; in U.S. since 1937. Educ.: Vienna, Austria (MD), Bellevue Hosp.; N.Y. Psychoanalytic Inst. Clinical prof., psychiatry, NYU; mem. staff and faculty, Long Island Jewish Medical Center. Specialist in dance therapy; authority on psychological effects of Holocaust on survivors and their children. Founder and head, Child Development Research; Holocaust Child Survivor Studies; Internatl. Study of the Organized Persecution of Children. Au. or ed.: *Children During the Nazi Reign: Psychological Perspectives on the Interview Process* (1994); *Sexuality, Body Movement and the Rhythms of Development* (1995); *The Last Witness: The Child Survivor of the Holocaust* (1996); *Children Surviving Persecution: An International Study of Trauma and Healing* (1998).

KLUTZNICK, PHILIP M., business executive, communal leader; b. Kansas City, Mo., July 9, 1907; d. Chicago, Ill., Aug. 14, 1999. Educ.: U. Kansas, U. Nebraska, Creighton U. (LLB). Asst. corp. counsel, Omaha, Neb., 1933–35; special asst. to U.S. attorney genl. on slum clearance and housing, 1935–36; genl. counsel, Omaha Housing Authority, 1938–41; commissioner, Federal Public Housing Authority, 1944–46. Real-estate investor and developer, chmn., Urban Investment and Development Corp., Amer. Bank and Trust Co.; pres., Oak Brook Utility Co.; limited partner, Salomon Brothers. Mem., U.S. delegations to UN, 1957, 1961, 1962; U.S. rep., with rank of ambassador, to UN-ECSOC, 1961–63; U.S. sec. commerce, 1980–81. Pres., B'nai B'rith Internatl., 1953–59, hon. pres., 1959–; pres., World Jewish Cong., 1977–79, hon. pres., 1979–. Mem: bds. of Creighton U., Roosevelt U., Natl. Jewish Welfare Bd., Boy Scouts of Amer.; founder, Inst. for Jewish Policy Planning. Recipient: Ralph Bunche peace award.

KOMAROVSKY, MIRRA, sociologist; b. Baku, Russia, Feb. 4, 1905; d. NYC, Jan 30, 1999; in U.S. since 1922. Educ.: Barnard Coll., Columbia U. (PhD). Asst. prof., sociology, Skidmore Coll., 1927–29; research asst., assoc., Yale U. Inst. of Human Relations, 1931–32; instr., Barnard Coll., 1936–45, asst. prof., 1945–47, assoc. prof., 1948–53, prof.,

1954–73, dept. chmn., 1949–62, 1965–68, chmn., women's studies program, 1978. Au.: *Leisure, A Suburban Study* (1934); *The Unemployed Man and His Family* (1940); *Women in the Modern World: Their Education and Their Dilemmas* (1953); *Blue-Collar Marriage* (1964); *Dilemmas of Masculinity* (1976); *Women in College: Shaping New Feminine Identities* (1985). Recipient: Distinguished Alumna Award, Barnard Coll.; Burgess Award, Natl. Council on Family Relations; Career of Distinguished Scholarship Award, Sociological Research Assn.

MINDEL, NISSAN, rabbi, author; b. Rezenke, Latvia, Mar. 20, 1912; d. NYC (Brooklyn), June 26, 1999; in U.S. since 1940. Educ.: Yeshiva Tomchei Tmimim (ordination); Manchester U., England; Columbia U. (PhD). Dir., Merkos L'Inyonei Chinuch (educational org. of Chabad), 1941–; personal sec. to last two rebbes of Lubavitch. Au. books on history and philosophy of Chabad; translated *Liqqutei Amarim Tanya*, basic text of Chabad, into English.

MONTAGU, ASHLEY (Israel Ehrenberg), anthropologist; b. London, England, June 28, 1905; d. Princeton, N.J., Nov. 26, 1999; in U.S. since 1930. Educ.: U. London, U. Florence, Columbia U. (PhD). Research assoc., British Museum of Natural History, 1926–27; curator, physical anthropology, Wellcome Historical Medical Museum, 1929–30; asst. prof., anatomy, NYU, 1931–38; assoc. prof., Hahnemann Medical Coll. and Hosp., Philadelphia, 1938–49; chmn., dept. of anthropology, Rutgers U., 1949–55. Produced, financed, wrote, and directed film *One World or None*, 1946, on implications of atomic power. Responsible for drafting UNESCO statement on race, 1949. Au. of over 60 books, incl.: *Coming into Being Among the Australian Aborigines* (1937); *Man's Most Dangerous Myth: The Fallacy of Race* (1942); *Introduction to Physical Anthropology* (1945); *On Being Human* (1950); *Statement on Race* (1952); *The Natural Superiority of Women* (1953); *Anthropology and Human Nature* (1957); *Human Heredity* (1959); *Race, Science, and Humanity* (1963); *Man's Evolution* (1965); *The Anatomy of Swearing* (1967); *Immortality, Religion, and Morals* (1971); *Touching* (1971); *The Elephant Man* (1971); *The Nature of Human Aggression*

(1976); *What We Know About Race* (1987). Recipient: Distinguished Service Award, Assn, for Childbirth at Home Internatl.; Humanistic Award, Rollo May Inst. for Humanistic Studies.

MOSSE, GEORGE L., historian; b. Berlin, Germany, Sept. 20, 1918; d. Madison, Wis., Jan. 22, 1999; in U.S. since 1939. Educ.: Cambridge U. (England); Haverford Coll.; Harvard U. (PhD). Instr., asst. prof., assoc. prof., history, U. Iowa, 1944–55; assoc. prof., prof., U. Wisconsin, 1955–89 (Bascom prof., 1964–83; Bascom-Weinstein prof. of Jewish studies, 1983–89); prof. emer., 1989–; Koebner prof., Hebrew U., Jerusalem, 1979–86; prof. emer., 1986–; inaugural Shapiro sr. scholar-in-residence, U.S. Holocaust Memorial Museum, 1989; A. D. White prof.-at-large, Cornell U., 1993–. Au. of over two dozen books, incl.: *The Crisis of German Ideology* (1964); *Nazi Culture: Intellectual, Cultural and Social Life in the Third Reich* (1966); *Germans and Jews* (1970); *The Nationalization of the Masses, Political Symbols and Mass Movements in Germany* (1975); *Nazism* (1978); *Towards the Final Solution: A History of European Racism* (1978); *German Jews Beyond Judaism* (1985); *Nationalism and Sexuality: Respectability and Abnormal Sexuality in Modern Europe* (1985); *Confronting the Nation: Jewish and Western Nationalism* (1993); *The Fascist Revolution: Toward a General Theory of Fascism* (1999). Coeditor, *Journal of Contemporary History,* 1966–. Recipient: Goethe Institute medal; Leo Baeck Institute medal; award for scholarly distinction, Amer. Historical Assn.

PRITZKER, JAY, real-estate developer, philanthropist; b. Chicago, Ill., Aug 26, 1922; d. Chicago, Ill., Jan. 23, 1999. Educ.: Northwestern U. (BSc, JD). Served U.S. Navy, WWII. Asst. custodian, Alien Property Admin, 1947; partner, Pritzker & Pritzker, 1948–. Bought first Hyatt hotel in 1957, eventually amassing a chain of 182 hotels; chmn., Hyatt Corp., Hyatt Internatl., Marmon Group, Inc. Life trustee, U. Chicago. Established Pritzker Architectural Prize; founded Nancy Friend Pritzker Laboratory for study of clinical depression, Stanford U.

RESNICK, PEARL, philanthropist; b. Okna, Russia, Jan. 3, 1912; d. Palm Beach, Fla., Dec. 13, 1999; in U.S. since 1923. Together with husband, a real-estate developer, established Jack and Pearl Resnick Film Division of Simon Wiesenthal Center; Jack and Pearl Resnick Gerontology Center, Jack and Pearl Resnick Fellowship, and academic chair in brain-tumor research at Albert Einstein Coll. of Medicine, Yeshiva U., whose Resnick Campus was named for them in 1990. Mem.: bd. overseers, Albert Einstein Coll. of Medicine, bds. of Yeshiva U., Jewish Theological Sem. of America, Hebrew Home for the Aged (Riverdale), Bar-Ilan U.

ROSE, FREDERICK P., real-estate developer, philanthropist; b. NYC, Nov. 16, 1923; d. Rye, N.Y., Sept. 14, 1999. Educ.: Yale U. (Bachelor of Civil Engineering). Served U.S. Navy (construction battalions), WWII. V.-pres., Rose Associates, 1946–60, pres., 1960–80, chmn., 1980–; v.- chmn., N.Y. Facilities Devel. Corp., 1970–75. Donated more than $95 million to a variety of causes and projects, incl. Rose Main Reading Room of N. Y. Public Library, Rose Center for Earth and Space at Amer. Museum of Natural Hist. (Hayden Planetarium). Initiated Amer. Jewish Com. Kosovo relief fund. Pres., Fed. of Jewish Philanthropies of N.Y., 1974–77, bd. chmn., 1981–83, hon. bd. chmn, 1983–; mem., publs. com., *Commentary* magazine, 1964–, chmn., 1979–84; bd. mem. of 35 orgs. Recipient: Yale medal; NYU Urban Leadership award.

SAFRA, EDMUND J., banker, philanthropist; b. Beirut, Lebanon., Aug. 6, 1932; d. Monte Carlo, Monaco, Dec. 3, 1999. Associated with series of Safra family private banks: Beirut, 1948–52; Banco Safra, São Paulo, Brazil, 1955–56; Trade Development Bank, Geneva, 1956–83; Republic New York, Safra Republic Holdings, 1966–. Rated no. 199 on *Forbes* magazine's list of world's billionaires. Major donor to U.S. Memorial Holocaust Museum; Sephardic studies and Latin American studies at Harvard U.; Sephardic studies at Yeshiva U.; banking studies at U. Penn.; Sephardic educ. institutions in many U.S. cities.

SELIGSON, DAVID, rabbi; b. NYC, June 10, 1907; d. NYC, Aug. 3, 1999. Educ.: Yeshiva Coll., Columbia U., Hebrew Union Coll. (ordination, DHL, DD.). Served U.S. Army (chaplain) in Burma and India, WWII. Rabbi: Ventnor City, N.J., 1933–35; Birmingham, Eng., 1935–

40; Port Chester, N.Y., 1940–42; Central Synagogue, NYC, 1945–72, emer., 1972–. Pres.: N.Y. Assn. of Reform Rabbis, 1952–54, N.Y Bd. of Rabbis, 1954–55. Mem., bd. of govs., HUC, Zionist Org. of Amer.

SILVERSTEIN, SHEL (Shelby), author, composer; b. Chicago, Ill., Sept. 25, 1930; d. Key West, Fla., May 10, 1999. Served U.S. Army in Japan and Korea (correspondent for *Stars and Stripes)*. Cartoonist, writer, *Playboy* magazine. Au. of best-selling children's books, incl.: *Uncle Shelby's Story of Lafcadio, the Lion Who Shot Back* (1963); *The Giving Tree* (1964); *Where the Sidewalk Ends* (1974); *A Light in the Attic* (1981). Composed hit song, "A Boy Named Sue" (1969).

SISKEL, GENE, film critic; b. Chicago, Ill., Jan. 26, 1946; d. Evanston, Ill., Feb. 20, 1999. Educ.: Yale U. Film critic: Chicago *Tribune*, 1969–, WBBM-TV, 1974–, CBS "This Morning," 1990–; host, "Nightwatch," WTTW-TV, 1979–80; co-host: "Sneak Previews," PBS, 1977–82, "At the Movies," syndicated TV, 1982–86, "Siskel and Ebert," syndicated TV, 1986–. Au. (with Roger Ebert): *The Future of the Movies* (1991). Emmy awards, 1979, 1980. Established fund to send Chicago Jewish teens to visit Israel.

STEIN, HERBERT, economist, government official; b. Detroit, Mich., Aug. 27, 1916; d. Washington, D.C., Sept. 8, 1999. Educ.: Williams Coll., U. Chicago (PhD). Economist: FDIC, 1938–40; Natl. Defense Adv. Comm., 1940–41; Wage and Price Bd., 1941–44; Office of War Mobilization and Reconversion, 1945; Com. for Economic Devel., 1945–67 (assoc. dir. research, 1948–56, dir. research, 1956–66, v.-pres. and chief economist, 1966–67); sr. fellow, Brookings Institution, 1967–69; mem., Pres.'s Council of Economic Advisers, 1969–72, chmn., 1972–74; A. Willis Robertson prof. of economics, U. Va., 1974–84; adj. scholar, Amer. Enterprise Inst., 1975–77, sr. fellow, 1977–; weekly columnist, "The Economy Today," Scripps Howard newspapers, 1974–80; mem. bd. of contributors, *Wall Street Journal,* 1974–. Au: *Jobs and Markets* (1946); *The Fiscal Revolution in America* (1969); *Economic Planning and the Improvement of Public Policy* (1975); *Presidential Economics* (1984); *Governing the $5 Trillion Economy* (1989). Recipient: Pabst postwar employment award, first prize; Center for Advanced Study in Behavioral Sciences fellowship.

STEINBERG, SAUL, artist; b. Romanic-Sarat, Romania, June 15, 1914; d. NYC, May 12, 1999; in U.S. since 1942. Educ.: Bucharest U.; Regio Politecnico, Faculta de Architettura, Milan, Italy (Doctor of Architecture). Served U.S. Navy, 1943–45 (drew anti-Nazi cartoons dropped behind enemy lines). Cartoonist for *Bertoldo* magazine, Milan, 1936–39; practicing architect, 1939–41; free-lance cartoonist, mainly for *New Yorker* magazine (85 covers and 642 drawings), 1941–. First one-man show, Wakefield Gallery, 1943, followed by inclusion in Museum of Modern Art show, "Fourteen Americans," 1946, and numerous subsequent shows. Best known for 1976 *New Yorker* cover depicting New Yorker's view of the world — everything beyond Hudson River is insignificant. Au.: *All in Line* (1945); *The New World* (1965); *The Discovery of America* (1993). Recipient: Chevalier des Arts et des Lettres, France; gold medal, Amer. Acad. of Arts and Letters.

TANNENWALD, THEODORE, JR., public official, communal worker; b. Valatie, N.Y., July 28, 1916; d. Washington, D.C., Jan. 17, 1999; Educ.: Brown U., Harvard U. (LLB). Assoc., Weil, Gotshal & Manges (New York), 1939–42, partner, 1947–65; prin. legal consultant, Lend Lease Admin., 1942; acting asst. chief, foreign funds control div., U.S. State Dept., 1942–43; special consultant to sec. of war, 1943–45; consultant to sec. of defense, 1945–49; counsel to special asst. to the pres., 1950–51; exec. office of the pres., 1951–53; special counsel to Moreland Comm., 1955–58; N.Y mem., Tri-State Tax Comm., 1958–59; judge, U.S. Tax Court, 1965–81, chief judge, 1981–83, sr. judge, 1983–. Chmn., bd. of govs., Hebrew Union Coll.-Jewish Inst. of Religion, 1978–81, hon. chmn, 1981–; mem., natl. exec. com. and bd. of govs., Amer. Jewish Com.

TISHMAN, RITA V., philanthropist; b. NYC, May 3, 1907; d. NYC, Jan. 21, 1999. Educ.: Smith Coll. Awarded civilian medal of merit by Pres. Roosevelt for leading war bond drive, N.Y. State women's div., 1946; active in numerous civil rights, human rights causes; pres., N.Y. section, Natl. Council of Jewish Women; bd. mem., hon. chmn., United Jewish Appeal; bd. mem., Amer. Jewish Com., Anti-Defamation League, which created annual Rita. V. Tishman award for civil rights in her honor. Recipient: Hannah G. Solomon award, National Council of Jewish Women; Appeal for Human Relations award, Amer. Jewish Com.

WEINBERG, YAAKOV, rabbi, yeshiva head; b. NYC, Jan. 2, 1923; d. Baltimore, Md., July 1, 1999. Educ.: Yeshiva Chaim Berlin, Brooklyn, N.Y. Instr. of Talmud, Ner Israel Rabbinical Coll., Baltimore, Md., 1945–65, dean of *kollel* (graduate program), 1953–65, dean (Toronto branch), 1965–71, assoc. dean, (Baltimore), 1971–87, dean, 1987–. Mem. rabbinical adv. bds.: Torah Umesorah-Natl. Soc. for Hebrew Day Schools; Torah Schools for Israel-Chinuch Atzmai.

WOLF, ERIC R., anthropologist; b. Vienna, Austria, Feb. 1, 1923; d. Irvington, N.Y., Mar. 7, 1999; in U.S. since 1940. Served US Army, WWII. Educ.: Queens Coll., Columbia U. (PhD). Asst. prof., anthropology, U. Ill., 1952-55; U. Va., 1955–58; visiting asst. prof., Yale U., 1958–59; assoc. prof., U. Chicago, 1959–61; prof., U. Mich., 1965–71; distinguished prof., Herbert H. Lehman Coll. and Graduate Center, City U. of N.Y., 1971–. Au.: *Sons of the Shaking Earth* (1958); *Anthropology* (1964); *Peasants* (1968); *Peasant Wars of the Twentieth Century* (1969); *Europe and the People Without History* (1982); *Envisioning Power: Ideologies of Dominance and Crisis* (1999). Recipient: McArthur Found. "genius grant"; Guggenheim fellowship; NIH career award; NEH sr. fellowship.

ZAKIM, LEONARD, communal professional; b. Clifton, N.J., Nov. 17, 1953; d. Boston, Mass., Dec. 2, 1999. Educ.: American U., New Eng. School of Law. Civil rights dir., Anti-Defamation League New England region, 1979–1984; dir., 1984–. Pioneered "World of Difference" tolerance-educ. program, worked to better Jewish relations with blacks and Catholics, established Lenny Fund to fight poverty and bigotry. Recipient: Knight of St. Gregory (bestowed by Pope John Paul II).

Calendars

SUMMARY JEWISH CALENDAR, 5760–5764 (Sept. 1999–Aug. 2004)

HOLIDAY	5760	5761	5762	5763	5764
Rosh Ha-shanah, 1st day	Sa Sept. 11	Sa Sept. 30	T Sept. 18	Sa Sept. 7	Sa Sept. 27
Rosh Ha-shanah, 2nd day	S Sept. 12	S Oct. 1	W Sept. 19	S Sept. 8	S Sept. 28
Fast of Gedaliah	M Sept. 13	M Oct. 2	Th Sept. 20	M Sept. 9	M Sept. 29
Yom Kippur	M Sept. 20	M Oct. 9	Th Sept. 27	M Sept. 16	M Oct. 6
Sukkot, 1st day	Sa Sept. 25	Sa Oct. 14	T Oct. 2	Sa Sept. 21	S Oct. 11
Sukkot, 2nd day	S Sept. 26	S Oct. 15	W Oct. 3	S Sept. 22	F Oct. 12
Hosha'na' Rabbah	F Oct. 1	F Oct. 20	M Oct. 8	F Sept. 27	Sa Oct. 17
Shemini 'Azeret	Sa Oct. 2	Sa Oct. 21	T Oct. 9	Sa Sept. 28	S Oct. 18
Simhat Torah	S Oct. 3	S Oct. 22	W Oct. 10	S Sept. 29	M Oct. 19
New Moon, Heshwan, 1st day	M Oct. 10	M Oct. 29	Th Oct. 17	M Oct. 6	T Oct. 26
New Moon, Heshwan, 2nd day	T Oct. 11	T Oct. 30	F Oct. 18	T Oct. 7	W Oct. 27
New Moon, Kislew, 1st day	W Nov. 9	W Nov. 28	F Nov. 16	W Nov. 5	W Nov. 25
New Moon, Kislew, 2nd day	Sa Nov. 10			Sa Nov. 6	Sa Nov. 26
Hanukkah, 1st day	Sa Dec. 4	F Dec. 22	M Dec. 10	Sa Nov. 30	Sa Dec. 20
New Moon, Ṭevet, 1st day	Th Dec. 9	W Dec. 27	Sa Dec. 15	Th Dec. 5	Th Dec. 25
New Moon, Ṭevet, 2nd day	F Dec. 10		S Dec. 16	F Dec. 6	F Dec. 26
Fast of 10th of Ṭevet	S Dec. 19	F Jan. 5 (2001)	T Dec. 25	S Dec. 15	S Jan. 4 (2004)

	2000	2001	2002	2003	2004
New Moon, Shevat	Sa Jan. 8	Th Jan. 25	M Jan. 14	Sa Jan. 4	Sa Jan. 24
Hamishshah-ʿasar bi-Shevat	Sa Jan. 22	Th Feb. 8	M Jan. 28	Sa Jan. 18	Sa Feb. 7
New Moon, Adar I, 1st day	S Feb. 6			S Feb. 2	
New Moon, Adar I, 2nd day	M Feb. 7			M Feb. 3	
New Moon, Adar II, 1st day	T Mar. 7	F Feb. 23	T Feb. 12	T Mar. 4	S Feb. 22
New Moon, Adar II, 2nd day	W Mar. 8	Sa Feb. 24	W Feb. 13	W Mar. 5	M Feb. 23
Fast of Esther	M Mar. 20	Th Mar. 8	M Feb. 25	M Mar. 17	Th Mar. 4
Purim	T Mar. 21	F Mar. 9	T Feb. 26	T Mar. 18	S Mar. 7
Shushan Purim	W Mar. 22	Sa Mar. 10	W Feb. 27	W Mar. 19	M Mar. 8
New Moon, Nisan	Th Apr. 6	S Mar. 25	Th Mar. 14	Th Apr. 3	T Mar. 23
Passover, 1st day	Th Apr. 20	S Apr. 8	Th Mar. 28	Th Apr. 17	T Apr. 6
Passover, 2nd day	F Apr. 21	M Apr. 9	F Mar. 29	F Apr. 18	W Apr. 7
Passover, 7th day	W Apr. 26	Sa Apr. 14	W Apr. 3	W Apr. 23	M Apr. 12
Passover, 8th day	Th Apr. 27	S Apr. 15	Th Apr. 4	Th Apr. 24	T Apr. 13
Holocaust Memorial Day	T May 2	F Apr. 20*	T Apr. 9	T Apr. 29	S Apr. 18
New Moon, Iyar, 1st day	F May 5	M Apr. 23	F Apr. 12	F May 2	W Apr. 21
New Moon, Iyar, 2nd day	Sa May 6	T Apr. 24	Sa Apr. 13	Sa May 3	Th Apr. 22
Israel Independence Day	W May 10	Sa Apr. 28†	W Apr. 17	W May 7	M Apr. 26
Lag Ba-ʿomer	T May 23	F May 11	T Apr. 30	T May 20	S May 9
Jerusalem Day	F June 2*	M May 21	F May 10*	F May 30*	W May 19
New Moon, Siwan	S June 4	W May 23	S May 12	S June 1	F May 21
Shavuʿot, 1st day	F June 9	M May 28	F May 17	F June 6	W May 26
Shavuʿot, 2nd day	Sa June 10	T May 29	Sa May 18	Sa June 7	Th May 27
New Moon, Tammuz, 1st day	M July 3	Th June 21	M June 10	M June 30	Sa June 19
New Moon, Tammuz, 2nd day	T July 4	F June 22	T June 11	T July 1	S June 20
Fast of 17th of Tammuz	Th July 20	S July 8	Th June 27	Th July 17	T July 6
New Moon, Av	W Aug. 2	Sa July 21	W July 10	W July 30	M July 19
Fast of 9th of Av	Th Aug. 10	S July 29	Th July 18	Th Aug. 7	T July 27
New Moon, Elul, 1st day	Th Aug. 31	S Aug. 19	Th Aug. 8	Th Aug. 28	T Aug. 17
New Moon, Elul, 2nd day	F Sept. 1	M Aug. 20	F Aug. 9	F Aug. 29	W Aug. 18

*Observed Thursday, a day earlier, to avoid conflict with the Sabbath.

†Observed Thursday, two days earlier, to avoid conflict with the Sabbath.

CONDENSED MONTHLY CALENDAR
(1999–2002)

1999, Jan. 18–Feb. 16] SHEVAṬ (30 DAYS) [5759

Civil Date	Day of the Week	Jewish Date	SABBATHS, FESTIVALS, FASTS	PENTATEUCHAL READING	PROPHETICAL READING
Jan. 18	M	Shevaṭ 1	New Moon	Num. 28:1–15	
23	Sa	6	Bo'	Exod. 10:1–13:16	Jeremiah 46:13–28
30	Sa	13	Be-shallaḥ (Shabbat Shirah)	Exod. 13:17–17:16	Judges 4:4–5:31 *Judges 5:1–31*
Feb. 1	M	15	Ḥamishah-'asar bi-Shevaṭ		
6	Sa	20	Yitro	Exod. 18:1–20:23	Isaiah 6:1–7:6; 9:5–6 *Isaiah 6:1–13*
13	Sa	27	Mishpaṭim (Shabbat Sheḳalim)	Exod. 21:1–24:18 Exod. 30:11–16	II Kings 12:1–17 *II Kings 11:17–12:17*
16	T	30	New Moon, first day	Num. 28:1–15	

Italics are for Sephardi Minhag.

1999, Feb. 17–Mar. 17] ADAR (29 DAYS) [5759

Civil Date	Day of the Week	Jewish Date	SABBATHS, FESTIVALS, FASTS	PENTATEUCHAL READING	PROPHETICAL READING
Feb. 17	W	Adar 1	New Moon, second day	Num. 28:1–15	
20	Sa	4	Terumah	Exod. 25:1–27:19	I Kings 5:26–6:13
27	Sa	11	Teẓawweh (Shabbat Zakhor)	Exod. 27:20–30:10 Deut. 25:17–19	I Samuel 15:2–34 *I Samuel 15:1–34*
Mar. 1	M	13	Fast of Esther	Exod. 32:11–14 Exod. 34:1–10 (morning and afternoon)	Isaiah 55:6–56:8 (afternoon only)
2	T	14	Purim	Exod. 17:8–16	Book of Esther (night before and in the morning)
3	W	15	Shushan Purim		
6	Sa	18	Ki tissa' (Shabbat Parah)	Exod. 30:11–34:35 Num. 19:1–22	Ezekiel 36:16–38 *Ezekiel 36:16–36*
13	Sa	25	Wa-yakhel, Peḳude (Shabbat Ha-ḥodesh)	Exod. 35:1–40:38 Exod. 12:1–20	Ezekiel 45:16–46:18 *Ezekiel 45:18–46:15*

Italics are for Sephardi Minhag.

1999, Mar. 18–April 16]   NISAN (30 DAYS)   [5759

Civil Date	Day of the Week	Jewish Date	SABBATHS, FESTIVALS, FASTS	PENTATEUCHAL READING	PROPHETICAL READING
Mar. 18	Th	Nisan 1	New Moon	Num. 28:1–15	
20	Sa	3	Wa-yikra'	Levit. 1:1–5:26	Isaiah 43:21–44:24
27	Sa	10	Ẓaw (Shabbat Ha-gadol)	Levit. 6:1–8:36	Malachi 3:4–24
31	W	14	Fast of Firstborn		
Apr. 1	Th	15	Passover, first day	Exod. 12:21–51 Num. 28:16–25	Joshua 5:2–6:1, 27
2	F	16	Passover, second day	Levit. 22:26–23:44 Num. 28:16–25	II Kings 23:1–9, 21–25
3	Sa	17	Ḥol Ha-mo'ed, first day	Exod. 33:12–34:26 Num. 28:19–25	Ezekiel 37:1–14
4	S	18	Ḥol Ha-mo'ed, second day	Exod. 13:1–16 Num. 28:19–25	Ezekiel 45:16–46:18
5	M	19	Ḥol Ha-mo'ed, third day	Exod. 22:24–23:19 Num. 28:19–25	
6	T	20	Ḥol Ha-mo'ed, fourth day	Num. 9:1–14 Num. 28:19–25	
7	W	21	Passover, seventh day	Exod. 13:17–15:26 Num. 28:19–25	II Samuel 22:1–51
8	Th	22	Passover, eighth day	Deut. 15:19–16:17 Num. 28:19–25	Isaiah 10:32–12:6
10	Sa	24	Shemini	Levit. 9:1–11:47 Num. 28:19–25	II Samuel 6:1–7:17 *II Samuel 6:1–19*
13	T	27	Holocaust Memorial Day		
16	F	30	New Moon	Num. 28:1–15	

Italics are for Sephardi Minhag.

1999, Apr. 17–May 15]   IYAR (29 DAYS)   [5759

Civil Date	Day of the Week	Jewish Date	SABBATHS, FESTIVALS, FASTS	PENTATEUCHAL READING	PROPHETICAL READING
Apr. 17	Sa	Iyar 1	Tazria', Mezora'; New Moon, second day	Levit. 12:1–15:33 Num. 28:9–15	Isaiah 66:1–24
21	W	5	Israel Independence Day		
24	Sa	8	Aḥare mot, Kedoshim	Levit. 16:1–20:27	Amos 9:7–15 *Ezekiel 20:2–20*
May 1	Sa	15	Emor	Levit. 21:1–24:23	Ezekiel 44:15–31
4	T	18	Lag Ba-'omer		
8	Sa	22	Be-har, Be-ḥuḳḳotai	Levit. 25:1–27:34	Jeremiah 16:19–17:14
14	F	28	Jerusalem Day*		
15	Sa	29	Be-midbar	Num. 1:1–4:20	I Samuel 20:18–42

*Observed May 13, to avoid conflict with the Sabbath.

*Italics are for
Sephardi Minhag.*

1999, May 16–June 14]   SIWAN (30 DAYS)   [5759

Civil Date	Day of the Week	Jewish Date	SABBATHS, FESTIVALS, FASTS	PENTATEUCHAL READING	PROPHETICAL READING
May 16	S	Siwan 1	New Moon	Num. 28:1–15	
21	F	6	Shavu'ot, first day	Exod. 19:1–20:23 Num. 28:26–31	Ezekiel 1:1–28 Ezekiel 3:12
22	Sa	7	Shavu'ot, second day	Deut. 15:19–16:17 Num. 28:26–31	Habbakuk 3:1–19 *Habbakuk 2:20–3:19*
29	Sa	14	Naso'	Num. 4:21–7:89	Judges 13:2–25
June 5	Sa	21	Be-ha'alotekha	Num. 8:1–12:16	Zechariah 2:14–4:7
12	Sa	28	Shelaḥ lekha	Num. 13:1–15:41	Joshua 2:1–24
14	M	30	New Moon, first day	Num. 28:1–15	

Italics are for Sephardi Minhag.

1999, June 15–July 13]   TAMMUZ (29 DAYS)   [5759

Civil Date	Day of the Week	Jewish Date	SABBATHS, FESTIVALS, FASTS	PENTATEUCHAL READING	PROPHETICAL READING
June 15	T	Tammuz 1	New Moon, second day	Num. 28:1–15	
19	Sa	5	Ḳoraḥ	Num. 16:1–18:32	I Samuel 11:14–12:22
26	Sa	12	Ḥuḳḳat, Balaḳ	Num. 19:1–25:9	Micah 5:6–6:8
July 1	Th	17	Fast of 17th of Tammuz	Exod. 32:11–14 Exod. 34:1–10 (morning and afternoon)	Isaiah 55:6–56:8 (afternoon only)
3	Sa	19	Pineḥas	Num. 25:10–30:1	Jeremiah 1:1–2:3
10	Sa	26	Maṭṭot, Mas‘e	Num. 30:2–36:13	Jeremiah 2:4–28 Jeremiah 3:4 *Jeremiah 2:4–28* *Jeremiah 4:1–2*

Italics are for
Sephardi Minhag.

1999, July 14–Aug. 12]   AV (30 DAYS)   [5759

Civil Date	Day of the Week	Jewish Date	SABBATHS, FESTIVALS, FASTS	PENTATEUCHAL READING	PROPHETICAL READING
July 14	W	Av 1	New Moon	Num. 28:1–15	
17	Sa	4	Devarim (Shabbat Ḥazon)	Deut. 1:1–3:22	Isaiah 1:1–27
22	Th	9	Fast of 9th of Av	Morning: Deut. 4:25–40 Afternoon: Exod. 32:11–14 Exod. 34:1–10	(Lamentations is read the night before) Jeremiah 8:13–9:23 (morning) Isaiah 55:6–56:8 (afternoon)
24	Sa	11	Wa-etḥannan (Shabbat Naḥamu)	Deut. 3:23–7:11	Isaiah 40:1–26
31	Sa	18	'Eḳev	Deut. 7:12–11:25	Isaiah 49:14–51:3
Aug. 7	Sa	25	Re'eh	Deut. 11:26–16:17	Isaiah 54:11–55:5
12	Th	30	New Moon, first day	Num. 28:1–15	

Italics are for Sephardi Minhag.

1999, Aug. 13–Sept. 10]   ELUL (29 DAYS)   [5759

Civil Date	Day of the Week	Jewish Date	SABBATHS, FESTIVALS, FASTS	PENTATEUCHAL READING	PROPHETICAL READING
Aug. 13	F	Elul 1	New Moon, second day	Num. 28:1–15	
14	Sa	2	Shofeṭim (Shabbat Ḥazon)	Deut. 16:18–21:9	Isaiah 51:12–52:12
21	Sa	9	Ki teẓe'	Deut. 21:10–25:19	Isaiah 54:1–10
28	Sa	16	Ki tavo'	Deut. 26:1–29:8	Isaiah 60:1–22
Sept. 4	Sa	23	Niẓẓavim, Wa-yelekh	Deut. 29:9–30:20	Isaiah 61:10–63:9

*Italics are for
Sephardi Minhag.*

1999, Sept. 11–Oct. 10]   TISHRI (30 DAYS)   [5760

Civil Date	Day of the Week	Jewish Date	SABBATHS, FESTIVALS, FASTS	PENTATEUCHAL READING	PROPHETICAL READING
Sept. 11	Sa	Tishri 1	Rosh Ha-shanah, first day	Gen. 21:1–34 Num. 29:1–6	I Samuel 1:1–2:10
12	S	2	Rosh Ha-shanah, second day	Gen. 22:1–24 Num. 29:1–6	Jeremiah 31:2–20
13	M	3	Fast of Gedaliah	Exod. 32:11–14 Exod. 34:1–10 (morning and afternoon)	Isaiah 55:6–56:8 (afternoon only)
18	Sa	8	Ha'azinu (Shabbat Shuvah)	Deut. 32:1–52	Hosea 14:2–10 Micah 7:18–20 Joel 2:15–27 *Hosea 14:2–10* *Micah 7:18–20*
20	M	10	Yom Kippur	Morning: Levit. 16:1–34 Num. 29:7–11 Afternoon: Levit. 18:1–30	Isaiah 57:14–58:14 Jonah 1:1–4:11 Micah 7:18–20
25	Sa	15	Sukkot, first day	Levit. 22:26–23:44 Num. 29:12–16	Zechariah 14:1–21
26	S	16	Sukkot, second day	Levit. 22:26–23:44 Num. 29:12–16	I Kings 8:2–21
27-30	M-Th	17–20	Ḥol Ha-mo'ed	M Num. 29:17–25 T Num. 29:20–28 W Num. 29:23–31 Th Num. 29:26–34	
Oct. 1	F	21	Hosha'na' Rabbah	Num. 29:26–34	
2	Sa	22	Shemini 'Aẓeret	Deut. 14:22–16:17 Num. 29:35–30:1	I Kings 8:54–66
3	S	23	Simḥat Torah	Deut. 33:1–34:12 Gen. 1:1–2:3 Num. 29:35–30:1	Joshua 1:1–18 *Joshua 1:1–9*
9	Sa	29	Be-re'shit	Gen. 1:1–6:8	I Samuel 20:18–42
10	S	30	New Moon, first day	Num. 28:1–15	

Italics are for Sephardi Minhag.

1999, Oct. 11–Nov. 9] HESHWAN (30 DAYS) [5760

Civil Date	Day of the Week	Jewish Date	SABBATHS, FESTIVALS, FASTS	PENTATEUCHAL READING	PROPHETICAL READING
Oct. 11	M	Heshwan 1	New Moon, second day	Num. 28:1–15	
16	Sa	6	Noaḥ	Gen. 6:9–11:32	Isaiah 54:1–55:5 *Isaiah 54:1–10*
23	Sa	13	Lekh lekha	Gen. 12:1–17:27	Isaiah 40:27–41:16
30	Sa	20	Wa-yera'	Gen. 18:1–22:24	II Kings 4:1–37 *II Kings 4:1–23*
Nov. 6	Sa	27	Ḥayye Sarah	Gen. 23:1–25:18	I Kings 1:1–31
9	T	30	New Moon, first day	Num. 28:1–15	

*Italics are for
Sephardi Minhag.*

1999, Nov. 10–Dec. 9]　　　KISLEW (30 DAYS)　　　[5760

Civil Date	Day of the Week	Jewish Date	SABBATHS, FESTIVALS, FASTS	PENTATEUCHAL READING	PROPHETICAL READING
Nov. 10	W	Kislew 1	New Moon, second day	Num. 28:1–15	
13	Sa	4	Toledot	Gen. 25:19–28:9	Malachi 1:1–2:7
20	Sa	11	Wa-yeze'	Gen. 28:10–32:3	Hosea 12:13–14:10 *Hosea 11:7–12:12*
27	Sa	18	Wa-yishlah	Gen. 32:4–36:43	Hosea 11:7–12:12 *Obadiah 1:1–21*
Dec. 4	Sa	25	Wa-yeshev; Hanukkah, first day	Gen. 37:1–40:23 Num. 7:1–17	Zechariah 2:14–4:7
5–8	S–W	26–29	Hanukkah, second to fifth days	S　Num. 7:18–29 M　Num. 7:24–35 T　Num. 7:30–41 W　Num. 7:36–47	
9	Th	30	New Moon, first day; Hanukkah, sixth day	Num. 28:1–15 Num. 7:42–47	

Italics are for Sephardi Minhag.

1999, Dec. 10–Jan. 7, 2000] ṬEVET (29 DAYS) [5760

Civil Date	Day of the Week	Jewish Date	SABBATHS, FESTIVALS, FASTS	PENTATEUCHAL READING	PROPHETICAL READING
Dec. 10	F	Ṭevet 1	New Moon, second day; Ḥanukkah, seventh day	Num. 28:1–15 Num. 7:48–53	
11	Sa	2	Miḳeẓ; Ḥanukkah, eighth day	Gen. 41:1–44:17 Num. 7:54–8.4	I Kings 7:40–50
18	Sa	9	Wa-yiggash	Gen. 44:18–47:27	Ezekiel 37:15–28
19	S	10	Fast of 10th of Ṭevet	Exod. 32:11–14 Exod. 34:1–10 (morning and afternoon)	Isaiah 55:6–56:8 (afternoon only)
25	Sa	16	Wa-yeḥi	Gen. 47:28–50:26	I Kings 2:1–12
Jan. 1	Sa	23	Shemot	Exod. 1:1–6:1	Isaiah 27:6–28:13 Isaiah 29:22–23 *Jeremiah 1:1–2:3*

Italics are for Sephardi Minhag.

2000, Jan. 8 – Feb. 6] SHEVAṬ (30 DAYS) [5760

Civil Date	Day of the Week	Jewish Date	SABBATHS, FESTIVALS, FASTS	PENTATEUCHAL READING	PROPHETICAL READING
Jan. 8	Sa	Shevaṭ 1	Wa-'era'; New Moon	Exod. 6:2–9:35 Num. 28:9–15	Isaiah 66:1–24
15	Sa	8	Bo'	Exod. 10:1–13:16	Jeremiah 46:13–28
22	Sa	15	Be-shallaḥ (Shabbat Shirah); Ḥamishah 'asar bi-Shevaṭ	Exod. 13:17–17:16	Judges 4:4–5:31 *Judges 5:1–31*
29	Sa	22	Yitro	Exod. 18:1–20:23	Isaiah 6:1–7:6; 9:5–6 *Isaiah 6:1–13*
Feb. 5	Sa	29	Mishpaṭim	Exod. 21:1–24:18	I Samuel 20:18–42
6	S	30	New Moon, first day	Num. 28:1–15	

Italics are for
Sephardi Minhag.

Civil Date	Day of the Week	Jewish Date	SABBATHS, FESTIVALS, FASTS	PENTATEUCHAL READING	PROPHETICAL READING
Feb. 7	M	Adar I 1	New Moon, second day	Num. 28:1 – 15	
12	Sa	6	Terumah	Exod. 25:1 – 27:19	I Kings 5:26 – 6:13
19	Sa	13	Teẓawweh	Exod. 27:20 – 30:10	Ezekiel 43:10 – 27
26	Sa	20	Ki tissa'	Exod. 30:11 – 34:35	I Kings 18:1 – 39 *I Kings 18:20 – 39*
Mar. 4	Sa	27	Wa-yaḵhel (Shabbat Sheḵalim)	Exod. 35:1 – 38:20 Exod. 30:11 – 16	II Kings 12:1 – 17 *II Kings 11:17 – 12:17*
7	T	30	New Moon, first day	Num. 28:1 – 15	

Italics are for Sephardi Minhag.

2000, Mar. 8–Apr. 5]   ADAR II (29 DAYS)   [5760

Civil Date	Day of the Week	Jewish Date	SABBATHS, FESTIVALS, FASTS	PENTATEUCHAL READING	PROPHETICAL READING
Mar. 8	W	Adar II 1	New Moon, second day	Num. 28:1–15	
11	Sa	4	Peḳude	Exod. 38:21–40:38	I Kings 7:51–8:21 *I Kings 7:40–50*
18	Sa	11	Wa-yiḳra' (Shabbat Zakhor)	Levit. 1:1–5:26 Deut. 25:17–19	I Samuel 15:2–34 *I Samuel 15:1–34*
20	M	13	Fast of Esther	Exod. 32:11–14 Exod. 34:1–10 (morning and afternoon)	Isaiah 55:6–56:8 (afternoon only)
21	T	14	Purim	Exod. 17:8–16	Book of Esther (night before and in the morning)
22	W	15	Shushan Purim		
25	Sa	18	Ẓaw (Shabbat Parah)	Levit. 6:1–8:36 Num. 19:1–22	Ezekiel 36:16–38 *Ezekiel 36:16–36*
Apr. 1	Sa	25	Shemini (Shabbat Ha-ḥodesh)	Levit. 9:1–11:47 Exod. 12:1–20	Ezekiel 45:16–46:18 *Ezekiel 45:18–46:15*

Italics are for Sephardi Minhag.

2000, Apr. 6–May 5] **NISAN (30 DAYS)** [5760

Civil Date	Day of the Week	Jewish Date	SABBATHS, FESTIVALS, FASTS	PENTATEUCHAL READING	PROPHETICAL READING
Apr. 6	Th	Nisan 1	New Moon	Num. 28:1–15	
8	Sa	3	Tazria'	Levit. 12:1–13:59	II Kings 4:42–5:19
15	Sa	10	Mezora' (Shabbat Ha-gadol)	Levit. 14:1–15:33	Malachi 3:4–24
19	W	14	Fast of Firstborn		
20	Th	15	Passover, first day	Exod. 12:21–51 Num. 28:16–25	Joshua 5:2–6:1, 27
21	F	16	Passover, second day	Levit. 22:26–23:44 Num. 28:16–25	II Kings 23:1–9, 21–25
22	Sa	17	Hol Ha-mo'ed, first day	Exod. 33:12–34:26 Num. 28:19–25	Ezekiel 37:1–14
23	S	18	Hol Ha-mo'ed, second day	Exod. 13:1–16 Num. 28:19–25	
24	M	19	Hol Ha-mo'ed, third day	Exod. 22:24–23:19 Num. 28:19–25	
25	T	20	Hol Ha-mo'ed, fourth day	Num. 9:1–14 Num. 28:19–25	
26	W	21	Passover, seventh day	Exod. 13:17–15:26 Num. 28:19–25	II Samuel 22:1–51
27	Th	22	Passover, eighth day	Deut. 15:19–16:17 Num. 28:19–25	Isaiah 10:32–12:6
29	Sa	24	Aḥare mot	Levit 16:1–18:30	Amos 9:7–15 *Ezekiel 22:1–16*
May 2	T	27	Holocaust Memorial Day		
5	F	30	New Moon, first day	Num. 28:1–15	

Italics are for Sephardi Minhag.

2000, May 6–June 3] IYAR (29 DAYS) [5760

Civil Date	Day of the Week	Jewish Date	SABBATHS, FESTIVALS, FASTS	PENTATEUCHAL READING	PROPHETICAL READING
May 6	Sa	Iyar 1	Ķedoshim; New Moon, second day	Levit. 19:1–20:27 Num. 28:9–15	Isaiah 66:1–24
10	W	5	Israel Independence Day		
13	Sa	8	Emor	Levit. 21:1–24:23	Ezekiel 44:15–31
20	Sa	15	Be-har	Levit 25:1–26:2	Jeremiah 32:6–27
23	T	18	Lag Ba-'omer		
27	Sa	22	Be-ḥukķotai	Levit. 26:3–27:34	Jeremiah 16:19–17:14
June 2	F	28	Jerusalem Day*		
3	Sa	29	Be-midbar	Num. 1:1–4:20	I Samuel 20:18–42

*Observed June 1, to avoid conflict with the Sabbath.

*Italics are for
Sephardi Minhag.*

2000, June 4–July 3] SIWAN (30 DAYS) [5760

Civil Date	Day of the Week	Jewish Date	SABBATHS, FESTIVALS, FASTS	PENTATEUCHAL READING	PROPHETICAL READING
June 4	S	Siwan 1	New Moon	Num. 28:1–15	
9	F	6	Shavu'ot, first day	Exod. 19:1–20:23 Num. 28:26–31	Ezekiel 1:1–28, 3:12
10	Sa	7	Shavu'ot, second day	Deut. 15:19–16:17 Num. 28:26–31	Habbakuk 3:1–19 *Habbakuk 2:20–3:19*
17	Sa	14	Naso'	Num. 4:21–7:89	Judges 13:2–25
24	Sa	21	Be-ha'alotekha	Num. 8:1–12:16	Zechariah 2:14–4:7
July 1	Sa	28	Shelaḥ lekha	Num. 13:1–15:41	Joshua 2:1–24
3	M	30	New Moon, first day	Num. 28:1–15	

*Italics are for
Sephardi Minhag.*

2000, July 4–Aug. 1] TAMMUZ (29 DAYS) [5760

Civil Date	Day of the Week	Jewish Date	SABBATHS, FESTIVALS, FASTS	PENTATEUCHAL READING	PROPHETICAL READING
July 4	T	Tammuz 1	New Moon, second day	Num. 28:1–15	
8	Sa	5	Ḳorah	Num. 16:1–18:32	I Samuel 11:14–12:22
15	Sa	12	Ḥuḳḳat, Balaḳ	Num. 19:1–25:9	Micah 5:6–6:8
20	Th	17	Fast of 17th of Tammuz	Exod. 32:11–14 Exod. 34:1–10 (morning and afternoon)	Isaiah 55:6–56:8 (afternoon only)
22	Sa	19	Pineḥas	Num. 25:10–30:1	Jeremiah 1:1–2:3
29	Sa	26	Maṭṭot, Masʿe	Num. 30:2–36:13	Jeremiah 2:4–28 Jeremiah 3:4 *Jeremiah 2:4–28* *Jeremiah 4:1–2*

Italics are for Sephardi Minhag.

2000, Aug. 2 – Aug. 31]   AV (30 DAYS)   [5760

Civil Date	Day of the Week	Jewish Date	SABBATHS, FESTIVALS, FASTS	PENTATEUCHAL READING	PROPHETICAL READING
Aug. 2	W	Av 1	New Moon	Num. 28:1–15	
5	Sa	4	Devarim (Shabbat Ḥazon)	Deut. 1:1–3:22	Isaiah 1:1–27
10	Th	9	Fast of 9th of Av	Morning: Deut. 4:25–40 Afternoon: Exod. 32:11–14 Exod. 34:1–10	(Lamentations is read the night before) Jeremiah 8:13–9:23 (morning) Isaiah 55:6–56:8 (afternoon)
12	Sa	11	Wa-ethannan (Shabbat Naḥamu)	Deut. 3:23–7:11	Isaiah 40:1–26
19	Sa	18	'Eḳev	Deut. 7:12–11:25	Isaiah 49:14–51:3
26	Sa	25	Re'eh	Deut. 11:26–16:17	Isaiah 54:11–55:5
31	Th	30	New Moon, first day	Num. 28:1–15	

Italics are for Sephardi Minhag.

2000, Sept. 1 – Sept. 29]   ELUL (29 DAYS)   [5760

Civil Date	Day of the Week	Jewish Date	SABBATHS, FESTIVALS, FASTS	PENTATEUCHAL READING	PROPHETICAL READING
Sept. 1	F	Elul 1	New Moon, second day	Num. 28:1–15	
2	Sa	2	Shofeṭim	Deut. 16:18–21:9	Isaiah 51:12–52:12
9	Sa	9	Ki teẕe'	Deut. 21:10–25:19	Isaiah 54:1–10
16	Sa	16	Ki tavo'	Deut. 26:1–29:8	Isaiah 60:1–22
23	Sa	23	Niẕẕavim, Wa-yelekh	Deut. 29:9–30:20	Isaiah 61:10–63:9

Italics are for
Sephardi Minhag.

2000, Sept. 30–Oct. 29]   TISHRI (30 DAYS)   [5761

Civil Date	Day of the Week	Jewish Date	SABBATHS, FESTIVALS, FASTS	PENTATEUCHAL READING	PROPHETICAL READING
Sept. 30	Sa	Tishri 1	Rosh Ha-shanah, first day	Gen. 21:1–34 Num. 29:1–6	I Samuel 1:1–2:10
Oct. 1	S	2	Rosh Ha-shanah, second day	Gen. 22:1–24 Num. 29:1–6	Jeremiah 31:2–20
2	M	3	Fast of Gedaliah	Exod. 32:11–14 Exod. 34:1–10 (morning and afternoon)	Isaiah 55:6–56:8 (afternoon only)
7	Sa	8	Ha'azinu (Shabbat Shuvah)	Deut. 32:1–52	Hosea 14:2–10 Micah 7:18–20 Joel 2:15–27 *Hosea 14:2–10* *Micah 7:18–20*
9	M	10	Yom Kippur	Morning: Levit. 16:1–34 Num. 29:7–11 Afternoon: Levit. 18:1–30	Isaiah 57:14–58:14 Jonah: 1:1–4:11 Micah 7:18–20
14	Sa	15	Sukkot, first day	Levit. 22:26–23:44 Num. 29:12–16	Zechariah 14:1–21
15	S	16	Sukkot, second day	Levit. 22:26–23:44 Num. 29:12–16	I Kings 8:2–21
16–19	M–Th	17–20	Ḥol Ha-mo'ed	M: Num. 29:17–25 T: Num. 29:20–28 W: Num. 29:23–31 Th: Num. 29:26–34	
20	F	21	Hosha'na' Rabbah	Num. 29:26–34	
21	Sa	22	Shemini 'Azeret	Deut. 14:22–16:17 Num. 29:35–30:1	I Kings 8:54–66
22	S	23	Simḥat Torah	Deut. 33:1–34:12 Gen. 1:1–2:3 Num. 29:35–30:1	Joshua 1:1–18 *Joshua 1:1–9*
28	Sa	29	Be-re'shit	Gen. 1:1–6:8	I Samuel 20:18–42
29	S	30	New Moon, first day	Num. 28:1–15	

Italics are for
Sephardi Minhag.

2000, Oct. 30–Nov. 27]   ḤESHWAN (29 DAYS)   [5761

Civil Date	Day of the Week	Jewish Date	SABBATHS, FESTIVALS, FASTS	PENTATEUCHAL READING	PROPHETICAL READING
Oct. 30	M	Ḥeshwan 1	New Moon, second day	Num. 28:1–15	
Nov. 4	Sa	6	Noaḥ	Gen. 6:9–11:32	Isaiah 54:1–55:5 *Isaiah 54:1–10*
11	Sa	13	Lekh lekha	Gen. 12:1–17:27	Isaiah 40:27–41:16
18	Sa	20	Wa-yera'	Gen. 18:1–22:24	II Kings 4:1–37 *II Kings 4:1–23*
25	Sa	27	Ḥayye Sarah	Gen. 23:1–25:18	I Kings 1:1–31

Italics are for
Sephardi Minhag.

2000, Nov. 28 – Dec. 26]　　KISLEW (29 DAYS)　　[5761

Civil Date	Day of the Week	Jewish Date	SABBATHS, FESTIVALS, FASTS	PENTATEUCHAL READING	PROPHETICAL READING
Nov. 28	T	Kislew 1	New Moon	Num. 28:1–15	
Dec. 2	Sa	5	Toledot	Gen. 25:19–28:9	Malachi 1:1–2:7
9	Sa	12	Wa-yeze'	Gen. 28:10–32:3	Hosea 12:13–14:10 *Hosea 11:7–12:12*
16	Sa	19	Wa-yishlaḥ	Gen. 32:4–36:43	Hosea 11:7–12:12 *Obadiah 1:1–21*
22	F	25	Hanukkah, first day	Num. 7:1–17	
23	Sa	26	Wa-yeshev; Hanukkah, second day	Gen. 37:1–40:23 Num. 7:18–23	Zechariah 2:14–4:7
24–26	S–T	27–29	Hanukkah, third to fifth days	S Num. 7:24–35 M Num. 7:30–41 T Num. 7:36–47	

*Italics are for
Sephardi Minhag.*

2000, Dec. 27–Jan. 24, 2001] ṬEVET (29 DAYS) [5761

Civil Date	Day of the Week	Jewish Date	SABBATHS, FESTIVALS, FASTS	PENTATEUCHAL READING	PROPHETICAL READING
Dec. 27	W	Ṭevet 1	New Moon; Ḥanukkah, sixth day	Num. 28:1–15 Num. 7:42–47	
28	Th	2	Ḥanukkah, seventh day	Num. 7:48–53	
29	F	3	Ḥanukkah, eighth day	Num. 7:54–8:4	
30	Sa	4	Mi-ḳeẓ	Gen. 41:1–44:17	I Kings 3:15–4:1
2001 Jan. 5	F	10	Fast of 10th of Ṭevet	Exod. 32:11–14 Exod. 34:1–10 (morning and afternoon)	Isaiah 55:6–56:8 (afternoon only)
6	Sa	11	Wa-yiggash	Gen. 44:18–47:27	Ezekiel 37:15–28
13	Sa	18	Wa-yeḥi	Gen. 47:28–50:26	I Kings 2:1–12
20	Sa	25	Shemot	Exod. 1:1–6:1	Isaiah 27:6–28:13 Isaiah 29:22–23 *Jeremiah 1:1–2:3*

Italics are for Sephardi Minhag.

2001, Jan. 25 – Feb. 23]   SHEVAṬ (30 DAYS)   [5761

Civil Date	Day of the Week	Jewish Date	SABBATHS, FESTIVALS, FASTS	PENTATEUCHAL READING	PROPHETICAL READING
Jan. 25	Th	Shevaṭ 1	New Moon	Num. 28: 1–15	
27	Sa	3	Wa-'era'	Exod. 6:2–9:35	Ezekiel 28:25–29:21
Feb. 3	Sa	10	Bo'	Exod. 10:1–13:16	Jeremiah 46:13–28
8	Th	15	Ḥamishah 'asar Bi-Shevaṭ		
10	Sa	17	Be-shallaḥ (Shabbat Shirah)	Exod. 13:17–17:16	Judges 4:4–5:31 *Judges 5:1–31*
17	Sa	24	Yitro	Exod. 18:1–20:23	Isaiah 6:1–7:6; 9:5–6 *Isaiah 6:1–13*
23	F	30	New Moon, first day	Num. 28:1–15	

Italics are for Sephardi Minhag.

2001, Feb. 24–Mar. 24]   ADAR (29 DAYS)   [5761

Civil Date	Day of the Week	Jewish Date	SABBATHS, FESTIVALS, FASTS	PENTATEUCHAL READING	PROPHETICAL READING
Feb. 24	Sa	Adar 1	Mishpaṭim, New Moon, second day (Shabbat Sheḳalim)	Exod. 21:1–24:18 Num. 28:9–15 Exod. 30:11–16	II Kings 12:1–17 *II Kings 11:17–12:17*
Mar. 3	Sa	8	Terumah (Shabbat Zakhor)	Exod. 25:1–27:19 Deut. 25:17–19	I Samuel 15:2–34 *I Samuel 15:1–34*
8	Th	13	Fast of Esther	Exod. 32:11–14 Exod. 34:1–10 (morning and afternoon)	Isaiah 55:6–56:8 (afternoon only)
9	F	14	Purim	Exod. 17:8–16	Book of Esther (night before and in the morning)
10	Sa	15	Teẓawweh Shùshan Purim	Exod. 27:20–30:10	Ezekiel 43:10–27
17	Sa	22	Ki tissa' (Shabbat Parah)	Exod. 30:11–34:35 Num. 19:1–22	Ezekiel 36:16–38 *Ezekiel 36:16–36*
24	Sa	29	Wa-yaḳhel-Peḳude (Shabbat Ha-ḥodesh)	Exod. 35:1–40:38 Exod. 12:1–20	Ezekiel 45:16–46:18 *Ezekiel 45:18–46:15*

Italics are for Sephardi Minhag.

2001, Mar. 25–Apr. 23]   NISSAN (30 DAYS)   [5761

Civil Date	Day of the Week	Jewish Date	SABBATHS, FESTIVALS, FASTS	PENTATEUCHAL READING	PROPHETICAL READING
Mar. 25	S	Nissan 1	New Moon	Num. 28:1–15	
31	Sa	7	Wa-yiḳra'	Levit. 1:1–5:26	Isaiah 43:21–44:24
Apr. 5	Th	12	Fast of Firstborn		
7	Sa	14	Ẓaw (Shabbat Ha-gadol)	Levit. 6:1–8:36	Malachi 3:4–24
8	S	15	Passover, first day	Exod. 12:21–51 Num. 28:16–25	Joshua 5:2–6:1,27
9	M	16	Passover, second day	Levit. 22:26–23:44 Num. 28:16–25	II Kings 23:1–9, 21–25
10	T	17	Ḥol Ha–mo 'ed, first day	Exod. 13:1–16 Num. 28:19–25	
11	W	18	Ḥol Ha–mo'ed second day	Exod. 22:24–23:19, Num. 28:19–25	
12	Th	19	Ḥol Ha–mo'ed, third day	Exod. 34:1–26 Num. 28:19–25	
13	F	20	Ḥol Ha–mo'ed, fourth day	Num. 9:1–14 Num. 28:19–25	
14	Sa	21	Passover, seventh day	Exod. 13:17–15:26 Num. 28:19–25	II Samuel 22:1–51
15	S	22	Passover, eighth day	Deut. 15:19–16:17 Num. 28:19–25	Isaiah 10:32–12:6
20	F	27*	Holocaust Memorial Day		
21	Sa	28	Shemini	Levit. 9:1–11:47	II Samuel 6:1–7:17 *II Samuel 6:1–19*
23	M	30	New Moon, first day	Num. 28:1–15	

*Observed April 26, to avoid conflict with the Sabbath.

Italics are for Sephardi Minhag.

2001, Apr. 24 – May 22]   IYAR (29 DAYS)   [5761

Civil Date	Day of the Week	Jewish Date	SABBATHS, FESTIVALS, FASTS	PENTATEUCHAL READING	PROPHETICAL READING
Apr. 24	T	Iyar 1	New Moon, second day	Num. 28:1–15	
28	Sa	5**	Tazria', Mezora'	Levit. 12:1–15:33	II Kings 7:3–20
May 5	Sa	12	Aḥare mot, Ḳedoshim	Levit.16:1–20:27	Amos 9:7–15 *Ezekiel 20:2–20*
11	F	18	Lag Ba-ʿomer		
12	Sa	19	Emor	Levit. 21:1–24:23	Ezekiel 44:15–31
19	Sa	26	Be-har, Be-ḥuḳḳotai	Levit. 25:1–27:34	Jeremiah 16:19–17:14
21	M	28	Jerusalem Day		

** Also Israel Independence Day, observed April 26 to avoid conflict with the Sabbath.

Italics are for Sephardi Minhag.

2001 May 23 – Jun. 21]   SIWAN (30 DAYS)   [5761

Civil Date	Day of the Week	Jewish Date	SABBATHS, FESTIVALS, FASTS	PENTATEUCHAL READING	PROPHETICAL READING
May 23	W	Siwan 1	New Moon	Num. 28:1–15	
26	Sa	4	Be-midbar	Num. 1:1–4:20	Hosea 2:1–22
28	M	6	Shavu'ot, first day	Exod. 19:1–20:23 Num. 28:26–31	Ezekiel 1:1–28; 3:12
29	T	7	Shavu'ot, second day	Deut. 15:19–16:17 Num. 28:26–31	Habbakuk 3:1–19 *Habbakuk 2:20–3:19*
June 2	Sa	11	Naso'	Num. 4:21–7:89	Judges 13:2–25
9	Sa	18	Be-ha'alotekha	Num. 8:1–12:16	Zechariah 2:14–4:7
16	Sa	25	Shelaḥ lekha	Num. 13:1–15:41	Joshua 2:1–24
21	Th	30	New Moon, first day	Num. 28:1–15	

Italics are for Sephardi Minhag.

Civil Date	Day of the Week	Jewish Date	SABBATHS, FESTIVALS, FASTS	PENTATEUCHAL READING	PROPHETICAL READING
June 22	F	Tammuz 1	New Moon, second day	Num. 28:1–15	
23	Sa	2	Ḳoraḥ	Num. 16:1–18:32	I Samuel 11:14–12:22
30	Sa	9	Ḥuḳḳat	Num. 19:1–22:1	Judges 11:1–33
July 7	Sa	16	Balaḳ	Num. 22:2–25:9	Micah 5:6–6:8
8	S	17	Fast of 17th of Tammuz	Exod. 32:11–14 Exod. 34:1–10 (morning and afternoon)	Isaiah 55:6–56:8 (afternoon only)
14	Sa	23	Pineḥas	Num. 25:10–30:1	Jeremiah 1:1–2:3

Italics are for Sephardi Minhag.

Civil Date	Day of the Week	Jewish Date	SABBATHS, FESTIVALS, FASTS	PENTATEUCHAL READING	PROPHETICAL READING
July 21	Sa	Av 1	Maṭṭot, Masʿe New Moon	Num. 30:2–36:13 Num. 28:9–15	Jeremiah 2:4–28; 3:4 *Jeremiah 2:4–28; 4:1–2*
28	Sa	8	Devarim (Shabbat Hazon)	Deut. 1:1–3:22	Isaiah 1:1–27
29	S	9	Fast of 9th of Av	Morning: Deut. 4:25–40 Afternoon: Exod. 32:11–14 34:1–10	(Lamentations is read the night before) Jeremiah 8:13–9:23 (morning) Isaiah 55:6–56:8 (afternoon)
Aug. 4	Sa	15	Wa-ethannan (Shabbat Naḥamu)	Deut. 3:23–7:11	Isaiah 40:1–26
11	Sa	22	ʿEḳev	Deut. 7:12–11:25	Isaiah 49:14–51:3
18	Sa	29	Re'eh	Deut. 11:26–16:17	I Samuel 20:18–42
19	S	30	New Moon, first day	Num. 28:1–15	

Italics are for Sephardi Minhag.

2001, Aug. 20–Sept. 17]   ELUL (29 DAYS)   [5761

Civil Date	Day of the Week	Jewish Date	SABBATHS, FESTIVALS, FASTS	PENTATEUCHAL READING	PROPHETICAL READING
Aug 20	M	Elul 1	New Moon, second day	Num. 28:1–15	
25	Sa	6	Shofeṭim	Deut. 16:18–21:9	Isaiah 51:12–52:12
Sept 1	Sa	13	Ki Teze'	Deut. 21:10–25:19	Isaiah 54:1–55:5
8	Sa	20	Ki Tavo'	Deut. 26:1–29:8	Isaiah 60:1–22
15	Sa	27	Niẓẓavim	Deut. 29:9–30:20	Isaiah 61:10–63:9

Italics are for
Sephardi Minhag.

2001, Sept. 18–Oct. 17]   TISHRI (30 DAYS)   [5762

Civil Date	Day of the Week	Jewish Date	SABBATHS, FESTIVALS, FASTS	PENTATEUCHAL READING	PROPHETICAL READING
Sept. 18	T	Tishri 1	Rosh Ha-shanah, first day	Gen. 21:1–34 Num. 29:1–6	1 Sam. 1:1–2:10
19	W	2	Rosh Ha-shanah second day	Gen. 22:1–24 Num. 29:1–6	Jeremiah 3:2–20
20	Th	3	Fast of Gedaliah	Exod. 32:11–14 34:1–10 (morning & afternoon)	Isaiah 55:6–56:8 (afternoon only)
22	Sa	5	Wa-yelekh (Shabbat Shuvah)	Deut. 31:1–30	Hosea 14:2–10 Micah 7:18–20 Joel 2:15–27 *Hosea 14:2–10* *Micah 7:18–20*
27	Th	10	Yom Kippur	Morning: Levit. 16:1–34 Num. 29:7–11 Afternoon: Levit. 18:1–30	Isaiah 57:14–58:14 Jonah 1:1–4:11 Micah 7:18–20
29	Sa	12	Ha'azinu	Deut. 32:1–52	II Samuel 22:1–51
Oct 2	T	15	Sukkot, first day	Levit. 22:26–23:44 Num. 29:12–16	Zechariah 14:1–21
3	W	16	Sukkot, second day	Levit. 22:26–23:44 Num. 29:12–16	I Kings 8:2–21
4–7	Th–S	17–20	Ḥol Ha-mo'ed	Th Num. 29:17–25 F Num. 29: 20–28 Sa Exod. 33:12–34:26, Num. 29:26–34 S Num. 29:26–34	Ezekiel 38:18–39:16
8	M	21	Hosha'na' Rabbah	Num. 29:26–34	
9	T	22	Shemini 'Aẓeret	Deut. 14:22–16:17 Num. 29:35–30:1	I Kings 8:54–66
10	W	23	Simḥat Torah	Deut. 33:1–34:12 Gen. 1:1–2:3 Num. 29:35–30:1	Joshua 1:1–18 *Joshua 1:1–9*
13	Sa	26	Be-re'shit	Gen. 1:1–6:8	Isaiah 42:5–43:10 *Isaiah 42:5–21*
17	W	30	New Moon first day	Num. 28:1–15	

Italics are for
Sephardi Minhag.

2001, Oct. 18 – Nov. 15]   ḤESHWAN (29 DAYS)   [5762

Civil Date	Day of the Week	Jewish Date	SABBATHS, FESTIVALS, FASTS	PENTATEUCHAL READING	PROPHETICAL READING
Oct. 18	Th	Ḥeshwan 1	New Moon, second day	Num. 28:1–15	
20	Sa	3	Noaḥ	Gen. 6:9–11:32	Isaiah 54:1–55:5 *Isaiah 54:1–10*
27	Sa	10	Lekh lekha	Gen. 12:1–17:27	Isaiah 40:27–41:16
Nov. 3	Sa	17	Wa-yera'	Gen. 18:1–22:24	II Kings 4:1–37 *II Kings 4:1–23*
10	Sa	24	Ḥayye Sarah	Gen. 23:1–25:18	I Kings 1:1–31

Italics are for Sephardi Minhag.

2001, Nov. 16–Dec. 15]   KISLEW (30 DAYS)   [5762

Civil Date	Day of the Week	Jewish Date	SABBATHS, FESTIVALS, FASTS	PENTATEUCHAL READING	PROPHETICAL READING
Nov. 16	F	Kislew 1	New Moon	Num. 28:1–15	
17	Sa	2	Toledot	Gen. 25:19–28:9	Malachi 1:1–2:7
24	Sa	9	Wa-yeze'	Gen. 28:10–32:3	Hosea 12:13–14:10 *Hosea 11:7–12:12*
Dec. 1	Sa	16	Wa-yishlah	Gen. 32:4–36:43	Hosea 11:7–12:12 *Obadiah 1:1–21*
8	Sa	23	Wa-yeshev	Gen. 37:1–40:23	Amos 2:6–3:8
10–14	M–F	25–29	Hanukkah, first to fifth days	M Num. 7:1–17 T Num. 7:18–29 W Num. 7:24–35 Th Num. 7:30–41 F Num. 7:36–47	
15	Sa	30	Mikez; New Moon, first day; Hanukkah, sixth day	Gen. 41:1–44:17 Num. 28:9–15 Num. 7:42–47	Zechariah 2:14–4:7 *Zechariah 2:14–4:7* *Isaiah 66:1, 24* *Isaiah 20:18,42*

*Italics are for
Sephardi Minhag.*

2001, Dec. 16–Jan. 13, 2002]   ṬEVET (29 DAYS)   [5762

Civil Date	Day of the Week	Jewish Date	SABBATHS, FESTIVALS, FASTS	PENTATEUCHAL READING	PROPHETICAL READING
Dec. 16	S	Ṭevet 1	New Moon, second day; Ḥanukkah, seventh day	Num. 28:1–15 Num. 7:48–53	
17	M	2	Ḥanukkah, eighth day	Num. 7:54–8:4	
22	Sa	7	Wa-yiggash	Gen. 44:18–47:27	Ezekiel 37:15–28
25	T	10	Fast of 10th of Ṭevet	Exod. 32:11–14; 34:1–10 (morning and afternoon)	Isaiah 55:6–56:8 (afternoon only)
29	Sa	14	Wa-yeḥi	Gen. 47:28–50:26	I Kings 2:1–12
2002 Jan. 5	Sa	21	Shemot	Exod. 1:1–6:1	Isaiah 27:6–28:13; 29:22–23 *Jeremiah 1:1–2:3*
12	Sa	28	Wa-’era’	Exod. 6:2–9:35	Ezekiel 28:25–29:21

*Italics are for
Sephardi Minhag.*

Index

Abadi, Moussa, 312–13
Abadi, Odette, 312–13
Abargil, Linor, 482
Abd Rabbo, Yasir, 459
Abdullah II, King, 189, 192, 199, 203, 232, 305, 319, 452, 467, 468
Abeles, Peter, 415
Abella, Irving, 278, 287
Abenhaim, Lucien, 287
Abraham Fund, 512
Abramovici, Charlotte, 103*n*
Abramovici, Jean, 103*n*
Abrams, Elliot, 209, 210
Abrams, Jeanne, 10*n*
Abrams, Stanley, 103*n*
Abramson, Glenda, 298
Academy for Jewish Religion, 538
Acheson, Dean, 62
Ackerman, Walter, 78, 93, 94
Adamkus, Valdas, 401
Adler, Cyrus, 3, 5, 6, 7, 8, 10, 11, 15, 16, 17, 25, 26, 38
Adler, Elkan, 24
Adler, Rodney, 415
Adler, Taffy, 426
Afn Shvel, 579
Agbrallah, Abdallah, 457
Agenda: Jewish Education, 579
Agronsky, Martin, 587
Agudath Israel of America, 175, 178, 181, 223, 224, 229, 526
Agudath Israel World Organization, 317, 527
Aharoni, Zvi, 300
Ain, Steve, 277
Aish Hatorah, 557
Akenson, Donald Harman, 286
Akron Jewish News, 583
Ala, Abu, 453

Albert Einstein College of Medicine, 546
Albright, Madeleine, 202, 203, 204, 206, 207, 235, 381, 453, 456, 461
ALEPH, 527
Algemeiner Journal, 579
Alhadeff, Vic, 413
Allan, Jani, 419
Almaliah, Shimon, 465
Al-Marayati, Salam, 170, 171, 235
Alper, Howard, 287
Alpha Epsilon Pi Fraternity, 549
Altmann, Manfred, 302
Altschuler, David, 240, 241
Altschuler, Mordechai, 138*n*
Alyagon, Oded, 473
Am Kolel Judaic Resource Center, 527
Amaudruz, Gaston-Armand, 335
AMC Cancer Research Center, 551
Amcha for Tsedakah, 551
Amedi, Avner, 477
America-Israel Cultural Foundation, 512
America-Israel Friendship League, 512
American Academy for Jewish Research, 504
American Associates, Ben-Gurion University of the Negev, 512
American Association of Jews from the Former USSR, 549
American Association of Rabbis, 527
American Committee for Shaare Zedek Jerusalem Medical Center, 512
American Committee for Shenkar College in Israel, 512
American Committee for the Beer-Sheva Foundation, 513
American Committee for the Weizmann Institute of Science, 513
American Conference of Cantors, 534
American Council for Judaism, 48–49, 499

American Federation of Jews from Central Europe, 549
American Friends of Alyn Hospital, 513
American Friends of Assaf Harofeh Medical Center, 513
American Friends of Bar-Ilan University, 513
American Friends of Beth Hatefutsoth, 513
American Friends of Herzog Hospital/ Ezrath Nashim, 513
American Friends of Likud, 514
American Friends of Neve Shalom/Wahat Al-Salam, 514
American Friends of Rabin Medical Center, 514
American Friends of Rambam Medical Center, 514
American Friends of Tel Aviv University, 514
American Friends of the Tel Aviv Museum of Art, 515
American Friends of the Alliance Israélite Universelle, 524
American Friends of the Hebrew University, 514
American Friends of the Israel Museum, 514
American Friends of the Israel Philharmonic Orchestra, 514
American Friends of the Open University of Israel, 515
American Friends of the Shalom Hartman Institute, 515
American Gathering of Holocaust Survivors, 185, 504
American Guild of Judaic Art, 504
American Israel Public Affairs Committee (AIPAC), 157, 168, 198, 232, 233, 234, 237, 515
American Israelite, 583
American Jewish Press Association, 504
American Jewish Archives Journal, 583
American Jewish Committee, 17–21, 23, 27, 28, 35, 48, 49, 51, 52, 53, 55, 56, 59, 60, 62, 65, 67–68, 75, 76, 88, 155, 159, 165, 166, 170, 171, 174, 180, 181, 182, 184, 211, 214, 231, 347, 351, 372, 373, 377, 386, 392, 393, 406, 407, 499

American Jewish Conference on Soviet Jewry, 88
American Jewish Conference, 47, 48
American Jewish Congress, 152, 166, 172, 174, 176, 181, 182, 500
American Jewish Correctional Chaplains Association, 551
American Jewish Historical Society, 4, 63n, 504
American Jewish History, 577
American Jewish Joint Distribution Committee (JDC), 27, 159, 239, 293, 386, 392, 395, 403, 524
American Jewish League for Israel, 515
American Jewish Periodical Center, 540
American Jewish Philanthropic Fund, 524
American Jewish Public Relations Society, 556
American Jewish Society for Service, 551
American Jewish Times Outlook, 583
American Jewish World Service, 159, 216, 525
American Jewish World, 578
American Jewish Year Book, 3–102, 579
American ORT, 525
American Physicians Fellowship for Medicine in Israel, 515
American Rabbi, 574
American Red Magen David for Israel, 516
American Sephardi Federation, 504
American Society for Jewish Music, 505
American Society for Technion-Israel Institute of Technology, 516
American Society for the Protection of Nature in Israel, 516
American Society for Yad Vashem, 516
American Society of the University of Haifa, 516
American Students to Activate Pride, 527
American Veterans of Israel, 549
American Zionist Movement, 516
American-Israel Environmental Council, 515
American-Israeli Lighthouse, 515
Americans for a Safe Israel, 236, 516
Americans for Peace Now, 157, 230, 517
Amir, Yigal, 460, 479
Amit, 517
Amit, 579

Ampal-American Israel Corporation, 517
Amsellem, Moise, 277
Ancell, Nathan S., 587
Anderman, Benjamin, 103n
Angel, Marc, 86
Annan, Kofi, 161, 197
Anpilov, Viktor, 397
Anti-Defamation League (ADL), 52, 150, 155, 162, 164, 165, 166, 167, 169, 171, 177, 181, 216, 372, 374, 383, 400, 500
Antonescu, Ion, 391
Anzel, Erez, 287
Apple, Raymond, 414
Arad, Uzi, 191, 200
Arafat, Suha, 153, 236, 237
Arafat, Yasir, 153, 174, 175, 189, 190, 193, 194, 195, 196, 197, 199, 200, 202, 203, 205, 236, 268, 306, 318, 418, 451, 452, 453, 455, 456, 458, 459
Arens, Moshe, 428, 429, 441
Ariel, Meir, 483
Arizona Jewish Post, 574
Aronson, David, 415
ARZA/World Union, North America, 229, 517
Ashcroft, John, 179
Askénazi, Léon, 316
Asmal, Kadar, 425
Assad, Bashar al-, 190, 454
Assad, Hafez al-, 189, 190, 191, 192, 199, 200, 203, 204, 454, 461, 462, 463
Association for Jewish Studies, 527
Association for Modern Orthodox Day Schools in North America, 226
Association for the Social Scientific Study of Jewry, 527
Association of Jewish Aging Services, 551
Association of Jewish Book Publishers, 505
Association of Jewish Center Professionals, 551
Association of Jewish Community Organization Personnel, 551
Association of Jewish Community Relations Workers, 500
Association of Jewish Family and Children's Agencies, 552
Association of Jewish Libraries, 505
Association of Orthodox Jewish Scientists, 528

Association of Yugoslav Jews in the United States, 549
Attias, Jean-Christophe, 316
Auerbach, Jerold S., 48n
Aufbau, 579
Australia/Israel & Jewish Affairs Council (AIJAC), 406, 407, 412, 413
Avi Chai Foundation, 212
Aviv, Diana, 155, 156
Avner, Uri, 132n
Avotaynu, 578
Axworthy, Lloyd, 268
Azeri, Yigal, 360
Azrieli, David, 287
Azure, 575

Bachi, Roberto, 105n
Baeck, Leo, 353
Baggio, Roberto, 318
Bailey, Ann, 287
Bakshi-Doron, Eliyahu, 472
Balinsky, Clara, 286
Baltimore Hebrew University, 538
Baltimore Institute for Jewish Communal Service, 538
Baltimore Jewish Times, 577
Band, Arnold J., 76, 78, 87
Bandel, Ehud, 472
Baneshik, Percy, 426
Barak, Aharon, 474, 481
Barak, Ehud, 153, 162, 190, 192, 197, 199–205, 230, 231, 232, 233, 236, 237, 270, 290, 306, 318, 339, 340, 388, 398, 407, 408, 418, 427–471, 473, 479, 482
Barak, Navah, 439
Baraka, Mohammed, 445
Baram, Uzi, 447, 455
Baranovski, Dmitri Matti, 270
Bardossy, Laszlo, 383
Barer, Robert, 300
Barford, Wanda, 301
Barkashov, Aleksandr, 399
Barnea, Noam, 464
Baron, Alexander, 302
Baron, Salo W., 47, 68–69
Barr, Roseanne, 209
Bart, Lionel, 302
Bar-Zohar, Michael, 374
Basayev, Shamil 397

Bassan, Esther, 103n
Bassat, Nina, 411, 413
Battersby, John, 418
Bauer, Gary, 152
Bauer, Gerd, 349
Bauer, Julien, 286
Baum, David, 302
Baum, Phil, 162
Baum, Shlomo, 482
Baumgartner, Michael, 274
Baumhorn, Lipot, 383, 385
Bayme, Steven, 214
Beaudoin, Louis, 270
Bebe, Pauline, 316
Beckman, Morris, 300
Beerman, Leonard, 171
Begin, Benny, 433, 434, 435, 438, 441, 443
Begin, Menachem, 98, 433, 481
Beilin, Yossi, 269, 300, 367, 433, 441, 447, 456, 464
Beinart, Peter, 212
Beinish, Dorit, 479
Beit-Hallahmi, Benjamin, 132n
Belin, David W., 587
Belling, Suzanna, 425
Bellon, Loleh, 316
Bellow, Corrine, 302
Beloff, Max Lord, 301
Ben Ali, Zine El Abidine, 305
Ben Noui, Omar, 342
Ben-Ami, Shlomo, 430, 441, 445, 447, 457, 458, 474
Benatoff, Cobi, 328
Ben-Chorin, Shalom, 362, 363
Ben-David, Joseph, 279
Ben-David, Lenny, 193
Bendheim, Jack, 232, 233
Ben-Eliezer, Binyamin, 447
Ben-Gal, Avigdor, 481
Ben-Gurion, David, 61, 68, 390
Ben-Hur, Oded, 401
Benigni, Roberto, 326
Ben-Itto, Hadassa, 382
Benizri, Shlomo, 402, 447, 471
Benjamin N. Cardozo School of Law, 547
Bennett, John, 410
Benotto, Mary Lou, 279
Bensimon, Doris, 136n
Bensoussan, David, 284, 286

Ben-Tsur, Eitan, 158
Berclaz, René-Louis, 335
Berezovsky, Boris, 402, 403
Berger, Graenum, 588
Berger, Yossi, 414
Berggruen, Heinz, 362
Bergier, Jean-François, 332
Berkowitz, Henry, 37
Berlin, Charles, 78
Berman, Saul, 225, 226
Bernard Revel Graduate School, 547
Bernard, Paul, 314
Bernstein, David, 413
Bernstein, Edgar, 72, 73
Bernstein, Herman, 25, 64
Bernstein, Lionel, 425
Bernstein, Zalman C., 588
Berrin, Shani, 297
Betar Zionist Youth Organization, 517
Bethlehem, Marlene, 416, 417, 421
Biden, Joseph, 155
Bingham, Theodore A., 22
Bin-Laden, Osama, 154
Birnbaum, David, 287
Bishara, Azmi, 433, 438, 442, 445
Bitton-Jackson, Livia, 300
Blacker, Harry, 302
Blair, Tony, 289, 290, 429
Blank, Victor, 301
Blau, Joseph L., 64
Blaustein, Jacob, 61, 84
Blech, Harry, 302
Bleich, Yaacov, 402
Blet, Pierre, 173
Bloch, Rolf, 336
Bloch-Bauer, Ferdinand, 370
Blocher, Christoph, 329, 333, 334, 335
Block, Richard, 356
Bloomfield, Sara, 217
Blumenthal, Michael, 360, 361, 362, 363
Blumer, Marilyn, 287
B'nei Akiva, 522
B'nai B'rith, 173, 181, 374, 391, 552
B'nai Brith Canada, 279, 282, 557
B'nai B'rith International Jewish Monthly, 575
B'nai B'rith Klutznick National Jewish Museum, 505
B'nai B'rith Youth Organization, 528

Bnai Zion, 549
Bober, Robert, 316
Bogue, Donald J., 66
Boteach, Shmuel, 209, 297
Bouchard, Gerard, 284
Bouchard, Lucien, 276
Bourque, Pierre, 276
Bousquet, René, 307
Bouteflika, Abd al-Aziz, 200, 453
Boys Town Jerusalem Foundation of America, 517
Braham, Mark, 300
Bramson Ort College, 539
Brandeis University National Women's Committee, 556
Brandeis University, 539
Brandeis-Bardin Institute, 539
Brandt, Henry, 352
Brauman, Ron, 285, 315
Bräutigam, Otto, 344
Brenner, Michael, 363
Brett, Lily, 414
Brickner, Barnett, 66
Bridges, 584
Brith Abraham, 550
Brith Sholom, 550
Brivati, Brian, 300
Brodbar, Jay, 275
Bronfman, Charles R., 210, 212, 239, 240, 241, 277
Bronfman, Edgar, 186, 215, 330
Bronfman, Roman, 442, 449
Brooks, Matthew, 151
Brotman, Shari L., 127*n*
Brovender, Chaim, 297
Brown, David, 286
Brown, Michael, 286
Brownback, Sam, 182
Brozik, Karl, 184
Bruk, Shirley, 140*n*, 425
Brumlik, Micha, 346
Brunner, Alois, 310
Buber, Martin, 84, 363
Bubis, Ignatz, 345, 346, 347, 351, 354
Buchanan, Patrick, 151, 152
Buettner, Thomas, 103*n*
Buffalo Jewish Review, 579
Bulawko, Henry, 316
Burdi, George, 271

Burg, Avraham, 447, 453, 482
Burg, Yosef, 482
Burke, Allan, 302
Busch, Isidor, 5
Bush, George W., 151, 152, 179
Bush, Jeb, 178
Bushinsky, Aviv, 194
Buzek, Jerzy, 388

Cahan, Abraham, 36
Call, 579
Callahan, Sonny, 160
Camera-Committee for Accuracy in Middle East Reporting in America, 517
Campbell, Graeme, 410
Campbell, Menzies, 290
Canadian Friends of Cali & Amal, 558
Canadian Friends of the Hebrew University of Jerusalem, 558
Canadian Jewish Congress (CJC), 272, 273, 280, 558
Canadian Jewish Herald, 585
Canadian Jewish News, 586
Canadian Jewish Outlook, 586
Canadian Young Judaea, 558
Canadian Zionist Federation, 559
Cantors Assembly, 528
Capital Communiqué, 575
Caplan, David, 267
Caplan, Elinor, 267
Cardin, Benjamin, 179
Carey, George, 290
Carmi, Gad, 476
Carol II, King, 391
Carr, Judy Feld, 286
Carville, James, 199, 429
Cassidy, Edward Cardinal, 172, 414, 324, 325
Cassim, Layla, 422
Castan, Ron, 415
Castro, Fidel, 271
CCAR Journal, 579
Ceauşescu, Nicolae, 390
Center for Christian-Jewish Understanding, 528
Center for Jewish Community Studies, 500
Center for Judaic Studies, 539
Center for Middle East Peace and Development, 232

Center for Russian Jewry with Student Struggle for Soviet Jewry/SSSJ, 500
Central California Jewish Heritage, 574
Central Conference of American Rabbis (CCAR), 49, 150, 219, 278, 528
Central Yiddish Culture Organization (CYCO), 505
Chabad-Lubavitch, 226–27, 283, 314, 323, 384, 403
Chadwick, James, 271
Chambers, Gretta, 273
Charest, Jean, 284
Charleston Jewish Journal, 585
Charlotte Jewish News, 583
Charness, Susan, 287
Chaskalson, Arthur, 417, 426
Chenkin, Alvin, 92, 588
Cherne, Leo, 588
Chernin, Albert D., 89*n*
Chernomyrdin, Viktor, 398
Chicago Jewish News, 576
Chicago Jewish Star, 576
Chirac, Jacques, 303, 306, 465
Chiswick, Barry, 92
Chopra, Deepak, 209
Chrétien, Jean, 267, 268, 275
Christie, Douglas, 271
Christopher, Warren, 200, 201
Chronicle, 576
Ciampi, Carlo Azeglio, 317, 318, 328
Ciralsky, Adam, 168
Circle, 579
City of Hope National Medical Center and Beckman Research Institute, 552
Ciurinskas, Kazys, 186, 400
CLAL, 528
Clendinnen, Inge, 415
Cleveland College of Jewish Studies, 539
Cleveland Jewish News, 583
Clinton, Bill, 149, 151, 156, 159, 161, 165, 175, 178, 188, 193, 194, 195, 196, 197, 199, 200, 201, 202, 203, 204, 205, 206, 216, 232, 233, 234, 374, 427, 429, 452, 453, 458, 459, 461, 462
Clinton, Hillary Rodham, 152, 153, 201, 202, 235, 236, 388, 393
Coalition for the Advancement of Jewish Education, 528

Coalition on the Environment & Jewish Life, 500
Coats, Dan, 182
Codreanu, Corneliu Zelea, 391
Cohen, Alfred, 182
Cohen, Amnon, 475
Cohen, Frances, 137*n*
Cohen, Leah, 110*n*
Cohen, Lewis, 300
Cohen, Malcolm, 297
Cohen, Matt, 286, 288
Cohen, Moïse, 314
Cohen, Naomi W., 17*n*, 19*n*, 22*n*, 26*n*, 48, 48*n*, 52*n*, 60*n*, 62*n*
Cohen, Percy, 302
Cohen, Ran, 447
Cohen, Samuel, 588
Cohen, Steven M., 89, 92, 96, 112*n*
Cohen, William, 188
Cohen, Yitzhak, 447
Cohn-Bendit, Daniel, 304
Cole, Tim, 300
Collins, Doug, 271
Collins, Kenneth, 300
Commentary, 65, 212, 217, 579
Commission on Jewish Education, 536
Commission on Social Action and Public Policy (United Synagogue), 536
Commission on Social Action of Reform Judaism, 500
Community Review, 584
Community, 577
Conference of Presidents of Major American Jewish Organizations, 162, 169, 191, 229, 233, 238, 373, 501
Conference on Jewish Material Claims Against Germany, 69, 183, 184, 525
Conference on Jewish Social Studies, 505
Congregation Bina, 505
Congress for Jewish Culture, 505
Congress Monthly, 579
Congress of Secular Jewish Organizations, 529
Connecticut Jewish Ledger, 575
Conservative Judaism, 579
Constantinescu, Emil, 390, 391
Consultative Council of Jewish Organizations-CCJO, 501
Contemporary Jewish Record, 43

Contemporary Jewry, 584
Conversion to Judaism Resource Center, 529
Cook, Robin, 291, 294
Cooley, Thomas M., 22
Cooney, Mike, 151
Cooper, Abraham, 162
Coordinating Board of Jewish Organizations, 501
Corinaldi, Michael, 113*n*
Cornwell, John, 173, 325
Corren, Asher, 294
Cotler, Irwin, 267
Council for Jewish Education, 529
Council of Jewish Federations (CJF), 155, 210, 239
Council of Jewish Organizations in Civil Service, Inc., 501
Crombie, Tony, 302
Csurka, Istvan, 382, 383

Dadon, Kotel, 375
Dahlan, Mohammed, 194
Dais, 586
D'Alema, Massimo, 317, 318
Dalin, David, 22*n,* 83, 89, 90
Damary, Yigal, 480
D'Amato, Alfonse, 330
Damri, Musa, 476
Danby, Michael, 407
Daoud, Abu, 234
Daube, David, 588
David, Misa, 394
Davidson, Israel, 34
Davies, Lynne, 415
Davis, Dennis, 424
Davis, Gray, 163, 166, 184, 350
Dawidowicz, Lucy, 61, 72, 74, 80, 90–91, 94
Dayan, Tiki, 437
Dayan, Yael, 448
De Beer, Joop, 142*n*
De Rothschild, Alphonse, 370
De Rothschild, Batsheva, 483
De Rothschild, Éric, 313
De Rothschild, Louis, 370
De Saint Cheron, Michaël, 315
De Villiers, Philippe, 304
Deane, William, 414
Decol, René Daniel, 136*n*

Deeb, Ali Hassan, 465
Deep South Jewish Voice, 574
Degen, Michael, 361
Delisle, Esther, 284
DellaPergola, Sergio, 91, 100, 101, 104*n,* 105*n,* 107*n,* 108*n,* 110*n,* 112*n,* 114*n,* 129*n,* 132*n,* 133*n,* 135*n,* 136*n,* 137*n,* 138*n,* 141*n,* 144*n,* 214
Delmaire, Jean-Marie, 315
Demirel, Suleiman, 453
Demjanjuk, John, 187
Deri, Arye, 427, 434, 442, 445, 448, 449, 476, 477
Deroo, Delphine, 316
Detroit Jewish News, 577
Deutch, John, 168
Devins, Rita, 271
Di Yiddishe Heim, 582
Diamond, Stanley, 278
DiCastro, Sandro, 323
Dick, Moshe, 358
Dickson, Gerry, 301
Diepgen, Eberhard, 345, 347, 348, 362
Dillingham, William, 20
Dimson, Gladys, 301
Diner, Dan, 358
Dinin, Samuel, 49
Dinnerstein, Leonard, 23*n,* 33, 33*n*
Directions, 586
Discherheit, Esther, 361
Donath, Gitel, 286
D'Ormesson, Jean, 307–08
Dos Yiddishe Vort, 583
Downer, Alexander, 406, 408
Drachsler, Julius, 66
Drai, Pierre, 311
Dreifuss, Ruth, 329, 336, 337
Dreyfus, Alfred, 6
Druckman, Haim, 441
Dubb, Allie A., 140*n*
Dubbin, Sam, 179
Dubiel, Helmut, 360
Duke, David, 152
Dulberg, Moshe, 317
Dunner, Pini, 295
Duvdevani, Yehuda, 418
Dye, Nancy Schrom, 28*n*
Dzieduszycka, Malgorzata, 387
Dzurinda, Mikulas, 392

Eagleburger, Lawrence, 185
Ecker, Janet, 280–81
Eckstein, Yechiel, 174
Edah, 225, 226, 529
Edelstein, Yuli, 449
Edwards, Chet, 179
Eggeleton, Art, 270
Ehrenberg, Yizhak, 356
Ehrentrau, Dayan, 295
Einstein, Albert, 35, 40, 208
Eisen, Arnold, 100
Eisenmann, Peter, 347
Eitan, Michael, 438
Eitan, Rafael, 444
Eizenstat, Stuart, 184
El'Herfi, Salman, 418
Elaine Kaufman Cultural Center, 505
Elazar, Daniel J., 78, 79, 82, 589
Elbogen, Ismar, 46, 78
Eliezri, Elie, 386
Elkana, Yehuda, 385
Elkin, Judith Laikin, 101
Elkus, Abram I., 20
Elsässer, Jürgen, 345, 360
Emunah of America, 518
Engel, Robert, 288
Englander, David, 302
Englander, Nathan, 301
Epstein, Jerome, 221
Epstein, Seymour, 287
Eran, Oded, 459
Eslin, Jean-Claude, 314
Etter, Roger, 334
Even, Judith, 103n, 138n

Fadiman, Clifton, 589
Fagan, Cary, 286
Falwell, Jerry, 174
Farber, Bernie, 273
Farber, Roberta Rosenberg, 114n
Farhi, Morris, 301
Farrakhan, Louis, 169, 292
Fassbinder, Werner, 341
Fast, Jacob, 274
Fatchett, Derek, 290
Federated Council of Israel Institutions, 518
Federation of Jewish Men's Clubs, 529
Feinberg Graduate School, Weizmann Institute of Science, 539

Feingold, Henry, 83
Feingold, Russell, 150
Feinstein, Dianne, 150, 166
Feldbrill, Victor, 287
Feldstein, Jack, 414
Fenech, Georges, 307
Ferguson, Laurie, 407
Ferguson, Niall, 300
Festeryga, William, 280
Feuchtwanger, Lion, 363
Fichman, Niv, 285
Finchter, Yehiel Shai, 457
Fine, Morris, 51, 57, 57n, 65, 76, 78, 89
Fineberg, S. Andhil, 57
Finestein, Israel, 300
Finestone, Sheila, 267
Fini, Gianfranco, 317
Finkel, Shimon, 483
Finkelstein, Arthur, 199, 437
Finkelstein, Maxyne, 277
Finkiel, Emmanuel, 315
Finn, Ralph, 302
Firman, Bert, 302
Fischer, Bobby, 381
Fischer, Joschka, 338, 340
Fischer, Peter, 353
Fischer, Tim, 407
Fischman, Sheila, 286
Fishberg, Mollie, 302
Fishman, Sylvia Barack, 87, 95
Fitch, Ed, 287
Flatow, Alisa, 154
Flatow, Stephen, 154
Fleischer, Tzvi, 413
Fleischman, Cyrille, 316
Fogel, Semadar, 114n
Foley, Mark, 167, 195
Foltin, Richard, 182
Förberbock, Max, 359
Ford, Henry, 33
Forget, Celine, 282
Forverts, 579
Forward, 36, 153, 214, 579
Foschi, Enzo, 321
Foundation for Ethnic Understanding, 168
Foundation for Jewish Camping, 213
Foxman, Abraham, 152, 169, 170
Fradkin, Arnold, 287
Franco, Shiran, 468

Frank, Anne, 217
Frank, Leo, 23
Frankel, Glenn, 425
Frankfurter, Felix, 84
Franklin, Selwyn, 414
Free Sons of Israel, 550
Freilich, Emanuel, 302
Freitag, Henry, 282
Frejka, Tomas, 114n
Frenkel, Jacob, 469, 470
Fresco, Nadine, 316
Freund-Rosenthal, Miriam, 589
Frey, Gerhard, 343, 344
Friedenwald, Herbert, 17–19, 22, 25
Friedlander, Albert, 297
Friedman, Elyse, 286
Friedman, Murray, 89, 89n, 90
Friedman, Rosemary, 300
Friedman, Thomas L., 193
Friends of Pioneering Israel, 559
Friends of the Israel Defense Forces, 518
Frister, Roman, 300
Fritsche, Klaus-Dieter, 341
Fry, Helen, 300
Fry, Varian, 315

Gabai, Shlomo, 476
Gabriel, Joyce, 300
Gaddin, Russell, 417, 421
Gadecki, Stanislaw, 387
Gaensler, Brian, 415
Galili, Nir, 481
Galimir, Felix, 589
Galinski, Heinz, 346
Gampel, Eli Meir, 353, 354
Ganchrow, Mandell, 225, 228
Garaudy, Roger, 292
Gassman-Sherr, Rosalie, 301
Gaster, Theodor H., 43
Gaubert, Patrick, 306
Gee, Maurice, 301
Gejdenson, Samuel, 161
Gelman, Zakhar, 399
Gentile, Giovanni, 318
George, Götz, 359
Georgiou, Petro, 407
Gephardt, Richard, 170, 171, 235
Gershuni, Doli, 476
Gershuni, Uri, 476

Gerstein, Erez, 464
Gerz, Jochen, 347
Gesher Foundation, 518
Gideon, Yehoshua, 451
Gilbert, Arthur, 301
Gilboa, Eytan, 92
Gilman, Benjamin, 157, 161
Gilman, Sander L., 426
Gimzauskas, Kazys, 400
Ginsberg, Peter, 286
Ginzberg, Louis, 16, 35
Gisel, Pierre, 316
Gitai, Amos, 285
Giuliani, Rudolph, 153
Givat Haviva Educational Foundation, 518
Glanville, Brian, 300
Glatstein, Jacob, 85
Glazer, Nathan, 63–64, 75, 92, 93
Glickman, Leonard, 156
Glustron, Chana, 418
Godfrey, Paul, 287
Godfrey, Sheldon, 287
Golani, Motti, 299
Gold, Alan, 167
Gold, Bernard, 415
Gold, Nora, 286
Goldberg, Alf, 300
Goldberg, Jacqueline, 140n, 425
Goldberg, S.P., 82
Goldblatt, David, 425
Goldbloom, Sam, 415
Goldbloom, Victor, 287
Goldhar, Maxwell, 287
Goldman, Hy, 287
Goldstein, Alice, 130n, 139n
Goldstein, Cyril, 426
Goldstein, David, 287
Goldstein, Elyse, 286
Goldstein, Joshua R., 114n
Goldstein, Judith, 19n
Goldstein, Sidney, 84, 113n, 127n, 130n, 139n
Goldstone, Richard, 425
Golinkin, David, 35n
Goncz, Arpad, 382, 383
Gonen, Anat, 114
Goodman, Jerry, 73, 80
Goodman, Tamir, 224
Gorbachev, Mikhail, 396

Gordimer, Nadine, 426
Gordis, Daniel, 209
Gordon, Joseph, 58
Gore, Al, 152, 155, 179, 180, 198, 231, 241
Goren, Arthur A., 65, 65n
Gottesman, Eli, 284–85
Goujon, Anne, 142n
Gould, Milton, 589
Govrin, Yosef, 300
Graetz, Heinrich, 43
Graf, Jürgen, 334, 335
Gramm, Phil, 150
Grass, Günter, 346
Gratz College, 4, 539
Gray, Herb, 276, 421
Green, Doreen, 287
Green, Ryan, 183
Green, Shawn, 208
Greenberg, Lawrence, 288
Greenberg, Lorry, 287
Greenberg, Stanley, 199, 429, 432
Greenebaum, Gary, 171
Greenstone, Julius, 14, 37
Grieve, John, 292
Griffiths, Richard, 299
Griliches, Zvi, 590
Groner, Oscar, 75
Gross, Heinrich, 367, 368
Grossman, Jack, 287
Grossman, Lawrence, 93, 94
Gruber, Michael, 187
Gruen, George E., 80, 98
Grumberg, Jean-Claude, 315
Grunewald, Hans Isaak, 363
Grunfeld, Henry, 302
Gudelis, Antanas, 411
Guigou, Élisabeth, 307, 311
Gusinsky, Vladimir, 399, 402
Guttman, Frank, 287

Habibie, B.J., 405
Habonim-Dror North America, 518
Hadarom, 580
Hadas-Lebel, Mireille, 316
Hadassah Magazine, 580
Hadassah, The Women's Zionist Organiza-
    tion of America, 153, 236, 518
Hadassah-WIZO Organization of Canada,
    559

Hadoar, 580
Hague, William, 290
Haider, Jörg, 292, 354, 365, 366, 367, 469
Hain, Peter, 291
Hajdenberg, Henri, 305
Hakohen, Menachem, 391
Halevi, Jehuda, 43
Halikah, Miki, 480
Halpert, Marta, 372
Halter, Marek, 316
Halvorson, Ken, 282
Handlin, Mary, 46, 50, 64
Handlin, Oscar, 21, 46, 50, 64
Handy, Robert T., 38n
Hanegbi, Tsachi, 432, 441
Hanson, Pauline, 405, 410
Hanus, George, 211
Hare, David, 299
Hargov, Udi, 480
Harris, Cyril, 417, 420, 422, 423, 424, 425
Harris, David A., 155, 170, 171, 184
Harris, Mike, 267, 280
Harrisberg, Judith, 426
Harrow, Benjamin, 35
Har-Shefi, Margalit, 479
Hashomer Hatzair, 519, 559
Hass, Amira, 300
Hassan II, King, 189, 199, 277, 453, 454
Hassan, Crown Prince, 467
Hatch, Orrin, 152, 178, 181
Hatter, Maurice, 301
Hausfeld, Michael, 350, 351
Havel, Vaclav, 376, 378, 381
Hawatmeh, Naif, 453, 467
Hayo, Manfred, 349
Hayoun, Maurice-Ruben, 315
Hebrew College, 540
Hebrew Seminary of the Deaf, 540
Hebrew Theological College, 540
Hebrew Union College-Jewish Institute of
    Religion, 77, 218, 227, 540
Hebrew Watchman, 585
Hecht, Thomas, 271
Heideman, Richard D., 173, 391
Heilman, Samuel, 226
Heller, Joseph, 590
Heller, Maxmillian, 13
Hemed, Ya'akov, 450
Hendel, Zvi, 441

Henig, Monty, 302
Herberg, Will, 63
Heritage Florida Jewish News, 576
Heritage-Southwest Jewish Press, 574
Hermalin, David, 13
Hershkopf (Banki), Judith, 69–70
Herzberg, Hanna, 363
Herzog, Roman, 361
Heschel, Abraham Joshua, 70, 85
Heskes, Irene, 590
Hess, Leon, 590
Hess, Rudolf, 344
Hevesi, Alan, 349
HIAS (Hebrew Immigrant Aid Society), 39, 156, 159, 525
Hier, Marvin, 173, 325
Higham, John, 53, 70
Hill, Heather, 405
Hillel-The Foundation for Jewish Campus Life, 75, 212, 213, 529
Hilsner, Leopold, 381
Himmelfarb, Milton, 65, 66, 67, 76, 78, 89, 90
Hindlip, Lord, 370
Hirsch, Ammiel, 229
Hirsch, Emil G., 37
Histadruth Ivrith of America, 506
Hoenlein, Malcolm, 170
Hoffberger, Jerold C., 590
Holocaust Center of the United Jewish Federation of Greater Pittsburgh, 506
Holocaust Memorial Center, 506
Holocaust Memorial Resource & Education Center of Central Florida, 506
Holocaust Museum and Learning Center in Memory of Gloria Goldstein, 506
Homel, David, 286
Homolka, Walter, 355, 362
Hooker, Bernard, 301
Hoon, Geoff, 291
Hoover, Herbert, 40
Horbulin, Volodymyr, 402
Horenczyk, Gabriel, 112*n*
Horowitz, Sara, 286
Hoss, Selim al-, 204, 464
Howard, Dorothy Zalcman, 284
Howard, John, 405, 407, 414, 415
Huldai, Ron, 479
Humanistic Judaism, 577

Hummel, Craig, 423
Huntington, Samuel P., 146*n*
Hussein, King, 157, 189, 191, 200, 205, 305, 454, 467
Hussein, Saddam, 189, 198, 206, 319, 432, 467
Husseini, Faisal, 458
Hutchinson, Tim, 182
Hyamson, Moses, 34
Hyman, Joe, 302

I.A.J.E. Newsletter, 580
Icke, David, 273, 419
Illiana News, 576
Indech, Jonah, 301
Index to Jewish Periodicals, 583
Indiana Jewish Post and Opinion, 576
Indikt, Adam, 413
Indyk, Martin, 169, 193, 198, 206, 235
Inglehart, Ronald, 146*n*
Institute for Computers in Jewish Life, 529
Institute for Jewish Policy Research, 295
Institute for Public Affairs (UOJCA), 535
Institute of Traditional Judaism, 541
Intermountain Jewish News, 575
International Association of Jewish Genealogical Societies, 506
International Association of Jewish Vocational Services, 552
International Council on Jewish Social and Welfare Services, 552
International Federation of Secular Humanistic Jews, 530
International Institute for Secular Humanistic Judaism, 530
International Jewish Committee on Interreligious Consultations (IJCIC), 173, 324, 325
International Jewish Correspondence (IJC), 559
International Jewish Media Association, 506
International League for the Repatriation of Russian Jews, Inc, 501
International Network of Children of Jewish Holocaust Survivors, 507
Interns for Peace, 519
Irving, David, 409
Isaac, Jules, 69

Isaacs, Abram S., 6
Isarescu, Mugur, 390
Israel Cancer Research Fund, 519
Israel Humanitarian Foundation, 519
Israel Policy Forum (IPF), 231, 232, 233, 237, 519
Israël, Gérard, 316
Istook, Ernest, 177, 178
Itzik, Dalia, 447, 448

Jabara, Hussnia, 441, 444
Jabloner, Clemens, 368
Jackson, Andrew, 18
Jackson, Henry, 88
Jackson, Jesse, 168, 169
Jackson, Michael, 208
Jacksonville Jewish News, 576
Jacob Rader Marcus Center of the American Jewish Archives, 507
Jacob, Walter, 355
Jacobs, Jeremy, 296
Jacobs, Joseph, 5, 6, 25, 30
Jacobs, Malvern, 279
Jacobs, Maurice, 45
Jacobs, Robert, 172
Jacobson, Gaynor, 590
Jacobson, Howard, 301
Jacobson, Kenneth, 162
Jacobson, Nathan, 591
Jacoby, Ingrid, 300
Jahshan, Khalil, 170
Jakobovits, Lord Immanuel, 302
Janner, Lord, 294
JBI Voice, 580
Jeffords, Jim, 167
Jerusalem Foundation, 520
Jerusalem Letter/Viewpoints, 584
Jewish Publication Society, 506
Jewish Action, 580
Jewish Advocate, 577
Jewish Agency, 239, 240
Jewish Book Annual, 580
Jewish Book Council, 507
Jewish Book World, 580
Jewish Braille Institute of America, 553
Jewish Braille Review, 580
Jewish Bulletin of Northern California, 574
Jewish Chautauqua Society, 530
Jewish Children's Adoption Network, 553

Jewish Chronicle (Mass.), 577
Jewish Chronicle (N.J.), 578
Jewish Chronicle of Pittsburgh, 584
Jewish Civic Press (Ga.), 576
Jewish Civic Press (La.), 577
Jewish Community Centers Association of North America, 165, 213, 553
Jewish Community Chronicle, 574
Jewish Community News (Calif.), 574
Jewish Community News (Ill.), 576
Jewish Community News (N.J.), 578
Jewish Community Voice, 578
Jewish Council for Public Affairs (JCPA), 158, 159, 210, 212, 229, 241, 501
Jewish Currents, 580
Jewish Education in Media, 530
Jewish Education News, 580
Jewish Educational Service of North America (JESNA), 211, 530
Jewish Educators Assembly, 537
Jewish Exponent, 584
Jewish Federation News, 583
Jewish Federation of Greater Kansas City, 210
Jewish Federation of Metropolitan Chicago, 241
Jewish Federation's Los Angeles Museum of the Holocaust (Martyrs Memorial), 507
Jewish Foundation for the Righteous, 525
Jewish Free Press, 586
Jewish Frontier, 580
Jewish Fund for Justice, 553
Jewish Funders Network, 554
Jewish Guide to Boston & New England, 577
Jewish Herald, 580
Jewish Herald-Voice, 585
Jewish Heritage Project, 507
Jewish Immigrant Aid Services of Montreal (JIAS), 559
Jewish Institute for National Security Affairs, 520
Jewish Institute for the Blind-Jerusalem, 520
Jewish Journal (Fla.), 576
Jewish Journal (Long Island), 580
Jewish Journal (N.J.), 578
Jewish Journal (Ohio), 583
Jewish Journal of Greater Los Angeles, 574
Jewish Journal of San Antonio, 585

Jewish Journal/North of Boston, 577
Jewish Labor Bund, 550
Jewish Labor Committee, 501
Jewish Leader, 575
Jewish Ledger, 580
Jewish Museum, 507
Jewish National Fund of Canada, 559
Jewish National Fund, 191, 238, 423, 520
Jewish News (Calif.), 574
Jewish News (La.), 577
Jewish News of Greater Phoenix, 574
Jewish Observer of Central New York, 580
Jewish Observer, 224, 580
Jewish Outreach Institute, 214
Jewish Peace Fellowship, 502
Jewish Peace Lobby, 520
Jewish Political Studies Review, 584
Jewish Post & News, 586
Jewish Post of NY, 580
Jewish Press (Brooklyn), 580
Jewish Press (Neb.), 578
Jewish Press of Pinellas County, 576
Jewish Press of Tampa, 576
Jewish Publication Society, 3, 4, 5, 9, 12, 15,16, 17, 24–25, 27, 38, 45, 51, 52, 65, 507
Jewish Quarterly Review, 584
Jewish Reconstructionist Federation, 223, 530
Jewish Reporter, 578
Jewish Review, 584
Jewish Social Services Professionals Association, 554
Jewish Social Studies, 575
Jewish Spectator, 578
Jewish Sports Review, 575
Jewish Standard (N.J.), 578
Jewish Standard (Toronto), 586
Jewish Star, 578
Jewish State, 578
Jewish Teachers Association, 531
Jewish Telegraphic Agency Community News Reporter, 580
Jewish Telegraphic Agency Daily News Bulletin, 580
Jewish Telegraphic Agency Weekly News Digest, 580
Jewish Telegraphic Agency, 152, 157, 186, 585

Jewish Theological Seminary of America, 77, 87, 222, 542
Jewish Transcript, 585
Jewish Tribune (N.Y.), 581
Jewish Tribune (Toronto), 586
Jewish Veteran, 575
Jewish Voice, 575
Jewish Voice & Opinion, 578
Jewish Voice of Greater Monmouth County, 578
Jewish Voice of Rhode Island, 585
Jewish War Veterans of the United States of America, 502
Jewish Week, 220, 238, 581
Jewish Welfare Board Jewish Chaplains Council, 553
Jewish Western Bulletin, 586
Jewish Women International, 554
Jewish World, 581
Jocum, Simon, 418
Joel, Richard, 213
Joffe, Isaac, 420
Johnson, Keith, 419
Johnson, Lyndon, 74
Jona, Alwynne Beryl, 415
Jones, Jeremy, 409
Joseph, Samuel, 12*n*
Joskowicz, Menachem, 388, 389
Jospin, Lionel, 303, 306, 311
Jost, Hans-Ulrich, 337
Jouffa, Yves, 316
Journal of Jewish Communal Service, 578
Journal of Jewish Education, 581
Journal of Psychology and Judaism, 586
JTS Magazine, 581
Judah L. Magnes Museum-Jewish Museum of the West, 508
Judaica Captioned Film Center, 508
Judaism, 581
Judt, Tony, 216
JUF News & Guide to Jewish Living in Chicago, 576
Junod, Pascal, 334
JWB, 27, 28, 44, 74

Kacer, Kathy, 286
Kaczyne, Alter, 328
Kaczyne-Reale, Shulamit, 328
Kadima, 537

Kadish, Benjamin, 165
Kagan, Elie, 316
Kahalani, Avigdor, 444
Kahn, Jean, 314
Kahn, Jeffrey, 172
Kahn, Michèle, 316
Kalejs, Konrad, 293, 294, 411
Kalichman, Peter, 277
Kallen, Horace, 85
Kamenetz, Rodger, 210
Kaminer, Phyllis, 591
Kaminetsky, Joseph, 591
Kammerdiener, Don, 174
Kansas City Jewish Chronicle, 577
Kaplan, Hyman, 30
Kaplan, Jacob, 45
Kaplan, Mendel, 418
Kaplin, Casriel, 296
Kaplun, Arik, 285
Karlikow, Abraham, 57, 79
Kashrus Faxletter, 581
Kashrus Magazine, 581
Kasic, Kaspar, 359
Kasrils, Ronnie, 426
Kassie, Lynne, 287
Katriuk, Vladimir, 273, 274
Katsav, Moshe, 441
Katz, Danny, 481
Katz, Elihu, 132n, 133n
Katz, Roman, 185
Katz, Yossi, 459
Katznelson, Shulamith, 483
Kaye, Emmanuel, 301
Kayyam, Juliette, 171
Keal, Minna, 301
Kedem, Perry, 132n
Kedmi, Ya'akov, 436, 439
Kelemen, Katalin, 384
Keller, Ro'i, 465
Keller, Rudolf, 334, 337
Kellman, Joseph A.G., 55, 591
Kellner, Menachem, 301
Kelman, Ruth, 287
Kemp, David, 411
Kennedy, Ruby Jo, 66, 66n
Kenrick, Donald, 300
Kentucky Jewish Post and Opinion, 577
Keren Or, 520
Kerry, John, 182

Kessler, David, 302
Kestenbaum, Jonathan, 298
Kestenberg, Judith S., 591
Keysar, Ariella, 113n
Khair, Boris, 402
Khamenei, Ali, 468
Khatami, Mohammad, 468
Kidwa, Mohammed al-, 197
Kimmel, A. Earl, 287
Kinsey, Alfred, 64
Kirby, James, 300
Kirienko, Sergei, 398
Kirshner, Florence, 288
Kiryas Joel, 176
Kisluk, Serge, 274
Kissinger, Henry, 216
Klaff, Vivian, 114n
Klarsfeld, Serge, 310
Klaus, Vaclav, 376
Klebold, Dylan, 163
Klein Halevi, Yossi, 100
Klein, A.G. 415
Klein, A.M., 286
Klein, Claude, 315
Klein, George, 288
Klein, Morton, 233, 234, 235
Klein, Nancy, 66n
Klein, Théo, 316
Klemperer, Victor, 360
Klestil, Thomas, 364, 372, 381
Klima, Ivan, 381
Klima, Viktor, 364, 366, 367, 372
Klopstock, Yifat, 103n
Klutznick, Philip M., 591
Knox, Katharine, 300
Kobzon, Iosif, 402
Koch, Ed, 153
Kock, Manfred, 357
Koenigsberg, Alex, 287
Kohanski, Alexander S., 47n
Kohl, Helmut, 339
Kohler, Kaufmann, 37
Kohler, Max, 20
Kohn, Leo, 353
Kohr, Howard, 232
Kol Hat'nua, 581
Komarovsky, Mirra, 591
Komoroczy, Geza, 385
Kopelowitz, Seymour, 417, 426

Korey, William, 198, 199
Korman, Edward, 185, 331
Korn, Neer, 414
Kosmin, Barry A., 113n, 140n, 242n, 425
Kottelat, Jean-Jacques, 334
Kovac, Michal, 392
Kozlowski, Stefan Zdzislaw, 350
Kraft, Louis, 44
Kramer, Leib, 288
Krauskopf, Joseph, 37
Krausz, Herman, 277
Krebs, John, 301
Krivchun, Nikita, 399
Krochmal, Nachman, 43
Krygier, Rivon, 316
Kubrick, Stanley, 300
Kuchma, Leonid, 398
Kulanu, 531
Kultur un Lebn, 581
Kumermann, Daniel, 378
Kune, Gabriel, 414
Kupfermann, Moshe, 360
Kurdybelski, Jan, 272
Kushner, Tony, 298, 299, 300
Kussner, Sheila, 287
Kuznets, Simon, 12n
Kwasniewski, Aleksander, 386
Kwinter, Monte, 267

La Voix Sépharade, 586
Labor Zionist Alliance, 520
Labour Zionist Alliance of Canada, 559
Ladd, Everett Carll, 87
Lafontaine, Oskar, 338
Lamishpaha, 581
Lamm, Norman, 225, 226, 227
Lancz, Tibor, 384
Landau, Philippe, 315
Landau, Ronnie S., 300
Landes, Richard, 175
Landry, Bernard, 271
Landver, Sofa, 428
Landy, Keith, 272
Lang, Berel, 96
Lang, Slobodan, 375
Lapid, Yosef "Tommy," 442, 443
Lapin, Shmuel, 85
Lappin, Elena, 301
Largent, Steve, 174, 175

LaRouche, Lyndon, 409, 410
Las Vegas Israelite, 578
Lauck, Gary, 166
Lauder, Ronald, 169, 191, 238, 388, 463
Lautenberg, Frank, 154
Lawton, Clive, 298
Layton, Irving, 285
Lazerzon, Avraham Yosef, 472
Le Pen, Jean-Marie, 304, 305
League for Human Rights, 558
League for Yiddish, 508
Leavitt, Julian, 27, 29
Leavitt, Michael, 151
Lee, Carol Ann, 300
Lehman, Herbert, 84
Leibler, Mark, 413
Leipman, Flora, 302
Leo Baeck Institute, 508
Leon, Tony, 426
Lerer, Nava, 113n
Leridon, Henri, 114n
Lerman, Antony, 137n
Lerman, Miles, 217
Lermer, Arthur, 286
Lerner, Anne Lapidus, 87–88
Lerner, Gad, 328
Lerner, Susana, 136n
Leshem, Elazar, 108n
Lesthaeghe, Ron, 117n
Levenson, Geoffrey, 426
Levenson, Michael, 279
Levi Hospital, 554
Levi-Montaleini, Rita, 328
Levin Epstein, N., 138n
Levin, Arthur, 302
Levin, Hanoch, 483
Levin, Itamar, 380
Levin, Mark, 155
Levin, Salmond S., 301
Levine, Allan, 286
Levinsohn, Hana, 132n, 133n
Levinson, Nathan Peter, 358
Levitas, Ilya, 402
Lévy, Albert, 307
Levy, David, 319, 367, 418, 433, 435, 447, 453, 455, 457, 469
Levy, Ernest, 300
Levy, Joel, 357
Levy, Martha Washington, 14

Levy, Michael Abraham Lord, 291
Levy, Richard, 219, 220
Levy, Shlomit, 132n, 133n
Levy, Uriah P., 15
Levy, Yitzhak, 441, 447, 459, 460
Leyris, Raymond, 312
Liberles, Robert, 68n
Libeskind, Daniel, 347, 360, 363
Libman, Charles, 310
Libman, Robert, 283
Lichtblau, Albert, 361
Lichtenstein, Rachel, 300
Lieberman, Avigdor, 439, 441, 442, 444, 449
Lieberman, Joseph, 175, 182
Lieberman, Michael, 150
Liebman, Charles S., 76–77, 79, 82, 86, 132n, 209
Lightman, Bernard, 286
Likutim, 581
Lileikis, Aleksandras, 187, 400
Lilith, 581
Linfield, Harry, 31–33, 54
Lior, Dov, 460
Lipkin-Shahak, Amnon, 430, 431, 448
Lipman, Maureen, 300
Lipset, Seymour Martin, 75, 87
Lipstadt, Deborah, 41, 43
Litzka, Gerhard, 367
Living Traditions, 508
Livingston, Bob, 152
Livnat, Limor, 437, 441
Lloyd, Tony, 290
Lockhart, Joe, 162
Loeb, Jacques, 23
London, Hannah, 34
Long Island Jewish World, 581
Lookstein, Haskel, 41, 41n
Lopez, Moses, 4n
Lorenz, Mitzi, 302
Los Angeles Jewish Times, 575
Louvish, Misha, 79, 80
Lowenthal, Gerhart, 415
Lowy, Frederick, 287
Lubner, Gerald, 426
Lubotzky, Alex, 431
Luchins, David, 229
Lufty, Allan, 274
Lukashenka, Aleksandr, 398
Lundström, Hans, 116n

Lutz, Wolfgang, 114n, 116n, 117n, 118n, 142n
Luzhkov, Yuri, 398, 402
Luzzatto, Amos, 325
Lyons, Henry, 169

Maalot, 543
Maccabi USA/Sports for Israel, 520
Maccoby, Deborah, 300
Maccoby, Hyam, 300
Macias, Enrico, 312
Mack, Connie, 154
Madonna, 209
Maggiore, Giuseppe, 318
Magnus, Katie, 4
Magonet, Jonathan, 301
Mahmeed, Hashem, 448
Maimonides, Moses, 43
Makashov, Albert, 399, 401
Malka, Avi, 341
Malloth, Anton, 378
Malovany, Joseph, 380
Malthête, Jean-François, 315
Mandel, Ralph, 98, 99
Mandela, Nelson, 416, 418, 422, 423, 425
Mandlbaum, Zorin, 374
Manhattan Jewish Sentinel, 581
Maor, Anat, 449
Marchi, Sergio, 269
Marcus, Gill, 417, 426
Marcus, Jacob Rader, 45
Markovits, Andy, 360
Maron, Malka, 286
Marrus, Michael, 275
Marshall, Louis, 20, 23, 48
Martini, Carlo Maria Cardinal, 324
Martyrdom and Resistance, 581
Masaryk, Tomas Garrigue, 381
Mashaal, Khaled, 468
Massalhe, Nawaf, 448
Massarik, Fred, 84
Mathys, Michael, 334
Matia, Paul, 187
Mattéoli, Jean, 310
Max Weinreich Center for Advanced Jewish Studies, 512
Mayne, Seymour, 286
Mazen, Abu, 457, 458
Mazon: A Jewish Response to Hunger, 554

Mbeki, Thabo, 416, 417, 418, 421, 422, 423
McBride, Joseph, 301
McCain, John, 151
McCarthy, Joseph, 56
McDermott, Katherine, 296
McFarland, Steve, 183
McFarlane, Quinn, 273
McGuinness, Martin, 289
McIntosh, David, 186
McKane, Richard, 301
McLellan, Anne, 267
Meciar, Vladimir, 392
Medalie, Leon, 426
Mégret, Bruno, 304, 305
Mehta, Zubin, 327
Meir, Golda, 74
Melchior, Michael, 230, 473, 448
Memmi, Albert, 361
Memorial Foundation for Jewish Culture, 508
Mendelsohn, Nathan Saul, 287
Mendes-Flohr, Paul, 47n
Mengele, Josef, 333, 350, 359
Menitoff, Paul, 150
Menuhin, Yehudi Lord, 301
Mercaz USA, 521
Meretz USA, 521
Meridor, Dan, 430, 431, 435
Mesivta Yeshiva Rabbi Chaim Berlin Rabbinical Academy, 543
Messale, Adissu, 428
MetroWest Jewish Reporter, 577
Michelson, Albert A., 35
Midstream, 581
Mihaileanu, Radu, 328
Mikalson, Poshi, 163
Mikulski, Barbara, 182
Miljavac, Paval, 375
Miller, Monte Kim, 475
Miller, Stephen, 137n
Milo, Roni, 430, 431
Milosevic, Slobodan, 198
Milunovic, Dobrivoje, 163
Minczeles, Henri, 315
Mindel, Nissan, 592
Minerbi, Yitzhak, 485
Mintz, Alan, 96
Mintzberg, Henry, 287
Mishal, Nissim, 434

Mitterand, François, 307–08, 345
Mizrachi Organization of Canada, 560
Mizrahi, Moshe, 478
Mizrahi, Viktor, 386
Mock, Karen, 282
Modern Judaism, 583
Mofaz, Shaul, 481
Mohammad, Mahmoud Mohammad Issa, 270
Mohammed VI, King, 189
Moïse, Penina, 15
Molnar, George, 415
Moment, 575
Monitor, 576
Montagu, Ashley, 592
Morais, Stanley, 269
Moratinos, Miguel Angel, 192
Mordechai, Yitzhak, 231, 430, 431, 432, 433, 434, 435, 438, 447
Morgenstern, Moshe, 295
Morgenthau, Hans, 62
Morgenthau, Robert M., 370
Morris, Brian, 268
Mortara, Edgardo, 325
Moscati, Maria Luisa, 328
Moscovitch, Allan, 276
Mosès, Emmanuel, 316
Moses, Lewis, 287
Mosès, Stéphane, 316
Mosse, George, 592
Moussa, Amre, 466
Moynihan, Daniel Patrick, 182, 201
Mozes, Arnon, 478
Mubarak, Hosni, 199, 203, 305, 452, 466
Muhammad, Imam W. Deen, 172
Museum of Jewish Heritage—A Living Memorial to the Holocaust, 240, 508
Museum of Tolerance of the Simon Wiesenthal Center, 509
Muslim Public Affairs Council, 170
Mussolini, Benito, 42
Muszynski, Henryk Josef, 357
Muzicant, Ariel, 365, 366, 368, 372
Myers, Baruch, 393, 394
Myrdal, Gunnar, 53

Na'amat USA, 521
Na'amat Woman, 581
Nachama, Andreas, 353, 355, 356

Nadler, Allan, 280
Nadler, Jerrold, 166, 180, 181, 186
Nadon, Marc, 273
Nador, George, 301
Nagato, Mollo, 464
Nahon, Gérard, 316
Nahshon, Edna, 301
Nahum, Maya, 316
Nasatir, Steven, 241
National Association of Jewish Chaplains, 554
National Association of Jewish Legislators, 502
National Association of Temple Administrators, 534
National Association of Temple Educators, 535
National Center for the Hebrew Language, 509
National Committee for Furtherance of Jewish Education, 531
National Committee for Labor Israel, 521
National Community Relations Committee, Canadian Jewish Congress, 560
National Conference of Synagogue Youth, 536
National Conference on Soviet Jewry, 73, 155, 502
National Council of Jewish Women of Canada, 560
National Council of Jewish Women, 181, 554
National Council of Young Israel, 531
National Foundation for Jewish Culture, 509
National Havurah Committee, 532
National Institute for Jewish Hospice, 555
National Jewish Children's Leukemia Foundation, 555
National Jewish Coalition, 183
National Jewish Commission on Law and Public Affairs (COLPA), 502
National Jewish Committee on Scouting, 532
National Jewish Democratic Council, 151, 153, 180, 502
National Jewish Girl Scout Committee, 532
National Jewish Hospitality Committee, 532

National Jewish Medical and Research Center, 555
National Jewish Post and Opinion, 577
National Jewish/Catholic Coalition, 173
National Museum of American Jewish Military History, 502
National Trade Union Council for Human Rights, 502
National Yiddish Book Center, 509
Nattel, Lillian, 286
Naumann, Michael, 347, 348
Naveh, Danny, 458
Near East Report, 576
Ner Israel Rabbinical College, 543
Netanyahu, Benjamin, 190, 191, 192, 193, 195, 199, 200, 201, 204, 205, 231, 232, 233, 330, 339, 340, 398, 407, 427, 428, 429, 430, 431, 432, 434, 435, 436, 437, 438, 439, 440, 441, 444, 451, 452, 454, 455, 463, 464, 465, 467, 477
Netanyahu, Sara, 477
Neuwirthova, Vida, 380
New Israel Fund, 231, 521
New Jersey Jewish News, 579
New Menorah, 584
New Mexico Jewish Link, 579
New York UJA-Federation, 210, 229, 239, 241
News and Views, 586
Niebuhr, Reinhold, 85
Nimrodi, Ofer, 478
Nixon, Richard, 74
North American Alliance for Jewish Youth, 557
North American Association of Synagogue Executives, 537
North American Boards of Rabbis (NABOR), 227, 379
North American Conference on Ethiopian Jewry (NACOEJ), 526
North American Federation of Temple Brotherhoods, 535
Norton, Eleanor Holmes, 166
Notelovitz, Jack, 424
Notelowitz, Mark, 421
Novick, Peter, 67, 217
Nugent, Peter, 407
Nussbaum, Felix, 357
Nussbaum, Moshe, 287

Observer, 585
Ocalan, Abdullah, 340
Ochs, Adolph S., 18
O'Connor, John Cardinal, 172
Odeh, Mohammed Daoud, 306
Odenheimer, Micha Z., 99
Odynsky, Wasyl, 274
Ofek, Avraham, 372
Offmann, Marian, 354
Ohio Jewish Chronicle, 584
Olmert, Ehud, 435, 450, 453
Olomeinu-Our World, 582
Oppenheim, Samson, 25
Oppenheimer, Peter, 298
Orange County Jewish Heritage, 575
Orbach, Eitan, 480
Orban, Viktor, 382, 383, 385
Oren, Uri, 417
Oron, Haim, 448
Orsten, Elisabeth M., 300
ORT Canada, 560
ORT, 159
Orthodox Jewish Archives, 509
Osrin, Myra, 425
Ottawa Jewish Bulletin, 586
Ovadia, Moni, 327
Owen, Ron, 411
Ozar Hatorah, 532
Ozols, Karlis, 411

Paikin, Marnie, 287
Pakn-Treger, 577
Paltiel, Ari, 103*n*
Papo, Michael, 376
Papon, Maurice, 309–10, 333
Pardes Progressive Association of Reform
    Day Schools, 532
Parfitt, Tudor, 424
Partnership for Jewish Life, 213
Pasqua, Charles, 304, 306
Passover Directory, 582
Paul, Wolfgang, 367
Pavey, Roger, 281
Pavlat, Leo, 380
Pearce, Keith, 300
PEC Israel Economic Corporation, 521
PEF Israel Endowment Funds, 521
Pelavin, Mark, 179
Peled, Yossi, 436

Pelossof, Dalia Rabin, 431, 479
Peres, Shimon, 271, 433, 435, 441, 447, 453,
    456, 467
Peretz, Amir, 442, 444
Peretz, Isaac Leib, 24
Perkins, Maureen, 4*n*
Perlman, Selig, 63, 63*n*
Perlmutter, Philip, 83
Perlow, Yaakov, 223, 224
Pétain, Philippe, 308
Peterson, Jim, 277
Petitdemange, Guy, 314
Petkovski, Tito, 386
P'eylim-Lev L'achim, 532
Phillips, Alec, 301
Phillips, Bruce A., 92, 128*n*, 213
Pianka, Max, 302
Picard, Jean-Claude, 313
Pierre-Bloch, Jean, 316
Pikan, Tali, 317
Pink, Irving, 287
Pinto, Diana, 361
Plantin, Jean, 308
Plotnick, Stan, 276
Poale Agudath Israel of America, 522
Podins, Eduards, 274
Polgar, Klara, 381
Polgar, Laszlo, 381
Pollard, Jonathan, 161, 162
Pool, Lea, 285
Pope John Paul II, 172, 173, 324, 325, 386,
    387, 389, 475
Pope John XXIII, 69, 173, 325
Pope Pius IX, 325
Pope Pius XII, 173, 324–25
Porat, Hanan, 441
Poraz, Avraham, 442
Porges, Nenad, 375
Posner, Barry, 287
Post, Marlene, 236
Povarsky, David, 483
Preminger, Otto, 359
Pridan, Rafi, 478
Priebke, Erich, 321
Primakov, Yevgeny, 155, 396, 398, 403
Primor, Avi, 339, 340
Prinz, Cristopher, 114*n*
Pritzker, Jay, 592
Prlincevic, Chedar, 395

Pro Israel, 522
Proceedings of the American Academy for Jewish Research, 582
Prodi, Romano, 317
Prooftexts, 577
Proskauer, Joseph M., 48, 49, 85
Prutschi, Manuel, 287
Putin, Vladimir, 396, 397, 398, 403
Pyne, Christopher, 406, 407

Qaddafi, Muammar, 318
Quezada, Mordechai, 284

Raab, Earl, 83
Raab, Elizabeth, 286
Rabbi Isaac Elchanan Theological Seminary, 548
Rabbinical Alliance of America, 532
Rabbinical Assembly (RA), 150, 209, 222, 532
Rabbinical College of Telshe, 544
Rabbinical Council of America, 226, 533
Rabin, Leah, 439, 479
Rabin, Yitzhak, 200, 201, 202, 203, 431, 444, 453, 458, 460, 479
Rabinovich, Itamar, 191
Rabinovich, Vadim, 402
Rabinovitch, Robert, 287
Rabinowicz, Baruch, 388, 389
Rabinowitz, Ian, 297
Rabinyan, Dorit, 299
Raffel, Martin, 158
Rakoczy, Tadeusz, 390
Ramer, Bruce, 347
Ramon, Haim, 230, 430, 445, 447, 463
Raphael, Adam, 302
Raphael, Frederic, 300
Raphael, Yitzhak, 483
Rapoport, Louis, 300
Rappaport, Amir, 191
Rappaport, Charles, 302
Rappaz, Henri, 334
Rashi, 43
Raskin, Mendel, 283
Raslan, Rana, 481
Rassinier, Paul, 305, 316
Ratajczak, Dariusz, 387, 388
Ratner, Joel, 177
Rau, Johannes, 351

Raviv, Avishai, 479
Raviv, Gilad, 476
Ravvin, Norman, 281
Raymers, Abraham, 23
Rayner, John D., 301
RCA Record, 582
Rebhun, Uzi, 114*n*, 129*n*, 130*n*, 133*n*, 214
Recanati, Rafael, 483
Reconstructionism Today, 584
Reconstructionist Rabbinical Association, 530
Reconstructionist Rabbinical College, 77, 227, 544
Reconstructionist, 584
Reemtsma, Jan Philipp, 349
Reform Judaism, 582
Reich, Seymour, 173, 325
Reich-Ranicki, Marcel, 361
Reinharz, Jehuda, 47*n*
Religious Action Center of Reform Judaism, 150, 178, 179, 181, 183
Religious Zionists of America, 522
Renewal Magazine, 585
Reno, Janet, 166, 188
Reporter, 582
Republican Jewish Coalition, 151, 153, 503
Research Foundation for Jewish Immigration, 509
Resnick, Pearl, 592
Response: A Contemporary Jewish Review, 582
Ressam, Ahmed, 154
Re'uth Women's Social Service, 526
Rhode Island Jewish Herald, 585
Rhode Island Jewish Historical Notes, 585
Rickenbach, Franz, 337
Ridgeway, Aden, 407
Ripoll, Bernie, 407
Ritterband, Paul, 138*n*
Robinson, Ira, 284
Rodley, Nigel, 301
Roeh, Ilan, 463, 464
Rohrlich, Ruby, 300
Ro'i, Y., 138*n*
Roitman, Paul, 316
Ronald S. Lauder Foundation, 357, 380, 388, 391, 394
Ronen, Moshe, 275
Ronen, Nehama, 442

Roosevelt, Eleanor, 62
Roosevelt, Franklin D., 44, 173
Roosevelt, Theodore, 13
Rose, Frederick P., 593
Rose, Gerald, 287
Rose, Joe, 415
Rosen, Harold, 300
Rosenbaum, Eli, 187
Rosenbaum, Yankel, 97
Rosenberg, Ethel, 56–57
Rosenberg, Herby, 422
Rosenberg, Julius, 56–57
Rosenblum, Pnina, 442
Rosenfarb, Chava, 286
Rosenne, Shabtai, 81
Rosenthal, Erich, 65, 66, 67, 76
Rosh, Lea, 361
Ross, Dennis, 193, 202, 461
Rotchin, Glenn, 286
Roth, Lewis, 157
Rothschild, Walter, 356
Ruabdeh, Abd a-Rauf, 467
Ruben, David-Hillel, 297
Rubenstein, Colin, 406, 407, 413
Rubin, James, 192, 195
Rubinstein, Amnon, 482
Rubinstein, Elyakim, 160, 434, 450, 473, 479, 481
Rubinstein, William D., 140n
Rudin, A. James, 174
Rudolf, Anthony, 300
Rudolf, Germar, 292
Ruff, Charles, 162
Ruml, Jan, 376
Rushton, Colin, 300
Ruskay, John, 210
Russian Forward, 582
Russian Jewish Congress, 155
Rutelli, Francesco, 320

Saadiah Gaon, 43
Sabah, Michel, 474
Sacks, Jonathan, 295, 296, 297
Sadat, Anwar, 200
Sadun, Elvio, 318
Saenger, Hanns, 426
Saevecke, Theodor, 321
Safire, William, 152
Safra, Edmond J., 337, 593

Sagall, Jonathan, 285
Sagi, Dalia, 103n
Saguy, Uri, 462
Saideman, Seymour, 375
Sakic, Dinko, 376
Salamander, Rachel, 363
Sallon, Ralph, 302
Samuel, Maurice, 85
San Diego Jewish Press Heritage, 575
San Diego Jewish Times, 575
Sanderson, Warren, 142n
Sandler, Alan, 277, 287
Saperstein, David, 150, 151, 177, 183
Sarfati, Georges-Elia, 315
Sarid, Yossi, 367, 445, 447, 451, 459
Sarna, Jonathan D., 3n, 5n, 17n, 22n, 38n, 66n
Sarraute, Nathalie, 316
Saunders, John, 414
Saveth, Edward N., 44
Sawoniuk, Anthony, 293
Scalfaro, Oscar Luigi, 317, 320
Schama, Simon, 300
Schargenheim, Felice, 359
Schatz, Zohara, 483
Schechter, Solomon, 14
Scheckner, Jeffrey, 113n
Scheier, Libby, 286
Scherbov, Sergei, 142n
Schiele, Egon, 370
Schiff, Jacob, 18
Schifferli, Pierre, 334
Schilly, Otto, 341
Schimmel, Betty, 300
Schirmacher, Frank, 360
Schmelz, Usiel O., 91, 101, 103n, 107n, 114n, 115n, 132n, 135n, 141n
Schmelzer, Menahem, 78
Schmidt, Maria, 383
Schmool, Marlena, 137n
Schneerson, Menachem M., 226
Schneid, Otto, 285
Schneider Children's Medical Center of Israel, 522
Schneiderman, Harry, 18, 28, 29, 30, 33, 34, 36, 37, 45, 50
Schneiderman, N.N., 286
Schneiderman, Rose, 28
Schneid-Ofseyer, Miriam, 285

Schneier, Marc, 168, 227
Schochet, Yitzhak, 295
Schocken, Amos, 478
Schoenberg, Philip E., 14n
Schoenfeld, Gabriel, 217
Schoeps, Julius, 355, 356
Scholem, Gershom, 363
Schönbohm, Jörg, 344
Schorsch, Ismar, 222, 227
Schröder, Gerhard, 338, 339, 340, 346, 347, 349, 350, 351
Schröder, Richard, 348
Schudrich, Michael, 388
Schulweis, Harold, 150, 229
Schüssel, Wolfgang, 364
Schuster, Rudolf, 392
Schusterman, Charles, 210
Schwartz, Fred, 390
Schwarzfeld, Elias, 12
Sciacca, Con, 407
Scranton Federation Reporter, 584
Seale, Patrick, 461
Sebel, Harry, 415
Secter, Harvey, 287
Security Affairs, 576
Segal, George, 372
Segre, Daniele, 327
Seiple, Robert, 183
Seixas, Gershom, 15
Seksik, Laurent, 316
Sela, Beni, 476
Seldin, Ruth R., 89, 95
Seligman, Ben, 54
Seligson, David, 593
Sephardic Educational Center, 509
Sephardic House, 510
Sephardic Jewish Brotherhood of America, 550
Serota, Nicholas, 301
Setton, Dan, 359
Sha'ath, Nabil, 454
Shafir, Shlomo, 59
Shain, Milton, 140n, 425, 426
Shalem Center, 503
Shalom (Fla.), 576
Shalom (Halifax), 586
Shalom Center, 503
Shalom L.A., 575
Shalom, Silvan, 441

Shapira, Anita, 100
Shapiro, Bernard, 287
Shapiro, Leon, 73, 80, 88, 91
Shara, Farouk al-, 200, 203, 204, 268, 427, 461, 462
Sharansky, Natan, 230, 436, 439, 444, 447, 449, 460
Shargel, Baila, 35n
Sharon, Ariel, 205, 237, 305, 318, 319, 339, 340, 398, 432, 463, 467, 481, 439, 441, 445, 450, 451
Sheinbein, Samuel, 159–161, 480
Sheldon, Peter, 297
Shepherd, Naomi, 300
Sher, Neal, 168
Sherman, Kenneth, 286
Sheskin, Ira, 243
Shilowa, Mbhazima, 418
Shimoni, Gideon, 73
Shindler, Colin, 301
Shitreet, Meir, 441, 450
Shlomo, Nur, 482
Sh'ma, 577
Shoah Visual History Foundation, 218
Shochat, Avraham, 447, 470
Shofar, 585
Shoshi, Zalman, 482
Shoval, Zalman, 192
Shrage, Barry, 240
Shrum, Robert, 429, 437
Shultz, George, 204
Shuval, Judith T., 108n
Sichrovsky, Peter, 354
Sidon, Karol, 379, 380
Sieff, David, 301
Siegel, Seymour, 85
Sifrin, Geoff, 425
Silberman, Charles, 93, 95
Silberman, Lou, 78
Silbert, Marlene, 425
Silkin, Jon, 301
Silvain, Gérard, 315
Silverstein, Shel, 593
Silverstone, Jack, 274, 277
Simhon, Shalom, 447
Simmons, Godfrey, 300
Simon Wiesenthal Center, 159, 162, 163, 173, 187, 272, 325, 411, 510
Sinclair, Iain, 300

Sinclair, Sidney, 415
Singer, Aca, 395
Singer, David, 89
Singer, Israel, 351
Sirota, Marvin, 103n
Siskel, Gene, 593
Sitruk, Joseph, 306, 314
Sivan, Eyal, 285, 315, 359
Skirball Cultural Center, 510
Sklare, Marshall, 67, 67n
Skuratov, Yuri, 399
Skyte, Heinz, 300
Slansky, Rudolf, 58
Slawson, John, 53
Sliwinski, Krzystof, 387
Slouschz, Nahum, 24
Smith, Gordon, 155, 167
Smith, Lamar, 156, 157
Smith, Mervyn, 417
Smith, Stephen, 425
Smorgon, Eric, 415
Sobel, Zvi, 132n
Society for Humanistic Judaism, 533
Society for the History of Czechoslovak
    Jews, 510
Society of Friends of Touro Synagogue, 510
Society of Israel Philatelists, 522
Solender, Stephen, 229, 239, 240, 241
Soltes, Mordecai, 36
Sommer, Evelyn, 421
Sonnino, Aldo, 328
Soros, George, 385
Southeastern Virginia Jewish News, 585
Spanier, Allen, 287
Speaker, 579
Specter, Arlen, 150, 157
Spertus Institute of Jewish Studies, 544
Spertus Museum, 510
Spielberg, Steven, 214, 218, 347
Sprecher, Hannah, 35n
Sroka, Ghila, 287
St. Louis Jewish Light, 578
Stalin, Josef, 58
Stark Jewish News, 584
Starr, Kenneth, 150
State of Israel Bonds (Canada), 560
State of Israel Bonds, 522
Stavans, Ilan, 301
Steg, Ady, 311

Stein, Herbert, 593
Stein, Herman, 64
Steinberg, Saul, 594
Steinhardt, Michael, 210, 212, 213, 277
Steinhorn, E.J., 424
Steinitz, Sharon, 457
Steinsaltz, Adin, 209, 421
Stelmach, Nahum, 483
Stepashin, Sergei, 396, 398
Stern, Fritz, 362
Stern, Horace, 38
Stern, Kenneth, 162, 165
Stern, Marc, 176
Stern, Moshe, 279
Stern, Sasha, 297
Stern, Vivien, 301
Stoessel, Haim, 483
Stoiber, Edmund, 348
Stoll, Louise, 240
Stolpe, Manfred, 342
Stone, Deborah, 413
Stoyanov, Peter, 374, 375
Straus, Oscar, 37
Strauss, Leo, 85
Straw, Jack, 291, 292, 294
Student Struggle for Soviet Jewry, 88
Studies in Bibliography and Booklore, 584
Studies in Contemporary Jewry, 213
Suissa, Eli, 447, 448, 449
Sulzberger, Cyrus, 14, 20
Sulzberger, Mayer, 16, 20, 37
Sundin, Jules, 287
Survivors of the Shoah Visual History
    Foundation, 511
Susser, Bernard, 209
Sussman, Lance, 220
Svonkin, Stuart, 52, 52n, 53n, 55n, 57n
Switon, Kazimierez, 387, 388
Synagogue Light and Kosher Life, 582
Szadaj, Jakub, 389
Szold, Henrietta, 6, 7, 8, 9, 15, 16, 17, 26

Tabachnik, Eldred, 291
Taft, William Howard, 19
Tal, David, 472
Tal, Dorit, 103n
Tamir, Yuli, 448, 471
Tanenbaum Center for Interreligious Un-
    derstanding, 183

Tannenwald, Theodore Jr., 594
Tarifi, Jamil, 458
Tatz, Colin, 414
Tauchner, Maximilian, 363
Tavenas, François, 284
Taylor, Jeffrey, 175
Tekiah, 533
Teller, Charles J., 27
Temkin, Sefton, 86
Tendler, Moses, 225
Tenet, George, 168, 194
Tennéfeld, Meinhard, 362
Terrail, Alain, 307
Teutsch, David, 227
Teva Learning Center, 533
Texas Jewish Post, 585
Thanks to Scandinavia, 526
Theodor Herzl Foundation, 523
Thibaud, Paul, 314
Thomas, Gordon, 300
Tichon, Dan, 400
Tikkun, 575
Tisch, James, 241
Tishman, Rita V., 594
Tivoni, Erez, 475
Toaff, Elio, 320, 323, 326, 387
Toben, Frederick, 409, 410
Tobias, Phillip, 426
Tobin, Gary, 92, 214
Todovov, Tzevetan, 300
Toledo Jewish News, 584
Tolts, Mark, 113n, 114n, 138n
Torah Schools for Israel-Chinuch Atzmai, 533
Torah Umesorah, 226, 533
Torczyner, Jim L., 127n
Tordai, Peter, 384
Touro College, 544
Touro National Heritage Trust, 510
Toval, Shaul, 137n
Trachtenberg, Joshua, 48
Tradition, 582
Trajkovski, Boris, 386
Traves, Thomas Donald, 287
Trigano, Shmuel, 314, 316
Triguboff, Harry, 415
Trimble, David, 289
Troper, Harold, 286
Tsomet-Techiya USA, 523

Tudjman, Franjo, 375, 376
Tulchinsky, Gerald, 286
Tulsa Jewish Review, 584
Tutu, Desmond, 417, 425
Twain, Mark, 9
Twigg, Stephen, 298
Tyndall, John, 292
Tzur, Ya'akov, 478

UIA Federations Canada, 277
UN Watch, 503
Union for Traditional Judaism, 534
Union of American Hebrew Congregations (UAHC), 8, 9, 86, 218, 219, 220, 534
Union of Councils for Soviet Jews, 98, 503
Union of Orthodox Jewish Congregations of America, 8, 9, 153, 175, 178, 179, 180, 181, 225, 229, 236, 317, 535
Union of Orthodox Rabbis of the United States and Canada, 536
Union of Sephardic Congregations, 536
United Charity Institutions of Jerusalem, 523
United Israel Appeal (UIA), 210, 239, 523
United Jewish Appeal (UJA), 168, 210, 239
United Jewish Communities (UJC), 156, 165, 210, 215, 239, 242, 244–45, 277, 526
United Lubavitcher Yeshivoth, 536
United Order True Sisters, 555
United States Holocaust Memorial Museum, 217–18, 511
United Synagogue of Conservative Judaism, 221, 222, 536
United Synagogue Review, 582
United Synagogue Youth, 537
University of Judaism, 545
Unser Tsait, 582
Urofsky, Melvin, 47n
US/Israel Women to Women, 523

Vaad Mishmereth Stam, 537
Vadnai, Gabriel, 313
Valiani, Leo, 328
Valkavickas, Vincas, 186, 400
Valman, Nadia, 299
Valori, Giancarlo Elia, 328
Van de Kaa, Dirk, 117n
Van Wissen, Leo, 142n

Vandernoot, Joseph, 302
Vanik, Charles, 88
Vanunu, Mordechai, 482
Vasile, Radu, 390
Vaughan, Frankie, 302
Vaupel, James W., 116*n*
Velmans, Edith, 299
Vero, Tamas, 384
Victor, Herschel, 287
Viewpoint Magazine, 582
Vigevani, Alberto, 328
Vilnai, Matan, 430, 441, 448, 480
Violante, Luciano, 320
Vital, David, 300
Voghera, Giorgio, 328
Vogt, Arthur, 336
Voice of the Dutchess Jewish Community, 582
Volcker, Paul, 186, 331
Volunteers for Israel, 523

Wagner, Erica, 301
Waks, Moishe, 355, 356
Waksberg, Joseph, 113*n*
Waldman, Morris, 28
Walfish, Barry, 285
Walker, Ned, 206, 207
Wallenberg, Raoul, 383
Wallerstein, Immanuel, 146*n*
Walser, Martin, 345, 346, 362
Washington Institute for Jewish Leadership & Values, 537
Washington Jewish Week, 577
Washtenaw Jewish News, 578
Wasserstein, Bernard, 298
Watts, Irene, 286
Waxman, Al, 286
Waxman, Chaim I., 114*n*
Weill, Anne, 337
Weinberg, Yaakov, 594
Weinberg, Yehuda David, 287
Weinreich, Max, 84
Weinroth, Ya'akov, 477
Weiser, Ron, 413
Weiss, Abner, 423
Weiss, Avi, 226
Weiss, Branco, 337
Weiss, Mel, 350

Weiss, Shevach, 390
Weiz, Daniel, 270
Weizman, Ezer, 306, 453, 467
Wenger, Beth, 39
Wertheimer, Jack, 94, 212, 225
Werzberger, Alex, 282
Wesker, Arnold, 301
West Coast Talmudical Seminary, 545
Western States Jewish History, 575
Wiebe, Robert, 8, 8*n*
Wiesel, Elie, 172, 216, 315
Wiesenthal, Simon, 378
Wieviorka, Annette, 315
Wigoder, Geoffrey, 325, 483
Wilder, Joseph, 287
Wilkomirski, Binjamin, 299
Williams, Bill, 300
Williams, Norman, 302
Williams, Randy, 183
Williams, Robin, 217
Wilstein Institute of Jewish Policy Studies, 511
Winner, David, 300
Wisconsin Jewish Chronicle, 585
Wiseman, Shloime, 281
Wistrich, Robert S., 299, 372
Witti, Michael, 352
Wolf, Arnold Jacob, 220
Wolf, Eric R., 594
Wolf, John, 302
Wolf, Leonid, 402
Wolf, Simon, 9,10,15, 20, 37
Wolfe, Rose, 287
Wolfson, Harry A., 85
Wolnek, Stephen, 228
Women of Reform Judaism, 535
Women's American ORT, 525
Women's League for Conservative Judaism, 538
Women's League for Israel, 523
Women's League Outlook Magazine, 582
Woocher, Jonathan, 86
Workmen's Circle/Arbeter Ring, 550
World Confederation of United Zionists, 523
World Congress of Gay, Lesbian, & Bisexual Jewish Organizations, 503
World Council of Conservative/Masorti Synagogues, 538

World Council of Jewish Communal Service, 555
World Jewish Congress, 168, 186, 215, 216, 319, 330, 351, 503
World of Lubavitch, 586
World Union for Progressive Judaism, 355, 356, 384
World Zionist Organization-American Section, 523
Wright, Tamara, 301
Wust, Lissy, 359
Wyman, David, 44, 44n
Wyoming Valley Jewish Reporter, 582

Yakobovich, Yevgeny, 476
Yanofsky, Joel, 286
Yaron, Zvi, 81
Yatom, Danny, 453
Yearbook of the Central Conference of American Rabbis, 582
Yehoshua, A.B., 328
Yeltsin, Boris, 155, 396, 397, 398, 403, 469
Yeshiva Torah Vodaath, 545
Yeshiva University Museum, 511
Yeshiva University, 76, 225, 226, 227, 546
Yiddish, 582
Yiddishe Kultur, 583
Yiddisher Kemfer, 583
Yiddisher Kultur Farband-Ykuf, 511
Yidishe Shprakh, 583
Yishai, Eli, 447, 449, 451
YIVO Bleter, 583
YIVO Institute for Jewish Research, 511

Yoffie, Eric, 218, 219, 220, 221, 228
Yosef, Ovadia, 431, 445, 451, 473
Young Judaea, 519
Young Judaean, 583
Young, David, 267
Youth Renewal Fund, 524
Yugntruf: Yiddish Youth Magazine, 583
Yugntruf-Youth for Yiddish, 512

Zakim, Leonard, 594
Zakka, Najib, 315
Zana, Tony, 465
Zarecki, Mark, 276
Ze'evi, Rehavam, 441
Zeman, Milos, 376
Zeta Beta Tau Fraternity, 550
Zevi, Bruno, 318
Zhirinovsky, Vladimir, 397, 398
Zimmerman, Sheldon, 227
Zinker, Alexander, 449
Ziok, Ilona, 359
Zionist Organization of America (ZOA), 169, 233, 234, 235, 524
Zissels, Iosif, 402
Zlotnik, Hania, 103n, 118n
Zogby, James, 169, 170, 171
Zogby, Joseph, 169, 235
Zoltai, Gusztav, 384
Zukunft, 583
Zundel, Ernst, 271
Zwiebel, David, 175
Zyuganov, Gennady, 399